HOW TO USE THE BLUE BOOK

FINDING A VEHICLE

There are two sections in this book, the Automobile or Car section up front and the Truck & Van Section in the back. The Truck & Van section is marked by black tabs on each page. Within each section, the makes are listed alphabetically and models are listed by size within each make. Model years are listed oldest to newest.

EQUIPMENT ADJUSTMENTS

To get the most accurate value, you will need to add or deduct from the base value depending on the equipment. "Adds" and "Deducts" appear underneath individual vehicles and in separate Equipment Schedules. A value in parentheses represents a "Deduct". More generic equipment adjustments appear in the Equipment Schedules. Schedules for cars are at the front of the book. Equipment schedules for trucks and vans are at the back of the book.

You should always add or subtract for each item that is listed separately, even if it is part of a package that you have already added for or if it was considered original standard equipment. If an equipment item is listed both underneath the vehicle listing and in the Equipment Schedule, use the value underneath the vehicle listing because it is specific to that vehicle.

MILEAGE

Mileage must also be taken into consideration to derive the most accurate valuation of a used vehicle. On page 9 we have listed an "acceptable" range of mileage for each model year. The range does not represent the average mileage driven for the model year but the point of resistence where value can be affected. As a vehicle gets older, condition is more important than mileage. Vehicles with more miles may sometimes be worth more than lower mileage vehicles if its condition is better. It is important to note that the values we list are intended for vehicles within the acceptable mileage range.

P9-CAL-655

5

HOW TO USE THE BLUE BOOK

ABBREVIATIONS USED IN THIS BOOK

VIN — Vehicle Identification Number. The VIN may vary depending on model, engine, transmission and option packages.

W.B. — Wheelbase. This is the distance from the center of the front wheel to the center of the rear wheel.

CID/L — Engine size displacement in cubic inches or liters.

List — This is the original suggested suggested retail price of the vehicle when it was sold new, including destination charges and equipment as indicated on the equipment schedule.

Trucks — Trucks listed in this guide have a smooth exterior with the rear wheel wells inside the bed. Value adjustments for models with the rear wheel wells on the outside of the bed can be found on the Truck Equipment Schedules under the Stepside listing.

Premium Sound — This refers to an upgraded sound system (Bose, JBL, Infinity, etc.) not simply a CD changer, equalizer or an aftermarket receiver.

VEHICLE IDENTIFICATION NUMBERS (VINs)

If you are not sure of the year or model of a vehicle, you can often determine them from the Vehicle Identification Number or VIN. Using VINs can get a bit technical. If you already know the year and the model of the vehicle you can skip this information.

Under 1995 Lincoln, you will see the heading "1995 LINCOLN - 1LN(LM81W)-S-#." What this means is that all 1995 Lincolns have a VIN starting with 1LN and have an S in the 10th position. The fourth through eighth positions determine the specific Linoln model and are marked by parentheses. The hyphens indicate positions which can be ignored and the # symbol represents the individual vehicle's serial number.

Please note that we do not have room in this guidebook to list all the VIN information. There are some VINs that you cannot decode using the information provided. Also there are some VINs that indicate two or more possible models. In these cases you must determine the particular model by inspecting the vehicle.

TIPS ON BUYING A USED CAR

DEALER vs PRIVATE PARTY

There are advantages and disadvantages to buying a car from a dealer vs a Private Party. With a dealer, you may get a warranty and some dealerships offer certification programs for late model vehicles that will extend the original factory warranty. While buying from a dealership provides security, buying from a Private Party can save you money. When buying from a private party, ask for all repair and maintenance records and contact information of the previous owner in case you have questions later.

TRADING-IN YOUR VEHICLE

If you are trading your vehicle to a dealer, be sure to check the Trade-In Value and the Private Party Value of your vehicle. You may find it to your benefit to sell the vehicle yourself.

CHECKING OUT A USED VEHICLE

If you are contacting a private party, be sure to ask why they are selling the vehicle. Ask them to describe the condition of the vehicle and how it was used (daily, as a second car, kids car). Ask if they have all of the repair and maintenance records for the vehicle. Ask if you can take the car to a mechanic for an inspection. This is extremely important as private party sales are "As Is" and once you have bought the vehicle, it's yours. If your state requires a smog certificate, insist that the vehicle pass a smog test before buying the car. Smog checks are the current owner's responsibility. Also be certain the vehicle's registration is current and paid to date. It can be costly to reinstate an expired registration. Registration fees vary from state to state, be sure to consult your state's Department of Motor Vehicles.

— Write down the VIN. For a fee, services such as CARFAX can provide you with the vehicle's history (www.kbb.com/carfax).

— Stand away from the vehicle and look at its body panels. Do they all match in color? Do they line up?

— Check the tires for wear. Uneven tire wear, balding on the sides or in the middle, could indicate the need for an alignment or a costly repair to the vehicle's suspension.

— Open the trunk, hood and doors. Look for paint specks or over spray, a sign that all or part of the vehicle has been repainted. If the vehicle has been repainted it is often a sign of some previous damage.

— Check the radiator fluid. If it is very dark or has oil droplets in it, there is a good chance the vehicle has a cracked head gasket meaning that coolant and oil are mixing together.

— Look at the condition of the rubber on each foot pedal and the leather on the steering wheel. Do they show heavy wear? Heavy wear in a low mileage vehicle may indicate that the vehicle has seen more mileage then the odometer indicates.

TIPS ON BUYING A USED CAR

— Spend as much time as you can inside the vehicle. Feel the seat, and we mean really feel it. Take a good long time to sit, because really, the seat is one of the most important parts of the vehicle.

— What about the steering wheel? Is it too high up or too close to the dash? When adjusted comfortably, does it cut off any or all the gauges? Look at the layout of the radio and heater controls. Can they be easily adjusted without taking your eyes off the road? Look over your shoulders, are there any blind spots that you cannot compensate for by using your mirrors? Climb into the seats, front and back. Is there enough legroom and headroom? Do the headrests come up far enough? Do they touch your head or are they raked back at an angle away from you? Does the seatbelt have an adjustable anchor or does it cut into your neck? Check to see how far the rear windows roll down. Some models have windows that only go down a few inches or are sealed in place and don't roll down at all. Take your time to explore all these areas.

— Then take it for a drive. How does it sound? A prolonged tapping could be the valves needing adjustment or a bad hydraulic lifter. Pump the brake pedal a few times and then press hard with your foot. If it slowly sinks all the way to the floor, there is either a leak in the line or the master cylinder/brake booster is dying. Shift into gear. If the vehicle is an automatic, the transmission should engage immediately and shifts should be crisp and quick. With your foot firmly on the brake, shift from drive to reverse; clunks or grinding noises could indicate a worn or broken engine/transmission mount, bad U-joints or differential wear.

— As you drive along, does the steering wheel shake or vibrate? It shouldn't. Vibration in the steering wheel can mean anything from an unbalanced wheel to a loose steering rack. Cars with ABS (anti-lock brakes) will have a slight pulsating action in the brake pedal when the brakes are applied with some force. Cars without ABS should not have a pulsating brake pedal.

— We also recommend that you contact your local Department of Motor Vehicles. Ask them what forms are required to transfer the vehicle title as well as any other required information. For example, some states require a smog certificate while others require the bill of sale from the current owner.

— Lastly, whatever you do, get it in WRITING. This means if you settle with a private party, write up a contract stating what you are paying for the vehicle and under what terms it is to be delivered. Likewise with a dealer, any work they promise to do or options they intend to add, get it in writing before you close the deal.

MILEAGE RANGES

ACCEPTABLE MILEAGE RANGES

The following are acceptable mileage ranges for each model year. They do **not** represent the average miles driven. Rather, they represent an accepted mileage range as demonstrated by market research. If a vehicle's mileage is outside of the accepted range, dollar adjustments may be necessary. Mileage higher than shown on the guidelines below can expect to encounter resistance from a buyer.

YEAR	ACCEPTABLE MILEAGE RANGE
1990 – 1991	99,000 – 104,000
1992	95,000 – 100,000
1993	92,000 – 97,000
1994	89,000 – 94,000
1995	86,000 – 91,000
1996	83,000 – 88,000
1997	80,000 – 85,000
1998	77,000 – 82,000
1999	71,000 – 76,000
2000	65,000 – 70,000
2001	55,000 – 60,000
2002	43,000 – 48,000
2003	29,000 – 34,000
2004	13,000 – 18,000

PRIVATE PARTY & RETAIL EQUIPMENT VALUE CONVERSION

Use the chart below to convert Trade-In Equipment Values to Private Party and Retail Values. Simply find your total Trade-In Equipment Value under the Trade-In (TI) column then follow across to the Private Party and Retail (PP/R) column. This new figure will be your Private Party or Retail Equipment Value.

TI	PP/R	TI	PP/R	TI	PP/R	TI	PP/R	TI	PP/R
25	35	225	300	425	565	625	835	825	1100
50	65	250	335	450	600	650	865	850	1135
75	100	275	365	475	635	675	900	875	1165
100	135	300	400	500	665	700	935	900	1200
125	165	325	435	525	700	725	965	925	1235
150	200	350	465	550	735	750	1000	950	1265
175	235	375	500	575	765	775	1035	975	1300
200	265	400	535	600	800	800	1065	1000	1335

1990 –1991 FACTORY EQUIP. TRADE-IN VALUES

Equipment	1	2	3	4	5	6
Automatic Trans	—	—	100	—	*	150
Power Steering	*	*	*	*	*	50
Air Conditioning	*	*	*	*	*	50
GROUP TOTAL	*	*	100	*	*	250
Cassette	*	*	*	50	25	25
Power Windows	*	*	*	25	0	0
Power Door Locks	*	*	25	25	0	0
Tilt Wheel	*	*	25	25	25	0
Cruise Control	*	*	25	25	25	0
BOTH GROUPS	*	*	175	150	75	275
CD (Single Disc)	50	50	50	50	50	25
CD (Multi Disc)	100	100	100	100	100	75
Leather	*	100	100	50	25	25
Sun Roof (Flip-up)	*	—	50	50	25	25
Sun Roof (Sliding)	*	50	50	50	50	25
Moon Roof (Sldng)	*	75	75	75	50	25
T-Bar Roof	—	—	200	200	—	100
Alloy Wheels	*	*	25	25	25	25
Premium Wheels	75	75	50	50	50	25
Third Seat (Wagon)	100	50	50	50	50	50
DEDUCT FOR:						
Manual Trans	—	(100)	*	(175)	(150)	*
w/o Power Steering	—	—	—	(50)	(50)	(50)
w/o Air Cond.	(125)	(125)	(75)	(75)	(50)	(50)
w/o AM/FM Stereo	(25)	(25)	(25)	(25)	0	0
w/o Power Windows	—	(25)	—	(25)	—	—
w/o Pwr Door Locks	—	(25)	—	(25)	—	—

* — EQUIPMENT INCLUDED IN BASE PRICE

1992 FACTORY EQUIPMENT TRADE-IN VALUES

Equipment	1	2	3	4	5	6
Automatic Trans	—	—	—	—	*	175
Power Steering	*	*	*	*	*	*
Air Conditioning	*	*	*	*	*	*
Power Windows	*	*	*	*	0	0
Power Door Locks	*	*	*	*	0	0
Tilt Wheel	*	*	*	*	25	0
Cruise Control	*	*	*	*	25	0
Cassette	*	*	*	*	25	25
GROUP TOTAL	*	*	*	*	75	200
Power Seat	*	*	25	25	0	—
Dual Power Seats	*	*	25	25	25	—
ABS (4 Wheel)	*	*	50	50	25	0
CD (Single Disc)	50	50	50	50	50	25
CD (Multi Disc)	100	100	100	100	100	75
Premium Sound	25	25	25	25	25	25
Integrated Phone	0	0	0	0	—	—
Leather	*	*	100	50	25	25
Sun Roof (Flip-up)	—	—	50	50	25	25
Sun Roof (Sliding)	*	50	50	50	50	25
Moon Roof (Sldng)	*	100	75	75	50	25
T-Bar Roof	—	—	225	225	—	100
Rear Spoiler	—	—	0	0	0	0
Alloy Wheels	*	*	25	25	25	25
Premium Wheels	100	100	50	50	50	25
Roof Rack (Wagon)	25	25	25	25	0	0
Third Seat (Wagon)	125	50	50	50	50	50
DEDUCT FOR:						
Manual Trans	—	—	—	—	(200)	*
w/o Power Steering	—	—	—	(50)	(50)	(50)
w/o Air Cond	(150)	(150)	(100)	(100)	(50)	(50)
w/o AM/FM Stereo	(25)	(25)	(25)	(25)	0	0
w/o Power Windows	—	(25)	—	(25)	—	—
w/o Pwr Door Locks	—	(25)	—	(25)	—	—
w/o Tilt Wheel	—	(50)	—	(50)	—	—
w/o Cruise Control	—	(25)	—	(25)	—	—
w/o Leather	(100)	(100)	—	—	—	—
w/o Sun/Moon Roof	(225)	—	—	—	—	—

* — EQUIPMENT INCLUDED IN BASE PRICE

SEE PAGE 9 FOR PVT PARTY & RETAIL EQUIPMENT

1993 FACTORY EQUIPMENT TRADE-IN VALUES

Equipment	1	2	3	4	5	6
Automatic Trans	—	—	—	—	*	200
Power Steering	*	*	*	*	*	*
Air Conditioning	*	*	*	*	*	*
Power Windows	*	*	*	*	0	0
Power Door Locks	*	*	*	*	0	0
Tilt Wheel	*	*	*	*	25	0
Cruise Control	*	*	*	*	25	0
Cassette	*	*	*	*	25	25
GROUP TOTAL	*	*	*	*	75	225
Power Seat	*	*	25	25	0	—
Dual Power Seats	*	*	25	25	25	—
ABS (4 Wheel)	*	*	50	50	25	0
CD (Single Disc)	50	50	50	50	25	25
CD (Multi Disc)	125	125	125	125	100	75
Premium Sound	25	25	25	25	25	25
Integrated Phone	0	0	0	0	—	—
Leather	*	*	100	50	25	25
Sun Roof (Flip-up)	—	—	50	50	25	25
Sun Roof (Sliding)	*	50	50	50	50	25
Moon Roof (Sldng)	*	125	75	75	50	25
T-Bar Roof	—	—	250	250	—	100
Rear Spoiler	—	—	0	0	0	0
Alloy Wheels	*	*	25	25	25	25
Premium Wheels	125	125	75	75	50	25
Roof Rack (Wagon)	25	25	25	25	0	0
Third Seat (Wagon)	175	75	75	75	50	50
DEDUCT FOR:						
Manual Trans	—	—	—	—	(250)	*
w/o Power Steering	—	—	—	(50)	(50)	(50)
w/o Air Cond	(175)	(175)	(125)	(125)	(50)	(50)
w/o AM/FM Stereo	(25)	(25)	(25)	(25)	0	0
w/o Power Windows	—	(25)	—	(25)	—	—
w/o Pwr Door Locks	—	(25)	—	(25)	—	—
w/o Tilt Wheel	—	(50)	—	(50)	—	—
w/o Cruise Control	—	(25)	—	(25)	—	—
w/o Leather	(100)	(100)	—	—	—	—
w/o Sun/Moon Roof	(275)	—	—	—	—	—

* — EQUIPMENT INCLUDED IN BASE PRICE

1994 FACTORY EQUIPMENT TRADE-IN VALUES

Equipment	1	2	3	4	5	6
Automatic Trans	—	—	—	—	*	225
Power Steering	*	*	*	*	*	*
Air Conditioning	*	*	*	*	*	*
Power Windows	*	*	*	*	25	0
Power Door Locks	*	*	*	*	0	0
Tilt Wheel	*	*	*	*	25	0
Cruise Control	*	*	*	*	25	0
Cassette	*	*	*	*	25	25
GROUP TOTAL	*	*	*	*	100	250
Power Seat	*	*	25	25	0	—
Dual Power Seats	*	*	25	25	25	—
ABS (4 Wheel)	*	*	50	50	25	0
CD (Single Disc)	50	50	50	50	50	25
CD (Multi Disc)	150	150	150	150	100	75
Premium Sound	25	25	25	25	25	25
Integrated Phone	75	75	50	50	—	—
Leather	*	*	100	75	25	25
Sun Roof (Flip-up)	—	—	50	50	25	25
Sun Roof (Sliding)	*	50	50	50	50	25
Moon Roof (Sldng)	*	150	100	100	75	50
T-Bar Roof	—	—	275	275	—	100
Rear Spoiler	—	—	0	0	0	0
Alloy Wheels	*	*	25	25	25	25
Premium Wheels	150	150	100	100	50	25
Roof Rack (Wagon)	25	25	25	25	0	0
Third Seat (Wagon)	225	100	100	100	50	50
DEDUCT FOR:						
Manual Trans	—	—	—	—	(300)	*
w/o Power Steering	—	—	—	(50)	(50)	(50)
w/o Air Cond	(200)	(200)	(150)	(150)	(50)	(50)
w/o AM/FM Stereo	(25)	(25)	(25)	(25)	0	0
w/o Power Windows	—	(50)	—	(50)	—	—
w/o Pwr Door Locks	—	(25)	—	(25)	—	—
w/o Tilt Wheel	—	(50)	—	(50)	—	—
w/o Cruise Control	—	(25)	—	(25)	—	—
w/o Leather	(100)	(100)	—	—	—	—
w/o Sun/Moon Roof	(300)	—	—	—	—	—

* — EQUIPMENT INCLUDED IN BASE PRICE

1995 FACTORY EQUIPMENT TRADE-IN VALUES

Equipment	1	2	3	4	5	6
Automatic Trans	—	—	—	—	*	250
Power Steering	*	*	*	*	*	*
Air Conditioning	*	*	*	*	*	*
Power Windows	*	*	*	*	50	0
Power Door Locks	*	*	*	*	0	0
Tilt Wheel	*	*	*	*	25	0
Cruise Control	*	*	*	*	25	0
Cassette	*	*	*	*	25	25
GROUP TOTAL	*	*	*	*	125	275
Power Seat	*	*	25	25	0	0
Dual Power Seats	*	*	25	25	25	0
ABS (4 Wheel)	*	*	50	50	25	0
CD (Single Disc)	75	75	75	75	50	25
CD (Multi Disc)	175	175	175	175	125	100
Premium Sound	50	50	25	25	25	25
Integrated Phone	100	100	75	75	—	—
Leather	*	*	125	100	25	25
Sun Roof (Flip-up)	—	—	50	50	25	25
Sun Roof (Sliding)	*	75	50	50	50	25
Moon Roof (Sldng)	*	175	125	125	100	75
T-Bar Roof	—	—	300	300	—	125
Rear Spoiler	25	25	25	25	25	25
Alloy Wheels	*	*	25	25	25	25
Premium Wheels	175	175	125	125	75	25
Roof Rack (Wagon)	25	25	25	25	0	0
Third Seat (Wagon)	275	125	125	125	75	75
DEDUCT FOR:						
Manual Trans	—	—	—	—	(350)	*
w/o Power Steering	—	—	—	(75)	(50)	(50)
w/o Air Cond	(225)	(225)	(175)	(175)	(75)	(75)
w/o AM/FM Stereo	(25)	(25)	(25)	(25)	0	0
w/o Power Windows	—	(75)	—	(75)	—	—
w/o Pwr Door Locks	—	(25)	—	(25)	—	—
w/o Tilt Wheel	—	(50)	—	(50)	—	—
w/o Cruise Control	—	(25)	—	(25)	—	—
w/o Leather	(125)	(125)	—	—	—	—
w/o Sun/Moon Roof	(325)	—	—	—	—	—

* — EQUIPMENT INCLUDED IN BASE PRICE

1996 FACTORY EQUIPMENT TRADE-IN VALUES

Equipment	1	2	3	4	5	6
Automatic Trans	—	—	—	—	*	275
Power Steering	*	*	*	*	*	*
Air Conditioning	*	*	*	*	*	*
Power Windows	*	*	*	*	75	25
Power Door Locks	*	*	*	*	0	0
Tilt Wheel	*	*	*	*	50	0
Cruise Control	*	*	*	*	25	0
Cassette	*	*	*	*	25	25
GROUP TOTAL	*	*	*	*	175	325
Power Seat	*	*	25	25	0	0
Dual Power Seats	*	*	25	25	25	0
ABS (4 Wheel)	*	*	50	50	25	0
CD (Single Disc)	100	100	100	100	50	50
CD (Multi Disc)	200	200	200	200	150	125
Premium Sound	75	75	25	25	25	25
Integrated Phone	125	125	100	100	—	—
Navigation System	225	—	—	—	—	—
Leather	*	*	150	125	25	25
Sun Roof (Flip-up)	—	—	50	50	25	25
Sun Roof (Sliding)	*	100	75	75	50	25
Moon Roof (Sldng)	*	200	150	150	125	100
T-Bar Roof	—	—	325	325	—	—
Rear Spoiler	25	25	25	25	25	25
Alloy Wheels	*	*	50	50	25	25
Premium Wheels	225	225	150	150	100	50
Roof Rack (Wagon)	25	25	25	25	0	0
Third Seat (Wagon)	325	150	150	150	100	100
DEDUCT FOR:						
Manual Trans	—	—	—	—	(375)	*
w/o Power Steering	—	—	—	(100)	(50)	(50)
w/o Air Cond	(250)	(250)	(200)	(200)	(100)	(100)
w/o AM/FM Stereo	(25)	(25)	(25)	(25)	0	0
w/o Power Windows	—	(100)	—	(100)	—	—
w/o Pwr Door Locks	—	(25)	—	(25)	—	—
w/o Tilt Wheel	—	(75)	—	(75)	—	—
w/o Cruise Control	—	(25)	—	(25)	—	—
w/o Leather	(150)	(150)	—	—	—	—
w/o Sun/Moon Roof	(350)	—	—	—	—	—

* — EQUIPMENT INCLUDED IN BASE PRICE

SEE PAGE 9 FOR PVT PARTY & RETAIL EQUIPMENT

1997 FACTORY EQUIPMENT TRADE-IN VALUES

Equipment	1	2	3	4	5	6
Automatic Trans	—	—	—	—	*	300
Power Steering	*	*	*	*	*	*
Air Conditioning	*	*	*	*	*	*
Power Windows	*	*	*	*	100	50
Power Door Locks	*	*	*	*	25	0
Tilt Wheel	*	*	*	*	75	25
Cruise Control	*	*	*	*	25	0
Cassette	*	*	*	*	50	25
GROUP TOTAL	*	*	*	*	275	400
Power Seat	*	*	25	25	0	0
Dual Power Seats	*	*	50	50	25	0
ABS (4 Wheel)	*	*	75	75	25	25
CD (Single Disc)	125	125	125	125	75	75
CD (Multi Disc)	225	225	225	225	175	150
Premium Sound	100	100	50	50	50	50
Integrated Phone	150	150	125	125	—	—
Navigation System	275	—	—	—	—	—
Leather	*	*	175	150	25	25
Sun Roof (Flip-up)	—	—	50	50	25	25
Sun Roof (Sliding)	*	125	100	100	75	50
Moon Roof (Sldng)	*	225	175	175	150	125
T-Bar Roof	—	—	—	375	—	—
Imitation Conv Top	—	75	—	25	—	—
Rear Spoiler	25	25	25	25	25	25
Alloy Wheels	*	*	75	75	50	25
Premium Wheels	275	275	175	175	125	75
Roof Rack (Wagon)	25	25	25	25	0	0
Third Seat (Wagon)	375	175	175	175	125	125
DEDUCT FOR:						
Manual Trans	—	—	—	—	(400)	*
w/o Power Steering	—	—	—	(125)	(75)	(75)
w/o Air Cond	(275)	(275)	(225)	(225)	(125)	(125)
w/o AM/FM Stereo	(25)	(25)	(25)	(25)	0	0
w/o Power Windows	—	(125)	—	(125)	—	—
w/o Pwr Door Locks	—	(25)	—	(25)	—	—
w/o Tilt Wheel	—	(100)	—	(100)	—	—
w/o Cruise Control	—	(25)	—	(25)	—	—
w/o Leather	(175)	(175)	—	—	—	—
w/o Sun/Moon Roof	(375)	—	—	—	—	—

* — EQUIPMENT INCLUDED IN BASE PRICE

1998 FACTORY EQUIPMENT TRADE-IN VALUES

Equipment	1	2	3	4	5	6
Automatic Trans	—	—	—	—	*	300
Power Steering	*	*	*	*	*	*
Air Conditioning	*	*	*	*	*	*
Power Windows	*	*	*	*	125	75
Power Door Locks	*	*	*	*	50	25
Tilt Wheel	*	*	*	*	100	50
Cruise Control	*	*	*	*	50	25
Cassette	*	*	*	*	75	50
GROUP TOTAL	*	*	*	*	400	525
Power Seat	*	*	50	50	25	25
Dual Power Seats	*	*	75	75	50	25
ABS (4 Wheel)	*	*	100	100	50	50
CD (Single Disc)	150	150	150	150	100	100
CD (Multi Disc)	250	250	250	250	200	175
Premium Sound	125	125	75	75	75	75
Integrated Phone	175	175	150	150	—	—
Navigation System	300	—	—	—	—	—
Leather	*	*	200	175	50	25
Sun Roof (Flip-up)	—	—	50	50	25	25
Sun Roof (Sliding)	*	150	125	125	100	75
Moon Roof (Sldng)	*	250	200	200	175	150
Imitation Conv Top	—	100	—	50	—	—
Rear Spoiler	25	25	25	25	25	25
Alloy Wheels	*	*	100	100	75	50
Premium Wheels	300	300	200	200	150	100
Roof Rack (Wagon)	25	25	25	25	0	0
Third Seat (Wagon)	400	200	200	200	150	150
DEDUCT FOR:						
Manual Trans	—	—	—	—	(425)	*
w/o Power Steering	—	—	—	(150)	(100)	(100)
w/o Air Cond	(325)	(325)	(250)	(250)	(150)	(150)
w/o AM/FM Stereo	(50)	(50)	(50)	(50)	(25)	(25)
w/o Power Windows	—	(150)	—	(150)	—	—
w/o Pwr Door Locks	—	(50)	—	(50)	—	—
w/o Tilt Wheel	—	(125)	—	(125)	—	—
w/o Cruise Control	—	(25)	—	(25)	—	—
w/o Leather	(200)	(200)	—	—	—	—
w/o Sun/Moon Roof	(425)	—	—	—	—	—

* — EQUIPMENT INCLUDED IN BASE PRICE

SEE PAGE 9 FOR PVT PARTY & RETAIL EQUIPMENT

1999 FACTORY EQUIPMENT TRADE-IN VALUES

Equipment	1	2	3	4	5	6
Automatic Trans	—	—	—	—	*	350
Power Steering	*	*	*	*	*	*
Air Conditioning	*	*	*	*	*	*
Power Windows	*	*	*	*	125	75
Power Door Locks	*	*	*	*	50	25
Tilt Wheel	*	*	*	*	100	50
Cruise Control	*	*	*	*	50	25
Cassette	*	*	*	*	75	50
GROUP TOTAL	*	*	*	*	400	575
Power Seat	*	*	50	50	25	25
Dual Power Seats	*	*	100	100	50	25
ABS (4 Wheel)	*	*	100	100	50	50
CD (Single Disc)	150	150	150	150	100	100
CD (Multi Disc)	275	275	275	275	225	200
Premium Sound	150	150	100	100	75	75
Integrated Phone	200	200	150	150	—	—
Navigation System	325	—	—	—	—	—
Leather	*	*	250	200	75	50
Sun Roof (Flip-up)	—	—	75	75	25	25
Sun Roof (Sliding)	*	200	150	150	125	100
Moon Roof (Sldng)	*	325	250	250	200	175
Imitation Conv Top	—	125	—	75	—	—
Rear Spoiler	50	50	50	50	50	50
Alloy Wheels	*	*	100	100	75	50
Premium Wheels	325	325	225	225	150	100
Roof Rack (Wagon)	50	50	50	50	25	25
Third Seat (Wagon)	425	225	225	225	175	175
DEDUCT FOR:						
Manual Trans	—	—	—	—	(450)	*
w/o Power Steering	—	—	—	(175)	(125)	(100)
w/o Air Cond	(400)	(400)	(300)	(300)	(200)	(200)
w/o AM/FM Stereo	(50)	(50)	(50)	(50)	(25)	(25)
w/o Power Windows	—	(175)	—	(175)	—	—
w/o Pwr Door Locks	—	(50)	—	(50)	—	—
w/o Tilt Wheel	—	(150)	—	(150)	—	—
w/o Cruise Control	—	(50)	—	(50)	—	—
w/o Leather	(250)	(250)	—	—	—	—
w/o Sun/Moon Roof	(500)	—	—	—	—	—

* — EQUIPMENT INCLUDED IN BASE PRICE

2000 FACTORY EQUIPMENT TRADE-IN VALUES

Equipment	1	2	3	4	5	6
Automatic Trans	—	—	—	—	*	400
Power Steering	*	*	*	*	*	*
Air Conditioning	*	*	*	*	*	*
Power Windows	*	*	*	*	150	75
Power Door Locks	*	*	*	*	50	25
Tilt Wheel	*	*	*	*	100	50
Cruise Control	*	*	*	*	50	25
Cassette	*	*	*	*	75	50
GROUP TOTAL	*	*	*	*	425	625
Power Seat	*	*	50	50	25	25
Dual Power Seats	*	*	125	125	50	25
ABS (4 Wheel)	*	*	100	100	50	50
CD (Single Disc)	175	175	175	175	125	100
CD (Multi Disc)	300	300	300	300	250	225
Premium Sound	175	175	125	125	75	75
Integrated Phone	225	225	175	175	—	—
Navigation System	350	350	350	—	—	—
Leather	*	*	300	225	100	75
Sun Roof (Flip-up)	—	—	100	100	25	25
Sun Roof (Sliding)	*	250	200	200	150	125
Moon Roof (Sldng)	*	400	300	300	250	200
Imitation Conv Top	—	150	—	100	—	—
Rear Spoiler	75	75	75	75	75	75
Alloy Wheels	*	*	100	100	75	50
Premium Wheels	350	350	250	250	175	100
Roof Rack (Wagon)	75	75	75	75	50	50
Third Seat (Wagon)	450	250	250	250	200	200
DEDUCT FOR:						
Manual Trans	—	—	—	—	(475)	*
w/o Power Steering	—	—	—	(200)	(150)	(100)
w/o Air Cond	(475)	(475)	(350)	(350)	(250)	(250)
w/o AM/FM Stereo	(75)	(75)	(75)	(75)	(25)	(25)
w/o Power Windows	—	(200)	—	(200)	—	—
w/o Pwr Door Locks	—	(75)	—	(75)	—	—
w/o Tilt Wheel	—	(175)	—	(175)	—	—
w/o Cruise Control	—	(75)	—	(75)	—	—
w/o Leather	(300)	(300)	—	—	—	—
w/o Sun/Moon Roof	(550)	—	—	—	—	—

* — EQUIPMENT INCLUDED IN BASE PRICE

SEE PAGE 9 FOR PVT PARTY & RETAIL EQUIPMENT

2001 FACTORY EQUIPMENT TRADE-IN VALUES

Equipment	1	2	3	4	5	6
Automatic Trans	—	—	—	—	*	450
Power Steering	*	*	*	*	*	*
Air Conditioning	*	*	*	*	*	*
Power Windows	*	*	*	*	175	75
Power Door Locks	*	*	*	*	50	25
Tilt Wheel	*	*	*	*	100	50
Cruise Control	*	*	*	*	50	25
Cassette	*	*	*	*	75	50
GROUP TOTAL	*	*	*	*	450	675
Power Seat	*	*	50	50	25	25
Dual Power Seats	*	*	150	150	50	25
ABS (4 Wheel)	*	*	100	100	50	50
CD (Single Disc)	200	200	200	200	150	100
CD (Multi Disc)	325	325	325	325	275	250
Premium Sound	200	200	150	150	100	75
Integrated Phone	250	250	200	200	—	—
Navigation System	400	400	400	—	—	—
Leather	*	*	350	250	125	100
Sun Roof (Flip-up)	—	—	125	125	50	50
Sun Roof (Sliding)	*	300	250	250	175	150
Moon Roof (Sldng)	*	475	350	350	300	250
Imitation Conv Top	—	200	—	125	—	—
Rear Spoiler	100	100	100	100	100	100
Alloy Wheels	*	*	100	100	75	50
Premium Wheels	400	400	275	275	200	100
Roof Rack (Wagon)	100	100	100	100	50	50
Third Seat (Wagon)	475	275	275	275	225	225
DEDUCT FOR:						
Manual Trans	—	—	—	—	(500)	*
w/o Power Steering	—	—	—	(225)	(175)	(100)
w/o Air Cond	(550)	(550)	(425)	(425)	(300)	(300)
w/o AM/FM Stereo	(100)	(100)	(100)	(100)	(50)	(25)
w/o Power Windows	—	(225)	—	(225)	—	—
w/o Pwr Door Locks	—	(100)	—	(100)	—	—
w/o Tilt Wheel	—	(200)	—	(200)	—	—
w/o Cruise Control	—	(100)	—	(100)	—	—
w/o Leather	(350)	(350)	—	—	—	—
w/o Sun/Moon Roof	(600)	—	—	—	—	—

* — EQUIPMENT INCLUDED IN BASE PRICE

2002 FACTORY EQUIPMENT TRADE-IN VALUES

Equipment	1	2	3	4	5	6
Automatic Trans	—	—	—	—	*	475
Power Steering	*	*	*	*	*	*
Air Conditioning	*	*	*	*	*	*
Power Windows	*	*	*	*	200	100
Power Door Locks	*	*	*	*	75	25
Tilt Wheel	*	*	*	*	100	75
Cruise Control	*	*	*	*	75	25
Cassette	*	*	*	*	100	75
GROUP TOTAL	*	*	*	*	550	775
Power Seat	*	*	75	75	25	25
Dual Power Seats	*	*	175	175	75	25
ABS (4 Wheel)	*	*	125	125	75	50
CD (Single Disc)	225	225	225	225	175	125
CD (Multi Disc)	350	350	350	350	300	275
Premium Sound	225	225	175	175	125	75
Integrated Phone	275	275	225	225	—	—
Navigation System	450	450	450	450	—	—
Leather	*	*	400	300	150	125
Sun Roof (Flip-up)	—	—	150	150	75	75
Sun Roof (Sliding)	*	350	300	300	200	175
Moon Roof (Sldng)	*	550	425	425	350	300
Imitation Conv Top	—	250	—	150	—	—
Rear Spoiler	100	100	100	100	100	100
Alloy Wheels	*	*	125	125	100	75
Premium Wheels	450	450	300	300	225	125
Roof Rack (Wagon)	100	100	100	100	50	50
Third Seat (Wagon)	500	300	300	300	250	250
DEDUCT FOR:						
Manual Trans	—	—	—	—	(525)	*
w/o Power Steering	—	—	—	(250)	(200)	(125)
w/o Air Cond	(625)	(625)	(500)	(500)	(350)	(350)
w/o AM/FM Stereo	(125)	(125)	(125)	(125)	(75)	(25)
w/o Power Windows	—	(250)	—	(250)	—	—
w/o Pwr Door Locks	—	(125)	—	(125)	—	—
w/o Tilt Wheel	—	(250)	—	(225)	—	—
w/o Cruise Control	—	(125)	—	(125)	—	—
w/o Leather	(400)	(400)	—	—	—	—
w/o Sun/Moon Roof	(650)	—	—	—	—	—

* — EQUIPMENT INCLUDED IN BASE PRICE

SEE PAGE 9 FOR PVT PARTY & RETAIL EQUIPMENT

2003 FACTORY EQUIPMENT TRADE-IN VALUES

Equipment	1	2	3	4	5	6
Automatic Trans	—	—	—	—	*	500
Power Steering	*	*	*	*	*	*
Air Conditioning	*	*	*	*	*	*
Power Windows	*	*	*	*	225	125
Power Door Locks	*	*	*	*	100	50
Tilt Wheel	*	*	*	*	125	100
Cruise Control	*	*	*	*	100	50
Cassette	*	*	*	*	125	100
GROUP TOTAL	*	*	*	*	675	925
Power Seat	*	*	100	100	50	25
Dual Power Seats	*	*	200	200	100	50
ABS (4 Wheel)	*	*	150	150	100	50
CD (Single Disc)	250	250	250	250	200	150
CD (Multi Disc)	400	400	400	400	325	300
Premium Sound	250	250	200	200	150	100
Integrated Phone	300	300	250	250	—	—
Video/DVD	500	500	500	500	500	500
Navigation System	500	500	500	500	—	—
Leather	*	*	475	350	200	150
Sun Roof (Flip-up)	—	—	200	200	100	100
Sun Roof (Sliding)	*	425	350	350	250	200
Moon Roof (Sldng)	*	625	500	500	400	350
Imitation Conv Top	—	300	—	200	—	—
Rear Spoiler	100	100	100	100	100	100
Alloy Wheels	*	*	150	150	125	100
Premium Wheels	500	500	350	350	250	150
Roof Rack (Wagon)	100	100	100	100	50	50
Third Seat (Wagon)	525	350	350	350	275	275
DEDUCT FOR:						
Manual Trans	—	—	—	—	(550)	*
w/o Power Steering	—	—	—	(275)	(225)	(150)
w/o Air Cond	(700)	(700)	(575)	(575)	(400)	(400)
w/o AM/FM Stereo	(150)	(150)	(150)	(150)	(100)	(50)
w/o Power Windows	—	(275)	—	(275)	—	—
w/o Pwr Door Locks	—	(150)	—	(150)	—	—
w/o Tilt Wheel	—	(300)	—	(250)	—	—
w/o Cruise Control	—	(150)	—	(150)	—	—
w/o Leather	(475)	(475)	—	—	—	—
w/o Sun/Moon Roof	(700)	—	—	—	—	—

* — EQUIPMENT INCLUDED IN BASE PRICE

22   SEE PAGE 9 FOR PVT PARTY & RETAIL EQUIPMENT

2004 FACTORY EQUIPMENT TRADE-IN VALUES

Equipment	1	2	3	4	5	6
Automatic Trans	—	—	—	—	*	525
Power Steering	*	*	*	*	*	*
Air Conditioning	*	*	*	*	*	*
Power Windows	*	*	*	*	250	150
Power Door Locks	*	*	*	*	125	75
Tilt Wheel	*	*	*	*	150	125
Cruise Control	*	*	*	*	125	75
Cassette	*	*	*	*	150	125
GROUP TOTAL	*	*	*	*	800	1075
Power Seat	*	*	125	125	75	25
Dual Power Seats	*	*	225	225	125	75
ABS (4 Wheel)	*	*	175	175	125	75
CD (Single Disc)	275	275	275	275	225	175
CD (Multi Disc)	450	450	450	450	350	325
Premium Sound	275	275	225	225	175	125
Integrated Phone	350	350	275	275	—	—
Video/DVD	500	500	500	500	500	500
Navigation System	550	550	550	550	—	—
Leather	*	*	550	400	250	175
Sun Roof (Flip-up)	—	—	250	250	125	125
Sun Roof (Sliding)	*	500	400	400	300	250
Moon Roof (Sldng)	*	700	575	575	450	400
Imitation Conv Top	—	—	—	250	—	—
Rear Spoiler	100	100	100	100	100	100
Alloy Wheels	*	*	175	175	150	125
Premium Wheels	550	550	400	400	275	175
Roof Rack (Wagon)	100	100	100	100	50	50
Third Seat (Wagon)	550	400	400	400	300	300
DEDUCT FOR:						
Manual Trans	—	—	—	—	(575)	*
w/o Power Steering	—	—	—	(300)	(250)	(175)
w/o Air Cond	(775)	(775)	(650)	(650)	(450)	(450)
w/o AM/FM Stereo	(175)	(175)	(175)	(175)	(125)	(75)
w/o Power Windows	—	(300)	—	(300)	—	—
w/o Pwr Door Locks	—	(175)	—	(175)	—	—
w/o Tilt Wheel	—	(350)	—	(275)	—	—
w/o Cruise Control	—	(175)	—	(175)	—	—
w/o Leather	(550)	(550)	—	—	—	—
w/o Sun/Moon Roof	(750)	—	—	—	—	—

* — EQUIPMENT INCLUDED IN BASE PRICE

SEE PAGE 9 FOR PVT PARTY & RETAIL EQUIPMENT

Body	Type	VIN	List	Trade-In Fair	Trade-In Good	Pvt-Party Good	Retail Excellent

Automobile Section

ACURA

1990 ACURA — JH4(DB164)–L–#

INTEGRA—4-Cyl.—Equipment Schedule 3
W.B. 100.4", 102.4" (4D); 1.8 Liter.

Body	Type	VIN	List	Fair	Good	Good	Excellent
RS Sedan 4D		DB164	13145	875	1225	2075	3350
RS Hatchback 2D		DA944	12970	900	1275	2125	3425
LS Sedan 4D		DB165	14840	950	1375	2375	3875
LS Hatchback 2D		DA945	14020	950	1375	2375	3875
GS Sedan 4D		DB166	16245	1050	1500	2575	4075
GS Hatchback 2D		DA946	16120	1050	1500	2575	4075
Manual Trans (Sedan)	3,5			**(100)**	**(100)**	**(135)**	**(135)**

LEGEND—V6—Equipment Schedule 1
W.B. 106.5", 108.7" (4D); 2.7 Liter.

Body	Type	VIN	List	Fair	Good	Good	Excellent
Sedan 4D		KA464	24580	1425	1900	3100	4775
Coupe 2D		KA324	25855	1425	1900	3125	4825
L Sedan 4D		KA465	26995	1700	2225	3500	5275
L Coupe 2D		KA325	28420	1700	2225	3525	5325
LS Sedan 4D		KA467	30705	1800	2325	3625	5450
LS Coupe 2D		KA327	31785	1800	2325	3650	5475
Manual Trans (Sedan)	1,5			**(200)**	**(200)**	**(265)**	**(265)**

1991 ACURA — JH4(DB164)–M–#

INTEGRA—4-Cyl.—Equipment Schedule 3
W.B. 100.4", 102.4" (4D); 1.8 Liter.

Body	Type	VIN	List	Fair	Good	Good	Excellent
RS Sedan 4D		DB164	13870	1000	1450	2500	4000
RS Hatchback 2D		DA944	12970	1025	1475	2550	4050
LS Sedan 4D		DB165	15565	1125	1575	2700	4275
LS Hatchback 2D		DA945	14845	1125	1575	2700	4275
LS Special H'Back 2D		DA939	14985	1175	1625	2750	4325
GS Sedan 4D		DB166	17470	1300	1775	2925	4525
GS Hatchback 2D		DA946	16945	1300	1775	2925	4525
Manual Trans (Sedan)	3,5			**(175)**	**(175)**	**(235)**	**(235)**

LEGEND—V6—Equipment Schedule 1
W.B. 111.4", 114.6" (4D); 3.2 Liter.

Body	Type	VIN	List	Fair	Good	Good	Excellent
Sedan 4D		KA763	27910	2825	3450	4950	7025
L Sedan 4D		KA765	29910	3325	4025	5625	7850
L Coupe 2D		KA825	32010	3400	4100	5700	7975
LS Sedan 4D		KA767	34510	3500	4200	5825	8125
LS Coupe 2D		KA827	36610	3575	4275	5925	8225
Manual Trans (Sedan)	1,5			**(200)**	**(200)**	**(265)**	**(265)**

NSX—V6—Equipment Schedule 2
W.B. 99.6"; 3.0 Liter.

Body	Type	VIN	List	Fair	Good	Good	Excellent
Sport Coupe 2D		NA126	64600	15400	17375	21400	27200

1992 ACURA — JH4(DB164)–N–#

INTEGRA—4-Cyl.—Equipment Schedule 3
W.B. 100.4", 102.4" (4D); 1.7 Liter, 1.8 Liter.

Body	Type	VIN	List	Fair	Good	Good	Excellent
RS Sedan 4D		DB164	14335	1225	1675	2800	4425
RS Hatchback 2D		DA944	13410	1275	1750	2900	4500
LS Sedan 4D		DB165	16065	1450	1925	3125	4775
LS Hatchback 2D		DA945	15315	1450	1925	3125	4800
GS Sedan 4D		DB166	18025	1625	2125	3350	5075
GS Hatchback 2D		DA946	17485	1625	2125	3350	5075
GS-R Hatchback 2D		DB238	18255	1725	2250	3475	5225
Manual Trans (Sedan)	3,5			**(125)**	**(125)**	**(165)**	**(165)**

VIGOR—5-Cyl.—Equipment Schedule 1
W.B. 110.4"; 2.5 Liter.

Body	Type	VIN	List	Fair	Good	Good	Excellent
LS Sedan 4D		CC264	24340	2350	2925	4350	6300
GS Sedan 4D		CC265	26325	2600	3225	4675	6725
w/o Leather				0	0	0	0
Manual Trans				**(250)**	**(250)**	**(335)**	**(335)**

LEGEND—V6—Equipment Schedule 1
W.B. 111.4", 114.6" (4D); 3.2 Liter.

Body	Type	VIN	List	Fair	Good	Good	Excellent
Sedan 4D		KA763	28575	3325	4025	5600	7825
L Sedan 4D		KA765	30975	3900	4650	6325	8700

1992 ACURA

Body	Type	VIN	List	Trade-In Fair	Good	Pvt-Party Good	Retail Excellent
L Coupe 2D		KA825	32425	4050	4825	6550	8975
LS Sedan 4D		KA767	35475	4125	4900	6625	9075
LS Coupe 2D		KA827	36825	4275	5075	6825	9300
Manual Trans (Sedan)		1,5		**(250)**	**(250)**	**(335)**	**(335)**
NSX—V6—Equipment Schedule 2							
W.B. 99.6"; 3.0 Liter.							
Sport Coupe 2D		NA126	67600	16950	19050	23300	29400

1993 ACURA — JH4(DA944)-P-#

INTEGRA—4-Cyl.—Equipment Schedule 3
W.B. 100.4", 102.4" (4D); 1.7 Liter, 1.8 Liter.

Body	Type	VIN	List	Trade-In Fair	Good	Pvt-Party Good	Retail Excellent
RS Sedan 2D		DA944	14045	1550	2075	3300	5075
RS Sedan 4D		DB164	14970	1500	1975	3225	4950
LS Sedan 2D		DA945	15950	1775	2300	3600	5400
LS Sedan 4D		DB165	16700	1750	2275	3550	5325
LS Special Sedan 2D		DA948	17450	1775	2300	3600	5400
GS Sedan 2D		DA946	18120	1975	2525	3850	5700
GS Sedan 4D		DB166	18660	1975	2525	3850	5700
GS-R Sedan 2D		DB238	18625	2100	2675	4000	5875
Manual Trans (Sedan)		3,5		**(150)**	**(150)**	**(200)**	**(200)**
VIGOR—5-Cyl.—Equipment Schedule 1							
W.B. 110.4"; 2.5 Liter.							
LS Sedan 4D		CC264	25380	2775	3400	4900	7000
GS Sedan 4D		CC266	27865	3075	3725	5275	7475
w/o Leather		4		0	0	0	0
Manual Trans		5		**(300)**	**(300)**	**(400)**	**(400)**
LEGEND—V6—Equipment Schedule 1							
W.B. 111.4", 114.6" (4D); 3.2 Liter.							
Sedan 4D		KA763	30365	3900	4650	6325	8700
LS Sedan 4D		KA766	33865	4550	5375	7150	9700
L Coupe 2D		KA826	35915	4775	5625	7450	10050
LS Sedan 4D		KA767	36865	4800	5650	7500	10100
LS Coupe 2D		KA827	39315	5050	5900	7750	10400
Manual Trans (Sedan)		1,5		**(300)**	**(300)**	**(400)**	**(400)**
NSX—V6—Equipment Schedule 2							
W.B. 99.6"; 3.0 Liter.							
Sport Coupe 2D		NA126	73250	18575	20825	25200	31600

1994 ACURA — JH4(DB764)-R-#

INTEGRA—4-Cyl.—Equipment Schedule 3
W.B. 101.2", 103.1" (4D); 1.8 Liter.

Body	Type	VIN	List	Trade-In Fair	Good	Pvt-Party Good	Retail Excellent
RS Sedan 4D		DB764	16695	2000	2550	3650	5250
RS Sport Coupe 2D		DC444	15935	2100	2650	3750	5375
LS Sedan 4D		DB765	18565	2275	2850	4000	5675
LS Sport Coupe 2D		DC445	18565	2325	2900	4075	5750
GS-R Sedan 4D		DB858	20345	2650	3250	4475	6225
GS-R Sport Coupe 2D		DC238	20015	2700	3300	4525	6300
Manual Trans (Sedan)		3,5		**(175)**	**(175)**	**(235)**	**(235)**
VIGOR—5-Cyl.—Equipment Schedule 1							
W.B. 110.4"; 2.5 Liter.							
LS Sedan 4D		CC264	27485	3250	3900	5500	7700
GS Sedan 4D		CC266	29485	3575	4275	5900	8175
w/o Leather		4		0	0	0	0
Manual Trans		5		**(350)**	**(350)**	**(465)**	**(465)**
LEGEND—V6—Equipment Schedule 1							
W.B. 111.4", 114.6" (4D); 3.2 Liter.							
L Sedan 4D		KA766	36485	5225	6125	8000	10650
L Coupe 2D		KA826	38085	5550	6450	8375	11150
LS Sedan 4D		KA767	38985	5525	6425	8375	11150
LS Coupe 2D		KA827	41885	5825	6800	8750	11550
GS Sedan 4D		KA768	41085	5775	6725	8675	11450
Manual Trans		1,5		**(350)**	**(350)**	**(465)**	**(465)**
NSX—V6—Equipment Schedule 2							
W.B. 99.6"; 3.0 Liter.							
Sport Coupe 2D		NA126	77200	20350	22750	27300	33900

1995 ACURA — JH4(DB764)-S-#

INTEGRA—4-Cyl.—Equipment Schedule 3
W.B. 101.2", 103.1" (4D); 1.8 Liter.

Body	Type	VIN	List	Trade-In Fair	Good	Pvt-Party Good	Retail Excellent
RS Sedan 4D		DB764	17390	2450	3050	4200	5875
RS Sport Coupe 2D		DC444	16630	2550	3150	4300	6000
LS Sedan 4D		DB765	20110	2750	3375	4550	6300

1995 ACURA

Body	Type	VIN	List	Trade-In Fair	Trade-In Good	Pvt-Party Good	Retail Excellent
	LS Sport Coupe 2D	DC445	19310	2825	3450	4650	6425
	Special Ed Sedan 4D	DB766	21610	2775	3400	4575	6325
	Special Ed Coupe 2D	DC446	21060	2875	3525	4725	6500
	GS-R Sedan 4D	DB858	21100	3150	3825	5075	6900
	GS-R Sport Coupe 2D	DC238	20770	3250	3900	5175	7025
	Manual Trans (Sedan)	3,5		**(200)**	**(200)**	**(265)**	**(265)**

TL—5-Cyl.—Equipment Schedule 1
W.B. 111.8"; 2.5 Liter.

Body	Type	VIN	List	Trade-In Fair	Trade-In Good	Pvt-Party Good	Retail Excellent
	2.5 Sedan 4D	UA265	30370	4250	5050	6825	9350

LEGEND—V6—Equipment Schedule 1
W.B. 111.4", 114.6" (4D); 3.2 Liter.

Body	Type	VIN	List	Trade-In Fair	Trade-In Good	Pvt-Party Good	Retail Excellent
	L Sedan 4D	KA766	38220	5975	6925	8925	11750
	L Coupe 2D	KA826	39820	6375	7375	9400	12350
	SE Sedan 4D	KA769	39320	6125	7100	9100	11950
	LS Sedan 4D	KA767	40120	6300	7325	9325	12250
	LS Coupe 2D	KA827	43620	6675	7725	9800	12750
	GS Sedan 4D	KA768	42420	6575	7600	9650	12600
	Manual Trans (Sedan)	1,5		**(400)**	**(400)**	**(535)**	**(535)**

NSX-T—V6—Equipment Schedule 2
W.B. 99.6"; 3.0 Liter.

Body	Type	VIN	List	Trade-In Fair	Trade-In Good	Pvt-Party Good	Retail Excellent
	T-Targa 2D	NA128	85225	24475	27350	32400	39800

1996 ACURA — JH4(DB764)—T–#

INTEGRA—4-Cyl.—Equipment Schedule 3
W.B. 101.2", 103.1" (4D); 1.8 Liter.

Body	Type	VIN	List	Trade-In Fair	Trade-In Good	Pvt-Party Good	Retail Excellent
	RS Sedan 4D	DB764	18080	2975	3625	4825	6600
	RS Sport Coupe 2D	DC444	17320	3050	3700	4925	6725
	LS Sedan 4D	DB765	20870	3300	3975	5225	7050
	LS Sport Coupe 2D	DC445	20070	3375	4075	5325	7175
	Special Ed Sedan 4D	DB766	22370	3300	4000	5225	7075
	Special Ed Coupe 2D	DC446	21820	3425	4125	5375	7225
	GS-R Sedan 4D	DB858	21820	3725	4450	5725	7675
	GS-R Sport Coupe 2D	DC238	21520	3825	4550	5875	7825
	Manual Trans (Sedan)	3,5		**(200)**	**(200)**	**(265)**	**(265)**

TL—5-Cyl.—Equipment Schedule 1
W.B. 111.8"; 2.5 Liter.

Body	Type	VIN	List	Trade-In Fair	Trade-In Good	Pvt-Party Good	Retail Excellent
	2.5 Sedan 4D	UA265	30370	4875	5700	7600	10250

TL—V6—Equipment Schedule 1
W.B. 111.8"; 3.2 Liter.

Body	Type	VIN	List	Trade-In Fair	Trade-In Good	Pvt-Party Good	Retail Excellent
	3.2 Sedan 4D	UA365	35920	5625	6525	8550	11400

RL—V6—Equipment Schedule 1
W.B. 114.6"; 3.5 Liter.

Body	Type	VIN	List	Trade-In Fair	Trade-In Good	Pvt-Party Good	Retail Excellent
	3.5 Sedan 4D	KA964	41435	6775	7800	9900	12850
	Traction Control	5,6		**225**	**225**	**300**	**300**

NSX—V6—Equipment Schedule 2
W.B. 99.6"; 3.0 Liter.

Body	Type	VIN	List	Trade-In Fair	Trade-In Good	Pvt-Party Good	Retail Excellent
	Sport Coupe 2D	NA126	83725	24200	27075	32000	39200
	T-Targa 2D	NA128	87725	26600	29750	34800	42500

1997 ACURA — JH4(DC444)—V–#

INTEGRA—4-Cyl.—Equipment Schedule 3
W.B. 101.2", 103.1" (4D); 1.8 Liter.

Body	Type	VIN	List	Trade-In Fair	Trade-In Good	Pvt-Party Good	Retail Excellent
	RS Sport Coupe 2D	DC444	17335	3650	4375	5650	7500
	LS Sedan 4D	DB765	20885	3900	4650	5950	7900
	LS Sport Coupe 2D	DC445	20085	4000	4750	6075	8025
	GS Sedan 4D	DB766	22385	4225	5025	6325	8350
	GS Sport Coupe 2D	DC446	21835	4325	5100	6450	8475
	GS-R Sedan 4D	DB858	21835	4350	5125	6500	8525
	GS-R Sport Coupe 2D	DC238	21535	4475	5275	6650	8700
	Type R Sport Cpe 2D	DC238	23535	****	****	****	9750
	Manual Trans (Sedan)	3,5		**(200)**	**(200)**	**(265)**	**(265)**

CL—4-Cyl.—Equipment Schedule 1
W.B. 106.9"; 2.2 Liter.

Body	Type	VIN	List	Trade-In Fair	Trade-In Good	Pvt-Party Good	Retail Excellent
	2.2 Coupe 2D	YA125	24395	4575	5400	7250	9850
	Manual Trans			**(425)**	**(425)**	**(565)**	**(565)**

CL—V6—Equipment Schedule 1
W.B. 106.9"; 3.0 Liter.

Body	Type	VIN	List	Trade-In Fair	Trade-In Good	Pvt-Party Good	Retail Excellent
	3.0 Coupe 2D	YA225	26895	5150	6025	7950	10650

TL—5-Cyl.—Equipment Schedule 1
W.B. 111.8"; 2.5 Liter.

Body	Type	VIN	List	Trade-In Fair	Trade-In Good	Pvt-Party Good	Retail Excellent
	2.5 Sedan 4D	UA265	30935	5575	6475	8500	11350

TL—V6—Equipment Schedule 1
W.B. 111.8"; 3.2 Liter.

1997 ACURA

Body	Type	VIN	List	Trade-In Fair	Trade-In Good	Pvt-Party Good	Retail Excellent
3.2 Sedan 4D		UA365	33385	6350	7350	9450	12500
	Traction Control			275	275	365	365
RL—V6—Equipment Schedule 1							
W.B. 114.6"; 3.5 Liter.							
3.5 Sedan 4D		KA964	41435	7600	8725	10950	14100
	Traction Control			275	275	365	365
NSX—V6—Equipment Schedule 2							
W.B. 99.6"; 3.0 Liter, 3.2 Liter.							
Sport Coupe 2D		NA123	84725	26400	29575	34600	42100
T-Targa 2D		NA126	88725	29000	32350	37600	45600

1998 ACURA — JH4(DC444)–W–#

Body	Type	VIN	List	Trade-In Fair	Trade-In Good	Pvt-Party Good	Retail Excellent
INTEGRA—4-Cyl.—Equipment Schedule 3							
W.B. 101.2", 103.1" (4D); 1.8 Liter.							
RS Sport Coupe 2D		DC444	17435	4325	5100	6400	8350
LS Sedan 4D		DB765	21235	4600	5450	6750	8725
LS Sport Coupe 2D		DC445	20435	4725	5550	6875	8875
GS Sedan 4D		DB766	22635	4950	5800	7150	9200
GS Sport Coupe 2D		DC446	22085	5050	5925	7275	9325
GS-R Sedan 4D		DB858	22035	5100	5975	7325	9375
GS-R Sport Coupe 2D		DC238	21735	5200	6100	7475	9550
Type R Sport Cpe 2D		DC231	23500	****	****	****	10650
	Manual Trans (Sedan)	3,5		(200)	(200)	(265)	(265)
CL—4-Cyl.—Equipment Schedule 1							
W.B. 106.9"; 2.3 Liter.							
2.3 Coupe 2D		YA325	24595	5350	6250	8100	10800
	Manual Trans	1		(450)	(450)	(600)	(600)
CL—V6—Equipment Schedule 1							
W.B. 106.9"; 3.0 Liter.							
3.0 Coupe 2D		YA225	27095	5975	6925	8875	11650
TL—5-Cyl.—Equipment Schedule 1							
W.B. 111.8"; 2.5 Liter.							
2.5 Sedan 4D		UA265	31135	6400	7425	9475	12450
TL—V6—Equipment Schedule 1							
W.B. 111.8"; 3.2 Liter.							
3.2 Sedan 4D		UA364	33585	7275	8350	10500	13600
	Traction Control			300	300	400	400
RL—V6—Equipment Schedule 1							
W.B. 114.6"; 3.5 Liter.							
3.5 Sedan 4D		KA964	41635	8650	9900	12100	15300
	Traction Control			300	300	400	400
NSX—V6—Equipment Schedule 2							
W.B. 99.6"; 3.0 Liter, 3.2 Liter.							
Sport Coupe 2D		NA123	84725	29100	32450	37500	45200
T-Targa 2D		NA126	88725	31775	35425	40700	48900

1999 ACURA — (JH4or19U)(DB765)–X–#

Body	Type	VIN	List	Trade-In Fair	Trade-In Good	Pvt-Party Good	Retail Excellent
INTEGRA—4-Cyl.—Equipment Schedule 3							
W.B. 101.2", 103.1" (4D); 1.8 Liter.							
LS Sedan 4D		DB765	21255	5425	6325	7675	9800
LS Sport Coupe 2D		DC445	20455	5550	6450	7825	9925
GS Sedan 4D		DB766	22655	5750	6700	8100	10200
GS Sport Coupe 2D		DC446	22105	5875	6850	8225	10400
GS-R Sedan 4D		DB858	22855	5950	6900	8325	10500
GS-R Sport Coupe 2D		DC238	22555	6100	7075	8500	10700
	Manual Trans (Sedan)	3,5		(225)	(225)	(300)	(300)
CL—4-Cyl.—Equipment Schedule 1							
W.B. 106.9"; 2.3 Liter.							
2.3 Coupe 2D		YA325	24355	6325	7350	9325	12250
	Manual Trans			(500)	(500)	(665)	(665)
CL—V6—Equipment Schedule 1							
W.B. 106.9"; 3.0 Liter.							
3.0 Coupe 2D		YA225	26605	7075	8150	10200	13250
TL—V6—Equipment Schedule 1							
W.B. 108.1"; 3.2 Liter.							
3.2 Sedan 4D		UA564	28405	8875	10175	12100	15050
RL—V6—Equipment Schedule 1							
W.B. 114.6"; 3.5 Liter.							
3.5 Sedan 4D		KA964	42355	10125	11525	13800	17300
NSX—V6—Equipment Schedule 2							
W.B. 99.6"; 3.0 Liter, 3.2 Liter.							
Sport Coupe 2D		NA123	84745	33225	37050	42300	50500
T-Targa 2D		NA126	88745	36375	40500	46000	54700

2000 ACURA

Body	Type	VIN	List	Trade-In Fair	Good	Pvt-Party Good	Retail Excellent

2000 ACURA — (JH4or19U)(DB765)-Y-#

INTEGRA—4-Cyl.—Equipment Schedule 3
W.B. 101.2", 103.1" (4D); 1.8 Liter.

LS Sedan 4D		DB765	21355	6325	7350	8750	11000
LS Sport Coupe 2D		DC445	20555	6475	7500	8925	11200
GS Sedan 4D		DB766	22755	6675	7700	9150	11400
GS Sport Coupe 2D		DC446	22205	6825	7850	9300	11600
GS-R Sedan 4D		DB859	22955	6925	8000	9450	11750
GS-R Sport Coupe 2D		DC239	22655	7100	8175	9650	12000
Type R Sport Cpe 2D		DC231	24805	****	****	****	13450
Manual Trans (Sedan)		3,5		(250)	(250)	(335)	(335)

TL—V6—Equipment Schedule 1
W.B. 108.1"; 3.2 Liter.

3.2 Sedan 4D		UA566	28855	10375	11800	13800	16950

RL—V6—Equipment Schedule 1
W.B. 114.6"; 3.5 Liter.

3.5 Sedan 4D		KA965	42455	12475	14100	16750	20700

NSX—V6—Equipment Schedule 2
W.B. 99.6"; 3.0 Liter, 3.2 Liter.

Sport Coupe 2D		NA123	84745	37525	41850	47300	56100
T-Targa 2D		NA126	88745	41100	45700	51500	60700

2001 ACURA — JH4or19U(DB765)-1-#

INTEGRA—4-Cyl.—Equipment Schedule 3
W.B. 101.2", 103.1" (4D); 1.8 Liter.

LS Sedan 4D		DB765	21480	7400	8500	9975	12350
LS Sport Coupe 2D		DC445	20680	7550	8700	10200	12600
GS Sedan 4D		DB766	22880	7700	8850	10350	12750
GS Sport Coupe 2D		DC446	22330	7900	9075	10600	13000
GS-R Sedan 4D		DB859	23080	8075	9250	10750	13200
GS-R Sport Coupe 2D		DC239	22780	8225	9425	11000	13450
Type R Sport Cpe 2D		DC231	24930	****	****	****	15000
Manual Trans (Sedan)		3,5		(275)	(275)	(365)	(365)

CL—V6—Equipment Schedule 1
W.B. 106.9"; 3.2 Liter.

3.2 Coupe 2D		YA424	28460	10275	11675	14050	17600
3.2 Type S Coupe 2D		YA426	30810	11575	13100	15600	19300

TL—V6—Equipment Schedule 1
W.B. 108.1"; 3.2 Liter.

3.2 Sedan 4D		UA566	29030	12050	13675	15800	19150

RL—V6—Equipment Schedule 1
W.B. 114.6"; 3.5 Liter.

3.5 Sedan 4D		KA965	42630	14600	16475	19200	23500

NSX—V6—Equipment Schedule 2
W.B. 99.6"; 3.0 Liter, 3.2 Liter.

Sport Coupe 2D		NA123	84845	42325	47125	52800	62000
T-Targa 2D		NA126	88845	46275	51450	57400	67100

2002 ACURA — JH4or19U(DC548)-2-#

RSX—4-Cyl.—Equipment Schedule 3
W.B. 101.2"; 2.0 Liter.

Sport Coupe 2D		DC548	21330	10175	11575	13200	15850
Type S Sport Cpe 2D		DC530	23650	11425	12950	14650	17400

CL—V6—Equipment Schedule 1
W.B. 106.9"; 3.2 Liter.

3.2 Coupe 2D		YA424	28510	11800	13400	15900	19700
3.2 Type S Coupe 2D		YA426	30860	13300	15025	17600	21600

TL—V6—Equipment Schedule 1
W.B. 108.1"; 3.2 Liter.

3.2 Sedan 4D		UA566	29360	13875	15700	17850	21400
3.2 Type S Sedan 4D		UA568	31710	14925	16800	19050	22800

RL—V6—Equipment Schedule 1
W.B. 114.6"; 3.5 Liter.

3.5 Sedan 4D		KA965	43630	16850	18950	21800	26300

NSX-T—V6—Equipment Schedule 2
W.B. 99.6"; 3.0 Liter, 3.2 Liter.

Targa 2D		NA126	89745	47900	53275	59100	68800

2003 ACURA — JH4or19U(DC548)-3-#

RSX—4-Cyl.—Equipment Schedule 3
W.B. 101.2"; 2.0 Liter.

2003 ACURA

Body	Type	VIN	List	Trade-In Fair	Trade-In Good	Pvt-Party Good	Retail Excellent
Sport Coupe 2D		DC548	21375	**11675**	**13200**	**14750**	**17400**
Type S Sport Cpe 2D		DC530	23770	**13050**	**14775**	**16350**	**19200**
CL—V6—Equipment Schedule 1							
W.B. 106.9"; 3.2 Liter.							
3.2 Coupe 2D		YA424	28700	**13525**	**15275**	**17800**	**21700**
3.2 Type S Coupe 2D		YA426	31050	**15075**	**17000**	**19700**	**23800**
TL—V6—Equipment Schedule 1							
W.B. 108.1"; 3.2 Liter.							
3.2 Sedan 4D		UA566	29480	**15900**	**17850**	**20100**	**23800**
3.2 Type S Sedan 4D		UA568	31830	**16950**	**19050**	**21400**	**25200**
RL—V6—Equipment Schedule 1							
W.B. 114.6"; 3.5 Liter.							
3.5 Sedan 4D		KA965	43650	**19300**	**21600**	**24600**	**29400**
NSX-T—V6—Equipment Schedule 2							
W.B. 99.6"; 3.0 Liter, 3.2 Liter.							
Targa 2D		NA126	89765	**53275**	**59125**	**65100**	**75200**

2004 ACURA — JH4or19U(DC548)-4-#

Body	Type	VIN	List	Trade-In Fair	Trade-In Good	Pvt-Party Good	Retail Excellent
RSX—4-Cyl.—Equipment Schedule 3							
W.B. 101.2"; 2.0 Liter.							
Sport Coupe 2D		DC548	21470	**13500**	**15225**	**16800**	**19600**
Type S Sport Cpe 2D		DC530	23865	**15025**	**16950**	**18600**	**21600**
TL—V6—Equipment Schedule 1							
W.B. 107.9"; 3.2 Liter.							
3.2 Sedan 4D		UA566	33195	**22175**	**24775**	**27300**	**31600**
TSX—4-Cyl.—Equipment Schedule 3							
W.B. 105.1"; 2.4 Liter.							
Sedan 4D		CL958	26990	**17100**	**19200**	**21400**	**25100**
RL—V6—Equipment Schedule 1							
W.B. 114.6"; 3.5 Liter.							
3.5 Sedan 4D		KA965	46100	**21975**	**24575**	**27700**	**32700**
NSX-T—V6—Equipment Schedule 2							
W.B. 99.6"; 3.0 Liter, 3.2 Liter.							
Targa 2D		NA126	89765				

ALFA ROMEO

1990 ALFA ROMEO — ZAR(BA564)-L-#

Body	Type	VIN	List	Trade-In Fair	Trade-In Good	Pvt-Party Good	Retail Excellent
SPIDER—4-Cyl.—Equipment Schedule 6							
W.B. 88.6"; 2.0 Liter.							
Graduate Conv 2D		BA564	18320	**2900**	**3550**	**5050**	**7150**
Veloce Convertible 2D		BC558	22320	**3200**	**3875**	**5425**	**7600**
Quadrifoglio Conv 2D		BC545	24325	**3275**	**3925**	**5525**	**7725**
Hard Top/Soft Top				**100**	**100**	**135**	**135**

1991 ALFA ROMEO — ZAR(BB32G)-M-#

Body	Type	VIN	List	Trade-In Fair	Trade-In Good	Pvt-Party Good	Retail Excellent
SPIDER—4-Cyl.—Equipment Schedule 6							
W.B. 88.6"; 2.0 Liter.							
Convertible 2D		BB32G	22320	**3025**	**3700**	**5300**	**7525**
Veloce Convertible 2D		BB32N	23325	**3325**	**4025**	**5700**	**8050**
Hard Top/Soft Top				**100**	**100**	**135**	**135**
164—V6—Equipment Schedule 3							
W.B. 104.7"; 3.0 Liter.							
Sedan 4D		EA33A	25525	**900**	**1300**	**2400**	**4000**
L Sedan 4D		EA33L	28525	**1025**	**1450**	**2625**	**4275**
S Sedan 4D		EA33E	29875	**1500**	**2000**	**3300**	**5100**

1992 ALFA ROMEO — ZAR(BB32G)-N-#

Body	Type	VIN	List	Trade-In Fair	Trade-In Good	Pvt-Party Good	Retail Excellent
SPIDER—4-Cyl.—Equipment Schedule 6							
W.B. 88.6"; 2.0 Liter.							
Convertible 2D		BB32G	22654	**3625**	**4350**	**6075**	**8500**
Veloce Convertible 2D		BB32N	24704	**3975**	**4725**	**6550**	**9075**
Hard Top/Soft Top				**100**	**100**	**135**	**135**
164—V6—Equipment Schedule 3							
W.B. 104.7"; 3.0 Liter.							
L Sedan 4D		EA33L	29885	**1225**	**1700**	**3000**	**4775**
S Sedan 4D		EA33E	35385	**1825**	**2350**	**3775**	**5700**

Body	Type	VIN	List	Trade-In Fair	Good	Pvt-Party Good	Retail Excellent

1993 ALFA ROMEO — ZAR(BB32G)-P-#

SPIDER—4-Cyl.—Equipment Schedule 6
W.B. 88.6"; 2.0 Liter.

Convertible 2D		BB32G	23174	4300	5075	6925	9525
Veloce Convertible 2D		BB32N	25265	4675	5525	7450	10150
Hard Top/Soft Top				100	100	135	135

164—V6—Equipment Schedule 3
W.B. 104.7"; 3.0 Liter.

L Sedan 4D		EA33L	30635	1500	2025	3400	5325
S Sedan 4D		EA33E	35385	2200	2775	4275	6350

1994 ALFA ROMEO — ZAR(BB32G)-R-#

SPIDER—4-Cyl.—Equipment Schedule 6
W.B. 88.6"; 2.0 Liter.

Convertible 2D		BB32G	24095	5000	5850	7825	10600
Veloce Ce Conv 2D		BB32N	28015	5425	6325	8375	11300
Hard Top/Soft Top				100	100	135	135

164—V6—Equipment Schedule 3
W.B. 104.7"; 3.0 Liter.

LS Sedan 4D		ED33E	35315	2675	3275	4925	7175
Q Sedan 4D		ED33R	38115	2875	3525	5175	7500

1995 ALFA ROMEO — ZAR(ED33E)-S-#

164—V6—Equipment Schedule 3
W.B. 104.7"; 3.0 Liter.

LS Sedan 4D		ED33E	36600	3975	4725	6625	9250
Q Sedan 4D		ED33R	39400	4850	5700	7675	10450

AUDI

1990 AUDI — WAU(EA58A)-L-#

80—4-Cyl.—Equipment Schedule 3
W.B. 100.2"; 2.0 Liter.

Sedan 4D		EA58A	19235	750	1050	1950	3275

AUDI—5-Cyl.—Equipment Schedule 3
W.B. 99.9" (80 & 90 Quattro), 100.2" (90 Sed), 105.6" (100), 105.9" (100 Quattro); 2.3 Liter.

80 Quattro Sedan 4D		FC58A	23135	950	1375	2475	4050
90 Sedan 4D		GC58A	24910	950	1375	2475	4025
90 Quattro 20V Sed 4D		HE58A	27835	1425	1900	3150	4850
100 Sedan 4D		BC544	27235	900	1250	2325	3875
100 Quattro Sedan 4D		CC544	29805	1375	1875	3125	4850

QUATTRO—5-Cyl.—Equipment Schedule 1
W.B. 100.4"; 2.3 Liter.

Coupe 2D		GC58B	30085	2775	3400	4850	6875

200—5-Cyl. Turbo—Equipment Schedule 1
W.B. 105.6", 105.9" (Quattro); 2.2 Liter.

Sedan 4D		FE544	33740	1225	1675	2875	4550
Quattro Sedan 4D		GE544	36140	1925	2450	3800	5675
Quattro Wagon 4D		HE544	37265	2150	2725	4100	6050

QUATTRO—V8—Equipment Schedule 1
W.B. 106.4"; 3.6 Liter.

Sedan 4D		KE544	47785	3325	4025	5650	7900

1991 AUDI — WAU(EC58A)-M-#

AUDI—5-Cyl.—Equipment Schedule 3
W.B. 99.9" (80 & 90 Quattro), 100.3" (80 & 90 Sed), 105.6" (100), 105.9" (100 Quattro); 2.3 Liter.

80 Sedan 4D		EC58A	21400	925	1325	2450	4050
80 Quattro Sedan 4D		FC58A	25165	1100	1550	2775	4500
90 Sedan 4D		GC58A	26045	1100	1550	2775	4475
90 Quattro 20V Sed 4D		HE58A	28935	1700	2225	3550	5400
100 Sedan 4D		BC544	28505	1025	1450	2625	4275
100 Quattro Sedan 4D		CC544	30865	1675	2200	3550	5400
Manual Trans				(100)	(100)	(135)	(135)

QUATTRO—5-Cyl.—Equipment Schedule 1
W.B. 100.4"; 2.3 Liter.

Coupe 2D		GE58B	31345	3300	4000	5550	7725

Body	Type	VIN	List	Trade-In Fair	Trade-In Good	Pvt-Party Good	Retail Excellent
200—5-Cyl. Turbo—Equipment Schedule 1							
W.B. 105.6", 106.1" (Quattro); 2.2 Liter.							
Sedan 4D		FD544	34935	1500	2000	3300	5100
Quattro Sedan 4D		GD544	42755	2300	2875	4350	6350
Quattro Wagon 4D		HD544	42755	2600	3225	4700	6800
QUATTRO—V8—Equipment Schedule 1							
W.B. 106.4": 3.6 Liter.							
Sedan 4D		KE544	50555	3950	4700	6450	8925
Manual Trans				(200)	(200)	(265)	(265)

1992 AUDI — WAU(ED58A)-N-#

Body	Type	VIN	List	Trade-In Fair	Trade-In Good	Pvt-Party Good	Retail Excellent
80—5-Cyl.—Equipment Schedule 3							
W.B. 100.2", 99.9" (Quattro); 2.3 Liter.							
Sedan 4D		ED58A	23055	1025	1475	2700	4400
Quattro Sedan 4D		FD58A	26655	1350	1825	3150	4950
Manual Trans				(125)	(125)	(165)	(165)
100—V6—Equipment Schedule 3							
W.B. 105.8", 106.0" (Quattro); 2.8 Liter.							
Sedan 4D		AK54A	28105	1600	2100	3475	5350
S Sedan 4D		BK54A	30305	1800	2325	3750	5700
CS Sedan 4D		DK54A	33305	2225	2775	4275	6325
CS Quattro Sedan 4D		EK54A	36805	2700	3300	4900	7075
CS Quattro Wagon 4D		FK54A	41205	3350	4050	5725	8075
Manual Trans				(125)	(125)	(165)	(165)
S4—5-Cyl. Turbo—Equipment Schedule 1							
W.B. 106.0"; 2.2 Liter.							
Quattro Sedan 4D		HP54A	44155	4975	5825	7800	10550
QUATTRO—V8—Equipment Schedule 1							
W.B. 106.4": 4.2 Liter.							
Sedan 4D		BW84C	53505	5200	6100	8100	10900

1993 AUDI — WAU(BK58C)-P-#

Body	Type	VIN	List	Trade-In Fair	Trade-In Good	Pvt-Party Good	Retail Excellent
90—V6—Equipment Schedule 3							
W.B. 100.8", 102.2" (Quattro); 2.8 Liter.							
S Sedan 4D		BK58C	26295	1700	2225	3650	5625
CS Sedan 4D		DK58C	29145	1950	2475	3925	5925
CS Quattro Sedan 4D		EK58C	32695	2975	3625	5250	7500
Manual Trans				(150)	(150)	(200)	(200)
100—V6—Equipment Schedule 3							
W.B. 105.8", 106.0" (Quattro); 2.8 Liter.							
Sedan 4D		AK84A	30845	2025	2575	4050	6100
S Sedan 4D		BK84A	33695	2275	2850	4425	6525
CS Sedan 4D		DK84A	38195	2725	3350	5000	7225
CS Quattro Sedan 4D		EK848	41395	3350	4050	5750	8150
CS Quattro Wagon 4D		FK84A	44695	4100	4875	6700	9275
Manual Trans				(150)	(150)	(200)	(200)
S4—5-Cyl. Turbo—Equipment Schedule 1							
W.B. 106.0"; 2.2 Liter.							
Quattro Sedan 4D		HR84A	47295	6025	6975	9150	12200
QUATTRO—V8—Equipment Schedule 1							
W.B. 106.4": 4.2 Liter.							
Sedan 4D		BW84C	58945	6100	7075	9250	12300

1994 AUDI — WAU(BK88C)-R-#

Body	Type	VIN	List	Trade-In Fair	Trade-In Good	Pvt-Party Good	Retail Excellent
90—V6—Equipment Schedule 3							
W.B. 102.8", 102.2" (Quattro); 2.8 Liter.							
S Sedan 4D		BK88C	28265	2100	2700	4225	6350
CS Sedan 4D		DK88C	31215	2375	2950	4525	6725
CS Quattro Sedan 4D		EK88C	34865	3550	4250	6025	8475
Manual Trans				(175)	(175)	(235)	(235)
100—Equipment Schedule 3							
W.B. 105.8", 106.0" (Quattro); 2.8 Liter.							
S Sedan 4D		BK84A	35565	2825	3475	5150	7475
S Wagon 4D		CK84A	38515	3450	4150	5925	8400
CS Sedan 4D		DK84A	41015	3325	4025	5775	8200
CS Quattro Sedan 4D		EK84A	43465	4100	4875	6750	9350
CS Quattro Wagon 4D		FK84A	47465	4925	5775	7775	10550
Manual Trans				(175)	(175)	(235)	(235)
CABRIOLET—V6—Equipment Schedule 1							
W.B. 100.6"; 2.8 Liter.							
Convertible 2D		BL88G	39395	4325	5100	6975	9600

Body	Type	VIN	List	Trade-In Fair	Trade-In Good	Pvt-Party Good	Retail Excellent
S4—5-Cyl. Turbo—Equipment Schedule 1							
W.B. 106.0"; 2.2 Liter.							
Quattro Sedan 4D	HR84A	51615	**7150**	**8250**	**10600**	**13900**
QUATTRO—V-8—Equipment Schedule 1							
W.B. 106.4"; 4.2 Liter.							
Sedan 4D	BW84C	59145	**7075**	**8150**	**10450**	**13750**

1995 AUDI — WAU(BK88C)–S–#

Body	Type	VIN	List	Fair	Good	Good	Excellent
90—V6—Equipment Schedule 3							
W.B. 102.8", 102.2" (Quattro); 2.8 Liter.							
Sedan 4D	BK88C	26115	**2625**	**3250**	**4925**	**7225**
Sport Sedan 4D	DK88C	26515	**2875**	**3525**	**5250**	**7600**
Quattro AWD	C,E	......	**1325**	**1325**	**1765**	**1765**
Manual Trans		......	**(200)**	**(200)**	**(265)**	**(265)**
A6—V6—Equipment Schedule 3							
W.B. 105.8", 108.0" (Quattro); 2.8 Liter.							
Sedan 4D	FA84A	31045	**3625**	**4350**	**6150**	**8650**
Wagon 4D	HA84A	33615	**4325**	**5100**	**7000**	**9650**
Quattro AWD	G,J	......	**1325**	**1325**	**1765**	**1765**
Manual Trans		......	**(200)**	**(200)**	**(265)**	**(265)**
CABRIOLET—V6—Equipment Schedule 1							
W.B. 100.6"; 2.8 Liter.							
Convertible 2D	BL88G	36345	**4975**	**5825**	**7850**	**10650**
S6—5-Cyl. Turbo—Equipment Schedule 1							
W.B. 106.0"; 2.2 Liter.							
Quattro Sedan 4D	KA84A	45715	**8525**	**9750**	**12250**	**15800**
Quattro Wagon 4D	LA84A	48385	**9325**	**10650**	**13250**	**17000**

1996 AUDI — WAU(DA88D)–T–#

Body	Type	VIN	List	Fair	Good	Good	Excellent
A4—V6—Equipment Schedule 3							
W.B. 103.0"; 2.8 Liter.							
Sedan 4D	DA88D	26975	**4650**	**5500**	**7225**	**9700**
Quattro AWD	E	......	**1350**	**1350**	**1800**	**1800**
Manual Trans		......	**(200)**	**(200)**	**(265)**	**(265)**
A6—V6—Equipment Schedule 3							
W.B. 105.8"; 2.8 Liter.							
Sedan 4D	FA84A	32775	**4350**	**5125**	**7075**	**9800**
Wagon 4D	HA84A	34475	**5100**	**5975**	**8000**	**10850**
Quattro AWD	G,J	......	**1350**	**1350**	**1800**	**1800**
CABRIOLET—V6—Equipment Schedule 1							
W.B. 100.6"; 2.8 Liter.							
Convertible 2D	AA88G	37275	**5950**	**6900**	**9125**	**12200**

1997 AUDI — WAU(DA88A)–V–#

Body	Type	VIN	List	Fair	Good	Good	Excellent
A4—V6—Equipment Schedule 3							
W.B. 103.0"; 2.8 Liter.							
Sedan 4D	DA88A	28905	**5500**	**6425**	**8300**	**11000**
Quattro AWD	C,E	......	**1375**	**1375**	**1835**	**1835**
Manual Trans		......	**(200)**	**(200)**	**(265)**	**(265)**
4-Cyl. 1.8L Turbo	B	......	**(975)**	**(975)**	**(1300)**	**(1300)**
A6—V6—Equipment Schedule 3							
W.B. 105.8"; 2.8 Liter.							
Sedan 4D	FA84A	33100	**5175**	**6050**	**8175**	**11150**
Wagon 4D	HA84A	34900	**5950**	**6900**	**9150**	**12250**
Quattro AWD	G,J	......	**1375**	**1375**	**1835**	**1835**
A8—V8—Equipment Schedule 1							
W.B. 113.0"; 3.7 Liter, 4.2 Liter.							
Sedan 4D	AF84D	57400	**9375**	**10700**	**14050**	**18650**
Quattro AWD Sed 4D	AG84D	65000	**11525**	**13050**	**16650**	**21700**
CABRIOLET—V6—Equipment Schedule 1							
W.B. 100.6"; 2.8 Liter.							
Convertible 2D	AA88G	38800	**6925**	**8000**	**10350**	**13750**

1998 AUDI — WAU(DD68D)–W–#

Body	Type	VIN	List	Fair	Good	Good	Excellent
A4—V6—Equipment Schedule 3							
W.B. 103.0"; 2.8 Liter.							
Sedan 4D	DD68D	29965	**6475**	**7500**	**9325**	**12050**
Avant Wagon 4D	FD68D	30965	**6900**	**7975**	**9850**	**12600**
Quattro AWD	G,C,E	......	**1400**	**1400**	**1865**	**1865**
Manual Trans		......	**(200)**	**(200)**	**(265)**	**(265)**
4-Cyl. 1.8L Turbo	B	......	**(1025)**	**(1025)**	**(1365)**	**(1365)**

1998 AUDI

Body	Type	VIN	List	Trade-In Fair	Good	Pvt-Party Good	Retail Excellent
A6—V6—Equipment Schedule 3							
W.B. 105.8", 108.7" (Sed); 2.8 Liter.							
Sedan 4D		AA74A	34250	7275	8375	10250	13050
Wagon 4D		JA84A	38050	8125	9325	11350	14250
Quattro AWD		B,J		1400	1400	1865	1865
A8—V8—Equipment Schedule 1							
W.B. 113.0"; 3.7 Liter, 4.2 Liter.							
Sedan 4D		AF74D	57900	10900	12375	15700	20400
Quattro AWD Sed 4D		BG74D	65500	13250	14975	18550	23600
CABRIOLET—V6—Equipment Schedule 1							
W.B. 100.6"; 2.8 Liter.							
Convertible 2D		AA88G	38800	8075	9250	11650	15100

1999 AUDI — WAU(DD38D)–X–#

Body	Type	VIN	List	Trade-In Fair	Good	Pvt-Party Good	Retail Excellent
A4—V6—Equipment Schedule 3							
W.B. 103.0"; 2.8 Liter.							
Sedan 4D		DD38D	28890	7625	8750	10850	13900
Quattro AWD		C,E		1450	1450	1935	1935
Manual Trans				(225)	(225)	(300)	(300)
4-Cyl. 1.8L Turbo		B		(1175)	(1175)	(1565)	(1565)
A4 AVANT QUATTRO AWD—V6—Equipment Schedule 3							
W.B. 102.6"; 2.8 Liter.							
Wagon 4D		GD38D	31540	8750	10025	12200	15400
Manual Trans				(225)	(225)	(300)	(300)
4-Cyl. 1.8L Turbo		B		(1175)	(1175)	(1565)	(1565)
A6—V6—Equipment Schedule 3							
W.B. 108.7"; 2.8 Liter.							
Sedan 4D		AA24D	34250	8725	9975	12000	15050
Quattro AWD		B		1450	1450	1935	1935
A6 AVANT QUATTRO AWD—V6—Equipment Schedule 3							
W.B. 108.6"; 2.8 Liter.							
Wagon 4D		DA24D	37100	9900	11225	13400	16650
A8—V8—Equipment Schedule 1							
W.B. 113.0"; 3.7 Liter, 4.2 Liter.							
Sedan 4D		AF34D	57900	12725	14400	17950	23000
Quattro AWD Sed 4D		BG34D	65500	15400	17375	21200	26700

2000 AUDI — (WAUorTRU)(AH28D)–Y–#

Body	Type	VIN	List	Trade-In Fair	Good	Pvt-Party Good	Retail Excellent
A4—V6—Equipment Schedule 3							
W.B. 103.0"; 2.8 Liter.							
Sedan 4D		AH28D	30390	9025	10325	12600	16100
Quattro AWD		D		1475	1475	1965	1965
Manual Trans				(250)	(250)	(335)	(335)
4-Cyl. 1.8L Turbo		C		(1325)	(1325)	(1765)	(1765)
A4 AVANT QUATTRO AWD—V6—Equipment Schedule 3							
W.B. 102.6"; 2.8 Liter.							
Wagon 4D		KH28D	33140	10275	11700	14150	17750
Manual Trans				(250)	(250)	(335)	(335)
4-Cyl. 1.8L Turbo		C		(1325)	(1325)	(1765)	(1765)
S4 QUATTRO AWD—V6 Turbo—Equipment Schedule 3							
W.B. 102.6"; 2.7 Liter.							
2.7T Sedan 4D		DD68D	39625	14025	15800	18550	22700
A6—V6—Equipment Schedule 3							
W.B. 108.7"; 2.8 Liter.							
Sedan 4D		BH24B	34475	10375	11800	13950	17350
Quattro AWD		G,J		1475	1475	1965	1965
A6 AVANT QUATTRO AWD—V6—Equipment Schedule 3							
W.B. 108.6"; 2.8 Liter.							
Wagon 4D		LH24B	37425	11700	13250	15550	19100
A6 QUATTRO AWD—V6 Turbo—Equipment Schedule 3							
W.B. 108.7"; 2.7 Liter.							
2.7T Sedan 4D		ED24B	39075	13100	14825	17200	20900
A6 QUATTRO AWD—V8—Equipment Schedule 3							
W.B. 108.6"; 4.2 Liter.							
4.2 Sedan 4D		ZL54B	49425	17525	19675	22400	26800
A8 QUATTRO AWD—V8—Equipment Schedule 1							
W.B. 113.4", 118.5" (L); 4.2 Liter.							
Sedan 4D		FL54D	62525	17850	20075	24100	30000
L Sedan 4D		FL54D	68425	20450	22850	27200	33500
TT—4-Cyl. Turbo—Equipment Schedule 2							
W.B. 95.4", 95.6"; 1.8 Liter							
Coupe 2D		TC28N	31025	9550	10900	13150	16550
Quattro AWD		U		1475	1475	1965	1965

Body	Type	VIN	List	Trade-In Fair	Trade-In Good	Pvt-Party Good	Retail Excellent

2001 AUDI — (WAUorTRU)(AH68D)-1-#

A4—V6—Equipment Schedule 3
W.B. 103.0"; 2.8 Liter.

Sedan 4D		AH68D	30890	**10650**	**12150**	**14750**	**18600**
Quattro AWD		C,E	------	**1500**	**1500**	**2000**	**2000**
Manual Trans			------	**(275)**	**(275)**	**(365)**	**(365)**
4-Cyl. 1.8L Turbo		C	------	**(1475)**	**(1475)**	**(1965)**	**(1965)**

A4 AVANT QUATTRO AWD—V6—Equipment Schedule 3
W.B. 102.6"; 2.8 Liter.

Wagon 4D		KH68D	33640	**12050**	**13675**	**16400**	**20400**
Manual Trans			------	**(275)**	**(275)**	**(365)**	**(365)**
4-Cyl. 1.8L Turbo		C	------	**(1475)**	**(1475)**	**(1965)**	**(1965)**

S4 QUATTRO AWD—V6 Turbo—Equipment Schedule 3
W.B. 102.6"; 2.7 Liter.

2.7T Sedan 4D		RD58D	39450	**16275**	**18325**	**21200**	**25600**
2.7T Avant Wagon 4D		XD68D	41050	**17525**	**19675**	**22700**	**27300**

A6—V6—Equipment Schedule 3
W.B. 108.7"; 2.8 Liter.

Sedan 4D		BH54B	34950	**12325**	**13975**	**16300**	**19950**
Quattro AWD		G,J	------	**1500**	**1500**	**2000**	**2000**

A6 AVANT QUATTRO AWD—V6—Equipment Schedule 3
W.B. 108.6"; 2.8 Liter.

Wagon 4D		LH54B	37900	**13775**	**15550**	**18000**	**21900**

A6 QUATTRO AWD—V6 Turbo—Equipment Schedule 3
W.B. 108.7"; 2.7 Liter.

2.7T Sedan 4D		ED54B	40050	**15300**	**17275**	**19850**	**24000**
Sport Pkg			------	**425**	**425**	**565**	**565**

ALLROAD QUATTRO AWD—V6 Turbo—Equipment Sch 1
W.B. 108.5"; 2.7 Liter.

2.7T Wagon 4D		YP54B	43450	**19000**	**21300**	**24200**	**28700**

A6 QUATTRO AWD—V8—Equipment Schedule 3
W.B. 108.6"; 4.2 Liter.

4.2 Sedan 4D		ZL54B	49950	**20250**	**22650**	**25500**	**30200**
Sport Pkg			------	**425**	**425**	**565**	**565**

A8 QUATTRO AWD—V8—Equipment Schedule 1
W.B. 113.4", 118.5" (L); 4.2 Liter.

Sedan 4D		FL54D	62750	**20725**	**23225**	**27600**	**33900**
L Sedan 4D		ML54D	68450	**23625**	**26400**	**30900**	**37600**

S8 QUATTRO AWD—V8—Equipment Schedule 1
W.B. 113.4"; 4.2 Liter.

Sedan 4D		GU54D	73050	**28225**	**31575**	**36300**	**43700**

TT—4-Cyl. Turbo—Equipment Schedule 2
W.B. 95.4"; 1.8 Liter.

Coupe 2D		SC58N	31750	**11125**	**12625**	**15050**	**18750**
Roadster 2D		TT58N	33750	**12525**	**14150**	**16700**	**20500**
Power Folding Roof			------	**400**	**400**	**535**	**535**
Quattro AWD			------	**1500**	**1500**	**2000**	**2000**

TT QUATTRO AWD—4-Cyl. HO Turbo—Equipment Schedule 2
W.B. 95.4"; 1.8 Liter.

Coupe 2D		WT58N	36650	**13625**	**15400**	**18050**	**22100**
Roadster 2D		UT58N	39450	**15075**	**17000**	**19800**	**24000**

2002 AUDI — (WAUorTRU)(JT58E)-2-#

A4—V6—Equipment Schedule 3
W.B. 104.3"; 3.0 Liter.

Sedan 4D		JT58E	31965	**14075**	**15850**	**18250**	**22000**
Sport Pkg			------	**325**	**325**	**435**	**435**
Quattro AWD		L	------	**1525**	**1525**	**2035**	**2035**
5-Spd Manual Trans			------	**(300)**	**(300)**	**(400)**	**(400)**
6-Spd Manual Trans			------	**0**	**0**	**0**	**0**
4-Cyl. 1.8L Turbo		C	------	**(1625)**	**(1625)**	**(2165)**	**(2165)**

A4 AVANT QUATTRO AWD—V6—Equipment Schedule 3
W.B. 104.3"; 3.0 Liter.

Wagon 4D		VT58E	34715	**15600**	**17625**	**20100**	**24000**
Sport Pkg			------	**325**	**325**	**435**	**435**
5-Spd Manual Trans			------	**(300)**	**(300)**	**(400)**	**(400)**
6-Spd Manual Trans			------	**0**	**0**	**0**	**0**
4-Cyl. 1.8L Turbo		C	------	**(1625)**	**(1625)**	**(2165)**	**(2165)**

S4 QUATTRO AWD—V6 Turbo—Equipment Schedule 3
W.B. 102.6"; 2.7 Liter.

2.7T Sedan 4D		RD68D	39475	**18900**	**21225**	**24300**	**29100**
2.7T Avant Wagon 4D		XD68D	41075	**20250**	**22650**	**25800**	**30700**

Body	Type	VIN	List	Trade-In Fair	Good	Pvt-Party Good	Retail Excellent
A6—V6—Equipment Schedule 3							
W.B. 108.7"; 3.0 Liter.							
Sedan 4D		JT54B	35975	**14500**	**16375**	**18900**	**22900**
Quattro AWD		L		**1525**	**1525**	**2035**	**2035**
A6 AVANT QUATTRO AWD—V6—Equipment Schedule 3							
W.B. 108.6"; 3.0 Liter.							
Wagon 4D		VT54B	38925	**16125**	**18150**	**20700**	**25000**
A6 QUATTRO AWD—V6 Turbo—Equipment Schedule 3							
W.B. 108.7"; 3.0 Liter.							
2.7T Sedan 4D		LD54B	40325	**17850**	**20075**	**22800**	**27200**
Sport Pkg				**450**	**450**	**600**	**600**
ALLROAD QUATTRO AWD—V6 Turbo—Equipment Sch 1							
W.B. 108.5"; 2.7 Liter.							
2.7T Wagon 4D		YD54B	43325	**21700**	**24375**	**27400**	**32300**
A6 QUATTRO AWD—V8—Equipment Schedule 3							
W.B. 108.6"; 4.2 Liter.							
4.2 Sedan 4D		ML54B	50225	**23225**	**26025**	**29000**	**34100**
Sport Pkg				**450**	**450**	**600**	**600**
S6 AVANT QUATTRO AWD—V8—Equipment Schedule 1							
W.B. 108.6"; 4.2 Liter.							
Wagon 4D		XU54B	61375	**27650**	**30900**	**34200**	**39800**
A8 QUATTRO AWD—V8—Equipment Schedule 1							
W.B. 113.4", 118.5" (L); 4.2 Liter.							
Sedan 4D		FL44D	62775	**24000**	**26775**	**31400**	**38300**
L Sedan 4D		ML44D	67775	**27075**	**30250**	**35000**	**42300**
S8 QUATTRO AWD—V8—Equipment Schedule 1							
W.B. 113.4"; 4.2 Liter.							
Sedan 4D		GU44D	74775	**32150**	**35800**	**40900**	**48800**
TT—4-Cyl. Turbo—Equipment Schedule 2							
W.B. 95.4"; 1.8 Liter.							
Coupe 2D		SC28N	31775	**13150**	**14875**	**17500**	**21600**
Roadster 2D		TC28N	33775	**14700**	**16600**	**19400**	**23600**
Power Folding Roof				**400**	**400**	**535**	**535**
TT QUATTRO AWD—4-Cyl. Turbo—Equipment Schedule 2							
W.B. 95.4"; 1.8 Liter.							
180 Coupe 2D		WX28N	33595	**14500**	**16375**	**19100**	**23300**
TT QUATTRO AWD—4-Cyl. HO Turbo—Equipment Schedule 2							
W.B. 95.6"; 1.8 Liter.							
225 Coupe 2D		WT28N	36675	**15900**	**17900**	**20700**	**25200**
225 Roadster 2D		UT28N	39475	**17525**	**19675**	**22600**	**27200**
225 ALMS Comm Cpe		WT28N	40245	**18425**	**20725**	**23600**	**28300**
2003 AUDI — (WAU,WUA,WA1orTRU)(JT58E)-3-#							
A4—V6—Equipment Schedule 3							
W.B. 104.3", 104.5" (Cabriolet); 3.0 Liter.							
Sedan 4D		JT58E	32250	**16600**	**18675**	**21200**	**25200**
Cabriolet 2D		AT28H	42160	**24775**	**27550**	**30600**	**35600**
Sport Pkg				**350**	**350**	**465**	**465**
Quattro AWD		L		**1550**	**1550**	**2065**	**2065**
5-Spd Manual Trans				**(300)**	**(300)**	**(400)**	**(400)**
6-Spd Manual Trans				**0**	**0**	**0**	**0**
4-Cyl. 1.8L Turbo		C		**(1775)**	**(1775)**	**(2365)**	**(2365)**
A4 AVANT QUATTRO AWD—V6—Equipment Schedule 3							
W.B. 104.3"; 3.0 Liter.							
Wagon 4D		VT58E	35000	**18250**	**20550**	**23100**	**27400**
Sport Pkg				**350**	**350**	**465**	**465**
5-Spd Manual Trans				**(300)**	**(300)**	**(400)**	**(400)**
6-Spd Manual Trans				**0**	**0**	**0**	**0**
4-Cyl. 1.8L Turbo		C		**(1775)**	**(1775)**	**(2365)**	**(2365)**
A6—V6—Equipment Schedule 3							
W.B. 108.7"; 3.0 Liter.							
Sedan 4D		JT54B	36360	**17100**	**19200**	**22000**	**26300**
Quattro AWD		L		**1550**	**1550**	**2065**	**2065**
A6 AVANT QUATTRO AWD—V6—Equipment Schedule 3							
W.B. 108.6"; 3.0 Liter.							
Wagon 4D		VT54B	39310	**18825**	**21125**	**24000**	**28500**
A6 QUATTRO AWD—V6 Turbo—Equipment Schedule 3							
W.B. 108.7"; 2.7 Liter.							
2.7T Wagon 4D		LD54B	41510	**20725**	**23225**	**26100**	**30900**
ALLROAD QUATTRO AWD—V6 Turbo—Equipment Schedule 1							
W.B. 108.5"; 2.7 Liter.							
2.7T Wagon 4D		YD54B	45110	**24875**	**27850**	**30900**	**36200**

2003 AUDI

Body	Type	VIN	List	Trade-In Fair	Good	Pvt-Party Good	Retail Excellent
A6 QUATTRO AWD—V8—Equipment Schedule 3							
W.B. 108.6"; 4.2 Liter.							
4.2 Sedan 4D		ML54B	48460	**26600**	**29750**	**32900**	**38300**
Sport Pkg				475	475	635	635
S6 AVANT QUATTRO AWD—V8—Equipment Schedule 1							
W.B. 108.6"; 4.2 Liter.							
Wagon 4D		XU54B	61060	**31500**	**35125**	**38500**	**44400**
RS6 QUATTRO AWD—V8 Bi Turbo—Equipment Schedule 1							
W.B. 108.6"; 4.2 Liter.							
Sedan 4D		PV54B	84660				
A8 QUATTRO AWD—V8—Equipment Schedule 1							
W.B. 113.4", 118.5" (L); 4.2 Liter.							
Sedan 4D		FL44D	62860	**27650**	**30900**	**35800**	**43200**
L Sedan 4D		ML44D	67860	**31100**	**34750**	**39700**	**47500**
S8 QUATTRO AWD—V8—Equipment Schedule 1							
W.B. 113.4"; 4.2 Liter.							
Sedan 4D		GU44D	74460	**36575**	**40800**	**46000**	**54300**
TT—4-Cyl. Turbo—Equipment Schedule 2							
W.B. 95.4"; 1.8 Liter.							
Coupe 2D		SC28N	33145	**15700**	**17675**	**20500**	**25000**
Roadster 2D		TC28N	35145	**17375**	**19500**	**22500**	**27100**
Power Folding Roof				400	400	535	535
TT QUATTRO AWD—4-Cyl. HO Turbo—Equipment Schedule 2							
W.B. 95.4"; 1.8 Liter.							
Coupe 2D		WT28N	36845	**18775**	**21025**	**24100**	**28800**
Roadster 2D		UT28N	39645	**20450**	**22950**	**26000**	**31000**

2004 AUDI — (WAU,WA1 or TRU)(JT58E)-4-#

Body	Type	VIN	List	Trade-In Fair	Good	Pvt-Party Good	Retail Excellent
A4—V6—Equipment Schedule 3							
W.B. 104.3", 104.5" (Cabriolet); 3.0 Liter.							
Sedan 4D		JT58E	31840	**19775**	**22175**	**25000**	**29500**
Cabriolet 2D		AT48H	42490	**28600**	**31875**	**34900**	**40300**
Sport Pkg				375	375	500	500
Ultra Sport Pkg				1000	1000	1335	1335
Quattro AWD		L		1575	1575	2100	2100
5-Spd Manual Trans				0	0	0	0
6-Spd Manual Trans				(300)	(300)	(400)	(400)
4-Cyl. 1.8L Turbo		C		(1900)	(1900)	(2535)	(2535)
A4 AVANT QUATTRO AWD—V6—Equipment Schedule 3							
W.B. 104.3"; 3.0 Liter.							
Wagon 4D		VT58E	35480	**21600**	**24200**	**27000**	**31700**
Sport Pkg				375	375	500	500
Ultra Sport Pkg				1000	1000	1335	1335
6-Spd Manual Trans				0	0	0	0
4-Cyl. 1.8L Turbo		C		(1900)	(1900)	(2535)	(2535)
S4 QUATTRO AWD—V8—Equipment Schedule 1							
W.B. 104.3"; 4.2 Liter.							
Sedan 4D		PL58E	47490	**28900**	**32250**	**36300**	**42800**
Cabriolet 2D		RL48H	55720				
S4 AVANT QUATTRO AWD—V8—Equipment Schedule 1							
W.B. 104.3"; 4.2 Liter.							
Wagon 4D		XL68E	48490	**30525**	**33975**	**38100**	**44700**
A6—V6—Equipment Schedule 3							
W.B. 108.7"; 3.0 Liter.							
Sedan 4D		JT54B	36640	**20350**	**22750**	**25800**	**30600**
Quattro AWD		L		1575	1575	2100	2100
A6 AVANT QUATTRO AWD—V6—Equipment Schedule 3							
W.B. 108.6"; 3.0 Liter.							
Wagon 4D		VT54B	40840	**22275**	**24875**	**27900**	**32900**
A6 QUATTRO AWD—V6 Turbo—Equipment Schedule 3							
W.B. 108.7"; 2.7 Liter.							
2.7T Sedan 4D		LD54B	42840	**24200**	**27075**	**30100**	**35300**
2.7T S-Line Sedan 4D		CD64B	43870	**24575**	**27550**	**30600**	**35900**
ALLROAD QUATTRO AWD—V6 Turbo—Equipment Schedule 3							
W.B. 108.5"; 2.7 Liter.							
2.7T Wagon 4D		YD54B	40640	**28500**	**31775**	**33700**	**37800**
ALLROAD QUATTRO AWD—V8—Equipment Schedule 1							
W.B. 108.5"; 4.2 Liter.							
4.2 Wagon 4D		YL64B	47640	**30825**	**34375**	**37600**	**43500**
A8 QUATTRO AWD—V8—Equipment Schedule 3							
W.B. 108.6"; 4.2 Liter.							
4.2 Sedan 4D		ML54B	49690	**30525**	**34075**	**37400**	**43200**
Sport Pkg				500	500	665	665

Body	Type	VIN	List	Trade-In Fair	Good	Pvt-Party Good	Retail Excellent
A8 QUATTRO AWD—V8—Equipment Schedule 1							
W.B. 121.1"; 4.2 Liter.							
L Sedan 4D		ML44E	69190				
TT—4-Cyl. Turbo—Equipment Schedule 2							
W.B. 95.4"; 1.8 Liter.							
Coupe 2D		SC28N	33940	**19500**	**21900**	**25200**	**30300**
Roadster 2D		TC28N	35940	**21300**	**23900**	**27300**	**32500**
Power Folding Roof				400	400	535	535
TT QUATTRO AWD—4-Cyl. HO Turbo—Equipment Schedule 2							
W.B. 95.6"; 1.8 Liter.							
Coupe 2D		WT28N	37390	**22850**	**25525**	**28900**	**34400**
Roadster 2D		UT28N	40190	**24575**	**27550**	**31000**	**36600**
TT QUATTRO AWD—V6—Equipment Schedule 2							
W.B. 95.6"; 3.2 Liter.							
Coupe 2D		WF28N	40590				
Roadster 2D		UF28N	43590				

BMW

1990 BMW — WB(AorS)(AK031)–L–#

Body	Type	VIN	List	Trade-In Fair	Good	Pvt-Party Good	Retail Excellent
3 SERIES—6-Cyl.—Equipment Schedule 1							
W.B. 101.2"; 2.5 Liter.							
325i Sedan 2D		AA231	25695	**1325**	**1800**	**3125**	**4925**
325i Sedan 4D		AD231	26495	**1475**	**1950**	**3300**	**5150**
325is Sedan 2D		AA231	29995	**1825**	**2350**	**3800**	**5750**
325iX 4WD Sedan 2D		AB031	30995	**2200**	**2775**	**4250**	**6300**
325iX 4WD Sedan 4D		AE031	31795	**2275**	**2850**	**4350**	**6400**
325i Convertible 2D		BB231	34895	**2350**	**2925**	**4450**	**6550**
M3—4-Cyl.—Equipment Schedule 1							
W.B. 101.0"; 2.3 Liter.							
Sedan 2D		AK031	35295	**5200**	**6100**	**8000**	**10700**
5 SERIES—6-Cyl.—Equipment Schedule 1							
W.B. 108.7"; 2.5 Liter, 3.5 Liter.							
525i Sedan 4D		HC231	34245	**2775**	**3400**	**5025**	**7225**
535i Sedan 4D		HD231	42495	**3425**	**4150**	**5875**	**8275**
Manual Trans				**(350)**	**(350)**	**(465)**	**(465)**
7 SERIES—6-Cyl.—Equipment Schedule 1							
W.B. 111.5", 116.0" (iL); 3.5 Liter.							
735i Sedan 4D		GB431	49995	**3175**	**3850**	**5525**	**7875**
735iL Sedan 4D		GC431	53995	**3550**	**4250**	**6025**	**8475**
Manual Trans				**(350)**	**(350)**	**(465)**	**(465)**
7 SERIES—V12—Equipment Schedule 1							
W.B. 116.0"; 5.0 Liter.							
750iL Sedan 4D		GC831	71845	**3850**	**4575**	**6375**	**8900**

1991 BMW — WB(AorS)(AJ931)–M–#

Body	Type	VIN	List	Trade-In Fair	Good	Pvt-Party Good	Retail Excellent
3 SERIES—4-Cyl.—Equipment Schedule 1							
W.B. 101.0" (M3), 101.2"; 1.8 Liter, 2.3 Liter.							
318i Sedan 4D		AJ931	20275	**950**	**1350**	**2650**	**4425**
318is Sedan 2D		AF931	21875	**1000**	**1450**	**2725**	**4525**
318i Convertible 2D		BA731	28875	**1550**	**2075**	**3500**	**5450**
M3 Sedan 2D		AK031	36275	**6000**	**6950**	**9075**	**12050**
3 SERIES—6-Cyl.—Equipment Schedule 1							
W.B. 101.2"; 2.5 Liter.							
325i Sedan 2D		AA231	26700	**1550**	**2075**	**3500**	**5450**
325i Sedan 4D		AD231	27500	**1725**	**2250**	**3725**	**5700**
325iX 4WD Sedan 2D		AB031	32200	**2575**	**3200**	**4800**	**7025**
325iX 4WD Sedan 4D		AE031	33000	**2675**	**3275**	**4925**	**7175**
325i Convertible 2D		BB231	35650	**2725**	**3350**	**5025**	**7300**
5 SERIES—6-Cyl.—Equipment Schedule 1							
W.B. 108.7"; 2.5 Liter, 3.5 Liter, 3.6 Liter.							
525i Sedan 4D		HC231	35600	**3250**	**3900**	**5700**	**8100**
535i Sedan 4D		HD231	43625	**4000**	**4750**	**6650**	**9300**
M5 Sedan 4D		HD931	58450	**6300**	**7300**	**9650**	**12900**
Traction Control				**100**	**100**	**135**	**135**
Manual Trans (Ex M5)				**(375)**	**(375)**	**(500)**	**(500)**
7 SERIES—6-Cyl.—Equipment Schedule 1							
W.B. 111.5", 116.0" (iL); 3.5 Liter.							
735i Sedan 4D		GB431	51925	**3725**	**4450**	**6300**	**8825**
735iL Sedan 4D		GC431	56025	**4150**	**4925**	**6850**	**9525**
Traction Control				**100**	**100**	**135**	**135**

1991 BMW

Body	Type	VIN	List	Trade-In Fair	Good	Pvt-Party Good	Retail Excellent
7 SERIES—V12—Equipment Schedule 1							
W.B. 116.0"; 5.0 Liter.							
750iL Sedan 4D		GC831	75875	**4475**	**5275**	**7275**	**10050**
8 SERIES—V12—Equipment Schedule 1							
W.B. 105.7"; 5.0 Liter.							
850i Sedan 2D		EG231	75100	**10550**	**12050**	**15150**	**19600**
Traction Control				**100**	**100**	**135**	**135**

1992 BMW — WB(AorS)(CA531)–N–#

Body	Type	VIN	List	Trade-In Fair	Good	Pvt-Party Good	Retail Excellent
3 SERIES—4-Cyl.—Equipment Schedule 1							
W.B. 101.2" (Conv), 106.3"; 1.8 Liter.							
318i Sedan 4D		CA531	23275	**1700**	**2225**	**3775**	**5850**
318is Coupe 2D		BE531	23975	**1775**	**2300**	**3850**	**5950**
318i Convertible 2D		BA731	29245	**2475**	**3075**	**4750**	**7025**
w/o Leather				**0**	**0**	**0**	**0**
3 SERIES—6-Cyl.—Equipment Schedule 1							
W.B. 101.2" (Conv), 106.3"; 2.5 Liter.							
325i Sedan 4D		CB431	30265	**2700**	**3300**	**5000**	**7325**
325is Coupe 2D		BF431	30275	**2650**	**3250**	**4950**	**7275**
325i Convertible 2D		BB231	37495	**3850**	**4575**	**6475**	**9100**
Manual Trans (Sedan)				**(325)**	**(325)**	**(435)**	**(435)**
5 SERIES—6-Cyl.—Equipment Schedule 1							
W.B. 108.7"; 2.5 Liter, 3.5 Liter, 3.6 Liter.							
525i Sedan 4D		HD631	37975	**3775**	**4500**	**6375**	**9000**
525i Touring Wagon 4D		HJ631	40175	**3700**	**4425**	**6300**	**8875**
535i Sedan 4D		HD231	45725	**4650**	**5500**	**7525**	**10350**
M5 Sedan 4D		HD931	58600	**7375**	**8475**	**11000**	**14550**
Traction Control				**125**	**125**	**165**	**165**
Manual Trans (Ex M5)				**(425)**	**(425)**	**(565)**	**(565)**
7 SERIES—6-Cyl.—Equipment Schedule 1							
W.B. 111.5", 116.0" (iL); 3.5 Liter.							
735i Sedan 4D		GB431	54665	**4175**	**4950**	**6900**	**9575**
735iL Sedan 4D		GC431	58625	**4650**	**5500**	**7525**	**10350**
Traction Control				**125**	**125**	**165**	**165**
7 SERIES—V12—Equipment Schedule 1							
W.B. 116.0"; 5.0 Liter.							
750iL Sedan 4D		GC831	79875	**5075**	**5950**	**8075**	**11000**
8 SERIES—V12—Equipment Schedule 1							
W.B. 105.7"; 5.0 Liter.							
850i Coupe 2D		EG231	81500	**12250**	**13875**	**17200**	**22000**

1993 BMW — WB(AorS)(CA531)–P–#

Body	Type	VIN	List	Trade-In Fair	Good	Pvt-Party Good	Retail Excellent
3 SERIES—4-Cyl.—Equipment Schedule 1							
W.B. 106.3"; 1.8 Liter.							
318i Sedan 4D		CA531	25420	**2075**	**2625**	**4275**	**6525**
318is Coupe 2D		BE531	26520	**2100**	**2650**	**4300**	**6550**
w/o Leather				**0**	**0**	**0**	**0**
Manual Trans (Sedan)				**(350)**	**(350)**	**(465)**	**(465)**
3 SERIES—6-Cyl.—Equipment Schedule 1							
W.B. 101.2" (Conv), 106.3"; 2.5 Liter.							
325i Sedan 4D		CB431	32055	**3150**	**3800**	**5650**	**8125**
325is Coupe 2D		BF431	32205	**3100**	**3750**	**5575**	**8075**
325iC Convertible 2D		BB131	36725	**4450**	**5225**	**7275**	**10100**
Manual Trans (Sedan)				**(350)**	**(350)**	**(465)**	**(465)**
5 SERIES—6-Cyl.—Equipment Schedule 1							
W.B. 108.7"; 2.5 Liter, 3.4 Liter, 3.6 Liter.							
525i Sedan 4D		HD631	38355	**4400**	**5175**	**7225**	**10050**
525i Touring Wagon 4D		HJ631	41505	**4300**	**5075**	**7075**	**9850**
535i Sedan 4D		HD231	45755	**5375**	**6300**	**8475**	**11500**
M5 Sedan 4D		HD931	63300	**8525**	**9750**	**12450**	**16250**
Traction Control				**150**	**150**	**200**	**200**
Manual Trans (Ex M5)				**(475)**	**(475)**	**(635)**	**(635)**
7 SERIES—V8—Equipment Schedule 1							
W.B. 111.5", 116.0" (iL); 4.0 Liter.							
740i Sedan 4D		GD432	55705	**5375**	**6300**	**8475**	**11500**
740iL Sedan 4D		GD832	59705	**5650**	**6550**	**8950**	**12250**
Traction Control				**150**	**150**	**200**	**200**
7 SERIES—V12—Equipment Schedule 1							
W.B. 116.0"; 5.0 Liter.							
750iL Sedan 4D		GC832	84305	**6425**	**7450**	**9800**	**13100**
8 SERIES—V12—Equipment Schedule 1							
W.B. 105.7"; 5.0 Liter.							
850Ci Coupe 2D		EG232	86400	**13975**	**15800**	**19300**	**24500**

1994 BMW

Body Type	VIN	List	Trade-In Fair	Good	Pvt-Party Good	Retail Excellent
1994 BMW — WB(AorS)(CA632)-R-#						
3 SERIES—4-Cyl.—Equipment Schedule 1						
W.B. 106.3"; 1.8 Liter.						
318i Sedan 4D	CA632	26720	3575	4300	5975	8350
318is Coupe 2D	BE632	27845	3575	4300	5975	8350
318i Convertible 2D	BK632	31945	4750	5600	7475	10100
w/o Leather			0	0	0	0
Hard Top (Conv)			400	400	535	535
Rollover Pkg (Conv)			250	250	335	335
Manual Trans (Sedan)			(375)	(375)	(500)	(500)
3 SERIES—6-Cyl.—Equipment Schedule 1						
W.B. 106.3"; 2.5 Liter.						
325i Sedan 4D	CB432	33350	4750	5600	7475	10100
325is Coupe 2D	BF432	33550	4725	5550	7425	10050
325i Convertible 2D	BJ632	40150	6875	7925	10200	13350
Hard Top (Conv)			400	400	535	535
Rollover Pkg (Conv)			250	250	335	335
Traction Control			175	175	235	235
Manual Trans (Sedan)			(375)	(375)	(500)	(500)
5 SERIES—6-Cyl.—Equipment Schedule 1						
W.B. 108.7"; 2.5 Liter.						
525i Sedan 4D	HD632	39775	5350	6250	8450	11500
525i Touring Wagon 4D	HJ632	41050	5175	6050	8250	11300
Traction Control			175	175	235	235
w/o Premium Pkg			(550)	(550)	(735)	(735)
Manual Trans			(525)	(525)	(700)	(700)
5 SERIES—V8—Equipment Schedule 1						
W.B. 108.7"; 3.0 Liter, 4.0 Liter.						
530i Sedan 4D	HE232	43050	6300	7300	9650	12900
530i Touring Wagon 4D	HK232	46250	6075	7025	9350	12600
540i Sedan 4D	HE632	48950	7200	8275	10750	14250
Traction Control (Sedan)			175	175	235	235
7 SERIES—V8—Equipment Schedule 1						
W.B. 111.5", 116.0" (iL); 4.0 Liter.						
740i Sedan 4D	GD432	57400	6250	7225	9550	12800
740iL Sedan 4D	GD832	61400	6425	7450	10050	13600
Traction Control			175	175	235	235
7 SERIES—V12—Equipment Schedule 1						
W.B. 116.0"; 5.0 Liter.						
750iL Sedan 4D	GC832	87400	7425	8550	11100	14650
8 SERIES—V8—Equipment Schedule 1						
W.B. 105.7"; 4.0 Liter.						
840Ci Coupe 2D	EF632	69850	13875	15700	19150	24200
8 SERIES—V12—Equipment Schedule 1						
W.B. 105.7"; 5.0 Liter, 5.6 Liter.						
850Ci Coupe 2D	EG232	88500	15750	17700	21500	27000
850CSi Coupe 2D	EG932	101500	20925	23425	27900	34600
1995 BMW — WB(AorS)(CG632)-S-#						
3 SERIES—4-Cyl.—Equipment Schedule 1						
W.B. 106.3"; 1.8 Liter.						
318ti H'Back Coupe 2D	CG632	25295	2700	3325	4850	6950
318i Sedan 4D	CA632	27645	4300	5075	6875	9375
318is Coupe 2D	BE632	29690	4275	5075	6850	9350
318i Convertible 2D	BK632	33965	5575	6475	8450	11250
w/o Leather			0	0	0	0
Sport Pkg			275	275	365	365
Hard Top (Conv)			425	425	565	565
Rollover Pkg (Conv)			275	275	365	365
Manual Trans (Sedan)			(400)	(400)	(535)	(535)
3 SERIES—6-Cyl.—Equipment Schedule 1						
W.B. 106.3"; 2.5 Liter.						
325i Sedan 4D	CB432	34120	5575	6475	8450	11250
325is Coupe 2D	BF432	34220	5525	6425	8400	11200
325i Convertible 2D	BJ632	40970	7900	9075	11400	14750
Sport Pkg			275	275	365	365
Hard Top (Conv)			425	425	565	565
Rollover Pkg (Conv)			275	275	365	365
Traction Control			200	200	265	265
Manual Trans (Sedan)			(400)	(400)	(535)	(535)
M3—6-Cyl.—Equipment Schedule 1						
W.B. 106.7"; 3.0 Liter.						

1995 BMW

Body	Type	VIN	List	Trade-In Fair	Trade-In Good	Pvt-Party Good	Retail Excellent
Sedan 2D		BF932	38845	**8100**	**9300**	**11600**	**14950**
5 SERIES—6-Cyl.—Equipment Schedule 1							
W.B. 108.7"; 2.5 Liter.							
525i Sedan 4D		HD632	40195	**6100**	**7075**	**9425**	**12700**
525i Touring Wagon 4D		HJ632	42795	**5925**	**6900**	**9200**	**12450**
Traction Control				**200**	**200**	**265**	**265**
w/o Premium Pkg				**(625)**	**(625)**	**(835)**	**(835)**
Manual Trans				**(575)**	**(575)**	**(765)**	**(765)**
5 SERIES—V8—Equipment Schedule 1							
W.B. 108.7"; 3.0 Liter, 4.0 Liter.							
530i Sedan 4D		HE232	44320	**7100**	**8200**	**10700**	**14200**
530i Touring Wagon 4D		HK232	47520	**6900**	**7975**	**10450**	**13900**
540i Sedan 4D		HE632	48420	**8175**	**9375**	**12000**	**15750**
Traction Control				**200**	**200**	**265**	**265**
7 SERIES—V8—Equipment Schedule 1							
W.B. 115.4", 120.9" (iL); 4.0 Liter.							
740i Sedan 4D		GF632	59370	**8000**	**9175**	**11900**	**15800**
740iL Sedan 4D		GJ632	61470	**8175**	**9375**	**12450**	**16650**
Traction Control				**200**	**200**	**265**	**265**
7 SERIES—V12—Equipment Schedule 1							
W.B. 120.9"; 5.4 Liter.							
750iL Sedan 4D		GK232	89770	**10275**	**11700**	**14800**	**19150**
8 SERIES—V8—Equipment Schedule 1							
W.B. 105.7"; 4.0 Liter.							
840Ci Coupe 2D		EF632	71670	**15600**	**17575**	**21200**	**26500**
8 SERIES—V12—Equipment Schedule 1							
W.B. 105.7"; 5.4 Liter, 5.6 Liter.							
850Ci Coupe 2D		EG432	90150	**17100**	**19200**	**23000**	**28700**
850CSi Coupe 2D		EG932	104650	**23225**	**26025**	**30600**	**37500**
1996 BMW — WBA(CG732)-T-#							
3 SERIES—4-Cyl.—Equipment Schedule 1							
W.B. 106.3"; 1.9 Liter.							
318ti H'Back Coupe 2D		CG732	26180	**3400**	**4100**	**5700**	**7975**
318i Sedan 4D		CD732	30120	**5100**	**5975**	**7875**	**10550**
318is Coupe 2D		BE732	30995	**5075**	**5950**	**7825**	**10500**
318i Convertible 2D		BH732	35745	**6500**	**7500**	**9575**	**12550**
w/o Leather				**0**	**0**	**0**	**0**
Sport Pkg				**300**	**300**	**400**	**400**
Hard Top (Conv)				**450**	**450**	**600**	**600**
Rollover Pkg (Conv)				**300**	**300**	**400**	**400**
Traction Control				**225**	**225**	**300**	**300**
Manual Trans (Sedan)				**(425)**	**(425)**	**(565)**	**(565)**
3 SERIES—6-Cyl.—Equipment Schedule 1							
W.B. 106.3"; 2.8 Liter.							
328i Sedan 4D		CD132	36410	**6500**	**7500**	**9575**	**12550**
328is Coupe 2D		BG132	36500	**6450**	**7475**	**9525**	**12500**
328i Convertible 2D		BK832	42875	**9025**	**10325**	**12700**	**16250**
Sport Pkg				**300**	**300**	**400**	**400**
Hard Top (Conv)				**450**	**450**	**600**	**600**
Rollover Pkg (Conv)				**300**	**300**	**400**	**400**
Traction Control				**225**	**225**	**300**	**300**
Manual Trans (Sedan)				**(425)**	**(425)**	**(565)**	**(565)**
M3—6-Cyl.—Equipment Schedule 1							
W.B. 106.7"; 3.2 Liter.							
Coupe 2D		BG932	41205	**9275**	**10550**	**12950**	**16500**
Z3—4-Cyl.—Equipment Schedule 1							
W.B. 96.3"; 1.9 Liter.							
Roadster 2D		CH732	31445	**5450**	**6350**	**8275**	**11050**
Hard Top				**450**	**450**	**600**	**600**
Traction Control				**225**	**225**	**300**	**300**
7 SERIES—V8—Equipment Schedule 1							
W.B. 120.9"; 4.4 Liter.							
740iL Sedan 4D		GJ832	63060	**9175**	**10475**	**13800**	**18300**
7 SERIES—V12—Equipment Schedule 1							
W.B. 120.9"; 5.4 Liter.							
750iL Sedan 4D		GK232	92630	**11525**	**13050**	**16350**	**21000**
8 SERIES—V8—Equipment Schedule 1							
W.B. 105.7"; 4.4 Liter.							
840Ci Coupe 2D		EF832	76670	**17425**	**19575**	**23300**	**28900**
8 SERIES—V12—Equipment Schedule 1							
W.B. 105.7"; 5.4 Liter.							
850Ci Coupe 2D		EG432	95460	**19300**	**21600**	**25600**	**31600**

1997 BMW

Body	Type	VIN	List	Trade-In Fair	Trade-In Good	Pvt-Party Good	Retail Excellent

1997 BMW — WBA(CG732)-V-#

3 SERIES—4-Cyl.—Equipment Schedule 1
W.B. 106.3"; 1.9 Liter.

318ti H'Back Coupe 2D		CG732	26535	4200	5000	6700	9125
318i Sedan 4D		CC932	30745	6075	7025	9025	11900
318is Coupe 2D		BE732	31645	6000	6950	8975	11850
318i Convertible 2D		BH732	36145	7550	8700	10850	14000
w/o Leather				0	0	0	0
Sport Pkg				325	325	435	435
Hard Top (Conv)				475	475	635	635
Rollover Pkg (Conv)				325	325	435	435
Manual Trans (Sedan)				(425)	(425)	(565)	(565)

3 SERIES—6-Cyl.—Equipment Schedule 1
W.B. 106.3"; 2.8 Liter.

328i Sedan 4D		CD332	36845	7550	8700	10850	14000
328is Coupe 2D		BG132	36935	7500	8650	10800	13950
328i Convertible 2D		BK832	42935	10275	11700	14250	17950
Sport Pkg				325	325	435	435
Hard Top (Conv)				475	475	635	635
Rollover Pkg (Conv)				325	325	435	435
Manual Trans (Sedan)				(425)	(425)	(565)	(565)

M3—6-Cyl.—Equipment Schedule 1
W.B. 106.3"; 3.2 Liter.

Sedan 4D		CD932	45400	11125	12625	15150	19000
Coupe 2D		BG932	44200	10550	12000	14500	18200

Z3—4-Cyl.—Equipment Schedule 1
W.B. 96.3"; 1.9 Liter.

Roadster 2D		CH732	31695	6400	7425	9450	12400
Hard Top				475	475	635	635

Z3—6-Cyl.—Equipment Schedule 1
W.B. 96.3"; 2.8 Liter.

Roadster 2D		CJ332	37445	7850	9025	11250	14400
Hard Top				475	475	635	635

5 SERIES—6-Cyl.—Equipment Schedule 1
W.B. 111.4"; 2.8 Liter.

528i Sedan 4D		DD532	43895	9600	10950	13800	17800
w/o Premium Pkg				(775)	(775)	(1035)	(1035)
Manual Trans				(675)	(675)	(900)	(900)

5 SERIES—V8—Equipment Schedule 1
W.B. 111.4"; 4.4 Liter.

540i Sedan 4D		DE632	50470	12325	13975	17150	21700

7 SERIES—V8—Equipment Schedule 1
W.B. 115.4", 120.9"; 4.4 Liter.

740i Sedan 4D		GF832	61420	10175	11575	14750	19150
740iL Sedan 4D		GJ832	65370	10325	11750	15250	20100

7 SERIES—V12—Equipment Schedule 1
W.B. 120.9"; 5.4 Liter.

750iL Sedan 4D		GK232	93370	12900	14600	18000	22900

8 SERIES—V8—Equipment Schedule 1
W.B. 105.7"; 4.4 Liter.

840Ci Coupe 2D		EF832	77970	19300	21700	25600	31500

8 SERIES—V12—Equipment Schedule 1
W.B. 105.7"; 5.4 Liter.

850Ci Coupe 2D		EG432	96800	21400	24000	28200	34500

1998 BMW — WBA(CG832)-W-#

3 SERIES—4-Cyl.—Equipment Schedule 1
W.B. 106.3"; 1.9 Liter.

318ti Coupe 2D		CG832	26685	5100	5975	7725	10200
318i Sedan 4D		CC032	31045	7125	8225	10200	13000
w/o Leather				0	0	0	0
Sport Pkg				350	350	465	465
Manual Trans (Sedan)				(425)	(425)	(565)	(565)

3 SERIES—6-Cyl.—Equipment Schedule 1
W.B. 106.3"; 2.5 Liter, 2.8 Liter.

323is Coupe 2D		BF832	32370	7325	8425	10350	13250
323i Convertible 2D		BJ832	38995	10275	11700	13900	17300
328i Sedan 4D		CD432	36770	8750	10025	12100	15200
328is Coupe 2D		BG232	36870	8725	9975	12050	15150
328i Convertible 2D		BK832	44495	11750	13300	15700	19300
Sport Pkg				350	350	465	465
Hard Top (Conv)				500	500	665	665

1998 BMW

Body	Type	VIN	List	Trade-In Fair	Trade-In Good	Pvt-Party Good	Retail Excellent
	Rollover Pkg (Conv)	....		350	350	465	465
	Manual Trans (Sedan)	....		(425)	(425)	(565)	(565)

M3—6-Cyl.—Equipment Schedule 1
W.B. 106.7"; 3.2 Liter.

Body	Type	VIN	List	Fair	Good	Good	Excellent
Sedan 4D		CD032	43840	12625	14300	16750	20500
Coupe 2D		BG932	42640	12000	13575	15950	19600
Convertible 2D		BK033	46470	13525	15300	17850	21800
Hard Top (Conv)		....		500	500	665	665

Z3—4-Cyl.—Equipment Schedule 1
W.B. 96.3"; 1.9 Liter.

| Roadster 2D | | CH732 | 32120 | 7525 | 8675 | 10600 | 13550 |
| Hard Top | | .... | | 500 | 500 | 665 | 665 |

Z3—6-Cyl.—Equipment Schedule 1
W.B. 96.3"; 2.8 Liter, 3.2 Liter.

Roadster 2D		CJ332	37445	9050	10325	12450	15600
M Roadster 2D		CK932	42770	11175	12675	15000	18500
Hard Top		....		500	500	665	665

5 SERIES—6-Cyl.—Equipment Schedule 1
W.B. 111.4"; 2.8 Liter.

528i Sedan 4D		DD632	43895	10900	12375	15200	19300
w/o Premium Pkg		....		(800)	(800)	(1065)	(1065)
Sport Pkg		....		625	625	835	835
Manual Trans		5		(725)	(725)	(965)	(965)

5 SERIES—V8—Equipment Schedule 1
W.B. 111.4"; 4.4 Liter.

| 540i Sedan 4D | | DE632 | 51070 | 13925 | 15750 | 18800 | 23400 |
| Sport Pkg | | .... | | 625 | 625 | 835 | 835 |

7 SERIES—V8—Equipment Schedule 1
W.B. 115.4", 120.9" (iL); 4.4 Liter.

| 740i Sedan 4D | | GF832 | 62070 | 11700 | 13250 | 16400 | 20900 |
| 740iL Sedan 4D | | GJ832 | 66070 | 11850 | 13450 | 16950 | 21900 |

7 SERIES—V12—Equipment Schedule 1
W.B. 120.9"; 5.4 Liter.

| 750iL Sedan 4D | | GK232 | 92670 | 14650 | 16500 | 19950 | 25100 |

1999 BMW — (4UorWB)(SorA)(CG833)-X-#

3 SERIES—4-Cyl.—Equipment Schedule 1
W.B. 106.3"; 1.9 Liter.

| 318ti Coupe 2D | | CG833 | 26270 | 7525 | 8675 | 10300 | 12900 |
| w/o Leather | | .... | | 0 | 0 | 0 | 0 |

3 SERIES—6-Cyl.—Equipment Schedule 1
W.B. 106.3", 107.3" (Sedan); 2.5 Liter, 2.8 Liter.

323i Sedan 4D		AM332	30670	11050	12525	14500	17600
323is Coupe 2D		BF833	32645	10075	11475	13400	16350
323i Convertible 2D		BJ833	37695	13500	15225	17400	20900
328i Sedan 4D		AM633	37670	12950	14700	16800	20300
328is Coupe 2D		BG233	37145	11700	13250	15300	18550
328i Convertible 2D		BK833	43045	15175	17100	19400	23100
Sport Pkg		....		400	400	535	535
Hard Top (Conv)		....		525	525	700	700
Rollover Pkg (Conv)		....		375	375	500	500
Manual Trans (Sedan)		....		(475)	(475)	(635)	(635)

M3—6-Cyl.—Equipment Schedule 1
W.B. 106.3", 106.7" (Coupe); 3.2 Liter.

Coupe 2D		BG933	41695	15450	17425	19800	23550
Convertible 2D		BK033	48145	17375	19500	22000	26100
Hard Top (Conv)		....		525	525	700	700

Z3—6-Cyl.—Equipment Schedule 1
W.B. 96.3", 96.8" (M); 2.5 Liter, 2.8 Liter, 3.2 Liter.

Coupe 2D		CK533	38045	11750	13300	15350	18600
2.3 Roadster 2D		CH933	33120	9800	11175	13050	16000
2.8 Roadster 2D		CH333	37745	12050	13675	15700	19000
M Coupe 2D		CM933	42670	13775	15550	17750	21300
M Roadster 2D		CK933	43270	14450	16325	18600	22300
Hard Top (Roadster)		....		525	525	700	700

5 SERIES—6-Cyl.—Equipment Schedule 1
W.B. 111.4"; 2.8 Liter.

528i Sedan 4D		DM633	42945	12625	14300	17300	21700
528iT Wagon 4D		DP633	44745	11850	13450	16350	20600
w/o Premium Pkg		....		(850)	(850)	(1135)	(1135)
Sport Pkg		....		725	725	965	965
Manual Trans		....		(800)	(800)	(1065)	(1065)

1999 BMW

Body	Type	VIN	List	Trade-In Fair	Trade-In Good	Pvt-Party Good	Retail Excellent
5 SERIES—V8—Equipment Schedule 1							
W.B. 111.4"; 4.4 Liter.							
540i Sedan 4D		DN633	51670	16175	18250	21600	26600
540iT Wagon 4D		DR633	54050	15300	17225	20400	25200
Sport Pkg				725	725	965	965
7 SERIES—V8—Equipment Schedule 1							
W.B. 115.4"; 120.9" (iL); 4.4 Liter.							
740i Sedan 4D		GG833	62970	14600	16475	19850	24900
740iL Sedan 4D		GH833	66970	15025	16900	20600	26100
Sport Pkg				725	725	965	965
7 SERIES—V12—Equipment Schedule 1							
W.B. 120.9"; 5.4 Liter.							
750iL Sedan 4D		GJ033	92670	18000	20250	24000	29600

2000 BMW — (4UorWB)(SorA)(AM334)-Y-#

Body	Type	VIN	List	Trade-In Fair	Trade-In Good	Pvt-Party Good	Retail Excellent
3 SERIES—6-Cyl.—Equipment Schedule 1							
W.B. 107.3"; 2.5 Liter, 2.8 Liter.							
323i Sedan 4D		AM334	32680	12775	14450	16450	19800
323i Wagon 4D		AR334	32985	12675	14350	16350	19700
323Ci Coupe 2D		BM334	34280	13500	15225	17350	20700
323Ci Convertible 2D		BR334	38285	17375	19500	21900	25800
328i Sedan 4D		AM534	37670	14925	16800	19000	22700
328Ci Coupe 2D		BM534	38335	15450	17425	19700	23300
Hard Top (Conv)				550	550	735	735
Premium Pkg				400	400	535	535
Sport Pkg				450	450	600	600
Sport Premium Pkg				550	550	735	735
Manual Trans (Sedan)				(500)	(500)	(665)	(665)
Z3—6-Cyl.—Equipment Schedule 1							
W.B. 96.3"; 2.5 Liter, 2.8 Liter.							
Coupe 2D		CK534	38395	13525	15300	17400	20800
2.3 Roadster 2D		CH933	34470	11375	12900	14850	17950
2.8 Roadster 2D		CH334	38445	13925	15750	17850	21300
Hard Top (Roadster)				550	550	735	735
M—6-Cyl.—Equipment Schedule 1							
W.B. 96.8"; 3.2 Liter.							
Coupe 2D		CM934	42670	15850	17800	20200	23900
Roadster 2D		CK934	43270	16600	18675	21000	24900
Hard Top (Roadster)				550	550	735	735
Z8—V8—Equipment Schedule 1							
W.B. 98.9"; 5.0 Liter.							
Roadster 2D		EJ134	130670	****	****	****	82600
5 SERIES—6-Cyl.—Equipment Schedule 1							
W.B. 111.4"; 2.8 Liter.							
528i Sedan 4D		DM634	44595	14550	16425	19600	24300
528iT Wagon 4D		DP634	46545	13675	15450	18600	23100
w/o Premium Pkg				(875)	(875)	(1165)	(1165)
Sport Pkg				825	825	1100	1100
Manual Trans				(875)	(875)	(1165)	(1165)
5 SERIES—V8—Equipment Schedule 1							
W.B. 111.4"; 4.4 Liter.							
540i Sedan 4D		DN634	52970	18675	20925	24500	29800
540iT Wagon 4D		DR634	55350	17525	19675	23000	28200
Sport Pkg				825	825	1100	1100
M5—V8—Equipment Schedule 1							
W.B. 111.4"; 5.0 Liter.							
Sedan 4D		DE934	72070	30425	33900	37900	44400
7 SERIES—V8—Equipment Schedule 1							
W.B. 115.4"; 120.9" (iL); 4.4 Liter.							
740i Sedan 4D		GG834	64670	19875	22375	25900	31400
740iL Sedan 4D		GH834	66970	20550	23050	27000	32900
Sport Pkg				825	825	1100	1100
7 SERIES—V12—Equipment Schedule 1							
W.B. 120.9"; 5.4 Liter.							
750iL Sedan 4D		GJ034	95270	23900	26700	30500	36600

2001 BMW — WBAorWBS(AV334)-1-#

Body	Type	VIN	List	Trade-In Fair	Trade-In Good	Pvt-Party Good	Retail Excellent
3 SERIES—6-Cyl.—Equipment Schedule 1							
W.B. 107.3"; 2.5 Liter, 3.0 Liter.							
325i Sedan 4D		AV334	30060	14700	16550	18700	22300
325xi AWD Sedan 4D		AV334	31810	15450	17425	19600	23200
325Ci Coupe 2D		BN334	32060	15500	17475	19700	23300
325Cic Convertible 2D		BS334	38010	19775	22175	24700	28900

2001 BMW

Body Type	VIN	List	Trade-In Fair	Good	Pvt-Party Good	Retail Excellent
325iT Wagon 4D	AW334	32470	14600	16475	18600	22200
325xiT AWD Wagon 4D	AW334	34220	15025	16900	19050	22700
330i Sedan 4D	AV534	37100	17100	19200	21500	25300
330xi AWD Sedan 4D	AV534	41030	17850	20075	22500	26400
330Ci Coupe 2D	BN534	39335	17750	19975	22300	26200
330Cic Convertible 2D	BS534	44245	21600	24200	26700	31100
Hard Top (Conv)			575	575	765	765
Premium Pkg			450	450	600	600
Sport Pkg			500	500	665	665
Manual Trans (Sedan)			(525)	(525)	(700)	(700)
M3—6-Cyl.—Equipment Schedule 1						
W.B. 107.5"; 3.2 Liter.						
Coupe 2D	BL934	46045	24475	27350	30100	34900
Convertible 2D	BR934	54045	28125	31500	34500	39800
Hard Top (Conv)			575	575	765	765
Z3—6-Cyl.—Equipment Schedule 1						
W.B. 96.3"; 2.5 Liter, 3.0 Liter.						
2.5i Roadster 2D	CN334	33215	13150	14875	16900	20300
3.0i Coupe 2D	CK734	39845	15600	17575	19800	23400
3.0i Roadster 2D	CN534	39745	15975	18000	20300	24000
Hard Top (Roadster)			575	575	765	765
M—6-Cyl.—Equipment Schedule 1						
W.B. 96.8"; 3.2 Liter.						
Coupe 2D	CN934	45635	18100	20350	22800	26800
Roadster 2D	CL934	46635	18900	21225	23700	27800
Hard Top (Roadster)			575	575	765	765
Z8—V8—Equipment Schedule 1						
W.B. 98.6"; 5.0 Liter.						
Roadster 2D	EJ134	130745	****	****	****	90500
5 SERIES—6-Cyl.—Equipment Schedule 1						
W.B. 111.4"; 2.5 Liter, 3.0 Liter.						
525i Sedan 4D	DT334	40195	19100	21400	24300	28900
525iT Wagon 4D	DS334	41995	18100	20350	23100	27600
530i Sedan 4D	DT534	44345	21025	23625	26600	31500
w/o Premium Pkg			(900)	(900)	(1200)	(1200)
Sport Pkg			925	925	1235	1235
Manual Trans			(950)	(950)	(1265)	(1265)
5 SERIES—V8—Equipment Schedule 1						
W.B. 111.4"; 4.4 Liter.						
540i Sedan 4D	DN634	51670	23700	26500	29700	34800
540iT Wagon 4D	DR634	54050	22475	25150	28200	33300
Sport Pkg			925	925	1235	1235
M5—V8—Equipment Schedule 1						
W.B. 111.4"; 5.0 Liter.						
Sedan 4D	DE934	69970	36675	40900	44400	51000
7 SERIES—V8—Equipment Schedule 1						
W.B. 115.4", 120.9" (iL); 4.4 Liter.						
740i Sedan 4D	GG834	63470	22550	25250	29000	34800
740iL Sedan 4D	GH834	67470	23425	26300	30300	36600
Sport Pkg			925	925	1235	1235
7 SERIES—V12—Equipment Schedule 1						
W.B. 120.9"; 5.4 Liter.						
750iL Sedan 4D	GJ034	92670	26975	30150	34200	40500
Sport Pkg			300	300	400	400

2002 BMW — WBA,WBS,4USor5UM(ET374)-2-#

Body Type	VIN	List	Trade-In Fair	Good	Pvt-Party Good	Retail Excellent
3 SERIES—6-Cyl.—Equipment Schedule 1						
W.B. 107.3"; 2.5 Liter, 3.0 Liter.						
325i Sedan 4D	ET374	32465	16850	18950	21200	25000
325xi AWD Sedan 4D	EU334	34215	17675	19875	22200	26000
325Ci Coupe 2D	BN334	34465	17750	19975	22300	26100
325Cic Convertible 2D	BS534	39470	22475	25150	27700	32200
325iT Wagon 4D	EN334	34865	16750	18875	21100	24900
325xiT AWD Wagon 4D	EP334	36615	17275	19400	21700	25500
330i Sedan 4D	EV534	38410	19500	21900	24300	28300
330xi AWD Sedan 4D	EW534	40160	20450	22850	25200	29500
330Ci Coupe 2D	BN534	39410	20350	22750	25200	29400
330Cic Convertible 2D	BS534	46820	24375	27275	29900	34600
Hard Top (Conv)			600	600	800	800
Premium Pkg			500	500	665	665
Sport Pkg			550	550	735	735
Manual Trans (Sedan)			(550)	(550)	(735)	(735)

Body Type	VIN	List	Trade-In Fair	Trade-In Good	Pvt-Party Good	Retail Excellent
M3—6-Cyl.—Equipment Schedule 1						
W.B. 107.5"; 3.2 Liter.						
Coupe 2D	BL934	49745	28025	31300	34100	39200
Convertible 2D	BR934	55545	31675	35325	38300	43800
Z3—6-Cyl.—Equipment Schedule 1						
W.B. 96.3"; 2.5 Liter, 3.0 Liter.						
2.5i Roadster 2D	CN334	34370	15225	17125	19300	22800
3.0i Coupe 2D	CK734	39920	17850	20075	22400	26200
3.0i Roadster 2D	CN534	39820	18325	20650	22900	26900
Hard Top (Roadster)			600	600	800	800
M—6-Cyl.—Equipment Schedule 1						
W.B. 96.8"; 3.2 Liter.						
Coupe 2D	CN934	45635	20650	23125	25600	29900
Roadster 2D	CL934	46635	21600	24200	26700	31000
Hard Top (Roadster)			600	600	800	800
Z8—V8—Equipment Schedule 1						
W.B. 98.6"; 5.0 Liter.						
Roadster 2D	EJ134	132745	****	****	****	98600
5 SERIES—6-Cyl.—Equipment Schedule 1						
W.B. 111.4"; 2.5 Liter, 3.0 Liter.						
525i Sedan 4D	DT434	41070	21700	24375	27400	32300
525iT Wagon 4D	DS334	42870	20650	23125	26000	30800
530i Sedan 4D	DT634	44670	23900	26700	29800	34900
w/o Premium Pkg			(925)	(925)	(1235)	(1235)
Sport Pkg			1000	1000	1335	1335
Manual Trans			(1025)	(1025)	(1365)	(1365)
5 SERIES—V8—Equipment Schedule 1						
W.B. 111.4"; 4.4 Liter.						
540i Sedan 4D	DN634	53145	26875	29950	33200	38800
540iT Wagon 4D	DR634	55545	25450	28425	31600	37000
Sport Pkg			1000	1000	1335	1335
M5—V8—Equipment Schedule 1						
W.B. 111.4"; 5.0 Liter.						
Sedan 4D	DE934	72645	41100	45800	49300	56100
7 SERIES—V8—Equipment Schedule 1						
W.B. 117.7", 123.2" (Li); 4.4 Liter.						
745i Sedan 4D	GL634	68495	38300	42725	46800	54100
745Li Sedan 4D	GN634	72495	39450	43975	48400	56100

2003 BMW — WBA,WBSor4US(EV334)-3-#

Body Type	VIN	List	Trade-In Fair	Trade-In Good	Pvt-Party Good	Retail Excellent
3 SERIES—6-Cyl.—Equipment Schedule 1						
W.B. 107.3"; 2.5 Liter, 3.0 Liter.						
325i Sedan 4D	EV334	32270	19300	21700	23900	27800
325xi AWD Sedan 4D	EU334	34020	20250	22650	25000	29000
325Ci Coupe 2D	BN334	34070	20350	22750	25200	29200
325Cic Convertible 2D	BS334	40120	25450	28425	31000	35600
325iT Wagon 4D	EN334	33820	19300	21600	23800	27700
325xiT AWD Wagon 4D	EP334	35570	19775	22175	24400	28400
330i Sedan 4D	EV934	39070	22275	24875	27300	31600
330xi AWD Sedan 4D	EW534	40820	23125	25925	28300	32700
330Ci Coupe 2D	BN534	40070	23125	25925	28300	32700
330Cic Convertible 2D	BS534	44870	27550	30725	33400	38200
Hard Top (Conv)			625	625	835	835
Premium Pkg			550	550	735	735
Sport Pkg			350	350	465	465
Performance Pkg			500	500	665	665
Manual Trans (Sedan)			(575)	(575)	(765)	(765)
M3—6-Cyl.—Equipment Schedule 1						
W.B. 107.5"; 3.2 Liter.						
Coupe 2D	BL934	49345	31875	35525	38400	43700
Convertible 2D	BR934	55195	35425	39450	42400	48100
Hard Top (Conv)			625	625	835	835
Z4—6-Cyl.—Equipment Schedule 1						
W.B. 98.2"; 2.5 Liter, 3.0 Liter.						
2.5i Roadster 2D	BT334	37690	21300	23900	26200	30400
3.0i Roadster 2D	BT534	43215	24200	27075	29600	34100
Sport Pkg			350	350	465	465
Premium Pkg			550	550	735	735
Z8—V8—Equipment Schedule 1						
W.B. 98.6"; 4.8 Liter, 5.0 Liter.						
Roadster 2D	EJ134	134295	****	****	****	106700
Alpina Roadster 2D	EJ134	139295				

Body Type	VIN	List	Trade-In Fair	Trade-In Good	Pvt-Party Good	Retail Excellent
5 SERIES—6-Cyl.—Equipment Schedule 1						
W.B. 111.4"; 2.5 Liter, 3.0 Liter.						
525i Sedan 4D	DT334	41770	24675	27650	30600	35800
525iT Wagon 4D	DS334	43470	23525	26300	29400	34400
530i Sedan 4D	DT534	45370	26975	30150	33300	38800
w/o Premium Pkg		------	(950)	(950)	(1265)	(1265)
Sport Pkg		------	1075	1075	1435	1435
Manual Trans		------	(700)	(700)	(935)	(935)
5 SERIES—V8—Equipment Schedule 1						
W.B. 111.4"; 4.4 Liter.						
540i Sedan 4D	DN634	52495	30425	33900	37200	43000
540iT Wagon 4D	DR634	56085	28800	32150	35400	41000
Sport Pkg		------	1075	1075	1435	1435
M5—V8—Equipment Schedule 1						
W.B. 111.4"; 5.0 Liter.						
Sedan 4D	DE934	73195	45800	50975	54400	61300
7 SERIES—V8—Equipment Schedule 1						
W.B. 117.7", 123.2" (Li); 4.4 Liter.						
745i Sedan 4D	GL634	70895	42900	47800	51900	59400
745Li Sedan 4D	GN634	73195	44350	49350	53800	61600
7 SERIES—V12—Equipment Schedule 1						
W.B. 123.2"; 6.0 Liter.						
760Li Sedan 4D	GN834	118195	70375	78050	83400	93700

2004 BMW — WBA,WBSor4US(EV334)–4–#

Body Type	VIN	List	Trade-In Fair	Trade-In Good	Pvt-Party Good	Retail Excellent
3 SERIES—6-Cyl.—Equipment Schedule 1						
W.B. 107.3"; 2.5 Liter, 3.0 Liter.						
325i Sedan 4D	EV334	33265	22375	25050	27600	32000
325xi AWD Sedan 4D	EU334	35015	23425	26200	28700	33100
325Ci Coupe 2D	BD334	34570	23425	26300	28800	33200
325Cic Convertible 2D	BW334	40720	29000	32350	35000	40000
325iT Wagon 4D	EN334	34815	22275	24950	27500	31900
325xiT AWD Wagon 4D	EP334	36565	22850	25625	28100	32500
330i Sedan 4D	EV534	39270	25525	28500	31100	35800
330xi AWD Sedan 4D	EW534	41020	26500	29675	32300	37000
330Ci Coupe 2D	BD534	40770	26500	29675	32300	37000
330Cic Convertible 2D	BW534	45570	31200	34850	37600	42800
Hard Top (Conv)			650	650	865	865
Premium Pkg			575	575	765	765
Sport Pkg			375	375	500	500
Performance Pkg			500	500	665	665
5-Spd Manual Trans (Sedan)			(600)	(600)	(800)	(800)
M3—6-Cyl.—Equipment Schedule 1						
W.B. 107.5"; 3.2 Liter.						
Coupe 2D	BL934	51340				
Convertible 2D	BR934	56595				
Hard Top (Conv)						
Z4—6-Cyl.—Equipment Schedule 1						
W.B. 98.2"; 2.5 Liter, 3.0 Liter.						
2.5i Roadster 2D	BT334	37790	24575	27450	30000	34600
3.0i Roadster 2D	BT534	43315	27650	30900	33500	38400
Sport Pkg		------	375	375	500	500
Premium Pkg		------	575	575	765	765
5 SERIES—6-Cyl.—Equipment Schedule 1						
W.B. 113.7"; 2.5 Liter, 3.0 Liter.						
525i Sedan 4D	NA535	43670	29850	33300	36400	42000
530i Sedan 4D	NA735	48670	32250	36000	39300	45000
Sport Pkg		------	1150	1150	1535	1535
Manual Trans (ex SMG)		------	(725)	(725)	(965)	(965)
5 SERIES—V8—Equipment Schedule 1						
W.B. 113.7"; 4.4 Liter.						
545i Sedan 4D	NB335	54995	38025	42325	45700	52000
Sport Pkg		------	1150	1150	1535	1535
6 SERIES—V8—Equipment Schedule 1						
W.B. 109.4"; 4.4 Liter.						
645Ci Coupe 2D	EH734	69995				
645Cic Convertible 2D	EK734	76995				
Sport Pkg						
7 SERIES—V8—Equipment Schedule 1						
W.B. 117.7", 123.2" (Li); 4.4 Liter.						
745i Sedan 4D	GL634	69195	48200	53575	57600	65300
745Li Sedan 4D	GN634	73195	49825	55400	59600	67700
Sport Pkg		------	375	375	500	500

46   DEDUCT FOR RECONDITIONING   0105

Body	Type	VIN	List	Trade-In Fair	Good	Pvt-Party Good	Retail Excellent

7 SERIES—V12—Equipment Schedule 1
W.B. 123.2"; 6.0 Liter.

| 760i Sedan 4D | GL834 | 111795 | | | | |
| 760Li Sedan 4D | GN834 | 117795 | | | | |

BUICK

1990 BUICK — 1G4(NV54U)-L-#

SKYLARK—4-Cyl.—Equipment Schedule 5
W.B. 103.4"; 2.5 Liter.

Type	VIN	List	Fair	Good	Pvt Good	Retail
Sedan 4D	NV54U	11811	400	575	1025	1750
Coupe 2D	NV14U	11821	400	575	1025	1750
Custom Sedan 4D	NC54U	13063	400	575	1025	1750
Custom Coupe 2D	NJ14U	13063	400	575	1025	1750
Luxury Sedan 4D	ND54U	14585	425	625	1075	1850
Gran Sport Coupe 2D	NM14U	14375	475	675	1150	1975
Gran Touring Pkg			50	50	65	65
4-Cyl. 2.3L Quad 4	D		100	100	135	135
V6 3.3 Liter	N		125	125	165	165

CENTURY—V6—Equipment Schedule 4
W.B. 104.9"; 3.3 Liter.

Custom Sedan 4D	AH54N	16076	525	750	1250	2100
Custom Coupe 2D	AH14N	16061	525	750	1250	2100
Custom Wagon 4D	AH84N	17931	550	800	1350	2225
Limited Sedan 4D	AL54N	16760	625	900	1500	2475
Limited Wagon 4D	AL84N	18708	575	825	1350	2225
4-Cyl. 2.5 Liter	R		(150)	(150)	(200)	(200)

REGAL—V6—Equipment Schedule 4
W.B. 107.5"; 3.1 Liter.

Custom Coupe 2D	WB14T	16405	600	850	1500	2600
Limited Coupe 2D	WD14T	17356	625	900	1550	2700
Gran Touring Pkg			50	50	65	65
Gran Sport Pkg			75	75	100	100
V6 3.8 Liter	L		150	150	200	200

LeSABRE—V6—Equipment Schedule 4
W.B. 110.8"; 3.8 Liter.

Coupe 2D	HP14C	17919	550	800	1350	2250
Custom Sedan 4D	HP54C	17929	675	925	1550	2575
Limited Sedan 4D	HR54C	19366	675	925	1550	2575
Limited Coupe 2D	HR14C	19161	600	850	1425	2350
Gran Touring Pkg			50	50	65	65

ELECTRA—V6—Equipment Schedule 4
W.B. 110.8"; 3.8 Liter.

Limited Sedan 4D	CX54C	21784	475	675	1175	2025
Park Ave Sedan 4D	CW54C	23125	525	750	1300	2175
T Type Sedan 4D	CF54C	24265	475	700	1225	2075
Park Ave Ultra Sed 4D	CU54C	28375	650	900	1525	2600
Gran Touring Pkg			50	50	65	65

ESTATE—V8—Equipment Schedule 2
W.B. 115.9"; 5.0 Liter.

| Wagon 4D | BR84Y | 21130 | 575 | 825 | 1400 | 2350 |

RIVIERA—V6—Equipment Schedule 2
W.B. 108.0"; 3.8 Liter.

| Coupe 2D | EZ14C | 25985 | 850 | 1200 | 2100 | 3425 |
| Gran Touring Pkg | | | 50 | 50 | 65 | 65 |

REATTA—V6—Equipment Schedule 2
W.B. 98.5"; 3.8 Liter.

| Coupe 2D | EC14C | 28885 | 1425 | 1900 | 3100 | 4750 |
| Convertible 2D | EC34C | 35545 | 2600 | 3225 | 4600 | 6600 |

1991 BUICK — 1G4(NV54U)-M-#

SKYLARK—4-Cyl.—Equipment Schedule 5
W.B. 103.4"; 2.5 Liter.

Sedan 4D	NV54U	12036	450	650	1150	1975
Coupe 2D	NV14U	12136	450	650	1150	1975
Custom Sedan 4D	NC54U	13653	450	650	1150	1975
Custom Coupe 2D	NJ14U	13653	450	650	1150	1975
Luxury Sedan 4D	ND54U	15335	475	700	1225	2075
Gran Sport Coupe 2D	NM14U	15135	550	775	1325	2225
Gran Touring Pkg			50	50	65	65
4-Cyl. 2.3L Quad 4	D		125	125	135	135

Body	Type	VIN	List	Trade-In Fair	Trade-In Good	Pvt-Party Good	Retail Excellent
	V6 3.3 Liter	N		125	125	165	165
CENTURY—V6—Equipment Schedule 4							
W.B. 104.8"; 3.3 Liter.							
	Special Sedan 4D	AG54N	15798	600	850	1425	2400
	Custom Sedan 4D	AH54N	16805	600	850	1425	2400
	Custom Coupe 2D	AH14N	16800	600	850	1425	2400
	Custom Wagon 4D	AH84N	18865	625	900	1500	2525
	Limited Sedan 4D	AL54N	17786	725	1025	1700	2800
	Limited Wagon 4D	AL84N	19656	650	900	1525	2575
	4-Cyl. 2.5 Liter	R		(150)	(150)	(200)	(200)
REGAL—V6—Equipment Schedule 4							
W.B. 107.5"; 3.1 Liter.							
	Custom Sedan 4D	WB54T	17295	825	1150	1975	3250
	Custom Coupe 2D	WB14T	17075	700	975	1750	2975
	Limited Sedan 4D	WD54T	18501	775	1100	1950	3250
	Limited Coupe 2D	WD14T	18116	725	1025	1825	3075
	Gran Touring Pkg			50	50	65	65
	Gran Sport Pkg			75	75	100	100
	V6 3.8 Liter	L		150	150	200	200
LeSABRE—V6—Equipment Schedule 4							
W.B. 110.8"; 3.8 Liter.							
	Coupe 2D	HP14C	19019	650	900	1525	2600
	Custom Sedan 4D	HP54C	19024	775	1075	1775	2925
	Limited Sedan 4D	HR54C	20481	775	1075	1775	2925
	Limited Coupe 2D	HR14C	20276	675	950	1600	2700
	Gran Touring Pkg			50	50	65	65
PARK AVENUE—V6—Equipment Schedule 4							
W.B. 110.8"; 3.8 Liter.							
	Sedan 4D	CW53L	25594	1050	1500	2550	4025
	Ultra Sedan 4D	CU53L	28000	1400	1875	3025	4625
	Gran Touring Pkg			50	50	65	65
	V6 3.8L Supercharged	1		175	175	235	235
ROADMASTER—V8—Equipment Schedule 4							
W.B. 115.9"; 5.0 Liter.							
	Estate Wagon 4D	BR83E	24642	2225	2775	4075	5875
RIVIERA—V6—Equipment Schedule 2							
W.B. 108.0"; 3.8 Liter.							
	Coupe 2D	EZ13L	26250	1000	1450	2550	4150
	Gran Touring Pkg			50	50	65	65
REATTA—V6—Equipment Schedule 2							
W.B. 98.5"; 3.8 Liter.							
	Coupe 2D	EC14C	29880	1775	2300	3600	5400
	Convertible 2D	EC34C	36545	3175	3850	5400	7600

1992 BUICK — 1G4(NJ543)-N-#

Body	Type	VIN	List	Trade-In Fair	Trade-In Good	Pvt-Party Good	Retail Excellent
SKYLARK—4-Cyl.—Equipment Schedule 5							
W.B. 103.4"; 2.3 Liter.							
	Sedan 4D	NJ543	15180	575	825	1400	2350
	Coupe 2D	NJ143	15180	550	800	1375	2300
	V6 3.3 Liter	N		150	150	200	200
SKYLARK—V6—Equipment Schedule 5							
W.B. 103.4"; 3.3 Liter.							
	Gran Sport Sedan 4D	NM54N	17175	700	1000	1650	2725
	Gran Sport Coupe 2D	NM14N	17175	700	1000	1650	2725
CENTURY—V6—Equipment Schedule 4							
W.B. 104.9"; 3.3 Liter.							
	Special Sedan 4D	AG54N	16337	675	950	1600	2700
	Custom Sedan 4D	AH54N	16897	675	950	1600	2700
	Custom Coupe 2D	AH14N	16627	675	925	1575	2650
	Custom Wagon 4D	AH84N	17375	750	1025	1725	2850
	Limited Sedan 4D	AL54N	17894	850	1200	2000	3250
	Limited Wagon 4D	AL84N	18969	750	1050	1775	2900
	4-Cyl. 2.5 Liter	R		(175)	(175)	(235)	(235)
REGAL—V6—Equipment Schedule 4							
W.B. 107.5"; 3.1 Liter.							
	Custom Sedan 4D	WB54T	18370	900	1300	2325	3875
	Custom Coupe 2D	WB14T	18050	800	1125	2050	3400
	Limited Sedan 4D	WD54T	19700	900	1300	2350	3900
	Limited Coupe 2D	WD14T	19315	825	1150	2100	3475
	Gran Sport Sedan 4D	WF54L	21098	1025	1475	2600	4175
	Gran Sport Coupe 2D	WF14L	20333	925	1325	2400	3950
	Gran Touring Pkg			75	75	100	100
	V6 3.8 Liter	L		175	175	235	235

1992 BUICK

Body	Type	VIN	List	Trade-In Fair	Trade-In Good	Pvt-Party Good	Retail Excellent
LeSABRE—V6—Equipment Schedule 4							
W.B. 110.8"; 3.8 Liter.							
Custom Sedan 4D		HP53L	19615	775	1075	1850	3075
Limited Sedan 4D		HR53L	21695	1175	1625	2725	4275
Gran Touring Pkg				75	75	100	100
PARK AVENUE—V6—Equipment Schedule 4							
W.B. 110.8"; 3.8 Liter.							
Sedan 4D		CW53L	26569	1400	1875	3025	4625
Gran Touring Pkg				75	75	100	100
PARK AVENUE—V6 Supercharged—Equipment Schedule 4							
W.B. 110.8"; 3.8 Liter.							
Ultra Sedan 4D		CU531	29380	1800	2325	3550	5275
Gran Touring Pkg				75	75	100	100
ROADMASTER—V8—Equipment Schedule 2							
W.B. 115.9"; 5.7 Liter.							
Sedan 4D		BN537	24255	1550	2075	3250	4900
Limited Sedan 4D		BT537	25835	1725	2250	3425	5125
Estate Wagon 4D		BR837	25110	2700	3300	4675	6625
RIVIERA—V6—Equipment Schedule 2							
W.B. 108.0"; 3.8 Liter.							
Coupe 2D		EZ13L	27080	1250	1725	2975	4700
Gran Touring Pkg				75	75	100	100

1993 BUICK — 1G4(NV543)-P-#

Body	Type	VIN	List	Trade-In Fair	Trade-In Good	Pvt-Party Good	Retail Excellent
SKYLARK—4-Cyl.—Equipment Schedule 5							
W.B. 103.4"; 2.3 Liter.							
Custom Sedan 4D		NV543	14260	650	900	1550	2650
Custom Coupe 2D		NV143	14260	625	900	1525	2600
Limited Sedan 4D		NJ543	15180	675	925	1600	2700
Limited Coupe 2D		NJ143	15180	650	900	1550	2650
V6 3.3 Liter		N		175	175	235	235
SKYLARK—V6—Equipment Schedule 5							
W.B. 103.4"; 3.3 Liter.							
Gran Sport Sedan 4D		NM54N	17065	825	1150	1900	3100
Gran Sport Coupe 2D		NM14N	17065	825	1150	1900	3100
CENTURY—V6—Equipment Schedule 4							
W.B. 104.9"; 3.3 Liter.							
Special Sedan 4D		AG54N	16627	775	1100	1850	3025
Special Wagon 4D		AG84N	17681	825	1150	1900	3100
Custom Sedan 4D		AH55N	18955	775	1100	1850	3025
Custom Coupe 2D		AH15N	17958	750	1050	1775	2925
Custom Wagon 4D		AH85N	20597	850	1200	2000	3250
Limited Sedan 4D		AL55N	19468	975	1400	2300	3650
4-Cyl. 2.2 Liter		4		(200)	(200)	(265)	(265)
REGAL—V6—Equipment Schedule 4							
W.B. 107.5"; 3.1 Liter.							
Custom Sedan 4D		WB54T	18195	1025	1450	2625	4275
Custom Coupe 2D		WB14T	17875	900	1300	2425	4025
Limited Sedan 4D		WD54T	20045	1050	1500	2700	4325
Limited Coupe 2D		WD14T	19780	950	1350	2475	4075
Gran Sport Sedan 4D		WF54L	21103	1225	1700	2925	4600
Gran Sport Coupe 2D		WF14L	20823	1100	1550	2725	4400
Gran Touring Pkg				100	100	135	135
V6 3.8 Liter		L		200	200	265	265
LeSABRE—V6—Equipment Schedule 4							
W.B. 110.8"; 3.8 Liter.							
90th Anny Sedan 4D		HP53L	19554	900	1275	2175	3575
Custom Sedan 4D		HP53L	21651	900	1275	2175	3575
Limited Sedan 4D		HR53L	23886	1475	1950	3125	4775
Gran Touring Pkg				100	100	135	135
PARK AVENUE—V6—Equipment Schedule 4							
W.B. 110.8"; 3.8 Liter.							
Sedan 4D		CW53L	26640	1800	2325	3550	5300
Gran Touring Pkg				100	100	135	135
PARK AVENUE—V6 Supercharged—Equipment Schedule 4							
W.B. 110.8"; 3.8 Liter.							
Ultra Sedan 4D		CU531	29995	2250	2800	4125	6000
Gran Touring Pkg				100	100	135	135
ROADMASTER—V8—Equipment Schedule 2							
W.B. 115.9"; 5.7 Liter.							
Sedan 4D		BN537	25895	1950	2475	3750	5525
Limited Sedan 4D		BT537	26235	2100	2675	3925	5750
Estate Wagon 4D		BR837	27895	3200	3875	5325	7400

Body	Type	VIN	List	Trade-In Fair	Good	Pvt-Party Good	Retail Excellent
RIVIERA—V6—Equipment Schedule 2							
W.B. 108.0"; 3.8 Liter.							
Coupe 2D		EZ13L	28125	**1600**	**2100**	**3500**	**5400**
Gran Touring Pkg				**100**	**100**	**135**	**135**

1994 BUICK — 1G4(NV553)-R-#

Body	Type	VIN	List	Trade-In Fair	Good	Pvt-Party Good	Retail Excellent
SKYLARK—4-Cyl.—Equipment Schedule 5							
W.B. 103.4"; 2.3 Liter.							
Custom Sedan 4D		NV553	14914	**750**	**1050**	**1825**	**3025**
Custom Coupe 2D		NV153	14914	**725**	**1025**	**1775**	**2975**
Limited Sedan 4D		NJ553	16684	**775**	**1075**	**1850**	**3075**
V6 3.1 Liter		M		**200**	**200**	**265**	**265**
SKYLARK—V6—Equipment Schedule 5							
W.B. 103.4"; 3.1 Liter.							
Gran Sport Sedan 4D		NM55M	18784	**900**	**1300**	**2175**	**3525**
Gran Sport Coupe 2D		NM15M	18784	**900**	**1300**	**2175**	**3525**
CENTURY—V6—Equipment Schedule 4							
W.B. 104.9"; 3.1 Liter.							
Special Sedan 4D		AG55M	17325	**900**	**1275**	**2150**	**3475**
Special Wagon 4D		AG85M	18175	**925**	**1325**	**2225**	**3600**
Custom Sedan 4D		AH55M	19686	**900**	**1275**	**2150**	**3475**
4-Cyl. 2.2 Liter		4		**(225)**	**(225)**	**(300)**	**(300)**
REGAL—V6—Equipment Schedule 4							
W.B. 107.5"; 3.1 Liter.							
Custom Sedan 4D		WB55M	19672	**1200**	**1650**	**2925**	**4675**
Custom Coupe 2D		WB15M	19372	**1075**	**1525**	**2725**	**4425**
Limited Sedan 4D		WD55L	21242	**1300**	**1775**	**3000**	**4725**
Gran Sport Sedan 4D		WF55L	21724	**1500**	**2000**	**3275**	**5050**
Gran Sport Coupe 2D		WF15L	21442	**1350**	**1825**	**3075**	**4800**
Gran Touring Pkg				**100**	**100**	**135**	**135**
V6 3.8 Liter		L		**200**	**200**	**265**	**265**
LeSABRE—V6—Equipment Schedule 4							
W.B. 110.8"; 3.8 Liter.							
Custom Sedan 4D		HP52L	22541	**1050**	**1500**	**2625**	**4200**
Limited Sedan 4D		HR52L	24995	**1775**	**2300**	**3550**	**5300**
Gran Touring Pkg				**100**	**100**	**135**	**135**
PARK AVENUE—V6—Equipment Schedule 4							
W.B. 110.8"; 3.8 Liter.							
Sedan 4D		CW52L	27624	**2200**	**2775**	**4100**	**5975**
Gran Touring Pkg				**100**	**100**	**135**	**135**
PARK AVENUE—V6 Supercharged—Equipment Schedule 4							
W.B. 110.8"; 3.8 Liter.							
Ultra Sedan 4D		CU521	32324	**2700**	**3300**	**4725**	**6725**
Gran Touring Pkg				**100**	**100**	**135**	**135**
ROADMASTER—V8—Equipment Schedule 2							
W.B. 115.9"; 5.7 Liter.							
Sedan 4D		BN52P	27224	**2350**	**2925**	**4275**	**6175**
Limited Sedan 4D		BT52P	27734	**2525**	**3125**	**4500**	**6400**
Estate Wagon 4D		BR82P	29078	**3725**	**4475**	**6000**	**8200**

1995 BUICK — (1or2)G4(NV55D)-S-#

Body	Type	VIN	List	Trade-In Fair	Good	Pvt-Party Good	Retail Excellent
SKYLARK—4-Cyl.—Equipment Schedule 5							
W.B. 103.4"; 2.3 Liter.							
Custom Sedan 4D		NV55D	16070	**900**	**1250**	**2125**	**3475**
Custom Coupe 2D		NV15D	16070	**875**	**1225**	**2100**	**3425**
Gran Sport Pkg				**100**	**100**	**135**	**135**
V6 3.1 Liter		M		**225**	**225**	**300**	**300**
CENTURY—V6—Equipment Schedule 4							
W.B. 104.9"; 3.1 Liter.							
Special Sedan 4D		AG55M	19171	**1025**	**1475**	**2550**	**4100**
Special Wagon 4D		AG85M	19989	**1075**	**1525**	**2650**	**4200**
Custom Sedan 4D		AH55M	18865	**1025**	**1475**	**2550**	**4100**
4-Cyl. 2.2 Liter		4		**(250)**	**(250)**	**(335)**	**(335)**
REGAL—V6—Equipment Schedule 4							
W.B. 107.5"; 3.1 Liter.							
Custom Sedan 4D		WB52M	20650	**1425**	**1900**	**3275**	**5125**
Custom Coupe 2D		WB12M	20333	**1300**	**1775**	**3075**	**4850**
Limited Sedan 4D		WD52L	22243	**1525**	**2050**	**3350**	**5200**
Gran Sport Sedan 4D		WF52L	22878	**1775**	**2300**	**3655**	**5525**
Gran Sport Coupe 2D		WF12L	19995	**1575**	**2100**	**3400**	**5250**
Gran Touring Pkg				**100**	**100**	**135**	**135**
V6 3.8 Liter		L		**200**	**200**	**265**	**265**

1995 BUICK

Body	Type	VIN	List	Trade-In Fair	Trade-In Good	Pvt-Party Good	Retail Excellent
LeSABRE—V6—Equipment Schedule 4							
W.B. 110.8"; 3.8 Liter.							
Custom Sedan 4D		HP52L	23481	1300	1775	3000	4725
Limited Sedan 4D		HR52L	26050	2100	2700	4025	5925
Gran Touring Pkg				100	100	135	135
PARK AVENUE—V6—Equipment Schedule 4							
W.B. 110.8"; 3.8 Liter.							
Sedan 4D		CW52K	28879	2675	3275	4700	6725
Gran Touring Pkg				100	100	135	135
PARK AVENUE—V6 Supercharged—Equipment Schedule 4							
W.B. 110.8"; 3.8 Liter.							
Ultra Sedan 4D		CU521	33719	3200	3875	5375	7525
Gran Touring Pkg				100	100	135	135
ROADMASTER—V8—Equipment Schedule 2							
W.B. 115.9"; 5.7 Liter.							
Sedan 4D		BN52P	28425	2800	3425	4875	6900
Limited Sedan 4D		BT52P	29930	2975	3625	5100	7150
Estate Wagon 4D		BR82P	30365	4300	5075	6700	9050
RIVIERA—V6—Equipment Schedule 2							
W.B. 113.8"; 3.8 Liter.							
Coupe 2D		GD12K	28857	1425	1900	3325	5300
V6 3.8L Supercharged		1		275	275	365	365

1996 BUICK — (1,2or3)G4(NJ52T)—T-#

Body	Type	VIN	List	Trade-In Fair	Trade-In Good	Pvt-Party Good	Retail Excellent
SKYLARK—4-Cyl.—Equipment Schedule 5							
W.B. 103.4"; 2.4 Liter.							
Custom Sedan 4D		NJ52T	15995	1000	1450	2525	4075
Custom Coupe 2D		NJ12T	15995	975	1425	2500	4025
Gran Sport Pkg				100	100	135	135
V6 3.1 Liter		M		250	250	335	335
CENTURY—V6—Equipment Schedule 4							
W.B. 104.9"; 3.1 Liter.							
Sedan 4D		AG55M	18235	1250	1725	2900	4525
Wagon 4D		AG85M	19040	1325	1800	2975	4625
4-Cyl. 2.2 Liter		4		(275)	(275)	(365)	(365)
REGAL—V6—Equipment Schedule 4							
W.B. 107.5"; 3.1 Liter.							
Custom Sedan 4D		WB52M	20280	1700	2225	3700	5700
Custom Coupe 2D		WB12M	19985	1575	2100	3475	5375
Limited Sedan 4D		WD52K	21735	1850	2375	3800	5750
Gran Sport Sedan 4D		WF52K	22340	2100	2675	4100	6100
Gran Sport Coupe 2D		WF12K	21495	1900	2425	3850	5800
Gran Touring Pkg				100	100	135	135
V6 3.8 Liter		K		200	200	265	265
LeSABRE—V6—Equipment Schedule 4							
W.B. 110.8"; 3.8 Liter.							
Custom Sedan 4D		HP52K	22345	1650	2150	3500	5350
Limited Sedan 4D		HR52K	25975	2550	3175	4600	6650
Gran Touring Pkg				100	100	135	135
PARK AVENUE—V6—Equipment Schedule 4							
W.B. 110.8"; 3.8 Liter.							
Sedan 4D		CW52K	28845	3200	3875	5400	7575
Gran Touring Pkg				100	100	135	135
PARK AVENUE—V6 Supercharged—Equipment Schedule 4							
W.B. 110.8"; 3.8 Liter.							
Ultra Sedan 4D		CU521	33460	3775	4500	6125	8400
Gran Touring Pkg				100	100	135	135
ROADMASTER—V8—Equipment Schedule 2							
W.B. 115.9"; 5.7 Liter.							
Sedan 4D		BN52P	28590	3300	4000	5550	7725
Limited Sedan 4D		BT52P	30125	3475	4175	5750	7975
Estate Wagon 4D		BR82P	30230	4900	5750	7500	9975
RIVIERA—V6—Equipment Schedule 2							
W.B. 113.8"; 3.8 Liter.							
Coupe 2D		GD12K	30715	2000	2550	4150	6325
V6 3.8L Supercharged		1		300	300	400	400

1997 BUICK — (1,2or3)G4(NJ52T)—V-#

Body	Type	VIN	List	Trade-In Fair	Trade-In Good	Pvt-Party Good	Retail Excellent
SKYLARK—4-Cyl.—Equipment Schedule 5							
W.B. 103.4"; 2.4 Liter.							
Custom Sedan 4D		NJ52T	16495	1200	1650	2850	4525
Custom Coupe 2D		NJ12T	16495	1175	1625	2825	4500
Gran Sport Pkg				100	100	135	135

1997 BUICK

Body	Type	VIN	List	Trade-In Fair	Trade-In Good	Pvt-Party Good	Retail Excellent
V6 3.1 Liter		M	......	250	250	335	335
CENTURY—V6—Equipment Schedule 4							
W.B. 109.0"; 3.1 Liter.							
Custom Sedan 4D		WS52M	18590	1850	2375	3675	5500
Limited Sedan 4D		WY52M	19965	2350	2925	4300	6225
REGAL—V6—Equipment Schedule 4							
W.B. 109.0"; 3.8 Liter.							
LS Sedan 4D		WB52K	21095	2525	3125	4500	6400
Gran Touring Pkg			......	100	100	135	135
REGAL—V6 Supercharged—Equipment Schedule 4							
W.B. 109.0"; 3.8 Liter.							
GS Sedan 4D		WF521	23495	3675	4400	5800	7875
LeSABRE—V6—Equipment Schedule 4							
W.B. 110.8"; 3.8 Liter.							
Custom Sedan 4D		HP52K	25040	2100	2650	4075	6100
Limited Sedan 4D		HR52K	26170	3075	3725	5300	7500
Gran Touring Pkg			......	100	100	135	135
PARK AVENUE—V6—Equipment Schedule 4							
W.B. 113.8"; 3.8 Liter.							
Sedan 4D		CW52K	30660	4000	4750	6425	8775
Gran Touring Pkg			......	100	100	135	135
PARK AVENUE—V6 Supercharged—Equipment Schedule 4							
W.B. 113.8"; 3.8 Liter.							
Ultra Sedan 4D		CU521	35660	4600	5425	7125	9600
Gran Touring Pkg			......	100	100	135	135
RIVIERA—V6—Equipment Schedule 2							
W.B. 113.8"; 3.8 Liter.							
Coupe 2D		GD22K	31375	2750	3375	5200	7700
V6 3.8L Supercharged		1	......	325	325	435	435

1998 BUICK — (1,2or3)G4(NJ52M)–W–#

Body	Type	VIN	List	Trade-In Fair	Trade-In Good	Pvt-Party Good	Retail Excellent
SKYLARK—V6—Equipment Schedule 5							
W.B. 103.4"; 3.1 Liter.							
Custom Sedan 4D		NJ52M	16755	1500	1975	3200	4925
CENTURY—V6—Equipment Schedule 4							
W.B. 109.0"; 3.1 Liter.							
Custom Sedan 4D		WS52M	19185	2250	2800	4200	6150
Limited Sedan 4D		WY52M	20545	2800	3425	4875	6900
REGAL—V6—Equipment Schedule 4							
W.B. 109.0"; 3.8 Liter.							
LS Sedan 4D		WB52K	21495	2975	3625	5075	7125
Gran Touring Pkg			......	100	100	135	135
REGAL—V6 Supercharged—Equipment Schedule 4							
W.B. 109.0"; 3.8 Liter.							
GS Sedan 4D		WF521	24240	4200	5000	6375	8450
LeSABRE—V6—Equipment Schedule 4							
W.B. 110.8"; 3.8 Liter.							
Custom Sedan 4D		HP52K	23265	2625	3250	4700	6800
Limited Sedan 4D		HR52K	26395	3725	4450	6025	8275
Gran Touring Pkg			......	100	100	135	135
PARK AVENUE—V6—Equipment Schedule 4							
W.B. 113.8"; 3.8 Liter.							
Sedan 4D		CW52K	31340	4675	5525	7175	9600
Gran Touring Pkg			......	100	100	135	135
PARK AVENUE—V6 Supercharged—Equipment Schedule 4							
W.B. 113.8"; 3.8 Liter.							
Ultra Sedan 4D		CU521	36215	5325	6225	7950	10450
Gran Touring Pkg			......	100	100	135	135
RIVIERA—V6 Supercharged—Equipment Schedule 2							
W.B. 113.8"; 3.8 Liter.							
Coupe 2D		GD221	33165	3725	4450	6375	9050

1999 BUICK — (1,2or3)G4(WS52M)–X–#

Body	Type	VIN	List	Trade-In Fair	Trade-In Good	Pvt-Party Good	Retail Excellent
CENTURY—V6—Equipment Schedule 4							
W.B. 109.0"; 3.1 Liter.							
Custom Sedan 4D		WS52M	19755	2825	3475	4975	7075
Limited Sedan 4D		WY52M	21125	3475	4175	5725	7950
REGAL—V6—Equipment Schedule 4							
W.B. 109.0"; 3.8 Liter.							
LS Sedan 4D		WB52K	22255	3525	4225	5775	8025
Gran Touring Pkg			......	125	125	165	165
REGAL—V6 Supercharged—Equipment Schedule 4							
W.B. 109.0"; 3.8 Liter.							

Body Type	VIN	List	Trade-In Fair	Good	Pvt-Party Good	Retail Excellent
GS Sedan 4D	WF521	24955	4950	5800	7275	9475
LeSABRE—V6—Equipment Schedule 4						
W.B. 110.8". 3.8 Liter.						
Custom Sedan 4D	HP52K	23535	3300	3950	5575	7825
Limited Sedan 4D	HR52K	26605	4550	5375	7075	9550
Gran Touring Pkg			125	125	165	165
PARK AVENUE—V6—Equipment Schedule 4						
W.B. 113.8". 3.8 Liter.						
Sedan 4D	CW52K	31800	5650	6550	8375	11000
Gran Touring Pkg			125	125	165	165
PARK AVENUE—V6 Supercharged—Equipment Schedule 4						
W.B. 113.8". 3.8 Liter.						
Ultra Sedan 4D	CU521	36695	6375	7375	9275	12000
Gran Touring Pkg			125	125	165	165
RIVIERA—V6 Supercharged—Equipment Schedule 2						
W.B. 113.8". 3.8 Liter.						
Coupe 2D	GD221	35830	4725	5550	7725	10700

2000 BUICK — (1,2or3)G4(WS52J)-Y-#

Body Type	VIN	List	Trade-In Fair	Good	Pvt-Party Good	Retail Excellent
CENTURY—V6—Equipment Schedule 4						
W.B. 109.0". 3.1 Liter.						
Custom Sedan 4D	WS52J	20592	3575	4300	5900	8150
Limited Sedan 4D	WY52J	22727	4325	5100	6750	9125
Century 2000 Pkg			300	300	400	400
REGAL—V6—Equipment Schedule 4						
W.B. 109.0". 3.8 Liter.						
LS Sedan 4D	WB52K	22780	4225	5025	6700	9100
Gran Touring Pkg			150	150	200	200
REGAL—V6 Supercharged—Equipment Schedule 4						
W.B. 109.0". 3.8 Liter.						
GS Sedan 4D	WF521	25625	5825	6800	8350	10700
LeSABRE—V6—Equipment Schedule 4						
W.B. 112.2". 3.8 Liter.						
Custom Sedan 4D	HP54K	24115	4325	5100	6750	9075
Limited Sedan 4D	HR54K	27310	5775	6725	8450	11000
Gran Touring Pkg			150	150	200	200
PARK AVENUE—V6—Equipment Schedule 4						
W.B. 113.8". 3.8 Liter.						
Sedan 4D	CW52K	32395	6725	7775	9700	12550
Gran Touring Pkg			150	150	200	200
PARK AVENUE—V6 Supercharged—Equipment Schedule 4						
W.B. 113.8". 3.8 Liter.						
Ultra Sedan 4D	CU521	37470	7550	8700	10700	13700
Gran Touring Pkg			150	150	200	200

2001 BUICK — (1or2)G4(WS52J)-2-#

Body Type	VIN	List	Trade-In Fair	Good	Pvt-Party Good	Retail Excellent
CENTURY—V6—Equipment Schedule 4						
W.B. 109.0". 3.1 Liter.						
Custom Sedan 4D	WS52J	20870	4475	5250	6975	9450
Limited Sedan 4D	WY52J	23471	5250	6150	7950	10500
REGAL—V6—Equipment Schedule 4						
W.B. 109.0". 3.8 Liter.						
LS Sedan 4D	WB52K	23445	5100	5975	7800	10400
Abboud Pkg			175	175	235	235
Gran Touring Pkg			175	175	235	235
REGAL—V6 Supercharged—Equipment Schedule 4						
W.B. 109.0". 3.8 Liter.						
GS Sedan 4D	WF521	26695	6900	7950	9650	12200
Abboud Pkg			175	175	235	235
LeSABRE—V6—Equipment Schedule 4						
W.B. 112.2". 3.8 Liter.						
Custom Sedan 4D	HP54K	24762	5400	6300	8100	10650
Limited Sedan 4D	HR54K	29451	7000	8100	9925	12700
Gran Touring Pkg			175	175	235	235
PARK AVENUE—V6—Equipment Schedule 4						
W.B. 113.8". 3.8 Liter.						
Sedan 4D	CW52K	33700	8075	9250	11350	14450
Gran Touring Pkg			175	175	235	235
PARK AVENUE—V6 Supercharged—Equipment Schedule 4						
W.B. 113.8". 3.8 Liter.						
Ultra Sedan 4D	CU521	38210	9025	10325	12450	15650
Gran Touring Pkg			175	175	235	235

Body Type	VIN	List	Trade-In Fair	Trade-In Good	Pvt-Party Good	Retail Excellent

2002 BUICK — (1or2)G4(WS52J)-2-#

CENTURY—V6—Equipment Schedule 4
W.B. 109.0"; 3.1 Liter.

Type	VIN	List	Fair	Good	Good	Excellent
Custom Sedan 4D	WS52J	21325	5525	6425	8300	11000
Limited Sedan 4D	WY52J	23895	6400	7425	9325	12150

REGAL—V6—Equipment Schedule 4
W.B. 109.0"; 3.8 Liter.

Type	VIN	List	Fair	Good	Good	Excellent
LS Sedan 4D	WB52K	23840	6200	7175	9175	12050
Abboud Pkg			200	200	265	265
Gran Touring Pkg			200	200	265	265

REGAL—V6 Supercharged—Equipment Schedule 4
W.B. 109.0"; 3.8 Liter.

Type	VIN	List	Fair	Good	Good	Excellent
GS Sedan 4D	WF521	27895	8125	9325	11200	13950
Abboud Pkg			200	200	265	265

LeSABRE—V6—Equipment Schedule 4
W.B. 112.2"; 3.8 Liter.

Type	VIN	List	Fair	Good	Good	Excellent
Custom Sedan 4D	HP54K	24975	6750	7800	9750	12600
Limited Sedan 4D	HR54K	30675	8575	9800	11800	14900

PARK AVENUE—V6—Equipment Schedule 4
W.B. 113.8"; 3.8 Liter.

Type	VIN	List	Fair	Good	Good	Excellent
Sedan 4D	CW52K	34165	9700	11050	13300	16650
Gran Touring Pkg			200	200	265	265

PARK AVENUE—V6 Supercharged—Equipment Schedule 4
W.B. 113.8"; 3.8 Liter.

Type	VIN	List	Fair	Good	Good	Excellent
Ultra Sedan 4D	CU521	38675	10700	12150	14500	18000
Gran Touring Pkg			200	200	265	265

2003 BUICK — (1or2)G4(WS52J)-3-#

CENTURY—V6—Equipment Schedule 4
W.B. 109.0"; 3.1 Liter.

Type	VIN	List	Fair	Good	Good	Excellent
Sedan 4D	WS52J	21685	6850	7900	9800	12600
Limited Sedan 4D	WY52J	24180	7825	8975	10950	13900

REGAL—V6—Equipment Schedule 4
W.B. 109.0"; 3.8 Liter.

Type	VIN	List	Fair	Good	Good	Excellent
LS Sedan 4D	WB52K	24230	7550	8700	10850	13950
Abboud Pkg			200	200	265	265
Gran Touring Pkg			225	225	300	300

REGAL—V6 Supercharged—Equipment Schedule 4
W.B. 109.0"; 3.8 Liter.

Type	VIN	List	Fair	Good	Good	Excellent
GS Sedan 4D	WF521	28175	9700	11100	13050	16100
Abboud Pkg			200	200	265	265

LeSABRE—V6—Equipment Schedule 4
W.B. 112.2"; 3.8 Liter.

Type	VIN	List	Fair	Good	Good	Excellent
Custom Sedan 4D	HP52K	25730	8475	9700	11700	14750
Limited Sedan 4D	HR54K	31360	10475	11900	14000	17300
Celebration Edition			500	500	665	665

PARK AVENUE—V6—Equipment Schedule 4
W.B. 113.8"; 3.8 Liter.

Type	VIN	List	Fair	Good	Good	Excellent
Sedan 4D	CW54K	34615	11675	13200	15650	19300
Gran Touring Pkg			225	225	300	300

PARK AVENUE—V6 Supercharged—Equipment Schedule 4
W.B. 113.8"; 3.8 Liter.

Type	VIN	List	Fair	Good	Good	Excellent
Ultra Sedan 4D	CU541	39915	12775	14450	16950	20700

2004 BUICK — (1or2)G4(WS52J)-4-#

CENTURY—V6—Equipment Schedule 4
W.B. 109.0"; 3.1 Liter.

Type	VIN	List	Fair	Good	Good	Excellent
Sedan 4D	WS52J	22415	8525	9750	11800	14900
Limited Sedan 4D	WY52J	23220	9600	10950	13050	16250

REGAL—V6—Equipment Schedule 4
W.B. 109.0"; 3.8 Liter.

Type	VIN	List	Fair	Good	Good	Excellent
LS Sedan 4D	WB52K	24895	9375	10700	13100	16600
Abboud Pkg			200	200	265	265
Gran Touring Pkg			250	250	335	335

REGAL—V6 Supercharged—Equipment Schedule 4
W.B. 109.0"; 3.8 Liter.

Type	VIN	List	Fair	Good	Good	Excellent
GS Sedan 4D	WF521	28345	11675	13200	15400	18850
Abboud Pkg			200	200	265	265

LeSABRE—V6—Equipment Schedule 4
W.B. 112.2"; 3.8 Liter.

Type	VIN	List	Fair	Good	Good	Excellent
Custom Sedan 4D	HP54K	26470	10650	12150	14400	17900

Body Type	VIN	List	Trade-In Fair	Trade-In Good	Pvt-Party Good	Retail Excellent
Limited Sedan 4D	HR54K	32245	12875	14550	17000	20700
Celebration Edition			500	500	665	665
PARK AVENUE—V6—Equipment Schedule 4						
W.B. 113.8"; 3.8 Liter.						
Sedan 4D	CW52K	35545	14100	15900	18600	22700
Gran Touring Pkg			250	250	335	335
PARK AVENUE—V6 Supercharged—Equipment Schedule 4						
W.B. 113.8"; 3.8 Liter.						
Ultra Sedan 4D	CU521	40720	15300	17225	19850	24100

CADILLAC

1990 CADILLAC — 1G6(EL133)-L-#

Body Type	VIN	List	Trade-In Fair	Trade-In Good	Pvt-Party Good	Retail Excellent
ELDORADO—V8—Equipment Schedule 2						
W.B. 108.0"; 4.5 Liter.						
Coupe 2D	EL133	30875	1025	1475	2575	4125
Biarritz Coupe 2D	EL133	34055	1175	1625	2750	4375
Touring Coupe 2D	EL133	32400	1100	1550	2700	4325
SEVILLE—V8—Equipment Schedule 2						
W.B. 108.0"; 4.5 Liter.						
Sedan 4D	KS533	33755	1225	1675	2825	4450
STS Touring Sedan 4D	KY533	36870	1500	2000	3225	4925
DeVILLE—V8—Equipment Schedule 2						
W.B. 110.8", 113.8" (Sed); 4.5 Liter.						
Sedan 4D	CD533	29931	925	1325	2450	4025
Coupe 2D	CD133	29351	850	1175	2150	3600
FLEETWOOD—V8—Equipment Schedule 2						
W.B. 110.8", 113.8" (Sed); 4.5 Liter.						
Sedan 4D	CB533	34090	975	1425	2550	4175
Coupe 2D	CB133	33510	975	1425	2550	4175
FLEETWOOD SIXTY SPECIAL—V8—Equipment Schedule 2						
W.B. 113.8"; 4.5 Liter.						
Sedan 4D	CS533	37530	950	1350	2475	4075
BROUGHAM—V8—Equipment Schedule 2						
W.B. 121.5"; 5.7 Liter.						
Sedan 4D	DW547	30128	900	1300	2375	3925
V8 5.0 Liter	Y		(200)	(200)	(265)	(265)
ALLANTE'—V8—Equipment Schedule 2						
W.B. 99.4"; 4.5 Liter.						
Convertible Coupe 2D	VS338	51550	4450	5225	6975	9450
Hard Top	R		1100	1100	1465	1465

1991 CADILLAC — 1G6(EL13B)-M-#

Body Type	VIN	List	Trade-In Fair	Trade-In Good	Pvt-Party Good	Retail Excellent
ELDORADO—V8—Equipment Schedule 2						
W.B. 108.0"; 4.9 Liter.						
Coupe 2D	EL13B	32380	1275	1750	2950	4650
Biarritz Coupe 2D	EL13B	35005	1475	1950	3225	4975
Touring Coupe 2D	EL13B	33875	1400	1875	3150	4875
SEVILLE—V8—Equipment Schedule 2						
W.B. 108.0"; 4.9 Liter.						
Sedan 4D	KS53B	34975	1500	2025	3300	5050
STS Touring Sedan 4D	KY53B	37715	1875	2400	3750	5600
DeVILLE—V8—Equipment Schedule 2						
W.B. 110.8", 113.8" (Sed); 4.9 Liter.						
Sedan 4D	CD53B	31925	1100	1550	2750	4475
Coupe 2D	CD13B	31675	975	1400	2575	4225
Touring Sedan 4D	CD53B	34375	1375	1875	3150	4950
FLEETWOOD—V8—Equipment Schedule 2						
W.B. 110.8", 113.8" (Sed); 4.9 Liter.						
Sedan 4D	CB53B	36095	1200	1650	2925	4650
Coupe 2D	CB13B	35845	1200	1650	2925	4650
FLEETWOOD SIXTY SPECIAL—V8—Equipment Schedule 2						
W.B. 113.8"; 4.9 Liter.						
Sedan 4D	CG53B	38925	1100	1550	2800	4525
BROUGHAM—V8—Equipment Schedule 2						
W.B. 121.5"; 5.7 Liter.						
Sedan 4D	DW547	31375	1075	1525	2725	4425
V8 5.0 Liter	E		(200)	(200)	(265)	(265)
ALLANTE'—V8—Equipment Schedule 2						
W.B. 99.4"; 4.5 Liter.						
Convertible Coupe 2D	VS338	55250	5350	6250	8225	11050

Body	Type	VIN	List	Trade-In Fair	Good	Pvt-Party Good	Retail Excellent
Hard Top		R		1150	1150	1535	1535

1992 CADILLAC — 1G6(EL13B)-N-#

ELDORADO—V8—Equipment Schedule 2
W.B. 108.0"; 4.9 Liter.

Coupe 2D		EL13B	33720	1975	2525	3875	5750
Touring Coupe 2D		EL13B	35570	2125	2700	4075	6025

SEVILLE—V8—Equipment Schedule 2
W.B. 111.0"; 4.9 Liter.

Sedan 4D		KS53B	36225	1800	2325	3675	5575
STS Touring Sedan 4D		KY53D	38575	2125	2700	4125	6125

DeVILLE—V8—Equipment Schedule 2
W.B. 110.8", 113.8 (Sed); 4.9 Liter.

Sedan 4D		CD53B	32910	1375	1875	3200	5050
Coupe 2D		CD13B	32910	1225	1675	3000	4800
Touring Sedan 4D		CT53B	35790	1700	2225	3625	5575

FLEETWOOD—V8—Equipment Schedule 2
W.B. 110.8", 113.8 (Sed); 4.9 Liter.

Sedan 4D		CB53B	37530	1525	2050	3425	5325
Coupe 2D		CB13B	37530	1525	2050	3425	5325

FLEETWOOD SIXTY SPECIAL—V8—Equipment Schedule 2
W.B. 113.8"; 4.9 Liter.

Sedan 4D		CG53B	40460	1500	2025	3375	5275

BROUGHAM—V8—Equipment Schedule 2
W.B. 121.5"; 5.7 Liter.

Sedan 4D		DW547	32910	1300	1775	3100	4900
d'Elegance				125	125	165	165
V8 5.0 Liter		E		(225)	(225)	(300)	(300)

ALLANTE'—V8—Equipment Schedule 2
W.B. 99.4"; 4.5 Liter.

Convertible Coupe 2D		VS338	58470	6250	7250	9350	12400
Hard Top		R		1325	1325	1765	1765

1993 CADILLAC — 1G6(EL12B)-P-#

ELDORADO—V8—Equipment Schedule 2
W.B. 108.0"; 4.6 Liter, 4.9 Liter.

Coupe 2D		EL12B	35240	2425	3025	4500	6525
Sport Coupe 2D		EL12Y	38240	2825	3450	5000	7125
Touring Coupe 2D		EL129	39590	2900	3550	5100	7250

SEVILLE—V8—Equipment Schedule 2
W.B. 111.0"; 4.6 Liter, 4.9 Liter.

Sedan 4D		KS52B	38240	2825	3475	5025	7175
STS Touring Sedan 4D		KY529	42590	3700	4425	6100	8475

DeVILLE—V8—Equipment Schedule 2
W.B. 110.8", 113.8 (Sed); 4.9 Liter.

Sedan 4D		CD53B	34160	1775	2300	3775	5750
Coupe 2D		CD13B	35085	1600	2100	3550	5525
Touring Sedan 4D		CT53B	36910	2125	2700	4225	6325

FLEETWOOD—V8—Equipment Schedule 2
W.B. 121.5"; 5.7 Liter.

Sedan 4D		DW527	35160	3075	3725	5400	7700
Brougham Pkg				275	275	365	365

SIXTY SPECIAL—V8—Equipment Schedule 2
W.B. 113.8"; 4.9 Liter.

Sedan 4D		CB53B	38400	2025	2575	4075	6150

ALLANTE—V8—Equipment Schedule 2
W.B. 99.4"; 4.6 Liter.

Convertible Coupe 2D		VS339	61675	10475	11900	14650	18650
Hard Top				1500	1500	2000	2000

1994 CADILLAC — 1G6(EL12Y)-R-#

ELDORADO—V8—Equipment Schedule 2
W.B. 108.0"; 4.6 Liter.

Coupe 2D		EL12Y	38565	2975	3650	5200	7425
Touring Coupe 2D		ET129	41215	3550	4250	5900	8225

SEVILLE—V8—Equipment Schedule 2
W.B. 111.0"; 4.6 Liter.

SLS Sedan 4D		KS52Y	42265	3400	4100	5750	8100
STS Touring Sedan 4D		KY529	45515	4350	5125	6950	9500

DeVILLE—V8—Equipment Schedule 2
W.B. 113.8"; 4.6 Liter, 4.9 Liter.

Sedan 4D		KD52B	34400	2400	3000	4475	6500

1994 CADILLAC

Body	Type	VIN	List	Trade-In Fair	Good	Pvt-Party Good	Retail Excellent
	Concours Sedan 4D	KF52Y	37215	3175	3850	5425	7650
FLEETWOOD—V8—Equipment Schedule 2							
W.B. 121.5"; 5.7 Liter.							
	Sedan 4D	DW52P	35185	3675	4400	6200	8700
	Brougham Pkg			300	300	400	400

1995 CADILLAC — 1G6(EL12Y)-S-#

Body	Type	VIN	List	Trade-In Fair	Good	Pvt-Party Good	Retail Excellent
ELDORADO—V8—Equipment Schedule 2							
W.B. 108.0"; 4.6 Liter.							
	Coupe 2D	EL12Y	39505	3675	4400	6100	8500
	Touring Coupe 2D	ET129	42170	4325	5100	6900	9425
SEVILLE—V8—Equipment Schedule 2							
W.B. 111.0"; 4.6 Liter.							
	SLS Sedan 4D	KS52Y	43220	4075	4850	6675	9225
	STS Touring Sedan 4D	KY529	46570	5125	6000	7975	10750
DeVILLE—V8—Equipment Schedule 2							
W.B. 113.8"; 4.6 Liter, 4.9 Liter.							
	Sedan 4D	KD52B	36320	3050	3700	5300	7550
	Concours Sedan 4D	KF52Y	40035	3875	4600	6325	8750
FLEETWOOD—V8—Equipment Schedule 2							
W.B. 121.5"; 5.7 Liter.							
	Sedan 4D	DW52P	37015	4400	5175	7175	9925
	Brougham Pkg			325	325	435	435

1996 CADILLAC — 1G6(EL12Y)-T-#

Body	Type	VIN	List	Trade-In Fair	Good	Pvt-Party Good	Retail Excellent
ELDORADO—V8—Equipment Schedule 2							
W.B. 108.0"; 4.6 Liter.							
	Coupe 2D	EL12Y	41020	4475	5275	7150	9800
	Touring Coupe 2D	ET129	43635	5200	6075	8075	10850
SEVILLE—V8—Equipment Schedule 2							
W.B. 111.0"; 4.6 Liter.							
	SLS Sedan 4D	KS52Y	44420	4900	5725	7725	10500
	STS Touring Sedan 4D	KY529	48135	6050	7000	9175	12200
DeVILLE—V8—Equipment Schedule 2							
W.B. 113.8"; 4.6 Liter.							
	Sedan 4D	KD52Y	37420	3850	4575	6325	8800
	Concours Sedan 4D	KF52Y	41135	4725	5550	7450	10100
FLEETWOOD—V8—Equipment Schedule 2							
W.B. 121.5"; 5.7 Liter.							
	Sedan 4D	DW52P	38420	5250	6150	8325	11400
	Brougham Pkg			350	350	465	465

1997 CADILLAC — (Wor1)(GorO)6(VR52R)-V-#

Body	Type	VIN	List	Trade-In Fair	Good	Pvt-Party Good	Retail Excellent
CATERA—V6—Equipment Schedule 2							
W.B. 107.4"; 3.0 Liter.							
	Sedan 4D	VR52R	33635	1975	2525	4300	6675
ELDORADO—V8—Equipment Schedule 2							
W.B. 108.0"; 4.6 Liter.							
	Coupe 2D	EL12Y	39883	5475	6375	8425	11350
	Touring Coupe 2D	ET129	42060	6250	7250	9400	12500
SEVILLE—V8—Equipment Schedule 2							
W.B. 111.0"; 4.6 Liter.							
	SLS Sedan 4D	KS52Y	41883	5875	6850	9025	12100
	STS Touring Sedan 4D	KY529	45660	7125	8225	10550	13850
DeVILLE—V8—Equipment Schedule 2							
W.B. 113.8"; 4.6 Liter.							
	Sedan 4D	KD54Y	38445	4775	5625	7575	10300
	d'Elegance Sedan 4D	KE54Y	40660	5250	6150	8150	11000
	Concours Sedan 4D	KF549	42660	5725	6675	8725	11650

1998 CADILLAC — (Wor1)(GorO)6(VR52R)-W-#

Body	Type	VIN	List	Trade-In Fair	Good	Pvt-Party Good	Retail Excellent
CATERA—V6—Equipment Schedule 2							
W.B. 107.4"; 3.0 Liter.							
	Sedan 4D	VR52R	34250	2700	3325	5225	7800
ELDORADO—V8—Equipment Schedule 2							
W.B. 108.0"; 4.6 Liter.							
	Coupe 2D	EL12Y	39945	6700	7750	9900	12950
	Touring Coupe 2D	ET129	43360	7550	8700	10950	14150
SEVILLE—V8—Equipment Schedule 2							
W.B. 112.2"; 4.6 Liter.							
	SLS Sedan 4D	KS52Y	43160	6950	8050	9600	12000
	STS Touring Sedan 4D	KY529	47660	8350	9575	11250	13850

1998 CADILLAC

Body	Type	VIN	List	Trade-In Fair	Trade-In Good	Pvt-Party Good	Retail Excellent
DeVILLE—V8—Equipment Schedule 2							
W.B. 113.8"; 4.6 Liter.							
Sedan 4D		KD54Y	39145	**5950**	**6900**	**8900**	**11750**
d'Elegance Sedan 4D		KE54Y	41960	**6500**	**7500**	**9550**	**12500**
Concours Sedan 4D		KF549	42960	**6975**	**8075**	**10200**	**13200**

1999 CADILLAC — (Wor1)(Gor0)6(VR52R)-X-#

Body	Type	VIN	List	Trade-In Fair	Trade-In Good	Pvt-Party Good	Retail Excellent
CATERA—V6—Equipment Schedule 2							
W.B. 107.5"; 3.0 Liter.							
Sedan 4D		VR52R	34820	**3725**	**4475**	**6625**	**9550**
Sport Sedan 4D		VR54R	35615	**3925**	**4675**	**6900**	**9850**
ELDORADO—V8—Equipment Schedule 2							
W.B. 108.0"; 4.6 Liter.							
Coupe 2D		EL12Y	40690	**8275**	**9475**	**11900**	**15350**
Touring Coupe 2D		ET129	44165	**9275**	**10550**	**13050**	**16700**
SEVILLE—V8—Equipment Schedule 2							
W.B. 112.2"; 4.6 Liter.							
SLS Sedan 4D		KS52Y	44025	**8225**	**9425**	**11150**	**13800**
STS Touring Sedan 4D		KY529	48520	**9800**	**11175**	**12950**	**15850**
DeVILLE—V8—Equipment Schedule 2							
W.B. 113.8"; 4.6 Liter.							
Sedan 4D		KD54Y	40085	**7325**	**8425**	**10650**	**13850**
d'Elegance Sedan 4D		KE54Y	43400	**8025**	**9200**	**11450**	**14800**
Concours Sedan 4D		KF549	43900	**8600**	**9850**	**12150**	**15500**

2000 CADILLAC — (Wor1)(Gor0)6(VR52R)-Y-#

Body	Type	VIN	List	Trade-In Fair	Trade-In Good	Pvt-Party Good	Retail Excellent
CATERA—V6—Equipment Schedule 2							
W.B. 107.5"; 3.0 Liter.							
Sedan 4D		VR52R	31500	**5300**	**6200**	**8100**	**10850**
Sport Sedan 4D		VR54R	33500	**5525**	**6425**	**8400**	**11200**
ELDORADO—V8—Equipment Schedule 2							
W.B. 108.0"; 4.6 Liter.							
ESC Coupe 2D		EL12Y	39790	**9800**	**11175**	**13650**	**17250**
ETC Coupe 2D		ET129	43365	**10950**	**12425**	**15000**	**18750**
SEVILLE—V8—Equipment Schedule 2							
W.B. 112.2"; 4.6 Liter.							
SLS Sedan 4D		KS52Y	44550	**9850**	**11225**	**13100**	**16100**
STS Touring Sedan 4D		KY529	49150	**11625**	**13150**	**15200**	**18450**
DeVILLE—V8—Equipment Schedule 2							
W.B. 115.3"; 4.6 Liter.							
Sedan 4D		KD54Y	40955	**8875**	**10175**	**12600**	**16100**
DHS Sedan 4D		KE54Y	45370	**11750**	**13350**	**16000**	**19850**
DTS Sedan 4D		KF549	45370	**12425**	**14075**	**16750**	**20700**

2001 CADILLAC — (Wor1)(Gor0)6(VR52R)-1-#

Body	Type	VIN	List	Trade-In Fair	Trade-In Good	Pvt-Party Good	Retail Excellent
CATERA—V6—Equipment Schedule 2							
W.B. 107.4"; 3.0 Liter.							
Sedan 4D		VR52R	31945	**7125**	**8225**	**10450**	**13700**
Sport Sedan 4D		VR54R	34455	**7400**	**8500**	**10750**	**14000**
ELDORADO—V8—Equipment Schedule 2							
W.B. 108.0"; 4.6 Liter.							
ESC Coupe 2D		EL12Y	40756	**12200**	**13825**	**16600**	**20700**
ETC Coupe 2D		ET129	44331	**13500**	**15225**	**18100**	**22400**
SEVILLE—V8—Equipment Schedule 2							
W.B. 112.2"; 4.6 Liter.							
SLS Sedan 4D		KS52Y	42655	**11950**	**13525**	**15700**	**19050**
STS Touring Sedan 4D		KY529	48765	**13875**	**15700**	**17900**	**21500**
DeVILLE—V8—Equipment Schedule 2							
W.B. 115.3"; 4.6 Liter.							
Sedan 4D		KD54Y	42000	**11200**	**12475**	**15200**	**19200**
DHS Sedan 4D		KE54Y	46987	**14250**	**16075**	**19000**	**23400**
DTS Sedan 4D		KF549	46987	**15025**	**16900**	**19850**	**24400**

2002 CADILLAC — 1G6(EL12Y)-2-#

Body	Type	VIN	List	Trade-In Fair	Trade-In Good	Pvt-Party Good	Retail Excellent
ELDORADO—V8—Equipment Schedule 2							
W.B. 108.0"; 4.6 Liter.							
ESC Coupe 2D		EL12Y	42610	**15175**	**17100**	**20300**	**25000**
ETC Coupe 2D		ET129	45745	**16500**	**18575**	**21900**	**26800**
ECS Coupe 2D		ET129	48405	**16850**	**18950**	**22200**	**27100**
SEVILLE—V8—Equipment Schedule 2							
W.B. 112.2"; 4.6 Liter.							
SLS Sedan 4D		KS52Y	44269	**14650**	**16500**	**18950**	**22800**

Body	Type	VIN	List	Trade-In Fair	Good	Pvt-Party Good	Retail Excellent
STS Touring Sedan 4D	KY529		49825	16750	18875	21500	25600

DeVILLE—V8—Equipment Schedule 2
W.B. 115.3"; 4.6 Liter.

Sedan 4D	KD54Y		43070	13625	15400	18450	22900
DHS Sedan 4D	KE54Y		48000	17275	19400	22700	27600
DTS Sedan 4D	KF549		48000	18100	20350	23600	28600

2003 CADILLAC — 1G6(DM57N)-3-#

CTS—V6—Equipment Schedule 2
W.B. 113.4"; 3.2 Liter.

Sedan 4D	DM57N		29990	17100	19200	22300	26900
Luxury Sport Pkg				700	700	935	935

SEVILLE—V8—Equipment Schedule 2
W.B. 112.2"; 4.6 Liter.

SLS Sedan 4D	KS54Y		45270	18100	20350	23100	27600
STS Touring Sedan 4D	KY549		51175	20450	22850	25800	30600

DeVILLE—V8—Equipment Schedule 2
W.B. 115.3"; 4.6 Liter.

Sedan 4D	KD54Y		43995	16500	18575	22000	27100
DHS Sedan 4D	KE54Y		48825	20550	23050	26600	32200
DTS Sedan 4D	KF549		48825	21400	24000	27600	33100

2004 CADILLAC — 1G6(DM57N)-4-#

CTS—V6—Equipment Schedule 2
W.B. 113.4"; 3.2 Liter.

Sedan 4D	DM57N		33155	18775	21025	24400	29500
Luxury Sport Pkg				750	750	1000	1000
V6 3.6 Liter		7		600	600	800	800

CTS-V—V8—Equipment Schedule 2
W.B. 113.4"; 5.7 Liter.

Sedan 4D	DN57S		49995	33500	37350	41200	47600

SEVILLE—V8—Equipment Schedule 2
W.B. 112.2"; 4.6 Liter.

SLS Sedan 4D	KS52Y		47955	22475	25150	28500	33800

DeVILLE—V8—Equipment Schedule 2
W.B. 115.3"; 4.6 Liter.

Sedan 4D	KD54Y		45445	20350	22750	26500	32400
DHS Sedan 4D	KE54Y		50595	24575	27550	31500	37600
DTS Sedan 4D	KF549		50595	25625	28600	32500	38800

XLR—V8—Equipment Schedule 1
W.B. 105.7"; 4.6 Liter.

Hardtop Conv 2D	YV34A		76200				

CHEVROLET

1990 CHEVROLET — 1G1(JC54G)-L-#

CAVALIER—4-Cyl.—Equipment Schedule 5
W.B. 101.2"; 2.2 Liter.

VL Sedan 4D	JC54G		9994	250	325	725	1300
VL Coupe 2D	JC14G		9794	250	325	725	1300
VL Wagon 4D	JC84G		10382	300	400	800	1425
Sedan 4D	JC54G		10748	300	400	800	1425
Coupe 2D	JC14G		10548	300	400	800	1425
Wagon 4D	JC84G		10805	300	400	800	1425
RS Sport Pkg				50	50	65	65
V6 3.1 Liter		T		100	100	135	135

CAVALIER—V6—Equipment Schedule 5
W.B. 101.2"; 3.1 Liter.

Z24 Sport Coupe 2D	JF14T		13115	500	725	1225	2100

CORSICA—4-Cyl.—Equipment Schedule 5
W.B. 103.4"; 2.2 Liter.

LT Notchback Sed 4D	LT54G		11240	325	475	900	1575
LT Hatchback Sed 4D	LT64G		11640	325	475	900	1575
V6 3.1 Liter		T		125	125	165	165

CORSICA—V6—Equipment Schedule 5
W.B. 103.4"; 3.1 Liter.

LTZ Sedan 4D	LT54T		13760	475	700	1225	2075

BERETTA—4-Cyl.—Equipment Schedule 5
W.B. 103.4"; 2.2 Liter.

Coupe 2D	LV14G		12065	400	600	1050	1800
V6 3.1 Liter		T		125	125	165	165

1990 CHEVROLET

Body Type	VIN	List	Trade-In Fair	Good	Pvt-Party Good	Retail Excellent
BERETTA—4-Cyl. Quad 4—Equipment Schedule 5						
W.B. 103.4"; 2.3 Liter.						
GTZ Coupe 2D	LZ14A	14715	600	875	1450	2400
Manual Trans			0	0	0	0
BERETTA—V6—Equipment Schedule 5						
W.B. 103.4"; 3.1 Liter.						
GT Coupe 2D	LW14T	13465	550	775	1300	2175
CELEBRITY—V6—Equipment Schedule 4						
W.B. 104.9"; 3.1 Liter.						
Wagon 4D	AW84T	15764	425	625	1100	1900
4-Cyl. 2.5 Liter	R		(150)	(150)	(200)	(200)
LUMINA—V6—Equipment Schedule 4						
W.B. 107.5"; 3.1 Liter.						
Sedan 4D	WL54T	15225	475	675	1275	2225
Coupe 2D	WL14T	14920	450	625	1225	2125
Euro Sedan 4D	WN54T	15900	575	825	1500	2575
Euro Coupe 2D	WN14T	15595	575	825	1500	2575
4-Cyl. 2.5 Liter			(250)	(250)	(335)	(335)
CAMARO—V6—Equipment Schedule 4						
W.B. 101.0"; 3.1 Liter.						
RS Coupe 2D	FP23T	13731	850	1175	2000	3250
V8 5.0 Liter	E		200	200	265	265
CAMARO—V8—Equipment Schedule 4						
W.B. 101.0"; 5.0 Liter.						
RS Convertible 2D	FP33E	19474	1950	2500	3725	5450
IROC-Z Spt Cpe 2D	FP23F	17628	1100	1550	2825	4575
IROC-Z Conv 2D	FP33F	22789	1800	2325	3750	5675
Manual Trans			(100)	(100)	(135)	(135)
V8 5.7 Liter TPI	8		250	250	335	335
CAPRICE—V8—Equipment Schedule 4						
W.B. 116.0"; 5.0 Liter.						
Sedan 4D	BL54E	15990	375	550	1000	1750
Classic Sedan 4D	BN54E	17177	475	700	1225	2075
Classic Wagon 4D	BN84Y	17786	525	750	1275	2125
Classic Brhm Sed 4D	BU54E	19214	525	750	1300	2175
Clsc Brhm LS Sed 4D	BU54E	20524	550	775	1350	2250
CORVETTE—V8—Equipment Schedule 2						
W.B. 96.2"; 5.7 Liter.						
Hatchback Coupe 2D	YY248	33444	4775	5625	7600	10350
Convertible 2D	YY348	38729	5650	6550	8700	11700
ZR1 H'Back Coupe 2D	YZ23J	59555	12575	14200	17700	22700
Glass Roof Panel			250	250	335	335
Dual Roof Panels			300	300	400	400
Hard Top			200	200	265	265
Handling Pkg			50	50	65	65
6-Spd Manual Trans			0	0	0	0

1991 CHEVROLET — 1G1(JC54G)-M-#

Body Type	VIN	List	Trade-In Fair	Good	Pvt-Party Good	Retail Excellent
CAVALIER—4-Cyl.—Equipment Schedule 5						
W.B. 101.3"; 2.2 Liter.						
VL Sedan 4D	JC54G	10252	300	400	825	1475
VL Coupe 2D	JC14G	9977	300	400	825	1475
VL Wagon 4D	JC84G	10742	325	475	925	1625
RS Sedan 4D	JC54G	10915	325	475	925	1625
RS Coupe 2D	JC14G	10715	325	475	925	1625
RS Wagon 4D	JC84G	11455	325	475	925	1625
V6 3.1 Liter	T		125	125	165	165
CAVALIER—V6—Equipment Schedule 5						
W.B. 101.3"; 3.1 Liter.						
RS Convertible 2D	JF34T	16929	900	1250	2025	3250
Z24 Coupe 2D	JF14T	13700	600	875	1450	2425
CORSICA—4-Cyl.—Equipment Schedule 5						
W.B. 103.4"; 2.2 Liter.						
LT Notchback Sed 4D	LT54G	11845	400	575	1025	1800
LT Hatchback Sed 4D	LT64G	12520	400	575	1025	1800
V6 3.1 Liter	T		125	125	165	165
BERETTA—4-Cyl.—Equipment Schedule 5						
W.B. 103.4"; 2.2 Liter.						
Coupe 2D	LV14G	12140	475	700	1225	2075
V6 3.1 Liter	T		125	125	165	165
BERETTA—4-Cyl. Quad 4—Equipment Schedule 5						
W.B. 103.4"; 2.3 Liter.						
GTZ Coupe 2D	LZ14A	15545	700	1000	1650	2725

1991 CHEVROLET

Body	Type	VIN	List	Trade-In Fair	Trade-In Good	Pvt-Party Good	Retail Excellent
Manual Trans			......	0	0	0	0
V6 3.1 Liter		T	......	125	125	165	165
BERETTA—V6—Equipment Schedule 4							
W.B. 103.4"; 3.1 Liter.							
GT Coupe 2D		LW14T	14145	625	900	1500	2525
LUMINA—V6—Equipment Schedule 4							
W.B. 107.5"; 3.1 Liter, 3.4 Liter.							
Sedan 4D		WL54T	15200	550	800	1475	2525
Coupe 2D		WL14T	15095	525	750	1400	2425
Euro Sedan 4D		WN54T	16060	675	950	1700	2900
Euro Coupe 2D		WN14T	16055	675	950	1700	2900
Z34 Coupe 2D		WP14X	18455	875	1225	2100	3425
Manual Trans				(50)	(50)	(65)	(65)
4-Cyl. 2.5 Liter		R		(275)	(275)	(365)	(365)
CAMARO—V6—Equipment Schedule 4							
W.B. 101.0"; 3.1 Liter.							
RS Coupe 2D		FP23T	14496	950	1350	2275	3650
RS Convertible 2D		FP33T	20134	1625	2125	3300	5000
Manual Trans				(175)	(175)	(235)	(235)
V8 5.0 Liter		E		225	225	300	300
CAMARO—V8—Equipment Schedule 4							
W.B. 101.0"; 5.0 Liter.							
Z28 Coupe 2D		FP23F	18276	1325	1800	2925	4525
Z28 Convertible 2D		FP33F	23504	2275	2850	4175	6025
Manual Trans				(100)	(100)	(135)	(135)
V8 5.7 Liter TPI		8		250	250	335	335
CAPRICE—V8—Equipment Schedule 4							
W.B. 115.9"; 5.0 Liter.							
Sedan 4D		BL53E	18040	650	900	1575	2700
Classic Sedan 4D		BN53E	19938	825	1150	1975	3200
Wagon 4D		BL83E	19590	1300	1775	2875	4450
LTZ Pkg				50	50	65	65
CORVETTE—V8—Equipment Schedule 2							
W.B. 96.2"; 5.7 Liter.							
Hatchback Coupe 2D		YY248	33990	5250	6150	8175	11050
Convertible 2D		YY348	40305	6200	7175	9375	12500
ZR1 H'Back Coupe 2D		YZ238	64668	13725	15500	19050	24200
Glass Roof Panel				250	250	335	335
Dual Roof Panels				300	300	400	400
Handling Pkg				50	50	65	65
Hard Top				225	225	300	300
6-Spd Manual Trans				0	0	0	0

1992 CHEVROLET — 1G1(JC544)-N-#

Body	Type	VIN	List	Trade-In Fair	Trade-In Good	Pvt-Party Good	Retail Excellent
CAVALIER—4-Cyl.—Equipment Schedule 5							
W.B. 101.3"; 2.2 Liter.							
VL Sedan 4D		JC544	11046	300	450	900	1575
VL Coupe 2D		JC144	10946	300	450	900	1575
VL Wagon 4D		JC844	11651	375	525	1000	1750
RS Sedan 4D		JC544	11914	375	550	1025	1800
RS Coupe 2D		JC144	11714	375	550	1025	1800
RS Wagon 4D		JC844	12419	400	575	1050	1850
RS Convertible 2D		JC344	17720	875	1225	2025	3250
V6 3.1 Liter		T		150	150	200	200
CAVALIER—V6—Equipment Schedule 5							
W.B. 101.3"; 3.1 Liter.							
Z24 Coupe 2D		JF14T	14710	700	1000	1650	2750
Z24 Convertible 2D		JF34T	20020	1025	1450	2425	3875
CORSICA—4-Cyl.—Equipment Schedule 5							
W.B. 103.4"; 2.2 Liter.							
LT Sedan 4D		LT534	12834	450	625	1150	1975
V6 3.1 Liter		T		150	150	200	200
BERETTA—4-Cyl.—Equipment Schedule 5							
W.B. 103.4"; 2.2 Liter.							
Coupe 2D		LV134	12834	525	750	1325	2225
GT Coupe 2D		LW134	14410	625	900	1500	2525
V6 3.1 Liter		T		150	150	200	200
BERETTA—4-Cyl. Quad—Equipment Schedule 5							
W.B. 103.4"; 2.3 Liter.							
GTZ Coupe 2D		LZ13A	16620	800	1125	1850	3025
Manual Trans				0	0	0	0
V6 3.1 Liter		T		150	150	200	200

1992 CHEVROLET

Body	Type	VIN	List	Trade-In Fair	Good	Pvt-Party Good	Retail Excellent
LUMINA—V6—Equipment Schedule 4							
W.B. 107.5"; 3.1 Liter.							
Sedan 4D	WL54T	15850	**575**	**825**	**1525**	**2700**
Coupe 2D	WL14T	15745	**525**	**750**	**1475**	**2575**
Euro Sedan 4D	WN54T	16860	**725**	**1025**	**1850**	**3150**
Euro Coupe 2D	WN14T	16755	**725**	**1025**	**1850**	**3150**
Z34 Coupe 2D	WP14X	19580	**900**	**1300**	**2375**	**3900**
Manual Trans			(75)	(75)	(100)	(100)
4-Cyl. 2.5 Liter	R		(325)	(325)	(435)	(435)
V6 3.4 Liter	X		175	175	235	235
CAMARO—V6—Equipment Schedule 4							
W.B. 101.0"; 3.1 Liter.							
RS Coupe 2D	FP23T	14132	**1125**	**1575**	**2700**	**4275**
RS Convertible 2D	FP33T	19960	**1950**	**2500**	**3775**	**5550**
Manual Trans			(225)	(225)	(300)	(300)
V8 5.0 Liter	E		250	250	335	335
CAMARO—V8—Equipment Schedule 4							
W.B. 101.0"; 5.0 Liter.							
Z28 Coupe 2D	FP23F	18112	**1675**	**2200**	**3400**	**5125**
Z28 Convertible 2D	FP33F	23405	**2750**	**3375**	**4775**	**6775**
Manual Trans			(125)	(125)	(165)	(165)
V8 5.7 Liter TPI	8		275	275	365	365
CAPRICE—V8—Equipment Schedule 4							
W.B. 115.9"; 5.0 Liter.							
Sedan 4D	BL53E	19018	**800**	**1125**	**1950**	**3200**
Classic Sedan 4D	BN53E	21746	**975**	**1425**	**2450**	**3925**
Wagon 4D	BL83E	20433	**1650**	**2150**	**3325**	**5025**
LTZ Pkg			75	75	100	100
V6 4.3 Liter	Z		(125)	(125)	(165)	(165)
V8 5.7 Liter	7		125	125	165	165
CORVETTE—V8—Equipment Schedule 2							
W.B. 96.2"; 5.7 Liter.							
Hatchback Coupe 2D	YY23P	35270	**5850**	**6825**	**8925**	**11900**
Convertible 2D	YY33P	41780	**6925**	**8000**	**10250**	**13550**
ZR1 H'Back Coupe 2D	YZ23J	72378	**15600**	**17575**	**21300**	**26800**
Glass Roof Panel			250	250	335	335
Dual Roof Panels			300	300	400	400
Hard Top			275	275	365	365
Suspension Pkg			75	75	100	100
6-Spd Manual Trans			25	25	35	35

1993 CHEVROLET — 1G1(JC544)-P-#

Body	Type	VIN	List	Trade-In Fair	Good	Pvt-Party Good	Retail Excellent
CAVALIER—4-Cyl.—Equipment Schedule 5							
W.B. 101.3"; 2.2 Liter.							
VL Sedan 4D	JC544	10667	**350**	**500**	**1000**	**1800**
VL Coupe 2D	JC144	10567	**350**	**500**	**1000**	**1800**
VL Wagon 4D	JC844	11287	**400**	**600**	**1125**	**1975**
RS Sedan 4D	JC544	11335	**450**	**625**	**1175**	**2075**
RS Coupe 2D	JC144	11235	**450**	**625**	**1175**	**2075**
RS Wagon 4D	JC844	12035	**475**	**675**	**1225**	**2125**
RS Convertible 2D	JC344	17110	**975**	**1400**	**2300**	**3650**
V6 3.1 Liter	T		175	175	235	235
CAVALIER—V6—Equipment Schedule 5							
W.B. 101.3"; 3.1 Liter.							
Z24 Coupe 2D	JF14T	14215	**825**	**1150**	**1975**	**3200**
Z24 Convertible 2D	JF34T	20020	**1225**	**1675**	**2750**	**4275**
CORSICA—4-Cyl.—Equipment Schedule 5							
W.B. 103.4"; 2.2 Liter.							
LT Sedan 4D	LT534	13230	**500**	**725**	**1300**	**2225**
V6 3.1 Liter	T		175	175	235	235
BERETTA—4-Cyl.—Equipment Schedule 5							
W.B. 103.4"; 2.2 Liter.							
Coupe 2D	LV134	13230	**600**	**875**	**1500**	**2525**
GT Coupe 2D	LW134	14830	**725**	**1025**	**1725**	**2850**
V6 3.1 Liter	T		175	175	235	235
BERETTA—4-Cyl. Quad 4—Equipment Schedule 5							
W.B. 103.4"; 2.3 Liter.							
GTZ Coupe 2D	LZ13A	17025	**900**	**1275**	**2100**	**3400**
Manual Trans			0	0	0	0
V6 3.1 Liter	T		175	175	235	235
LUMINA—V6—Equipment Schedule 4							
W.B. 107.5"; 3.1 Liter.							
Sedan 4D	WL54T	15550	**625**	**900**	**1675**	**2925**

1993 CHEVROLET

Body	Type	VIN	List	Trade-In Fair	Good	Pvt-Party Good	Retail Excellent
Coupe 2D		WL14T	15735	550	800	1550	2750
Euro Sedan 4D		WN54T	17040	800	1125	2075	3475
Euro Coupe 2D		WN14T	16810	800	1125	2075	3475
Z34 Coupe 2D		WP14X	19370	1000	1450	2575	4175
Manual Trans				(100)	(100)	(135)	(135)
4-Cyl. 2.2 Liter		4		(375)	(375)	(500)	(500)
V6 3.4 Liter		X		200	200	265	265
CAMARO—V6—Equipment Schedule 4							
W.B. 101.1"; 3.4 Liter.							
Coupe 2D		FP22S	16385	1500	2025	3200	4850
Manual Trans				(275)	(275)	(365)	(365)
CAMARO—V8—Equipment Schedule 4							
W.B. 101.1"; 5.7 Liter.							
Z28 Coupe 2D		FP22P	20125	2175	2750	4025	5850
CAPRICE CLASSIC—V8—Equipment Schedule 4							
W.B. 115.9"; 5.0 Liter.							
Sedan 4D		BL53E	19223	950	1350	2400	3925
LS Sedan 4D		BN53E	20950	1225	1675	2800	4425
Wagon 4D		BL83E	21318	2025	2575	3850	5650
LTZ Pkg				100	100	135	135
V8 5.7 Liter		7		150	150	200	200
CORVETTE—V8—Equipment Schedule 2							
W.B. 96.2"; 5.7 Liter.							
Coupe 2D		YY23P	36230	6525	7550	9750	12850
Convertible 2D		YY33P	42830	7750	8900	11350	14750
ZR1 Coupe 2D		YZ2JP	66828	17525	19675	23600	29400
Anniversary Edition				700	700	935	935
Glass Roof Panel				250	250	335	335
Dual Roof Panels				300	300	400	400
Hard Top (Convertible)				325	325	435	435
Suspension Pkg				100	100	135	135
6-Spd Manual Trans				50	50	65	65

1994 CHEVROLET — 1G1(JC544)–R–#

Body	Type	VIN	List	Trade-In Fair	Good	Pvt-Party Good	Retail Excellent
CAVALIER—4-Cyl.—Equipment Schedule 5							
W.B. 101.3"; 2.2 Liter.							
VL Sedan 4D		JC544	11082	400	600	1150	2075
VL Coupe 2D		JC144	10932	400	600	1150	2075
Wagon 4D		JC844	12375	550	800	1450	2475
RS Sedan 4D		JC544	11790	525	750	1350	2350
RS Coupe 2D		JC144	11685	525	750	1350	2350
RS Convertible 2D		JC344	17470	1100	1550	2650	4175
V6 3.1 Liter		T		200	200	265	265
CAVALIER—V6—Equipment Schedule 5							
W.B. 101.3"; 3.1 Liter.							
Z24 Coupe 2D		JF14T	14965	950	1350	2275	3650
Z24 Convertible 2D		JF34T	20965	1475	1950	3075	4675
CORSICA—4-Cyl.—Equipment Schedule 5							
W.B. 103.4"; 2.2 Liter.							
LT Sedan 4D		LD554	13630	575	825	1475	2525
V6 3.1 Liter		M		200	200	265	265
BERETTA—4-Cyl.—Equipment Schedule 5							
W.B. 103.4"; 2.2 Liter.							
Coupe 2D		LV154	13455	700	975	1700	2850
V6 3.1 Liter		M		200	200	265	265
BERETTA—4-Cyl. Quad 4—Equipment Schedule 5							
W.B. 103.4"; 2.3 Liter.							
Z26 Coupe 2D		LW15A	15795	1000	1450	2475	3950
Manual Trans				0	0	0	0
V6 3.1 Liter		M		200	200	265	265
LUMINA—V6—Equipment Schedule 4							
W.B. 107.5"; 3.1 Liter.							
Sedan 4D		WL54T	16645	700	975	1900	3275
Euro Sedan 4D		WN54T	17815	900	1275	2400	4000
Euro Coupe 2D		WN14T	17625	900	1275	2400	4000
Z34 Coupe 2D		WP14X	19835	1125	1575	2800	4500
V6 3.4 Liter		X		225	225	300	300
CAMARO—V6—Equipment Schedule 4							
W.B. 101.1"; 3.4 Liter.							
Coupe 2D		FP22S	16250	1825	2350	3600	5325
Convertible 2D		FP32S	22021	2825	3450	4850	6825
Manual Trans				(325)	(325)	(435)	(435)

1994 CHEVROLET

Body	Type	VIN	List	Trade-In Fair	Good	Pvt-Party Good	Retail Excellent
CAMARO—V8—Equipment Schedule 4							
W.B. 101.1"; 5.7 Liter.							
Z28 Coupe 2D		FP22P	19900	2600	3225	4550	6475
Z28 Convertible 2D		FP32P	25351	3900	4625	6200	8400
CAPRICE CLASSIC—V8—Equipment Schedule 4							
W.B. 115.9"; 4.3 Liter.							
Sedan 4D		BL52W	20698	1150	1600	2775	4425
LS Sedan 4D		BN52W	22010	1500	2025	3250	4950
Wagon 4D		BL82P	22703	2425	3025	4375	6300
V8 5.7 Liter		P		175	175	235	235
IMPALA SS—V8—Equipment Schedule 2							
W.B. 115.9"; 5.7 Liter.							
Sedan 4D		BN52P	23355	5500	6400	8175	10800
CORVETTE—V8—Equipment Schedule 2							
W.B. 96.2"; 5.7 Liter.							
Coupe 2D		YY22P	37345	7275	8375	10700	13950
Convertible 2D		YY32P	44120	8650	9900	12400	15950
ZR1 Coupe 2D		YZ22J	67993	19500	21900	25900	32000
Glass Roof Panel				250	250	335	335
Dual Roof Panels				300	300	400	400
Hard Top (Convertible)				375	375	500	500
Suspension Pkg				125	125	165	165
6-Spd Manual Trans				75	75	100	100

1995 CHEVROLET — (1or2)G1(JC524)-S-#

Body	Type	VIN	List	Trade-In Fair	Good	Pvt-Party Good	Retail Excellent
CAVALIER—4-Cyl.—Equipment Schedule 5							
W.B. 104.1"; 2.2 Liter, 2.3 Liter.							
Sedan 4D		JC524	12030	625	900	1575	2725
Coupe 2D		JC124	11825	625	900	1575	2725
LS Sedan 4D		JF524	12950	825	1150	2025	3300
LS Convertible 2D		JF324	17695	1725	2250	3425	5100
Z24 Coupe 2D		JF12D	14385	900	1300	2250	3650
CORSICA—4-Cyl.—Equipment Schedule 5							
W.B. 103.4"; 2.2 Liter.							
Sedan 4D		LD554	14385	675	950	1700	2900
V6 3.1 Liter		M		225	225	300	300
BERETTA—4-Cyl.—Equipment Schedule 5							
W.B. 103.4"; 2.2 Liter.							
Coupe 2D		LV154	14045	825	1150	1975	3275
V6 3.1 Liter		M		225	225	300	300
BERETTA—V6—Equipment Schedule 5							
W.B. 103.4"; 3.1 Liter.							
Z26 Coupe 2D		LW15M	16790	1175	1625	2750	4325
LUMINA—V6—Equipment Schedule 4							
W.B. 107.5"; 3.1 Liter.							
Sedan 4D		WL52M	16837	950	1375	2200	3475
LS Sedan 4D		WN52M	17712	1150	1600	2625	4075
V6 3.4 Liter		X		250	250	335	335
MONTE CARLO—V6—Equipment Schedule 4							
W.B. 107.5"; 3.1 Liter, 3.4 Liter.							
LS Coupe 2D		WW12M	17512	1100	1550	2550	3975
Z34 Coupe 2D		WX12X	19495	1400	1875	2950	4475
CAMARO—V6—Equipment Schedule 4							
W.B. 101.1".							
Coupe 2D		FP22S	17536	2200	2775	4050	5900
Convertible 2D		FP32S	22781	3300	3950	5400	7475
Manual Trans				(375)	(375)	(500)	(500)
V6 3.8 Liter		K		200	200	265	265
CAMARO—V8—Equipment Schedule 4							
W.B. 101.1"; 5.7 Liter.							
Z28 Coupe 2D		FP22P	21236	3075	3725	5150	7175
Z28 Convertible 2D		FP32P	26388	4475	5275	6900	9225
CAPRICE CLASSIC—V8—Equipment Schedule 4							
W.B. 115.9"; 4.3 Liter.							
Sedan 4D		BL52W	21798	1475	1950	3225	4975
Wagon 4D		BL82P	24373	2875	3525	4975	7025
V8 5.7 Liter		P		200	200	265	265
IMPALA SS—V8—Equipment Schedule 2							
W.B. 115.9"; 5.7 Liter.							
Sedan 4D		BL52P	24385	6250	7225	9125	11900
CORVETTE—V8—Equipment Schedule 2							
W.B. 96.2"; 5.7 Liter.							
Coupe 2D		YY22P	37955	8100	9300	11650	15100

1995 CHEVROLET

Body	Type	VIN	List	Trade-In Fair	Trade-In Good	Pvt-Party Good	Retail Excellent
Convertible 2D		YY32P	44835	9600	10950	13500	17250
ZR1 Coupe 2D		YZ22J	68603	21600	24300	28400	34800
Glass Roof Panel				250	250	335	335
Dual Roof Panels				300	300	400	400
Hard Top (Convertible)				425	425	565	565
Suspension Pkg				150	150	200	200
6-Spd Manual Trans				100	100	135	135

1996 CHEVROLET — (1,2or4)G1(JC524)–T–#

CAVALIER—4-Cyl.—Equipment Schedule 5
W.B. 104.1"; 2.2 Liter, 2.4 Liter.

Body	Type	VIN	List	Fair	Good	Pvt Good	Excellent
Sedan 4D		JC524	12872	750	1050	1925	3250
Coupe 2D		JC124	12672	750	1050	1925	3250
LS Sedan 4D		JF524	13395	950	1375	2450	3975
LS Convertible 2D		JF324	17995	2050	2600	3850	5625
Z24 Coupe 2D		JF12T	15490	1075	1525	2675	4250
CORSICA—4-Cyl.—Equipment Schedule 5							
W.B. 103.4"; 2.2 Liter.							
Sedan 4D		LD554	14885	800	1125	2025	3350
V6 3.1 Liter		M		250	250	335	335
BERETTA—4-Cyl.—Equipment Schedule 5							
W.B. 103.4"; 2.2 Liter.							
Coupe 2D		LV154	14545	925	1325	2400	3925
V6 3.1 Liter		M		250	250	335	335
BERETTA—V6—Equipment Schedule 5							
W.B. 103.4"; 3.1 Liter.							
Z26 Coupe 2D		LW15M	17190	1400	1875	3050	4700
LUMINA—V6—Equipment Schedule 4							
W.B. 107.5"; 3.1 Liter.							
Sedan 4D		WL52M	17863	1200	1650	2700	4225
LS Sedan 4D		WN52M	18812	1450	1925	3025	4550
V6 3.4 Liter		X		275	275	365	365
MONTE CARLO—V6—Equipment Schedule 4							
W.B. 107.5"; 3.1 Liter, 3.4 Liter.							
LS Coupe 2D		WW12M	18012	1400	1875	2975	4500
Z34 Coupe 2D		WX12X	19995	1725	2250	3375	5000
CAMARO—V6—Equipment Schedule 4							
W.B. 101.1"; 3.8 Liter.							
Coupe 2D		FP22K	18411	2625	3250	4600	6575
Convertible 2D		FP32K	23796	3750	4500	6000	8175
RS Coupe 2D		FP22K	20911	3175	3850	5300	7400
RS Convertible 2D		FP32K	25246	4300	5075	6675	8950
Manual Trans				(400)	(400)	(535)	(535)
CAMARO—V8—Equipment Schedule 4							
W.B. 101.1"; 5.7 Liter.							
Z28 Coupe 2D		FP22P	21951	3575	4300	5800	7975
Z28 Convertible 2D		FP32P	27016	5100	5975	7650	10150
SS Pkg				1350	1350	1800	1800
CAPRICE CLASSIC—V8—Equipment Schedule 4							
W.B. 115.9"; 4.3 Liter.							
Sedan 4D		BL52W	21495	1850	2375	3750	5650
Wagon 4D		BL82P	22995	3400	4100	5650	7850
V8 5.7 Liter		P		200	200	265	265
IMPALA SS—V8—Equipment Schedule 2							
W.B. 115.9"; 5.7 Liter.							
Sedan 4D		BL52P	24995	7025	8100	10150	13050
CORVETTE—V8—Equipment Schedule 2							
W.B. 96.2"; 5.7 Liter.							
Coupe 2D		YY22P	38400	9050	10325	12800	16400
Convertible 2D		YY32P	46235	10650	12150	14800	18700
Collector Edition				725	725	965	965
Grand Sport				2000	2000	2665	2665
Glass Roof Panel				250	250	335	335
Dual Roof Panels				300	300	400	400
Hard Top (Convertible)				475	475	635	635
Suspension Pkg				175	175	235	235
6-Spd Manual Trans				125	125	165	165
V8 5.7 Liter LT4		5		1000	1000	1335	1335

1997 CHEVROLET — (1,2or4)G1(JC524)–V–#

CAVALIER—4-Cyl.—Equipment Schedule 5
W.B. 104.1"; 2.2 Liter, 2.4 Liter.

Body	Type	VIN	List	Fair	Good	Pvt Good	Excellent
Sedan 4D		JC524	13357	900	1300	2400	4000

1997 CHEVROLET

Body	Type	VIN	List	Trade-In Fair	Trade-In Good	Pvt-Party Good	Retail Excellent
Coupe 2D		JC124	13157	900	1300	2400	4000
RS Coupe 2D		JC124	14070	1075	1525	2700	4350
LS Sedan 4D		JF524	13880	1150	1600	2800	4475
LS Convertible 2D		JF324	18265	2375	2950	4300	6200
Z24 Coupe 2D		JF12T	15760	1350	1825	3025	4725
MALIBU—V6—Equipment Schedule 5							
W.B. 107.0"; 3.1 Liter.							
Sedan 4D		ND52M	16390	1000	1450	2725	4550
LS Sedan 4D		NE52M	18715	1275	1750	3125	5000
4-Cyl. 2.4 Liter		T		(200)	(200)	(265)	(265)
LUMINA—V6—Equipment Schedule 4							
W.B. 107.5"; 3.1 Liter.							
Sedan 4D		WL52M	18485	1525	2050	3175	4775
LS Sedan 4D		WL52M	19695	1800	2325	3475	5125
LTZ Sedan 4D		WN52M	20200	1850	2375	3550	5200
V6 3.4 Liter		X		300	300	400	400
MONTE CARLO—V6—Equipment Schedule 4							
W.B. 107.5"; 3.1 Liter, 3.4 Liter.							
LS Coupe 2D		WW12M	18220	1750	2275	3425	5075
Z34 Coupe 2D		WX12X	20495	2100	2700	3900	5625
CAMARO—V6—Equipment Schedule 4							
W.B. 101.1"; 3.8 Liter.							
Coupe 2D		FP22K	18786	3100	3750	5200	7300
Convertible 2D		FP32K	24341	4300	5075	6675	8975
RS Coupe 2D		FP22K	20541	3725	4450	5975	8175
RS Convertible 2D		FP32K	25741	4900	5725	7400	9800
Manual Trans				(425)	(425)	(565)	(565)
CAMARO—V8—Equipment Schedule 4							
W.B. 101.1"; 5.7 Liter.							
Z28 Coupe 2D		FP22P	22721	4175	4950	6525	8800
Z28 Convertible 2D		FP32P	28091	5775	6725	8475	11050
SS Pkg				1450	1450	1935	1935
CORVETTE—V8—Equipment Schedule 2							
W.B. 104.5"; 5.7 Liter.							
Coupe 2D		YY22G	38365	11475	13000	15850	19950
Glass Roof Panel				250	250	335	335
Dual Roof Panels				300	300	400	400
Suspension Pkg				200	200	265	265
6-Spd Manual Trans				150	150	200	200

1998 CHEVROLET—(1,2or4)(C,GorY)1(MR226)–W–

Body	Type	VIN	List	Trade-In Fair	Trade-In Good	Pvt-Party Good	Retail Excellent
METRO—3-Cyl.—Equipment Schedule 6							
W.B. 93.1"; 1.0 Liter.							
Coupe 2D		MR226	10110	900	1300	2125	3400
METRO—4-Cyl.—Equipment Schedule 6							
W.B. 93.1"; 1.3 Liter.							
LSi Sedan 4D		MR522	11800	1475	1950	3025	4525
LSi Coupe 2D		MR222	10910	1075	1525	2550	4000
PRIZM—4-Cyl.—Equipment Schedule 6							
W.B. 97.0"; 1.8 Liter.							
Sedan 4D		SK528	15248	2050	2600	3800	5525
LSi Sedan 4D		SK528	16208	2200	2775	4000	5750
CAVALIER—4-Cyl.—Equipment Schedule 6							
W.B. 104.1"; 2.2 Liter, 2.4 Liter.							
Sedan 4D		JC524	13705	1100	1550	2725	4400
Coupe 2D		JC124	13505	1100	1550	2725	4400
RS Coupe 2D		JC124	14945	1375	1850	3050	4750
LS Sedan 4D		JF524	14750	1500	1975	3200	4925
LS Convertible 2D		JF324		2475	3075	4400	6275
Z24 Coupe 2D		JF12T	16490	1650	2175	3400	5150
Z24 Convertible 2D		JF32T	20690	2775	3400	4750	6700
MALIBU—V6—Equipment Schedule 5							
W.B. 107.0"; 3.1 Liter.							
Sedan 4D		ND52M	16690	1300	1775	3125	5000
LS Sedan 4D		NE52M	18995	1650	2150	3550	5475
4-Cyl. 2.4 Liter		T		(200)	(200)	(265)	(265)
LUMINA—V6—Equipment Schedule 4							
W.B. 107.5"; 3.1 Liter.							
Sedan 4D		WL52M	18785	1950	2475	3625	5275
LS Sedan 4D		WL52M	20020	2175	2750	3900	5625
LTZ Sedan 4D		WN52M	20520	2275	2850	4050	5750
V6 3.8 Liter		K		300	300	400	400

Body	Type	VIN	List	Trade-In Fair	Good	Pvt-Party Good	Retail Excellent

MONTE CARLO—V6—Equipment Schedule 4
W.B. 107.5"; 3.1 Liter, 3.8 Liter.

LS Coupe 2D		WW12M	18570	2125	2700	3900	5575
Z34 Coupe 2D		WX12K	20845	2575	3200	4400	6150

CAMARO—V6—Equipment Schedule 4
W.B. 101.1"; 3.8 Liter.

Coupe 2D		FP22K	19196	3675	4400	5825	7925
Convertible 2D		FP32K	24771	4950	5800	7375	9650
T-Bar Roof				425	425	565	565
Manual Trans				(450)	(450)	(600)	(600)

CAMARO—V8—Equipment Schedule 4
W.B. 101.1"; 5.7 Liter.

Z28 Coupe 2D		FP22G	22571	4875	5700	7275	9550
Z28 Convertible 2D		FP32G	27975	6600	7625	9325	11900
T-Bar Roof				425	425	565	565
SS Pkg				1550	1550	2065	2065

CORVETTE—V8—Equipment Schedule 2
W.B. 104.5"; 5.7 Liter.

Coupe 2D		YY22G	38565	12775	14450	17050	21000
Convertible 2D		YY32G	45295	15300	17275	20100	24500
Glass Roof Panel				250	250	335	335
Dual Roof Panels				300	300	400	400
Suspension Pkg				200	200	265	265
6-Spd Manual Trans				150	150	200	200

1999 CHEVROLET — (1,2or3)(C,GorY)1(MR226)-X-

METRO—3-Cyl.—Equipment Schedule 6
W.B. 93.1"; 1.0 Liter.

Coupe 2D		MR226	10488	1025	1475	2525	4000

METRO—4-Cyl.—Equipment Schedule 6
W.B. 93.1"; 1.3 Liter.

LSi Sedan 4D		MR522	12187	1750	2275	3375	5000
LSi Sedan 4D		MR222	11285	1300	1775	2850	4400

PRIZM—4-Cyl.—Equipment Schedule 6
W.B. 97.1"; 1.8 Liter.

Sedan 4D		SK528	13828	2450	3050	4325	6175
LSi Sedan 4D		SK528	15269	2675	3275	4550	6425

CAVALIER—4-Cyl.—Equipment Schedule 5
W.B. 104.1"; 2.2 Liter, 2.4 Liter.

Sedan 4D		JC524	13876	1475	1950	3225	4975
Coupe 2D		JC124	13776	1425	1900	3175	4925
RS Coupe 2D		JC124	15216	1750	2275	3550	5350
LS Sedan 4D		JF524	14921	1900	2425	3750	5575
Z24 Coupe 2D		JF12T	17261	2100	2675	3975	5825
Z24 Convertible 2D		JF32T	20861	3375	4075	5500	7550

MALIBU—V6—Equipment Schedule 5
W.B. 107.5"; 3.1 Liter.

Sedan 4D		ND52M,J	17080	1725	2250	3750	5775
LS Sedan 4D		NE52M,J	19445	2125	2700	4225	6325
4-Cyl. 2.4 Liter		T		(250)	(250)	(335)	(335)

LUMINA—V6—Equipment Schedule 4
W.B. 107.5"; 3.1 Liter, 3.8 Liter.

Sedan 4D		WL52M	18982	2350	2925	4150	5925
LS Sedan 4D		WL52M	20480	2650	3250	4500	6300
LTZ Sedan 4D		WN52K	20920	2750	3375	4650	6475

MONTE CARLO—V6—Equipment Schedule 4
W.B. 107.5"; 3.1 Liter, 3.8 Liter.

LS Coupe 2D		WW12M	19070	2600	3225	4450	6250
Z34 Coupe 2D		WX12K	21095	3100	3750	5050	6900

CAMARO—V6—Equipment Schedule 4
W.B. 101.1"; 3.8 Liter.

Coupe 2D		FP22K	19221	4475	5275	6825	9075
Convertible 2D		FP32K	24796	5925	6900	8575	11050
T-Bar Roof				500	500	665	665
Manual Trans				(500)	(500)	(665)	(665)

CAMARO—V8—Equipment Schedule 4
W.B. 101.1"; 5.7 Liter.

Z28 Coupe 2D		FP22G	22996	5950	6900	8600	11100
Z28 Convertible 2D		FP32G	28385	7900	9075	10900	13650
T-Bar Roof				500	500	665	665
SS Pkg				1775	1775	2365	2365

CORVETTE—V8—Equipment Schedule 2
W.B. 104.5"; 5.7 Liter.

1999 CHEVROLET

Body	Type	VIN	List	Trade-In Fair	Good	Pvt-Party Good	Retail Excellent
Hard Top 2D		YY12G	39082	12525	14150	16700	20500
Coupe 2D		YY22G	39476	14200	16025	18650	22900
Convertible 2D		YY32G	45884	17100	19200	22200	26700
Glass Roof Panel				275	275	365	365
Dual Roof Panels				350	350	465	465
Suspension Pkg				250	250	335	335
6-Spd Manual Trans				175	175	235	235

2000 CHEVROLET — (1,2or3)(C,GorY)1(MR226)–Y–

METRO—3-Cyl.—Equipment Schedule 6
W.B. 93.1"; 1.0 Liter.

Body	Type	VIN	List	Fair	Good	Good	Excellent
Coupe 2D		MR226	10680	1275	1750	2850	4450

METRO—4-Cyl.—Equipment Schedule 6
W.B. 93.1"; 1.3 Liter.

| LSi Sedan 4D | | MR522 | 12395 | 2100 | 2700 | 3875 | 5550 |
| LSi Coupe 2D | | MR222 | 11530 | 1600 | 2100 | 3250 | 4875 |

PRIZM—4-Cyl.—Equipment Schedule 6
W.B. 97.1"; 1.8 Liter.

| Sedan 4D | | SK528 | 14246 | 2975 | 3625 | 4975 | 6900 |
| LSi Sedan 4D | | SK528 | 16272 | 3225 | 3900 | 5250 | 7225 |

CAVALIER—4-Cyl.—Equipment Schedule 5
W.B. 104.1"; 2.2 Liter, 2.4 Liter.

Sedan 4D		JC524	14275	2225	2775	4075	5925
Coupe 2D		JC124	14175	2150	2725	4025	5850
LS Sedan 4D		JF524	15220	2700	3325	4675	6600
Z24 Coupe 2D		JF12T	17560	2950	3600	4950	6900
Z24 Convertible 2D		JF32T	21025	4400	5175	6650	8775

MALIBU—V6—Equipment Schedule 5
W.B. 107.0"; 3.1 Liter.

| Sedan 4D | | ND52J | 16995 | 2300 | 2875 | 4500 | 6700 |
| LS Sedan 4D | | NE52J | 19625 | 2750 | 3375 | 5050 | 7300 |

LUMINA—V6—Equipment Schedule 4
W.B. 107.5"; 3.1 Liter.

| Sedan 4D | | WL52J | 19350 | 2925 | 3575 | 4900 | 6800 |

IMPALA—V6—Equipment Schedule 4
W.B. 110.5"; 3.4 Liter, 3.8 Liter.

| Sedan 4D | | WF52E | 19787 | 4550 | 5375 | 6975 | 9325 |
| LS Sedan 4D | | WH52K | 22925 | 5400 | 6300 | 8000 | 10450 |

MONTE CARLO—V6—Equipment Schedule 4
W.B. 110.5"; 3.4 Liter, 3.8 Liter.

| LS Coupe 2D | | WW12E | 20090 | 4675 | 5525 | 7150 | 9100 |
| SS Coupe 2D | | WX12K | 22295 | 6050 | 7000 | 8550 | 10900 |

CAMARO—V6—Equipment Schedule 4
W.B. 101.1"; 3.8 Liter.

Coupe 2D		FP22K	19360	5425	6325	8000	10400
Convertible 2D		FP32K	25490	7075	8150	9925	12600
T-Bar Roof				575	575	765	765
Manual Trans				(525)	(525)	(700)	(700)

CAMARO—V8—Equipment Schedule 4
W.B. 101.1"; 5.7 Liter.

Z28 Coupe 2D		FP22G	23515	7200	8275	10100	12750
Z28 Convertible 2D		FP32G	28900	9300	10600	12600	15550
T-Bar Roof				575	575	765	765
SS Pkg				2000	2000	2665	2665

CORVETTE—V8—Equipment Schedule 2
W.B. 104.5"; 5.7 Liter.

Hard Top 2D		YY12G	39205	15125	17050	19950	24400
Coupe 2D		YY22G	40085	17050	19150	22200	26900
Convertible 2D		YY32G	46510	20350	22750	26100	31300
Glass Roof Panel				300	300	400	400
Dual Roof Panels				400	400	535	535
Suspension Pkg				275	275	365	365
6-Spd Manual Trans				200	200	265	265

2001 CHEVROLET — (1or2)(C,GorY)(MR522)–1–#

METRO—4-Cyl.—Equipment Schedule 6
W.B. 93.1"; 1.3 Liter.

| LSi Sedan 4D | | MR522 | 12915 | 2675 | 3275 | 4525 | 6375 |

PRIZM—4-Cyl.—Equipment Schedule 6
W.B. 97.0"; 1.8 Liter.

| Sedan 4D | | SK528 | 14460 | 3575 | 4275 | 5700 | 7775 |
| LSi Sedan 4D | | SK528 | 16525 | 3875 | 4600 | 6050 | 8125 |

2001 CHEVROLET

Body	Type	VIN	List	Trade-In Fair	Trade-In Good	Pvt-Party Good	Retail Excellent
CAVALIER—4-Cyl.—Equipment Schedule 5							
W.B. 104.1"; 2.2 Liter, 2.4 Liter.							
Sedan 4D		JC524	14480	2825	3450	4875	6875
Coupe 2D		JC124	14380	2725	3350	4775	6775
LS Sedan 4D		JF524	15375	3350	4050	5500	7550
Z24 Coupe 2D		JF12T	17665	3625	4350	5800	7900
MALIBU—V6—Equipment Schedule 5							
W.B. 107.0"; 3.1 Liter.							
Sedan 4D		ND52J	17595	3000	3675	5425	7825
LS Sedan 4D		NE52J	19875	3500	4200	6000	8475
LUMINA—V6—Equipment Schedule 4							
W.B. 107.5"; 3.1 Liter.							
Sedan 4D		WL52J	19490	3675	4400	5825	7900
IMPALA—V6—Equipment Schedule 4							
W.B. 110.5"; 3.4 Liter, 3.8 Liter.							
Sedan 4D		WF52E	20271	5550	6450	8175	10700
LS Sedan 4D		WH52K	23825	6475	7500	9275	11900
MONTE CARLO—V6—Equipment Schedule 4							
W.B. 110.5"; 3.4 Liter, 3.8 Liter.							
LS Coupe 2D		WW12E	20410	5625	6525	8100	10400
SS Coupe 2D		WX15K	23000	7100	8200	9850	12400
CAMARO—V6—Equipment Schedule 4							
W.B. 101.1"; 3.8 Liter.							
Coupe 2D		FP22K	19635	6525	7525	9300	11900
Convertible 2D		FP32K	25760	8350	9575	11400	14250
T-Bar Roof		------		650	650	865	865
RS				275	275	365	365
Manual Trans		------		(550)	(550)	(735)	(735)
CAMARO—V8—Equipment Schedule 4							
W.B. 101.1"; 5.7 Liter.							
Z28 Coupe 2D		FP22G	23935	8600	9850	11700	14600
Z28 Convertible 2D		FP32G	29325	10900	12325	14350	17500
T-Bar Roof		------		650	650	865	865
SS Pkg				2225	2225	2965	2965
CORVETTE—V8—Equipment Schedule 4							
W.B. 104.5"; 5.7 Liter.							
Coupe 2D		YY22G	40475	18900	21225	24300	29200
Z06 Hard Top 2D		YY12G	47500	22375	25050	28400	33700
Convertible 2D		YY32G	47000	22550	25250	28500	33900
Glass Roof Panel				325	325	435	435
Dual Roof Panels				450	450	600	600
Suspension Pkg				300	300	400	400
6-Spd Manual Trans				225	225	300	300

2002 CHEVROLET — (1or2)(GorY)1(SK528)-2-#

Body	Type	VIN	List	Trade-In Fair	Trade-In Good	Pvt-Party Good	Retail Excellent
PRIZM—4-Cyl.—Equipment Schedule 6							
W.B. 97.0"; 1.8 Liter.							
Sedan 4D		SK528	14815	4275	5075	6550	8750
LSi Sedan 4D		SK528	16880	4600	5425	6925	9175
CAVALIER—4-Cyl.—Equipment Schedule 5							
W.B. 104.1"; 2.2 Liter, 2.4 Liter.							
Sedan 4D		JC524	15280	3575	4300	5800	8000
Coupe 2D		JC124	15180	3475	4175	5700	7875
LS Sedan 4D		JF524	16330	4175	4950	6475	8725
LS Coupe 2D		JS124	16230	4000	4775	6300	8550
LS Sport Sedan 4D		JF52F	17700	4375	5150	6725	9000
LS Sport Coupe 2D		JS12F	17600	4250	5050	6575	8825
Z24 Sedan 4D		JH52T	17900	4600	5425	6975	9300
Z24 Coupe 2D		JF12T	17800	4475	5275	6850	9125
MALIBU—V6—Equipment Schedule 5							
W.B. 107.0"; 3.1 Liter.							
Sedan 4D		ND52J	18120	3900	4650	6300	9250
LS Sedan 4D		NE52J	20325	4475	5250	7200	9900
IMPALA—V6—Equipment Schedule 4							
W.B. 110.5"; 3.4 Liter, 3.8 Liter.							
Sedan 4D		WF52E	20820	6750	7800	9600	12350
LS Sedan 4D		WH52K	24270	7750	8900	10800	13700
MONTE CARLO—V6—Equipment Schedule 4							
W.B. 110.5"; 3.4 Liter, 3.8 Liter.							
LS Coupe 2D		WW12E	20920	6775	7800	9500	12050
SS Coupe 2D		WX12K	23470	8450	9650	11400	14200
CAMARO—V6—Equipment Schedule 4							
W.B. 101.1"; 3.8 Liter.							

Body	Type	VIN	List	Trade-In Fair	Trade-In Good	Pvt-Party Good	Retail Excellent
Coupe 2D		FP22K	20640	7825	8975	10900	13750
Convertible 2D		FP32K	26650	9850	11225	13200	16300
T-Bar Roof				725	725	965	965
RS				300	300	400	400
Manual Trans				(575)	(575)	(765)	(765)
CAMARO—V8—Equipment Schedule 4							
W.B. 101.1"; 5.7 Liter.							
Z28 Coupe 2D		FP22G	24770	10175	11575	13600	16700
Z28 Convertible 2D		FP32G	30165	12625	14300	16450	19850
35th Annv Coupe 2D		FP22G	27270	11225	12775	14850	18100
35th Annv Conv 2D		FP32G	32665	13675	15450	17650	21200
T-Bar Roof				725	725	965	965
SS Pkg				2425	2425	3235	3235
CORVETTE—V8—Equipment Schedule 2							
W.B. 104.5"; 5.7 Liter.							
Coupe 2D		YY22G	41650	21025	23525	26600	31600
Z06 Hard Top 2D		YY12G	50350	24775	27750	31000	36500
Convertible 2D		YY32G	48175	24950	27925	31200	36700
Glass Roof Panel				350	350	465	465
Dual Roof Panels				500	500	665	665
Suspension Pkg				325	325	435	435
6-Spd Manual Trans				250	250	335	335

2003 CHEVROLET — (1or2)G1(JC52F)-3-#

CAVALIER—4-Cyl.—Equipment Schedule 5
W.B. 104.1"; 2.2 Liter.

Body	Type	VIN	List	Fair	Good	Good	Excellent
Sedan 4D		JC52F	15520	4550	5375	6900	9125
Coupe 2D		JC12F	15370	4450	5225	6750	8975
LS Sedan 4D		JF52F	16920	5175	6050	7600	9925
LS Coupe 2D		JF12F	16770	5050	5900	7450	9750
LS Sport Sedan 4D		JH52F	18120	5400	6300	7875	10200
LS Sport Coupe 2D		JH12F	17970	5250	6150	7700	10050
MALIBU—V6—Equipment Schedule 5							
W.B. 107.0"; 3.1 Liter.							
Sedan 4D		ND52J	18290	5100	5975	7950	10700
LS Sedan 4D		NE52J	20575	5700	6625	8600	11400
IMPALA—V6—Equipment Schedule 4							
W.B. 110.5"; 3.4 Liter, 3.8 Liter.							
Sedan 4D		WF52K	21350	8225	9425	11300	14100
LS Sedan 4D		WH52K	24460	9325	10650	12600	15550
MONTE CARLO—V6—Equipment Schedule 4							
W.B. 110.5"; 3.4 Liter, 3.8 Liter.							
LS Coupe 2D		WW12K	21350	8225	9425	11250	13950
SS Coupe 2D		WX12K	23665	9975	11375	13300	16250
CORVETTE—V8—Equipment Schedule 2							
W.B. 104.5"; 5.7 Liter.							
Coupe 2D		YY22G	43895	23425	26300	29300	34400
Z06 Hard Top 2D		YY12S	51155	27550	30825	34100	39600
Convertible 2D		YY32G	50370	27750	31000	34200	39700
50th Anniversary				3000	3000	4000	4000
Glass Roof Panel				375	375	500	500
Dual Roof Panels				550	550	735	735
Suspension Pkg				350	350	465	465
6-Spd Manual Trans				275	275	365	365

2004 CHEVROLET — (1,2orK)(GorL)1(TD526)-4-#

AVEO—4-Cyl.—Equipment Schedule 6
W.B. 97.6"; 1.6 Liter.

Body	Type	VIN	List	Fair	Good	Good	Excellent
SVM Sedan 4D		TD526	9995	4325	5100	6275	8075
SVM Hatchback 4D		TD626	9995	4325	5100	6275	8075
Sedan 4D		TD526	11690	4950	5800	7000	8875
Hatchback 4D		TD626	11690	4950	5800	7000	8875
LS Sedan 4D		TJ526	12585	5350	6250	7475	9375
LS Hatchback 4D		TJ626	12585	5350	6250	7475	9375
CAVALIER—4-Cyl.—Equipment Schedule 5							
W.B. 104.1"; 2.2 Liter.							
Sedan 4D		JC52F	15995	6125	7100	8725	11200
Coupe 2D		JC12F	15975	5975	6925	8575	11000
LS Sedan 4D		JF52F	17230	6800	7825	9500	12050
LS Coupe 2D		JF12F	17030	6650	7675	9350	11900
LS Sport Sedan 4D		JH52F	18635	7025	8100	9800	12400
LS Sport Coupe 2D		JH12F	18435	6875	7925	9600	12150

Body	Type	VIN	List	Trade-In Fair	Trade-In Good	Pvt-Party Good	Retail Excellent
CLASSIC—4-Cyl.—Equipment Schedule 5							
W.B. 107.0" 2.2 Liter.							
Sedan 4D		ND52F	19380	**5900**	**6875**	**9250**	**12550**
MALIBU—V6—Equipment Schedule 5							
W.B. 106.3", 112.3" (MAXX); 3.5 Liter.							
Sedan 4D		ZS52F	18995				
MAXX Hatchback 4D		ZS638	21725				
LS Sedan 4D		ZT528	20995				
LS MAXX H'Back 4D		ZT638	22225				
LT Sedan 4D		ZU528	23495				
LT MAXX H'Back 4D		ZU668	24725				
4-Cyl. 2.2 Liter		F					
IMPALA—V6—Equipment Schedule 4							
W.B. 110.5"; 3.4 Liter, 3.8 Liter.							
Sedan 4D		WF52E	22150	**9975**	**11375**	**13400**	**16450**
LS Sedan 4D		WH52K	25000	**11175**	**12725**	**14800**	**18050**
IMPALA—V6 Supercharged—Equipment Schedule 4							
W.B. 110.5"; 3.8 Liter.							
SS Sedan 4D		WP521	27995	**14600**	**16475**	**18700**	**22400**
MONTE CARLO—V6—Equipment Schedule 4							
W.B. 110.5"; 3.4 Liter, 3.8 Liter.							
LS Coupe 2D		WW12E	22075	**10075**	**11475**	**13550**	**16650**
SS Coupe 2D		WX12K	24225	**12050**	**13625**	**15800**	**19200**
MONTE CARLO—V6 Supercharged—Equipment Schedule 4							
W.B. 110.5"; 3.8 Liter.							
SS Coupe 2D		WZ121	27795	**13000**	**14725**	**16950**	**20400**
CORVETTE—V8—Equipment Schedule 2							
W.B. 104.5"; 5.7 Liter.							
Coupe 2D		YY22G	44535	**25825**	**28900**	**32000**	**37200**
Z06 Hard Top 2D		YY12S	52385	**30425**	**33900**	**37200**	**42800**
Convertible 2D		YY32G	51535	**30525**	**34075**	**37300**	**43000**
Commemorative Ed				600	600	800	800
Glass Roof Panel				400	400	535	535
Dual Roof Panels				575	575	765	765
Handling Pkg				375	375	500	500
6-Spd Manual Trans				300	300	400	400

CHRYSLER

1990 CHRYSLER — (1C3orZC2)–(J41K)–L–#

Body	Type	VIN	List	Trade-In Fair	Trade-In Good	Pvt-Party Good	Retail Excellent
LeBARON—4-Cyl.—Equipment Schedule 4							
W.B. 100.3", 100.4" (Conv); 2.5 Liter.							
Highline Coupe 2D		J41K	14561	**475**	**700**	**1200**	**2025**
Highline Conv 2D		J45K	17061	**675**	**925**	**1550**	**2575**
4-Cyl. 2.5 Liter Turbo				**0**	**0**	**0**	**0**
V6 3.0 Liter		3		**200**	**200**	**265**	**265**
LeBARON—V6—Equipment Schedule 4							
W.B. 100.3", 100.4" (Conv), 103.3" (Sed); 3.0 Liter.							
Sedan 4D		A563	16660	**775**	**1075**	**1725**	**2800**
Premium Coupe 2D		J513	17205	**525**	**750**	**1300**	**2175**
Premium Conv 2D		J553	20060	**900**	**1300**	**2050**	**3250**
GT Coupe 2D		J413	16742	**525**	**750**	**1300**	**2175**
GT Convertible 2D		J453	18816	**850**	**1200**	**1950**	**3100**
Manual Trans				**(100)**	**(100)**	**(135)**	**(135)**
4-Cyl. 2.5 Liter Turbo		J		**0**	**0**	**0**	**0**
LeBARON—4-Cyl. Turbo—Equipment Schedule 4							
W.B. 100.3", 100.4" (Conv); 2.2 Liter, 2.5 Liter.							
GTC Coupe 2D		J41C	18703	**675**	**925**	**1550**	**2575**
GTC Convertible 2D		J45C	20871	**975**	**1400**	**2200**	**3425**
Manual Trans				**(100)**	**(100)**	**(135)**	**(135)**
NEW YORKER—V6— Equipment Schedule 4							
W.B. 104.3"; 3.3 Liter.							
Salon Sedan 4D		C46R	18632	**725**	**1025**	**1650**	**2725**
Landau Sedan 4D		C66R	20986	**925**	**1325**	**2125**	**3350**
FIFTH AVE—V6—Equipment Schedule 4							
W.B. 109.3"; 3.3 Liter.							
Sedan 4D		Y66R	23992	**1025**	**1475**	**2325**	**3600**
IMPERIAL—V6—Equipment Schedule 4							
W.B. 109.3"; 3.3 Liter.							
Sedan 4D		Y56R	25545	**1300**	**1775**	**2800**	**4275**
TC—4-Cyl. Turbo—Equipment Schedule 2							
W.B. 93.3"; 2.2 Liter.							

Body	Type	VIN	List	Trade-In Fair	Trade-In Good	Pvt-Party Good	Retail Excellent
Convertible 2D		R120	35550	2600	3225	4600	6600
V6 3.0 Liter		S		0	0	0	0

1991 CHRYSLER — (1C3orZC2)–(J41K)–M–#

LeBARON—4-Cyl.—Equipment Schedule 4
W.B. 100.3"; 2.5 Liter.

Body	Type	VIN	List	Fair	Good	Good	Excellent
Highline Coupe 2D		J41K	15389	550	800	1375	2300
Highline Conv 2D		J45K	18021	775	1075	1775	2925
Manual Trans				(175)	(175)	(235)	(235)
4-Cyl. 2.5 Liter Turbo		J		0	0	0	0
V6 3.0 Liter		3		200	200	265	265

LeBARON—V6—Equipment Schedule 4
W.B. 100.3", 103.3" (Sed); 3.0 Liter.

Sedan 4D		A563	16915	900	1250	2025	3250
Premium LX Coupe 2D		J513	16580	625	900	1500	2525
Premium LX Conv 2D		J553	20235	1025	1475	2475	3900
GTC Coupe 2D		J413	16655	700	1000	1650	2750
GTC Convertible 2D		J453	19160	900	1300	2100	3350
Manual Trans				(100)	(100)	(135)	(135)
4-Cyl.		K		(150)	(150)	(200)	(200)
4-Cyl. 2.5 Liter Turbo		J		0	0	0	0

NEW YORKER—V6—Equipment Schedule 4
W.B. 104.3"; 3.3 Liter.

Salon Sedan 4D		C66R	18990	850	1175	1950	3150

FIFTH AVE—V6—Equipment Schedule 4
W.B. 109.3"; 3.8 Liter.

Sedan 4D		Y66R	23405	1225	1700	2750	4250

IMPERIAL—V6—Equipment Schedule 2
W.B. 109.3"; 3.3 Liter, 3.8 Liter.

Sedan 4D		Y56L	27515	1550	2075	3200	4775

TC—V6—Equipment Schedule 2
W.B. 93.0"; 3.0 Liter.

Convertible 2D		S120	37570	2525	3125	4675	6850

1992 CHRYSLER — (1or3)C3–(A46K)–N–#

LeBARON—4-Cyl.—Equipment Schedule 4
W.B. 100.5", 103.5" (Sed); 2.5 Liter.

Sedan 4D		A46K	15253	775	1100	1825	2975
Landau Sedan 4D		A56K	16195	825	1150	1900	3075
Coupe 2D		U41K	14767	625	900	1525	2575
Convertible 2D		U45K	18631	875	1225	2025	3275
Manual Trans				(225)	(225)	(300)	(300)
4-Cyl. 2.5 Liter Turbo		J		25	25	35	35
V6 3.0 Liter		3		225	225	300	300

LeBARON—V6—Equipment Schedule 4
W.B. 100.5", 103.5" (Sed); 3.0 Liter.

LX Sedan 4D		A763	16624	975	1425	2275	3600
LX Coupe 2D		U513	16894	725	1025	1700	2800
LX Convertible 2D		U553	20930	1175	1625	2700	4175
GTC Coupe 2D		U413	17356	825	1150	1900	3100
GTC Convertible 2D		U453	20177	1000	1450	2425	3875
4-Cyl. 2.5 Liter Turbo		J		25	25	35	35

NEW YORKER—V6—Equipment Schedule 4
W.B. 104.5"; 3.3 Liter.

Salon Sedan 4D		C66R	20134	950	1375	2250	3575

FIFTH AVE—V6—Equipment Schedule 4
W.B. 109.5"; 3.3 Liter, 3.8 Liter.

Sedan 4D		V66R	23906	1500	2000	3100	4675

IMPERIAL—V6—Equipment Schedule 2
W.B. 109.6"; 3.8 Liter.

Sedan 4D		V56L	29063	1875	2400	3575	5250

1993 CHRYSLER — (1or3)C3–(U41K)–P–#

LeBARON—4-Cyl.—Equipment Schedule 4
W.B. 100.6", 103.5" (Sed); 2.5 Liter.

Coupe 2D		U41K	15594	725	1025	1700	2850
Convertible 2D		U45K	19569	975	1400	2300	3650
LE Sedan 4D		A36K	15774	900	1250	2075	3300
Manual Trans				(275)	(275)	(365)	(365)
V6 3.0 Liter		3		250	250	335	335

LeBARON—V6—Equipment Schedule 4
W.B. 100.6", 103.5" (Sed); 3.0 Liter.

1993 CHRYSLER

Body	Type	VIN	List	Trade-In Fair	Trade-In Good	Pvt-Party Good	Retail Excellent
Landau Sedan 4D		A563	17689	1025	1475	2475	3925
LX Coupe 2D		U513	17351	825	1150	1950	3150
LX Convertible 2D		U553	21675	1375	1850	2925	4500
GTC Coupe 2D		U413	18040	900	1300	2175	3475
GTC Convertible 2D		U453	21015	1125	1575	2650	4150
CONCORDE—V6—Equipment Schedule 4							
W.B. 113.0'; 3.3 Liter.							
Sedan 4D		L56T	19718	1375	1850	2950	4525
V6 3.5 Liter		F		150	150	200	200
NEW YORKER—V6—Equipment Schedule 4							
W.B. 104.5'; 3.3 Liter.							
Salon Sedan 4D		C66R	20000	1100	1550	2625	4100
FIFTH AVE—V6—Equipment Schedule 4							
W.B. 109.6'; 3.3 Liter, 3.8 Liter.							
Sedan 4D		V66R	22723	1800	2325	3450	5100
IMPERIAL—V6—Equipment Schedule 2							
W.B. 109.6'; 3.8 Liter.							
Sedan 4D		V56L	29991	2200	2775	4000	5750

1994 CHRYSLER — (1or3)C3–(A363)–R–#

Body	Type	VIN	List	Trade-In Fair	Trade-In Good	Pvt-Party Good	Retail Excellent
LeBARON—V6—Equipment Schedule 4							
W.B. 100.6', 103.5" (Sed); 3.0 Liter.							
LE Sedan 4D		A363	17226	1075	1525	2600	4100
Landau Sedan 4D		A563	18438	1200	1650	2750	4300
GTC/LX Convertible 2D		U453	18239	1325	1800	2900	4500
4-Cyl. 2.5 Liter		K		(225)	(225)	(300)	(300)
CONCORDE—V6—Equipment Schedule 4							
W.B. 113.0'; 3.3 Liter.							
Sedan 4D		L56T	21017	1600	2100	3300	4975
V6 3.5 Liter		F		225	225	300	300
NEW YORKER—V6—Equipment Schedule 2							
W.B. 113.0'; 3.5 Liter.							
Sedan 4D		D46F	26126	1575	2100	3300	5025
LHS—V6—Equipment Schedule 2							
W.B. 113.0'; 3.5 Liter.							
Sedan 4D		D56F	30868	2050	2600	3875	5700

1995 CHRYSLER — (1,2or4)C3–(U42Y)–S–#

Body	Type	VIN	List	Trade-In Fair	Trade-In Good	Pvt-Party Good	Retail Excellent
SEBRING—4-Cyl.—Equipment Schedule 4							
W.B. 103.7'; 2.0 Liter.							
LX Coupe 2D		U42Y	17636	2050	2600	3700	5300
Manual Trans				(375)	(375)	(500)	(500)
V6 2.5 Liter		H,N		325	325	435	435
SEBRING—V6—Equipment Schedule 4							
W.B. 103.7'; 2.5 Liter.							
LXi Coupe 2D		U52H,N	20548	2500	3100	4275	6000
CIRRUS—V6—Equipment Schedule 4							
W.B. 108.0'; 2.5 Liter.							
LX Sedan 4D		J56H,N	17970	1500	2025	3150	4725
LXi				100	100	135	135
4-Cyl. 2.4 Liter		X		(275)	(275)	(365)	(365)
LeBARON—V6—Equipment Schedule 4							
W.B. 100.6'; 3.0 Liter.							
GTC/LX Convertible 2D		U453	18709	1525	2050	3225	4900
CONCORDE—V6—Equipment Schedule 4							
W.B. 113.0'; 3.3 Liter.							
Sedan 4D		D56T	21085	1900	2425	3700	5475
V6 3.5 Liter		F		250	250	335	335
NEW YORKER—V6—Equipment Schedule 2							
W.B. 113.0'; 3.5 Liter.							
Sedan 4D		C46F	26191	1925	2450	3775	5625
LHS—V6—Equipment Schedule 2							
W.B. 113.0'; 3.5 Liter.							
Sedan 4D		C56F	30190	2400	3000	4400	6325

1996 CHRYSLER — (1,2or4)C3–(U42Y)–T–#

Body	Type	VIN	List	Trade-In Fair	Trade-In Good	Pvt-Party Good	Retail Excellent
SEBRING—4-Cyl.—Equipment Schedule 4							
W.B. 103.7', 106.0" (Conv); 2.0 Liter, 2.4 Liter.							
LX Coupe 2D		U42Y	18418	2400	2975	4125	5825
JX Convertible 2D		L45X	19995	3400	4100	5400	7300
Manual Trans				(400)	(400)	(535)	(535)
V6 2.5 Liter		H,N		350	350	465	465

1996 CHRYSLER

Body	Type	VIN	List	Trade-In Fair	Trade-In Good	Pvt-Party Good	Retail Excellent
SEBRING—V6—Equipment Schedule 4							
W.B. 103.7", 106.0" (Conv); 2.5 Liter.							
LXi Coupe 2D		U52N	20685	2875	3525	4775	6575
JXi Convertible 2D		L55H	25210	3850	4575	5900	7900
CIRRUS—V6—Equipment Schedule 4							
W.B. 108.0"; 2.5 Liter.							
LX Sedan 4D		J56H	18895	1850	2375	3550	5200
LXi				100	100	135	135
4-Cyl. 2.4 Liter		X		(300)	(300)	(400)	(400)
CONCORDE—V6—Equipment Schedule 4							
W.B. 113.0"; 3.3 Liter.							
LX Sedan 4D		D56T	19995	2225	2775	4100	5950
LXi				100	100	135	135
V6 3.5 Liter		F		250	250	335	335
NEW YORKER—V6—Equipment Schedule 2							
W.B. 113.0"; 3.5 Liter.							
Sedan 4D		C46F	27895	2325	2900	4325	6300
LHS—V6—Equipment Schedule 2							
W.B. 113.0"; 3.5 Liter.							
Sedan 4D		C56F	30850	2850	3500	5000	7075

1997 CHRYSLER — (1,2,3or4)C3–(U42Y)–V–#

Body	Type	VIN	List	Trade-In Fair	Trade-In Good	Pvt-Party Good	Retail Excellent
SEBRING—4-Cyl.—Equipment Schedule 4							
W.B. 103.7", 106.0" (Conv); 2.0 Liter, 2.4 Liter.							
LX Coupe 2D		U42Y	18541	2775	3400	4650	6450
JX Convertible 2D		L45X	21560	3875	4600	6000	8025
JXi Convertible 2D		L55X	25195	3950	4700	6100	8100
Manual Trans				(425)	(425)	(565)	(565)
V6 2.5 Liter		H,N		375	375	500	500
SEBRING—V6—Equipment Schedule 4							
W.B. 103.7"; 2.5 Liter.							
LXi Coupe 2D		U52N	21555	3300	4000	5325	7250
CIRRUS—V6—Equipment Schedule 4							
W.B. 108.0"; 2.5 Liter.							
LX Sedan 4D		J56H	19265	2250	2800	4025	5775
LXi				100	100	135	135
4-Cyl. 2.4 Liter		X		(325)	(325)	(435)	(435)
CONCORDE—V6—Equipment Schedule 4							
W.B. 113.0"; 3.5 Liter.							
LX Sedan 4D		D56F	20985	2600	3225	4575	6525
LXi				100	100	135	135
LHS—V6—Equipment Schedule 2							
W.B. 113.0"; 3.5 Liter.							
Sedan 4D		C56F	30850	3400	4100	5700	7950

1998 CHRYSLER — (1,2,3or4)C3–(U49Y)–W–#

Body	Type	VIN	List	Trade-In Fair	Trade-In Good	Pvt-Party Good	Retail Excellent
SEBRING—4-Cyl.—Equipment Schedule 4							
W.B. 103.7", 106.0" (Conv); 2.0 Liter, 2.4 Liter.							
LX Coupe 2D		U49Y	18850	3300	3950	5175	6975
JX Convertible 2D		L45X	21985	4475	5275	6600	8625
JXi Convertible 2D		L55X	25575	4550	5375	6725	8725
Limited				300	300	400	400
Manual Trans				(450)	(450)	(600)	(600)
V6 2.5 Liter		H,N		425	425	565	565
SEBRING—V6—Equipment Schedule 4							
W.B. 103.7"; 2.5 Liter.							
LXi Coupe 2D		U59N	21310	3875	4600	5900	7800
CIRRUS—V6—Equipment Schedule 4							
W.B. 108.0"; 2.5 Liter.							
LXi Sedan 4D		J56H	19995	3025	3700	4825	6550
CONCORDE—V6—Equipment Schedule 4							
W.B. 113.0"; 2.7 Liter.							
LX Sedan 4D		D46R	21855	2950	3600	4950	6900
LXi				100	100	135	135
V6 3.2 Liter		J		250	250	335	335

1999 CHRYSLER — (1,2,3or4)C3–(U42Y)–X–#

Body	Type	VIN	List	Trade-In Fair	Trade-In Good	Pvt-Party Good	Retail Excellent
SEBRING—4-Cyl.—Equipment Schedule 4							
W.B. 103.7"; 2.0 Liter.							
LX Coupe 2D		U42Y	19390	3975	4725	6025	7950
Manual Trans				(500)	(500)	(665)	(665)
V6 2.5 Liter		N		300	300	400	400

0105

1999 CHRYSLER

Body	Type	VIN	List	Trade-In Fair	Trade-In Good	Pvt-Party Good	Retail Excellent
SEBRING—V6—Equipment Schedule 4							
W.B. 103.7", 106.0" (Conv); 2.5 Liter.							
LXi Coupe 2D		U52N	21860	4750	5575	6900	8950
JX Convertible 2D		L45H	24505	5650	6550	8000	10200
JXi Convertible 2D		L55H	26820	6075	7025	8500	10750
Limited				325	325	435	435
CIRRUS—V6—Equipment Schedule 4							
W.B. 108.0"; 2.5 Liter.							
LXi Sedan 4D		J56H	19995	3775	4500	5725	7575
CONCORDE—V6—Equipment Schedule 4							
W.B. 113.0"; 2.7 Liter.							
LX Sedan 4D		D46R	22115	3650	4375	5825	7950
LXi				125	125	165	165
V6 3.2 Liter		J		300	300	400	400
300M—V6—Equipment Schedule 2							
W.B. 113.0"; 3.5 Liter.							
Sedan 4D		E66G	29445	6100	7075	8750	11300
LHS—V6—Equipment Schedule 2							
W.B. 113.0"; 3.5 Liter.							
Sedan 4D		C56G	29445	4900	5750	7375	9700

2000 CHRYSLER — (1,2,3or4)C3–(U42N)–Y–#

Body	Type	VIN	List	Trade-In Fair	Trade-In Good	Pvt-Party Good	Retail Excellent
SEBRING—V6—Equipment Schedule 4							
W.B. 103.7", 106.0" (Conv); 2.5 Liter.							
LX Coupe 2D		U42N	19635	5100	5975	7375	9475
LXi Coupe 2D		U52N	22015	5700	6625	8075	10250
JX Convertible 2D		L45H	24790	6675	7700	9225	11150
JXi Convertible 2D		L55H	27105	7125	8225	9800	12200
Limited				350	350	465	465
CIRRUS—4-Cyl.—Equipment Schedule 4							
W.B. 108.0"; 2.0 Liter, 2.4 Liter.							
LX Sedan 4D		J46B	17675	3550	4250	5475	7300
Manual Trans				(475)	(475)	(635)	(635)
CIRRUS—V6—Equipment Schedule 4							
W.B. 108.0"; 2.5 Liter.							
LXi Sedan 4D		J56H	20480	4650	5500	6800	8750
CONCORDE—V6—Equipment Schedule 4							
W.B. 113.0"; 2.7 Liter, 3.2 Liter.							
LX Sedan 4D		D46R	22550	4475	5275	6850	9125
LXi Sedan 4D		D36J	26480	5100	5975	7550	9900
300M—V6—Equipment Schedule 2							
W.B. 113.0"; 3.5 Liter.							
Sedan 4D		E66G	29690	7225	8300	10150	12800
LHS—V6—Equipment Schedule 2							
W.B. 113.0"; 3.5 Liter.							
Sedan 4D		C56G	28695	5850	6825	8525	11050

2001 CHRYSLER — 1C(4or8)–(Y4BB)–1–#

Body	Type	VIN	List	Trade-In Fair	Trade-In Good	Pvt-Party Good	Retail Excellent
PT CRUISER—4-Cyl.—Equipment Schedule 4							
W.B. 103.0"; 2.4 Liter.							
Sport Wagon 4D		Y4BB	18325	5775	6725	8200	10450
Limited Sport Wag 4D		Y4BB	20685	6375	7400	8900	11250
Touring				275	275	365	365
SEBRING—4-Cyl.—Equipment Schedule 4							
W.B. 103.7", 108.0" (Sed); 2.4 Liter.							
LX Sedan 4D		L46G	18520	4425	5200	6525	8525
LX Coupe 2D		G42G	20495	5675	6600	8075	10250
V6 2.7/3.0 Liter		R,H		600	600	800	800
SEBRING—V6—Equipment Schedule 4							
W.B. 103.7", 106.0" (Conv), 108.0" (Sed); 2.7 Liter, 3.0 Liter.							
LXi Sedan 4D		L66R	21405	5650	6575	7975	10150
LXi Coupe 2D		G62H	22885	6775	7800	9325	11700
LX Convertible 2D		L55U	24945	7825	8975	10550	13100
LXi Convertible 2D		L65U	27405	8350	9575	11200	13750
Limited Convertible 2D		L65U	29490	8925	10225	11900	14550
CONCORDE—V6—Equipment Schedule 4							
W.B. 113.0"; 2.7 Liter, 3.2 Liter.							
LX Sedan 4D		D46R	22995	5425	6325	8025	10500
LXi Sedan 4D		D36J	27240	6150	7125	8850	11400
300M—V6—Equipment Schedule 2							
W.B. 113.0"; 3.5 Liter.							
Sedan 4D		E66G	30170	8575	9800	11750	14700

Body	Type	VIN	List	Trade-In Fair	Trade-In Good	Pvt-Party Good	Retail Excellent
LHS—V6—Equipment Schedule 2							
W.B. 113.0"; 3.5 Liter.							
Sedan 4D		C56G	29210	**7025**	**8100**	**9975**	**12700**
PROWLER—V6—Equipment Schedule 1							
W.B. 113.3"; 3.5 Liter.							
Roadster 2D		W65G	45400	**23625**	**26400**	**30000**	**35700**

2002 CHRYSLER–(1,2,3or4)C(3,4or8)–(Y48B)–2–#

Body	Type	VIN	List	Trade-In Fair	Trade-In Good	Pvt-Party Good	Retail Excellent
PT CRUISER—4-Cyl.—Equipment Schedule 4							
W.B. 103.0"; 2.4 Liter.							
Sport Wagon 4D		Y48B	18395	**6900**	**7950**	**9500**	**11900**
Touring Sport Wag 4D		Y58B	19540	**7250**	**8325**	**9900**	**12350**
Limited Sport Wag 4D		Y68B	21655	**7550**	**8700**	**10250**	**12750**
Dream Cruiser Wag 4D		Y68B	23395	**8225**	**9425**	**11050**	**13650**
Woodie Edition				**300**	**300**	**400**	**400**
SEBRING—4-Cyl.—Equipment Schedule 4							
W.B. 103.7", 106.0" (Conv), 108.0" (Sed); 2.4 Liter.							
LX Sedan 4D		L46X	18535	**5500**	**6400**	**7825**	**9975**
LX Coupe 2D		G42G	20615	**6750**	**7800**	**9325**	**11700**
LX Convertible 2D		L55G	23905	**9150**	**10425**	**12100**	**14800**
V6 2.7/3.0 Liter		R,H		**650**	**650**	**865**	**865**
SEBRING—V6—Equipment Schedule 4							
W.B. 103.7", 106.0" (Conv), 108.0" (Sed); 2.7 Liter, 3.0 Liter.							
LXi Sedan 4D		L56R	20875	**6850**	**7900**	**9375**	**11700**
LXi Coupe 2D		G52H	23130	**8025**	**9200**	**10800**	**13350**
LXi Convertible 2D		L55R	26755	**9700**	**11100**	**12750**	**15500**
GTC Convertible 2D		L75R	25875	**9050**	**10325**	**12000**	**14700**
Limited Convertible 2D		L65R	29390	**10325**	**11750**	**13500**	**16300**
CONCORDE—V6—Equipment Schedule 4							
W.B. 113.0"; 2.7 Liter, 3.5 Liter.							
LX Sedan 4D		D46R	22995	**6575**	**7600**	**9400**	**12100**
LXi Sedan 4D		D36M	25600	**7425**	**8525**	**10350**	**13150**
Limited Sedan 4D		D56G	28495	**7825**	**8975**	**10850**	**13700**
300M—V6—Equipment Schedule 2							
W.B. 113.0"; 3.5 Liter.							
Sedan 4D		E66G	28995	**10175**	**11575**	**13700**	**16900**
Special Sedan 4D		E76K	32595	**10500**	**11950**	**14000**	**17300**
PROWLER—V6—Equipment Schedule 1							
W.B. 113.0"; 3.5 Liter.							
Roadster 2D		W65G	45400	**26100**	**29175**	**32800**	**38700**

2003 CHRYSLER–(1,2,3or4)C(3,4or8)–(Y48B)–3–

Body	Type	VIN	List	Trade-In Fair	Trade-In Good	Pvt-Party Good	Retail Excellent
PT CRUISER—4-Cyl.—Equipment Schedule 4							
W.B. 103.0"; 2.4 Liter.							
Sport Wagon 4D		Y48B	18815	**8300**	**9525**	**11050**	**13500**
Touring Sport Wag 4D		Y58B	19940	**8700**	**9925**	**11450**	**13950**
Limited Sport Wag 4D		Y68B	22180	**9050**	**10325**	**11900**	**14450**
Woodie Edition				**300**	**300**	**400**	**400**
PT CRUISER—4-Cyl. HO Turbo—Equipment Schedule 4							
W.B. 103.0"; 2.4 Liter.							
GT Sport Wagon 4D		Y78G	23170	**11625**	**13150**	**14450**	**16800**
Dream Cruiser				**600**	**600**	**800**	**800**
SEBRING—4-Cyl.—Equipment Schedule 4							
W.B. 103.7", 106.0" (Conv), 108.0" (Sed); 2.4 Liter.							
LX Sedan 4D		L46X	19930	**6825**	**7850**	**9275**	**11500**
LX Coupe 2D		G42G	21560	**8025**	**9200**	**10750**	**13250**
LX Convertible 2D		L45X	24560	**10600**	**12100**	**13800**	**16600**
V6 2.7/3.0 Liter		U,R		**700**	**700**	**935**	**935**
SEBRING—V6—Equipment Schedule 4							
W.B. 103.7", 106.0" (Conv), 108.0" (Sed); 2.7 Liter, 3.0 Liter.							
LXi Sedan 4D		L56R	21295	**8300**	**9525**	**11050**	**13450**
LXi Coupe 2D		G52H	23835	**9475**	**10800**	**12450**	**15100**
GTC Convertible 2D		L75R	26160	**10550**	**12000**	**13700**	**16450**
LXi Convertible 2D		L55T	27410	**11275**	**12825**	**14550**	**17400**
Limited Convertible 2D		L65R	30045	**11950**	**13525**	**15300**	**18300**
CONCORDE—V6—Equipment Schedule 4							
W.B. 113.0"; 2.7 Liter, 3.5 Liter.							
LX Sedan 4D		D46R	23510	**8025**	**9200**	**11050**	**13800**
LXi Sedan 4D		D36M	26240	**8925**	**10225**	**12150**	**15050**
Limited Sedan 4D		D56G	29135	**9325**	**10650**	**12600**	**15600**
300M—V6—Equipment Schedule 2							
W.B. 113.0"; 3.5 Liter.							
Sedan 4D		E66G	29245	**12100**	**13725**	**15950**	**19400**

2003 CHRYSLER

Body	Type	VIN	List	Trade-In Fair	Good	Pvt-Party Good	Retail Excellent
Special Sedan 4D		E76K	32895	12475	14100	16350	19850

2004 CHRYSLER—(1,2,3or4)C(3,4or8)—(Y48B)—4—#

PT CRUISER—4-Cyl.—Equipment Schedule 4
W.B. 103.0"; 2.4 Liter.

Sport Wagon 4D		Y48B	19515	9975	11325	12850	15450
Touring Sport Wag 4D		Y58B	20585	10375	11800	13350	16000
Limited Sport Wag 4D		Y68B	22825	10750	12200	13800	16450
4-Cyl. 2.4L Turbo		8		950	950	1265	1265

PT CRUISER—4-Cyl. HO Turbo—Equipment Schedule 4
W.B. 103.0"; 2.4 Liter.

GT Sport Wagon 4D		Y78G	26245	13525	15300	16600	19150

SEBRING—4-Cyl.—Equipment Schedule 4
W.B. 103.7", 106.0" (Conv), 108.0" (Sed); 2.4 Liter.

Sedan 4D		L66R	19360	8275	9475	10900	13250
Coupe 2D		G42G	22305	9900	11225	13000	15800
Convertible 2D		L45J	25570	12325	13975	15900	19000
LX Sedan 4D		L46X	19500	8475	9700	11200	13600
LX Convertible 2D		L45X	25215	12725	14400	16300	19500
V6 2.7 Liter		T,R		750	750	1000	1000

SEBRING—V6—Equipment Schedule 4
W.B. 103.7", 106.0" (Conv), 108.0" (Sed); 2.7 Liter, 3.0 Liter.

LXi Sedan 4D		L56R	21840	10125	11525	13100	15750
LXi Convertible 2D		L55T	28140	13450	15175	17200	20400
GTC Convertible 2D		L75R	27045	12625	14250	16200	19400
Touring Sedan 4D		L56R	21200	10475	11900	13500	16200
Touring Convertible 2D		L55T	28370	13625	15400	17400	20600
Limited Sedan 4D		L66R	23240	11425	12950	14600	17350
Limited Coupe 2D		G52H	24580	12250	13875	15750	18850
Limited Convertible 2D		L65R	31180	14100	15925	17950	21300

CONCORDE—V6—Equipment Schedule 4
W.B. 113.0"; 2.7 Liter, 3.5 Liter.

LX Sedan 4D		D46R	24130	9750	11125	13100	16150
LXi Sedan 4D		D36M	26860	10850	12300	14350	17500
Limited Sedan 4D		D56G	29755	11225	12775	14850	18050

300M—V6—Equipment Schedule 2
W.B. 113.0"; 3.5 Liter.

Sedan 4D		E66G	29865	14600	16475	18900	22800
Special Sedan 4D		E76K	33295	14975	16850	19400	23300

CROSSFIRE—V6—Equipment Schedule 1
W.B. 94.5"; 3.2 Liter.

Coupe 2D		N69L	35570	19150	21500	23900	28000

DAEWOO

1999 DAEWOO — KLA(TA226)-X-#

LANOS—4-Cyl.—Equipment Schedule 6
W.B. 99.0"; 1.6 Liter.

S Hatchback 2D		TA226	9699	850	1200	1900	3025
S Sedan 4D		TA526	10399	950	1350	2100	3300
SE Hatchback 2D		TB226	11300	1025	1450	2275	3525
SE Sedan 4D		TB526	11600	1050	1500	2375	3650
SX Hatchback 2D		TC226	11669	1050	1500	2325	3600
SX Sedan 4D		TC526	11969	1075	1525	2475	3875

NUBIRA—4-Cyl.—Equipment Schedule 5
W.B. 101.0"; 2.0 Liter.

SX Sedan 4D		JA52C	13300	975	1425	2425	3900
SX Hatchback 4D		JA62Z	13300	950	1350	2250	3600
SX Wagon 4D		JA82Z	13900	1025	1475	2500	3975
CDX Sedan 4D		JB52Z	14610	1150	1600	2675	4175
CDX Hatchback 4D		JB62Z	14610	1100	1550	2600	4075
CDX Wagon 4D		JB82Z	15210	1200	1650	2700	4225

LEGANZA—4-Cyl.—Equipment Schedule 5
W.B. 105.1"; 2.2 Liter.

SE Sedan 4D		VB692	15590	1225	1700	2750	4250
SX Sedan 4D		VA692	16910	1650	2150	3250	4800
CDX Sedan 4D		VA692	18910	1975	2525	3650	5250

2000 DAEWOO — KLA(TA226)-Y-#

LANOS—4-Cyl.—Equipment Schedule 6
W.B. 99.2"; 1.6 Liter.

Body	Type	VIN	List	Trade-In Fair	Good	Pvt-Party Good	Retail Excellent
S Hatchback 2D		TA226	9699	1000	1450	2275	3575
S Sedan 4D		TA526	10479	1125	1575	2600	4000
SE Hatchback 2D		TB226	11230	1250	1725	2725	4175
SE Sedan 4D		TC526	12049	1375	1850	2825	4300

NUBIRA—4-Cyl.—Equipment Schedule 5
W.B. 101.2"; 2.0 Liter.

SE Sedan 4D		JC52Z	12885	1300	1775	2850	4425
CDX Sedan 4D		JB52Z	14755	1500	2025	3125	4700
CDX Wagon 4D		JB82Z	15355	1575	2100	3225	4800

LEGANZA—4-Cyl.—Equipment Schedule 5
W.B. 105.1"; 2.2 Liter.

SE Sedan 4D		VB692	14865	1650	2150	3275	4875
SX Sedan 4D		VA692	17065	2100	2675	3825	5475
CDX Sedan 4D		VA692	19065	2500	3100	4275	6000

2001 DAEWOO — KLA(TA226)-1-#

LANOS—4-Cyl.—Equipment Schedule 6
W.B. 99.2"; 1.6 Liter.

S Hatchback 2D		TA226	10329	1250	1725	2775	4300
S Sedan 4D		TA526	11229	1450	1925	3000	4525
Sport Hatchback 2D		TB226	13429	1575	2100	3175	4725

NUBIRA—4-Cyl.—Equipment Schedule 5
W.B. 101.2"; 2.0 Liter.

SE Sedan 4D		JC52Z	13329	1725	2250	3400	5075
CDX Sedan 4D		JB52Z	15429	1975	2525	3700	5400
CDX Wagon 4D		JB82Z	16029	2075	2625	3800	5500

LEGANZA—4-Cyl.—Equipment Schedule 5
W.B. 105.1"; 2.2 Liter.

SE Sedan 4D		VB692	15429	2200	2775	3950	5700
SX Sedan 4D		VA692	17929	2700	3300	4550	6325
CDX Sedan 4D		VA692	19429	3150	3800	5050	6900

2002 DAEWOO — KLA(TA226)-2-#

LANOS—4-Cyl.—Equipment Schedule 6
W.B. 99.2"; 1.6 Liter.

S Hatchback 2D		TA226	10644	1650	2175	3300	4950
S Sedan 4D		TA526	11544	1850	2375	3525	5175
Sport Hatchback 2D		TB226	13494	2025	2575	3725	5400

NUBIRA—4-Cyl.—Equipment Schedule 5
W.B. 101.2"; 2.0 Liter.

| SE Sedan 4D | | JC52Z | 13844 | 2250 | 2825 | 4075 | 5825 |
| CDX Wagon 4D | | JB82Z | 15294 | 2625 | 3250 | 4500 | 6300 |

LEGANZA—4-Cyl.—Equipment Schedule 5
W.B. 105.1"; 2.2 Liter.

| SE Sedan 4D | | VB692 | 16094 | 2900 | 3550 | 4825 | 6700 |
| CDX Sedan 4D | | VA692 | 19094 | 3900 | 4650 | 6000 | 8000 |

DAEWOO — No Longer Produced

DODGE

1990 DODGE — (1orJ)B(3or4)-(L18D)-L-#

OMNI AMERICA—4-Cyl.—Equipment Schedule 6
W.B. 99.1"; 2.2 Liter.

| Hatchback 4D | | L18D | 8689 | 375 | 550 | 925 | 1575 |

COLT—4-Cyl.—Equipment Schedule 6
W.B. 93.7", 93.9" (H'Back, AWD); 1.5 Liter, 1.6 Liter, 1.8 Liter.

Hatchback 2D		U14X	8331	375	525	950	1625
GL Hatchback 2D		U24X	9582	375	525	950	1625
GT Hatchback 2D		U34X	10767	475	700	1175	1975
DL Wagon 4D		V31X	10935	400	575	1000	1725
DL AWD Wagon 4D		W31T	12505	525	750	1225	2075

COLT VISTA—4-Cyl.—Equipment Schedule 6
W.B. 103.3", 103.5" (AWD); 2.0 Liter.

| Wagon 4D | | G39V | 13652 | 625 | 900 | 1425 | 2350 |
| AWD Wagon 4D | | H39V | 14619 | 625 | 900 | 1475 | 2425 |

SHADOW—4-Cyl.—Equipment Schedule 5
W.B. 97.0"; 2.5 Liter.

Hatchback Coupe 2D		P24D	10525	325	475	900	1575
Hatchback Sedan 4D		P48D	10725	325	475	900	1575
ES Pkg				50	50	65	65
4-Cyl. 2.5 Liter Turbo		J		50	50	65	65

1990 DODGE

Body	Type	VIN	List	Trade-In Fair	Trade-In Good	Pvt-Party Good	Retail Excellent
DAYTONA—4-Cyl.—Equipment Schedule 4							
W.B. 97.0"; 2.5 Liter.							
Hatchback 2D		G24K	12589	625	900	1550	2650
ES Hatchback 2D		G44K	13789	675	925	1600	2725
4-Cyl. 2.5 Liter Turbo		C,J		0	0	0	0
V6 3.0 Liter		3		200	200	265	265
DAYTONA—4-Cyl. Turbo—Equipment Schedule 4							
W.B. 97.0"; 2.5 Liter.							
ES Hatchback 2D		G44J	15218	750	1025	1775	2975
Shelby Hatchback 2D		G74J	16066	750	1050	1825	3025
SPIRIT—4-Cyl.—Equipment Schedule 5							
W.B. 103.3"; 2.5 Liter.							
Sedan 4D		A46K	12418	400	575	1000	1725
LE Sedan 4D		A56K	13656	425	625	1050	1800
4-Cyl. 2.5 Liter Turbo		J		0	0	0	0
V6 3.0 Liter		3		150	150	200	200
SPIRIT—4-Cyl. Turbo—Equipment Schedule 5							
W.B. 103.3"; 2.5 Liter.							
ES Sedan 4D		A76J	14956	500	725	1225	2075
V6 3.0 Liter		3		200	200	265	265
DYNASTY—V6—Equipment Schedule 4							
W.B. 104.3"; 3.0 Liter, 3.3 Liter.							
Sedan 4D		C46U	15944	575	825	1350	2250
LE Sedan 4D		C56U	16661	650	900	1500	2475
4-Cyl. 2.5 Liter		H,K		(150)	(150)	(200)	(200)
MONACO—V6—Equipment Schedule 4							
W.B. 106.0"; 3.0 Liter.							
LE Sedan 4D		B56U	17154	275	375	875	1575
ES Sedan 4D		B60U	19353	325	475	900	1800

1991 DODGE — (1orJ)B(3or4)–(U14A)–M–#

Body	Type	VIN	List	Trade-In Fair	Trade-In Good	Pvt-Party Good	Retail Excellent
COLT—4-Cyl.—Equipment Schedule 6							
W.B. 93.9"; 1.5 Liter.							
Hatchback 2D		U14A	8247	425	625	1075	1850
GL Hatchback 2D		U24A	9143	425	625	1075	1850
COLT VISTA—4-Cyl.—Equipment Schedule 6							
W.B. 103.3", 103.5" (AWD); 2.0 Liter.							
Wagon 4D		G39V	13695	700	1000	1625	2700
AWD Wagon 4D		H49V	14462	750	1025	1675	2750
SHADOW—4-Cyl.—Equipment Schedule 5							
W.B. 97.0"; 2.2 Liter, 2.5 Liter.							
America H'Back 2D		P24D	9786	375	525	950	1675
America H'Back 4D		P28D	10086	400	575	1025	1750
Highline H'Back 2D		P44D	10702	400	575	1025	1750
Highline H'Back 4D		P48D	11002	400	575	1025	1750
Highline Conv 2D		P45K	14758	600	850	1425	2350
ES Hatchback 2D		P64K	12178	450	650	1125	1925
ES Hatchback 4D		P68K	12478	475	675	1150	1975
ES Convertible 2D		P65K	15871	600	850	1425	2350
4-Cyl. 2.5 Liter Turbo		J		50	50	65	65
DAYTONA—4-Cyl.—Equipment Schedule 4							
W.B. 97.0"; 2.5 Liter.							
Hatchback 2D		G24K	12428	725	1025	1775	2975
ES Hatchback 2D		G44K	14011	750	1050	1850	3075
4-Cyl. 2.5 Liter Turbo		J		0	0	0	0
V6 3.0 Liter		3		200	200	265	265
DAYTONA—4-Cyl. Turbo—Equipment Schedule 4							
W.B. 97.0"; 2.5 Liter.							
Shelby H'Back 2D		G74J	15752	850	1200	2100	3400
DAYTONA—V6—Equipment Schedule 4							
W.B. 97.0"; 3.0 Liter.							
IROC H'Back 2D		G743	15687	900	1300	2200	3575
4-Cyl. 2.5 Liter Turbo		J		0	0	0	0
SPIRIT—4-Cyl.—Equipment Schedule 5							
W.B. 103.3"; 2.5 Liter.							
Sedan 4D		A46K	12852	450	650	1150	1975
LE Sedan 4D		A56K	14211	475	700	1225	2075
4-Cyl. 2.5 Liter Turbo		J		0	0	0	0
V6 3.0 Liter		3		175	175	235	235
SPIRIT—4-Cyl. Turbo—Equipment Schedule 5							
W.B. 103.3"; 2.2 Liter, 2.5 Liter.							
ES Sedan 4D		A76J	15542	575	825	1400	2350
R/T Sedan 4D		A66A	18285	900	1250	2025	3250

1991 DODGE

Body	Type	VIN	List	Trade-In Fair	Trade-In Good	Pvt-Party Good	Retail Excellent
Manual Trans (R/T)				**0**	**0**	**0**	**0**
V6 3.0 Liter (ES)	3			**200**	**200**	**265**	**265**
DYNASTY—V6—Equipment Schedule 4							
W.B. 104.3"; 3.0 Liter, 3.3 Liter.							
Sedan 4D	C46U	16741		**675**	**925**	**1550**	**2600**
LE Sedan 4D	C56U	17341		**750**	**1050**	**1750**	**2850**
4-Cyl. 2.5 Liter	K			**(150)**	**(150)**	**(200)**	**(200)**
MONACO—V6—Equipment Schedule 4							
W.B. 106.0".							
LE Sedan 4D	B56U	16461		**300**	**450**	**975**	**1800**
ES Sedan 4D	B66U	18060		**375**	**550**	**1150**	**2075**
STEALTH—V6—Equipment Schedule 4							
W.B. 97.2"; 3.0 Liter.							
Coupe 2D	D44S	18484		**1175**	**1625**	**2925**	**4675**
ES Coupe 2D	D54B	20121		**1375**	**1875**	**3200**	**5050**
R/T Coupe 2D	D64B	24483		**1800**	**2325**	**3750**	**5700**
Auto Trans				**100**	**100**	**135**	**135**
STEALTH—V6 Turbo—Equipment Schedule 4							
W.B. 97.2"; 3.0 Liter.							
R/T AWD Coupe 2D	E74C	30438		**2950**	**3600**	**5225**	**7500**

1992 DODGE — (1,3orJ)B3–(U14A)–N–#

Body	Type	VIN	List	Trade-In Fair	Trade-In Good	Pvt-Party Good	Retail Excellent
COLT—4-Cyl.—Equipment Schedule 6							
W.B. 93.9"; 1.5 Liter.							
Hatchback 2D	U14A	8640		**475**	**700**	**1225**	**2100**
GL Hatchback 2D	U24A	9304		**500**	**725**	**1250**	**2125**
SHADOW—4-Cyl.—Equipment Schedule 5							
W.B. 97.0"; 2.2 Liter, 2.5 Liter.							
America Hatchback 2D	P24D	10210		**375**	**550**	**1025**	**1800**
America Hatchback 4D	P28D	10610		**400**	**600**	**1075**	**1900**
Highline Hatchback 2D	P44D	11188		**425**	**625**	**1100**	**1925**
Highline Hatchback 4D	P48D	11588		**450**	**625**	**1150**	**1975**
Highline Convertible 2D	P45K	15399		**650**	**900**	**1525**	**2600**
ES Hatchback 2D	P64K	12854		**500**	**725**	**1250**	**2125**
ES Hatchback 4D	P68K	13176		**525**	**750**	**1300**	**2175**
ES Convertible 2D	P65K	16627		**650**	**900**	**1525**	**2600**
4-Cyl. 2.5 Liter Turbo	J			**75**	**75**	**100**	**100**
V6 3.0 Liter	3			**125**	**125**	**165**	**165**
DAYTONA—4-Cyl.—Equipment Schedule 4							
W.B. 97.2"; 2.5 Liter.							
Hatchback 2D	W24K	12918		**875**	**1225**	**2125**	**3475**
ES Hatchback 2D	W44K	13959		**900**	**1300**	**2200**	**3600**
V6 3.0 Liter	3			**225**	**225**	**300**	**300**
DAYTONA—4-Cyl.—Equipment Schedule 4							
W.B. 97.2"; 3.0 Liter.							
IROC Hatchback 2D	W743	15254		**1100**	**1550**	**2700**	**4275**
4-Cyl. 2.5 Liter Turbo	J			**0**	**0**	**0**	**0**
DAYTONA—4-Cyl. Turbo—Equipment Schedule 4							
W.B. 97.2"; 2.2 Liter.							
IROC R/T Hatchback 2D	W64A	20093		**1475**	**1950**	**3150**	**4800**
SPIRIT—4-Cyl.—Equipment Schedule 5							
W.B. 103.5"; 2.5 Liter.							
Sedan 4D	A46K	13343		**500**	**725**	**1250**	**2125**
LE Sedan 4D	A56K	14846		**550**	**775**	**1350**	**2250**
4-Cyl. 2.5 Liter Turbo	J			**25**	**25**	**35**	**35**
V6 3.0 Liter	3			**225**	**225**	**300**	**300**
SPIRIT—4-Cyl. Turbo—Equipment Schedule 5							
W.B. 103.5"; 2.2 Liter, 2.5 Liter.							
ES Sedan 4D	A76J	16314		**650**	**900**	**1525**	**2575**
R/T Sedan 4D	A66A	19159		**975**	**1400**	**2250**	**3575**
Manual Trans (R/T)				**0**	**0**	**0**	**0**
V6 3.0 Liter	3			**225**	**225**	**300**	**300**
DYNASTY—V6—Equipment Schedule 4							
W.B. 104.5"; 3.0 Liter, 3.3 Liter.							
Sedan 4D	C463	17006		**775**	**1075**	**1775**	**2925**
LE Sedan 4D	C563	17658		**875**	**1225**	**2025**	**3250**
4-Cyl. 2.5 Liter	K			**(175)**	**(175)**	**(235)**	**(235)**
MONACO—V6—Equipment Schedule 4							
W.B. 106.0"; 3.0 Liter.							
LE Sedan 4D	B56U	16673		**400**	**575**	**1175**	**2125**
ES Sedan 4D	B66U	18883		**475**	**700**	**1375**	**2425**
STEALTH—V6—Equipment Schedule 4							
W.B. 97.2"; 3.0 Liter.							

Body Type	VIN	List	Trade-In Fair	Good	Pvt-Party Good	Retail Excellent
Coupe 2D	D44S	19525	**1500**	**2025**	**3400**	**5325**
ES Coupe 2D	D54B	21428	**1775**	**2300**	**3750**	**5725**
R/T Coupe 2D	D64B	25868	**2250**	**2825**	**4375**	**6450**
Auto Trans			**125**	**125**	**165**	**165**
STEALTH—V6 Turbo—Equipment Schedule 2						
W.B. 97.2"; 3.0 Liter.						
R/T AWD Coupe 2D	E74C	32096	**3575**	**4300**	**6050**	**8475**
VIPER—V10—Equipment Schedule 2						
W.B. 96.2"; 8.0 Liter.						
RT/10 Roadster 2D	R65E	50700	**16700**	**18775**	**22800**	**28500**

1993 DODGE — (1,3orJ)B3-(A11A)-P-#

Body Type	VIN	List	Trade-In Fair	Good	Pvt-Party Good	Retail Excellent
COLT—4-Cyl.—Equipment Schedule 6						
W.B. 96.1", 98.4" (4D); 1.5 Liter, 1.8 Liter.						
Sedan 2D	A11A	9260	**625**	**900**	**1500**	**2525**
Sedan 4D	A26A	10902	**775**	**1075**	**1775**	**2900**
GL Sedan 2D	A21A	10376	**700**	**975**	**1600**	**2700**
GL Sedan 4D	A46C	12260	**825**	**1150**	**1900**	**3075**
SHADOW—4-Cyl.—Equipment Schedule 5						
W.B. 97.2"; 2.2 Liter, 2.5 Liter.						
Hatchback Sedan 4D	P28D	11023	**450**	**650**	**1200**	**2100**
Hatchback 2D	P24D	10623	**425**	**625**	**1150**	**2025**
Highline Convertible 2D	P25K	15970	**750**	**1025**	**1750**	**2900**
ES Hatchback Sedan 4D	P68K	12146	**600**	**850**	**1475**	**2475**
ES Hatchback 2D	P64K	11746	**575**	**825**	**1425**	**2425**
ES Convertible 2D	P65K	16109	**750**	**1025**	**1775**	**2925**
V6 3.0 Liter	3		**150**	**150**	**200**	**200**
DAYTONA—4-Cyl.—Equipment Schedule 4						
W.B. 97.2"; 2.5 Liter.						
Hatchback 2D	W24K	13500	**1025**	**1475**	**2575**	**4150**
ES Hatchback 2D	W44K	14556	**1100**	**1550**	**2700**	**4275**
V6 3.0 Liter	3		**250**	**250**	**335**	**335**
DAYTONA—V6—Equipment Schedule 4						
W.B. 97.2"; 3.0 Liter.						
IROC Hatchback 2D	W743	15980	**1450**	**1925**	**3150**	**4825**
DAYTONA—4-Cyl. Turbo—Equipment Schedule 4						
W.B. 97.2"; 2.2 Liter.						
IROC R/T Hatchback 2D	W64A	21436	**1800**	**2325**	**3600**	**5350**
SPIRIT—4-Cyl.—Equipment Schedule 5						
W.B. 103.5"; 2.5 Liter.						
Highline Sedan 4D	A46K	13455	**550**	**800**	**1425**	**2350**
ES Sedan 4D	A56K	15827	**725**	**1025**	**1700**	**2800**
4-Cyl. Flexible Fuel	V		**0**	**0**	**0**	**0**
V6 3.0 Liter	3		**275**	**275**	**365**	**365**
INTREPID—V6—Equipment Schedule 4						
W.B. 113.0"; 3.3 Liter.						
Sedan 4D	D46T	18005	**1050**	**1500**	**2525**	**3975**
ES Sedan 4D	D56T	19520	**1325**	**1800**	**2875**	**4450**
V6 3.5 Liter	F		**200**	**200**	**265**	**265**
DYNASTY—V6—Equipment Schedule 4						
W.B. 104.5"; 3.0 Liter, 3.3 Liter.						
Sedan 4D	C463	17535	**900**	**1250**	**2075**	**3300**
LE Sedan 4D	C563	18228	**975**	**1425**	**2300**	**3650**
4-Cyl. 2.5 Liter	K		**(200)**	**(200)**	**(265)**	**(265)**
STEALTH—V6—Equipment Schedule 4						
W.B. 97.2"; 3.0 Liter.						
Coupe 2D	M44H	20863	**1950**	**2475**	**3975**	**6025**
ES Coupe 2D	M54J	22974	**2225**	**2775**	**4350**	**6475**
R/T Coupe 2D	M64J	27766	**2775**	**3400**	**5075**	**7325**
Auto Trans			**150**	**150**	**200**	**200**
STEALTH—V6 Turbo—Equipment Schedule 2						
W.B. 97.2"; 3.0 Liter.						
R/T AWD Coupe 2D	N74K	34350	**4275**	**5075**	**6900**	**9525**
VIPER—V10—Equipment Schedule 2						
W.B. 96.2"; 8.0 Liter.						
RT/10 Roadster 2D	R65E	53300	**17525**	**19675**	**23700**	**29700**

1994 DODGE — (1,3orJ)B3-(A11A)-R-#

Body Type	VIN	List	Trade-In Fair	Good	Pvt-Party Good	Retail Excellent
COLT—4-Cyl.—Equipment Schedule 6						
W.B. 96.1", 98.4" (4D); 1.5 Liter, 1.8 Liter.						
Sedan 2D	A11A	10779	**725**	**1025**	**1725**	**2850**
Sedan 4D	A36C	13248	**875**	**1225**	**2025**	**3275**
ES Sedan 2D	A21A	11876	**775**	**1100**	**1850**	**3025**

1994 DODGE

Body	Type	VIN	List	Trade-In Fair	Trade-In Good	Pvt-Party Good	Retail Excellent
ES Sedan 4D		A46C	13824	900	1300	2150	3425
SHADOW—4-Cyl.—Equipment Schedule 5							
W.B. 97.2"; 2.2 Liter, 2.5 Liter.							
Hatchback Sedan 4D		P28D	11452	525	750	1400	2400
Hatchback 2D		P24D	11052	500	725	1325	2300
ES H'Back Sedan 4D		P68K	12614	675	950	1650	2800
ES Hatchback 2D		P64K	12214	675	925	1625	2750
V6 3.0 Liter		3		175	175	235	235
SPIRIT—4-Cyl.—Equipment Schedule 5							
W.B. 103.5"; 2.5 Liter.							
Sedan 4D		A46K	14154	625	900	1575	2700
4-Cyl. Flexible Fuel		V		0	0	0	0
V6 3.0 Liter		3		300	300	400	400
INTREPID—V6—Equipment Schedule 4							
W.B. 113.0"; 3.3 Liter.							
Sedan 4D		D46T	19106	1225	1700	2800	4375
ES Sedan 4D		D56T	21423	1550	2075	3225	4850
V6 3.5 Liter		F		225	225	300	300
STEALTH—V6—Equipment Schedule 4							
W.B. 97.2"; 3.0 Liter.							
Coupe 2D		M44H	23659	2400	2975	4600	6825
R/T Coupe 2D		M64J	26404	2700	3325	5025	7300
Auto Trans				175	175	235	235
STEALTH—V6 Turbo—Equipment Schedule 2							
W.B. 97.2"; 3.0 Liter.							
R/T AWD Coupe 2D		N74K	38785	5000	5850	7850	10650
VIPER—V10—Equipment Schedule 2							
W.B. 96.2"; 8.0 Liter.							
RT/10 Roadster 2D		R65E	58500	18325	20650	24700	30700

1995 DODGE — (1,4orJ)B3–(S27C)–S–#

Body	Type	VIN	List	Trade-In Fair	Trade-In Good	Pvt-Party Good	Retail Excellent
NEON—4-Cyl.—Equipment Schedule 6							
W.B. 104.0"; 2.0 Liter.							
Sedan 4D		S27C	12195	650	900	1500	2475
Highline Sedan 4D		S47C	12443	750	1050	1700	2750
Highline Coupe 2D		S41C	12443	725	1025	1625	2700
Sport Sedan 4D		S67C	14393	900	1275	2025	3200
Sport Coupe 2D		S61C	14693	975	1425	2225	3475
Competition Pkg				50	50	65	65
AVENGER—4-Cyl.—Equipment Schedule 4							
W.B. 103.7"; 2.0 Liter.							
Coupe 2D		U42Y	16309	1850	2375	3475	5050
Manual Trans				(375)	(375)	(500)	(500)
AVENGER—V6—Equipment Schedule 4							
W.B. 103.7"; 2.5 Liter.							
ES Coupe 2D		U52H,N	18260	2300	2875	4025	5700
SPIRIT—4-Cyl.—Equipment Schedule 5							
W.B. 103.5"; 2.5 Liter.							
Sedan 4D		A46K	14828	750	1025	1850	3100
V6 3.0 Liter		3		325	325	435	435
STRATUS—4-Cyl.—Equipment Schedule 4							
W.B. 108.0"; 2.0 Liter, 2.4 Liter.							
Sedan 4D		J46C	15230	875	1225	2050	3300
STRATUS—V6—Equipment Schedule 4							
W.B. 108.0"; 2.5 Liter.							
ES Sedan 4D		J56H,N	17800	1375	1850	3000	4650
Manual Trans				(375)	(375)	(500)	(500)
4-Cyl. 2.0L/2.4 Liter		C,X		(275)	(275)	(365)	(365)
INTREPID—V6—Equipment Schedule 4							
W.B. 113.0"; 3.3 Liter.							
Sedan 4D		D46T	19232	1500	1975	3175	4825
ES Sedan 4D		D56T	21379	1825	2350	3575	5300
V6 3.3L Flexible Fuel		U		0	0	0	0
V6 3.5 Liter		F		250	250	335	335
STEALTH—V6—Equipment Schedule 4							
W.B. 97.2"; 3.0 Liter.							
Hatchback 2D		M84H	24572	2875	3525	5250	7625
R/T Hatchback 2D		M44J	27756	3250	3900	5700	8125
Auto Trans				200	200	265	265
STEALTH—V6 Turbo—Equipment Schedule 2							
W.B. 97.2"; 3.0 Liter.							
R/T AWD H'Back 2D		N74K	39178	5750	6700	8800	11800

Body	Type	VIN	List	Trade-In Fair	Good	Pvt-Party Good	Retail Excellent

VIPER—V10—Equipment Schedule 2
W.B. 96.2"; 8.0 Liter.

| RT/10 Roadster 2D | | R65E | 60500 | 19300 | 21600 | 25700 | 31900 |

1996 DODGE — (1,4orJ)B3–(S27C)–T–#

NEON—4-Cyl.—Equipment Schedule 6
W.B. 104.0"; 2.0 Liter.

Sedan 4D		S27C	11730	800	1125	1800	2900
Coupe 2D		S22C	11230	775	1075	1725	2800
Highline Sedan 4D		S47C	12735	900	1275	2025	3200
Highline Coupe 2D		S42C	12535	875	1225	1950	3100
Sport Sedan 4D		S67C	14165	1050	1500	2350	3650
Sport Coupe 2D		S62C	13965	1175	1625	2625	4025

AVENGER—4-Cyl.—Equipment Schedule 4
W.B. 103.7"; 2.0 Liter.

| Coupe 2D | | U41B | 17008 | 2175 | 2750 | 3900 | 5550 |
| Manual Trans | | | | (400) | (400) | (535) | (535) |

AVENGER—V6—Equipment Schedule 4
W.B. 103.7"; 2.5 Liter.

ES Coupe 2D		U51H,N	19190	2700	3300	4500	6250
Manual Trans				(400)	(400)	(535)	(535)
4-Cyl. 2.0 Liter		B		(250)	(250)	(335)	(335)

STRATUS—4-Cyl.—Equipment Schedule 5
W.B. 108.0"; 2.0 Liter, 2.4 Liter.

| Sedan 4D | | J46C | 15820 | 1025 | 1475 | 2500 | 3975 |

STRATUS—V6—Equipment Schedule 4
W.B. 108.0"; 2.5 Liter.

ES Sedan 4D		J56H,N	18720	1650	2175	3400	5125
Manual Trans				(400)	(400)	(535)	(535)
4-Cyl. 2.0L/2.4 Liter		C,X		(300)	(300)	(400)	(400)

INTREPID—V6—Equipment Schedule 4
W.B. 113.0"; 3.3 Liter.

Sedan 4D		D46T	18995	1775	2300	3525	5250
ES Sedan 4D		D56F	22810	2125	2700	3975	5775
V6 3.5 Liter		F		250	250	335	335

STEALTH—V6—Equipment Schedule 4
W.B. 97.2"; 3.0 Liter.

Hatchback 2D		M84J	25651	3450	4150	6000	8550
R/T Hatchback 2D		M54J	29207	3850	4575	6450	9075
Auto Trans				200	200	265	265

STEALTH—V6 Turbo—Equipment Schedule 2
W.B. 97.2"; 3.0 Liter.

| R/T AWD H'Back 2D | | N74K | 35355 | 6600 | 7625 | 9850 | 13000 |

VIPER—V10—Equipment Schedule 2
W.B. 96.2"; 8.0 Liter.

| RT/10 Roadster 2D | | R65E | 63100 | 20350 | 22750 | 27000 | 33200 |
| GTS Coupe 2D | | R69E | 66700 | 22475 | 25150 | 29700 | 36400 |

1997 DODGE — (1or4)B3–(S27C)–V–#

NEON—4-Cyl.—Equipment Schedule 6
W.B. 104.0"; 2.0 Liter.

Sedan 4D		S27C	12430	950	1350	2175	3425
Coupe 2D		S22C	12230	900	1300	2100	3350
Highline Sedan 4D		S47C	13170	1050	1500	2475	3900
Highline Coupe 2D		S42C	12970	1025	1450	2325	3650

AVENGER—V6—Equipment Schedule 4
W.B. 103.7"; 2.5 Liter.

Coupe 2D		U42N	18857	2900	3550	4800	6650
ES Coupe 2D		U52N	19971	3100	3750	5025	6900
Manual Trans				(425)	(425)	(565)	(565)
4-Cyl. 2.0 Liter		Y		(275)	(275)	(365)	(365)

STRATUS—4-Cyl.—Equipment Schedule 5
W.B. 108.0"; 2.0 Liter, 2.4 Liter.

| Sedan 4D | | J46C | 16545 | 1325 | 1800 | 2900 | 4475 |

STRATUS—V6—Equipment Schedule 4
W.B. 108.0"; 2.5 Liter.

ES Sedan 4D		J56H	19390	2050	2600	3875	5700
Manual Trans				(425)	(425)	(565)	(565)
4-Cyl. 2.0L/2.4 Liter		C		(325)	(325)	(435)	(435)

INTREPID—V6—Equipment Schedule 4
W.B. 113.0"; 3.3 Liter.

| Sedan 4D | | D46T | 19955 | 2100 | 2675 | 3950 | 5800 |
| ES Sedan 4D | | D56F | 23460 | 2500 | 3100 | 4450 | 6350 |

1997 DODGE

Body	Type	VIN	List	Trade-In Fair	Trade-In Good	Pvt-Party Good	Retail Excellent
V6 3.5 Liter		F		250	250	335	335
VIPER—V10—Equipment Schedule 2							
W.B. 96.2"; 8.0 Liter.							
GTS Coupe 2D		R69E	69300	23800	26600	31200	38000

1998 DODGE — (1,2or4)B3-(S47C)-W-#

Body	Type	VIN	List	Fair	Good	Good	Excellent
NEON—4-Cyl.—Equipment Schedule 6							
W.B. 104.0"; 2.0 Liter.							
Highline Sedan 4D		S47C	12855	1300	1775	2750	4200
Highline Coupe 2D		S42C	12655	1250	1725	2700	4150
Competition Sedan 4D		S27C	14660	1775	2300	3325	4850
Competition Coupe 2D		S22Y	14480	1725	2250	3300	4800
R/T or Sport Pkg				50	50	65	65
AVENGER—V6—Equipment Schedule 4							
W.B. 103.7"; 2.5 Liter.							
Coupe 2D		U42N	18685	3400	4100	5325	7150
ES Coupe 2D		U52N	20525	3625	4350	5600	7475
Manual Trans				(450)	(450)	(600)	(600)
4-Cyl. 2.0 Liter		Y		(300)	(300)	(400)	(400)
STRATUS—4-Cyl.—Equipment Schedule 6							
W.B. 108.0"; 2.0 Liter, 2.4 Liter.							
Sedan 4D		J46C	16425	1675	2200	3375	5050
STRATUS—V6—Equipment Schedule 4							
W.B. 108.0"; 2.5 Liter.							
ES Sedan 4D		J56H	19000	2500	3100	4425	6300
4-Cyl. 2.4 Liter		X		(350)	(350)	(465)	(465)
INTREPID—V6—Equipment Schedule 4							
W.B. 113.0"; 2.7 Liter, 3.2 Liter.							
Sedan 4D		D46R	20235	2400	2975	4375	6325
ES Sedan 4D		D56J	23015	2825	3450	4900	6925
VIPER—V10—Equipment Schedule 2							
W.B. 96.2"; 8.0 Liter.							
RT/10 Roadster 2D		R65E	64700	22950	25725	30000	36500
GTS Coupe 2D		R69E	67900	25525	28500	33100	40000

1999 DODGE — (1,2or4)B3-(S47C)-X-#

Body	Type	VIN	List	Fair	Good	Good	Excellent
NEON—4-Cyl.—Equipment Schedule 6							
W.B. 104.0"; 2.0 Liter.							
Highline Sedan 4D		S47C	13320	1575	2100	3125	4600
Highline Coupe 2D		S42C	13120	1500	2025	3050	4525
Competition Sedan 4D		S27C	14985	2125	2700	3775	5350
Competition Coupe 2D		S22Y	14805	2100	2650	3700	5275
R/T or Sport Pkg				75	75	100	100
AVENGER—V6—Equipment Schedule 4							
W.B. 103.7"; 2.5 Liter.							
Coupe 2D		U42N	19665	4125	4900	6200	8125
ES Coupe 2D		U52N	20975	4400	5175	6500	8500
Manual Trans				(500)	(500)	(665)	(665)
4-Cyl. 2.0 Liter		Y		(350)	(350)	(465)	(465)
STRATUS—4-Cyl.—Equipment Schedule 5							
W.B. 108.0"; 2.0 Liter, 2.4 Liter.							
Sedan 4D		J46C	16865	2225	2775	4050	5850
STRATUS—V6—Equipment Schedule 4							
W.B. 108.0"; 2.5 Liter.							
ES Sedan 4D		J56H	19495	3175	3850	5275	7325
INTREPID—V6—Equipment Schedule 4							
W.B. 113.0"; 2.7 Liter, 3.2 Liter.							
Sedan 4D		D46R	20495	3000	3675	5150	7300
ES Sedan 4D		D56J	23340	3500	4200	5750	7975
VIPER—V10—Equipment Schedule 2							
W.B. 96.2"; 8.0 Liter.							
RT/10 Roadster 2D		R65E	66425	25825	28900	33300	40100
GTS Coupe 2D		R69E	68925	28700	32075	36800	44100
Competition Group				2350	2350	3135	3135

2000 DODGE — (1,2or4)B3-(S46C)-Y-#

Body	Type	VIN	List	Fair	Good	Good	Excellent
NEON—4-Cyl.—Equipment Schedule 6							
W.B. 105.0"; 2.0 Liter.							
Highline Sedan 4D		S46C	13890	1700	2225	3450	5175
ES Sedan 4D		S56C	14680	2275	2850	4125	5925
AVENGER—V6—Equipment Schedule 4							
W.B. 103.7"; 2.5 Liter.							

0105

Body	Type	VIN	List	Trade-In Fair	Trade-In Good	Pvt-Party Good	Retail Excellent
Coupe 2D		U42N	18840	4925	5775	7175	9275
ES Coupe 2D		U52N	21130	5200	6100	7500	9650
STRATUS—4-Cyl.—Equipment Schedule 5							
W.B. 108.0"; 2.0 Liter, 2.4 Liter.							
SE Sedan 4D		J46C	17525	2875	3525	4900	6850
STRATUS—V6—Equipment Schedule 4							
W.B. 108.0"; 2.5 Liter.							
SE Sedan 4D		J56H	20655	4000	4750	6300	8500
INTREPID—V6—Equipment Schedule 4							
W.B. 113.0"; 2.7 Liter, 3.2 Liter, 3.5 Liter.							
Sedan 4D		D46R	20950	3750	4500	6125	8425
ES Sedan 4D		D56J	22530	4325	5100	6775	9150
R/T Sedan 4D		D76V	24995	5875	6850	8525	11050
VIPER—V10—Equipment Schedule 2							
W.B. 96.2"; 8.0 Liter.							
RT/10 Roadster 2D		R65E	70925	28800	32150	36800	43900
GTS Coupe 2D		R69E	73425	32150	35800	40700	48300
Competition Group				2650	2650	3530	3530

2001 DODGE — (1,2or4)B3—(S46C)—1—#

Body	Type	VIN	List	Trade-In Fair	Trade-In Good	Pvt-Party Good	Retail Excellent
NEON—4-Cyl.—Equipment Schedule 6							
W.B. 105.0"; 2.0 Liter.							
Highline Sedan 4D		S46C	14275	2250	2800	4100	5950
ES Sedan 4D		S56C	15095	2875	3525	4875	6800
Competition Sedan 4D		S66C	15155	2925	3575	4925	6850
R/T Sedan 4D		S66F	16845	3325	4025	5400	7375
STRATUS—4-Cyl.—Equipment Schedule 4							
W.B. 103.7", 108.0" (Sed); 2.4 Liter.							
SE Sedan 4D		J46X	18425	3675	4400	5875	8025
SE Coupe 2D		G42X	19230	5675	6600	8075	10250
Manual Trans				(550)	(550)	(735)	(735)
V6 2.7/3.0 Liter		U,H		600	600	800	800
STRATUS—V6—Equipment Schedule 4							
W.B. 103.7", 108.0" (Sed); 2.7 Liter, 3.0 Liter.							
ES Sedan 4D		J56U	21010	4925	5775	7450	9850
R/T Coupe 2D		G52H	22115	7050	8125	9700	12100
INTREPID—V6—Equipment Schedule 4							
W.B. 113.0"; 2.7 Liter, 3.2 Liter, 3.5 Liter.							
SE Sedan 4D		D46R	21395	4600	5450	7225	9750
ES Sedan 4D		D56J	23090	5225	6125	7925	10500
R/T Sedan 4D		D66V	25460	6950	8050	9850	12600
VIPER—V10—Equipment Schedule 2							
W.B. 96.2"; 8.0 Liter.							
RT/10 Roadster 2D		R65E	67950	32075	35700	40300	47700
GTS Coupe 2D		R69E	70450	35700	39750	44500	52400
Competition Group				2950	2950	3930	3930

2002 DODGE — (1,2or4)B3—(S26C)—2—#

Body	Type	VIN	List	Trade-In Fair	Trade-In Good	Pvt-Party Good	Retail Excellent
NEON—4-Cyl.—Equipment Schedule 6							
W.B. 105.0"; 2.0 Liter.							
S Sedan 4D		S26C	10570	2825	3450	4850	6825
Sedan 4D		S26C	13805	2975	3650	5050	7025
SXT Sedan 4D		S66C	14130	3400	4100	5500	7525
ACR Sedan 4D		S66F	14795	3375	4075	5475	7500
SE Sedan 4D		S46C	15330	3400	4100	5500	7525
ES Sedan 4D		S56C	15860	3700	4425	5825	7925
R/T Sedan 4D		S76F	16680	4175	4975	6400	8550
STRATUS—4-Cyl.—Equipment Schedule 4							
W.B. 103.7", 108.0" (Sed); 2.4 Liter.							
SE Sedan 4D		L46X	18290	4650	5500	7100	9425
SE Coupe 2D		G42X	19340	6750	7800	9325	11700
SXT Sedan 4D		L66X	19345	5025	5875	7500	9900
SXT Coupe 2D		G42G	19695	7150	8250	9800	12250
Manual Trans				(575)	(575)	(765)	(765)
V6 2.7/3.0 Liter		R,H		650	650	865	865
STRATUS—V6—Equipment Schedule 4							
W.B. 103.7", 108.0" (Sed); 2.7 Liter, 3.0 Liter.							
ES Sedan 4D		J56U	21255	6075	7025	8825	11450
R/T Sedan 4D		L76R	22150	7050	8125	9975	12700
R/T Coupe 2D		G52H	22360	8275	9475	11100	13700
INTREPID—V6—Equipment Schedule 4							
W.B. 113.0"; 2.7 Liter, 3.5 Liter.							
SE Sedan 4D		D46R	21230	5700	6625	8550	11300

Body	Type	VIN	List	Trade-In Fair	Trade-In Good	Pvt-Party Good	Retail Excellent
ES Sedan 4D		D56J	23155	6375	7375	9300	12150
SXT Sedan 4D		D66G	24170	7075	8150	9925	12600
R/T Sedan 4D		D66V	27240	8275	9475	11400	14350
VIPER—V10—Equipment Schedule 2							
W.B. 96.2"; 8.0 Liter.							
RT/10 Roadster 2D		R65E	75500	35325	39350	44100	51600
GTS Coupe 2D		R69E	76000	39350	43775	48700	56700
Competition Group				3225	3225	4300	4300

2003 DODGE — (1,2or4)B3–(S46C)–3–#

NEON—4-Cyl.—Equipment Schedule 6
W.B. 105.0"; 2.0 Liter.

Body	Type	VIN	List	Trade-In Fair	Trade-In Good	Pvt-Party Good	Retail Excellent
SE Sedan 4D		S46C	14100	4500	5300	6675	8700
SXT Sedan 4D		S66C	14295	4500	5300	6675	8700
R/T Sedan 4D		S76F	17250	5350	6250	7650	9800
NEON—4-Cyl. Turbo—Equipment Schedule 6							
W.B. 105.0"; 2.4 Liter.							
SRT-4 Sedan 4D		S66S	19965	9975	11375	13050	15750
STRATUS—4-Cyl.—Equipment Schedule 4							
W.B. 103.7", 108.0" (Sed); 2.4 Liter.							
SE Sedan 4D		L46X	18470	5925	6900	8500	10950
SE Coupe 2D		G42G	20680	8025	9200	10750	13250
SXT Sedan 4D		L46X	18340	6300	7300	8925	11400
Manual Trans				(600)	(600)	(800)	(800)
V6 2.7/3.0 Liter		R,H		700	700	935	935
STRATUS—V6—Equipment Schedule 4							
W.B. 103.7", 108.0" (Sed); 2.7 Liter, 3.0 Liter.							
ES Sedan 4D		J56U	21980	7475	8600	10400	13150
R/T Sedan 4D		L76R	22340	8525	9750	11600	14500
R/T Coupe 2D		G52H	23175	9700	11050	12650	15350
INTREPID—V6—Equipment Schedule 4							
W.B. 113.0"; 2.7 Liter, 3.5 Liter.							
SE Sedan 4D		D46R	21720	7025	8100	10100	12950
ES Sedan 4D		D56J	25515	7775	8925	10950	13900
SXT Sedan 4D		D66G	24335	8575	9800	11600	14450
VIPER—V10—Equipment Schedule 2							
W.B. 98.8"; 8.3 Liter.							
SRT-10 Roadster 2D		R65Z	83795	54150	60200	65300	74400

2004 DODGE — (1,2or4)B3–(S46C)–4–#

NEON—4-Cyl.—Equipment Schedule 6
W.B. 105.0"; 2.0 Liter.

Body	Type	VIN	List	Trade-In Fair	Trade-In Good	Pvt-Party Good	Retail Excellent
SE Sedan 4D		S46C	14745	5800	6775	8075	10150
SXT Sedan 4D		S66C	15115	5825	6800	8100	10200
R/T Sedan 4D		S76F	17895	6750	7800	9175	11400
NEON—4-Cyl. HO Turbo—Equipment Schedule 6							
W.B. 105.0"; 2.4 Liter.							
SRT-4 Sedan 4D		S66S	20995	11750	13300	15000	17900
STRATUS—4-Cyl.—Equipment Schedule 4							
W.B. 103.7", 108.0" (Sed); 2.4 Liter.							
SXT Sedan 4D		L66X	19155	7950	9125	10800	13450
SXT Coupe 2D		G42G	20535	9900	11225	13000	15800
SE Sedan 4D		L46X	20315	7525	8675	10350	12950
Manual Trans				(625)	(625)	(835)	(835)
V6 2.7 Liter		T		750	750	1000	1000
STRATUS—V6—Equipment Schedule 4							
W.B. 103.7", 108.0" (Sed); 2.7 Liter, 3.0 Liter.							
ES Sedan 4D		J56M	22600	9225	10500	12500	15450
R/T Sedan 4D		L76R	23135	10325	11750	13800	16900
R/T Coupe 2D		G52H	23030	11675	13200	15050	18100
INTREPID—V6—Equipment Schedule 4							
W.B. 113.0"; 2.7 Liter, 3.5 Liter.							
SE Sedan 4D		D46R	22270	8725	9975	12050	15100
ES Sedan 4D		D56J	26065	9500	10850	12950	16200
SXT Sedan 4D		D66G	24485	10375	11800	13750	16750
VIPER—V10—Equipment Schedule 2							
W.B. 98.8"; 8.3 Liter.							
SRT/10 Roadster 2D		R65Z	84795				

Body	Type	VIN	List	Trade-In Fair	Good	Pvt-Party Good	Retail Excellent

EAGLE

1990 EAGLE — (1,4orJ)E3C(U36X)-L-#

SUMMIT—4-Cyl.—Equipment Schedule 6
W.B. 96.7"; 1.5 Liter, 1.6 Liter.

Body	Type	VIN	List	Fair	Good	Good	Excellent
Sedan 4D		U36X	10634	500	725	1200	2025
DL Sedan 4D		U36X	11120	500	725	1200	2025
LX Sedan 4D		U46X	11804	500	725	1200	2025
ES Sedan 4D		U56Y	12665	525	750	1225	2075

TALON—4-Cyl.—Equipment Schedule 4
W.B. 97.2"; 2.0 Liter.

Coupe 2D		S44R	14944	450	650	1225	2125

TALON—4-Cyl. Turbo—Equipment Schedule 4
W.B. 97.2"; 2.0 Liter.

TSi Coupe 2D		S54U	16702	625	900	1550	2650
TSi AWD Coupe 2D		T64U	18386	800	1125	1900	3100
Manual Trans				0	0	0	0

PREMIER—V6—Equipment Schedule 4
W.B. 106.0"; 3.0 Liter.

LX Sedan 4D		B56U	17746	275	375	875	1575
ES Sedan 4D		B66U	19039	325	475	1000	1800
ES Ltd Sedan 4D		B66U	20737	375	525	1050	1900

1991 EAGLE — (1,4orJ)E3C(U36A)-M-#

SUMMIT—4-Cyl.—Equipment Schedule 6
W.B. 93.9", 96.7" (Sed); 1.5 Liter.

Sedan 4D		U36A	10454	550	800	1350	2225
Hatchback Coupe 2D		U14A	8506	450	625	1100	1850
ES Sedan 4D		U56A	11212	575	825	1350	2250
ES Hatchback Coupe 2D		U24A	9402	500	725	1200	2025

TALON—4-Cyl.—Equipment Schedule 4
W.B. 97.2"; 2.0 Liter.

Coupe 2D		S44R	14906	550	800	1500	2600
Auto Trans				100	100	135	135

TALON—4-Cyl. Turbo—Equipment Schedule 4
W.B. 97.2"; 2.0 Liter.

TSi Coupe 2D		S54U	16525	750	1050	1875	3150
TSi AWD Coupe 2D		T64U	18429	925	1325	2350	3875
Auto Trans				100	100	135	135

PREMIER—V6—Equipment Schedule 4
W.B. 106.0"; 3.0 Liter.

LX Sedan 4D		B56U	16249	300	450	975	1800
ES Sedan 4D		B66U	18061	375	550	1125	2025
ES Ltd Sedan 4D		B66U	19975	400	600	1200	2125

1992 EAGLE — (1,4orJ)E3C(U36A)-N-#

SUMMIT—4-Cyl.—Equipment Schedule 6
W.B. 93.9", 96.7" (Sed), 99.2" (Wag); 1.5 Liter, 1.8 Liter, 2.4 Liter.

Sedan 4D		U36A	10661	650	900	1500	2525
Hatchback 2D		U14A	8640	500	725	1225	2100
ES Sedan 4D		U56A	11419	675	925	1550	2600
ES Hatchback 2D		U24A	10057	550	800	1350	2250
DL Wagon 3D		V20D	12806	1100	1550	2550	3975
LX Wagon 3D		V50D	13262	1175	1625	2675	4150
AWD Wagon 3D		W40D	14878	1425	1900	2975	4500

TALON—4-Cyl.—Equipment Schedule 4
W.B. 97.2"; 2.0 Liter.

Coupe 2D		S44R	15854	675	950	1750	3025
Auto Trans				125	125	165	165

TALON—4-Cyl. Turbo—Equipment Schedule 4
W.B. 97.2"; 2.0 Liter.

TSi Coupe 2D		S54U	17375	875	1225	2150	3575
TSi AWD Coupe 2D		T64U	19382	1075	1525	2675	4250
Auto Trans				125	125	165	165

PREMIER—V6—Equipment Schedule 4
W.B. 106.0"; 3.0 Liter.

LX Sedan 4D		B56U	17016	375	550	1150	2100
ES Sedan 4D		B66U	18743	475	675	1325	2350
ES Ltd Sedan 4D		B66U	20712	525	750	1425	2525

1993 EAGLE

Body	Type	VIN	List	Trade-In Fair	Trade-In Good	Pvt-Party Good	Retail Excellent

1993 EAGLE — (1,4orJ)E3–(A36B)–P–#

SUMMIT—4-Cyl.—Equipment Schedule 6
W.B. 96.1", 98.4" (Sed), 99.2" (Wag); 1.5 Liter, 1.8 Liter, 2.4 Liter.

Body	Type	VIN	List	Fair	Good	Good	Excellent
DL Sedan 4D		A36B	10902	825	1150	1875	3025
DL Coupe 2D		A11B	9260	650	900	1525	2575
ES Sedan 4D		A46B	12260	850	1175	1925	3100
ES Coupe 2D		A21B	9888	700	1000	1650	2725
DL Wagon 3D		B20B	12926	1325	1800	2850	4375
LX Wagon 3D		B50B	14060	1450	1925	3025	4550
AWD Wagon 3D		C40B	15010	1675	2200	3325	4950

VISION—V6—Equipment Schedule 4
W.B. 113.0"; 3.3 Liter, 3.5 Liter.

ESi Sedan 4D		D56T	18725	1025	1450	2475	3925
TSi Sedan 4D		D66F	21935	1175	1625	2700	4225

TALON—4-Cyl.—Equipment Schedule 4
W.B. 97.2"; 1.8 Liter, 2.0 Liter.

DL Coupe 2D		F34B	13910	725	1025	1900	3250
ES Coupe 2D		F44E	16243	825	1150	2125	3575
Auto Trans				150	150	200	200

TALON—4-Cyl. Turbo—Equipment Schedule 4
W.B. 97.2"; 2.0 Liter.

TSi Coupe 2D		F54F	17749	1000	1450	2575	4175
TSi AWD Coupe 2D		G64F	20034	1325	1800	3000	4675
Auto Trans				150	150	200	200

1994 EAGLE — (1,4orJ)E3–(A11A)–R–#

SUMMIT—4-Cyl.—Equipment Schedule 6
W.B. 96.1", 98.4" (Sed), 99.2" (Wag); 1.5 Liter, 1.8 Liter, 2.4 Liter.

DL Coupe 2D		A11A	10779	750	1025	1750	2900
LX Sedan 4D		A36C	13248	900	1300	2125	3400
ES Sedan 4D		A46C	13824	925	1325	2175	3475
ES Coupe 2D		A21A	11876	800	1125	1875	3075
ESi Sedan 4D		A46C	14607	1050	1500	2525	3975
ESi Coupe 2D		A31C	12524	900	1250	2075	3300
DL Wagon 3D		B30C	14565	1525	2050	3150	4725
LX Wagon 3D		B50G	16233	1700	2225	3375	5025
AWD Wagon 3D		C40G	16285	1950	2500	3675	5375

VISION—V6—Equipment Schedule 4
W.B. 113.0"; 3.3 Liter, 3.5 Liter.

ESi Sedan 4D		D56T	20272	1175	1625	2725	4300
TSi Sedan 4D		D66F	23737	1425	1900	3050	4675

TALON—4-Cyl.—Equipment Schedule 4
W.B. 97.2"; 1.8 Liter, 2.0 Liter.

DL Coupe 2D		F34B	14080	850	1200	2325	3925
ES Coupe 2D		F44E	16438	975	1425	2600	4250
Auto Trans				175	175	235	235

TALON—4-Cyl. Turbo—Equipment Schedule 4
W.B. 97.2"; 2.0 Liter.

TSi Coupe 2D		F54F	18479	1225	1675	2925	4650
TSi AWD Coupe 2D		G64F	20270	1600	2100	3400	5200
Auto Trans				175	175	235	235

1995 EAGLE — (1,4orJ)E3–(A11A)–S–#

SUMMIT—4-Cyl.—Equipment Schedule 6
W.B. 96.1", 98.4" (Sed), 99.2" (Wag); 1.5 Liter, 1.8 Liter, 2.4 Liter.

DL Coupe 2D		A11A	11878	850	1200	2025	3275
LX Sedan 4D		A36C	13553	1025	1475	2500	3950
ESi Sedan 4D		A46C	15497	1225	1700	2775	4325
ESi Coupe 2D		A31C	13257	1000	1450	2425	3900
DL Wagon 3D		B30C	15799	1800	2325	3475	5125
LX Wagon 3D		B50G	17305	2025	2575	3775	5475
AWD Wagon 3D		C50G	18461	2250	2825	4050	5800

VISION—V6—Equipment Schedule 4
W.B. 113.0"; 3.3 Liter.

ESi Sedan 4D		D56T	20232	1400	1875	3050	4700
TSi Sedan 4D		D66F	23406	1700	2225	3425	5150
V6 3.5 Liter		F		250	250	335	335

TALON—4-Cyl.—Equipment Schedule 4
W.B. 98.8"; 2.0 Liter.

ESi Coupe 2D		K44Y	16927	1775	2300	3525	5275
Auto Trans				200	200	265	265

Body	Type	VIN	List	Trade-In Fair	Good	Pvt-Party Good	Retail Excellent
TALON—4-Cyl. Turbo—Equipment Schedule 4							
W.B. 98.8"; 2.0 Liter.							
TSi Coupe 2D		K54F	19270	**2300**	**2875**	**4200**	**6075**
TSi AWD Coupe 2D		L54F	20758	**2725**	**3350**	**4725**	**6700**
Auto Trans				**200**	**200**	**265**	**265**

1996 EAGLE — (J,2or4)E3-(A31A)-T-#

Body	Type	VIN	List	Trade-In Fair	Good	Pvt-Party Good	Retail Excellent
SUMMIT—4-Cyl.—Equipment Schedule 6							
W.B. 96.1", 98.4" (Sed), 99.2" (Wag); 1.5 Liter, 1.8 Liter, 2.4 Liter.							
DL Coupe 2D		A31A	12271	**975**	**1425**	**2450**	**3925**
LX Sedan 4D		A56C	14474	**1225**	**1700**	**2775**	**4350**
ESi Sedan 4D		A46C	16411	**1500**	**1975**	**3100**	**4700**
ESi Coupe 2D		A41A	13759	**1200**	**1650**	**2725**	**4275**
DL Wagon 3D		B30C	16347	**2100**	**2675**	**3875**	**5600**
LX Wagon 3D		B50G	17873	**2350**	**2925**	**4150**	**5925**
AWD Wagon 3D		C60G	19009	**2600**	**3225**	**4500**	**6300**
VISION—V6—Equipment Schedule 4							
W.B. 113.0"; 3.3 Liter.							
ESi Sedan 4D		D56T	19795	**1650**	**2175**	**3400**	**5100**
TSi Sedan 4D		D66F	24385	**2050**	**2600**	**3875**	**5675**
V6 3.5 Liter		F		**250**	**250**	**335**	**335**
TALON—4-Cyl.—Equipment Schedule 4							
W.B. 98.8"; 2.0 Liter.							
Hatchback 2D		K24Y	15954	**2100**	**2675**	**3950**	**5775**
ESi Hatchback 2D		K44Y	17563	**2225**	**2775**	**4100**	**5975**
Auto Trans				**200**	**200**	**265**	**265**
TALON—4-Cyl. Turbo—Equipment Schedule 4							
W.B. 98.8"; 2.0 Liter.							
TSi Hatchback 2D		K54F	20140	**2800**	**3425**	**4850**	**6850**
TSi AWD H'Back 2D		L54F	21695	**3300**	**3950**	**5400**	**7500**
Auto Trans				**200**	**200**	**265**	**265**

1997 EAGLE — (2or4)E3-(D56F)-V-#

Body	Type	VIN	List	Trade-In Fair	Good	Pvt-Party Good	Retail Excellent
VISION—V6—Equipment Schedule 4							
W.B. 113.0"; 3.5 Liter.							
ESi Sedan 4D		D56F	20855	**1975**	**2525**	**3825**	**5650**
TSi Sedan 4D		D66F	25035	**2400**	**3000**	**4350**	**6275**
TALON—4-Cyl.—Equipment Schedule 4							
W.B. 98.8"; 2.0 Liter.							
Hatchback 2D		K24Y	16701	**2600**	**3225**	**4600**	**6575**
ESi Hatchback 2D		K44Y	17587	**2750**	**3375**	**4800**	**6825**
Auto Trans				**200**	**200**	**265**	**265**
TALON—4-Cyl. Turbo—Equipment Schedule 4							
W.B. 98.8"; 2.0 Liter.							
TSi Hatchback 2D		K54F	20164	**3375**	**4075**	**5575**	**7700**
TSi AWD H'Back 2D		L54F	21666	**3900**	**4625**	**6200**	**8400**
Auto Trans				**200**	**200**	**265**	**265**

1998 EAGLE — 4E3-(K24Y)-W-#

Body	Type	VIN	List	Trade-In Fair	Good	Pvt-Party Good	Retail Excellent
TALON—4-Cyl.—Equipment Schedule 4							
W.B. 98.8"; 2.0 Liter.							
Hatchback 2D		K24Y	16400	**3150**	**3825**	**5250**	**7300**
ESi Hatchback 2D		K44Y	18550	**3325**	**4025**	**5475**	**7550**
Auto Trans				**200**	**200**	**265**	**265**
TALON—4-Cyl. Turbo—Equipment Schedule 4							
W.B. 98.8"; 2.0 Liter.							
TSi Hatchback 2D		K54F	21000	**4000**	**4775**	**6300**	**8500**
TSi AWD H'Back 2D		L54F	22110	**4550**	**5375**	**6925**	**9225**
Auto Trans				**200**	**200**	**265**	**265**

FORD

1990 FORD — (1FA,KNJor1ZV)(PT05H)-L-#

Body	Type	VIN	List	Trade-In Fair	Good	Pvt-Party Good	Retail Excellent
FESTIVA—4-Cyl.—Equipment Schedule 6							
W.B. 90.2"; 1.3 Liter.							
L Hatchback 2D		PT05H	6824	**275**	**375**	**800**	**1425**
L Plus Hatchback 2D		PT06H	8455	**300**	**425**	**850**	**1500**
LX Hatchback 2D		PT07H	8989	**325**	**475**	**900**	**1575**
ESCORT—4-Cyl.—Equipment Schedule 6							
W.B. 94.2"; 1.9 Liter.							
Pony Hatchback 2D		PP909	7948	**375**	**525**	**900**	**1500**

Body	Type	VIN	List	Trade-In Fair	Trade-In Good	Pvt-Party Good	Retail Excellent
LX Hatchback 2D		PP919	9277	375	525	900	1550
LX Hatchback 4D		PP959	9607	375	550	925	1575
LX Wagon 4D		PP989	10208	425	625	1025	1725
GT Hatchback 2D		PP93J	10928	400	575	975	1675

TEMPO—4-Cyl.—Equipment Schedule 5
W.B. 99.9"; 2.3 Liter.

Body	Type	VIN	List	Trade-In Fair	Trade-In Good	Pvt-Party Good	Retail Excellent
GL Sedan 2D		PP31X	11293	300	425	850	1475
GL Sedan 4D		PP36X	11442	300	425	850	1475
GLS Sedan 2D		PP33S	12110	300	425	850	1475
GLS Sedan 4D		PP38S	12258	300	450	875	1500
LX Sedan 4D		PP37X	12415	300	450	875	1500
AWD Sedan 4D		PP39S	12578	375	550	1000	1750

MUSTANG—4-Cyl.—Equipment Schedule 4
W.B. 100.5"; 2.3 Liter.

Body	Type	VIN	List	Trade-In Fair	Trade-In Good	Pvt-Party Good	Retail Excellent
LX Sedan 2D		CP40A	11341	675	925	1600	2700
LX Hatchback 2D		CP41A	11847	675	925	1600	2700
LX Convertible 2A		CP44A	16926	925	1325	2175	3475

MUSTANG—V8—Equipment Schedule 4
W.B. 100.5"; 5.0 Liter.

Body	Type	VIN	List	Trade-In Fair	Trade-In Good	Pvt-Party Good	Retail Excellent
LX Sport Sedan 2D		CP40E	14135	1100	1550	2600	4075
LX Sport Hatchback 2D		CP41E	14978	1125	1575	2650	4150
LX Sport Conv 2D		CP44E	20154	1500	1975	3125	4750
Manual Trans				(100)	(100)	(135)	(135)

MUSTANG—V8—Equipment Schedule 4
W.B. 100.5"; 5.0 Liter.

Body	Type	VIN	List	Trade-In Fair	Trade-In Good	Pvt-Party Good	Retail Excellent
GT Hatchback 2D		CP42E	16015	1175	1625	2700	4250
GT Convertible 2D		CP45E	20297	1625	2125	3300	4975
Manual Trans				0	0	0	0

PROBE—4-Cyl.—Equipment Schedule 5
W.B. 99.0"; 2.2 Liter.

Body	Type	VIN	List	Trade-In Fair	Trade-In Good	Pvt-Party Good	Retail Excellent
GL Hatchback 2D		PT20C	13434	450	650	1225	2125

PROBE—V6—Equipment Schedule 5
W.B. 99.0"; 3.0 Liter.

Body	Type	VIN	List	Trade-In Fair	Trade-In Good	Pvt-Party Good	Retail Excellent
LX Hatchback 2D		PT21U	14852	600	850	1500	2525

PROBE—4-Cyl. Turbo—Equipment Schedule 5
W.B. 99.0"; 2.2 Liter.

Body	Type	VIN	List	Trade-In Fair	Trade-In Good	Pvt-Party Good	Retail Excellent
GT Hatchback 2D		PT22L	16570	600	850	1500	2525
Manual Trans				0	0	0	0

TAURUS—V6—Equipment Schedule 4
W.B. 106.0"; 3.0 Liter.

Body	Type	VIN	List	Trade-In Fair	Trade-In Good	Pvt-Party Good	Retail Excellent
L Sedan 4D		CP50U	15510	475	675	1150	1975
L Wagon 4D		CP55U	16421	625	900	1475	2425
GL Sedan 4D		CP52U	16054	525	750	1250	2100
GL Wagon 4D		CP57U	16892	650	900	1500	2525
LX Sedan 4D		CP53U	16991	575	825	1375	2300
LX Wagon 4D		CP584	18582	750	1025	1675	2750
SHO Sedan 4D		CP54Y	22088	750	1025	1675	2750
4-Cyl. 2.5 Liter		D		(150)	(150)	(200)	(200)
V6 3.8 Liter		4		100	100	135	135

THUNDERBIRD—V6—Equipment Schedule 4
W.B. 113.0"; 3.8 Liter.

Body	Type	VIN	List	Trade-In Fair	Trade-In Good	Pvt-Party Good	Retail Excellent
Coupe 2D		PP604	16473	475	700	1300	2250
LX Coupe 2D		PP624	17723	600	850	1500	2575

THUNDERBIRD—V6 Supercharged—Equipment Schedule 4
W.B. 113.0"; 3.8 Liter.

Body	Type	VIN	List	Trade-In Fair	Trade-In Good	Pvt-Party Good	Retail Excellent
Super Coupe 2D		PP64R	21413	850	1200	2000	3350

CROWN VICTORIA—V8—Equipment Schedule 4
W.B. 114.3"; 5.0 Liter, 5.8 Liter.

Body	Type	VIN	List	Trade-In Fair	Trade-In Good	Pvt-Party Good	Retail Excellent
S Sedan 4D		CP72F	17760	500	725	1250	2125
Sedan 4D		CP73F	18388	550	775	1350	2250
Wagon 4D		CP76F	18799	500	725	1250	2125
LX Sedan 4D		CP74F	19025	700	975	1625	2725
LX Wagon 4D		CP77F	18549	575	825	1400	2350
Country Squire Wag 4D		CP78F	19052	575	825	1400	2350
Country Sq LX Wag 4D		CP79F	19802	600	850	1425	2400

1991 FORD — (1FA,KNJor1ZV)—(T05H)—M—#

FESTIVA—4-Cyl.—Equipment Schedule 6
W.B. 90.2"; 1.3 Liter.

Body	Type	VIN	List	Trade-In Fair	Trade-In Good	Pvt-Party Good	Retail Excellent
L Hatchback 2D		T05H	7150	300	450	900	1575
GL Hatchback 2D		T06H	8844	325	475	950	1675

ESCORT—4-Cyl.—Equipment Schedule 6
W.B. 98.4"; 1.8 Liter, 1.9 Liter.

Body	Type	VIN	List	Trade-In Fair	Good	Pvt-Party Good	Retail Excellent
Pony Hatchback 2D		P10J	8586	500	725	1150	1900
LX Hatchback 2D		P11J	10011	500	725	1150	1925
LX Hatchback 4D		P14J	10439	525	750	1200	1975
LX Wagon 4D		P15J	11024	575	825	1300	2125
GT Hatchback 2D		P128	12593	550	775	1250	2075

TEMPO—4-Cyl.—Equipment Schedule 5
W.B. 99.9"; 2.3 Liter.

Body	Type	VIN	List	Fair	Good	Good	Excellent
L Sedan 2D		P30X	10141	250	325	700	1250
L Sedan 4D		P35X	10284	250	325	725	1300
GL Sedan 2D		P31X	11376	350	500	925	1625
GL Sedan 4D		P36X	11526	350	500	925	1625
GLS Sedan 2D		P33S	12193	350	500	925	1625
GLS Sedan 4D		P38S	12341	375	525	950	1675
LX Sedan 4D		P37X	12498	375	525	950	1675
AWD Sedan 4D		P39S	12662	450	650	1150	1975

MUSTANG—4-Cyl.—Equipment Schedule 4
W.B. 100.5"; 2.3 Liter.

Body	Type	VIN	List	Fair	Good	Good	Excellent
LX Sedan 2D		P40M	12321	750	1050	1825	3025
LX Hatchback 2D		P41M	12827	750	1050	1825	3025
LX Convertible 2D		P44M	18271	1050	1500	2550	4050
Manual Trans				(175)	(175)	(235)	(235)

MUSTANG—V8—Equipment Schedule 4
W.B. 100.5"; 5.0 Liter.

Body	Type	VIN	List	Fair	Good	Good	Excellent
LX 5.0L Sedan 2D		P40E	15609	1300	1775	2875	4475
LX 5.0L H'Back 2D		P41E	16394	1375	1850	2975	4550
LX 5.0L Conv 2D		P44E	21016	1750	2275	3475	5200
Manual Trans				(100)	(100)	(135)	(135)

MUSTANG—V8—Equipment Schedule 4
W.B. 100.5"; 5.0 Liter.

Body	Type	VIN	List	Fair	Good	Good	Excellent
GT Hatchback 2D		P42E	17373	1400	1875	3025	4650
GT Convertible 2D		P45E	21638	1925	2450	3700	5475

PROBE—4-Cyl.—Equipment Schedule 5
W.B. 99.0"; 2.2 Liter.

Body	Type	VIN	List	Fair	Good	Good	Excellent
GL Hatchback 2D		T20C	13680	550	775	1450	2525

PROBE—V6—Equipment Schedule 5
W.B. 99.0"; 3.0 Liter.

Body	Type	VIN	List	Fair	Good	Good	Excellent
LX Hatchback 2D		T21U	15281	700	975	1750	2975

PROBE—4-Cyl. Turbo—Equipment Schedule 5
W.B. 99.0"; 2.2 Liter.

Body	Type	VIN	List	Fair	Good	Good	Excellent
GT Hatchback 2D		T22L	17016	700	975	1750	2975
Manual Trans				0	0	0	0

TAURUS—V6—Equipment Schedule 4
W.B. 106.0"; 3.0 Liter.

Body	Type	VIN	List	Fair	Good	Good	Excellent
L Sedan 4D		P50U	16075	550	775	1350	2250
L Wagon 4D		P55U	16986	725	1025	1700	2800
GL Sedan 4D		P52U	16595	600	875	1450	2425
GL Wagon 4D		P57U	17482	750	1050	1775	2900
LX Sedan 4D		P53U	18218	675	925	1575	2650
LX Wagon 4D		P58U	19808	850	1200	1975	3200
SHO Sedan 4D		P54Y	22551	850	1200	1975	3200
4-Cyl. 2.5 Liter		N		(150)	(150)	(200)	(200)
V6 3.8 Liter		4		100	100	135	135

THUNDERBIRD—V6—Equipment Schedule 4
W.B. 113.0"; 3.8 Liter.

Body	Type	VIN	List	Fair	Good	Good	Excellent
Coupe 2D		P604	16548	575	825	1500	2600
LX Coupe 2D		P624	18219	700	975	1725	2925
V8 5.0 Liter		T		250	350	335	335

THUNDERBIRD—V6 Supercharged—Equipment Schedule 4
W.B. 113.0"; 3.8 Liter.

Body	Type	VIN	List	Fair	Good	Good	Excellent
Super Coupe 2D		P64R	22079	975	1425	2475	4000

CROWN VICTORIA—V8—Equipment Schedule 4
W.B. 114.3"; 5.0 Liter, 5.8 Liter.

Body	Type	VIN	List	Fair	Good	Good	Excellent
S Sedan 4D		P72F	18776	600	850	1450	2425
Sedan 4D		P73F	19403	650	900	1525	2600
Wagon 4D		P76F	19274	600	850	1450	2425
LX Sedan 4D		P74F	20039	825	1150	1950	3150
LX Wagon 4D		P77F	20024	675	950	1600	2700
Country Squire Wag 4D		P78F	19256	675	950	1600	2700
Country Sq LX Wag 4D		P79F	20276	700	975	1625	2725

1992 FORD — (1FA,KNJor1ZV)–(T05H)–N–#

FESTIVA—4-Cyl.—Equipment Schedule 6
W.B. 90.2"; 1.3 Liter.

1992 FORD

Body	Type	VIN	List	Trade-In Fair	Good	Pvt-Party Good	Retail Excellent
L Hatchback 2D		T05H	7548	350	500	975	1750
GL Hatchback 2D		T06H	9138	400	575	1075	1900
ESCORT—4-Cyl.—Equipment Schedule 6							
W.B. 98.4"; 1.8 Liter, 1.9 Liter.							
Pony Hatchback 2D		P10J	9883	500	725	1150	1925
LX Sedan 4D		P13J	11177	550	775	1275	2100
LX Hatchback 2D		P11J	10437	525	750	1225	2025
LX Hatchback 4D		P14J	10865	550	775	1275	2100
LX Wagon 4D		P15J	11449	625	900	1425	2300
GT Hatchback 2D		P128	12800	600	850	1375	2225
LX-E Sedan 4D		P168	12862	600	850	1375	2225
TEMPO—4-Cyl.—Equipment Schedule 5							
W.B. 99.9"; 2.3 Liter.							
GL Sedan 2D		P31X	11808	375	525	975	1725
GL Sedan 4D		P36X	11958	375	550	1000	1750
LX Sedan 4D		P37X	12936	400	600	1075	1850
V6 3.0 Liter		U		150	150	200	200
TEMPO—V6—Equipment Schedule 5							
W.B. 99.9"; 3.0 Liter.							
GLS Sedan 2D		P33U	13656	475	700	1225	2075
GLS Sedan 4D		P38U	13804	525	750	1300	2175
MUSTANG—4-Cyl.—Equipment Schedule 4							
W.B. 100.5"; 2.3 Liter.							
LX Sedan 2D		P40M	12343	850	1200	2100	3400
LX Hatchback 2D		P41M	12849	875	1225	2100	3425
LX Convertible 2D		P44M	18873	1325	1800	2950	4550
Manual Trans				(225)	(225)	(300)	(300)
MUSTANG—V8—Equipment Schedule 4							
W.B. 100.5"; 5.0 Liter.							
LX 5.0L Sedan 2D		P40E	15825	1575	2100	3275	4950
LX 5.0L H'Back 2D		P41E	16610	1650	2175	3375	5075
LX 5.0L Conv 2D		P44E	21496	2175	2750	4050	5900
Manual Trans				(125)	(125)	(165)	(165)
MUSTANG—V8—Equipment Schedule 4							
W.B. 100.5"; 5.0 Liter.							
GT Hatchback 2D		P42E	17645	1750	2275	3500	5225
GT Convertible 2D		P45E	21997	2350	2925	4275	6175
PROBE—4-Cyl.—Equipment Schedule 5							
W.B. 99.0"; 2.2 Liter.							
GL Hatchback 2D		T20C	14140	650	900	1675	2900
PROBE—V6—Equipment Schedule 5							
W.B. 99.0"; 3.0 Liter.							
LX Hatchback 2D		T21U	15140	825	1150	2075	3425
PROBE—4-Cyl. Turbo—Equipment Schedule 5							
W.B. 99.0"; 2.2 Liter.							
GT Hatchback 2D		T22L	16740	825	1150	2075	3425
Manual Trans				0	0	0	0
TAURUS—V6—Equipment Schedule 4							
W.B. 106.0"; 3.0 Liter.							
L Sedan 4D		P50U	17164	625	900	1525	2575
L Wagon 4D		P55U	18197	850	1175	1975	3200
GL Sedan 4D		P52U	17619	700	1000	1650	2750
GL Wagon 4D		P57U	18629	875	1225	2025	3275
LX Sedan 4D		P53U	18660	775	1100	1825	2975
LX Wagon 4D		P584	20349	975	1400	2275	3600
SHO Sedan 4D		P54Y	24262	975	1400	2275	3600
V6 3.8 Liter		4		125	125	165	165
THUNDERBIRD—V6—Equipment Schedule 4							
W.B. 113.0"; 3.8 Liter.							
Coupe 2D		P604	17676	650	900	1700	2925
LX Coupe 2D		P624	18278	775	1100	1975	3300
V8 5.0 Liter		T		275	275	365	365
THUNDERBIRD—V6 Supercharged—Equipment Schedule 4							
W.B. 113.0"; 3.8 Liter.							
Super Coupe 2D		P64R	23052	1175	1625	2775	4425
THUNDERBIRD—V8—Equipment Schedule 4							
W.B. 113.0"; 5.0 Liter.							
Sport Coupe 2D		P60T	19787	900	1250	2200	3650
CROWN VICTORIA—V8—Equipment Schedule 4							
W.B. 114.4"; 4.6 Liter.							
Sedan 4D		P73W	21051	875	1225	2100	3400
LX Sedan 4D		P74W	22259	1050	1500	2600	4125
Touring Sedan 4D		P75W	24842	1125	1575	2700	4250

Body	Type	VIN	List	Trade-In Fair	Trade-In Good	Pvt-Party Good	Retail Excellent

1993 FORD — (1FA,KNJor1ZV)–(T05H)–P–#

FESTIVA—4-Cyl.—Equipment Schedule 6
W.B. 90.2"; 1.3 Liter.

Body	Type	VIN	List	Fair	Good	Good	Excellent
L Hatchback 2D		T05H	7548	400	575	1075	1925
GL Hatchback 2D		T06H	9027	450	650	1200	2100

ESCORT—4-Cyl.—Equipment Schedule 6
W.B. 98.4"; 1.8 Liter, 1.9 Liter.

Hatchback 2D		P10J	9883	550	775	1275	2100
LX Sedan 4D		P13J	11423	625	900	1425	2350
LX Hatchback 2D		P11J	10746	575	825	1350	2225
LX Hatchback 4D		P14J	11179	625	900	1425	2350
LX Wagon 4D		P15J	11749	700	1000	1575	2600
GT Hatchback 2D		P128	12800	675	950	1525	2525
LX-E Sedan 4D		P168	12862	675	950	1525	2525

TEMPO—4-Cyl.—Equipment Schedule 6
W.B. 99.9"; 2.3 Liter.

GL Sedan 2D		P31X	11599	400	575	1075	1900
GL Sedan 4D		P36X	11599	425	625	1125	1975
LX Sedan 4D		P37X	13605	475	675	1225	2100
V6 3.0 Liter		U		175	175	235	235

MUSTANG—4-Cyl.—Equipment Schedule 4
W.B. 100.5"; 2.3 Liter.

LX Sedan 2D		P40M	12847	975	1425	2500	4025
LX Hatchback 2D		P41M	13352	1000	1450	2525	4050
LX Convertible 2D		P44M	19706	1625	2125	3350	5075
Manual Trans				(275)	(275)	(365)	(365)

MUSTANG—V8—Equipment Schedule 4
W.B. 100.5"; 5.0 Liter.

LX 5.0L Sedan 2D		P40E	16345	1925	2450	3700	5475
LX 5.0L H'Back 2D		P41E	17129	2000	2550	3825	5625
LX 5.0L Conv 2D		P44E	22145	2625	3250	4600	6575
Manual Trans				(150)	(150)	(200)	(200)

MUSTANG—V8—Equipment Schedule 4
W.B. 100.5"; 5.0 Liter.

GT Hatchback 2D		P42E	18165	2100	2700	3975	5800
GT Convertible 2D		P45E	22662	2800	3425	4850	6850
Cobra Hatchback 2D		P42D	19935	3025	3700	5125	7175

PROBE—4-Cyl.—Equipment Schedule 5
W.B. 102.9"; 2.0 Liter.

Hatchback 2D		T20A	15119	550	800	1500	2600
SE Pkg				100	100	135	135

PROBE—V6—Equipment Schedule 5
W.B. 102.9"; 2.5 Liter.

GT Hatchback 2D		T22B	17687	900	1275	2200	3600

TAURUS—V6—Equipment Schedule 4
W.B. 106.0"; 3.0 Liter, 3.2 Liter.

GL Sedan 4D		P52U	17675	750	1025	1750	2900
GL Wagon 4D		P57U	18840	950	1275	2250	3600
LX Sedan 4D		P53U	19291	900	1275	2100	3350
LX Wagon 4D		P584	21181	1125	1575	2650	4150
SHO Sedan 4D		P54Y	25960	1375	1875	2950	4500
Manual Trans				(275)	(275)	(365)	(365)
V6 3.0L Flexible Fuel		1		0	0	0	0
V6 3.8 Liter		4		150	150	200	200

THUNDERBIRD—V6—Equipment Schedule 4
W.B. 113.0"; 3.8 Liter.

LX Coupe 2D		P624	15833	750	1050	1975	3350
V8 5.0 Liter		T		300	300	400	400

THUNDERBIRD—V6 Supercharged—Equipment Schedule 4
W.B. 113.0"; 3.8 Liter.

Super Coupe 2D		P64R	23120	1425	1900	3150	4875

CROWN VICTORIA—V8—Equipment Schedule 4
W.B. 114.4"; 4.6 Liter.

Sedan 4D		P73W	21247	975	1400	2475	4025
LX Sedan 4D		P74W	23180	1250	1725	2900	4525

1994 FORD — (1FA,KNJor1ZV)–(T05H)–R–#

ASPIRE—4-Cyl.—Equipment Schedule 6
W.B. 90.7", 93.9" (5D); 1.3 Liter.

Hatchback 2D		T05H	9660	350	500	950	1675
Hatchback 4D		T06H	10525	525	750	1300	2175
SE Hatchback 2D		T07H	10315	500	725	1225	2100

1994 FORD

Body	Type	VIN	List	Trade-In Fair	Trade-In Good	Pvt-Party Good	Retail Excellent
ESCORT—4-Cyl.—Equipment Schedule 6							
W.B. 98.4"; 1.8 Liter, 1.9 Liter.							
Hatchback 2D		P10J	10510	600	875	1425	2350
LX Sedan 4D		P13J	11885	700	1000	1625	2700
LX Hatchback 2D		P11J	11225	650	900	1500	2525
LX Hatchback 4D		P14J	11660	700	1000	1625	2700
LX Wagon 4D		P15J	12215	825	1150	1850	2975
GT Hatchback 2D		P128	12675	775	1100	1775	2900
TEMPO—4-Cyl.—Equipment Schedule 5							
W.B. 99.9"; 2.3 Liter.							
GL Sedan 2D		P31X	12065	450	625	1225	2125
GL Sedan 4D		P36X	12065	475	700	1300	2250
LX Sedan 4D		P37X	13350	525	750	1400	2400
V6 3.0 Liter		U		200	200	265	265
MUSTANG—V6—Equipment Schedule 4							
W.B. 101.3"; 3.8 Liter.							
Coupe 2D		P404	16455	1500	2000	3225	4950
Convertible 2D		P444	22840	2100	2675	4050	6025
Manual Trans				(325)	(325)	(435)	(435)
MUSTANG—V8—Equipment Schedule 4							
W.B. 101.3"; 5.0 Liter.							
GT Coupe 2D		P42T	19950	2500	3100	4450	6350
GT Convertible 2D		P45T	24640	3375	4075	5575	7700
Cobra Coupe 2D		P42D	22425	4350	5125	6800	9150
Cobra Convertible 2D		P45D	26845	5200	6100	7875	10400
PROBE—4-Cyl.—Equipment Schedule 5							
W.B. 102.8"; 2.0 Liter.							
Hatchback 2D		T20A	15975	725	1025	1850	3150
SE Pkg				100	100	135	135
PROBE—V6—Equipment Schedule 5							
W.B. 102.8"; 2.5 Liter.							
GT Hatchback 2D		T22B	19105	1100	1550	2700	4300
GT Plus Pkg				100	100	135	135
TAURUS—V6—Equipment Schedule 4							
W.B. 106.0"; 3.0 Liter, 3.2 Liter.							
GL Sedan 4D		P52U	18280	850	1200	2075	3350
GL Wagon 4D		P57U	19360	1100	1550	2675	4200
LX Sedan 4D		P53U	19825	1025	1450	2500	3975
LX Wagon 4D		P584	21630	1375	1850	2975	4550
SHO Sedan 4D		P54Y	25240	1625	2125	3300	4950
Manual Trans				(325)	(325)	(435)	(435)
V6 3.0L Flexible Fuel		1		0	0	0	0
V6 3.8 Liter		4		175	175	235	235
THUNDERBIRD—V6—Equipment Schedule 4							
W.B. 113.0"; 3.8 Liter.							
LX Coupe 2D		P624	17325	900	1275	2400	4000
V8 4.6 Liter		W		300	300	400	400
THUNDERBIRD—V6 Supercharged—Equipment Schedule 4							
W.B. 113.0"; 3.8 Liter.							
Super Coupe 2D		P64R	23525	1725	2250	3575	5400
CROWN VICTORIA—V8—Equipment Schedule 4							
W.B. 114.4"; 4.6 Liter.							
Sedan 4D		P73W	19345	1125	1575	2775	4450
LX Sedan 4D		P74W	20995	1500	2000	3275	5025

1995 FORD — (K,1,2,3or4)(FA,NJorZV)-(T05H)-S-#

Body	Type	VIN	List	Trade-In Fair	Trade-In Good	Pvt-Party Good	Retail Excellent
ASPIRE—4-Cyl.—Equipment Schedule 6							
W.B. 90.7", 93.9" (5D); 1.3 Liter.							
Hatchback 2D		T05H	9860	425	625	1100	1900
Hatchback 4D		T06H	10425	625	900	1475	2425
SE Hatchback 2D		T07H	10535	600	850	1425	2350
ESCORT—4-Cyl.—Equipment Schedule 6							
W.B. 98.4"; 1.8 Liter, 1.9 Liter.							
Hatchback 2D		P10J	11115	675	950	1575	2650
LX Sedan 4D		P13J	12390	825	1150	1900	3075
LX Hatchback 2D		P11J	11785	750	1025	1725	2850
LX Hatchback 4D		P14J	12220	825	1150	1900	3075
LX Wagon 4D		P15J	12775	900	1300	2125	3400
GT Hatchback 2D		P128	13530	900	1275	2075	3300
CONTOUR—4-Cyl.—Equipment Schedule 6							
W.B. 106.5"; 2.0 Liter.							
GL Sedan 4D		P653	15470	675	925	1700	2900
LX Sedan 4D		P663	16655	750	1025	1850	3100

Body	Type	VIN	List	Trade-In Fair	Trade-In Good	Pvt-Party Good	Retail Excellent
	V6 2.5 Liter	L		200	200	265	265
CONTOUR—V6—Equipment Schedule 5							
W.B. 106.5"; 2.5 Liter.							
	SE Sedan 4D	P67L	18355	950	1350	2400	3925
MUSTANG—V6—Equipment Schedule 4							
W.B. 101.3"; 3.8 Liter.							
	Coupe 2D	P404	17550	1850	2375	3700	5525
	Convertible 2D	P444	23610	2450	3050	4550	6650
	Hard Top (Conv)			500	500	665	665
	Manual Trans			(375)	(375)	(500)	(500)
MUSTANG—V8—Equipment Schedule 4							
W.B. 101.3"; 5.0 Liter.							
	GTS Coupe 2D	P42T	19080	2325	2900	4300	6250
	GT Coupe 2D	P42T	20710	2925	3575	5025	7050
	GT Convertible 2D	P45T	25400	3875	4600	6200	8450
	Cobra Coupe 2D	P42D	23060	4950	5800	7500	9975
	Cobra Convertible 2D	P45D	27365	5900	6875	8700	11400
	Hard Top (Conv)			500	500	665	665
PROBE—4-Cyl.—Equipment Schedule 5							
W.B. 102.8"; 2.0 Liter.							
	Hatchback 2D	T20A	15890	900	1300	2375	3950
	SE Pkg			100	100	135	135
PROBE—V6—Equipment Schedule 5							
W.B. 102.8"; 2.5 Liter.							
	GT Hatchback 2D	T22B	19485	1400	1875	3125	4825
TAURUS—V6—Equipment Schedule 4							
W.B. 106.0"; 3.0 Liter, 3.2 Liter.							
	GL Sedan 4D	P52U	18295	975	1425	2475	4000
	GL Wagon 4D	P57U	19390	1375	1850	3000	4625
	SE Sedan 4D	P52U	19165	1025	1450	2550	4075
	LX Sedan 4D	P53U	20290	1225	1675	2800	4400
	LX Wagon 4D	P584	22090	1600	2100	3300	5000
	SHO Sedan 4D	P54Y	26465	1900	2425	3650	5400
	Manual Trans			(375)	(375)	(500)	(500)
	V6 3.0L Flexible Fuel	1		0	0	0	0
	V6 3.8 Liter	4		200	200	265	265
THUNDERBIRD—V6—Equipment Schedule 4							
W.B. 113.0"; 3.8 Liter.							
	LX Coupe 2D	P624	17895	1050	1500	2725	4475
	V8 4.6 Liter	W		300	300	400	400
THUNDERBIRD—V6 Supercharged—Equipment Schedule 4							
W.B. 113.0"; 3.8 Liter.							
	Super Coupe 2D	P64R	24195	2075	2625	4000	5950
CROWN VICTORIA—V8—Equipment Schedule 4							
W.B. 114.4"; 4.6 Liter.							
	Sedan 4D	P73W	21315	1375	1875	3175	4975
	LX Sedan 4D	P74W	23365	1800	2325	3675	5575

1996 FORD — (K,1,2or3)(NJ,FAorZV)—(T05H)—T–#

Body	Type	VIN	List	Fair	Good	Good	Excellent
ASPIRE—4-Cyl.—Equipment Schedule 6							
W.B. 90.7", 93.9" (5D); 1.3 Liter.							
	Hatchback 2D	T05H	10225	525	750	1300	2225
	Hatchback 4D	T06H	11090	725	1025	1700	2800
ESCORT—4-Cyl.—Equipment Schedule 6							
W.B. 98.4"; 1.8 Liter, 1.9 Liter.							
	Hatchback 4D	P10J	11615	800	1125	1850	3025
	LX Sedan 4D	P13J	12890	950	1350	2200	3525
	LX Hatchback 2D	P11J	12335	875	1225	2025	3275
	LX Hatchback 4D	P14J	12720	950	1350	2200	3525
	LX Wagon 4D	P15J	13275	1050	1500	2525	3975
	GT Hatchback 2D	P128	14040	1050	1500	2500	3950
CONTOUR—4-Cyl.—Equipment Schedule 5							
W.B. 106.5"; 2.0 Liter.							
	GL Sedan 4D	P653	15980	800	1125	2050	3400
	LX Sedan 4D	P663	16995	900	1250	2200	3650
	V6 2.5 Liter	L		200	200	265	265
CONTOUR—V6—Equipment Schedule 5							
W.B. 106.5"; 2.5 Liter.							
	SE Sedan 4D	P67L	18865	1100	1550	2725	4350
MUSTANG—V6—Equipment Schedule 4							
W.B. 101.3"; 3.8 Liter.							
	Coupe 2D	P404	18485	2250	2800	4225	6175
	Convertible 2D	P444	23935	2825	3475	5100	7325

1996 FORD

Body Type	VIN	List	Trade-In Fair	Trade-In Good	Pvt-Party Good	Retail Excellent
Manual Trans			(400)	(400)	(535)	(535)
MUSTANG—V8—Equipment Schedule 4						
W.B. 101.3"; 4.6 Liter.						
GT Coupe 2D	P42X	21740	3400	4100	5650	7825
GT Convertible 2D	P45X	26430	4425	5200	6875	9250
Cobra Coupe 2D	P47V	26645	5575	6475	8275	10900
Cobra Convertible 2D	P46V	29415	6625	7650	9575	12400
PROBE—4-Cyl.—Equipment Schedule 5						
W.B. 102.8"; 2.0 Liter.						
SE Hatchback 2D	T20A	16240	1175	1625	2850	4550
PROBE—V6—Equipment Schedule 5						
W.B. 102.8"; 2.5 Liter.						
GT Hatchback 2D	T22B	19545	1800	2325	3625	5475
TAURUS—V6—Equipment Schedule 4						
W.B. 108.5"; 3.0 Liter.						
G Sedan 4D	P51U	18545	950	1350	2425	3975
GL Sedan 4D	P52U	19390	1100	1550	2700	4300
GL Wagon 4D	P57U	20470	1525	2050	3250	4950
LX Sedan 4D	P53S	21680	1375	1875	3050	4700
LX Wagon 4D	P58S	22700	1800	2325	3575	5325
V6 3.0L Flexible Fuel	1,2		0	0	0	0
TAURUS—V8—Equipment Schedule 4						
W.B. 108.5"; 3.4 Liter.						
SHO Sedan 4D	P54N	27805	3000	3675	5075	7050
THUNDERBIRD—V6—Equipment Schedule 4						
W.B. 113.0"; 3.8 Liter.						
LX Coupe 2D	P624	17995	1325	1800	3150	5000
V8 4.6 Liter	W		300	300	400	400
CROWN VICTORIA—V8—Equipment Schedule 4						
W.B. 114.4"; 4.6 Liter.						
Sedan 4D	P73W	21780	1725	2250	3650	5600
LX Sedan 4D	P74W	23895	2175	2750	4200	6225

1997 FORD — (K,1,2or3)(NJ,FAorZV)–(T05H)–V–#

Body Type	VIN	List	Trade-In Fair	Trade-In Good	Pvt-Party Good	Retail Excellent
ASPIRE—4-Cyl.—Equipment Schedule 6						
W.B. 90.7", 93.9" (5D); 1.3 Liter.						
Hatchback 2D	T05H	10655	625	900	1550	2650
Hatchback 4D	T06H	11285	850	1200	2025	3275
ESCORT—4-Cyl.—Equipment Schedule 6						
W.B. 98.4"; 2.0 Liter.						
Sedan 4D	P10P	12225	825	1150	2275	3925
LX Sedan 4D	P13P	12975	900	1300	2500	4150
LX Wagon 4D	P15P	13630	1025	1475	2700	4400
CONTOUR—4-Cyl.— Equipment Schedule 5						
W.B. 106.5"; 2.0 Liter.						
Sedan 4D	P653	16015	850	1200	2300	3900
GL Sedan 4D	P653	16945	950	1375	2525	4125
LX Sedan 4D	P663	17480	1050	1500	2675	4300
V6 2.5 Liter	L		200	200	265	265
CONTOUR—V6—Equipment Schedule 5						
W.B. 106.5"; 2.5 Liter.						
SE Sedan 4D	P67L	19350	1400	1875	3125	4850
MUSTANG—V6—Equipment Schedule 4						
W.B. 101.3"; 3.8 Liter.						
Coupe 2D	P404	18810	2700	3300	4775	6875
Convertible 2D	P444	23710	3300	3975	5700	8075
Manual Trans			(425)	(425)	(565)	(565)
MUSTANG—V8—Equipment Schedule 4						
W.B. 101.3"; 4.6 Liter.						
GT Coupe 2D	P42X	20790	3925	4675	6300	8650
GT Convertible 2D	P45X	27010	5025	5875	7600	10150
Cobra Coupe 2D	P47V	27195	6250	7250	9125	11850
Cobra Convertible 2D	P46V	29995	7400	8500	10500	13500
PROBE—4-Cyl.—Equipment Schedule 5						
W.B. 102.8"; 2.0 Liter.						
Hatchback 2D	T20A	16235	1600	2100	3450	5300
PROBE—V6—Equipment Schedule 5						
W.B. 102.8"; 2.5 Liter.						
GT Hatchback 2D	T22B	18735	2250	2825	4250	6250
GTS Pkg			100	100	135	135
TAURUS—V6—Equipment Schedule 4						
W.B. 108.5"; 3.0 Liter.						
G Sedan 4D	P51U	19005	1125	1575	2775	4450

DEDUCT FOR RECONDITIONING 0105

1997 FORD

Body	Type	VIN	List	Trade-In Fair	Trade-In Good	Pvt-Party Good	Retail Excellent
GL Sedan 4D		P52U	19785	1375	1875	3100	4800
GL Wagon 4D		P57U	20995	1850	2375	3675	5475
LX Sedan 4D		P53S	22880	1675	2200	3450	5225
LX Wagon 4D		P58S	23985	2100	2700	4000	5850
V6 3.0L Flexible Fuel		1,2		0	0	0	0
TAURUS—V8—Equipment Schedule 4							
W.B. 108.5"; 3.4 Liter.							
SHO Sedan 4D		P54N	28220	3450	4150	5650	7750
THUNDERBIRD—V6—Equipment Schedule 4							
W.B. 113.0"; 3.8 Liter.							
LX Coupe 2D		P624	18395	1650	2175	3625	5625
V8 4.6 Liter		W		300	300	400	400
CROWN VICTORIA—V8—Equipment Schedule 4							
W.B. 114.4"; 4.6 Liter.							
Sedan 4D		P73W	21425	2150	2725	4250	6350
LX Sedan 4D		P73440	23440	2650	3250	4825	7000

1998 FORD — (1,2or3)FA–(P10P)–W–#

Body	Type	VIN	List	Trade-In Fair	Trade-In Good	Pvt-Party Good	Retail Excellent
ESCORT—4-Cyl.—Equipment Schedule 6							
W.B. 98.4"; 2.0 Liter.							
LX Sedan 4D		P10P	12490	950	1375	2575	4275
SE Sedan 4D		P13P	12995	1075	1525	2750	4500
SE Wagon 4D		P15P	14195	1250	1725	3000	4750
ZX2 Coupe 2D		P113	14325	1400	1875	3175	4950
CONTOUR—4-Cyl.—Equipment Schedule 5							
W.B. 106.5"; 2.0 Liter.							
Sedan 4D		P653	15980	1075	1525	2700	4350
GL Sedan 4D		P653	17305	1225	1700	2900	4575
LX Sedan 4D		P653	17760	1375	1850	3050	4750
SE Sedan 4D		P663	19475	1500	1975	3200	4925
V6 2.5 Liter		L		200	200	265	265
CONTOUR—V6—Equipment Schedule 5							
W.B. 106.5"; 2.5 Liter.							
SVT Sedan 4D		P68G	22900	3050	3700	5100	7050
Manual Trans				0	0	0	0
MUSTANG—V6—Equipment Schedule 4							
W.B. 101.3"; 3.8 Liter.							
Coupe 2D		P404	17805	3200	3875	5350	7450
Convertible 2D		P444	22305	3875	4600	6300	8700
Manual Trans				(450)	(450)	(600)	(600)
MUSTANG—V8—Equipment Schedule 4							
W.B. 101.3"; 4.6 Liter.							
GT Coupe 2D		P42X	21605	4600	5425	7100	9525
GT Convertible 2D		P45X	25605	5725	6675	8475	11100
Cobra Coupe 2D		P47V	26155	7100	8175	10050	12750
Cobra Convertible 2D		P46V	28955	8350	9575	11500	14500
TAURUS—V6—Equipment Schedule 4							
W.B. 108.5"; 3.0 Liter.							
LX Sedan 4D		P52U	19255	1750	2275	3525	5275
SE Sedan 4D		P52U	19995	2100	2675	3925	5750
SE Wagon 4D		P57U	21655	2550	3175	4500	6375
V6 3.0 Liter 24V		S		200	200	265	265
V6 3.0L Flexible Fuel		1,2		0	0	0	0
TAURUS—V8—Equipment Schedule 4							
W.B. 108.5"; 3.4 Liter.							
SHO Sedan 4D		P54N	29470	4025	4800	6275	8400
CROWN VICTORIA—V8—Equipment Schedule 4							
W.B. 114.7"; 4.6 Liter.							
Sedan 4D		P73W	21725	2700	3300	4875	7050
LX Sedan 4D		P74W	23740	3200	3875	5500	7750

1999 FORD — (1,2or3)FA–(P10P)–X–#

Body	Type	VIN	List	Trade-In Fair	Trade-In Good	Pvt-Party Good	Retail Excellent
ESCORT—4-Cyl.—Equipment Schedule 6							
W.B. 98.4"; 2.0 Liter.							
LX Sedan 4D		P10P	12665	1075	1525	2800	4575
SE Sedan 4D		P13P	13350	1275	1750	3075	4875
SE Wagon 4D		P15P	13550	1550	2075	3400	5250
ZX2 Coupe 2D		P113	13705	1650	2150	3500	5350
S/R Pkg				250	250	335	335
CONTOUR—4-Cyl.—Equipment Schedule 5							
W.B. 106.5"; 2.0 Liter.							
LX Sedan 4D		P653	15810	1525	2050	3325	5100
SE Sedan 4D		P663	17305	1750	2275	3575	5400

Body	Type	VIN	List	Trade-In Fair	Good	Pvt-Party Good	Retail Excellent
V6 2.5 Liter		L		250	250	335	335
CONTOUR—V6—Equipment Schedule 5							
W.B. 106.5"; 2.5 Liter.							
SVT Sedan 4D		P68G	23200	3825	4550	6025	8150
Manual Trans				0	0	0	0
MUSTANG—V6—Equipment Schedule 4							
W.B. 101.3"; 3.8 Liter.							
Coupe 2D		P404	18360	3600	4325	5700	7725
Convertible 2D		P444	22960	4475	5250	6900	9250
Manual Trans				(500)	(500)	(665)	(665)
MUSTANG—V8—Equipment Schedule 4							
W.B. 101.3"; 4.6 Liter.							
GT Coupe 2D		P42X	22760	5250	6150	7750	10150
GT Convertible 2D		P45X	26760	6575	7600	9325	11900
Cobra Coupe 2D		P47V	27995	8175	9375	11150	13850
Cobra Convertible 2D		P46V	31995	9600	10950	12800	15750
TAURUS—V6—Equipment Schedule 4							
W.B. 108.5"; 3.0 Liter.							
LX Sedan 4D		P52U	18670	2225	2775	4125	6025
SE Sedan 4D		P53U	18995	2650	3250	4625	6575
SE Wagon 4D		P58U	19995	3150	3825	5225	7275
V6 3.0 Liter 24V		S		250	250	335	335
V6 3.0L Flexible Fuel		2		0	0	0	0
TAURUS—V8—Equipment Schedule 4							
W.B. 108.5"; 3.4 Liter.							
SHO Sedan 4D		P54N	29550	4850	5700	7250	9550
CROWN VICTORIA—V8—Equipment Schedule 4							
W.B. 114.7"; 4.6 Liter.							
Sedan 4D		P73W	22510	3325	4025	5725	8100
LX Sedan 4D		P74W	24530	3925	4675	6425	8900

2000 FORD — (1,2or3)FA–(P33P)–Y–#

Body	Type	VIN	List	Trade-In Fair	Good	Pvt-Party Good	Retail Excellent
FOCUS—4-Cyl.—Equipment Schedule 6							
W.B. 103.0"; 2.0 Liter.							
LX Sedan 4D		P33P	13335	2575	3200	4400	6150
SE Sedan 4D		P34P	13980	2950	3600	4825	6650
SE Wagon 4D		P36P	15795	3250	3900	5175	7025
Sony Special Edition				100	100	135	135
4-Cyl. 2.0 Liter 16V		3		150	150	200	200
FOCUS—4-Cyl. 16V—Equipment Schedule 6							
W.B. 103.0"; 2.0 Liter.							
ZX3 Hatchback 2D		P313	13075	2975	3650	4950	6850
ZTS Sedan 4D		P383	15580	3400	4100	5375	7250
Kona Limited Edition				100	100	135	135
ESCORT—4-Cyl.—Equipment Schedule 6							
W.B. 98.4"; 2.0 Liter.							
Sedan 4D		P13P	12440	1575	2100	3475	5375
ZX2 Coupe 2D		P113	12970	1975	2525	3925	5875
S/R Pkg				275	275	365	365
CONTOUR—V6—Equipment Schedule 5							
W.B. 106.5"; 2.5 Liter.							
SE Sedan 4D		P66L	17265	2150	2725	4100	6050
SE Sport Sedan 4D		P66L	18195	3100	3750	5200	7275
SVT Sedan 4D		P68G	23250	4725	5550	7125	9425
Manual Trans (SVT)				0	0	0	0
4-Cyl. 2.0 Liter		Z,3		(275)	(275)	(365)	(365)
MUSTANG—V6—Equipment Schedule 4							
W.B. 101.3"; 3.8 Liter.							
Coupe 2D		P404	18410	4350	5125	6600	8750
Convertible 2D		P444	23260	5350	6275	8025	10550
Manual Trans				(525)	(525)	(700)	(700)
MUSTANG—V8—Equipment Schedule 4							
W.B. 101.3"; 4.6 Liter.							
GT Coupe 2D		P42X	22905	6250	7250	8925	11450
GT Convertible 2D		P45X	27160	7750	8900	10700	13500
TAURUS—V6—Equipment Schedule 4							
W.B. 108.5"; 3.0 Liter.							
LX Sedan 4D		P52U	18995	2825	3475	4925	6925
SE Sedan 4D		P53U	19295	3300	4000	5475	7550
SE Wagon 4D		P58U	20450	3900	4625	6150	8325
SES Sedan 4D		P55U	20290	3300	4000	5475	7550
SES Wagon 4D		P55U	20870	3900	4625	6150	8325
SEL Sedan 4D		P56U	21565	3575	4275	5750	7900

Body	Type	VIN	List	Trade-In Fair	Good	Pvt-Party Good	Retail Excellent
V6 3.0 Liter 24V		S		275	275	365	365
V6 3.0L Flexible Fuel		2		0	0	0	0

CROWN VICTORIA—V8—Equipment Schedule 4
W.B. 114.7"; 4.6 Liter.

Body	Type	VIN	List	Fair	Good	Good	Excellent
Sedan 4D		P73W	22610	4150	4925	6775	9350
LX Sedan 4D		P74W	24725	4825	5675	7575	10250

2001 FORD — (1,2or3)FA-(P33P)-1-#

FOCUS—4-Cyl.—Equipment Schedule 6
W.B. 103.0"; 2.0 Liter.

Body	Type	VIN	List	Fair	Good	Good	Excellent
LX Sedan 4D		P33P	13645	3175	3850	5125	7000
SE Sedan 4D		P34P	14505	3575	4300	5625	7525
SE Wagon 4D		P363	16700	3900	4650	6000	7975
Street Edition				175	175	235	235
4-Cyl. 2.0 Liter 16V		3		150	150	200	200

FOCUS—4-Cyl. 16V—Equipment Schedule 6
W.B. 103.0"; 2.0 Liter.

Body	Type	VIN	List	Fair	Good	Good	Excellent
ZX3 Hatchback 2D		P313	13385	3625	4350	5725	7750
ZTS Sedan 4D		P383	15725	4075	4850	6200	8175
Street Edition				175	175	235	235
S2 Feature Car				175	175	235	235
ZTW				300	300	400	400
Traction Control				300	300	400	400

ESCORT—4-Cyl.—Equipment Schedule 6
W.B. 98.4"; 2.0 Liter.

Body	Type	VIN	List	Fair	Good	Good	Excellent
Sedan 4D		P13P	14230	2050	2600	4050	6100

ZX2—4-Cyl.—Equipment Schedule 6
W.B. 98.4"; 2.0 Liter.

Body	Type	VIN	List	Fair	Good	Good	Excellent
Coupe 2D		P113	13310	2450	3050	4525	6625

MUSTANG—V6—Equipment Schedule 4
W.B. 101.3"; 3.8 Liter.

Body	Type	VIN	List	Fair	Good	Good	Excellent
Coupe 2D		P404	18195	5250	6150	7700	10050
Convertible 2D		P444	23610	6425	7450	9300	12050
Manual Trans				(550)	(550)	(735)	(735)

MUSTANG—V8—Equipment Schedule 4
W.B. 101.3"; 4.6 Liter.

Body	Type	VIN	List	Fair	Good	Good	Excellent
GT Coupe 2D		P42X	23830	7425	8525	10300	13050
GT Convertible 2D		P45X	28265	9100	10375	12300	15200
Bullit Coupe 2D		P42X	26830	8850	10125	11900	14700
Cobra Coupe 2D		P47V	29205	11175	12725	14650	17750
Cobra Convertible 2D		P46V	33205	12900	14600	16650	19950

TAURUS—V6—Equipment Schedule 4
W.B. 108.5"; 3.0 Liter.

Body	Type	VIN	List	Fair	Good	Good	Excellent
LX Sedan 4D		P52U	19455	3575	4300	5850	8075
SE Sedan 4D		P53U	19635	4125	4900	6475	8750
SE Wagon 4D		P58U	20790	4750	5600	7225	9600
SES Sedan 4D		P55U	20650	4125	4900	6475	8750
SES Wagon 4D		P55S	21225	4750	5600	7225	9600
SEL Sedan 4D		P56U	22135	4400	5175	6800	9125
V6 3.0 Liter 24V		S		300	300	400	400
V6 3.0L Flexible Fuel		2		0	0	0	0

CROWN VICTORIA—V8—Equipment Schedule 4
W.B. 114.7"; 4.6 Liter.

Body	Type	VIN	List	Fair	Good	Good	Excellent
Sedan 4D		P73W	22620	5175	6050	8100	10950
LX Sedan 4D		P74W	24735	5925	6900	8975	11950

2002 FORD — (1,2or3)FA-(P33P)-2-#

FOCUS—4-Cyl.—Equipment Schedule 6
W.B. 103.0"; 2.0 Liter.

Body	Type	VIN	List	Fair	Good	Good	Excellent
LX Sedan 4D		P33P	13220	3975	4725	6100	8125
SE Sedan 4D		P34P	14810	4450	5225	6625	8700
SE Wagon 4D		P36P	17015	4775	5625	7025	9150
4-Cyl. 2.0 Liter 16V		3		150	150	200	200

FOCUS—4-Cyl. 16V—Equipment Schedule 6
W.B. 103.0"; 2.0 Liter.

Body	Type	VIN	List	Fair	Good	Good	Excellent
ZX3 Hatchback 2D		P313	13700	4475	5275	6750	8900
ZTS Sedan 4D		P383	15730	4975	5825	7250	9375
ZX5 Hatchback 4D		P373	16105	5250	6150	7600	9800
SVT Hatchback 2D		P395	17995	6150	7125	8350	10300
ZTW Wagon 4D		P383	18195	5500	6400	7850	10050

ESCORT—4-Cyl.—Equipment Schedule 6
W.B. 98.4"; 2.0 Liter.

Body	Type	VIN	List	Fair	Good	Good	Excellent
Sedan 4D		P13P	14450	2700	3300	4900	7100

2002 FORD

Body	Type	VIN	List	Trade-In Fair	Good	Pvt-Party Good	Retail Excellent
ZX2—4-Cyl.—Equipment Schedule 6							
W.B. 98.4"; 2.0 Liter.							
Coupe 2D		P113	13655	**3150**	**3800**	**5400**	**7650**
MUSTANG—V6—Equipment Schedule 4							
W.B. 101.3"; 3.8 Liter.							
Coupe 2D		P404	18635	**6375**	**7375**	**9075**	**11600**
Convertible 2D		P444	23955	**7700**	**8850**	**10850**	**13800**
Manual Trans				**(575)**	**(575)**	**(765)**	**(765)**
MUSTANG—V8—Equipment Schedule 4							
W.B. 101.3"; 4.6 Liter.							
GT Coupe 2D		P42X	24175	**8750**	**10025**	**11950**	**14950**
GT Convertible 2D		P45X	28430	**10650**	**12150**	**14100**	**17300**
TAURUS—V6—Equipment Schedule 4							
W.B. 108.5"; 3.0 Liter.							
LX Sedan 4D		P52U	19445	**4525**	**5350**	**7025**	**9450**
SE Sedan 4D		P53U	20070	**5125**	**6000**	**7725**	**10200**
SE Wagon 4D		P58U	22005	**5800**	**6775**	**8525**	**11100**
SES Sedan 4D		P55U	21085	**5125**	**6000**	**7725**	**10200**
SEL Sedan 4D		P56S	22995	**5675**	**6600**	**8350**	**10900**
SEL Wagon 4D		P59S	23265	**6000**	**6950**	**8725**	**11350**
V6 3.0 Liter 24V		S		**325**	**325**	**435**	**435**
V6 3.0L Flexible Fuel		2		**0**	**0**	**0**	**0**
CROWN VICTORIA—V8—Equipment Schedule 4							
W.B. 114.7"; 4.6 Liter.							
Sedan 4D		P73W	23435	**6500**	**7500**	**9750**	**12900**
LX Sedan 4D		P74W	27025	**7325**	**8425**	**10700**	**13950**
THUNDERBIRD—V8—Equipment Schedule 2							
W.B. 107.2"; 3.9 Liter.							
Soft Top Conv 2D		P60A	35495	**16025**	**18050**	**20500**	**24500**
Hard Top				**875**	**875**	**1165**	**1165**

2003 FORD — (1,2or3)FA—(P33P)-3-#

Body	Type	VIN	List	Trade-In Fair	Good	Pvt-Party Good	Retail Excellent
FOCUS—4-Cyl.—Equipment Schedule 6							
W.B. 103.0"; 2.0 Liter, 2.3 Liter.							
LX Sedan 4D		P33P	13505	**5100**	**5975**	**7275**	**9300**
SE Sedan 4D		P34P	15175	**5600**	**6500**	**7850**	**9925**
SE Wagon 4D		P36F	17525	**5950**	**6900**	**8275**	**10400**
4-Cyl. 2.3 Liter 16V		Z		**150**	**150**	**200**	**200**
FOCUS—4-Cyl. 16V—Equipment Schedule 6							
W.B. 103.0"; 2.0 Liter, 2.3 Liter.							
ZX3 Hatchback 2D		P313	13990	**5650**	**6550**	**7975**	**10150**
ZX5 Hatchback 4D		P373	15900	**6475**	**7500**	**8875**	**11100**
ZTS Sedan 4D		P383	16095	**6175**	**7150**	**8525**	**10650**
ZTW Wagon 4D		P363	17870	**6775**	**7800**	**9225**	**11400**
ZX3 SVT Hatchback 2D		P395	19100	**7475**	**8600**	**9700**	**11650**
ZX5 SVT Hatchback 4D		P375	19600	**8600**	**9850**	**11050**	**13150**
ZX2—4-Cyl.—Equipment Schedule 6							
W.B. 98.4"; 2.0 Liter.							
Coupe 2D		P113	14250	**4125**	**4900**	**6450**	**8700**
MUSTANG—V6—Equipment Schedule 4							
W.B. 101.3"; 3.8 Liter.							
Coupe 2D		P404	18915	**7775**	**8925**	**10600**	**13250**
Convertible 2D		P444	24585	**9300**	**10600**	**12650**	**15800**
Manual Trans				**(600)**	**(600)**	**(800)**	**(800)**
MUSTANG—V8—Equipment Schedule 4							
W.B. 101.3"; 4.6 Liter.							
GT Coupe 2D		P42X	24785	**10425**	**11850**	**13800**	**16950**
GT Convertible 2D		P45X	29060	**12475**	**14100**	**16200**	**19600**
Mach I Coupe 2D		P42R	29810	**12825**	**14500**	**16600**	**19950**
MUSTANG—V8 Supercharged—Equipment Schedule 4							
W.B. 101.3"; 4.6 Liter.							
Cobra Coupe 2D		P48Y	33750	**18000**	**20250**	**22600**	**26600**
Cobra Convertible 2D		P49Y	37995	**19875**	**22375**	**24900**	**29200**
10th Anniversary Edition				**300**	**300**	**400**	**400**
TAURUS—V6—Equipment Schedule 4							
W.B. 108.5"; 3.0 Liter.							
LX Sedan 4D		P52U	20230	**5750**	**6700**	**8425**	**10950**
SE Sedan 4D		P53U	20345	**6400**	**7425**	**9175**	**11750**
SE Wagon 4D		P58U	21995	**7125**	**8225**	**9975**	**12650**
SES Sedan 4D		P55U	21670	**6400**	**7425**	**9175**	**11750**
SEL Sedan 4D		P56S	23570	**6975**	**8075**	**9850**	**12550**
SEL Wagon 4D		P59U	23820	**7050**	**8125**	**9900**	**12600**
V6 3.0 Liter 24V		S		**350**	**350**	**465**	**465**

Body	Type	VIN	List	Trade-In Fair	Trade-In Good	Pvt-Party Good	Retail Excellent
V6 3.0L Flexible Fuel		2		0	0	0	0
CROWN VICTORIA—V8—Equipment Schedule 4							
W.B. 114.7"; 4.6 Liter.							
Sedan 4D		P73W	24510	8175	9375	11750	15150
LX Sedan 4D		P74W	27780	9100	10375	12800	16300
THUNDERBIRD—V8—Equipment Schedule 2							
W.B. 107.2"; 3.9 Liter.							
Soft Top Conv 2D		P60A	36895	18425	20725	23300	27600
007 Hard Top Conv 2D		P62A	43995				
Hard Top				950	950	1265	1265

2004 FORD — (1,2or3)FA–(P333)–4–#

Body	Type	VIN	List	Trade-In Fair	Trade-In Good	Pvt-Party Good	Retail Excellent
FOCUS—4-Cyl.—Equipment Schedule 6							
W.B. 103.0"; 2.0 Liter.							
LX Sedan 4D		P333	14640	6450	7475	8700	10750
SE Wagon 4D		P363	17675	7400	8500	9850	12000
4-Cyl. 2.0/2.3L 16V		P		150	150	200	200
FOCUS—4-Cyl. 16V—Equipment Schedule 6							
W.B. 103.0"; 2.0 Liter, 2.3 Liter.							
ZX3 Hatchback 2D		P313	14180	7025	8100	9475	11650
ZX5 Hatchback 4D		P373	15580	7950	9125	10500	12750
SE Sedan 4D		P34Z	15460	7150	8250	9525	11650
ZTS Sedan 4D		P38Z	16080	7600	8725	10100	12300
ZTW Wagon 4D		P35Z	18290	8300	9525	10900	13200
SVT Hatchback 2D		P395	19375	9025	10325	11400	13400
SVT Hatchback 4D		P375	19630	10275	11675	12850	15000
MUSTANG—V6—Equipment Schedule 4							
W.B. 101.3"; 3.8 Liter.							
Coupe 2D		P404	19160	9700	11100	12950	15900
Convertible 2D		P444	24895	11425	12950	15200	18700
Manual Trans				(625)	(625)	(835)	(835)
MUSTANG—V8—Equipment Schedule 4							
W.B. 101.3"; 4.6 Liter.							
GT Coupe 2D		P42X	24685	12625	14250	16450	19950
GT Convertible 2D		P45X	29025	14825	16700	18950	22700
Mach 1 Coupe 2D		P42R	30260	15175	17100	19400	23100
MUSTANG—V8 Supercharged—Equipment Schedule 4							
W.B. 101.3"; 4.6 Liter.							
Cobra Coupe 2D		P48Y	35200	20925	23425	26000	30300
Cobra Convertible 2D		P49Y	39575	23050	25825	28400	32900
TAURUS—V6—Equipment Schedule 4							
W.B. 108.5"; 3.0 Liter.							
LX Sedan 4D		P52U	20720	7325	8425	10200	12900
SE Sedan 4D		P53U	20855	8025	9200	11050	13800
SE Wagon 4D		P58S	22290	8800	10075	11950	14900
SES Sedan 4D		P55S	22040	8025	9200	11050	13800
SEL Sedan 4D		P56S	23965	8700	9925	11800	14700
SEL Wagon 4D		P59U	24115	8725	9975	11850	14750
V6 3.0 Liter 24V		S		375	375	500	500
V6 3.0L Flexible Fuel		2		0	0	0	0
CROWN VICTORIA—V8—Equipment Schedule 4							
W.B. 114.7"; 4.6 Liter.							
Sedan 4D		P73W	24345	10375	11800	14450	18350
LX Sedan 4D		P74W	27370	11325	12875	15550	19600
THUNDERBIRD—V8—Equipment Schedule 2							
W.B. 107.2"; 3.9 Liter.							
Soft Top Conv 2D		P60A	37530	21225	23800	26600	31200
Pacific Coast Conv 2D		P63A	43995				
Hard Top				1025	1025	1365	1365

GEO

1990 GEO — (1Y,JGorJ8)1(MS246)–L–#

Body	Type	VIN	List	Trade-In Fair	Trade-In Good	Pvt-Party Good	Retail Excellent
METRO—3-Cyl.—Equipment Schedule 6							
W.B. 89.2", 93.1" (4D); 1.0 Liter.							
XFi Hatchback 2D		MS246	6551	175	250	600	1125
Hatchback 2D		MS246	7921	175	225	575	1075
Hatchback 4D		MS646	8221	175	250	600	1125
LSi Hatchback 2D		MR246	8721	200	300	650	1225
LSi Hatchback 4D		MR646	9021	250	325	700	1300
LSi Convertible 2D		MR346	10966	300	425	850	1500

1990 GEO

Body	Type	VIN	List	Trade-In Fair	Good	Pvt-Party Good	Retail Excellent
STORM—4-Cyl.—Equipment Schedule 6							
W.B. 96.5"; 1.6 Liter.							
2+2 Coupe 2D		RF236	11395	300	425	900	1675
GSi Coupe 2D		RT235	12655	400	600	1150	2025
PRIZM—4-Cyl.—Equipment Schedule 6							
W.B. 95.7"; 1.6 Liter.							
Notchback Sedan 4D		SK516	11849	450	625	1200	2100
Hatchback Sedan 4D		SK616	12059	450	625	1200	2100
GSi N'Back Sedan 4D		SL515	13294	500	725	1300	2250
GSi Hatchback 4D		SL615	13529	525	750	1375	2350
LSi Pkg		-------		100	100	135	135

1991 GEO — (1Y,JGorJ8)1(MS246)—M—#

Body	Type	VIN	List	Trade-In Fair	Good	Pvt-Party Good	Retail Excellent
METRO—3-Cyl.—Equipment Schedule 6							
W.B. 89.2", 93.1" (4D); 1.0 Liter.							
XFi Hatchback 2D		MS246	7361	200	300	650	1225
Hatchback 2D		MR246	8031	200	275	625	1175
Hatchback 4D		MR646	8231	200	300	650	1225
LSi Hatchback 2D		MR246	9031	250	325	700	1300
LSi Hatchback 4D		MR646	9231	275	350	775	1400
LSi Convertible 2D		MR336	10966	325	475	900	1575
STORM—4-Cyl.—Equipment Schedule 6							
W.B. 96.5"; 1.6 Liter.							
2+2 Coupe 2D		RF236	11685	350	500	1075	1975
Hatchback Coupe 2D		RF436	11720	375	550	1150	2075
GSi 2+2 Coupe 2D		RT235	13410	475	675	1325	2350
PRIZM—4-Cyl.—Equipment Schedule 6							
W.B. 95.7"; 1.6 Liter.							
Notchback Sedan 4D		SK546	11555	525	750	1350	2300
Hatchback Sedan 4D		SK646	11992	525	750	1350	2300
GSi N'Back Sedan 4D		SL545	13599	575	825	1450	2475
GSi Hatchback 4D		SL645	13949	600	875	1500	2575
LSi Pkg		-------		100	100	135	135

1992 GEO — (1Y,JGorJ8)1(MS246)—N—#

Body	Type	VIN	List	Trade-In Fair	Good	Pvt-Party Good	Retail Excellent
METRO—3-Cyl.—Equipment Schedule 6							
W.B. 89.2", 93.1" (4D); 1.0 Liter.							
XFi Hatchback 2D		MS246	7585	225	300	700	1300
Hatchback 2D		MR246	8305	200	300	675	1250
Hatchback 4D		MR646	8705	225	300	700	1300
LSi Hatchback 2D		MR246	9505	275	350	775	1425
LSi Hatchback 4D		MR646	9905	300	425	875	1550
LSi Convertible 2D		MR336	11275	375	525	1000	1750
STORM—4-Cyl.—Equipment Schedule 6							
W.B. 96.5"; 1.6 Liter, 1.8 Liter.							
2+2 Coupe 2D		RF236	12560	450	625	1275	2300
Hatchback Coupe 2D		RF436	13330	475	675	1350	2400
GSi 2+2 Coupe 2D		RT238	14530	575	825	1550	2725
PRIZM—4-Cyl.—Equipment Schedule 6							
W.B. 95.7"; 1.6 Liter.							
Sedan 4D		SK546	11995	575	825	1500	2575
GSi Sedan 4D		SL545	14135	650	900	1600	2750
LSi Pkg		-------		125	125	165	165

1993 GEO — (1Y,JGorJ8)1(MS246)—P—#

Body	Type	VIN	List	Trade-In Fair	Good	Pvt-Party Good	Retail Excellent
METRO—3-Cyl.—Equipment Schedule 6							
W.B. 89.2", 93.1" (4D); 1.0 Liter.							
XFi Hatchback 2D		MS246	7296	250	325	750	1400
Hatchback 2D		MR246	8016	225	300	725	1350
Hatchback 4D		MR646	8505	250	325	750	1400
LSi Hatchback 2D		MR246	9505	300	400	875	1550
LSi Hatchback 4D		MR646	9905	325	475	925	1675
LSi Convertible 2D		MR336	10749	400	600	1100	1925
STORM—4-Cyl.—Equipment Schedule 6							
W.B. 96.5"; 1.6 Liter, 1.8 Liter.							
2+2 Coupe 2D		RF236	12620	550	800	1550	2750
GSi 2+2 Coupe 2D		RT238	14585	700	1000	1900	3250
PRIZM—4-Cyl.—Equipment Schedule 6							
W.B. 97.1"; 1.6 Liter, 1.8 Liter.							
Sedan 4D		SK536	11662	650	900	1625	2800
LSi Sedan 4D		SL536	12482	775	1075	1900	3150

1994 GEO

Body	Type	VIN	List	Trade-In Fair	Good	Pvt-Party Good	Retail Excellent

1994 GEO — (1Y,JGorJ8)1(MS246)–R–#

METRO—3-Cyl.—Equipment Schedule 6
W.B. 89.2", 93.1" (5D); 1.0 Liter.

XFi Hatchback 2D		MS246	7791	275	350	850	1550
Hatchback 2D		MR246	8511	250	325	825	1500
Hatchback 4D		MR646	9011	275	375	875	1575

PRIZM—4-Cyl.—Equipment Schedule 6
W.B. 97.1"; 1.6 Liter, 1.8 Liter.

Sedan 4D		SK536	12480	750	1050	1900	3200
LSi Sedan 4D		SK536	13410	875	1225	2125	3525

1995 GEO — (JG,2Cor1Y)1(MR226)–S–#

METRO—3-Cyl.—Equipment Schedule 6
W.B. 93.1"; 1.0 Liter.

Hatchback 2D		MR226	9481	300	425	875	1550
LSi Hatchback 2D		MR226	9781	400	575	1050	1850
4-Cyl. 1.3 Liter		9		100	100	135	135

METRO—4-Cyl.—Equipment Schedule 6
W.B. 93.1"; 1.3 Liter.

Sedan 4D		MR529	10741	575	825	1425	2400
LSi Sedan 4D		MR529	11141	625	900	1500	2525

PRIZM—4-Cyl.—Equipment Schedule 6
W.B. 97.1"; 1.6 Liter, 1.8 Liter.

Sedan 4D		SK526	13435	900	1250	2200	3650
LSi Sedan 4D		SK526	14260	975	1425	2525	4075

1996 GEO — (1Yor2C)1(MR226)–T–#

METRO—3-Cyl.—Equipment Schedule 6
W.B. 93.1"; 1.0 Liter.

Coupe 2D		MR226	9988	375	550	1050	1850
LSi Coupe 2D		MR226	10271	475	700	1250	2125
4-Cyl. 1.3 Liter		9		100	100	135	135

METRO—4-Cyl.—Equipment Schedule 6
W.B. 93.1"; 1.3 Liter.

Sedan 4D		MR529	11026	700	975	1650	2750
LSi Sedan 4D		MR529	11426	750	1050	1775	2925

PRIZM—4-Cyl.—Equipment Schedule 6
W.B. 97.1"; 1.6 Liter, 1.8 Liter.

Sedan 4D		SK526	14300	1025	1475	2625	4250
LSi Sedan 4D		SK526	15010	1175	1625	2825	4500

1997 GEO — (1Yor2C)1(MR226)–V–#

METRO—3-Cyl.—Equipment Schedule 6
W.B. 93.1"; 1.0 Liter.

Coupe 2D		MR226	10185	500	725	1300	2225

METRO—4-Cyl.—Equipment Schedule 6
W.B. 93.1"; 1.3 Liter.

LSi Sedan 4D		MR529	11546	900	1300	2125	3425
LSi Coupe 2D		MR229	10606	675	950	1625	2725

PRIZM—4-Cyl.—Equipment Schedule 6
W.B. 97.1"; 1.6 Liter, 1.8 Liter.

Sedan 4D		SK526	14375	1325	1800	3000	4700
LSi Sedan 4D		SK526	15020	1500	1975	3200	4925

HONDA

1990 HONDA — (1HGorJHM)(ED836)–L–#

CIVIC—4-Cyl.—Equipment Schedule 6
W.B. 90.6", 98.4" (3D, 4D); 1.5 Liter, 1.6 Liter.

CRX HF Hatchback 2D		ED836	9390	850	1200	2025	3275
CRX Hatchback 2D		ED835	9655	900	1275	2100	3400
CRX Si Hatchback 2D		ED936	11375	1025	1475	2500	3950
Hatchback 2D		ED634	6880	775	1075	1825	3025
Wagon 4D		EE275	10570	900	1250	2100	3350
DX Sedan 4D		ED354	9685	925	1325	2200	3525
DX Hatchback 2D		ED635	8940	775	1075	1825	3025
Si Hatchback 2D		ED736	10490	950	1375	2250	3600
LX Sedan 4D		ED355	10695	925	1325	2200	3525
EX Sedan 4D		ED456	11370	975	1425	2425	3900

1990 HONDA

Body	Type	VIN	List	Trade-In Fair	Trade-In Good	Pvt-Party Good	Retail Excellent
4WD Wagon 4D		EE476	12655	950	1375	2250	3600
ACCORD—4-Cyl.—Equipment Schedule 3							
W.B. 107.1"; 2.2 Liter.							
DX Sedan 4D		CB764	13340	975	1425	2425	3900
DX Coupe 2D		CB724	13140	1025	1475	2525	4000
LX Sedan 4D		CB765	15890	1125	1575	2675	4175
LX Coupe 2D		CB725	15690	1225	1700	2775	4350
EX Sedan 4D		CB766	17390	1175	1625	2700	4250
EX Coupe 2D		CB726	17390	1275	1750	2850	4425
Manual Trans				(175)	(175)	(235)	(235)
PRELUDE—4-Cyl.—Equipment Schedule 3							
W.B. 101.1"; 2.0 Liter, 2.1 Liter.							
2.0 S Coupe 2D		BA411	14955	900	1275	2125	3425
2.0 Si Coupe 2D		BA412	15955	950	1350	2250	3600
Si Coupe 2D		BA413	17975	1000	1450	2450	3925
Si 4WS Coupe 2D		BA414	19460	1000	1450	2450	3925
Si ALB Coupe 2D		BA415	19560	1000	1450	2450	3925

1991 HONDA — (1HGorJHM)(ED836)–M–#

Body	Type	VIN	List	Trade-In Fair	Trade-In Good	Pvt-Party Good	Retail Excellent
CIVIC—4-Cyl.—Equipment Schedule 6							
W.B. 98.4", 90.6" (CRX); 1.5 Liter, 1.6 Liter.							
CRX HF H'Back 2D		ED836	9405	975	1400	2400	3875
CRX Hatchback 2D		ED835	9670	1025	1450	2475	3950
CRX Si Hatchback 2D		ED936	11390	1225	1700	2800	4375
Hatchback 2D		ED634	7155	900	1275	2100	3400
Wagon 4D		EE275	10585	1000	1450	2450	3925
DX Sedan 4D		ED354	9750	1050	1500	2575	4050
DX Hatchback 2D		ED635	9005	900	1275	2125	3425
Si Hatchback 2D		ED736	10555	1100	1550	2650	4175
LX Sedan 4D		ED355	10760	1050	1500	2575	4075
EX Sedan 4D		ED456	11455	1175	1625	2725	4275
4WD Wagon 4D		EE476	12670	1100	1550	2625	4125
ACCORD—4-Cyl.—Equipment Schedule 3							
W.B. 107.1"; 2.2 Liter.							
DX Sedan 4D		CB764	13555	1175	1625	2750	4350
DX Coupe 2D		CB724	13355	1225	1700	2825	4450
LX Sedan 4D		CB765	16105	1400	1875	3075	4725
LX Coupe 2D		CB725	15905	1500	1975	3200	4875
LX Wagon 4D		CB985	18325	1450	1925	3125	4775
EX Sedan 4D		CB766	17805	1450	1925	3125	4775
EX Coupe 2D		CB726	17605	1525	2050	3250	4950
EX Wagon 4D		CB986	20075	1725	2250	3475	5200
SE Sedan 4D		CB768	19805	1500	1975	3175	4850
Manual Trans				(175)	(175)	(235)	(235)
PRELUDE—4-Cyl.—Equipment Schedule 3							
W.B. 101.0"; 2.0 Liter.							
2.0 Si Coupe 2D		BA412	15955	1150	1600	2775	4450
Si Coupe 2D		BA413	18175	1225	1700	2900	4550
Si 4WS Coupe 2D		BA414	19460	1225	1700	2900	4550
Si ALB Coupe 2D		BA415	19710	1225	1700	2900	4550
Auto Trans				100	100	135	135

1992 HONDA — (1HGorJHM)(EH234)–N–#

Body	Type	VIN	List	Trade-In Fair	Trade-In Good	Pvt-Party Good	Retail Excellent
CIVIC—4-Cyl.—Equipment Schedule 6							
W.B. 101.3", 103.2" (Sed); 1.5 Liter, 1.6 Liter.							
CX Hatchback 2D		EH234	8190	875	1225	2100	3425
DX Sedan 4D		EG854	10845	1325	1800	2950	4550
DX Hatchback 2D		EH235	9940	1050	1500	2575	4125
VX Hatchback 2D		EH240	10640	1225	1675	2800	4400
Si Hatchback 2D		EH338	11990	1425	1900	3075	4725
LX Sedan 4D		EG855	11675	1350	1825	2975	4600
EX Sedan 4D		EH959	13865	1500	2000	3200	4850
ACCORD—4-Cyl.—Equipment Schedule 3							
W.B. 107.1"; 2.2 Liter.							
DX Sedan 4D		CB764	14265	1475	1950	3150	4800
DX Coupe 2D		CB724	14065	1500	2000	3200	4850
LX Sedan 4D		CB765	16865	1775	2300	3525	5275
LX Coupe 2D		CB725	16665	1800	2325	3625	5450
LX Wagon 4D		CB985	18490	1800	2325	3600	5350
EX Sedan 4D		CB767	19285	1825	2350	3625	5425
EX Coupe 2D		CB727	19085	1925	2450	3750	5575
EX Wagon 4D		CB987	20940	2100	2700	3975	5800
Manual Trans				(225)	(225)	(300)	(300)

1992 HONDA

PRELUDE—4-Cyl.—Equipment Schedule 3
W.B. 100.4"; 2.2 Liter, 2.3 Liter.

Body	Type	VIN	List	Fair	Good	Good	Excellent
S Coupe 2D		BA814	16540	2000	2550	3850	5675
Si Coupe 2D		BB215	19540	2200	2775	4100	6000
Si 4WS Coupe 2D		BB216	21860	2200	2775	4100	6000
Auto Trans				125	125	165	165

1993 HONDA — (1HGorJHM)(EH235)-P-#

CIVIC—4-Cyl.—Equipment Schedule 6
W.B. 101.3", 103.2" (2D, 4D); 1.5 Liter, 1.6 Liter.

Body	Type	VIN	List	Fair	Good	Good	Excellent
CX Hatchback 2D		EH235	8730	975	1400	2450	3950
DX Sedan 4D		EG854	11385	1550	2075	3275	4950
DX Coupe 2D		EJ214	10680	1350	1825	2975	4600
DX Hatchback 2D		EH236	10430	1225	1700	2825	4450
VX Hatchback 2D		EH237	11130	1450	1925	3100	4750
Si Hatchback 2D		EH338	12530	1675	2200	3425	5150
LX Sedan 4D		EG855	12215	1600	2100	3300	5000
EX Sedan 4D		EH959	15430	1800	2325	3575	5325
EX Coupe 2D		EJ115	12730	1775	2300	3525	5275

CIVIC del SOL—4-Cyl.—Equipment Schedule 6
W.B. 93.3"; 1.5 Liter, 1.6 Liter.

Body	Type	VIN	List	Fair	Good	Good	Excellent
S Coupe 2D		EG114	13530	1550	2075	3250	4900
Si Coupe 2D		EH616	15330	1800	2325	3550	5275

ACCORD—4-Cyl.—Equipment Schedule 3
W.B. 107.1"; 2.2 Liter.

Body	Type	VIN	List	Fair	Good	Good	Excellent
DX Sedan 4D		CB764	15030	1750	2275	3550	5325
DX Coupe 2D		CB724	14830	1775	2300	3575	5350
LX Sedan 4D		CB765	17630	2100	2700	4025	5900
LX Coupe 2D		CB725	17430	2125	2700	4125	6100
LX Wagon 4D		CB985	19055	2175	2750	4100	6000
10th Anny Sedan 4D		CB769	18780	2100	2675	4000	5875
EX Sedan 4D		CB767	20050	2225	2775	4175	6125
EX Coupe 2D		CB727	19850	2275	2850	4275	6275
EX Wagon 4D		CB987	21505	2525	3125	4500	6475
SE Sedan 4D		CB768	22050	2250	2825	4200	6125
SE Coupe 2D		CB728	21850	2175	2750	4100	6000
Manual Trans				(275)	(275)	(365)	(365)

PRELUDE—4-Cyl.—Equipment Schedule 3
W.B. 100.4"; 2.2 Liter, 2.3 Liter.

Body	Type	VIN	List	Fair	Good	Good	Excellent
S Coupe 2D		BA814	17330	2400	2975	4375	6300
Si Coupe 2D		BB215	20330	2650	3250	4675	6700
Si 4WS Coupe 2D		BB216	22650	2650	3250	4675	6700
VTEC Coupe 2D		BB117	23020	2975	3650	5125	7225
Auto Trans				150	150	200	200

1994 HONDA — (1HGorJHM)(EH235)-R-#

CIVIC—4-Cyl.—Equipment Schedule 6
W.B. 101.3", 103.2" (2D, 4D); 1.5 Liter, 1.6 Liter.

Body	Type	VIN	List	Fair	Good	Good	Excellent
CX Hatchback 2D		EH235	9750	1100	1550	2700	4300
DX Sedan 4D		EG854	12100	1825	2350	3625	5375
DX Coupe 2D		EJ212	11570	1575	2100	3300	5025
DX Hatchback 2D		EH236	11150	1475	1950	3150	4825
VX Hatchback 2D		EH237	11850	1675	2200	3425	5150
Si Hatchback 2D		EH338	13520	1975	2525	3825	5625
LX Sedan 4D		EG855	13300	1875	2400	3650	5425
EX Sedan 4D		EH959	16090	2125	2700	4000	5850
EX Coupe 2D		EJ112	13950	2100	2650	3925	5750

del SOL—4-Cyl.—Equipment Schedule 6
W.B. 93.3"; 1.5 Liter, 1.6 Liter.

Body	Type	VIN	List	Fair	Good	Good	Excellent
S Coupe 2D		EG114	14450	1850	2375	3600	5325
Si Coupe 2D		EH616	16450	2100	2700	3925	5725
VTEC Coupe 2D		EG217	17850	2300	2875	4175	6025

ACCORD—4-Cyl.—Equipment Schedule 3
W.B. 106.9"; 2.2 Liter.

Body	Type	VIN	List	Fair	Good	Good	Excellent
DX Sedan 4D		CD562	15430	1975	2525	3775	5550
DX Coupe 2D		CD722	15230	1975	2525	3775	5550
LX Sedan 4D		CD563	18330	2400	3000	4325	6225
LX Coupe 2D		CD723	18130	2400	3000	4425	6400
LX Wagon 4D		CE182	19280	2500	3100	4450	6325
EX Sedan 4D		CD565	20850	2550	3175	4525	6500
EX Coupe 2D		CD725	20650	2575	3200	4625	6650
EX Wagon 4D		CE189	21850	2825	3475	4875	6850
Manual Trans				(325)	(325)	(435)	(435)

Body	Type	VIN	List	Trade-In Fair	Trade-In Good	Pvt-Party Good	Retail Excellent
PRELUDE—4-Cyl.—Equipment Schedule 3							
W.B. 100.4"; 2.2 Liter, 2.3 Liter.							
S Coupe 2D		BA814	18450	**2800**	**3425**	**4900**	**6975**
Si Coupe 2D		BB215	21750	**3100**	**3750**	**5275**	**7450**
4WS Coupe 2D		BB216	24510	**3100**	**3750**	**5275**	**7450**
VTEC Coupe 2D		BB117	24850	**3475**	**4175**	**5750**	**8000**
Auto Trans				175	175	235	235

Body	Type	VIN	List	Trade-In Fair	Trade-In Good	Pvt-Party Good	Retail Excellent
CIVIC—4-Cyl.—Equipment Schedule 6							
W.B. 101.3", 103.2" (2D, 4D); 1.5 Liter, 1.6 Liter.							
CX Hatchback 2D		EH235	10130	**1375**	**1850**	**3050**	**4725**
DX Sedan 4D		EG854	12360	**2100**	**2700**	**4000**	**5850**
DX Coupe 2D		EJ212	11970	**1875**	**2400**	**3700**	**5500**
DX Hatchback 2D		EH236	11480	**1725**	**2250**	**3500**	**5275**
VX Hatchback 2D		EH237	12180	**1975**	**2525**	**3825**	**5650**
Si Hatchback 2D		EH338	13920	**2300**	**2875**	**4250**	**6150**
LX Sedan 4D		EG855	13700	**2175**	**2750**	**4050**	**5925**
EX Sedan 4D		EH959	16580	**2525**	**3125**	**4500**	**6425**
EX Coupe 2D		EJ112	14410	**2425**	**3025**	**4400**	**6300**
del SOL—4-Cyl.—Equipment Schedule 6							
W.B. 93.3"; 1.5 Liter, 1.6 Liter.							
S Coupe 2D		EG114	15160	**2175**	**2750**	**4000**	**5800**
Si Coupe 2D		EH616	17330	**2475**	**3075**	**4375**	**6250**
VTEC Coupe 2D		EG217	19580	**2700**	**3300**	**4625**	**6550**
ACCORD—4-Cyl.—Equipment Schedule 3							
W.B. 106.9"; 2.2 Liter.							
DX Sedan 4D		CD562	15930	**2400**	**2975**	**4300**	**6175**
LX Sedan 4D		CD563	18880	**2875**	**3525**	**4925**	**6900**
LX Coupe 2D		CD723	18680	**2850**	**3500**	**5025**	**7150**
LX Wagon 4D		CE182	19840	**2975**	**3625**	**5025**	**7025**
EX Sedan 4D		CD565	21440	**3075**	**3725**	**5200**	**7300**
EX Coupe 2D		CD725	21240	**3050**	**3700**	**5250**	**7450**
EX Wagon 4D		CE189	22470	**3350**	**4050**	**5500**	**7575**
Manual Trans				**(375)**	**(375)**	**(500)**	**(500)**
V6 2.7 Liter				375	375	500	500
PRELUDE—4-Cyl.—Equipment Schedule 3							
W.B. 100.4"; 2.2 Liter, 2.3 Liter.							
S Coupe 2D		BA814	19930	**3275**	**3925**	**5525**	**7725**
Si Coupe 2D		BB215	22580	**3575**	**4300**	**5925**	**8225**
SE Coupe 2D		BB217	23780	**3575**	**4300**	**5925**	**8225**
VTEC Coupe 2D		BB117	25730	**4000**	**4775**	**6450**	**8850**
Auto Trans				200	200	265	265

Body	Type	VIN	List	Trade-In Fair	Trade-In Good	Pvt-Party Good	Retail Excellent
CIVIC—4-Cyl.—Equipment Schedule 6							
W.B. 103.2"; 1.6 Liter.							
CX Hatchback 2D		EJ632	10360	**2050**	**2600**	**3725**	**5375**
DX Sedan 4D		EJ652	12630	**2825**	**3475**	**4725**	**6525**
DX Coupe 2D		EJ612	12280	**2600**	**3225**	**4425**	**6200**
DX Hatchback 2D		EJ634	11630	**2425**	**3025**	**4225**	**5950**
HX Coupe 2D		EJ712	13480	**2925**	**3575**	**4825**	**6650**
LX Sedan 4D		EJ650	13980	**2925**	**3575**	**4825**	**6650**
EX Sedan 4D		EJ854	16660	**3300**	**3975**	**5275**	**7200**
EX Coupe 2D		EJ814	15330	**3225**	**3900**	**5175**	**7075**
del SOL—4-Cyl.—Equipment Schedule 6							
W.B. 93.3"; 1.6 Liter.							
S Coupe 2D		EH614	15475	**2525**	**3125**	**4475**	**6350**
Si Coupe 2D		EH616	17695	**2800**	**3425**	**4800**	**6775**
VTEC Coupe 2D		EG217	19995	**3050**	**3700**	**5125**	**7150**
ACCORD—4-Cyl.—Equipment Schedule 3							
W.B. 106.9"; 2.2 Liter.							
DX Sedan 4D		CD562	16280	**2850**	**3500**	**4900**	**6900**
Anniversary Ed Sed 4D		CD568	17390	**3025**	**3700**	**5100**	**7125**
LX Sedan 4D		CD563	19270	**3425**	**4125**	**5600**	**7700**
LX Coupe 2D		CD723	19070	**3375**	**4075**	**5675**	**7925**
LX Wagon 4D		CE182	20170	**3500**	**4200**	**5700**	**7825**
EX Sedan 4D		CD565	21780	**3625**	**4350**	**5925**	**8150**
EX Coupe 2D		CD725	21580	**3575**	**4300**	**5950**	**8275**
EX Wagon 4D		CE189	22810	**3900**	**4650**	**6200**	**8400**
Manual Trans		1,5,7		**(400)**	**(400)**	**(535)**	**(535)**
V6 2.7 Liter				425	425	565	565

1996 HONDA

Body	Type	VIN	List	Trade-In Fair	Trade-In Good	Pvt-Party Good	Retail Excellent
PRELUDE—4-Cyl.—Equipment Schedule 3							
W.B. 100.4"; 2.2 Liter, 2.3 Liter.							
S Coupe 2D		BA814	20340	3800	4525	6200	8575
Si Coupe 2D		BB215	23035	4175	4950	6650	9100
VTEC Coupe 2D		BB117	26260	4625	5475	7250	9800
Auto Trans				200	200	265	265

1997 HONDA — (1HG,2HGorJHM)(EJ632)–V–#

Body	Type	VIN	List	Trade-In Fair	Trade-In Good	Pvt-Party Good	Retail Excellent
CIVIC—4-Cyl.—Equipment Schedule 6							
W.B. 103.2"; 1.6 Liter.							
CX Hatchback 2D		EJ632	10945	2400	3000	4200	5925
DX Sedan 4D		EJ652	13030	3275	3925	5225	7125
DX Coupe 2D		EJ612	12675	3000	3675	4950	6800
DX Hatchback 2D		EJ634	12195	2825	3450	4700	6525
HX Coupe 2D		EJ712	13795	3350	4050	5350	7275
LX Sedan 4D		EJ657	15045	3350	4050	5350	7275
EX Sedan 4D		EJ854	16875	3775	4500	5850	7875
EX Coupe 2D		EJ814	15645	3700	4425	5750	7750
del SOL—4-Cyl.—Equipment Schedule 6							
W.B. 93.3"; 1.6 Liter.							
S Coupe 2D		EH614	15475	2925	3575	4950	6900
Si Coupe 2D		EH616	17695	3225	3900	5300	7325
VTEC Coupe 2D		EG217	19995	3500	4200	5675	7750
ACCORD—4-Cyl.—Equipment Schedule 3							
W.B. 106.9"; 2.2 Liter.							
DX Sedan 4D		CD562	16295	3400	4100	5600	7700
LX Sedan 4D		CD563	19385	4000	4775	6325	8575
LX Coupe 2D		CD723	19185	3950	4700	6400	8800
LX Wagon 4D		CE182	20285	4100	4875	6425	8700
Special Edition 4D		CD560	20795	4000	4775	6325	8575
Special Edition 2D		CD720	20595	3950	4700	6400	8800
EX Sedan 4D		CD565	21895	4250	5050	6725	9125
EX Coupe 2D		CD725	21695	4175	4975	6725	9225
EX Wagon 4D		CE189	22925	4525	5350	6950	9300
Manual Trans		1,5,7		(425)	(425)	(565)	(565)
V6 2.7 Liter				475	475	635	635
PRELUDE—4-Cyl.—Equipment Schedule 3							
W.B. 101.8"; 2.2 Liter.							
Coupe 2D		BB614	23595	5225	6125	7850	10350
Type SH Coupe 2D		BB615	26095	5700	6650	8425	11000
Auto Trans				200	200	265	265

1998 HONDA — (1HG,2HGorJHM)(EJ632)–W–#

Body	Type	VIN	List	Trade-In Fair	Trade-In Good	Pvt-Party Good	Retail Excellent
CIVIC—4-Cyl.—Equipment Schedule 6							
W.B. 103.2"; 1.6 Liter.							
CX Hatchback 2D		EJ632	11045	2825	3475	4725	6550
DX Sedan 4D		EJ652	13130	3750	4500	5800	7775
DX Coupe 2D		EJ612	12975	3500	4200	5525	7450
DX Hatchback 2D		EJ634	12495	3300	4000	5300	7200
HX Coupe 2D		EJ712	13795	3875	4600	5925	7925
LX Sedan 4D		EJ657	15145	3900	4625	5975	7975
EX Sedan 4D		EJ854	16875	4325	5100	6500	8575
EX Coupe 2D		EJ814	15645	4250	5050	6400	8450
ACCORD—4-Cyl.—Equipment Schedule 3							
W.B. 105.1", 106.9" (Sed); 2.3 Liter.							
DX Sedan 4D		CF864	16295	4400	5175	6375	8200
LX Sedan 4D		CG564	19485	5100	5975	7225	9175
LX Coupe 2D		CG324	19485	5025	5875	7275	9375
EX Sedan 4D		CG565	21995	5350	6275	7650	9800
EX Coupe 2D		CG325	21995	5275	6175	7650	9900
Manual Trans		1,3,5,7		(450)	(450)	(600)	(600)
4-Cyl. 2.3L ULEV				0	0	0	0
V6 3.0 Liter VTEC				525	525	700	700
PRELUDE—4-Cyl.—Equipment Schedule 3							
W.B. 101.8"; 2.2 Liter.							
Coupe 2D		BB614	23695	6025	6975	8775	11400
Type SH Coupe 2D		BB615	26195	6525	7550	9375	12100
Auto Trans				200	200	265	265

1999 HONDA — (1HG,2HGorJHM)(EJ632)–X–#

CIVIC—4-Cyl.—Equipment Schedule 6
W.B. 103.2"; 1.6 Liter.

1999 HONDA

Body	Type	VIN	List	Trade-In Fair	Trade-In Good	Pvt-Party Good	Retail Excellent
CX Hatchback 2D		EJ632	11065	3350	4050	5375	7300
DX Sedan 4D		EJ652	13200	4425	5200	6625	8700
DX Coupe 2D		EJ612	12995	4150	4925	6300	8350
DX Hatchback 2D		EJ634	12515	3900	4650	6025	8050
VP Sedan 4D		EJ661	15045	4650	5500	6900	9050
HX Coupe 2D		EJ712	13815	4500	5325	6750	8850
LX Sedan 4D		EJ657	15245	4625	5475	6900	9025
EX Sedan 4D		EJ854	17145	5125	6000	7500	9700
EX Coupe 2D		EJ814	15865	5025	5875	7350	9525
Si Coupe 2D		EM115	17860	6525	7550	9125	11500
ACCORD—4-Cyl.—Equipment Schedule 3							
W.B. 105.1", 106.9" (Sed); 2.3 Liter.							
DX Sedan 4D		CF864	16415	5075	5950	7175	9100
LX Sedan 4D		CG564	19605	6100	7075	8400	10450
LX Coupe 2D		CG324	19605	5975	6925	8425	10700
EX Sedan 4D		CG565	22115	6375	7400	8875	11200
EX Coupe 2D		CG325	22115	6300	7325	8875	11300
Manual Trans		1,3,5		(500)	(500)	(665)	(665)
4-Cyl. 2.3L ULEV				0	0	0	0
V6 3.0 Liter VTEC				600	600	800	800
PRELUDE—4-Cyl.—Equipment Schedule 3							
W.B. 101.8"; 2.2 Liter.							
Coupe 2D		BB614	23865	7075	8150	10050	12850
Type SH Coupe 2D		BB615	26365	7675	8800	10750	13700
Auto Trans				225	225	300	300

2000 HONDA — (1HG,2HGorJHM)(ZE137)-Y-#

Body	Type	VIN	List	Trade-In Fair	Trade-In Good	Pvt-Party Good	Retail Excellent
INSIGHT—3-Cyl. HYBRID—Equipment Schedule 3							
W.B. 94.5"; 1.0 Liter.							
Hatchback 2D		ZE137	20495	5975	6925	8425	10700
CIVIC—4-Cyl.—Equipment Schedule 6							
W.B. 103.2"; 1.6 Liter.							
CX Hatchback 2D		EJ632	11165	3950	4700	6075	8100
DX Sedan 4D		EJ652	13300	5150	6025	7475	9650
DX Coupe 2D		EJ612	13095	4875	5700	7150	9300
DX Hatchback 2D		EJ634	12615	4600	5425	6825	8925
VP Sedan 4D		EJ661	15145	5450	6350	7825	10050
HX Coupe 2D		EJ712	13915	5250	6150	7600	9800
LX Sedan 4D		EJ657	15145	5475	6375	7850	10100
EX Sedan 4D		EJ854	17245	6025	6975	8500	10800
EX Coupe 2D		EJ814	15965	5850	6825	8300	10600
Si Coupe 2D		EM115	17960	7550	8700	10250	12750
ACCORD—4-Cyl.—Equipment Schedule 3							
W.B. 105.1", 106.9" (Sed); 2.3 Liter.							
DX Sedan 4D		CF864	16565	5850	6825	8100	10200
LX Sedan 4D		CG564	19755	7175	8250	9650	11900
LX Coupe 2D		CG324	19755	7025	8100	9700	12150
SE Sedan 4D		CG567	20905	7500	8625	10050	12350
EX Sedan 4D		CG565	22265	7500	8650	10250	12750
EX Coupe 2D		CG325	22265	7425	8525	10200	12800
Manual Trans				(525)	(525)	(700)	(700)
4-Cyl. 2.3L ULEV				0	0	0	0
V6 3.0 Liter VTEC				675	675	900	900
PRELUDE—4-Cyl.—Equipment Schedule 3							
W.B. 101.8"; 2.2 Liter.							
Coupe 2D		BB614	23915	8225	9425	11400	14450
Type SH Coupe 2D		BB615	26415	8925	10225	12250	15350
Auto Trans				250	250	335	335
S2000—4-Cyl.—Equipment Schedule 2							
W.B. 94.5"; 2.0 Liter.							
Convertible 2D		AP114	32415	12900	14600	16200	19100
Hard Top				700	700	935	935

2001 HONDA — (1HGorJHM)(ZE135)-1-#

Body	Type	VIN	List	Trade-In Fair	Trade-In Good	Pvt-Party Good	Retail Excellent
INSIGHT—3-Cyl. HYBRID—Equipment Schedule 3							
W.B. 94.5"; 1.0 Liter.							
Hatchback 2D		ZE135	20620	6900	7950	9500	11900
CIVIC—4-Cyl.—Equipment Schedule 6							
W.B. 103.1"; 1.7 Liter.							
DX Sedan 4D		ES152	13400	6250	7225	8425	10350
DX Coupe 2D		EM212	13200	5925	6900	8075	9975
HX Coupe 2D		EM217	14000	6325	7350	8550	10500
LX Sedan 4D		ES155	15450	6625	7650	8875	10900

2001 HONDA

Body	Type	VIN	List	Trade-In Fair	Good	Pvt-Party Good	Retail Excellent
LX Coupe 2D		EM215	15250	6500	7500	8700	10700
EX Sedan 4D		ES257	17350	7250	8325	9575	11650
EX Coupe 2D		EM219	16850	7025	8100	9350	11400
GX Sedan 4D		EN264	20670				

ACCORD—4-Cyl.—Equipment Schedule 3
W.B. 105.1", 106.9" (Sed); 2.3 Liter.

DX Sedan 4D		CF864	16640	6800	7825	9225	11400
VP Sedan 4D		CF866	17640	7000	8100	9475	11700
LX Sedan 4D		CG564	20030	8400	9600	11100	13550
LX Coupe 2D		CG324	20030	8225	9425	11100	13750
EX Sedan 4D		CG565	22640	8750	10025	11750	14450
EX Coupe 2D		CG325	22640	8650	9900	11700	14500
Manual Trans	1,5			(550)	(550)	(735)	(735)
4-Cyl. 2.3L ULEV/SULEV				0	0	0	0
V6 3.0 Liter VTEC				750	750	1000	1000

PRELUDE—4-Cyl.—Equipment Schedule 3
W.B. 101.8"; 2.2 Liter.

Coupe 2D		BB614	24040	9550	10900	13000	16200
Type SH Coupe 2D		BB615	26540	10325	11750	13900	17250
Auto Trans				275	275	365	365

S2000—4-Cyl.—Equipment Schedule 2
W.B. 94.5"; 2.0 Liter.

| Convertible 2D | | AP114 | 32740 | 14550 | 16425 | 18050 | 21000 |
| Hard Top | | | | 725 | 725 | 965 | 965 |

2002 HONDA — (1HG,SHHorJHM)(ZE135)-2-#

INSIGHT—3-Cyl. HYBRID—Equipment Schedule 3
W.B. 94.5"; 1.0 Liter.

| Hatchback 2D | | ZE135 | 21720 | 7900 | 9075 | 10650 | 13200 |

CIVIC—4-Cyl.—Equipment Schedule 6
W.B. 101.2", 103.1" (Sed & Cpe); 1.7 Liter, 2.0 Liter.

DX Sedan 4D		ES151	13450	7100	8200	9425	11450
DX Coupe 2D		EM212	13250	6825	7850	9075	11100
HX Coupe 2D		EM217	14050	7250	8325	9575	11650
LX Sedan 4D		ES155	15550	7600	8725	9975	12100
LX Coupe 2D		EM215	15850	7475	8600	9850	11950
EX Sedan 4D		ES257	17450	8275	9475	10800	13000
EX Coupe 2D		EM219	16950	8075	9250	10500	12650
Si Hatchback 2D		EP335	19440	7775	8925	10600	13200

ACCORD—4-Cyl.—Equipment Schedule 3
W.B. 105.1", 106.9" (Sed); 2.3 Liter.

DX Sedan 4D		CF864	16740	7900	9075	10500	12850
VP Sedan 4D		CF866	17740	8125	9325	10800	13200
LX Sedan 4D		CG564	20130	9800	11175	12700	15300
LX Coupe 2D		CG324	20130	9600	10950	12700	15500
SE Sedan 4D		CG567	21290	10125	11525	13100	15750
SE Coupe 2D		CG320	21290	10375	11800	13400	16050
EX Sedan 4D		CG566	22740	10225	11625	13400	16200
EX Coupe 2D		CG325	22740	10025	11425	13350	16350
Manual Trans	1,5			(575)	(575)	(765)	(765)
4-Cyl. 2.3L ULEV/SULEV				0	0	0	0
V6 3.0 Liter VTEC				825	825	1100	1100

S2000—4-Cyl.—Equipment Schedule 2
W.B. 94.5"; 2.0 Liter.

| Convertible 2D | | AP114 | 32840 | 16375 | 18425 | 20100 | 23200 |
| Hard Top | | | | 750 | 750 | 1000 | 1000 |

2003 HONDA — (1HG,SHHorJHM)(ZE135)-3-#

INSIGHT—3-Cyl. HYBRID—Equipment Schedule 3
W.B. 94.5"; 1.0 Liter.

| Hatchback 2D | | ZE135 | 21740 | 9050 | 10325 | 11900 | 14450 |

CIVIC—4-Cyl.—Equipment Schedule 6
W.B. 101.2", 103.1" (Sed & Cpe), 103.2" (Hybrid); 1.3 Liter, 1.7 Liter, 2.0 Liter.

DX Sedan 4D		ES151	13470	8125	9325	10400	12400
DX Coupe 2D		EM212	13270	7850	9025	10150	12050
HX Coupe 2D		EM217	14170	8300	9525	10650	12600
LX Sedan 4D		ES155	15670	8750	10025	11200	13200
LX Coupe 2D		EM215	15470	8600	9850	10950	12950
EX Sedan 4D		ES257	17520	9475	10800	11950	14050
EX Coupe 2D		EM219	17270	9225	10500	11650	13800
Si Hatchback 2D		EP335	19460	8875	10175	11700	14250
Hybrid Sedan 4D		ES956	19990	11100	12575	13700	15850

2003 HONDA

Body	Type	VIN	List	Trade-In Fair	Trade-In Good	Pvt-Party Good	Retail Excellent
ACCORD—4-Cyl.—Equipment Schedule 3							
W.B. 105.1", 107.9" (Sed); 2.4 Liter.							
DX Sedan 4D		CM551	17060	8925	10225	11750	14250
LX Sedan 4D		CM564	20460	11325	12875	14400	17050
LX Coupe 2D		CM712	20560	11275	12825	14500	17300
EX Sedan 4D		CM556	22860	12050	13625	15250	18100
EX Coupe 2D		CM716	22960	11675	13200	15100	18200
5-Spd Manual Trans	1,5			(600)	(600)	(800)	(800)
6-Spd Manual Trans				0	0	0	0
V6 3.0 Liter VTEC				900	900	1200	1200
S2000—4-Cyl.—Equipment Schedule 2							
W.B. 94.5"; 2.0 Liter.							
Convertible 2D		AP114	33060	18425	20725	22300	25400
Hard Top				775	775	1035	1035

2004 HONDA — (1HG,SHHorJHM)(ZE135)–4–#

Body	Type	VIN	List	Trade-In Fair	Trade-In Good	Pvt-Party Good	Retail Excellent
INSIGHT—3-Cyl. Hybrid—Equipment Schedule 3							
W.B. 94.5"; 1.0 Liter.							
Hatchback 2D		ZE135	21870	10325	11750	13350	16000
CIVIC—4-Cyl.—Equipment Schedule 6							
W.B. 101.2", 103.1" (Sed & Cpe); 1.3 Liter, 1.7 Liter, 2.0 Liter.							
DX Sedan 4D		ES151	13500	9300	10600	11600	13550
Value Sedan 4D		ES163	14900	9550	10900	11900	13850
Value Coupe 2D		EM221	13900	9025	10325	11300	13200
HX Coupe 2D		EM217	14200	9475	10800	11800	13800
LX Sedan 4D		ES155	15650	9975	11375	12450	14450
LX Coupe 2D		EM215	15650	9850	11225	12250	14250
EX Sedan 4D		ES257	17750	10750	12200	13300	15400
EX Coupe 2D		EM219	17350	10475	11900	12950	15000
Si Hatchback 2D		EP335	19560	10125	11525	13050	15600
Hybrid Sedan 4D		ES956	20140	12475	14100	15200	17400
GX Sedan 4D		EN264	21250				
ACCORD—4-Cyl.—Equipment Schedule 3							
W.B. 105.1", 107.9" (Sed); 2.4 Liter.							
DX Sedan 4D		CM551	17190	10550	12050	13600	16200
LX Sedan 4D		CM553	20590	13250	14975	16550	19400
LX Coupe 2D		CM712	20690	13250	14925	16650	19600
EX Sedan 4D		CM556	22990	14025	15800	17500	20500
EX Coupe 2D		CM716	23090	13575	15350	17350	20600
5-Spd Manual Trans	1,5			(625)	(625)	(835)	(835)
6-Spd Manual Trans				0	0	0	0
V6 3.0 Liter VTEC				950	950	1265	1265
S2000—4-Cyl.—Equipment Schedule 2							
W.B. 94.5"; 2.2 Liter.							
Convertible 2D		AP214	33290	20825	23325	25000	28300
Hard Top				800	800	1065	1065

HYUNDAI

1990 HYUNDAI — KMH(VF12J)–L–#

Body	Type	VIN	List	Trade-In Fair	Trade-In Good	Pvt-Party Good	Retail Excellent
EXCEL—4-Cyl.—Equipment Schedule 6							
W.B. 93.7"; 1.5 Liter.							
Sedan 4D		VF12J	8344	275	350	775	1400
Hatchback 2D		VD12J	7244	225	300	675	1250
GL Sedan 4D		VF22J	9559	300	425	850	1500
GL Hatchback 4D		VA22J	9279	300	425	850	1500
GS Hatchback 2D		VD32J	8604	275	375	800	1425
GLS Sedan 4D		VF32J	9789	325	475	900	1575
SONATA—4-Cyl.—Equipment Schedule 5							
W.B. 104.3"; 2.4 Liter.							
Sedan 4D		BF22S	12104	200	275	700	1350
GLS Sedan 4D		BF32S	14119	250	325	825	1500
V6 3.0 Liter		T		100	100	135	135

1991 HYUNDAI — (KMHor2HM)(VF12J)–M–#

Body	Type	VIN	List	Trade-In Fair	Trade-In Good	Pvt-Party Good	Retail Excellent
EXCEL—4-Cyl.—Equipment Schedule 6							
W.B. 93.8"; 1.5 Liter.							
Sedan 4D		VF12J	9100	275	375	800	1425
Hatchback 2D		VD12J	7965	250	325	700	1300
GL Sedan 4D		VF22J	9755	300	450	900	1575
GL SE Sedan 4D		VF22J	8875	300	450	900	1575

Body	Type	VIN	List	Trade-In Fair	Good	Pvt-Party Good	Retail Excellent
GS Hatchback 2D		VD32J	8785	300	400	825	1475
GS SE Hatchback 2D		VD32J	7745	300	400	825	1475
GLS Sedan 4D		VF32J	10110	325	475	950	1675
SCOUPE—4-Cyl.—Equipment Schedule 6							
W.B. 93.8"; 1.5 Liter.							
Coupe 2D		VE12J	10030	300	400	825	1475
SE Coupe 2D		VE22J	10095	325	475	925	1625
LS Coupe 2D		VE32J	10815	425	625	1100	1900
SONATA—4-Cyl.—Equipment Schedule 5							
W.B. 104.3"; 2.4 Liter.							
Sedan 4D		BF12S	12540	225	300	775	1475
SE Sedan 4D		BF22S	12320	225	300	775	1475
GLS Sedan 4D		BF32S	15090	275	375	900	1625
GLS SE Sedan 4D		BF32T	15320	275	375	900	1625
V6 3.0 Liter		T		150	150	200	200

Body	Type	VIN	List	Trade-In Fair	Good	Pvt-Party Good	Retail Excellent
EXCEL—4-Cyl.—Equipment Schedule 6							
W.B. 93.8"; 1.5 Liter.							
Sedan 4D		VF12J	9490	275	375	825	1475
Hatchback 2D		VD12J	8390	225	300	700	1300
GS Hatchback 2D		VD32J	9034	300	400	850	1500
GL Sedan 4D		VF22J	9934	325	475	900	1625
SCOUPE—4-Cyl.—Equipment Schedule 6							
W.B. 93.8"; 1.5 Liter.							
Coupe 2D		VE22J	10569	300	450	900	1625
LS Coupe 2D		VE32J	11174	475	675	1225	2100
ELANTRA—4-Cyl.—Equipment Schedule 6							
W.B. 98.4"; 1.6 Liter.							
Sedan 4D		JF22R	11155	375	525	1025	1800
GLS Sedan 4D		JF32R	12051	475	675	1225	2100
SONATA—4-Cyl.—Equipment Schedule 5							
W.B. 104.3"; 2.0 Liter.							
Sedan 4D		BF22S	13130	250	325	875	1625
GLS Sedan 4D		BF32S	15125	300	450	1000	1850
V6 3.0 Liter		T		225	225	300	300

Body	Type	VIN	List	Trade-In Fair	Good	Pvt-Party Good	Retail Excellent
EXCEL—4-Cyl.—Equipment Schedule 6							
W.B. 93.8"; 1.5 Liter.							
Sedan 4D		VF12J	9534	275	375	825	1500
Hatchback 2D		VD12J	8634	200	300	700	1300
GS Hatchback 2D		VD32J	9174	300	400	875	1550
GL Sedan 4D		VF22J	10074	325	475	925	1675
SCOUPE—4-Cyl.—Equipment Schedule 6							
W.B. 93.8"; 1.5 Liter.							
Coupe 2D		VE22N	10879	475	700	1275	2175
LS Coupe 2D		VE32N	11414	675	925	1600	2700
SCOUPE—4-Cyl. Turbo—Equipment Schedule 6							
W.B. 93.8"; 1.5 Liter.							
Coupe 2D		VE32N	12669	825	1150	1925	3150
ELANTRA—4-Cyl.—Equipment Schedule 6							
W.B. 98.4"; 1.6 Liter, 1.8 Liter.							
Sedan 4D		JF22R	11749	400	600	1125	1975
GLS Sedan 4D		JF32M	12214	525	750	1350	2300
SONATA—4-Cyl.—Equipment Schedule 5							
W.B. 104.3"; 2.0 Liter.							
Sedan 4D		BF22F	13554	300	400	1000	1925
GLS Sedan 4D		BF32F	14954	375	525	1175	2175
V6 3.0 Liter		T		275	275	365	365

Body	Type	VIN	List	Trade-In Fair	Good	Pvt-Party Good	Retail Excellent
EXCEL—4-Cyl.—Equipment Schedule 6							
W.B. 93.8"; 1.5 Liter.							
Hatchback 2D		VD12J	9140	250	325	825	1500
GL Sedan 4D		VF22J	9659	375	550	1075	1925
GS Hatchback 2D		VD32J	9659	325	475	1000	1800
SCOUPE—4-Cyl.—Equipment Schedule 6							
W.B. 93.8"; 1.5 Liter.							
Coupe 2D		VE22N	11409	550	800	1450	2475
LS Coupe 2D		VE32N	11889	750	1050	1825	3025

1994 HYUNDAI

Body	Type	VIN	List	Trade-In Fair	Good	Pvt-Party Good	Retail Excellent
SCOUPE—4-Cyl. Turbo—Equipment Schedule 6							
W.B. 93.8"; 1.5 Liter.							
Coupe 2D		VE32N	13189	**900**	**1300**	**2175**	**3525**
ELANTRA—4-Cyl.—Equipment Schedule 5							
W.B. 98.4"; 1.6 Liter, 1.8 Liter.							
Sedan 4D		JF22R	12674	**475**	**675**	**1275**	**2225**
GLS Sedan 4D		JF32M	13392	**600**	**875**	**1500**	**2600**
SONATA—4-Cyl.—Equipment Schedule 5							
W.B. 104.3"; 2.0 Liter.							
Sedan 4D		BF22F	13984	**375**	**525**	**1225**	**2300**
GLS Sedan 4D		BF32F	15384	**475**	**675**	**1425**	**2600**
V6 3.0 Liter		T	......	**325**	**325**	**435**	**435**

1995 HYUNDAI — KMH(VD14N)—S–#

Body	Type	VIN	List	Trade-In Fair	Good	Pvt-Party Good	Retail Excellent
ACCENT—4-Cyl.—Equipment Schedule 6							
W.B. 94.5"; 1.5 Liter.							
L Hatchback 2D		VD14N	9674	**450**	**625**	**1175**	**2075**
Hatchback 2D		VD14N	10310	**575**	**825**	**1425**	**2425**
Sedan 4D		VF14N	10834	**675**	**950**	**1625**	**2725**
SCOUPE—4-Cyl.—Equipment Schedule 6							
W.B. 93.8"; 1.5 Liter.							
Coupe 2D		VE12N	11905	**675**	**925**	**1650**	**2800**
LS Coupe 2D		VE32N	12735	**875**	**1225**	**2100**	**3400**
SCOUPE—4-Cyl. Turbo—Equipment Schedule 6							
W.B. 93.8"; 1.5 Liter.							
Coupe 2D		VE32N	14045	**1025**	**1475**	**2550**	**4050**
ELANTRA—4-Cyl.—Equipment Schedule 5							
W.B. 98.4"; 1.6 Liter, 1.8 Liter.							
Sedan 4D		JF13M	13149	**550**	**800**	**1475**	**2525**
SE Sedan 4D		JF23M	13848	**625**	**900**	**1600**	**2725**
GLS Sedan 4D		JF33M	14032	**700**	**1000**	**1750**	**2925**
SONATA—4-Cyl.—Equipment Schedule 5							
W.B. 106.3"; 2.0 Liter.							
Sedan 4D		CF14F	14614	**350**	**500**	**1275**	**2425**
GL Sedan 4D		CF24F	15334	**300**	**400**	**1250**	**2525**
V6 3.0 Liter		T	......	**375**	**375**	**500**	**500**
SONATA—V6—Equipment Schedule 5							
W.B. 106.3"; 3.0 Liter.							
GLS Sedan 4D		CF34T	17804	**775**	**1100**	**2225**	**3875**

1996 HYUNDAI — KMH(VD14N)–T–#

Body	Type	VIN	List	Trade-In Fair	Good	Pvt-Party Good	Retail Excellent
ACCENT—4-Cyl.—Equipment Schedule 6							
W.B. 94.5"; 1.5 Liter.							
L Hatchback 2D		VD14N	8690	**550**	**775**	**1400**	**2400**
Hatchback 2D		VD14N	10770	**700**	**975**	**1675**	**2800**
Sedan 4D		VF14N	11270	**800**	**1125**	**1900**	**3100**
GT Hatchback 2D		VD34N	11679	**900**	**1300**	**2125**	**3425**
ELANTRA—4-Cyl.—Equipment Schedule 5							
W.B. 100.4"; 1.8 Liter.							
Sedan 4D		JF24M	13434	**925**	**1325**	**2225**	**3575**
Wagon 4D		JW24M	14334	**1225**	**1700**	**2775**	**4300**
GLS Sedan 4D		JF34M	14679	**1100**	**1550**	**2600**	**4100**
GLS Wagon 4D		JW34M	15329	**1450**	**1925**	**3050**	**4625**
SONATA—4-Cyl.—Equipment Schedule 5							
W.B. 106.3"; 2.0 Liter.							
Sedan 4D		CF14F	15204	**550**	**775**	**1725**	**3200**
GL Sedan 4D		CF24F	16104	**450**	**650**	**1700**	**3275**
V6 3.0 Liter		T	......	**425**	**425**	**565**	**565**
SONATA—V6—Equipment Schedule 5							
W.B. 106.3"; 3.0 Liter.							
GLS Sedan 4D		CF34T	18404	**1000**	**1450**	**2700**	**4500**

1997 HYUNDAI — KMH(VD14N)–V–#

Body	Type	VIN	List	Trade-In Fair	Good	Pvt-Party Good	Retail Excellent
ACCENT—4-Cyl.—Equipment Schedule 6							
W.B. 94.5"; 1.5 Liter.							
L Hatchback 2D		VD14N	9014	**675**	**950**	**1650**	**2800**
GS Hatchback 2D		VD34N	11419	**850**	**1175**	**2000**	**3275**
GL Sedan 4D		VF24N	11819	**925**	**1325**	**2225**	**3575**
GT Hatchback 2D		VD34N	12139	**1050**	**1500**	**2550**	**4025**
ELANTRA—4-Cyl.—Equipment Schedule 5							
W.B. 100.4"; 1.8 Liter.							
Sedan 4D		JF24M	13659	**1100**	**1550**	**2625**	**4125**

1997 HYUNDAI

Body	Type	VIN	List	Trade-In Fair	Trade-In Good	Pvt-Party Good	Retail Excellent
Wagon 4D		JW24M	14559	1500	1975	3075	4650
GLS Sedan 4D		JF34M	14879	1350	1825	2900	4475
GLS Wagon 4D		JW34M	15529	1700	2225	3375	5025
TIBURON—4-Cyl.—Equipment Schedule 5							
W.B. 97.4"; 1.8 Liter, 2.0 Liter.							
Coupe 2D		JG24M	15609	1400	1875	3100	4800
FX Coupe 2D		JG34F	17539	1700	2225	3475	5225
SONATA—4-Cyl.—Equipment Schedule 5							
W.B. 106.3"; 2.0 Liter.							
Sedan 4D		CF24F	15964	1050	1500	2625	4175
GL Sedan 4D		CF24F	16764	950	1375	2575	4250
V6 3.0 Liter		T		475	475	635	635
SONATA—V6—Equipment Schedule 5							
W.B. 106.3"; 3.0 Liter.							
GLS Sedan 4D		CF34T	18964	1750	2275	3475	5175

1998 HYUNDAI — KMH(VD14N)-W-#

Body	Type	VIN	List	Trade-In Fair	Trade-In Good	Pvt-Party Good	Retail Excellent
ACCENT—4-Cyl.—Equipment Schedule 6							
W.B. 94.5"; 1.5 Liter.							
L Hatchback 2D		VD14N	9534	850	1175	2000	3275
GS Hatchback 2D		VD34N	11328	1000	1450	2450	3925
GL Sedan 4D		VF24N	11728	1125	1575	2650	4150
GSi Hatchback 2D		VD34N	12573	1350	1825	2900	4450
ELANTRA—4-Cyl.—Equipment Schedule 5							
W.B. 100.4"; 1.8 Liter.							
Sedan 4D		JF24M	13728	1350	1825	2950	4525
Wagon 4D		JW24M	14628	1775	2300	3450	5125
GLS Sedan 4D		JF34M	15023	1600	2100	3275	4925
GLS Wagon 4D		JW34M	15673	2025	2575	3775	5475
TIBURON—4-Cyl.—Equipment Schedule 5							
W.B. 97.4"; 2.0 Liter.							
Coupe 2D		JG24F	16217	1875	2400	3700	5525
FX Coupe 2D		JG34F	17717	2225	2775	4125	6000
SE Pkg				100	100	135	135
SONATA—4-Cyl.—Equipment Schedule 5							
W.B. 106.3"; 2.0 Liter.							
Sedan 4D		CF24F	15984	1450	1925	3125	4775
GL Sedan 4D		CF24F	16784	1275	1750	3050	4825
V6 3.0 Liter		T		525	525	700	700
SONATA—V6—Equipment Schedule 5							
W.B. 106.3"; 3.0 Liter.							
GLS Sedan 4D		CF34T	18984	2200	2775	4025	5800

1999 HYUNDAI — KMH(VD14N)-X-#

Body	Type	VIN	List	Trade-In Fair	Trade-In Good	Pvt-Party Good	Retail Excellent
ACCENT—4-Cyl.—Equipment Schedule 6							
W.B. 94.5"; 1.5 Liter.							
L Hatchback 2D		VD14N	9434	975	1425	2475	3975
GS Hatchback 2D		VD34N	12129	1225	1700	2800	4375
GL Sedan 4D		VF24N	12129	1475	1950	3075	4675
Sport Pkg				175	175	235	235
ELANTRA—4-Cyl.—Equipment Schedule 5							
W.B. 100.4"; 2.0 Liter.							
GL Sedan 4D		JF24F	12734	2125	2700	3925	5700
GL Wagon 4D		JW24F	13634	2650	3250	4525	6350
GLS Sedan 4D		JF34F	13934	2475	3075	4325	6150
GLS Wagon 4D		JW34F	14434	2875	3525	4825	6700
TIBURON—4-Cyl.—Equipment Schedule 5							
W.B. 97.4"; 2.0 Liter.							
Coupe 2D		JG24F	16229	2325	2900	4300	6250
FX Coupe 2D		JG34F	17729	2725	3350	4775	6800
SONATA—4-Cyl.—Equipment Schedule 5							
W.B. 106.3"; 2.4 Liter.							
Sedan 4D		WF24S	16234	3125	3775	4975	6725
V6 2.5 Liter		V		600	600	800	800
SONATA—V6—Equipment Schedule 5							
W.B. 106.3"; 2.5 Liter.							
GLS Sedan 4D		WF34V	18234	4200	5000	6100	7825

2000 HYUNDAI — KMH(CF35G)-Y-#

Body	Type	VIN	List	Trade-In Fair	Trade-In Good	Pvt-Party Good	Retail Excellent
ACCENT—4-Cyl.—Equipment Schedule 6							
W.B. 96.1"; 1.5 Liter.							
L Hatchback 2D		CF35G	9434	1950	2475	3525	5075

2000 HYUNDAI

Body	Type	VIN	List	Trade-In Fair	Good	Pvt-Party Good	Retail Excellent
GS Hatchback 2D		CG35G	10784	2250	2825	3900	5500
GL Sedan 4D		CG45G	10884	2550	3175	4250	5875
ELANTRA—4-Cyl.—Equipment Schedule 5							
W.B. 100.4"; 2.0 Liter.							
GLS Sedan 4D		JF34F	12984	3000	3675	5000	6900
GLS Wagon 4D		JW34F	13684	3400	4100	5450	7450
TIBURON—4-Cyl.—Equipment Schedule 5							
W.B. 97.4"; 2.0 Liter.							
Coupe 2D		JG24F	15184	3575	4300	5800	7975
SONATA—4-Cyl.—Equipment Schedule 5							
W.B. 106.3"; 2.4 Liter.							
Sedan 4D		WF14S	15934	3750	4500	5725	7600
V6 2.5 Liter		V		675	675	900	900
SONATA—V6—Equipment Schedule 5							
W.B. 106.3"; 2.5 Liter.							
GLS Sedan 4D		WF34V	17934	5000	5850	7000	8825

2001 HYUNDAI — KMH(CF35G)-1-#

Body	Type	VIN	List	Trade-In Fair	Good	Pvt-Party Good	Retail Excellent
ACCENT—4-Cyl.—Equipment Schedule 5							
W.B. 96.1"; 1.5 Liter, 1.6 Liter.							
L Hatchback 2D		CF35G	10184	2425	3025	4125	5750
GS Hatchback 2D		CH35C	10584	2800	3425	4550	6250
GL Sedan 4D		CG45C	10884	3150	3800	4950	6675
ELANTRA—4-Cyl.—Equipment Schedule 5							
W.B. 102.7"; 2.0 Liter.							
GLS Sedan 4D		JF35D	13784	3600	4325	5750	7825
GT Hatchback 4D		JF35D	15234	4125	4900	6350	8500
TIBURON—4-Cyl.—Equipment Schedule 5							
W.B. 97.4"; 2.0 Liter.							
Coupe 2D		JG25D	15734	4375	5150	6800	9150
SONATA—4-Cyl.—Equipment Schedule 5							
W.B. 106.3"; 2.4 Liter.							
Sedan 4D		WF15S	15934	4525	5350	6650	8650
V6 2.5 Liter		V		750	750	1000	1000
SONATA—V6—Equipment Schedule 5							
W.B. 106.3"; 2.5 Liter.							
GLS Sedan 4D		WF35V	17934	5925	6900	8075	9975
XG300—V6—Equipment Schedule 3							
W.B. 108.3"; 3.0 Liter.							
Sedan 4D		FU45D	23934	5800	6775	8775	11650
L Sedan 4D		FU45D	25434	6075	7025	9075	12000

2002 HYUNDAI — KMH(CF35G)-2-#

Body	Type	VIN	List	Trade-In Fair	Good	Pvt-Party Good	Retail Excellent
ACCENT—4-Cyl.—Equipment Schedule 6							
W.B. 96.1"; 1.5 Liter, 1.6 Liter.							
L Hatchback 2D		CF35G	10244	3025	3700	4850	6575
GS Hatchback 2D		CH35C	10744	3425	4150	5325	7100
GL Sedan 4D		CG45C	11144	3825	4550	5750	7575
ELANTRA—4-Cyl.—Equipment Schedule 5							
W.B. 102.7"; 2.0 Liter.							
GLS Sedan 4D		DN45D	13794	4300	5075	6600	8800
GT Hatchback 4D		DN55D	15294	4850	5700	7250	9525
SONATA—4-Cyl.—Equipment Schedule 5							
W.B. 106.3"; 2.4 Liter.							
Sedan 4D		WF15S	16494	5475	6375	7725	9850
V6 2.7 Liter		H		650	650	865	865
SONATA—V6—Equipment Schedule 5							
W.B. 106.3"; 2.7 Liter.							
GLS Sedan 4D		WF35H	17994	6975	8075	9300	11350
LX Sedan 4D		WF35H	19319	7400	8500	9750	11800
XG350—V6—Equipment Schedule 3							
W.B. 108.3"; 3.5 Liter.							
Sedan 4D		FU45E	24494	7750	8900	10950	13950
L Sedan 4D		FU45E	26094	8025	9200	11300	14350

2003 HYUNDAI — KMH(CF35C)-3-#

Body	Type	VIN	List	Trade-In Fair	Good	Pvt-Party Good	Retail Excellent
ACCENT—4-Cyl.—Equipment Schedule 6							
W.B. 96.1"; 1.6 Liter.							
Hatchback 2D		CF35C	10745	3875	4600	5700	7375
GL Hatchback 2D		CG35C	11144	4325	5100	6200	7950
GL Sedan 4D		CG45C	11544	4725	5550	6675	8475

2003 HYUNDAI

Body	Type	VIN	List	Trade-In Fair	Good	Pvt-Party Good	Retail Excellent
ELANTRA—4-Cyl.—Equipment Schedule 5							
W.B. 102.7"; 2.0 Liter.							
GLS Sedan 4D		DN45D	13794	5200	6075	7550	9800
GT Sedan 4D		DN55D	15444	5150	6025	7875	10500
GT Hatchback 4D		DN55D	15444	5775	6750	8250	10550
TIBURON—4-Cyl.—Equipment Schedule 3							
W.B. 99.6"; 2.0 Liter.							
Coupe 2D		HM65D	16494	7100	8175	10150	12950
5-Spd Manual Trans				(550)	(550)	(735)	(735)
TIBURON—V6—Equipment Schedule 3							
W.B. 99.6"; 2.7 Liter.							
GT Coupe 2D		HN65F	19244	7850	9025	11000	13950
5-Spd Manual Trans				(550)	(550)	(735)	(735)
6-Spd Manual Trans				0	0	0	0
SONATA—4-Cyl.—Equipment Schedule 5							
W.B. 106.3"; 2.4 Liter.							
Sedan 4D		WF15S	16494	6550	7575	8875	11000
V6 2.7 Liter		H		700	700	935	935
SONATA—V6—Equipment Schedule 5							
W.B. 106.3"; 2.7 Liter.							
GLS Sedan 4D		WF35H	18094	8225	9425	10600	12650
LX Sedan 4D		WF35H	19319	8650	9900	11100	13200
XG350—V6—Equipment Schedule 3							
W.B. 108.3"; 3.5 Liter.							
Sedan 4D		FU45E	24494	9100	10375	12500	15650
L Sedan 4D		FU45E	26094	9375	10700	12800	16050

2004 HYUNDAI — KMH(CF35C)–4–#

Body	Type	VIN	List	Trade-In Fair	Good	Pvt-Party Good	Retail Excellent
ACCENT—4-Cyl.—Equipment Schedule 6							
W.B. 96.1"; 1.6 Liter.							
Hatchback 2D		CF35C	11289	4750	5600	6550	8150
GL Hatchback 2D		CG35C	11439	5225	6125	7125	8775
GL Sedan 4D		CG45C	11839	5700	6625	7650	9375
GT Hatchback 2D		CG45C	11939	5925	6900	7950	9700
ELANTRA—4-Cyl.—Equipment Schedule 5							
W.B. 102.7"; 2.0 Liter.							
GLS Sedan 4D		DN45D	14639	6175	7150	8600	10850
GT Sedan 4D		DN55D	16189	6125	7100	8925	11600
GT Hatchback 4D		DN55D	16189	6800	7825	9325	11650
TIBURON—4-Cyl.—Equipment Schedule 3							
W.B. 99.6"; 2.0 Liter.							
Coupe 2D		HM65D	18439	8525	9750	11750	14850
5-Spd Manual Trans				(575)	(575)	(765)	(765)
TIBURON—V6—Equipment Schedule 3							
W.B. 99.6"; 2.7 Liter.							
GT Coupe 2D		HN65F	19639	9325	10650	12750	15950
GT Special Ed Cpe 2D		HN65F	20987				
5-Spd Manual Trans				(575)	(575)	(765)	(765)
6-Spd Manual Trans				0	0	0	0
SONATA—4-Cyl.—Equipment Schedule 5							
W.B. 106.3"; 2.4 Liter.							
Sedan 4D		WF15S	17339	8025	9200	10500	12700
V6 2.7 Liter		H		750	750	1000	1000
SONATA—V6—Equipment Schedule 5							
W.B. 106.3"; 2.7 Liter.							
GLS Sedan 4D		WF35H	19339	9800	11175	12400	14550
LX Sedan 4D		WF35H	20339	10275	11675	12900	15100
XG350—V6—Equipment Schedule 3							
W.B. 108.3"; 3.5 Liter.							
Sedan 4D		FU45E	24589	10900	12325	14600	18000
L Sedan 4D		FU45E	26189	11175	12725	15000	18450

INFINITI

1990 INFINITI — JNK(HF14)C–L–#

Body	Type	VIN	List	Trade-In Fair	Good	Pvt-Party Good	Retail Excellent
M30—V6—Equipment Schedule 1							
W.B. 103.0"; 3.0 Liter.							
Coupe 2D		HF14	23850	1100	1550	2700	4275
Q45—V8—Equipment Schedule 1							
W.B. 113.2"; 4.5 Liter.							
Sedan 4D		NG01	38350	1175	1625	2925	4675

EQUIPMENT & MILEAGE PAGE 9 TO 23

1990 INFINITI

Body	Type	VIN	List	Trade-In Fair	Good	Pvt-Party Good	Retail Excellent
	Touring Pkg			100	100	135	135

1991 INFINITI — JN(KorX)(CP01P)–M–#

G20—4-Cyl.—Equipment Schedule 1
W.B. 104.0"; 2.0 Liter.

Sedan 4D		CP01P	18650	1175	1625	2800	4475
Manual Trans				(200)	(200)	(265)	(265)

M30—V6—Equipment Schedule 1
W.B. 103.0"; 3.0 Liter.

Coupe 2D		HF14C	24885	1300	1775	2975	4650
Convertible 2D		HF16C	31385	2375	2950	4375	6350

Q45—V8—Equipment Schedule 1
W.B. 113.2"; 4.5 Liter.

Sedan 4D		NG01C	40385	1375	1875	3250	5125
Active Suspension				250	250	335	335
Touring Pkg				125	125	165	165
Traction Control				100	100	135	135

1992 INFINITI — JN(KorX)(CP01P)–N–#

G20—4-Cyl.—Equipment Schedule 1
W.B. 104.0"; 2.0 Liter.

Sedan 4D		CP01P	19585	1375	1875	3100	4825
Manual Trans				(250)	(250)	(335)	(335)

M30—V6—Equipment Schedule 1
W.B. 103.0"; 3.0 Liter.

Coupe 2D		HF14C	25385	1500	2025	3300	5050
Convertible 2D		HF16C	33385	2825	3450	4950	7050

Q45—V8—Equipment Schedule 1
W.B. 113.2"; 4.5 Liter.

Sedan 4D		NG01C	42385	1350	1825	3325	5375
Active Suspension				325	325	435	435
Touring Pkg				175	175	235	235
Traction Control				125	125	165	165

1993 INFINITI — JNK(CP01P)–P–#

G20—4-Cyl.—Equipment Schedule 1
W.B. 100.4"; 2.0 Liter.

Sedan 4D		CP01P	22750	1650	2150	3475	5300
Manual Trans				(300)	(300)	(400)	(400)

J30—V6—Equipment Schedule 1
W.B. 108.7"; 3.0 Liter.

Sedan 4D		AY21D	34450	2700	3300	4800	6900
Touring Pkg				225	225	300	300

Q45—V8—Equipment Schedule 1
W.B. 113.2"; 4.5 Liter.

Sedan 4D		NG01C	45850	1400	1875	3550	5775
Active Suspension				400	400	535	535
Touring Pkg				225	225	300	300
Traction Control				150	150	200	200

1994 INFINITI — JNK(CP01D)–R–#

G20—4-Cyl.—Equipment Schedule 1
W.B. 100.4"; 2.0 Liter.

Sedan 4D		CP01D	25625	1950	2500	3900	5800
Touring				175	175	235	235
Manual Trans				(350)	(350)	(465)	(465)

J30—V6—Equipment Schedule 1
W.B. 108.7"; 3.0 Liter.

Sedan 4D		AY21D	37400	3150	3800	5350	7550
Touring				275	275	365	365

Q45—V8—Equipment Schedule 1
W.B. 113.2"; 4.5 Liter.

Sedan 4D		NG01C	50900	1800	2325	4175	6650
Active Suspension				475	475	635	635
Touring				275	275	365	365
Traction Control				175	175	235	235

1995 INFINITI — JNK(CP01D)–S–#

G20—4-Cyl.—Equipment Schedule 1
W.B. 100.4"; 2.0 Liter.

Sedan 4D		CP01D	26625	2325	2900	4400	6425

1995 INFINITI

Body	Type	VIN	List	Trade-In Fair	Good	Pvt-Party Good	Retail Excellent
	Touring			200	200	265	265
	Manual Trans			(400)	(400)	(535)	(535)
J30—V6—Equipment Schedule 1							
W.B. 108.7"; 3.0 Liter.							
	Sedan 4D	AY21D	39000	3625	4350	6000	8325
	Touring			325	325	435	435
Q45—V8—Equipment Schedule 1							
W.B. 113.4"; 4.5 Liter.							
	Sedan 4D	NG01D	52850	2375	2950	4950	7600
	Active Suspension			550	550	735	735
	Touring			325	325	435	435
	Traction Control			200	200	265	265

1996 INFINITI — JNK(CP01D)–T–#

Body	Type	VIN	List	Trade-In Fair	Good	Pvt-Party Good	Retail Excellent
G20—4-Cyl.—Equipment Schedule 1							
W.B. 100.4"; 2.0 Liter.							
	Sedan 4D	CP01D	27630	2775	3400	5000	7175
	Touring			200	200	265	265
	Manual Trans			(450)	(450)	(600)	(600)
I30—V6—Equipment Schedule 1							
W.B. 106.3"; 3.0 Liter.							
	Sedan 4D	CA21D	32000	3650	4375	6050	8400
	Touring			350	350	465	465
	Manual Trans			(450)	(450)	(600)	(600)
J30—V6—Equipment Schedule 1							
W.B. 108.7"; 3.0 Liter.							
	Sedan 4D	AY21D	40400	4175	4975	6700	9175
	Touring			350	350	465	465
Q45—V8—Equipment Schedule 1							
W.B. 113.4"; 4.5 Liter.							
	Sedan 4D	NG01D	54000	3125	3775	5950	8825
	Touring			350	350	465	465
	Traction Control			225	225	300	300

1997 INFINITI — JNK(CA01D)–V–#

Body	Type	VIN	List	Trade-In Fair	Good	Pvt-Party Good	Retail Excellent
I30—V6—Equipment Schedule 1							
W.B. 106.3"; 3.0 Liter.							
	Sedan 4D	CA21D	30395	4225	5025	6800	9300
	Touring			375	375	500	500
	Manual Trans			(475)	(475)	(635)	(635)
J30—V6—Equipment Schedule 1							
W.B. 108.7"; 3.0 Liter.							
	Sedan 4D	AY21D	36245	4825	5675	7525	10200
	Touring			375	375	500	500
Q45—V8—Equipment Schedule 1							
W.B. 111.4"; 4.1 Liter.							
	Sedan 4D	BY31D	48395	7075	8150	10700	14300
	Touring			375	375	500	500

1998 INFINITI — JNK(CA21D)–W–#

Body	Type	VIN	List	Trade-In Fair	Good	Pvt-Party Good	Retail Excellent
I30—V6—Equipment Schedule 1							
W.B. 106.3"; 3.0 Liter.							
	Sedan 4D	CA21D	30695	5350	6250	8100	10800
	Touring			425	425	565	565
	Manual Trans			(500)	(500)	(665)	(665)
Q45—V8—Equipment Schedule 1							
W.B. 111.4"; 4.1 Liter.							
	Sedan 4D	BY31D	48395	8450	9650	12100	15650
	Touring			425	425	565	565

1999 INFINITI — JNK(CP11A)–X–#

Body	Type	VIN	List	Trade-In Fair	Good	Pvt-Party Good	Retail Excellent
G20—4-Cyl.—Equipment Schedule 1							
W.B. 102.4"; 2.0 Liter.							
	Sedan 4D	CP11A	23820	5200	6075	8000	10700
	Touring			250	250	335	335
	Manual Trans			(550)	(550)	(735)	(735)
I30—V6—Equipment Schedule 1							
W.B. 106.3"; 3.0 Liter.							
	Sedan 4D	CA21A	30725	6325	7350	9325	12250
	Limited Sedan 4D	CA21A	31625	6375	7400	9425	12350
	Touring			500	500	665	665
	Manual Trans			(550)	(550)	(735)	(735)

1999 INFINITI

Body Type	VIN	List	Trade-In Fair	Good	Pvt-Party Good	Retail Excellent
Q45—V8—Equipment Schedule 1						
W.B. 111.4"; 4.1 Liter.						
Sedan 4D	BY31A	48725	9850	11225	13800	17600
Touring			500	500	665	665

2000 INFINITI — JNK(CP11A)-Y-#

Body Type	VIN	List	Trade-In Fair	Good	Pvt-Party Good	Retail Excellent
G20—4-Cyl.—Equipment Schedule 1						
W.B. 102.4"; 2.0 Liter.						
Sedan 4D	CP11A	24220	6175	7150	9200	12100
Touring			275	275	365	365
Manual Trans			(600)	(600)	(800)	(800)
I30—V6—Equipment Schedule 1						
W.B. 108.3"; 3.0 Liter.						
Sedan 4D	CA21A	29990	9300	10600	12350	15050
Touring			550	550	735	735
Q45—V8—Equipment Schedule 1						
W.B. 111.4"; 4.1 Liter.						
Sedan 4D	BY31A	49420	11525	13050	15900	19950
Touring			550	550	735	735
Anniversary Edition			350	350	465	465

2001 INFINITI — JNK(CP11A)-1-#

Body Type	VIN	List	Trade-In Fair	Good	Pvt-Party Good	Retail Excellent
G20—4-Cyl.—Equipment Schedule 1						
W.B. 102.4"; 2.0 Liter.						
Sedan 4D	CP11A	24220	7275	8375	10550	13750
Touring			300	300	400	400
Manual Trans			(650)	(650)	(865)	(865)
I30—V6—Equipment Schedule 1						
W.B. 108.3"; 3.0 Liter.						
Sedan 4D	CA31A	29990	10900	12325	14100	17050
Touring			600	600	800	800
Q45—V8—Equipment Schedule 1						
W.B. 111.4"; 4.1 Liter.						
Sedan 4D	BY31A	49420	13575	15350	18400	22800
Touring			600	600	800	800

2002 INFINITI — JNK(CP11A)-2-#

Body Type	VIN	List	Trade-In Fair	Good	Pvt-Party Good	Retail Excellent
G20—4-Cyl.—Equipment Schedule 1						
W.B. 102.4"; 2.0 Liter.						
Sedan 4D	CP11A	24340	8600	9850	12150	15550
Sport Pkg			325	325	435	435
Manual Trans			(675)	(675)	(900)	(900)
I35—V6—Equipment Schedule 1						
W.B. 108.3"; 3.5 Liter.						
Sedan 4D	DA31A	29295	11525	13050	14950	17950
Sport Pkg			650	650	865	865
Q45—V8—Equipment Schedule 1						
W.B. 113.0"; 4.5 Liter.						
Sedan 4D	BF01A	51045	21025	23625	28000	34600
Sport Pkg			650	650	865	865
Premium Pkg			1625	1625	2165	2165

2003 INFINITI — JNK(CV51E)-3-#

Body Type	VIN	List	Trade-In Fair	Good	Pvt-Party Good	Retail Excellent
G35—V6—Equipment Schedule 1						
W.B. 112.2"; 3.5 Liter.						
Sedan 4D	CV51E	29495	18250	20550	22700	26400
Coupe 2D	CV54E	32945	21500	24100	26400	30500
Sport Pkg			350	350	465	465
I35—V6—Equipment Schedule 1						
W.B. 108.3"; 3.5 Liter.						
Sedan 4D	DA31A	30995	15800	17750	19700	22900
Sport Pkg			700	700	935	935
M45—V8—Equipment Schedule 1						
W.B. 110.2"; 4.5 Liter.						
Sedan 4D	AY41E	43845	23700	26500	29600	34700
Q45—V8—Equipment Schedule 1						
W.B. 113.0"; 4.5 Liter.						
Sedan 4D	BF01A	52545	24575	27450	32200	39300
Premium Sedan 4D	BF01A	62145	28225	31575	36400	43900

2004 INFINITI

2004 INFINITI — JNK(CV51E)-4-#

G35—V6—Equipment Schedule 1
W.B. 112.2"; 3.5 Liter.

Sedan 4D		CV51E	31690	20825	23325	25500	29600
AWD Sedan 4D		CV51E	33490	22375	25050	27400	31500
Coupe 2D		CV54E	33140	24300	27175	29600	33900

I35—V6—Equipment Schedule 1
W.B. 108.3"; 3.5 Liter.

Sedan 4D		DA31A	31190	18100	20350	22300	25800

M45—V8—Equipment Schedule 1
W.B. 110.2"; 4.5 Liter.

Sedan 4D		AY41E	44840	26500	29675	32700	38000

Q45—V8—Equipment Schedule 1
W.B. 113.0"; 4.5 Liter.

Sedan 4D		BF01A	52990				
Premium Sedan 4D		BF01A	62190				
Journey Pkg			------				

ISUZU

1990 ISUZU — JABRT(435)-L-#

IMPULSE—4-Cyl.—Equipment Schedule 6
W.B. 96.5"; 1.6 Liter.

XS Coupe 2D		435	13313	300	425	900	1675

1991 ISUZU — JABRT(536)-M-#

STYLUS—4-Cyl.—Equipment Schedule 6
W.B. 96.5"; 1.6 Liter.

S Sedan 4D		536	10728	375	550	975	1675
XS Sedan 4D		535	12348	500	725	1225	2075

IMPULSE—4-Cyl.—Equipment Schedule 6
W.B. 96.5"; 1.6 Liter.

XS Coupe 2D		235	13363	350	500	1075	1975
XS Hatchback 2D		435	13668	450	625	1250	2225

IMPULSE AWD—4-Cyl. Turbo—Equipment Schedule 6
W.B. 96.5"; 1.6 Liter.

RS Coupe 2D		234	16073	475	675	1325	2350

1992 ISUZU — JABRT(536)-N-#

STYLUS—4-Cyl.—Equipment Schedule 6
W.B. 96.5"; 1.6 Liter, 1.8 Liter.

S Sedan 4D		536	10798	425	625	1100	1900
RS Sedan 4D		538	11838	525	750	1300	2175

IMPULSE—4-Cyl.—Equipment Schedule 6
W.B. 96.5"; 1.8 Liter.

XS Coupe 2D		238	13588	425	625	1250	2250
XS Hatchback 2D		438	14188	525	750	1475	2575

IMPULSE AWD—4-Cyl. Turbo—Equipment Schedule 6
W.B. 96.5"; 1.6 Liter.

RS Coupe 2D		234	16018	575	825	1525	2700

1993 ISUZU — JABRT(536)-P-#

STYLUS—4-Cyl.—Equipment Schedule 6
W.B. 96.5"; 1.6 Liter.

S Sedan 4D		536	11168	500	725	1250	2125

JAGUAR

1990 JAGUAR — SAJ(FY17)4-L-#

XJ6—6-Cyl.—Equipment Schedule 1
W.B. 113.0"; 4.0 Liter.

Sedan 4D		FY17	40200	1525	2050	3375	5250
Sovereign Sedan 4D		HY17	43500	1925	2450	3900	5850
Vanden Plas Sedan 4D		KY17	48500	2050	2600	4050	6075
Vanden Plas Majestic 4D		MY17	53500	2275	2850	4375	6450

XJS—V12—Equipment Schedule 2
W.B. 102.0"; 5.3 Liter.

Coupe 2D		NW58	48500	2050	2600	4050	6075

1990 JAGUAR

Body	Type	VIN	List	Trade-In Fair	Good	Pvt-Party Good	Retail Excellent
Collection Rouge Cpe 2D		TW58	51500	2400	3000	4525	6675
Convertible 2D		NW48	57500	3525	4225	6000	8475
XJS CLASSIC—V12—Equipment Schedule 2							
W.B. 102.0"; 5.3 Liter.							
Coupe 2D		NW58	48500	2075	2625	4100	6150
Collection Rouge Cpe 2D		TW58	51500	2475	3075	4625	6775
Collection Conv 2D		TW48	57500	4400	5175	7075	9750

1991 JAGUAR — SAJ(FY17)4-M-#

Body	Type	VIN	List	Trade-In Fair	Good	Pvt-Party Good	Retail Excellent
XJ6—6-Cyl.—Equipment Schedule 1							
W.B. 113.0"; 4.0 Liter.							
Sedan 4D		FY17	40425	1925	2450	3950	6000
Sovereign Sedan 4D		HY17	45425	2350	2925	4500	6700
Vanden Plas Sedan 4D		KY17	50425	2500	3100	4700	6925
XJS—V12—Equipment Schedule 2							
W.B. 102.0"; 5.3 Liter.							
Coupe 2D		NW58	53580	2500	3100	4700	6925
Convertible 2D		NW48	64180	4250	5050	7000	9750

1992 JAGUAR — SAJ(FY17)4-N-#

Body	Type	VIN	List	Trade-In Fair	Good	Pvt-Party Good	Retail Excellent
XJ6—6-Cyl.—Equipment Schedule 1							
W.B. 113.0"; 4.0 Liter.							
Sedan 4D		FY17	45080	2275	2850	4500	6750
Sovereign Sedan 4D		HY17	50080	2775	3400	5125	7500
Vanden Plas Sedan 4D		KY17	55080	3000	3675	5450	7900
Majestic Sedan 4D		MY17	60080	3300	3950	5775	8275
XJS—V12—Equipment Schedule 2							
W.B. 102.0"; 5.3 Liter.							
Coupe 2D		NW58	61080	3075	3725	5525	7975
Convertible 2D		NW48	68080	5475	6375	8625	11700

1993 JAGUAR — SAJ(HW174)-P-#

Body	Type	VIN	List	Trade-In Fair	Good	Pvt-Party Good	Retail Excellent
XJ6—6-Cyl.—Equipment Schedule 1							
W.B. 113.0"; 4.0 Liter.							
Sedan 4D		HW174	51830	3325	4025	5925	8525
Vanden Plas Sedan 4D		KW174	57330	3650	4375	6300	9000
XJS—6-Cyl.—Equipment Schedule 2							
W.B. 102.0"; 4.0 Liter.							
Coupe 2D		NW574	50330	3650	4375	6300	8975
Convertible 2D		NW474	57330	5725	6675	8925	12100
Manual Trans				(300)	(300)	(400)	(400)
XJ—V12—Equipment Schedule 1							
W.B. 102.0", 113.0" (XJ12); 6.0 Liter.							
XJ12 Sedan 4D		MW134	72330	3525	4225	6175	8825
XJR-S Coupe 2D		SW534	73600	5500	6425	8675	11750
XJR-S Convertible 2D		SW434	80700	6675	7700	10150	13550

1994 JAGUAR — SAJ(HX174)-R-#

Body	Type	VIN	List	Trade-In Fair	Good	Pvt-Party Good	Retail Excellent
XJ6—6-Cyl.—Equipment Schedule 1							
W.B. 113.0"; 4.0 Liter.							
Sedan 4D		HX174	52330	4000	4775	6900	9750
Vanden Plas Sedan 4D		KX174	59980	4425	5200	7375	10300
XJS—6-Cyl.—Equipment Schedule 2							
W.B. 102.0"; 4.0 Liter.							
Coupe 2D		NX574	50330	4475	5250	7400	10300
2+2 Convertible 2D		NX474	60530	6750	7800	10250	13750
Manual Trans				(350)	(350)	(465)	(465)
XJS—V12—Equipment Schedule 2							
W.B. 102.0"; 6.0 Liter.							
Coupe 2D		NX534	70530	6175	7150	9550	12850
2+2 Convertible 2D		NX234	80530	7725	8875	11500	15150
XJ12—V12—Equipment Schedule 1							
W.B. 102.0"; 6.0 Liter.							
Sedan 4D		MX134	72330	4300	5075	7225	10200

1995 JAGUAR — SAJ(HX174)-S-#

Body	Type	VIN	List	Trade-In Fair	Good	Pvt-Party Good	Retail Excellent
XJ6—6-Cyl.—Equipment Schedule 1							
W.B. 113.0"; 4.0 Liter.							
Sedan 4D		HX174	54030	4450	5225	7400	10350
Vanden Plas Sedan 4D		KX174	62780	5475	6375	8700	11900
Traction Control				200	200	265	265

1995 JAGUAR

Body	Type	VIN	List	Trade-In Fair	Good	Pvt-Party Good	Retail Excellent
XJR—6-Cyl. Supercharged—Equipment Schedule 1							
W.B. 113.0"; 4.0 Liter.							
Sedan 4D		PX114	65580	6825	7850	10400	13900
XJS—6-Cyl.—Equipment Schedule 2							
W.B. 102.0"; 4.0 Liter.							
Coupe 2D		NX574	53980	5400	6300	8700	11950
2+2 Convertible 2D		NX274	62130	7900	9075	11750	15550
XJS—V12—Equipment Schedule 2							
W.B. 102.0"; 6.0 Liter.							
Coupe 2D		NX534	72930	7275	8350	11000	14650
2+2 Convertible 2D		NX234	83130	8975	10275	13100	17100
XJ12—V12—Equipment Schedule 1							
W.B. 113.0"; 6.0 Liter.							
Sedan 4D		MX134	77830	4750	5600	7825	10900

1996 JAGUAR — SAJ(HX174)–T–#

Body	Type	VIN	List	Trade-In Fair	Good	Pvt-Party Good	Retail Excellent
XJ6—6-Cyl.—Equipment Schedule 1							
W.B. 113.0", 117.9" (Vanden Plas); 4.0 Liter.							
Sedan 4D		HX174	56900	5525	6425	8850	12200
Vanden Plas Sedan 4D		KX674	65000	7600	8725	11400	15150
Traction Control				225	225	300	300
XJR—6-Cyl. Supercharged—Equipment Schedule 1							
W.B. 113.0"; 4.0 Liter.							
Sedan 4D		PX114	66850	8300	9525	12350	16200
XJS—6-Cyl.—Equipment Schedule 2							
W.B. 102.0"; 4.0 Liter.							
2+2 Convertible 2D		NX274	62150	9225	10500	13500	17650
XJ12—V12—Equipment Schedule 1							
W.B. 117.9"; 6.0 Liter.							
Sedan 4D		MX634	79950	8400	9600	12400	16250

1997 JAGUAR — SAJ(HX124)–V–#

Body	Type	VIN	List	Trade-In Fair	Good	Pvt-Party Good	Retail Excellent
XJ6—6-Cyl.—Equipment Schedule 1							
W.B. 113.0", 117.9" (L & Vanden Plas); 4.0 Liter.							
Sedan 4D		HX124	54980	7025	8100	10800	14500
L Sedan 4D		HX624	59980	7350	8450	11200	15000
Vanden Plas Sedan 4D		KX624	64380	9150	10425	13350	17450
Traction Control				275	275	365	365
XJR—6-Cyl. Supercharged—Equipment Schedule 1							
W.B. 113.0"; 4.0 Liter.							
Sedan 4D		PX114	67980	10025	11425	14500	18800
XK8—V8—Equipment Schedule 2							
W.B. 101.9", 109.9" (Conv); 4.0 Liter.							
Coupe 2D		GX574	65480	12150	13775	16400	20400
Convertible 2D		GX274	70480	14075	15850	18800	23200
Traction Control				275	275	365	365

1998 JAGUAR — SAJ(HX124)–W–#

Body	Type	VIN	List	Trade-In Fair	Good	Pvt-Party Good	Retail Excellent
XJ8—V8—Equipment Schedule 1							
W.B. 113.0", 117.9" (L & Vanden Plas); 4.0 Liter.							
Sedan 4D		HX124	55330	8750	10025	12650	16400
L Sedan 4D		HX624	60330	9550	10900	13600	17450
Vanden Plas Sedan 4D		KX624	64380	10900	12375	15200	19300
Traction Control				300	300	400	400
XJR—V8 Supercharged—Equipment Schedule 1							
W.B. 113.0"; 4.0 Liter.							
Sedan 4D		PX184	67980	13775	15550	18600	23200
XK8—V8—Equipment Schedule 2							
W.B. 101.9"; 4.0 Liter.							
Coupe 2D		GX524	65480	14300	16125	18800	22900
Convertible 2D		GX224	70480	16375	18425	21300	25700
Traction Control				300	300	400	400

1999 JAGUAR — SAJ(HX104)–X–#

Body	Type	VIN	List	Trade-In Fair	Good	Pvt-Party Good	Retail Excellent
XJ8—V8—Equipment Schedule 1							
W.B. 113.0", 117.9" (L & Vanden Plas); 4.0 Liter.							
Sedan 4D		HX104	55780	11275	12825	15500	19500
L Sedan 4D		HX604	60830	12200	13825	16600	20700
Vanden Plas Sedan 4D		KX604	64880	13825	15650	18600	22900
Traction Control				325	325	435	435
XJR—V8 Supercharged—Equipment Schedule 1							
W.B. 113.0"; 4.0 Liter.							

1999 JAGUAR

Body	Type	VIN	List	Trade-In Fair	Good	Pvt-Party Good	Retail Excellent
Sedan 4D		PX184	69030	**17050**	**19150**	**22300**	**27200**
XK8—V8—Equipment Schedule 2							
W.B. 101.9"; 4.0 Liter.							
Coupe 2D		GX504	66330	**17175**	**19300**	**22300**	**26900**
Convertible 2D		GX204	71330	**19500**	**21900**	**25000**	**30000**
Traction Control				325	325	435	435

2000 JAGUAR — SAJ(DorJ)(A01C)-Y-#

S-TYPE—V6—Equipment Schedule 1
W.B. 114.5"; 3.0 Liter.

Sedan 4D		A01C	44980	**12375**	**14025**	**16400**	**20100**
Sport Pkg				200	200	265	265

S-TYPE—V8—Equipment Schedule 1
W.B. 114.5"; 4.0 Liter.

Sedan 4D		A01D	48580	**14075**	**15850**	**18400**	**22300**
Sport Pkg				200	200	265	265

XJ8—V8—Equipment Schedule 1
W.B. 113.0", 117.9" (L & Vanden Plas); 4.0 Liter.

Sedan 4D		A14C	56245	**14150**	**15975**	**18750**	**23000**
L Sedan 4D		A23C	61295	**15175**	**17100**	**19950**	**24400**
Vanden Plas Sedan 4D		A24C	65345	**17100**	**19200**	**22300**	**26900**

XJR—V8 Supercharged—Equipment Schedule 1
W.B. 113.0"; 4.0 Liter.

Sedan 4D		A15B	69145	**20550**	**23050**	**26300**	**31500**

XJ8—V8 Supercharged—Equipment Schedule 1
W.B. 113.0"; 4.0 Liter.

Vanden Plas Sedan 4D		A14B	81245	**26025**	**29100**	**32700**	**38700**

XK8—V8—Equipment Schedule 2
W.B. 101.9"; 4.0 Liter.

Coupe 2D		A41C	66795	**20450**	**22950**	**26100**	**31200**
Convertible 2D		A42C	71795	**23125**	**25925**	**29300**	**34700**

XKR—V8 Supercharged—Equipment Schedule 2
W.B. 101.9"; 4.0 Liter.

Coupe 2D		A41B	77395	**25150**	**28125**	**31700**	**37300**
Convertible 2D		A42B	82395	**27850**	**31100**	**34800**	**40900**

2001 JAGUAR — SAJD(A01C)-1-#

S-TYPE—V6—Equipment Schedule 1
W.B. 114.5"; 3.0 Liter.

Sedan 4D		A01C	46250	**14875**	**16750**	**19400**	**23400**
Sport Pkg				225	225	300	300

S-TYPE—V8—Equipment Schedule 1
W.B. 114.5"; 4.0 Liter.

Sedan 4D		A01D	49950	**16700**	**18775**	**21500**	**25800**
Sport Pkg				225	225	300	300

XJ8—V8—Equipment Schedule 1
W.B. 113.0", 117.9" (L & Vanden Plas); 4.0 Liter.

Sedan 4D		A14C	56950	**17625**	**19775**	**22700**	**27200**
L Sedan 4D		A23C	62950	**18675**	**20925**	**23900**	**28600**
Vanden Plas Sedan 4D		A24C	68250	**21025**	**23525**	**26600**	**31600**

XJR—V8 Supercharged—Equipment Schedule 1
W.B. 113.0"; 4.0 Liter.

Sedan 4D		A15B	69930	**24675**	**27650**	**30900**	**36400**

XJ8—V8 Supercharged—Equipment Schedule 1
W.B. 117.9"; 4.0 Liter.

Vanden Plas Sedan 4D		A25B	83950	**30825**	**34375**	**38000**	**44300**

XK8—V8—Equipment Schedule 2
W.B. 101.9"; 4.0 Liter.

Coupe 2D		A41C	69750	**24200**	**27075**	**30500**	**36200**
Convertible 2D		A42C	74750	**27075**	**30250**	**33900**	**39900**

XKR—V8 Supercharged—Equipment Schedule 2
W.B. 101.9"; 4.0 Liter.

Coupe 2D		A41B	80750	**29375**	**32825**	**36600**	**42900**
Convertible 2D		A42B	85750	**32350**	**36100**	**40100**	**46800**
Silverstone Coupe 2D		A41B	97500	********	********	********	**59100**
Silverstone Conv 2D		A42B	97500	********	********	********	**62800**

2002 JAGUAR — SAJ-(A51D)-2-#

X-TYPE AWD—V6—Equipment Schedule 2
W.B. 106.7"; 2.5 Liter, 3.0 Liter.

2.5L Sedan 4D		A51D	34370	**11525**	**13050**	**15650**	**19500**
2.5L Sport Sedan 4D		A53D	36370	**12250**	**13875**	**16450**	**20400**

Body	Type	VIN	List	Trade-In Fair	Trade-In Good	Pvt-Party Good	Retail Excellent
3.0L Sedan 4D		A51C	39095	13825	15650	18350	22500
3.0L Sport Sedan 4D		A53C	41095	14500	16375	19100	23300
Manual Trans				(825)	(825)	(1100)	(1100)

S-TYPE—V6—Equipment Schedule 1
W.B. 114.5"; 3.0 Liter.

Sedan 4D		A01C	46320	17950	20150	23000	27600
Sport Sedan 4D		A03N	48320	18675	20925	24100	28900
Manual Trans				(825)	(825)	(1100)	(1100)

S-TYPE—V8—Equipment Schedule 1
W.B. 114.5"; 4.0 Liter.

| Sedan 4D | | A01D | 49975 | 19875 | 22375 | 25300 | 30100 |
| Sport Sedan 4D | | A03P | 51975 | 20550 | 23050 | 26100 | 31000 |

XJ8—V8—Equipment Schedule 1
W.B. 113.0"; 4.0 Liter.

| Sedan 4D | | A14C | 56975 | 21500 | 24100 | 27200 | 32200 |

XJ SPORT—V8—Equipment Schedule 1
W.B. 113.0"; 4.0 Liter.

| Sedan 4D | | A14C | 59975 | 21600 | 24300 | 27400 | 32400 |

VANDEN PLAS—V8—Equipment Schedule 1
W.B. 117.9"; 4.0 Liter.

| Sedan 4D | | A24C | 68975 | 25250 | 28225 | 31500 | 37000 |

XJR—V8 Supercharged—Equipment Schedule 1
W.B. 113.0"; 4.0 Liter.

| Sedan 4D | | A15B | 72475 | 29275 | 32725 | 36200 | 42100 |
| 100 Sedan 4D | | A15B | | 32250 | 36000 | 39600 | 45900 |

XJ SUPER—V8 Supercharged—Equipment Schedule 1
W.B. 117.9"; 4.0 Liter.

| Sedan 4D | | A25B | 79975 | 36000 | 40125 | 43900 | 50600 |

XK8—V8—Equipment Schedule 2
W.B. 101.9"; 4.0 Liter.

| Coupe 2D | | A41C | 69975 | 28600 | 31875 | 35600 | 41800 |
| Convertible 2D | | A42C | 74975 | 31775 | 35425 | 39400 | 45900 |

XKR—V8 Supercharged—Equipment Schedule 2
W.B. 101.9"; 4.0 Liter.

Coupe 2D		A41B	82975	34275	38200	42200	49100
Convertible 2D		A42B	87975	37525	41850	46100	53300
100 Coupe 2D		A41B	84000	****	****	****	66600

X-TYPE AWD—V6—Equipment Schedule 2
W.B. 106.7"; 2.5 Liter, 3.0 Liter.

2.5L Sedan 4D		A51D	29950	13925	15750	18600	22800
3.0L Sedan 4D		A51C	36950	16475	18525	21400	26000
Sport Pkg				700	700	935	935
Manual Trans				(900)	(900)	(1200)	(1200)

S-TYPE—V6—Equipment Schedule 1
W.B. 114.5"; 3.0 Liter.

Sedan 4D		A01T	44975	20925	23425	26500	31400
Sport Sedan 4D		A03T	46975	21600	24300	27600	32700
Manual Trans				(900)	(900)	(1200)	(1200)

S-TYPE—V8—Equipment Schedule 1
W.B. 114.5"; 4.2 Liter.

| Sedan 4D | | A01U | 49975 | 23050 | 25825 | 28900 | 34100 |
| Sport Sedan 4D | | A03U | 51975 | 23800 | 26600 | 29800 | 35000 |

S-TYPE R—V8 Supercharged—Equipment Schedule 1
W.B. 114.5"; 4.2 Liter.

| Sedan 4D | | A03V | 62400 | 30525 | 34075 | 37500 | 43500 |

XJ8—V8—Equipment Schedule 1
W.B. 113.0"; 4.0 Liter.

| Sedan 4D | | A14C | 56975 | 25450 | 28425 | 31500 | 36700 |

XJ SPORT—V8—Equipment Schedule 1
W.B. 113.0"; 4.0 Liter.

| Sedan 4D | | A12C | 59975 | 25625 | 28600 | 31700 | 36900 |

VANDEN PLAS—V8—Equipment Schedule 1
W.B. 117.9"; 4.0 Liter.

| Sedan 4D | | A24C | 68975 | 29675 | 33125 | 36300 | 42000 |

XJR—V8 Supercharged—Equipment Schedule 1
W.B. 113.0"; 4.0 Liter.

| Sedan 4D | | A15B | 72475 | 33975 | 37825 | 41300 | 47300 |

XJ SUPER—V8 Supercharged—Equipment Schedule 1
W.B. 117.9"; 4.0 Liter.

| Sedan 4D | | A25B | 79975 | 41275 | 45975 | 49600 | 56500 |

2003 JAGUAR

Body	Type	VIN	List	Trade-In Fair	Good	Pvt-Party Good	Retail Excellent
XK8—V8—Equipment Schedule 2							
W.B. 101.9"; 4.2 Liter.							
Coupe 2D		A41U	69975	32825	36575	40500	47100
Convertible 2D		A42U	74975	36300	40425	44400	51500
XKR—V8 Supercharged—Equipment Schedule 2							
W.B. 101.9"; 4.2 Liter.							
Coupe 2D		A41V	81975	39075	43500	47600	54900
Convertible 2D		A42V	86975	42625	47425	51700	59400
Handling Pkg				2000	2000	2665	2665

2004 JAGUAR — SAJ–(A51D)–4–#

Body	Type	VIN	List	Trade-In Fair	Good	Pvt-Party Good	Retail Excellent
X-TYPE AWD—V6—Equipment Schedule 2							
W.B. 106.7"; 2.5 Liter, 3.0 Liter.							
2.5L Sedan 4D		A51D	30520	17525	19675	22900	27800
3.0L Sedan 4D		A51C	33995	20250	22650	26000	31200
Sport Pkg				950	950	1265	1265
Manual Trans				(950)	(950)	(1265)	(1265)
S-TYPE—V6—Equipment Schedule 1							
W.B. 114.5"; 3.0 Liter.							
Sedan 4D		A01T	44995	25150	28125	31400	37000
Sport Sedan 4D		A03T	46195	25925	29000	32500	38400
Manual Trans				(950)	(950)	(1265)	(1265)
S-TYPE—V8—Equipment Schedule 1							
W.B. 114.5"; 4.2 Liter.							
Sedan 4D		A01U	49995	27450	30625	34100	39800
Sport Sedan 4D		A03U	51195	28225	31575	35000	40900
S-TYPE R—V8 Supercharged—Equipment Schedule 1							
W.B. 114.5"; 4.2 Liter.							
Sedan 4D		A03V	63120	35625	39650	43400	49900
XJ8—V8—Equipment Schedule 1							
W.B. 119.4"; 4.2 Liter.							
Sedan 4D		A71C	59995	30525	33975	37200	43000
VANDEN PLAS—V8—Equipment Schedule 1							
W.B. 119.4"; 4.2 Liter.							
Sedan 4D		A74C	68995				
XJR—V8 Supercharged—Equipment Schedule 1							
W.B. 119.4"; 4.2 Liter.							
Sedan 4D		A73B	74995				
XK8—V8—Equipment Schedule 2							
W.B. 101.9"; 4.2 Liter.							
Coupe 2D		A41C	69995				
Convertible 2D		A42C	74995				
XKR—V8 Supercharged—Equipment Schedule 2							
W.B. 101.9"; 4.2 Liter.							
Coupe 2D		A41B	82995				
Convertible 2D		A42B	87995				
Handling Pkg							

KIA

1994 KIA — KNA(FA121)–R–#

Body	Type	VIN	List	Trade-In Fair	Good	Pvt-Party Good	Retail Excellent
SEPHIA—4-Cyl.—Equipment Schedule 6							
W.B. 98.4"; 1.6 Liter.							
RS Sedan 4D		FA121	10130	375	525	975	1725
LS Sedan 4D		FA121	10674	450	650	1150	1975
GS Sedan 4D		FA121	11420	550	775	1325	2225

1995 KIA — KNA(FA121)–S–#

Body	Type	VIN	List	Trade-In Fair	Good	Pvt-Party Good	Retail Excellent
SEPHIA—4-Cyl.—Equipment Schedule 6							
W.B. 98.4"; 1.6 Liter, 1.8 Liter.							
RS Sedan 4D		FA121	10140	450	650	1150	1975
LS Sedan 4D		FA121	10730	550	775	1325	2225
GS Sedan 4D		FA121	11630	650	900	1500	2525

1996 KIA — KNA(FA125)–T–#

Body	Type	VIN	List	Trade-In Fair	Good	Pvt-Party Good	Retail Excellent
SEPHIA—4-Cyl.—Equipment Schedule 6							
W.B. 98.4"; 1.6 Liter, 1.8 Liter.							
RS Sedan 4D		FA125	11040	550	800	1375	2300
LS Sedan 4D		FA125	11980	650	900	1525	2575
GS Sedan 4D		FA125	12880	775	1075	1775	2900

1997 KIA

Body	Type	VIN	List	Trade-In Fair	Trade-In Good	Pvt-Party Good	Retail Excellent
1997 KIA — KNA(FA125)–V–#							
SEPHIA—4-Cyl.—Equipment Schedule 6							
W.B. 98.4"; 1.6 Liter, 1.8 Liter.							
RS Sedan 4D		FA125	11350	**700**	**1000**	**1650**	**2725**
LS Sedan 4D		FA125	12190	**800**	**1125**	**1825**	**2975**
GS Sedan 4D		FA125	13250	**900**	**1300**	**2100**	**3350**
1998 KIA — KNA(FB121)–W–#							
SEPHIA—4-Cyl.—Equipment Schedule 6							
W.B. 100.8"; 1.8 Liter.							
Sedan 4D		FB121	11605	**1025**	**1475**	**2525**	**4000**
LS Sedan 4D		FB121	12345	**1125**	**1575**	**2675**	**4175**
1999 KIA — KNA(FB121)–X–#							
SEPHIA—4-Cyl.—Equipment Schedule 6							
W.B. 100.8"; 1.8 Liter.							
Sedan 4D		FB121	11605	**1300**	**1775**	**2900**	**4500**
LS Sedan 4D		FB121	12345	**1450**	**1925**	**3075**	**4675**
2000 KIA — KNA(FA121)–Y–#							
SEPHIA—4-Cyl.—Equipment Schedule 6							
W.B. 100.8"; 1.8 Liter.							
Sedan 4D		FA121	11605	**1650**	**2175**	**3350**	**5050**
LS Sedan 4D		FA121	12345	**1825**	**2350**	**3550**	**5250**
SPECTRA—4-Cyl.—Equipment Schedule 6							
W.B. 100.8"; 1.8 Liter.							
GS Sedan 4D		FB161	11245	**2425**	**3025**	**4125**	**5725**
GSX Sedan 4D		FB161	13445	**2700**	**3325**	**4475**	**6125**
2001 KIA — KNA(DC123)–1–#							
RIO—4-Cyl.—Equipment Schedule 6							
W.B. 94.9"; 1.5 Liter.							
Sedan 4D		DC123	10175	**2250**	**2800**	**4125**	**6000**
SEPHIA—4-Cyl.—Equipment Schedule 6							
W.B. 100.8"; 1.8 Liter.							
Sedan 4D		FB121	11945	**2400**	**2975**	**4250**	**6075**
LS Sedan 4D		FB121	12645	**2575**	**3200**	**4475**	**6300**
SPECTRA—4-Cyl.—Equipment Schedule 6							
W.B. 100.8"; 1.8 Liter.							
GS Hatchback 4D		FB161	12345	**2950**	**3600**	**4775**	**6500**
GSX Hatchback 4D		FB161	13645	**3300**	**3950**	**5150**	**6925**
OPTIMA—4-Cyl.—Equipment Schedule 5							
W.B. 106.3"; 2.4 Liter.							
LX Sedan 4D		GD126	16599	**3650**	**4375**	**5750**	**7775**
SE Sedan 4D		GD126	18899	**4575**	**5400**	**6850**	**8975**
V6 2.5 Liter				**750**	**750**	**1000**	**1000**
2002 KIA — KNA(DC123)–2–#							
RIO—4-Cyl.—Equipment Schedule 6							
W.B. 94.9"; 1.5 Liter.							
Sedan 4D		DC123	10660	**2800**	**3425**	**4850**	**6850**
Cinco Wagon 4D		DC163	11630	**3075**	**3725**	**5150**	**7175**
SPECTRA—4-Cyl.—Equipment Schedule 6							
W.B. 100.8"; 1.8 Liter.							
Sedan 4D		FB121	12450	**3400**	**4100**	**5325**	**7175**
GS Hatchback 4D		FB161	12850	**3575**	**4275**	**5525**	**7400**
LS Sedan 4D		FB121	13090	**3725**	**4475**	**5700**	**7600**
GSX Hatchback 4D		FB161	14090	**3900**	**4650**	**5925**	**7825**
OPTIMA—4-Cyl.—Equipment Schedule 5							
W.B. 106.3"; 2.4 Liter.							
LX Sedan 4D		GD126	16244	**4475**	**5275**	**6750**	**8925**
SE Sedan 4D		GD126	17894	**5500**	**6400**	**7925**	**10200**
V6 2.7 Liter		8		**825**	**825**	**1100**	**1100**
2003 KIA — KNA(DC125)–3–#							
RIO—4-Cyl.—Equipment Schedule 6							
W.B. 94.9"; 1.6 Liter.							
Sedan 4D		DC125	10495	**3575**	**4300**	**5675**	**7650**
Cinco Wagon 4D		DC165	11995	**3875**	**4600**	**6000**	**8025**

2003 KIA

Body	Type	VIN	List	Trade-In Fair	Good	Pvt-Party Good	Retail Excellent
SPECTRA—4-Cyl.—Equipment Schedule 6							
W.B. 100.8"; 1.8 Liter.							
Sedan 4D		FB121	12715	**4250**	**5050**	**6225**	**8050**
GS Hatchback 4D		FB161	13140	**4425**	**5200**	**6400**	**8250**
LS Sedan 4D		FB121	13320	**4575**	**5400**	**6600**	**8475**
GSX Hatchback 4D		FB161	14360	**4775**	**5625**	**6850**	**8725**
OPTIMA—4-Cyl.—Equipment Schedule 5							
W.B. 106.3"; 2.4 Liter.							
LX Sedan 4D		GD126	16915	**5475**	**6375**	**7825**	**10050**
SE Sedan 4D		GD126	18590	**6550**	**7575**	**9100**	**11400**
V6 2.7 Liter		8		**900**	**900**	**1200**	**1200**

2004 KIA — KNA(DC125)—4-#

Body	Type	VIN	List	Trade-In Fair	Good	Pvt-Party Good	Retail Excellent
RIO—4-Cyl.—Equipment Schedule 6							
W.B. 94.9"; 1.6 Liter.							
Sedan 4D		DC125	11030	**4450**	**5225**	**6525**	**8500**
Cinco Wagon 4D		DC165	12655	**4750**	**5575**	**6900**	**8900**
SPECTRA—4-Cyl.—Equipment Schedule 6							
W.B. 100.8"; 1.8 Liter.							
Sedan 4D		FB121	13320	**5125**	**6000**	**7125**	**8925**
GS Hatchback 4D		FB121	13580	**5300**	**6200**	**7325**	**9150**
LS Sedan 4D		FB121	13590	**5475**	**6375**	**7500**	**9350**
LX Sedan 4D		FB121	14120	**5550**	**6450**	**7600**	**9450**
EX Sedan 4D		FB121	14290	**5625**	**6525**	**7675**	**9550**
GSX Hatchback 4D		FB161	14630	**5700**	**6625**	**7775**	**9650**
OPTIMA—4-Cyl.—Equipment Schedule 5							
W.B. 106.3"; 2.4 Liter.							
LX Sedan 4D		GD126	16960	**6825**	**7850**	**9300**	**11600**
EX Sedan 4D		GD126	18635	**8000**	**9175**	**10700**	**13200**
V6 2.7 Liter		8		**950**	**950**	**1265**	**1265**
AMANTI—V6—Equipment Schedule 3							
W.B. 110.2"; 3.5 Liter.							
Sedan 4D		LD124	25535	**14725**	**16650**	**18650**	**22100**

LEXUS

1990 LEXUS — JT8(VV22T)–L–#

Body	Type	VIN	List	Trade-In Fair	Good	Pvt-Party Good	Retail Excellent
ES 250—V6—Equipment Schedule 1							
W.B. 102.4"; 2.5 Liter.							
Sedan 4D		VV22T	24050	**1275**	**1750**	**2900**	**4525**
Manual Trans				**(200)**	**(200)**	**(265)**	**(265)**
LS 400—V8—Equipment Schedule 1							
W.B. 110.8"; 4.0 Liter.							
Sedan 4D		UF11E	38650	**3200**	**3875**	**5600**	**8000**
Traction Control				**100**	**100**	**135**	**135**

1991 LEXUS — JT8(VV22T)–M–#

Body	Type	VIN	List	Trade-In Fair	Good	Pvt-Party Good	Retail Excellent
ES 250—V6—Equipment Schedule 1							
W.B. 102.4"; 2.5 Liter.							
Sedan 4D		VV22T	24500	**1500**	**2000**	**3225**	**4950**
Manual Trans				**(200)**	**(200)**	**(265)**	**(265)**
LS 400—V8—Equipment Schedule 1							
W.B. 110.8"; 4.0 Liter.							
Sedan 4D		UF11E	41650	**3675**	**4400**	**6275**	**8825**
Traction Control				**100**	**100**	**135**	**135**

1992 LEXUS — JT8(VK13T)–N–#

Body	Type	VIN	List	Trade-In Fair	Good	Pvt-Party Good	Retail Excellent
ES 300—V6—Equipment Schedule 1							
W.B. 103.1"; 3.0 Liter.							
Sedan 4D		VK13T	28650	**3050**	**3700**	**5250**	**7425**
Manual Trans				**(250)**	**(250)**	**(335)**	**(335)**
SC 300—6-Cyl.—Equipment Schedule 1							
W.B. 105.9"; 3.0 Liter.							
Sport Coupe 2D		JZ31C	35000	**4175**	**4950**	**6850**	**9500**
Traction Control				**125**	**125**	**165**	**165**
SC 400—V8—Equipment Schedule 1							
W.B. 105.9"; 4.0 Liter.							
Sport Coupe 2D		UZ30C	39100	**4850**	**5700**	**7725**	**10550**
Traction Control				**125**	**125**	**165**	**165**
LS 400—V8—Equipment Schedule 1							
W.B. 110.8"; 4.0 Liter.							

1992 LEXUS

Body	Type	VIN	List	Trade-In Fair	Good	Pvt-Party Good	Retail Excellent
Sedan 4D		UF11E	43600	4075	4850	6825	9550
	Traction Control			125	125	165	165

1993 LEXUS — JT8(VK13T)-P-#

ES 300—V6—Equipment Schedule 1
W.B. 103.1"; 3.0 Liter.

Sedan 4D		VK13T	31030	3625	4350	5975	8300
	Manual Trans			(300)	(300)	(400)	(400)

GS 300—6-Cyl.—Equipment Schedule 1
W.B. 109.4"; 3.0 Liter.

Sedan 4D		JS47E	40130	6525	7550	9600	12600
	Traction Control			150	150	200	200

SC 300—6-Cyl.—Equipment Schedule 1
W.B. 105.9"; 3.0 Liter.

Sport Coupe 2D		JZ31C	38730	4825	5675	7675	10500
	Traction Control			150	150	200	200

SC 400—V8—Equipment Schedule 1
W.B. 105.9"; 4.0 Liter.

Sport Coupe 2D		UZ30C	42730	5600	6500	8700	11700
	Traction Control			150	150	200	200

LS 400—V8—Equipment Schedule 1
W.B. 110.8"; 4.0 Liter.

Sedan 4D		UF11E	48030	4600	5425	7500	10400
	Traction Control			150	150	200	200

1994 LEXUS — JT8(GK13T)-R-#

ES 300—V6—Equipment Schedule 1
W.B. 103.1"; 3.0 Liter.

Sedan 4D		GK13T	31070	4250	5050	6750	9200

GS 300—6-Cyl.—Equipment Schedule 1
W.B. 109.4"; 3.0 Liter.

Sedan 4D		JS47E	40370	7400	8500	10650	13800
	Traction Control			175	175	235	235

SC 300—6-Cyl.—Equipment Schedule 1
W.B. 105.9"; 3.0 Liter.

Sport Coupe 2D		JZ31C	39370	5600	6500	8700	11750
	Traction Control			175	175	235	235

SC 400—V8—Equipment Schedule 1
W.B. 105.9"; 4.0 Liter.

Sport Coupe 2D		UZ30C	45570	6425	7450	9800	13050
	Traction Control			175	175	235	235

LS 400—V8—Equipment Schedule 1
W.B. 110.8"; 4.0 Liter.

Sedan 4D		UF11E	50370	5200	6100	8350	11450
	Traction Control			175	175	235	235

1995 LEXUS — JT8(GK13T)-S-#

ES 300—V6—Equipment Schedule 1
W.B. 103.1"; 3.0 Liter.

Sedan 4D		GK13T	34180	4900	5750	7575	10200

GS 300—6-Cyl.—Equipment Schedule 1
W.B. 109.4"; 3.0 Liter.

Sedan 4D		JS47E	45380	8300	9525	11750	15000
	Traction Control			200	200	265	265

SC 300—6-Cyl.—Equipment Schedule 1
W.B. 105.9"; 3.0 Liter.

Sport Coupe 2D		JZ31C	44980	6500	7500	9900	13200
	Traction Control			200	200	265	265

SC 400—V8—Equipment Schedule 1
W.B. 105.9"; 4.0 Liter.

Sport Coupe 2D		UZ30C	49780	7425	8550	11050	14600
	Traction Control			200	200	265	265

LS 400—V8—Equipment Schedule 1
W.B. 112.2"; 4.0 Liter.

Sedan 4D		UF22E	52680	6425	7450	10050	13650
	Traction Control			200	200	265	265

1996 LEXUS — JT8(BF12G)-T-#

ES 300—V6—Equipment Schedule 1
W.B. 103.1"; 3.0 Liter.

Sedan 4D		BF12G	34895	5650	6575	8525	11300

1996 LEXUS

Body	Type	VIN	List	Trade-In Fair	Good	Pvt-Party Good	Retail Excellent
GS 300—6-Cyl.—Equipment Schedule 1							
W.B. 109.4"; 3.0 Liter.							
Sedan 4D		BD42S	48445	**9300**	**10600**	**12950**	**16350**
Traction Control			....	**225**	**225**	**300**	**300**
SC 300—6-Cyl.—Equipment Schedule 1							
W.B. 105.9"; 3.0 Liter.							
Sport Coupe 2D		CD32Z	47695	**7575**	**8700**	**11300**	**14950**
Traction Control			....	**225**	**225**	**300**	**300**
SC 400—V8—Equipment Schedule 1							
W.B. 105.9"; 4.0 Liter.							
Sport Coupe 2D		CH32Y	53845	**8600**	**9850**	**12550**	**16350**
Traction Control			....	**225**	**225**	**300**	**300**
LS 400—V8—Equipment Schedule 1							
W.B. 112.2"; 4.0 Liter.							
Sedan 4D		BH33F	54445	**7500**	**8625**	**11400**	**15250**
Traction Control			....	**225**	**225**	**300**	**300**

1997 LEXUS — JT8(BF22G)-V-#

Body	Type	VIN	List	Trade-In Fair	Good	Pvt-Party Good	Retail Excellent
ES 300—V6—Equipment Schedule 1							
W.B. 105.1"; 3.0 Liter.							
Sedan 4D		BF22G	33045	**7100**	**8200**	**10350**	**13500**
GS 300—6-Cyl.—Equipment Schedule 1							
W.B. 109.4"; 3.0 Liter.							
Sedan 4D		BD42S	48595	**10375**	**11800**	**14200**	**17800**
Traction Control			....	**275**	**275**	**365**	**365**
SC 300—6-Cyl.—Equipment Schedule 1							
W.B. 105.9"; 3.0 Liter.							
Sport Coupe 2D		CD32Z	43445	**8850**	**10125**	**12900**	**16850**
Traction Control			....	**275**	**275**	**365**	**365**
SC 400—V8—Equipment Schedule 1							
W.B. 105.9"; 4.0 Liter.							
Sport Coupe 2D		CH32Y	52295	**9925**	**11275**	**14200**	**18400**
Traction Control			....	**275**	**275**	**365**	**365**
LS 400—V8—Equipment Schedule 1							
W.B. 112.2"; 4.0 Liter.							
Sedan 4D		BH28F	54495	**10225**	**11625**	**14950**	**19600**
Traction Control			....	**275**	**275**	**365**	**365**

1998 LEXUS — JT8(BF28G)-W-#

Body	Type	VIN	List	Trade-In Fair	Good	Pvt-Party Good	Retail Excellent
ES 300—V6—Equipment Schedule 1							
W.B. 105.1"; 3.0 Liter.							
Sedan 4D		BF28G	33935	**8350**	**9575**	**11700**	**14950**
GS 300—6-Cyl.—Equipment Schedule 1							
W.B. 110.2"; 3.0 Liter.							
Sedan 4D		BD68S	40025	**11275**	**12825**	**15200**	**18850**
GS 400—V8—Equipment Schedule 1							
W.B. 110.2"; 4.0 Liter.							
Sedan 4D		BH68X	46315	**13350**	**15075**	**17700**	**21700**
SC 300—6-Cyl.—Equipment Schedule 1							
W.B. 105.9"; 3.0 Liter.							
Sport Coupe 2D		CD32Z	44565	**10275**	**11675**	**14700**	**19000**
Traction Control			....	**300**	**300**	**400**	**400**
SC 400—V8—Equipment Schedule 1							
W.B. 105.9"; 4.0 Liter.							
Sport Coupe 2D		CH32Y	54315	**11475**	**13000**	**16150**	**20600**
Traction Control			....	**300**	**300**	**400**	**400**
LS 400—V8—Equipment Schedule 1							
W.B. 112.2"; 4.0 Liter.							
Sedan 4D		BH28F	54515	**11800**	**13400**	**16650**	**21300**

1999 LEXUS — JT8(BF28G)-X-#

Body	Type	VIN	List	Trade-In Fair	Good	Pvt-Party Good	Retail Excellent
ES 300—V6—Equipment Schedule 1							
W.B. 105.1"; 3.0 Liter.							
Sedan 4D		BF28G	34235	**9800**	**11175**	**13450**	**16850**
Coach Edition			....	**225**	**225**	**300**	**300**
GS 300—6-Cyl.—Equipment Schedule 1							
W.B. 110.2"; 3.0 Liter.							
Sedan 4D		BD68S	40580	**13150**	**14875**	**17400**	**21300**
GS 400—V8—Equipment Schedule 1							
W.B. 110.2"; 4.0 Liter.							
Sedan 4D		BH68X	47020	**15600**	**17625**	**20400**	**24700**

Body	Type	VIN	List	Trade-In Fair	Trade-In Good	Pvt-Party Good	Retail Excellent
SC 300—6-Cyl.—Equipment Schedule 1							
W.B. 105.9"; 3.0 Liter.							
Sport Coupe 2D		CD32Z	46640	11750	13300	16500	21100
Traction Control				325	325	435	435
SC 400—V8—Equipment Schedule 1							
W.B. 105.9"; 4.0 Liter.							
Sport Coupe 2D		CH32Y	56830	13250	14975	18350	23100
Traction Control				325	325	435	435
LS 400—V8—Equipment Schedule 1							
W.B. 112.2"; 4.0 Liter.							
Sedan 4D		BH28F	55220	13825	15650	19150	24200
2000 LEXUS — JT8(BF28G)-Y-#							
ES 300—V6—Equipment Schedule 1							
W.B. 105.1"; 3.0 Liter.							
Sedan 4D		BF28G	34785	11325	12875	15250	18900
Platinum Series				350	350	465	465
GS 300—6-Cyl.—Equipment Schedule 1							
W.B. 110.2"; 3.0 Liter.							
Sedan 4D		BD68S	40880	14975	16850	19700	24100
Platinum Series				350	350	465	465
GS 400—V8—Equipment Schedule 1							
W.B. 110.2"; 4.0 Liter.							
Sedan 4D		BH68X	47520	17850	20075	23100	27900
Platinum Series				350	350	465	465
SC 300—6-Cyl.—Equipment Schedule 1							
W.B. 105.9"; 3.0 Liter.							
Sport Coupe 2D		CD32Z	47140	13525	15275	18650	23600
Traction Control				350	350	465	465
SC 400—V8—Equipment Schedule 1							
W.B. 105.9"; 4.0 Liter.							
Sport Coupe 2D		CH32Y	57530	15350	17325	20900	26200
Traction Control				350	350	465	465
LS 400—V8—Equipment Schedule 1							
W.B. 112.2"; 4.0 Liter.							
Sedan 4D		BH28F	55420	16125	18150	21900	27400
Platinum Series				350	350	465	465
2001 LEXUS — JT(8orH)(BF28G)-1-#							
ES 300—V6—Equipment Schedule 1							
W.B. 105.1"; 3.0 Liter.							
Sedan 4D		BF28G	34935	13050	14775	17350	21200
Coach Edition				275	275	365	365
IS 300—6-Cyl.—Equipment Schedule 1							
W.B. 105.1"; 3.0 Liter.							
Sedan 4D		BD182	34055	13250	14925	17350	21000
GS 300—6-Cyl.—Equipment Schedule 1							
W.B. 110.2"; 3.0 Liter.							
Sedan 4D		BD68S	41780	17050	19150	22200	26800
GS 430—V8—Equipment Schedule 1							
W.B. 110.2"; 4.3 Liter.							
Sedan 4D		BN68X	50580	20350	22750	25900	31000
LS 430—V8—Equipment Schedule 1							
W.B. 115.2"; 4.3 Liter.							
Sedan 4D		BN30F	54550	26200	29275	33000	39200
Ultra Luxury Pkg				2800	2800	3730	3730
2002 LEXUS — JT(8orH)(BF30G)-2-#							
ES 300—V6—Equipment Schedule 1							
W.B. 105.1"; 3.0 Liter.							
Sedan 4D		BF30G	33640	16175	18250	20900	25200
IS 300—6-Cyl.—Equipment Schedule 1							
W.B. 105.1"; 3.0 Liter.							
Sedan 4D		BD192	33655	15125	17050	19600	23500
Sport Cross H'Back 4D		ED192	35195	15300	17225	19800	23700
Manual Trans				(500)	(500)	(665)	(665)
GS 300—6-Cyl.—Equipment Schedule 1							
W.B. 110.2"; 3.0 Liter.							
Sedan 4D		BD69S	41840	19300	21700	24800	29700
SportDesign Edition				825	825	1100	1100
GS 430—V8—Equipment Schedule 1							
W.B. 110.2"; 4.3 Liter.							

Body	Type	VIN	List	Trade-In Fair	Trade-In Good	Pvt-Party Good	Retail Excellent
Sedan 4D		BL69S	48980	23050	25825	29100	34500
LS 430—V8—Equipment Schedule 1							
W.B. 115.2"; 4.3 Liter.							
Sedan 4D		BN30F	56080	29575	33025	37000	43400
Ultra Luxury Pkg				2875	2875	3830	3830
SC 430—V8—Equipment Schedule 1							
W.B. 103.1"; 4.3 Liter.							
Convertible 2D		FN48Y	59030	31400	35050	39000	45600

2003 LEXUS — JT(8orH)(BF30G)-3-#

Body	Type	VIN	List	Trade-In Fair	Trade-In Good	Pvt-Party Good	Retail Excellent
ES 300—V6—Equipment Schedule 1							
W.B. 107.1"; 3.0 Liter.							
Sedan 4D		BF30G	33780	18250	20550	23300	27700
IS 300—6-Cyl.—Equipment Schedule 1							
W.B. 105.1"; 3.0 Liter.							
Sedan 4D		BD192	32485	17100	19200	21800	25900
Sport Cross H'Back 4D		ED192	32525	17275	19400	22000	26100
SportDesign				800	800	1065	1065
Manual Trans				(500)	(500)	(665)	(665)
GS 300—6-Cyl.—Equipment Schedule 1							
W.B. 110.2"; 3.0 Liter.							
Sedan 4D		BD69S	40960	21700	24375	27500	32500
SportDesign				1400	1400	1865	1865
GS 430—V8—Equipment Schedule 1							
W.B. 110.2"; 4.3 Liter.							
Sedan 4D		BL69S	48400	25725	28800	32200	37600
LS 430—V8—Equipment Schedule 1							
W.B. 115.2"; 4.3 Liter.							
Sedan 4D		BN30F	56600	33400	37250	41400	48300
Ultra Luxury Pkg				2950	2950	3930	3930
SC 430—V8—Equipment Schedule 1							
W.B. 103.1"; 4.3 Liter.							
Convertible 2D		FN48Y	62600	35800	39925	44100	51100

2004 LEXUS — JT(8orH)(BA30G)-4-#

Body	Type	VIN	List	Trade-In Fair	Trade-In Good	Pvt-Party Good	Retail Excellent
ES 330—V6—Equipment Schedule 1							
W.B. 107.1"; 3.3 Liter.							
Sedan 4D		BA30G	32350	20250	22650	25500	30200
IS 300—6-Cyl.—Equipment Schedule 1							
W.B. 105.1"; 3.0 Liter.							
Sedan 4D		BD192	32815	19575	21975	24600	28900
Sport Cross H'Back 4D		ED192	32855	19775	22175	24800	29100
Manual Trans				(500)	(500)	(665)	(665)
GS 300—6-Cyl.—Equipment Schedule 1							
W.B. 110.2"; 3.0 Liter.							
Sedan 4D		BD68S	41010	24575	27450	30600	36000
GS 430—V8—Equipment Schedule 1							
W.B. 110.2"; 4.3 Liter.							
Sedan 4D		BL69S	48450	29000	32350	35700	41500
LS 430—V8—Equipment Schedule 1							
W.B. 115.2"; 4.3 Liter.							
Sedan 4D		BN30F	55750				
Ultra Luxury Pkg							
SC 430—V8—Equipment Schedule 1							
W.B. 103.1"; 4.3 Liter.							
Convertible 2D		FN48Y	63200				

LINCOLN

1990 LINCOLN — 1LN(LM81F)-L-#

Body	Type	VIN	List	Trade-In Fair	Trade-In Good	Pvt-Party Good	Retail Excellent
TOWN CAR—V8—Equipment Schedule 2							
W.B. 117.4"; 5.0 Liter.							
Sedan 4D		LM81F	31218	875	1225	2200	3650
Signature Sedan 4D		LM82F	32721	900	1300	2425	4000
Cartier Dsgnr Sed 4D		LM83F	34300	950	1350	2475	4050
MARK VII—V8—Equipment Schedule 2							
W.B. 108.5"; 5.0 Liter.							
Bill Blass Sedan 2D		CM92E	29801	750	1050	1900	3200
LSC Sedan 2D		CM93E	30023	750	1050	1925	3250
Special Edition Pkg				50	50	65	65

1990 LINCOLN

Body	Type	VIN	List	Trade-In Fair	Good	Pvt-Party Good	Retail Excellent
CONTINENTAL—V6—Equipment Schedule 2							
W.B. 109.0"; 3.8 Liter.							
Sedan 4D		LM974	31352	675	925	1775	3075
Signature Sedan 4D		LM984	31901	700	1000	1875	3200

1991 LINCOLN — 1LN(LM81W)–M–#

Body	Type	VIN	List	Trade-In Fair	Good	Pvt-Party Good	Retail Excellent
TOWN CAR—V8—Equipment Schedule 2							
W.B. 117.4"; 4.6 Liter.							
Executive Sedan 4D		LM81W	31908	1025	1450	2625	4275
Signature Sedan 4D		LM82W	33566	1100	1550	2750	4475
Cartier Dsgnr Sed 4D		LM83W	35084	1125	1575	2825	4525
MARK VII—V8—Equipment Schedule 2							
W.B. 108.5"; 5.0 Liter.							
Bill Blass Sedan 2D		CM92E	30942	900	1275	2350	3925
LSC Sedan 2D		CM93E	30818	900	1275	2375	3950
Special Edition Pkg				50	50	65	65
CONTINENTAL—V6—Equipment Schedule 2							
W.B. 109.0"; 3.8 Liter.							
Executive Sedan 4D		LM974	32175	800	1125	2100	3525
Signature Sedan 4D		LM984	32700	850	1200	2300	3875

1992 LINCOLN — 1LN(LM81W)–N–#

Body	Type	VIN	List	Trade-In Fair	Good	Pvt-Party Good	Retail Excellent
TOWN CAR—V8—Equipment Schedule 2							
W.B. 117.4"; 4.6 Liter.							
Executive Sedan 4D		LM81W	33585	1225	1675	2975	4775
Signature Sedan 4D		LM82W	35968	1375	1875	3200	5050
Cartier Dsgnr Sed 4D		LM83W	36930	1450	1925	3300	5125
MARK VII—V8—Equipment Schedule 2							
W.B. 108.5"; 5.0 Liter.							
Bill Blass Designer 2D		CM92E	32746	1075	1525	2750	4475
LSC Sedan 2D		CM93E	32622	1100	1550	2775	4500
Special Edition Pkg				75	75	100	100
CONTINENTAL—V6—Equipment Schedule 2							
W.B. 109.0"; 3.8 Liter.							
Executive Sedan 4D		LM974	34237	900	1275	2450	4125
Signature Sedan 4D		LM984	34843	950	1350	2550	4250

1993 LINCOLN — 1LN(LM81W)–P–#

Body	Type	VIN	List	Trade-In Fair	Good	Pvt-Party Good	Retail Excellent
TOWN CAR—V8—Equipment Schedule 2							
W.B. 117.4"; 4.6 Liter.							
Executive Sedan 4D		LM81W	35350	1525	2050	3450	5400
Signature Sedan 4D		LM82W	36654	1775	2300	3775	5750
Cartier Dsgnr Sed 4D		LM83W	38171	1825	2350	3850	5850
CONTINENTAL—V6—Equipment Schedule 2							
W.B. 109.0"; 3.8 Liter.							
Executive Sedan 4D		LM974	33918	1050	1500	2825	4625
Signature Sedan 4D		LM984	35909	1125	1575	2925	4750
MARK VIII—V8—Equipment Schedule 2							
W.B. 113.0"; 4.6 Liter.							
Coupe 2D		LM91V	37230	1375	1850	2975	4600

1994 LINCOLN — 1LN(LM81W)–R–#

Body	Type	VIN	List	Trade-In Fair	Good	Pvt-Party Good	Retail Excellent
TOWN CAR—V8—Equipment Schedule 2							
W.B. 117.4"; 4.6 Liter.							
Executive Sedan 4D		LM81W	35930	1950	2475	4025	6150
Signature Sedan 4D		LM82W	37230	2225	2775	4400	6600
Cartier Dsgnr Sed 4D		LM83W	38725	2275	2850	4500	6700
CONTINENTAL—V6—Equipment Schedule 2							
W.B. 109.0"; 3.8 Liter.							
Executive Sedan 4D		LM974	34375	1375	1850	3300	5300
Signature Sedan 4D		LM984	36225	1450	1925	3400	5425
MARK VIII—V8—Equipment Schedule 2							
W.B. 113.0"; 4.6 Liter.							
Coupe 2D		LM91V	38675	1650	2175	3350	5050

1995 LINCOLN — 1LN(LM81W)–S–#

Body	Type	VIN	List	Trade-In Fair	Good	Pvt-Party Good	Retail Excellent
TOWN CAR—V8—Equipment Schedule 2							
W.B. 117.4"; 4.6 Liter.							
Executive Sedan 4D		LM81W	37595	2175	2750	4425	6700
Signature Sedan 4D		LM82W	39695	2550	3150	4875	7225
Cartier Sedan 4D		LM83W	41825	2600	3225	4950	7325

1995 LINCOLN

Body	Type	VIN	List	Trade-In Fair	Trade-In Good	Pvt-Party Good	Retail Excellent
Spinnaker Edition				75	75	100	100

CONTINENTAL—V8—Equipment Schedule 2
W.B. 109.0"; 4.6 Liter.

| | Sedan 4D | LM97V | 41375 | 1975 | 2525 | 3950 | 5925 |

MARK VIII—V8—Equipment Schedule 2
W.B. 113.0"; 4.6 Liter.

| | Coupe 2D | LM91V | 39425 | 2100 | 2675 | 3900 | 5700 |
| | LSC | | | 200 | 200 | 265 | 265 |

1996 LINCOLN — 1LN(LM81W)–T–#

TOWN CAR—V8—Equipment Schedule 2
W.B. 117.4"; 4.6 Liter.

	Executive Sedan 4D	LM81W	38120	2700	3325	5200	7700
	Signature Sedan 4D	LM82W	40170	3150	3800	5700	8300
	Cartier Sedan 4D	LM83W	42600	3200	3875	5775	8400

CONTINENTAL—V8—Equipment Schedule 2
W.B. 109.0"; 4.6 Liter.

| | Sedan 4D | LM97V | 42440 | 2700 | 3300 | 4875 | 7050 |

MARK VIII—V8—Equipment Schedule 2
W.B. 113.0"; 4.6 Liter.

| | Coupe 2D | LM91V | 40290 | 2675 | 3275 | 4650 | 6600 |
| | LSC | | | 200 | 200 | 265 | 265 |

1997 LINCOLN — 1LN(LM81W)–V–#

TOWN CAR—V8—Equipment Schedule 2
W.B. 117.4"; 4.6 Liter.

	Executive Sedan 4D	LM81W	38720	3425	4150	6225	9000
	Signature Sedan 4D	LM82W	41080	3900	4625	6775	9650
	Cartier Sedan 4D	LM83W	43870	3975	4725	6900	9800

CONTINENTAL—V8—Equipment Schedule 2
W.B. 109.0"; 4.6 Liter.

| | Sedan 4D | LM97V | 37850 | 3550 | 4250 | 6025 | 8475 |

MARK VIII—V8—Equipment Schedule 2
W.B. 113.0"; 4.6 Liter.

| | Coupe 2D | LM91V | 36950 | 3400 | 4100 | 5625 | 7800 |
| | LSC | | | 200 | 200 | 265 | 265 |

1998 LINCOLN — 1LN(LM81W)–W–#

TOWN CAR—V8—Equipment Schedule 2
W.B. 117.7"; 4.6 Liter.

	Executive Sedan 4D	LM81W	38330	5625	6525	7850	9900
	Signature Sedan 4D	LM82W	40150	6125	7100	8475	10600
	Cartier Sedan 4D	LM83W	42500	6250	7250	8600	10750

CONTINENTAL—V8—Equipment Schedule 2
W.B. 109.0"; 4.6 Liter.

| | Sedan 4D | LM97V | 38500 | 4625 | 5475 | 7225 | 9750 |

MARK VIII—V8—Equipment Schedule 2
W.B. 113.0"; 4.6 Liter.

| | Coupe 2D | LM91V | 37500 | 4475 | 5275 | 6900 | 9250 |
| | LSC | | | 200 | 200 | 265 | 265 |

1999 LINCOLN — 1LN(LM81W)–X–#

TOWN CAR—V8—Equipment Schedule 2
W.B. 117.7"; 4.6 Liter.

	Executive Sedan 4D	LM81W	38995	6825	7875	9325	11600
	Signature Sedan 4D	LM82W	40995	7475	8600	10100	12450
	Cartier Sedan 4D	LM83W	43495	7825	8975	10500	12900

CONTINENTAL—V8—Equipment Schedule 2
W.B. 109.0"; 4.6 Liter.

| | Sedan 4D | LM97V | 38995 | 5850 | 6825 | 8800 | 11650 |

2000 LINCOLN — 1LN(HM81W)–Y–#

TOWN CAR—V8—Equipment Schedule 2
W.B. 117.7", 123.7" (L Pkg); 4.6 Liter.

	Executive Sedan 4D	HM81W	39300	3400	9600	11300	13850
	Signature Sedan 4D	HM82W	41300	9150	10425	12150	14850
	Cartier Sedan 4D	HM83W	43800	9700	11100	12800	15600
	L Pkg			1825	1825	2435	2435
	Touring Pkg			150	150	200	200

CONTINENTAL—V8—Equipment Schedule 2
W.B. 117.7".

Body	Type	VIN	List	Trade-In Fair	Good	Pvt-Party Good	Retail Excellent
Sedan 4D		HM97V	39550	7275	8375	10350	13250

LS—V6—Equipment Schedule 2
W.B. 114.5"; 3.0 Liter.

Sedan 4D		HM86S	31450	7575	8700	10650	13550
Sport Pkg			------	150	150	200	200
Manual Trans			------	(600)	(600)	(800)	(800)

LS—V8—Equipment Schedule 2
W.B. 114.5"; 3.9 Liter.

| Sedan 4D | | HM87A | 35225 | 9500 | 10850 | 12900 | 16050 |
| Sport Pkg | | | ------ | 150 | 150 | 200 | 200 |

2001 LINCOLN — 1LN(HM81W)-1-#

TOWN CAR—V8—Equipment Schedule 2
W.B. 117.7", 123.7" (L); 4.6 Liter.

Executive Sedan 4D	HM81W	39865	10375	11800	13700	16700
Executive L Sed 4D	HM84W	44225	12625	14300	16300	19600
Signature Sedan 4D	HM82W	42035	11225	12775	14700	17800
Signature Touring 4D	HM82W	42745	11375	12900	14850	17950
Cartier Sedan 4D	HM83W	44420	12050	13625	15600	18800
Cartier L Sedan 4D	HM85W	49230	14725	16650	18800	22400

CONTINENTAL—V8—Equipment Schedule 2
W.B. 109.0"; 4.6 Liter.

| Sedan 4D | HM97V | 40100 | 9300 | 10600 | 12850 | 16200 |

LS—V6—Equipment Schedule 2
W.B. 114.5"; 3.0 Liter.

Sedan 4D	HM86S	32250	9500	10850	13100	16450
Sport Pkg		------	175	175	235	235
Manual Trans		------	(650)	(650)	(865)	(865)

LS—V8—Equipment Schedule 2
W.B. 114.5"; 3.9 Liter.

| Sedan 4D | HM87A | 36280 | 11625 | 13150 | 15550 | 19200 |
| Sport Pkg | | ------ | 175 | 175 | 235 | 235 |

2002 LINCOLN — 1LN(HM81W)-2-#

TOWN CAR—V8—Equipment Schedule 2
W.B. 117.7", 123.7" (L); 4.6 Liter.

Executive Sedan 4D	HM81W	40540	12900	14600	16700	20200
Executive L Sed 4D	HM84W	44600	15350	17325	19700	23400
Signature Sedan 4D	HM82W	42710	13825	15650	17850	21400
Signature Touring 4D	HM82W	43420	14025	15800	18050	21600
Cartier Sedan 4D	HM83W	45095	14875	16750	19050	22800
Cartier L Sedan 4D	HM85W	49605	17675	19875	22300	26200

CONTINENTAL—V8—Equipment Schedule 2
W.B. 109.0"; 4.6 Liter.

| Sedan 4D | HM97V | 38555 | 11800 | 13400 | 15950 | 19800 |

LS—V6—Equipment Schedule 2
W.B. 114.5"; 3.0 Liter.

Sedan 4D	HM86S	33455	12000	13575	16250	20300
LSE Sedan 4D	HM86S	38135	13350	15075	17850	22000
Manual Trans			(675)	(675)	(900)	(900)

LS—V8—Equipment Schedule 2
W.B. 114.5"; 3.9 Liter.

| Sedan 4D | HM87A | 37630 | 14300 | 16125 | 18950 | 23200 |
| LSE Sedan 4D | HM87A | 41180 | 15300 | 17225 | 20100 | 24500 |

2003 LINCOLN — 1LN(HM81W)-3-#

TOWN CAR—V8—Equipment Schedule 2
W.B. 117.7", 123.7" (L); 4.6 Liter.

Executive Sedan 4D	HM81W	41140	15650	17625	20100	24000
Executive L Sed 4D	HM84W	45115	18325	20650	23100	27400
Signature Sedan 4D	HM82W	43600	16700	18775	21300	25300
Cartier Sedan 4D	HM83W	46110	17950	20150	22700	26900
Cartier L Sedan 4D	HM85W	51570	20825	23325	26000	30500
Limited Edition		------	500	500	665	665

LS—V6—Equipment Schedule 2
W.B. 114.5"; 3.0 Liter.

| Sedan 4D | HM86S | 34495 | 15275 | 17175 | 20300 | 24900 |

LS—V8—Equipment Schedule 2
W.B. 114.5"; 3.9 Liter.

| Sedan 4D | HM87A | 40695 | 17750 | 19975 | 23100 | 28100 |

Body	Type	VIN	List	Trade-In Fair	Good	Pvt-Party Good	Retail Excellent

TOWN CAR—V8—Equipment Schedule 2
W.B. 117.7", 123.7" (L); 4.6 Liter.

Body	Type	VIN	List	Fair	Good	Good	Excellent
Signature Sedan 4D		HM82W	41815	20450	22850	25700	30400
Executive L Sed 4D		HM84W	45790	22175	24775	27700	32500
Ultimate Sedan 4D		HM83W	44925	21900	24475	27500	32300
Ultimate L Sedan 4D		HM85W	50470	24875	27850	30800	35900

LS—V6—Equipment Schedule 2
W.B. 114.5"; 3.0 Liter.

| Sedan 4D | | HM86S | 32495 | 18825 | 21125 | 23500 | 27600 |

LS—V8—Equipment Schedule 2
W.B. 114.5"; 3.9 Liter.

| Sedan 4D | | HM87A | 40095 | 21600 | 24200 | 26600 | 30900 |
| LSE Sedan 4D | | HM87A | 43490 | 22750 | 25450 | 27900 | 32400 |

MAZDA

1990 MAZDA — (JM1or1YV)(BG232)-L-#

323—4-Cyl.—Equipment Schedule 6
W.B. 96.5"; 1.6 Liter.

| Hatchback 2D | | BG232 | 7913 | 475 | 700 | 1175 | 1975 |
| SE Hatchback 2D | | BG232 | 9643 | 550 | 775 | 1300 | 2125 |

PROTEGE'—4-Cyl.—Equipment Schedule 6
W.B. 98.4"; 1.8 Liter.

SE Sedan 4D		BG224	11103	550	775	1400	2400
LX Sedan 4D		BG222	12063	600	875	1500	2575
4WD Sedan 4D		BG228	12753	675	950	1625	2750

626—4-Cyl.—Equipment Schedule 4
W.B. 101.4"; 2.2 Liter.

DX Sedan 4D		GD221	14488	650	900	1575	2700
LX Sedan 4D		GD221	15738	700	1000	1700	2850
LX Touring Sedan 4D		GD241	15938	750	1025	1775	2925

626—4-Cyl. Turbo—Equipment Schedule 4
W.B. 101.4"; 2.2 Liter.

| GT Touring Sedan 4D | | GD244 | 17508 | 775 | 1100 | 1875 | 3075 |

MX-6—4-Cyl.—Equipment Schedule 4
W.B. 99.0"; 2.2 Liter.

| DX Coupe 2D | | GD312 | 14298 | 650 | 900 | 1575 | 2700 |
| LX Coupe 2D | | GD312 | 15568 | 650 | 900 | 1575 | 2700 |

MX-6—4-Cyl. Turbo—Equipment Schedule 4
W.B. 99.0"; 2.2 Liter.

| GT Coupe 2D | | GD314 | 17828 | 650 | 900 | 1575 | 2700 |
| 4WS Coupe 2D | | GD314 | 18308 | 775 | 1075 | 1825 | 3025 |

MIATA—4-Cyl.—Equipment Schedule 6
W.B. 89.2"; 1.6 Liter.

MX-5 Convertible 2D		NA351	14069	900	1275	2125	3425
Auto Trans				0	0	0	0
Hard Top				300	300	400	400

RX-7—Rotary—Equipment Schedule 4
W.B. 95.7"; 1.3 Liter.

GTU Coupe 2D		FC331	19768	1050	1500	2675	4325
GTUs Coupe 2D		FC331	21318	1100	1550	2750	4450
Convertible 2D		FC352	28418	2200	2775	4200	6175
GXL Coupe 2D		FC331	23359	1150	1600	2825	4500
2+2 Seats		L		50	50	65	65

RX-7—Rotary Turbo—Equipment Schedule 4
W.B. 95.7"; 1.3 Liter.

| Coupe 2D | | FC332 | 26809 | 1350 | 1825 | 3050 | 4775 |
| Manual Trans | | | | 0 | 0 | 0 | 0 |

929—V6—Equipment Schedule 4
W.B. 106.7"; 3.0 Liter.

| Sedan 4D | | HC220 | 23579 | 900 | 1275 | 2200 | 3600 |
| S Sedan 4D | | HC224 | 25079 | 950 | 1350 | 2400 | 3925 |

1991 MAZDA — (JM1or1YV)(BG232)-M-#

323—4-Cyl.—Equipment Schedule 6
W.B. 96.5"; 1.6 Liter.

| Hatchback 2D | | BG232 | 8243 | 550 | 800 | 1350 | 2225 |
| SE Hatchback 2D | | BG234 | 9693 | 625 | 900 | 1475 | 2425 |

1991 MAZDA

Body	Type	VIN	List	Trade-In Fair	Good	Pvt-Party Good	Retail Excellent
PROTEGE—4-Cyl.—Equipment Schedule 4							
W.B. 98.4"; 1.8 Liter.							
DX Sedan 4D		BG224	11063	625	900	1550	2650
LX Sedan 4D		BG226	12393	700	975	1675	2800
4WD Sedan 4D		BG228	12783	800	1125	1925	3150
626—4-Cyl.—Equipment Schedule 4							
W.B. 101.4"; 2.2 Liter.							
DX Sedan 4D		GD222	14448	750	1050	1850	3075
LX Sedan 4D		GD222	15938	825	1150	1975	3250
LX Touring Sedan 4D		GD242	16338	850	1175	2025	3300
LE Sedan 4D		GD222	17269	925	1325	2250	3650
Manual Trans				(175)	(175)	(235)	(235)
626—4-Cyl. Turbo—Equipment Schedule 4							
W.B. 101.4"; 2.2 Liter.							
GT Touring Sedan 4D		GD244	17938	900	1250	2125	3475
MX-6—4-Cyl.—Equipment Schedule 4							
W.B. 99.0"; 2.2 Liter.							
DX Coupe 2D		GD312	14384	750	1050	1850	3075
LX Coupe 2D		GD312	15938	750	1050	1850	3075
LE Coupe 2D		GD312	16549	750	1050	1850	3075
Manual Trans				(175)	(175)	(235)	(235)
MX-6—4-Cyl. Turbo—Equipment Schedule 4							
W.B. 99.0"; 2.2 Liter.							
GT Coupe 2D		GD314	18258	775	1075	1900	3150
MIATA—4-Cyl.—Equipment Schedule 6							
W.B. 89.2"; 1.6 Liter.							
MX-5 Convertible 2D		NA351	14499	1025	1475	2550	4075
MX-5 Spcl Ed Conv 2D		NA351	19548	1500	2025	3225	4900
Auto Trans				(25)	(25)	(35)	(35)
Hard Top				325	325	435	435
RX-7—Rotary—Equipment Schedule 4							
W.B. 95.7"; 1.3 Liter.							
Coupe 2D		FC331	20799	1325	1800	3125	4950
Convertible 2D		FC352	29199	2650	3250	4825	7000
RX-7—Rotary Turbo—Equipment Schedule 4							
W.B. 95.7"; 1.3 Liter.							
Coupe 2D		FC332	28149	1625	2125	3525	5450
929—V6—Equipment Schedule 4							
W.B. 106.7"; 3.0 Liter.							
Sedan 4D		HC222	23799	975	1425	2525	4075
S Sedan 4D		HC224	25299	1050	1500	2625	4225

1992 MAZDA — (JM1or1YV)(BG232)-N-#

Body	Type	VIN	List	Trade-In Fair	Good	Pvt-Party Good	Retail Excellent
323—4-Cyl.—Equipment Schedule 6							
W.B. 96.5"; 1.6 Liter.							
Hatchback 2D		BG232	8439	625	900	1500	2525
SE Hatchback 2D		BG232	10189	725	1025	1675	2750
MX-3—4-Cyl.—Equipment Schedule 6							
W.B. 96.3"; 1.6 Liter.							
Hatchback 2D		EC431	12630	1000	1450	2325	3650
MX-3—V6—Equipment Schedule 6							
W.B. 96.3"; 1.8 Liter.							
GS Hatchback 2D		EC432	15430	1425	1900	2975	4500
PROTEGE'—4-Cyl.—Equipment Schedule 6							
W.B. 98.4"; 1.8 Liter.							
DX Sedan 4D		BG224	11769	700	975	1725	2900
LX Sedan 4D		BG226	12889	775	1075	1875	3100
626—4-Cyl.—Equipment Schedule 4							
W.B. 101.4"; 2.2 Liter.							
DX Sedan 4D		GD22B	15685	875	1225	2125	3475
LX Sedan 4D		GD22B	16585	900	1300	2250	3650
Manual Trans				(225)	(225)	(300)	(300)
MX-6—4-Cyl.—Equipment Schedule 4							
W.B. 99.0"; 2.2 Liter.							
DX Coupe 2D		GD31B	15475	850	1200	2100	3425
LX Coupe 2D		GD31B	16575	900	1250	2150	3525
Manual Trans				(225)	(225)	(300)	(300)
MX-6—4-Cyl. Turbo—Equipment Schedule 4							
W.B. 99.0"; 2.2 Liter.							
GT Coupe 2D		GD31D	18895	900	1300	2350	3875
MIATA—4-Cyl.—Equipment Schedule 6							
W.B. 89.2"; 1.6 Liter.							
MX-5 Convertible 2D		NA351	15150	1250	1725	2875	4500

1992 MAZDA

Body	Type	VIN	List	Trade-In Fair	Good	Pvt-Party Good	Retail Excellent
Auto Trans		......	......	(75)	(75)	(100)	(100)
Hard Top		......	......	350	350	465	465
929—V6—Equipment Schedule 4							
W.B. 112.2"; 3.0 Liter.							
Sedan 4D		HD461	28150	**1800**	**2325**	**3675**	**5525**

1993 MAZDA — (JM1or1YV)(BG232)–P–#

Body	Type	VIN	List	Trade-In Fair	Good	Pvt-Party Good	Retail Excellent
323—4-Cyl.—Equipment Schedule 6							
W.B. 96.5"; 1.6 Liter.							
Hatchback 2D		BG232	9219	**750**	**1025**	**1725**	**2850**
SE Hatchback 2D		BG232	10889	**850**	**1175**	**1950**	**3150**
MX-3—4-Cyl.—Equipment Schedule 6							
W.B. 96.3"; 1.6 Liter.							
Hatchback 2D		EC431	13055	**1150**	**1600**	**2675**	**4150**
MX-3—V6—Equipment Schedule 6							
W.B. 96.3"; 1.8 Liter.							
GS Hatchback 2D		EC432	15825	**1700**	**2225**	**3350**	**4975**
Spcl Edition H'Back 2D		EC432	17660	**1700**	**2225**	**3350**	**4975**
PROTEGE'—4-Cyl.—Equipment Schedule 6							
W.B. 98.4"; 1.8 Liter.							
DX Sedan 4D		BG224	12374	**775**	**1100**	**1950**	**3250**
LX Sedan 4D		BG226	13539	**875**	**1225**	**2125**	**3475**
626—4-Cyl.—Equipment Schedule 4							
W.B. 102.8"; 2.0 Liter.							
DX Sedan 4D		GE22A	17495	**950**	**1375**	**2375**	**3875**
LX Sedan 4D		GE22A	17590	**1025**	**1450**	**2500**	**3975**
Manual Trans		......		**(275)**	**(275)**	**(365)**	**(365)**
626—V6—Equipment Schedule 4							
W.B. 102.8"; 2.5 Liter.							
ES Sedan 4D		GE22B	19875	**1425**	**1900**	**3050**	**4650**
Manual Trans		......		**(275)**	**(275)**	**(365)**	**(365)**
MX-6—4-Cyl.—Equipment Schedule 4							
W.B. 102.8"; 2.0 Liter.							
Coupe 2D		GE31A	18300	**975**	**1425**	**2450**	**3925**
Manual Trans		......		**(275)**	**(275)**	**(365)**	**(365)**
MX-6—V6—Equipment Schedule 4							
W.B. 102.8"; 2.5 Liter.							
LS Coupe 2D		GE31B	20575	**1225**	**1675**	**2775**	**4375**
Manual Trans		......		**(275)**	**(275)**	**(365)**	**(365)**
MIATA—4-Cyl.—Equipment Schedule 6							
W.B. 89.2"; 1.6 Liter.							
MX-5 Convertible 2D		NA351	15650	**1525**	**2050**	**3300**	**5025**
MX-5 Ltd Ed Conv 2D		NA351	22350	**2150**	**2725**	**4075**	**5975**
Auto Trans		......		**(125)**	**(125)**	**(165)**	**(165)**
Hard Top		......		**375**	**375**	**500**	**500**
RX-7—Rotary Turbo—Equipment Schedule 3							
W.B. 95.5"; 1.3 Liter.							
Coupe 2D		FD331	32850	**7000**	**8100**	**10400**	**13700**
Auto Trans		......		**(125)**	**(125)**	**(165)**	**(165)**
929—V6—Equipment Schedule 4							
W.B. 112.2"; 3.0 Liter.							
Sedan 4D		HD461	29550	**2125**	**2700**	**4100**	**6075**

1994 MAZDA — (JM1or1YV)(BG232)–R–#

Body	Type	VIN	List	Trade-In Fair	Good	Pvt-Party Good	Retail Excellent
323—4-Cyl.—Equipment Schedule 6							
W.B. 96.5"; 1.6 Liter.							
Hatchback 2D		BG232	10220	**850**	**1175**	**2000**	**3250**
MX-3—4-Cyl.—Equipment Schedule 6							
W.B. 96.3"; 1.6 Liter.							
Hatchback 2D		EC435	14840	**1350**	**1825**	**2900**	**4450**
MX-3—V6—Equipment Schedule 6							
W.B. 96.3"; 1.8 Liter.							
GS Hatchback 2D		EC436	17340	**1975**	**2525**	**3700**	**5400**
PROTEGE'—4-Cyl.—Equipment Schedule 6							
W.B. 98.4"; 1.8 Liter.							
Sedan 4D		BG224	10570	**675**	**950**	**1725**	**2975**
DX Sedan 4D		BG224	13070	**900**	**1250**	**2175**	**3600**
LX Sedan 4D		BG226	14770	**975**	**1400**	**2475**	**4000**
626—4-Cyl.—Equipment Schedule 4							
W.B. 102.8"; 2.0 Liter.							
DX Sedan 4D		GE22C	15450	**1025**	**1475**	**2550**	**4075**
LX Sedan 4D		GE22C	17735	**1100**	**1550**	**2650**	**4200**
Manual Trans		......		**(325)**	**(325)**	**(435)**	**(435)**

1994 MAZDA

Body	Type	VIN	List	Trade-In Fair	Trade-In Good	Pvt-Party Good	Retail Excellent
	V6 2.5 Liter	D		275	275	365	365
626—V6—Equipment Schedule 4							
W.B. 102.8"; 2.5 Liter.							
ES Sedan 4D		GE22D	22740	1725	2250	3450	5150
Manual Trans				(325)	(325)	(435)	(435)
MX-3—4-Cyl.—Equipment Schedule 4							
W.B. 102.8"; 2.0 Liter.							
Coupe 2D		GE31C	19540	1225	1675	2775	4375
Manual Trans				(325)	(325)	(435)	(435)
MX-6—V6—Equipment Schedule 4							
W.B. 102.8"; 2.5 Liter.							
LS Coupe 2D		GE31D	22690	1600	2100	3300	4975
Manual Trans				(325)	(325)	(435)	(435)
MIATA—4-Cyl.—Equipment Schedule 6							
W.B. 89.2"; 1.8 Liter.							
MX-5 Convertible 2D		NA353	17045	1700	2225	3475	5250
MX-5 M-Ed Conv 2D		NA353	21645	2375	2950	4325	6250
Auto Trans				0	0	0	0
Hard Top				400	400	535	535
RX-7—Rotary Turbo—Equipment Schedule 3							
W.B. 95.5"; 1.3 Liter.							
Coupe 2D		FD333	36395	8225	9425	11900	15450
Auto Trans				(150)	(150)	(200)	(200)
929—V6—Equipment Schedule 4							
W.B. 112.2"; 3.0 Liter.							
Sedan 4D		HD461	31895	2525	3125	4575	6650

1995 MAZDA — (JM1or1YV)(EC435)-S-#

Body	Type	VIN	List	Trade-In Fair	Trade-In Good	Pvt-Party Good	Retail Excellent
MX-3—4-Cyl.—Equipment Schedule 6							
W.B. 96.3"; 1.6 Liter.							
Hatchback 2D		EC435	15780	1525	2050	3175	4750
PROTEGE'—4-Cyl.—Equipment Schedule 6							
W.B. 98.4"; 1.5 Liter, 1.8 Liter.							
DX Sedan 4D		BA141	14010	900	1300	2150	3475
LX Sedan 4D		BA141	14980	1025	1450	2475	3950
ES Sedan 4D		BA142	16585	1225	1700	2775	4350
626—4-Cyl.—Equipment Schedule 4							
W.B. 102.8"; 2.0 Liter.							
DX Sedan 4D		GE22C	17630	1275	1750	2900	4525
LX Sedan 4D		GE22C	18635	1375	1875	3050	4700
Manual Trans				(375)	(375)	(500)	(500)
V6 2.5 Liter		D		325	325	435	435
626—V6—Equipment Schedule 4							
W.B. 102.8"; 2.5 Liter.							
ES Sedan 4D		GE22D	23935	2100	2650	3900	5725
Manual Trans				(375)	(375)	(500)	(500)
MX-6—4-Cyl.—Equipment Schedule 4							
W.B. 102.8"; 2.0 Liter.							
Coupe 2D		GE31C	20713	1500	2025	3225	4900
Manual Trans				(375)	(375)	(500)	(500)
MX-6—V6—Equipment Schedule 4							
W.B. 102.8"; 2.5 Liter.							
LS Coupe 2D		GE31D	22888	2050	2600	3875	5675
Manual Trans				(375)	(375)	(500)	(500)
MIATA—4-Cyl.—Equipment Schedule 6							
W.B. 89.2"; 1.8 Liter.							
MX-5 Convertible 2D		NA353	17940	2100	2650	3975	5875
MX-5 M-Ed Conv 2D		NA353	23970	2775	3400	4875	6900
Auto Trans				0	0	0	0
Hard Top				425	425	565	565
RX-7—Rotary Turbo—Equipment Schedule 3							
W.B. 95.5"; 1.3 Liter.							
Coupe 2D		FD333	37950	9475	10800	13450	17250
Auto Trans				(175)	(175)	(235)	(235)
MILLENIA—V6—Equipment Schedule 2							
W.B. 108.3"; 2.5 Liter.							
Sedan 4D		TA221	29335	2100	2650	4000	5900
MILLENIA—V6 Supercharged—Equipment Schedule 2							
W.B. 108.3"; 2.3 Liter.							
S Sedan 4D		TA222	32435	3275	3925	5450	7600
929—V6—Equipment Schedule 4							
W.B. 112.2"; 3.0 Liter.							
Sedan 4D		HD461	36235	2950	3600	5150	7350

Body	Type	VIN	List	Trade-In Fair	Trade-In Good	Pvt-Party Good	Retail Excellent

1996 MAZDA — JM1(BB141)–T–#

PROTEGE'—4-Cyl.—Equipment Schedule 6
W.B. 102.6"; 1.5 Liter, 1.8 Liter.

Body	Type	VIN	List	Fair	Good	Good	Excellent
DX Sedan 4D		BB141	13720	1050	1500	2600	4125
LX Sedan 4D		BB141	14590	1225	1700	2800	4400
ES Sedan 4D		BB142	15145	1500	2000	3150	4775

626—4-Cyl.—Equipment Schedule 4
W.B. 102.8"; 2.0 Liter.

DX Sedan 4D		GE22C	17960	1625	2125	3375	5100
LX Sedan 4D		GE22C	18945	1750	2275	3525	5275
Manual Trans				(400)	(400)	(535)	(535)
V6 2.5 Liter		D		350	350	465	465

626—V6—Equipment Schedule 4
W.B. 102.8"; 2.5 Liter.

| ES Sedan 4D | | GE22D | 24045 | 2525 | 3125 | 4475 | 6375 |
| Manual Trans | | | | (400) | (400) | (535) | (535) |

MX-6—4-Cyl.—Equipment Schedule 4
W.B. 102.8"; 2.0 Liter.

| Coupe 2D | | GE31C | 21745 | 1925 | 2450 | 3725 | 5525 |
| Manual Trans | | | | (400) | (400) | (535) | (535) |

MX-6—V6—Equipment Schedule 4
W.B. 102.8"; 2.5 Liter.

LS Coupe 2D		GE31D	24100	2550	3150	4500	6425
M-Edition Coupe 2D		GE31D	27600	2875	3525	4950	6925
Manual Trans				(400)	(400)	(535)	(535)

MIATA—4-Cyl.—Equipment Schedule 6
W.B. 89.2"; 1.8 Liter.

MX-5 Convertible 2D		NA353	18900	2550	3150	4575	6600
MX-5 M-Ed Conv 2D		NA353	25210	3300	3950	5500	7675
Auto Trans				0	0	0	0
Hard Top				450	450	600	600

MILLENIA—V6—Equipment Schedule 2
W.B. 108.3"; 2.5 Liter.

| Sedan 4D | | TA221 | 28445 | 2450 | 3050 | 4500 | 6500 |
| L Sedan 4D | | TA221 | 31845 | 2550 | 3150 | 4575 | 6625 |

MILLENIA—V6 Supercharged—Equipment Schedule 2
W.B. 108.3"; 2.3 Liter.

| S Sedan 4D | | TA222 | 34845 | 3800 | 4525 | 6150 | 8425 |

1997 MAZDA — JM1(BC141)–V–#

PROTEGE'—4-Cyl.—Equipment Schedule 6
W.B. 102.6"; 1.5 Liter, 1.8 Liter.

DX Sedan 4D		BC141	14170	1375	1850	2975	4575
LX Sedan 4D		BC141	15140	1550	2075	3225	4875
ES Sedan 4D		BC142	15745	1825	2350	3550	5225

626—4-Cyl.—Equipment Schedule 4
W.B. 102.8"; 2.0 Liter.

DX Sedan 4D		GE22C	18160	2075	2625	3925	5775
LX Sedan 4D		GE22C	19145	2200	2775	4100	5975
Manual Trans				(425)	(425)	(565)	(565)
V6 2.5 Liter		D		375	375	500	500

626—V6—Equipment Schedule 4
W.B. 102.8"; 2.5 Liter.

| ES Sedan 4D | | GE22D | 24245 | 3000 | 3675 | 5100 | 7125 |
| Manual Trans | | | | (425) | (425) | (565) | (565) |

MX-6—4-Cyl.—Equipment Schedule 4
W.B. 102.8"; 2.0 Liter.

| Coupe 2D | | GE31C | 22345 | 2400 | 2975 | 4325 | 6250 |
| Manual Trans | | | | (425) | (425) | (565) | (565) |

MX-6—V6—Equipment Schedule 4
W.B. 102.8"; 2.5 Liter.

| LS Coupe 2D | | GE31D | 25200 | 3125 | 3775 | 5200 | 7275 |
| Manual Trans | | | | (425) | (425) | (565) | (565) |

MIATA—4-Cyl.—Equipment Schedule 6
W.B. 89.2"; 1.8 Liter.

MX-5 Convertible 2D		NA353	20775	3050	3700	5250	7450
MX-5 STO-Ed Conv 2D		NA353	22970	3625	4350	5975	8250
MX-5 M-Ed Conv 2D		NA353	24935	3850	4575	6225	8550
Auto Trans				0	0	0	0
Hard Top				475	475	635	635

MILLENIA—V6—Equipment Schedule 2
W.B. 108.3"; 2.5 Liter.

0105

Body	Type	VIN	List	Trade-In Fair	Good	Pvt-Party Good	Retail Excellent
Sedan 4D		TA221	29445	2975	3650	5200	7400
L Sedan 4D		TA221	33445	3075	3725	5300	7500
MILLENIA—V6 Supercharged—Equipment Schedule 2							
W.B. 108.3"; 2.3 Liter.							
S Sedan 4D		TA222	37045	4425	5200	6925	9375

1998 MAZDA — JM1(BB141)-W-#

PROTEGE'—4-Cyl.—Equipment Schedule 6
W.B. 102.6"; 1.5 Liter, 1.8 Liter.

Body	Type	VIN	List	Fair	Good	Good	Excellent
DX Sedan 4D		BB141	14170	1675	2200	3400	5100
LX Sedan 4D		BB141	15140	1900	2425	3650	5350
ES Sedan 4D		BB142	15745	2200	2775	4000	5775
626—4-Cyl.—Equipment Schedule 4							
W.B. 105.1"; 2.0 Liter.							
DX Sedan 4D		GE22C	18690	2550	3175	4500	6375
LX Sedan 4D		GE22C	19395	2700	3300	4650	6575
Manual Trans				(450)	(450)	(600)	(600)
V6 2.5 Liter		D		425	425	565	565
626—V6—Equipment Schedule 4							
W.B. 105.1"; 2.5 Liter.							
ES Sedan 4D		GE22D	25495	3575	4275	5700	7750
Manual Trans				(450)	(450)	(600)	(600)
MILLENIA—V6—Equipment Schedule 2							
W.B. 108.3"; 2.5 Liter.							
Sedan 4D		TA221	33445	3725	4450	6050	8350
MILLENIA—V6 Supercharged—Equipment Schedule 2							
W.B. 108.3"; 2.3 Liter.							
S Sedan 4D		TA222	37045	5150	6025	7775	10300

1999 MAZDA — (Jor1)(M1orYV)(BJ222)-X-#

PROTEGE'—4-Cyl.—Equipment Schedule 6
W.B. 102.8"; 1.6 Liter, 1.8 Liter.

Body	Type	VIN	List	Fair	Good	Good	Excellent
DX Sedan 4D		BJ222	13995	2700	3325	4500	6200
LX Sedan 4D		BJ222	14725	2975	3625	4800	6525
ES Sedan 4D		BJ221	15375	3300	4000	5200	7000
626—4-Cyl.—Equipment Schedule 4							
W.B. 105.1"; 2.0 Liter.							
LX Sedan 4D		GF22C	19165	3225	3900	5325	7375
ES Sedan 4D		GF22C	20245	3800	4525	6000	8125
Manual Trans				(500)	(500)	(665)	(665)
V6 2.5 Liter		D		500	500	665	665
MIATA MX-5—4-Cyl.—Equipment Schedule 6							
W.B. 89.2"; 1.8 Liter.							
Convertible 2D		NB353	21420	5350	6275	8025	10550
10th Anniversary Conv		NB353	27325	7825	8975	10900	13800
Auto Trans				0	0	0	0
Hard Top				525	525	700	700
MILLENIA—V6—Equipment Schedule 2							
W.B. 108.3"; 2.5 Liter.							
Sedan 4D		TA221	28995	4950	5800	7625	10200
MILLENIA—V6 Supercharged—Equipment Schedule 2							
W.B. 108.3"; 2.3 Liter.							
S Sedan 4D		TA222	31495	6625	7650	9600	12500

2000 MAZDA — (Jor1)(M1orYV)(BJ222)-Y-#

PROTEGE'—4-Cyl.—Equipment Schedule 6
W.B. 102.8"; 1.6 Liter, 1.8 Liter.

Body	Type	VIN	List	Fair	Good	Good	Excellent
DX Sedan 4D		BJ222	13995	3300	3950	5150	6925
LX Sedan 4D		BJ222	14840	3575	4275	5500	7325
ES Sedan 4D		BJ221	15490	3950	4700	5950	7850
626—4-Cyl.—Equipment Schedule 4							
W.B. 105.1"; 2.0 Liter.							
LX Sedan 4D		GF22C	19695	3850	4575	6100	8275
ES Sedan 4D		GF22C	21095	4500	5300	6875	9150
Manual Trans				(525)	(525)	(700)	(700)
V6 2.5 Liter		D		550	550	735	735
MIATA MX-5—4-Cyl.—Equipment Schedule 6							
W.B. 89.2"; 1.8 Liter.							
Convertible 2D		NB353	22595	6300	7325	9150	11850
LS Convertible 2D		NB353	25345	7100	8200	10100	12900
Special Ed Conv 2D		NB353	25505	7425	8525	10400	13300
Auto Trans				0	0	0	0

Body	Type	VIN	List	Trade-In Fair	Trade-In Good	Pvt-Party Good	Retail Excellent
Hard Top				550	550	735	735
MILLENIA—V6—Equipment Schedule 2							
W.B. 108.3"; 2.5 Liter.							
Sedan 4D		TA221	25445	5875	6850	8775	11550
MILLENIA—V6 Supercharged—Equipment Schedule 2							
W.B. 108.3"; 2.3 Liter.							
S Sedan 4D		TA222	30445	7775	8925	11000	14050
Millennium Edition				200	200	265	265

2001 MAZDA — (Jor1)(M1orYV)(BJ222)-1-#

Body	Type	VIN	List	Trade-In Fair	Trade-In Good	Pvt-Party Good	Retail Excellent
PROTEGE'—4-Cyl.—Equipment Schedule 6							
W.B. 102.8"; 1.6 Liter, 2.0 Liter.							
DX Sedan 4D		BJ222	14095	3900	4650	5925	7825
LX Sedan 4D		BJ222	14895	4250	5050	6300	8250
ES Sedan 4D		BJ225	16015	4675	5525	6825	8800
MP3 Sedan 4D		BJ227	18500	6375	7400	8800	11050
626—4-Cyl.—Equipment Schedule 4							
W.B. 105.1"; 2.0 Liter.							
LX Sedan 4D		GF22C	20015	4600	5425	7025	9375
ES Sedan 4D		GF22C	21415	5350	6250	7900	10300
Manual Trans				(550)	(550)	(735)	(735)
V6 2.5 Liter		D		600	600	800	800
MIATA MX-5—4-Cyl.—Equipment Schedule 6							
W.B. 89.2"; 1.8 Liter.							
Convertible 2D		NB353	21660	7775	8925	10600	13200
LS Convertible 2D		NB353	24410	8650	9900	11600	14350
SE Convertible 2D		NB353	26195	9025	10325	12050	14850
Auto Trans				0	0	0	0
Hard Top				575	575	765	765
MILLENIA—V6—Equipment Schedule 2							
W.B. 108.3"; 2.5 Liter.							
Sedan 4D		TA221	28505	6950	8050	10150	13150
MILLENIA—V6 Supercharged—Equipment Schedule 2							
W.B. 108.3"; 2.3 Liter.							
S Sedan 4D		TA222	31505	9100	10375	12600	15950

2002 MAZDA — (Jor1)(M1orYV)(BJ222)-2-#

Body	Type	VIN	List	Trade-In Fair	Trade-In Good	Pvt-Party Good	Retail Excellent
PROTEGE'—4-Cyl.—Equipment Schedule 6							
W.B. 102.8"; 2.0 Liter.							
DX Sedan 4D		BJ222	14530	4650	5500	6800	8800
LX Sedan 4D		BJ222	15335	5025	5875	7225	9275
ES Sedan 4D		BJ221	16060	5500	6400	7750	9850
PROTEGE'5—4-Cyl.—Equipment Schedule 6							
W.B. 102.8"; 2.0 Liter.							
Hatchback 4D		BJ245	16815	7525	8675	9750	11650
626—4-Cyl.—Equipment Schedule 4							
W.B. 105.1"; 2.0 Liter.							
LX Sedan 4D		GF22C	20015	5550	6450	8150	10650
ES Sedan 4D		GF22C	22915	6350	7350	9125	11700
Manual Trans				(575)	(575)	(765)	(765)
V6 2.5 Liter		D		650	650	865	865
MIATA MX-5—4-Cyl.—Equipment Schedule 6							
W.B. 89.2"; 1.8 Liter.							
Convertible 2D		NB353	21660	9050	10325	12100	14900
LS Convertible 2D		NB353	24410	9975	11325	13150	16050
SE Convertible 2D		NB353	26275	10425	11850	13700	16600
Auto Trans				0	0	0	0
Hard Top				600	600	800	800
MILLENIA—V6—Equipment Schedule 2							
W.B. 108.3"; 2.5 Liter.							
Sedan 4D		TA221	28505	8275	9475	11700	15000
MILLENIA—V6 Supercharged—Equipment Schedule 2							
W.B. 108.3"; 2.3 Liter.							
S Sedan 4D		TA222	31505	10600	12100	14450	18000

2003 MAZDA — (Jor1)(M1orYV)(BJ225)-3-#

Body	Type	VIN	List	Trade-In Fair	Trade-In Good	Pvt-Party Good	Retail Excellent
PROTEGE'—4-Cyl.—Equipment Schedule 6							
W.B. 102.8"; 2.0 Liter.							
DX Sedan 4D		BJ225	14690	5500	6400	7650	9650
LX Sedan 4D		BJ225	15575	5850	6825	8100	10150
ES Sedan 4D		BJ225	16300	6375	7375	8700	10800

Body Type	VIN	List	Trade-In Fair	Good	Pvt-Party Good	Retail Excellent
PROTEGE'5—4-Cyl.—Equipment Schedule 6						
W.B. 102.8"; 2.0 Liter.						
Hatchback 4D	BJ245	17055	**8600**	**9850**	**10850**	**12700**
PROTEGE'—4-Cyl. Turbo—Equipment Schedule 6						
W.B. 102.8"; 1.8 Liter.						
Mazdaspeed Sedan 4D	BJ227	20500				
6—4-Cyl.—Equipment Schedule 4						
W.B. 103.3"; 2.3 Liter.						
i Sedan 4D	FP80C	19900	**9750**	**11125**	**13250**	**16500**
Sport Pkg			300	300	400	400
Manual Trans			(600)	(600)	(800)	(800)
6—V6—Equipment Schedule 4						
W.B. 105.3"; 3.0 Liter.						
s Sedan 4D	FP80D	22520	**11275**	**12825**	**14600**	**17550**
Sport Pkg			300	300	400	400
Manual Trans			(600)	(600)	(800)	(800)
MIATA MX-5—4-Cyl.—Equipment Schedule 6						
W.B. 89.2"; 1.8 Liter.						
Club Sport Conv 2D	NB353	20000				
Convertible 2D	NB353	22125	**10475**	**11900**	**13700**	**16500**
Shinsen Conv 2D	NB353	23625				
LS Convertible 2D	NB353	24905	**11425**	**12950**	**14800**	**17750**
SE Convertible 2D	NB353	26550				
Auto Trans			0	0	0	0
Hard Top			625	625	835	835

Body Type	VIN	List	Trade-In Fair	Good	Pvt-Party Good	Retail Excellent
3—4-Cyl.—Equipment Schedule 6						
W.B. 103.9"; 2.0 Liter, 2.3 Liter.						
i Sedan 4D	BK12F	14200	**9325**	**10650**	**12200**	**14750**
s Sedan 4D	BK123	16925	**11000**	**12475**	**14100**	**16850**
s Hatchback 4D	BK143	17415	**11425**	**12950**	**14600**	**17400**
6—4-Cyl.—Equipment Schedule 4						
W.B. 105.3"; 2.3 Liter.						
i Sedan 4D	FP80C	20120	**11475**	**13000**	**15250**	**18800**
i Hatchback 4D	FP84C	22165				
Sport Pkg			300	300	400	400
Manual Trans			(625)	(625)	(835)	(835)
6—V6—Equipment Schedule 4						
W.B. 105.3"; 3.0 Liter.						
s Sedan 4D	FP80D	22765	**13100**	**14825**	**16750**	**19950**
s Hatchback 4D	FP84D	24315				
s Wagon 4D	FP82D	23645				
Sport Pkg			300	300	400	400
Manual Trans			(625)	(625)	(835)	(835)
MIATA MX-5—4-Cyl.—Equipment Schedule 6						
W.B. 89.2"; 1.8 Liter.						
Convertible 2D	NB353	22388	**12100**	**13725**	**15650**	**18750**
LS Convertible 2D	NB353	25193	**13100**	**14825**	**16800**	**20100**
Auto Trans			0	0	0	0
Hard Top			650	650	865	865
MIATA—4-Cyl. Turbo—Equipment Schedule 6						
W.B. 89.2"; 1.8 Liter.						
Mazdaspeed Conv	NB354	26020				
RX-8—Rotary—Equipment Schedule 3						
W.B. 106.4"; 1.3 Liter.						
Coupe 4D	FE173	25700	**16700**	**18775**	**21500**	**25700**
Sport Pkg			500	500	665	665
Touring Pkg			700	700	935	935
Grand Touring Pkg			1000	1000	1335	1335

MERCEDES-BENZ

Body Type	VIN	List	Trade-In Fair	Good	Pvt-Party Good	Retail Excellent
MERCEDES—6-Cyl.—Equipment Schedule 1						
W.B. 104.9", 110.2" (300E, 300TE); 2.6 Liter, 3.0 Liter.						
190E 2.6 Sedan 4D	DA29D	32750	1475	1950	3125	4775
300E 2.6 Sedan 4D	EA26D	40200	2275	2850	4200	6075
300TE Wagon 4D	EA90D	49900	3475	4175	5725	7925
300TE 4-M 4WD Wag 4D	ED90D	56500	4175	4975	6625	9000
Manual Trans			(200)	(200)	(265)	(265)

1990 MERCEDES-BENZ

Body	Type	VIN	List	Trade-In Fair	Good	Pvt-Party Good	Retail Excellent
MERCEDES—6-Cyl.—Equipment Schedule 1							
W.B. 99.0", 106.9" (CE), 110.2" (E), 115.6" (SE), 121.1" (SEL); 3.0L.							
300E 3.0 Sedan 4D		EA30D	46200	2700	3325	4750	6750
300E 4-M 4WD Sed 4D		ED30D	53300	3750	4500	6075	8325
300CE Coupe 2D		EA51D	56450	3300	3950	5500	7650
300SE Sedan 4D		CA24E	54050	3400	4100	5625	7800
300SEL Sedan 4D		CA25D	57900	3575	4275	5800	8025
300SL Roadster 2D		FA61E	74250	6100	7075	9850	13650
Manual Trans				(200)	(200)	(265)	(265)
MERCEDES—5-Cyl. Turbo Diesel—Equipment Schedule 1							
W.B. 110.2"; 2.5 Liter.							
300D Sedan 4D		EB28E	39950	2900	3550	5275	7675
Leather				100	100	135	135
MERCEDES—6-Cyl. Turbo Diesel—Equipment Schedule 1							
W.B. 115.6", 121.1" (SDL); 3.5 Liter.							
350SD Sedan 4D		CB34E	53200	4375	5150	7150	9900
350SDL Sedan 4D		CB35D	57050	4750	5575	7625	10500
MERCEDES—V8—Equipment Schedule 1							
W.B. 99.0", 112.2" (SEC), 121.1" (SEL); 4.2L, 5.0L, 5.6L.							
420SEL Sedan 4D		CA35E	63800	3725	4450	6300	8875
560SEL Sedan 4D		CA39E	75550	4350	5125	7125	9900
560SEC Coupe 2D		CA45E	83050	5525	6425	8650	11700
500SL Roadster 2D		FA66E	85050	8850	10125	13400	17850

1991 MERCEDES-BENZ — WDB(DA28D)–M–#

Body	Type	VIN	List	Trade-In Fair	Good	Pvt-Party Good	Retail Excellent
MERCEDES—4-Cyl.—Equipment Schedule 1							
W.B. 104.9"; 2.3 Liter.							
190E 2.3 Sedan 4D		DA28D	31260	1675	2200	3775	5875
Leather				100	100	135	135
Manual Trans				(200)	(200)	(265)	(265)
MERCEDES—6-Cyl.—Equipment Schedule 1							
W.B. 104.9", 110.2" (300E, 300TE): 2.6 Liter, 3.0 Liter.							
190E 2.6 Sedan 4D		DA29D	34050	1750	2275	3550	5350
300E 2.6 Sedan 4D		EA26D	41350	2700	3300	4775	6825
300TE Wagon 4D		EA90D	52000	4050	4825	6550	8975
300TE 4-M 4WD Wag 4D		ED90D	59370	4900	5725	7575	10200
Leather				100	100	135	135
Slip Control				100	100	135	135
Manual Trans				(200)	(200)	(265)	(265)
MERCEDES—6-Cyl.—Equipment Schedule 1							
W.B. 99.0", 106.9" (CE), 110.2" (E), 115.6" (SE), 121.1" (SEL); 3.0L.							
300E 3.0 Sedan 4D		EA30D	47550	3200	3875	5425	7600
300E 4-M 4WD Sed 4D		ED30D	55000	4400	5175	6950	9450
300CE Coupe 2D		EA51D	57700	3850	4575	6275	8675
300SE Sedan 4D		CA24D	54250	3975	4725	6425	8825
300SEL Sedan 4D		CA25D	58150	4175	4950	6675	9125
300SL Roadster 2D		FA61E	79350	9225	10500	13900	18550
Slip Control				100	100	135	135
Manual Trans				(200)	(200)	(265)	(265)
MERCEDES—5-Cyl. Turbo Diesel—Equipment Schedule 1							
W.B. 110.2"; 2.5 Liter.							
300D Sedan 4D		EB28D	41350	3425	4125	6050	8675
Leather				100	100	135	135
MERCEDES—6-Cyl. Turbo Diesel—Equipment Schedule 1							
W.B. 115.6", 121.1" (SDL); 3.5 Liter.							
350SD Sedan 4D		CB34D	54250	5100	5975	8200	11300
350SDL Sedan 4D		CB35D	58150	5550	6450	8750	11950
MERCEDES—V8—Equipment Schedule 1							
W.B. 99.0", 112.2" (SEC), 121.1" (SEL); 4.2L, 5.0L, 5.6L.							
420SEL Sedan 4D		CA35E	64800	4325	5100	7125	9925
560SEL Sedan 4D		CA39E	76750	5050	5900	8050	11050
560SEC Coupe 2D		CA45E	84550	6375	7375	9800	13100
500SL Roadster 2D		FA66E	90700	9425	10750	14250	19000
Slip Control				100	100	135	135

1992 MERCEDES-BENZ — WDB(DA28D)–N–#

Body	Type	VIN	List	Trade-In Fair	Good	Pvt-Party Good	Retail Excellent
MERCEDES—4-Cyl.—Equipment Schedule 1							
W.B. 104.9"; 2.3 Liter.							
190E 2.3 Sedan 4D		DA28D	30200	1900	2425	4100	6325
Leather				100	100	135	135
Manual Trans				(250)	(250)	(335)	(335)
MERCEDES—5-Cyl. Turbo Diesel—Equipment Schedule 1							
W.B. 110.2"; 2.5 Liter.							

Body	Type	VIN	List	Trade-In Fair	Trade-In Good	Pvt-Party Good	Retail Excellent
300D Sedan 4D		EB28D	43300	**3900**	**4625**	**6675**	**9450**
Leather				**100**	**100**	**135**	**135**

MERCEDES—6-Cyl.—Equipment Schedule 1
W.B. 104.9", 110.2" (300E, 300TE); 2.6 Liter, 3.0 Liter.

Body	Type	VIN	List	Trade-In Fair	Trade-In Good	Pvt-Party Good	Retail Excellent
190E 2.6 Sedan 4D		DA29D	35250	**2100**	**2650**	**3975**	**5875**
300E 2.6 Sedan 4D		EA26D	43300	**3225**	**3900**	**5425**	**7600**
300TE Wagon 4D		EA90D	55250	**4850**	**5700**	**7500**	**10150**
300TE 4-M 4WD Wag 4D		ED90D	61450	**5750**	**6700**	**8700**	**11500**
Leather				**100**	**100**	**135**	**135**
Slip Control				**125**	**125**	**165**	**165**
Manual Trans				**(250)**	**(250)**	**(335)**	**(335)**

MERCEDES—6-Cyl.—Equipment Schedule 1
W.B. 99.0", 106.9" (CE), 110.2" (E), 119.7" (SE); 3.0 Liter.

Body	Type	VIN	List	Trade-In Fair	Trade-In Good	Pvt-Party Good	Retail Excellent
300E 3.0 Sedan 4D		EA30D	49850	**3800**	**4525**	**6175**	**8500**
300E 4-M 4WD Sed 4D		ED30D	58450	**5050**	**5925**	**7775**	**10400**
300CE Coupe 2D		EA51D	60750	**4750**	**5600**	**7450**	**10050**
300SE Sedan 4D		GA32D	71850	**7900**	**9075**	**11400**	**14750**
300SL Roadster 2D		FA61E	84850	**9325**	**10650**	**14100**	**18850**
Slip Control				**125**	**125**	**165**	**165**
Manual Trans				**(250)**	**(250)**	**(335)**	**(335)**

MERCEDES—6-Cyl. Turbo Diesel—Equipment Schedule 1
W.B. 119.7"; 3.5 Liter.

Body	Type	VIN	List	Trade-In Fair	Trade-In Good	Pvt-Party Good	Retail Excellent
300SD Sedan 4D		GB34E	69750	**7950**	**9125**	**11850**	**15650**

MERCEDES—V8—Equipment Schedule 1
W.B. 99.0", 110.2" (E), 119.7" (SE), 123.6" (SEL); 4.2L, 5.0L.

Body	Type	VIN	List	Trade-In Fair	Trade-In Good	Pvt-Party Good	Retail Excellent
400E Sedan 4D		EA34E	56150	**4600**	**5450**	**7100**	**9525**
400SE Sedan 4D		GA42D	78250	**7850**	**9025**	**11250**	**14450**
500E Sedan 4D		EA36E	82150	**10500**	**11950**	**14600**	**18500**
500SEL Sedan 4D		GA51E	96850	**8700**	**9925**	**12300**	**15700**
500SL Roadster 2D		FA66E	99950	**10275**	**11675**	**15300**	**20400**
Slip Control (400)				**125**	**125**	**165**	**165**

MERCEDES—V12—Equipment Schedule 1
W.B. 123.6"; 6.0 Liter.

Body	Type	VIN	List	Trade-In Fair	Trade-In Good	Pvt-Party Good	Retail Excellent
600SEL Sedan 4D		GA57E	132650	**7125**	**8225**	**10950**	**14750**

1993 MERCEDES-BENZ — WDB(DA28D)–P–#

MERCEDES—4-Cyl.—Equipment Schedule 1
W.B. 104.9"; 2.3 Liter.

Body	Type	VIN	List	Trade-In Fair	Trade-In Good	Pvt-Party Good	Retail Excellent
190E 2.3 Sedan 4D		DA28D	33930	**2175**	**2750**	**4550**	**6975**
Leather				**100**	**100**	**135**	**135**
Manual Trans				**(300)**	**(300)**	**(400)**	**(400)**

MERCEDES—5-Cyl. Turbo Diesel—Equipment Schedule 1
W.B. 110.2"; 2.5 Liter.

Body	Type	VIN	List	Trade-In Fair	Trade-In Good	Pvt-Party Good	Retail Excellent
300D Sedan 4D		EB28E	46115	**4600**	**5450**	**7650**	**10700**
Leather				**100**	**100**	**135**	**135**

MERCEDES—6-Cyl.—Equipment Schedule 1
W.B. 104.9", 110.2 (300E, 300TE); 2.6L, 2.8L, 3.0L, 3.2L.

Body	Type	VIN	List	Trade-In Fair	Trade-In Good	Pvt-Party Good	Retail Excellent
190E 2.6 Sedan 4D		DA29D	36865	**2475**	**3075**	**4500**	**6550**
300E 2.8 Sedan 4D		EA28E	46115	**3800**	**4525**	**6200**	**8525**
300TE Wagon 4D		EA92E	56365	**5700**	**6625**	**8600**	**11400**
300TE 4-M 4WD Wag 4D		ED90D	63100	**6675**	**7725**	**9850**	**12850**
Leather				**100**	**100**	**135**	**135**
Slip Control				**150**	**150**	**200**	**200**
Manual Trans				**(300)**	**(300)**	**(400)**	**(400)**

MERCEDES—6-Cyl.—Equipment Schedule 1
W.B. 99.0", 106.9" (CE), 110.2" (E), 119.7" (SE); 3.0 Liter, 3.2 Liter.

Body	Type	VIN	List	Trade-In Fair	Trade-In Good	Pvt-Party Good	Retail Excellent
300E 3.2 Sedan 4D		EA32E	50300	**4475**	**5250**	**7025**	**9525**
300E 4-M 4WD Sed 4D		ED32D	59100	**5775**	**6725**	**8700**	**11500**
300CE Coupe 2D		EA52E	61400	**5750**	**6700**	**8700**	**11500**
300CE Cabriolet 2D		EA66E	76900	**13000**	**14725**	**17800**	**22400**
300SE Sedan 4D		GA32E	72000	**8800**	**10075**	**12500**	**16050**
300SL Roadster 2D		FA61E	85800	**9550**	**10900**	**14500**	**19400**
Slip Control				**150**	**150**	**200**	**200**
Manual Trans				**(300)**	**(300)**	**(400)**	**(400)**

MERCEDES—6-Cyl. Turbo Diesel—Equipment Schedule 1
W.B. 119.7"; 3.5 Liter.

Body	Type	VIN	List	Trade-In Fair	Trade-In Good	Pvt-Party Good	Retail Excellent
300SD Sedan 4D		GB34E	70300	**9175**	**10475**	**13400**	**17500**

MERCEDES—V8—Equipment Schedule 1
W.B. 110.2" (E), 115.9" (SEC), 123.6" (SEL); 4.2L, 5.0L.

Body	Type	VIN	List	Trade-In Fair	Trade-In Good	Pvt-Party Good	Retail Excellent
400E Sedan 4D		EA34E	56800	**4950**	**5800**	**7925**	**10850**
400SEL Sedan 4D		GA43E	81200	**8575**	**9800**	**12500**	**16250**
500E Sedan 4D		EA36E	81700	**11475**	**13050**	**16200**	**20700**
500SEL Sedan 4D		GA51E	97800	**9325**	**10650**	**13450**	**17400**

Body	Type	VIN	List	Trade-In Fair	Good	Pvt-Party Good	Retail Excellent
500SEC Coupe 2D		GA70E	102300	13100	14825	18200	23000
500SL Roadster 2D		FA67E	100200	11125	12625	16500	21900
Slip Control (400)				150	150	200	200

MERCEDES—V12—Equipment Schedule 1
W.B. 99.0", 115.9" (SEC), 123.6" (SEL); 6.0 Liter.

Body	Type	VIN	List	Trade-In Fair	Good	Pvt-Party Good	Retail Excellent
600SEL Sedan 4D		GA57E	133100	8125	9325	12300	16300
600SEC Coupe 2D		GA76E	136100	10125	11525	14850	19400
600SL Roadster 2D		FA72E	132900	11275	12825	16700	22100

1994 MERCEDES-BENZ — WDB(HA22E)–R–#

C-CLASS—4-Cyl.—Equipment Schedule 1
W.B. 105.9"; 2.2 Liter.

Body	Type	VIN	List	Trade-In Fair	Good	Pvt-Party Good	Retail Excellent
C220 Sedan 4D		HA22E	31085	3875	4600	6625	9375

C-CLASS—6-Cyl.—Equipment Schedule 1
W.B. 105.9"; 2.8 Liter.

C280 Sedan 4D		HA28E	37105	4000	4750	6900	9850
Slip Control				175	175	235	235

E-CLASS—6-Cyl.—Equipment Schedule 1
W.B. 106.9", 110.2" (4D); 3.2 Liter.

E320 Sedan 4D		EA32E	42975	4725	5550	7825	10950
E320 Coupe 2D		EA52E	62075	6600	7625	10200	13800
E320 Cabriolet 2D		EA66E	77775	14400	16275	19950	25200
E320 Wagon 4D		EA92E	46675	6500	7500	10050	13550
Slip Control				175	175	235	235
Sport Pkg				300	300	400	400

E-CLASS—V8—Equipment Schedule 1
W.B. 110.2"; 4.2 Liter.

E420 Sedan 4D		EA34E	51475	6050	7000	9350	12600
Slip Control				175	175	235	235

S-CLASS—6-Cyl.—Equipment Schedule 1
W.B. 119.7"; 3.2 Liter.

S320 Sedan 4D		GA32E	71075	8100	9300	12050	15950
Slip Control				175	175	235	235

S-CLASS—6-Cyl. Turbo Diesel—Equipment Schedule 1
W.B. 119.7"; 3.5 Liter.

S350D Sedan 4D		GB34E	71075	10475	11900	15000	19400

S-CLASS—V8—Equipment Schedule 1
W.B. 115.9", 123.6" (S420, S500 4D); 4.2 Liter, 5.0 Liter.

S420 Sedan 4D		GA43E	81675	9550	10900	14000	18350
S500 Sedan 4D		GA51E	97875	10275	11675	14900	19400
S500 Coupe 2D		GA70E	102375	14400	16225	20100	25400
Slip Control				175	175	235	235

S-CLASS—V12—Equipment Schedule 1
W.B. 115.9", 123.6" (4D); 6.0 Liter.

S600 Sedan 4D		GA57E	134475	9375	10700	13850	18300
S600 Coupe 2D		GA76E	136775	11675	13200	16700	21600

SL-CLASS—6-Cyl.—Equipment Schedule 1
W.B. 99.0"; 3.2 Liter.

SL320 Roadster 2D		FA63E	85675	9975	11375	15150	20300
Slip Control				175	175	235	235

SL-CLASS—V8—Equipment Schedule 1
W.B. 99.0"; 5.0 Liter.

SL500 Roadster 2D		FA67E	101275	12250	13875	18000	23700

SL-CLASS—V12—Equipment Schedule 1
W.B. 99.0"; 6.0 Liter.

SL600 Roadster 2D		FA76E	123575	12325	13975	18050	23700

1995 MERCEDES-BENZ — WDB(HA22E)–S–#

C-CLASS—4-Cyl.—Equipment Schedule 1
W.B. 105.9"; 2.2 Liter.

C220 Sedan 4D		HA22E	32000	4450	5225	7400	10350
Traction Control				200	200	265	265

C-CLASS—6-Cyl.—Equipment Schedule 1
W.B. 105.9"; 2.8 Liter, 3.6 Liter.

C280 Sedan 4D		HA28E	38400	4725	5550	7925	11150
C36 Sedan 4D		HM36E	50500	8125	9325	12200	16150
Slip Control				200	200	265	265

E-CLASS—6-Cyl.—Equipment Schedule 1
W.B. 106.9", 110.2" (4D); 3.2 Liter.

E320 Sedan 4D		EA32E	43975	5525	6425	8900	12300
E320 Coupe 2D		EA52E	63475	7725	8875	11650	15550
E320 Cabriolet 2D		EA66E	79475	16275	18325	22300	27900
E320 Wagon 4D		EA92E	49600	7475	8600	11350	15100

Body	Type	VIN	List	Trade-In Fair	Trade-In Good	Pvt-Party Good	Retail Excellent
	Slip Control			200	200	265	265
	Sport Pkg			325	325	435	435
E-CLASS—6-Cyl. Diesel—Equipment Schedule 1							
W.B. 110.2"; 3.0 Liter.							
E300D Sedan 4D		EB31E	43100	6375	7375	9975	13600
E-CLASS—V8—Equipment Schedule 1							
W.B. 110.2"; 4.2 Liter.							
E420 Sedan 4D		EA34E	52975	5650	6550	9300	13000
	Slip Control			200	200	265	265
S-CLASS—6-Cyl.—Equipment Schedule 1							
W.B. 119.7", 123.6" (LWB); 3.2 Liter.							
S320 SWB Sedan 4D		GA32E	63175	8850	10125	13000	17100
S320 LWB Sedan 4D		GA33E	66375	9175	10475	13450	17600
	Slip Control			200	200	265	265
S-CLASS—6-Cyl. Turbo Diesel—Equipment Schedule 1							
W.B. 119.7"; 3.5 Liter.							
S350D Sedan 4D		GB34E	66375	11850	13450	16750	21500
S-CLASS—V8—Equipment Schedule 1							
W.B. 115.9", 123.6" (4D); 4.2 Liter, 5.0 Liter.							
S420 Sedan 4D		GA43E	76075	9100	10375	13400	17600
S500 Sedan 4D		GA51E	89675	10275	11675	15200	20100
S500 Coupe 2D		GA70E	94075	14775	16700	20800	26600
S-CLASS—V12—Equipment Schedule 1							
W.B. 115.9", 123.6" (4D); 6.0 Liter.							
S600 Sedan 4D		GA57E	133775	10800	12250	15700	20400
S600 Coupe 2D		GA76E	136775	13300	15025	18800	24200
SL-CLASS—6-Cyl.—Equipment Schedule 1							
W.B. 99.0"; 3.2 Liter.							
SL320 Roadster 2D		FA63E	78775	11525	13150	16300	20900
	Slip Control			200	200	265	265
SL-CLASS—V8—Equipment Schedule 1							
W.B. 99.0"; 5.0 Liter.							
SL500 Roadster 2D		FA67E	91675	13775	15550	19050	24100
SL-CLASS—V12—Equipment Schedule 1							
W.B. 99.0"; 6.0 Liter.							
SL600 Roadster 2D		FA76E	123175	14400	16275	19850	25100

1996 MERCEDES-BENZ — WDB(HA22E)-T-#

Body	Type	VIN	List	Trade-In Fair	Trade-In Good	Pvt-Party Good	Retail Excellent
C-CLASS—4-Cyl.—Equipment Schedule 1							
W.B. 105.9"; 2.2 Liter.							
C220 Sedan 4D		HA22E	33055	5100	5975	8325	11500
	Traction Control			225	225	300	300
C-CLASS—6-Cyl.—Equipment Schedule 1							
W.B. 105.9"; 2.8 Liter, 3.6 Liter.							
C280 Sedan 4D		HA28E	37815	5375	6300	8575	11700
C36 Sedan 4D		HM36E	51595	8875	10175	12900	16800
	Slip Control			225	225	300	300
	Sport Pkg			350	350	465	465
E-CLASS—6-Cyl.—Equipment Schedule 1							
W.B. 111.5"; 3.2 Liter.							
E320 Sedan 4D		JF55F	45165	8350	9575	12250	16050
	Slip Control			225	225	300	300
E-CLASS—6-Cyl. Diesel—Equipment Schedule 1							
W.B. 111.5"; 3.0 Liter.							
E300D Sedan 4D		JF20F	42465	8650	9900	12800	16900
S-CLASS—6-Cyl.—Equipment Schedule 1							
W.B. 119.2", 123.6" (LWB); 3.2 Liter.							
S320 SWB Sedan 4D		GA32E	63295	9700	11100	13900	17950
S320 LWB Sedan 4D		GA33E	66495	9975	11325	14200	18300
	Slip Control			225	225	300	300
S-CLASS—V8—Equipment Schedule 1							
W.B. 115.9", 123.6" (4D); 4.2 Liter, 5.0 Liter.							
S420 Sedan 4D		GA43E	74495	10750	12200	15500	20200
S500 Sedan 4D		GA51E	88095	11900	13500	17300	22600
S500 Coupe 2D		GA70E	92495	16750	18875	23300	29600
S-CLASS—V12—Equipment Schedule 1							
W.B. 115.9", 123.6" (4D); 6.0 Liter.							
S600 Sedan 4D		GA57E	130895	12475	14100	17900	23100
S600 Coupe 2D		GA76E	133895	15300	17225	21300	27200
SL-CLASS—6-Cyl.—Equipment Schedule 1							
W.B. 99.0"; 3.2 Liter.							
SL320 Roadster 2D		FA63F	78895	12875	14550	17850	22700
	Slip Control			225	225	300	300

Body	Type	VIN	List	Trade-In Fair	Good	Pvt-Party Good	Retail Excellent
Sport Pkg			....	1475	1475	1965	1965

SL-CLASS—V8—Equipment Schedule 1
W.B. 99.0"; 5.0 Liter.

| SL500 Roadster 2D | | FA67F | 90495 | 15600 | 17575 | 21200 | 26600 |
| Sport Pkg | | | | 1475 | 1475 | 1965 | 1965 |

SL-CLASS—V12—Equipment Schedule 1
W.B. 99.0"; 6.0 Liter.

| SL600 Roadster 2D | | FA76F | 122595 | 16275 | 18325 | 22100 | 27600 |
| Sport Pkg | | | | 1475 | 1475 | 1965 | 1965 |

1997 MERCEDES-BENZ — WDB(HA23E)-V-#

C-CLASS—4-Cyl.—Equipment Schedule 1
W.B. 105.9"; 2.3 Liter.

| C230 Sedan 4D | | HA23E | 33235 | 5575 | 6475 | 8900 | 12250 |
| Traction Control | | | | 275 | 275 | 365 | 365 |

C-CLASS—6-Cyl.—Equipment Schedule 1
W.B. 105.9"; 2.8 Liter, 3.6 Liter.

C280 Sedan 4D		HA28E	37985	6100	7075	9525	12900
C36 Sedan 4D		HM36E	52520	10175	11575	14500	18650
Slip Control				275	275	365	365
Sport Pkg				375	375	500	500

E-CLASS—6-Cyl.—Equipment Schedule 1
W.B. 111.5"; 3.2 Liter.

| E320 Sedan 4D | | JF55F | 46485 | 9600 | 10950 | 13800 | 17800 |
| Slip Control | | | | 275 | 275 | 365 | 365 |

E-CLASS—6-Cyl. Diesel—Equipment Schedule 1
W.B. 111.5"; 3.0 Liter.

| E300D Sedan 4D | | JF20F | 42475 | 9900 | 11225 | 14450 | 18850 |

E-CLASS—V8—Equipment Schedule 1
W.B. 111.5"; 4.2 Liter.

| E420 Sedan 4D | | JF72F | 51585 | 10550 | 12000 | 15650 | 20600 |
| Sport Pkg | | | | 625 | 625 | 835 | 835 |

S-CLASS—6-Cyl.—Equipment Schedule 1
W.B. 119.7", 123.6" (LWB); 3.2 Liter.

S320 SWB Sedan 4D		GA32G	63895	11050	12525	15550	19850
S320 LWB Sedan 4D		GA33G	67195	11275	12825	15850	20200
Slip Control				275	275	365	365

S-CLASS—V8—Equipment Schedule 1
W.B. 115.9", 123.6" (4D); 4.2 Liter, 5.0 Liter.

S420 Sedan 4D		GA43G	75795	12725	14400	17950	22900
S500 Sedan 4D		GA51G	89795	13875	15700	19800	25400
S500 Coupe 2D		GA70G	93795	19100	21400	26100	32800

S-CLASS—V12—Equipment Schedule 1
W.B. 115.9", 123.6" (4D); 6.0 Liter.

| S600 Sedan 4D | | GA57G | 133895 | 14400 | 16275 | 20400 | 26100 |
| S600 Coupe 2D | | GA76G | 136495 | 17525 | 19675 | 24100 | 30400 |

SL-CLASS—6-Cyl.—Equipment Schedule 1
W.B. 99.0"; 3.2 Liter.

SL320 Roadster 2D		FA63F	80195	14400	16275	19800	24900
Slip Control				275	275	365	365
Sport Pkg				1450	1450	1935	1935

SL-CLASS—V8—Equipment Schedule 1
W.B. 99.0"; 5.0 Liter.

| SL500 Roadster 2D | | FA67F | 91795 | 17675 | 19875 | 23800 | 29600 |
| Sport Pkg | | | | 625 | 625 | 835 | 835 |

SL-CLASS—V12—Equipment Schedule 1
W.B. 99.0"; 6.0 Liter.

| SL600 Roadster 2D | | FA76F | 125895 | 18525 | 20825 | 24700 | 30500 |
| Sport Pkg | | | | 1600 | 1600 | 2135 | 2135 |

1998 MERCEDES-BENZ — WDB(KK47F)-W-#

SLK-CLASS—4-Cyl. Supercharged—Equipment Schedule 1
W.B. 94.5"; 2.3 Liter.

| SLK230 Roadster 2D | | KK47F | 40295 | 10275 | 11675 | 14400 | 18400 |

C-CLASS—4-Cyl.—Equipment Schedule 1
W.B. 105.9" 2.3 Liter.

| C230 Sedan 4D | | HA23G | 33235 | 6675 | 7725 | 10150 | 13550 |
| Slip Control | | | | 300 | 300 | 400 | 400 |

C-CLASS—V6—Equipment Schedule 1
W.B. 105.9"; 2.8 Liter.

| C280 Sedan 4D | | HA29G | 37985 | 7075 | 8150 | 10550 | 13900 |
| Sport Pkg | | | | 425 | 425 | 565 | 565 |

Body	Type	VIN	List	Trade-In Fair	Good	Pvt-Party Good	Retail Excellent
C-CLASS—V8—Equipment Schedule 1							
W.B. 105.9"; 4.3 Liter.							
C43 Sedan 4D		HA33G	53345	**13350**	**15075**	**18000**	**22400**
CLK-CLASS—V6—Equipment Schedule 1							
W.B. 105.9"; 3.2 Liter.							
CLK320 Coupe 2D		LJ65G	41555	**11175**	**12675**	**15250**	**19150**
E-CLASS—V6—Equipment Schedule 1							
W.B. 111.5"; 3.2 Liter.							
E320 Sedan 4D		JF65F	47205	**11125**	**12625**	**15400**	**19500**
E320 4Matic Sedan 4D		JF82F	49955	**12000**	**13575**	**16400**	**20600**
E320 Wagon 4D		JH65F	49900	**11850**	**13450**	**16250**	**20400**
E320 4Matic Wagon 4D		JH82F	52650	**12675**	**14350**	**17300**	**21600**
E-CLASS—6-Cyl. Turbo Diesel—Equipment Schedule 1							
W.B. 111.5"; 3.0 Liter.							
E300TD Sedan 4D		JF25F	45200	**12950**	**14650**	**17900**	**22700**
E-CLASS—V8—Equipment Schedule 1							
W.B. 111.5"; 4.3 Liter.							
E430 Sedan 4D		JF70F	52305	**12525**	**14150**	**17600**	**22600**
Sport Pkg				**650**	**650**	**865**	**865**
CL-CLASS—V8—Equipment Schedule 1							
W.B. 115.9"; 5.0 Liter.							
CL500 Coupe 2D		GA70G	92495	**21700**	**24375**	**28900**	**35500**
CL-CLASS—V12—Equipment Schedule 1							
W.B. 115.9"; 6.0 Liter.							
CL600 Coupe 2D		GA76G	135895	**20075**	**22550**	**26900**	**33200**
S-CLASS—6-Cyl.—Equipment Schedule 1							
W.B. 119.7", 123.6" (LWB); 3.2 Liter.							
S320 SWB Sedan 4D		GA32G	64595	**12675**	**14350**	**17300**	**21600**
S320 LWB Sedan 4D		GA33G	67895	**12950**	**14700**	**17600**	**22000**
S-CLASS—V8—Equipment Schedule 1							
W.B. 123.6"; 4.2 Liter, 5.0 Liter.							
S420 Sedan 4D		GA43G	75795	**14825**	**16700**	**20200**	**25200**
S500 Sedan 4D		GA51G	89795	**16025**	**18050**	**22000**	**27700**
S-CLASS—V12—Equipment Schedule 1							
W.B. 123.6"; 6.0 Liter.							
S600 Sedan 4D		GA57G	135845	**16700**	**18775**	**22800**	**28600**
SL-CLASS—V8—Equipment Schedule 1							
W.B. 99.0"; 5.0 Liter.							
SL500 Roadster 2D		FA67F	81495	**20150**	**22650**	**26300**	**32000**
Sport Pkg				**1650**	**1650**	**2200**	**2200**
SL-CLASS—V12—Equipment Schedule 1							
W.B. 99.0"; 6.0 Liter.							
SL600 Roadster 2D		FA76F	127695	**21125**	**23700**	**27500**	**33300**
Sport Pkg				**1650**	**1650**	**2200**	**2200**

Body	Type	VIN	List	Trade-In Fair	Good	Pvt-Party Good	Retail Excellent
SLK-CLASS—4-Cyl. Supercharged—Equipment Schedule 1							
W.B. 94.5"; 2.3 Liter.							
SLK230 Roadster 2D		KK47F	41495	**13000**	**14725**	**17350**	**21300**
Sport Pkg				**725**	**725**	**965**	**965**
Manual Trans				**(500)**	**(500)**	**(665)**	**(665)**
C-CLASS—4-Cyl. Supercharged—Equipment Schedule 1							
W.B. 105.9"; 2.3 Liter.							
C230 Sedan 4D		HA24G	34795	**9025**	**10325**	**12600**	**15950**
Sport Pkg				**500**	**500**	**665**	**665**
C-CLASS—V6—Equipment Schedule 1							
W.B. 105.9"; 2.8 Liter.							
C280 Sedan 4D		HA29G	38630	**8400**	**9600**	**12200**	**15850**
Sport Pkg				**500**	**500**	**665**	**665**
C-CLASS—V8—Equipment Schedule 1							
W.B. 105.9"; 4.3 Liter.							
C43 Sedan 4D		HA33G	53595	**14550**	**16425**	**19700**	**24600**
CLK-CLASS—V6—Equipment Schedule 1							
W.B. 105.9"; 3.2 Liter.							
CLK320 Coupe 2D		LJ65G	42485	**13250**	**14925**	**17750**	**22000**
CLK320 Cabriolet 2D		LK65G	47795	**17850**	**20075**	**23200**	**28200**
CLK-CLASS—V8—Equipment Schedule 1							
W.B. 105.9"; 4.3 Liter.							
CLK430 Coupe 2D		LJ70G	49785	**13925**	**15750**	**19400**	**24600**
E-CLASS—V6—Equipment Schedule 1							
W.B. 111.5"; 3.2 Liter.							
E320 Sedan 4D		JF65F	47905	**13200**	**14875**	**17850**	**22300**
E320 AWD Sedan 4D		JF82F	50695	**14150**	**15975**	**19050**	**23600**

Body	Type	VIN	List	Trade-In Fair	Good	Pvt-Party Good	Retail Excellent
E320 Wagon 4D		JH65F	48905	14025	15800	18850	23400
E320 AWD Wagon 4D		JH82F	51695	14975	16850	19950	24700

E-CLASS—6-Cyl. Turbo Diesel—Equipment Schedule 1
W.B. 111.5"; 3.0 Liter.

Body	Type	VIN	List	Trade-In Fair	Good	Pvt-Party Good	Retail Excellent
E300TD Sedan 4D		JF25F	45430	15025	16900	20400	25500

E-CLASS—V8—Equipment Schedule 1
W.B. 111.5"; 4.3 Liter, 5.5 Liter.

Body	Type	VIN	List	Trade-In Fair	Good	Pvt-Party Good	Retail Excellent
E430 Sedan 4D		JF70F	53005	13525	15275	19000	24300
E55 Sedan 4D		JF744	69695	20250	22650	27200	33600
Sport Pkg (E430)				725	725	965	965

CL-CLASS—V8—Equipment Schedule 1
W.B. 115.9"; 5.0 Liter.

Body	Type	VIN	List	Trade-In Fair	Good	Pvt-Party Good	Retail Excellent
CL500 Coupe 2D		GA70G	93795	24200	27075	31900	39000

CL-CLASS—V12—Equipment Schedule 1
W.B. 115.9"; 6.0 Liter.

Body	Type	VIN	List	Trade-In Fair	Good	Pvt-Party Good	Retail Excellent
CL600 Coupe 2D		GA76G	140495	23325	26100	30700	37700

S-CLASS—6-Cyl.—Equipment Schedule 1
W.B. 119.7", 123.6" (LWB); 3.2 Liter.

Body	Type	VIN	List	Trade-In Fair	Good	Pvt-Party Good	Retail Excellent
S320 SWB Sedan 4D		GA32G	65345	15125	17050	20200	24900
S320 LWB Sedan 4D		GA33G	68595	15600	17575	20700	25500

S-CLASS—V8—Equipment Schedule 1
W.B. 123.6"; 4.2 Liter, 5.0 Liter.

Body	Type	VIN	List	Trade-In Fair	Good	Pvt-Party Good	Retail Excellent
S420 Sedan 4D		GA43G	75795	16375	18425	22200	27600
S500 Sedan 4D		GA51G	89795	18000	20250	24500	30600
Grand Edition (S500)				250	250	335	335

S-CLASS—V12—Equipment Schedule 1
W.B. 123.6"; 6.0 Liter.

Body	Type	VIN	List	Trade-In Fair	Good	Pvt-Party Good	Retail Excellent
S600 Sedan 4D		GA57G	137845	19400	21800	26200	32500

SL-CLASS—V8—Equipment Schedule 1
W.B. 99.0"; 5.0 Liter.

Body	Type	VIN	List	Trade-In Fair	Good	Pvt-Party Good	Retail Excellent
SL500 Roadster 2D		FA68F	82695	22850	25625	29600	35600
Sport Pkg				1700	1700	2265	2265

SL-CLASS—V12—Equipment Schedule 1
W.B. 99.0"; 6.0 Liter.

Body	Type	VIN	List	Trade-In Fair	Good	Pvt-Party Good	Retail Excellent
SL600 Roadster 2D		FA76F	130095	24775	27750	31900	38200
Sport Pkg				1700	1700	2265	2265

SLK-CLASS—4-Cyl. Supercharged—Equipment Schedule 1
W.B. 94.5"; 2.3 Liter.

Body	Type	VIN	List	Trade-In Fair	Good	Pvt-Party Good	Retail Excellent
SLK230 Roadster 2D		KK47F	42495	15225	17125	19800	23900
Sport Pkg				800	800	1065	1065
designo Edition				475	475	635	635
Manual Trans				(500)	(500)	(665)	(665)

C-CLASS—4-Cyl. Supercharged—Equipment Schedule 1
W.B. 105.9"; 2.3 Liter.

Body	Type	VIN	List	Trade-In Fair	Good	Pvt-Party Good	Retail Excellent
C230 Sedan 4D		HA24G	34820	10750	12200	14550	18050
Sport Pkg				550	550	735	735

C-CLASS—V6—Equipment Schedule 1
W.B. 105.9"; 2.8 Liter.

Body	Type	VIN	List	Trade-In Fair	Good	Pvt-Party Good	Retail Excellent
C280 Sedan 4D		HA29G	39020	9975	11375	14150	18200
Sport Pkg				550	550	735	735

C-CLASS—V8—Equipment Schedule 1
W.B. 105.9"; 4.3 Liter.

Body	Type	VIN	List	Trade-In Fair	Good	Pvt-Party Good	Retail Excellent
C43 Sedan 4D		HA33G	53595	18525	20825	23900	28800

CLK-CLASS—V6—Equipment Schedule 1
W.B. 105.9"; 3.2 Liter.

Body	Type	VIN	List	Trade-In Fair	Good	Pvt-Party Good	Retail Excellent
CLK320 Coupe 2D		LJ65G	43505	15550	17525	20400	25100
CLK320 Cabriolet 2D		LK65G	48695	20650	23125	26600	32000
designo Edition				475	475	635	635

CLK-CLASS—V8—Equipment Schedule 1
W.B. 105.9"; 4.3 Liter.

Body	Type	VIN	List	Trade-In Fair	Good	Pvt-Party Good	Retail Excellent
CLK430 Coupe 2D		LJ70G	51005	18100	20350	23700	28800
CLK430 Cabriolet 2D		LK70G	56195	23325	26100	29000	34000
designo Edition				475	475	635	635

E-CLASS—V6—Equipment Schedule 1
W.B. 111.5"; 3.2 Liter.

Body	Type	VIN	List	Trade-In Fair	Good	Pvt-Party Good	Retail Excellent
E320 Sedan 4D		JF65G	48825	15500	17475	20700	25500
E320 AWD Sedan 4D		JF82G	51625	16600	18675	22000	26900
E320 Wagon 4D		JH65F	49675	16475	18525	21800	26700
E320 AWD Wagon 4D		JH82F	52475	17525	19675	23000	28100
designo Edition				475	475	635	635

Body	Type	VIN	List	Trade-In Fair	Trade-In Good	Pvt-Party Good	Retail Excellent
E-CLASS—V8—Equipment Schedule 1							
W.B. 111.5"; 4.3 Liter, 5.5 Liter.							
E430 Sedan 4D		JF70G	54175	17375	19500	22900	28100
E430 AWD Sedan 4D		JF83G	56975	17625	19775	23300	28700
E55 Sedan 4D		JF74G	71395	25250	28225	32400	38800
Sport Pkg (E430)				800	800	1065	1065
designo Edition				475	475	635	635
CL-CLASS—V8—Equipment Schedule 1							
W.B. 113.6"; 5.0 Liter.							
CL500 Coupe 2D		PJ75J	87145	38200	42625	47200	55100
S-CLASS—V8—Equipment Schedule 1							
W.B. 121.5"; 4.3 Liter, 5.0 Liter.							
S430 Sedan 4D		NG70J	70295	25150	28125	32200	38000
S500 Sedan 4D		NG75J	79445	28425	31775	36100	42900
Sport Pkg				1750	1750	2335	2335
designo Edition				900	900	1200	1200
SL-CLASS—V8—Equipment Schedule 1							
W.B. 99.0"; 5.0 Liter.							
SL500 Roadster 2D		FA68F	84195	26200	29275	33400	39800
Sport Pkg				1750	1750	2335	2335
designo Edition				900	900	1200	1200
SL-CLASS—V12—Equipment Schedule 1							
W.B. 99.0"; 6.0 Liter.							
SL600 Roadster 2D		FA76F	132145	29000	32350	36700	43600
Sport Pkg				1750	1750	2335	2335
designo Edition				900	900	1200	1200

2001 MERCEDES-BENZ — WDB(KK49F)-1-#

Body	Type	VIN	List	Trade-In Fair	Trade-In Good	Pvt-Party Good	Retail Excellent
SLK-CLASS—4-Cyl. Supercharged—Equipment Schedule 1							
W.B. 94.5"; 2.3 Liter.							
SLK230 Roadster 2D		KK49F	40495	17675	19875	22600	26900
Sport Pkg				875	875	1165	1165
designo Edition				600	600	800	800
Manual Trans				(500)	(500)	(665)	(665)
SLK-CLASS—V6—Equipment Schedule 1							
W.B. 94.5"; 3.2 Liter.							
SLK320 Roadster 2D		KK65F	45495	20150	22650	25500	30200
Sport Pkg				875	875	1165	1165
designo Edition				600	600	800	800
Manual Trans				(500)	(500)	(665)	(665)
C-CLASS—V6—Equipment Schedule 1							
W.B. 106.9"; 2.6 Liter, 3.2 Liter.							
C240 Sedan 4D		RF61G	34610	13100	14825	17300	21100
C320 Sedan 4D		RF64G	40310	16025	18050	20700	25000
Sport Pkg				600	600	800	800
Manual Trans				(500)	(500)	(665)	(665)
CLK-CLASS—V6—Equipment Schedule 1							
W.B. 105.9"; 3.2 Liter.							
CLK320 Coupe 2D		LJ65G	42595	20725	23225	26000	30500
CLK320 Cabriolet 2D		LK65G	49545	26400	29575	32600	38000
designo Edition				600	600	800	800
CLK-CLASS—V8—Equipment Schedule 1							
W.B. 105.9"; 4.3 Liter, 5.5 Liter.							
CLK430 Coupe 2D		LJ70G	50295	21300	23900	27600	33100
CLK430 Cabriolet 2D		LK70G	57145	27175	30325	33600	39100
CLK55 Coupe 2D		LJ74G	68045	27350	30525	34800	41700
designo Edition				925	925	1235	1235
E-CLASS—V6—Equipment Schedule 1							
W.B. 111.5"; 3.2 Liter.							
E320 Sedan 4D		JF65F	48495	20650	23125	26100	30900
E320 AWD Sedan 4D		JF82F	51345	21800	24475	27500	32400
E320 Wagon 4D		JH65F	49295	21600	24300	27300	32200
E320 AWD Wagon 4D		JH82F	52145	22850	25625	28700	33800
Sport Pkg				875	875	1165	1165
designo Edition				600	600	800	800
E-CLASS—V8—Equipment Schedule 1							
W.B. 111.5"; 4.3 Liter, 5.5 Liter.							
E430 Sedan 4D		JF70F	53845	20250	22650	26500	32200
E430 AWD Sedan 4D		JF83G	56695	20450	22950	26900	32700
E55 Sedan 4D		JF744	70945	29275	32725	37200	44200
Sport Pkg				875	875	1165	1165
designo Edition				600	600	800	800

2001 MERCEDES-BENZ

Body	Type	VIN	List	Trade-In Fair	Good	Pvt-Party Good	Retail Excellent
CL-CLASS—V8—Equipment Schedule 1							
W.B. 113.6"; 5.0 Liter, 5.5 Liter.							
CL500 Coupe 2D		PJ75J	89145	43675	48575	53500	61900
CL55 Coupe 2D		PJ73J	100145	49250	54725	60400	70000
Sport Pkg				1800	1800	2400	2400
designo Edition				925	925	1235	1235
CL-CLASS—V12—Equipment Schedule 1							
W.B. 113.6"; 6.0 Liter.							
CL600 Coupe 2D		PJ78J	119145	50775	56450	63400	74500
Sport Pkg				1800	1800	2400	2400
designo Edition				925	925	1235	1235
S-CLASS—V8—Equipment Schedule 1							
W.B. 121.5"; 4.3 Liter, 5.0 Liter, 5.5 Liter.							
S430 Sedan 4D		NG70J	71445	29175	32550	36700	43300
S500 Sedan 4D		NG75J	80595	32825	36575	41200	48700
S55 Sedan 4D		NG73J	98645	44075	49050	54400	63400
Sport Pkg				1800	1800	2400	2400
designo Edition				925	925	1235	1235
S-CLASS—V12—Equipment Schedule 1							
W.B. 121.5"; 6.0 Liter.							
S600 Sedan 4D		NG78J	115985	41100	45800	52000	61900
Sport Pkg				1800	1800	2400	2400
designo Edition				925	925	1235	1235
SL-CLASS—V8—Equipment Schedule 1							
W.B. 99.0"; 5.0 Liter.							
SL500 Roadster 2D		FA68F	84445	29850	33300	37700	44700
Sport Pkg				1800	1800	2400	2400
designo Edition				925	925	1235	1235
SL-CLASS—V12—Equipment Schedule 1							
W.B. 99.0"; 6.0 Liter.							
SL600 Roadster 2D		FA76F	129595	33600	37450	42100	49600
designo Edition				925	925	1235	1235

2002 MERCEDES-BENZ — WDB(KK49F)-2-#

Body	Type	VIN	List	Trade-In Fair	Good	Pvt-Party Good	Retail Excellent
SLK-CLASS—4-Cyl. Supercharged—Equipment Schedule 1							
W.B. 94.5"; 2.3 Liter.							
SLK230 Roadster 2D		KK49F	41345	20450	22850	25600	30200
Sport Pkg				950	950	1265	1265
designo Edition				725	725	965	965
Manual Trans				(500)	(500)	(665)	(665)
SLK-CLASS—V6—Equipment Schedule 1							
W.B. 94.5"; 3.2 Liter.							
SLK320 Roadster 2D		KK65F	46745	23125	25925	28900	34000
Sport Pkg				950	950	1265	1265
designo Edition				725	725	965	965
Manual Trans				(500)	(500)	(665)	(665)
SLK-CLASS—V6 Supercharged—Equipment Schedule 1							
W.B. 94.5"; 3.2 Liter.							
SLK32 Roadster 2D		KK66F	55545	26775	29950	33100	38700
designo Edition				725	725	965	965
C-CLASS—4-Cyl. Supercharged—Equipment Schedule 1							
W.B. 106.9"; 2.3 Liter.							
C230 Sport Coupe 2D		RN47J	29490	12300	13925	16150	19600
Manual Trans				(500)	(500)	(665)	(665)
C-CLASS—V6—Equipment Schedule 1							
W.B. 106.9"; 2.6 Liter, 3.2 Liter.							
C240 Sedan 4D		RF61J	33680	15350	17325	19950	24100
C320 Sedan 4D		RF64J	38780	18575	20825	23700	28200
C320 Wagon 4D		RH64J	40280	19300	21700	24600	29200
Sport Pkg				650	650	865	865
Manual Trans				(500)	(500)	(665)	(665)
C-CLASS—V6 Supercharged—Equipment Schedule 1							
W.B. 106.9"; 3.2 Liter.							
C32 Sedan 4D		RF65J	50545	24375	27275	30400	35600
CLK-CLASS—V6—Equipment Schedule 1							
W.B. 105.9"; 3.2 Liter.							
CLK320 Coupe 2D		LJ65G	44565	23700	26500	29400	34300
CLK320 Cabriolet 2D		LK65G	50245	29950	33500	36700	42300
Sport Pkg				950	950	1265	1265
designo Edition				725	725	965	965
CLK-CLASS—V8—Equipment Schedule 1							
W.B. 105.9"; 4.3 Liter, 5.5 Liter.							
CLK430 Coupe 2D		LJ70G	52265	25150	28125	32200	38400

Body	Type	VIN	List	Trade-In Fair	Good	Pvt-Party Good	Retail Excellent
CLK430 Cabriolet 2D	LK70G	57945	31675	35325	38800	44900
CLK55 Coupe 2D	LJ74G	69095	31675	35425	40000	47500
CLK55 Cabriolet 2D	LK74G	79645	35800	39850	44400	51900
designo Edition			950	950	1265	1265

E-CLASS—V6—Equipment Schedule 1
W.B. 111.5"; 3.2 Liter.

E320 Sedan 4D	JF65J	50280	23625	26400	29600	34700
E320 AWD Sedan 4D	JF82J	53130	25900	27925	31000	36300
E320 Wagon 4D	JH65J	51080	24775	27750	30800	36100
E320 AWD Wagon 4D	JH82J	53130	26100	29115	32400	37800
Sport Pkg			950	950	1265	1265
designo Edition			725	725	965	965

E-CLASS—V8—Equipment Schedule 1
W.B. 111.5"; 4.3 Liter, 5.5 Liter.

E430 Sedan 4D	JF70J	55680	23625	26400	30600	37100
E430 AWD Sedan 4D	JF83J	58530	24000	26775	31100	37600
E55 Sedan 4D	JF74J	71995	33900	37725	42500	50200
Sport Pkg (E430)			950	950	1265	1265
designo Edition			950	950	1265	1265

CL-CLASS—V8—Equipment Schedule 1
W.B. 113.6"; 5.0 Liter, 5.5 Liter.

CL500 Coupe 2D	PJ75J	92395	49625	55200	60400	69400
CL55 Coupe 2D	PJ73J	105145	55775	61925	67800	78000
Sport Pkg			1850	1850	2465	2465
designo Edition			950	950	1265	1265

CL-CLASS—V12—Equipment Schedule 1
W.B. 113.6"; 6.0 Liter.

CL600 Coupe 2D	PJ78J	120895	57500	63850	71000	82900
Sport Pkg			1850	1850	2465	2465
designo Edition			950	950	1265	1265

S-CLASS—V8—Equipment Schedule 1
W.B. 121.5"; 4.3 Liter, 5.0 Liter, 5.5 Liter.

S430 Sedan 4D	NG70J	72495	33800	37625	42000	49300
S500 Sedan 4D	NG75J	81845	37625	41950	46900	55000
S55 Sedan 4D	NG73J	101145	50200	55775	61400	71000
Sport Pkg			1850	1850	2465	2465
designo Edition			950	950	1265	1265

S-CLASS—V12—Equipment Schedule 1
W.B. 121.5"; 6.0 Liter.

S600 Sedan 4D	NG78J	117545	46950	52125	58800	69400
Sport Pkg			1850	1850	2465	2465
designo Edition			950	950	1265	1265

SL-CLASS—V8—Equipment Schedule 1
W.B. 99.0"; 5.0 Liter.

SL500 Roadster 2D	FA68F	85445	34175	38100	42800	50400
Sport Pkg			1850	1850	2465	2465
Silver Arrow Edition			2300	2300	3065	3065

SL-CLASS—V12—Equipment Schedule 1
W.B. 99.0"; 6.0 Liter.

SL600 Roadster 2D	FA76F	132195	38875	43300	48300	56400
Silver Arrow Edition			2300	2300	3065	3065

2003 MERCEDES-BENZ — WDB(KK49F)-3-#

SLK-CLASS—4-Cyl. Supercharged—Equipment Schedule 1
W.B. 94.5"; 2.3 Liter.

SLK230 Roadster 2D	KK49F	40265	23625	26400	29300	34100
Sport Pkg			1000	1000	1335	1335
Manual Trans			(500)	(500)	(665)	(665)

SLK-CLASS—V6—Equipment Schedule 1
W.B. 94.5"; 3.2 Liter.

SLK320 Roadster 2D	KK65F	45715	26400	29475	32300	37200
Sport Pkg			1000	1000	1335	1335
designo Edition			825	825	1100	1100
Manual Trans			(500)	(500)	(665)	(665)

SLK-CLASS—V6 Supercharged—Equipment Schedule 1
W.B. 94.5"; 3.2 Liter.

SLK32 Roadster 2D	KK66F	56115	30425	33900	36900	42200
designo Edition			825	825	1100	1100

C-CLASS—4-Cyl. Supercharged—Equipment Schedule 1
W.B. 106.9"; 1.8 Liter.

C230 Sport Sedan 4D	RF40J	30310	15300	17275	19700	23600
C230 Sport Coupe 2D	RN40J	28270	14450	16325	18550	22100
Manual Trans			(500)	(500)	(665)	(665)

Body	Type	VIN	List	Trade-In Fair	Good	Pvt-Party Good	Retail Excellent
C-CLASS—V6—Equipment Schedule 1							
W.B. 106.9"; 2.6 Liter, 3.2 Liter.							
C240 Sedan 4D		RF61J	32165	18000	20250	22600	26600
C240 4Matic Sedan 4D		RH61J	33965	18675	20925	23400	27500
C240 Wagon 4D		RF81J	33544	18675	20925	23400	27500
C240 4Matic Wagon 4D		RH81J	35544	19775	22175	24600	28800
C320 Sedan 4D		RF64J	38790	21500	24100	26600	31000
C320 4Matic Sedan 4D		RF84J	40045	22275	24950	27600	32100
C320 Coupe 2D		RN64J	30620	16850	18950	21300	25200
C320 Wagon 4D		RH64J	38840	22275	24950	27600	32100
C320 4Matic Wagon 4D		RH84J	40640	23050	25825	28400	33000
Sport Pkg		-------	-------	1000	1000	1335	1335
Manual Trans		-------	-------	(500)	(500)	(665)	(665)
C-CLASS—V6 Supercharged—Equipment Schedule 1							
W.B. 106.9"; 3.2 Liter.							
C32 Sedan 4D		RF65J	52065	27750	31000	33900	39000
CLK-CLASS—V6—Equipment Schedule 1							
W.B. 105.9", 106.9" (Coupe); 3.2 Liter.							
CLK320 Coupe 2D		TJ65J	44565	27075	30250	32800	37500
CLK320 Cabriolet 2D		LK65G	50615	33900	37725	40600	46200
Sport Pkg		-------	-------	1000	1000	1335	1335
designo Edition		-------	-------	825	825	1100	1100
CLK-CLASS—V8—Equipment Schedule 1							
W.B. 105.9", 106.9" (Coupe); 4.3 Liter, 5.0 Liter, 5.5 Liter.							
CLK430 Cabriolet 2D		LK70G	58315	36950	41100	44900	51600
CLK500 Coupe 2D		TJ75J	52865	29750	33225	37500	44500
CLK55 Coupe 2D		TJ76H	69470	36950	41100	46200	54300
designo Edition		-------	-------	975	975	1300	1300
E-CLASS—V6—Equipment Schedule 1							
W.B. 111.5"; 3.2 Liter.							
E320 Sedan 4D		UF65J	49165	28500	31775	33900	38200
E320 Wagon 4D		JH65J	55415	28125	31500	34300	39500
E320 4Matic Wagon 4D		JH82J	55415	29675	33125	36000	41300
Sport Pkg		-------	-------	1000	1000	1335	1335
E-CLASS—V8—Equipment Schedule 1							
W.B. 112.4"; 5.0 Liter.							
E500 Sedan 4D		UF70J	57065	33700	37525	41300	47800
Sport Pkg		-------	-------	1000	1000	1335	1335
E-CLASS—V8 Supercharged—Equipment Schedule 1							
W.B. 112.4"; 5.5 Liter.							
E55 Sedan 4D		UF72J	76720	50500	56150	61800	71400
CL-CLASS—V8—Equipment Schedule 1							
W.B. 113.6"; 5.0 Liter.							
CL500 Coupe 2D		PJ75J	93315	56450	62700	68100	77800
Sport Pkg		-------	-------	1900	1900	2535	2535
designo Edition		-------	-------	975	975	1300	1300
CL-CLASS—V8 Supercharged—Equipment Schedule 1							
W.B. 113.6"; 5.5 Liter.							
CL55 Coupe 2D		PJ74J	115265	63075	70075	76100	87100
designo Edition		-------	-------	975	975	1300	1300
CL-CLASS—V12—Equipment Schedule 1							
W.B. 113.6"; 5.5 Liter.							
CL600 Coupe 2D		PJ76J	127265	65000	72100	79700	92300
Sport Pkg		-------	-------	1900	1900	2535	2535
designo Edition		-------	-------	975	975	1300	1300
S-CLASS—V8—Equipment Schedule 1							
W.B. 121.5"; 4.3 Liter, 5.0 Liter.							
S430 Sedan 4D		NG70J	73265	39075	43500	48300	56300
S430 4Matic Sedan 4D		NG83J	76165	39750	44250	49400	57900
S500 Sedan 4D		NG75J	82665	43400	48200	53600	62400
S500 4Matic Sedan 4D		NG84J	85565	45025	50025	55400	64400
Sport Pkg		-------	-------	1900	1900	2535	2535
designo Edition		-------	-------	975	975	1300	1300
S-CLASS—V8 Supercharged—Equipment Schedule 1							
W.B. 100.8"; 5.5 Liter.							
S55 Sedan 4D		NG74J	107165	57025	63275	69100	79400
designo Edition		-------	-------	975	975	1300	1300
S-CLASS—V12—Equipment Schedule 1							
W.B. 121.5"; 5.8 Liter.							
S600 Sedan 4D		NG76J	121205	53475	59325	66300	77800
Sport Pkg		-------	-------	1900	1900	2535	2535
designo Edition		-------	-------	975	975	1300	1300

2003 MERCEDES-BENZ

Body	Type	VIN	List	Trade-In Fair	Good	Pvt-Party Good	Retail Excellent
SL-CLASS—V8—Equipment Schedule 1							
W.B. 100.8"; 5.0 Liter.							
SL500 Roadster 2D		SK75F	87655	59900	66425	71000	80000
Sport Pkg				1900	1900	2535	2535
designo Edition				975	975	1300	1300
SL-CLASS—V8 Supercharged—Equipment Schedule 1							
W.B. 100.8"; 5.5 Liter.							
SL55 Roadster 2D		SK74F	114915	74200	82375	87500	97900
designo Edition				975	975	1300	1300

2004 MERCEDES BENZ — WDB(KK49F)-4-#

Body	Type	VIN	List	Trade-In Fair	Good	Pvt-Party Good	Retail Excellent
SLK-CLASS—4-Cyl. Supercharged—Equipment Schedule 1							
W.B. 94.5"; 2.3 Liter.							
SLK230 Roadster 2D		KK49F	40320	27550	30725	33600	38800
Sport Pkg				1050	1050	1400	1400
designo Edition				925	925	1235	1235
Manual Trans				(500)	(500)	(665)	(665)
SLK-CLASS—V6—Equipment Schedule 1							
W.B. 94.5"; 3.2 Liter.							
SLK320 Roadster 2D		KK65F	47330	30425	33900	36900	42100
Sport Pkg				1050	1050	1400	1400
designo Edition				925	925	1235	1235
Manual Trans				(500)	(500)	(665)	(665)
SLK-CLASS—V6 Supercharged—Equipment Schedule 1							
W.B. 94.5"; 3.2 Liter.							
SLK32 Roadster 2D		KK66F	56170				
designo Edition							
C-CLASS—4-Cyl. Supercharged—Equipment Schedule 1							
W.B. 106.9"; 1.8 Liter.							
C230 Sport Sedan 4D		RF40J	33180	18575	20825	23500	27800
C230 Sport Coupe 2D		RN47J	30090	17425	19575	22000	25900
Manual Trans				(500)	(500)	(665)	(665)
C-CLASS—V6—Equipment Schedule 1							
W.B. 106.9"; 2.6 Liter, 3.2 Liter.							
C240 Sedan 4D		RF61J	33920	21300	23900	26500	31000
C240 4Matic Sedan 4D		RF81J	35120	22175	24775	27500	32100
C240 Wagon 4D		RH61J	35290	22475	25150	27800	32400
C240 4Matic Wagon 4D		RH81J	36490	23325	26100	28800	33400
C320 Sedan 4D		RF64J	39270	25150	28125	30800	35700
C320 4Matic Sedan 4D		RF94J	40470	26025	29100	31900	36800
C320 Coupe 2D		RN64J	29610	20075	22550	25200	29500
C320 Wagon 4D		RH64J	40640	26025	29100	31900	36800
C320 4Matic Wagon 4D		RH84J	41840	26775	29950	32700	37700
Sport Pkg				1050	1050	1400	1400
Manual Trans				(500)	(500)	(665)	(665)
C-CLASS—V6 Supercharged—Equipment Schedule 1							
W.B. 106.9"; 3.2 Liter.							
C32 Sedan 4D		RF65J	53120				
CLK-CLASS—V6—Equipment Schedule 1							
W.B. 106.9"; 3.2 Liter.							
CLK320 Coupe 2D		TJ65J	46480	31100	34750	37300	42400
CLK320 Cabriolet 2D		LK65G	52120				
designo Edition				925	925	1235	1235
CLK-CLASS—V8—Equipment Schedule 1							
W.B. 106.9"; 5.0 Liter, 5.5 Liter.							
CLK500 Coupe 2D		TJ75J	54520				
CLK500 Cabriolet 2D		TK75G	61570				
CLK55 Coupe 2D		TJ76H	70620				
CLK55 Cabriolet 2D		LJ74G	80220				
designo Edition							
E-CLASS—V6—Equipment Schedule 1							
W.B. 112.4"; 3.2 Liter.							
E320 Sedan 4D		UF65J	49410	32725	36475	38700	43300
E320 Wagon 4D		JH65J	51910	32350	36100	39100	44600
Sport Pkg				1050	1050	1400	1400
designo Edition				925	925	1235	1235
E-CLASS—V8—Equipment Schedule 1							
W.B. 112.4"; 5.0 Liter.							
E500 Sedan 4D		UF70J	58510	39925	44550	48600	55900
E500 4Matic Wagon 4D		UH83J	63210	38775	43100	48500	57100
Sport Pkg				1050	1050	1400	1400
designo Edition				1000	1000	1335	1335

Body	Type	VIN	List	Trade-In Fair	Good	Pvt-Party Good	Retail Excellent
E-CLASS—V8 Supercharged—Equipment Schedule 1							
W.B. 112.4"; 5.5 Liter.							
E55 Sedan 4D		UF76J	80070				
designo Edition							
CL-CLASS—V8—Equipment Schedule 1							
W.B. 113.6"; 5.0 Liter.							
CL500 Coupe 2D		PJ75J	94520				
Sport Pkg							
designo Edition							
CL-CLASS—V8 Supercharged—Equipment Schedule 1							
W.B. 113.6"; 5.5 Liter.							
CL55 Coupe 2D		PJ74J	119520				
designo Edition							
CL-CLASS—V12 Twin Turbo—Equipment Schedule 1							
W.B. 113.6"; 5.5 Liter.							
CL600 Coupe 2D		PJ76J	129320				
Sport Pkg							
designo Edition							
S-CLASS—V8—Equipment Schedule 1							
W.B. 121.5"; 4.3 Liter, 5.0 Liter.							
S430 Sedan 4D		NG70J	74320	45800	50875	56100	65000
S430 4Matic Sedan 4D		NG83J	78220	46475	51750	57300	66600
S500 Sedan 4D		NG75J	83770	50400	55975	61600	71300
S500 4Matic Sedan 4D		NG84J	86970	52125	57900	63600	73500
Sport Pkg				1950	1950	2600	2600
designo Edition				1000	1000	1335	1335
S-CLASS—V8 Supercharged—Equipment Schedule 1							
W.B. 121.5"; 5.5 Liter.							
S55 Sedan 4D		NG74J	111870				
designo Edition							
S-CLASS—V12 Twin Turbo—Equipment Schedule 1							
W.B. 121.5"; 5.5 Liter.							
S600 Sedan 4D		NG76J	124260				
Sport Pkg							
designo Edition							
SL-CLASS—V8—Equipment Schedule 1							
W.B. 100.8"; 5.0 Liter.							
SL500 Roadster 2D		SK75F	89800				
Sport Pkg							
designo Edition							
SL-CLASS—V8 Supercharged—Equipment Schedule 1							
W.B. 100.8"; 5.5 Liter.							
SL55 Roadster 2D		SK74F	121450				
designo Edition							
SL-CLASS—V12 Bi-Turbo—Equipment Schedule 1							
W.B. 100.8"; 5.5 Liter.							
SL600 Roadster 2D		SK76F	128550				
Sport Pkg							
designo Edition							

MERCURY

1990 MERCURY — 1ME(PM31X)–L–#

Body	Type	VIN	List	Trade-In Fair	Good	Pvt-Party Good	Retail Excellent
TOPAZ—4-Cyl.—Equipment Schedule 5							
W.B. 99.9"; 2.3 Liter.							
GS Sedan 2D		PM31X	11817	275	350	750	1350
GS Sedan 4D		PM36X	11974	275	350	750	1350
LS Sedan 4D		PM37X	13353	300	400	800	1425
XR5 Sedan 2D		PM33S	12816	275	350	750	1350
LTS Sedan 4D		PM38S	13560	325	475	900	1575
All Wheel Drive Pkg				250	250	335	335
SABLE—V6—Equipment Schedule 4							
W.B. 106.0"; 3.0 Liter.							
GS Sedan 4D		CM50U	16448	525	750	1250	2100
GS Wagon 4D		CM55U	17345	675	950	1550	2575
LS Sedan 4D		CM53U	17093	600	875	1425	2350
LS Wagon 4D		CM58U	18064	750	1025	1675	2750
V6 3.8 Liter		4		100	100	135	135
COUGAR—V6—Equipment Schedule 4							
W.B. 113.0"; 3.8 Liter.							
LS Coupe 2D		PM604	16668	600	850	1500	2575

1990 MERCURY

Body	Type	VIN	List	Trade-In Fair	Trade-In Good	Pvt-Party Good	Retail Excellent
COUGAR—V6 Supercharged—Equipment Schedule 4							
W.B. 113.0"; 3.8 Liter.							
XR7 Coupe 2D		PM62R	21236	925	1325	2225	3575
GRAND MARQUIS—V8—Equipment Schedule 4							
W.B. 114.3"; 5.0 Liter.							
GS Sedan 4D		CM74F	18915	425	625	1100	1925
GS Colony Park Wag 4D		CM78F	19650	450	650	1175	2025
LS Sedan 4D		CM75F	19415	550	775	1350	2300
LS Colony Park Wag 4D		CM79F	20222	525	750	1300	2175

1991 MERCURY — (1,3or6)M(E,AorP)(PM10J)–M–#

Body	Type	VIN	List	Trade-In Fair	Trade-In Good	Pvt-Party Good	Retail Excellent
TRACER—4-Cyl.—Equipment Schedule 6							
W.B. 98.4"; 1.8 Liter, 1.9 Liter.							
Notchback 4D		PM10J	10730	475	700	1150	1900
Wagon 4D		PM15J	11516	550	775	1250	2075
LTS Notchback 4D		PM148	12745	575	825	1325	2175
CAPRI—4-Cyl.—Equipment Schedule 6							
W.B. 94.7"; 1.6 Liter.							
Convertible 2D		PT01Z	14172	625	900	1550	2700
Hard Top				325	325	435	435
CAPRI—4-Cyl. Turbo—Equipment Schedule 6							
W.B. 94.7"; 1.6 Liter.							
XR2 Convertible 2D		PT036	16285	750	1025	1800	3025
Hard Top				325	325	435	435
TOPAZ—4-Cyl.—Equipment Schedule 5							
W.B. 99.9"; 2.3 Liter.							
GS Sedan 2D		PM31X	11900	300	425	850	1475
GS Sedan 4D		PM36X	12057	300	450	875	1500
LS Sedan 4D		PM37X	13436	325	475	900	1575
XR5 Sedan 2D		PM33S	12899	300	450	875	1500
LTS Sedan 4D		PM38S	13644	400	575	1025	1750
Four Wheel Drive Pkg				275	275	365	365
SABLE—V6—Equipment Schedule 4							
W.B. 106.0"; 3.0 Liter.							
GS Sedan 4D		CM50U	16748	600	875	1450	2425
GS Wagon 4D		CM55U	17643	775	1100	1825	2975
LS Sedan 4D		CM53U	17225	700	975	1625	2725
LS Wagon 4D		CM58U	18195	850	1200	1975	3200
V6 3.8 Liter		4		100	100	135	135
COUGAR—V6—Equipment Schedule 4							
W.B. 113.0"; 3.8 Liter.							
LS Coupe 2D		PM604	16890	700	975	1725	2925
V8 5.0 Liter		T		250	250	335	335
COUGAR—V8—Equipment Schedule 4							
W.B. 113.0"; 5.0 Liter.							
XR-7 Coupe 2D		PM62T	22166	1150	1600	2725	4325
GRAND MARQUIS—V8—Equipment Schedule 4							
W.B. 114.3"; 5.0 Liter.							
GS Sedan 4D		CM74F	19917	525	750	1325	2250
GS Colony Park Wag 4D		CM78F	20109	550	775	1375	2350
LS Sedan 4D		CM75F	20417	675	925	1600	2725
LS Colony Park Wag 4D		CM79F	20681	625	900	1500	2575

1992 MERCURY — (1,3or6)M(E,AorP)(PM10J)–N–#

Body	Type	VIN	List	Trade-In Fair	Trade-In Good	Pvt-Party Good	Retail Excellent
TRACER—4-Cyl.—Equipment Schedule 6							
W.B. 98.4"; 1.8 Liter, 1.9 Liter.							
Notchback 4D		PM10J	11168	525	750	1250	2075
Wagon 4D		PM15J	11928	600	875	1375	2250
LTS Notchback 4D		PM148	13157	650	900	1500	2425
CAPRI—4-Cyl.—Equipment Schedule 6							
W.B. 94.7"; 1.6 Liter.							
Convertible 2D		CT01Z	15644	650	900	1650	2850
Hard Top				350	350	465	465
CAPRI—4-Cyl. Turbo—Equipment Schedule 6							
W.B. 94.7"; 1.6 Liter.							
XR2 Convertible 2D		CT036	17625	775	1100	1950	3250
Hard Top				350	350	465	465
TOPAZ—4-Cyl.—Equipment Schedule 5							
W.B. 99.9"; 2.3 Liter.							
GS Sedan 2D		PM31X	12332	300	450	900	1550
GS Sedan 4D		PM36X	12498	350	500	950	1675
LS Sedan 4D		PM37X	13878	375	550	1000	1750
V6 3.0 Liter		U		150	150	200	200

1992 MERCURY

Body Type	VIN	List	Trade-In Fair	Good	Pvt-Party Good	Retail Excellent
TOPAZ—V6—Equipment Schedule 5						
W.B. 99.9"; 3.0 Liter.						
XR5 Sedan 2D	PM33U	14456	500	725	1225	2100
LTS Sedan 4D	PM38U	15248	525	750	1325	2225
SABLE—V6—Equipment Schedule 4						
W.B. 106.0"; 3.0 Liter.						
GS Sedan 4D	CM50U	17917	700	1000	1650	2750
GS Wagon 4D	CM55U	18895	900	1275	2100	3350
LS Sedan 4D	CM53U	18510	825	1150	1900	3100
LS Wagon 4D	CM58U	19537	1000	1450	2425	3875
V6 3.8 Liter	4		125	125	165	165
COUGAR—V6—Equipment Schedule 4						
W.B. 113.0"; 3.8 Liter.						
LS Coupe 2D	PM604	17790	775	1100	1975	3300
V8 5.0 Liter	T		275	275	365	365
COUGAR—V8—Equipment Schedule 4						
W.B. 113.0"; 5.0 Liter.						
XR-7 Coupe 2D	PM62T	23384	1400	1875	3100	4775
GRAND MARQUIS—V8—Equipment Schedule 4						
W.B. 114.4"; 4.6 Liter.						
GS Sedan 4D	CM74W	21450	925	1325	2200	3525
LS Sedan 4D	CM75W	21878	1100	1550	2650	4150

1993 MERCURY — (1,3or6)M(E,AorP)(PM10J)–P–#

Body Type	VIN	List	Trade-In Fair	Good	Pvt-Party Good	Retail Excellent
TRACER—4-Cyl.—Equipment Schedule 6						
W.B. 98.4"; 1.8 Liter, 1.9 Liter.						
Sedan 4D	PM10J	11289	600	875	1400	2300
Wagon 4D	PM15J	12116	700	975	1550	2575
LTS Notchback 4D	PM148	12398	750	1050	1700	2750
CAPRI—4-Cyl.—Equipment Schedule 6						
W.B. 94.7"; 1.6 Liter.						
Convertible 2D	CT01Z	15874	700	1000	1850	3150
Hard Top			375	375	500	500
CAPRI—4-Cyl. Turbo—Equipment Schedule 6						
W.B. 94.7"; 1.6 Liter.						
XR2 Convertible 2D	CT036	17625	850	1200	2150	3575
Hard Top			375	375	500	500
TOPAZ—4-Cyl.—Equipment Schedule 5						
W.B. 99.9"; 2.3 Liter.						
GS Sedan 2D	PM31X	12141	325	475	950	1725
GS Sedan 4D	PM36X	12181	400	600	1100	1925
V6 3.0 Liter	U		175	175	235	235
SABLE—V6—Equipment Schedule 4						
W.B. 106.0"; 3.0 Liter.						
GS Sedan 4D	LM50U	18909	825	1150	1950	3150
GS Wagon 4D	LM55U	20019	1025	1450	2475	3925
LS Sedan 4D	LM53U	20379	925	1325	2200	3525
LS Wagon 4D	LM58U	21406	1225	1675	2750	4275
V6 3.8 Liter	4		150	150	200	200
COUGAR—V8—Equipment Schedule 4						
W.B. 113.0"; 5.0 Liter.						
XR-7 Coupe 2D	PM62T	17833	950	1350	2475	4050
V6 3.8 Liter	4		(125)	(125)	(165)	(165)
GRAND MARQUIS—V8—Equipment Schedule 4						
W.B. 114.4"; 4.6 Liter.						
GS Sedan 4D	LM74W	23420	1100	1550	2650	4175
LS Sedan 4D	LM75W	24184	1375	1875	3000	4625

1994 MERCURY — (1,3or6)M(E,AorP)(PM10J)–R–#

Body Type	VIN	List	Trade-In Fair	Good	Pvt-Party Good	Retail Excellent
TRACER—4-Cyl.—Equipment Schedule 6						
W.B. 98.4"; 1.8 Liter, 1.9 Liter.						
Sedan 4D	PM10J	11350	700	975	1600	2650
Wagon 4D	PM15J	11620	800	1125	1800	2925
LTS Notchback 4D	PM148	13660	875	1225	2000	3200
CAPRI—4-Cyl.—Equipment Schedule 6						
W.B. 94.7"; 1.6 Liter.						
Convertible 2D	CT01Z	13565	825	1150	2125	3600
CAPRI—4-Cyl. Turbo—Equipment Schedule 6						
W.B. 94.7"; 1.6 Liter.						
XR2 Convertible 2D	CT036	15275	950	1375	2525	4125
TOPAZ—4-Cyl.—Equipment Schedule 5						
W.B. 99.9"; 2.3 Liter.						
GS Sedan 2D	PM31X	12585	400	575	1125	2025

Body	Type	VIN	List	Trade-In Fair	Good	Pvt-Party Good	Retail Excellent
GS Sedan 4D	PM36X	12625	475	700	1300	2250
V6 3.0 Liter	U		200	200	265	265

SABLE—V6—Equipment Schedule 4
W.B. 106.0"; 3.0 Liter.

GS Sedan 4D	LM50U	19230	950	1350	2275	3650
GS Wagon 4D	LM55U	20390	1200	1650	2750	4325
LS Sedan 4D	LM53U	21625	1075	1525	2600	4125
LS Wagon 4D	LM58U	22735	1500	1975	3125	4725
LTS Pkg			100	100	135	135
V6 3.8 Liter	4		175	175	235	235

COUGAR—V8—Equipment Schedule 4
W.B. 113.0"; 4.6 Liter.

| XR-7 Coupe 2D | LM62W | 18360 | 1200 | 1650 | 2875 | 4575 |
| V6 3.8 Liter | 4 | | (150) | (150) | (200) | (200) |

GRAND MARQUIS—V8—Equipment Schedule 4
W.B. 114.4"; 4.6 Liter.

| GS Sedan 4D | LM74W | 21130 | 1375 | 1850 | 2975 | 4600 |
| LS Sedan 4D | LM75W | 23130 | 1675 | 2175 | 3400 | 5100 |

1995 MERCURY — (1ME,2MEor3MA)(SM10J)–S–#

TRACER—4-Cyl.—Equipment Schedule 6
W.B. 98.4"; 1.8 Liter, 1.9 Liter.

Sedan 4D	SM10J	12040	800	1125	1850	3025
Wagon 4D	SM15J	12310	900	1300	2100	3350
LTS Notchback 4D	SM148	14445	975	1425	2300	3650

MYSTIQUE—4-Cyl.—Equipment Schedule 6
W.B. 106.5"; 2.0 Liter.

GS Sedan 4D	LM653	16060	600	875	1575	2725
LS Sedan 4D	LM663	17920	750	1050	1875	3150
Young America Edition			200	200	265	265
V6 2.5 Liter	L		200	200	265	265

SABLE—V6—Equipment Schedule 4
W.B. 106.0"; 3.0 Liter.

GS Sedan 4D	LM50U	19710	1100	1550	2700	4250
GS Wagon 4D	LM55U	20860	1450	1925	3100	4750
LS Sedan 4D	LM53U	21450	1325	1800	2950	4575
LS Wagon 4D	LM58U	22550	1800	2325	3525	5250
LTS Pkg			100	100	135	135
V6 3.8 Liter	4		200	200	265	265

COUGAR—V8—Equipment Schedule 4
W.B. 113.0"; 4.6 Liter.

| XR-7 Coupe 2D | LM62W | 18960 | 1450 | 1925 | 3250 | 5050 |
| V6 3.8 Liter | 4 | | (150) | (150) | (200) | (200) |

GRAND MARQUIS—V8—Equipment Schedule 4
W.B. 114.4"; 4.6 Liter.

| GS Sedan 4D | LM74W | 22130 | 1650 | 2175 | 3400 | 5150 |
| LS Sedan 4D | LM75W | 24335 | 2025 | 2575 | 3850 | 5675 |

1996 MERCURY — (1,2or3)M(EorA)–(M10J)–T–#

TRACER—4-Cyl.—Equipment Schedule 6
W.B. 98.4"; 1.8 Liter, 1.9 Liter.

Sedan 4D	M10J	12540	925	1325	2175	3475
Wagon 4D	M15J	12810	1050	1500	2525	3975
LTS Notchback 4D	M148	14945	1200	1650	2700	4200

MYSTIQUE—4-Cyl.—Equipment Schedule 5
W.B. 106.5"; 2.0 Liter.

GS Sedan 4D	M653	16570	750	1025	1925	3250
LS Sedan 4D	M663	19280	900	1250	2200	3650
V6 2.5 Liter	L		200	200	265	265

SABLE—V6—Equipment Schedule 4
W.B. 108.5"; 3.0 Liter.

G Sedan 4D	M51U	18910	1100	1550	2700	4300
GS Sedan 4D	M50U	19755	1250	1725	2900	4525
GS Wagon 4D	M55U	20775	1625	2125	3350	5100
LS Sedan 4D	M53S	21995	1500	2000	3200	4900
LS Wagon 4D	M58S	23055	2050	2600	3875	5675

COUGAR—V8—Equipment Schedule 4
W.B. 113.0"; 4.6 Liter.

| XR-7 Coupe 2D | M62W | 18445 | 1750 | 2275 | 3675 | 5625 |
| V6 3.8 Liter | 4 | | (150) | (150) | (200) | (200) |

GRAND MARQUIS—V8—Equipment Schedule 4
W.B. 114.4"; 4.6 Liter.

| GS Sedan 4D | M74W | 22595 | 2075 | 2625 | 3925 | 5800 |

1996 MERCURY

Body	Type	VIN	List	Trade-In Fair	Trade-In Good	Pvt-Party Good	Retail Excellent
LS Sedan 4D		M75W	24785	2425	3025	4400	6325

1997 MERCURY — (1,2or3)ME–(M10P)–V–#

TRACER—4-Cyl.—Equipment Schedule 6
W.B. 98.4"; 2.0 Liter.

GS Sedan 4D		M10P	12355	700	1000	1975	3425
LS Sedan 4D		M13P	13200	850	1175	2325	3950
LS Wagon 4D		M15P	13855	1050	1500	2700	4400

MYSTIQUE—4-Cyl.—Equipment Schedule 5
W.B. 106.5"; 2.0 Liter.

Sedan 4D		M653	16105	825	1150	2125	3600
Sedan 4D		M653	17605	900	1300	2400	4000
LS Sedan 4D		M663	19920	1050	1500	2675	4300
V6 2.5 Liter		L		200	200	265	265

SABLE—V6—Equipment Schedule 5
W.B. 108.5"; 3.0 Liter.

GS Sedan 4D		M50U	20295	1525	2050	3300	5050
GS Wagon 4D		M55U	20295	1950	2500	3825	5650
LS Sedan 4D		M53S	23350	1800	2325	3625	5400
LS Wagon 4D		M58S	23350	2425	3025	4375	6300

COUGAR—V8—Equipment Schedule 4
W.B. 113.0"; 4.6 Liter.

XR-7 Sedan 2D		M62W	19685	2100	2700	4175	6250
V6 3.8 Liter		4		(150)	(150)	(200)	(200)

GRAND MARQUIS—V8—Equipment Schedule 4
W.B. 114.4"; 4.6 Liter.

GS Sedan 4D		M74W	23140	2550	3150	4550	6575
LS Sedan 4D		M75W	25330	2925	3575	5050	7125

1998 MERCURY — (1,2or3)ME–(M10P)–W–#

TRACER—4-Cyl.—Equipment Schedule 6
W.B. 98.4"; 2.0 Liter.

GS Sedan 4D		M10P	12565	875	1225	2375	4025
LS Sedan 4D		M13P	13125	975	1425	2625	4300
LS Wagon 4D		M15P	14620	1300	1775	3025	4775

MYSTIQUE—4-Cyl.—Equipment Schedule 5
W.B. 106.5"; 2.0 Liter.

Sedan 4D		M653	16105	1025	1475	2650	4275
Sedan 4D		M653	18230	1150	1600	2800	4475

MYSTIQUE—V6—Equipment Schedule 5
W.B. 106.5"; 2.5 Liter

LS Sedan 4D		M66L	19295	1525	2050	3275	5000

SABLE—V6—Equipment Schedule 4
W.B. 108.5"; 3.0 Liter.

GS Sedan 4D		M50U	19995	1950	2475	3750	5525
LS Sedan 4D		M53U	20995	2225	2775	4075	5925
LS Wagon 4D		M58U	22835	2875	3525	4875	6825
V6 3.0 Liter 24V		S		200	200	265	265

GRAND MARQUIS—V8—Equipment Schedule 4
W.B. 114.7"; 4.6 Liter.

GS Sedan 4D		M74W	22495	3100	3750	5200	7275
LS Sedan 4D		M75W	24395	3525	4225	5725	7875

1999 MERCURY — (1,2or3)(MEorZW)–(M10P)–X–#

TRACER—4-Cyl.—Equipment Schedule 6
W.B. 98.4"; 2.0 Liter.

GS Sedan 4D		M10P	12740	1000	1450	2700	4425
LS Sedan 4D		M13P	13485	1200	1650	2950	4725
LS Wagon 4D		M15P	14690	1600	2100	3425	5275

MYSTIQUE—4-Cyl.—Equipment Schedule 5
W.B. 106.5"; 2.0 Liter.

GS Sedan 4D		M653	17740	1625	2125	3425	5225

MYSTIQUE—V6—Equipment Schedule 5
W.B. 106.5"; 2.5 Liter.

LS Sedan 4D		M66L	19095	2100	2675	3975	5850

SABLE—V6—Equipment Schedule 4
W.B. 108.5"; 3.0 Liter.

GS Sedan 4D		M50U	18995	2500	3100	4475	6375
LS Sedan 4D		M53U	20095	2775	3400	4800	6775
LS Wagon 4D		M58U	21195	3525	4225	5700	7775
V6 3.0 Liter 24V		S		250	250	335	335

1999 MERCURY

Body	Type	VIN	List	Trade-In Fair	Trade-In Good	Pvt-Party Good	Retail Excellent
COUGAR—V6—Equipment Schedule 4							
W.B. 106.4"; 2.5 Liter.							
Coupe 2D		T61L	18630	**3500**	**4200**	**5750**	**7950**
Manual Trans			....	(275)	(275)	(365)	(365)
4-Cyl. 2.0 Liter		3	....	(450)	(450)	(600)	(600)
GRAND MARQUIS—V8—Equipment Schedule 4							
W.B. 114.7"; 4.6 Liter.							
GS Sedan 4D		M74W	22825	**3825**	**4550**	**6125**	**8375**
LS Sedan 4D		M75W	24725	**4325**	**5100**	**6725**	**9050**

2000 MERCURY — (1,2or3)(MEorZW)–(M653)–Y–#

Body	Type	VIN	List	Trade-In Fair	Trade-In Good	Pvt-Party Good	Retail Excellent
MYSTIQUE—4-Cyl.—Equipment Schedule 5							
W.B. 106.5"; 2.0 Liter.							
GS Sedan 4D		M653	17495	**2250**	**2825**	**4250**	**6200**
MYSTIQUE—V6—Equipment Schedule 5							
W.B. 106.5"; 2.5 Liter.							
LS Sedan 4D		M66L	18795	**2775**	**3400**	**4850**	**6875**
SABLE—V6—Equipment Schedule 4							
W.B. 108.5"; 3.0 Liter.							
GS Sedan 4D		M50U	19395	**3200**	**3875**	**5325**	**7425**
GS Wagon 4D		M58U	21195	**3825**	**4550**	**6050**	**8225**
LS Sedan 4D		M53U	20495	**3450**	**4150**	**5650**	**7750**
V6 3.0 Liter 24V		S	....	275	275	365	365
SABLE—V6 24V—Equipment Schedule 4							
W.B. 108.5"; 3.0 Liter.							
LS Premium Sedan 4D		M55S	21795	**3975**	**4725**	**6275**	**8450**
LS Premium Wagon 4D		M59S	22895	**4650**	**5500**	**7050**	**9325**
COUGAR—V6—Equipment Schedule 4							
W.B. 106.4"; 2.5 Liter.							
Coupe 2D		T61L	18880	**4200**	**5000**	**6625**	**8975**
Manual Trans			....	(300)	(300)	(400)	(400)
4-Cyl. 2.0 Liter		3	....	(475)	(475)	(635)	(635)
GRAND MARQUIS—V8—Equipment Schedule 4							
W.B. 114.7"; 4.6 Liter.							
GS Sedan 4D		M74W	23020	**4675**	**5525**	**7200**	**9650**
LS Sedan 4D		M75W	24920	**5225**	**6125**	**7875**	**10400**

2001 MERCURY — (1or2)(MEorZW)–(M50U)–1–#

Body	Type	VIN	List	Trade-In Fair	Trade-In Good	Pvt-Party Good	Retail Excellent
SABLE—V6—Equipment Schedule 4							
W.B. 108.5"; 3.0 Liter.							
GS Sedan 4D		M50U	19785	**4000**	**4775**	**6350**	**8650**
GS Wagon 4D		M58U	21585	**4725**	**5550**	**7175**	**9525**
LS Sedan 4D		M53U	20885	**4275**	**5075**	**6650**	**8950**
V6 3.0 Liter 24V		S	....	300	300	400	400
V6 3.0L Flex Fuel		2	....	0	0	0	0
SABLE—V6 24V—Equipment Schedule 4							
W.B. 108.5"; 3.0 Liter.							
LS Premium Sedan 4D		M55S	22185	**4850**	**5700**	**7325**	**9700**
LS Premium Wagon 4D		M59S	23285	**5650**	**6575**	**8250**	**10750**
COUGAR—V6—Equipment Schedule 4							
W.B. 106.4"; 2.5 Liter.							
Coupe 2D		T61L	18545	**5925**	**6900**	**8425**	**10750**
C2 Coupe 2D		T61L	20660	**6525**	**7550**	**9150**	**11550**
Zn Coupe 2D		T61L	21645	**6775**	**7800**	**9400**	**11850**
Manual Trans			....	(325)	(325)	(435)	(435)
4-Cyl. 2.0 Liter		3	....	(500)	(500)	(665)	(665)
GRAND MARQUIS—V8—Equipment Schedule 4							
W.B. 114.7"; 4.6 Liter.							
GS Sedan 4D		M74W	23460	**5775**	**6725**	**8600**	**11300**
LS Sedan 4D		M75W	25360	**6375**	**7400**	**9300**	**12100**

2002 MERCURY — (1or2)(MEorZW)–(M50U)–2–#

Body	Type	VIN	List	Trade-In Fair	Trade-In Good	Pvt-Party Good	Retail Excellent
SABLE—V6—Equipment Schedule 4							
W.B. 108.5"; 3.0 Liter.							
GS Sedan 4D		M50U	20255	**5050**	**5925**	**7625**	**10150**
GS Wagon 4D		M58U	21665	**5825**	**6800**	**8550**	**11150**
SABLE—V6 24V—Equipment Schedule 4							
W.B. 108.5"; 3.0 Liter.							
LS Premium Sedan 4D		M55S	22680	**5925**	**6900**	**8650**	**11250**
LS Premium Wagon 4D		M59S	23845	**6850**	**7900**	**9750**	**12450**
COUGAR—V6—Equipment Schedule 4							
W.B. 106.4"; 2.5 Liter.							

Body	Type	VIN	List	Trade-In Fair	Good	Pvt-Party Good	Retail Excellent
Coupe 2D		M61L	18490	7025	8100	9750	12300
Sport Coupe 2D		M62L	18990	7550	8700	10400	13000
C2 Coupe 2D		M62L	19505	7700	8850	10550	13200
Xr Coupe 2D		M62L	19940	8000	9175	10900	13550
Manual Trans				(350)	(350)	(465)	(465)
4-Cyl. 2.0 Liter		3		(525)	(525)	(700)	(700)
35th Anniversary Ed				200	200	265	265

GRAND MARQUIS—V8—Equipment Schedule 4
W.B. 114.7"; 4.6 Liter.

GS Sedan 4D		M74W	24325	7150	8250	10250	13250
LS Sedan 4D		M75W	27800	7850	9025	11100	14150
LSE Sedan 4D		M75W	29305	8525	9750	11850	15000

2003 MERCURY — (1or2)ME—(M50U)-3-#

SABLE—V6—Equipment Schedule 4
W.B. 108.5"; 3.0 Liter.

| GS Sedan 4D | | M50U | 20770 | 6350 | 7350 | 9100 | 11650 |
| GS Wagon 4D | | M58U | 22180 | 7225 | 8300 | 10150 | 12800 |

SABLE—V6 24V—Equipment Schedule 4
W.B. 108.5"; 3.0 Liter.

| LS Premium Sedan 4D | | M55S | 23145 | 7275 | 8350 | 10200 | 12850 |
| LS Premium Wagon 4D | | M59S | 24310 | 8300 | 9525 | 11400 | 14200 |

GRAND MARQUIS—V8—Equipment Schedule 4
W.B. 114.7"; 4.6 Liter.

GS Sedan 4D		M74W	24875	8925	10225	12350	15550
LS Sedan 4D		M75W	28605	9700	11050	13200	16450
LSE Sedan 4D		M75W	30110	10425	11850	14050	17400
Limited Edition				500	500	665	665

MARAUDER—V8—Equipment Schedule 2
W.B. 114.7"; 4.6 Liter.

| Sedan 4D | | M75V | 34495 | 14100 | 15925 | 18200 | 21800 |

2004 MERCURY — (1or2)ME—(M50U)-4-#

SABLE—V6—Equipment Schedule 4
W.B. 108.5"; 3.0 Liter.

| GS Sedan 4D | | M50U | 21595 | 8025 | 9200 | 11050 | 13800 |
| GS Wagon 4D | | M58U | 22595 | 8925 | 10225 | 12100 | 15000 |

SABLE—V6 24V—Equipment Schedule 4
W.B. 108.5"; 3.0 Liter.

| LS Premium Sedan 4D | | M55S | 23895 | 8975 | 10275 | 12150 | 15050 |
| LS Premium Wagon 4D | | M59S | 24795 | 10125 | 11525 | 13550 | 16600 |

GRAND MARQUIS—V8—Equipment Schedule 4
W.B. 114.7"; 4.6 Liter.

GS Sedan 4D		M74W	24695	11175	12675	15100	18750
LS Sedan 4D		M75W	29595	11950	13525	16050	19800
Limited Edition				500	500	665	665

MARAUDER—V8—Equipment Schedule 2
W.B. 114.7"; 4.6 Liter.

| Sedan 4D | | M79V | 34495 | 16850 | 18950 | 21400 | 25400 |

MERKUR

MINI

2002 MINI — WMW(RC334)-2-#

COOPER—4-Cyl.—Equipment Schedule 3
W.B. 97.1"; 1.6 Liter.

| Hatchback 2D | | RC334 | 16850 | 11275 | 12825 | 14600 | 17450 |
| Sport Pkg | | | | 550 | 550 | 735 | 735 |

COOPER S—4-Cyl. Supercharged—Equipment Schedule 3
W.B. 97.1"; 1.6 Liter.

| Hatchback 2D | | RE334 | 19850 | 13300 | 15025 | 16900 | 20100 |
| Sport Pkg | | | | 550 | 550 | 735 | 735 |

2003 MINI — WMW(RC334)-3-#

COOPER—4-Cyl.—Equipment Schedule 3
W.B. 97.1"; 1.6 Liter.

| Hatchback 2D | | RC334 | 18575 | 12875 | 14550 | 16200 | 19150 |
| Sport Pkg | | | | 600 | 600 | 800 | 800 |

Body	Type	VIN	List	Trade-In Fair	Good	Pvt-Party Good	Retail Excellent

COOPER S—4-Cyl. Supercharged—Equipment Schedule 3
W.B. 97.1"; 1.6 Liter.

Hatchback 2D	RE334	20325	**15025**	**16950**	**18700**	**21900**
Sport Pkg			**600**	**600**	**800**	**800**

2004 MINI — WMW(RC334)–4–#

COOPER—4-Cyl.—Equipment Schedule 3
W.B. 97.1"; 1.6 Liter.

Hatchback 2D	RC334	18299				
Sport Pkg						

COOPER S—4-Cyl. Supercharged—Equipment Schedule 3
W.B. 97.1"; 1.6 Liter.

Hatchback 2D	RE334	19999				
Sport Pkg						

MITSUBISHI

1990 MITSUBISHI — (JA3,4A3orKPH)(VD12J)–L–#

PRECIS—4-Cyl.—Equipment Schedule 6
W.B. 93.8"; 1.5 Liter.

Hatchback 2D	VD12J	7540	225	300	675	1250
RS Hatchback 2D	VD22J	8640	275	375	800	1425

MIRAGE—4-Cyl.—Equipment Schedule 6
W.B. 93.9", 96.7" (Sed); 1.5 Liter.

VL Hatchback 2D	CU14X	8310	325	475	975	1750
Sedan 4D	CU26X	10155	400	575	1075	1925
Hatchback 2D	CU24X	9435	400	575	1075	1925
exe Hatchback 2D	CU24X	8637	400	600	1125	1975
RS Sedan 4D	CU36X	9807	475	675	1225	2125
RS Hatchback 2D	CU34X	10384	450	650	1200	2100
SE Sedan 4D	CU46X	9927	475	675	1225	2125
SE Hatchback 2D	CU44X	9077	475	675	1225	2125

ECLIPSE—4-Cyl.—Equipment Schedule 4
W.B. 97.2"; 1.8 Liter, 2.0 Liter.

Coupe 2D	CS34T	12526	450	650	1225	2125
GS Coupe 2D	CS44T	13501	525	750	1350	2300
GS 16V DOHC Cpe 2D	CS44R	14341	600	850	1500	2525
Auto Trans			100	100	135	135

ECLIPSE—4-Cyl. Turbo—Equipment Schedule 4
W.B. 97.2"; 2.0 Liter.

GS DOHC Coupe 2D	CS54U	16301	700	1000	1700	2850
GSX Coupe 2D	CT54U	17924	975	1425	2425	3900
Manual Trans			0	0	0	0

GALANT—4-Cyl.—Equipment Schedule 4
W.B. 102.4"; 2.0 Liter.

Sedan 4D	CR46V	14041	550	800	1425	2425
LS Sedan 4D	CR56V	15069	675	950	1625	2750
GS Sport Sedan 4D	CR56R	16769	825	1150	1975	3250
GSX Sport Sedan 4D	CX56R	17469	900	1250	2100	3400

SIGMA—V6—Equipment Schedule 4
W.B. 102.4"; 3.0 Liter.

Sedan 4D	XB46S	18177	550	800	1500	2650

1991 MITSUBISHI — (JA3,4A3orKPH)(VD12J)–M–#

PRECIS—4-Cyl.—Equipment Schedule 6
W.B. 93.8"; 1.5 Liter.

Hatchback 2D	VD12J	7107	250	325	700	1300
RS Hatchback 2D	VD22J	8761	300	400	825	1475

MIRAGE—4-Cyl.—Equipment Schedule 6
W.B. 93.9", 96.7" (Sed); 1.5 Liter, 1.6 Liter.

VL Hatchback 2D	CU14X	8508	375	550	1075	1925
Sedan 4D	CU26X	10190	450	625	1200	2100
Hatchback 2D	CU24X	9303	450	625	1225	2125
Special Ed H'Back 2D	CU24X	8652	450	650	1250	2175
LS Sedan 4D	CU36X	10977	550	775	1425	2425
GS DOHC Sedan 4D	CU56Y	12115	450	650	1250	2175

ECLIPSE—4-Cyl.—Equipment Schedule 4
W.B. 97.2"; 1.8 Liter, 2.0 Liter.

Coupe 2D	CS34T	12655	550	775	1450	2525
GS Coupe 2D	CS44T	13697	625	900	1600	2750
GS 16V DOHC Cpe 2D	CS44R	14597	700	1000	1775	3025

Body	Type	VIN	List	Trade-In Fair	Trade-In Good	Pvt-Party Good	Retail Excellent
Auto Trans				100	100	135	135
ECLIPSE—4-Cyl. Turbo—Equipment Schedule 4							
W.B. 97.2"; 2.0 Liter.							
GS DOHC Coupe 2D		CS54U	16697	825	1150	2050	3350
GSX Coupe 2D		CT64U	18357	1150	1600	2725	4325
Auto Trans				100	100	135	135
GALANT—4-Cyl.—Equipment Schedule 4							
W.B. 102.4"; 2.0 Liter.							
Sedan 4D		CR46V	14098	675	925	1650	2800
LS Sedan 4D		CR56V	15741	775	1100	1925	3200
GS Sport Sedan 4D		CR56R	16144	950	1375	2400	3900
GSR Sport Sedan 4D		CR56R	17714	1025	1450	2525	4025
GSX Sport Sedan 4D		CX56R	18104	1025	1450	2525	4025
Manual Trans				(175)	(175)	(235)	(235)
GALANT—4-Cyl. Turbo—Equipment Schedule 4							
W.B. 102.4"; 2.0 Liter.							
VR-4 Sport Sedan 4D		CX56U	22145	1225	1700	2825	4425
3000GT—V6—Equipment Schedule 4							
W.B. 97.2"; 3.0 Liter.							
Coupe 2D		XD54B	21161	2025	2575	4000	6000
SL Coupe 2D		XD64B	25092	2475	3075	4600	6725
Auto Trans				100	100	135	135
3000GT—V6 Turbo—Equipment Schedule 2							
W.B. 97.2"; 3.0 Liter.							
VR-4 Coupe 2D		XE74C	32265	4475	5250	7150	9800
Manual Trans				0	0	0	0

1992 MITSUBISHI — (JA3,4A3orKPH)(VD11J)–N–#

Body	Type	VIN	List	Trade-In Fair	Trade-In Good	Pvt-Party Good	Retail Excellent
PRECIS—4-Cyl.—Equipment Schedule 6							
W.B. 93.8"; 1.5 Liter.							
Hatchback 2D		VD11J	8436	225	300	700	1300
MIRAGE—4-Cyl.—Equipment Schedule 6							
W.B. 93.9", 96.7" (Sed); 1.5 Liter, 1.6 Liter.							
VL Hatchback 2D		CU14A	8823	425	625	1200	2125
Special Ed H'Back 2D		CU14A	8927	425	625	1200	2125
Sedan 4D		CU26A	10605	500	725	1350	2350
Hatchback 2D		CU24A	9638	525	750	1375	2400
LS Sedan 4D		CU36A	11120	625	900	1600	2750
GS DOHC Sedan 4D		CU56Y	12530	550	800	1475	2575
EXPO—4-Cyl.—Equipment Schedule 6							
W.B. 99.2" (LRV), 107.1"; 1.8 Liter, 2.4 Liter.							
LRV Wagon 3D		CV20D	12639	1150	1600	2625	4075
LRV Sport Wagon 3D		CW40D	13459	1250	1725	2775	4275
LRV Sport AWD Wag 3D		CW40D	15359	1475	1950	3025	4575
Wagon 4D		CY29W	14692	1500	2000	3075	4625
SP Wagon 4D		CY59W	15652	1675	2200	3300	4925
SP AWD Wagon 4D		CZ59W	16982	1950	2475	3625	5275
ECLIPSE—4-Cyl.—Equipment Schedule 4							
W.B. 97.2"; 1.8 Liter, 2.0 Liter.							
Coupe 2D		CS34T	12894	625	900	1650	2850
GS Coupe 2D		CS44T	14396	750	1050	1925	3250
GS 16V DOHC Cpe 2D		CS44R	15336	850	1200	2125	3525
Auto Trans				125	125	165	165
ECLIPSE—4-Cyl. Turbo—Equipment Schedule 4							
W.B. 97.2"; 2.0 Liter.							
GS DOHC Coupe 2D		CS54U	17477	975	1400	2475	4025
GSX Coupe 2D		CT64U	19217	1400	1875	3075	4725
Auto Trans				125	125	165	165
GALANT—4-Cyl.—Equipment Schedule 4							
W.B. 102.4"; 2.0 Liter.							
Sedan 4D		CR46V	15487	775	1100	1950	3250
LS Sedan 4D		CR56V	15979	900	1300	2250	3650
GS Sport Sedan 4D		CR56R	17109	1125	1575	2700	4300
GSR Sport Sedan 4D		CR56R	17859	1225	1675	2800	4425
GSX Sport Sedan 4D		CX56R	18899	1225	1700	2850	4475
Manual Trans (Ex GSR)				(225)	(225)	(300)	(300)
GALANT—4-Cyl. Turbo—Equipment Schedule 4							
W.B. 102.4"; 2.0 Liter.							
VR-4 Sport Sedan 4D		CX56U	22868	1500	2025	3225	4900
3000GT—V6—Equipment Schedule 4							
W.B. 97.2"; 3.0 Liter.							
Coupe 2D		XD54B	21826	2550	3150	4700	6900
SL Coupe 2D		XD64B	26577	3100	3750	5425	7750

Body	Type	VIN	List	Trade-In Fair	Trade-In Good	Pvt-Party Good	Retail Excellent
	Auto Trans			125	125	165	165
3000GT—V6 Turbo—Equipment Schedule 2							
W.B. 97.2"; 3.0 Liter.							
VR-4 Coupe 2D		XE74C	34288	5325	6225	8275	11200
DIAMANTE—V6—Equipment Schedule 4							
W.B. 107.1"; 3.0 Liter.							
Sedan 4D		XC47S	21375	1025	1450	2600	4200
LS Sedan 4D		XC57B	26007	1500	1975	3250	5000
	Euro-Handling Pkg			300	300	400	400

1993 MITSUBISHI — (JA3,4A3orKPH)(VD12J)–P–#

Body	Type	VIN	List	Trade-In Fair	Trade-In Good	Pvt-Party Good	Retail Excellent
PRECIS—4-Cyl.—Equipment Schedule 6							
W.B. 93.8"; 1.5 Liter.							
Hatchback 2D		VD12J	8360	200	300	700	1300
MIRAGE—4-Cyl.—Equipment Schedule 6							
W.B. 96.1", 98.4" (Sed); 1.5 Liter, 1.8 Liter.							
S Sedan 4D		CA26A	11208	600	850	1525	2700
S Coupe 2D		CA11A	8822	425	625	1250	2225
ES Sedan 4D		CA36C	11986	550	800	1500	2650
ES Coupe 2D		CA21A	10708	475	700	1350	2400
LS Sedan 4D		CA46C	13252	625	900	1600	2800
LS Coupe 2D		CA31A	11472	550	775	1475	2600
EXPO—4-Cyl.—Equipment Schedule 6							
W.B. 99.2" (LRV), 107.1"; 1.8 Liter, 2.4 Liter.							
LRV Wagon 3D		CB20C	12988	1400	1875	2950	4500
LRV Sport Wagon 3D		CB40G	15494	1500	2025	3125	4675
LRV AWD Wagon 3D		CC20G	14728	1775	2300	3425	5075
Wagon 4D		CD49G	15213	1800	2325	3475	5100
AWD Wagon 4D		CE49G	16533	2200	2775	3950	5700
SP Wagon 4D		CD59G	17211	2025	2575	3750	5425
SP AWD Wagon 4D		CE59G	18561	2275	2850	4075	5800
ECLIPSE—4-Cyl.—Equipment Schedule 4							
W.B. 97.2"; 1.8 Liter, 2.0 Liter.							
Coupe 2D		CF34B	13399	750	1050	1950	3300
GS Coupe 2D		CF44B	15350	900	1300	2375	3950
GS 16V DOHC Cpe 2D		CF44E	16280	1025	1450	2600	4200
	Auto Trans			150	150	200	200
ECLIPSE—4-Cyl. Turbo—Equipment Schedule 4							
W.B. 97.2"; 2.0 Liter.							
GS DOHC Coupe 2D		CF54F	18442	1175	1625	2825	4500
GSX AWD Coupe 2D		CG64F	21162	1675	2200	3450	5225
	Auto Trans			150	150	200	200
GALANT—4-Cyl.—Equipment Schedule 4							
W.B. 102.4"; 2.0 Liter.							
S Sedan 4D		CH46D	16024	900	1300	2375	3925
ES Sedan 4D		CH56D	16704	1050	1500	2675	4275
LS Sport Sedan 4D		CH56D	17734	1375	1875	3075	4775
	Manual Trans			(275)	(275)	(365)	(365)
3000GT—V6—Equipment Schedule 4							
W.B. 97.2"; 3.0 Liter.							
Coupe 2D		BM54J	24102	3100	3750	5475	7850
SL Coupe 2D		BM64J	29152	3725	4475	6300	8825
	Auto Trans			150	150	200	200
3000GT—V6 Turbo—Equipment Schedule 2							
W.B. 97.2"; 3.0 Liter.							
VR-4 Coupe 2D		BN74K	37693	6250	7225	9425	12600
DIAMANTE—V6—Equipment Schedule 4							
W.B. 107.1"; 107.2" (Wag); 3.0 Liter.							
ES Luxury Sedan 4D		BP47H	22842	1225	1700	2950	4650
LS Luxury Sedan 4D		BP57J	30293	1800	2325	3650	5525
Wagon 4D		XC49S	22869	1075	1525	2725	4425
	Euro-Handling Pkg			325	325	435	435

1994 MITSUBISHI — (JA3,4A3orKPH)(VD12J)–R–#

Body	Type	VIN	List	Trade-In Fair	Trade-In Good	Pvt-Party Good	Retail Excellent
PRECIS—4-Cyl.—Equipment Schedule 6							
W.B. 93.8"; 1.5 Liter.							
Hatchback 2D		VD12J		250	325	825	1500
MIRAGE—4-Cyl.—Equipment Schedule 6							
W.B. 96.1", 98.4" (Sed); 1.5 Liter, 1.8 Liter.							
S Sedan 4D		EA26A	12928	700	975	1800	3075
S Coupe 2D		EA11A	10548	525	750	1450	2575
ES Sedan 4D		EA36C	13488	675	950	1775	3075
ES Coupe 2D		EA21A	11918	575	825	1550	2725

Body	Type	VIN	List	Trade-In Fair	Good	Pvt-Party Good	Retail Excellent
LS Sedan 4D		EA46C	15754	775	1075	1975	3300
LS Coupe 2D		EA31C	13104	675	925	1750	3025

EXPO—4-Cyl.—Equipment Schedule 6
W.B. 99.2" (LRV), 107.1"; 1.8 Liter, 2.4 Liter.

LRV Wagon 3D		EB30C	14627	1650	2150	3300	4900
LRV Sport Wagon 3D		EB40G	17244	1800	2325	3475	5125
Wagon 4D		ED59G	18635	2100	2675	3875	5575
AWD Wagon 4D		EE59G	18869	2525	3125	4375	6175

ECLIPSE—4-Cyl.—Equipment Schedule 4
W.B. 97.2"; 1.8 Liter, 2.0 Liter.

Coupe 2D		CF34B	13686	900	1275	2400	4000
GS Coupe 2D		CF44B	16037	1075	1525	2725	4450
GS 16V DOHC Cpe 2D		CF44E	16711	1250	1725	2975	4700
Auto Trans				175	175	235	235

ECLIPSE—4-Cyl. Turbo—Equipment Schedule 4
W.B. 97.2"; 2.0 Liter.

GS DOHC Coupe 2D		CF54F	18949	1475	1950	3250	5025
GSX AWD Coupe 2D		CG64F	21689	2025	2575	3900	5800
Auto Trans				175	175	235	235

GALANT—4-Cyl.—Equipment Schedule 4
W.B. 103.7"; 2.4 Liter.

S Sedan 4D		AJ46G	16204	900	1250	2425	4075
ES Sedan 4D		AJ56G	17195	1050	1500	2700	4450
LS Sport Sedan 4D		AJ56G	18635	1400	1875	3200	5025
GS DOHC Sedan 4D		AJ56L	21697	1475	1950	3275	5100
Manual Trans				(325)	(325)	(435)	(435)

3000GT—V6—Equipment Schedule 4
W.B. 97.2"; 3.0 Liter.

Coupe 2D		AM54J	27645	3700	4425	6300	8875
SL Coupe 2D		AM64J	32120	4425	5200	7200	9925
Auto Trans				175	175	235	235

3000GT—V6 Turbo—Equipment Schedule 2
W.B. 97.2"; 3.0 Liter.

VR-4 Coupe 2D		BN74K	41370	7150	8250	10650	14000

DIAMANTE—V6—Equipment Schedule 4
W.B. 107.1", 107.2" (Wag); 3.0 Liter.

ES Luxury Sedan 4D		AP47H	25995	1500	2025	3325	5150
LS Luxury Sedan 4D		AP57J	32970	2125	2700	4125	6100
Wagon 4D		AC49S	26320	1350	1825	3125	4900
Traction Control				150	150	200	200

1995 MITSUBISHI — (J,4or6)(A3orMM)A(A26A)–S–

MIRAGE—4-Cyl.—Equipment Schedule 6
W.B. 96.1", 98.4" (Sed); 1.5 Liter, 1.8 Liter.

S Sedan 4D		A26A	13707	825	1150	2100	3525
S Coupe 2D		A11A	11563	625	900	1700	2975
ES Sedan 4D		A36C	14627	825	1150	2125	3575
ES Coupe 2D		A21A	13367	700	975	1825	3150
LS Coupe 2D		A31C	14696	825	1150	2100	3525

EXPO—4-Cyl.—Equipment Schedule 6
W.B. 107.1"; 2.4 Liter.

Wagon 4D		D59G	17894	2425	3025	4275	6050
AWD Wagon 4D		E59G	19364	2850	3500	4800	6675

ECLIPSE—4-Cyl.—Equipment Schedule 4
W.B. 98.8"; 2.0 Liter.

RS Coupe 2D		K34Y	15891	1850	2375	3625	5400
GS Coupe 2D		K44Y	18544	2375	2950	4275	6175
Auto Trans				200	200	265	265

ECLIPSE—4-Cyl. Turbo—Equipment Schedule 4
W.B. 98.8"; 2.0 Liter.

GS-T Coupe 2D		K54F	20419	2600	3225	4550	6500
GSX Coupe 2D		L54F	23349	3200	3875	5300	7350
Auto Trans				200	200	265	265

GALANT—4-Cyl.—Equipment Schedule 4
W.B. 103.7"; 2.4 Liter.

S Sedan 4D		J46G	17017	1075	1525	2825	4600
ES Sedan 4D		J56G	19089	1350	1825	3150	5000
LS Sedan 4D		J56G	20689	1650	2150	3550	5475
Manual Trans				(375)	(375)	(500)	(500)

3000GT—V6—Equipment Schedule 4
W.B. 97.2"; 3.0 Liter.

Coupe 2D		M84J	28920	4325	5100	7150	9925
SL Coupe 2D		M54J	34220	5125	6000	8150	11150

Body Type	VIN	List	Trade-In Fair	Trade-In Good	Pvt-Party Good	Retail Excellent
SL Spyder Conv 2D	V65J	57969	10275	11675	14500	18600
Auto Trans			200	200	265	265

3000GT—V6 Turbo—Equipment Schedule 2
W.B. 97.2"; 3.0 Liter.

VR-4 Coupe 2D	N74K	43520	8125	9325	11850	15450
VR-4 Spyder Conv 2D	W75K	64919	12425	14075	17200	21700

DIAMANTE—V6—Equipment Schedule 4
W.B. 107.1", 107.2" (Wag); 3.0 Liter.

ES Luxury Sedan 4D	P47H	28370	1875	2400	3825	5750
LS Luxury Sedan 4D	P57J	35720	2550	3175	4650	6775
Wagon 4D	P49H	28720	1650	2175	3575	5475
Traction Control			175	175	235	235

1996 MITSUBISHI — (Jor4)A3A(A26A)–T–#

MIRAGE—4-Cyl.—Equipment Schedule 4
W.B. 96.1", 98.4" (Sed); 1.5 Liter, 1.8 Liter.

S Sedan 4D	A26A	14834	950	1375	2525	4150
S Coupe 2D	A11A	12422	775	1075	2075	3525
LS Coupe 2D	A31C	14924	950	1375	2525	4200

ECLIPSE—4-Cyl.—Equipment Schedule 4
W.B. 98.8"; 2.0 Liter, 2.4 Liter.

Coupe 2D	K34Y	15135	1975	2525	3825	5650
RS Coupe 2D	K34Y	16281	2300	2875	4225	6100
GS Coupe 2D	K44Y	19310	2875	3525	4950	6925
GS Spyder Conv 2+2	X35G	21227	3600	4325	5800	7975
Auto Trans			200	200	265	265

ECLIPSE—4-Cyl. Turbo—Equipment Schedule 4
W.B. 98.8"; 2.0 Liter.

GS-T Coupe 2D	K54F	21360	3150	3800	5225	7300
GS-T Spyder Conv 2+2	X55F	25410	4350	5125	6725	9025
GSX Coupe 2D	L54F	24330	3775	4500	6025	8175
Auto Trans			200	200	265	265

GALANT—4-Cyl.—Equipment Schedule 4
W.B. 103.7"; 2.4 Liter.

S Sedan 4D	J46G	18535	1425	1900	3300	5225
ES Sedan 4D	J56G	20210	1700	2225	3675	5650
LS Sedan 4D	J56G	23280	2050	2600	4075	6150
Manual Trans			(400)	(400)	(535)	(535)

3000GT—V6—Equipment Schedule 4
W.B. 97.2"; 3.0 Liter.

Coupe 2D	M84J	31110	5050	5925	8100	11100
SL Coupe 2D	M54J	36250	5925	6900	9200	12400
SL Spyder Conv 2D	V65J	58600	11625	13150	16150	20400
Auto Trans			200	200	265	265

3000GT—V6 Turbo—Equipment Schedule 2
W.B. 97.2"; 3.0 Liter.

VR-4 Coupe 2D	N74K	46878	9175	10475	13150	17000
VR-4 Spyder Conv 2D	W75K	65740	13825	15650	18850	23600

DIAMANTE—V6—Equipment Schedule 4
W.B. 107.1"; 3.0 Liter.

ES Luxury Sedan 4D	P47H	27540	2300	2875	4400	6475

1997 MITSUBISHI–(J,4or6)(A3orMM)A(Y26A)–V–#

MIRAGE—4-Cyl.—Equipment Schedule 6
W.B. 95.1", 98.4" (Sed); 1.5 Liter, 1.8 Liter.

DE Sedan 4D	Y26A	13390	1325	1800	2900	4475
DE Coupe 2D	Y11A	11962	1050	1500	2575	4075
LS Sedan 4D	Y36C	14907	1375	1875	3000	4575
LS Coupe 2D	Y31C	14547	1375	1850	2975	4550

ECLIPSE—4-Cyl.—Equipment Schedule 4
W.B. 98.8"; 2.0 Liter, 2.4 Liter.

Coupe 2D	K24Y	15821	2500	3100	4500	6425
RS Coupe 2D	K34Y	18219	2825	3475	4900	6900
GS Coupe 2D	K44Y	20623	3475	4175	5700	7850
GS Spyder Conv 2D	X35G	22411	4250	5050	6625	8900
Auto Trans			200	200	265	265

ECLIPSE—4-Cyl. Turbo—Equipment Schedule 4
W.B. 98.8"; 2.0 Liter.

GS-T Coupe 2D	K54F	22440	3750	4500	6025	8200
GS-T Spyder Conv 2D	X55F	26800	5050	5925	7575	10050
GSX Coupe 2D	L54F	24490	4425	5200	6825	9125
Auto Trans			200	200	265	265

1997 MITSUBISHI

Body	Type	VIN	List	Trade-In Fair	Good	Pvt-Party Good	Retail Excellent
GALANT—4-Cyl.—Equipment Schedule 4							
W.B. 103.7"; 2.4 Liter.							
DE Sedan 4D		J46G	17964	1750	2275	3550	5350
ES Sedan 4D		J56G	18535	2075	2625	3925	5775
LS Sedan 4D		J56G	24400	2400	3000	4375	6300
Manual Trans				(425)	(425)	(565)	(565)
3000GT—V6—Equipment Schedule 4							
W.B. 97.2"; 3.0 Liter.							
Coupe 2D		M44H	28400	5825	6800	9125	12350
SL Coupe 2D		M84J	34460	6825	7850	10300	13750
Auto Trans				200	200	265	265
3000GT—V6 Turbo—Equipment Schedule 2							
W.B. 97.2"; 3.0 Liter.							
VR-4 Coupe 2D		N74K	45060	10275	11700	14550	18600
DIAMANTE—V6—Equipment Schedule 4							
W.B. 107.1"; 3.5 Liter.							
ES Luxury Sedan 4D		P37P	26370	2250	2825	4400	6525
LS Luxury Sedan 4D		P47P	30460	3050	3700	5350	7625

1998 MITSUBISHI—(J,4or6)(A3orMM)A(Y26A)-W-#

Body	Type	VIN	List	Trade-In Fair	Good	Pvt-Party Good	Retail Excellent
MIRAGE—4-Cyl.—Equipment Schedule 6							
W.B. 95.1", 98.4" (Sed); 1.5 Liter, 1.8 Liter.							
DE Sedan 4D		Y26A	13660	1650	2150	3300	4950
DE Coupe 2D		Y11A	12130	1375	1850	2950	4525
LS Sedan 4D		Y36C	15320	1775	2300	3450	5100
LS Coupe 2D		Y31C	14750	1725	2250	3400	5050
ECLIPSE—4-Cyl.—Equipment Schedule 4							
W.B. 98.8"; 2.0 Liter, 2.4 Liter.							
RS Coupe 2D		K24Y	17775	3425	4125	5600	7675
GS Coupe 2D		K44Y	19245	4125	4900	6400	8625
GS Spyder Conv 2D		X35G	22311	4950	5800	7400	9750
Auto Trans				200	200	265	265
ECLIPSE—4-Cyl. Turbo—Equipment Schedule 4							
W.B. 98.8"; 2.0 Liter.							
GS-T Coupe 2D		K54F	22380	4425	5200	6775	9025
GS-T Spyder Conv 2D		X55F	27080	5825	6800	8475	10950
GSX Coupe 2D		L54F	25740	5100	5975	7600	9975
Auto Trans				200	200	265	265
GALANT—4-Cyl.—Equipment Schedule 4							
W.B. 103.7"; 2.4 Liter.							
DE Sedan 4D		J46G	18222	2250	2800	4150	6050
ES Sedan 4D		J56G	18870	2575	3200	4525	6475
LS Sedan 4D		J56G	25730	2975	3625	5025	7025
Manual Trans				(450)	(450)	(600)	(600)
3000GT—V6—Equipment Schedule 4							
W.B. 97.2"; 3.0 Liter.							
Coupe 2D		M44H	28240	6775	7800	10200	13500
SL Coupe 2D		M84J	35660	7850	9025	11450	14950
Auto Trans				200	200	265	265
3000GT—V6 Turbo—Equipment Schedule 2							
W.B. 97.2"; 3.0 Liter.							
VR-4 Coupe 2D		N74K	46700	11625	13150	16000	20200
DIAMANTE—V6—Equipment Schedule 4							
W.B. 107.1"; 3.5 Liter.							
ES Luxury Sedan 4D		P37P	28120	2875	3525	5100	7275
LS Luxury Sedan 4D		P47P	33520	3725	4475	6100	8425

1999 MITSUBISHI — (J,4or6)(A3orMM)A(Y26A)-X-

Body	Type	VIN	List	Trade-In Fair	Good	Pvt-Party Good	Retail Excellent
MIRAGE—4-Cyl.—Equipment Schedule 6							
W.B. 95.1", 98.4" (Sed); 1.5 Liter, 1.8 Liter.							
DE Sedan 4D		Y26A	14405	1975	2525	3750	5475
DE Coupe 2D		Y11A	12455	1625	2125	3300	5000
LS Sedan 4D		Y36C	15432	2100	2675	3900	5650
LS Coupe 2D		Y31C	15025	2075	2625	3850	5600
ECLIPSE—4-Cyl.—Equipment Schedule 4							
W.B. 98.8"; 2.0 Liter, 2.4 Liter.							
RS Coupe 2D		K34Y	18474	3975	4725	6275	8475
GS Coupe 2D		K44Y	20214	4775	5625	7225	9550
GS Spyder Conv 2D		X35G	22836	5725	6675	8325	10800
Auto Trans				225	225	300	300
ECLIPSE—4-Cyl. Turbo—Equipment Schedule 4							
W.B. 98.8"; 2.0 Liter.							
GS-T Coupe 2D		K54F	23645	5100	5975	7575	9925

1999 MITSUBISHI

Body	Type	VIN	List	Trade-In Fair	Good	Pvt-Party Good	Retail Excellent
	GS-T Spyder Conv 2D	X55F	27395	6750	7800	9550	12200
	GSX Coupe 2D	L54F	26985	5925	6900	8575	11100
	Auto Trans			225	225	300	300
GALANT—4-Cyl.—Equipment Schedule 4							
W.B. 103.7"; 2.4 Liter.							
	DE Sedan 4D	A36G	17425	3000	3675	4800	6525
	ES Sedan 4D	A46G	18425	3375	4075	5250	7025
	V6 3.0 Liter	L		600	600	800	800
GALANT—V6—Equipment Schedule 4							
W.B. 103.7"; 3.0 Liter.							
	LS Sedan 4D	A56L	24685	5175	6050	7400	9425
	GTZ Sedan 4D	A46L	24785	5025	5875	7425	9700
3000GT—V6—Equipment Schedule 4							
W.B. 97.2"; 3.0 Liter.							
	Coupe 2D	M44H	25920	7350	8450	10850	14200
	SL Coupe 2D	M84J	33870	9425	10750	13300	16950
	Auto Trans			225	225	300	300
3000GT—V6 Turbo—Equipment Schedule 2							
W.B. 97.2"; 3.0 Liter.							
	VR-4 Coupe 2D	N74K	45070	13675	15450	18350	22700
DIAMANTE—V6—Equipment Schedule 4							
W.B. 107.1"; 3.5 Liter.							
	Luxury Sedan 4D	P37P	27669	3675	4400	6000	8300
	Traction Control			275	275	365	365

2000 MITSUBISHI — (J,4or6)(A3orMM)A(Y26A)–Y–

Body	Type	VIN	List	Trade-In Fair	Good	Pvt-Party Good	Retail Excellent
MIRAGE—4-Cyl.—Equipment Schedule 6							
W.B. 95.1", 98.4" (Sed); 1.5 Liter, 1.8 Liter.							
	DE Sedan 4D	Y26A	14412	2400	3000	4275	6100
	DE Coupe 2D	Y11A	13062	2000	2550	3800	5550
	LS Sedan 4D	Y36C	17372	2550	3150	4425	6275
	LS Coupe 2D	Y31C	15032	2500	3100	4375	6225
ECLIPSE—4-Cyl.—Equipment Schedule 4							
W.B. 100.8"; 2.4 Liter.							
	RS Coupe 2D	C34G	18932	4475	5250	6575	8575
	GS Coupe 2D	C44G	20482	5350	6275	7650	9800
	Auto Trans			250	250	335	335
ECLIPSE—V6—Equipment Schedule 4							
W.B. 100.8"; 3.0 Liter.							
	GT Coupe 2D	C84L	21622	5725	6675	8425	11000
	Traction Control			300	300	400	400
	Auto Trans			250	250	335	335
GALANT—4-Cyl.—Equipment Schedule 4							
W.B. 103.7"; 2.4 Liter.							
	DE Sedan 4D	A36G	17792	3600	4325	5525	7350
	ES Sedan 4D	A46G	18692	4000	4775	6025	7900
	V6 3.0 Liter	L		675	675	900	900
GALANT—V6—Equipment Schedule 4							
W.B. 103.7"; 3.0 Liter.							
	LS Sedan 4D	A56L	24292	6050	7000	8400	10550
	GTZ Sedan 4D	A46L	24192	5850	6825	8425	10850
DIAMANTE—V6—Equipment Schedule 4							
W.B. 107.1"; 3.5 Liter.							
	ES Sedan 4D	P57P	25467	4575	5400	7075	9475
	LS Sedan 4D	P67P	28367	5675	6600	8350	10900

2001 MITSUBISHI–(J,4or6)(A3orMM)A(Y11A)–1–#

Body	Type	VIN	List	Trade-In Fair	Good	Pvt-Party Good	Retail Excellent
MIRAGE—4-Cyl.—Equipment Schedule 6							
W.B. 95.1", 98.4" (Sed); 1.5 Liter, 1.8 Liter.							
	DE Coupe 2D	Y11A	13277	2450	3050	4375	6275
	ES Sedan 4D	Y26C	14147	2925	3575	4950	6900
	LS Sedan 4D	Y36C	14997	3050	3700	5100	7050
	LS Coupe 2D	Y31C	15237	3000	3675	5050	7000
ECLIPSE—4-Cyl.—Equipment Schedule 4							
W.B. 100.8"; 2.4 Liter.							
	RS Coupe 2D	C31G	18507	5350	6275	7650	9800
	GS Coupe 2D	C41G	19317	6375	7375	8825	11100
	GS Spyder Conv 2D	E35G	23927	6950	8025	9900	12600
	Auto Trans			275	275	365	365
ECLIPSE—V6—Equipment Schedule 4							
W.B. 100.8"; 3.0 Liter.							
	GT Coupe 2D	C81H	21467	6750	7800	9600	12350
	GT Spyder Conv 2D	E55H	25927	8100	9300	11450	14700

EQUIPMENT & MILEAGE PAGE 9 TO 23

2001 MITSUBISHI

Body	Type	VIN	List	Trade-In Fair	Trade-In Good	Pvt-Party Good	Retail Excellent
	Auto Trans			275	275	365	365
	Traction Control			325	325	435	435
GALANT—4-Cyl.—Equipment Schedule 4							
W.B. 103.7"; 2.4 Liter.							
DE Sedan 4D		A36G	18077	4375	5150	6450	8400
ES Sedan 4D		A46G	18927	4825	5675	6975	8975
V6 3.0 Liter		H		750	750	1000	1000
GALANT—V6—Equipment Schedule 4							
W.B. 103.7"; 3.0 Liter.							
LS Sedan 4D		A56H	24427	7075	8150	9600	11900
GTZ Sedan 4D		A46H	24527	6875	7925	9600	12200
DIAMANTE—V6—Equipment Schedule 4							
W.B. 107.1"; 3.5 Liter.							
ES Sedan 4D		P57P	25907	5650	6575	8325	10900
LS Sedan 4D		P67P	28927	6875	7925	9750	12450

2002 MITSUBISHI—(J,4or6)(A3orMM)A(Y11A)-2-#

Body	Type	VIN	List	Trade-In Fair	Trade-In Good	Pvt-Party Good	Retail Excellent
MIRAGE—4-Cyl.—Equipment Schedule 6							
W.B. 95.1"; 1.5 Liter, 1.8 Liter.							
DE Coupe 2D		Y11A	13362	3000	3675	5100	7100
LS Coupe 2D		Y31C	15332	3625	4350	5800	7900
LANCER—4-Cyl.—Equipment Schedule 6							
W.B. 102.4"; 2.0 Liter.							
ES Sedan 4D		J26E	15242	4875	5700	7025	9075
LS Sedan 4D		J36E	16442	5125	6000	7350	9400
OZ Rally Sedan 4D		J86E	16832	5875	6850	8150	10250
ECLIPSE—4-Cyl.—Equipment Schedule 4							
W.B. 100.8"; 2.4 Liter.							
RS Coupe 2D		C31G	18642	6425	7450	8900	11200
GS Coupe 2D		C41G	19512	7550	8700	10200	12600
GS Spyder Conv 2D		E35G	24172	8175	9375	11350	14250
Auto Trans				300	300	400	400
ECLIPSE—V6—Equipment Schedule 4							
W.B. 100.8"; 3.0 Liter.							
GT Coupe 2D		C81H	21702	7950	9125	11050	13900
GT Spyder Conv 2D		E55H	26152	9425	10750	13050	16500
Auto Trans				300	300	400	400
Traction Control				350	350	465	465
GALANT—4-Cyl.—Equipment Schedule 4							
W.B. 103.7"; 2.4 Liter.							
DE Sedan 4D		A36G	18262	5275	6175	7500	9600
ES Sedan 4D		A46G	19072	5775	6725	8100	10200
LS Sedan 4D		A46G	21672	6475	7500	8900	11150
V6 3.0 Liter		L		825	825	1100	1100
GALANT—V6—Equipment Schedule 4							
W.B. 103.7"; 3.0 Liter.							
GTZ Sedan 4D		A46H	24712	8025	9200	11000	13750
DIAMANTE—V6—Equipment Schedule 4							
W.B. 107.1"; 3.5 Liter.							
ES Sedan 4D		P57P	26247	6950	8025	9850	12550
VR-X Sedan 4D		P67P	27557	7625	8750	10600	13400
LS Sedan 4D		P67P	29007	8300	9525	11400	14250

2003 MITSUBISHI — (J,4or6)(A3orMM)A(J26E)-3-#

Body	Type	VIN	List	Trade-In Fair	Trade-In Good	Pvt-Party Good	Retail Excellent
LANCER—4-Cyl.—Equipment Schedule 6							
W.B. 102.4"; 2.0 Liter.							
ES Sedan 4D		J26E	14587	5700	6650	7925	9925
LS Sedan 4D		J36E	16617	6000	6950	8250	10300
OZ Rally Sedan 4D		J86E	16317	6825	7850	9150	11250
LANCER AWD—4-Cyl. Turbo—Equipment Schedule 4							
W.B. 103.1"; 2.0 Liter.							
Evolution Sedan 4D		H86F	29582	17850	20075	22800	27300
ECLIPSE—4-Cyl.—Equipment Schedule 4							
W.B. 100.8"; 2.4 Liter.							
RS Coupe 2D		C34G	18717	7600	8725	10200	12500
GS Coupe 2D		C44G	19617	8850	10125	11600	14050
GS Spyder Conv 2D		E45G	24397	9500	10850	12750	15800
Auto Trans				300	300	400	400
ECLIPSE—V6—Equipment Schedule 4							
W.B. 100.8"; 3.0 Liter.							
GT Coupe 2D		C84H	21807	9225	10500	12450	15400
GT Spyder Conv 2D		E85H	26477	10900	12325	14750	18300
GTS Coupe 2D		C74H	24777	11900	13500	15100	17950

Body Type	VIN	List	Trade-In Fair	Good	Pvt-Party Good	Retail Excellent
GTS Spyder Conv 2D	E75H	28847	11575	13100	15600	19300
Auto Trans			300	300	400	400
Traction Control			400	400	535	535

GALANT—4-Cyl.—Equipment Schedule 4
W.B. 103.7"; 2.4 Liter.

DE Sedan 4D	A36G	18347	6350	7350	8675	10750
ES Sedan 4D	A46G	19157	6900	7950	9300	11400
LS Sedan 4D	A46G	21757	7650	8775	10200	12450
V6 3.0 Liter	H		900	900	1200	1200

GALANT—V6—Equipment Schedule 4
W.B. 103.7"; 3.0 Liter.

GTZ Sedan 4D	A46H	25047	9325	10650	12400	15100

DIAMANTE—V6—Equipment Schedule 4
W.B. 107.1"; 3.5 Liter.

ES Sedan 4D	P57P	26557	8350	9575	11350	14050
VR-X Sedan 4D	P87P	27677	9100	10375	12200	15000
LS Sedan 4D	P67P	29027	9850	11225	13050	15950

LANCER—4-Cyl.—Equipment Schedule 4
W.B. 102.4"; 2.0 Liter, 2.4 Liter.

ES Sedan 4D	J26E	14172	6725	7775	9000	11050
LS Sedan 4D	J36E	16572	7025	8100	9375	11450
LS Wagon 4D	D29F	17172	7350	8450	9750	11850
OZ Rally Sedan 4D	J86E	16372	7900	9075	10300	12500
Ralliart Sedan 4D	J66F	18572				
Ralliart Wagon 4D	D69F	19772				

LANCER AWD—4-Cyl. Turbo—Equipment Schedule 4
W.B. 102.4"; 2.0 Liter.

Evolution RS Sedan 4D	H36D	27374				
Evolution Sedan 4D	H86D	30574				

ECLIPSE—4-Cyl.—Equipment Schedule 4
W.B. 100.8"; 2.4 Liter.

RS Coupe 2D	C34G	18892	9100	10375	11850	14250
GS Coupe 2D	C44G	19892	10425	11850	13400	16000
GS Spyder Conv 2D	E45G	24892	11125	12625	14700	17950
Auto Trans			300	300	400	400

ECLIPSE—V6—Equipment Schedule 4
W.B. 100.8"; 3.0 Liter.

GT Coupe 2D	C84H	22092	10800	12250	14300	17500
GT Spyder Conv 2D	E85H	26992	12625	14300	16800	20600
GTS Coupe 2D	C74H	25092	13775	15550	17350	20400
GTS Spyder Conv 2D	E75H	29372	13350	15075	17750	21800
Auto Trans			300	300	400	400

GALANT—4-Cyl.—Equipment Schedule 4
W.B. 108.3"; 2.4 Liter.

DE Sedan 4D	A36G	18592	10475	11900	13600	16300
ES Sedan 4D	A46G	19592	11050	12525	14250	17100

GALANT—V6—Equipment Schedule 4
W.B. 108.3"; 3.8 Liter.

LS Sedan 4D	A46H	21592	13575	15350	17100	20100
GTS Sedan 4D	A46H	26292	13725	15500	17550	20900

DIAMANTE—V6—Equipment Schedule 4
W.B. 107.1"; 3.5 Liter.

ES Sedan 4D	P57P	25594	10125	11525	13400	16300
VR-X Sedan 4D	P87P	27414	10900	12375	14300	17350
LS Sedan 4D	P67P	28214	11700	13250	15200	18400

NISSAN

SENTRA—4-Cyl.—Equipment Schedule 6
W.B. 95.7"; 1.6 Liter.

Sedan 2D	GB22B	8384	450	650	1200	2075
XE Sedan 2D	GB22B	9634	525	750	1325	2250
XE Sedan 4D	GB21B	10834	525	750	1325	2250
XE Sport Coupe 2D	GB24B	12084	525	750	1300	2225
XE Wagon 4D	GB25B	11584	525	750	1325	2250
SE Sport Coupe 2D	GB24B	13384	650	900	1525	2600

STANZA—4-Cyl.—Equipment Schedule 5
W.B. 100.4"; 2.4 Liter.

Body	Type	VIN	List	Trade-In Fair	Trade-In Good	Pvt-Party Good	Retail Excellent
	XE Sedan 4D	FU21P	13335	550	775	1400	2400
	GXE Sedan 4D	FU21P	15835	625	900	1525	2600
PULSAR NX—4-Cyl.—Equipment Schedule 6							
W.B. 95.7"; 1.6 Liter.							
	XE H'Back Coupe 2D	GN34C	13334	600	850	1400	2300
240SX—4-Cyl.—Equipment Schedule 5							
W.B. 97.4"; 2.4 Liter.							
	XE Coupe 2D	HS34P	15164	825	1150	1950	3200
	SE Fastback 2D	HS36P	15414	850	1175	2000	3275
AXXESS—4-Cyl.—Equipment Schedule 6							
W.B. 102.8"; 2.4 Liter.							
	XE Wagon 4D	HM15P	15109	975	1425	2225	3475
	SE Wagon 4D	HM15P	17009	1025	1450	2300	3575
	4WD	J		250	250	335	335
MAXIMA—V6—Equipment Schedule 4							
W.B. 104.3"; 3.0 Liter.							
	GXE Sedan 4D	HJ01P	17959	975	1400	2475	4025
	SE Sedan 4D	HJ01P	19939	975	1400	2475	4025
300ZX—V6—Equipment Schedule 3							
W.B. 96.5"; 101.2" (2+2); 3.0 Liter.							
	GS Coupe 2D	RZ24A	28960	2700	3300	4800	6900
	GS 2+2 Coupe 2D	RZ26A	30160	2850	3500	5050	7200
300ZX—V6 Turbo—Equipment Schedule 3							
W.B. 96.5"; 3.0 Liter.							
	Coupe 2D	CZ24A	34060	3500	4200	5875	8200

1991 NISSAN — (1N4orJN1)(EB32A)-M-#

Body	Type	VIN	List	Trade-In Fair	Trade-In Good	Pvt-Party Good	Retail Excellent
SENTRA—4-Cyl.—Equipment Schedule 6							
W.B. 95.7"; 1.6 Liter, 2.0 Liter.							
	E Sedan 2D	EB32A	9099	525	750	1350	2300
	E Sedan 4D	EB31B	10000	525	750	1350	2300
	XE Sedan 4D	EB31B	10370	600	875	1500	2525
	XE Sedan 4D	EB31B	10035	600	875	1500	2525
	SE Sedan 2D	EB32A	10855	600	850	1475	2475
	SE-R Sedan 2D	GB32A	11245	825	1150	1975	3200
	GXE Sedan 4D	EB31B	12325	750	1025	1750	2900
STANZA—4-Cyl.—Equipment Schedule 6							
W.B. 100.4"; 2.4 Liter.							
	XE Sedan 4D	FU21P	13900	650	900	1600	2750
	GXE Sedan 4D	FU21P	16300	725	1025	1800	3025
NX—4-Cyl.—Equipment Schedule 6							
W.B. 95.7"; 1.6 Liter, 2.0 Liter.							
	1600 Hatchback Cpe 2D	EB34C	12240	875	1225	1950	3100
	2000 Hatchback Cpe 2D	GB34C	14120	1000	1450	2275	3575
240SX—4-Cyl.—Equipment Schedule 5							
W.B. 97.4"; 2.4 Liter.							
	Coupe 2D	MS34P	15539	925	1325	2350	3875
	Fastback 2D	MS36P	15789	950	1350	2400	3900
	SE Coupe 2D	MS34P	17579	950	1350	2400	3900
	SE Fastback 2D	MS36P	17764	950	1375	2425	3925
	LE Fastback 2D	MS36P	18664	950	1350	2400	3900
MAXIMA—V6—Equipment Schedule 3							
W.B. 104.3"; 3.0 Liter.							
	GXE Sedan 4D	HJ01P	18974	1100	1550	2725	4375
	SE Sedan 4D	HJ01P	20994	1125	1575	2775	4450
	Manual Trans			(175)	(175)	(235)	(235)
300ZX—V6—Equipment Schedule 3							
W.B. 96.5"; 101.2" (2+2); 3.0 Liter.							
	Coupe 2D	RZ24A	30175	3175	3850	5500	7800
	2+2 Coupe 2D	RZ26A	31375	3375	4075	5750	8125
300ZX—V6 Turbo—Equipment Schedule 3							
W.B. 96.5"; 3.0 Liter.							
	Coupe 2D	CZ24A	34575	4100	4875	6700	9250

1992 NISSAN — (1N4orJN1)(EB32A)-N-#

Body	Type	VIN	List	Trade-In Fair	Trade-In Good	Pvt-Party Good	Retail Excellent
SENTRA—4-Cyl.—Equipment Schedule 6							
W.B. 95.7"; 1.6 Liter, 2.0 Liter.							
	E Sedan 2D	EB32A	9645	600	850	1500	2600
	E Sedan 4D	EB31B	10700	600	875	1525	2650
	XE Sedan 2D	EB32A	11175	675	950	1675	2850
	XE Sedan 4D	EB31B	11860	675	950	1675	2850
	SE Sedan 2D	EB32A	12155	675	925	1650	2800
	SE-R Sedan 2D	GB32A	13445	900	1300	2200	3575

Body	Type	VIN	List	Trade-In Fair	Good	Pvt-Party Good	Retail Excellent
GXE Sedan 4D		EB31B	13250	825	1150	1975	3250
STANZA—4-Cyl.—Equipment Schedule 5							
W.B. 100.4"; 2.4 Liter.							
XE Sedan 4D		FU21P	14000	750	1050	1875	3150
GXE Sedan 4D		FU21P	17370	850	1200	2100	3475
SE Sedan 4D		FU21P	17825	900	1300	2350	3875
NX—4-Cyl.—Equipment Schedule 5							
W.B. 95.7"; 1.6 Liter, 2.0 Liter.							
1600 H'Back Cpe 2D		EB34C	12900	975	1400	2425	3525
2000 H'Back Cpe 2D		GB34C	14630	1175	1625	2675	4150
240SX—4-Cyl.—Equipment Schedule 5							
W.B. 97.4"; 2.4 Liter.							
Coupe 2D		MS34P	16495	1100	1550	2700	4300
Fastback 2D		MS36P	16765	1150	1600	2750	4375
SE Coupe 2D		MS34P	18665	1150	1600	2750	4375
SE Fastback 2D		MS36P	18865	1175	1625	2775	4400
SE Convertible 2D		MS36A	22295	1875	2400	3675	5475
LE Fastback 2D		MS36P	19025	1150	1600	2750	4375
MAXIMA—V6—Equipment Schedule 4							
W.B. 104.3"; 3.0 Liter.							
GXE Sedan 4D		HJ01P	19995	1375	1850	3075	4800
SE Sedan 4D		EJ01P	22050	1450	1925	3200	4950
Manual Trans				(225)	(225)	(300)	(300)
300ZX—V6—Equipment Schedule 3							
W.B. 96.5", 101.2" (2+2); 3.0 Liter.							
Coupe 2D		RZ24H	31490	3850	4575	6350	8850
2+2 Coupe 2D		RZ26H	32740	4075	4850	6675	9250
300ZX—V6 Turbo—Equipment Schedule 3							
W.B. 96.5"; 3.0 Liter.							
Coupe 2D		CZ24H	36190	4900	5750	7700	10450

1993 NISSAN — (1N4orJN1)(EB32A)-P-#

Body	Type	VIN	List	Trade-In Fair	Good	Pvt-Party Good	Retail Excellent
SENTRA—4-Cyl.—Equipment Schedule 6							
W.B. 95.7"; 1.6 Liter, 2.0 Liter.							
E Sedan 2D		EB32A	10310	675	950	1700	2900
E Sedan 4D		EB31P	11760	700	1000	1750	2975
XE Sedan 2D		EB32A	11850	775	1075	1900	3150
XE Sedan 4D		EB31P	12540	775	1100	1925	3200
SE Sedan 2D		EB32A	12845	775	1075	1900	3150
SE-R Sedan 2D		EB32A	14400	1025	1450	2525	4025
GXE Sedan 4D		EB31C	14495	900	1300	2200	3575
NX—4-Cyl.—Equipment Schedule 6							
W.B. 95.7"; 1.6 Liter, 2.0 Liter.							
1600 Coupe 2D		EB34C	13285	1125	1575	2625	4075
2000 Coupe 2D		GB36C	15920	1425	1900	3000	4525
240SX—4-Cyl.—Equipment Schedule 5							
W.B. 97.4"; 2.4 Liter.							
Coupe 2D		MS34P	16785	1375	1875	3075	4775
Fastback 2D		MS36P	17500	1425	1900	3150	4850
SE Coupe 2D		MS34P	19245	1425	1900	3150	4850
SE Fastback 2D		MS36P	19705	1475	1950	3200	4900
SE Convertible 2D		MS36A	23545	2250	2825	4200	6125
ALTIMA—4-Cyl.—Equipment Schedule 4							
W.B. 103.1"; 2.4 Liter.							
XE Sedan 4D		BU31F	16229	825	1150	2150	3650
GXE Sedan 4D		BU31F	16199	825	1150	2275	3875
SE Sedan 4D		BU31F	17699	950	1350	2525	4175
GLE Sedan 4D		BU31F	18699	1225	1675	2925	4650
Manual Trans				(275)	(275)	(365)	(365)
MAXIMA—V6—Equipment Schedule 4							
W.B. 104.3"; 3.0 Liter.							
GXE Sedan 4D		HJ01F	23525	1650	2175	3500	5325
SE Sedan 4D		EJ01F	23310	1800	2325	3675	5550
Manual Trans				(275)	(275)	(365)	(365)
300ZX—V6—Equipment Schedule 3							
W.B. 96.5", 101.2" (2+2); 3.0 Liter.							
Coupe 2D		RZ24H	30445	4550	5375	7275	9925
2+2 Coupe 2D		RZ26H	33875	4850	5700	7650	10400
Convertible 2D		RZ27H	36920	5700	6625	8700	11650
300ZX—V6 Turbo—Equipment Schedule 3							
W.B. 96.5"; 3.0 Liter.							
Coupe 2D		CZ24H	37440	5775	6725	8800	11750

1994 NISSAN

1994 NISSAN — (1N4orJN1)(EB32A)-R-#

SENTRA—4-Cyl.—Equipment Schedule 6
W.B. 95.7"; 1.6 Liter, 2.0 Liter.

Body Type	VIN	List	Fair	Good	Good	Excellent
E Sedan 2D	EB32A	11924	775	1100	1950	3275
E Sedan 4D	EB31P	12474	825	1150	2025	3350
XE Sedan 2D	EB32A	12479	875	1225	2125	3525
XE Sedan 4D	EB31P	12679	900	1250	2175	3575
Limited Ed Sedan 2D	EB32A	13029	950	1375	2425	3950
Limited Ed Sedan 4D	EB31P	13249	1000	1450	2525	4075
SE Sedan 2D	EB32A	13974	900	1250	2175	3575
SE-R Sedan 2D	GB32A	15174	1150	1600	2725	4325
GXE Sedan 4D	EB31C	15049	1025	1450	2550	4075

240SX—4-Cyl.—Equipment Schedule 5
W.B. 97.4"; 2.4 Liter.

SE Convertible 2D	MS36A	25344	2700	3300	4775	6850

ALTIMA—4-Cyl.—Equipment Schedule 5
W.B. 103.1"; 2.4 Liter.

XE Sedan 4D	BU31F	16904	950	1375	2600	4300
GXE Sedan 4D	BU31F	17264	975	1400	2625	4325
SE Sedan 4D	BU31F	19384	1150	1600	2900	4675
GLE Sedan 4D	BU31F	19559	1500	2000	3325	5175
Manual Trans			(325)	(325)	(435)	(435)

MAXIMA—V6—Equipment Schedule 4
W.B. 104.3"; 3.0 Liter.

GXE Sedan 4D	HJ01F	22579	2025	2575	3950	5900
SE Sedan 4D	EJ01F	24614	2175	2750	4175	6175
Manual Trans			(325)	(325)	(435)	(435)

300ZX—V6—Equipment Schedule 3
W.B. 96.5", 101.2" (2+2); 3.0 Liter.

Coupe 2D	RZ24D	34079	5300	6200	8225	11100
2+2 Coupe 2D	RZ26D	36869	5650	6550	8650	11550
Convertible 2D	RZ27D	41259	6550	7575	9800	12950

300ZX—V6 Turbo—Equipment Schedule 3
W.B. 96.5"; 3.0 Liter.

Coupe 2D	CZ24D	40479	6650	7675	9900	13050

1995 NISSAN — (1N4orJN1)(AB41D)-S-#

SENTRA—4-Cyl.—Equipment Schedule 6
W.B. 99.8"; 1.6 Liter.

Sedan 4D	AB41D	11389	1200	1650	2750	4325
XE Sedan 4D	AB41D	13139	1325	1800	2900	4500
GXE Sedan 4D	AB41D	13839	1450	1925	3050	4650
GLE Sedan 4D	AB41D	14839	1725	2250	3425	5100

200SX—4-Cyl.—Equipment Schedule 6
W.B. 99.8"; 1.6 Liter, 2.0 Liter.

Coupe 2D	AB42D	13874	1350	1825	2925	4500
SE Coupe 2D	AB42D	14674	1475	1950	3100	4700
SE-R Coupe 2D	BB42D	15674	1700	2225	3400	5100

240SX—4-Cyl.—Equipment Schedule 5
W.B. 99.4"; 2.4 Liter.

Coupe 2D	AS44D	19758	2525	3125	4550	6575
SE Coupe 2D	AS44D	22439	2975	3650	5150	7300

ALTIMA—4-Cyl.—Equipment Schedule 5
W.B. 103.1"; 2.4 Liter.

XE Sedan 4D	BU31D	17848	1175	1625	2975	4825
GXE Sedan 4D	BU31D	18218	1200	1650	3000	4850
SE Sedan 4D	BU31D	20089	1475	1950	3325	5250
GLE Sedan 4D	BU31D	20279	1825	2350	3800	5775
Manual Trans			(375)	(375)	(500)	(500)

MAXIMA—V6—Equipment Schedule 4
W.B. 106.3"; 3.0 Liter.

GXE Sedan 4D	CA21D	21989	2475	3075	4575	6675
SE Sedan 4D	CA21D	22989	2700	3300	4850	6975
GLE Sedan 4D	CA21D	25209	3225	3900	5500	7750
Manual Trans			(375)	(375)	(500)	(500)

300ZX—V6—Equipment Schedule 3
W.B. 96.5", 101.2" (2+2); 3.0 Liter.

Coupe 2D	RZ24D	35399	6075	7050	9225	12300
2+2 Coupe 2D	RZ26D	38189	6425	7450	9650	12750
Convertible 2D	RZ27D	42579	7475	8600	10950	14250

300ZX—V6 Turbo—Equipment Schedule 3
W.B. 96.5"; 3.0 Liter.

Body	Type	VIN	List	Trade-In Fair	Trade-In Good	Pvt-Party Good	Retail Excellent
Coupe 2D		CZ24D	41799	**7550**	**8700**	**11050**	**14400**

1996 NISSAN — (1N4or3N1)(AB41D)–T–#

SENTRA—4-Cyl.—Equipment Schedule 6
W.B. 99.8"; 1.6 Liter.

Sedan 4D		AB41D	11904	**1475**	**1950**	**3100**	**4725**
XE Sedan 4D		AB41D	13934	**1575**	**2100**	**3275**	**4925**
GXE Sedan 4D		AB41D	14864	**1725**	**2250**	**3425**	**5100**
GLE Sedan 4D		AB41D	15634	**2050**	**2600**	**3850**	**5600**

200SX—4-Cyl.—Equipment Schedule 6
W.B. 99.8"; 1.6 Liter, 2.0 Liter.

Coupe 2D		AB42D	14303	**1600**	**2100**	**3300**	**4950**
SE Coupe 2D		SE24D	15274	**1725**	**2250**	**3425**	**5100**
SE-R Coupe 2D		BB42D	16474	**2025**	**2575**	**3800**	**5525**

240SX—4-Cyl.—Equipment Schedule 5
W.B. 99.4"; 2.4 Liter.

Coupe 2D		AS44D	20563	**2975**	**3650**	**5175**	**7350**
SE Coupe 2D		AS44D	23454	**3525**	**4225**	**5850**	**8125**

ALTIMA—4-Cyl.—Equipment Schedule 4
W.B. 103.1"; 2.4 Liter.

XE Sedan 4D		BU31D	18783	**1500**	**2000**	**3450**	**5450**
GXE Sedan 4D		BU31D	19533	**1500**	**2025**	**3475**	**5475**
SE Sedan 4D		BU31D	20534	**1825**	**2350**	**3875**	**5925**
GLE Sedan 4D		BU31D	21404	**2200**	**2775**	**4325**	**6450**
Manual Trans				**(400)**	**(400)**	**(535)**	**(535)**

MAXIMA—V6—Equipment Schedule 4
W.B. 106.3"; 3.0 Liter.

GXE Sedan 4D		CA21D	23084	**2950**	**3600**	**5200**	**7450**
SE Sedan 4D		CA21D	24084	**3200**	**3875**	**5525**	**7825**
GLE Sedan 4D		CA21D	26684	**3750**	**4500**	**6200**	**8600**
Manual Trans				**(400)**	**(400)**	**(535)**	**(535)**

300ZX—V6—Equipment Schedule 3
W.B. 96.5", 101.2" (2+2); 3.0 Liter.

Coupe 2D		RZ24D	37844	**6950**	**8025**	**10250**	**13550**
2+2 Coupe 2D		RZ26D	40594	**7325**	**8425**	**10750**	**14050**
Convertible 2D		RZ27D	45084	**8475**	**9700**	**12150**	**15700**

300ZX—V6 Turbo—Equipment Schedule 3
W.B. 96.5"; 3.0 Liter.

Coupe 2D		CZ24D	44384	**8575**	**9800**	**12250**	**15800**

1997 NISSAN–(1N4or3N1)(AB41D)–V–

SENTRA—4-Cyl.—Equipment Schedule 6
W.B. 99.8"; 1.6 Liter.

Sedan 4D		AB41D	11919	**1800**	**2325**	**3525**	**5250**
XE Sedan 4D		AB41D	14069	**1925**	**2450**	**3700**	**5450**
GXE Sedan 4D		AB41D	15219	**2100**	**2650**	**3900**	**5675**
GLE Sedan 4D		AB41D	16069	**2400**	**3000**	**4300**	**6150**

200SX—4-Cyl.—Equipment Schedule 6
W.B. 99.8"; 1.6 Liter, 2.0 Liter.

Coupe 2D		AB42D	14418	**1950**	**2475**	**3725**	**5475**
SE Coupe 2D		AB42D	15769	**2075**	**2625**	**3875**	**5650**
SE-R Coupe 2D		BB42D	17169	**2375**	**2950**	**4250**	**6075**

240SX—4-Cyl.—Equipment Schedule 5
W.B. 99.4"; 2.4 Liter.

Coupe 2D		AS44D	20628	**3550**	**4250**	**5900**	**8225**
SE Coupe 2D		AS44D	23269	**4125**	**4900**	**6625**	**9075**
LE Coupe 2D		AS44D	25719	**4175**	**4950**	**6675**	**9125**

ALTIMA—4-Cyl.—Equipment Schedule 4
W.B. 103.1"; 2.4 Liter.

XE Sedan 4D		BU31D	18798	**1925**	**2450**	**4000**	**6150**
GXE Sedan 4D		BU31D	19548	**1950**	**2475**	**4050**	**6200**
SE Sedan 4D		BU31D	20549	**2275**	**2850**	**4500**	**6700**
GLE Sedan 4D		BU31D	21419	**2675**	**3275**	**4925**	**7200**
Manual Trans				**(425)**	**(425)**	**(565)**	**(565)**

MAXIMA—V6—Equipment Schedule 4
W.B. 106.3"; 3.0 Liter.

GXE Sedan 4D		CA21D	23669	**3500**	**4200**	**5950**	**8350**
SE Sedan 4D		CA21D	24719	**3800**	**4525**	**6300**	**8775**
GLE Sedan 4D		CA21D	27319	**4375**	**5150**	**7000**	**9575**
Manual Trans				**(425)**	**(425)**	**(565)**	**(565)**

Body	Type	VIN	List	Trade-In Fair	Trade-In Good	Pvt-Party Good	Retail Excellent

1998 NISSAN — (1N4or3N1)(AB41D)-W-#

SENTRA—4-Cyl.—Equipment Schedule 6
W.B. 99.8"; 1.6 Liter, 2.0 Liter.

Body	Type	VIN	List	Fair	Good	Good	Excellent
	Sedan 4D	AB41D	11989	2125	2700	4000	5825
	XE Sedan 4D	AB41D	14189	2275	2850	4175	6050
	GXE Sedan 4D	AB41D	15389	2450	3050	4375	6275
	GLE Sedan 4D	AB41D	16239	2825	3450	4825	6775
	SE Sedan 4D	AB41D	17239	2975	3650	5025	6975

200SX—4-Cyl.—Equipment Schedule 6
W.B. 99.8"; 1.6 Liter, 2.0 Liter.

Body	Type	VIN	List	Fair	Good	Good	Excellent
	Coupe 2D	AB42D	14638	2300	2875	4200	6075
	SE Coupe 2D	AB42D	15889	2425	3025	4350	6250
	SE-R Coupe 2D	BB42D	17239	2775	3400	4775	6725

240SX—4-Cyl.—Equipment Schedule 5
W.B. 99.4"; 2.4 Liter.

Body	Type	VIN	List	Fair	Good	Good	Excellent
	Coupe 2D	AS44D	20648	4175	4975	6750	9250
	SE Coupe 2D	AS44D	23289	4825	5675	7500	10150
	LE Coupe 2D	AS44D	25739	4875	5700	7550	10200

ALTIMA—4-Cyl.—Equipment Schedule 4
W.B. 103.1"; 2.4 Liter.

Body	Type	VIN	List	Fair	Good	Good	Excellent
	XE Sedan 4D	DL01D	18179	2900	3550	4975	6975
	GXE Sedan 4D	DL01D	18480	2925	3575	5000	7025
	SE Sedan 4D	DL01D	19780	3325	4025	5500	7575
	GLE Sedan 4D	DL01D	20380	3725	4450	5925	8100
	Manual Trans			(450)	(450)	(600)	(600)

MAXIMA—V6—Equipment Schedule 4
W.B. 106.3"; 3.0 Liter.

Body	Type	VIN	List	Fair	Good	Good	Excellent
	GXE Sedan 4D	CA21D	23739	4175	4975	6725	9225
	SE Sedan 4D	CA21D	24989	4525	5350	7150	9700
	GLE Sedan 4D	CA21D	27389	5100	5975	7825	10450
	Manual Trans			(450)	(450)	(600)	(600)

1999 NISSAN — (1N4,JN1or3N1)(AB41D)-X-#

SENTRA—4-Cyl.—Equipment Schedule 6
W.B. 99.8"; 1.6 Liter, 2.0 Liter.

Body	Type	VIN	List	Fair	Good	Good	Excellent
	XE Sedan 4D	AB41D	13319	2725	3350	4750	6725
	GXE Sedan 4D	AB41D	14719	2900	3550	4950	6925
	SE Sedan 4D	BB41D	15719	3475	4175	5650	7725

ALTIMA—4-Cyl.—Equipment Schedule 4
W.B. 103.1"; 2.4 Liter.

Body	Type	VIN	List	Fair	Good	Good	Excellent
	XE Sedan 4D	DL01D	18209	3425	4150	5675	7825
	GXE Sedan 4D	DL01D	18510	3475	4175	5700	7875
	SE Sedan 4D	DL01D	19810	3925	4675	6250	8500
	GLE Sedan 4D	DL01D	20510	4375	5150	6775	9075
	Manual Trans			(500)	(500)	(665)	(665)

MAXIMA—V6—Equipment Schedule 4
W.B. 106.3"; 3.0 Liter.

Body	Type	VIN	List	Fair	Good	Good	Excellent
	GXE Sedan 4D	CA21D	23769	5000	5850	7725	10400
	SE Sedan 4D	CA21D	25019	5475	6375	8325	11100
	GLE Sedan 4D	CA21D	27419	6050	7000	9000	11850
	Manual Trans			(500)	(500)	(665)	(665)

2000 NISSAN — (1N4,JN1or3N1)(CB51D)-Y-#

SENTRA—4-Cyl.—Equipment Schedule 6
W.B. 99.8"; 1.8 Liter, 2.0 Liter.

Body	Type	VIN	List	Fair	Good	Good	Excellent
	XE Sedan 4D	CB51D	12169	3300	3950	5400	7475
	GXE Sedan 4D	CB51D	14019	3425	4150	5600	7675
	CA Sedan 4D	DB51D	15319	3850	4575	6050	8175
	SE Sedan 4D	BB51D	15419	4025	4800	6300	8475

ALTIMA—4-Cyl.—Equipment Schedule 4
W.B. 103.1"; 2.4 Liter.

Body	Type	VIN	List	Fair	Good	Good	Excellent
	XE Sedan 4D	DL01D	18459	4750	5575	7050	9250
	GXE Sedan 4D	DL01D	18659	4800	5650	7125	9300
	SE Sedan 4D	DL01D	19960	5300	6200	7700	9975
	GLE Sedan 4D	DL01D	20910	5775	6750	8275	10600
	Manual Trans			(525)	(525)	(700)	(700)

MAXIMA—V6—Equipment Schedule 4
W.B. 108.3"; 3.0 Liter.

Body	Type	VIN	List	Fair	Good	Good	Excellent
	GXE Sedan 4D	CA31A	23269	6925	8000	9650	12200
	SE Sedan 4D	CA31A	24669	7525	8675	10350	13000
	GLE Sedan 4D	CA31A	26769	8100	9300	11050	13750

Body	Type	VIN	List	Trade-In Fair	Trade-In Good	Pvt-Party Good	Retail Excellent
	Manual Trans			(525)	(525)	(700)	(700)

2001 NISSAN — (1N4,JN1or3N1)(CB51D)-1-#

SENTRA—4-Cyl.—Equipment Schedule 6
W.B. 99.8"; 1.8 Liter, 2.0 Liter.

Body	Type	VIN	List	Fair	Good	Good	Excellent
	XE Sedan 4D	CB51D	13368	4175	4975	6300	8300
	GXE Sedan 4D	CB51D	14019	4350	5125	6500	8525
	CA Sedan 4D	DB51D	15319	4800	5650	7025	9125
	SE Sedan 4D	BB51D	15419	4975	5825	7225	9325

ALTIMA—4-Cyl.—Equipment Schedule 4
W.B. 103.1"; 2.4 Liter.

	XE Sedan 4D	DL01D	18459	5625	6525	8100	10400
	GXE Sedan 4D	DL01D	18659	5700	6625	8175	10500
	SE Sedan 4D	DL01D	19960	6250	7225	8800	11250
	GLE Sedan 4D	DL01D	20190	6800	7825	9450	11950
	LE			175	175	235	235
	Manual Trans			(550)	(550)	(735)	(735)

MAXIMA—V6—Equipment Schedule 4
W.B. 108.3"; 3.0 Liter.

	GXE Sedan 4D	CA31D	23469	8175	9375	11100	13800
	SE Sedan 4D	CA31D	24869	8925	10225	11950	14750
	SE 20th Anniv Sed 4D	CA31A	28169	9700	11100	12900	15800
	GLE Sedan 4D	CA31D	26969	9500	10850	12650	15500
	Manual Trans			(550)	(550)	(735)	(735)

2002 NISSAN — (1N4,JN1or3N1)(CB51D)-2-#

SENTRA—4-Cyl.—Equipment Schedule 6
W.B. 99.8"; 1.8 Liter, 2.5 Liter.

	XE Sedan 4D	CB51D	13588	4900	5750	7175	9300
	GXE Sedan 4D	CB51D	14289	5075	5950	7375	9525
	CA Sedan 4D	DB51D	15439	5600	6500	7975	10200
	SE-R Sedan 4D	AB51A	16539	6175	7150	8475	10550
	SE-R Spec V Sedan 4D	AB51A	17539	7250	8325	9750	11950

ALTIMA—4-Cyl.—Equipment Schedule 4
W.B. 110.2"; 2.5 Liter.

	2.5 Sedan 4D	AL11D	17869	8725	9975	11600	14200
	2.5 S Sedan 4D	AL11D	19389	9150	10425	12100	14750
	2.5 SL Sedan 4D	AL11D	23239	9750	11125	12800	15500
	Manual Trans			(575)	(575)	(765)	(765)

ALTIMA—V6—Equipment Schedule 4
W.B. 110.2"; 3.5 Liter.

	3.5 SE Sedan 4D	BL11D	23689	10375	11800	13550	16300
	Manual Trans			(575)	(575)	(765)	(765)

MAXIMA—V6—Equipment Schedule 4
W.B. 108.3"; 3.5 Liter.

	GXE Sedan 4D	CA31D	25239	9650	11000	12750	15650
	SE Sedan 4D	CA31D	25989	10500	11950	13800	16750
	GLE Sedan 4D	CA31D	27639	11100	12575	14500	17500

2003 NISSAN — (1N4,JN1or3N1)(CB51D)-3-#

SENTRA—4-Cyl.—Equipment Schedule 6
W.B. 99.8"; 1.8 Liter, 2.5 Liter.

	XE Sedan 4D	CB51D	13888	5750	6700	8050	10150
	GXE Sedan 4D	CB51D	14639	5925	6900	8200	10300
	Limited Sedan 4D	AB51D	17139	6500	7500	8900	11100
	SE-R Sedan 4D	AB51D	16739	7125	8225	9425	11450
	SE-R Spec V Sed 4D	AB51D	17739	8300	9525	10800	13000

ALTIMA—4-Cyl.—Equipment Schedule 4
W.B. 110.2"; 2.5 Liter.

	2.5 Sedan 4D	AL11D	17689	10075	11475	13000	15600
	2.5 S Sedan 4D	AL11D	19539	10550	12000	13550	16200
	2.5 SL Sedan 4D	AL11D	23539	11175	12725	14300	17000
	Manual Trans			(600)	(600)	(800)	(800)

ALTIMA—V6—Equipment Schedule 4
W.B. 110.2"; 3.5 Liter.

	3.5 SE Sedan 4D	BL11D	23689	11900	13500	15100	17900
	Manual Trans			(600)	(600)	(800)	(800)

MAXIMA—V6—Equipment Schedule 4
W.B. 108.3"; 3.5 Liter.

	GXE Sedan 4D	DA31D	25439	11125	12625	14450	17400
	SE Sedan 4D	DA31D	26189	12100	13725	15550	18600
	GLE Sedan 4D	DA31D	28089	12675	14350	16250	19400

Body	Type	VIN	List	Trade-In Fair	Trade-In Good	Pvt-Party Good	Retail Excellent
350Z—V6—Equipment Schedule 3							
W.B. 104.3"; 3.5 Liter.							
Coupe 2D		AZ34D	26809	16850	18950	21000	24600
Enthusiast Coupe 2D		AZ34D	29759	17750	19975	22100	25800
Performance Cpe 2D		AZ34D	30969	18525	20825	23000	26900
Touring Coupe 2D		AZ34D	32129	19150	21500	23700	27600
Track Coupe 2D		AZ34D	34619	20450	22850	25200	29300

2004 NISSAN—(1N4,JN1or3N1)(CB51D)-4-#

Body	Type	VIN	List	Trade-In Fair	Trade-In Good	Pvt-Party Good	Retail Excellent
SENTRA—4-Cyl.—Equipment Schedule 6							
W.B. 99.8"; 1.8 Liter, 2.5 Liter.							
Sedan 4D		CB51D	12740	6775	7800	9125	11250
1.8 S Sedan 4D		CB51D	14740	6925	8000	9300	11450
2.5 S Sedan 4D		AB51D	17360	7300	8400	9750	11950
SE-R Sedan 4D		AB51D	17640	8275	9475	10700	12750
SE-R Spec V Sed 4D		AB51D	17840	9550	10900	12200	14450
ALTIMA—4-Cyl.—Equipment Schedule 4							
W.B. 110.2"; 2.5 Liter.							
2.5 Sedan 4D		AL11D	17890	11800	13400	14950	17600
2.5 S Sedan 4D		AL11D	19740	12300	13925	15500	18250
2.5 SL Sedan 4D		AL11D	23740	12950	14700	16250	19100
Manual Trans				(625)	(625)	(835)	(835)
ALTIMA—V6—Equipment Schedule 4							
W.B. 110.2"; 3.5 Liter.							
3.5 SE Sedan 4D		BL11D	23790	13725	15500	17150	20100
Manual Trans				(625)	(625)	(835)	(835)
MAXIMA—V6—Equipment Schedule 4							
W.B. 111.2"; 3.5 Liter.							
SE Sedan 4D		BA41E	27490	17950	20150	21900	25100
SL Sedan 4D		BA41E	29440	19150	21500	23200	26600
350Z—V6—Equipment Schedule 3							
W.B. 104.3"; 3.5 Liter.							
Coupe 2D		AZ34D	26910	19150	21500	23600	27500
Enthusiast Coupe 2D		AZ34D	29860	20150	22650	24900	28800
Enthusiast Roadster		AZ36A	35360	22550	25450	28100	32800
Performance Cpe 2D		AZ34D	31070	21025	23525	25800	29900
Track Coupe 2D		AZ34D	34720	22950	25725	28000	32400
Touring Coupe 2D		AZ34D	33820	21600	24300	26600	30700
Touring Roadster 2D		AZ36A	37730	24000	26875	29700	34400

OLDSMOBILE

1990 OLDSMOBILE — 1G3(NL54U)-L-#

Body	Type	VIN	List	Trade-In Fair	Trade-In Good	Pvt-Party Good	Retail Excellent
CALAIS—4-Cyl.—Equipment Schedule 5							
W.B. 103.4"; 2.5 Liter.							
Sedan 4D		NL54U	11680	400	575	1025	1750
Coupe 2D		NL14U	11680	400	575	1025	1750
S Sedan 4D		NF54U	12680	450	650	1125	1900
S Coupe 2D		NF14U	12680	450	650	1125	1900
Quad 442 Spt Perf Pkg				50	50	65	65
4-Cyl. 2.3L Quad 4		A,D		100	100	135	135
CALAIS—4-Cyl. Quad 4—Equipment Schedule 5							
W.B. 103.4"; 2.3 Liter.							
SL Sedan 4D		NT54D	14440	450	650	1125	1925
SL Coupe 2D		NT14D	14340	450	650	1125	1925
International Sed 4D		NK54A	15420	500	725	1225	2100
International Cpe 2D		NK14A	15320	500	725	1225	2100
V6 3.3 Liter		N		125	125	165	165
CIERA—V6—Equipment Schedule 4							
W.B. 104.9"; 3.3 Liter.							
Sedan 4D		AL54N	15020	525	750	1250	2100
S Sedan 4D		AJ54N	16135	525	750	1275	2125
S Coupe 2D		AJ14N	15420	525	750	1250	2100
S Cruiser Wagon 4D		AJ84N	16654	575	825	1350	2250
SL Sedan 4D		AM54N	16300	600	850	1400	2300
SL Cruiser Wagon 4D		AM84N	16780	600	850	1425	2350
International Sed 4D		AS54N	18325	675	950	1550	2575
International Cpe 2D		AS14N	17420	625	900	1475	2425
4-Cyl. 2.5 Liter		R		(150)	(150)	(200)	(200)
CUTLASS SUPREME—V6—Equipment Schedule 4							
W.B. 107.5"; 3.1 Liter.							

1990 OLDSMOBILE

Body Type	VIN	List	Trade-In Fair	Good	Pvt-Party Good	Retail Excellent
Sedan 4D	WH54T	16862	625	900	1525	2650
Coupe 2D	WH14T	16657	600	850	1500	2575
Convertible Cpe 2D	WT14T	22002	1100	1550	2625	4150
SL Sedan 4D	WS54T	18617	625	900	1600	2725
SL Coupe 2D	WS14T	18402	600	875	1500	2600
International Sed 4D	WR54T	19195	725	1025	1775	2975
International Cpe 2D	WR14T	19120	700	975	1725	2900
4-Cyl. 2.3L Quad 4	D,A		(200)	(200)	(265)	(265)
EIGHTY EIGHT—V6—Equipment Schedule 4						
W.B. 110.8"; 3.8 Liter.						
Royale Sedan 4D	HN54C	17999	525	750	1275	2125
Royale Coupe 2D	HN14C	17794	550	800	1350	2250
Royale Brhm Sedan 4D	HY54C	19305	625	900	1500	2475
Royale Brhm Coupe 2D	HY14C	19090	600	850	1425	2350
CUSTOM CRUISER—V8—Equipment Schedule 4						
W.B. 116.0"; 5.0 Liter.						
Wagon 4D	BP84Y	20337	525	750	1300	2175
NINETY EIGHT—V6—Equipment Schedule 4						
W.B. 110.8"; 3.8 Liter.						
Regency Sedan 4D	CX54C	22613	525	750	1300	2175
Regency Brhm Sedan 4D	CW54C	23054	575	825	1400	2350
Touring Sedan 4D	CV54C	27345	675	950	1600	2700
TORONADO—V6—Equipment Schedule 2						
W.B. 108.0"; 3.8 Liter.						
Coupe 2D	EZ14C	24609	850	1175	2050	3350
Trofeo Coupe 2D	EV14C	25545	900	1250	2125	3475

1991 OLDSMOBILE — 1G3(NL54U)–M–#

Body Type	VIN	List	Trade-In Fair	Good	Pvt-Party Good	Retail Excellent
CALAIS—4-Cyl.—Equipment Schedule 5						
W.B. 103.4"; 2.5 Liter.						
Sedan 4D	NL54U	12793	450	650	1175	2025
Coupe 2D	NL14U	12753	450	650	1175	2025
S Sedan 4D	NF54U	13310	525	750	1300	2175
S Coupe 2D	NF14U	13210	525	750	1300	2175
Quad 442 Sport Pkg			50	50	65	65
4-Cyl. 2.3L Quad 4	A,D		100	100	135	135
CALAIS—4-Cyl. Quad 4—Equipment Schedule 5						
W.B. 103.4"; 2.3 Liter.						
SL Sedan 4D	NT54D	15650	525	750	1300	2225
SL Coupe 2D	NT14D	15550	525	750	1300	2225
International Sed 4D	NK54A	16850	575	825	1425	2400
International Cpe 2D	NK14A	16750	575	825	1425	2400
V6 3.3 Liter	N		125	125	165	165
CIERA—V6—Equipment Schedule 4						
W.B. 104.9"; 3.3 Liter.						
Sedan 4D	AL54N	15605	600	850	1425	2400
S Sedan 4D	AJ54N	15945	600	850	1450	2425
S Coupe 2D	AJ14N	16345	600	850	1425	2400
S Cruiser Wagon 4D	AJ84N	16935	650	900	1525	2600
SL Sedan 4D	AM54N	17165	675	950	1575	2650
SL Cruiser Wagon 4D	AM84N	17955	675	950	1600	2700
4-Cyl. 2.5 Liter	R		(150)	(150)	(200)	(200)
CUTLASS SUPREME—V6—Equipment Schedule 4						
W.B. 107.5"; 3.1 Liter, 3.4 Liter.						
Sedan 4D	WH54T	16812	725	1025	1800	3025
Coupe 2D	WH14T	16607	700	975	1725	2925
Convertible Cpe 2D	WT34T	22047	1375	1850	3000	4625
SL Sedan 4D	WS54T	18407	750	1050	1875	3150
SL Coupe 2D	WS14T	18232	700	1000	1750	2975
International Sed 4D	WR54T	20685	850	1200	2100	3425
International Cpe 2D	WR14T	20510	825	1150	2000	3300
Manual Trans			(50)	(50)	(65)	(65)
4-Cyl. 2.3L Quad 4	D		(225)	(225)	(300)	(300)
V6 3.4 Liter	X		150	150	200	200
EIGHTY EIGHT—V6—Equipment Schedule 4						
W.B. 110.8"; 3.8 Liter.						
Royale Sedan 4D	HN54C	18969	625	900	1500	2475
Royale Coupe 2D	HN14C	18764	650	900	1525	2600
Royale Brhm Sedan 4D	HY54C	20596	700	1025	1725	2850
Royale Brhm Coupe 2D	HY14C	20381	675	950	1600	2700
CUSTOM CRUISER—V8—Equipment Schedule 4						
W.B. 115.9"; 5.0 Liter.						
Wagon 4D	BP83E	23668	1475	1950	3100	4725

EQUIPMENT & MILEAGE PAGE 9 TO 23

1991 OLDSMOBILE

Body	Type	VIN	List	Trade-In Fair	Good	Pvt-Party Good	Retail Excellent
NINETY EIGHT—V6—Equipment Schedule 4							
W.B. 110.8"; 3.8 Liter.							
Regency Elite Sedan 4D		CW53L	25129	875	1225	2050	3300
Touring Sedan 4D		CV53L	29175	1075	1525	2575	4075
TORONADO—V6—Equipment Schedule 2							
W.B. 108.0"; 3.8 Liter.							
Coupe 2D		EZ13L	25579	975	1425	2500	4050
Trofeo Coupe 2D		EV13L	27075	1050	1500	2600	4175

1992 OLDSMOBILE — (1or3)G3(NL543)–N–#

Body	Type	VIN	List	Trade-In Fair	Good	Pvt-Party Good	Retail Excellent
ACHIEVA—4-Cyl.—Equipment Schedule 5							
W.B. 103.4"; 2.3 Liter.							
S Sedan 4D		NL543	14675	450	650	1175	2025
S Coupe 2D		NL143	14575	450	625	1150	1975
SL Sedan 4D		NF54D	15900	525	750	1325	2225
SL Coupe 2D		NF14D	15800	500	725	1250	2125
SCX Coupe 2D		NL14A	16495	575	825	1400	2350
SC Pkg				75	75	100	100
V6 3.3 Liter		N		150	150	200	200
CIERA—V6—Equipment Schedule 4							
W.B. 104.9"; 3.3 Liter.							
S Sedan 4D		AL54N	15855	600	875	1450	2425
S Cruiser Wagon 4D		AJ84N	16900	700	975	1600	2700
SL Sedan 4D		AM54N	18230	700	1000	1650	2725
SL Cruiser Wagon 4D		AM84N	18730	725	1025	1675	2750
4-Cyl. 2.5 Liter		R		(175)	(175)	(235)	(235)
CUTLASS SUPREME—V6—Equipment Schedule 4							
W.B. 107.5"; 3.1 Liter.							
S Sedan 4D		WH54T	17425	850	1175	2100	3475
S Coupe 2D		WH14T	17220	800	1125	2025	3350
Convertible Cpe 2D		WT34T	23205	1650	2150	3400	5125
International Sed 4D		WR54T	22740	975	1425	2525	4075
International Cpe 2D		WR14T	22575	925	1325	2400	3950
SL Pkg				75	75	100	100
Manual Trans				(75)	(75)	(100)	(100)
V6 3.4 Liter		X		175	175	235	235
EIGHTY EIGHT—V6—Equipment Schedule 4							
W.B. 110.8"; 3.8 Liter.							
Royale Sedan 4D		HN53L	20502	575	825	1450	2475
Royale LS Sedan 4D		HY53L	21950	600	875	1500	2600
CUSTOM CRUISER—V8—Equipment Schedule 4							
W.B. 115.9"; 5.0 Liter.							
Wagon 4D		BP83E	23983	1850	2375	3625	5350
V8 5.7 Liter		7		125	125	165	165
NINETY EIGHT—V6—Equipment Schedule 4							
W.B. 110.7"; 3.8 Liter.							
Regency Sedan 4D		CX53L	25943	1050	1500	2575	4050
Reg Elite Sed 4D		CW53L	26795	1100	1550	2625	4150
Touring Sedan 4D		CV53L	29595	1500	2025	3200	4825
V6 3.8L Supercharged		1		225	225	300	300
TORONADO—V6—Equipment Schedule 2							
W.B. 108.0"; 3.8 Liter.							
Coupe 2D		EZ13L	26539	1050	1500	2700	4350
Trofeo Coupe 2D		EV13L	27895	1150	1600	2800	4500

1993 OLDSMOBILE — (1or3)G3(NL543)–P–#

Body	Type	VIN	List	Trade-In Fair	Good	Pvt-Party Good	Retail Excellent
ACHIEVA—4-Cyl.—Equipment Schedule 5							
W.B. 103.4"; 2.3 Liter.							
S Sedan 4D		NL543	15009	550	775	1375	2350
S Coupe 2D		NL143	14909	525	750	1325	2250
SL Sedan 4D		NF54D	16254	625	900	1525	2600
SL Coupe 2D		NF14D	16154	600	875	1500	2525
SC Pkg				100	100	135	135
SCX Pkg				200	200	265	265
V6 3.3 Liter		N		175	175	235	235
CIERA—V6—Equipment Schedule 4							
W.B. 104.9"; 3.3 Liter.							
S Sedan 4D		AG54N	16234	700	975	1625	2725
SL Sedan 4D		AM55N	18964	775	1075	1775	2925
4-Cyl. 2.2 Liter		4		(200)	(200)	(265)	(265)
CUTLASS SUPREME—V6—Equipment Schedule 4							
W.B. 107.5"; 3.1 Liter.							
S Sedan 4D		WH54T	17175	950	1375	2500	4075

1993 OLDSMOBILE

Body	Type	VIN	List	Trade-In Fair	Trade-In Good	Pvt-Party Good	Retail Excellent
S Coupe 2D		WH14T	17010	900	1300	2375	3950
Convertible Cpe 2D		WT34T	23574	1950	2500	3825	5675
International Sed 4D		WR54T	23744	1150	1600	2800	4500
International Cpe 2D		WR14T	23579	1075	1525	2700	4375
SL Pkg				100	100	135	135
V6 3.4 Liter		X		200	200	265	265

CUTLASS CRUISER—V6—Equipment Schedule 4
W.B. 104.9"; 3.3 Liter.

Body	Type	VIN	List	Fair	Good	Good	Excellent
S Wagon 4D		AJ84N	16934	750	1050	1775	2900
SL Wagon 4D		AM85N	19464	775	1100	1825	2975
4-Cyl. 2.2 Liter		4		(200)	(200)	(265)	(265)

EIGHTY EIGHT—V6—Equipment Schedule 4
W.B. 110.8"; 3.8 Liter.

Body	Type	VIN	List	Fair	Good	Good	Excellent
Royale Sedan 4D		HN53L	21251	675	950	1700	2900
Royale LS Sedan 4D		HY53L	22504	725	1025	1825	3075
LSS Pkg				100	100	135	135

NINETY EIGHT—V6—Equipment Schedule 4
W.B. 110.8"; 3.8 Liter.

Body	Type	VIN	List	Fair	Good	Good	Excellent
Regency Sedan 4D		CX53L	25839	1375	1850	2975	4600
Reg Elite Sed 4D		CW53L	27599	1450	1925	3100	4750
Touring Sedan 4D		CV53L	30299	1975	2525	3800	5575
V6 3.8L Supercharged		1		275	275	365	365

1994 OLDSMOBILE — (1or3)G3(NL553)–R–#

ACHIEVA—4-Cyl.—Equipment Schedule 5
W.B. 103.4"; 2.3 Liter.

Body	Type	VIN	List	Fair	Good	Good	Excellent
S Sedan 4D		NL553	16045	625	900	1575	2700
S Coupe 2D		NL153	15945	600	875	1500	2600
SL Sedan 4D		NF55A	18715	725	1025	1750	2925
SC Coupe 2D		NF15A	18715	700	975	1700	2850
V6 3.1 Liter		M		200	200	265	265

CIERA—V6—Equipment Schedule 4
W.B. 104.9"; 3.1 Liter.

Body	Type	VIN	List	Fair	Good	Good	Excellent
S Sedan 4D		AG55M	17725	775	1075	1850	3075
4-Cyl. 2.2 Liter		4		(225)	(225)	(300)	(300)

CUTLASS SUPREME—V6—Equipment Schedule 4
W.B. 107.5"; 3.1 Liter.

Body	Type	VIN	List	Fair	Good	Good	Excellent
S Sedan 4D		WH55M	18827	1125	1575	2800	4500
S Coupe 2D		WH15M	18662	1050	1500	2700	4350
Convertible Cpe 2D		WT35M	25800	2275	2850	4250	6225
V6 3.4 Liter		X		225	225	300	300

CUTLASS CRUISER—V6—Equipment Schedule 4
W.B. 104.9"; 3.1 Liter.

Body	Type	VIN	List	Fair	Good	Good	Excellent
S Wagon 4D		AJ85M	18757	825	1150	1975	3250

EIGHTY EIGHT—V6—Equipment Schedule 4
W.B. 110.8"; 3.8 Liter.

Body	Type	VIN	List	Fair	Good	Good	Excellent
Royale Sedan 4D		HN52L	22480	825	1150	2050	3400
Royale LS Sedan 4D		HY52L	23450	875	1225	2175	3600
LSS Pkg				100	100	135	135

NINETY EIGHT—V6—Equipment Schedule 4
W.B. 110.8"; 3.8 Liter.

Body	Type	VIN	List	Fair	Good	Good	Excellent
Regency Sedan 4D		CX52L	26695	1700	2225	3450	5175
Reg Elite Sed 4D		CW53L	28600	1825	2350	3625	5400
V6 3.8L Supercharged		1		300	300	400	400

1995 OLDSMOBILE — (1or2)G3(NL55D)–S–#

ACHIEVA—4-Cyl.—Equipment Schedule 5
W.B. 103.4"; 2.3 Liter.

Body	Type	VIN	List	Fair	Good	Good	Excellent
S Sedan 4D		NL55D	14750	750	1050	1850	3100
S Coupe 2D		NL15D	14750	725	1025	1800	3025
V6 3.1 Liter		M		225	225	300	300

CIERA—V6—Equipment Schedule 4
W.B. 104.9"; 3.1 Liter.

Body	Type	VIN	List	Fair	Good	Good	Excellent
SL Sedan 4D		AJ55M	16595	925	1325	2350	3875
SL Wagon 4D		AJ85M	17595	950	1350	2375	3900
4-Cyl. 2.2 Liter		4		(250)	(250)	(335)	(335)

CUTLASS SUPREME—V6—Equipment Schedule 4
W.B. 107.5"; 3.1 Liter.

Body	Type	VIN	List	Fair	Good	Good	Excellent
S Sedan 4D		WH52M	18995	1375	1875	3175	4975
S Coupe 2D		WH12M	18995	1250	1725	3000	4775
Convertible 2D		WT32M	26531	2650	3250	4725	6800
V6 3.4 Liter		X		250	250	335	335

1995 OLDSMOBILE

Body	Type	VIN	List	Trade-In Fair	Good	Pvt-Party Good	Retail Excellent
EIGHTY EIGHT—V6—Equipment Schedule 4							
W.B. 110.8"; 3.8 Liter.							
Royale Sedan 4D		HN52K	20995	950	1375	2525	4125
Royale LS Sedan 4D		HY52K	23295	1025	1475	2675	4325
LSS Pkg				100	100	135	135
V6 3.8L Supercharged		1		325	325	435	435
NINETY EIGHT—V6—Equipment Schedule 4							
W.B. 110.7"; 3.8 Liter.							
Reg Elite Sed 4D		CX52K	26695	2250	2800	4200	6125
V6 3.8L Supercharged		1		325	325	435	435
AURORA—V8—Equipment Schedule 2							
W.B. 113.8"; 4.0 Liter.							
Sedan 4D		GR52C	31995	1650	2175	3450	5250

1996 OLDSMOBILE — (1or2)G3(NL52T)-T-#

Body	Type	VIN	List	Trade-In Fair	Good	Pvt-Party Good	Retail Excellent
ACHIEVA—4-Cyl.—Equipment Schedule 5							
W.B. 103.4"; 2.4 Liter.							
SL Sedan 4D		NL52T	15790	900	1250	2175	3600
SC Coupe 2D		NL12T	15790	850	1200	2125	3525
V6 3.1 Liter		M		250	250	335	335
CIERA—V6—Equipment Schedule 4							
W.B. 104.9"; 3.1 Liter.							
SL Sedan 4D		AJ55M	15305	1050	1500	2650	4225
SL Wagon 4D		AJ85M	17995	1075	1525	2675	4250
4-Cyl. 2.2 Liter		4		(275)	(275)	(365)	(365)
CUTLASS SUPREME—V6—Equipment Schedule 4							
W.B. 107.5"; 3.1 Liter.							
SL Sedan 4D		WH52M	17995	1650	2175	3575	5500
SL Coupe 2D		WH12M	17995	1525	2050	3425	5325
V6 3.4 Liter		X		275	275	365	365
EIGHTY EIGHT—V6—Equipment Schedule 4							
W.B. 110.8"; 3.8 Liter.							
Sedan 4D		HN52K	21370	1225	1675	2950	4700
LS Sedan 4D		HN52K	23400	1700	1825	3125	4925
LSS Sedan 4D		HY52K	26600	2100	2700	4075	6050
V6 3.8L Supercharged		1		350	350	465	465
NINETY EIGHT—V6—Equipment Schedule 4							
W.B. 110.7"; 3.8 Liter.							
Reg Elite Sed 4D		CX52K	28800	2725	3350	4850	6900
AURORA—V8—Equipment Schedule 2							
W.B. 113.8"; 4.0 Liter.							
Sedan 4D		GR62C	35000	2100	2675	4050	6025

1997 OLDSMOBILE — (1or2)G3(NL52T)-V-#

Body	Type	VIN	List	Trade-In Fair	Good	Pvt-Party Good	Retail Excellent
ACHIEVA—4-Cyl.—Equipment Schedule 5							
W.B. 103.4"; 2.4 Liter.							
SL Sedan 4D		NL52T	15750	1025	1475	2650	4275
SC Coupe 2D		NL12T	15950	1000	1450	2575	4200
V6 3.1 Liter		M		250	250	335	335
CUTLASS—V6—Equipment Schedule 4							
W.B. 107.0"; 3.1 Liter.							
Sedan 4D		WH52T	18170	1650	2150	3400	5175
GLS Sedan 4D		WH52M	19225	2000	2550	3850	5675
CUTLASS SUPREME—V6—Equipment Schedule 4							
W.B. 107.5"; 3.1 Liter.							
SL Sedan 4D		WH52M	19500	2025	2575	4050	6100
SL Coupe 2D		WH12M	19500	1900	2425	3900	5925
EIGHTY EIGHT—V6—Equipment Schedule 4							
W.B. 110.8"; 3.8 Liter.							
Sedan 4D		HN52K	23100	1600	2100	3525	5450
LS Sedan 4D		HN52K	24400	1750	2275	3700	5650
LSS—V6—Equipment Schedule 4							
W.B. 110.8"; 3.8 Liter.							
Sedan 4D		HY52K	28300	2600	3225	4725	6850
V6 3.8L Supercharged		1		375	375	500	500
REGENCY—V6—Equipment Schedule 4							
W.B. 110.8"; 3.8 Liter.							
Sedan 4D		HC52K	28600	2800	3425	4975	7125
AURORA—V8—Equipment Schedule 2							
W.B. 113.8"; 4.0 Liter.							
Sedan 4D		GR62C	36400	2725	3350	4925	7100

1998 OLDSMOBILE

Body	Type	VIN	List	Trade-In Fair	Good	Pvt-Party Good	Retail Excellent
1998 OLDSMOBILE — (1or2)G3(NL52T)–W–#							
ACHIEVA—4-Cyl.—Equipment Schedule 5							
W.B. 103.4"; 2.4 Liter.							
SL Sedan 4D		NL52T	18340	1425	1900	3125	4825
V6 3.1 Liter		M		250	250	335	335
CUTLASS—V6—Equipment Schedule 4							
W.B. 107.0"; 3.1 Liter.							
GL Sedan 4D		NB52M	18950	2050	2600	3875	5675
GLS Sedan 4D		NG52M	19950	2425	3025	4350	6225
INTRIGUE—V6—Equipment Schedule 4							
W.B. 109.0"; 3.8 Liter.							
Sedan 4D		WH52K	21250	2250	2800	4225	6175
GL Sedan 4D		WS52K	22650	2550	3150	4550	6575
GLS Sedan 4D		WX52K	24660	3000	3675	5125	7225
EIGHTY EIGHT—V6—Equipment Schedule 4							
W.B. 110.8"; 3.8 Liter.							
Sedan 4D		HN52K	23400	2100	2675	4100	6100
LS Sedan 4D		HN52K	24800	2250	2825	4300	6300
LSS—V6—Equipment Schedule 4							
W.B. 110.8"; 3.8 Liter.							
Sedan 4D		HY52K	28700	3200	3875	5400	7575
V6 3.8L Supercharged		1		425	425	565	565
REGENCY—V6—Equipment Schedule 4							
W.B. 110.8"; 3.8 Liter.							
Sedan 4D		HC52K	29000	3400	4100	5675	7875
AURORA—V8—Equipment Schedule 2							
W.B. 113.8"; 4.0 Liter.							
Sedan 4D		GR62C	36625	3500	4200	5825	8100
1999 OLDSMOBILE — (1or2)G3(NK52T)–X–#							
ALERO—4-Cyl.—Equipment Schedule 5							
W.B. 107.0"; 2.4 Liter.							
GX Sedan 4D		NK52T	16850	1800	2325	3750	5700
GX Coupe 2D		NK12T	16850	1700	2225	3625	5575
GL Sedan 4D		NL52T	18745	2225	2775	4225	6250
GL Coupe 2D		NL12T	19180	2100	2675	4075	6075
V6 3.4 Liter		E		225	225	300	300
ALERO—V6—Equipment Schedule 4							
W.B. 107.0"; 3.4 Liter.							
GLS Sedan 4D		NF52E	21400	3025	3700	5175	7325
GLS Coupe 2D		NF12E	21400	2875	3525	5025	7125
CUTLASS—V6—Equipment Schedule 4							
W.B. 107.0"; 3.1 Liter.							
GL Sedan 4D		NB52M	19325	2600	3225	4575	6525
GLS Sedan 4D		NG52M	20250	3050	3700	5100	7125
INTRIGUE—V6—Equipment Schedule 4							
W.B. 109.0"; 3.5 Liter, 3.8 Liter.							
GX Sedan 4D		WH52K	21735	2875	3525	5050	7150
GL Sedan 4D		WS52K	23135	3225	3900	5425	7600
GLS Sedan 4D		WX52H	25505	3775	4500	6100	8350
EIGHTY EIGHT—V6—Equipment Schedule 4							
W.B. 110.8"; 3.8 Liter.							
Sedan 4D		HN52K	24170	2675	3275	4850	7000
LS Sedan 4D		HN52K	25720	2850	3500	5100	7275
LSS—V6—Equipment Schedule 4							
W.B. 110.8"; 3.8 Liter.							
Sedan 4D		HY52K	29720	3925	4675	6350	8700
V6 3.8L Supercharged		1		500	500	665	665
AURORA—V8—Equipment Schedule 2							
W.B. 113.8"; 4.0 Liter.							
Sedan 4D		GR62C	36899	4000	4775	6575	9075
2000 OLDSMOBILE — (1or2)G3(NK52T)–Y–#							
ALERO—4-Cyl.—Equipment Schedule 5							
W.B. 107.0"; 2.4 Liter.							
GX Sedan 4D		NK52T	16995	2325	2900	4450	6550
GX Coupe 2D		NK12T	16995	2200	2775	4300	6400
GL Sedan 4D		NL52T	18185	2775	3400	4975	7150
GL Coupe 2D		NL12T	18185	2675	3275	4850	7000
V6 3.4 Liter		E		250	250	335	335

2000 OLDSMOBILE

Body	Type	VIN	List	Trade-In Fair	Good	Pvt-Party Good	Retail Excellent
ALERO—V6—Equipment Schedule 4							
W.B. 107.0"; 3.4 Liter.							
GLS Sedan 4D		NF52E	21900	3700	4425	6050	8350
GLS Coupe 2D		NF12E	21900	3550	4250	5875	8150
INTRIGUE—V6—Equipment Schedule 4							
W.B. 109.0"; 3.5 Liter.							
GX Sedan 4D		WH52H	22650	3675	4400	6000	8300
GL Sedan 4D		WS52H	24280	4025	4800	6425	8775
GLS Sedan 4D		WX52H	26280	4650	5500	7175	9600
Sterling Edition				100	100	135	135

2001 OLDSMOBILE — 1G3(NK52T)-1-#

Body	Type	VIN	List	Trade-In Fair	Good	Pvt-Party Good	Retail Excellent
ALERO—4-Cyl.—Equipment Schedule 5							
W.B. 107.0"; 2.4 Liter.							
GX Sedan 4D		NK52T	17785	2950	3600	5275	7575
GX Coupe 2D		NK12T	17785	2800	3425	5100	7400
GL Sedan 4D		NL52T	19195	3425	4150	5850	8225
GL Coupe 2D		NL12T	19195	3300	4000	5700	8075
V6 3.4 Liter		E		275	275	365	365
ALERO—V6—Equipment Schedule 4							
W.B. 107.0"; 3.4 Liter.							
GLS Sedan 4D		NF52E	22540	4475	5250	7025	9525
GLS Coupe 2D		NF12E	22765	4300	5075	6850	9325
INTRIGUE—V6—Equipment Schedule 4							
W.B. 109.0"; 3.5 Liter.							
GX Sedan 4D		WH52H	22540	4575	5400	7150	9650
GL Sedan 4D		WS52H	24750	5000	5850	7625	10200
GLS Sedan 4D		WX52H	27115	5675	6600	8425	11050
AURORA—V6—Equipment Schedule 2							
W.B. 112.2"; 3.5 Liter.							
Sedan 4D		GR64H	31579	7400	8500	10450	13350
AURORA—V8—Equipment Schedule 2							
W.B. 112.2"; 4.0 Liter.							
Sedan 4D		GS64C	35314	8600	9850	11850	14950

2002 OLDSMOBILE — 1G3(NK52T)-2-#

Body	Type	VIN	List	Trade-In Fair	Good	Pvt-Party Good	Retail Excellent
ALERO—4-Cyl.—Equipment Schedule 5							
W.B. 107.0"; 2.2 Liter.							
GX Sedan 4D		NK52T	18055	3725	4475	6300	8800
GX Coupe 2D		NK12T	18055	3575	4275	6100	8600
GL Sedan 4D		NL52T	20040	4275	5075	6900	9475
GL Coupe 2D		NL12T	20265	4150	4925	6775	9325
V6 3.4 Liter		E		300	300	400	400
ALERO—V6—Equipment Schedule 4							
W.B. 107.0"; 3.4 Liter.							
GLS Sedan 4D		NF52E	22675	5375	6300	8175	10900
GLS Coupe 2D		NF12E	22900	5200	6075	7975	10650
INTRIGUE—V6—Equipment Schedule 4							
W.B. 109.0"; 3.5 Liter.							
GX Sedan 4D		WH52H	23427	5675	6600	8500	11250
GL Sedan 4D		WS52H	25012	6125	7100	9025	11800
GLS Sedan 4D		WX52H	28502	6875	7925	9900	12750
AURORA—V6—Equipment Schedule 2							
W.B. 112.2"; 3.5 Liter.							
Sedan 4D		GR64H	31665	9375	10700	13000	16350
AURORA—V8—Equipment Schedule 2							
W.B. 112.2"; 4.0 Liter.							
Sedan 4D		GS64C	35660	10700	12150	14500	18050

2003 OLDSMOBILE — 1G3(NK52F)-3-#

Body	Type	VIN	List	Trade-In Fair	Good	Pvt-Party Good	Retail Excellent
ALERO—4-Cyl.—Equipment Schedule 5							
W.B. 107.0"; 2.2 Liter.							
GX Sedan 4D		NK52F	18335	4725	5550	7425	10050
GX Coupe 2D		NK12F	18335	4550	5375	7200	9800
GL Sedan 4D		NL52F	20175	5300	6200	8075	10750
GL Coupe 2D		NL12F	20175	5175	6050	7950	10600
V6 3.4 Liter		E		300	300	400	400
ALERO—V6—Equipment Schedule 4							
W.B. 107.0"; 3.4 Liter.							
GLS Sedan 4D		NF52E	22755	6525	7525	9500	12350
GLS Coupe 2D		NF12E	23005	6300	7325	9250	12050

2003 OLDSMOBILE

Body	Type	VIN	List	Trade-In Fair	Good	Pvt-Party Good	Retail Excellent
AURORA—V8—Equipment Schedule 2							
W.B. 112.2"; 4.0 Liter.							
Sedan 4D		GS64C	34775	**13525**	**15300**	**18000**	**22100**

2004 OLDSMOBILE — 1G3(NK52F)-4-#

Body	Type	VIN	List	Fair	Good	Good	Excellent
ALERO—4-Cyl.—Equipment Schedule 5							
W.B. 107.0"; 2.2 Liter.							
GX Sedan 4D		NK52F	18825	**6300**	**7325**	**9325**	**12250**
GX Coupe 2D		NK12F	18825	**6150**	**7125**	**9125**	**12000**
GL Sedan 4D		NL52F	20775	**6925**	**8000**	**10050**	**13000**
GL Coupe 2D		NL12F	20775	**6800**	**7825**	**9900**	**12850**
V6 3.4 Liter		E		**300**	**300**	**400**	**400**
ALERO—V6—Equipment Schedule 4							
W.B. 107.0"; 3.4 Liter.							
GLS Sedan 4D		NF52E	23425	**8275**	**9475**	**11600**	**14750**
GLS Coupe 2D		NF12E	23675	**8025**	**9200**	**11350**	**14500**

PEUGEOT

1990 PEUGEOT — VF3(DA131)-L-#

Body	Type	VIN	List	Fair	Good	Good	Excellent
PEUGEOT—4-Cyl.—Equipment Schedule 3							
W.B. 105.1"; 1.9 Liter.							
405 DL Sportswagon 4D		DA131	17040	**175**	**225**	**750**	**1500**
405 S Sportswagon 4D		DA232	19545	**275**	**375**	**950**	**1850**

1991 PEUGEOT — VF3(DA131)-M-#

Body	Type	VIN	List	Fair	Good	Good	Excellent
PEUGEOT—4-Cyl.—Equipment Schedule 3							
W.B. 105.1", 114.2" (505); 1.9 Liter, 2.2 Liter.							
405 DL Sedan 4D		DA131	16350	**125**	**200**	**750**	**1550**
405 DL Sportswagon 4D		DA231	17040	**200**	**275**	**875**	**1725**
405 S Sedan 4D		DA132	18750	**275**	**350**	**975**	**1925**
405 S Sportswagon 4D		DA232	19545	**300**	**450**	**1100**	**2100**
405 Mi 16 Sedan 4D		DB133	22140	**425**	**625**	**1350**	**2475**
505 DL Wagon 4D		BF221	19640	**325**	**475**	**1150**	**2175**
505 SW8 Wagon 4D		BF327	21450	**600**	**875**	**1700**	**3025**
Auto Trans				**100**	**100**	**135**	**135**
PEUGEOT—4-Cyl. Turbo—Equipment Schedule 3							
W.B. 114.2"; 2.2 Liter.							
505 SW8 Wagon 4D		BE328	26500	**850**	**1200**	**2300**	**3900**
Auto Trans				**100**	**100**	**135**	**135**

PLYMOUTH

1990 PLYMOUTH — (1P3,JP3orJP4)(XL18D)-L-#

Body	Type	VIN	List	Fair	Good	Good	Excellent
HORIZON AMERICA—4-Cyl.—Equipment Schedule 6							
W.B. 99.1"; 2.2 Liter.							
America Hatchback 4D		XL18D	8689	**375**	**550**	**925**	**1575**
COLT—4-Cyl.—Equipment Schedule 6							
W.B. 93.7", 93.9" (4WD, H'Back); 1.5 Liter, 1.6 Liter, 1.8 Liter.							
Hatchback 2D		CU14X	8331	**375**	**525**	**950**	**1625**
GL Hatchback 2D		CU24X	9582	**375**	**525**	**950**	**1625**
GT Sedan 4D		CU34X	10767	**450**	**625**	**1100**	**1850**
DL Wagon 4D		CV31X	10935	**400**	**575**	**1000**	**1725**
DL 4WD Wagon 4D		CW31T	12505	**525**	**750**	**1225**	**2075**
COLT VISTA—4-Cyl.—Equipment Schedule 6							
W.B. 103.3", 103.5" (4WD); 2.0 Liter.							
Wagon 4D		CG39V	13652	**625**	**900**	**1425**	**2350**
4WD Wagon 4D		CH34V	14619	**625**	**900**	**1475**	**2425**
SUNDANCE—4-Cyl.—Equipment Schedule 5							
W.B. 97.0"; 2.2 Liter, 2.5 Liter.							
Liftback Coupe 2D		XP24D	10585	**325**	**475**	**900**	**1575**
Liftback Sedan 4D		XP28D	10785	**325**	**475**	**900**	**1575**
4-Cyl. 2.5 Liter Turbo		J		**50**	**50**	**65**	**65**
LASER—4-Cyl.—Equipment Schedule 4							
W.B. 97.2"; 1.8 Liter, 2.0 Liter.							
Liftback Coupe 2D		CS34T	12890	**400**	**600**	**1150**	**2025**
RS Liftback Coupe 2D		CS44R	14130	**475**	**700**	**1275**	**2225**
Auto Trans				**100**	**100**	**135**	**135**
4-Cyl. 1.8 Liter (RS)		T		**(150)**	**(150)**	**(200)**	**(200)**

1990 PLYMOUTH

Body	Type	VIN	List	Trade-In Fair	Good	Pvt-Party Good	Retail Excellent
LASER—4-Cyl. Turbo—Equipment Schedule 4							
W.B. 97.2"; 2.0 Liter.							
RS Liftback Coupe 2D		CS44J	16135	550	775	1400	2400
Manual Trans				0	0	0	0
ACCLAIM—4-Cyl.—Equipment Schedule 5							
W.B. 103.3"; 2.5 Liter.							
Sedan 4D		XA46K	12318	400	575	1000	1725
LE Sedan 4D		XA56K	13626	425	625	1050	1800
4-Cyl. 2.5 Liter Turbo		J		0	0	0	0
V6 3.0 Liter		3		150	150	200	200
ACCLAIM—V6—Equipment Schedule 5							
W.B. 103.3"; 3.0 Liter.							
LX Sedan 4D		XA763	15064	625	900	1425	2350

1991 PLYMOUTH — (1P3,JP3orJP4)(CU14A)–M–#

Body	Type	VIN	List	Trade-In Fair	Good	Pvt-Party Good	Retail Excellent
COLT—4-Cyl.—Equipment Schedule 6							
W.B. 93.9"; 1.5 Liter.							
Hatchback 2D		CU14A	8247	425	625	1075	1850
GL Hatchback 2D		CU24A	9559	425	625	1075	1850
COLT VISTA—4-Cyl.—Equipment Schedule 6							
W.B. 103.3", 103.5" (4WD); 2.0 Liter.							
Wagon 4D		CG39V	13695	700	1000	1625	2700
4WD Wagon 4D		EH31V	14662	750	1025	1675	2750
SUNDANCE—4-Cyl.—Equipment Schedule 6							
W.B. 97.0"; 2.2 Liter, 2.5 Liter.							
America Sedan 4D		XP28D	10086	400	575	1025	1750
America Coupe 2D		XP24D	9786	375	525	950	1675
Highline Sedan 4D		XP48D	11002	400	575	1025	1750
Highline Coupe 2D		XP44D	10702	400	575	1025	1750
RS Sedan 4D		XP68K	12228	475	675	1150	1975
RS Coupe 2D		XP64K	11902	450	650	1125	1925
4-Cyl. 2.5 Liter Turbo		J		50	50	65	65
LASER—4-Cyl.—Equipment Schedule 4							
W.B. 97.2"; 1.8 Liter, 2.0 Liter.							
Liftback Coupe 2D		CS34T	12958	500	725	1375	2400
RS Liftback Coupe 2D		CS44R	14966	575	825	1500	2650
Auto Trans				100	100	135	135
LASER—4-Cyl. Turbo—Equipment Schedule 4							
W.B. 97.2"; 2.0 Liter.							
RS Liftback Coupe 2D		CS44U	16150	625	900	1625	2800
Auto Trans				100	100	135	135
ACCLAIM—4-Cyl.—Equipment Schedule 5							
W.B. 103.3"; 2.5 Liter.							
Sedan 4D		XA46K	12752	450	650	1150	1975
LE Sedan 4D		XA56K	14166	475	700	1225	2075
V6 3.0 Liter		3		175	175	235	235
ACCLAIM—V6—Equipment Schedule 5							
W.B. 103.3"; 3.0 Liter.							
LX Sedan 4D		XA763	15666	700	1000	1650	2725

1992 PLYMOUTH — (1,3,4orJ)P3(CU14A)–N–#

Body	Type	VIN	List	Trade-In Fair	Good	Pvt-Party Good	Retail Excellent
COLT—4-Cyl.—Equipment Schedule 6							
W.B. 93.9"; 1.5 Liter.							
Hatchback 2D		CU14A	8640	475	700	1225	2100
GL Hatchback 2D		CU24A	9304	500	725	1250	2125
COLT VISTA—4-Cyl.—Equipment Schedule 6							
W.B. 99.2"; 1.8 Liter, 2.4 Liter.							
Wagon 3D		CV20D	12426	1200	1650	2700	4150
SE Wagon 3D		CV50D	13262	1300	1775	2825	4350
AWD Wagon 3D		CW40D	14381	1500	2000	3075	4625
SUNDANCE—4-Cyl.—Equipment Schedule 6							
W.B. 97.0"; 2.2 Liter, 2.5 Liter.							
America Sedan 4D		XP28D	10610	400	600	1075	1900
America H'Back 2D		XP24D	10210	375	550	1025	1800
Highline Sedan 4D		XP48D	11588	450	625	1150	1975
Highline H'Back 2D		XP44D	11188	425	625	1100	1925
SUNDANCE—V6—Equipment Schedule 5							
W.B. 97.0"; 3.0 Liter.							
Duster Hatchback 2D		XP643	11924	525	750	1325	2225
Duster Sedan 4D		XP683	12324	575	825	1400	2350
4-Cyl. 2.5 Liter		K		(150)	(150)	(200)	(200)
LASER—4-Cyl.—Equipment Schedule 4							
W.B. 97.2"; 1.8 Liter, 2.0 Liter.							

Body	Type	VIN	List	Trade-In Fair	Trade-In Good	Pvt-Party Good	Retail Excellent
Hatchback 2D		CS34T	13398	600	875	1575	2750
RS Hatchback 2D		CS44R	15631	700	975	1800	3075
Auto Trans				125	125	165	165
LASER—4-Cyl. Turbo—Equipment Schedule 4							
W.B. 97.2"; 2.0 Liter.							
RS Hatchback 2D		CS44U	17110	750	1050	1925	3250
RS AWD Hatchback 2D		CT44U	19152	1075	1525	2675	4250
Auto Trans				125	125	165	165
ACCLAIM—4-Cyl.—Equipment Schedule 5							
W.B. 103.5"; 2.5 Liter.							
Sedan 4D		XA46K	13343	500	725	1250	2125
V6 3.0 Liter		3		225	225	300	300

1993 PLYMOUTH — (1,3,4orJ)P3–(A11A)–P–#

Body	Type	VIN	List	Trade-In Fair	Trade-In Good	Pvt-Party Good	Retail Excellent
COLT—4-Cyl.—Equipment Schedule 6							
W.B. 96.1", 98.4" (4D); 1.5 Liter, 1.8 Liter.							
Sedan 2D		A11A	9260	625	900	1500	2525
Sedan 4D		A26A	10902	775	1075	1775	2900
GL Sedan 2D		A21A	9888	700	975	1600	2700
GL Sedan 4D		A46C	12260	825	1150	1900	3075
COLT VISTA—4-Cyl.—Equipment Schedule 6							
W.B. 99.2"; 1.8 Liter, 2.4 Liter.							
Wagon 3D		B20C	12926	1450	1925	3000	4525
SE Wagon 3D		B50G	14060	1550	2075	3175	4750
AWD Wagon 3D		C40C	15010	1800	2325	3450	5100
SUNDANCE—4-Cyl.—Equipment Schedule 5							
W.B. 97.2"; 2.2 Liter, 2.5 Liter.							
Hatchback 2D		P24D	10623	425	625	1150	2025
Sedan 4D		P28D	11023	450	650	1200	2100
SUNDANCE—V6—Equipment Schedule 5							
W.B. 97.2"; 3.0 Liter.							
Duster Hatchback 2D		P643	12440	600	875	1500	2525
Duster Sedan 4D		P683	12840	650	900	1550	2650
4-Cyl. 2.5 Liter		K		(175)	(175)	(235)	(235)
LASER—4-Cyl.—Equipment Schedule 4							
W.B. 97.2"; 1.8 Liter, 2.0 Liter.							
Hatchback 2D		F34B	13876	750	1025	1925	3275
RS Hatchback 2D		F44E	16273	850	1175	2150	3600
Auto Trans				150	150	200	200
LASER—4-Cyl. Turbo—Equipment Schedule 4							
W.B. 97.2"; 2.0 Liter.							
RS Hatchback 2D		F44F	17680	900	1275	2350	3925
RS AWD H'Back 2D		G44F	19784	1325	1800	3000	4675
Auto Trans				150	150	200	200
ACCLAIM—4-Cyl.—Equipment Schedule 5							
W.B. 103.5"; 2.5 Liter.							
Sedan 4D		A46K	13455	550	800	1400	2350
V6 3.0 Liter		3		275	275	365	365
4-Cyl. 2.5L Flexible Fuel		V		0	0	0	0

1994 PLYMOUTH — (1,3,4orJ)P3–(A11A)–R–#

Body	Type	VIN	List	Trade-In Fair	Trade-In Good	Pvt-Party Good	Retail Excellent
COLT—4-Cyl.—Equipment Schedule 6							
W.B. 96.1", 98.4" (4D); 1.5 Liter, 1.8 Liter.							
Sedan 2D		A11A	10779	725	1025	1725	2850
Sedan 4D		A36C	13428	875	1225	2025	3275
GL Sedan 2D		A21A	11400	775	1100	1850	3025
GL Sedan 4D		A46C	13824	900	1300	2150	3425
COLT VISTA—4-Cyl.—Equipment Schedule 6							
W.B. 99.2"; 1.8 Liter, 2.4 Liter.							
Wagon 3D		B30C	14565	1675	2200	3325	4950
SE Wagon 3D		B50G	16233	1825	2350	3500	5150
AWD Wagon 3D		C40G	16777	2100	2650	3850	5550
SUNDANCE—4-Cyl.—Equipment Schedule 5							
W.B. 97.2"; 2.2 Liter, 2.5 Liter.							
Hatchback 2D		P24D	11052	500	725	1325	2300
Sedan 4D		P28D	11452	525	750	1400	2400
SUNDANCE—V6—Equipment Schedule 5							
W.B. 97.2"; 3.0 Liter.							
Duster Hatchback 2D		P643	13008	700	975	1700	2850
Duster Sedan 4D		P683	13408	750	1025	1775	2975
4-Cyl. 2.5 Liter		K		(200)	(200)	(265)	(265)
LASER—4-Cyl.—Equipment Schedule 4							
W.B. 97.2"; 1.8 Liter, 2.0 Liter.							

1994 PLYMOUTH

Body	Type	VIN	List	Trade-In Fair	Good	Pvt-Party Good	Retail Excellent
Hatchback 2D		F34B	14042	900	1250	2375	3975
RS Hatchback 2D		F44E	16353	1000	1450	2600	4250
Auto Trans				175	175	235	235
LASER—4-Cyl. Turbo—Equipment Schedule 4							
W.B. 97.2"; 2.0 Liter.							
RS Hatchback 2D		F44F	17887	1050	1500	2725	4425
RS AWD H'Back 2D		G44F	20015	1600	2100	3400	5200
Auto Trans				175	175	235	235
ACCLAIM—4-Cyl.—Equipment Schedule 5							
W.B. 103.5"; 2.5 Liter.							
Sedan 4D		A46K	14154	625	900	1575	2700
V6 3.0 Liter		3		300	300	400	400
4-Cyl. 2.5L Flexible Fuel		V		0	0	0	0

1995 PLYMOUTH — (1,3,4orJ)P3–(S27C)–S–#

Body	Type	VIN	List	Trade-In Fair	Good	Pvt-Party Good	Retail Excellent
NEON—4-Cyl.—Equipment Schedule 6							
W.B. 104.0"; 2.0 Liter.							
Sedan 4D		S27C	12195	650	900	1500	2475
Highline Sedan 4D		S47C	12443	750	1050	1700	2750
Highline Coupe 2D		S41C	12443	725	1025	1625	2700
Sport Sedan 4D		S67C	14393	900	1275	2025	3200
Sport Coupe 2D		S61C	14693	975	1425	2225	3475
ACCLAIM—4-Cyl.—Equipment Schedule 5							
W.B. 103.5"; 2.5 Liter.							
Sedan 4D		A46K	14828	750	1025	1850	3100
V6 3.0 Liter		3		325	325	435	435

1996 PLYMOUTH — (1or3)P3–(S27C)–T–#

Body	Type	VIN	List	Trade-In Fair	Good	Pvt-Party Good	Retail Excellent
NEON—4-Cyl.—Equipment Schedule 6							
W.B. 104.0"; 2.0 Liter.							
Sedan 4D		S27C	11730	800	1125	1800	2900
Coupe 2D		S22C	11230	775	1075	1725	2800
Highline Sedan 4D		S47C	12735	900	1275	2025	3200
Highline Coupe 2D		S42C	12535	875	1225	1950	3100
Sport Sedan 4D		S67C	14165	1050	1500	2350	3650
Sport Coupe 2D		S62C	13965	1175	1625	2625	4025
BREEZE—4-Cyl.—Equipment Schedule 5							
W.B. 108.0"; 2.0 Liter.							
Sedan 4D		J46C	15645	825	1150	1975	3250

1997 PLYMOUTH — (1or3)P3–(S27C)–V–#

Body	Type	VIN	List	Trade-In Fair	Good	Pvt-Party Good	Retail Excellent
NEON—4-Cyl.—Equipment Schedule 6							
W.B. 104.0"; 2.0 Liter.							
Sedan 4D		S27C	12430	950	1350	2175	3425
Coupe 2D		S22C	12230	900	1300	2100	3350
Highline Sedan 4D		S47C	13170	1050	1500	2475	3900
Highline Coupe 2D		S42C	12970	1025	1450	2325	3650
BREEZE—4-Cyl.—Equipment Schedule 5							
W.B. 108.0"; 2.0 Liter.							
Sedan 4D		J46C	16380	1025	1475	2525	4025
PROWLER—V6—Equipment Schedule 1							
W.B. 113.0"; 3.5 Liter.							
Roadster 2D		W65F	39000	15400	17375	20800	26000

1998 PLYMOUTH — (1or3)P3–(S47C)–W–#

Body	Type	VIN	List	Trade-In Fair	Good	Pvt-Party Good	Retail Excellent
NEON—4-Cyl.—Equipment Schedule 6							
W.B. 104.0"; 2.0 Liter.							
Highline Sedan 4D		S47C	12855	1300	1775	2750	4200
Highline Coupe 2D		S42C	12655	1250	1725	2700	4150
Competition Sedan 4D		S27C	14660	1775	2300	3325	4850
Competition Coupe 2D		S22C	14480	1725	2250	3300	4800
Expresso or Style				50	50	65	65
BREEZE—4-Cyl.—Equipment Schedule 5							
W.B. 108.0"; 2.0 Liter, 2.4 Liter.							
Sedan 4D		J46C	16260	1375	1875	2950	4500
Expresso				50	50	65	65

1999 PLYMOUTH — (1or3)P3(EorH)(S47C)–X–#

Body	Type	VIN	List	Trade-In Fair	Good	Pvt-Party Good	Retail Excellent
NEON—4-Cyl.—Equipment Schedule 6							
W.B. 104.0"; 2.0 Liter.							
Highline Sedan 4D		S47C	13320	1575	2100	3125	4600

Body	Type	VIN	List	Trade-In Fair	Good	Pvt-Party Good	Retail Excellent
Highline Coupe 2D		S42C	13120	1500	2025	3050	4525
Competition Sedan 4D		S27C	14985	2125	2700	3775	5350
Competition Coupe 2D		S22C	14805	2100	2650	3700	5275
Expresso or Style				75	75	100	100

BREEZE—4-Cyl.—Equipment Schedule 5
W.B. 108.0"; 2.0 Liter, 2.4 Liter.

| Sedan 4D | | J46C | 16700 | 1850 | 2375 | 3550 | 5225 |
| Expresso | | | | 75 | 75 | 100 | 100 |

PROWLER—V6—Equipment Schedule 1
W.B. 113.3"; 3.5 Liter.

| Roadster 2D | | W65G | 40000 | 19100 | 21400 | 24900 | 30200 |

2000 PLYMOUTH — (1or3)P3(EorH)(S46C)-Y-#

NEON—4-Cyl.—Equipment Schedule 6
W.B. 105.0"; 2.0 Liter.

| Highline Sedan 4D | | S46C | 13890 | 1700 | 2225 | 3450 | 5175 |
| LX Sedan 4D | | S46C | 14680 | 2275 | 2850 | 4125 | 5925 |

BREEZE—4-Cyl.—Equipment Schedule 5
W.B. 108.0"; 2.0 Liter, 2.4 Liter.

| Sedan 4D | | J46C | 17525 | 2475 | 3075 | 4325 | 6125 |

PROWLER—V6—Equipment Schedule 1
W.B. 113.3"; 3.5 Liter.

| Roadster 2D | | W65G | 43500 | 21225 | 23800 | 27400 | 32900 |

2001 PLYMOUTH — 1P3(EorH)(S46C)-1-#

NEON—4-Cyl.—Equipment Schedule 6
W.B. 105.0"; 2.0 Liter.

| Highline Sedan 4D | | S46C | 14275 | 2250 | 2800 | 4100 | 5950 |
| LX Sedan 4D | | S46C | 15095 | 2875 | 3525 | 4875 | 6800 |

PONTIAC

1990 PONTIAC — (1GorKL)2(TX246)-L-#

LeMANS—4-Cyl.—Equipment Schedule 6
W.B. 99.2"; 1.6 Liter, 2.0 Liter.

VL Aerocoupe 2D		TX246	7876	250	325	750	1350
LE Aerocoupe 2D		TN246	9763	350	500	950	1675
LE Sedan 4D		TN546	10113	400	575	1025	1800
GSE Aerocoupe 2D		TS24K	11079	400	575	1025	1800

SUNBIRD—4-Cyl.—Equipment Schedule 5
W.B. 101.2"; 2.0 Liter.

LE Sedan 4D		JB54K	10925	300	425	850	1475
LE Coupe 2D		JB14K	10825	300	425	850	1475
LE Convertible 2D		JB34K	15534	525	750	1325	2225
SE Coupe 2D		JD14K	11230	300	425	850	1475
4-Cyl. 2.0 Liter Turbo		M		50	50	65	65

SUNBIRD—4-Cyl. Turbo—Equipment Schedule 5
W.B. 101.2"; 2.0 Liter.

| GT Coupe 2D | | JU14M | 13334 | 325 | 475 | 900 | 1550 |
| 4-Cyl. 2.0 Liter | | K | | (50) | (50) | (65) | (65) |

GRAND AM—4-Cyl.—Equipment Schedule 5
W.B. 103.4"; 2.5 Liter.

LE Sedan 4D		NE54U	12429	475	700	1200	2025
LE Coupe 2D		NE14U	12229	475	700	1200	2025
4-Cyl. 2.3L Quad 4		D		100	100	135	135

GRAND AM—4-Cyl. Quad 4—Equipment Schedule 5
W.B. 103.4"; 2.3 Liter.

| SE Sedan 4D | | NW54A | 16159 | 625 | 900 | 1475 | 2425 |
| SE Coupe 2D | | NW14A | 15859 | 600 | 875 | 1425 | 2350 |

FIREBIRD—V6—Equipment Schedule 4
W.B. 101.0"; 3.1 Liter.

| Hatchback 2D | | FS23T | 14027 | 900 | 1275 | 2100 | 3400 |
| V8 5.0 Liter | | E | | 200 | 200 | 265 | 265 |

FIREBIRD—V8—Equipment Schedule 4
W.B. 101.0"; 5.0 Liter.

Formula H'Back 2D		FS23E	16603	1025	1475	2525	4000
Trans Am H'Back 2D		FW23F	18468	1175	1625	2700	4250
Manual Trans				(100)	(100)	(135)	(135)
V8 5.0 Liter TPI		F		50	50	65	65
V8 5.7 Liter TPI		8		250	250	335	335

1990 PONTIAC

Body	Type	VIN	List	Trade-In Fair	Trade-In Good	Pvt-Party Good	Retail Excellent
FIREBIRD—V8—Equipment Schedule 4							
W.B. 101.0"; 5.7 Liter.							
GTA Hatchback 2D	FW238	23759	**1400**	**1875**	**3000**	**4575**
Manual Trans			**(100)**	**(100)**	**(135)**	**(135)**
V8 5.0 Liter TPI	F		**(50)**	**(50)**	**(65)**	**(65)**
6000—V6—Equipment Schedule 4							
W.B. 104.9"; 3.1 Liter.							
LE Sedan 4D	AF54T	15114	**500**	**725**	**1225**	**2100**
LE Wagon 4D	AF84T	16849	**500**	**725**	**1225**	**2100**
SE Sedan 4D	AJ54T	17359	**600**	**875**	**1450**	**2400**
SE Wagon 4D	AJ84T	18959	**600**	**875**	**1450**	**2400**
AWD			**250**	**250**	**335**	**335**
4-Cyl. 2.5 Liter	R		**(150)**	**(150)**	**(200)**	**(200)**
GRAND PRIX—V6—Equipment Schedule 4							
W.B. 107.5"; 3.1 Liter.							
LE Sedan 4D	WJ54T	16064	**450**	**650**	**1250**	**2175**
LE Coupe 2D	WJ14T	16044	**425**	**625**	**1175**	**2075**
SE Coupe 2D	WP14T	18139	**525**	**750**	**1400**	**2400**
STE Sedan 4D	WT54T	19634	**700**	**1000**	**1725**	**2900**
4-Cyl. Quad 4	D		**(200)**	**(200)**	**(265)**	**(265)**
V6 3.1 Liter Turbo			**250**	**250**	**335**	**335**
BONNEVILLE—V6—Equipment Schedule 4							
W.B. 110.8"; 3.8 Liter.							
LE Sedan 4D	HX54C	17473	**425**	**625**	**1100**	**1900**
SE Sedan 4D	HZ54C	19649	**600**	**850**	**1425**	**2400**
SSE Sedan 4D	HY54C	24499	**750**	**1050**	**1775**	**2900**

1991 PONTIAC — (1GorKL)2(TX246)-M-#

Body	Type	VIN	List	Trade-In Fair	Trade-In Good	Pvt-Party Good	Retail Excellent
LeMANS—4-Cyl.—Equipment Schedule 6							
W.B. 99.2"; 1.6 Liter.							
VL Aerocoupe 2D	TX246	8206	**275**	**350**	**775**	**1400**
LE Aerocoupe 2D	TN246	9523	**375**	**525**	**1000**	**1750**
LE Sedan 4D	TN546	9973	**425**	**625**	**1100**	**1925**
SUNBIRD—4-Cyl.—Equipment Schedule 5							
W.B. 101.2"; 2.0 Liter.							
Sedan 4D	JC54K	10424	**450**	**625**	**1125**	**1925**
Coupe 2D	JC14K	10324	**450**	**625**	**1125**	**1925**
LE Sedan 4D	JB54K	11184	**450**	**650**	**1150**	**1975**
LE Coupe 2D	JB14K	11084	**450**	**650**	**1150**	**1975**
LE Convertible 2D	JB34K	16054	**850**	**1175**	**1925**	**3100**
SE Coupe 2D	JD14K	12334	**475**	**675**	**1175**	**2025**
V6 3.1 Liter	T		**125**	**125**	**165**	**165**
SUNBIRD—V6—Equipment Schedule 5							
W.B. 101.2"; 3.1 Liter.							
GT Coupe 2D	JU14T	14084	**625**	**900**	**1500**	**2475**
GRAND AM—4-Cyl.—Equipment Schedule 5							
W.B. 103.4"; 2.5 Liter.							
Sedan 4D	NG54U	12089	**475**	**700**	**1225**	**2100**
Coupe 2D	NG14U	11889	**475**	**700**	**1225**	**2100**
LE Sedan 4D	NE54U	13039	**575**	**825**	**1400**	**2350**
LE Coupe 2D	NE14U	12839	**575**	**825**	**1400**	**2350**
4-Cyl. 2.3L Quad 4	A,D		**100**	**100**	**135**	**135**
GRAND AM—4-Cyl. Quad 4—Equipment Schedule 5							
W.B. 103.4"; 2.3 Liter.							
SE Sedan 4D	NW54A	17539	**750**	**1050**	**1750**	**2850**
SE Coupe 2D	NW14A	17339	**700**	**1000**	**1650**	**2725**
Manual Trans			**0**	**0**	**0**	**0**
FIREBIRD—V6—Equipment Schedule 4							
W.B. 101.0"; 3.1 Liter.							
Hatchback 2D	FS23T	14624	**1025**	**1450**	**2500**	**4000**
Convertible 2D	FS33T	21033	**1750**	**2275**	**3475**	**5175**
Manual Trans			**(175)**	**(175)**	**(235)**	**(235)**
V8 5.0 Liter	E		**225**	**225**	**300**	**300**
FIREBIRD—V8—Equipment Schedule 4							
W.B. 101.0"; 5.0 Liter.							
Formula H'Back 2D	FS23F	17174	**1225**	**1700**	**2825**	**4425**
Trans Am H'Back 2D	FW23F	19174	**1475**	**1900**	**3050**	**4675**
Trans Am Conv 2D	FW33F	25054	**2425**	**3025**	**4375**	**6275**
Manual Trans			**(100)**	**(100)**	**(135)**	**(135)**
V8 5.7 Liter TPI	8		**250**	**250**	**335**	**335**
FIREBIRD—V8—Equipment Schedule 4							
W.B. 101.0"; 5.7 Liter.							
GTA Hatchback 2D	FW238	24999	**1650**	**2175**	**3375**	**5100**

1991 PONTIAC

Body	Type	VIN	List	Trade-In Fair	Good	Pvt-Party Good	Retail Excellent
Manual Trans				(100)	(100)	(135)	(135)
V8 5.0 Liter TPI		F		(50)	(50)	(65)	(65)
6000—V6—Equipment Schedule 4							
W.B. 104.9"; 3.1 Liter.							
LE Sedan 4D		AF54T	15628	600	850	1450	2425
LE Wagon 4D		AF84T	18314	600	850	1450	2425
SE Sedan 4D		AJ54T	18879	700	1000	1650	2750
4-Cyl. 2.5 Liter		R		(150)	(150)	(200)	(200)
GRAND PRIX—V6—Equipment Schedule 4							
W.B. 107.5"; 3.1 Liter.							
LE Sedan 4D		WH54T	15869	525	750	1425	2475
SE Sedan 4D		WJ54T	16992	650	900	1625	2800
SE Coupe 2D		WJ14T	16379	625	900	1575	2725
GT Coupe 2D		WP14T	19639	775	1100	1950	3250
STE Sedan 4D		WT54T	20479	825	1150	2000	3300
GTP Pkg				125	125	165	165
Manual Trans				(50)	(50)	(65)	(65)
4-Cyl. 2.3L Quad 4		D		(225)	(225)	(300)	(300)
V6 3.4 Liter		X		150	150	200	200
BONNEVILLE—V6—Equipment Schedule 4							
W.B. 110.8"; 3.8 Liter.							
LE Sedan 4D		HX54C	18548	500	725	1275	2175
SE Sedan 4D		HZ54C	20999	700	975	1650	2750
SSE Sedan 4D		HY54C	25799	900	1250	2100	3350

1992 PONTIAC — (1G,JGorKL)2(TX246)-N-#

Body	Type	VIN	List	Trade-In Fair	Good	Pvt-Party Good	Retail Excellent
LeMANS—4-Cyl.—Equipment Schedule 6							
W.B. 99.2"; 1.6 Liter.							
VL Aerocoupe 2D		TX246	8702	275	350	775	1425
SE Aerocoupe 2D		TN246	10025	400	575	1050	1850
SE Sedan 4D		TN546	10740	450	650	1175	2025
SUNBIRD—4-Cyl.—Equipment Schedule 5							
W.B. 101.3"; 2.0 Liter.							
LE Sedan 4D		JC54H	11435	525	750	1300	2175
LE Coupe 2D		JC14H	11325	525	750	1300	2175
SE Sedan 4D		JB54H	12195	550	775	1350	2250
SE Coupe 2D		JB14H	12095	550	775	1350	2250
SE Convertible 2D		JB34H	17060	950	1350	2175	3475
V6 3.1 Liter		T		150	150	200	200
SUNBIRD—V6—Equipment Schedule 5							
W.B. 101.3"; 3.1 Liter.							
GT Coupe 2D		JD14T	14535	725	1025	1700	2800
GRAND AM—4-Cyl.—Equipment Schedule 5							
W.B. 103.4"; 2.3 Liter.							
SE Sedan 4D		NE543	13859	725	1025	1700	2800
SE Coupe 2D		NE143	13759	725	1025	1700	2800
GT Sedan 4D		NW54A	15659	825	1150	1925	3100
GT Coupe 2D		NW14A	15559	800	1125	1850	3025
Manual Trans				0	0	0	0
V6 3.3 Liter		N		150	150	200	200
FIREBIRD—V6—Equipment Schedule 4							
W.B. 101.0"; 3.1 Liter.							
Hatchback 2D		FS23T	15070	1225	1675	2800	4400
Convertible 2D		FS33T	21940	2100	2650	3900	5725
Manual Trans				(225)	(225)	(300)	(300)
V8 5.0 Liter		H		250	250	335	335
FIREBIRD—V8—Equipment Schedule 4							
W.B. 101.0"; 5.0 Liter.							
Formula H'Back 2D		FS23E	17940	1500	2000	3200	4850
Trans Am H'Back 2D		FW23F	19840	1775	2300	3525	5250
Trans Am Conv 2D		FW33F	25610	2875	3525	4950	6950
Manual Trans				(125)	(125)	(165)	(165)
V8 5.7 Liter TPI		8		275	275	365	365
FIREBIRD—V8—Equipment Schedule 4							
W.B. 101.0"; 5.7 Liter.							
GTA Hatchback 2D		FW238	26370	2075	2625	3900	5725
Manual Trans				(125)	(125)	(165)	(165)
V8 5.0 Liter TPI		F		(75)	(75)	(100)	(100)
GRAND PRIX—V6—Equipment Schedule 4							
W.B. 107.5"; 3.1 Liter.							
LE Sedan 4D		WH54T	16575	600	875	1600	2800
SE Sedan 4D		WJ54T	17875	750	1025	1900	3200
SE Coupe 2D		WJ14T	16753	700	975	1800	3075

Body	Type	VIN	List	Trade-In Fair	Trade-In Good	Pvt-Party Good	Retail Excellent
GT Coupe 2D		WP14T	20845	900	1275	2325	3875
STE Sedan 4D		WT54T	22140	950	1350	2425	3975
GTP Pkg				75	75	100	100
Manual Trans				(75)	(75)	(100)	(100)
V6 3.4 Liter		X		175	175	235	235

BONNEVILLE—V6—Equipment Schedule 4
W.B. 110.8"; 3.8 Liter.

Body	Type	VIN	List	Fair	Good	Good	Excellent
SE Sedan 4D		HX53L	19677	700	1000	1725	2900
SSE Sedan 4D		HZ53L	24554	950	1375	2375	3875
V6 3.8L Supercharged		1		225	225	300	300

BONNEVILLE—V6 Supercharged—Equipment Schedule 4
W.B. 110.8"; 3.8 Liter.

Body	Type	VIN	List	Fair	Good	Good	Excellent
SSEi Sedan 4D		HY521	28600	1675	2200	3375	5050

1993 PONTIAC — (1G,JGorKL)2(TX246)-P-#

LeMANS—4-Cyl.—Equipment Schedule 6
W.B. 99.2"; 1.6 Liter.

Body	Type	VIN	List	Fair	Good	Good	Excellent
VL Aerocoupe 2D		TX246	8806	275	350	800	1475
SE Aerocoupe 2D		TN246	10329	400	600	1100	1925
SE Sedan 4D		TN546	11129	475	675	1225	2100

SUNBIRD—4-Cyl.—Equipment Schedule 5
W.B. 101.3"; 2.0 Liter.

Body	Type	VIN	List	Fair	Good	Good	Excellent
LE Sedan 4D		JC54H	11097	600	850	1475	2475
LE Coupe 2D		JC14H	11097	600	850	1475	2475
SE Coupe 2D		JB54H	12095	625	900	1525	2600
SE Coupe 2D		JB14H	12095	625	900	1525	2600
SE Convertible 2D		JB34H	17118	1050	1500	2525	3975
V6 3.1 Liter		T		175	175	235	235

SUNBIRD—V6—Equipment Schedule 5
W.B. 101.3"; 3.1 Liter.

Body	Type	VIN	List	Fair	Good	Good	Excellent
GT Coupe 2D		JD14T	14535	825	1150	1975	3200

GRAND AM—4-Cyl.—Equipment Schedule 5
W.B. 103.4"; 2.3 Liter.

Body	Type	VIN	List	Fair	Good	Good	Excellent
SE Sedan 4D		NE543	14484	850	1175	2000	3250
SE Coupe 2D		NE143	14384	850	1175	2000	3250
GT Sedan 4D		NW54A	15884	950	1350	2225	3575
GT Coupe 2D		NW14A	15784	900	1300	2125	3425
Manual Trans				0	0	0	0
V6 3.3 Liter		N		175	175	235	235

FIREBIRD—V6—Equipment Schedule 4
W.B. 101.2"; 3.4 Liter.

Body	Type	VIN	List	Fair	Good	Good	Excellent
Hatchback 2D		FS22S	16710	1500	2025	3200	4850
Manual Trans				(275)	(275)	(365)	(365)

FIREBIRD—V8—Equipment Schedule 4
W.B. 101.2"; 5.7 Liter.

Body	Type	VIN	List	Fair	Good	Good	Excellent
Formula H'Back 2D		FV22P	19815	2175	2750	4025	5850
Trans Am H'Back 2D		FV22P	22480	2550	3150	4500	6375

GRAND PRIX—V6—Equipment Schedule 4
W.B. 107.5"; 3.1 Liter.

Body	Type	VIN	List	Fair	Good	Good	Excellent
LE Sedan 4D		WH54T	16245	700	1000	1900	3250
SE Sedan 4D		WJ54T	17545	850	1200	2175	3650
SE Coupe 2D		WJ14T	16680	800	1125	2075	3475
GT Coupe 2D		WP14T	20845	1025	1475	2650	4275
STE Sedan 4D		WT54T	22140	1100	1550	2750	4425
GTP Pkg				100	100	135	135
Manual Trans				(100)	(100)	(135)	(135)
V6 3.4 Liter		X		200	200	265	265

BONNEVILLE—V6—Equipment Schedule 4
W.B. 110.8"; 3.8 Liter.

Body	Type	VIN	List	Fair	Good	Good	Excellent
SE Sedan 4D		HX53L	20522	850	1175	2075	3400
SSE Sedan 4D		HZ53L	25399	1200	1650	2775	4400
V6 3.8L Supercharged		1		275	275	365	365

BONNEVILLE—V6 Supercharged—Equipment Schedule 4
W.B. 110.8"; 3.8 Liter.

Body	Type	VIN	List	Fair	Good	Good	Excellent
SSEi Sedan 4D		HY521	29999	2025	2575	3850	5625

1994 PONTIAC — (1G,JGorKL)2(JB54H)-R-#

SUNBIRD—4-Cyl.—Equipment Schedule 5
W.B. 101.3"; 2.0 Liter.

Body	Type	VIN	List	Fair	Good	Good	Excellent
LE Sedan 4D		JB54H	11519	675	950	1650	2800
LE Coupe 2D		JB14H	11519	675	950	1650	2800
LE Convertible 2D		JB34H	17279	1200	1650	2750	4300
V6 3.1 Liter		T		200	200	265	265

Body	Type	VIN	List	Trade-In Fair	Good	Pvt-Party Good	Retail Excellent
SUNBIRD—V6—Equipment Schedule 5							
W.B. 101.3"; 3.1 Liter.							
SE Coupe 2D		JL14T	14179	800	1125	1950	3200
GRAND AM—4-Cyl.—Equipment Schedule 5							
W.B. 103.4"; 2.3 Liter.							
SE Sedan 4D		NE553	14484	950	1375	2375	3875
SE Coupe 2D		NE153	14384	950	1375	2375	3875
GT Sedan 4D		NW55A	16354	1075	1525	2600	4100
GT Coupe 2D		NW15A	16254	1025	1475	2525	4000
Manual Trans				0	0	0	0
V6 3.1 Liter		M		200	200	265	265
FIREBIRD—V6—Equipment Schedule 4							
W.B. 101.1"; 3.4 Liter.							
Hatchback 2D		FS22S	16735	1825	2350	3600	5325
Convertible 2D		FS32S	22444	2900	3550	4950	6925
Manual Trans				(325)	(325)	(435)	(435)
FIREBIRD—V8—Equipment Schedule 4							
W.B. 101.1"; 5.7 Liter.							
Formula H'Back 2D		FV22P	19615	2600	3225	4550	6475
Formula Convertible 2D		FV32P	25544	3925	4675	6250	8450
Trans Am H'Back 2D		FV22P	21005	3000	3675	5100	7100
Trans Am GT H'Back 2D		FV22P	22505	3300	3950	5400	7475
Trans Am GT Conv 2D		FV32P	27744	4600	5425	7050	9400
GRAND PRIX—V6—Equipment Schedule 4							
W.B. 107.5"; 3.1 Liter.							
SE Sedan 4D		WJ52M	17094	975	1425	2575	4225
SE Coupe 2D		WJ16M	17295	925	1325	2475	4100
GT/GTP Pkg				100	100	135	135
V6 3.4 Liter		X		225	225	300	300
BONNEVILLE—V6—Equipment Schedule 4							
W.B. 110.8"; 3.8 Liter.							
SE Sedan 4D		HX52L	21627	975	1425	2525	4075
SSE Sedan 4D		HZ52L	26459	1500	2025	3250	4950
SLE Pkg				150	150	200	200
BONNEVILLE—V6 Supercharged—Equipment Schedule 4							
W.B. 110.8"; 3.8 Liter.							
SSEi Sedan 4D		HZ521	29141	2225	2775	4100	5975

1995 PONTIAC — (1G,JGorKL)2(JB524)-S-#

Body	Type	VIN	List	Trade-In Fair	Good	Pvt-Party Good	Retail Excellent
SUNFIRE—4-Cyl.—Equipment Schedule 5							
W.B. 104.1"; 2.2 Liter, 2.3 Liter.							
SE Sedan 4D		JB524	12989	775	1100	1950	3250
SE Coupe 2D		JB124	12839	750	1050	1875	3150
SE Convertible 2D		JB324	18034	1800	2325	3550	5250
GT Coupe 2D		JD12D	14824	975	1400	2450	3950
GRAND AM—4-Cyl.—Equipment Schedule 5							
W.B. 103.4"; 2.3 Liter.							
SE Sedan 4D		NE55D	15084	1125	1575	2700	4250
SE Coupe 2D		NE15D	14984	1125	1575	2700	4250
GT Sedan 4D		NW55D	16204	1300	1775	2900	4500
GT Coupe 2D		NW15D	16104	1225	1700	2800	4400
Manual Trans				0	0	0	0
V6 3.1 Liter		M		225	225	300	300
FIREBIRD—V6—Equipment Schedule 4							
W.B. 101.1"; 3.4 Liter.							
Hatchback 2D		FS22S	17764	2200	2775	4050	5900
Convertible 2D		FS32S	23214	3375	4075	5525	7600
Manual Trans				(375)	(375)	(500)	(500)
V6 3.8 Liter		K		200	200	265	265
FIREBIRD—V8—Equipment Schedule 4							
W.B. 101.1"; 5.7 Liter.							
Formula H'Back 2D		FV22P	21450	3075	3725	5150	7175
Formula Convertible 2D		FV32P	26404	4500	5325	6925	9275
Trans Am H'Back 2D		FV22P	22344	3550	4250	5725	7875
Trans Am Conv 2D		FV32P	28414	5200	6100	7800	10250
GRAND PRIX—V6—Equipment Schedule 4							
W.B. 107.5"; 3.1 Liter.							
SE Sedan 4D		WJ52M	17589	1175	1625	2900	4650
SE Coupe 2D		WJ16M	17919	1100	1550	2800	4525
GT/GTP Pkg				100	100	135	135
V6 3.4 Liter		X		250	250	335	335
BONNEVILLE—V6—Equipment Schedule 4							
W.B. 110.8"; 3.8 Liter.							

Body	Type	VIN	List	Trade-In Fair	Good	Pvt-Party Good	Retail Excellent
SE Sedan 4D		HX52K	21584	1225	1675	2900	4600
SSE Sedan 4D		HZ52K	26389	1900	2425	3775	5625
SLE Pkg				150	150	200	200
V6 3.8L Supercharged (SE)		1		325	325	435	435

BONNEVILLE—V6 Supercharged—Equipment Schedule 4
W.B. 110.8"; 3.8 Liter.

| SSEi Sedan 4D | | HZ521 | 27556 | 2650 | 3250 | 4675 | 6675 |

1996 PONTIAC — (1,2,3or4)G2(JB524)-T-#

SUNFIRE—4-Cyl.—Equipment Schedule 5
W.B. 104.1"; 2.2 Liter, 2.4 Liter.

SE Sedan 4D		JB524	13514	900	1300	2350	3900
SE Coupe 2D		JB124	13344	900	1250	2200	3650
SE Convertible 2D		JB324	18229	2125	2700	3975	5775
GT Coupe 2D		JD12T	15299	1125	1575	2725	4350

GRAND AM—4-Cyl.—Equipment Schedule 5
W.B. 103.8"; 2.4 Liter.

SE Sedan 4D		NE52T	15624	1375	1875	3025	4675
SE Coupe 2D		NE12T	15624	1375	1875	3025	4675
GT Sedan 4D		NW52T	16794	1525	2050	3250	4925
GT Coupe 2D		NW12T	16794	1500	1975	3175	4825
Manual Trans				0	0	0	0
V6 3.1 Liter		M		250	250	335	335

FIREBIRD—V6—Equipment Schedule 4
W.B. 101.1"; 3.8 Liter.

Coupe 2D		FS22K	19408	2625	3250	4600	6575
Convertible 2D		FS32K	23739	3875	4600	6175	8375
Manual Trans				(400)	(400)	(535)	(535)

FIREBIRD—V8—Equipment Schedule 4
W.B. 101.1"; 5.7 Liter.

Formula Coupe 2D		FV22P	22363	3575	4300	5800	7975
Formula Conv 2D		FV32P	26579	5125	6000	7700	10200
Trans Am Coupe 2D		FV22P	22709	4125	4900	6450	8725
Trans Am Conv 2D		FV32P	28659	5875	6850	8625	11250
Ram Air Handling Pkg				925	925	1235	1235

GRAND PRIX—V6—Equipment Schedule 4
W.B. 107.5"; 3.1 Liter.

SE Sedan 4D		WJ52M	18049	1475	1950	3325	5200
SE Coupe 2D		WJ12M	18899	1375	1875	3225	5100
GT/GTP Pkg				100	100	135	135
V6 3.4 Liter		X		275	275	365	365

BONNEVILLE—V6—Equipment Schedule 4
W.B. 110.8"; 3.8 Liter.

SE Sedan 4D		HX52K	22374	1550	2075	3375	5225
SSE Sedan 4D		HZ52K	27149	2325	2900	4350	6325
SLE Pkg				150	150	200	200
V6 3.8L Supercharged (SE)		1		350	350	465	465

BONNEVILLE—V6 Supercharged—Equipment Schedule 4
W.B. 110.8"; 3.8 Liter.

| SSEi Sedan 4D | | HZ521 | 28491 | 3125 | 3775 | 5300 | 7450 |

1997 PONTIAC — (1,2,3or4)G2(JB524)-V-#

SUNFIRE—4-Cyl.—Equipment Schedule 5
W.B. 104.1"; 2.2 Liter, 2.4 Liter.

SE Sedan 4D		JB524	14079	1050	1500	2700	4350
SE Coupe 2D		JB124	13939	1025	1475	2650	4300
SE Convertible 2D		JB324	19399	2525	3125	4500	6400
GT Coupe 2D		JD12T	15859	1375	1850	3075	4775

GRAND AM—4-Cyl.—Equipment Schedule 5
W.B. 103.8"; 2.4 Liter.

SE Sedan 4D		NE52T	15969	1650	2150	3400	5175
SE Coupe 2D		NE12T	15969	1650	2150	3400	5175
GT Sedan 4D		NW52T	17209	1800	2325	3625	5400
GT Coupe 2D		NW12T	17209	1750	2275	3550	5325
Manual Trans				0	0	0	0
V6 3.1 Liter		M		250	250	335	335

FIREBIRD—V6—Equipment Schedule 4
W.B. 101.1"; 3.8 Liter.

Coupe 2D		FS22K	19209	3100	3750	5200	7300
Convertible 2D		FS32K	24374	4450	5225	6850	9175
Manual Trans				(425)	(425)	(565)	(565)

FIREBIRD—V8—Equipment Schedule 4
W.B. 101.1"; 5.7 Liter.

1997 PONTIAC

Body	Type	VIN	List	Trade-In Fair	Good	Pvt-Party Good	Retail Excellent
	Formula Coupe 2D	FV22P	21179	4175	4950	6525	8800
	Formula Conv 2D	FV32P	26979	5800	6775	8550	11150
	Trans Am Coupe 2D	FV22P	23339	4750	5600	7250	9650
	Trans Am Conv 2D	FV32P	28899	6575	7600	9450	12200
	Ram Air Handling Pkg			975	975	1300	1300
GRAND PRIX—V6—Equipment Schedule 4							
W.B. 110.5"; 3.8 Liter.							
	SE Sedan 4D	WJ52K	19249	1850	2375	3850	5850
	GT Sedan 4D	WP52K	20359	2625	3250	4675	6700
	GT Coupe 2D	WP12K	20029	2275	2850	4375	6450
	GTP Pkg			100	100	135	135
	V6 3.1 Liter	M		(250)	(250)	(335)	(335)
	V6 3.8L Supercharged	1		375	375	500	500
BONNEVILLE—V6—Equipment Schedule 4							
W.B. 110.8"; 3.8 Liter.							
	SE Sedan 4D	HX52K	22914	2000	2550	3975	5975
	SSE Sedan 4D	HZ52K	27769	2825	3475	5025	7175
	SLE			150	150	200	200
	V6 3.8L Superchrgd (SE)	1		375	375	500	500
BONNEVILLE—V6 Supercharged—Equipment Schedule 4							
W.B. 110.8"; 3.8 Liter.							
	SSEi Sedan 4D	HZ521	29111	3675	4400	6025	8325

1998 PONTIAC — (1,2,3or4)G2(JB524)-W-#

SUNFIRE—4-Cyl.—Equipment Schedule 5							
W.B. 104.1"; 2.2 Liter, 2.4 Liter.							
	SE Sedan 4D	JB524	14425	1350	1825	3025	4700
	SE Coupe 2D	JB124	14425	1300	1775	2975	4650
	SE Convertible 2D	JB324	19995	2950	3600	4950	6900
	GT Coupe 2D	JD12T	16805	1650	2175	3400	5150
GRAND AM—4-Cyl.—Equipment Schedule 5							
W.B. 103.4"; 2.4 Liter.							
	SE Sedan 4D	NE52T	16359	2000	2550	3825	5625
	SE Coupe 2D	NE12T	16209	2000	2550	3825	5625
	GT Sedan 4D	NW52T	17809	2175	2750	4025	5850
	GT Coupe 2D	NW12T	17659	2100	2700	3950	5775
	Manual Trans			0	0	0	0
	V6 3.1 Liter	M		250	250	335	335
FIREBIRD—V6—Equipment Schedule 4							
W.B. 101.1"; 3.8 Liter.							
	Coupe 2D	FS22K	20380	3675	4400	5825	7925
	Convertible 2D	FS32K	25545	5100	5975	7550	9900
	T-Bar Roof			425	425	565	565
	Manual Trans			(450)	(450)	(600)	(600)
FIREBIRD—V8—Equipment Schedule 4							
W.B. 101.1"; 5.7 Liter.							
	Formula Coupe 2D	FV22P	23290	4875	5700	7275	9550
	Trans Am Coupe 2D	FV22P	26400	5575	6475	8100	10500
	Trans Am Conv 2D	FV32P	30140	7450	8575	10350	13050
	T-Bar Roof			425	425	565	565
	Ram Air Handling Pkg			1025	1025	1365	1365
GRAND PRIX—V6—Equipment Schedule 4							
W.B. 110.5"; 3.8 Liter.							
	SE Sedan 4D	WJ52K	19885	2250	2800	4350	6425
	GT Sedan 4D	WP52K	21215	3100	3750	5200	7300
	GT Coupe 2D	WP12K	20965	2700	3325	4900	7075
	GTP Pkg			100	100	135	135
	V6 3.1 Liter	M		(250)	(250)	(335)	(335)
	V6 3.8L Supercharged	1		425	425	565	565
BONNEVILLE—V6—Equipment Schedule 4							
W.B. 110.8"; 3.8 Liter.							
	SE Sedan 4D	HX52K	23215	2525	3125	4575	6650
	SSE Sedan 4D	HZ52K	29895	3475	4175	5750	7975
	SLE Pkg			150	150	200	200
BONNEVILLE—V6 Supercharged—Equipment Schedule 4							
W.B. 110.8"; 3.8 Liter.							
	SSEi Sedan 4D	HZ521	31165	4375	5150	6825	9175

1999 PONTIAC — (1,2,3or4)G2(JB524)-X-#

SUNFIRE—4-Cyl.—Equipment Schedule 5							
W.B. 104.1"; 2.2 Liter, 2.4 Liter.							
	SE Sedan 4D	JB524	14685	1750	2275	3550	5350
	SE Coupe 2D	JB124	14685	1675	2200	3475	5275

Body	Type	VIN	List	Trade-In Fair	Trade-In Good	Pvt-Party Good	Retail Excellent
	GT Coupe 2D	JD12T	17065	2150	2725	4050	5925
	GT Convertible 2D	JB32T	21655	3625	4350	5775	7875
GRAND AM—4-Cyl.—Equipment Schedule 5							
W.B. 106.7"; 2.4 Liter.							
	SE Sedan 4D	NE52T	16995	2700	3300	4575	6425
	SE Coupe 2D	NE12T	16595	2700	3300	4550	6400
	V6 3.4 Liter	E		300	300	400	400
GRAND AM—V6—Equipment Schedule 5							
W.B. 107.0"; 3.4 Liter.							
	GT Sedan 4D	NW52E	19995	3675	4400	5625	7450
	GT Coupe 2D	NW12E	19595	3375	4075	5425	7375
FIREBIRD—V6—Equipment Schedule 4							
W.B. 101.1"; 3.8 Liter.							
	Coupe 2D	FS22K	20540	4475	5275	6825	9075
	Convertible 2D	FS32K	26465	6150	7125	8800	11350
	T-Bar Roof			500	500	665	665
	Manual Trans			(500)	(500)	(665)	(665)
FIREBIRD—V8—Equipment Schedule 4							
W.B. 101.1"; 5.7 Liter.							
	Formula Coupe 2D	FV22G	23930	5725	6900	8600	11100
	Trans Am Coupe 2D	FV22G	27040	6825	7875	9600	12250
	Trans Am Conv 2D	FV32G	31110	8875	10175	12050	15000
	T-Bar Roof			500	500	665	665
	Ram Air Handling Pkg			1175	1175	1565	1565
GRAND PRIX—V6—Equipment Schedule 4							
W.B. 110.5"; 3.8 Liter.							
	SE Sedan 4D	WJ52K	20210	3000	3675	5050	7025
	GT Sedan 4D	WP52K	21705	3975	4725	6050	8025
	GT Coupe 2D	WP12K	21555	3575	4275	5700	7775
	V6 3.1 Liter	M		(250)	(250)	(335)	(335)
GRAND PRIX—V6 Supercharged—Equipment Schedule 4							
W.B. 110.5"; 3.8 Liter.							
	GTP Sedan 4D	WR521	24470	4975	5825	7375	9650
	GTP Coupe 2D	WR121	24320	4750	5600	7125	9375
BONNEVILLE—V6—Equipment Schedule 4							
W.B. 110.8"; 3.8 Liter.							
	SE Sedan 4D	HX52K	23715	3150	3800	5400	7625
	SSE Sedan 4D	HZ52K	30715	4475	5275	6975	9425
	SLE Pkg			175	175	235	235
BONNEVILLE—V6 Supercharged—Equipment Schedule 4							
W.B. 110.8"; 3.8 Liter.							
	SSEi Sedan 4D	HZ521	31665	5500	6425	8100	10550

2000 PONTIAC — (1,2,3or4)G2(JB524)-Y-#

Body	Type	VIN	List	Trade-In Fair	Trade-In Good	Pvt-Party Good	Retail Excellent
SUNFIRE—4-Cyl.—Equipment Schedule 5							
W.B. 104.1"; 2.2 Liter, 2.4 Liter.							
	SE Sedan 4D	JB524	15120	2475	3075	4350	6200
	SE Coupe 2D	JB124	15020	2400	2975	4250	6075
	GT Coupe 2D	JD12T	17530	2975	3625	4950	6850
	GT Convertible 2D	JD32T	22120	4575	5400	6825	8950
GRAND AM—4-Cyl.—Equipment Schedule 5							
W.B. 107.0"; 2.4 Liter.							
	SE Sedan 4D	NE52T	17540	3300	3950	5325	7325
	SE Coupe 2D	NE12T	17240	3250	3900	5275	7275
	V6 3.4 Liter	E		325	325	435	435
GRAND AM—V6—Equipment Schedule 5							
W.B. 107.0"; 3.4 Liter.							
	GT Sedan 4D	NW52E	20385	4400	5175	6500	8475
	GT Coupe 2D	NW12E	20085	4075	4850	6300	8375
FIREBIRD—V6—Equipment Schedule 4							
W.B. 101.1"; 3.8 Liter.							
	Coupe 2D	FS22K	20535	5425	6325	8000	10400
	Convertible 2D	FS32K	26460	7325	8425	10200	12900
	T-Bar Roof			575	575	765	765
	Manual Trans			(525)	(525)	(700)	(700)
FIREBIRD—V8—Equipment Schedule 4							
W.B. 101.1"; 5.7 Liter.							
	Formula Coupe 2D	FV22G	24055	7200	8275	10100	12750
	Trans Am Coupe 2D	FV22G	27165	8225	9425	11300	14050
	Trans Am Conv 2D	FV32G	31235	10425	11850	13850	17050
	T-Bar Roof			575	575	765	765
	Ram Air Handling Pkg			1325	1325	1765	1765

2000 PONTIAC

Body	Type	VIN	List	Trade-In Fair	Good	Pvt-Party Good	Retail Excellent
GRAND PRIX—V6—Equipment Schedule 4							
W.B. 110.5"; 3.8 Liter.							
SE Sedan 4D		WJ52J	20610	**3675**	**4400**	**5875**	**8025**
GT Sedan 4D		WP52K	22105	**4750**	**5600**	**7000**	**9125**
GT Coupe 2D		WP12K	21955	**4300**	**5075**	**6600**	**8825**
V6 3.1 Liter		J		**(250)**	**(250)**	**(335)**	**(335)**
GRAND PRIX—V6 Supercharged—Equipment Schedule 4							
W.B. 110.5"; 3.8 Liter.							
GTP Sedan 4D		WR521	24870	**5875**	**6850**	**8475**	**10900**
GTP Coupe 2D		WR121	24720	**5650**	**6550**	**8175**	**10600**
BONNEVILLE—V6—Equipment Schedule 4							
W.B. 112.2"; 3.8 Liter.							
SE Sedan 4D		HX52K	24295	**4550**	**5375**	**7300**	**9975**
SLE Sedan 4D		HY52K	27995	**5450**	**6350**	**8325**	**11150**
SSEi Sedan 4D		HZ52K	32250	**7450**	**8575**	**10450**	**13300**
V6 3.8L Supercharged		1		**550**	**550**	**735**	**735**

2001 PONTIAC — (1,2or3)G(2or7)(JB524)–1–#

Body	Type	VIN	List	Trade-In Fair	Good	Pvt-Party Good	Retail Excellent
SUNFIRE—4-Cyl.—Equipment Schedule 5							
W.B. 104.1"; 2.2 Liter, 2.4 Liter.							
SE Sedan 4D		JB524	15650	**3100**	**3750**	**5125**	**7125**
SE Coupe 2D		JB124	15395	**3000**	**3675**	**5050**	**7025**
GT Coupe 2D		JD12T	17625	**3650**	**4375**	**5775**	**7850**
GRAND AM—4-Cyl.—Equipment Schedule 5							
W.B. 107.0"; 2.4 Liter.							
SE Sedan 4D		NE52T	17800	**3975**	**4725**	**6225**	**8350**
SE Coupe 2D		NE12T	17500	**3900**	**4650**	**6150**	**8275**
V6 3.4 Liter		E		**350**	**350**	**465**	**465**
GRAND AM—V6—Equipment Schedule 5							
W.B. 107.0"; 3.4 Liter.							
GT Sedan 4D		NW52E	21110	**5225**	**6125**	**7500**	**9650**
GT Coupe 2D		NW12E	20810	**4900**	**5750**	**7300**	**9575**
FIREBIRD—V6—Equipment Schedule 4							
W.B. 101.1"; 3.8 Liter.							
Coupe 2D		FS22K	20810	**6525**	**7525**	**9300**	**11900**
Convertible 2D		FS32K	26735	**8650**	**9900**	**11750**	**14650**
T-Bar Roof				**650**	**650**	**865**	**865**
Manual Trans				**(550)**	**(550)**	**(735)**	**(735)**
75th Anniversary				**500**	**500**	**665**	**665**
FIREBIRD—V8—Equipment Schedule 4							
W.B. 101.1"; 5.7 Liter.							
Formula Coupe 2D		FV22K	24480	**8600**	**9850**	**11700**	**14600**
Trans Am Coupe 2D		FV22G	27590	**9750**	**11125**	**13050**	**16100**
Trans Am Conv 2D		FV32G	31660	**12100**	**13725**	**15850**	**19150**
T-Bar Roof				**650**	**650**	**865**	**865**
Ram Air Handling Pkg				**1475**	**1475**	**1965**	**1965**
75th Anniversary				**500**	**500**	**665**	**665**
NHRA Pkg				**275**	**275**	**365**	**365**
GRAND PRIX—V6—Equipment Schedule 4							
W.B. 110.5"; 3.1 Liter, 3.8 Liter.							
SE Sedan 4D		WJ52J	21135	**4500**	**5300**	**6900**	**9250**
GT Sedan 4D		WP52K	22615	**5700**	**6650**	**8150**	**10450**
GT Coupe 2D		WP12K	22465	**5175**	**6050**	**7700**	**10150**
Special Edition				**175**	**175**	**235**	**235**
GRAND PRIX—V6 Supercharged—Equipment Schedule 4							
W.B. 110.5"; 3.8 Liter.							
GTP Sedan 4D		WR521	26135	**6950**	**8025**	**9800**	**12450**
GTP Coupe 2D		WR121	25935	**6675**	**7700**	**9425**	**12050**
Special Edition				**175**	**175**	**235**	**235**
BONNEVILLE—V6—Equipment Schedule 4							
W.B. 112.2"; 3.8 Liter.							
SE Sedan 4D		HX52K	25730	**5600**	**6500**	**8625**	**11550**
SLE Sedan 4D		HY52K	28700	**6575**	**7600**	**9750**	**12800**
BONNEVILLE—V6 Supercharged—Equipment Schedule 4							
W.B. 112.2"; 3.8 Liter.							
SSEi Sedan 4D		HZ521	33070	**9025**	**10325**	**12300**	**15300**

2002 PONTIAC — (1or2)G2(JB524)–2–#

Body	Type	VIN	List	Trade-In Fair	Good	Pvt-Party Good	Retail Excellent
SUNFIRE—4-Cyl.—Equipment Schedule 5							
W.B. 104.1"; 2.2 LIter, 2.4 Liter.							
SE Sedan 4D		JB524	16545	**3875**	**4600**	**6125**	**8275**
SE Coupe 2D		JB124	16045	**3800**	**4525**	**6025**	**8175**
GT Coupe 2D		JD12T	18205	**4500**	**5300**	**6850**	**9075**

2002 PONTIAC

Body Type	VIN	List	Trade-In Fair	Good	Pvt-Party Good	Retail Excellent
GRAND AM—4-Cyl.—Equipment Schedule 5						
W.B. 107.0"; 2.2 Liter.						
SE Sedan 4D	NE52T	18360	**4850**	**5700**	**7275**	**9600**
SE Coupe 2D	NE12T	18210	**4750**	**5600**	**7175**	**9475**
V6 3.4 Liter	E		**375**	**375**	**500**	**500**
GRAND AM—V6—Equipment Schedule 5						
W.B. 107.0"; 3.4 Liter.						
GT Sedan 4D	NW52E	21425	**6250**	**7250**	**8700**	**11000**
GT Coupe 2D	NW12E	21275	**5875**	**6850**	**8475**	**10900**
FIREBIRD—V6—Equipment Schedule 4						
W.B. 101.1"; 3.8 Liter.						
Coupe 2D	FS22K	21115	**7825**	**8975**	**10900**	**13750**
Convertible 2D	FS32K	27205	**10125**	**11525**	**13550**	**16650**
T-Bar Roof			**725**	**725**	**965**	**965**
GT Pkg			**300**	**300**	**400**	**400**
Manual Trans			**(575)**	**(575)**	**(765)**	**(765)**
FIREBIRD—V8—Equipment Schedule 4						
W.B. 101.1"; 5.7 Liter.						
Formula Coupe 2D	FV22G	26235	**10175**	**11575**	**13650**	**16700**
Trans Am Coupe 2D	FV22G	28265	**11475**	**13050**	**15100**	**18400**
Trans Am Conv 2D	FV32G	32335	**14025**	**15800**	**18050**	**21600**
Collector Ed Cpe 2D	FV22G	31265	**12675**	**14350**	**16500**	**19950**
Collector Ed Conv 2D	FV32G	35335	**15075**	**17000**	**19300**	**22900**
T-Bar Roof			**725**	**725**	**965**	**965**
NHRA Pkg			**300**	**300**	**400**	**400**
Ram Air Handling Pkg			**1625**	**1625**	**2165**	**2165**
GRAND PRIX—V6—Equipment Schedule 4						
W.B. 110.5"; 3.1 Liter, 3.8 Liter.						
SE Sedan 4D	WJ52J	21575	**5550**	**6450**	**8250**	**10850**
GT Sedan 4D	WP52K	23695	**6900**	**7950**	**9600**	**12100**
GT Coupe 2D	WP12K	23545	**6300**	**7300**	**9100**	**11750**
40th Anniversary Edition			**125**	**125**	**165**	**165**
GRAND PRIX—V6 Supercharged—Equipment Schedule 4						
W.B. 110.5"; 3.8 Liter.						
GTP Sedan 4D	WR521	26415	**8275**	**9475**	**11400**	**14300**
GTP Coupe 2D	WR121	26235	**7950**	**9125**	**11000**	**13850**
40th Anniversary Edition			**125**	**125**	**165**	**165**
BONNEVILLE—V6—Equipment Schedule 4						
W.B. 112.2"; 3.8 Liter.						
SE Sedan 4D	HX52K	25625	**6900**	**7975**	**10250**	**13550**
SLE Sedan 4D	HY52K	29545	**8025**	**9200**	**11550**	**14950**
BONNEVILLE—V6 Supercharged—Equipment Schedule 4						
W.B. 112.2"; 3.8 Liter.						
SSEi Sedan 4D	HZ521	33605	**10850**	**12300**	**14400**	**17600**

2003 PONTIAC — (1or5)G2orY2(JB12F)-3-#

Body Type	VIN	List	Trade-In Fair	Good	Pvt-Party Good	Retail Excellent
SUNFIRE—4-Cyl.—Equipment Schedule 5						
W.B. 104.1"; 2.2 Liter.						
Coupe 2D	JB12F	15435	**4775**	**5625**	**7125**	**9325**
VIBE—4-Cyl.—Equipment Schedule 6						
W.B. 102.4"; 1.8 Liter.						
Sport Wagon 4D	SL628	16900	**7425**	**8550**	**10150**	**12600**
GT Sport Wagon	SN62L	19900	**7550**	**8700**	**10250**	**12700**
AWD Sport Wagon 4D	SM628	20100	**7950**	**9125**	**10700**	**13200**
GRAND AM—4-Cyl.—Equipment Schedule 5						
W.B. 107.0"; 2.2 Liter.						
SE Sedan 4D	NE52F	18465	**5925**	**6900**	**8475**	**10850**
V6 3.4 Liter	E		**400**	**400**	**535**	**535**
GRAND AM—V6—Equipment Schedule 5						
W.B. 107.0"; 3.4 Liter.						
GT Sedan 4D	NW52E	21640	**7475**	**8600**	**10100**	**12450**
GT Coupe 2D	NW12E	21640	**7050**	**8125**	**9800**	**12350**
GRAND PRIX—V6—Equipment Schedule 4						
W.B. 110.5"; 3.1 Liter, 3.8 Liter.						
SE Sedan 4D	WK52J	22140	**6900**	**7950**	**9850**	**12600**
GT Sedan 4D	WP52K	23990	**8350**	**9575**	**11350**	**14050**
Wide Track Sport Pkg			**400**	**400**	**535**	**535**
GRAND PRIX—V6 Supercharged—Equipment Schedule 4						
W.B. 110.5"; 3.8 Liter.						
GTP Sedan 4D	WR521	26800	**9850**	**11225**	**13250**	**16350**
BONNEVILLE—V6—Equipment Schedule 4						
W.B. 112.2"; 3.8 Liter.						
SE Sedan 4D	HX52K	26665	**8600**	**9850**	**12250**	**15750**

2003 PONTIAC

Body	Type	VIN	List	Trade-In Fair	Good	Pvt-Party Good	Retail Excellent
SLE Sedan 4D		HY52K	29855	**9800**	**11175**	**13650**	**17300**

BONNEVILLE—V6 Supercharged—Equipment Schedule 4
W.B. 112.2"; 3.8 Liter.

| SSEi Sedan 4D | | HZ541 | 34085 | **13050** | **14775** | **16850** | **20300** |

2004 PONTIAC — (1,2,5or6)G2orY2(JB12F)-4-#

SUNFIRE—4-Cyl.—Equipment Schedule 5
W.B. 104.1"; 2.2 Liter.

| Coupe 2D | | JB12F | 16695 | | | | |

VIBE—4-Cyl.—Equipment Schedule 6
W.B. 102.4" 1.8 Liter.

Sport Wagon 4D		SL628	17045	**9050**	**10325**	**11950**	**14500**
GT Sport Wagon		SN62L	19995	**9225**	**10500**	**12100**	**14700**
AWD Sport Wagon 4D		SM628	20345	**9600**	**10950**	**12550**	**15150**

GRAND AM—4-Cyl.—Equipment Schedule 5
W.B. 107.0"; 2.2 Liter.

| SE Sedan 4D | | NE52F | 18545 | **7550** | **8700** | **10450** | **13150** |
| V6 3.4 Liter | | E | | **425** | **425** | **565** | **565** |

GRAND AM—V6—Equipment Schedule 5
W.B. 107.0"; 3.4 Liter.

| GT Sedan 4D | | NW52E | 22450 | **9275** | **10550** | **12250** | **14900** |
| GT Coupe 2D | | NW12E | 22450 | **8800** | **10075** | **11900** | **14750** |

GRAND PRIX—V6—Equipment Schedule 4
W.B. 110.5"; 3.8 Liter.

| GT Sedan 4D | | WP522 | 22395 | **10225** | **11625** | **13600** | **16700** |

GRAND PRIX—V6 Supercharged—Equipment Schedule 4
W.B. 110.5"; 3.8 Liter.

| GTP Sedan 4D | | WR524 | 26495 | **11800** | **13400** | **15750** | **19300** |

BONNEVILLE—V6—Equipment Schedule 4
W.B. 112.2"; 3.8 Liter.

| SE Sedan 4D | | HX52K | 27570 | **11125** | **12625** | **15250** | **19200** |
| SLE Sedan 4D | | HY52K | 30420 | **12375** | **14025** | **16750** | **20800** |

BONNEVILLE—V8—Equipment Schedule 4
W.B. 112.2"; 4.6 Liter.

| GXP Sedan 4D | | HZ54Y | 35995 | **13500** | **15225** | **18400** | **23000** |

GTO—V8—Equipment Schedule 2
W.B. 109.8"; 5.7 Liter.

| Coupe 2D | | VX13G | 33495 | | | | |

PORSCHE

1990 PORSCHE — WPO(AB294)-L-#

944—4-Cyl.—Equipment Schedule 1
W.B. 94.5"; 3.0 Liter.

| S2 Coupe 2D | | AB294 | 45675 | **2800** | **3425** | **5000** | **7150** |
| S2 Cabriolet 2D | | BA294 | 52375 | **5375** | **6300** | **8325** | **11200** |

911 CARRERA 2—6-Cyl.—Equipment Schedule 1
W.B. 89.4"; 3.6 Liter.

Coupe 2D		AB296	59655	**11375**	**12900**	**16800**	**22200**
Targa 2D		BB296	61055	**11175**	**12675**	**16550**	**21900**
Cabriolet 2D		CB296	67950	**14400**	**16275**	**20700**	**26900**
Full Leather				**100**	**100**	**135**	**135**
Tiptronic Auto Trans				**300**	**300**	**400**	**400**

911 CARRERA 4—6-Cyl.—Equipment Schedule 1
W.B. 89.4"; 3.6 Liter.

AWD Coupe 2D		AB296	71005	**12525**	**14150**	**18250**	**23900**
AWD Targa 2D		BB296	72405	**12310**	**13925**	**17950**	**23500**
AWD Cabriolet 2D		CB296	79305	**14025**	**15800**	**20300**	**26300**
Full Leather				**100**	**100**	**135**	**135**

928—V8—Equipment Schedule 1
W.B. 98.4"; 5.0 Liter.

| S4 Coupe 2D | | JB292 | 76050 | **8075** | **9250** | **11700** | **15250** |

1991 PORSCHE — WPO(AB294)-M-#

944—4-Cyl.—Equipment Schedule 1
W.B. 94.5"; 3.0 Liter.

| S2 Coupe 2D | | AB294 | 47290 | **3250** | **3900** | **5600** | **7925** |
| S2 Cabriolet 2D | | CB294 | 54290 | **6150** | **7125** | **9350** | **12500** |

911 CARRERA 2—6-Cyl.—Equipment Schedule 1
W.B. 89.5"; 3.6 Liter.

| Coupe 2D | | AB296 | 64850 | **12325** | **13975** | **18100** | **23800** |

Body	Type	VIN	List	Trade-In Fair	Trade-In Good	Pvt-Party Good	Retail Excellent
Targa 2D		BB296	66350	12050	13675	17750	23400
Cabriolet 2D		CB296	73450	15600	17625	22300	28800
Full Leather		------		100	100	135	135
Tiptronic Auto Trans		------		325	325	435	435

911 CARRERA 4—6-Cyl.—Equipment Schedule 1
W.B. 89.5"; 3.6 Liter.

AWD Coupe 2D		AB296	73550	13525	15300	19700	25600
AWD Targa 2D		BB296	75050	13300	15025	19300	25200
AWD Cabriolet 2D		CB296	82150	15175	17100	21800	28300
Full Leather		------		100	100	135	135

911 TURBO—6-Cyl. Turbo—Equipment Schedule 1
W.B. 89.4"; 3.3 Liter.

Coupe 2D		AA296	97800	19875	22275	27700	35400

928—V8—Equipment Schedule 1
W.B. 98.4"; 5.0 Liter.

S4 Coupe 2D		AA292	79050	9850	11225	14850	19800
GT Coupe 2D		AA292	79500	9850	11225	14850	19800

1992 PORSCHE — WPO(AA296)-N-#

968—4-Cyl.—Equipment Schedule 1
W.B. 94.5"; 3.0 Liter.

Coupe 2D		AA296	48350	6525	7525	9750	12900
Cabriolet 2D		CA296	56850	9500	10850	13600	17450
Tiptronic Auto Trans		------		375	375	500	500

911 CARRERA 2—6-Cyl.—Equipment Schedule 1
W.B. 89.4"; 3.6 Liter.

America Roadster 2D		CB296	91750	****	****	****	40700
Coupe 2D		AB296	67750	13675	15450	19800	25800
Targa 2D		BB296	69350	13450	15175	19500	25400
Cabriolet 2D		CB296	76750	16850	18950	23800	30500
Full Leather		------		100	100	135	135
Tiptronic Auto Trans		------		375	375	500	500

911 CARRERA 4—6-Cyl.—Equipment Schedule 1
W.B. 89.4"; 3.6 Liter.

AWD Coupe 2D		AB296	77780	14825	16700	21200	27600
AWD Targa 2D		BB296	79380	14600	16475	20900	27200
AWD Cabriolet 2D		CB296	86780	16850	18950	23900	30800
Full Leather		------		100	100	135	135

911 TURBO—6-Cyl. Turbo—Equipment Schedule 1
W.B. 89.4"; 3.3 Liter.

Coupe 2D		AA296	101675	21900	24475	30200	38200

1993 PORSCHE — WPO(AA296)-P-#

968—4-Cyl.—Equipment Schedule 1
W.B. 94.5"; 3.0 Liter.

Coupe 2D		AA296	47157	7500	8625	11000	14350
Cabriolet 2D		CA296	58800	10900	12325	15200	19400
Tiptronic Auto Trans		------		425	425	565	565

911 CARRERA 2—6-Cyl.—Equipment Schedule 1
W.B. 89.4"; 3.6 Liter.

RS America Coupe 2D		AB296	62742	14200	16025	20400	26600
America Roadster 2D		CB296	94301	****	****	****	42500
Coupe 2D		AB296	69941	15125	17050	21600	27900
Targa 2D		BB296	71551	14825	16700	21200	27600
Cabriolet 2D		CB296	79141	18100	20350	25300	32400
Full Leather		------		100	100	135	135
Tiptronic Auto Trans		------		425	425	565	565

911 CARRERA 4 AWD—6-Cyl.—Equipment Schedule 1
W.B. 89.4"; 3.6 Liter.

Coupe 2D		AB296	80151	16275	18325	22900	29500
Targa 2D		BB296	81761	15975	18000	22700	29200
Cabriolet 2D		CB296	89351	18575	20825	26000	33300
Full Leather		------		100	100	135	135

928 GTS—V8—Equipment Schedule 1
W.B. 98.4"; 5.4 Liter.

Coupe 2D		AA292	85085	16275	18325	22900	29500

1994 PORSCHE — WPO(AA296)-R-#

968—4-Cyl.—Equipment Schedule 1
W.B. 94.5"; 3.0 Liter.

Coupe 2D		AA296	43887	8525	9750	12250	15850
Cabriolet 2D		CA296	55530	12300	13925	16900	21300

1994 PORSCHE

Body	Type	VIN	List	Trade-In Fair	Trade-In Good	Pvt-Party Good	Retail Excellent
	Tiptronic Auto Trans			475	475	635	635
911 CARRERA 2—6-Cyl.—Equipment Schedule 1							
W.B. 89.4"; 3.6 Liter.							
	RS America Coupe 2D	AB296	55525	15600	17575	22100	28500
	Coupe 2D	AB296	65715	16700	18775	23500	30200
	Cabriolet 2D	CB296	74915	19575	21975	27100	34400
	Carrera 2 Speedster	CB296	70916	****	****	****	43900
	Full Leather			100	100	135	135
	Tiptronic Auto Trans			475	475	635	635
911 CARRERA 4 AWD—6-Cyl.—Equipment Schedule 1							
W.B. 89.4"; 3.6 Liter.							
	Coupe 2D	AB296	81551	18200	20450	25400	32400
	Full Leather			100	100	135	135
911 TURBO 3.6—6-Cyl. Turbo—Equipment Schedule 1							
W.B. 89.4"; 3.6 Liter.							
	Coupe 2D	AC296	101825	27350	30525	36900	45900
928 GTS—V8—Equipment Schedule 1							
W.B. 98.4"; 5.4 Liter.							
	Coupe 2D	AA292	85085	18000	20250	25200	32000

1995 PORSCHE — WPO(AA296)-S-#

Body	Type	VIN	List	Trade-In Fair	Trade-In Good	Pvt-Party Good	Retail Excellent
968—4-Cyl.—Equipment Schedule 1							
W.B. 94.5"; 3.0 Liter.							
	Coupe 2D	AA296	43887	9550	10900	13500	17300
	Cabriolet 2D	CA296	55530	13675	15450	18600	23200
	Tiptronic Auto Trans			525	525	700	700
911 CARRERA—6-Cyl.—Equipment Schedule 1							
W.B. 89.4"; 3.6 Liter.							
	Coupe 2D	AA299	63055	17625	19775	24700	31600
	Cabriolet 2D	CA299	71355	20350	22750	28000	35400
	Full Leather			125	125	165	165
	Hard Top (Cabriolet)			425	425	565	565
	Aero Kit			1625	1625	2165	2165
	Tiptronic Auto Trans			525	525	700	700
911 CARRERA 4 AWD—6-Cyl.—Equipment Schedule 1							
W.B. 89.4"; 3.6 Liter.							
	Coupe 2D	AA299	70055	18675	20925	25900	32900
	Cabriolet 2D	CA299	78355	21700	24375	29900	37700
	Full Leather			125	125	165	165
	Hard Top (Cabriolet)			425	425	565	565
	Aero Kit			1625	1625	2165	2165
928 GTS—V8—Equipment Schedule 1							
W.B. 98.4"; 5.4 Liter.							
	Coupe 2D	AA292	85085	19875	22375	27500	34700

1996 PORSCHE — WPO(AA299)-T-#

Body	Type	VIN	List	Trade-In Fair	Trade-In Good	Pvt-Party Good	Retail Excellent
911 CARRERA—6-Cyl.—Equipment Schedule 1							
W.B. 89.5"; 3.6 Liter.							
	Coupe 2D	AA299	67043	19500	21900	27000	34200
	Targa 2D	DA299	74043	21500	24100	29500	37100
	Cabriolet 2D	CA299	76293	22175	24775	30100	37800
	Full Leather			150	150	200	200
	Hard Top (Cabriolet)			450	450	600	600
	Aero Kit			1700	1700	2265	2265
	Tiptronic Auto Trans			550	550	735	735
911 CARRERA 4 AWD—6-Cyl.—Equipment Schedule 1							
W.B. 89.5"; 3.6 Liter.							
	Coupe 2D	AA299	73393	20450	22950	28100	35500
	4S Coupe 2D	AA299	76289	22175	24775	30300	38200
	Cabriolet 2D	CA299	82643	23900	26700	32400	40700
	Full Leather			150	150	200	200
	Hard Top (Cabriolet)			450	450	600	600
	Aero Kit			1700	1700	2265	2265
911 TURBO—6-Cyl. Turbo—Equipment Schedule 1							
W.B. 89.5"; 3.6 Liter.							
	Coupe 2D	AC299	115050	40800	45400	53100	64400

1997 PORSCHE — WPO(CA298)-V-#

Body	Type	VIN	List	Trade-In Fair	Trade-In Good	Pvt-Party Good	Retail Excellent
BOXSTER—6-Cyl.—Equipment Schedule 1							
W.B. 95.1"; 2.5 Liter.							
	Cabriolet 2D	CA298	43086	12300	13925	17000	21500
	Full Leather			175	175	235	235

Body	Type	VIN	List	Trade-In Fair	Good	Pvt-Party Good	Retail Excellent
Hard Top				475	475	635	635
Aero Kit				1775	1775	2365	2365
Sport Touring Pkg				1475	1475	1965	1965
Tiptronic Auto Trans				575	575	765	765
911 CARRERA—6-Cyl.—Equipment Schedule 1							
W.B. 89.5"; 3.6 Liter.							
Coupe 2D		AA299	67063	21025	23525	28700	36200
S Coupe 2D		AA299	67063	21600	24200	29500	37000
Targa 2D		DA299	74063	23700	26500	32100	40000
Cabriolet 2D		CA299	76313	24000	26875	32400	40400
Full Leather				175	175	235	235
Hard Top (Cabriolet)				475	475	635	635
Aero Kit				1775	1775	2365	2365
Tiptronic Auto Trans				575	575	765	765
911 CARRERA 4 AWD—6-Cyl.—Equipment Schedule 1							
W.B. 89.5"; 3.6 Liter.							
4S Coupe 2D		AA299	76313	24300	27175	32900	41200
Cabriolet 2D		CA299	81663	26300	29375	35300	44000
Full Leather				175	175	235	235
Hard Top (Cabriolet)				475	475	635	635
Aero Kit				1775	1775	2365	2365
911 TURBO—6-Cyl. Turbo—Equipment Schedule 1							
W.B. 89.5"; 3.6 Liter.							
Coupe 2D		AC299	105765	44650	49625	57500	69300
S Coupe 2D		AC299	153365	****	****	****	87000

1998 PORSCHE — WPO(CA298)-W-#

Body	Type	VIN	List	Trade-In Fair	Good	Pvt-Party Good	Retail Excellent
BOXSTER—6-Cyl.—Equipment Schedule 1							
W.B. 95.2"; 2.5 Liter.							
Cabriolet 2D		CA298	44316	13875	15700	18500	22800
Full Leather				200	200	265	265
Hard Top				500	500	665	665
Aero Kit				1825	1825	2435	2435
Sport Touring Pkg				1525	1525	2035	2035
Tiptronic Auto Trans				625	625	835	835
911 CARRERA—6-Cyl.—Equipment Schedule 1							
W.B. 89.4"; 3.6 Liter.							
S Coupe 2D		AA299	67461	22475	25150	30000	37100
Targa 2D		DA299	74461	24875	27850	32800	40300
Cabriolet 2D		CA299	76711	24950	27925	32900	40400
Full Leather				200	200	265	265
Hard Top (Cabriolet)				500	500	665	665
Aero Kit				1825	1825	2435	2435
Tiptronic Auto Trans				625	625	835	835
911 CARRERA 4 AWD—6-Cyl.—Equipment Schedule 1							
W.B. 89.4"; 3.6 Liter.							
4S Coupe 2D		AA299	76711	25350	28325	33700	41500
Cabriolet 2D		CA299	82061	27550	30725	36200	44400
Full Leather				200	200	265	265
Hard Top (Cabriolet)				500	500	665	665
Aero Kit				1825	1825	2435	2435

1999 PORSCHE — WPO(CA298)-X-#

Body	Type	VIN	List	Trade-In Fair	Good	Pvt-Party Good	Retail Excellent
BOXSTER—6-Cyl.—Equipment Schedule 1							
W.B. 95.2"; 2.5 Liter.							
Cabriolet 2D		CA298	44316	14875	16750	19600	24000
Full Leather				250	250	335	335
Hard Top				550	550	735	735
Aero Kit				1950	1950	2600	2600
Sport Touring Pkg				1600	1600	2135	2135
Tiptronic Auto Trans				725	725	965	965
911 CARRERA—6-Cyl.—Equipment Schedule 1							
W.B. 92.6"; 3.4 Liter.							
Coupe 2D		AA299	70815	26500	29675	33600	39900
Cabriolet 2D		CA299	80245	29375	32825	37100	43900
Full Leather				250	250	335	335
Hard Top (Cabriolet)				550	550	735	735
Aero Kit				1950	1950	2600	2600
Tiptronic Auto Trans				725	725	965	965
911 CARRERA 4 AWD—6-Cyl.—Equipment Schedule 1							
W.B. 92.6"; 3.4 Liter.							
Coupe 2D		AA299	75980	29575	33025	37500	44600
Cabriolet 2D		CA299	85420	32075	35700	40400	47800

1999 PORSCHE

Body	Type	VIN	List	Trade-In Fair	Trade-In Good	Pvt-Party Good	Retail Excellent
	Full Leather		-------	250	250	335	335
	Hard Top (Cabriolet)		-------	550	550	735	735
	Aero Kit		-------	1950	1950	2600	2600
	Tiptronic Auto Trans		-------	725	725	965	965

2000 PORSCHE — WPO(CA298)–Y–#

BOXSTER—6-Cyl.—Equipment Schedule 1
W.B. 95.2"; 2.7 Liter, 3.2 Liter.

Body	Type	VIN	List	Trade-In Fair	Trade-In Good	Pvt-Party Good	Retail Excellent
	Cabriolet 2D	CA298	44745	16125	18150	21000	25500
	S Cabriolet 2D	CB298	53245	20450	22950	26200	31300
	Full Leather		-------	300	300	400	400
	Hard Top		-------	575	575	765	765
	Aero Kit		-------	2075	2075	2765	2765
	Sport Touring Pkg		-------	1675	1675	2235	2235
	Tiptronic Auto Trans		-------	825	825	1100	1100

911 CARRERA—6-Cyl.—Equipment Schedule 1
W.B. 92.6"; 3.4 Liter.

Body	Type	VIN	List	Trade-In Fair	Trade-In Good	Pvt-Party Good	Retail Excellent
	Coupe 2D	AA299	71375	29950	33500	37500	44300
	Cabriolet 2D	CA299	80755	33300	37150	41500	48600
	Full Leather		-------	300	300	400	400
	Hard Top (Cabriolet)		-------	575	575	765	765
	Aero Kit		-------	2075	2075	2765	2765
	Tiptronic Auto Trans		-------	825	825	1100	1100

911 CARRERA 4 AWD—6-Cyl.—Equipment Schedule 1
W.B. 92.6"; 3.4 Liter.

Body	Type	VIN	List	Trade-In Fair	Trade-In Good	Pvt-Party Good	Retail Excellent
	Coupe 2D	AA299	76805	33225	37050	41700	49100
	Cabriolet 2D	CA299	86185	35960	40025	44800	52700
	Full Leather		-------	300	300	400	400
	Hard Top (Cabriolet)		-------	575	575	765	765
	Aero Kit		-------	2075	2075	2765	2765
	Millennium Pkg		-------	4650	4650	6200	6200
	Tiptronic Auto Trans		-------	825	825	1100	1100

2001 PORSCHE — WPO(CA298)–1–#

BOXSTER—6-Cyl.—Equipment Schedule 1
W.B. 95.2"; 2.7 Liter, 3.2 Liter.

Body	Type	VIN	List	Trade-In Fair	Trade-In Good	Pvt-Party Good	Retail Excellent
	Cabriolet 2D	CA298	42865	17750	19975	23000	27600
	S Cabriolet 2D	CB298	50965	22550	25250	28500	33800
	Full Leather		-------	350	350	465	465
	Hard Top		-------	600	600	800	800
	Aero Kit		-------	2200	2200	2935	2935
	Sport Touring Pkg		-------	1750	1750	2335	2335
	Tiptronic Auto Trans		-------	900	900	1200	1200

911 CARRERA—6-Cyl.—Equipment Schedule 1
W.B. 92.6"; 3.4 Liter.

Body	Type	VIN	List	Trade-In Fair	Trade-In Good	Pvt-Party Good	Retail Excellent
	Coupe 2D	AA299	70275	33900	37725	41900	48900
	Cabriolet 2D	CA299	79775	37525	41850	46300	53700
	Full Leather		-------	350	350	465	465
	Hard Top (Cabriolet)		-------	600	600	800	800
	Aero Kit		-------	2200	2200	2935	2935
	Tiptronic Auto Trans		-------	900	900	1200	1200

911 CARRERA 4 AWD—6-Cyl.—Equipment Schedule 1
W.B. 92.6"; 3.4 Liter.

Body	Type	VIN	List	Trade-In Fair	Trade-In Good	Pvt-Party Good	Retail Excellent
	Coupe 2D	AA299	75320	37250	41475	46200	54000
	Cabriolet 2D	CA299	84820	40325	44825	49700	57900
	Full Leather		-------	350	350	465	465
	Hard Top (Cabriolet)		-------	600	600	800	800
	Aero Kit		-------	2200	2200	2935	2935
	Tiptronic Auto Trans		-------	900	900	1200	1200

911 TURBO AWD—6-Cyl. Turbo—Equipment Schedule 1
W.B. 92.6"; 3.6 Liter.

Body	Type	VIN	List	Trade-In Fair	Trade-In Good	Pvt-Party Good	Retail Excellent
	Coupe 2D	AB299	111765	58750	65175	70900	81100
	Full Leather		-------	350	350	465	465
	Aero Kit		-------	2200	2200	2935	2935
	Tiptronic Auto Trans		-------	900	900	1200	1200

2002 PORSCHE — WPO(CA298)–2–#

BOXSTER—6-Cyl.—Equipment Schedule 1
W.B. 95.2"; 2.7 Liter, 3.2 Liter.

Body	Type	VIN	List	Trade-In Fair	Trade-In Good	Pvt-Party Good	Retail Excellent
	Cabriolet 2D	CA298	43365	19775	22175	25200	30200
	S Cabriolet 2D	CB298	52365	25050	28025	31400	37000
	Full Leather		-------	400	400	535	535

Body	Type	VIN	List	Trade-In Fair	Trade-In Good	Pvt-Party Good	Retail Excellent
Hard Top			———	625	625	835	835
Aero Kit			———	2325	2325	3100	3100
Sport Touring Pkg			———	1825	1825	2435	2435
Tiptronic Auto Trans			———	975	975	1300	1300

911 CARRERA—6-Cyl.—Equipment Schedule 1
W.B. 92.6"; 3.6 Liter.

Body	Type	VIN	List	Trade-In Fair	Trade-In Good	Pvt-Party Good	Retail Excellent
Coupe 2D		AA299	73450	38100	42425	46600	53900
Targa 2D		AA299	75965	41950	46650	51100	58800
Cabriolet 2D		CA299	83150	42250	46950	51400	59100
Full Leather			———	400	400	535	535
Hard Top (Cabriolet)			———	625	625	835	835
Aero Kit			———	2325	2325	3100	3100
Tiptronic Auto Trans			———	975	975	1300	1300

911 CARRERA 4 AWD—6-Cyl.—Equipment Schedule 1
W.B. 92.6"; 3.6 Liter.

Body	Type	VIN	List	Trade-In Fair	Trade-In Good	Pvt-Party Good	Retail Excellent
4S Coupe 2D		AA299	80965	41675	46375	51000	59000
Cabriolet 2D		CA299	88750	45025	50025	54900	63400
Full Leather			———	400	400	535	535
Hard Top (Cabriolet)			———	625	625	835	835
Aero Kit			———	2325	2325	3100	3100
Tiptronic Auto Trans			———	975	975	1300	1300

911 TURBO AWD—6-Cyl. Turbo—Equipment Schedule 1
W.B. 92.6"; 3.6 Liter.

Body	Type	VIN	List	Trade-In Fair	Trade-In Good	Pvt-Party Good	Retail Excellent
Coupe 2D		AB299	115765	65375	72575	78200	88700
Full Leather			———	400	400	535	535
Aero Kit			———	2325	2325	3100	3100
Tiptronic Auto Trans			———	975	975	1300	1300

911 TURBO—6-Cyl. Turbo—Equipment Schedule 1
W.B. 92.6"; 3.6 Liter.

Body	Type	VIN	List	Trade-In Fair	Trade-In Good	Pvt-Party Good	Retail Excellent
GT2 Coupe 2D		AB299	180665				

2003 PORSCHE — WPO(CA298)-3-#

BOXSTER—6-Cyl.—Equipment Schedule 1
W.B. 95.2"; 2.7 Liter, 3.2 Liter.

Body	Type	VIN	List	Trade-In Fair	Trade-In Good	Pvt-Party Good	Retail Excellent
Cabriolet 2D		CA298	45485	22275	24875	28100	33300
S Cabriolet 2D		CB298	54485	28025	31300	34800	40600
Full Leather			———	475	475	635	635
Hard Top			———	650	650	865	865
Aero Kit			———	2425	2425	3235	3235
Sport Touring Pkg			———	1900	1900	2535	2535
Tiptronic Auto Trans			———	1050	1050	1400	1400

911 CARRERA—6-Cyl.—Equipment Schedule 1
W.B. 92.6"; 3.6 Liter.

Body	Type	VIN	List	Trade-In Fair	Trade-In Good	Pvt-Party Good	Retail Excellent
Coupe 2D		AA299	72435	42725	47525	51800	59400
Targa 2D		BA299	79835	46950	52125	56600	64700
Cabriolet 2D		CA299	82235	47125	52425	56900	65000
Full Leather			———	475	475	635	635
Hard Top (Cabriolet)			———	650	650	865	865
Aero Kit			———	2425	2425	3235	3235
Tiptronic Auto Trans			———	1050	1050	1400	1400

911 CARRERA 4 AWD—6-Cyl.—Equipment Schedule 1
W.B. 92.6"; 3.6 Liter.

Body	Type	VIN	List	Trade-In Fair	Trade-In Good	Pvt-Party Good	Retail Excellent
4S Coupe 2D		AA299	82565	46375	51650	56400	64800
Cabriolet 2D		CA299	87835	50100	55675	60700	69400
Full Leather			———	475	475	635	635
Hard Top (Cabriolet)			———	650	650	865	865
Aero Kit			———	2425	2425	3235	3235
Tiptronic Auto Trans			———	1050	1050	1400	1400

911 TURBO AWD—6-Cyl. Turbo—Equipment Schedule 1
W.B. 92.6"; 3.6 Liter.

Body	Type	VIN	List	Trade-In Fair	Trade-In Good	Pvt-Party Good	Retail Excellent
Coupe 2D		AB299	118265	72375	80350	85800	96600
Full Leather			———	475	475	635	635
Aero Kit			———	2425	2425	3235	3235
Tiptronic Auto Trans			———	1050	1050	1400	1400

911 TURBO—6-Cyl. Turbo—Equipment Schedule 1
W.B. 92.6"; 3.6 Liter.

Body	Type	VIN	List	Trade-In Fair	Trade-In Good	Pvt-Party Good	Retail Excellent
GT2 Coupe 2D		AB299	183765				

2004 PORSCHE — WPO(CA298)-4-#

BOXSTER—6-Cyl.—Equipment Schedule 1
W.B. 95.1"; 2.7 Liter, 3.2 Liter.

Body	Type	VIN	List	Trade-In Fair	Trade-In Good	Pvt-Party Good	Retail Excellent
Cabriolet 2D		CA298	45485	25525	28500	32000	37600
S Cabriolet 2D		CB298	54485	31775	35425	39100	45300

Body	Type	VIN	List	Trade-In Fair	Good	Pvt-Party Good	Retail Excellent
Special Edition				2000	2000	2665	2665
Full Leather				550	550	735	735
Hard Top				675	675	900	900
Aero Kit				2525	2525	3365	3365
Tiptronic Auto Trans				1125	1125	1500	1500

911 CARRERA—6-Cyl.—Equipment Schedule 1
W.B. 92.5", 92.6" (Targa); 3.6 Liter.

Body	Type	VIN	List	Fair	Good	Good	Excellent
Coupe 2D		AA299	72435				
Targa 2D		BA299	79835				
Cabriolet 2D		CA299	82235				
40th Anniversary Ed							
Full Leather							
Hard Top (Cabriolet)							
Aero Kit							
Tiptronic Auto Trans							

911 CARRERA 4 AWD—6-Cyl.—Equipment Schedule 1
W.B. 92.5"; 3.6 Liter.

Body	Type	VIN	List	Fair	Good	Good	Excellent
Cabriolet 2D		CA299	86285				
4S Coupe 2D		AA299	84165				
4S Cabriolet 2D		CA299	93965				
Full Leather							
Hard Top							
Aero Kit							
Tiptronic Auto Trans							

911 TURBO AWD—6-Cyl. Turbo—Equipment Schedule 1
W.B. 92.5"; 3.6 Liter.

Body	Type	VIN	List	Fair	Good	Good	Excellent
Coupe 2D		AB299	120465				
Cabriolet 2D		CB299	130265				
Full Leather							
Aero Kit							
Tiptronic Auto Trans							

911 TURBO—6-Cyl. Turbo—Equipment Schedule 1
W.B. 92.7"; 3.6 Liter.

Body	Type	VIN	List	Fair	Good	Good	Excellent
GT2 Coupe 2D		AB299	193765				

911—6-Cyl.—Equipment Schedule 1
W.B. 92.7"; 3.6 Liter.

Body	Type	VIN	List	Fair	Good	Good	Excellent
GT3 Coupe 2D		AC299	101965				

CARRERA GT—V10—Equipment Schedule 1
W.B. 107.5"; 5.7 Liter.

Body	Type	VIN	List	Fair	Good	Good	Excellent
Roadster 2D		AB299	446165				

SAAB

1990 SAAB — YS3(AJ45D)–L–#

900—4-Cyl.—Equipment Schedule 3
W.B. 99.1"; 2.0 Liter.

Body	Type	VIN	List	Fair	Good	Good	Excellent
Sedan 4D		AJ45D	18478	450	625	1325	2400
Hatchback 2D		AJ35D	17958	450	625	1325	2400
S Sedan 4D		AK45D	22508	675	925	1750	3025
S Hatchback 2D		AK35D	21958	675	925	1750	3025

900—4-Cyl. Turbo—Equipment Schedule 3
W.B. 99.1"; 2.0 Liter.

Body	Type	VIN	List	Fair	Good	Good	Excellent
Sedan 4D		AL45L	27008	900	1300	2375	3900
Hatchback 2D		AL35L	26458	900	1300	2375	3925
Convertible 2D		AL75L	33958	2250	2800	4175	6100
Spcl Performance Group				300	300	400	400

9000—4-Cyl.—Equipment Schedule 2
W.B. 105.2"; 2.0 Liter.

Body	Type	VIN	List	Fair	Good	Good	Excellent
S Sedan 4D		CK48D	26378	850	1175	2125	3525
S Hatchback 4D		CK58D	25878	825	1150	2075	3425
Manual Trans				(200)	(200)	(265)	(265)
4-Cyl. 2.3 Liter		B		100	100	135	135

9000—4-Cyl. Turbo—Equipment Schedule 2
W.B. 105.2"; 2.0 Liter.

Body	Type	VIN	List	Fair	Good	Good	Excellent
Hatchback 4D		CL58L	32878	1100	1550	2700	4350
CD Sedan 4D		CL48L	33378	1175	1625	2800	4475
Manual Trans				(200)	(200)	(265)	(265)

1991 SAAB — YS3(AK45E)–M–#

900—4-Cyl.—Equipment Schedule 3
W.B. 99.1"; 2.1 Liter.

1991 SAAB

Body	Type	VIN	List	Trade-In Fair	Good	Pvt-Party Good	Retail Excellent
Sedan 4D		AK45E	19812	450	625	1350	2475
Hatchback 2D		AK35E	19292	450	625	1350	2475
S Sedan 4D		AK45E	23992	725	1025	1925	3300
S Hatchback 2D		AK35E	23442	725	1025	1925	3300
S Convertible 2D		AK75E	29292	1750	2275	3600	5450
900—4-Cyl. Turbo—Equipment Schedule 3							
W.B. 99.1"; 2.0 Liter.							
Hatchback 2D		AL35L	27292	1000	1450	2600	4225
Convertible 2D		AL75L	34292	2625	3250	4725	6825
SE Convertible 2D		AL75L	35792	2700	3300	4800	6900
Spcl Performance Group				325	325	435	435
9000—4-Cyl.—Equipment Schedule 2							
W.B. 105.2"; 2.3 Liter.							
Hatchback 4D		CK58B	24077	1075	1525	2725	4450
S Hatchback 4D		CK58B	28177	1100	1550	2775	4500
CD Sedan 4D		CK48B	29412	1225	1700	2950	4675
Manual Trans				(100)	(100)	(135)	(135)
9000—4-Cyl. Turbo—Equipment Schedule 2							
W.B. 105.2"; 2.3 Liter.							
Hatchback 4D		CL58M	34177	1650	2175	3525	5375
CD Sedan 4D		CL48M	34412	1775	2300	3675	5575
Manual Trans				(100)	(100)	(135)	(135)

1992 SAAB — YS3(AK45E)-N-#

Body	Type	VIN	List	Trade-In Fair	Good	Pvt-Party Good	Retail Excellent
900—4-Cyl.—Equipment Schedule 3							
W.B. 99.1"; 2.1 Liter.							
Sedan 4D		AK45E	20435	475	700	1500	2750
Hatchback 2D		AK35E	19835	475	700	1500	2750
S Sedan 4D		AK45E	24435	800	1125	2250	3875
S Hatchback 2D		AK35E	23835	800	1125	2250	3875
S Convertible 2D		AK75E	31035	2025	2575	3975	5950
900—4-Cyl. Turbo—Equipment Schedule 3							
W.B. 99.1"; 2.0 Liter.							
Hatchback 2D		AL35L	29085	1100	1550	2775	4500
Convertible 2D		AL75L	35785	3050	3700	5300	7525
9000—4-Cyl.—Equipment Schedule 2							
W.B. 105.2"; 2.3 Liter.							
Hatchback 4D		CK58B	26175	1375	1850	3175	5000
S Hatchback 4D		CK58B	29425	1400	1875	3225	5050
CD Sedan 4D		CK48B	30635	1525	2050	3375	5250
Manual Trans				(250)	(250)	(335)	(335)
9000—4-Cyl. Turbo—Equipment Schedule 2							
W.B. 105.2"; 2.3 Liter.							
Hatchback 4D		CL58M	37375	2075	2625	4050	6075
CD Sedan 4D		CL48M	37135	2175	2750	4225	6300
CD Griffin Ed Sedan 4D		CL48M	42635	2400	2975	4500	6600
Manual Trans				(250)	(250)	(335)	(335)

1993 SAAB — YS3(AK45E)-P-#

Body	Type	VIN	List	Trade-In Fair	Good	Pvt-Party Good	Retail Excellent
900—4-Cyl.—Equipment Schedule 3							
W.B. 99.1"; 2.1 Liter.							
S Sedan 4D		AK45E	21400	900	1300	2525	4275
S Hatchback 2D		AK35E	20785	900	1300	2525	4275
S Convertible 2D		AK75E	32600	2350	2925	4450	6550
900—4-Cyl. Turbo—Equipment Schedule 3							
W.B. 99.1"; 2.0 Liter.							
Hatchback 2D		AL35L	30995	1275	1750	3100	4950
Convertible 2D		AL75L	37500	3550	4250	5975	8375
9000—4-Cyl.—Equipment Schedule 2							
W.B. 105.2"; 2.3 Liter.							
CS Hatchback 4D		CK68B	28570	1975	2525	4000	6075
CD Sedan 4D		CK48B	27670	1825	2350	3850	5850
CSE Hatchback 4D		CK58B	32420	2250	2800	4375	6475
CDE Sedan 4D		CK48B	32190	2250	2825	4375	6475
Manual Trans				(300)	(300)	(400)	(400)
4-Cyl. 2.3 Liter Turbo		M		1000	1000	1335	1335
9000—4-Cyl. Turbo—Equipment Schedule 2							
W.B. 105.2"; 2.3 Liter.							
Aero Hatchback 4D		CL68M	38695	2925	3575	5225	7500
Manual Trans				(150)	(150)	(200)	(200)

Body	Type	VIN	List	Trade-In Fair	Good	Pvt-Party Good	Retail Excellent

1994 SAAB — YS3(DM35B)-R-#

900—4-Cyl.—Equipment Schedule 3
W.B. 99.1" (Conv), 102.4"; 2.1 Liter, 2.3 Liter.

Body	Type	VIN	List	Fair	Good	Good	Excellent
S Coupe 2D		DM35B	22750	775	1075	2300	4050
S Hatchback 4D		DM55B	21450	700	975	2175	3900
S Convertible 2D		AK75E	33735	2750	3375	5050	7300
V6 2.5 Liter		V		300	300	400	400

900—V6—Equipment Schedule 3
W.B. 102.4"; 2.5 Liter.

SE Hatchback 4D		DM55V	27450	1500	2000	3425	5375
Auto Trans				175	175	235	235

900—4-Cyl. Turbo—Equipment Schedule 3
W.B. 99.1"; 2.0 Liter.

SE Coupe 2D		DN35L	27740	1500	2000	3425	5375
Convertible 2D		AL75L	38875	4125	4900	6750	9300
Commem Ed Conv 2D		AL75T	40875	4225	5025	6850	9425

9000—4-Cyl.—Equipment Schedule 2
W.B. 105.2"; 2.3 Liter.

CS Hatchback 4D		CM68B	30670	2000	2550	4075	6175
CD Sedan 4D		CM48B	32775	1850	2375	3900	5975
CSE Hatchback 4D		CM68B	34450	2300	2875	4475	6650
CDE Sedan 4D		CM48B	34090	2275	2850	4450	6600
Manual Trans				(350)	(350)	(465)	(465)
4-Cyl. 2.3 Liter Turbo		M		1125	1125	1500	1500

9000—4-Cyl. Turbo—Equipment Schedule 2
W.B. 105.2"; 2.3 Liter.

Aero Hatchback 4D		CN68M	39150	3275	3925	5700	8100
Manual Trans				(175)	(175)	(235)	(235)
Traction Control				175	175	235	235

1995 SAAB — YS3(DD35B)-S-#

900—4-Cyl.—Equipment Schedule 3
W.B. 102.4"; 2.3 Liter.

S Coupe 2D		DD35B	24545	1025	1475	2875	4775
S Hatchback 4D		DD55B	24225	925	1325	2700	4575
S Convertible 2D		DD75B	33465	2875	3525	5200	7525
Auto Trans				200	200	265	265

900—V6—Equipment Schedule 3
W.B. 102.4"; 2.5 Liter.

SE Hatchback 4D		DF55V	29150	1950	2500	4050	6175
Auto Trans				200	200	265	265

900—4-Cyl. Turbo—Equipment Schedule 3
W.B. 102.4"; 2.0 Liter.

SE Coupe 2D		DF35N	29460	1950	2500	4050	6175
SE Convertible 2D		DF78N	39990	4050	4825	6675	9250
Auto Trans				200	200	265	265
V6 2.5 Liter		V		325	325	435	435

9000—4-Cyl. Light Pressure Turbo—Equipment Schedule 3
W.B. 105.2"; 2.3 Liter.

CS Hatchback 4D		CD68U	32695	2500	3100	4775	7050
Manual Trans				(400)	(400)	(535)	(535)

9000—4-Cyl. Turbo—Equipment Schedule 2
W.B. 105.2"; 2.3 Liter.

Aero Hatchback 4D		CH68M,R	41770	3950	4700	6600	9250
Manual Trans				(200)	(200)	(265)	(265)

9000—V6—Equipment Schedule 2
W.B. 105.2"; 3.0 Liter.

CSE Hatchback 4D		CF68W	39120	3025	3700	5450	7850
CDE Sedan 4D		CF48W	39465	2950	3600	5325	7725
Manual Trans				(400)	(400)	(535)	(535)
4-Cyl. 2.3 Liter Turbo				0	0	0	0

1996 SAAB — YS3(DD35B)-T-#

900—4-Cyl.—Equipment Schedule 3
W.B. 102.4"; 2.3 Liter.

S Coupe 2D		DD35B	24490	1525	2050	3600	5700
S Hatchback 4D		DD55B	25190	1375	1875	3400	5475
S Convertible 2D		DD75B	34490	3575	4275	6100	8600
Auto Trans				200	200	265	265

900—4-Cyl. Turbo—Equipment Schedule 3
W.B. 102.4"; 2.0 Liter.

1996 SAAB

Body	Type	VIN	List	Trade-In Fair	Trade-In Good	Pvt-Party Good	Retail Excellent
SE Coupe 2D		DF35N	29490	2550	3175	4850	7150
SE Hatchback 4D		DF55N	30190	2500	3100	4775	7050
SE Convertible 2D		DF75N	40490	4900	5750	7725	10500
Auto Trans				200	200	265	265
V6 2.5 Liter		V		350	350	465	465

9000—4-Cyl. Light Pressure Turbo—Equipment Schedule 2
W.B. 105.2"; 2.3 Liter.

Body	Type	VIN	List	Trade-In Fair	Trade-In Good	Pvt-Party Good	Retail Excellent
CS Hatchback 4D		CD68U	32695	3125	3775	5625	8100
Manual Trans		5		(450)	(450)	(600)	(600)

9000—4-Cyl. Turbo—Equipment Schedule 2
W.B. 105.2"; 2.3 Liter.

Body	Type	VIN	List	Trade-In Fair	Trade-In Good	Pvt-Party Good	Retail Excellent
Aero Hatchback 4D		CH58M,R	42735	4775	5625	7675	10550
Manual Trans		5		(200)	(200)	(265)	(265)

9000—V6—Equipment Schedule 2
W.B. 105.2"; 3.0 Liter.

Body	Type	VIN	List	Trade-In Fair	Trade-In Good	Pvt-Party Good	Retail Excellent
CSE Hatchback 4D		CF68W	40690	3700	4425	6325	8950
Manual Trans		M		(450)	(450)	(600)	(600)
4-Cyl. 2.3 Liter Turbo		M		0	0	0	0

1997 SAAB — YS3(DD35B)-V-#

900—4-Cyl.—Equipment Schedule 3
W.B. 102.4"; 2.3 Liter.

Body	Type	VIN	List	Trade-In Fair	Trade-In Good	Pvt-Party Good	Retail Excellent
S Coupe 2D		DD35B	25520	2200	2775	4500	6850
S Hatchback 4D		DD55B	26520	2025	2575	4275	6575
S Convertible 2D		DD75B	35520	4375	5150	7150	9900
Auto Trans				200	200	265	265

900—4-Cyl. Turbo—Equipment Schedule 3
W.B. 102.4"; 2.0 Liter.

Body	Type	VIN	List	Trade-In Fair	Trade-In Good	Pvt-Party Good	Retail Excellent
SE Coupe 2D		DF35N	30520	3300	3950	5800	8350
SE Hatchback 4D		DF55N	31520	3200	3875	5700	8225
SE Convertible 2D		DF75N	41520	5875	6850	8975	12000
Auto Trans				200	200	265	265
V6 2.5 Liter		V		375	375	500	500

9000—4-Cyl. Light Pressure Turbo—Equipment Schedule 2
W.B. 105.2"; 2.3 Liter.

Body	Type	VIN	List	Trade-In Fair	Trade-In Good	Pvt-Party Good	Retail Excellent
CS Hatchback 4D		CD68U	35360	3875	4600	6600	9350
Manual Trans				(475)	(475)	(635)	(635)

9000—4-Cyl. Turbo—Equipment Schedule 2
W.B. 105.2"; 2.3 Liter.

Body	Type	VIN	List	Trade-In Fair	Trade-In Good	Pvt-Party Good	Retail Excellent
Aero Hatchback 4D		CH68M	43065	5725	6675	8925	12050
Manual Trans				(200)	(200)	(265)	(265)

9000—V6—Equipment Schedule 2
W.B. 105.2"; 3.0 Liter.

Body	Type	VIN	List	Trade-In Fair	Trade-In Good	Pvt-Party Good	Retail Excellent
CSE Hatchback 4D		CF68W	41020	4475	5275	7375	10200
Manual Trans		5		(475)	(475)	(635)	(635)
4-Cyl. 2.3 Liter Turbo		U		0	0	0	0

1998 SAAB — YS3(DD55B)-W-#

900—4-Cyl.—Equipment Schedule 3
W.B. 102.4"; 2.3 Liter.

Body	Type	VIN	List	Trade-In Fair	Trade-In Good	Pvt-Party Good	Retail Excellent
S Hatchback 4D		DD55B	27505	2700	3300	5100	7525
S Convertible 2D		DD75B	36945	5275	6175	8175	11050
Auto Trans				200	200	265	265

900—4-Cyl. Turbo—Equipment Schedule 3
W.B. 102.4"; 2.0 Liter.

Body	Type	VIN	List	Trade-In Fair	Trade-In Good	Pvt-Party Good	Retail Excellent
S Coupe 2D		DD35N	25050	3150	3800	5625	8100
SE Coupe 2D		DF35N	31545	4050	4825	6750	9375
SE Hatchback 4D		DF55N	32545	3975	4725	6625	9275
SE Convertible 2D		DF75N	42745	6950	8050	10200	13350
Auto Trans				200	200	265	265

9000—4-Cyl. Turbo—Equipment Schedule 2
W.B. 105.2"; 2.3 Liter.

Body	Type	VIN	List	Trade-In Fair	Trade-In Good	Pvt-Party Good	Retail Excellent
CSE Hatchback 4D		CF68M	40175	5350	6275	8400	11400
Manual Trans		5		(500)	(500)	(665)	(665)

1999 SAAB — YS3(DD38N)-X-#

9-3—4-Cyl. Turbo—Equipment Schedule 3
W.B. 102.6"; 2.0 Liter.

Body	Type	VIN	List	Trade-In Fair	Trade-In Good	Pvt-Party Good	Retail Excellent
Hatchback 2D		DD38N	26225	4150	4925	6750	9300
Hatchback 4D		DD58N	26725	4350	5125	7000	9600
Convertible 2D		DD78N	38725	7950	9125	11250	14400
SE Hatchback 4D		DF58N	33275	5425	6325	8275	11050

Body Type	VIN	List	Trade-In Fair	Good	Pvt-Party Good	Retail Excellent
SE Convertible 2D	DF78N	44570	9150	10425	12650	16050
Auto Trans			225	225	300	300
4-Cyl. 2.0L HO Turbo	P		300	300	400	400
9-3—4-Cyl. HO Turbo—Equipment Schedule 3						
W.B. 102.6"; 2.3 Liter.						
Viggen Coupe 2D	DP35G	38325	9175	10475	12700	16100
9-5—V6 Turbo—Equipment Schedule 2						
W.B. 106.4"; 3.0 Liter.						
Sedan 4D	ED48Z	35640	6525	7550	9900	13200
Wagon 4D	ED58Z	37475	7025	8100	10500	13850
SE Sedan 4D	EF48Z	37825	7275	8375	10800	14200
Manual Trans			(550)	(550)	(735)	(735)
4-Cyl. 2.3L Turbo	E		(1175)	(1175)	(1565)	(1565)

2000 SAAB — YS3(DD35H)-Y-#

Body Type	VIN	List	Trade-In Fair	Good	Pvt-Party Good	Retail Excellent
9-3—4-Cyl. Turbo—Equipment Schedule 3						
W.B. 102.6"; 2.0 Liter.						
Hatchback 2D	DD35H	27675	5200	6100	8125	11000
Hatchback 4D	DD55H	28175	5450	6350	8400	11300
Convertible 2D	DD75H	41225	9475	10800	13100	16550
Auto Trans	8		250	250	335	335
9-3—4-Cyl. HO Turbo—Equipment Schedule 3						
W.B. 102.6"; 2.0 Liter, 2.3 Liter.						
SE Hatchback 4D	DF55K	33670	6700	7750	9900	12900
SE Convertible 2D	DF75K	44770	10850	12300	14750	18400
Viggen Hatchback 2D	DP35G	38325	10900	12375	14850	18500
Viggen Hatchback 4D	DP55G	38325	9800	11175	13550	17050
Viggen Convertible 2D	DP75G	45570	13525	15300	18150	22400
Auto Trans	8		250	250	335	335
9-5—4-Cyl. Turbo—Equipment Schedule 2						
W.B. 106.4", 106.6" (Wagon); 2.3 Liter.						
Sedan 4D	ED48E	35300	7900	9075	11600	15200
Wagon 4D	ED58E	35300	8475	9700	12300	16000
Gary Fisher Edition			750	750	1000	1000
Manual Trans	5		(600)	(600)	(800)	(800)
9-5—4-Cyl. HO Turbo—Equipment Schedule 2						
W.B. 106.4", 106.6" (Wagon); 2.3 Liter.						
Aero Sedan 4D	EH48G	41550	9900	11225	13950	17850
Aero Wagon 4D	EH58G	44145	10700	12150	14950	18900
Manual Trans	5		(600)	(600)	(800)	(800)
9-5—V6 Turbo—Equipment Schedule 2						
W.B. 106.4", 106.6" (Wagon); 3.0 Liter.						
SE Sedan 4D	EF48Z	38325	8750	10025	12600	16350
SE Wagon 4D	EF58Z	38325	9275	10550	13250	17050

2001 SAAB — YS3(DD35H)-1-#

Body Type	VIN	List	Trade-In Fair	Good	Pvt-Party Good	Retail Excellent
9-3—4-Cyl. Turbo—Equipment Schedule 3						
W.B. 102.6"; 2.0 Liter.						
Hatchback 2D	DD35H	27070	6550	7575	9850	13000
Hatchback 4D	DD55H	27570	6825	7850	10100	13300
Auto Trans			275	275	365	365
9-3—4-Cyl. HO Turbo—Equipment Schedule 3						
W.B. 102.6"; 2.0 Liter, 2.3 Liter.						
SE Hatchback 4D	DF55K	33170	8275	9475	11800	15150
SE Convertible 2D	DF75K	40570	12775	14450	17050	21000
Viggen Hatchback 2D	DP35G	38570	12875	14550	17200	21200
Viggen Hatchback 4D	DP55G	38570	11675	13200	15750	19600
Viggen Convertible 2D	DP75G	45570	15800	17750	20700	25300
Auto Trans			275	275	365	365
9-5—4-Cyl. Turbo—Equipment Schedule 2						
W.B. 106.4"; 2.3 Liter.						
Sedan 4D	ED48E	34570	9550	10900	13700	17650
Wagon 4D	ED58E	35270	10175	11575	14400	18450
Manual Trans			(650)	(650)	(865)	(865)
9-5—4-Cyl. HO Turbo—Equipment Schedule 2						
W.B. 106.4"; 2.3 Liter.						
Aero Sedan 4D	EH48G	40750	11750	13300	16200	20400
Aero Wagon 4D	EH58G	41450	12625	14300	17300	21700
Manual Trans			(650)	(650)	(865)	(865)
9-5—V6 Turbo—Equipment Schedule 2						
W.B. 106.4"; 3.0 Liter.						
SE Sedan 4D	EF48Z	39225	10500	11950	14800	18850
SE Wagon 4D	EF58Z	39925	11100	12575	15450	19600

2002 SAAB

Body	Type	VIN	List	Trade-In Fair	Good	Pvt-Party Good	Retail Excellent

2002 SAAB — YS3(DF55K)-2-#

9-3—4-Cyl. Turbo—Equipment Schedule 3
W.B. 102.6"; 2.0 Liter.

Body	Type	VIN	List	Fair	Good	Good	Excellent
SE Hatchback 4D		DF55K	29820	10075	11475	14050	17800
SE Convertible 2D		DF75K	41820	15025	16950	19800	24100
Auto Trans				300	300	400	400

9-3—4-Cyl. HO Turbo—Equipment Schedule 3
W.B. 102.6"; 2.3 Liter.

Viggen Hatchback 2D		DP35G	38720	15125	17050	19850	24200
Viggen Hatchback 4D		DP55G	38720	13825	15600	18350	22600
Viggen Convertible 2D		DP75G	45620	18325	20650	23800	28800

9-5—4-Cyl. Turbo—Equipment Schedule 2
W.B. 106.4"; 2.3 Liter.

Linear Sedan 4D		EB49E	35820	11475	13000	16000	20400
Linear Wagon 4D		EB59E	36520	12150	13775	16850	21300
Manual Trans		5		(675)	(675)	(900)	(900)

9-5—4-Cyl. HO Turbo—Equipment Schedule 2
W.B. 106.4"; 2.3 Liter.

Aero Sedan 4D		EH49G	40475	13825	15650	18800	23500
Aero Wagon 4D		EH59G	41175	14825	16700	19950	24800
Manual Trans		5		(675)	(675)	(900)	(900)

9-5—V6 Turbo—Equipment Schedule 2
W.B. 106.4"; 3.0 Liter.

| Arc Sedan 4D | | ED49Z | 39275 | 12475 | 14100 | 17250 | 21700 |
| Arc Wagon 4D | | ED59Z | 39975 | 13100 | 14825 | 17900 | 22500 |

2003 SAAB — YS3(FB45S)-3-#

9-3—4-Cyl. Turbo—Equipment Schedule 3
W.B. 105.3"; 2.0 Liter.

| Linear Sedan 4D | | FB45S | 26525 | 13000 | 14725 | 17300 | 21200 |
| Auto Trans | | | | 300 | 300 | 400 | 400 |

9-3—4-Cyl. HO Turbo—Equipment Schedule 3
W.B. 102.6", 105.3" (Sed); 2.0 Liter.

Arc Sedan 4D		FD46Y	30620	15225	17125	19800	23900
Vector Sedan 4D		FF46Y	33120	16275	18325	21000	25200
SE Convertible 2D		DF75K	40620	19675	22075	25000	29700
Auto Trans				300	300	400	400

9-5—4-Cyl. Turbo—Equipment Schedule 2
W.B. 106.4"; 2.3 Liter.

Linear Sedan 4D		EB49E	35920	13775	15550	18800	23600
Linear Wagon 4D		EB59E	36620	14500	16375	19700	24600
Manual Trans				(700)	(700)	(935)	(935)

9-5—4-Cyl. HO Turbo—Equipment Schedule 2
W.B. 106.4"; 2.3 Liter.

Aero Sedan 4D		EH49G	40575	16375	18425	21900	27000
Aero Wagon 4D		EH59G	41275	17425	19575	23000	28300
Manual Trans				(700)	(700)	(935)	(935)

9-5—V6 Turbo—Equipment Schedule 2
W.B. 106.4"; 3.0 Liter.

| Arc Sedan 4D | | ED49Z | 39275 | 14875 | 16750 | 20200 | 25100 |
| Arc Wagon 4D | | ED59Z | 39975 | 15600 | 17575 | 20900 | 25900 |

2004 SAAB — YS3(FB45S)-4-#

9-3—4-Cyl. Turbo—Equipment Schedule 3
W.B. 105.3"; 2.0 Liter.

| Linear Sedan 4D | | FB45S | 26765 | 15900 | 17900 | 20800 | 25200 |
| Auto Trans | | | | 300 | 300 | 400 | 400 |

9-3—4-Cyl. HO Turbo—Equipment Schedule 3
W.B. 105.3"; 2.0 Liter.

Arc Sedan 4D		FD46Y	30860	18250	20550	23400	28100
Arc Convertible 2D		FD75Y	40670	24475	27350	30500	35900
Aero Sedan 4D		FF45Y	34710	19000	21300	24400	29200
Aero Convertible 2D		FH76Y	43175	25250	28225	31400	36800
Auto Trans				300	300	400	400

9-5—4-Cyl. Turbo—Equipment Schedule 2
W.B. 106.4"; 2.3 Liter.

Linear Wagon 4D		EB59E	34225	17525	19675	23300	28700
Arc Sedan 4D		ED49G	36455	17850	20075	23700	29100
Arc Wagon 4D		ED59G	37165	18675	20925	24700	30100
Manual Trans				(725)	(725)	(965)	(965)

0105

Body	Type	VIN	List	Trade-In Fair	Good	Pvt-Party Good	Retail Excellent

9-5—4-Cyl. Turbo—Equipment Schedule 2
W.B. 106.4"; 2.3 Liter.

Aero Sedan 4D		EH49G	41490	19500	21900	25500	31100
Aero Wagon 4D		EH59G	42195	20650	23125	26900	32500
Manual Trans				(725)	(725)	(965)	(965)

SATURN

1991 SATURN — 1G8Z(F549)–M–#

SATURN—4-Cyl.—Equipment Schedule 6
W.B. 99.2", 102.4" (4D); 1.9 Liter.

SL Sedan 4D		F549	9045	475	675	1225	2100
SL1 Sedan 4D		G549	9645	600	850	1475	2475
SL2 Sedan 4D		J547	11345	700	1000	1700	2850
SC Coupe 2D		G147	12825	750	1050	1800	2975

1992 SATURN — 1G8Z(F549)–N–#

SATURN—4-Cyl.—Equipment Schedule 6
W.B. 99.2", 102.4" (4D); 1.9 Liter.

SL Sedan 4D		F549	9265	500	725	1250	2125
SL1 Sedan 4D		G549	10065	650	900	1525	2600
SL2 Sedan 4D		J547	11465	800	1125	1850	3025
SC Coupe 2D		G147	12945	850	1175	1975	3200

1993 SATURN — 1G8Z(F559)–P–#

SATURN—4-Cyl.—Equipment Schedule 6
W.B. 99.2", 102.4" (4D); 1.9 Liter.

SL Sedan 4D		F559	10325	550	800	1375	2300
SL1 Sedan 4D		G559	11125	750	1025	1725	2850
SL2 Sedan 4D		J557	12625	900	1275	2075	3300
SC1 Coupe 2D		E159	12125	800	1125	1850	3025
SC2 Coupe 2D		G157	13925	950	1350	2200	3525
SW1 Wagon 4D		G859	12025	850	1175	1950	3150
SW2 Wagon 4D		J857	13325	950	1375	2250	3575

1994 SATURN — 1G8Z(F559)–R–#

SATURN—4-Cyl.—Equipment Schedule 6
W.B. 99.2", 102.4" (4D); 1.9 Liter.

SL Sedan 4D		F559	11210	625	900	1500	2525
SL1 Sedan 4D		G559	12010	850	1175	1950	3150
SL2 Sedan 4D		J557	13010	1000	1450	2325	3650
SC1 Coupe 2D		E159	12910	900	1300	2100	3350
SC2 Coupe 2D		G157	14110	1075	1525	2550	4000
SW1 Wagon 4D		G859	12910	950	1350	2175	3475
SW2 Wagon 4D		J857	13810	1100	1550	2575	4050

1995 SATURN — 1G8Z(F528)–S–#

SATURN—4-Cyl.—Equipment Schedule 6
W.B. 99.2", 102.4" (4D); 1.9 Liter.

SL Sedan 4D		F528	11260	750	1025	1700	2800
SL1 Sedan 4D		G528	12260	950	1375	2225	3525
SL2 Sedan 4D		J527	13260	1175	1625	2675	4125
SC1 Coupe 2D		E128	13130	1050	1500	2500	3925
SC2 Coupe 2D		G127	14260	1300	1775	2825	4350
SW1 Wagon 4D		G828	12960	1100	1550	2575	4000
SW2 Wagon 4D		J827	13960	1325	1800	2850	4375

1996 SATURN — 1G8Z(F528)–T–#

SATURN—4-Cyl.—Equipment Schedule 6
W.B. 99.2", 102.4" (4D); 1.9 Liter.

SL Sedan 4D		F528	11805	850	1200	2025	3275
SL1 Sedan 4D		G528	12705	1100	1550	2625	4100
SL2 Sedan 4D		J527	13605	1400	1875	2975	4500
SC1 Coupe 2D		E128	13505	1250	1725	2775	4300
SC2 Coupe 2D		G127	14605	1525	2050	3150	4725
SW1 Wagon 4D		G828	13305	1325	1800	2850	4400
SW2 Wagon 4D		J827	14205	1550	2075	3200	4775

Body Type	VIN	List	Trade-In Fair	Trade-In Good	Pvt-Party Good	Retail Excellent

1997 SATURN — 1G8Z(F528)-V-#

SATURN—4-Cyl.—Equipment Schedule 6
W.B. 102.4"; 1.9 Liter.

Body Type	VIN	List	Fair	Good	Good	Excellent
SL Sedan 4D	F528	11925	1025	1475	2500	3950
SL1 Sedan 4D	G528	12925	1400	1875	2950	4500
SL2 Sedan 4D	J527	13825	1700	2225	3325	4925
SC1 Coupe 2D	E128	13825	1525	2050	3150	4700
SC2 Coupe 2D	G127	15025	1875	2400	3525	5150
SW1 Wagon 4D	G828	13525	1600	2100	3225	4775
SW2 Wagon 4D	J827	14425	1900	2425	3575	5200

1998 SATURN — 1G8Z(F528)-W-#

SATURN—4-Cyl.—Equipment Schedule 6
W.B. 102.4"; 1.9 Liter.

Body Type	VIN	List	Fair	Good	Good	Excellent
SL Sedan 4D	F528	11995	1325	1800	2850	4400
SL1 Sedan 4D	G528	12695	1725	2250	3350	4975
SL2 Sedan 4D	J527	13195	2100	2650	3800	5450
SC1 Coupe 2D	E128	13995	1875	2400	3525	5150
SC2 Coupe 2D	G127	15295	2250	2800	3975	5675
SW1 Wagon 4D	G828	13695	1950	2475	3625	5250
SW2 Wagon 4D	J827	14695	2275	2850	4025	5725

1999 SATURN — 1G8Z(F528)-X-#

SATURN—4-Cyl.—Equipment Schedule 6
W.B. 102.4"; 1.9 Liter.

Body Type	VIN	List	Fair	Good	Good	Excellent
SL Sedan 4D	F528	11995	1625	2125	3300	4925
SL1 Sedan 4D	G528	12695	2100	2650	3825	5525
SL2 Sedan 4D	J527	13195	2500	3100	4325	6075
SC1 Coupe 2D	E128	13345	2250	2800	4025	5750
SC1 Coupe 3D	E128	13845	2275	2850	4075	5800
SC2 Coupe 2D	G127	14945	2700	3300	4525	6325
SC2 Coupe 3D	G127	15445	2725	3350	4600	6400
SW1 Wagon 4D	G828	13695	2325	2900	4100	5850
SW2 Wagon 4D	J827	14695	2700	3325	4575	6375

2000 SATURN — 1G8(JorZ)(F528)-Y-#

SATURN—4-Cyl.—Equipment Schedule 6
W.B. 102.4"; 1.9 Liter.

Body Type	VIN	List	Fair	Good	Good	Excellent
SL Sedan 4D	F528	12085	1975	2525	3750	5500
SL1 Sedan 4D	G528	12885	2475	3075	4325	6150
SL2 Sedan 4D	J527	13335	2925	3575	4875	6750
SC1 Coupe 3D	N128	12975	2700	3300	4600	6450
SC2 Coupe 3D	R127	15585	3225	3900	5200	7125
SW2 Wagon 4D	J827	14730	3200	3875	5175	7100

SATURN L-SERIES—4-Cyl.—Equipment Schedule 3
W.B. 106.5"; 2.2 Liter.

Body Type	VIN	List	Fair	Good	Good	Excellent
LS Sedan 4D	R52F	16700	3500	4200	5475	7350
LS1 Sedan 4D	T52F	18150	3950	4700	6000	7950
LW1 Wagon 4D	U82F	19375	4300	5075	6375	8375
Manual Trans			(525)	(525)	(700)	(700)

SATURN L-SERIES—V6—Equipment Schedule 3
W.B. 106.5"; 3.0 Liter.

Body Type	VIN	List	Fair	Good	Good	Excellent
LS2 Sedan 4D	W52R	20575	5050	5925	7300	9375
LW2 Wagon 4D	W82R	21800	5375	6300	7675	9850

2001 SATURN — 1G8(JorZ)(F528)-1-#

SATURN—4-Cyl.—Equipment Schedule 6
W.B. 102.4"; 1.9 Liter.

Body Type	VIN	List	Fair	Good	Good	Excellent
SL Sedan 4D	F528	11995	2725	3350	4600	6425
SL1 Sedan 4D	G528	12910	3300	3950	5225	7125
SL2 Sedan 4D	J527	13360	3775	4500	5825	7775
SC1 Coupe 3D	N128	13960	3525	4225	5525	7450
SC2 Coupe 3D	R127	16110	4100	4875	6225	8200
SW2 Wagon 4D	J827	14755	4075	4850	6200	8175

SATURN L-SERIES—4-Cyl.—Equipment Schedule 3
W.B. 106.5"; 2.2 Liter.

Body Type	VIN	List	Fair	Good	Good	Excellent
L100 Sedan 4D	R52F	16245	4250	5050	6375	8400
L200 Sedan 4D	T52F	18210	4750	5575	6950	9025
LW200 Wagon 4D	U82F	19335	5100	5975	7400	9500
Manual Trans			(550)	(550)	(735)	(735)

Body	Type	VIN	List	Trade-In Fair	Trade-In Good	Pvt-Party Good	Retail Excellent
SATURN L-SERIES—V6—Equipment Schedule 3							
W.B. 106.5"; 3.0 Liter.							
L300 Sedan 4D		W52R	19995	5950	6900	8375	10600
LW300 Wagon 4D		W82R	21860	6325	7350	8800	11100

2002 SATURN — 1G8(JorZ)(F528)-2-#

Body	Type	VIN	List	Trade-In Fair	Trade-In Good	Pvt-Party Good	Retail Excellent
SATURN—4-Cyl.—Equipment Schedule 6							
W.B. 102.4"; 1.9 Liter.							
SL Sedan 4D		F528	11995	3375	4075	5400	7325
SL1 Sedan 4D		G528	13275	3950	4700	6050	8050
SL2 Sedan 4D		J527	13800	4500	5300	6675	8725
SC1 Coupe 3D		N128	14325	4225	5025	6350	8375
SC2 Coupe 3D		R127	16545	4875	5700	7100	9200
SATURN L-SERIES—4-Cyl.—Equipment Schedule 3							
W.B. 106.5"; 2.2 Liter.							
L100 Sedan 4D		R52F	16870	5125	6000	7450	9600
L200 Sedan 4D		T52F	19070	5675	6600	8075	10250
LW200 Wagon 4D		U82F	20515	6075	7050	8550	10800
Manual Trans				(575)	(575)	(765)	(765)
SATURN L-SERIES—V6—Equipment Schedule 3							
W.B. 106.5"; 3.0 Liter.							
L300 Sedan 4D		W52R	20920	7000	8100	9600	12000
LW300 Wagon 4D		W82R	22850	7425	8525	10100	12550

2003 SATURN — 1G8(AF54F)-3-#

Body	Type	VIN	List	Trade-In Fair	Trade-In Good	Pvt-Party Good	Retail Excellent
ION—4-Cyl.—Equipment Schedule 6							
W.B. 103.2"; 2.2 Liter.							
1 Sedan 4D		AF54F	12955	5425	6325	7775	9975
2 Sedan 4D		AZ52F	14075	5925	6900	8350	10600
3 Sedan 4D		AK52F	15575	6375	7375	8875	11200
2 Quad Coupe 2D		AM12F	14595	6925	8000	9525	11900
3 Quad Coupe 2D		AV12F	16095	7400	8500	10050	12500
SATURN L-SERIES—4-Cyl.—Equipment Schedule 3							
W.B. 106.5"; 2.2 Liter.							
L200 Sedan 4D		JT54F	19040	6775	7800	9250	11450
LW200 Wagon 4D		JU84F	20850	7225	8300	9750	12050
Manual Trans				(600)	(600)	(800)	(800)
SATURN L-SERIES—V6—Equipment Schedule 3							
W.B. 106.5"; 3.0 Liter.							
L300 Sedan 4D		JW54R	21255	8225	9425	10950	13400
LW300 Wagon 4D		JW84R	23185	8650	9900	11400	13900

2004 SATURN — 1G8(AF54F)-4-#

Body	Type	VIN	List	Trade-In Fair	Trade-In Good	Pvt-Party Good	Retail Excellent
ION—4-Cyl.—Equipment Schedule 6							
W.B. 103.2"; 2.2 Liter.							
1 Sedan 4D		AF54F	10995	6400	7425	8775	10950
2 Sedan 4D		AZ52F	14750	6950	8025	9425	11650
3 Sedan 4D		AK52F	16275	7450	8575	9975	12300
2 Quad Coupe 2D		AM12F	14850	8075	9250	10700	13050
3 Quad Coupe 2D		AV12F	16800	8575	9800	11300	13750
ION—4-Cyl. Supercharged—Equipment Schedule 6							
W.B. 103.5"; 2.0 Liter.							
Red Line Quad Cpe 2D		AY12P	20950				
SATURN L-SERIES—4-Cyl.—Equipment Schedule 3							
W.B. 106.5"; 2.2 Liter.							
L300 Sedan 4D		JC54F	16995	8225	9425	10900	13250
L300 Wagon 4D		JC84F	19045	8725	9975	11450	13850
SATURN L-SERIES—V6—Equipment Schedule 3							
W.B. 106.5"; 3.0 Liter.							
L300 Sedan 4D		JD54R	21410	9800	11175	12700	15300
L300 Wagon 4D		JD84R	23560	10275	11675	13250	15900

SCION

2004 SCION — JT(KorL)(KT624)-4-#

Body	Type	VIN	List	Trade-In Fair	Trade-In Good	Pvt-Party Good	Retail Excellent
xA—4-Cyl.—Equipment Schedule 6							
W.B. 93.3"; 1.5 Liter.							
Hatchback 4D		KT624	12965	8650	9900	10750	12500
xB—4-Cyl.—Equipment Schedule 6							
W.B. 98.4"; 1.5 Liter.							
Sport Wagon 4D		KT324	14165	10075	11475	12450	14350

Body	Type	VIN	List	Trade-In Fair	Trade-In Good	Pvt-Party Good	Retail Excellent

STERLING

1990 STERLING — SAXXS(43H)–L–#

827—V6—Equipment Schedule 1
W.B. 108.6"; 2.7 Liter.

Body	Type	VIN	List	Fair	Good	Good	Excellent
S Sedan 4D		43H	24010	325	475	1075	1975
Si Sedan 4D		43H	26960	375	525	1125	2075
SL Sedan 4D		83H	28960	450	625	1275	2300
SLi Hatchback 4D		55H	28960	475	675	1350	2400
Oxford Ed Sedan 4D		43H	29960	525	750	1475	2575
Manual Trans				(200)	(200)	(265)	(265)

1991 STERLING — SAXXS(43H)–M–#

827—V6—Equipment Schedule 1
W.B. 108.6"; 2.7 Liter.

Body	Type	VIN	List	Fair	Good	Good	Excellent
Si Sedan 4D		43H,K	26960	400	600	1250	2250
SL Sedan 4D		83H,K	28960	500	725	1450	2575
SLi Hatchback 4D		56H,K	28960	525	750	1500	2650
Manual Trans				(200)	(200)	(265)	(265)

SUBARU

1990 SUBARU — JF(1or2)(KA722)–L–#

JUSTY—3-Cyl.—Equipment Schedule 6
W.B. 90.0"; 1.2 Liter.

Body	Type	VIN	List	Fair	Good	Good	Excellent
DL Hatchback 2D		KA722	6261	250	325	700	1300
GL Hatchback 2D		KA732	7646	275	350	775	1400
GL 4WD Hatchback 2D		KA83A	8346	300	400	825	1475
GL 4WD Hatchback 4D		KD83A	8551	300	400	825	1475

LOYALE—4-Cyl.—Equipment Schedule 4
W.B. 97.2", 97.0 (Wag). 1.8 Liter.

Body	Type	VIN	List	Fair	Good	Good	Excellent
Sedan 4D		AC422	9694	600	850	1400	2300
Coupe 2D		AG421	9994	600	850	1400	2300
Wagon 4D		AN422	10394	550	800	1350	2225
Touring Wagon 4D		AK422	11094	675	925	1525	2525
4WD				475	475	635	635
4-Cyl. 1.8 Liter Turbo		5		0	0	0	0

LOYALE 4WD—4-Cyl.—Equipment Schedule 4
W.B. 97.2"; 1.8 Liter.

Body	Type	VIN	List	Fair	Good	Good	Excellent
RS Coupe 2D		AG57B	11419	1000	1450	2275	3575
4-Cyl. 1.8 Liter Turbo		5		0	0	0	0

LEGACY—4-Cyl.—Equipment Schedule 4
W.B. 101.6"; 2.2 Liter.

Body	Type	VIN	List	Fair	Good	Good	Excellent
Sedan 4D		BC622	12444	550	800	1425	2425
Wagon 4D		BJ622	12994	700	1000	1700	2850
L Sedan 4D		BC632	14639	575	825	1450	2475
L Wagon 4D		BJ632	15189	700	1000	1700	2850
LS Sedan 4D		BC642	15844	625	900	1550	2650
LS Wagon 4D		BJ642	16394	775	1075	1825	3025
4WD				475	475	635	635

LEGACY 4WD—4-Cyl.—Equipment Schedule 4
W.B. 101.6"; 2.2 Liter.

Body	Type	VIN	List	Fair	Good	Good	Excellent
L+ Sedan 4D		BC552	17204	875	1225	2075	3350
L+ Wagon 4D		BJ552	17804	1000	1450	2450	3925

1991 SUBARU — JF(1or2)(KA722)–M–#

JUSTY—3-Cyl.—Equipment Schedule 6
W.B. 90.0"; 1.2 Liter.

Body	Type	VIN	List	Fair	Good	Good	Excellent
Hatchback 2D		KA722	6390	250	325	750	1350
GL Hatchback 2D		KA732	7794	275	375	800	1425
GL 4WD H'Back 2D		KA83A	8594	300	425	850	1500
GL 4WD H'Back 4D		KD83A	8694	300	425	850	1500

LOYALE—4-Cyl.—Equipment Schedule 4
W.B. 97.0", 97.2" (Sed); 1.8 Liter.

Body	Type	VIN	List	Fair	Good	Good	Excellent
Sedan 4D		AC422	9894	700	975	1575	2600
Wagon 4D		AN422	10694	675	925	1550	2575
4WD				550	550	735	735
Auto Trans				150	150	200	200

Body	Type	VIN	List	Trade-In Fair	Trade-In Good	Pvt-Party Good	Retail Excellent
LEGACY—4-Cyl.—Equipment Schedule 4							
W.B. 101.6"; 2.2 Liter.							
L Sedan 4D		BC632	15259	675	950	1675	2850
L Wagon 4D		BJ632	15859	825	1150	1975	3275
LS Sedan 4D		BC652	18164	750	1025	1825	3075
LS Wagon 4D		BJ652	18764	900	1275	2150	3525
LSi Sedan 4D		BC652	19094	750	1050	1850	3100
4WD		C		550	550	735	735
Manual Trans				(175)	(175)	(235)	(235)
LEGACY 4WD—4-Cyl. Turbo—Equipment Schedule 4							
W.B. 101.6"; 2.2 Liter.							
Sport Sedan 4D		BC67C	19294	1025	1475	2550	4050
Manual Trans				(175)	(175)	(235)	(235)
XT—4-Cyl.—Equipment Schedule 4							
W.B. 97.0"; 1.8 Liter.							
GL Coupe 2D		AX432	13833	775	1100	1775	2850
Auto Trans				150	150	200	200
XT6—6-Cyl.—Equipment Schedule 4							
W.B. 97.0"; 2.7 Liter.							
Coupe 2D		AX842	17873	1025	1450	2300	3600
4WD Coupe 2D		AX942	18713	1100	1550	2550	3950
Auto Trans				150	150	200	200

1992 SUBARU — (JF1,JF2,4S3or4S4)(KA722)–N–#

Body	Type	VIN	List	Trade-In Fair	Trade-In Good	Pvt-Party Good	Retail Excellent
JUSTY—3-Cyl.—Equipment Schedule 6							
W.B. 90.0"; 1.2 Liter.							
Hatchback 2D		KA722	7090	250	325	775	1400
GL Hatchback 2D		KA732	8494	300	400	850	1500
GL AWD H'Back 2D		KA832	9294	300	450	900	1575
GL AWD H'Back 4D		KD83A	9394	300	450	900	1575
LOYALE—4-Cyl.—Equipment Schedule 4							
W.B. 97.0", 97.2" (Sed); 1.8 Liter.							
Sedan 4D		AC422	10244	775	1100	1800	2925
Wagon 4D		AN422	11094	775	1100	1825	2975
AWD		5		625	625	835	835
Auto Trans				175	175	235	235
LEGACY—4-Cyl.—Equipment Schedule 4							
W.B. 101.6"; 2.2 Liter.							
L Sedan 4D		BC632	16229	775	1100	1950	3250
L Wagon 4D		BJ632	16729	925	1325	2375	3900
LS Sedan 4D		BC652	19744	875	1225	2125	3525
LS Wagon 4D		BJ652	20244	1050	1500	2600	4150
LSi Sedan 4D		BC652	21144	900	1250	2175	3575
4WD		6		625	625	835	835
Manual Trans				(225)	(225)	(300)	(300)
LEGACY 4WD—4-Cyl. Turbo—Equipment Schedule 4							
W.B. 101.6"; 2.2 Liter.							
Sport Sedan 4D		BC672	21029	1250	1725	2875	4500
LE Touring Wagon		BJ672	22090	1500	1975	3175	4825
Manual Trans				(225)	(225)	(300)	(300)
SVX AWD—6-Cyl.—Equipment Schedule 4							
W.B. 102.8"; 3.3 Liter.							
Sport Coupe 2D		CX343	25445	2100	2675	4150	6225
Touring Pkg				325	325	435	435

1993 SUBARU — (JF1,JF2,4S3or4S4)(KA722)–P–#

Body	Type	VIN	List	Trade-In Fair	Trade-In Good	Pvt-Party Good	Retail Excellent
JUSTY—3-Cyl.—Equipment Schedule 6							
W.B. 90.0"; 1.2 Liter.							
Hatchback 2D		KA722	7783	250	325	775	1425
GL Hatchback 2D		KA732	9558	300	400	875	1550
GL AWD H'Back 2D		KA832	10358	325	475	925	1675
GL AWD H'Back 4D		KD83A	9923	325	475	925	1675
LOYALE—4-Cyl.—Equipment Schedule 4							
W.B. 97.0", 97.2" (Sed); 1.8 Liter.							
Sedan 4D		AC422	10923	900	1275	2075	3300
Wagon 4D		AN422	11794	900	1300	2125	3400
AWD				700	700	935	935
Auto Trans				200	200	265	265
IMPREZA—4-Cyl.—Equipment Schedule 5							
W.B. 99.2"; 1.8 Liter.							
Sedan 4D		GC214	11444	650	900	1650	2850
L Sedan 4D		GC224	14244	775	1075	1925	3200
L Wagon 4D		GF244	14644	950	1375	2425	3950

Body Type	VIN	List	Trade-In Fair	Good	Pvt-Party Good	Retail Excellent
LS Sedan 4D	GC254	16144	975	1400	2450	3975
LS Wagon 4D	GF254	16544	1125	1575	2700	4300
AWD			700	700	935	935
LEGACY—4-Cyl.—Equipment Schedule 4						
W.B. 101.6"; 2.2 Liter.						
L Sedan 4D	BC633	17495	900	1275	2350	3900
L Wagon 4D	BJ633	18195	1075	1525	2700	4325
LS Sedan 4D	BC653	19595	1000	1450	2575	4175
LS Wagon 4D	BJ653	20295	1250	1725	2925	4600
AWD			700	700	935	935
Manual Trans			(275)	(275)	(365)	(365)
LEGACY AWD—4-Cyl.—Equipment Schedule 4						
W.B. 101.6"; 2.2 Liter.						
LSi Sedan 4D	BC653	22095	1725	2250	3525	5300
LSi Wagon 4D	BJ653	23095	2075	2625	3925	5800
LEGACY AWD—4-Cyl. Turbo—Equipment Schedule 4						
W.B. 101.6"; 2.2 Liter.						
Sport Sedan 4D	BC673	21295	1500	2025	3275	5000
Touring Wagon 4D	BJ673	23095	1775	2300	3575	5350
Manual Trans			(275)	(275)	(365)	(365)
SVX AWD—6-Cyl.—Equipment Schedule 4						
W.B. 102.8"; 3.3 Liter.						
Special Edition Cpe 2D	CX343	34445	2650	3250	4875	7100

Body Type	VIN	List	Trade-In Fair	Good	Pvt-Party Good	Retail Excellent
JUSTY—3-Cyl.—Equipment Schedule 6						
W.B. 90.0"; 1.2 Liter.						
DL Hatchback 2D	KA722	8194	275	350	850	1550
GL AWD Hatchback 5D	KD83A	10048	350	500	1025	1850
LOYALE AWD—4-Cyl.—Equipment Schedule 4						
W.B. 96.9"; 1.8 Liter.						
Wagon 4D	AN52B	13998	1725	2250	3400	5050
Auto Trans			225	225	300	300
IMPREZA—4-Cyl.—Equipment Schedule 5						
W.B. 99.2"; 1.8 Liter.						
Sedan 4D	GC214	11645	750	1050	1925	3250
L Sedan 4D	GC224	15195	900	1250	2175	3600
L Wagon 4D	GF224	15595	1100	1550	2700	4300
AWD			775	775	1035	1035
IMPREZA AWD—4-Cyl.—Equipment Schedule 5						
W.B. 99.2"; 1.8 Liter.						
LS Sedan 4D	GC255	18995	2150	2725	3975	5775
LS Wagon 4D	GF255	19395	2425	3025	4350	6225
LEGACY—4-Cyl.—Equipment Schedule 4						
W.B. 101.6"; 2.2 Liter.						
L Sedan 4D	BC633	17395	1050	1500	2675	4325
L Wagon 4D	BJ633	18695	1350	1825	3075	4800
LS Sedan 4D	BC653	20145	1225	1700	2950	4650
LS Wagon 4D	BJ653	20845	1525	2050	3300	5100
AWD			775	775	1035	1035
Manual Trans			(325)	(325)	(435)	(435)
LEGACY AWD—4-Cyl.—Equipment Schedule 4						
W.B. 101.6"; 2.2 Liter.						
LSi Sedan 4D	BC653	22295	2100	2650	3975	5875
LSi Wagon 4D	BJ653	23295	2450	3050	4450	6400
LEGACY AWD—4-Cyl. Turbo—Equipment Schedule 4						
W.B. 101.6"; 2.2 Liter.						
Sport Sedan 4D	BC673	22645	1850	2375	3700	5550
Touring Wagon 4D	BJ673	23645	2100	2700	4025	5925
Manual Trans			(325)	(325)	(435)	(435)
SVX—6-Cyl.—Equipment Schedule 4						
W.B. 102.8"; 3.3 Liter.						
L Coupe 2D	CX323	24345	2000	2550	4100	6225
LS Coupe 2D	CX345	28995	2425	3025	4625	6850
LSi AWD Coupe 2D	CX355	34295	3225	3900	5625	8000

Body Type	VIN	List	Trade-In Fair	Good	Pvt-Party Good	Retail Excellent
IMPREZA—4-Cyl.—Equipment Schedule 5						
W.B. 99.2"; 1.8 Liter, 2.2 Liter.						
Sedan 4D	GC215	13420	900	1250	2325	3875
Coupe 2D	GM215	13715	775	1075	2000	3350
L Sedan 4D	GC235	15025	1025	1450	2575	4175
L Coupe 2D	GM235	15025	925	1325	2425	3975

Body Type	VIN	List	Trade-In Fair	Trade-In Good	Pvt-Party Good	Retail Excellent
AWD			825	825	1100	1100

IMPREZA AWD—4-Cyl.—Equipment Schedule 5
W.B. 99.2"; 1.8 Liter, 2.2 Liter.

Body Type	VIN	List	Fair	Good	Good	Excellent
L Wagon 4D	GF235	16425	2550	3150	4450	6300
L Sedan 4D	GC655	17470	2550	3175	4475	6325
LX Sedan 4D	GM655	17770	2375	2950	4250	6075
LX Wagon 4D	GF655	17870	2825	3475	4850	6800
Outback Wagon 4D	GF235	17225	3025	3700	5075	7050

LEGACY—4-Cyl.—Equipment Schedule 4
W.B. 103.5"; 2.2 Liter.

Body Type	VIN	List	Fair	Good	Good	Excellent
Sedan 4D	BD625	16517	1500	1975	3300	5100
L Sedan 4D	BD635	18264	1425	1900	3200	5000
L Wagon 4D	BK635	18964	1775	2300	3625	5500
AWD			825	825	1100	1100
Manual Trans (Sedan)			(375)	(375)	(500)	(500)

LEGACY AWD—4-Cyl.—Equipment Schedule 4
W.B. 103.5"; 2.2 Liter.

Body Type	VIN	List	Fair	Good	Good	Excellent
Brighton Wagon 4D	BK625	17643	2200	2775	4175	6150
Outback Wagon 4D	BK635	21095	3425	4150	5700	7950
LS Sedan 4D	BD655	21595	2425	3025	4475	6450
LS Wagon 4D	BK655	22295	2725	3350	4850	6925
LSi Sedan 4D	BD655	24095	2600	3225	4650	6700
LSi Wagon 4D	BK655	24795	2975	3650	5125	7275

SVX—6-Cyl.—Equipment Schedule 4
W.B. 102.8"; 3.3 Liter.

Body Type	VIN	List	Fair	Good	Good	Excellent
L Coupe 2D	CX335	27275	2475	3075	4750	7025
L AWD Coupe 2D	CX335	28775	3100	3750	5500	7925
LSi Coupe 2D	CX355	34825	3825	4550	6400	8975

1996 SUBARU — JF1or4S3(GM225)–T–#

IMPREZA AWD—4-Cyl.—Equipment Schedule 5
W.B. 99.2"; 1.8 Liter, 2.2 Liter.

Body Type	VIN	List	Fair	Good	Good	Excellent
Brighton Coupe 2D	GM225	13990	2125	2700	3975	5800
L Sedan 4D	GC435	16890	2600	3225	4525	6450
L Coupe 2D	GM435	16890	2400	2975	4300	6175
L Wagon 4D	GF435	16490	2925	3575	4950	6900
LX Sedan 4D	GC455	18290	2975	3625	5000	6925
LX Coupe 2D	GM455	18590	2750	3375	4725	6675
LX Wagon 4D	GF455	18690	3300	3950	5375	7450
Outback Wagon 4D	GF485	18890	3450	4150	5600	7675
2WD			(875)	(875)	(1165)	(1165)

LEGACY—4-Cyl.—Equipment Schedule 4
W.B. 103.5"; 2.2 Liter.

Body Type	VIN	List	Fair	Good	Good	Excellent
L Sedan 4D	BD335	18775	1775	2300	3700	5625
L Wagon 4D	BK335	19475	2125	2700	4150	6150
AWD	4		875	875	1165	1165
Manual Trans (Sedan)			(400)	(400)	(535)	(535)

LEGACY AWD—4-Cyl.—Equipment Schedule 4
W.B. 103.5"; 2.2 Liter, 2.5 Liter.

Body Type	VIN	List	Fair	Good	Good	Excellent
Brighton Wagon 4D	BK425	18075	2650	3250	4750	6875
Outback Wagon 4D	BG685	22490	4000	4750	6425	8800
LS Sedan 4D	BD455	22590	2900	3550	5100	7225
LS Wagon 4D	BK455	23290	3275	3925	5525	7750
GT Sedan 4D	BD675	22790	3125	3775	5325	7525
GT Wagon 4D	BK675	23490	3525	4225	5850	8125
LSi Sedan 4D	BD665	25290	3075	3725	5275	7475
LSi Wagon 4D	BK665	25990	3475	4175	5775	8050
4-Cyl. 2.5L (Outback)	6		250	250	335	335

SVX AWD—6-Cyl.—Equipment Schedule 4
W.B. 102.8"; 3.3 Liter.

Body Type	VIN	List	Fair	Good	Good	Excellent
L Coupe 2D	CX835	30490	3725	4450	6300	8875
LSi Coupe 2D	CX865	35990	4500	5300	7275	10050

1997 SUBARU — JF1or4S3(GM425)–V–#

IMPREZA AWD—4-Cyl.—Equipment Schedule 5
W.B. 99.2"; 1.8 Liter, 2.2 Liter.

Body Type	VIN	List	Fair	Good	Good	Excellent
Brighton Coupe 2D	GM425	15290	2550	3175	4500	6375
L Sedan 4D	GC435	17190	3050	3700	5100	7050
L Coupe 2D	GM435	17190	2825	3450	4800	6750
L Sport Wagon 4D	GF435	17590	3400	4100	5525	7550
Outback Sport Wagon	GF485	19290	3950	4700	6200	8325

LEGACY AWD—4-Cyl.—Equipment Schedule 4
W.B. 103.5"; 2.2 Liter, 2.5 Liter.

Body	Type	VIN	List	Trade-In Fair	Good	Pvt-Party Good	Retail Excellent
Brighton Wagon 4D		BK425	18490	3350	4050	5675	7925
L Sedan 4D		BD435	20490	3125	3775	5350	7575
L Wagon 4D		BK435	21190	3550	4250	5875	8175
Outback Wagon 4D		BG685	23790	4750	5575	7350	9900
Outback Ltd Wag 4D		BG685	25490	5050	5900	7700	10250
GT Sedan 4D		BD675	24090	4025	4800	6500	8900
GT Wagon 4D		BK675	24790	4450	5225	6950	9425
LSi Sedan 4D		BD665	25490	3925	4675	6375	8750
LSi Wagon 4D		BK665	26190	4325	5100	6850	9300
Manual Trans (Sedan)				**(425)**	**(425)**	**(565)**	**(565)**
SVX AWD—6-Cyl.—Equipment Schedule 4							
W.B. 102.8"; 3.3 Liter.							
L Coupe 2D		CX835	31120	4400	5175	7175	9925
LSi Coupe 2D		CX865	36740	5225	6125	8200	11150

1998 SUBARU — JF1or4S3(GC435)–W–#

IMPREZA AWD—4-Cyl.—Equipment Schedule 5
W.B. 99.2"; 2.2 Liter, 2.5 Liter.

Body	Type	VIN	List	Fair	Good	Good	Excellent
L Sedan 4D		GC435	17190	3575	4275	5675	7700
L Coupe 2D		GM435	17190	3300	3975	5350	7325
L Sport Wagon 4D		GF435	17590	3925	4675	6125	8200
Outback Sport Wag 4D		GF485	19290	4525	5350	6850	9025
2.5RS Coupe 2D		GM675	20490	4775	5625	7125	9350
LEGACY AWD—4-Cyl.—Equipment Schedule 4							
W.B. 103.5"; 2.2 Liter, 2.5 Liter.							
Brighton Wagon 4D		BK425	18524	3950	4700	6375	8725
L Sedan 4D		BD435	20490	3725	4450	6075	8400
L Wagon 4D		BK435	21190	4175	4975	6650	9050
Outback Wagon 4D		BG685	23790	5475	6375	8175	10800
Outback Ltd Wag 4D		BG685	25890	5825	6800	8625	11300
GT Sedan 4D		BD675	24090	4725	5550	7300	9800
GT Limited Sedan 4D		BE656	25390	4900	5725	7500	9975
GT Wagon 4D		BK675	24790	5150	6025	7800	10350
Manual Trans (Sedan)				**(450)**	**(450)**	**(600)**	**(600)**
Dual Power Moon Roofs				225	225	300	300

1999 SUBARU — JF1or4S3(GC435)–X–#

IMPREZA AWD—4-Cyl.—Equipment Schedule 5
W.B. 99.2"; 2.2 Liter, 2.5 Liter.

Body	Type	VIN	List	Fair	Good	Good	Excellent
L Sedan 4D		GC435	17190	4225	5025	6500	8675
L Coupe 2D		GM435	17190	3900	4650	6125	8225
L Sport Wagon 4D		GF435	17590	4625	5475	6975	9225
Outback Sport Wag 4D		GF485	19290	5325	6225	7800	10150
2.5RS Coupe 2D		GM675	20490	5625	6525	8125	10500
LEGACY AWD—4-Cyl.—Equipment Schedule 4							
W.B. 103.5"; 2.2 Liter, 2.5 Liter.							
Brighton Wagon 4D		BK425	18524	4650	5500	7275	9800
L Sedan 4D		BD435	20490	4375	5150	6900	9400
L Wagon 4D		BK435	21190	4925	5775	7575	10200
Outback Wagon 4D		BG686	23790	6375	7400	9300	12100
Outback Ltd Wag 4D		BG686	25890	6825	7850	9800	12650
GT Sedan 4D		BD675	24090	5525	6422	8275	10950
GT Limited Sedan 4D		BE656	25390	5700	6650	8500	11200
GT Wagon 4D		BK675	24790	6025	6975	8875	11600
Sport Util Sedan 4D		BD685	23890	6075	7025	8925	11650
Ltd Sport Util Sed 4D		BD685	26090	6650	7675	9600	12450
Manual Trans (Sedan)				**(500)**	**(500)**	**(665)**	**(665)**
Dual Moon Roofs				300	300	400	400

2000 SUBARU — JF1or4S3(GC435)–Y–#

IMPREZA AWD—4-Cyl.—Equipment Schedule 5
W.B. 99.2"; 2.2 Liter, 2.5 Liter.

Body	Type	VIN	List	Fair	Good	Good	Excellent
L Sedan 4D		GC435	17190	4975	5825	7375	9650
L Coupe 2D		GM435	17190	4625	5475	6975	9250
L Sport Wagon 4D		GF435	17590	5450	6350	7925	10250
Outback Sport Wag 4D		GF485	19390	6225	7200	8825	11300
2.5RS Sedan 4D		GC675	20590	6800	7825	9500	12050
2.5RS Coupe 2D		GM675	20590	6525	7550	9225	11700
LEGACY AWD—4-Cyl.—Equipment Schedule 4							
W.B. 104.3"; 2.5 Liter.							
Brighton Wagon 4D		BH625	19690	6375	7375	9075	11600
L Sedan 4D		BE635	20490	6050	7000	8700	11200

Body Type	VIN	List	Trade-In Fair	Good	Pvt-Party Good	Retail Excellent
L Wagon 4D	BH635	21190	6675	7700	9400	12000
GT Sedan 4D	BE645	24090	7350	8450	10200	12850
GT Limited Sedan 4D	BE656	25590	7550	8700	10450	13150
GT Wagon 4D	BH645	24990	7900	9075	10900	13650
Manual Trans (Sedan)			(525)	(525)	(700)	(700)
Dual Moon Roofs			375	375	500	500

OUTBACK AWD—4-Cyl.—Equipment Schedule 4
W.B. 104.3"; 2.5 Liter.

Body Type	VIN	List	Trade-In Fair	Good	Pvt-Party Good	Retail Excellent
Wagon 4D	BH666	23990	8300	9525	11400	14200
Limited Sedan 4D	BE686	26390	8600	9850	11700	14550
Limited Wagon 4D	BH686	27390	8750	10025	11900	14800
Dual Moon Roofs			375	375	500	500

2001 SUBARU — JF1or4S3(GC435)-1-#

IMPREZA AWD—4-Cyl.—Equipment Schedule 5
W.B. 99.2"; 2.2 Liter, 2.5 Liter.

Body Type	VIN	List	Trade-In Fair	Good	Pvt-Party Good	Retail Excellent
L Sedan 4D	GC435	17290	5775	6750	8375	10800
L Coupe 2D	GM435	17190	5450	6350	7950	10300
L Sport Wagon 4D	GF435	17690	6325	7350	8975	11600
Outback Sport Wag 4D	GF485	19490	7175	8250	9975	12600
2.5RS Sedan 4D	GC675	20790	7825	8975	10750	13450
2.5RS Coupe 2D	GM675	20790	7550	8700	10400	13100

LEGACY AWD—4-Cyl.—Equipment Schedule 4
W.B. 104.3"; 2.5 Liter.

Body Type	VIN	List	Trade-In Fair	Good	Pvt-Party Good	Retail Excellent
L Sedan 4D	BE635	20590	7050	8125	9900	12900
L Wagon 4D	BH635	21290	7725	8875	10700	13500
GT Sedan 4D	BE645	24190	8525	9750	11600	14450
GT Limited Sedan 4D	BE656	25690	8725	9975	11850	14750
GT Wagon 4D	BH645	25090	9150	10425	12300	15200
Manual Trans (Sedan)			(550)	(550)	(735)	(735)
Dual Moon Roofs			475	475	635	635

OUTBACK AWD—4-Cyl.—Equipment Schedule 4
W.B. 104.3"; 2.5 Liter.

Body Type	VIN	List	Trade-In Fair	Good	Pvt-Party Good	Retail Excellent
Wagon 4D	BH665	24190	9600	10950	12850	15850
Limited Sedan 4D	BE686	26490	9925	11275	13250	16250
Limited Wagon 4D	BH686	27590	10075	11475	13450	16450
Dual Moon Roofs			475	475	635	635

OUTBACK AWD—H6—Equipment Schedule 4
W.B. 104.3"; 3.0 Liter.

Body Type	VIN	List	Trade-In Fair	Good	Pvt-Party Good	Retail Excellent
L.L. Bean Wagon 4D	BH806	29990	10650	12150	14100	17300
VDC Wagon 4D	BH896	32390	11850	13450	15500	18800
Dual Moon Roofs			475	475	635	635

2002 SUBARU — JF1or4S3(GG655)-2-#

IMPREZA AWD—4-Cyl.—Equipment Schedule 5
W.B. 99.4"; 2.5 Liter.

Body Type	VIN	List	Trade-In Fair	Good	Pvt-Party Good	Retail Excellent
2.5 TS Sport Wagon 4D	GG655	18820	7325	8425	10150	12750
Outback Sport Wag 4D	GF485	20020	8275	9475	11250	13950
2.5RS Sedan 4D	GC675	20320	8975	10275	12050	14900

IMPREZA AWD—4-Cyl. Turbo—Equipment Schedule 4
W.B. 99.4"; 2.0 liter.

Body Type	VIN	List	Trade-In Fair	Good	Pvt-Party Good	Retail Excellent
WRX Sedan 4D	GD295	25520	12100	13725	15700	18850
WRX Sport Wagon 4D	GG295	25020	11800	13400	15400	18600

LEGACY AWD—4-Cyl.—Equipment Schedule 4
W.B. 104.3"; 2.5 Liter.

Body Type	VIN	List	Trade-In Fair	Good	Pvt-Party Good	Retail Excellent
L Sedan 4D	BE635	20620	8225	9425	11300	14100
L Wagon 4D	BH635	21320	8975	10275	12150	15000
GT Sedan 4D	BE645	24220	9850	11225	13150	16150
GT Limited Sedan 4D	BE656	26020	10075	11475	13450	16450
GT Wagon 4D	BH645	25120	10500	11950	13900	17000
Manual Trans (Sedan)			(575)	(575)	(765)	(765)
Dual Moon Roofs			575	575	765	765

OUTBACK AWD—4-Cyl.—Equipment Schedule 4
W.B. 104.3"; 2.5 Liter.

Body Type	VIN	List	Trade-In Fair	Good	Pvt-Party Good	Retail Excellent
Wagon 4D	BH665	24220	11000	12475	14500	17600
Limited Sedan 4D	BE686	26520	11375	12900	14950	18100
Limited Wagon 4D	BH686	27620	11525	13050	15050	18300
Dual Moon Roofs			575	575	765	765

OUTBACK AWD—H6—Equipment Schedule 4
W.B. 104.3"; 3.0 Liter.

Body Type	VIN	List	Trade-In Fair	Good	Pvt-Party Good	Retail Excellent
Sedan 4D	BE896	28520	11425	12950	14950	18150
L.L. Bean Wagon 4D	BH806	30020	12200	13825	15850	19150
VDC Sedan 4D	BH806	30920	12725	14400	16450	19800

2002 SUBARU

Body	Type	VIN	List	Trade-In Fair	Trade-In Good	Pvt-Party Good	Retail Excellent
VDC Wagon 4D		BH896	32420	**13525**	**15275**	**17400**	**20800**
Dual Moon Roofs				**575**	**575**	**765**	**765**

2003 SUBARU — JF1or4S3(GG655)-3-#

IMPREZA AWD—4-Cyl.—Equipment Schedule 5
W.B. 99.4"; 2.5 Liter.

2.5 TS Sport Wagon 4D		GG655	18920	**8450**	**9650**	**11400**	**14000**
Outback Sport Wag		GG685	20120	**9425**	**10750**	**12550**	**15300**
2.5RS Sedan 4D		GD675	20420	**10225**	**11625**	**13400**	**16250**

IMPREZA AWD—4-Cyl. Turbo—Equipment Schedule 4
W.B. 99.4"; 2.0 Liter.

WRX Sedan 4D		GD296	25720	**13575**	**15350**	**17350**	**20600**
WRX Sport Wagon 4D		GG296	25220	**13300**	**15025**	**17000**	**20300**

LEGACY AWD—4-Cyl.—Equipment Schedule 4
W.B. 104.3"; 2.5 Liter.

L Sedan 4D		BE635	20820	**9550**	**10900**	**12700**	**15650**
L Wagon 4D		BH635	21520	**10375**	**11800**	**13700**	**16700**
L Special Ed Sed 4D		BE635	21320	**9700**	**11100**	**12900**	**15850**
L Special Ed Wag 4D		BH635	22420	**10550**	**12000**	**13850**	**16900**
GT Sedan 4D		BE646	26320	**11275**	**12825**	**14750**	**17850**
GT Wagon 4D		BH646	27220	**12050**	**13625**	**15600**	**18800**
Manual Trans (Sedan)				**(600)**	**(600)**	**(800)**	**(800)**
Dual Moon Roofs				**675**	**675**	**900**	**900**

OUTBACK AWD—4-Cyl.—Equipment Schedule 4
W.B. 104.3"; 2.5 Liter.

Wagon 4D		BH675	24370	**12575**	**14200**	**16200**	**19500**
Limited Sedan 4D		BE686	26820	**12950**	**14650**	**16650**	**19950**
Limited Wagon 4D		BH686	27920	**13150**	**14875**	**16900**	**20300**
Dual Moon Roofs				**675**	**675**	**900**	**900**

OUTBACK AWD—H6—Equipment Schedule 4
W.B. 104.3"; 3.0 Liter.

Sedan 4D		BE896	29020	**13000**	**14725**	**16750**	**20100**
Wagon 4D		BH896	27520	**12425**	**14075**	**16100**	**19300**
L.L. Bean Wagon 4D		BH806	30520	**13875**	**15700**	**17750**	**21200**
VDC Sedan 4D		BE896	31420	**14450**	**16325**	**18450**	**21900**
VDC Wagon 4D		BH896	32920	**15300**	**17275**	**19500**	**23000**

2004 SUBARU — JF1or4S3(GG655)-4-#

IMPREZA AWD—4-Cyl.—Equipment Schedule 5
W.B. 99.4"; 2.5 Liter.

2.5 TS Sport Wagon 4D		GG655	19245	**9700**	**11050**	**12750**	**15500**
Outback Sport Wag		GG685	20445	**10750**	**12200**	**14000**	**16900**
2.5RS Sedan 4D		GD675	20745	**11625**	**13150**	**15000**	**18050**

IMPREZA AWD—4-Cyl. Turbo—Equipment Schedule 4
W.B. 99.4"; 2.0 Liter.

WRX Sedan 4D		GD296	26045	**15275**	**17175**	**19200**	**22700**
WRX Sport Wagon 4D		GG296	25545	**14925**	**16800**	**18850**	**22300**

IMPREZA AWD—4-Cyl. HO Turbo—Equipment Schedule 4
W.B. 100.0"; 2.5 Liter.

WRX STi Sedan 4D		GD706	31545	**20450**	**22950**	**25200**	**29200**

LEGACY AWD—4-Cyl.—Equipment Schedule 4
W.B. 104.3"; 2.5 Liter.

L Sedan 4D		BE635	21245	**11175**	**12725**	**14700**	**17850**
L Wagon 4D		BH635	21945	**12050**	**13675**	**15700**	**18950**
GT Sedan 4D		BE646	26645	**13100**	**14825**	**16950**	**20400**
GT Wagon 4D		BH646	27545	**13875**	**15700**	**17800**	**21300**
Manual Trans (Sedan)				**(625)**	**(625)**	**(835)**	**(835)**
Dual Moon Roofs				**775**	**775**	**1035**	**1035**

OUTBACK AWD—4-Cyl.—Equipment Schedule 4
W.B. 104.3"; 2.5 Liter.

Wagon 4D		BH675	24695	**14450**	**16325**	**18500**	**22000**
Limited Sedan 4D		BE686	27145	**14875**	**16750**	**18900**	**22500**
Limited Wagon 4D		BH686	28245	**15075**	**17000**	**19200**	**22800**
Dual Moon Roofs				**775**	**775**	**1035**	**1035**

OUTBACK AWD—H6—Equipment Schedule 4
W.B. 104.3"; 3.0 Liter.

Sedan 4D		BE896	29345	**14975**	**16850**	**19000**	**22600**
35th Anniv Wagon 4D		BH815	27645	**14350**	**16175**	**18300**	**21800**
L.L. Bean Wagon 4D		BH806	30845	**15900**	**17850**	**20100**	**23700**
VDC Sedan 4D		BE896	31545	**16500**	**18575**	**20800**	**24500**
VDC Wagon 4D		BH896	33045	**17425**	**19575**	**21800**	**25600**

1990 SUZUKI

Body	Type	VIN	List	Trade-In Fair	Good	Pvt-Party Good	Retail Excellent

SUZUKI

1990 SUZUKI — JS2(AE35S)-L-#

SWIFT—4-Cyl.—Equipment Schedule 6
W.B. 89.2", 93.1" (Sed); 1.3 Liter.

GA Sedan 4D		AE35S	7659	200	300	650	1225
GA Hatchback 2D		AC35S	6659	175	225	575	1075
GL Sedan 4D		AE35S	8159	225	300	675	1250
GL Hatchback 2D		AC35S	7059	225	300	675	1250
GS Sedan 4D		AE35S	8859	250	400	825	1475
GLX Hatchback 2D		AC35S	8059	250	325	700	1300
GT Hatchback 2D		AC34S	9659	350	500	950	1675

1991 SUZUKI — JS2(AE35S)-M-#

SWIFT—4-Cyl.—Equipment Schedule 6
W.B. 89.2", 93.1" (Sed); 1.3 Liter.

GA Sedan 4D		AE35S	7769	250	325	700	1300
GA Hatchback 2D		AE35S	6669	200	275	625	1175
GS Sedan 4D		AE35S	8869	300	450	900	1550
GT Hatchback 2D		AC34S	9669	400	575	1050	1850

1992 SUZUKI — JS2(AE34S)-N-#

SWIFT—4-Cyl.—Equipment Schedule 6
W.B. 89.2", 93.1" (Sed); 1.3 Liter.

GA Sedan 4D		AE34S	7984	275	375	825	1475
GA Hatchback 2D		AC34S	7184	225	300	700	1300
GA Limited Ed H'Back		AC34S	8484	225	300	700	1300
GS Sedan 4D		AE34S	9384	350	500	975	1725
GT Hatchback 2D		AC34S	9884	450	650	1200	2075

1993 SUZUKI — (JSor2S)2(AE34S)-P-#

SWIFT—4-Cyl.—Equipment Schedule 6
W.B. 89.2", 93.1" (Sed); 1.3 Liter.

GA Sedan 4D		AE34S	8299	300	425	900	1575
GA Hatchback 2D		AC34S	7599	250	325	775	1425
GS Sedan 4D		AE34S	9699	400	575	1075	1900
GT Hatchback 2D		AC34S	10299	525	750	1325	2250

1994 SUZUKI — (JSor2S)2(AE34S)-R-#

SWIFT—4-Cyl.—Equipment Schedule 6
W.B. 89.2", 93.1" (Sed); 1.3 Liter.

GA Sedan 4D		AE34S	8844	325	475	1000	1800
GA Hatchback 2D		AC34S	7864	300	400	900	1625
GS Sedan 4D		AE34S	10344	450	650	1225	2125
GT Hatchback 2D		AC34S	10974	600	850	1500	2575

1995 SUZUKI — (JSor2S)2(AB21H)-S-#

SWIFT—4-Cyl.—Equipment Schedule 6
W.B. 93.1"; 1.3 Liter.

Hatchback 2D		AB21H	9029	350	500	975	1725

ESTEEM—4-Cyl.—Equipment Schedule 6
W.B. 97.6"; 1.6 Liter.

GL Sedan 4D		GB31S	11789	575	825	1550	2725
GLX Sedan 4D		GB31S	14789	650	900	1700	2925

1996 SUZUKI — (JSor2S)2(AB21H)-T-#

SWIFT—4-Cyl.—Equipment Schedule 6
W.B. 93.1"; 1.3 Liter.

Hatchback 2D		AB21H	9359	450	625	1150	2025

ESTEEM—4-Cyl.—Equipment Schedule 6
W.B. 97.6"; 1.6 Liter.

GL Sedan 4D		GB31S	11989	675	925	1775	3100
GLX Sedan 4D		GB31S	13289	750	1050	1975	3350

1997 SUZUKI — (JSor2S)2(AB21H)-V-#

SWIFT—4-Cyl.—Equipment Schedule 6
W.B. 93.1"; 1.3 Liter.

Hatchback 2D		AB21H	9359	550	800	1425	2400

1997 SUZUKI

Body Type	VIN	List	Trade-In Fair	Trade-In Good	Pvt-Party Good	Retail Excellent
ESTEEM—4-Cyl.—Equipment Schedule 6						
W.B. 97.6"; 1.6 Liter.						
GL Sedan 4D	GB31S	13319	775	1100	2100	3575
GLX Sedan 4D	GB31S	14419	900	1250	2375	3975

1998 SUZUKI — (JSor2S)2(AB21H)-W-#

Body Type	VIN	List	Trade-In Fair	Trade-In Good	Pvt-Party Good	Retail Excellent
SWIFT—4-Cyl.—Equipment Schedule 6						
W.B. 93.1"; 1.3 Liter.						
Hatchback 2D	AB21H	9479	950	1375	2250	3575
ESTEEM—4-Cyl.—Equipment Schedule 6						
W.B. 97.6", 97.7" (Wag); 1.6 Liter.						
GL Sedan 4D	GB31S	12429	900	1300	2500	4200
GL Wagon 4D	GB31W	12929	1025	1475	2700	4450
GLX Sedan 4D	GB31S	13529	1025	1475	2700	4450
GLX Wagon 4D	GB31W	14029	1200	1650	2925	4675

1999 SUZUKI — (JSor2S)3(AB21H)-X-#

Body Type	VIN	List	Trade-In Fair	Trade-In Good	Pvt-Party Good	Retail Excellent
SWIFT—4-Cyl.—Equipment Schedule 6						
W.B. 93.1"; 1.3 Liter.						
Hatchback 2D	AB21H	9479	1100	1550	2625	4125
ESTEEM—4-Cyl.—Equipment Schedule 6						
W.B. 97.6"; 1.6 Liter, 1.8 Liter.						
GL Sedan 4D	GB31S	12629	1200	1650	3000	4850
GL Wagon 4D	GB31W	13129	1400	1875	3250	5100
GLX Sedan 4D	GB31S	13729	1400	1875	3250	5100
GLX Wagon 4D	GB31W	14229	1600	2100	3500	5400

2000 SUZUKI — (JSor2S)3(AB21H)-Y-#

Body Type	VIN	List	Trade-In Fair	Trade-In Good	Pvt-Party Good	Retail Excellent
SWIFT—4-Cyl.—Equipment Schedule 6						
W.B. 93.1"; 1.3 Liter.						
GA Hatchback 2D	AB21H	9499	1375	1850	2950	4525
GL Hatchback 2D	AB21H	10499	1550	2075	3225	4825
ESTEEM—4-Cyl.—Equipment Schedule 6						
W.B. 97.6"; 1.6 Liter, 1.8 Liter.						
GL Sedan 4D	GB31S	13349	1625	2125	3550	5525
GL Wagon 4D	GB31W	13849	1850	2375	3850	5825
GLX Sedan 4D	GB31S	14349	1850	2375	3850	5825
GLX Wagon 4D	GB31W	14849	2100	2650	4100	6125

2001 SUZUKI — (JSor2S)2(AB21H)-1-#

Body Type	VIN	List	Trade-In Fair	Trade-In Good	Pvt-Party Good	Retail Excellent
SWIFT—4-Cyl.—Equipment Schedule 6						
W.B. 93.1"; 1.3 Liter.						
GA Hatchback 2D	AB21H	9729	1675	2200	3400	5125
GL Hatchback 2D	AB21H	10729	1950	2475	3700	5450
ESTEEM—4-Cyl.—Equipment Schedule 6						
W.B. 97.6"; 1.8 Liter.						
GL Sedan 4D	GB41S	13679	2100	2700	4225	6350
GL Wagon 4D	GB41W	14179	2375	2950	4500	6675
GLX Sedan 4D	GB41S	14479	2375	2950	4500	6675
GLX Wagon 4D	GB41W	14979	2625	3250	4825	7000

2002 SUZUKI — JS2(RA41S)-2-#

Body Type	VIN	List	Trade-In Fair	Trade-In Good	Pvt-Party Good	Retail Excellent
AERIO—4-Cyl.—Equipment Schedule 6						
W.B. 97.6"; 2.0 Liter.						
S Sedan 4D	RA41S	13999	4175	4975	6500	8725
GS Sedan 4D	RA41S	14999	4525	5350	6900	9175
SX Wagon 4D	RC41H	14999	4875	5700	7300	9600
ESTEEM—4-Cyl.—Equipment Schedule 6						
W.B. 97.6"; 1.8 Liter.						
GL Sedan 4D	GB41S	13799	2700	3325	5000	7275
GL Wagon 4D	GB41W	14299	2975	3650	5300	7625
GLX Sedan 4D	GB41S	14799	2975	3650	5300	7625
GLX Wagon 4D	GB41W	15299	3275	3925	5625	7975

2003 SUZUKI — JS2(RA41S)-3-#

Body Type	VIN	List	Trade-In Fair	Trade-In Good	Pvt-Party Good	Retail Excellent
AERIO—4-Cyl.—Equipment Schedule 6						
W.B. 97.6"; 2.0 Liter.						
S Sedan 4D	RA41S	14094	4625	5475	6975	9225
GS Sedan 4D	RA41S	15294	5025	5875	7425	9700
SX Wagon 4D	RC41H	15594	5375	6300	7850	10200
AWD			550	550	735	735

220   DEDUCT FOR RECONDITIONING

0105

Body	Type	VIN	List	Trade-In Fair	Good	Pvt-Party Good	Retail Excellent

2004 SUZUKI — JS2orKL5(RA61S)-4-#

AERIO—4-Cyl.—Equipment Schedule 6
W.B. 97.6"; 2.3 Liter.

Body	Type	VIN	List	Fair	Good	Good	Excellent
S Sedan 4D		RA61S	13499	6200	7175	8300	10200
LX Sedan 4D		RA61S	15199	6575	7600	8750	10700
SX Wagon 4D		RC61H	15499	6950	8050	9250	11250
AWD				575	575	765	765

FORENZA—4-Cyl.—Equipment Schedule 3
W.B. 102.4"; 2.0 Liter.

S Sedan 4D		JD52Z	13799	6275	7275	8750	11100
LX Sedan 4D		JJ52Z	15699	6675	7700	9250	11600
EX Sedan 4D		JJ52Z	16499	6900	7950	9525	11950
Manual Trans				(625)	(625)	(835)	(835)

VERONA—6-Cyl.—Equipment Schedule 3
W.B. 106.3"; 2.5 Liter.

S Sedan 4D		VJ52L	16999	9425	10750	12400	15050
LX Sedan 4D		VJ52L	18299	9850	11225	12850	15600
EX Sedan 4D		VM52L	19999	10225	11625	13350	16150

TOYOTA

1990 TOYOTA — (1orJ)T2(EL31M)-L-#

TERCEL—4-Cyl.—Equipment Schedule 6
W.B. 93.7"; 1.5 Liter.

Base Liftback 2D		EL31M	7698	400	575	1075	1925
EZ Liftback 2D		EL36M	6963	325	475	975	1750
Liftback 2D		EL33M	9018	400	575	1075	1925
Coupe 2D		EL31F	9078	400	575	1075	1925
Deluxe Coupe 2D		EL32F	10238	525	750	1325	2250

COROLLA—4-Cyl.—Equipment Schedule 6
W.B. 95.7"; 1.6 Liter.

Sedan 4D		AE91A	10368	700	1000	1675	2800
Deluxe Sedan 4D		AE94A	10988	700	1000	1675	2800
Deluxe Wagon 4D		AE94K	11628	875	1225	2025	3275
Dlx All-Trac Sed 4D		AE94B	12008	800	1125	1875	3075
Dlx All-Trac Wag 4D		AE94M	13088	900	1300	2150	3425
LE Sedan 4D		AE97A	11338	750	1050	1775	2925
SR5 Sport Coupe 2D		AE96J	12688	850	1175	1975	3200
SR5 All-Trac Wag 4D		AE96W	14278	900	1275	2100	3350
GT-S Sport Coupe 2D		AE98J	14278	900	1250	2075	3300

CAMRY—4-Cyl.—Equipment Schedule 4
W.B. 102.4"; 2.0 Liter.

Sedan 4D		SV24E	14143	1000	1450	2475	3950
Deluxe Sedan 4D		SV21E	14732	1050	1500	2575	4075
Deluxe Wagon 4D		SV21W	15432	1150	1600	2700	4250
Dlx All-Trac Sed 4D		SV21J	16722	1275	1750	2850	4450
LE Sedan 4D		SV22E	16113	1225	1675	2775	4350
LE All-Trac Sed 4D		SV22J	18103	1375	1850	2975	4550
V6 2.5 Liter		V		100	100	135	135

CAMRY—V6—Equipment Schedule 4
W.B. 102.4"; 2.5 Liter.

LE Wagon 4D		VV22W	18133	1500	1975	3150	4775

CELICA—4-Cyl.—Equipment Schedule 4
W.B. 99.4"; 1.6 Liter, 2.2 Liter.

ST Sport Coupe 2D		AT86F	13673	1050	1500	2575	4075
GT Sport Coupe 2D		ST87F	15848	1125	1575	2700	4225
GT Liftback 2D		ST87N	16233	1225	1675	2775	4350
GT Convertible 2D		ST87K		1975	2525	3775	5550
GT-S Liftback 2D		ST85N	18258	1525	2050	3225	4875
Auto Trans				100	100	135	135

CELICA 4WD—4-Cyl. Turbo—Equipment Schedule 4
W.B. 99.4"; 2.0 Liter.

All-Trac Liftback 2D		ST88P	22263	1950	2500	3750	5500
Manual Trans				0	0	0	0

SUPRA—6-Cyl.—Equipment Schedule 4
W.B. 102.2"; 3.0 Liter.

Liftback 2D		MA70N	23875	1525	2050	3325	5125
Sport Roof				200	200	265	265
Auto Trans				100	100	135	135

1990 TOYOTA

Body	Type	VIN	List	Trade-In Fair	Trade-In Good	Pvt-Party Good	Retail Excellent
SUPRA—6-Cyl. Turbo—Equipment Schedule 4							
W.B. 102.2"; 3.0 Liter.							
Liftback 2D		MA71N	26215	2200	2775	4200	6175
Sport Roof				200	200	265	265
Auto Trans				100	100	135	135
CRESSIDA—6-Cyl.—Equipment Schedule 4							
W.B. 105.5"; 3.0 Liter.							
Luxury Sedan 4D		MX83E	21763	1500	2025	3250	4975

1991 TOYOTA — (1,4orJ)T(1,2orX)(EL46B)–M–#

Body	Type	VIN	List	Trade-In Fair	Trade-In Good	Pvt-Party Good	Retail Excellent
TERCEL—4-Cyl.—Equipment Schedule 6							
W.B. 93.7"; 1.5 Liter.							
Sedan 2D		EL46B	7728	450	625	1200	2100
DX Sedan 2D		EL43B	9288	600	850	1500	2575
DX Sedan 4D		EL43A	9388	675	925	1625	2750
LE Sedan 4D		EL44A	10878	675	925	1625	2750
COROLLA—4-Cyl.—Equipment Schedule 6							
W.B. 95.7"; 1.6 Liter.							
Sedan 4D		AE91A	10508	775	1100	1850	3025
Deluxe Sedan 4D		AE94A	11508	800	1125	1925	3150
Deluxe Wagon 4D		AE94K	12178	975	1400	2400	3875
Dlx All-Trac Wag 4D		AE94V	13878	1025	1475	2525	4000
LE Sedan 4D		AE97A	12477	850	1200	2050	3300
SR5 Sport Coupe 2D		AE96J	13048	925	1325	2225	3575
GT-S Sport Coupe 2D		AE98J	14638	975	1425	2425	3900
CAMRY—4-Cyl.—Equipment Schedule 4							
W.B. 102.4"; 2.0 Liter.							
Sedan 4D		SV24E	14513	1225	1675	2775	4375
Deluxe Sedan 4D		SV21E	15127	1300	1775	2900	4500
Deluxe Wagon 4D		SV21W	15837	1400	1900	3025	4650
Dlx All-Trac Sed 4D		SV21J	17107	1525	2050	3225	4900
LE Sedan 4D		SV22E	16242	1475	1950	3125	4775
LE All-Trac Sed 4D		SV22J	18232	1650	2150	3350	5075
Manual Trans				(175)	(175)	(235)	(235)
V6 2.5 Liter		V		150	150	200	200
CAMRY—V6—Equipment Schedule 4							
W.B. 102.4"; 2.5 Liter.							
LE Wagon 4D		VV22W	18483	1800	2325	3550	5275
MR2—4-Cyl.—Equipment Schedule 4							
W.B. 94.5"; 2.2 Liter.							
Coupe 2D		SW21M	16848	1375	1850	3000	4650
MR2—4-Cyl. Turbo—Equipment Schedule 6							
W.B. 94.5"; 2.0 Liter.							
Coupe 2D		SW22M	20178	1875	2400	3675	5475
CELICA—4-Cyl.—Equipment Schedule 4							
W.B. 99.4"; 1.6 Liter, 2.2 Liter.							
ST Sport Coupe 2D		AT86F	14323	1300	1775	2925	4550
GT Sport Coupe 2D		ST87F	16328	1375	1875	3050	4725
GT Liftback 2D		ST87N	16713	1475	1950	3175	4850
GT Convertible 2D		ST87K	21188	2325	2900	4275	6200
GT-S Liftback 2D		ST85N	18553	1825	2350	3625	5375
Auto Trans				100	100	135	135
CELICA AWD—4-Cyl. Turbo—Equipment Schedule 4							
W.B. 99.4"; 2.0 Liter.							
All-Trac Liftback 2D		ST88P	22673	2325	2900	4275	6175
SUPRA—6-Cyl.—Equipment Schedule 4							
W.B. 102.2"; 3.0 Liter.							
Liftback 2D		MA70M	24845	1850	2375	3800	5750
Auto Trans				100	100	135	135
SUPRA—6-Cyl. Turbo—Equipment Schedule 4							
W.B. 102.2"; 3.0 Liter.							
Liftback 2D		MA71M	28315	2575	3200	4725	6900
Sport Roof		N		225	225	300	300
Auto Trans				100	100	135	135
CRESSIDA—6-Cyl.—Equipment Schedule 4							
W.B. 105.5"; 3.0 Liter.							
Luxury Sedan 4D		MX83E	22473	1800	2325	3625	5450

1992 TOYOTA — (1,4orJ)(NorT)(1,2orX)(EL46B)–N

Body	Type	VIN	List	Trade-In Fair	Trade-In Good	Pvt-Party Good	Retail Excellent
TERCEL—4-Cyl.—Equipment Schedule 6							
W.B. 93.7"; 1.5 Liter.							
Sedan 2D		EL46B	8303	475	700	1325	2300
DX Sedan 2D		EL43B	9983	675	925	1675	2850

222   **DEDUCT FOR RECONDITIONING**

Body Type	VIN	List	Trade-In Fair	Trade-In Good	Pvt-Party Good	Retail Excellent
DX Sedan 4D	EL43A	10083	750	1050	1850	3100
LE Sedan 4D	EL44A	11253	775	1075	1900	3150
PASEO—4-Cyl.—Equipment Schedule 6						
W.B. 93.7"; 1.5 Liter.						
Coupe 2D	EL45F	11433	875	1225	2100	3400
COROLLA—4-Cyl.—Equipment Schedule 6						
W.B. 95.7"; 1.6 Liter.						
Sedan 4D	AE91A	11123	850	1175	2025	3300
Deluxe Sedan 4D	AE94A	12113	900	1300	2225	3600
Deluxe Wagon 4D	AE94K	12653	1150	1600	2725	4300
Dlx All-Trac Wag 4D	AE94V	14393	1225	1700	2825	4425
LE Sedan 4D	AE97A	13713	975	1425	2475	3975
CAMRY—4-Cyl.—Equipment Schedule 4						
W.B. 103.1"; 2.2 Liter.						
Deluxe Sedan 4D	SK11E	16713	1275	1750	3075	4900
Deluxe Wagon 4D	SK11V	18443	1500	2025	3375	5275
LE Sedan 4D	SK12E	17293	1375	1850	3175	5025
LE Wagon 4D	SK12V	19093	1550	2075	3450	5350
XLE Sedan 4D	SK13E	19143	1450	1925	3300	5125
Manual Trans			(225)	(225)	(300)	(300)
V6 3.0 Liter	V		225	225	300	300
CAMRY—V6—Equipment Schedule 4						
W.B. 103.1"; 3.0 Liter.						
SE Sedan 4D	VK14E	20538	1800	2325	3750	5700
Manual Trans			(225)	(225)	(300)	(300)
MR2—4-Cyl.—Equipment Schedule 6						
W.B. 94.5"; 2.2 Liter.						
Coupe 2D	SW21M	17813	1675	2200	3425	5150
MR2—4-Cyl. Turbo—Equipment Schedule 6						
W.B. 94.5"; 2.0 Liter.						
Coupe 2D	SW22M	21143	2300	2875	4225	6125
CELICA—4-Cyl.—Equipment Schedule 4						
W.B. 99.4"; 1.6 Liter, 2.2 Liter.						
ST Sport Coupe 2D	AT86F	15063	1575	2100	3300	5050
GT Sport Coupe 2D	ST87F	17733	1700	2225	3475	5225
GT Liftback 2D	ST87N	17818	1800	2325	3575	5350
GT Convertible 2D	ST87K	22313	2775	3400	4850	6900
GT-S Liftback 2D	ST85N	19353	2100	2700	4000	5850
Auto Trans			125	125	165	165
CELICA AWD—4-Cyl. Turbo—Equipment Schedule 4						
W.B. 99.4"; 2.0 Liter.						
All-Trac Liftback 2D	ST88P	23393	2750	3375	4825	6850
SUPRA—6-Cyl.—Equipment Schedule 4						
W.B. 102.2"; 3.0 Liter.						
Liftback 2D	MA70M	25575	2300	2875	4425	6500
Auto Trans			125	125	165	165
SUPRA—6-Cyl. Turbo—Equipment Schedule 4						
W.B. 102.2"; 3.0 Liter.						
Liftback 2D	MA71M	29045	3150	3825	5500	7800
Sport Roof			250	250	335	335
Auto Trans			125	125	165	165
CRESSIDA—6-Cyl.—Equipment Schedule 4						
W.B. 105.5"; 3.0 Liter.						
Luxury Sedan 4D	MX83E	23783	2100	2675	4025	5950

1993 TOYOTA — (1,4orJ)(NorT)(1,2orX)(EL46S)-P-#

Body Type	VIN	List	Trade-In Fair	Trade-In Good	Pvt-Party Good	Retail Excellent
TERCEL—4-Cyl.—Equipment Schedule 6						
W.B. 93.7"; 1.5 Liter.						
Sedan 2D	EL46S	9223	550	800	1500	2600
DX Sedan 2D	EL43S	11313	775	1075	1950	3250
DX Sedan 4D	EL43T	11413	875	1225	2125	3525
LE Sedan 4D	EL44T	12473	900	1250	2175	3575
PASEO—4-Cyl.—Equipment Schedule 6						
W.B. 93.7"; 1.5 Liter.						
Coupe 2D	EL45U	12663	975	1425	2475	3975
COROLLA—4-Cyl.—Equipment Schedule 6						
W.B. 97.0"; 1.6 Liter, 1.8 Liter.						
Sedan 4D	AE04E	12983	1075	1525	2600	4100
Deluxe Sedan 4D	AE09E	13823	1275	1750	2850	4450
Deluxe Wagon 4D	AE09W	14503	1650	2150	3325	5025
LE Sedan 4D	AE00E	15543	1425	1900	3050	4675
CAMRY—4-Cyl.—Equipment Schedule 4						
W.B. 103.2"; 2.2 Liter.						

0105

1993 TOYOTA

Body	Type	VIN	List	Trade-In Fair	Trade-In Good	Pvt-Party Good	Retail Excellent
Deluxe Sedan 4D		SK11E	17578	1500	2025	3450	5425
Deluxe Wagon 4D		SK11W	18908	1800	2325	3850	5875
LE Sedan 4D		SK12E	18233	1625	2125	3575	5575
LE Wagon 4D		SK12W	19553	1875	2400	3900	5975
XLE Sedan 4D		SK13E	20203	1700	2225	3700	5700
Manual Trans				(275)	(275)	(365)	(365)
V6 3.0 Liter		V		275	275	365	365

CAMRY—V6—Equipment Schedule 4
W.B. 103.2"; 3.0 Liter.

Body	Type	VIN	List	Trade-In Fair	Trade-In Good	Pvt-Party Good	Retail Excellent
SE Sedan 4D		VK14E	21188	2100	2700	4225	6325
Manual Trans				(275)	(275)	(365)	(365)

MR2—4-Cyl.—Equipment Schedule 6
W.B. 94.5"; 2.2 Liter.

| Coupe 2D | | SW21M | 20208 | 2075 | 2625 | 3900 | 5750 |

MR2—4-Cyl. Turbo—Equipment Schedule 6
W.B. 94.5"; 2.0 Liter.

| Coupe 2D | | SW22M | 24923 | 2775 | 3400 | 4825 | 6850 |

CELICA—4-Cyl.—Equipment Schedule 4
W.B. 99.4"; 1.6 Liter, 2.2 Liter.

ST Sport Coupe 2D		AT86F	15983	1925	2450	3775	5625
GT Sport Coupe 2D		ST87F	18108	2075	2625	3925	5800
GT Liftback 2D		ST87N	18333	2125	2700	4050	5925
GT Convertible 2D		ST87K	23903	3300	3950	5500	7675
GT-S Liftback 2D		ST85N	20863	2450	3050	4450	6375
Auto Trans				150	150	200	200

CELICA AWD—4-Cyl. Turbo—Equipment Schedule 4
W.B. 99.4"; 2.0 Liter.

| All-Trac Liftback 2D | | ST88P | 28623 | 3500 | 4200 | 5775 | 8025 |

SUPRA—6-Cyl.—Equipment Schedule 4
W.B. 100.4"; 3.0 Liter.

Liftback 2D		JA81L	34225	6875	7925	10100	13150
Sport Roof		J		275	275	365	365
Auto Trans				150	150	200	200

SUPRA—6-Cyl. Turbo—Equipment Schedule 4
W.B. 100.4"; 3.0 Liter.

Liftback 2D		JA82L	40225	10500	11950	14650	18600
Sport Roof		J		275	275	365	365
6-Spd Manual Trans				375	375	500	500

1994 TOYOTA — (1,4orJ)(NorT)(1,2orX)(EL46S)-R-#

TERCEL—4-Cyl.—Equipment Schedule 6
W.B. 93.7"; 1.5 Liter.

Body	Type	VIN	List	Trade-In Fair	Trade-In Good	Pvt-Party Good	Retail Excellent
Sedan 2D		EL46S	10223	650	900	1700	2925
DX Sedan 2D		EL43S	12028	900	1250	2200	3650
DX Sedan 4D		EL43T	12028	975	1425	2525	4075

PASEO—4-Cyl.—Equipment Schedule 6
W.B. 93.7"; 1.5 Liter.

| Coupe 2D | | EL45U | 13753 | 1150 | 1600 | 2750 | 4350 |

COROLLA—4-Cyl.—Equipment Schedule 6
W.B. 97.0"; 1.6 Liter, 1.8 Liter.

Sedan 4D		AE04B	13308	1225	1700	2825	4425
DX Sedan 4D		AE09B	14998	1500	2025	3200	4850
DX Wagon 4D		AE09V	15553	1950	2500	3750	5525
LE Sedan 4D		AE00B	18113	1700	2225	3425	5150

CAMRY—4-Cyl.—Equipment Schedule 4
W.B. 103.1"; 2.2 Liter.

DX Sedan 4D		SK11E	19293	1825	2350	3900	6000
DX Coupe 2D		SK11C	18963	1500	2000	3475	5500
DX Wagon 4D		SK11W	20703	2150	2725	4325	6500
LE Sedan 4D		SK12E	19613	1950	2500	4050	6175
LE Coupe 2D		SK12C	19323	1650	2150	3675	5725
LE Wagon 4D		SK12W	21003	2250	2800	4425	6625
XLE Sedan 4D		SK13E	21643	2050	2600	4150	6300
Manual Trans				(325)	(325)	(435)	(435)
V6 3.0 Liter		G		325	325	435	435

CAMRY—V6—Equipment Schedule 4
W.B. 103.1"; 3.0 Liter.

| SE Sedan 4D | | GK14E | 22913 | 2525 | 3125 | 4750 | 7000 |
| SE Coupe 2D | | GK14C | 22623 | 2250 | 2800 | 4425 | 6625 |

MR2—4-Cyl.—Equipment Schedule 6
W.B. 94.5"; 2.2 Liter.

| Coupe 2D | | SW21M | 23613 | 3050 | 3700 | 5125 | 7200 |

224   DEDUCT FOR RECONDITIONING

0105

1994 TOYOTA

Body	Type	VIN	List	Trade-In Fair	Trade-In Good	Pvt-Party Good	Retail Excellent
MR2—4-Cyl. Turbo—Equipment Schedule 6							
W.B. 94.5"; 2.0 Liter.							
Coupe 2D		SW22M	28663	3875	4600	6200	8425
CELICA—4-Cyl.—Equipment Schedule 4							
W.B. 99.9"; 1.8 Liter, 2.2 Liter.							
ST Sport Coupe 2D		AT00F	18628	2275	2850	4250	6175
ST Liftback 2D		AT00N	18968	2500	3100	4500	6475
GT Sport Coupe 2D		ST07F	20053	2525	3125	4500	6500
GT Liftback 2D		ST07N	20523	2600	3225	4625	6625
Auto Trans				175	175	235	235
SUPRA—6-Cyl.—Equipment Schedule 4							
W.B. 100.4"; 3.0 Liter.							
Liftback 2D		JA81L	36185	8025	9200	11450	14750
Sport Roof		J		300	300	400	400
Auto Trans				175	175	235	235
SUPRA—6-Cyl. Turbo—Equipment Schedule 4							
W.B. 100.4"; 3.0 Liter.							
Liftback 2D		JA82L	43185	12050	13625	16450	20600
Sport Roof		J		300	300	400	400
6-Spd Manual Trans				400	400	535	535

1995 TOYOTA — (1,4orJ)(NorT)(1,2,5orX)(EL55D)-S

Body	Type	VIN	List	Trade-In Fair	Trade-In Good	Pvt-Party Good	Retail Excellent
TERCEL—4-Cyl.—Equipment Schedule 6							
W.B. 93.7"; 1.5 Liter.							
Sedan 2D		EL55D	11535	1025	1475	2625	4225
DX Sedan 2D		EL56D	12685	1375	1875	3075	4775
DX Sedan 4D		EL56E	13125	1550	2075	3300	5050
PASEO—4-Cyl.—Equipment Schedule 6							
W.B. 93.7"; 1.5 Liter.							
Coupe 2D		EL45U	14725	1400	1875	3075	4725
COROLLA—4-Cyl.—Equipment Schedule 6							
W.B. 97.0"; 1.6 Liter, 1.8 Liter.							
Sedan 4D		AE04B	13782	1475	1950	3150	4825
DX Sedan 4D		AE09B	15552	1800	2325	3600	5350
DX Wagon 4D		AE09V	16527	2275	2850	4175	6050
LE Sedan 4D		AE00B	17075	2025	2575	3850	5675
CAMRY—4-Cyl.—Equipment Schedule 4							
W.B. 103.1"; 2.2 Liter.							
DX Sedan 4D		SK11E	19815	2175	2750	4400	6650
DX Coupe 2D		SK11C	19430	1800	2325	3925	6075
LE Sedan 4D		SK12E	19955	2300	2875	4550	6825
LE Coupe 2D		SK12C	19665	1975	2525	4150	6325
LE Wagon 4D		SK12W	21365	2650	3250	4975	7325
XLE Sedan 4D		SK13E	22015	2400	3000	4675	6950
Manual Trans				(375)	(375)	(500)	(500)
V6 3.0 Liter		G		375	375	500	500
CAMRY—V6—Equipment Schedule 4							
W.B. 103.1"; 3.0 Liter.							
SE Sedan 4D		GK14E	23895	2925	3575	5325	7725
SE Coupe 2D		GK14C	23605	2650	3250	4975	7325
MR2—4-Cyl.—Equipment Schedule 6							
W.B. 94.5"; 2.2 Liter.							
Coupe 2D		SW21M	24655	3575	4300	5800	8000
MR2—4-Cyl. Turbo—Equipment Schedule 6							
W.B. 94.5"; 2.0 Liter.							
Coupe 2D		SW22N	29755	4500	5325	6975	9350
CELICA—4-Cyl.—Equipment Schedule 6							
W.B. 99.9"; 1.8 Liter, 2.2 Liter.							
ST Sport Coupe 2D		AT00F	19410	2700	3300	4775	6850
ST Liftback 2D		AT00N	19760	2925	3575	5100	7200
GT Sport Coupe 2D		ST07F	20925	2950	3600	5100	7225
GT Liftback 2D		ST07N	21415	3025	3700	5200	7350
GT Convertible 2D		ST07K	25635	4475	5250	6950	9400
Auto Trans				200	200	265	265
AVALON—V6—Equipment Schedule 4							
W.B. 107.1"; 3.0 Liter.							
XL Sedan 4D		GB10E	23155	2675	3275	4850	7025
XLS Sedan 4D		GB11E	27085	3700	4425	6175	8650
SUPRA—6-Cyl.—Equipment Schedule 4							
W.B. 100.4"; 3.0 Liter.							
SE Liftback 2D		JA81L	31497	8575	9800	12100	15400
Liftback 2D		JA81L	37297	9150	10425	12800	16250
Sport Roof		J		325	325	435	435

0105

EQUIPMENT & MILEAGE PAGE 9 TO 23   225

Body	Type	VIN	List	Trade-In Fair	Trade-In Good	Pvt-Party Good	Retail Excellent
Auto Trans				200	200	265	265
SUPRA—6-Cyl. Turbo—Equipment Schedule 4							
W.B. 100.4"; 3.0 Liter.							
Liftback 2D		JA82L	46997	13525	15300	18250	22700
Sport Roof		J		325	325	435	435
6-Spd Manual Trans				425	425	565	565

1996 TOYOTA — (4T,JTor1N)(1,2,5orX)(AC52L)–T–#

Body	Type	VIN	List	Trade-In Fair	Trade-In Good	Pvt-Party Good	Retail Excellent
TERCEL—4-Cyl.—Equipment Schedule 6							
W.B. 93.7"; 1.5 Liter.							
Sedan 2D		AC52L	11981	1225	1700	2950	4650
DX Sedan 2D		AC52L	13458	1650	2150	3425	5225
DX Sedan 4D		BC52L	13768	1850	2375	3700	5550
PASEO—4-Cyl.—Equipment Schedule 6							
W.B. 93.7"; 1.5 Liter.							
Coupe 2D		CC52H	14383	1650	2175	3425	5175
COROLLA—4-Cyl.—Equipment Schedule 6							
W.B. 97.0"; 1.6 Liter, 1.8 Liter.							
Sedan 4D		BA02E	14538	1700	2225	3450	5200
DX Sedan 4D		BB02E	15448	2100	2700	3975	5800
DX Wagon 4D		EB02E	16598	2650	3250	4625	6575
CAMRY—4-Cyl.—Equipment Schedule 6							
W.B. 103.1"; 2.2 Liter.							
DX Sedan 4D		BG12K	19848	2600	3225	5000	7400
DX Coupe 2D		CG12K	19458	2175	2750	4475	6775
LE Sedan 4D		BG12K	20588	2700	3325	5125	7550
LE Coupe 2D		CG12K	20298	2375	2950	4700	7050
LE Wagon 4D		EG12K	22028	3100	3750	5600	8100
XLE Sedan 4D		BG12K	22698	2825	3475	5275	7725
Manual Trans				(400)	(400)	(535)	(535)
V6 3.0 Liter		F		425	425	565	565
CAMRY—V6—Equipment Schedule 4							
W.B. 103.1"; 3.0 Liter.							
SE Sedan 4D		BF12K	24538	3400	4100	5975	8550
SE Coupe 2D		CF12K	24248	3100	3750	5600	8100
CELICA—4-Cyl.—Equipment Schedule 4							
W.B. 99.9"; 1.8 Liter, 2.2 Liter.							
ST Sport Coupe 2D		CB02T	19638	3150	3825	5400	7600
ST Liftback 2D		DB02T	19998	3425	4125	5725	8000
GT Sport Coupe 2D		CG02T	21183	3450	4150	5750	8050
GT Liftback 2D		DG02T	21693	3550	4250	5875	8150
GT Convertible 2D		FG02T	25893	5100	5975	7775	10350
Auto Trans				200	200	265	265
AVALON—V6—Equipment Schedule 4							
W.B. 107.1"; 3.0 Liter.							
XL Sedan 4D		BF12B	23838	3150	3800	5500	7825
XLS Sedan 4D		BF12B	27868	4250	5050	6900	9550
SUPRA—6-Cyl.—Equipment Schedule 4							
W.B. 100.4"; 3.0 Liter.							
Liftback 2D		DD82A	39020	10425	11850	14300	17950
Sport Roof				350	350	465	465
Auto Trans				200	200	265	265
SUPRA—6-Cyl. Turbo—Equipment Schedule 4							
W.B. 100.4"; 3.0 Liter.							
Liftback 2D		DE82A	50820	15225	17125	20200	24800

1997 TOYOTA—(4T,JTor1N)(1,2,5orX)(AC52L)–V–#

Body	Type	VIN	List	Trade-In Fair	Trade-In Good	Pvt-Party Good	Retail Excellent
TERCEL—4-Cyl.—Equipment Schedule 6							
W.B. 93.7"; 1.5 Liter.							
CE Sedan 2D		AC52L	12508	2050	2600	3900	5725
CE Sedan 4D		BC52L	13968	2350	2925	4275	6150
Limited Edition				25	25	35	35
PASEO—4-Cyl.—Equipment Schedule 6							
W.B. 93.7"; 1.5 Liter.							
Coupe 2D		CC52H	14553	2025	2575	3850	5675
Convertible 2D		FC52H	18073	3000	3675	5075	7050
COROLLA—4-Cyl.—Equipment Schedule 6							
W.B. 97.0"; 1.6 Liter, 1.8 Liter.							
Sedan 4D		BA02E	15028	2025	2575	3875	5700
CE Sedan 4D		BA02E	15063	2225	2775	4125	6000
DX Sedan 4D		BB02E	16445	2500	3100	4475	6375
CAMRY—4-Cyl.—Equipment Schedule 4							
W.B. 105.1"; 2.2 Liter.							

1997 TOYOTA

Body	Type	VIN	List	Trade-In Fair	Good	Pvt-Party Good	Retail Excellent
CE Sedan 4D		BG22K	19918	3550	4250	5500	7350
LE Sedan 4D		BG22K	20288	3675	4400	5650	7500
XLE Sedan 4D		BG22K	22228	3825	4550	5825	7725
Manual Trans				(425)	(425)	(565)	(565)
V6 3.0 Liter		F		475	475	635	635
CELICA—4-Cyl.—Equipment Schedule 4							
W.B. 99.9"; 1.8 Liter, 2.2 Liter.							
ST Sport Coupe 2D		CB02T	19703	3725	4450	6125	8500
ST Liftback 2D		DB02T	20063	4000	4750	6475	8900
GT Liftback 2D		DG02T	21893	4150	4925	6650	9100
GT Convertible 2D		FG02T	26093	5800	6775	8675	11400
Auto Trans				200	200	265	265
AVALON—V6—Equipment Schedule 4							
W.B. 107.1"; 3.0 Liter.							
XL Sedan 4D		BF12B	23958	3700	4425	6250	8750
XLS Sedan 4D		BF12B	27468	4900	5725	7775	10600
SUPRA—6-Cyl.—Equipment Schedule 4							
W.B. 100.4"; 3.0 Liter.							
Ltd Edition LBack 2D		DD82A	30340	11700	13250	15800	19600
Sport Roof		P		375	375	500	500
Auto Trans				200	200	265	265
SUPRA—6-Cyl. Turbo—Equipment Schedule 4							
W.B. 100.4"; 3.0 Liter.							
Ltd Edition L'Back 2D		DE82A	39040	18200	20450	23500	28400
6-Spd Manual Trans				475	475	635	635

1998 TOYOTA–(4T,JTor1N)(1,2,5orX)(AC52L)–W–#

Body	Type	VIN	List	Trade-In Fair	Good	Pvt-Party Good	Retail Excellent
TERCEL—4-Cyl.—Equipment Schedule 6							
W.B. 93.7"; 1.5 Liter.							
CE Sedan 4D		AC52L	13110	2425	3025	4375	6300
COROLLA—4-Cyl.—Equipment Schedule 6							
W.B. 97.0"; 1.8 Liter.							
VE Sedan 4D		BR12E	13443	2450	3050	4300	6075
CE Sedan 4D		BR12E	14208	2700	3325	4600	6425
LE Sedan 4D		BR12E	15218	3000	3675	4950	6825
CAMRY—4-Cyl.—Equipment Schedule 4							
W.B. 105.2"; 2.2 Liter.							
CE Sedan 4D		BG22K	20464	4200	5000	6300	8225
LE Sedan 4D		BG22K	20858	4325	5100	6425	8400
XLE Sedan 4D		BG22K	23279	4500	5325	6650	8675
Manual Trans				(450)	(450)	(600)	(600)
V6 3.0 Liter		F		525	525	700	700
CELICA—4-Cyl.—Equipment Schedule 4							
W.B. 99.9"; 2.2 Liter.							
GT Sport Coupe 2D		CG02T	20531	4400	5175	6950	9475
GT Liftback 2D		DG02T	21701	4725	5550	7375	9925
GT Convertible 2D		FG02T	24970	6525	7550	9525	12400
Auto Trans				200	200	265	265
AVALON—V6—Equipment Schedule 4							
W.B. 107.1"; 3.0 Liter.							
XL Sedan 4D		BF18B	24698	4375	5150	7000	9575
XLS Sedan 4D		BF18B	28548	5650	6575	8625	11500
SUPRA—6-Cyl.—Equipment Schedule 4							
W.B. 100.4"; 3.0 Liter.							
Liftback 2D		DD82A	31338	13200	14875	17450	21400
Sport Roof		P		425	425	565	565
SUPRA—6-Cyl. Turbo—Equipment Schedule 4							
W.B. 100.4"; 3.0 Liter.							
Liftback 2D		DE82A	40728	20150	22650	25800	31000
6-Spd Manual Trans				500	500	665	665

1999 TOYOTA–(J,1,2or4)(NorT)(X,1,2or5)(BR12E)–X

Body	Type	VIN	List	Trade-In Fair	Good	Pvt-Party Good	Retail Excellent
COROLLA—4-Cyl.—Equipment Schedule 6							
W.B. 97.0"; 1.8 Liter.							
VE Sedan 4D		BR12E	13588	2925	3575	4875	6750
CE Sedan 4D		BR12E	14278	3250	3900	5225	7150
LE Sedan 4D		BR12E	15288	3575	4275	5650	7600
CAMRY—4-Cyl.—Equipment Schedule 4							
W.B. 105.2"; 2.2 Liter.							
CE Sedan 4D		BG22K	19444	5000	5850	7175	9225
LE Sedan 4D		BG22K	20218	5125	6000	7350	9400
XLE Sedan 4D		BG22K	23178	5375	6300	7650	9750
Manual Trans				(500)	(500)	(665)	(665)

1999 TOYOTA

Body	Type	VIN	List	Trade-In Fair	Trade-In Good	Pvt-Party Good	Retail Excellent
V6 3.0 Liter		F		600	600	800	800
SOLARA—4-Cyl.—Equipment Schedule 4							
W.B. 105.1"; 2.2 Liter.							
SE Coupe 2D		CG22P	19858	4725	5550	7125	9425
Manual Trans				(500)	(500)	(665)	(665)
V6 3.0 Liter		F		600	600	800	800
SOLARA—V6—Equipment Schedule 4							
W.B. 105.1"; 3.0 Liter.							
SLE Coupe 2D		CF22P	25408	6025	6975	8700	11200
CELICA—4-Cyl.—Equipment Schedule 4							
W.B. 99.9"; 2.2 Liter.							
GT Liftback 2D		DG02T	22240	5575	6475	8400	11150
GT Convertible 2D		FG02T	25319	7600	8725	10850	13900
Auto Trans				225	225	300	300
AVALON—V6—Equipment Schedule 4							
W.B. 107.1"; 3.0 Liter.							
XL Sedan 4D		BF18B	24988	5200	6100	8100	10900
XLS Sedan 4D		BF18B	28998	6675	7725	9925	13100

2000 TOYOTA—(J,1,2or4)(NorT)(X,1,2or5)(BT123)—Y

Body	Type	VIN	List	Trade-In Fair	Trade-In Good	Pvt-Party Good	Retail Excellent
ECHO—4-Cyl.—Equipment Schedule 6							
W.B. 93.3"; 1.5 Liter.							
Sedan 4D		BT123	11945	3800	4525	5775	7650
Coupe 2D		AT123	11645	3575	4275	5500	7350
COROLLA—4-Cyl.—Equipment Schedule 6							
W.B. 97.0"; 1.8 Liter.							
VE Sedan 4D		BR12E	13603	3475	4175	5525	7500
CE Sedan 4D		BR12E	14653	3850	4575	5925	7950
LE Sedan 4D		BR12E	15523	4200	5000	6375	8450
CAMRY—4-Cyl.—Equipment Schedule 4							
W.B. 105.2"; 2.2 Liter.							
CE Sedan 4D		BG22K	19820	5875	6850	8175	10300
LE Sedan 4D		BG22K	20743	6050	7000	8400	10550
XLE Sedan 4D		BG22K	24423	6325	7350	8700	10900
Manual Trans				(525)	(525)	(700)	(700)
V6 3.0 Liter		F		675	675	900	900
SOLARA—4-Cyl.—Equipment Schedule 4							
W.B. 105.1"; 2.2 Liter.							
SE Coupe 2D		CG22P	20193	5550	6450	8100	10550
SE Convertible 2D		FG22P	25523	7350	8450	10200	12900
Manual Trans				(525)	(525)	(700)	(700)
V6 3.0 Liter		F		675	675	900	900
SOLARA—V6—Equipment Schedule 4							
W.B. 105.1"; 3.0 Liter.							
SLE Coupe 2D		CF22P	26293	7000	8100	9850	12500
SLE Convertible 2D		FF22P	30943	8850	10125	12000	14950
MR2 SPYDER—4-Cyl.—Equipment Schedule 4							
W.B. 96.5"; 1.8 Liter.							
Convertible 2D		FG320	23553	7950	9125	11050	13900
CELICA—4-Cyl.—Equipment Schedule 4							
W.B. 102.3"; 1.8 Liter.							
GT Liftback 2D		DR32T	17970	6450	7475	9025	11400
GT-S Liftback 2D		DY32T	21620	7575	8700	10350	12900
Auto Trans				250	250	335	335
AVALON—V6—Equipment Schedule 4							
W.B. 107.1"; 3.0 Liter.							
XL Sedan 4D		BF28B	25650	8975	10275	12150	15050
XLS Sedan 4D		BF28B	30210	10600	12100	14200	17500

2001 TOYOTA—(J,1,2or4)(NorT)(D,X,1or2)(BT123)—1

Body	Type	VIN	List	Trade-In Fair	Trade-In Good	Pvt-Party Good	Retail Excellent
ECHO—4-Cyl.—Equipment Schedule 6							
W.B. 93.3"; 1.5 Liter.							
Sedan 4D		BT123	11930	4475	5275	6575	8575
Coupe 2D		AT123	11400	4225	5025	6300	8250
COROLLA—4-Cyl.—Equipment Schedule 6							
W.B. 97.0"; 1.8 Liter.							
CE Sedan 4D		BR12E	13753	4650	5500	6875	8950
S Sedan 4D		BR12E	14343	5000	5850	7250	9375
LE Sedan 4D		BR12E	14863	5075	5950	7350	9475
PRIUS—4-Cyl. HYBRID—Equipment Schedule 3							
W.B. 100.4"; 1.5 Liter.							
Sedan 4D		BK12U	20450	9175	10475	12100	14700

0105

2001 TOYOTA

Body	Type	VIN	List	Trade-In Fair	Good	Pvt-Party Good	Retail Excellent
CAMRY—4-Cyl.—Equipment Schedule 4							
W.B. 105.1"; 2.2 Liter.							
CE Sedan 4D		BG22K	19733	**6900**	**7975**	**9375**	**11600**
LE Sedan 4D		BG22K	20895	**7100**	**8175**	**9600**	**11850**
XLE Sedan 4D		BG22K	24575	**7425**	**8550**	**9975**	**12300**
Manual Trans				**(550)**	**(550)**	**(735)**	**(735)**
V6 3.0 Liter		F		**750**	**750**	**1000**	**1000**
SOLARA—4-Cyl.—Equipment Schedule 4							
W.B. 105.1"; 2.2 Liter.							
SE Coupe 2D		CG22P	20245	**6525**	**7525**	**9275**	**11850**
SE Convertible 2D		FG22P	25575	**8525**	**9750**	**11600**	**14450**
Manual Trans				**(550)**	**(550)**	**(735)**	**(735)**
V6 3.0 Liter		F		**750**	**750**	**1000**	**1000**
SOLARA—V6—Equipment Schedule 4							
W.B. 105.1"; 3.0 Liter.							
SLE Coupe 2D		CF22P	25645	**8125**	**9325**	**11200**	**14000**
SLE Convertible 2D		FF22P	30995	**10175**	**11575**	**13550**	**16600**
MR2 SPYDER—4-Cyl.—Equipment Schedule 4							
W.B. 96.5"; 1.8 Liter.							
Convertible 2D		FG320	24065	**9175**	**10475**	**12550**	**15600**
CELICA—4-Cyl.—Equipment Schedule 4							
W.B. 102.3"; 1.8 Liter.							
GT Liftback 2D		DR32T	18285	**7550**	**8700**	**10300**	**12850**
GT-S Liftback 2D		DY32T	21935	**8850**	**10125**	**11850**	**14550**
Auto Trans				**275**	**275**	**365**	**365**
AVALON—V6—Equipment Schedule 4							
W.B. 107.1"; 3.0 Liter.							
XL Sedan 4D		BF28B	26325	**10375**	**11800**	**13800**	**16950**
XLS Sedan 4D		BF28B	30885	**12250**	**13875**	**16100**	**19600**

2002 TOYOTA—(J,1,2or4)(NorT)(D,X,1or2)(BT123)—2

Body	Type	VIN	List	Trade-In Fair	Good	Pvt-Party Good	Retail Excellent
ECHO—4-Cyl.—Equipment Schedule 6							
W.B. 93.3"; 1.5 Liter.							
Sedan 4D		BT123	12265	**5250**	**6150**	**7500**	**9600**
Coupe 2D		AT123	11675	**5000**	**5850**	**7200**	**9275**
COROLLA—4-Cyl.—Equipment Schedule 6							
W.B. 97.0"; 1.8 Liter.							
CE Sedan 4D		BR12E	13533	**5425**	**6325**	**7775**	**9975**
S Sedan 4D		BR12E	14073	**5775**	**6750**	**8200**	**10450**
LE Sedan 4D		BR12E	14443	**5875**	**6850**	**8300**	**10550**
PRIUS—4-Cyl. HYBRID—Equipment Schedule 3							
W.B. 100.4"; 1.5 Liter.							
Sedan 4D		BK12U	20480	**10425**	**11850**	**13500**	**16200**
CAMRY—4-Cyl.—Equipment Schedule 4							
W.B. 107.1"; 2.4 Liter.							
LE Sedan 4D		BE32K	20285	**9375**	**10700**	**12000**	**14250**
SE Sedan 4D		BE32K	21625	**9600**	**10950**	**12250**	**14500**
XLE Sedan 4D		BF32K	22780	**9975**	**11325**	**12650**	**15000**
Manual Trans				**(575)**	**(575)**	**(765)**	**(765)**
V6 3.0 Liter		F		**825**	**825**	**1100**	**1100**
SOLARA—4-Cyl.—Equipment Schedule 4							
W.B. 105.1"; 2.4 Liter.							
SE Coupe 2D		CE22P	20650	**7625**	**8750**	**10600**	**13350**
SE Convertible 2D		FE22P	25980	**9800**	**11175**	**13100**	**16150**
Manual Trans				**(575)**	**(575)**	**(765)**	**(765)**
V6 3.0 Liter		F		**825**	**825**	**1100**	**1100**
SOLARA—V6—Equipment Schedule 4							
W.B. 105.1"; 3.0 Liter.							
SLE Coupe 2D		CF22P	25160	**9425**	**10750**	**12650**	**15650**
SLE Convertible 2D		FF22P	31010	**11675**	**13200**	**15200**	**18450**
MR2 SPYDER—4-Cyl.—Equipment Schedule 4							
W.B. 96.5"; 1.8 Liter.							
Convertible 2D		FR320	25000	**10600**	**12100**	**14200**	**17500**
CELICA—4-Cyl.—Equipment Schedule 4							
W.B. 102.4"; 1.8 Liter.							
GT Liftback 2D		DR32T	18390	**8800**	**10075**	**11800**	**14500**
GT-S Liftback 2D		DY32T	22040	**10275**	**11675**	**13500**	**16350**
Auto Trans				**300**	**300**	**400**	**400**
AVALON—V6—Equipment Schedule 4							
W.B. 107.1"; 3.0 Liter.							
XL Sedan 4D		BF28B	26330	**12050**	**13625**	**15750**	**19050**
XLS Sedan 4D		BF28B	30890	**14075**	**15850**	**18200**	**21900**

Body	Type	VIN	List	Trade-In Fair	Trade-In Good	Pvt-Party Good	Retail Excellent
2003 TOYOTA—J,1,2or4(NorT)D,X,1or2(BT123)–3							
ECHO—4-Cyl.—Equipment Schedule 6							
W.B. 93.3"; 1.5 Liter.							
Sedan 4D		BT123	12375	**6150**	**7125**	**8425**	**10500**
Coupe 2D		AT123	11785	**5850**	**6825**	**8100**	**10150**
COROLLA—4-Cyl.—Equipment Schedule 6							
W.B. 102.4"; 1.8 Liter.							
CE Sedan 4D		BR32E	14055	**8275**	**9475**	**10650**	**12650**
S Sedan 4D		BR32E	15000	**8650**	**9900**	**11050**	**13100**
LE Sedan 4D		BR32E	15165	**8725**	**9975**	**11200**	**13250**
Sport Pkg				**100**	**100**	**135**	**135**
TRD Pkg				**200**	**200**	**265**	**265**
PRIUS—4-Cyl. Hybrid—Equipment Schedule 3							
W.B. 100.4"; 1.5 Liter.							
Sedan 4D		BK12U	20730	**11750**	**13300**	**14950**	**17700**
MATRIX—4-Cyl.—Equipment Schedule 6							
W.B. 102.4"; 1.8 Liter.							
Sport Wagon 4D		KR32E	15155	**8175**	**9375**	**10950**	**13450**
XR Sport Wagon 4D		KR32E	16665	**8350**	**9575**	**11150**	**13650**
XRS Sport Wagon 4D		KY32E	19235	**9100**	**10375**	**12000**	**14600**
4WD Sport Wagon 4D		LR32E	17600	**8700**	**9925**	**11500**	**14050**
4WD XR Sport Wag 4D		LR32E	18930	**8850**	**10125**	**11700**	**14250**
TRD Pkg				**400**	**400**	**535**	**535**
CAMRY—4-Cyl.—Equipment Schedule 4							
W.B. 107.1"; 2.4 Liter.							
LE Sedan 4D		BE30K	20285	**10850**	**12300**	**13500**	**15700**
SE Sedan 4D		BE30K	21625	**11100**	**12575**	**13800**	**16000**
XLE Sedan 4D		BF30K	22780	**11475**	**13050**	**14250**	**16500**
Manual Trans				**(600)**	**(600)**	**(800)**	**(800)**
V6 3.0 Liter		F		**900**	**900**	**1200**	**1200**
SOLARA—4-Cyl.—Equipment Schedule 4							
W.B. 105.1"; 2.4 Liter.							
SE Coupe 2D		CE22P	20650	**8875**	**10175**	**11950**	**14750**
SE Convertible 2D		FE22P	25980	**11225**	**12775**	**14650**	**17700**
Manual Trans				**(600)**	**(600)**	**(800)**	**(800)**
V6 3.0 Liter		F		**900**	**900**	**1200**	**1200**
SOLARA—V6—Equipment Schedule 4							
W.B. 105.1"; 3.0 Liter.							
SLE Coupe 2D		CF22P	25160	**10900**	**12325**	**14250**	**17300**
SLE Convertible 2D		FF22P	31010	**13250**	**14975**	**17000**	**20300**
MR2 SPYDER—4-Cyl.—Equipment Schedule 4							
W.B. 96.5"; 1.8 Liter.							
Convertible 2D		FR320	25055	**12150**	**13775**	**15900**	**19300**
CELICA—4-Cyl.—Equipment Schedule 4							
W.B. 102.4"; 1.8 Liter.							
GT Liftback 2D		DR32T	18610	**10125**	**11525**	**13200**	**15950**
GT-S Liftback 2D		DY32T	22455	**11750**	**13300**	**15050**	**18000**
Auto Trans				**300**	**300**	**400**	**400**
AVALON—V6—Equipment Schedule 4							
W.B. 107.1"; 3.0 Liter.							
XL Sedan 4D		BF28B	26330	**13725**	**15500**	**17600**	**21000**
XLS Sedan 4D		BF28B	27150	**15900**	**17900**	**20300**	**24100**
2004 TOYOTA—(J,1,2or4)(NorT)D,Xor1(BT123)–4–#							
ECHO—4-Cyl.—Equipment Schedule 6							
W.B. 93.3"; 1.5 Liter.							
Sedan 4D		BT123	12215	**7200**	**8275**	**9550**	**11650**
Coupe 2D		AT123	11685	**6900**	**7950**	**9200**	**11250**
COROLLA—4-Cyl.—Equipment Schedule 6							
W.B. 102.4"; 1.8 Liter.							
CE Sedan 4D		BR32E	14085	**9475**	**10800**	**11850**	**13850**
S Sedan 4D		BR32E	15030	**9900**	**11225**	**12350**	**14400**
LE Sedan 4D		BR32E	15295	**9975**	**11325**	**12450**	**14500**
PRIUS—4-Cyl. Hybrid—Equipment Schedule 3							
W.B. 106.3"; 1.5 Liter.							
Sedan 4D		KB20U	20510	**14025**	**15800**	**17650**	**20800**
MATRIX—4-Cyl.—Equipment Schedule 6							
W.B. 102.4"; 1.8 Liter.							
Sport Wagon 4D		KR32E	15185	**9800**	**11175**	**12650**	**15200**
XR Sport Wagon 4D		KR32E	16695	**9975**	**11325**	**12850**	**15400**
XRS Sport Wagon 4D		KY32E	19265	**10750**	**12200**	**13800**	**16400**
4WD Sport Wagon 4D		LR32E	17630	**10325**	**11750**	**13300**	**15900**

Body	Type	VIN	List	Trade-In Fair	Good	Pvt-Party Good	Retail Excellent
4WD XR Sport Wag 4D		LR32E	18960	10500	11950	13500	16100
Sport Pkg				400	400	535	535

CAMRY—4-Cyl.—Equipment Schedule 4
W.B. 107.1"; 2.4 Liter.

Body	Type	VIN	List	Trade-In Fair	Good	Pvt-Party Good	Retail Excellent
Sedan 4D		BE32K	19390	12250	13875	15000	17250
LE Sedan 4D		BE32K	20390	12625	14250	15400	17700
SE Sedan 4D		BE32K	21220	12875	14550	15700	18000
XLE Sedan 4D		BE32K	22810	13300	15025	16200	18600
Manual Trans				(625)	(625)	(835)	(835)
V6 3.0/3.3 Liter		F.A		950	950	1265	1265

SOLARA—4-Cyl.—Equipment Schedule 4
W.B. 107.2"; 2.4 Liter.

Body	Type	VIN	List	Trade-In Fair	Good	Pvt-Party Good	Retail Excellent
SE Coupe 2D		CE38P	20465	12050	13625	15050	17600
SE Sport Coupe 2D		CE38P	21960	13250	14925	16450	19150
SLE Coupe 2D		CE38P	23510	14100	15925	17500	20400
Manual Trans				(625)	(625)	(835)	(835)
V6 3.3 Liter		A		950	950	1265	1265

SOLARA—V6—Equipment Schedule 4
W.B. 107.2"; 3.3 Liter.

Body	Type	VIN	List	Trade-In Fair	Good	Pvt-Party Good	Retail Excellent
SE Convertible 2D		FA22P	26465	14600	16475	18050	20900
SLE Convertible 2D		FA22P	29965	16750	18875	20500	23700

MR2 SPYDER—4-Cyl.—Equipment Schedule 4
W.B. 96.5"; 1.8 Liter.

Body	Type	VIN	List	Trade-In Fair	Good	Pvt-Party Good	Retail Excellent
Convertible 2D		FR320	25410	13975	15800	18000	21600

CELICA—4-Cyl.—Equipment Schedule 4
W.B. 102.4"; 1.8 Liter.

Body	Type	VIN	List	Trade-In Fair	Good	Pvt-Party Good	Retail Excellent
GT Liftback 2D		DR32T	17905	11750	13300	15000	17900
GT-S Liftback 2D		DY32T	22570	13525	15275	17100	20200
Auto Trans				300	300	400	400

AVALON—V6—Equipment Schedule 4
W.B. 107.1"; 3.0 Liter.

Body	Type	VIN	List	Trade-In Fair	Good	Pvt-Party Good	Retail Excellent
XL Sedan 4D		BF28B	26560	15900	17850	20100	23700
XLS Sedan 4D		BF28B	31020	18200	20450	22900	27200

VOLKSWAGEN

1990 VOLKSWAGEN — (1,9orW)(BorV)W(BA230)–L

FOX—4-Cyl.—Equipment Schedule 6
W.B. 92.8"; 1.8 Liter.

Body	Type	VIN	List	Trade-In Fair	Good	Pvt-Party Good	Retail Excellent
Sedan 2D		BA230	8260	275	375	800	1425
GL Sedan 4D		GA230	9345	325	475	900	1575
GL Wagon 4D		DA230	9585	325	475	900	1575
GL Sport Sedan 2D		CA230	9630	325	475	900	1575

GOLF—4-Cyl.—Equipment Schedule 6
W.B. 97.3"; 1.8 Liter.

Body	Type	VIN	List	Trade-In Fair	Good	Pvt-Party Good	Retail Excellent
GL Hatchback 2D		BA21G	10095	550	800	1425	2400
GL Hatchback 4D		FA21G	10395	575	825	1425	2425
Wolfsburg Edition				25	25	35	35

GTI—4-Cyl.—Equipment Schedule 6
W.B. 97.3"; 1.8 Liter.

Body	Type	VIN	List	Trade-In Fair	Good	Pvt-Party Good	Retail Excellent
Hatchback 2D		HB21G	11120	625	900	1525	2600
Wolfsburg Edition				25	25	35	35

JETTA—4-Cyl.—Equipment Schedule 6
W.B. 97.3"; 1.8 Liter, 2.0 Liter.

Body	Type	VIN	List	Trade-In Fair	Good	Pvt-Party Good	Retail Excellent
GL Sedan 2D		MA21G	11120	725	1025	1725	2850
GL Sedan 4D		RA21G	11420	750	1050	1775	2925
Carat Sedan 4D		RB21G	12115	825	1150	1900	3100
GLI 16V Sedan 4D		TE21G	14875	975	1400	2275	3600
Wolfsburg Edition				25	25	35	35
4-Cyl. 1.6L Diesel		G		(200)	(200)	(265)	(265)

CABRIOLET—4-Cyl.—Equipment Schedule 6
W.B. 94.5"; 1.8 Liter.

Body	Type	VIN	List	Trade-In Fair	Good	Pvt-Party Good	Retail Excellent
Convertible 2D		CA515	16630	1000	1450	2450	3900
Bestseller Conv 2D		CA515	17325	1050	1500	2550	4025
Boutique Conv 2D		CA515	17885	1125	1575	2650	4150

PASSAT—4-Cyl.—Equipment Schedule 4
W.B. 103.3"; 2.0 Liter.

Body	Type	VIN	List	Trade-In Fair	Good	Pvt-Party Good	Retail Excellent
GL Sedan 4D		FB431	17085	675	925	1600	2725
GL Wagon 4D		GB431	17405	775	1100	1875	3075

CORRADO—4-Cyl. Supercharged—Equipment Schedule 3
W.B. 97.3"; 1.8 Liter.

Body	Type	VIN	List	Trade-In Fair	Good	Pvt-Party Good	Retail Excellent
Coupe 2D		DB450	18220	1050	1500	2575	4075

1991 VOLKSWAGEN

Body	Type	VIN	List	Trade-In Fair	Trade-In Good	Pvt-Party Good	Retail Excellent

1991 VOLKSWAGEN — (9orW)(BorV)W(BA230)–M

FOX—4-Cyl.—Equipment Schedule 6
W.B. 92.8"; 1.8 Liter.

Body	Type	VIN	List	Fair	Good	Good	Excellent
Sedan 2D		BA230	8405	300	425	850	1500
GL Sedan 4D		GA230	9595	350	500	950	1675
Wolfsburg Edition				25	25	35	35

GOLF—4-Cyl.—Equipment Schedule 6
W.B. 97.3"; 1.8 Liter.

GL Hatchback 2D		BA21G	10340	650	900	1575	2700
GL Hatchback 4D		FA21G	10640	675	925	1600	2725
Wolfsburg Edition				25	25	35	35

GTI—4-Cyl.—Equipment Schedule 6
W.B. 97.3"; 1.8 Liter, 2.0 Liter.

Hatchback 2D		DB21G	11355	725	1025	1750	2900
16V Hatchback 2D		HE21G	14060	900	1300	2175	3525
Wolfsburg Edition				25	25	35	35

JETTA—4-Cyl.—Equipment Schedule 6
W.B. 97.3"; 1.8 Liter, 2.0 Liter.

GL Sedan 2D		MA21G	11355	825	1150	1975	3200
GL Sedan 4D		RA21G	11655	850	1200	2025	3275
Carat Sedan 4D		RB21G	12370	900	1300	2125	3425
GLI 16V Sedan 4D		TE21G	15155	1100	1550	2650	4150
Wolfsburg Edition				25	25	35	35
4-Cyl. 1.6L Diesel		G		(200)	(200)	(265)	(265)

CABRIOLET—4-Cyl.—Equipment Schedule 6
W.B. 94.5"; 1.8 Liter.

Convertible 2D		CA515	17740	1175	1625	2700	4250
Carat Convertible 2D		CA515	19300	1250	1725	2825	4425
Etienne Aigner Conv 2D		EA515	19600	1350	1825	2950	4525
Power Top				50	50	65	65

PASSAT—4-Cyl.—Equipment Schedule 4
W.B. 103.3"; 2.0 Liter.

GL Sedan 4D		FB431	17355	775	1075	1875	3100
GL Wagon 4D		GB431	17760	900	1250	2100	3425
Manual Trans				(175)	(175)	(235)	(235)

CORRADO—4-Cyl. Supercharged—Equipment Schedule 3
W.B. 97.3"; 1.8 Liter.

Coupe 2D		DB450	19440	1300	1775	2925	4550

1992 VOLKSWAGEN–(9,3orW)(BorV)W(BA230)–N

FOX—4-Cyl.—Equipment Schedule 6
W.B. 92.8"; 1.8 Liter.

Sedan 2D		BA230	8770	325	475	925	1675
GL Sedan 4D		GA230	9990	400	575	1075	1900

GOLF—4-Cyl.—Equipment Schedule 6
W.B. 97.3"; 1.8 Liter.

GL Hatchback 2D		BA21G	11135	725	1025	1800	3025
GL Hatchback 4D		FA21G	11445	750	1050	1850	3100

GTI—4-Cyl.—Equipment Schedule 6
W.B. 97.3"; 1.8 Liter, 2.0 Liter.

Hatchback 2D		DB21G	12320	825	1150	1975	3275
16V Hatchback 2D		HE21G	15120	1025	1475	2550	4075

JETTA—4-Cyl.—Equipment Schedule 6
W.B. 97.3"; 1.8 Liter, 2.0 Liter.

GL Sedan 4D		RA21G	12580	950	1350	2375	3875
Carat Sedan 4D		SB21G	13600	1025	1450	2525	4025
GLI 16V Sedan 4D		TE21G	16690	1325	1800	2950	4550
4-Cyl. 1.6L Diesel		F		(225)	(225)	(300)	(300)

CABRIOLET—4-Cyl.—Equipment Schedule 6
W.B. 94.5"; 1.8 Liter.

Convertible 2D		CB515	18585	1375	1875	3000	4625
Carat Convertible 2D		DB515	20215	1500	2000	3175	4825
Wolfsburg Edition				50	50	65	65
Power Top				75	75	100	100

PASSAT—4-Cyl.—Equipment Schedule 4
W.B. 103.3"; 2.0 Liter.

CL Sedan 4D		EB431	16955	850	1175	2075	3400
GL Sedan 4D		FB431	18715	900	1275	2175	3575
GL Wagon 4D		GB431	19135	1025	1450	2525	4050
Manual Trans				(225)	(225)	(300)	(300)

CORRADO—4-Cyl. Supercharged—Equipment Schedule 3
W.B. 97.3"; 1.8 Liter.

Body	Type	VIN	List	Trade-In Fair	Good	Pvt-Party Good	Retail Excellent
G60 Coupe 2D		DB450	20230	1625	2125	3375	5100

CORRADO—V6—Equipment Schedule 3
W.B.97.3"; 2.8 Liter.

	SLC Coupe 2D		ED450	22210	2425	3025	4400	6325

1993 VOLKSWAGEN — (9orW)(BorV)W(BA230)–P

FOX—4-Cyl.—Equipment Schedule 6
W.B. 92.8"; 1.8 Liter.

Wolfsburg Sedan 2D	BA230	9065	375	525	1025	1850
Polo Sedan 2D	BA230	9285	375	525	1025	1850
Wolfsburg GL Sedan 4D	GA230	9895	450	650	1200	2100

GOLF III—4-Cyl.—Equipment Schedule 6
W.B. 97.4"; 2.0 Liter.

GL Hatchback 4D	FL21H	12830	1225	1700	2825	4450

JETTA III—4-Cyl.—Equipment Schedule 6
W.B. 97.4"; 2.0 Liter.

GL Sedan 4D	RL21H	14030	1225	1700	2825	4450

CABRIOLET—4-Cyl.—Equipment Schedule 6
W.B. 94.5"; 1.8 Liter.

Convertible 2D	AB515	19665	1625	2125	3325	5025
Classic Conv 2D	BB515	20320	1775	2300	3500	5225

PASSAT—4-Cyl.—Equipment Schedule 4
W.B. 103.3"; 2.0 Liter.

GL Sedan 4D	FB431	19125	850	1175	2300	3900
Manual Trans			(275)	(275)	(365)	(365)

PASSAT—V6—Equipment Schedule 4
W.B. 103.3"; 2.8 Liter.

GLX Sedan 4D	JD431	22395	1725	2250	3600	5450
GLX Wagon 4D	ND431	22825	1825	2350	3725	5625
Manual Trans			(275)	(275)	(365)	(365)

CORRADO—V6—Equipment Schedule 3
W.B. 97.3"; 2.8 Liter.

SLC Coupe 2D	ED450	23260	2925	3575	5050	7125

1994 VOLKSWAGEN — (9orW)(BorV)W(BA81H)–R

GOLF III—4-Cyl.—Equipment Schedule 6
W.B. 97.3"; 2.0 Liter.

GL Hatchback 2D	BA81H	13565	1425	1900	3100	4775
GL Hatchback 4D	FB21H	13140	1475	1950	3150	4825

JETTA III—4-Cyl.—Equipment Schedule 6
W.B. 97.3"; 2.0 Liter.

GL Sedan 4D	RB21H	14365	1475	1950	3150	4825
GLS Sedan 4D	SB81H	16090	1700	2225	3450	5200

JETTA III—V6—Equipment Schedule 6
W.B. 97.3"; 2.8 Liter.

GLX Sedan 4D	TS81H	20365	3125	3775	5225	7300

PASSAT—V6—Equipment Schedule 4
W.B. 103.3"; 2.8 Liter.

GLX Sedan 4D	JF431	24340	2100	2700	4125	6125
GLX Wagon 4D	NF431	24765	2250	2800	4275	6300
Manual Trans			(325)	(325)	(435)	(435)

CORRADO—V6—Equipment Schedule 3
W.B. 97.2"; 2.8 Liter.

SLC Coupe 2D	EF450	25540	3450	4150	5725	7975

1995 VOLKSWAGEN — (3VVorWVW)(JB81H)–S–#

GOLF III—4-Cyl.—Equipment Schedule 6
W.B. 97.3"; 2.0 Liter.

City Hatchback 4D	JB81H	11915	1375	1875	3075	4775
Hatchback 4D	KA81H	14590	1500	2025	3275	5000
GL Hatchback 2D	BA81H	14265	1675	2200	3450	5225
GL Hatchback 4D	FA81H	14590	1725	2250	3500	5275
Sport Hatchback 2D	BA81H	15640	2525	3125	4500	6425

GTI—V6—Equipment Schedule 6
W.B. 97.3"; 2.8 Liter.

Coupe 2D	HD81H	19265	3425	4150	5650	7800

JETTA III—4-Cyl.—Equipment Schedule 6
W.B. 97.3"; 2.0 Liter.

City Sedan 4D	VB81H	12915	1600	2100	3350	5100
Sedan 4D	PB81H	13865	1675	2200	3450	5225
GL Sedan 4D	RA81H	16065	2025	2575	3900	5725
GLS Sedan 4D	SB81H	17415	2225	2775	4125	6025

Body	Type	VIN	List	Trade-In Fair	Good	Pvt-Party Good	Retail Excellent
JETTA III—V6—Equipment Schedule 6							
W.B. 97.3"; 2.8 Liter.							
GLX Sedan 4D		TD81H	20365	**3575**	**4275**	**5800**	**7975**
CABRIO—4-Cyl.—Equipment Schedule 3							
W.B. 97.4"; 2.0 Liter.							
Convertible 2D		BC81E	21215	**3000**	**3675**	**5150**	**7300**
Manual Trans				**(200)**	**(200)**	**(265)**	**(265)**
PASSAT—4-Cyl.—Equipment Schedule 4							
W.B. 103.3"; 2.0 Liter.							
GLS Sedan 4D		CC83A	19215	**1225**	**1675**	**3025**	**4875**
Manual Trans				**(375)**	**(375)**	**(500)**	**(500)**
PASSAT—V6—Equipment Schedule 4							
W.B. 103.3"; 2.8 Liter.							
GLX Sedan 4D		EE83A	22080	**2550**	**3175**	**4700**	**6850**
GLX Wagon 4D		FE83A	22510	**2700**	**3300**	**4875**	**7050**
Manual Trans				**(375)**	**(375)**	**(500)**	**(500)**

1996 VOLKSWAGEN — (3VWorWVW)(FA81H)–T–#

Body	Type	VIN	List	Trade-In Fair	Good	Pvt-Party Good	Retail Excellent
GOLF—4-Cyl.—Equipment Schedule 6							
W.B. 97.4"; 2.0 Liter.							
GL Hatchback 4D		FA81H	14435	**1950**	**2500**	**3800**	**5625**
GTI Hatchback 2D		DA81H	16425	**2550**	**3150**	**4500**	**6450**
GOLF—4-Cyl. Turbo Diesel—Equipment Schedule 6							
W.B. 97.4"; 1.9 Liter.							
TDI Hatchback 4D		FF81H	15660	**2375**	**2950**	**4300**	**6225**
GOLF GTI VR6—V6—Equipment Schedule 6							
W.B. 97.4"; 2.8 Liter.							
Hatchback 2D		HD81H	20110	**3950**	**4700**	**6250**	**8425**
JETTA—4-Cyl.—Equipment Schedule 6							
W.B. 97.4"; 2.0 Liter.							
GL Sedan 4D		RA81H	15535	**2100**	**2675**	**3950**	**5775**
GLS Sedan 4D		SA81H	16725	**2350**	**2925**	**4275**	**6150**
Trek Edition		W		**50**	**50**	**65**	**65**
Wolfsburg Edition		P		**50**	**50**	**65**	**65**
JETTA—4-Cyl. Turbo Diesel—Equipment Schedule 6							
W.B. 97.4"; 1.9 Liter.							
TDI Sedan 4D		RF81H	16760	**2700**	**3300**	**4650**	**6600**
JETTA—V6—Equipment Schedule 6							
W.B. 97.4"; 2.8 Liter.							
GLX Sedan 4D		TD81H	21035	**3900**	**4625**	**6125**	**8275**
CABRIO—4-Cyl.—Equipment Schedule 3							
W.B. 97.2"; 2.0 Liter.							
Convertible 2D		BB81E	21260	**3375**	**4075**	**5675**	**7900**
Manual Trans				**(200)**	**(200)**	**(265)**	**(265)**
PASSAT—4-Cyl.—Equipment Schedule 4							
W.B. 103.3"; 2.0 Liter.							
GLS Sedan 4D		GC83A	19715	**1525**	**2050**	**3500**	**5500**
Manual Trans				**(400)**	**(400)**	**(535)**	**(535)**
PASSAT—4-Cyl. Turbo Diesel—Equipment Schedule 4							
W.B. 103.3"; 1.9 Liter.							
TDI Sedan 4D		GG83A	19905	**3200**	**3875**	**5525**	**7850**
TDI Wagon 4D		HG83A	20335	**3325**	**4025**	**5700**	**8050**
PASSAT—V6—Equipment Schedule 4							
W.B. 103.3"; 2.8 Liter.							
GLX Sedan 4D		EE83A	23115	**3050**	**3700**	**5375**	**7675**
GLX Wagon 4D		FE83A	23545	**3225**	**3900**	**5575**	**7900**
Manual Trans				**(400)**	**(400)**	**(535)**	**(535)**

1997 VOLKSWAGEN — (3VWorWVW)(FA81H)–V–#

Body	Type	VIN	List	Trade-In Fair	Good	Pvt-Party Good	Retail Excellent
GOLF—4-Cyl.—Equipment Schedule 6							
W.B. 97.4"; 2.0 Liter.							
GL Hatchback 4D		FA81H	14830	**2300**	**2875**	**4275**	**6200**
GTI Hatchback 2D		DA81H	16820	**2925**	**3575**	**5025**	**7050**
Jazz Edition		M		**50**	**50**	**65**	**65**
Trek Edition		L		**50**	**50**	**65**	**65**
K2 Edition		K		**50**	**50**	**65**	**65**
GOLF GTI VR6—V6—Equipment Schedule 6							
W.B. 97.4"; 2.8 Liter.							
Hatchback 2D		HD81H	20210	**4475**	**5275**	**6875**	**9175**
JETTA—4-Cyl.—Equipment Schedule 6							
W.B. 97.4"; 2.0 Liter.							
GL Sedan 4D		RA81H	15930	**2450**	**3050**	**4425**	**6350**
GT Sedan 4D		VA81H	16325	**2700**	**3300**	**4700**	**6700**

1997 VOLKSWAGEN

Body	Type	VIN	List	Trade-In Fair	Trade-In Good	Pvt-Party Good	Retail Excellent
GLS Sedan 4D		SA81H	17420	2975	3650	5100	7125
Trek Edition		W		50	50	65	65

JETTA—4-Cyl. Turbo Diesel—Equipment Schedule 6
W.B. 97.4"; 1.9 Liter.

Body	Type	VIN	List	Fair	Good	Good	Excellent
TDI Sedan 4D		RF81H	17105	3050	3700	5125	7175

JETTA—V6—Equipment Schedule 6
W.B. 97.4"; 2.8 Liter.

GLX Sedan 4D		TD81H	21055	4400	5175	6750	9000

CABRIO—4-Cyl.—Equipment Schedule 3
W.B. 97.4"; 2.0 Liter.

Convertible 2D		AA81E	20785	3825	4550	6250	8625
Highline Conv 2D		BA81E	23050	4200	5000	6625	8975
Manual Trans				(200)	(200)	(265)	(265)

PASSAT—4-Cyl. Turbo Diesel—Equipment Schedule 4
W.B. 103.3"; 1.9 Liter.

TDI Sedan 4D		GG83A	19930	3750	4500	6250	8700
TDI Wagon 4D		HG83A	20360	3900	4625	6425	8925

PASSAT—V6—Equipment Schedule 4
W.B. 103.3"; 2.8 Liter.

GLX Sedan 4D		EE83A	23190	3625	4350	6125	8575
GLX Wagon 4D		FE83A	23620	3800	4525	6300	8800
Manual Trans				(425)	(425)	(565)	(565)

1998 VOLKSWAGEN—(3VWorWVW)(FA81H)—W-#

GOLF—4-Cyl.—Equipment Schedule 6
W.B. 97.4"; 2.0 Liter.

GL Hatchback 2D		FA81H	14855	2700	3300	4750	6800
GTI Hatchback 2D		DA81H	17170	3375	4075	5575	7725
K2 Edition		K		50	50	65	65

GOLF GTI VR6—V6—Equipment Schedule 6
W.B. 97.4"; 2.8 Liter.

Hatchback 2D		HD81H	20735	5075	5950	7600	10050

NEW BEETLE—4-Cyl.—Equipment Schedule 6
W.B. 98.9"; 2.0 Liter.

Hatchback 2D		BB61C	15700	4050	4825	5950	7700

NEW BEETLE—4-Cyl. Turbo Diesel—Equipment Schedule 6
W.B. 98.9"; 1.9 Liter.

TDI Hatchback 2D		BF61C	16975	4950	5800	7000	8900

JETTA—4-Cyl.—Equipment Schedule 6
W.B. 97.4"; 2.0 Liter.

GL Sedan 4D		RA81H	15955	2875	3525	4975	7025
GT Sedan 4D		VA81H	16350	3150	3800	5275	7375
GLS Sedan 4D		SA81H	17445	3475	4175	5700	7850
K2 Edition		Y		50	50	65	65
Wolfsburg		P		50	50	65	65

JETTA—4-Cyl. Turbo Diesel—Equipment Schedule 6
W.B. 97.4"; 1.9 Liter.

TDI Sedan 4D		RF81H	17130	3525	4225	5725	7900

JETTA—V6—Equipment Schedule 6
W.B. 97.4"; 2.8 Liter.

GLX Sedan 4D		TD81H	21455	5000	5850	7500	9900

CABRIO—4-Cyl.—Equipment Schedule 3
W.B. 97.4"; 2.0 Liter.

GL Convertible 2D		AA81E	20835	4350	5125	6875	9300
GLS Convertible 2D		BA81E	23665	4775	5625	7300	9700
Manual Trans				(200)	(200)	(265)	(265)

PASSAT—4-Cyl. Turbo—Equipment Schedule 4
W.B. 106.4"; 1.8 Liter.

GLS Sedan 4D		MA63B	22325	4850	5700	7475	9975
GLS Wagon 4D		NA63B	22875	5025	5875	7650	10200
Manual Trans				(450)	(450)	(600)	(600)
V6 2.8 Liter		D		425	425	565	565

PASSAT—4-Cyl. Turbo Diesel—Equipment Schedule 4
W.B. 106.4"; 1.9 Liter.

GLS TDI Sedan 4D		MG63B	22575	5250	6150	7975	10550
Manual Trans				(450)	(450)	(600)	(600)

PASSAT—V6—Equipment Schedule 4
W.B. 106.4"; 2.8 Liter.

GLX Sedan 4D		PD63B	27825	7025	8100	10100	12950
Manual Trans				(450)	(450)	(600)	(600)

1999 VOLKSWAGEN

Body	Type	VIN	List	Trade-In Fair	Good	Pvt-Party Good	Retail Excellent

1999 VOLKSWAGEN — (3orW)VW(FB81H)–X–#

GOLF—4-Cyl.—Equipment Schedule 6
W.B. 97.4"; 2.0 Liter.

GL Hatchback 4D		FB81H	14855	3200	3875	5400	7575
Wolfsburg		J		75	75	100	100

GOLF GTI VR6—V6—Equipment Schedule 6
W.B. 97.4"; 2.8 Liter.

Hatchback 2D		HD81H	20735	5900	6875	8625	11200

NEW GOLF—4-Cyl.—Equipment Schedule 6
W.B. 98.9"; 2.0 Liter.

GL Hatchback 2D		BC31J	15425	4225	5025	6600	8875
GLS Hatchback 4D		GC31J	16875	4475	5250	6875	9200

NEW GOLF—4-Cyl. Turbo Diesel—Equipment Schedule 6
W.B. 98.9"; 1.9 Liter.

GL TDI H'Back 2D		BF31J	16720	5150	6025	7700	10150
GLS TDI H'Back 4D		GF31J	17925	5375	6300	7975	10400

NEW GTI—4-Cyl.—Equipment Schedule 6
W.B. 98.9"; 2.0 Liter.

GLS Hatchback 2D		DC31J	18025	5050	5925	7550	9975

NEW GTI—V6—Equipment Schedule 6
W.B. 98.9"; 2.8 Liter.

GLX Hatchback 2D		DE21J	22675	6875	7925	9750	12450

NEW BEETLE—4-Cyl.—Equipment Schedule 6
W.B. 98.9"; 2.0 Liter.

GL Hatchback 2D		BC21C	16425	4825	5675	6850	8700
GLS Hatchback 2D		CC21C	17375	5075	5950	7125	9025

NEW BEETLE—4-Cyl. Turbo—Equipment Schedule 6
W.B. 98.9"; 1.8 Liter.

GLS Hatchback 2D		CD21C	19525	5275	6175	7375	9300
GLX Hatchback 2D		DD21C	21425	5525	6425	7675	9650

NEW BEETLE—4-Cyl. Turbo Diesel—Equipment Schedule 6
W.B. 98.9"; 1.9 Liter.

GLS TDI H'Back 2D		CF21C	18425	5825	6800	8050	10050

JETTA—4-Cyl.—Equipment Schedule 6
W.B. 97.4"; 2.0 Liter.

GL Sedan 4D		RB81H	16205	3425	4125	5675	7850
Wolfsburg		P		75	75	100	100

JETTA—4-Cyl. Turbo Diesel—Equipment Schedule 6
W.B. 97.4"; 1.9 Liter.

TDI Sedan 4D		RF81H	17130	4175	4950	6550	8850

JETTA—V6—Equipment Schedule 6
W.B. 97.4"; 2.8 Liter.

GLX Sedan 4D		TD81H	21455	5800	6775	8525	11100

NEW JETTA—4-Cyl.—Equipment Schedule 6
W.B. 98.9"; 2.0 Liter.

GL Sedan 4D		RC29M	16400	4875	5700	7225	9450
GLS Sedan 4D		SC29M	16875	5200	6100	7500	9600

NEW JETTA—4-Cyl. Turbo Diesel—Equipment Schedule 6
W.B. 98.9"; 1.9 Liter.

GL TDI Sedan 4D		RF29M	17695	6175	7150	8575	10800
GLS TDI Sedan 4D		SF29M	17925	6300	7300	8700	10950

NEW JETTA VR6—V6—Equipment Schedule 6
W.B. 98.9"; 2.8 Liter.

GLS Sedan 4D		SE29M	20475	6750	7800	9300	11650
GLX Sedan 4D		TE29M	24025	6875	7925	9750	12450

CABRIO—4-Cyl.—Equipment Schedule 3
W.B. 97.4"; 2.0 Liter.

GL Convertible 2D		AB81E	20835	5100	5975	7800	10400
GLS Convertible 2D		BB81E	23665	5600	6500	8275	10850
Manual Trans				(250)	(250)	(335)	(335)

NEW CABRIO—4-Cyl.—Equipment Schedule 3
W.B. 97.4"; 2.0 Liter.

GL Convertible 2D		CB81E	22015	5550	6450	8325	11000
GLS Convertible 2D		DB81E	24700	5875	6850	8725	11450
Manual Trans				(250)	(250)	(335)	(335)

PASSAT—4-Cyl. Turbo—Equipment Schedule 4
W.B. 106.4"; 1.8 Liter.

GLS Sedan 4D		MA63B	22775	5675	6600	8475	11200
GLS Wagon 4D		NA63B	23325	5850	6825	8700	11400
Manual Trans				(500)	(500)	(665)	(665)
V6 2.8 Liter		D		500	500	665	665

Body	Type	VIN	List	Trade-In Fair	Trade-In Good	Pvt-Party Good	Retail Excellent
PASSAT—V6—Equipment Schedule 4							
W.B. 106.4"; 2.8 Liter.							
GLX Sedan 4D		UD63B	30300	8175	9375	11450	14550

2000 VOLKSWAGEN — (3orW)VW(BC21J)-Y-#

Body	Type	VIN	List	Fair	Good	Good	Excellent
GOLF—4-Cyl.—Equipment Schedule 6							
W.B. 98.9"; 2.0 Liter.							
GL Hatchback 2D		BC21J	15425	4950	5800	7450	9850
GLS Hatchback 4D		GC21J	16875	5200	6100	7775	10200
GOLF—4-Cyl. Turbo—Equipment Schedule 6							
W.B. 98.9"; 1.8 Liter.							
GLS Hatchback 4D		GH21J	18425	5650	6575	8275	10800
GOLF—4-Cyl. Turbo Diesel—Equipment Schedule 6							
W.B. 98.9"; 1.9 Liter.							
GL TDI H'Back 2D		BF21J	16720	6000	6950	8700	11250
GLS TDI H'Back 4D		GF21J	17295	6250	7250	9050	11550
GTI—4-Cyl.—Equipment Schedule 6							
W.B. 98.9"; 2.0 Liter.							
GLS Hatchback 2D		DC21J	18200	5875	6850	8550	11100
GTI—4-Cyl. Turbo—Equipment Schedule 6							
W.B. 98.9"; 1.8 Liter.							
GLS Hatchback 2D		DH21J	19750	7100	8200	10050	12700
GTI—V6—Equipment Schedule 6							
W.B. 98.9"; 2.8 Liter.							
GLX Hatchback 2D		DE21J	23145	7950	9125	11000	13800
NEW BEETLE—4-Cyl.—Equipment Schedule 6							
W.B. 98.9"; 2.0 Liter.							
GL Hatchback 2D		BC21C	16425	5675	6600	7800	9750
GLS Hatchback 2D		CC21C	17375	5950	6900	8125	10100
NEW BEETLE—4-Cyl. Turbo—Equipment Schedule 6							
W.B. 98.9"; 1.8 Liter.							
GLS Hatchback 2D		CD21C	19525	6200	7175	8425	10400
GLX Hatchback 2D		DD21C	21600	6475	7500	8750	10800
NEW BEETLE—4-Cyl. Turbo Diesel—Equipment Schedule 6							
W.B. 98.9"; 1.9 Liter.							
GLS TDI H'Back 2D		CF21C	18425	6825	7850	9150	11250
JETTA—4-Cyl.—Equipment Schedule 6							
W.B. 98.9"; 2.0 Liter.							
GL Sedan 4D		RC29M	17225	5650	6550	8125	10500
GLS Sedan 4D		SC29M	18175	6050	7000	8450	10650
JETTA—4-Cyl. Turbo—Equipment Schedule 6							
W.B. 98.9"; 1.8 Liter.							
GLS Sedan 4D		SD29M	19725	6475	7500	8950	11250
JETTA—4-Cyl. Turbo Diesel—Equipment Schedule 6							
W.B. 98.9"; 1.9 Liter.							
GL TDI Sedan 4D		RF29M	18520	7100	8175	9650	12000
GLS TDI Sedan 4D		SF29M	19225	7250	8325	9800	12150
JETTA—V6—Equipment Schedule 6							
W.B. 98.9"; 2.8 Liter.							
GLS Sedan 4D		SE29M	20475	7750	8900	10450	12900
GLX Sedan 4D		TE29M	24695	7900	9075	10950	13800
CABRIO—4-Cyl.—Equipment Schedule 3							
W.B. 97.4"; 2.0 Liter.							
GL Convertible 2D		CC21V	22015	6400	7425	9375	12250
GLS Convertible 2D		DC21V	24700	6800	7825	9850	12700
Manual Trans				(275)	(275)	(365)	(365)
PASSAT—4-Cyl. Turbo—Equipment Schedule 4							
W.B. 106.4"; 1.8 Liter.							
GLS Sedan 4D		MA23B	22800	6600	7625	9600	12500
GLS Wagon 4D		NA23B	23600	6825	7850	9850	12750
Manual Trans				(525)	(525)	(700)	(700)
V6 2.8 Liter		D		550	550	735	735
PASSAT—V6—Equipment Schedule 4							
W.B. 106.4"; 2.8 Liter.							
GLX Sedan 4D		PD23B	29255	9425	10750	12900	16200
GLX Wagon 4D		VD23B	30055	9650	11000	13150	16450
Manual Trans				(525)	(525)	(700)	(700)
PASSAT 4MOTION AWD—V6—Equipment Schedule 4							
W.B. 106.4"; 2.8 Liter.							
GLS Sedan 4D		TH23B	27050	9750	11125	13350	16650
GLS Wagon 4D		RH23B	27850	10275	11700	13950	17350
GLX Sedan 4D		UH23B	30905	10500	11950	14200	17600
GLX Wagon 4D		WH23B	31705	11125	12625	14950	18500

0105   **EQUIPMENT & MILEAGE PAGE 9 TO 23**   237

Body	Type	VIN	List	Trade-In Fair	Good	Pvt-Party Good	Retail Excellent

2001 VOLKSWAGEN — (3orW)VW(BK21J)–1–#

GOLF—4-Cyl.—Equipment Schedule 6
W.B. 98.9"; 2.0 Liter.

GL Hatchback 2D		BK21J	15425	5700	6650	8400	10950
GLS Hatchback 4D		GK21J	16875	6000	6950	8725	11350

GOLF—4-Cyl. Turbo—Equipment Schedule 6
W.B. 98.9"; 1.8 Liter.

GLS Hatchback 4D		GC21J	18425	6500	7500	9300	11950

GOLF—4-Cyl. Turbo Diesel—Equipment Schedule 6
W.B. 98.9"; 1.9 Liter.

GL TDI H'Back 2D		BP21J	16720	6900	7950	9800	12550
GLS TDI H'Back 4D		GP21J	17925	7150	8250	10100	12800

GTI—4-Cyl. Turbo—Equipment Schedule 6
W.B. 98.9"; 1.8 Liter.

GLS Hatchback 2D		DC21J	19800	8100	9300	11200	14050

GTI—V6—Equipment Schedule 6
W.B. 98.9"; 2.8 Liter.

GLX Hatchback 2D		PG21J	23425	9025	10325	12250	15200

NEW BEETLE—4-Cyl.—Equipment Schedule 6
W.B. 98.7"; 2.0 Liter.

GL Hatchback 2D		BK21C	16425	6575	7600	8850	10900
GLS Hatchback 2D		CK21C	17375	6900	7975	9250	11350

NEW BEETLE—4-Cyl. Turbo—Equipment Schedule 6
W.B. 98.7"; 1.8 Liter.

GLS Hatchback 2D		CD21C	19525	7150	8250	9525	11600
Sport Hatchback 2D		ED21C	21175	7275	8350	9650	11750
GLX Hatchback 2D		DD21C	21700	7500	8625	9900	12050

NEW BEETLE—4-Cyl. Turbo Diesel—Equipment Schedule 6
W.B. 98.7"; 1.9 Liter.

GLS TDI H'Back 2D		CP21C	18425	7850	9025	10300	12550

JETTA—4-Cyl.—Equipment Schedule 6
W.B. 98.9", 99.0" (Wag); 2.0 Liter.

GL Sedan 4D		RK29M	17225	6450	7475	9150	11650
GLS Sedan 4D		SK29M	18175	6925	8000	9500	11850
GLS Wagon 4D		SK21J	19150	7200	8275	9800	12200

JETTA—4-Cyl. Turbo—Equipment Schedule 6
W.B. 98.9"; 1.8 Liter.

GLS Sedan 4D		SD29M	19725	7425	8525	10100	12550
Wolfsburg Edition				100	100	135	135

JETTA—4-Cyl. Turbo Diesel—Equipment Schedule 6
W.B. 98.9"; 1.9 Liter.

GL TDI Sedan 4D		RP29M	18520	8100	9300	10850	13300
GLS TDI Sedan 4D		SP29M	19225	8275	9475	11050	13500

JETTA—V6—Equipment Schedule 6
W.B. 98.9", 99.0" (Wag); 2.8 Liter.

GLS Sedan 4D		SG29M	20475	8850	10125	11750	14350
GLS Wagon 4D		SG21J	21450	9050	10325	11950	14600
GLX Sedan 4D		TG29M	24825	8975	10275	12250	15300
GLX Wagon 4D		TG21J	25950	9225	10500	12550	15600

CABRIO—4-Cyl.—Equipment Schedule 3
W.B. 97.4"; 2.0 Liter.

GL Convertible 2D		BC21V	21625	7350	8450	10500	13550
GLS Convertible 2D		CC21V	22000	7750	8900	11000	14050
GLX Convertible 2D		DC21V	23700	8100	9300	11400	14550
Manual Trans				(300)	(300)	(400)	(400)

PASSAT—4-Cyl. Turbo—Equipment Schedule 4
W.B. 106.4"; 1.8 Liter.

GLS Sedan 4D		AD23B	23050	7675	8800	10950	14000
GLS Wagon 4D		HD23B	23850	7900	9075	11200	14250
Manual Trans				(550)	(550)	(735)	(735)
V6 2.8 Liter		H		600	600	800	800

NEW PASSAT—4-Cyl. Turbo—Equipment Schedule 4
W.B. 106.4"; 1.8 Liter.

GLS Sedan 4D		PD23B	23375	7900	9075	11200	14250
GLS Wagon 4D		VD23B	24175	8125	9325	11450	14600
Manual Trans				(550)	(550)	(735)	(735)
V6 2.8 Liter		H		600	600	800	800

PASSAT—V6—Equipment Schedule 4
W.B. 106.4"; 2.8 Liter.

GLX Sedan 4D		BH23B	29810	10800	12250	14550	18000
GLX Wagon 4D		JH23B	30610	11050	12525	14850	18350
Manual Trans				(550)	(550)	(735)	(735)

Body	Type	VIN	List	Trade-In Fair	Good	Pvt-Party Good	Retail Excellent
NEW PASSAT—V6—Equipment Schedule 4							
W.B. 106.4"; 2.8 Liter.							
GLX Sedan 4D		RD23B	30375	**10900**	**12325**	**14650**	**18150**
GLX Wagon 4D		WD23B	31175	**11125**	**12625**	**14950**	**18450**
Manual Trans				(550)	(550)	(735)	(735)
PASSAT 4MOTION AWD—V6—Equipment Schedule 4							
W.B. 106.4"; 2.8 Liter.							
GLS Sedan 4D		DH23B	27400	**11125**	**12625**	**14950**	**18450**
GLS Wagon 4D		KH23B	28200	**11700**	**13250**	**15600**	**19200**
GLX Sedan 4D		EH23B	31550	**11950**	**13525**	**15900**	**19500**
GLX Wagon 4D		LH23B	32360	**12675**	**14350**	**16750**	**20400**
NEW PASSAT 4MOTION AWD—V6—Equipment Schedule 4							
W.B. 106.4"; 2.8 Liter.							
GLS Sedan 4D		SH23B	27625	**11100**	**12575**	**14900**	**18400**
GLS Wagon 4D		XH23B	28425	**11675**	**13200**	**15550**	**19150**
GLX Sedan 4D		TH23B	32125	**12100**	**13725**	**16150**	**19800**
GLX Wagon 4D		YH23B	32925	**12775**	**14450**	**16850**	**20500**

2002 VOLKSWAGEN—(3,9orW)(BorV)W(BK12J)-2

Body	Type	VIN	List	Trade-In Fair	Good	Pvt-Party Good	Retail Excellent
GOLF—4-Cyl.—Equipment Schedule 6							
W.B. 98.9"; 2.0 Liter.							
GL Hatchback 2D		BK21J	15600	**6575**	**7600**	**9450**	**12200**
GL Hatchback 4D		FK21J	15800	**6750**	**7800**	**9650**	**12450**
GLS Hatchback 4D		GK21J	17150	**6900**	**7950**	**9800**	**12600**
GOLF—4-Cyl. Turbo Diesel—Equipment Schedule 6							
W.B. 98.9"; 1.9 Liter.							
GL TDI H'Back 2D		BP21J	16895	**7850**	**9025**	**10950**	**13800**
GL TDI H'Back 4D		FP21J	17095	**8000**	**9175**	**11050**	**13900**
GLS TDI H'Back 4D		GP21J	18200	**8175**	**9375**	**11350**	**14200**
GTI—4-Cyl. Turbo—Equipment Schedule 6							
W.B. 98.9"; 1.8 Liter.							
Hatchback 2D		DE61J	19460	**9225**	**10500**	**12100**	**15500**
337 Edition H'Back 2D		DE61J	22775	**9900**	**11225**	**13300**	**16400**
GTI VR6—V6—Equipment Schedule 6							
W.B. 98.9"; 2.8 Liter.							
Hatchback 2D		DH61J	20845	**10225**	**11625**	**13700**	**16850**
NEW BEETLE—4-Cyl.—Equipment Schedule 6							
W.B. 98.7"; 2.0 Liter.							
GL Hatchback 2D		BK21C	16450	**7575**	**8700**	**9975**	**12150**
GLS Hatchback 2D		CK21C	17400	**7950**	**9125**	**10400**	**12600**
NEW BEETLE—4-Cyl. Turbo—Equipment Schedule 6							
W.B. 98.7"; 1.8 Liter.							
GLS Hatchback 2D		CD21C	19750	**8225**	**9425**	**10700**	**12900**
Sport Hatchback 2D		ED21C	20800	**8350**	**9575**	**10900**	**13100**
GLX Hatchback 2D		DD21C	22050	**8600**	**9850**	**11200**	**13450**
S Hatchback 2D		FE21C	23905	**9700**	**11050**	**12450**	**14850**
NEW BEETLE—4-Cyl. Turbo Diesel—Equipment Schedule 6							
W.B. 98.7"; 1.9 Liter.							
GLS TDI H'Back 2D		CP21C	18450	**8975**	**10275**	**11600**	**13900**
JETTA—4-Cyl.—Equipment Schedule 6							
W.B. 98.9", 99.0" (Wag); 2.0 Liter.							
GL Sedan 4D		RK69M	17400	**7425**	**8525**	**10250**	**12900**
GL Wagon 4D		RK61J	18200	**7675**	**8800**	**10600**	**13300**
GLS Sedan 4D		SK69M	18450	**7950**	**9125**	**10650**	**13150**
GLS Wagon 4D		SK21J	19250	**8175**	**9375**	**10950**	**13550**
JETTA—4-Cyl. Turbo—Equipment Schedule 6							
W.B. 98.9", 99.0" (Wag); 1.8 Liter.							
GLS Sedan 4D		SE69M	20100	**8450**	**9650**	**11300**	**13800**
GLS Wagon 4D		SE61J	20900	**9025**	**10325**	**11900**	**14500**
JETTA—4-Cyl. Turbo Diesel—Equipment Schedule 6							
W.B. 98.9", 99.0" (Wag); 1.9 Liter.							
GL TDI Sedan 4D		RP69M	18695	**9175**	**10475**	**12100**	**14700**
GL TDI Wagon 4D		RP69M	19495	**9475**	**10800**	**12400**	**14950**
GLS TDI Sedan 4D		SP69M	19500	**9375**	**10700**	**12300**	**14900**
GLS TDI Wagon 4D		SP69M	20300	**9600**	**10950**	**12500**	**15050**
JETTA—V6—Equipment Schedule 6							
W.B. 98.9", 99.0" (Wag); 2.8 Liter.							
GLS Sedan 4D		SH69M	20750	**9975**	**11375**	**13100**	**15850**
GLS Wagon 4D		SH61J	21550	**10275**	**11675**	**13350**	**16100**
GLI Sedan 4D		VH69M	23500	**10425**	**11850**	**13600**	**16350**
GLX Sedan 4D		TH69M	25250	**10175**	**11575**	**13650**	**16850**
GLX Wagon 4D		TH61J	26050	**10425**	**11850**	**13900**	**17150**

2002 VOLKSWAGEN

Body	Type	VIN	List	Trade-In Fair	Good	Pvt-Party Good	Retail Excellent
CABRIO—4-Cyl.—Equipment Schedule 3							
W.B. 97.4"; 2.0 Liter.							
GL Convertible 2D		BC21V	21025	8400	9600	11750	14950
GLS Convertible 2D		CC21V	22025	8850	10125	12300	15500
GLX Convertible 2D		DC21V	23725	9225	10500	12700	16000
Manual Trans				(325)	(325)	(435)	(435)
PASSAT—4-Cyl. Turbo—Equipment Schedule 4							
W.B. 106.4"; 1.8 Liter.							
GLS Sedan 4D		PD63B	23375	9175	10475	12650	16000
GLS Wagon 4D		VD63B	24175	9425	10750	13000	16300
Manual Trans				(575)	(575)	(765)	(765)
V6 2.8 Liter		H		650	650	865	865
PASSAT—V6—Equipment Schedule 4							
W.B. 106.4"; 2.8 Liter.							
GLX Sedan 4D		RH63B	30375	12425	14075	16450	20200
GLX Wagon 4D		WH63B	31175	12675	14350	16800	20500
Manual Trans				(575)	(575)	(765)	(765)
PASSAT 4MOTION AWD—V6—Equipment Schedule 4							
W.B. 106.4"; 2.8 Liter.							
GLS Sedan 4D		SH63B	27625	12625	14250	16650	20400
GLS Wagon 4D		XH63B	28425	13200	14875	17350	21100
GLX Sedan 4D		TH63B	32125	13825	15600	18050	21900
GLX Wagon 4D		YH63B	32925	14500	16375	18850	22800
PASSAT 4MOTION AWD—W8—Equipment Schedule 4							
W.B. 106.4"; 4.0 Liter.							
Sedan 4D		UH63B	38450	17675	19875	22900	27700
Wagon 4D		ZH63B	39250	17750	19975	23000	27800

2003 VOLKSWAGEN — (3,9orW)(BorV)W(BK21J)-3

Body	Type	VIN	List	Trade-In Fair	Good	Pvt-Party Good	Retail Excellent
GOLF—4-Cyl.—Equipment Schedule 6							
W.B. 98.9"; 2.0 Liter.							
GL Hatchback 2D		BK21J	15870	7550	8700	10450	13200
GL Hatchback 4D		FK21J	16070	7725	8875	10650	13400
GLS Hatchback 4D		GK21J	18095	7900	9075	10850	13600
GOLF—4-Cyl. Turbo Diesel—Equipment Schedule 6							
W.B. 98.9"; 1.9 Liter.							
GL TDI H'Back 2D		BP21J	17295	8975	10275	12100	15000
GL TDI H'Back 4D		FP21J	17495	9100	10375	12250	15100
GLS TDI H'Back 4D		GP21J	19285	9300	10600	12500	15350
GTI—4-Cyl. Turbo—Equipment Schedule 6							
W.B. 98.9"; 1.8 Liter.							
Hatchback 2D		DE61J	19640	10425	11850	13800	16800
20th Anniv H'Back 2D		DE61J	23800	11325	12875	14900	18050
GTI VR6—V6—Equipment Schedule 6							
W.B. 98.9"; 2.8 Liter.							
Hatchback 2D		DH61J	22570	11525	13050	15000	18200
NEW BEETLE—4-Cyl.—Equipment Schedule 6							
W.B. 98.7", 98.8" (Conv) 2.0 Liter.							
GL Hatchback 2D		BK21C	16525	8725	9975	11200	13250
GL Convertible 2D		BK21Y	21025	13100	14825	16200	18750
GLS Hatchback 2D		CK21C	18390	9100	10375	11550	13700
GLS Convertible 2D		CK21Y	22425	14500	16375	17800	20500
NEW BEETLE—4-Cyl. Turbo—Equipment Schedule 6							
W.B. 98.7", 98.8" (Conv) 1.8 Liter.							
GL Hatchback 2D		BD21C	19025	9175	10475	11650	13800
GLS Hatchback 2D		CD21C	20430	9375	10700	11900	14050
GLS Convertible 2D		CD21Y	24675	14700	16600	18050	20800
GLX Hatchback 2D		DE21C	22215	9850	11225	12450	14650
GLX Convertible 2D		DD21Y	26125	16600	18675	20200	23100
S Hatchback 2D		FE21C	24115	11000	12475	13800	16150
NEW BEETLE—4-Cyl. Turbo Diesel—Equipment Schedule 6							
W.B. 98.7"; 1.9 Liter.							
GL TDI H'Back 2D		BP21C	17770	9975	11325	12600	14800
GLS TDI H'Back 2D		CP21C	19570	10275	11675	12900	15150
JETTA—4-Cyl.—Equipment Schedule 6							
W.B. 98.9", 99.0" (Wag); 2.0 Liter.							
GL Sedan 4D		RK69M	17675	8475	9700	11400	14000
GL Wagon 4D		RK61J	18475	8750	10025	11700	14400
GLS Sedan 4D		SK69M	19365	9025	10325	11750	14200
GLS Wagon 4D		SK61J	20165	9300	10600	12100	14600
JETTA—4-Cyl. Turbo—Equipment Schedule 6							
W.B. 98.9", 99.0" (Wag); 1.8 Liter.							
GL Sedan 4D		RE69M	19325	8850	10125	11800	14500

240 **DEDUCT FOR RECONDITIONING**

Body	Type	VIN	List	Trade-In Fair	Trade-In Good	Pvt-Party Good	Retail Excellent
GL Wagon 4D		RE61J	20125	9225	10500	12250	15000
Wolfsburg Sedan 4D		PE69M	20075	9425	10750	12250	14750
GLS Sedan 4D		SE29M	21015	9600	10950	12450	15000
GLS Wagon 4D		SE61J	21815	10225	11625	13150	15750
JETTA—4-Cyl. Turbo Diesel—Equipment Schedule 6							
W.B. 98.9"; 99.0" (Wag); 1.9 Liter.							
GL TDI Sedan 4D		RP69M	19065	10425	11850	13350	15900
GL TDI Wagon 4D		RP61J	19865	10700	12150	13700	16200
GLS TDI Sedan 4D		SP69M	20545	10600	12100	13600	16150
GLS TDI Wagon 4D		SP61J	21345	10850	12300	13800	16350
JETTA—V6—Equipment Schedule 6							
W.B. 98.9"; 2.8 Liter.							
GLI Sedan 4D		VH69M	23525	11750	13300	14950	17650
GLX Sedan 4D		TH69M	27515	11475	13000	15000	18200
PASSAT—4-Cyl. Turbo—Equipment Schedule 4							
W.B. 106.4"; 1.8 Liter.							
GL Sedan 4D		MD63B	23400	9600	10950	13050	16300
GL Wagon 4D		ND63B	24200	9925	11275	13500	16750
GLS Sedan 4D		PD63B	24535	10550	12050	14200	17550
GLS Wagon 4D		VD63B	27835	10900	12325	14550	17950
Manual Trans				(800)	(600)	(800)	(800)
V6 2.8 Liter		H		700	700	935	935
PASSAT—V6—Equipment Schedule 4							
W.B. 106.4"; 2.8 Liter.							
GLX Sedan 4D		RH63B	30400	14100	15925	18350	22100
GLX Wagon 4D		WH63B	31200	14400	16275	18650	22500
Manual Trans				(600)	(600)	(800)	(800)
PASSAT 4MOTION AWD—V6—Equipment Schedule 4							
W.B. 106.4"; 2.8 Liter.							
GLX Sedan 4D		TH63B	32150	15600	17625	20100	24000
GLX Wagon 4D		SH63B	32950	16375	18425	20900	25000
PASSAT 4MOTION AWD—W8—Equipment Schedule 4							
W.B. 106.4"; 4.0 Liter.							
Sedan 4D		UK63B	38475	19875	22375	25400	30300
Wagon 4D		ZK63B	39275	19975	22475	25500	30400

Body	Type	VIN	List	Trade-In Fair	Trade-In Good	Pvt-Party Good	Retail Excellent
GOLF—4-Cyl.—Equipment Schedule 6							
W.B. 98.9"; 2.0 Liter.							
GL Hatchback 2D		BK21J	16155	8725	9975	11700	14450
GL Hatchback 4D		FK21J	16355	8875	10175	11900	14700
GLS Hatchback 4D		GK21J	18715	9100	10375	12150	14950
GOLF—4-Cyl. Turbo Diesel—Equipment Schedule 6							
W.B. 98.9"; 1.9 Liter.							
GL TDI H'Back 4D		FP21J	17775				
GLS TDI H'Back 4D		GP21J	19895				
GTI—4-Cyl. Turbo—Equipment Schedule 6							
W.B. 98.9"; 1.8 Liter.							
Hatchback 2D		DE61J	19825	11800	13400	15300	18450
GTI VR6—V6—Equipment Schedule 6							
W.B. 98.9"; 2.8 Liter.							
Hatchback 2D		DH61J	22645	12950	14700	16650	19850
R32 AWD—V6—Equipment Schedule 3							
W.B. 99.1"; 3.2 Liter.							
Hatchback 2D		KG61J	29675				
NEW BEETLE—4-Cyl.—Equipment Schedule 6							
W.B. 98.7", 98.8" (Conv); 2.0 Liter.							
GL Hatchback 2D		BK21C	16905	10025	11425	12550	14550
GL Convertible 2D		BK21Y	21475	14725	16650	18000	20600
GLS Hatchback 2D		CK21C	19095	10475	11900	13000	15050
GLS Convertible 2D		CK21Y	23215	16275	18325	19800	22600
NEW BEETLE—4-Cyl. Turbo—Equipment Schedule 6							
W.B. 98.7", 98.8 (Conv); 1.8 Liter.							
GLS Hatchback 2D		CD21C	21055	10750	12200	13350	15450
GLS Convertible 2D		CD21Y	25395	16500	18575	20100	22800
S Hatchback 2D		FE21C	24425	12525	14150	15400	17750
NEW BEETLE—4-Cyl. Turbo—Equipment Schedule 6							
W.B. 98.7"; 1.9 Liter.							
GL TDI H'Back 2D		BP21C	18205				
GLS TDI H'Back 2D		CP21C	20335				
JETTA—4-Cyl.—Equipment Schedule 6							
W.B. 98.9", 99.0" (Wag); 2.0 Liter.							
GL Sedan 4D		RK29M	18005	9700	11100	12700	15350

2004 VOLKSWAGEN

Body	Type	VIN	List	Trade-In Fair	Trade-In Good	Pvt-Party Good	Retail Excellent
GL Wagon 4D		RK61J	19005	9975	11375	13050	15800
GLS Sedan 4D		SK29M	20035	10275	11675	13100	15550
GLS Wagon 4D		SK21J	21035	10550	12050	13500	16000
JETTA—4-Cyl. Turbo—Equipment Schedule 6							
W.B. 98.9", 99.0" (Wag); 1.8 Liter.							
GL Sedan 4D		SE69M	19485	10075	11475	13150	15900
GLS Sedan 4D		SE29M	21515	10900	12325	13800	16350
GLS Wagon 4D		SE61J	22515	11525	13050	14600	17250
GLI Sedan 4D		VH69M	24375	13250	14925	16550	19400
JETTA—4-Cyl. Turbo Diesel—Equipment Schedule 6							
W.B. 98.9", 99.0" (Wag); 1.9 Liter.							
GL TDI Sedan 4D		RP29M	19245				
GL TDI Wagon 4D		RP21J	20245				
GLS TDI Sedan 4D		SP69M	21055				
GLS TDI Wagon 4D		SP61J	22055				
JETTA—V6—Equipment Schedule 6							
W.B. 98.9"; 2.8 Liter.							
GLI Sedan 4D		VH29M	23785	13250	14925	16550	19400
PASSAT—4-Cyl. Turbo—Equipment Schedule 4							
W.B. 104.4"; 1.8 Liter.							
GL Sedan 4D		MD63B	23430	11225	12775	15000	18400
GL Wagon 4D		ND63B	24430	11625	13150	15400	18850
GLS Sedan 4D		PD63B	25030	12325	13975	16200	19800
GLS Wagon 4D		VD63B	26030	12625	14300	16600	20200
Manual Trans				(625)	(625)	(835)	(835)
PASSAT 4MOTION AWD—4-Cyl. Turbo—Equipment Schedule 4							
W.B. 106.4"; 1.8 Liter.							
GLS Sedan 4D		PD63B	26780	16275	18325	20700	24800
GLS Wagon 4D		VD63B	27780	16950	19050	21600	25600
Manual Trans				(625)	(625)	(835)	(835)
PASSAT—4-Cyl. Turbo Diesel—Equipment Schedule 4							
W.B. 106.4"; 2.0 Liter.							
GL TDI Sedan 4D		ME63B	23635				
GL TDI Wagon 4D		NE63B	24635				
GLS TDI Sedan 4D		PE63B	25235				
GLS TDI Wagon 4D		VE63B	26235				
Manual Trans							
PASSAT—V6—Equipment Schedule 4							
W.B. 106.4"; 2.8 Liter.							
GLX Sedan 4D		RH63B	31430	16175	18250	20700	24800
GLX Wagon 4D		WH63B	32430	16500	18575	21100	25200
Manual Trans				(625)	(625)	(835)	(835)
PASSAT 4MOTION AWD—V6—Equipment Schedule 4							
W.B. 106.4"; 2.8 Liter.							
GLX Sedan 4D		TH63B	33180	17850	20075	22600	26800
GLX Wagon 4D		YH63B	34180	18575	20825	23500	27800
PASSAT 4MOTION AWD—W8—Equipment Schedule 4							
W.B. 106.4"; 4.0 Liter.							
Sedan 4D		UK63B	39235	22475	25150	28300	33400
Wagon 4D		ZK63B	40235	22475	25150	28300	33500
Sport Pkg				375	375	500	500
PHAETON AWD—V8—Equipment Schedule 1							
W.B. 118.1"; 4.2 Liter.							
Sedan 4D		AF63D	65215				
4-Seater Pkg							
PHAETON AWD—W12—Equipment Schedule 1							
W.B. 118.1"; 6.0 Liter.							
Sedan 4D		AH63D	80515				
4-Seater Pkg							

VOLVO

1990 VOLVO — YV1(AA884)-L-#

Body	Type	VIN	List	Trade-In Fair	Trade-In Good	Pvt-Party Good	Retail Excellent
2 SERIES—4-Cyl.—Equipment Schedule 3							
W.B. 104.3"; 2.3 Liter.							
240 Sedan 4D		AA884	17735	1375	1875	3100	4825
240 Wagon 4D		AA885	18225	1675	2200	3475	5275
240 DL Sedan 4D		AA884	18000	1500	2000	3250	5000
240 DL Wagon 4D		AA885	19290	1700	2225	3525	5325
7 SERIES—4-Cyl.—Equipment Schedule 3							
W.B. 109.1"; 2.3 Liter.							
740 Sedan 4D		FA884	21035	1300	1775	2975	4650

Body	Type	VIN	List	Trade-In Fair	Good	Pvt-Party Good	Retail Excellent
740	Wagon 4D	FA885	21715	1525	2050	3300	5100
740 GL	Sedan 4D	FA884	22050	1300	1775	2975	4650
740 GL	Wagon 4D	FA885	22730	1525	2050	3300	5100
740 GLE	Sedan 4D	FA894	25790	1300	1775	2975	4650
740 GLE	Wagon 4D	FA895	26470	1525	2050	3300	5100

7 SERIES—4-Cyl. Turbo—Equipment Schedule 3
W.B. 109.1"; 2.3 Liter.

Body	Type	VIN	List	Fair	Good	Good	Excellent
740	Sedan 4D	FA874	26125	1500	2000	3250	5000
740	Wagon 4D	FA875	26805	1750	2275	3575	5375
760	Sedan 4D	GA874	34315	1650	2150	3450	5250
760	Wagon 4D	GA875	34315	2150	2725	4100	6050
780	Coupe 2D	HA872	40300	1400	1875	3125	4825

7 SERIES—V6—Equipment Schedule 3
W.B. 109.1"; 2.8 Liter.

Body	Type	VIN	List	Fair	Good	Good	Excellent
760 GLE	Sedan 4D	GA694	33535	700	1000	1850	3150
780 GLE	Coupe 2D	HA692	39085	1375	1850	3050	4750

1991 VOLVO — YV1(AA884)–M–#

240—4-Cyl.—Equipment Schedule 3
W.B. 104.3"; 2.3 Liter.

Body	Type	VIN	List	Fair	Good	Good	Excellent
	Sedan 4D	AA884	19680	1800	2325	3700	5600
	Wagon 4D	AA885	20175	2050	2600	4000	5975
	SE Wagon 4D	AA885	22915	2100	2650	4050	6025
	Manual Trans			(100)	(100)	(135)	(135)

740—4-Cyl.—Equipment Schedule 3
W.B. 109.1"; 2.3 Liter.

Body	Type	VIN	List	Fair	Good	Good	Excellent
	Sedan 4D	FA884	23135	1575	2100	3375	5200
	Wagon 4D	FA885	23815	1875	2400	3800	5700
	Manual Trans			(100)	(100)	(135)	(135)

740—4-Cyl. Turbo—Equipment Schedule 3
W.B. 109.1"; 2.3 Liter.

Body	Type	VIN	List	Fair	Good	Good	Excellent
	Sedan 4D	FA874	25190	1825	2350	3725	5625
	Wagon 4D	FA875	25870	2100	2675	4075	6075
	SE Sedan 4D	FA874	28335	1925	2450	3850	5750
	SE Wagon 4D	FA875	29015	2425	3025	4500	6575
	Coupe 2D	HA872	42325	1675	2200	3550	5400
	Manual Trans			(100)	(100)	(135)	(135)

940—4-Cyl.—Equipment Schedule 3
W.B. 109.1"; 2.3 Liter.

Body	Type	VIN	List	Fair	Good	Good	Excellent
GLE	Sedan 4D	JA894	28265	1750	2275	3625	5500
GLE	Wagon 4D	JA895	28945	1850	2375	3775	5700

940—4-Cyl. Turbo—Equipment Schedule 1
W.B. 109.1"; 2.3 Liter.

Body	Type	VIN	List	Fair	Good	Good	Excellent
	Sedan 4D	JA874	29675	2100	2675	4075	6075
	Wagon 4D	JA875	30355	2600	3225	4700	6825
	SE Sedan 4D	KA874	33330	2525	3125	4600	6700
	SE Wagon 4D	KA875	34010	2775	3400	4975	7125

1992 VOLVO — YV1(AS881)–N–#

240—4-Cyl.—Equipment Schedule 3
W.B. 104.3"; 2.3 Liter.

Body	Type	VIN	List	Fair	Good	Good	Excellent
	Sedan 4D	AS881	21215	2225	2775	4275	6300
	Wagon 4D	AW881	21715	2525	3125	4650	6775
GL	Sedan 4D	AS881	21890	2275	2850	4350	6400
	Manual Trans			(125)	(125)	(165)	(165)

740—4-Cyl.—Equipment Schedule 3
W.B. 109.1"; 2.3 Liter.

Body	Type	VIN	List	Fair	Good	Good	Excellent
	Sedan 4D	FS881	24680	1950	2475	3900	5875
	Wagon 4D	FW881	25360	2300	2875	4375	6425
GL	Wagon 4D	FW881	26070	2300	2875	4375	6425

740—4-Cyl. Turbo—Equipment Schedule 3
W.B. 109.1"; 2.3 Liter.

Body	Type	VIN	List	Fair	Good	Good	Excellent
	Wagon 4D	FW871	28190	2550	3175	4700	6850

940—4-Cyl.—Equipment Schedule 3
W.B. 109.1"; 2.3 Liter.

Body	Type	VIN	List	Fair	Good	Good	Excellent
GL	Sedan 4D	JS881	25390	2125	2700	4175	6200

940—4-Cyl. Turbo—Equipment Schedule 1
W.B. 109.1"; 2.3 Liter.

Body	Type	VIN	List	Fair	Good	Good	Excellent
	Sedan 4D	JS871	31190	2575	3200	4725	6875
	Wagon 4D	JW871	31870	3150	3800	5425	7700

960—6-Cyl.—Equipment Schedule 1
W.B. 109.1"; 3.0 Liter.

Body	Type	VIN	List	Fair	Good	Good	Excellent
	Sedan 4D	KS951	34370	1875	2400	3825	5750

1992 VOLVO

Body	Type	VIN	List	Trade-In Fair	Good	Pvt-Party Good	Retail Excellent
Wagon 4D		KW951	35050	2225	2775	4275	6300

1993 VOLVO — YV1(AS881)-P-#

240—4-Cyl.—Equipment Schedule 3
W.B. 104.3"; 2.3 Liter.

Sedan 4D		AS881	22215	2675	3275	4875	7050
Wagon 4D		AW881	23215	3000	3675	5300	7600
Manual Trans				(150)	(150)	(200)	(200)

850—5-Cyl.—Equipment Schedule 3
W.B. 104.9"; 2.4 Liter.

GLT Sedan 4D		LS551	24495	2000	2550	4025	6075
Manual Trans				(150)	(150)	(200)	(200)

940—4-Cyl.—Equipment Schedule 3
W.B. 109.1"; 2.3 Liter.

Sedan 4D		JS881	25390	2225	2775	4300	6375
Wagon 4D		JW881	26390	2500	3100	4650	6825

940—4-Cyl. Turbo—Equipment Schedule 1
W.B. 109.1"; 2.3 Liter.

Sedan 4D		JS871	28890	2725	3350	4975	7175
Wagon 4D		JW871	29890	3350	4050	5725	8100

960—6-Cyl.—Equipment Schedule 1
W.B. 109.1"; 2.9 Liter.

Sedan 4D		KS951	36070	2250	2825	4375	6450
Wagon 4D		KW951	37070	2700	3300	4925	7125

1994 VOLVO — YV1(LS551)-R-#

850—5-Cyl.—Equipment Schedule 3
W.B. 104.9"; 2.4 Liter.

Sedan 4D		LS551	24725	2425	3025	4625	6850
Wagon 4D		LW551	28120	2750	3375	5050	7325
Manual Trans				(175)	(175)	(235)	(235)

850—5-Cyl. Turbo—Equipment Schedule 1
W.B. 104.9"; 2.3 Liter.

Sedan 4D		LS571	31900	3300	4000	5725	8150
Wagon 4D		LW571	32900	3700	4425	6200	8700

940—4-Cyl.—Equipment Schedule 3
W.B. 109.1"; 2.3 Liter.

Sedan 4D		JS881	23325	2675	3275	4925	7175
Wagon 4D		JW881	24425	3000	3675	5350	7700

940—4-Cyl. Turbo—Equipment Schedule 1
W.B. 109.1"; 2.3 Liter.

Sedan 4D		JS871	27220	3275	3925	5675	8075
Wagon 4D		JW871	28220	3925	4675	6500	9050

960—6-Cyl.—Equipment Schedule 1
W.B. 109.1"; 2.9 Liter.

Sedan 4D		KS951	33875	2725	3350	5025	7300
Wagon 4D		KW951	34875	3275	3925	5675	8075

1995 VOLVO — YV1(LS551)-S-#

850—5-Cyl.—Equipment Schedule 3
W.B. 104.9"; 2.4 Liter.

Sedan 4D		LS551	25540	2175	2750	4400	6600
Wagon 4D		LW551	26840	2750	3375	5100	7475
GLT Sedan 4D		LS551	27570	2700	3300	5000	7325
GLT Wagon 4D		LW551	28870	3025	3700	5450	7850
Manual Trans				(200)	(200)	(265)	(265)

850—5-Cyl. Turbo—Equipment Schedule 1
W.B. 104.9"; 2.3 Liter.

Sedan 4D		LS571	32000	3950	4700	6600	9225
Wagon 4D		LW571	33300	4375	5150	7100	9800
T-5 R Sedan 4D		LS581	36005	4700	5525	7500	10250
T-5 R Wagon 4D		LW581	37555	5075	5950	8000	10850

940—4-Cyl.—Equipment Schedule 3
W.B. 109.1"; 2.3 Liter.

Sedan 4D		JS831	24315	3175	3850	5625	8075
Wagon 4D		JW831	25615	3600	4325	6175	8700
GL Sedan 4D		JS831	25295	3175	3850	5625	8075

940—4-Cyl. Turbo—Equipment Schedule 1
W.B. 109.1"; 2.3 Liter.

Sedan 4D		JS861	24820	3875	4600	6450	9050
Wagon 4D		JW861	26120	4600	5425	7400	10150

0105

1995 VOLVO

Body	Type	VIN	List	Trade-In Fair	Good	Pvt-Party Good	Retail Excellent
960—6-Cyl.—Equipment Schedule 1							
W.B. 109.1"; 2.9 Liter.							
Sedan 4D		KS961	30360	3300	3975	5750	8225
Wagon 4D		KW961	31660	3900	4625	6525	9125

1996 VOLVO — YV1(LS554)-T-#

Body	Type	VIN	List	Trade-In Fair	Good	Pvt-Party Good	Retail Excellent
850—5-Cyl.—Equipment Schedule 3							
W.B. 104.9"; 2.4 Liter.							
Sedan 4D		LS554	26620	2750	3375	5175	7600
Wagon 4D		LW554	27920	3375	4075	5950	8525
GLT Sedan 4D		LS554	29695	3275	3925	5775	8300
GLT Wagon 4D		LW554	30995	3725	4450	6325	8975
Manual Trans				(200)	(200)	(265)	(265)
850—5-Cyl. Turbo—Equipment Schedule 1							
W.B. 104.9"; 2.3 Liter.							
Sedan 4D		LS572	33145	4750	5575	7625	10450
Wagon 4D		LW572	34445	5200	6075	8150	11100
TLA Sedan 4D		LS572	37380	5525	6425	8575	11550
TLA Wagon 4D		LW572	38830	5925	6900	9100	12200
R Sedan 4D		LS572	38420	6025	6975	9200	12300
R Wagon 4D		LW572	39870	6500	7500	9800	12950
960—6-Cyl.—Equipment Schedule 1							
W.B. 109.1"; 2.9 Liter.							
Sedan 4D		KS960	34455	3975	4725	6675	9350
Wagon 4D		KW960	35755	4650	5500	7500	10300

1997 VOLVO — YV1(LS555)-V-#

Body	Type	VIN	List	Trade-In Fair	Good	Pvt-Party Good	Retail Excellent
850—5-Cyl.—Equipment Schedule 3							
W.B. 104.9"; 2.4 Liter.							
Sedan 4D		LS555	28180	3450	4150	6125	8800
Wagon 4D		LW555	29480	4125	4900	6925	9750
Manual Trans				(200)	(200)	(265)	(265)
850—5-Cyl. Turbo—Equipment Schedule 1							
W.B. 104.9"; 2.3 Liter, 2.4 Liter.							
GLT Sedan 4D		LS564	33525	5125	6000	8150	11150
GLT Wagon 4D		LW564	34825	5525	6425	8650	11700
T-5 Sedan 4D		LS564	36190	5650	6550	8750	11850
T-5 Wagon 4D		LW572	37490	6150	7125	9375	12600
R Sedan 4D		LS582	39180	6475	7500	9800	13050
R Wagon 4D		LW582	40630	6925	8000	10350	13750
960—6-Cyl.—Equipment Schedule 1							
W.B. 109.1"; 2.9 Liter.							
Sedan 4D		KS960	34795	4775	5625	7725	10650
Wagon 4D		KW960	36345	5550	6450	8700	11750
90 SERIES—6-Cyl.—Equipment Schedule 1							
W.B. 109.1"; 2.9 Liter.							
S90 Sedan 4D		KS960	34875	5050	5925	8075	11050
V90 Wagon 4D		KW960	36425	5875	6850	9100	12250

1998 VOLVO — YV1(LS553)-W-#

Body	Type	VIN	List	Trade-In Fair	Good	Pvt-Party Good	Retail Excellent
70 SERIES—5-Cyl.—Equipment Schedule 3							
W.B. 104.9"; 2.4 Liter.							
S70 Sedan 4D		LS553	28535	4675	5525	6975	9200
V70 Wagon 4D		LW553	29835	5400	6300	7850	10200
Manual Trans		4		(200)	(200)	(265)	(265)
70 SERIES—5-Cyl. Turbo—Equipment Schedule 1							
W.B. 104.9", 104.5" (AWD); 2.3 Liter, 2.4 Liter.							
C70 Coupe 2D		NK547	40545	8925	10225	12100	15000
C70 Convertible 2D		NC567	43570	10275	11700	13750	16850
S70 GLT Sedan 4D		LS564	33015	6375	7375	9025	11500
V70 GLT Wagon 4D		LW564	34315	7000	8100	9800	12400
S70 T-5 Sedan 4D		LS534	35560	7050	8125	9800	12450
V70 T-5 Wagon 4D		LW534	36860	7650	8775	10550	13250
V70 AWD Wagon 4D		LW564	36195	8225	9425	11250	14000
V70 XC AWD Wagon 4D		LZ564	38195	8400	9600	11600	14600
V70 R AWD Wagon 4D		LW524	41570	9650	11000	12900	15950
90 SERIES—6-Cyl.—Equipment Schedule 1							
W.B. 109.1"; 2.9 Liter.							
S90 Sedan 4D		KS960	34875	6050	7000	9225	12350
V90 Wagon 4D		KW960	36425	6925	8000	10250	13550

Body	Type	VIN	List	Trade-In Fair	Good	Pvt-Party Good	Retail Excellent

1999 VOLVO — YV1(LS55A)-X-#

70 SERIES—5-Cyl.—Equipment Schedule 3
W.B. 104.9"; 2.4 Liter.

S70 Sedan 4D		LS55A	28935	**5650**	**6575**	**8175**	**10550**
V70 Wagon 4D		LW55A	30235	**6475**	**7500**	**9175**	**11650**
Manual Trans		4		**(225)**	**(225)**	**(300)**	**(300)**

70 SERIES—5-Cyl. Turbo—Equipment Schedule 1
W.B. 104.5", 104.8" (XC), 104.9" (C70, S70/V70 GLT & T-5); 2.3 Liter, 2.4 Liter.

C70 LT Coupe 2D		NK56D	37570	**8725**	**9975**	**11800**	**14700**
C70 HT Coupe 2D		NK53D	40945	**10500**	**11950**	**13950**	**17100**
C70 Convertible 2D		NC56D	43970	**12050**	**13675**	**15800**	**19200**
S70 GLT Sedan 4D		LS56A	35105	**7625**	**8750**	**10550**	**13250**
V70 GLT Wagon 4D		LW56A	36405	**8350**	**9575**	**11400**	**14200**
S70 T-5 Sedan 4D		LS53A	37155	**8400**	**9600**	**11400**	**14250**
V70 T-5 Wagon 4D		LW53A	38455	**9100**	**10375**	**12300**	**15200**
S70 AWD Sedan 4D		LT56A	36985	**9025**	**10325**	**12200**	**15050**
V70 AWD Wagon 4D		LV56A	38285	**9700**	**11100**	**13000**	**16050**
V70 XC AWD Wag 4D		LZ56A	39460	**9925**	**11275**	**13450**	**16650**
V70 R AWD Wagon 4D		LV52A	41970	**11325**	**12875**	**14950**	**18200**

80 SERIES—6-Cyl.—Equipment Schedule 1
W.B. 109.9"; 2.9 Liter.

S80 2.9 Sedan 4D		TS97D	38790	**8025**	**9200**	**11400**	**14550**

80 SERIES—6-Cyl. Turbo—Equipment Schedule 1
W.B. 109.9"; 2.8 Liter.

S80 T-6 Sedan 4D		TS90D	43755	**9925**	**11275**	**13650**	**17100**

2000 VOLVO — YV1(VS252)-Y-#

40 SERIES—4-Cyl. Turbo—Equipment Schedule 3
W.B. 100.3"; 1.9 Liter.

S40 Sedan 4D		VS252	23475	**5775**	**6750**	**8200**	**10450**
V40 Wagon 4D		VW252	24475	**6850**	**7900**	**9450**	**11850**

70 SERIES—5-Cyl.—Equipment Schedule 3
W.B. 104.9"; 2.4 Liter.

S70 Sedan 4D		LS61J	29075	**6850**	**7900**	**9650**	**12300**
S70 SE Sedan 4D		LS61J	30075	**7000**	**8100**	**9850**	**12500**
V70 Wagon 4D		LW61J	30375	**7775**	**8925**	**10750**	**13550**
V70 SE Wagon 4D		LW61J	31575	**7950**	**9125**	**10950**	**13750**
Manual Trans		4		**(250)**	**(250)**	**(335)**	**(335)**

70 SERIES—5-Cyl. Turbo—Equipment Schedule 1
W.B. 104.5", 104.9" (C70, S70 & V70 ex. AWD); 2.3 Liter, 2.4 Liter.

C70 LT Coupe 2D		NK56D	36475	**10475**	**11900**	**13900**	**17050**
C70 LT Convertible 2D		NC56D	45675	**14100**	**15900**	**18200**	**21900**
C70 HT Coupe 2D		NK53D	40575	**12300**	**13925**	**16110**	**19500**
C70 HT Conv 2D		NC53D	47075	**15025**	**16900**	**19300**	**23000**
S70 GLT Sedan 4D		LS56D	34675	**9150**	**10425**	**12300**	**15250**
S70 GLT SE Sedan 4D		LS56D	33075	**9325**	**10650**	**12600**	**15600**
V70 GLT Wagon 4D		LW56D	35975	**9925**	**11275**	**13300**	**16350**
S70 T-5 Sedan 4D		LS53D	37275	**9925**	**11275**	**13300**	**16350**
S70 AWD Sedan 4D		LT56D	36575	**10600**	**12100**	**14100**	**17300**
V70 XC AWD Wag 4D		LZ56D	39075	**11625**	**13150**	**15450**	**18950**
V70 XC AWD SE Wag.		LZ56D	37575	**12150**	**13775**	**15900**	**19300**
V70 R AWD Wagon 4D		LV60D	42075	**13250**	**14925**	**17150**	**20600**

80 SERIES—6-Cyl.—Equipment Schedule 1
W.B. 109.9"; 2.9 Liter.

S80 2.9 Sedan 4D		TS94D	37775	**9700**	**11100**	**13400**	**16800**

80 SERIES—6-Cyl. Turbo—Equipment Schedule 1
W.B. 109.9"; 2.8 Liter.

S80 T-6 Sedan 4D		TS90D	42275	**11850**	**13450**	**15900**	**19600**

2001 VOLVO — YV1(VS295)-1-#

40 SERIES—4-Cyl. Turbo—Equipment Schedule 3
W.B. 100.9"; 1.9 Liter.

S40 Sedan 4D		VS295	24075	**6950**	**8050**	**9650**	**12150**
S40 SE Sedan 4D		VS295	28025	**8175**	**9375**	**11100**	**13750**
V40 Wagon 4D		VW295	25075	**8125**	**9325**	**11050**	**13700**
V40 SE Wagon 4D		VW295	29025	**9100**	**10375**	**12150**	**14900**

60 SERIES—5-Cyl.—Equipment Schedule 3
W.B. 106.9"; 2.4 Liter.

S60 2.4 Sedan 4D		RS61N	27075	**9550**	**10900**	**12750**	**15700**

60 SERIES—5-Cyl. Turbo—Equipment Schedule 3
W.B. 106.9"; 2.3 Liter, 2.4 Liter.

2001 VOLVO

Body	Type	VIN	List	Trade-In Fair	Good	Pvt-Party Good	Retail Excellent
S60 2.4T Sedan 4D		RS58P	30375	11050	12525	14500	17650
S60 T5 Sedan 4D		RS53D	32375	12250	13875	15900	19200

70 SERIES—5-Cyl.—Equipment Schedule 3
W.B. 108.5"; 2.4 Liter.

| V70 Wagon 4D | | SW61N | 30075 | 11175 | 12675 | 14800 | 18100 |

70 SERIES—5-Cyl. Turbo—Equipment Schedule 3
W.B. 104.9", 108.5" (V70 ex XC), 108.8" (XC); 2.3 Liter, 2.4 Liter.

C70 LT Convertible 2D		NC56D	44075	16375	18425	20800	24900
C70 HT Coupe 2D		NK53D	38475	14350	16175	18500	22200
C70 HT Conv 2D		NC53D	47075	17375	19500	22000	26100
V70 2.4T Wagon 4D		SW58D	35375	12675	14350	16550	20100
V70 T5 Wagon 4D		SW53D	36675	13400	15125	17400	20900
V70 XC AWD Wag 4D		SZ58D	37975	15125	17050	19400	23200

80 SERIES—6-Cyl.—Equipment Schedule 1
W.B. 109.9"; 2.9 Liter.

| S80 2.9 Sedan 4D | | TS94D | 38675 | 11675 | 13200 | 15700 | 19400 |

80 SERIES—6-Cyl. Turbo—Equipment Schedule 1
W.B. 109.9"; 2.8 Liter.

| S80 T-6A Sedan 4D | | TS90D | 42675 | 14025 | 15800 | 18400 | 22400 |
| S80 T-6 Executive 4D | | TS90D | 48075 | 15225 | 17125 | 19800 | 24000 |

2002 VOLVO — YV1(VS295)-2-#

40 SERIES—4-Cyl. Turbo—Equipment Schedule 3
W.B. 100.9"; 1.9 Liter.

| S40 Sedan 4D | | VS295 | 24525 | 8450 | 9650 | 11400 | 14200 |
| V40 Wagon 4D | | VW295 | 25525 | 9700 | 11100 | 12900 | 15850 |

60 SERIES—5-Cyl.—Equipment Schedule 3
W.B. 106.9"; 2.4 Liter.

| S60 2.4 Sedan 4D | | RS61N | 27750 | 11275 | 12825 | 14900 | 18150 |

60 SERIES—5-Cyl. Turbo—Equipment Schedule 3
W.B. 106.9"; 2.3 Liter, 2.4 Liter.

S60 2.4T Sedan 4D		RS58D	32250	12950	14700	16800	20300
S60 T5 Sedan 4D		RS53D	34650	14250	16075	18300	21900
S60 2.4T AWD Sed 4D		RH58D	34000	13675	15450	17650	21200

70 SERIES—5-Cyl.—Equipment Schedule 3
W.B. 108.5"; 2.4 Liter.

| V70 Wagon 4D | | SW61N | 30650 | 13250 | 14925 | 17250 | 20800 |

70 SERIES—5-Cyl. Turbo—Equipment Schedule 3
W.B. 104.9", 108.5" (V70 ex XC), 108.8" (XC); 2.3 Liter, 2.4 Liter.

C70 LT Convertible 2D		NC56D	44750	19000	21300	23900	28100
C70 HT Coupe 2D		NK53D	38150	16700	18775	21200	25200
C70 HT Conv 2D		NC53D	46750	20075	22550	25200	29500
V70 2.4T Wagon 4D		SW58D	36150	14875	16750	19100	22800
V70 2.4T AWD Wag 4D		SJ58D	37900	16375	18425	20800	24900
V70 T5 Wagon 4D		SW53D	38350	15750	17700	20200	24000
V70 XC AWD Wag 4D		SZ58D	38425	17525	19675	22200	26200

80 SERIES—6-Cyl.—Equipment Schedule 1
W.B. 109.9"; 2.9 Liter.

| S80 2.9 Sedan 4D | | TS94D | 38775 | 13875 | 15700 | 18300 | 22300 |

80 SERIES—6-Cyl. Turbo—Equipment Schedule 1
W.B. 109.9"; 2.9 Liter.

| S80 T-6 Sedan 4D | | TS90D | 42775 | 16475 | 18525 | 21300 | 25600 |
| S80 T-6 Executive 4D | | TS90D | 50575 | 17750 | 19975 | 22800 | 27200 |

2003 VOLVO — YV1(VS275)-3-#

40 SERIES—4-Cyl. Turbo—Equipment Schedule 3
W.B. 100.9"; 1.9 Liter.

| S40 Sedan 4D | | VS275 | 24560 | 10275 | 11700 | 13650 | 16600 |
| V40 Wagon 4D | | VW275 | 25560 | 11700 | 13250 | 15200 | 18400 |

60 SERIES—5-Cyl.—Equipment Schedule 3
W.B. 107.0"; 2.4 Liter.

| S60 2.4 Sedan 4D | | RS61T | 28030 | 13450 | 15175 | 17400 | 20900 |

60 SERIES—5-Cyl. Turbo—Equipment Schedule 3
W.B. 107.0"; 2.3 Liter, 2.4 Liter, 2.5 Liter.

S60 2.4T Sedan 4D		RS58D	31085	15300	17275	19600	23300
S60 2.5T AWD Sed 4D		RH59H	32835	16125	18150	20400	24300
S60 T5 Sedan 4D		RS53D	34685	16600	18675	21100	25100

70 SERIES—5-Cyl.—Equipment Schedule 3
W.B. 108.5"; 2.4 Liter.

| V70 Wagon 4D | | SW61T | 29530 | 15600 | 17625 | 20100 | 24000 |

70 SERIES—5-Cyl. Turbo—Equipment Schedule 1
W.B. 104.9", 108.5" (V70), 108.8" (XC70); 2.3 Liter, 2.4 Liter,
2.5 Liter.

Body Type	VIN	List	Trade-In Fair	Good	Pvt-Party Good	Retail Excellent
C70 LT Convertible 2D	NC63D	44785	21975	24575	27400	32000
C70 HT Conv 2D	NC62D	47785	23125	25925	28700	33400
V70 2.4T Wagon 4D	SW58D	31530	17425	19575	22100	26200
V70 2.5T AWD Wag 4D	SJ59H	33280	19100	21400	24000	28300
V70 T5 Wagon 4D	SW53D	35730	18425	20725	23300	27600
XC70 AWD Wagon 4D	SZ59H	34530	20250	22650	25300	29800

80 SERIES—6-Cyl.—Equipment Schedule 1
W.B. 109.9"; 2.9 Liter.

Body Type	VIN	List	Trade-In Fair	Good	Pvt-Party Good	Retail Excellent
S80 2.9 Sedan 4D	TS92D	39110	16500	18575	21400	25700

80 SERIES—6-Cyl. Turbo—Equipment Schedule 1
W.B. 109.9"; 2.9 Liter.

Body Type	VIN	List	Trade-In Fair	Good	Pvt-Party Good	Retail Excellent
S80 T6 Sedan 4D	TS91D	44595	19300	21700	24600	29300
S80 T6 Elite Sedan 4D	TS91Z	48880	20725	23225	26200	31000

2004 VOLVO — YV1(VS275)-4-#

40 SERIES—4-Cyl. Turbo—Equipment Schedule 3
W.B. 101.0"; 1.9 Liter.

Body Type	VIN	List	Trade-In Fair	Good	Pvt-Party Good	Retail Excellent
S40 Sedan 4D	VS275	25385	12775	14450	16600	20100
S40 LSE Sedan 4D	VS275	29530	14100	15925	18200	21800
V40 Wagon 4D	VW275	26385	14250	16075	18350	22000
V40 LSE Wagon 4D	VW275	30530	15600	17575	19850	23700

40 SERIES—5-Cyl.—Equipment Schedule 3
W.B. 103.9"; 2.4 Liter.

Body Type	VIN	List	Trade-In Fair	Good	Pvt-Party Good	Retail Excellent
S40 2.4i Sedan 4D	MS382	27170	14350	16175	18450	22100

40 SERIES—5-Cyl. Turbo—Equipment Schedule 3
W.B. 103.9"; 2.5 Liter.

Body Type	VIN	List	Trade-In Fair	Good	Pvt-Party Good	Retail Excellent
S40 T5 Sedan 4D	MS682	29970	15900	17900	20300	24000
S40 T5 AWD Sedan 4D	MH682		16700	18775	21100	25100

60 SERIES—5-Cyl.—Equipment Schedule 3
W.B. 106.9" 2.4 Liter.

Body Type	VIN	List	Trade-In Fair	Good	Pvt-Party Good	Retail Excellent
S60 2.4 Sedan 4D	RS61T	28645	16125	18150	20600	24800

60 SERIES—5-Cyl. Turbo—Equipment Schedule 3
W.B. 106.9", 107.0" (R); 2.3 Liter, 2.5 Liter.

Body Type	VIN	List	Trade-In Fair	Good	Pvt-Party Good	Retail Excellent
S60 2.5T Sedan 4D	RS59V	30295	18250	20550	23100	27400
S60 2.5T AWD Sed 4D	RH59H	32075	19100	21400	24100	28400
S60 T5 Sedan 4D	RS53D	34155	19575	21975	24600	29000
S60 R AWD Sedan 4D	RH52Y	39185	22175	24775	27600	32200

70 SERIES—5-Cyl.—Equipment Schedule 3
W.B. 108.5"; 2.4 Liter.

Body Type	VIN	List	Trade-In Fair	Good	Pvt-Party Good	Retail Excellent
V70 Wagon 4D	SW61T	30145	18675	20925	23600	27900

70 SERIES—5-Cyl. Turbo—Equipment Schedule 1
W.B. 104.9", 108.5" (V70), 108.8" (XC70); 2.3 Liter, 2.4 Liter, 2.5 Liter.

Body Type	VIN	List	Trade-In Fair	Good	Pvt-Party Good	Retail Excellent
C70 LT Convertible 2D	NC63D	40565	25525	28500	31500	36500
C70 HT Conv 2D	NC62D	43565	26775	29950	32800	38000
V70 2.5T Wagon 4D	SW59V	35070	20550	23050	25800	30400
V70 2.5T AWD Wag 4D	SJ59H	36895	22375	25050	27800	32600
V70 T5 Wagon 4D	SW53D	38145	21700	24375	27200	31900
V70 R AWD Wagon 4D	SJ52Y	40635	24100	26975	29800	34700
XC70 AWD Wagon 4D	SZ59H	38145	23625	26400	29300	34100

80 SERIES—6-Cyl.—Equipment Schedule 1
W.B. 109.9"; 2.9 Liter.

Body Type	VIN	List	Trade-In Fair	Good	Pvt-Party Good	Retail Excellent
S80 2.9 Sedan 4D	TS92D	39725	19775	22175	25100	29900

80 SERIES—6-Cyl. Turbo—Equipment Schedule 1
W.B. 109.9"; 2.5 Liter.

Body Type	VIN	List	Trade-In Fair	Good	Pvt-Party Good	Retail Excellent
S80 2.5T Sedan 4D	TR59V	38630	20450	22850	25900	30700
S80 2.5T AWD Sed 4D	TH59H	40380	21025	23525	26500	31400

80 SERIES—6-Cyl. Twin Turbo—Equipment Schedule 1
W.B. 109.9"; 2.9 Liter.

Body Type	VIN	List	Trade-In Fair	Good	Pvt-Party Good	Retail Excellent
S80 T6 Sedan 4D	TS91Z	45210				
S80 T6 Premier Sed 4D	TS91Z	49200				

Body	Type	VIN	List	Trade-In Fair	Good	Pvt-Party Good	Retail Excellent

Truck & Van Section

ACURA

1996 ACURA — JAE(DJ58V)–T–#

SLX 4WD—V6—Truck Equipment Schedule T3
Sport Utility 4D DJ58V 38420 **3575 4300 5950 8275**

1997 ACURA — JAE(DJ58V)–V–#

SLX 4WD—V6—Truck Equipment Schedule T3
Sport Utility 4D DJ58V 38735 **4175 4975 6750 9250**

1998 ACURA — JAE(DJ58X)–W–#

SLX 4WD—V6—Truck Equipment Schedule T3
Sport Utility 4D DJ58X 36735 **4975 5825 7650 10250**

1999 ACURA — JAE(DJ58X)–X–#

SLX 4WD—V6—Truck Equipment Schedule T3
Sport Utility 4D DJ58X 36755 **6075 7050 9025 11850**

2000 ACURA — No Production

2001 ACURA — 2HN(YD182)–1–#

MDX 4WD—V6—Truck Equipment Schedule T3
Sport Utility 4D YD182 34850 **16750 18875 21600 26000**
Touring Spt Util 4D YD186 37450 **18100 20350 23200 27700**

2002 ACURA — 2HN(YD182)–2–#

MDX 4WD—V6—Truck Equipment Schedule T3
Sport Utility 4D YD182 35180 **18825 21125 24000 28600**
Touring Spt Util 4D YD186 37780 **20350 22750 25700 30500**

2003 ACURA — 2HN(YD182)–3–#

MDX 4WD—V6—Truck Equipment Schedule T3
Sport Utility 4D YD182 36200 **21300 23900 26900 31800**
Touring Spt Util 4D YD186 38800 **22850 25625 28700 33800**

2004 ACURA — 2NH(YD182)–4–#

MDX 4WD—V6—Truck Equipment Schedule T3
Sport Utility 4D YD182 36945 **24300 27175 30300 35600**
Touring Spt Util 4D YD186 39545 **26025 29100 32300 37700**

BMW

2000 BMW — WBA(FB335)–Y–#

X5 AWD—V8—Truck Equipment Schedule T3
4.4i Sport Utility 4D FB335 49970 **21600 24200 27300 32400**
  Sport Pkg .... -------- **275 275 365 365**

2001 BMW — WBA(FA535)–1–#

X5 AWD—6-Cyl.—Truck Equipment Schedule T3
3.0i Sport Utility 4D FA535 42195 **20450 22950 25900 30800**
  Sport Pkg .... -------- **300 300 400 400**
X5 AWD—V8—Truck Equipment Schedule T3
4.4i Sport Utility 4D FB335 49970 **24375 27275 30400 35800**
  Sport Pkg .... -------- **300 300 400 400**

2002 BMW — 5UX(FA535)–2–#

X5 AWD—6-Cyl.—Truck Equipment Schedule T3
3.0i Sport Utility 4D FA535 42270 **23125 25925 29000 34100**
  Sport Pkg .... -------- **325 325 435 435**
X5 AWD—V8—Truck Equipment Schedule T3
4.4i Sport Utility 4D FB335 50045 **27450 30625 34000 39600**
4.6is Sport Utility 4D FB935 66845 **36000 40125 43900 50500**

TRUCKS & VANS

Body	Type	VIN	List	Trade-In Fair	Trade-In Good	Pvt-Party Good	Retail Excellent
Sport Pkg				325	325	435	435

2003 BMW — 5UX(FA535)-3-#

X5 AWD—6-Cyl.—Truck Equipment Schedule T3
| 3.0i Sport Utility 4D | FA535 | 42920 | 26200 | 29275 | 32400 | 37900 |
| Sport Pkg | | | 350 | 350 | 465 | 465 |

X5 AWD—V8—Truck Equipment Schedule T3
4.4i Sport Utility 4D	FB335	50645	30900	34475	37800	43800
4.6is Sport Utility 4D	FB935	67495	40225	44725	48600	55500
Sport Pkg			350	350	465	465

2004 BMW — USED DATA NOT YET AVAILABLE

BUICK

2002 BUICK — 3G5-(A03E)-2-#

RENDEZVOUS—V6—Truck Equipment Schedule T3
| CX Sport Utility 4D | A03E | 26279 | 8100 | 9300 | 11650 | 15050 |
| AWD | | | 900 | 900 | 1200 | 1200 |

RENDEZVOUS AWD—V6—Truck Equipment Schedule T3
| CXL Sport Utility 4D | B03E | 31502 | 9475 | 10800 | 13250 | 16850 |

2003 BUICK — 3G5-(A03E)-3-#

RENDEZVOUS—V6—Truck Equipment Schedule T3
CX Sport Utility 4D	A03E	26975	9700	11100	13550	17200
CXL Sport Utility 4D	B03E	30200	11175	12725	15250	19050
AWD			975	975	1300	1300

2004 BUICK — (3G5or5GA)-(A03E)-4-#

RENDEZVOUS—V6—Truck Equipment Schedule T3
CX Sport Utility 4D	A03E	26545	11625	13150	15850	19800
CXL Sport Utility 4D	A03E	26545	13200	14875	17600	21700
AWD			1050	1050	1400	1400
V6 3.6 Liter	B		400	400	535	535

RENDEZVOUS AWD—V6—Truck Equipment Schedule T3
| Ultra Sport Utility 4D | B037 | 39695 | 15500 | 17475 | 20300 | 24700 |

RAINIER AWD—6-Cyl.—Truck Equipment Schedule T1
CXL Sport Utility 4D	T13S	37895	14300	16125	19000	23300
2WD	S		(1550)	(1550)	(2065)	(2065)
V8 5.3 Liter	P		400	400	535	535

CADILLAC

1999 CADILLAC — 1GY-(K13R)-X-#

ESCALADE 4WD—V8—Truck Equipment Schedule T3
| Sport Utility 4D | K13R | 46525 | 11000 | 12475 | 15300 | 19400 |

2000 CADILLAC — 1GY-(K13R)-Y-#

ESCALADE 4WD—V8—Truck Equipment Schedule T3
| Sport Utility 4D | K13R | 46875 | 13525 | 15300 | 18250 | 22600 |

2001 CADILLAC — No Production

2002 CADILLAC — (1or3)GY-(K63N)-2-#

ESCALADE AWD—V8—Truck Equipment Schedule T3
Sport Utility 4D	K63N	51980	24375	27275	30600	36100
2WD	C		(1450)	(1450)	(1935)	(1935)
V8 5.3 Liter	T		(425)	(425)	(565)	(565)

ESCALADE EXT AWD—V8—Truck Equipment Schedule T3
| Sport Util Pickup 4D | K13N | 49990 | 25150 | 28125 | 30400 | 34800 |

2003 CADILLAC — (1or3)GY-(K63N)-3-#

ESCALADE AWD—V8—Truck Equipment Schedule T3
Sport Utility 4D	K63N	53975	27750	31000	34600	40400
2WD	C		(1500)	(1500)	(2000)	(2000)
V8 5.3 Liter	T		(450)	(450)	(600)	(600)

Body Type	VIN	List	Trade-In Fair	Trade-In Good	Pvt-Party Good	Retail Excellent
ESCALADE EXT AWD—V8—Truck Equipment Schedule T3						
Sport Util Pickup 4D	K63N	51215	28325	31675	33800	38200
ESCALADE ESV AWD—V8—Truck Equipment Schedule T3						
Sport Utility 4D	K66N	56160	31775	35425	39100	45200

2004 CADILLAC — (1or3)GY–(E63A)–4–#

Body Type	VIN	List	Trade-In Fair	Trade-In Good	Pvt-Party Good	Retail Excellent
SRX—V8—Truck Equipment Schedule T3						
Sport Utility 4D	E63A	46995	29000	32350	36100	42200
Luxury Performance			350	350	465	465
Power Third Seat			0	0	0	0
AWD			1050	1050	1400	1400
V6 3.6 Liter	7		(575)	(575)	(765)	(765)
ESCALADE AWD—V8—Truck Equipment Schedule T3						
Sport Utility 4D	K63N	55695	31675	35325	38900	45100
2WD	C		(1550)	(1550)	(2065)	(2065)
V8 5.3 Liter	T		(475)	(475)	(635)	(635)
ESCALADE EXT AWD—V8—Truck Equipment Schedule T3						
Sport Util Pickup 4D	K63N	52975	31775	35425	37500	42000
ESCALADE ESV AWD—V8—Truck Equipment Schedule T3						
Sport Utility 4D	K66N	58095				
Platinum Utility 4D	K66N	69730				

CHEVROLET/GMC

1990 CHEVY/GMC — 1G(C,T,BorD)–(T18Z)–L–#

Body Type	VIN	List	Trade-In Fair	Trade-In Good	Pvt-Party Good	Retail Excellent
S10 BLAZER/S15 JIMMY 4WD—V6—Truck Equipment Sch T1						
Sport Utility 2D	T18Z	16786	825	1150	1975	3250
2WD	S		(350)	(350)	(465)	(465)
BLAZER/JIMMY 4WD—V8—Truck Equipment Schedule T1						
Sport Utility 2D	V18K	18846	1025	1475	2550	4050
V8 6.2 Liter Diesel	C		(100)	(100)	(135)	(135)
SUBURBAN—V8—Truck Equipment Schedule T1						
R1500 Sport Utility	R16K	18279	950	1350	2500	4125
R2500 Sport Utility	R26K	19522	1025	1450	2625	4275
w/o Third Seat	V		(200)	(200)	(265)	(265)
4WD	V		500	500	665	665
V8 454/7.4 Liter	N		150	150	200	200
V8 6.2 Liter Diesel	C,J		(100)	(100)	(135)	(135)
APV—V6—Truck Equipment Schedule T2						
Cargo Minivan	U06D	13395	175	225	550	1050
LUMINA APV—V6—Truck Equipment Schedule T1						
Minivan	U06D	15300	300	425	825	1425
5 Passenger			(200)	(200)	(265)	(265)
ASTRO/SAFARI—4-Cyl.—Truck Equipment Schedule T2						
Cargo Minivan	M15E	12691	475	675	1150	1925
Extended Cargo	M19E	13898	500	725	1225	2075
AWD	L		250	250	335	335
V6 4.3 Liter	Z		200	200	265	265
ASTRO/SAFARI—V6—Truck Equipment Schedule T1						
Minivan	M15Z	15261	650	900	1500	2475
Extended Minivan	M19Z	16335	750	1025	1675	2725
5 Passenger			(200)	(200)	(265)	(265)
AWD	L		250	250	335	335
V6 4.3L High Output	B		100	100	135	135
SPORTVAN/RALLY WAGON—V8—Truck Equipment Sch T1						
G10 Passenger Van	G15H	17056	825	1150	1925	3150
G20 Passenger Van	G25H	17201	850	1175	2000	3250
G30 Passenger Van	G35K	19178	875	1225	2050	3300
5 Passenger			(200)	(200)	(265)	(265)
110" W.B.			0	0	0	0
146" W.B.			50	50	65	65
V6 4.3 Liter	Z		(200)	(200)	(265)	(265)
V8 454/7.4 Liter	N		100	100	135	135
V8 6.2 Liter Diesel	C,J		(100)	(100)	(135)	(135)
G-SERIES/VANDURA—V6—Truck Equipment Schedule T1						
G10 Cargo Van	G19Z	14506	775	1100	1725	2750
G20 Cargo Van	G29Z	14686	850	1175	1850	2925
G30 Cargo Van	G35Z	14953	875	1225	1925	3025
110" W.B.	5		0	0	0	0
146" W.B.	9		50	50	65	65
V8 5.0, 5.7 Liter	H,K		100	100	135	135

TRUCKS & VANS

Body Type	VIN	List	Trade-In Fair	Trade-In Good	Pvt-Party Good	Retail Excellent
V8 454/7.4 Liter	N		200	200	265	265
V8 6.2 Liter Diesel	C,J		(75)	(75)	(100)	(100)
S10/S15 PICKUP—4-Cyl.—Truck Equipment Schedule T2						
EL/Spcl Short Bed	S14E	8395	275	375	825	1475
Short Bed	S14E	9766	350	500	975	1725
Long Bed	S14E	9931	300	425	875	1550
Extended Cab	S19E	10716	550	800	1400	2350
4WD	T		500	500	665	665
V6 2.8 Liter	R		125	125	165	165
V6 4.3 Liter	Z		150	150	200	200
REGULAR CAB PICKUP—V8—Truck Equipment Schedule T1						
C1500 Short Bed	C14H	13465	1375	1850	2850	4325
C1500 Long Bed	C14H	13745	1275	1750	2725	4175
C2500 Long Bed	C24H	14370	1100	1550	2550	3925
C3500 Long Bed	C34K	15994	1175	1625	2625	4025
Work Truck/Special			(250)	(250)	(335)	(335)
4WD	K		500	500	665	665
V6 4.3 Liter	Z		(350)	(350)	(465)	(465)
V8 5.7 Liter	N		75	75	100	100
V8 454/7.4 Liter	N		150	150	200	200
V8 6.2 Liter Diesel	C,J		(100)	(100)	(135)	(135)
REGULAR CAB PICKUP—V8—Truck Equipment Schedule T3						
454SS Short Bed	C14N	18845	2975	3625	4925	6825
EXTENDED CAB PICKUP—V8—Truck Equipment Schedule T1						
C1500 Short Bed	C19H	14375	1625	2125	3200	4725
C1500 Long Bed	C19H	14655	1550	2075	3125	4625
C2500 Short Bed	C29H	15440	1750	2275	3350	4950
C2500 Long Bed	C29H	15720	1600	2100	3175	4675
C3500 Long Bed	C39K	17014	1600	2100	3175	4675
4WD	K		500	500	665	665
V6 4.3 Liter	Z		(350)	(350)	(465)	(465)
V8 5.7 Liter	N		75	75	100	100
V8 454/7.4 Liter	N		150	150	200	200
V8 6.2 Liter Diesel	C,J		(100)	(100)	(135)	(135)
BONUS CAB PICKUP—V8—Truck Equipment Schedule T1						
R3500 Long Bed	R34K	17544	1600	2100	3175	4675
4WD	V		500	500	665	665
V8 454/7.4 Liter	N		150	150	200	200
V8 6.2 Liter Diesel	C,J		(100)	(100)	(135)	(135)
CREW CAB PICKUP—V8—Truck Equipment Schedule T1						
R3500 Long Bed	R33K	18074	2100	2700	3850	5500
4WD	V		500	500	665	665
V8 454/7.4 Liter	N		150	150	200	200
V8 6.2 Liter Diesel	C,J		(100)	(100)	(135)	(135)

1991 CHEVY/GMC — 1G(C,T,BorD)–(T18Z)–M–#

Body Type	VIN	List	Trade-In Fair	Trade-In Good	Pvt-Party Good	Retail Excellent
S10 BLAZER/S15 JIMMY 4WD—V6—Truck Equipment Sch T1						
Sport Utility 2D	T18Z	17786	900	1275	2125	3425
Sport Utility 4D	T13Z	19426	1225	1675	2775	4350
2WD	S		(375)	(375)	(500)	(500)
BLAZER/JIMMY 4WD—V8—Truck Equipment Schedule T1						
Sport Utility 2D	V18K	19986	1200	1650	2775	4350
V8 6.2 Liter Diesel	C,J		(150)	(150)	(200)	(200)
SUBURBAN—V8—Truck Equipment Schedule T1						
R1500 Sport Utility	R16K	19244	1125	1575	2900	4675
R2500 Sport Utility	R26K	20661	1250	1725	3050	4875
w/o Third Seat			(225)	(225)	(300)	(300)
4WD	V		550	550	735	735
V8 454/7.4 Liter	N		150	150	200	200
V8 6.2 Liter Diesel	C,J		(150)	(150)	(200)	(200)
APV—V6—Truck Equipment Schedule T2						
Cargo Minivan	U06D	14102	200	275	625	1175
LUMINA APV—V6—Truck Equipment Schedule T2						
Minivan	U06D	16045	325	475	925	1625
5 Passenger			(225)	(225)	(300)	(300)
ASTRO/SAFARI—V6—Truck Equipment Schedule T2						
Cargo Minivan	M15Z	14081	525	750	1300	2175
Extended Cargo	M19Z	14751	575	825	1375	2300
AWD	L		275	275	365	365
V6 4.3L High Output	B		100	100	135	135
ASTRO/SAFARI—V6—Truck Equipment Schedule T1						
Minivan	M15Z	17145	750	1025	1700	2800
Extended Minivan	M19Z	17835	850	1175	1925	3100

0105

Body	Type	VIN	List	Trade-In Fair	Trade-In Good	Pvt-Party Good	Retail Excellent
5 Passenger				(225)	(225)	(300)	(300)
AWD		L		275	275	365	365
V6 4.3L High Output		B		100	100	135	135
SPORTVAN/RALLY WAGON—V8—Truck Equipment Sch T1							
G10 Passenger Van		G15H	18518	900	1300	2150	3475
G20 Passenger Van		G25H	18983	925	1325	2225	3575
G30 Passenger Van		G35K	20252	950	1375	2375	3875
5 Passenger				(225)	(225)	(300)	(300)
110" W.B.				0	0	0	0
146" W.B.		9		50	50	65	65
V6 4.3 Liter		Z		(225)	(225)	(300)	(300)
V8 454/7.4 Liter		N		100	100	135	135
V8 6.2 Liter Diesel		C,J		(100)	(100)	(135)	(135)
G-SERIES/VANDURA—V6—Truck Equipment Schedule T1							
G10 Cargo Van		G15Z	15486	900	1275	2000	3150
G20 Cargo Van		G25Z	15686	950	1350	2100	3300
G30 Cargo Van		G35Z	15456	975	1400	2175	3400
110" W.B.				0	0	0	0
146" W.B.		9		50	50	65	65
V8 5.0, 5.7 Liter		H,K		100	100	135	135
V8 454/7.4 Liter		N		225	225	300	300
V8 6.2 Liter Diesel		C,J		(75)	(75)	(100)	(100)
S10/SONOMA PICKUP—4-Cyl.—Truck Equipment Schedule T2							
EL/Spcl Short Bed		S14E	8832	300	450	900	1625
Short Bed		S14E	10150	400	600	1100	1925
Long Bed		S14E	10320	325	475	950	1725
Extended Cab		S19E	11420	650	900	1550	2650
4WD		T		500	550	735	735
V6 2.8 Liter		R		125	125	165	165
V6 4.3 Liter		Z		175	175	235	235
SONOMA PICKUP 4WD—V6 Turbo—Truck Equipment Sch T3							
Syclone Short Bed		T14Z	25970	6950	8050	10150	13100
REGULAR PICKUP—V8—Truck Equipment Schedule T1							
C1500 Short Bed		C14H	13125	1600	2100	3150	4625
C1500 Long Bed		C14H	15425	1500	2000	3000	4475
C2500 Short Bed		C24H	16065	1350	1825	2800	4250
C3500 Long Bed		C34K	18795	1400	1875	2875	4350
Work Truck/Special				(275)	(275)	(365)	(365)
4WD		K		550	550	735	735
V6 4.3 Liter		Z		(350)	(350)	(465)	(465)
V8 5.7 Liter		K		100	100	135	135
V8 454/7.4 Liter		N		150	150	200	200
V8 6.2 Liter Diesel		C,J		(150)	(150)	(200)	(200)
REGULAR CAB PICKUP—V8—Truck Equipment Schedule T3							
454SS Short Bed		C14N	20185	3425	4150	5525	7525
EXTENDED CAB PICKUP—V8—Truck Equipment Schedule T1							
C1500 Short Bed		C19H	16075	1925	2450	3550	5125
C1500 Long Bed		C19H	16565	1825	2350	3425	5000
C2500 Short Bed		C29H	17185	2100	2650	3800	5450
C2500 Long Bed		C29H	17465	1900	2425	3525	5125
C3500 Long Bed		C39K	19290	1900	2425	3525	5125
4WD		K		550	550	735	735
V6 4.3 Liter		Z		(350)	(350)	(465)	(465)
V8 5.7 Liter		K		100	100	135	135
V8 454/7.4 Liter		N		150	150	200	200
V8 6.2 Liter Diesel		C,J		(150)	(150)	(200)	(200)
BONUS CAB PICKUP—V8—Truck Equipment Schedule T1							
R3500 Long Bed		R34K	18592	1900	2425	3525	5125
4WD		V		550	550	735	735
V8 454/7.4 Liter		N		150	150	200	200
V8 6.2 Liter Diesel		C,J		(150)	(150)	(200)	(200)
CREW CAB PICKUP—V8—Truck Equipment Schedule T1							
R3500 Long Bed		R33K	19132	2500	3100	4325	6075
4WD		V		550	550	735	735
V8 454/7.4 Liter		N		150	150	200	200
V8 6.2 Liter Diesel		C,J		(150)	(150)	(200)	(200)
1992 CHEVY/GMC — 1G(C,T,N,BorD)—(T18Z)—N—#							
S10 BLAZER/JIMMY 4WD—V6—Truck Equipment Sch T1							
Sport Utility 2D		T18Z	18859	850	1175	2050	3350
Sport Utility 4D		T13Z	20229	1225	1675	2800	4400
2WD		S		(400)	(400)	(535)	(535)
V6 4.3L High Output		W		125	125	165	165

TRUCKS & VANS

1992 CHEVROLET/GMC

Body Type	VIN	List	Trade-In Fair	Good	Pvt-Party Good	Retail Excellent
JIMMY 4WD—V6 Turbo—Truck Equipment Schedule T3						
Typhoon Spt Util 2D	T18Z	33006	8725	9975	12400	15850
BLAZER/YUKON 4WD—V8—Truck Equipment Schedule T1						
Sport Utility 2D	K18K	21780	2225	2775	4125	6025
SUBURBAN—V8—Truck Equipment Schedule T1						
C1500 Sport Utility	C16K	20905	2025	2575	4025	6075
C2500 Sport Utility	C26K	22109	2150	2725	4225	6300
w/o Third Seat			(250)	(250)	(335)	(335)
4WD	K		650	650	865	865
V8 454/7.4 Liter	N		175	175	235	235
APV—V6—Truck Equipment Schedule T2						
Cargo Minivan	U06D	14905	175	225	575	1125
LUMINA APV—V6—Truck Equipment Schedule T1						
Minivan	U06D	16930	325	475	950	1675
5 Passenger			(250)	(250)	(335)	(335)
V6 3.8 Liter	L		75	75	100	100
ASTRO/SAFARI—V6—Truck Equipment Schedule T2						
Cargo Minivan	M15Z	14636	550	800	1375	2300
Extended Cargo	M19Z	15306	625	900	1500	2525
AWD	L		325	325	435	435
V6 4.3L High Output	W		125	125	165	165
ASTRO/SAFARI—V6—Truck Equipment Schedule T1						
Minivan	M15Z	16726	825	1150	1900	3075
Extended Minivan	M19Z	17416	900	1300	2125	3400
5 Passenger			(250)	(250)	(335)	(335)
AWD	L		325	325	435	435
V6 4.3L High Output	W		125	125	165	165
SPORTVAN/RALLY WAGON—V8—Truck Equipment Sch T1						
G10 Passenger Van	G15H	19266	975	1400	2425	3925
G20 Passenger Van	G25H	19456	1025	1450	2525	4025
G30 Passenger Van	G35K	20631	1050	1500	2600	4150
5 Passenger			(250)	(250)	(335)	(335)
110" W.B.			0	0	0	0
146" W.B.	9		75	75	100	100
V6 4.3 Liter	Z		(250)	(250)	(335)	(335)
V8 454/7.4 Liter	N		125	125	165	165
V8 6.2 Liter Diesel	C,J		(125)	(125)	(165)	(165)
G-SERIES/VANDURA—V6—Truck Equipment Schedule T1						
G10 Cargo Van	G15Z	16246	950	1350	2150	3400
G20 Cargo Van	G25Z	16486	1025	1450	2300	3600
G30 Cargo Van	G35Z	16206	1050	1500	2450	3875
110" W.B.			0	0	0	0
146" W.B.	9		75	75	100	100
V8 5.0, 5.7 Liter	H,K		125	125	165	165
V8 454/7.4 Liter	N		250	250	335	335
V8 6.2 Liter Diesel	C,J		(100)	(100)	(135)	(135)
S10/SONOMA PICKUP—4-Cyl.—Truck Equipment Schedule T2						
EL/Spcl Short Bed	S14A	9524	325	475	950	1725
Short Bed	S14A	10459	450	650	1200	2075
Long Bed	S14A	10759	375	525	1025	1800
Extended Cab	S19A	11959	725	1025	1725	2850
4WD	T		675	675	900	900
V6 2.8 Liter	E		150	150	200	200
V6 4.3 Liter	Z		200	200	265	265
V6 4.3L High Output	W		250	250	335	335
SONOMA PICKUP—V6—Truck Equipment Schedule T1						
GT Short Bed	S14W	16700	1150	1600	2675	4150
SONOMA PICKUP 4WD—V6 Turbo—Truck Equipment Sch T3						
Syclone Short Bed	T14Z	27465	7500	8625	10700	13750
REGULAR CAB PICKUP—V8—Truck Equipment Schedule T1						
C1500 Short Bed	C14H	16130	2475	3075	4200	5875
C1500 Long Bed	C14H	16430	2350	2925	4050	5700
C2500 Long Bed	C24H	17070	2275	2850	3975	5650
C3500 Long Bed	C34K	17895	2375	2950	4100	5750
Work Truck/Special			(325)	(325)	(435)	(435)
4WD	K		650	650	865	865
V6 4.3 Liter	Z		(375)	(375)	(500)	(500)
V8 5.7 Liter	K		150	150	200	200
V8 454/7.4 Liter	N		175	175	235	235
V8 6.2 Liter Diesel	C,J		(225)	(225)	(300)	(300)
V8 6.5L Turbo Diesel	F		325	325	435	435
REGULAR CAB PICKUP—V8—Truck Equipment Schedule T3						
454SS Short Bed	C14N	21180	4675	5525	7050	9300

0105

1992 CHEVROLET/GMC

Body Type	VIN	List	Trade-In Fair	Good	Pvt-Party Good	Retail Excellent
EXTENDED CAB PICKUP—V8—Truck Equipment Schedule T1						
C1500 Short Bed	C19H	17080	2900	3550	4775	6600
C1500 Long Bed	C19H	17370	2800	3425	4625	6400
C2500 Short Bed	C29H	18190	3150	3825	5100	6975
C2500 Long Bed	C29H	18470	2925	3575	4800	6625
C3500 Long Bed	C39K	18965	2950	3600	4825	6650
4WD	K		650	650	865	865
V6 4.3 Liter	Z		(375)	(375)	(500)	(500)
V8 5.7 Liter	K		150	150	200	200
V8 454/7.4 Liter	N		175	175	235	235
V8 6.2 Liter Diesel	C,J		(225)	(225)	(300)	(300)
CREW CAB PICKUP—V8—Truck Equipment Schedule T1						
C3500 Long Bed	C33K	19867	3625	4350	5700	7700
4WD	K		650	650	865	865
V8 454/7.4 Liter	N		175	175	235	235

1993 CHEVY/GMC — 1G(C,T,NorB)–(T18Z)–P–#

Body Type	VIN	List	Trade-In Fair	Good	Pvt-Party Good	Retail Excellent
S10 BLAZER/JIMMY 4WD—V6—Truck Equipment Sch T1						
Sport Utility 2D	T18Z	19129	825	1150	2050	3400
Sport Utility 4D	T13Z	20499	1250	1725	2900	4525
2WD			(425)	(425)	(565)	(565)
V6 4.3L High Output	W		150	150	200	200
JIMMY 4WD—V6 Turbo—Truck Equipment Schedule T3						
Typhoon Spt Util 2D	T18Z	29795	9425	10750	13200	16800
BLAZER/YUKON 4WD—V8—Truck Equipment Schedule T1						
Sport Utility 2D	K18K	22505	2625	3250	4650	6675
SUBURBAN—V8—Truck Equipment Schedule T1						
C1500 Sport Utility	C16K	21830	2400	2975	4525	6700
C2500 Sport Utility	C26K	23035	2550	3175	4750	6925
w/o Third Seat			(275)	(275)	(365)	(365)
4WD			750	750	1000	1000
V8 454/7.4 Liter	N		200	200	265	265
APV—V6—Truck Equipment Schedule T2						
Cargo Minivan	U06D	15225	175	250	650	1250
LUMINA APV—V6—Truck Equipment Schedule T2						
Minivan	U06D	17255	375	550	1075	1900
5 Passenger			(275)	(275)	(365)	(365)
V6 3.8 Liter	L		100	100	135	135
ASTRO/SAFARI—V6—Truck Equipment Schedule T2						
Cargo Minivan	M15Z	15336	625	900	1500	2575
Extended Cargo	M19Z	16006	725	1025	1725	2850
Dutch Doors			50	50	65	65
AWD			375	375	500	500
V6 4.3L High Output	W		150	150	200	200
ASTRO/SAFARI—V6—Truck Equipment Schedule T1						
Minivan	M15Z	17146	900	1300	2125	3425
Extended Minivan	M19Z	17836	1025	1475	2500	3950
5 Passenger			(275)	(275)	(365)	(365)
Dutch Doors			50	50	65	65
AWD	L		375	375	500	500
V6 4.3L High Output	W		150	150	200	200
SPORTVAN/RALLY WAGON—V8—Truck Equipment Sch T1						
G10 Passenger Van	G15H	18756	1050	1500	2625	4175
G20 Passenger Van	G25H	18946	1125	1575	2700	4300
G30 Passenger Van	G35K	20696	1225	1675	2825	4450
5 Passenger			(275)	(275)	(365)	(365)
110" W.B.			0	0	0	0
146" W.B.	9		100	100	135	135
V6 4.3 Liter	Z		(275)	(275)	(365)	(365)
V8 454/7.4 Liter	N		150	150	200	200
V8 6.2 Liter Diesel	C,J		(150)	(150)	(200)	(200)
G-SERIES/VANDURA—V6—Truck Equipment Schedule T1						
G10 Cargo Van	G15Z	16431	1050	1500	2475	3900
G20 Cargo Van	G25Z	16571	1125	1575	2600	4050
G30 Cargo Van	G35Z	16691	1200	1650	2700	4150
110" W.B.			0	0	0	0
146" W.B.	9		100	100	135	135
V8 5.0, 5.7 Liter	H,K		150	150	200	200
V8 454/7.4 Liter	N		275	275	365	365
V8 6.2 Liter Diesel	C,J		(125)	(125)	(165)	(165)
S10/SONOMA PICKUP—4-Cyl.—Truck Equipment Schedule T2						
EL/Special Short Bed	S14A	9547	375	550	1075	1900
Short Bed	S14A	10731	525	750	1325	2250

SEE BACK PAGES FOR TRUCK EQUIPMENT

TRUCKS & VANS

Body Type	VIN	List	Trade-In Fair	Trade-In Good	Pvt-Party Good	Retail Excellent
Long Bed	S14A	11031	400	600	1125	1975
Extended Cab	S19A	12231	825	1150	1925	3150
4WD	T		800	800	1065	1065
V6 2.8 Liter	R		175	175	235	235
V6 4.3 Liter	Z		225	225	300	300
V6 4.3L High Output	Z		275	275	365	365
REGULAR CAB PICKUP—V8—Truck Equipment Schedule T1						
1500 Short Bed	C14H	16120	2650	3250	4400	6100
1500 Long Bed	C14H	16420	2525	3125	4225	5875
2500 Long Bed	C24H	16885	2550	3150	4275	5925
3500 Long Bed	C34K	18624	2650	3250	4400	6100
Work Truck/Special			(375)	(375)	(500)	(500)
4WD	K		750	750	1000	1000
V6 4.3 Liter	Z		(400)	(400)	(535)	(535)
V8 5.7 Liter	K		175	175	235	235
V8 454/7.4 Liter	N		200	200	265	265
V8 6.2 Liter Diesel	C,J		(275)	(275)	(365)	(365)
V8 6.5L Turbo Diesel	F		375	375	500	500
REGULAR CAB PICKUP—V8—Truck Equipment Schedule T3						
454SS Short Bed	C14N	21835	5200	6075	7625	9925
EXTENDED CAB PICKUP—V8—Truck Equipment Schedule T1						
1500 Short Bed	C19H	17590	3225	3900	5125	6975
1500 Long Bed	C19H	17850	3075	3725	4950	6725
2500 Short Bed	C29H	18700	3525	4225	5550	7475
2500 Long Bed	C29H	18980	3275	3925	5175	7025
3500 Long Bed	C39K	20284	3300	3975	5225	7100
4WD	K		750	750	1000	1000
V6 4.3 Liter	Z		(400)	(400)	(535)	(535)
V8 5.7 Liter	K		175	175	235	235
V8 454/7.4 Liter	N		200	200	265	265
V8 6.2 Liter Diesel	C,J		(275)	(275)	(365)	(365)
V8 6.5L Turbo Diesel	F		375	375	500	500
CREW CAB PICKUP—V8—Truck Equipment Schedule T1						
3500 Long Bed	C33K	20604	4050	4825	6225	8250
4WD	K		750	750	1000	1000
V8 454/7.4 Liter	N		200	200	265	265
V8 6.5L Turbo Diesel	F		375	375	500	500

Body Type	VIN	List	Trade-In Fair	Trade-In Good	Pvt-Party Good	Retail Excellent
S10 BLAZER/JIMMY 4WD—V6—Truck Equipment Sch T1						
Sport Utility 2D	T18Z	19649	825	1150	2100	3575
Sport Utility 4D	T13Z	21377	1350	1825	3050	4775
2WD	S		(450)	(450)	(600)	(600)
V6 4.3L High Output	S		175	175	235	235
BLAZER/YUKON 4WD—V8—Truck Equipment Schedule T1						
Sport Utility 2D	K18K	23460	3050	3700	5225	7375
V8 6.5L Turbo Diesel	S		400	400	535	535
SUBURBAN—V8—Truck Equipment Schedule T1						
C1500 Sport Utility	C16K	21651	2800	3425	5100	7450
C2500 Sport Utility	C26K	22883	2975	3650	5350	7700
w/o Third Seat			(300)	(300)	(400)	(400)
4WD	K		850	850	1135	1135
V8 454/7.4 Liter	N		225	225	300	300
V8 6.5L Turbo Diesel	F		400	400	535	535
LUMINA—V6—Truck Equipment Schedule T2						
Cargo	U06G	16015	500	725	1325	2300
LUMINA—V6—Truck Equipment Schedule T1						
Passenger	U06D	18175	750	1050	1825	3025
5 Passenger			(300)	(300)	(400)	(400)
V6 3.8 Liter	L		100	100	135	135
ASTRO/SAFARI—V6—Truck Equipment Schedule T2						
Cargo Minivan	M15Z	15985	725	1025	1925	2925
Extended Cargo	M19Z	16458	850	1200	2050	3300
Dutch Doors			75	75	100	100
AWD	W		425	425	565	565
V6 4.3L High Output	W		175	175	235	235
ASTRO/SAFARI—V6—Truck Equipment Schedule T1						
Minivan	M15Z	17819	1050	1500	2550	4050
Extended Minivan	M19Z	18121	1225	1700	2775	4350
5 Passenger			(300)	(300)	(400)	(400)
Dutch Doors			75	75	100	100
AWD	W		425	425	565	565
V6 4.3L High Output	W		175	175	235	235

1994 CHEVROLET/GMC

Body	Type	VIN	List	Trade-In Fair	Trade-In Good	Pvt-Party Good	Retail Excellent
SPORTVAN/RALLY WAGON—V8—Truck Equipment Sch T1							
G20 Passenger Van	G25H	20344	1350	1825	3000	4675
G30 Passenger Van	G35K	21696	1450	1925	3150	4825
5 Passenger			(300)	(300)	(400)	(400)
146" W.B.	9		100	100	135	135
V6 4.3 Liter	Z		(300)	(300)	(400)	(400)
V8 454/7.4 Liter	N		175	175	235	235
V8 6.5 Liter Diesel	P		(175)	(175)	(235)	(235)
G-SERIES/VANDURA—V6—Truck Equipment Schedule T1							
G10 Cargo Van	G15Z	17544	1325	1675	2725	4225
G20 Cargo Van	G25Z	17534	1325	1800	2850	4375
G30 Cargo Van	G35Z	17661	1375	1875	2925	4475
110" W.B.			0	0	0	0
146" W.B.	9		100	100	135	135
V8 5.0, 5.7 Liter	H,K		175	175	235	235
V8 454/7.4 Liter	N		300	300	400	400
V8 6.5 Liter Diesel	P		(125)	(125)	(165)	(165)
S10/SONOMA PICKUP—4-Cyl.—Truck Equipment Schedule T2							
Short Bed	S144	10201	775	1075	1850	3075
Long Bed	S144	10501	650	900	1600	2725
Extended Cab	S194	12260	1075	1525	2600	4100
4WD	T		900	900	1200	1200
V6 4.3 Liter	Z		250	250	335	335
V6 4.3L High Output	W		300	300	400	400
REGULAR CAB PICKUP—V8—Truck Equipment Schedule T1							
1500 Short Bed	C14H	16322	2875	3525	4675	6400
1500 Long Bed	C14H	16602	2725	3350	4500	6175
2500 Long Bed	C24H	17579	2850	3500	4650	6375
3500 Long Bed	C34K	19313	2975	3625	4800	6525
Work Truck/Special			(400)	(400)	(535)	(535)
4WD	K		850	850	1135	1135
V6 4.3 Liter	Z		(425)	(425)	(565)	(565)
V8 5.7 Liter	K		200	200	265	265
V8 454/7.4 Liter	N		225	225	300	300
V8 6.5 Liter Diesel	P,Y		(325)	(325)	(435)	(435)
V8 6.5L Turbo Diesel	F,S		400	400	535	535
EXTENDED CAB PICKUP—V8—Truck Equipment Schedule T1							
1500 Short Bed	C19H	18319	3575	4300	5575	7475
1500 Long Bed	C19H	19162	3425	4125	5350	7200
2500 Short Bed	C29H	20107	3950	4700	6050	8050
2500 Long Bed	C29K	20995	3650	4375	5675	7650
3500 Long Bed	C39K	22547	3725	4450	5725	7650
4WD	K		850	850	1135	1135
V6 4.3 Liter	Z		(425)	(425)	(565)	(565)
V8 5.7 Liter	K		200	200	265	265
V8 454/7.4 Liter	N		225	225	300	300
V8 6.5 Liter Diesel	P,Y		(325)	(325)	(435)	(435)
V8 6.5L Turbo Diesel	F,S		400	400	535	535
CREW CAB PICKUP—V8—Truck Equipment Schedule T1							
3500 Long Bed	C33K	21652	4550	5375	6800	8900
4WD	K		850	850	1135	1135
V8 454/7.4 Liter	N		225	225	300	300
V8 6.5L Turbo Diesel	F,S		400	400	535	535

1995 CHEVY/GMC — 1G(C,T,NorB)–(T18W)–S–#

Body	Type	VIN	List	Trade-In Fair	Trade-In Good	Pvt-Party Good	Retail Excellent
BLAZER/JIMMY 4WD—V6—Truck Equipment Schedule T1							
Sport Utility 2D	T18W	20390	1400	1875	3200	5000
Sport Utility 4D	T13W	22438	2100	2700	4075	6050
2WD	S		(475)	(475)	(635)	(635)
TAHOE/YUKON 4WD—V8—Truck Equipment Schedule T1							
Sport Utility 2D	K18K	24215	2175	2750	4500	6900
Sport Utility 4D	K13K	29195	3175	4075	6000	8625
2WD	C		(475)	(475)	(635)	(635)
V8 6.5 Liter Turbo Diesel	S		425	425	565	565
SUBURBAN—V8—Truck Equipment Schedule T1							
C1500 Sport Utility	C16K	24264	3300	4000	5800	8300
C2500 Sport Utility	C26K	25497	3525	4225	6075	8600
w/o Third Seat			(325)	(325)	(435)	(435)
4WD	K		950	950	1265	1265
V8 454/7.4 Liter	N		250	250	335	335
V8 6.5 Liter Turbo Diesel	F		425	425	565	565
LUMINA—V6—Truck Equipment Schedule T2							
Cargo	U06D	16775	600	850	1525	2700

SEE BACK PAGES FOR TRUCK EQUIPMENT

Body	Type	VIN	List	Trade-In Fair	Good	Pvt-Party Good	Retail Excellent
LUMINA—V6—Truck Equipment Schedule T1							
Passenger		U06D	19625	875	1225	2125	3475
5 Passenger				(325)	(325)	(435)	(435)
V6 3.8 Liter		L		100	100	135	135
ASTRO/SAFARI—V6—Truck Equipment Schedule T2							
Cargo Minivan		M19W	18340	1250	1725	2850	4475
Dutch Doors				100	100	135	135
AWD		L		475	475	635	635
ASTRO/SAFARI—V6—Truck Equipment Schedule T1							
Minivan		M19W	19886	1800	2325	3525	5250
5 Passenger				(325)	(325)	(435)	(435)
Dutch Doors				100	100	135	135
AWD		L		475	475	635	635
SPORTVAN/RALLY WAGON—V8—Truck Equipment Sch T1							
G20 Passenger Van		G25H	21776	1575	2100	3350	5125
G30 Passenger Van		G35K	22595	1700	2225	3500	5300
5 Passenger				(325)	(325)	(435)	(435)
146" W.B.		9		100	100	135	135
V6 4.3 Liter		Z		(325)	(325)	(435)	(435)
V8 454/7.4 Liter		N		200	200	265	265
V8 6.5 Liter Diesel		Y		(200)	(200)	(265)	(265)
G-SERIES/VANDURA—V6—Truck Equipment Schedule T1							
G10 Cargo Van		G15Z	18588	1500	1975	3075	4650
G20 Cargo Van		G25Z	18578	1575	2100	3225	4825
G30 Cargo Van		G35Z	18732	1650	2150	3300	4900
110" W.B.				0	0	0	0
146" W.B.				100	100	135	135
V8 5.0, 5.7 Liter		H,K		200	200	265	265
V8 454/7.4 Liter		N		325	325	435	435
V8 6.5 Liter Diesel		Y		(125)	(125)	(165)	(165)
S10/SONOMA PICKUP—4-Cyl.—Truck Equipment Schedule T2							
Short Bed		S144	10820	900	1275	2150	3475
Long Bed		S144	11130	775	1075	1875	3100
Extended Cab		S194	12990	1300	1775	2875	4475
4WD		T		1000	1000	1335	1335
V6 4.3 Liter		Z		275	275	365	365
V6 4.3L High Output		W		325	325	435	435
REGULAR CAB PICKUP—V8—Truck Equipment Schedule T1							
1500 Short Bed		C14H	17217	3225	3900	5075	6850
1500 Long Bed		C14H	17497	3050	3700	4850	6575
2500 Long Bed		C24H	18679	3300	3950	5150	6925
3500 HD Long Bed		C34K	19803	3375	4075	5275	7075
Work Truck/Special				(425)	(425)	(565)	(565)
4WD		K		950	950	1265	1265
V6 4.3 Liter		Z		(450)	(450)	(600)	(600)
V8 5.7 Liter		K		225	225	300	300
V8 454/7.4 Liter		N		250	250	335	335
V8 6.5 Liter Diesel		P		(375)	(375)	(500)	(500)
V8 6.5L Turbo Diesel		S		425	425	565	565
EXTENDED CAB PICKUP—V8—Truck Equipment Schedule T1							
1500 Short Bed		C19H	19177	4025	4800	6125	8075
1500 Long Bed		C19H	19545	3875	4600	5850	7750
2500 Short Bed		C29H	21115	4475	5275	6650	8700
2500 Long Bed		C29H	21172	4350	5125	6475	8500
3500 HD Long Bed		C39K	23129	4200	4900	6300	8300
4WD		K		950	950	1265	1265
V6 4.3 Liter		Z		(450)	(450)	(600)	(600)
V8 5.7 Liter		K		225	225	300	300
V8 454/7.4 Liter		N		250	250	335	335
V8 6.5 Liter Diesel		P		(375)	(375)	(500)	(500)
V8 6.5L Turbo Diesel		S		425	425	565	565
CREW CAB PICKUP—V8—Truck Equipment Schedule T1							
3500 Long Bed		C33K	22389	5125	6000	7475	9650
4WD		K		950	950	1265	1265
V8 454/7.4 Liter		N		250	250	335	335
V8 6.5L Turbo Diesel		F,S		425	425	565	565

1996 CHEVY/GMC — 1G(C,K,NorT)–(T18W)–T–#

Body	Type	VIN	List	Trade-In Fair	Good	Pvt-Party Good	Retail Excellent
BLAZER/JIMMY 4WD—V6—Truck Equipment Schedule T1							
Sport Utility 2D		T18W	21694	1675	2200	3600	5525
Sport Utility 4D		T13W	23742	2475	3075	4550	6650
2WD				(500)	(500)	(665)	(665)

TRUCKS & VANS

Body	Type	VIN	List	Trade-In Fair	Trade-In Good	Pvt-Party Good	Retail Excellent
TAHOE/YUKON 4WD—V8—Truck Equipment Schedule T1							
Sport Utility 2D		K18R	26596	2700	3325	5250	7850
Sport Utility 4D		K13R	31079	4000	4775	6875	9700
2WD		C		(500)	(500)	(665)	(665)
V8 6.5L Turbo Diesel		S		450	450	600	600
SUBURBAN—V8—Truck Equipment Schedule T1							
C1500 Sport Utility		C16R	26709	3900	4650	6600	9300
C2500 Sport Utility		C26R	27942	4150	4925	6900	9600
w/o Third Seat				(350)	(350)	(465)	(465)
4WD		K		1050	1050	1400	1400
V8 454/7.4 Liter		J		275	275	365	365
V8 6.5L Turbo Diesel		F		450	450	600	600
LUMINA—V6—Truck Equipment Schedule T2							
Cargo		U06E	18415	700	1000	1875	3200
LUMINA—V6—Truck Equipment Schedule T1							
Passenger		U06E	20435	1000	1450	2550	4125
5 Passenger				(350)	(350)	(465)	(465)
ASTRO/SAFARI—V6—Truck Equipment Schedule T2							
Cargo/SL Cargo		M19V	19152	1525	2050	3275	5000
Dutch Doors				100	100	135	135
AWD		L		500	500	665	665
ASTRO/SAFARI—V6—Truck Equipment Schedule T1							
Minivan/SL Minivan		M19W	19736	2100	2700	3975	5800
5 Passenger				(350)	(350)	(465)	(465)
Dutch Doors				100	100	135	135
AWD		L		500	500	665	665
EXPRESS/SAVANA—V8—Truck Equipment Schedule T1							
1500 Passenger Van		G15M	23342	2225	2775	4200	6175
2500 Passenger Van		G25R	25767	2325	2900	4325	6300
3500 Passenger Van		G35R	25927	2475	3075	4500	6500
5 Passenger				(350)	(350)	(465)	(465)
155" W.B.		9		100	100	135	135
V6 4.3 Liter		W		(350)	(350)	(465)	(465)
V8 454/7.4 Liter		J		200	200	265	265
V8 6.5L Turbo Diesel		F		150	150	200	200
SPORTVAN/RALLY WAGON—V8—Truck Equipment Sch T1							
G30 Passenger Van		G35K	23451	2075	2625	4000	5925
146" W.B.				100	100	135	135
V8 454/7.4 Liter		N		200	200	265	265
V8 6.5 Turbo Diesel		Y		(225)	(225)	(300)	(300)
G-SERIES/SAVANA—V6—Truck Equip Schedule T1							
1500 Cargo Van		G15W	20214	2100	2700	4025	5950
2500 Cargo Van		G25W	20639	2225	2775	4175	6100
3500 Cargo Van		G35R	22019	2275	2850	4250	6200
155" W.B.		9		100	100	135	135
V8 5.0, 5.7 Liter		M,R		200	200	265	265
V8 454/7.4 Liter		J		350	350	465	465
V8 6.5L Turbo Diesel		F		250	250	335	335
G-SERIES/VANDURA—V8—Truck Equipment Schedule T1							
G30 Classic		G39K	20469	2100	2675	4025	5925
146" W.B.				100	100	135	135
V6 4.3 Liter		Z		(350)	(350)	(465)	(465)
V8 454/7.4 Liter		N		200	200	265	265
V8 6.5 Liter Diesel		Y		(125)	(125)	(165)	(165)
S10/SONOMA PICKUP—4-Cyl.—Truck Equipment Schedule T2							
Short Bed		S144	11755	1025	1450	2525	4025
Long Bed		S144	12065	900	1250	2150	3525
Extended Cab		S194	14470	1500	2025	3200	4825
Third Door				200	200	265	265
4WD		T		1100	1100	1465	1465
V6 4.3 Liter		X		300	300	400	400
V6 4.3L High Output		W		350	350	465	465
REGULAR CAB PICKUP—V8—Truck Equipment Schedule T1							
1500 Short Bed		C14M	18311	3600	4325	5575	7425
1500 Long Bed		C14M	18591	3425	4125	5325	7125
2500 Long Bed		C24M	19273	3750	4500	5725	7500
3500 Long Bed		C34R	20477	3875	4600	5850	7750
Work Truck/Special				(450)	(450)	(600)	(600)
4WD		K		1050	1050	1400	1400
V6 4.3 Liter		W		(450)	(450)	(600)	(600)
V8 5.7 Liter		R		250	250	335	335
V8 454/7.4 Liter		J		275	275	365	365
V8 6.5L Turbo Diesel		F,S		450	450	600	600

Body Type	VIN	List	Trade-In Fair	Good	Pvt-Party Good	Retail Excellent
EXTENDED CAB PICKUP—V8—Truck Equipment Schedule T1						
1500 Short Bed	C19M	20371	4550	5375	6750	8775
1500 Long Bed	C19M	20819	4350	5125	6450	8450
2500 Short Bed	C29M	21889	5050	5925	7350	9500
2500 HD Long Bed	C29M	21946	4900	5725	7125	9250
3500 Long Bed	C39R	23903	4750	5600	6975	9075
Third Door			225	225	300	300
4WD	K		1050	1050	1400	1400
V6 4.3 Liter	W		(450)	(450)	(600)	(600)
V8 5.7 Liter	R		250	250	335	335
V8 454/7.4 Liter	J		275	275	365	365
V8 6.5L Turbo Diesel	F,S		450	450	600	600
CREW CAB PICKUP—V8—Truck Equipment Schedule T1						
3500 Long Bed	C33R	23611	5775	6725	8225	10500
4WD	K		1050	1050	1400	1400
V8 454/7.4 Liter	J		275	275	365	365
V8 6.5L Turbo Diesel	F		450	450	600	600

1997 CHEVY/GMC — 1G(C,K,NorT)–T18W–V–#

Body Type	VIN	List	Trade-In Fair	Good	Pvt-Party Good	Retail Excellent
BLAZER/JIMMY 4WD—V6—Truck Equipment Schedule T1						
Sport Utility 2D	T18W	22631	2100	2650	4150	6250
Sport Utility 4D	T13W	24631	2900	3550	5150	7425
2WD	S		(525)	(525)	(700)	(700)
TAHOE/YUKON 4WD—V8—Truck Equipment Schedule T1						
Sport Utility 2D	K18R	27642	3400	4100	6175	8975
Sport Utility 4D	K13R	32125	4800	5650	7875	10950
2WD	C		(1175)	(1175)	(1565)	(1565)
V8 6.5L Turbo Diesel	S		475	475	635	635
SUBURBAN—V8—Truck Equipment Schedule T1						
C1500 Sport Utility	C16R	27350	4650	5500	7575	10450
C2500 Sport Utility	C26R	28583	4900	5750	7875	10800
w/o Third Seat			(375)	(375)	(500)	(500)
4WD	K		1150	1150	1535	1535
V8 454/7.4 Liter	J		300	300	400	400
V8 6.5L Turbo Diesel	F		475	475	635	635
VENTURE—V6—Truck Equipment Schedule T1						
Minivan	U03E	20495	2100	2650	3950	5825
Extended Minivan	X06E	21660	2475	3075	4450	6375
w/o 2nd Sliding Door			(475)	(475)	(635)	(635)
ASTRO/SAFARI—V6—Truck Equipment Schedule T2						
Cargo/SL Cargo	M19W	19583	1950	2475	3800	5650
Dutch Doors			100	100	135	135
AWD	L		525	525	700	700
ASTRO/SAFARI—V6—Truck Equipment Schedule T1						
Base/SLX Minivan	M19W	20167	2550	3150	4500	6450
5 Passenger			(375)	(375)	(500)	(500)
Dutch Doors			100	100	135	135
AWD	L		525	525	700	700
EXPRESS/SAVANA—V8—Truck Equipment Schedule T1						
1500 Passenger Van	G15M	23380	2725	3350	4875	6975
2500 Passenger Van	G25R	25411	2825	3475	5000	7125
3500 Passenger Van	G35R	25571	3000	3675	5175	7350
5 Passenger			(375)	(375)	(500)	(500)
155" W.B.	9		100	100	135	135
V6 4.3 Liter	W		(375)	(375)	(500)	(500)
V8 454/7.4 Liter	J		200	200	265	265
V8 6.5L Turbo Diesel	F		150	150	200	200
G-SERIES/SAVANA—V6—Truck Equipment Schedule T1						
1500 Cargo Van	G15W	20662	2625	3250	4675	6725
2500 Cargo Van	G25W	21087	2700	3325	4800	6875
3500 Cargo Van	G35R	22467	2775	3400	4900	6950
155" W.B.	9		100	100	135	135
V8 5.0, 5.7 Liter	M,R		200	200	265	265
V8 454/7.4 Liter	J		375	375	500	500
V8 6.5L Turbo Diesel	F		275	275	365	365
S10/SONOMA PICKUP—4-Cyl.—Truck Equipment Schedule T2						
Short Bed	S144	12008	1225	1700	2825	4450
Long Bed	S144	12308	1050	1700	2600	4150
Extended Cab	S194	14863	1800	2325	3550	5250
Third Door			200	200	265	265
4WD	T		1200	1200	1600	1600
V6 4.3 Liter	X		325	325	435	435
V6 4.3L High Output	W		375	375	500	500

Body Type	VIN	List	Trade-In Fair	Trade-In Good	Pvt-Party Good	Retail Excellent
REGULAR CAB PICKUP—V8—Truck Equipment Schedule T1						
1500 Short Bed	C14M	18837	4075	4850	6125	8075
1500 Long Bed	C14M	19137	3875	4600	5875	7750
2500 Long Bed	C24M	19819	4325	5100	6400	8375
3500 Long Bed	C34R	20807	4450	5225	6550	8550
Work Truck/Special			(475)	(475)	(635)	(635)
4WD	K		1150	1150	1535	1535
V6 4.3 Liter	W		(450)	(450)	(600)	(600)
V8 5.7 Liter	R		275	275	365	365
V8 454/7.4 Liter	J		300	300	400	400
V8 6.5L Turbo Diesel	F,S		475	475	635	635
EXTENDED CAB PICKUP—V8—Truck Equipment Schedule T1						
1500 Long Bed	C19M	20917	5150	6025	7450	9575
1500 Long Bed	C19M	21417	4925	5775	7150	9250
2500 Short Bed	C29M	22435	5700	6650	8100	10350
2500 HD Long Bed	C29M	22272	5500	6425	7875	10100
3500 Long Bed	C39R	24229	5400	6300	7750	9925
Third Door			250	250	335	335
4WD	K		1150	1150	1535	1535
V6 4.3 Liter	W		(450)	(450)	(600)	(600)
V8 5.7 Liter	R		275	275	365	365
V8 454/7.4 Liter	J		300	300	400	400
V8 6.5L Turbo Diesel	F,S		475	475	635	635
CREW CAB PICKUP—V8—Truck Equipment Schedule T1						
3500 Long Bed	C33R	23937	6500	7500	9075	11450
4WD	K		1150	1150	1535	1535
V8 454/7.4 Liter	J		300	300	400	400
V8 6.5L Turbo Diesel	F		475	475	635	635

1998 CHEVY/GMC—1G(C,K,NorT)—J186—W—#

Body Type	VIN	List	Trade-In Fair	Trade-In Good	Pvt-Party Good	Retail Excellent
TRACKER 4WD—4-Cyl.—Truck Equipment Schedule T2						
Sport Util Conv 2D	J186	15301	1225	1700	3025	4850
Sport Utility 4D	J136	16251	1925	2450	3850	5775
2WD	E		(525)	(525)	(700)	(700)
BLAZER/JIMMY 4WD—V6—Truck Equipment Schedule T1						
Sport Utility 2D	T18W	24166	2575	3200	4775	6975
Sport Utility 4D	T13W	25691	3450	4150	5850	8200
2WD	S		(575)	(575)	(765)	(765)
ENVOY 4WD—V6—Truck Equipment Schedule T3						
Sport Utility 4D	K13W	34650	6550	7575	9550	12450
TAHOE/YUKON 4WD—V8—Truck Equipment Schedule T1						
Sport Utility 2D	K18R	27670	4175	4950	7075	9975
Sport Utility 4D	K13R	32625	5700	6650	8925	12100
2WD	C		(1225)	(1225)	(1635)	(1635)
V8 6.5L Turbo Diesel	S		525	525	700	700
SUBURBAN—V8—Truck Equipment Schedule T1						
C1500 Sport Utility	C16R	27767	5525	6425	8550	11500
C2500 Sport Utility	C26R	29351	5775	6725	8850	11850
w/o Third Seat			(425)	(425)	(565)	(565)
4WD	K		1225	1225	1635	1635
V8 454/7.4 Liter	J		300	300	400	400
V8 6.5L Turbo Diesel	F		525	525	700	700
VENTURE—V6—Truck Equipment Schedule T2						
Cargo Minivan	G05E	21329	2125	2700	3975	5800
w/o 2nd Sliding Door			(500)	(500)	(665)	(665)
VENTURE—V6—Truck Equipment Schedule T1						
Minivan	U05E	21999	2575	3200	4500	6400
Extended Minivan	X09E	22829	3000	3675	5025	6975
w/o 2nd Sliding Door			(500)	(500)	(665)	(665)
ASTRO/SAFARI—V6—Truck Equipment Schedule T2						
Cargo/SL Cargo	M19W	19925	2400	2975	4300	6150
Dutch Doors			100	100	135	135
AWD	L		575	575	765	765
ASTRO/SAFARI—V6—Truck Equipment Schedule T1						
Base/SLX Minivan	M19W	21628	3050	3700	5100	7050
5 Passenger			(425)	(425)	(565)	(565)
Dutch Doors			100	100	135	135
AWD	L		575	575	765	765
EXPRESS/SAVANA—V8—Truck Equipment Schedule T1						
1500 Passenger Van	G15M	23871	3375	4075	5675	7900
2500 Passenger Van	G25R	25876	3475	4175	5775	8050
3500 Passenger Van	G35R	26165	3675	4400	6000	8275
5 Passenger			(425)	(425)	(565)	(565)

TRUCKS & VANS

1998 CHEVROLET/GMC

Body	Type	VIN	List	Trade-In Fair	Trade-In Good	Pvt-Party Good	Retail Excellent
155" W.B.		9		100	100	135	135
V6 4.3 Liter		W		(425)	(425)	(565)	(565)
V8 454/7.4 Liter		J		200	200	265	265
V8 6.5L Turbo Diesel		F		150	150	200	200
G-SERIES/SAVANA—V6—Truck Equipment Schedule T1							
1500 Cargo Van		G15W	21102	3250	3900	5375	7475
2500 Cargo Van		G25W	21527	3325	4025	5500	7600
3500 Cargo Van		G35R	23061	3425	4125	5600	7725
155" W.B.		9		100	100	135	135
V8 5.0, 5.7 Liter		M,R		200	200	265	265
V8 454/7.4 Liter		J		425	425	565	565
V8 6.5L Turbo Diesel		F		300	300	400	400
S10/SONOMA PICKUP—4-Cyl.—Truck Equipment Schedule T2							
Short Bed		S144	12508	1800	2325	3475	5125
Long Bed		S144	13172	2100	2100	3250	4850
Extended Cab		S194	15740	2450	3050	4250	6000
Third Door				200	200	265	265
4WD		T		1275	1275	1700	1700
V6 4.3 Liter		X		375	375	500	500
V6 4.3L High Output		W		425	425	565	565
REGULAR CAB PICKUP—V8—Truck Equipment Schedule T1							
1500 Short Bed		C14M	19250	4600	5425	6775	8800
1500 Long Bed		C14M	19550	4375	5150	6500	8500
2500 Long Bed		C24M	20232	4925	5775	7150	9250
3500 Long Bed		C34R	21419	5050	5925	7300	9400
Work Truck/Special				(525)	(525)	(700)	(700)
4WD		K		1225	1225	1635	1635
V6 4.3 Liter		W		(475)	(475)	(635)	(635)
V8 5.7 Liter		R		300	300	400	400
V8 454/7.4 Liter		J		300	300	400	400
V8 6.5L Turbo Diesel		F,S		525	525	700	700
EXTENDED CAB PICKUP—V8—Truck Equipment Schedule T1							
1500 Short Bed		C19M	21250	5800	6775	8225	10450
1500 Long Bed		C19M	22045	5575	6475	7925	10150
2500 Short Bed		C29M	22848	6450	7475	9000	11350
2500 HD Long Bed		C29M	22884	6225	7200	8700	11000
3500 Long Bed		C39R	24842	6100	7075	8575	10850
Third Door				250	250	335	335
4WD		K		1225	1225	1635	1635
V6 4.3 Liter		W		(475)	(475)	(635)	(635)
V8 5.7 Liter		R		300	300	400	400
V8 454/7.4 Liter		J		300	300	400	400
V8 6.5L Turbo Diesel		F,S		525	525	700	700
CREW CAB PICKUP—V8—Truck Equipment Schedule T1							
3500 Long Bed		C33R	24549	7300	8400	9975	12500
4WD		K		1225	1225	1635	1635
V8 454/7.4 Liter		J		300	300	400	400
V8 6.5L Turbo Diesel		F		525	525	700	700

1999 CHEVY/GMC—(1,2or3)(CorG)(A,CorN)—J186—X

Body	Type	VIN	List	Trade-In Fair	Trade-In Good	Pvt-Party Good	Retail Excellent
TRACKER 4WD—4-Cyl.—Truck Equipment Schedule T2							
Sport Util Conv 2D		J186	15095	1525	2050	3475	5425
Sport Utility 4D		J136	16295	2350	2925	4450	6500
2WD		E		(600)	(600)	(800)	(800)
BLAZER/JIMMY 4WD—V6—Truck Equipment Schedule T2							
Sport Utility 2D		T18W	22995	3150	3825	5550	7925
Sport Utility 4D		T13W	25945	4175	4975	6775	9300
2WD		S		(650)	(650)	(865)	(865)
ENVOY 4WD—V6—Truck Equipment Schedule T3							
Sport Utility 4D		K13W	34125	7725	8875	11000	14050
TAHOE/YUKON 4WD—V8—Truck Equipment Schedule T1							
Sport Utility 2D		K18R	27995	4800	5650	7950	11100
Sport Utility 4D		K13R	32950	6750	7800	10200	13700
2WD		C		(1300)	(1300)	(1735)	(1735)
V8 6.5L Turbo Diesel		C		600	600	800	800
YUKON DENALI 4WD—V8—Truck Equipment Schedule T3							
Sport Utility 4D		K13R	43505	10750	12200	15000	19050
SUBURBAN—V8—Truck Equipment Schedule T1							
C1500 Sport Utility		C16R	28267	6475	7500	9750	12950
C2500 Sport Utility		C26R	29851	6775	7800	10100	13350
w/o Third Seat				(500)	(500)	(665)	(665)
4WD		K		1400	1400	1865	1865
V8 454/7.4 Liter		J		350	350	465	465

DEDUCT FOR RECONDITIONING

0105

TRUCKS & VANS

Body Type	VIN	List	Trade-In Fair	Trade-In Good	Pvt-Party Good	Retail Excellent
V8 6.5L Turbo Diesel	F		600	600	800	800
VENTURE—V6—Truck Equipment Schedule T2						
Cargo Minivan 4D	G05E	22025	2650	3250	4600	6550
VENTURE—V6—Truck Equipment Schedule T1						
Minivan 4D	U05E	22625	3200	3875	5275	7300
Extended Minivan	X09E	23625	3700	4425	5850	7975
w/o 2nd Sliding Door			(550)	(550)	(735)	(735)
ASTRO/SAFARI—V6—Truck Equipment Schedule T2						
Cargo/SL Cargo	M19W	20268	2800	3425	4800	6775
Dutch Doors			150	150	200	200
AWD	L		675	675	900	900
ASTRO/SAFARI—V6—Truck Equipment Schedule T1						
Minivan/SL Minivan	M19W	21547	3725	4475	5900	8025
Dutch Doors			150	150	200	200
AWD	L		675	675	900	900
EXPRESS/SAVANA—V8—Truck Equipment Schedule T1						
1500 Passenger Van	G15M	24100	4225	5025	6750	9200
2500 Passenger Van	G25R	26105	4350	5125	6900	9350
3500 Passenger Van	G35M	26394	4550	5375	7125	9650
5 Passenger			(500)	(500)	(665)	(665)
155" W.B.	9		150	150	200	200
V6 4.3 Liter	W		(500)	(500)	(665)	(665)
V8 454/7.4 Liter			250	250	335	335
V8 6.5L Turbo Diesel	F,S		175	175	235	235
EXPRESS/SAVANA—V6—Truck Equipment Schedule T1						
1500 Cargo Van	G15M	21505	4000	4750	6350	8650
2500 Cargo Van	G25M	21955	4125	4900	6500	8800
3500 Cargo Van	G35M	23489	4250	5050	6650	8950
155" W.B.	9		150	150	200	200
V8 5.0, 5.7 Liter	M,R		250	250	335	335
V8 454/7.4 Liter			500	500	665	665
V8 6.5L Turbo Diesel	F,S		350	350	465	465
S10/SONOMA PICKUP—4-Cyl.—Truck Equipment Schedule T2						
Short Bed	S144	12658	2250	2800	4025	5775
Long Bed	S144	13322	2025	2575	3775	5475
Extended Cab	S194	15890	2975	3650	4925	6775
Third Door			225	225	300	300
4WD	T		1450	1450	1935	1935
V6 4.3 Liter	X		450	450	600	600
V6 4.3L High Output	W		500	500	665	665
SILVERADO/SIERRA REGULAR CAB—V8 (New)—Truck Sch T1						
1500 Short Bed	C14V	18390	5550	6450	7800	9900
1500 Long Bed	C14V	18690	5250	6150	7475	9475
2500 Long Bed	C24T	21601	6050	7000	8400	10550
2500 HD Long Bed	C24T	22445	6250	7225	8625	10800
4WD	K		1400	1400	1865	1865
V6 4.3 Liter	W		(550)	(550)	(735)	(735)
V8 5.3 Liter	T		325	325	435	435
V8 6.0 Liter	U		350	350	465	465
V8 6.5L Turbo Diesel	F,S		600	600	800	800
SILVERADO/SIERRA EXTENDED CAB—V8 (New)—Truck Sch T1						
1500 Short Bed	C19V	22635	7200	8275	9750	12100
1500 Long Bed	C19V	22935	6900	7975	9425	11700
2500 Short Bed	C29T	24051	7950	9125	10650	13100
2500 HD Short Bed	K29T	27995	8125	9325	10900	13350
2500 HD Long Bed	C29T	25195	7900	9075	10600	13050
4WD	K		1400	1400	1865	1865
V6 4.3 Liter	W		(550)	(550)	(735)	(735)
V8 5.3 Liter	T		325	325	435	435
V8 6.0 Liter	U		350	350	465	465
V8 6.5L Turbo Diesel	F,S		600	600	800	800
REGULAR CAB PICKUP—V8—Truck Equipment Schedule T1						
2500 HD Long Bed	C24R	21558	5800	6775	8200	10400
3500 Long Bed	C34R	21856	5725	6675	8100	10250
4WD	K		1400	1400	1865	1865
V8 454/7.4 Liter	J		350	350	465	465
V8 6.5L Turbo Diesel	F,S		600	600	800	800
EXTENDED CAB PICKUP—V8—Truck Equipment Schedule T1						
1500 Short Bed	C19M	23366	6625	7650	9150	11450
2500 HD Short Bed	K29M	26268	7550	8700	10250	12750
2500 HD Long Bed	C29M	23162	7125	8225	9800	12200
3500 Long Bed	C39R	25282	7075	8150	9700	12100
4WD	K		1400	1400	1865	1865

SEE BACK PAGES FOR TRUCK EQUIPMENT

TRUCKS & VANS

Body	Type	VIN	List	Trade-In Fair	Good	Pvt-Party Good	Retail Excellent
V8 5.7 Liter		R		325	325	435	435
V8 454/7.4 Liter		J		350	350	465	465
V8 6.5L Turbo Diesel		F,S		600	600	800	800
CREW CAB PICKUP—V8—Truck Equipment Schedule T1							
2500 Short Bed		C23R	24547	7700	8825	10400	12900
3500 Short Bed		C33J	26466	8575	9800	11400	14050
3500 Long Bed		C33R	24986	8300	9525	11200	13800
4WD		K		1400	1400	1865	1865
V8 454/7.4 Liter		J		350	350	465	465
V8 6.5L Turbo Diesel		F,S		600	600	800	800

2000 CHEVY/GMC—(1,2or3)(CorG)(1,CorN)—J186—Y

Body	Type	VIN	List	Trade-In Fair	Good	Pvt-Party Good	Retail Excellent
TRACKER 4WD—4-Cyl.—Truck Equipment Schedule T2							
Sport Util Conv 2D		J186	15425	1975	2525	4025	6100
Sport Utility 4D		J13C	16650	2875	3525	5100	7300
2WD		E		(675)	(675)	(900)	(900)
BLAZER/JIMMY 4WD—V6—Truck Equipment Schedule T1							
Sport Utility 2D		T18W	23495	3900	4625	6500	9075
Sport Utility 4D		T13W	26995	5050	5925	7875	10600
2WD		S		(725)	(725)	(965)	(965)
ENVOY 4WD—V6—Truck Equipment Schedule T3							
Sport Utility 4D		T13W	34695	9050	10325	12600	15900
TAHOE 4WD—V8 4.8L Engine (New)—Truck Equipment Sch T1							
Sport Utility 4D		K13V	29441	10275	11675	14300	18150
w/o Third Seat				(550)	(550)	(735)	(735)
2WD		C		(1350)	(1350)	(1800)	(1800)
V8 5.3 Liter		T		350	350	465	465
TAHOE 4WD—V8 5.7L Engine—Truck Equipment Schedule T1							
LT Sport Utility 4D		K13R	39544	8725	9975	12500	16150
2WD		C		(1350)	(1350)	(1800)	(1800)
YUKON 4WD—V8 (New)—Truck Equipment Schedule T1							
SLE Sport Utility 4D		K13V	35885	10275	11675	14300	18150
w/o Third Seat				(550)	(550)	(735)	(735)
2WD		C		(1350)	(1350)	(1800)	(1800)
V8 5.3 Liter		T		350	350	465	465
YUKON DENALI 4WD—V8—Truck Equipment Schedule T3							
Sport Utility 4D		K13R	44185	13250	14975	17850	22200
SUBURBAN—V8—Truck Equipment Schedule T1							
C1500 Sport Utility		C16T	27651	9425	10750	13150	16700
C2500 Sport Utility		C26U	29535	9750	11125	13550	17150
w/o Third Seat				(550)	(550)	(735)	(735)
4WD		K		1575	1575	2100	2100
YUKON XL—V8—Truck Equipment Schedule T1							
1500 Sport Utility		C13T	35178	9425	10750	13150	16700
2500 Sport Utility		C23U	36696	9750	11125	13550	17150
w/o Third Seat				(550)	(550)	(735)	(735)
4WD		K		1575	1575	2100	2100
VENTURE—V6—Truck Equipment Schedule T2							
Cargo Minivan 4D		U05E	22330	3275	3925	5400	7500
VENTURE—V6—Truck Equipment Schedule T1							
Minivan 4D		U05E	21230	3925	4675	6200	8375
Extended Minivan		X09E	24930	4500	5300	6875	9125
ASTRO/SAFARI—V6—Truck Equipment Schedule T2							
Cargo/SL Cargo		M19W	20635	3325	4025	5500	7600
Dutch Doors				200	200	265	265
AWD		L		750	750	1000	1000
ASTRO/SAFARI—V6—Truck Equipment Schedule T1							
Minivan/SL Minivan		M19W	21982	4525	5350	6900	9175
Dutch Doors				200	200	265	265
AWD		L		750	750	1000	1000
EXPRESS/SAVANA—V8—Truck Equipment Schedule T1							
1500 Passenger Van		G15M	24240	5275	6175	8075	10750
2500 Passenger Van		G25R	26245	5425	6325	8225	10950
3500 Passenger Van		G35R	26534	5650	6575	8500	11250
5 Passenger		9		(550)	(550)	(735)	(735)
155" W.B.				175	175	235	235
V6 4.3 Liter		W		(550)	(550)	(735)	(735)
V8 454/7.4 Liter		J		275	275	365	365
V8 6.5L Turbo Diesel		F		200	200	265	265
EXPRESS/SAVANA—V6—Truck Equipment Schedule T1							
1500 Cargo Van		G15W	21910	4950	5800	7500	9975
2500 Cargo Van		G25W	22360	5100	5975	7675	10200
3500 Cargo Van		G35R	23894	5250	6150	7900	10400

Body	Type	VIN	List	Trade-In Fair	Good	Pvt-Party Good	Retail Excellent
155" W.B.				175	175	235	235
V8 5.0, 5.7 Liter		M,R		275	275	365	365
V8 454/7.4 Liter		J		550	550	735	735
V8 6.5L Turbo Diesel		F		400	400	535	535

S10/SONOMA PICKUP—4-Cyl.—Truck Equipment Schedule T2

Body	Type	VIN	List	Fair	Good	Good	Excellent
Short Bed		S144	12610	2750	3375	4675	6525
Long Bed		S144	12661	2525	3125	4400	6225
Extended Cab		S194	15309	3600	4325	5675	7650
Third Door				250	250	335	335
4WD		T		1625	1625	2165	2165
V6 4.3 Liter		W		550	550	735	735

SILVERADO/SIERRA REGULAR CAB—V8 (New)—Truck Sch T1

Body	Type	VIN	List	Fair	Good	Good	Excellent
1500 Short Bed		C14V	18510	6375	7375	8725	10900
1500 Long Bed		C14V	18810	6050	7000	8350	10450
2500 Long Bed		C24T	21950	6925	8000	9400	11650
2500 HD Long Bed		C24T	23074	7125	8225	9650	11900
4WD		K		1575	1575	2100	2100
V6 4.3 Liter		W		(625)	(625)	(835)	(835)
V8 5.3 Liter		T		350	350	465	465
V8 6.0 Liter		U		400	400	535	535

SILVERADO/SIERRA EXTENDED CAB—V8 (New)—Truck Sch T1

Body	Type	VIN	List	Fair	Good	Good	Excellent
1500 Short Bed		C19V	22884	8225	9425	10950	13400
1500 Long Bed		C19V	23184	7900	9075	10550	12900
2500 Short Bed		C29T	24400	9100	10375	11950	14500
2500 HD Short Bed		C29T	28324	9300	10600	12200	14800
2500 HD Long Bed		C29T	25524	9050	10325	11900	14450
4WD		K		1575	1575	2100	2100
Fourth Door				275	275	365	365
V6 4.3 Liter		W		(625)	(625)	(835)	(835)
V8 5.3 Liter		T		350	350	465	465
V8 6.0 Liter		U		400	400	535	535

REGULAR CAB PICKUP—V8—Truck Equipment Schedule T1

Body	Type	VIN	List	Fair	Good	Good	Excellent
2500 HD Long Bed		C24R	21837	6675	7725	9200	11450
3500 Long Bed		C34R	22435	6650	7675	9150	11400
4WD		K		1575	1575	2100	2100
V8 454/7.4 Liter		J		400	400	535	535
V8 6.5L Turbo Diesel		F		675	675	900	900

EXTENDED CAB PICKUP—V8—Truck Equipment Schedule T1

Body	Type	VIN	List	Fair	Good	Good	Excellent
2500 HD Short Bed		K29R	26547	8700	9925	11500	14100
2500 HD Long Bed		C29R	23441	8275	9475	11050	13600
3500 Long Bed		C39R	25861	8275	9475	11050	13550
4WD		K		1575	1575	2100	2100
V8 454/7.4 Liter		J		400	400	535	535
V8 6.5L Turbo Diesel		F		675	675	900	900

CREW CAB PICKUP—V8—Truck Equipment Schedule T1

Body	Type	VIN	List	Fair	Good	Good	Excellent
2500 Short Bed		C23R	24826	8975	10275	11850	14450
3500 Short Bed		C33R	27045	9850	11225	12850	15600
3500 Long Bed		C33R	25565	9550	10900	12550	15200
4WD		K		1575	1575	2100	2100
V8 454/7.4 Liter		J		400	400	535	535
V8 6.5L Turbo Diesel		F		675	675	900	900

2001 CHEVY/GMC—(1,2or3)(CorG)(A,CorN)—J186–1

TRACKER 4WD—4-Cyl.—Truck Equipment Schedule T2

Body	Type	VIN	List	Fair	Good	Good	Excellent
Sport Util Conv 2D		J186	16760	2550	3175	4750	6950
Sport Utility 4D		J13C	17380	3575	4275	5950	8275
ZR2 Spt Utl Conv 2D		J78C	18835	3175	3850	5500	7775
ZR2 Sport Utility 4D		J734	21200	4400	5175	6900	9350
LT Sport Utility 4D		J634	21880	5000	5850	7600	10150
2WD		E		(750)	(750)	(1000)	(1000)
V6 2.5 Liter		4		600	600	800	800

BLAZER/JIMMY 4WD—V6—Truck Equipment Schedule T1

Body	Type	VIN	List	Fair	Good	Good	Excellent
Sport Utility 2D		T18W	23745	4850	5700	7675	10450
Sport Utility 4D		T13W	27345	6125	7100	9200	12150
2WD		S		(800)	(800)	(1065)	(1065)

TAHOE 4WD—V8—Truck Equipment Schedule T1

Body	Type	VIN	List	Fair	Good	Good	Excellent
Sport Utility 4D		K13V	31021	12050	13675	16450	20600
w/o Third Seat				(600)	(600)	(800)	(800)
2WD		C		(1400)	(1400)	(1865)	(1865)
V8 5.3 Liter		T		375	375	500	500

YUKON 4WD—V8—Truck Equipment Schedule T1

Body	Type	VIN	List	Fair	Good	Good	Excellent
SLE Sport Utility 4D		K13T	36128	12050	13675	16450	20600
w/o Third Seat				(600)	(600)	(800)	(800)

TRUCKS & VANS

Body	Type	VIN	List	Trade-In Fair	Good	Pvt-Party Good	Retail Excellent
2WD	C			(1400)	(1400)	(1865)	(1865)
V8 5.3 Liter	T,Z			375	375	500	500
YUKON DENALI 4WD—V8—Truck Equipment Schedule T3							
Sport Utility 4D	K13T	46680	17175	19300	22500	27300
SUBURBAN—V8—Truck Equipment Schedule T1							
C1500 Sport Utility	C16T	29428	11125	12625	15200	19050
C2500 Sport Utility	C26U	31287	11475	13050	15600	19500
w/o Third Seat			(600)	(600)	(800)	(800)
4WD	K		1750	1750	2335	2335
V8 8.1 Liter	G		450	450	600	600
YUKON XL—V8—Truck Equipment Schedule T1							
1500 Sport Utility	C13T	36287	11125	12625	15200	19050
2500 Sport Utility	C23U	37659	11475	13050	15600	19500
4WD	K		1750	1750	2335	2335
V8 8.1 Liter	G		450	450	600	600
YUKON XL DENALI AWD—V8—Truck Equipment Schedule T3							
1500 Sport Utility 4D	K16U	48185	19150	21500	24700	29600
VENTURE—V6—Truck Equipment Schedule T1							
Minivan 4D	U05E	21605	4900	5725	7350	9700
Extended Minivan	X09E	26085	5500	6425	8075	10500
ASTRO/SAFARI—V6—Truck Equipment Schedule T2							
Cargo/SL Cargo	M19W	21238	4075	4850	6400	8675
Dutch Doors			250	250	335	335
AWD	L		825	825	1100	1100
ASTRO/SAFARI—V6—Truck Equipment Schedule T2							
Minivan 3D	M19W	23886	5550	6450	8100	10550
Dutch Doors			250	250	335	335
AWD	L		825	825	1100	1100
EXPRESS/SAVANA VAN—V8—Truck Equipment Schedule T1							
1500 Passenger Van	G15M	24730	6625	7650	9700	12650
2500 Passenger Van	G25R	26735	6800	7825	9900	12850
3500 Passenger Van	G35R	27024	7025	8100	10200	13200
155" W.B.			200	200	265	265
V6 4.3 Liter	W		(600)	(600)	(800)	(800)
V8 8.1 Liter	G		300	300	400	400
V8 6.5L Turbo Diesel	F		225	225	300	300
EXPRESS/SAVANA VAN—V8—Truck Equipment Schedule T1							
1500 Cargo Van	G15W	22520	6175	7150	8975	11650
2500 Cargo Van	G25W	22650	6325	7350	9175	11850
3500 Cargo Van	G35M	24929	6525	7550	9400	12150
155" W.B.			200	200	265	265
V8 5.0, 5.7 Liter	M,R		300	300	400	400
V8 8.1 Liter	G		600	600	800	800
V8 6.5L Turbo Diesel	F		450	450	600	600
S10/SONOMA PICKUP—4-Cyl. Flex Fuel—Truck Equip Sch T2							
Short Bed	S145	12859	3425	4125	5475	7450
Long Bed	S145	13210	3150	3825	5150	7100
Extended Cab	S195	16203	4350	5125	6550	8675
Third Door			275	275	365	365
4WD	T		1800	1800	2400	2400
V6 4.3 Liter			600	600	800	800
S10/SONOMA CREW CAB 4WD—V6—Truck Equip Sch T1							
LS/SLS Short Bed	T13W	25369	7700	8850	10500	13050
SILVERADO/SIERRA REGULAR CAB—V8—Truck Equip Sch T1							
1500 Short Bed	C14V	19185	7425	8525	9925	12200
1500 Long Bed	C14V	19485	7025	8100	9500	11700
2500 Long Bed	C24U	23689	8025	9200	10650	13000
2500 HD Long Bed	C24U	24109	8225	9475	10950	13300
3500 Long Bed	C34U	25361	8300	9525	11000	13350
4WD	K		1750	1750	2335	2335
V6 4.3 Liter	W		(700)	(700)	(935)	(935)
V8 5.3 Liter			375	375	500	500
V8 8.1 Liter	G		450	450	600	600
V8 6.6L Turbo Diesel	1		5300	5300	7065	7065
SILVERADO/SIERRA EXTENDED CAB—V8—Truck Equip Sch T1							
1500 Short Bed	C19V	23589	9475	10800	12350	14900
1500 Long Bed	C19V	23889	9100	10375	11900	14400
2500 Short Bed	K29U	29039	10425	11850	13450	16100
2500 HD Short Bed	K29U	26614	10650	12150	13750	16400
2500 HD Long Bed	C29U	26859	10375	11800	13400	16050
3500 Long Bed	C39U	28141	10425	11850	13450	16100
4WD	K		1750	1750	2335	2335
V6 4.3 Liter	W		(700)	(700)	(935)	(935)

TRUCKS & VANS

Body	Type	VIN	List	Trade-In Fair	Good	Pvt-Party Good	Retail Excellent
V8 5.3 Liter		T		375	375	500	500
V8 8.1 Liter		G		450	450	600	600
V8 6.6L Turbo Diesel		1		5300	5300	7065	7065
SIERRA EXTENDED CAB PICKUP AWD—V8—Truck Equip Sch T1							
1500 C3 Short Bed		C19U	38995	15125	17050	18900	22200
SILVERADO/SIERRA CREW CAB—V8—Truck Equipment Sch T1							
1500 HD Short Bed		C13U	28912	10700	12150	13800	16450
2500 HD Short Bed		C23U	27984	11750	13300	15000	17800
2500 HD Long Bed		C23U	28284	11525	13050	14750	17500
3500 Long Bed		C33U	30766	11575	13100	14800	17600
4WD		K		1750	1750	2335	2335
V8 8.1 Liter		G		450	450	600	600
V8 6.6L Turbo Diesel		1		5300	5300	7065	7065

2002 CHEVY/GMC—1,2or3(CorG)A,CorN—(J18C)—2

Body	Type	VIN	List	Trade-In Fair	Good	Pvt-Party Good	Retail Excellent
TRACKER 4WD—4-Cyl.—Truck Equipment Schedule T2							
Sport Util Conv 2D		J18C	17415	3300	3975	5675	8025
Sport Utility 4D		J13C	18105	4425	5200	6950	9425
ZR2 Spt Utl Conv 2D		J78C	19395	3975	4725	6450	8875
ZR2 Sport Utility 4D		J734	21845	5200	6200	7975	10550
LT Sport Utility 4D		J634	22270	5950	6900	8750	11400
2WD		E		(825)	(825)	(1100)	(1100)
V6 2.5 Liter		4		650	650	865	865
BLAZER 4WD—V6—Truck Equipment Schedule T1							
Sport Utility 2D		T18W	23895	6000	6950	9150	12200
Sport Utility 4D		T13W	26130	7425	8525	10750	13950
2WD		S		(875)	(875)	(1165)	(1165)
TRAILBLAZER 4WD—6-Cyl.—Truck Equipment Schedule T1							
Sport Utility 4D		T1S3	28130	9800	11175	13700	17350
Extended Spt Util 4D		T16S	33610	11275	12825	14850	18050
2WD		S		(1450)	(1450)	(1935)	(1935)
ENVOY 4WD—6-Cyl.—Truck Equipment Schedule T1							
Sport Utility 4D		T13S	31770	9800	11175	13700	17350
2WD		S		(1450)	(1450)	(1935)	(1935)
ENVOY XL 4WD—6-Cyl.—Truck Equipment Schedule T1							
Sport Utility 4D		T16S	33820	11275	12825	14850	18050
2WD		S		(1450)	(1450)	(1935)	(1935)
TAHOE 4WD—V8—Truck Equipment Schedule T1							
Sport Utility 4D		K13V	36345	14150	15975	19000	23500
w/o Third Seat				(650)	(650)	(865)	(865)
2WD		C		(1450)	(1450)	(1935)	(1935)
V8 5.3 Liter		T,Z		400	400	535	535
YUKON 4WD—V8—Truck Equipment Schedule T1							
Sport Utility 4D		K13V	37000	14150	15975	19000	23500
w/o Third Seat		C		(650)	(650)	(865)	(865)
2WD		C		(1450)	(1450)	(1935)	(1935)
V8 5.3 Liter		T,Z		400	400	535	535
YUKON DENALI 4WD—V8—Truck Equipment Schedule T1							
Sport Utility 4D		K13U	47355	19775	22175	25400	30500
SUBURBAN—V8—Truck Equipment Schedule T1							
C1500 Sport Utility		C16T	35988	13150	14875	17550	21700
C2500 Sport Utility		C26U	37601	13525	15300	18100	22300
4WD		K		1925	1925	2565	2565
V8 8.1 Liter		G		500	500	665	665
YUKON XL—V8—Truck Equipment Schedule T1							
1500 Sport Utility		C13T	37047	13150	14875	17550	21700
2500 Sport Utility		C23U	38419	13525	15300	18100	22300
4WD		K		1925	1925	2565	2565
V8 8.1 Liter		G		500	500	665	665
YUKON XL DENALI AWD—V8—Truck Equipment Schedule T1							
1500 Sport Utility 4D		K16U	48890	21975	24575	27700	32900
VENTURE—V6—Truck Equipment Schedule T2							
Cargo Minivan 4D		U05E	24697	5175	6050	7725	10200
VENTURE—V6—Truck Equipment Schedule T1							
Minivan 4D		U03E	22035	6100	7075	8800	11400
Extended Minivan 4D		X03E	26255	6800	7825	9600	12250
5 Passenger				(650)	(650)	(865)	(865)
AWD				900	900	1200	1200
ASTRO/SAFARI—V6—Truck Equipment Schedule T2							
Cargo/SL Cargo		M19W	21768	5100	5975	7625	10100
Dutch Doors				300	300	400	400
AWD		L		900	900	1200	1200

0105

Body	Type	VIN	List	Trade-In Fair	Good	Pvt-Party Good	Retail Excellent
ASTRO/SAFARI—V6—Truck Equipment Schedule T1							
Minivan 3D		M19W	24416	6825	7875	9650	12300
Dutch Doors				300	300	400	400
AWD		L		900	900	1200	1200
EXPRESS/SAVANA VAN—V8—Truck Equipment Schedule T1							
1500 Passenger Van		G15M	25287	8300	9525	11750	15050
2500 Passenger Van		G25R	27292	8525	9750	12050	15350
3500 Passenger Van		G35R	27581	8750	10025	12300	15650
155" W.B.				225	225	300	300
V6 4.3 Liter		W		(650)	(650)	(865)	(865)
V8 8.1 Liter		G		325	325	435	435
V8 6.5L Turbo Diesel		F		250	250	335	335
EXPRESS/SAVANA VAN—V6—Truck Equipment Schedule T1							
1500 Cargo Van		G15W	22948	7725	8875	10850	13750
2500 Cargo Van		G25W	23078	7950	9125	11050	13950
3500 Cargo Van		G35R	25357	8175	9375	11350	14300
155" W.B.				225	225	300	300
V8 5.0, 5.7 Liter		M,R		325	325	435	435
V8 8.1 Liter		G		650	650	865	865
V8 6.5L Turbo Diesel		F		500	500	665	665
S10/SONOMA PICKUP—4-Cyl. Flex Fuel—Truck Equip Sch T2							
Short Bed		S145	14327	4200	5000	6425	8575
Long Bed		S145	15772	3900	4650	6100	8200
Extended Cab		S195	16309	5200	6100	7600	9850
4WD		T		1975	1975	2635	2635
V6 4.3 Liter				650	650	865	865
S10/SONOMA CREW CAB PICKUP 4WD—V6—Truck Sch T1							
LS/SLS Short Bed		T13W	24584	9150	10425	12150	14900
AVALANCHE 4WD—V8—Truck Equipment Schedule T1							
1500 Spt Util Pickup		C13T	33965	14150	15975	17700	20700
2500 Spt Util Pickup		C23G	35865	14975	16850	18650	21800
2WD				(875)	(875)	(1165)	(1165)
NorthFace Edition				850	850	1135	1135
SILVERADO/SIERRA REGULAR CAB—V8—Truck Equip Sch T1							
1500 Short Bed		C14V	20028	8650	9900	11350	13750
1500 Long Bed		C14V	20328	8275	9475	10900	13250
2500 Long Bed		C24U	24182	9325	10650	12150	14650
2500 HD Long Bed		C24U	24607	9600	10950	12450	14950
3500 Long Bed		C34U	29017	9650	11000	12500	15000
4WD				1925	1925	2565	2565
V6 4.3 Liter		W,X		(750)	(750)	(1000)	(1000)
V8 5.3 Liter		T		400	400	535	535
V8 8.1 Liter		G		500	500	665	665
V8 6.6L Turbo Diesel				5550	5550	7400	7400
SILVERADO/SIERRA EXTENDED CAB—V8—Truck Equip Sch T1							
1500 Short Bed		C19V	23952	10900	12375	13950	16600
1500 Long Bed		C19V	25052	10500	11950	13500	16100
2500 Short Bed		K29U	29407	11950	13525	15150	17950
2500 HD Short Bed		K29U	27177	12200	13825	15450	18250
2500 HD Long Bed		C29U	27452	11900	13500	15100	17850
3500 Long Bed		C39U	28734	11950	13525	15150	17950
Quadrasteer				850	850	1135	1135
4WD		K		1925	1925	2565	2565
V6 4.3 Liter		W,X		(750)	(750)	(1000)	(1000)
V8 5.3 Liter		T		400	400	535	535
V8 8.1 Liter		G		500	500	665	665
V8 6.6L Turbo Diesel				5550	5550	7400	7400
SIERRA DENALI EXT CAB PICKUP AWD—V8—Truck Sch T3							
1500 Short Bed		K69U	44105	17375	19500	21400	24900
SILVERADO/SIERRA CREW CAB PICKUP—V8—Truck Sch T1							
1500 HD Short Bed		C13U	29425	12300	13925	15550	18350
2500 HD Short Bed		C23U	28577	13450	15175	16850	19800
2500 HD Long Bed		C23U	28877	13200	14875	16550	19500
3500 Long Bed		C33U	30159	13250	14925	16650	19600
4WD		K		1925	1925	2565	2565
V8 8.1 Liter		G		500	500	665	665
V8 6.6L Turbo Diesel				5550	5550	7400	7400

2003 CHEVY/GMC–1,2or3(CorG)A,CorN–(J18C)–3

TRACKER 4WD—4-Cyl.—Truck Equipment Schedule T2							
Sport Util Conv 2D		J18C	17815	4275	5075	6675	9000
Sport Utility 4D		J13C	18505	5500	6400	8100	10550
ZR2 Spt Util Conv 2D		J78C	19675	5025	5875	7525	9925

TRUCKS & VANS

Body Type	VIN	List	Trade-In Fair	Trade-In Good	Pvt-Party Good	Retail Excellent
ZR2 Sport Utility 4D	J734	22125	6425	7450	9175	11750
LT Sport Utility 4D	J634	22550	7150	8250	10050	12650
2WD	E		(900)	(900)	(1200)	(1200)
V6 2.5 Liter	4		700	700	935	935
BLAZER 4WD—V6—Truck Equipment Schedule T1						
Sport Utility 2D	T18X	24705	7425	8550	10800	14000
Sport Utility 4D	T13X	26585	8975	10275	12550	15950
2WD			(950)	(950)	(1265)	(1265)
TRAILBLAZER 4WD—6-Cyl.—Truck Equipment Schedule T1						
Sport Utility 4D	T13S	28800	11475	13050	15650	19600
Extended Spt Util 4D	T16S	33510	13525	15300	17400	20800
2WD	S		(1500)	(1500)	(2000)	(2000)
V8 5.3 Liter	P		400	400	535	535
ENVOY 4WD—6-Cyl.—Truck Equipment Schedule T1						
Sport Utility 4D	T13S	30820	11475	13050	15650	19600
2WD	S		(1500)	(1500)	(2000)	(2000)
ENVOY XL 4WD—6-Cyl.—Truck Equipment Schedule T1						
Sport Utility 4D	T16S	33220	13525	15300	17400	20800
2WD	S		(1500)	(1500)	(2000)	(2000)
V8 5.3 Liter	P		400	400	535	535
TAHOE 4WD—V8—Truck Equipment Schedule T1						
Sport Utility 4D	K13V	37387	16600	18675	21900	26800
w/o Third Seat			(700)	(700)	(935)	(935)
2WD	C		(1500)	(1500)	(2000)	(2000)
V8 5.3 Liter	T,Z		400	400	535	535
YUKON 4WD—V8—Truck Equipment Schedule T1						
Sport Utility 4D	K13V	37920	16600	18675	21900	26800
w/o Third Seat			(700)	(700)	(935)	(935)
2WD	C		(1500)	(1500)	(2000)	(2000)
V8 5.3 Liter	T,Z		400	400	535	535
YUKON DENALI 4WD—V8—Truck Equipment Schedule T3						
Sport Utility 4D	K13U	49195	22650	25350	28800	34400
SUBURBAN—V8—Truck Equipment Schedule T1						
C1500 Sport Utility	C16T	37030	15500	17475	20400	24900
C2500 Sport Utility	C26U	38643	15925	17950	20900	25400
Quadrasteer			925	925	1235	1235
4WD	K		2100	2100	2800	2800
V8 8.1 Liter	G		550	550	735	735
YUKON XL—V8—Truck Equipment Schedule T1						
1500 Sport Utility	C13T	37967	15500	17475	20400	24900
2500 Sport Utility	C23U	39435	15925	17950	20900	25400
Quadrasteer			925	925	1235	1235
4WD	K		2100	2100	2800	2800
V8 8.1 Liter	G		550	550	735	735
YUKON XL DENALI AWD—V8—Truck Equipment Schedule T3						
1500 Sport Utility 4D	K16U	50859	25150	28125	31400	37000
VENTURE—V6—Truck Equipment Schedule T2						
Cargo Minivan 4D	U03E	22925	6600	7625	9300	11800
VENTURE—V6—Truck Equipment Schedule T1						
Minivan 4D	U03E	23139	7650	8775	10500	13150
Extended Minivan 4D	X03E	24509	8400	9600	11400	14100
5 Passenger			(700)	(700)	(935)	(935)
AWD	V		975	975	1300	1300
ASTRO/SAFARI—V6—Truck Equipment Schedule T2						
Cargo/SL Cargo 3D	M19X	21952	6425	7450	9125	11600
Dutch Doors			350	350	465	465
AWD	L		975	975	1300	1300
ASTRO/SAFARI—V6—Truck Equipment Schedule T1						
Minivan 3D	M19X	23801	8450	9650	11400	14150
Dutch Doors			350	350	465	465
AWD	L		975	975	1300	1300
EXPRESS/SAVANA VAN—V8—Truck Equipment Schedule T1						
1500 Passenger Van	G15X	27005	10475	11900	14300	17900
2500 Passenger Van	G25U	28000	10650	12150	14550	18200
3500 Passenger Van	G35U	28504	10950	12425	14900	18550
155" W.B.			250	250	335	335
AWD	H		975	975	1300	1300
V6 4.3 Liter	X		(700)	(700)	(935)	(935)
EXPRESS/SAVANA VAN—V6—Truck Equipment Schedule T1						
1500 Cargo Van	G15X	23265	9750	11125	13100	16200
2500 Cargo Van	G25X	23415	9975	11325	13300	16400
3500 Cargo Van	G35U	25969	10275	11675	13700	16800
155" W.B.			250	250	335	335

TRUCKS & VANS

Body Type	VIN	List	Fair	Good	Pvt-Party Good	Retail Excellent
V8 4.8, 5.3 Liter	T,V		350	350	465	465
V8 6.0 Liter	U		700	700	935	935
S10/SONOMA PICKUP—4-Cyl.—Truck Equipment Schedule T2						
Short Bed	S14H	14771	5200	6100	7500	9650
Long Bed	S14H	16216	4900	5750	7150	9275
Extended Cab	S19H	16593	6300	7325	8775	11100
4WD	T		2150	2150	2865	2865
V6 4.3 Liter	X		700	700	935	935
S10/SONOMA CREW CAB PICKUP 4WD—V6—Truck Equip Sch T1						
LS/SLS Short Bed	T13X	24404	10800	12250	13950	16800
SSR REGULAR CAB PICKUP—V8—Truck Equipment Schedule T3						
LS Convertible 2D	S14P	41995	28600	31875	34400	39200
AVALANCHE 4WD—V8—Truck Equipment Schedule T1						
1500 Spt Util Pickup	K13T	35139	16375	18425	20100	23100
2500 Spt Util Pickup	K23G	37039	17100	19200	21000	24200
North Face Edition			900	900	1200	1200
2WD	C		(950)	(950)	(1265)	(1265)
SILVERADO/SIERRA REGULAR CAB PICKUP—V8—Truck Sch T1						
1500 Short Bed	C14V	20726	10275	11675	13000	15400
1500 Long Bed	C14V	21026	9850	11225	12600	14950
2500 Long Bed	C24U	23627	11000	12475	13850	16350
2500 HD Long Bed	C24U	23877	11275	12825	14250	16750
3500 Long Bed	K34U	29317	11375	12900	14300	16850
Work Truck			(1275)	(1275)	(1700)	(1700)
4WD	K		2100	2100	2800	2800
V6 4.3 Liter	X		(800)	(800)	(1065)	(1065)
V8 5.3 Liter	T		400	400	535	535
V8 8.1 Liter	G		550	550	735	735
V8 6.6L Turbo Diesel	1		5800	5800	7730	7730
SILVERADO/SIERRA EXTENDED CAB PICKUP—V8—Truck Sch T1						
1500 Short Bed	C19V	24465	12725	14400	15900	18600
1500 Long Bed	C19V	25565	12300	13925	15350	18000
2500 Short Bed	K29U	29822	13825	15650	17200	19950
2500 HD Short Bed	K29U	26257	14100	15925	17500	20400
2500 HD Long Bed	C29U	26532	13825	15600	17150	19950
3500 Long Bed	C39U	28909	13825	15650	17200	19950
Quadrasteer			925	925	1235	1235
Work Truck			(1275)	(1275)	(1700)	(1700)
4WD	K		2100	2100	2800	2800
V6 4.3 Liter	X		(800)	(800)	(1065)	(1065)
V8 5.3 Liter	T		400	400	535	535
V8 8.1 Liter	G		550	550	735	735
V8 6.6L Turbo Diesel	1		5800	5800	7730	7730
SILVERADO SS EXTENDED CAB PICKUP AWD—V8—Truck Sch T3						
1500 Short Bed	K19U	39995	19100	21400	23200	26600
SIERRA DENALI EXT CAB PICKUP AWD—V8—Truck Sch T3						
1500 Short Bed	K19U	44995	19775	22175	24000	27600
SILVERADO/SIERRA CREW CAB PICKUP—V8—Truck Equip Sch T1						
1500 HD Short Bed	C31U	30442	14200	16025	17600	20400
2500 HD Short Bed	C23U	29277	15500	17475	19100	22100
2500 HD Long Bed	C23U	29577	15225	17125	18750	21700
3500 Long Bed	C33U	30714	15275	17175	18800	21800
Quadrasteer			925	925	1235	1235
4WD	K		2100	2100	2800	2800
V8 8.1 Liter	G		550	550	735	735
V8 6.6L Turbo Diesel	1		5800	5800	7730	7730

2004 CHEVY/GMC—(1,2or3)(CorG)(A,CorN)–J134–4

Body Type	VIN	List	Fair	Good	Pvt-Party Good	Retail Excellent
TRACKER 4WD—V6—Truck Equipment Schedule T2						
Sport Utility 4D	J134	21355	6800	7825	9475	12000
ZR2 Sport Utility 4D	J734	22705	7825	8975	10700	13350
LT Sport Utility 4D	J634	23105	8600	9850	11600	14400
2WD	E		(950)	(950)	(1265)	(1265)
BLAZER 4WD—V6—Truck Equipment Schedule T1						
Sport Utility 2D	T18X	25395	9150	10425	12800	16250
Sport Utility 4D	T13X	27345	10800	12250	14750	18450
2WD	S		(1000)	(1000)	(1335)	(1335)
TRAILBLAZER 4WD—6-Cyl.—Truck Equipment Schedule T1						
Sport Utility 4D	T13S	30045	13525	15275	18050	22300
Extended Spt Util 4D	T16S	32595	16125	18150	20400	24100
2WD	S		(1550)	(1550)	(2065)	(2065)
V8 5.3 Liter	P		400	400	535	535

Body	Type	VIN	List	Trade-In Fair	Good	Pvt-Party Good	Retail Excellent
ENVOY 4WD—6-Cyl.—Truck Equipment Schedule T1							
Sport Utility 4D		T13S	31745	13525	15275	18050	22300
2WD		S		(1550)	(1550)	(2065)	(2065)
ENVOY XL 4WD—6-Cyl.—Truck Equipment Schedule T1							
Sport Utility 4D		T16S	33845	16125	18150	20400	24100
2WD		S		(1550)	(1550)	(2065)	(2065)
V8 5.3 Liter		P		400	400	535	535
ENVOY XUV 4WD—6-Cyl.—Truck Equipment Schedule T1							
2WD		S					
V8 5.3 Liter		P					
TAHOE 4WD—V8—Truck Equipment Schedule T1							
Sport Utility 4D		K13V	38425	19575	21975	25400	30800
w/o Third Seat				(750)	(750)	(1000)	(1000)
2WD		C		(1550)	(1550)	(2065)	(2065)
V8 5.3 Liter		T,Z		400	400	535	535
YUKON 4WD—V8—Truck Equipment Schedule T1							
Sport Utility 4D		K13V	38785	19575	21975	25400	30800
w/o Third Seat				(750)	(750)	(1000)	(1000)
2WD		C		(1550)	(1550)	(2065)	(2065)
V8 5.3 Liter		T		400	400	535	535
YUKON DENALI AWD—V8—Truck Equipment Schedule T3							
Sport Utility 4D		K13U	50125	26025	29100	32700	38700
SUBURBAN—V8—Truck Equipment Schedule T1							
C1500 Sport Utility		C16T	37865	18325	20650	23800	28700
C2500 Sport Utility		C26U	39465	18825	21125	24300	29300
Quadrasteer				1000	1000	1335	1335
4WD		K		2275	2275	3035	3035
V8 8.1 Liter		G		575	575	765	765
YUKON XL—V8—Truck Equipment Schedule T1							
1500 Sport Utility		C13T	38775	18325	20650	23800	28700
2500 Sport Utility		C23U	40275	18825	21125	24300	29300
Quadrasteer				1000	1000	1335	1335
4WD		K		2275	2275	3035	3035
V8 8.1 Liter		G		575	575	765	765
YUKON XL DENALI AWD—V8—Truck Equipment Schedule T3							
1500 Sport Utility 4D		K16U	51775	28700	32075	35600	41500
VENTURE—V6—Truck Equipment Schedule T2							
Cargo Minivan 4D		U03E	23120	8450	9650	11400	14200
VENTURE—V6—Truck Equipment Schedule T1							
Minivan 4D		U03E	21995	9600	10950	12800	15750
Extended Minivan 4D		X09E	23570	10375	11800	13750	16750
5 Passenger				(750)	(750)	(1000)	(1000)
AWD		V		1050	1050	1400	1400
ASTRO/SAFARI—V6—Truck Equipment Schedule T2							
Cargo 3D		M19X	22965	8125	9325	11100	13800
Dutch Doors				375	375	500	500
AWD		L		1050	1050	1400	1400
ASTRO/SAFARI—V6—Truck Equipment Schedule T1							
Minivan 3D		M19X	24395	10425	11850	13800	16800
Dutch Doors				375	375	500	500
AWD		L		1050	1050	1400	1400
EXPRESS/SAVANA VAN—V8—Truck Equipment Schedule T1							
1500 Passenger Van		G15T	27280	13250	14925	17650	21800
2500 Passenger Van		G25U	28685	13500	15225	17950	22100
3500 Passenger Van		G35U	29089	13775	15550	18300	22500
155" W.B.		H		275	275	365	365
AWD				950	950	1265	1265
V6 4.3 Liter		X		(750)	(750)	(1000)	(1000)
EXPRESS/SAVANA VAN—V6—Truck Equipment Schedule T1							
1500 Cargo Van		G15X	23185	12325	13975	16200	19600
2500 Cargo Van		G25X	23965	12625	14250	16400	19850
3500 Cargo Van		G35U	27194	12900	14600	16750	20300
AWD				950	950	1265	1265
155" W.B.				275	275	365	365
V8 4.8, 5.3 Liter		V,T		375	375	500	500
V6 6.0 Liter		U		750	750	1000	1000
S10/SONOMA CREW CAB PICKUP 4WD—V6—Truck Sch T1							
LS/SLS Short Bed		T13X	25095	12900	14600	16400	19500
COLORADO/CANYON PICKUP—4-Cyl.—Truck Sch T2							
Short Bed		S148	16200	7125	8225	9750	12100
Extended Cab		S198	18545	8300	9525	11150	13700
Crew Cab		S138	20670	9475	10800	12500	15200
4WD				2325	2325	3100	3100

TRUCKS & VANS

Body	Type	VIN	List	Trade-In Fair	Trade-In Good	Pvt-Party Good	Retail Excellent
	5-Cyl. 3.5 Liter	6		200	200	265	265
SSR REGULAR CAB PICKUP—V8—Truck Equipment Schedule T3							
	Convertible 2D	S14P	41995				
AVALANCHE 4WD—V8—Truck Equipment Schedule T1							
1500 Spt Util Pickup		K13T	36100	18825	21125	22800	26000
2500 Spt Util Pickup		K22G	37935	19675	22075	23700	27100
2WD		C		(1000)	(1000)	(1335)	(1335)
SILVERADO/SIERRA REGULAR CAB PICKUP—V8—Truck Sch T1							
1500 Short Bed		C14V	23400	12250	13875	15200	17650
1500 Long Bed		C14V	23700	11750	13350	14700	17100
2500 Long Bed		C24U	26660	13000	14725	16150	18700
2500 HD Long Bed		C24U	26910	13300	15025	16450	19050
3500 Long Bed		K34U	30940	13400	15125	16550	19200
Work Truck				(1400)	(1400)	(1865)	(1865)
4WD		K		2275	2275	3035	3035
V6 4.3 Liter		X		(850)	(850)	(1135)	(1135)
V8 5.3 Liter		T		400	400	535	535
V8 8.1 Liter		G		575	575	765	765
V8 6.6L Turbo Diesel				6025	6025	8030	8030
SILVERADO/SIERRA EXTENDED CAB PICKUP—V8—Truck Sch T1							
1500 Short Bed		C19V	26260	14875	16750	18300	21100
1500 Long Bed		C19V	27360	14400	16275	17750	20500
2500 Short Bed		K29U	31615	16025	18050	19700	22700
2500 HD Short Bed		C29U	29160	16375	18425	20100	23100
2500 HD Long Bed		C29U	29460	15975	18000	19600	22600
3500 Long Bed		C39U	30400	16025	18050	19700	22700
Work Truck				(1400)	(1400)	(1865)	(1865)
Quadrasteer				1000	1000	1335	1335
4WD		K		2275	2275	3035	3035
V6 4.3 Liter		X		(850)	(850)	(1135)	(1135)
V8 5.3 Liter		T		400	400	535	535
V8 6.0 Liter (1500)		U		550	550	735	735
V8 8.1 Liter		G		575	575	765	765
V8 6.6L Turbo Diesel				6025	6025	8030	8030
SILVERADO SS EXTENDED CAB PICKUP AWD—V8—Truck Sch T1							
1500 Short Bed		K19N	40195	21700	24375	26100	29600
SILVERADO/SIERRA CREW CAB PICKUP—V8—Truck Sch T1							
1500 Short Bed		C13T	31020	16475	18525	20200	23200
2500 Short Bed		C23U	31540	17175	19300	21000	24100
2500 HD Short Bed		C23U	31460	17950	20150	21800	25000
2500 HD Long Bed		C23U	31160	17525	19675	21300	24500
3500 Long Bed		C33U	32400	17625	19775	21500	24700
Work Truck				(1400)	(1400)	(1865)	(1865)
Quadrasteer				1000	1000	1335	1335
4WD		K		2275	2275	3035	3035
V8 8.1 Liter		G		575	575	765	765
V8 6.6L Turbo Diesel		1,2		6025	6025	8030	8030

CHRYSLER TRUCKS

1990 CHRYSLER — (1,3orZ)C4(BY54R)–L–#

Body	Type	VIN	List	Trade-In Fair	Trade-In Good	Pvt-Party Good	Retail Excellent
TOWN & COUNTRY—V6—Truck Equipment Schedule T3							
Minivan		BY54R	25515	1225	1700	2725	4225
w/o Rear Air Conditioning				(100)	(100)	(135)	(135)

1991 CHRYSLER — (1,3orZ)C4(BY54R)–M–#

TOWN & COUNTRY—V6—Truck Equipment Schedule T3							
Minivan		BY54R	24425	1500	2025	3125	4675
5 Passenger				(225)	(225)	(300)	(300)
w/o Rear Air Conditioning				(100)	(100)	(135)	(135)

1992 CHRYSLER — (1or3)C4-(H54R)–N–#

TOWN & COUNTRY—V6—Truck Equipment Schedule T3							
Minivan		H54R	25161	1750	2275	3400	5050
5 Passenger				(250)	(250)	(335)	(335)
AWD		K		325	325	435	435
w/o Rear Air Conditioning				(125)	(125)	(165)	(165)

1993 CHRYSLER — (1or3)C4-(H54R)–P–#

TOWN & COUNTRY—V6—Truck Equipment Schedule T3							
Minivan		H54R	26078	2025	2575	3775	5475

Body	Type	VIN	List	Trade-In Fair	Good	Pvt-Party Good	Retail Excellent
	5 Passenger			(275)	(275)	(365)	(365)
	AWD	K		375	375	500	500
	w/o Rear Air Conditioning			(150)	(150)	(200)	(200)

1994 CHRYSLER — (1or3)C4-(H54L)-R-#

TOWN & COUNTRY—V6—Truck Equipment Schedule T3

Body	Type	VIN	List	Trade-In Fair	Good	Pvt-Party Good	Retail Excellent
	Minivan	H54L	27844	2325	2900	4175	5975
	5 Passenger			(300)	(300)	(400)	(400)
	w/o Rear Air Conditioning			(175)	(175)	(235)	(235)
	AWD	K		425	425	565	565

1995 CHRYSLER — (1or3)C4-(H54L)-S-#

TOWN & COUNTRY—V6—Truck Equipment Schedule T3

Body	Type	VIN	List	Trade-In Fair	Good	Pvt-Party Good	Retail Excellent
	Minivan	H54L	28240	2700	3300	4625	6525
	5 Passenger			(325)	(325)	(435)	(435)
	w/o Rear Air Conditioning			(200)	(200)	(265)	(265)
	AWD	K		475	475	635	635

1996 CHRYSLER — 1C4-(P55R)-T-#

TOWN & COUNTRY—V6—Truck Equipment Schedule T3

Body	Type	VIN	List	Trade-In Fair	Good	Pvt-Party Good	Retail Excellent
	LX Minivan	P55R	25850	3800	4525	6025	8175
	Minivan	P54R	28565	4000	4750	6275	8475
	LXi Minivan	P64L	30605	4300	5075	6625	8875
	5 Passenger			(350)	(350)	(465)	(465)
	w/o Quad Seating			(150)	(150)	(200)	(200)
	w/o 2nd Sliding Door			(450)	(450)	(600)	(600)
	w/o Rear Air Conditioning			(225)	(225)	(300)	(300)

1997 CHRYSLER — 1C4-(P55R)-V-#

TOWN & COUNTRY—V6—Truck Equipment Schedule T3

Body	Type	VIN	List	Trade-In Fair	Good	Pvt-Party Good	Retail Excellent
	SX Minivan	P55R	28070	4325	5100	6700	8975
	LX Minivan	P54R	28285	4550	5375	6950	9300
	LXi Minivan	P64L	32045	4875	5700	7350	9750
	5 Passenger			(375)	(375)	(500)	(500)
	w/o Quad Seating			(150)	(150)	(200)	(200)
	w/o Rear Air Conditioning			(250)	(250)	(335)	(335)
	AWD	T		525	525	700	700

1998 CHRYSLER — 1C4-(P55R)-W-#

TOWN & COUNTRY—V6—Truck Equipment Schedule T3

Body	Type	VIN	List	Trade-In Fair	Good	Pvt-Party Good	Retail Excellent
	SX Minivan	P55R	28150	5000	5850	7400	9700
	LX Minivan	P54R	28605	5225	6125	7700	10050
	LXi Minivan	P64L	32300	5600	6500	8100	10500
	w/o Quad Seating			(150)	(150)	(200)	(200)
	w/o Rear Air Conditioning			(250)	(250)	(335)	(335)
	AWD	T		575	575	765	765

1999 CHRYSLER — 1C4-(P55R)-X-#

TOWN & COUNTRY—V6—Truck Equipment Schedule T3

Body	Type	VIN	List	Trade-In Fair	Good	Pvt-Party Good	Retail Excellent
	SX Minivan	P55R	28855	6000	6950	8625	11100
	LX Minivan	P54R	29130	6200	7175	8825	11350
	LXi Minivan	P64L	31955	6675	7725	9425	12000
	Limited Minivan	P64L	34345	7575	8700	10500	13200
	w/o Rear Air Conditioning			(300)	(300)	(400)	(400)
	AWD	T		675	675	900	900

2000 CHRYSLER — 1C4-(J253)-Y-#

VOYAGER—V6—Truck Equipment Schedule T1

Body	Type	VIN	List	Trade-In Fair	Good	Pvt-Party Good	Retail Excellent
	Minivan 4D	J253	20895	3775	4500	6000	8150
	SE Minivan 4D	J453	23840	4275	5075	6600	8825
	Grand Minivan 4D	J243	22545	4525	5350	6900	9175
	SE Grand Minivan 4D	J443	24835	4900	5750	7350	9650
	5 Passenger			(550)	(550)	(735)	(735)
	w/o 2nd Sliding Door			(600)	(600)	(800)	(800)
	4-Cyl. 2.4 Liter	B		(1025)	(1025)	(1365)	(1365)

TOWN & COUNTRY—V6—Truck Equipment Schedule T3

Body	Type	VIN	List	Trade-In Fair	Good	Pvt-Party Good	Retail Excellent
	LX Minivan	P44R	26950	7275	8350	10150	12750
	LXi Minivan	P54L	31530	7900	9075	10900	13650
	Limited Minivan	P64L	34855	8875	10175	12000	14900
	w/o Rear Air Conditioning			(350)	(350)	(465)	(465)
	AWD	T		750	750	1000	1000

TRUCKS & VANS

TRUCKS & VANS

Body	Type	VIN	List	Trade-In Fair	Good	Pvt-Party Good	Retail Excellent
2001 CHRYSLER–1C(4or8)–(J24G)–1–#							
VOYAGER—V6—Truck Equipment Schedule T1							
Minivan		J24G	20770	**5125**	**6000**	**7625**	**10050**
LX Minivan		J54G	24165	**5675**	**6600**	**8250**	**10700**
5 Passenger				**(600)**	**(600)**	**(800)**	**(800)**
4-Cyl. 2.4 Liter		B		**(1125)**	**(1125)**	**(1500)**	**(1500)**
TOWN & COUNTRY—V6—Truck Equipment Schedule T3							
LX Minivan		P44G	26155	**8800**	**10075**	**11950**	**14850**
EX Minivan		P54L	26830	**9275**	**10550**	**12450**	**15350**
LXi Minivan		P64G	30705	**9500**	**10850**	**12700**	**15650**
Limited Minivan		P64L	35490	**10650**	**12150**	**14050**	**17200**
w/o Quad Seating				**(300)**	**(300)**	**(400)**	**(400)**
w/o Rear Air Conditioning				**(400)**	**(400)**	**(535)**	**(535)**
AWD		T		**825**	**825**	**1100**	**1100**
2002 CHRYSLER–1C(4or8)–(J15B)–2–#							
VOYAGER—V6—Truck Equipment Schedule T1							
eC Minivan		J15B	16995	**5025**	**5875**	**7550**	**9975**
Minivan		J253	19995	**6350**	**7350**	**9100**	**11650**
LX Minivan		J453	24060	**6925**	**8000**	**9800**	**12450**
5 Passenger				**(650)**	**(650)**	**(865)**	**(865)**
4-Cyl. 2.4 Liter		B		**(1225)**	**(1225)**	**(1635)**	**(1635)**
TOWN & COUNTRY—V6—Truck Equipment Schedule T3							
eL Minivan		P343	24330	**9300**	**10600**	**12500**	**15400**
LX Minivan		P443	27065	**10325**	**11750**	**13700**	**16700**
EX Minivan		P74L	26830	**10900**	**12325**	**14300**	**17400**
LXi Minivan		P543	30970	**11125**	**12625**	**14600**	**17750**
Limited Minivan		P64L	35990	**12325**	**13975**	**16100**	**19400**
w/o Quad Seating				**(325)**	**(325)**	**(435)**	**(435)**
w/o Rear Air Conditioning				**(425)**	**(425)**	**(565)**	**(565)**
AWD		T		**900**	**900**	**1200**	**1200**
2003 CHRYSLER–1C(4or8)–(J453)–3–#							
VOYAGER—V6—Truck Equipment Schedule T1							
LX Minivan		J453	24025	**8525**	**9750**	**11500**	**14250**
5 Passenger				**(700)**	**(700)**	**(935)**	**(935)**
4-Cyl. 2.4 Liter		B		**(1325)**	**(1325)**	**(1765)**	**(1765)**
TOWN & COUNTRY—V6—Truck Equipment Schedule T3							
Minivan		P24R	25975	**11475**	**13050**	**15000**	**18050**
eL Minivan		P343	24830	**11100**	**12575**	**14500**	**17500**
LX Minivan		P443	27010	**12150**	**13775**	**15750**	**18900**
EX Minivan		P74L	27235	**12825**	**14500**	**16500**	**19800**
LXi Minivan		P54L	34080	**13100**	**14825**	**16850**	**20200**
Limited Minivan		P64L		**14400**	**16275**	**18350**	**21800**
w/o Quad Seating				**(350)**	**(350)**	**(465)**	**(465)**
w/o Rear Air Conditioning				**(450)**	**(450)**	**(600)**	**(600)**
AWD		T		**975**	**975**	**1300**	**1300**
2004 CHRYSLER–(1or2)C(4or8)–(P45R)–4–#							
TOWN & COUNTRY—V6—Truck Equipment Schedule T3							
Minivan		P45R	23520	**12625**	**14300**	**16350**	**19700**
LX Minivan		P44R	27490	**14400**	**16225**	**18400**	**21900**
eX Minivan		P74L	30110	**15125**	**17050**	**19200**	**22800**
Touring Minivan		P54L	33245	**15750**	**17425**	**19600**	**23200**
Limited Minivan		P64L	38380	**16850**	**18950**	**21200**	**25000**
w/o Quad Seating				**(375)**	**(375)**	**(500)**	**(500)**
w/o Rear Air Conditioning				**(475)**	**(475)**	**(635)**	**(635)**
AWD		T		**1050**	**1050**	**1400**	**1400**
PACIFICA—V6—Truck Equipment Schedule T3							
Minivan		M684	30410	**14700**	**16600**	**19200**	**23300**
AWD		F		**1050**	**1050**	**1400**	**1400**

DODGE/PLYMOUTH

1990 DODGE/PLYM — (1orJ)BorP(4or7)–(M07Y)–L

Body	Type	VIN	List	Fair	Good	Good	Excellent
RAMCHARGER 4WD—V8—Truck Equipment Schedule T1							
AW150 S Sport Utility		M07Y	18030	**900**	**1300**	**2200**	**3575**
AW150 Sport Utility		M17Y	19359	**950**	**1375**	**2375**	**3875**
2WD		E		**(350)**	**(350)**	**(465)**	**(465)**

TRUCKS & VANS

Body	Type	VIN	List	Trade-In Fair	Good	Pvt-Party Good	Retail Excellent
	V8 5.9 Liter	Z		75	75	100	100
CARAVAN C/V—4-Cyl.—Truck Equipment Schedule T2							
	Minivan	-11K	11640	250	325	675	1225
	4-Cyl. 2.5 Liter Turbo	J		0	0	0	0
	V6 3.0 Liter	3		200	200	265	265
CARAVAN C/V—V6—Truck Equipment Schedule T2							
	Extended Minivan	-14R	13965	425	625	1075	1850
CARAVAN/VOYAGER—4-Cyl.—Truck Equipment Schedule T1							
	Minivan	-25K	13957	400	575	1025	1750
	SE Minivan	-45K	14637	400	600	1050	1800
	LE Minivan	-55K	17222	450	650	1125	1925
	5 Passenger			(200)	(200)	(265)	(265)
	4-Cyl. 2.5 Liter Turbo	J		0	0	0	0
	V6 3.0 Liter	3		200	200	265	265
CARAVAN/VOYAGER—4-Cyl. Turbo—Truck Equip Sch T1							
	ES/LX Minivan	-45J	18320	450	650	1125	1925
	5 Passenger			(200)	(200)	(265)	(265)
	V6 3.0 Liter	3		100	100	135	135
GRAND CARAVAN/VOYAGER—V6—Truck Equipment Sch T1							
	SE Minivan	-44R	16775	750	1025	1675	2750
	LE Minivan	-54R	18840	825	1150	1850	2975
RAM WAGON—V8—Truck Equipment Schedule T1							
	B150 Passenger Van	B15Y	16739	825	1150	1925	3150
	B250 Passenger Van	B25Y	17339	850	1200	2025	3275
	B350 Passenger Van	B35Z	17897	950	1350	2250	3600
	5 Passenger			(200)	(200)	(265)	(265)
	110" W.B.			0	0	0	0
	Maxi-Wagon	4		50	50	65	65
	V6 3.9 Liter	X		(200)	(200)	(265)	(265)
	V8 5.9 Liter	Z,5		25	25	35	35
VAN—6-Cyl.—Truck Equipment Schedule T1							
	B150 Cargo Van	B11X	13887	775	1100	1725	2750
	B250 Cargo Van	B21X	14317	850	1175	1850	2925
	110" W.B.			0	0	0	0
	Maxi-Van	4		50	50	65	65
	V8 5.2, 5.9 Liter	Y,Z		100	100	135	135
VAN—V8—Truck Equipment Schedule T1							
	B350 Cargo Van	B31Y	15847	900	1300	2050	3200
	Maxi-Van	4		50	50	65	65
	V8 5.9 Liter	Z		25	25	35	35
RAM 50 PICKUP—4-Cyl.—Truck Equipment Schedule T2							
	Short Bed	L24W	8700	250	325	775	1400
	Long Bed	L29W	9233	275	350	775	1425
	SE Short Bed	L44S	9425	300	450	900	1575
	Sport Cab	L25W	9739	450	625	1150	2025
	LE Sport Cab	L55S	11175	525	750	1325	2250
	4WD	M		500	500	665	665
	V6 3.0 Liter	S		200	200	265	265
RAM 50 PICKUP 4WD—V6—Truck Equipment Schedule T2							
	SE Sport Cab	M45S	13673	850	1200	2025	3275
DAKOTA PICKUP—4-Cyl.—Truck Equipment Schedule T2							
	S Short Bed	L16G	8310	400	600	1075	1900
	Short Bed	L26G	10065	450	650	1175	2025
	Conv Short Bed	L29G	14340	750	1025	1750	2900
	Long Bed	L26G	10210	400	575	1050	1850
	Club Cab	L23G	11090	650	900	1550	2650
	4WD	G		500	500	665	665
	V6 3.9 Liter	X		125	125	165	165
	V8 5.2 Liter	Y		150	150	200	200
DAKOTA PICKUP—V6—Truck Equipment Schedule T2							
	Sport Short Bed	L66X	12590	550	800	1400	2350
	Sport Convertible	L69X	15865	850	1175	1950	3150
	Sport Club Cab	L63X	13665	850	1175	1950	3150
	4WD	G		500	500	665	665
	V8 5.2 Liter	Y		125	125	165	165
REGULAR CAB PICKUP—V8—Truck Equipment Schedule T1							
	D150 S Short Bed	E06Y	13102	900	1300	2075	3250
	D150 S Long Bed	E06Y	13302	900	1300	2075	3250
	D150 Short Bed	E16Y	13931	950	1350	2100	3300
	D150 Long Bed	E16Y	14131	900	1300	2075	3250
	D250 Long Bed	E26Y	15006	975	1425	2200	3425
	D350 Long Bed	E36Z	15884	975	1425	2200	3425
	4WD			500	500	665	665

TRUCKS & VANS

Body Type	VIN	List	Trade-In Fair	Trade-In Good	Pvt-Party Good	Retail Excellent
V6 3.9 Liter	X		(350)	(350)	(465)	(465)
6-Cyl. 5.9L Turbo Dsl	8		2100	2100	2800	2800
V8 5.9 Liter	Z		75	75	100	100
CLUB CAB PICKUP—V8—Truck Equipment Schedule T1						
D150 Short Bed	E13Y	15584	975	1425	2200	3425
D150 Long Bed	E13Y	15784	925	1325	2100	3275
D250 Long Bed	E23Y	17109	1175	1625	2625	4050
4WD	M		500	500	665	665
V8 5.9 Liter	Z		75	75	100	100

1991 DODGE/PLYM — (1orJ)BorP(4or7)—(M07Y)—M

Body Type	VIN	List	Trade-In Fair	Trade-In Good	Pvt-Party Good	Retail Excellent
RAMCHARGER 4WD—V8—Truck Equipment Schedule T1						
AW150 S Sport Util 2D	M07Y	19022	1025	1450	2500	4000
AW150 Sport Util 2D	M17Y	20373	1050	1500	2575	4075
2WD	E		(375)	(375)	(500)	(500)
V8 5.9 Liter	Z		100	100	135	135
CARAVAN C/V—4-Cyl.—Truck Equipment Schedule T2						
Cargo Minivan	–11K	12806	275	350	750	1350
AWD	D		275	275	365	365
V6 3.0 Liter	3		225	225	300	300
CARAVAN C/V—V6—Truck Equipment Schedule T2						
Extended Minivan	–14R	14546	500	725	1225	2100
AWD	D		275	275	365	365
CARAVAN/VOYAGER—4-Cyl.—Truck Equipment Schedule T1						
Minivan	–25K	14989	475	675	1175	2025
SE Minivan	–45K	15722	475	700	1225	2075
LE Minivan	–55K	18165	525	750	1300	2175
5 Passenger			(225)	(225)	(300)	(300)
AWD	D		275	275	365	365
V6 3.0 Liter	3		225	225	300	300
V6 3.3 Liter	R		225	225	300	300
CARAVAN/VOYAGER—V6—Truck Equipment Schedule T1						
ES/LX Minivan	–25R	19660	775	1100	1800	2925
SE Grand Minivan	–44R	17472	875	1225	2000	3200
LE Grand Minivan	–54R	19775	925	1325	2150	3400
5 Passenger			(225)	(225)	(300)	(300)
AWD	D		275	275	365	365
RAM WAGON—V8—Truck Equipment Schedule T1						
B150 Passenger Van	B15Y	17511	900	1300	2150	3475
B250 Passenger Van	B25Y	18139	950	1350	2250	3600
B350 Passenger Van	B35Y	18808	1050	1500	2575	4075
5 Passenger			(225)	(225)	(300)	(300)
110" W.B.			0	0	0	0
Maxi-Wagon	4		50	50	65	65
V6 3.9 Liter	X		(225)	(225)	(300)	(300)
V8 5.9 Liter	Z		25	25	35	35
VAN—V6—Truck Equipment Schedule T1						
B150 Cargo Van	B11X	14881	900	1275	2000	3150
B250 Cargo Van	B21X	15122	950	1350	2100	3300
110" W.B.			0	0	0	0
Maxi-Van	4		50	50	65	65
V8 5.2, 5.9 Liter	Y,Z		100	100	135	135
VAN—V8—Truck Equipment Schedule T1						
B350 Cargo Van	B31Y	16622	1050	1500	2475	3875
Maxi-Van	4		50	50	65	65
V8 5.9 Liter	Z,5		25	25	35	35
RAM 50 PICKUP—4-Cyl.—Truck Equipment Schedule T2						
Short Bed	L24W	8358	300	400	850	1500
Long Bed	L24W	8889	300	425	875	1550
Sport Cab	L25W	9395	525	750	1300	2225
SE Short Bed	L44W	9067	375	525	1000	1750
LE Sport Cab	L55W	11296	600	875	1475	2475
4WD	M		550	550	735	735
V6 3.0 Liter	S		200	200	265	265
RAM 50 PICKUP 4WD—V6—Truck Equipment Schedule T2						
SE Sport Cab	M45S	13454	975	1425	2275	3600
DAKOTA PICKUP—4-Cyl.—Truck Equipment Schedule T2						
S Short Bed	L16G	9177	500	725	1275	2175
Short Bed	L26G	10622	550	775	1350	2300
Long Bed	L26G	10773	475	675	1225	2100
Club Cab	L23G	11691	775	1100	1850	3025
4WD	G		550	550	735	735
V6 3.9 Liter	X		125	125	165	165

TRUCKS & VANS

Body	Type	VIN	List	Trade-In Fair	Trade-In Good	Pvt-Party Good	Retail Excellent
V8 5.2 Liter		Y	......	175	175	235	235
DAKOTA PICKUP—V6—Truck Equipment Schedule T2							
Sport Short Bed	L66X	13324	675	925	1600	2700
Sport Club Cab	L63X	14443	975	1425	2300	3650
4WD		G	......	550	550	735	735
V8 5.2 Liter		Y	......	125	125	165	165
REGULAR CAB PICKUP—V8—Truck Equipment Schedule T1							
D150 S Short Bed	E06Y	13317	1025	1475	2225	3425
D150 S Long Bed	E06Y	13526	1025	1475	2225	3425
D150 Short Bed	E16Y	14694	1050	1500	2300	3525
D150 Long Bed	E16Y	14978	1025	1475	2225	3425
D250 Long Bed	E26Y	15581	1125	1575	2525	3875
D350 Long Bed	E36Z	17308	1125	1575	2525	3875
4WD		M	......	550	550	735	735
6-Cyl. 3.9 Liter		X	......	(350)	(350)	(465)	(465)
6-Cyl. 5.9L Turbo Dsl		8	......	2200	2200	2935	2935
V8 5.9 Liter		Z	......	100	100	135	135
CLUB CAB PICKUP—V8—Truck Equipment Schedule T1							
D150 Short Bed	E13Y	16463	1100	1550	2400	3650
D150 Long Bed	E13Y	16672	1050	1500	2275	3475
D250 Long Bed	E23Y	18059	1375	1875	2825	4250
4WD		M	......	550	550	735	735
V8 5.9 Liter		Z	......	100	100	135	135

1992 DODGE/PLYM — (1orJ)BorP(4or7)–(M07Y)–N

Body	Type	VIN	List	Trade-In Fair	Trade-In Good	Pvt-Party Good	Retail Excellent
RAMCHARGER 4WD—V8—Truck Equipment Schedule T1							
AW150 S Sport Util 2D	M07Y	20451	975	1425	2475	3975
AW150 Sport Util 2D	M17Y	21913	1050	1500	2575	4125
2WD		E	......	(400)	(400)	(535)	(535)
V8 5.9 Liter		Z	......	150	150	200	200
CARAVAN C/V—4-Cyl.—Truck Equipment Schedule T2							
Minivan	H11G	13360	250	325	700	1300
AWD		K	......	325	325	435	435
V6 3.0 Liter		3	......	250	250	335	335
V6 3.3 Liter		R	......	275	275	365	365
CARAVAN C/V—V6—Truck Equipment Schedule T2							
Extended Minivan	H14R	15749	525	750	1300	2175
AWD		K	......	325	325	435	435
V6 3.0 Liter		3	......	(100)	(100)	(135)	(135)
CARAVAN/VOYAGER—4-Cyl.—Truck Equipment Schedule T1							
Minivan	H25C	15379	475	675	1200	2075
SE Minivan	H45G	16926	475	700	1225	2100
5 Passenger			......	(250)	(250)	(335)	(335)
AWD		K	......	325	325	435	435
V6 3.0 Liter		3	......	250	250	335	335
V6 3.3 Liter		R	......	275	275	365	365
CARAVAN/VOYAGER—V6—Truck Equipment Schedule T1							
LE Minivan	H553	20785	850	1175	1950	3150
ES/LX Minivan	H553	21328	875	1225	2025	3250
Grand Minivan	H443	18723	900	1275	2075	3300
SE Grand Minivan	H44R	18908	950	1375	2225	3525
LE Grand Minivan	H54R	21505	1025	1475	2475	3900
ES Grand Minivan	H54R	22016	1025	1450	2425	3875
5 Passenger			......	(250)	(250)	(335)	(335)
AWD		K	......	325	325	435	435
RAM WAGON—V8—Truck Equipment Schedule T1							
B150 Passenger Van	B15Y	18152	950	1375	2400	3900
B250 Passenger Van	B25Y	18796	1025	1450	2525	4025
B350 Passenger Van	B35Z	19497	1175	1625	2750	4350
5 Passenger			......	(250)	(250)	(335)	(335)
110" W.B.			......	0	0	0	0
Maxi-Wagon		4	......	75	75	100	100
V6 3.9 Liter		X	......	(250)	(250)	(335)	(335)
V8 5.9 Liter		Z	......	50	50	65	65
VAN—V6—Truck Equipment Schedule T1							
B150 Cargo Van	B11X	16148	925	1325	2125	3350
B250 Cargo Van	B21X	16561	1000	1450	2275	3575
110" W.B.			......	0	0	0	0
Maxi-Van		4	......	75	75	100	100
V8 5.2, 5.9 Liter		Y,Z	......	125	125	165	165
VAN—V8—Truck Equipment Schedule T1							
B350 Cargo Van	B31Y	18428	1150	1600	2625	4075
Maxi-Van		4	......	75	75	100	100

TRUCKS & VANS

Body	Type	VIN	List	Trade-In Fair	Trade-In Good	Pvt-Party Good	Retail Excellent
V6 3.9 Liter		X		(250)	(250)	(335)	(335)
V8 5.9 Liter		Z		50	50	65	65
RAM 50 PICKUP—4-Cyl.—Truck Equipment Schedule T2							
Short Bed		L24W	8787	300	450	900	1575
Long Bed		L29W	9332	325	475	950	1675
SE Short Bed		L44W	9907	400	600	1075	1900
4WD		M		675	675	900	900
DAKOTA PICKUP—4-Cyl.—Truck Equipment Schedule T2							
S Short Bed		L16G	9659	475	700	1250	2125
Sport Short Bed		L66G	9934	525	750	1325	2250
Short Bed		L26G	11175	600	850	1450	2425
Long Bed		L26G	11458	500	725	1275	2175
Club Cab		L23G	12342	850	1200	2000	3250
4WD		G		675	675	900	900
V6 3.9 Liter		X		150	150	200	200
V8 5.2 Liter		Y		225	225	300	300
REGULAR CAB PICKUP—V8—Truck Equipment Schedule T1							
D150 Short Bed		E16Y	15949	1050	1500	2275	3475
D150 Long Bed		E16Y	16166	1025	1475	2225	3400
D250 Long Bed		E26Y	17107	1175	1625	2575	3900
D350 Long Bed		E36Z	17386	1175	1625	2575	3900
4WD		M		650	650	865	865
V6 3.9 Liter		X		(375)	(375)	(500)	(500)
6-Cyl. 5.9L Turbo Dsl		C		2500	2500	3335	3335
V8 5.9 Liter		Z		150	150	200	200
CLUB CAB PICKUP—V8—Truck Equipment Schedule T1							
D150 Short Bed		E13Y	17444	1150	1600	2525	3875
D150 Long Bed		E13Y	17663	1075	1525	2325	3525
D250 Long Bed		E23Y	18404	1450	1925	2875	4300
D350 Long Bed		E33C	23289	1500	2000	2975	4425
4WD		M		650	650	865	865
6-Cyl. 5.9L Turbo Dsl		C		2500	2500	3335	3335
V8 5.9 Liter		Z		150	150	200	200

1993 DODGE/PLYM — (1orJ)BorP(4or7)–(M07Y)–P

Body	Type	VIN	List	Trade-In Fair	Trade-In Good	Pvt-Party Good	Retail Excellent
RAMCHARGER 4WD—V8—Truck Equipment Schedule T1							
AW150 S Sport Util 2D		M07Y	21610	975	1425	2525	4100
AW150 Sport Util 2D		M17Y	23127	1050	1500	2675	4275
2WD		E		(425)	(425)	(565)	(565)
V8 5.9 Liter		Z		175	175	235	235
CARAVAN C/V—4-Cyl.—Truck Equipment Schedule T2							
Minivan		H11K	14106	250	325	750	1400
V6 3.0 Liter		3		275	275	365	365
CARAVAN C/V—V6—Truck Equipment Schedule T2							
Extended Minivan		H14R	18560	550	800	1425	2400
CARAVAN/VOYAGER—4-Cyl.—Truck Equipment Schedule T1							
Minivan		H25K	16071	500	725	1300	2225
SE Minivan		H45K	17498	525	750	1350	2300
5 Passenger				(275)	(275)	(365)	(365)
AWD		K		375	375	500	500
V6 3.0 Liter		3		275	275	365	365
V6 3.3 Liter		R		325	325	435	435
CARAVAN/VOYAGER—V6—Truck Equipment Schedule T1							
LE Minivan		H553	21381	950	1350	2225	3575
ES/LX Minivan		H553	21863	975	1400	2300	3650
Grand Minivan		H443	18140	1000	1450	2450	3900
SE Grand Minivan		H44R	18688	1075	1525	2575	4050
LE Grand Minivan		H54R	22324	1200	1650	2700	4225
ES Grand Minivan		H54R	22785	1175	1625	2700	4200
5 Passenger				(275)	(275)	(365)	(365)
AWD		K		375	375	500	500
RAM WAGON—V8—Truck Equipment Schedule T1							
B150 Passenger Van		B15Y	19145	1050	1500	2600	4150
B250 Passenger Van		B25Y	19789	1125	1575	2700	4300
B350 Passenger Van		B35Y	20490	1350	1825	2975	4625
5 Passenger				(275)	(275)	(365)	(365)
110" Minivan				0	0	0	0
Maxi-Wagon		4		100	100	135	135
V6 3.9 Liter		X		(275)	(275)	(365)	(365)
V8 5.9 Liter		Z		50	50	65	65
VAN—V6—Truck Equipment Schedule T1							
B150 Cargo Van		B11X	16933	1025	1450	2325	3650
B250 Cargo Van		B21X	17346	1100	1550	2600	4025

Body Type	VIN	List	Trade-In Fair	Trade-In Good	Pvt-Party Good	Retail Excellent
110" W.B.			**0**	**0**	**0**	**0**
Maxi-Van	4		100	100	135	135
V8 5.2, 5.9 Liter	Y,Z		150	150	200	200
VAN—V8—Truck Equipment Schedule T1						
B350 Cargo Van	B31Y	18626	1325	1800	2850	4375
Maxi-Van	4		100	100	135	135
V6 3.9 Liter	X		(275)	(275)	(365)	(365)
V8 5.9 Liter	Z		50	50	65	65
RAM 50 PICKUP—4-Cyl.—Truck Equipment Schedule T2						
Short Bed	S21G	9506	350	500	975	1750
Long Bed	S22G	10073	375	550	1050	1850
SE Short Bed	S41G	10676	475	675	1225	2100
4WD	T		800	800	1065	1065
DAKOTA PICKUP—4-Cyl.—Truck Equipment Schedule T2						
S Short Bed	L16G	9818	525	750	1350	2300
Sport Short Bed	L16G	10413	575	825	1425	2425
Short Bed	L26G	11844	650	900	1550	2650
Long Bed	L26G	12027	550	800	1425	2400
Club Cab	L23G	13096	925	1325	2200	3525
4WD	G		800	800	1065	1065
V6 3.9 Liter	X		175	175	235	235
V8 5.2 Liter	Y		275	275	365	365
REGULAR CAB PICKUP—V8—Truck Equipment Schedule T1						
D150 Short Bed	E16Y	16360	1100	1550	2325	3525
D150 Long Bed	E16Y	16577	1050	1500	2250	3425
D250 Long Bed	E26Y	17637	1250	1725	2650	3975
D350 Long Bed	E36Z	18155	1250	1725	2650	3975
4WD	M		750	750	1000	1000
V6 3.9 Liter	X		(400)	(400)	(535)	(535)
6-Cyl. 5.9L Turbo Dsl	C		2800	2800	3730	3730
V8 5.9 Liter	Z		175	175	235	235
CLUB CAB PICKUP—V8—Truck Equipment Schedule T1						
D150 Short Bed	E13Y	18294	1225	1700	2625	3950
D150 Long Bed	E13Y	18513	1175	1625	2550	3875
D250 Long Bed	E23Y	19454	1525	2050	3000	4425
D350 Long Bed	E33C	24339	1675	2200	3200	4650
4WD	M		750	750	1000	1000
6-Cyl. 5.9L Turbo Dsl	C		2800	2800	3730	3730
V8 5.9 Liter	Z		175	175	235	235

1994 DODGE/PLYM — (1orJ)BorP(4or7)–(H11K)–R

Body Type	VIN	List	Trade-In Fair	Trade-In Good	Pvt-Party Good	Retail Excellent
CARAVAN C/V—4-Cyl.—Truck Equipment Schedule T2						
Cargo Minivan	H11K	14972	275	350	850	1550
V6 3.0 Liter	3		300	300	400	400
CARAVAN C/V—V6—Truck Equipment Schedule T2						
Extended Minivan	H14R	17426	625	900	1575	2700
CARAVAN/VOYAGER—4-Cyl.—Truck Equipment Schedule T1						
Minivan	H25K	17135	575	825	1475	2525
5 Passenger			(300)	(300)	(400)	(400)
V6 3.0 Liter	3		300	300	400	400
CARAVAN/VOYAGER—V6—Truck Equipment Schedule T1						
SE Minivan	H453	19113	775	1100	1900	3150
LE Minivan	H553	22523	1075	1525	2600	4100
ES/LX Minivan	H553	23230	1125	1575	2675	4200
Grand Minivan	H243	19595	1175	1625	2700	4250
SE Grand Minivan	H44R	20278	1275	1750	2850	4425
LE Grand Minivan	H54R	23443	1400	1875	3000	4575
LS Grand Minivan	H54R	23952	1400	1875	3000	4575
5 Passenger			(300)	(300)	(400)	(400)
AWD	K		425	425	565	565
V6 3.8 Liter	L		100	100	135	135
RAM WAGON—V8—Truck Equipment Schedule T1						
B150 Passenger Van	B15Y	16643	1125	1575	2800	4500
B250 Passenger Van	B25Y	20412	1250	1725	2950	4675
B350 Passenger Van	B35Y	21113	1500	1975	3275	5050
5 Passenger			(300)	(300)	(400)	(400)
Maxi-Wagon	4		100	100	135	135
V6 3.9 Liter	X		(300)	(300)	(400)	(400)
V8 5.9 Liter	Z		50	50	65	65
VAN—V6—Truck Equipment Schedule T1						
B150 Cargo Van	B11X	17431	975	1425	2300	3650
B250 Cargo Van	B21X	17844	1075	1525	2550	4000
110" W.B.			0	0	0	0

TRUCKS & VANS

Body	Type	VIN	List	Trade-In Fair	Good	Pvt-Party Good	Retail Excellent
	Maxi-Van	4		100	100	135	135
	V8 5.2 Liter	Y		175	175	235	235
	V8 5.9 Liter	Z		300	300	400	400
VAN—V8—Truck Equipment Schedule T1							
	B350 Cargo Van	B31Y	19124	1325	1800	2875	4425
	Maxi-Van	4		100	100	135	135
	V8 5.9 Liter			50	50	65	65
DAKOTA PICKUP—4-Cyl.—Truck Equipment Schedule T2							
	WS Short Bed	L26G	10249	575	825	1475	2525
	WS Long Bed	L26G	11774	625	900	1525	2650
	Sport Short Bed	L26G	11237	625	900	1525	2650
	Short Bed	L26G	11927	700	1000	1725	2900
	Long Bed	L26G	12777	625	900	1525	2650
	4WD	G		900	900	1200	1200
	V6 3.9 Liter	X		200	200	265	265
	V8 5.2 Liter	Y		300	300	400	400
DAKOTA PICKUP—V6—Truck Equipment Schedule T2							
	Sport Club Cab	L23X	14537	1375	1875	2975	4550
	Club Cab	L23X	14794	1500	2000	3125	4725
	4WD	G		900	900	1200	1200
	V8 5.2 Liter	Y		175	175	235	235
REGULAR CAB PICKUP—V8—Truck Equipment Schedule T1							
	1500 Short Bed	C16Y	17265	2100	2675	3725	5250
	1500 Long Bed	C16Y	17537	1900	2425	3450	4950
	2500 Long Bed	C26Y	18205	2375	2950	4025	5650
	3500 Long Bed	C36Z	20706	2575	3200	4300	5925
	Work Special			(400)	(400)	(535)	(535)
	4WD	FM		850	850	1135	1135
	V6 3.9 Liter	X		(425)	(425)	(565)	(565)
	6-Cyl. 5.9L Turbo Dsl.	C		3100	3100	4130	4130
	V8 5.9 Liter	Z		200	200	265	265
	V10 8.0 Liter	W		175	175	235	235

1995 DODGE/PLYM — (1orJ)BorP(4or7)–(H11K)–S

Body	Type	VIN	List	Trade-In Fair	Good	Pvt-Party Good	Retail Excellent
CARAVAN C/V—4-Cyl.—Truck Equipment Schedule T2							
	Cargo Minivan	H11K	16705	300	450	1000	1850
	V6 3.0 Liter	3		325	325	435	435
CARAVAN C/V—V6—Truck Equipment Schedule T2							
	Extended Minivan	H14R	18245	750	1025	1850	3100
CARAVAN/VOYAGER—4-Cyl.—Truck Equipment Schedule T1							
	Minivan	H25K	17930	675	950	1725	2925
	5 Passenger			(325)	(325)	(435)	(435)
	V6 3.0 Liter	3		325	325	435	435
CARAVAN/VOYAGER—V6—Truck Equipment Schedule T1							
	SE Minivan	H453	20275	900	1300	2225	3650
	LE Minivan	H553	23940	1300	1775	2900	4500
	ES Minivan	H553	24895	1375	1875	3000	4625
	Grand Minivan	H243	20025	1425	1900	3075	4700
	SE Grand Minivan	H44R	20375	1500	2025	3200	4850
	LE Grand Minivan	H54R	24240	1650	2150	3325	5025
	ES Grand Minivan	H54R	25095	1650	2175	3350	5050
	5 Passenger			(325)	(325)	(435)	(435)
	AWD	K		475	475	635	635
	V6 3.8 Liter	L		100	100	135	135
RAM WAGON—V8—Truck Equipment Schedule T1							
	1500 Passenger Van	B15Y	17951	1375	1850	3150	4975
	2500 Passenger Van	B25Y	21627	1500	2000	3325	5150
	3500 Passenger Van	B35Y	22627	1750	2275	3650	5550
	5 Passenger			(325)	(325)	(435)	(435)
	Maxi-Wagon	4		100	100	135	135
	V6 3.9 Liter	X		(325)	(325)	(435)	(435)
	V8 5.9 Liter	Z		50	50	65	65
VAN—V6—Truck Equipment Schedule T1							
	1500 Cargo Van	B11X	18605	1225	1700	2775	4325
	2500 Cargo Van	B21X	18743	1375	1850	2925	4500
	110" W.B.			0	0	0	0
	Maxi-Van	4		100	100	135	135
	V8 5.2 Liter	Y		200	200	265	265
	V8 5.9 Liter	Z		325	325	435	435
VAN—V8—Truck Equipment Schedule T1							
	3500 Cargo Van	B31Y	20673	1650	2150	3300	4925
	Maxi-Van	4		100	100	135	135
	V8 5.9 Liter	Z		50	50	65	65

1995 DODGE/PLYMOUTH

Body	Type	VIN	List	Trade-In Fair	Good	Pvt-Party Good	Retail Excellent
DAKOTA PICKUP—4-Cyl.—Truck Equipment Schedule T2							
WS Short Bed	L26G	10975	675	950	1675	2850
WS Long Bed	L26G	12291	750	1025	1800	3025
Sport Short Bed	L26G	11489	750	1025	1800	3025
Short Bed	L26G	12710	825	1150	2000	3275
Long Bed	L26G	13921	750	1025	1800	3025
4WD	G		1000	1000	1335	1335
V6 3.9 Liter	X		225	225	300	300
V8 5.2 Liter	Y		325	325	435	435
DAKOTA PICKUP—V6—Truck Equipment Schedule T2							
Sport Club Cab	L23X	14722	1625	2125	3300	4925
Club Cab	L23X	16006	1775	2300	3450	5125
4WD	G		1000	1000	1335	1335
V8 5.2 Liter	Y		200	200	265	265
REGULAR CAB PICKUP—V8—Truck Equipment Schedule T1							
1500 Short Bed	C16Y	17594	2425	3025	4100	5700
1500 Long Bed	C16Y	17878	2200	2775	3825	5375
2500 Long Bed	C26Y	18851	2700	3325	4475	6125
3500 Long Bed	C36Z	21468	2950	3600	4725	6425
Work Special			(425)	(425)	(565)	(565)
4WD	F		950	950	1265	1265
V6 3.9 Liter	X		(450)	(450)	(600)	(600)
6-Cyl. 5.9L Turbo Dsl	C		3400	3400	4530	4530
V8 5.9 Liter	Z		225	225	300	300
V10 8.0 Liter	W		200	200	265	265
CLUB CAB PICKUP—V8—Truck Equipment Schedule T1							
1500 Short Bed	C13Y	20040	3400	4100	5300	7100
1500 Long Bed	C13Y	20321	3150	3825	5025	6775
2500 Short Bed	C23Z	21840	3900	4625	5925	7850
2500 Long Bed	C23Z	22046	3750	4500	5725	7600
3500 Long Bed	C33Z	23667	3900	4625	5925	7850
4WD	F		950	950	1265	1265
6-Cyl. 5.9L Turbo Dsl	C		3400	3400	4530	4530
V8 5.9 Liter	Z		225	225	300	300
V10 8.0 Liter	W		200	200	265	265

1996 DODGE/PLYM—(1,2or3)BorP(4or7)—(P253)—T

Body	Type	VIN	List	Trade-In Fair	Good	Pvt-Party Good	Retail Excellent
CARAVAN/VOYAGER—V6—Truck Equipment Schedule T1							
Minivan	P253	18510	1650	2150	3375	5100
SE Minivan	P453	21070	1975	2525	3825	5625
LE Minivan	P55R	24180	2550	3150	4500	6375
ES Minivan	P55R	25605	2625	3250	4575	6500
Grand Minivan	P243	19410	2125	2700	4000	5825
SE Grand Minivan	P443	21810	2400	3000	4325	6225
LE Grand Minivan	P54R	24670	2850	3500	4900	6875
ES Grand Minivan	P54R	26595	3150	3825	5225	7275
5 Passenger			(350)	(350)	(465)	(465)
w/o 2nd Sliding Door			(450)	(450)	(600)	(600)
4-Cyl. 2.4 Liter	B		(675)	(675)	(900)	(900)
V6 3.8 Liter	L		100	100	135	135
RAM WAGON—V8—Truck Equipment Schedule T1							
1500 Passenger Van	B15Y	19965	1650	2175	3575	5525
2500 Passenger Van	B24Y	21374	1825	2350	3800	5750
3500 Passenger Van	B34Y	22575	2100	2675	4125	6150
Maxi-Wagon			100	100	135	135
V6 3.9 Liter	X		(350)	(350)	(465)	(465)
V8 5.9 Liter	Z		50	50	65	65
RAM VAN—V6—Truck Equipment Schedule T1							
1500 Cargo Van	B11X	18460	1550	2075	3250	4900
2500 Cargo Van	B21X	18563	1675	2200	3375	5075
110" W.B.			0	0	0	0
Maxi-Van			100	100	135	135
V8 5.2 Liter	Y		200	200	265	265
V8 5.9 Liter	Z		350	350	465	465
RAM VAN—V8—Truck Equipment Schedule T1							
3500 Cargo Van	B31Y	21075	2025	2575	3800	5550
Maxi-Van			100	100	135	135
V8 5.9 Liter	Z		50	50	65	65
DAKOTA PICKUP—4-Cyl.—Truck Equipment Schedule T2							
WS Short Bed	L26G	11764	800	1125	1975	3275
WS Long Bed	L26G	12380	875	1225	2125	3475
Sport Short Bed	L26G	12440	875	1225	2125	3475
Short Bed	L26G	13665	950	1350	2375	3900

TRUCKS & VANS

Body Type	VIN	List	Trade-In Fair	Trade-In Good	Pvt-Party Good	Retail Excellent
Long Bed	L26X	14176	875	1225	2125	3475
4WD	G		1100	1100	1465	1465
V6 3.9 Liter	X		250	250	335	335
V8 5.2 Liter	Y		350	350	465	465
DAKOTA PICKUP—V6—Truck Equipment Schedule T2						
Sport Club Cab	L23X	15616	1900	2425	3650	5350
Club Cab	L23X	16746	2075	2625	3850	5600
4WD	G		1100	1100	1465	1465
V8 5.2 Liter	Y		200	200	265	265
REGULAR CAB PICKUP—V8—Truck Equipment Schedule T1						
1500 Short Bed	C16Y	18032	2825	3450	4575	6300
1500 Long Bed	C16Y	18316	2575	3200	4300	5925
2500 Long Bed	C26Y	19569	3150	3800	4975	6725
3500 Long Bed	C365	22286	3375	4075	5250	7050
Work Special			(450)	(450)	(600)	(600)
4WD	F		1050	1050	1400	1400
V6 3.9 Liter	X		(450)	(450)	(600)	(600)
6-Cyl. 5.9L Turbo Diesel	C		3700	3700	4930	4930
V8 5.9 Liter	Z		250	250	335	335
V10 8.0 Liter	W		225	225	300	300
CLUB CAB PICKUP—V8—Truck Equipment Schedule T1						
1500 Short Bed	C13Y	20190	3875	4600	5875	7775
1500 Long Bed	C13Y	20471	3625	4350	5600	7450
2500 Short Bed	C23Z	22958	4425	5200	6550	8575
2500 Long Bed	C23Z	23164	4250	5050	6325	8300
3500 Long Bed	C33Z	24685	4425	5200	6550	8575
4WD	F		1050	1050	1400	1400
6-Cyl. 5.9L Turbo Diesel	C		3700	3700	4930	4930
V8 5.9 Liter	Z,5		250	250	335	335
V10 8.0 Liter	W		225	225	300	300

Body Type	VIN	List	Trade-In Fair	Trade-In Good	Pvt-Party Good	Retail Excellent
CARAVAN/VOYAGER—V6—Truck Equipment Schedule T1						
Minivan	P253	19570	2000	2550	3850	5700
SE Minivan	P453	22495	2375	2950	4325	6250
LE Minivan	P55R	25715	2975	3625	5050	7050
ES Minivan	P55R	27055	3050	3700	5125	7175
Grand Minivan	P243	20565	2550	3150	4500	6450
SE Grand Minivan	P443	23325	2825	3450	4875	6875
LE Grand Minivan	P54R	26405	3300	4000	5475	7550
ES Grand Minivan	P54R	26995	3625	4350	5825	7975
5 Passenger			(375)	(375)	(500)	(500)
w/o 2nd Sliding Door			(475)	(475)	(635)	(635)
AWD	T		525	525	700	700
4-Cyl. 2.4 Liter	B		(725)	(725)	(965)	(965)
V6 3.8 Liter	L		100	100	135	135
RAM WAGON—V8—Truck Equipment Schedule T1						
1500 Passenger Van	B15Y	21192	2100	2650	4150	6250
2500 Passenger Van	B25Y	22555	2250	2800	4350	6450
3500 Passenger Van	B35Y	23755	2550	3150	4700	6875
Maxi-Wagon			100	100	135	135
V6 3.9 Liter	X		(375)	(375)	(500)	(500)
V8 5.9 Liter	Z		50	50	65	65
RAM VAN—V6—Truck Equipment Schedule T1						
1500 Cargo Van	B11X	19090	2000	2550	3800	5550
2500 Cargo Van	B21X	19295	2100	2700	3925	5725
110" W.B.			0	0	0	0
Maxi-Van			100	100	135	135
V8 5.2 Liter	Y		200	200	265	265
V8 5.9 Liter	Z		375	375	500	500
RAM VAN—V8—Truck Equipment Schedule T1						
3500 Cargo Van	B31Y	21885	2500	3100	4400	6275
Maxi-Van			100	100	135	135
V8 5.9 Liter	Z		50	50	65	65
DAKOTA PICKUP—4-Cyl.—Truck Equipment Schedule T1						
Short Bed	L26P	14959	2700	3325	4500	6250
Long Bed	L26P	15419	2600	3225	4375	6075
4WD	G		1200	1200	1600	1600
V6 3.9 Liter	X		250	250	335	335
V8 5.2 Liter	Y		375	375	500	500
DAKOTA PICKUP—V6—Truck Equipment Schedule T1						
Club Cab	L23X	18654	4000	4750	6075	8050
4WD	G		1200	1200	1600	1600

Body	Type	VIN	List	Trade-In Fair	Good	Pvt-Party Good	Retail Excellent
	V8 5.2 Liter	Y		200	200	265	265
REGULAR CAB PICKUP—V8—Truck Equipment Schedule T1							
1500 Short Bed		C16Y	18831	3300	4000	5200	6975
1500 Long Bed		C16Y	19116	3050	3700	4875	6600
2500 Long Bed		C26Z	21134	3650	4375	5600	7450
3500 Long Bed		C36Z	22619	3900	4625	5900	7775
Work Special				(475)	(475)	(635)	(635)
4WD		F		1150	1150	1535	1535
V6 3.9 Liter		X		(450)	(450)	(600)	(600)
6-Cyl. 5.9L Turbo Diesel		D		4000	4000	5330	5330
V8 5.9 Liter		5,Z		275	275	365	365
V10 8.0 Liter		W		225	225	300	300
CLUB CAB PICKUP—V8—Truck Equipment Schedule T1							
1500 Short Bed		C13Y	20914	4450	5225	6550	8550
1500 Long Bed		C13Y	21194	4175	4975	6275	8200
2500 Short Bed		C23Z	23139	5025	5875	7275	9375
2500 Long Bed		C23Z	23344	4825	5675	7025	9100
3500 Long Bed		C33Z	24964	5025	5875	7275	9375
4WD		F		1150	1150	1535	1535
6-Cyl. 5.9L Turbo Diesel		D		4000	4000	5330	5330
V8 5.9 Liter		5,Z		275	275	365	365
V10 8.0 Liter		W		225	225	300	300

1998 DODGE/PLYM—1(BorP)4—(S28Y)—W—#

Body	Type	VIN	List	Trade-In Fair	Good	Pvt-Party Good	Retail Excellent
DURANGO 4WD—V8—Truck Equipment Schedule T1							
SLT Sport Utility 4D		S28Y	28575	4250	5050	7225	10200
w/o Third Seat				(525)	(525)	(700)	(700)
V8 3.9 Liter		X		(575)	(575)	(765)	(765)
V8 5.9 Liter		Z		250	250	335	335
CARAVAN/VOYAGER—V6—Truck Equipment Schedule T1							
Minivan		P253	20535	2450	3050	4375	6250
SE Minivan		P453	22065	2850	3500	4850	6800
LE Minivan		P55R	25610	3500	4200	5625	7675
Grand Minivan		P243	20730	3050	3700	5100	7050
SE Grand Minivan		P443	23600	3325	4025	5425	7450
LE Grand Minivan		P54R	26605	3900	4625	6100	8200
ES Grand Minivan		P54R	27760	4225	5025	6500	8675
5 Passenger				(425)	(425)	(565)	(565)
w/o 2nd Sliding Door				(500)	(500)	(665)	(665)
AWD		T		575	575	765	765
4-Cyl. 2.4 Liter		B		(775)	(775)	(1035)	(1035)
V6 3.8 Liter		L		100	100	135	135
RAM WAGON—V8—Truck Equipment Schedule T1							
1500 Passenger Van		B15Y	21655	2600	3225	4850	7075
2500 Passenger Van		B25Y	23480	2750	3375	5050	7300
3500 Maxi Passenger		B35Y	26185	3075	3725	5400	7725
V6 3.9 Liter		X		(425)	(425)	(565)	(565)
V8 5.9 Liter		Z		50	50	65	65
RAM VAN—V6—Truck Equipment Schedule T1							
1500 Cargo Van		B11X	19440	2575	3200	4450	6275
110" W.B.				0	0	0	0
Maxi-Van				100	100	135	135
V8 5.2 Liter		Y		200	200	265	265
V8 5.9 Liter		Z		425	425	565	565
RAM VAN—V8—Truck Equipment Schedule T1							
2500 Cargo Van		B21Y	21375	3050	3700	5025	6900
3500 Cargo Van		B31Y	22545	3150	3800	5100	7025
Maxi-Van				100	100	135	135
V8 5.9 Liter		Z		50	50	65	65
DAKOTA PICKUP—4-Cyl.—Truck Equipment Schedule T1							
Short Bed		L26P	15235	3150	3800	4950	6650
R/T Short Bed		L26Z	19205	3775	4500	5700	7525
Long Bed		L26P	15695	3000	3675	4800	6475
4WD		G		1275	1275	1700	1700
V6 3.9 Liter		X		250	250	335	335
V8 5.2 Liter		Y		425	425	565	565
V8 5.9 Liter (ex. R/T)		Z		625	625	835	835
DAKOTA PICKUP—V6—Truck Equipment Schedule T1							
Club Cab		L22X	18430	4500	5325	6600	8550
R/T Club Cab		L22Z	21360	5050	5900	7225	9250
4WD		G		1275	1275	1700	1700
4-Cyl. 2.5 Liter		P		(300)	(300)	(400)	(400)
V8 5.2 Liter		Y		200	200	265	265

TRUCKS & VANS

1998 DODGE/PLYMOUTH

Body Type	VIN	List	Trade-In Fair	Good	Pvt-Party Good	Retail Excellent
V8 5.9 Liter (ex. R/T)	Z		**425**	**425**	**565**	**565**
REGULAR CAB PICKUP—V8—Truck Equipment Schedule T1						
1500 Short Bed	C16Y	19240	**3850**	**4575**	**5850**	**7750**
1500 Long Bed	C16Y	19525	**3550**	**4250**	**5500**	**7375**
2500 Long Bed	C26Z	21900	**4175**	**4975**	**6275**	**8225**
3500 Long Bed	C36Z	23190	**4450**	**5225**	**6550**	**8575**
Work Special			**(525)**	**(525)**	**(700)**	**(700)**
4WD	F		**1225**	**1225**	**1635**	**1635**
V6 3.9 Liter	X		**(475)**	**(475)**	**(635)**	**(635)**
6-Cyl. 5.9L Turbo Dsl	6,D		**4225**	**4225**	**5630**	**5630**
V8 5.9 Liter	5,Z		**300**	**300**	**400**	**400**
V10 8.0 Liter	W		**225**	**225**	**300**	**300**
CLUB CAB PICKUP—V8—Truck Equipment Schedule T1						
1500 Short Bed	C12Y	21365	**5050**	**5900**	**7275**	**9375**
1500 Long Bed	C12Y	21645	**4775**	**5625**	**6975**	**9050**
2500 Short Bed	C22Z	23680	**5675**	**6600**	**8075**	**10250**
2500 Long Bed	C22Z	23870	**5450**	**6350**	**7775**	**9925**
4WD	F		**1225**	**1225**	**1635**	**1635**
6-Cyl. 5.9L Turbo Dsl	6,D		**4225**	**4225**	**5630**	**5630**
V8 5.9 Liter	5,Z		**300**	**300**	**400**	**400**
V10 8.0 Liter	W		**225**	**225**	**300**	**300**
QUAD CAB PICKUP—V8—Truck Equipment Schedule T1						
1500 Short Bed	C13Y	22115	**5375**	**6300**	**7700**	**9900**
1500 Long Bed	C13Y	22395	**5100**	**5975**	**7400**	**9500**
2500 Short Bed	C23Z	24430	**6000**	**6950**	**8450**	**10700**
2500 Long Bed	C23Z	24620	**5775**	**6750**	**8175**	**10400**
3500 Long Bed	C33Z	26325	**6000**	**6950**	**8450**	**10700**
4WD	F		**1225**	**1225**	**1635**	**1635**
6-Cyl. 5.9L Turbo Dsl	6,D		**4225**	**4225**	**5630**	**5630**
V8 5.9 Liter	5,Z		**300**	**300**	**400**	**400**
V10 8.0 Liter	W		**225**	**225**	**300**	**300**

1999 DODGE/PLYM—(1,2,3or4)B4—(S28Y)—X—#

Body Type	VIN	List	Trade-In Fair	Good	Pvt-Party Good	Retail Excellent
DURANGO 4WD—V8—Truck Equipment Schedule T1						
SLT Sport Utility 4D	S28Y	29030	**5100**	**5975**	**8325**	**11550**
w/o Third Seat			**(600)**	**(600)**	**(800)**	**(800)**
2WD	R		**(650)**	**(650)**	**(865)**	**(865)**
V6 3.9 Liter	X		**(700)**	**(700)**	**(935)**	**(935)**
V8 5.9 Liter	Z		**300**	**300**	**400**	**400**
CARAVAN/VOYAGER—V6—Truck Equipment Schedule T1						
Minivan 4D	P253	21185	**3050**	**3700**	**5100**	**7100**
SE Minivan 4D	P453	22460	**3500**	**4200**	**5650**	**7725**
LE Minivan 4D	P55R	26280	**4275**	**5075**	**6550**	**8725**
Grand Minivan 4D	P243	22580	**3725**	**4475**	**5900**	**8025**
SE Grand Minivan 4D	P443	23455	**4050**	**4825**	**6300**	**8475**
LE Grand Minivan 4D	P54R	27275	**4700**	**5525**	**7050**	**9300**
ES Grand Minivan 4D	P54L	29485	**5075**	**5950**	**7500**	**9850**
5 Passenger			**(500)**	**(500)**	**(665)**	**(665)**
w/o 2nd Sliding Door			**(550)**	**(550)**	**(735)**	**(735)**
AWD	T		**675**	**675**	**900**	**900**
4-Cyl. 2.4 Liter	B		**(900)**	**(900)**	**(1200)**	**(1200)**
V6 3.8 Liter			**150**	**150**	**200**	**200**
RAM WAGON—V8—Truck Equipment Schedule T1						
1500 Passenger Van	B15Y	22000	**3225**	**3900**	**5675**	**8100**
2500 Passenger Van	B25Y	23725	**3425**	**4125**	**5900**	**8375**
3500 Maxi Passenger	B35Y	26430	**3725**	**4475**	**6300**	**8800**
V6 3.9 Liter	X		**(500)**	**(500)**	**(665)**	**(665)**
V8 5.9 Liter	Z		**100**	**100**	**135**	**135**
RAM VAN—V6—Truck Equipment Schedule T1						
1500 Cargo Van	B11X	19685	**3225**	**3900**	**5225**	**7200**
110" W.B.			**0**	**0**	**0**	**0**
Maxi-Van			**150**	**150**	**200**	**200**
V8 5.2 Liter	Y		**250**	**250**	**335**	**335**
V8 5.9 Liter	Z		**500**	**500**	**665**	**665**
RAM VAN—V8—Truck Equipment Schedule T1						
2500 Cargo Van	B21Y	21620	**3750**	**4500**	**5875**	**7925**
3500 Cargo Van	B31Y	22790	**3875**	**4600**	**6000**	**8050**
Maxi-Van			**150**	**150**	**200**	**200**
V8 5.9 Liter	Z		**100**	**100**	**135**	**135**
DAKOTA PICKUP—4-Cyl.—Truck Equipment Schedule T1						
Short Bed	L26P	15545	**3775**	**4500**	**5700**	**7500**
Long Bed	L26P	16005	**3600**	**4325**	**5500**	**7275**
R/T Short Bed	L26Z	19745	**4500**	**5325**	**6575**	**8500**

Body	Type	VIN	List	Trade-In Fair	Good	Pvt-Party Good	Retail Excellent
4WD		G		1450	1450	1935	1935
V6 3.9 Liter		X		300	300	400	400
V8 5.2 Liter		Y		500	500	665	665
V8 5.9 Liter (ex. R/T)		Z		725	725	965	965
DAKOTA PICKUP—V6—Truck Equipment Schedule T1							
Club Cab		L22X	18740	5300	6200	7500	9550
R/T Club Cab		L22Z	20215	5925	6900	8275	10400
4WD		G		1450	1450	1935	1935
4-Cyl. 2.5 Liter		P		(350)	(350)	(465)	(465)
V8 5.2 Liter		Y		250	250	335	335
V8 5.9 Liter (ex. R/T)		Z		500	500	665	665
REGULAR CAB PICKUP—V8—Truck Equipment Schedule T1							
1500 Short Bed		C16Y	19485	4275	5075	6350	8325
1500 Long Bed		C16Y	19770	3950	4700	6000	7925
2500 Long Bed		C26Z	22145	4700	5525	6875	8900
3500 Long Bed		C36Z	23935	4975	5825	7200	9275
Work Special				(675)	(675)	(900)	(900)
4WD		F		1400	1400	1865	1865
V6 3.9 Liter		X		(550)	(550)	(735)	(735)
6-Cyl. 5.9L Turbo Diesel		6		4425	4425	5900	5900
V8 5.9 Liter		5,Z		325	325	435	435
V10 8.0 Liter		W		250	250	335	335
CLUB CAB PICKUP—V8—Truck Equipment Schedule T1							
1500 Short Bed		C12Y	21515	5700	6650	8100	10250
1500 Long Bed		C12Y	21795	5425	6325	7725	9900
2500 Short Bed		C22Z	23330	6450	7450	8925	11250
2500 Long Bed		C22Z	23520	6175	7150	8625	10900
4WD		F		1400	1400	1865	1865
6-Cyl. 5.9L Turbo Diesel		6		4425	4425	5900	5900
V8 5.9 Liter		5,Z		325	325	435	435
V10 8.0 Liter		W		250	250	335	335
QUAD CAB PICKUP—V8—Truck Equipment Schedule T1							
1500 Short Bed		C13Y	22310	6125	7100	8575	10800
1500 Long Bed		C13Y	22590	5800	6775	8200	10400
2500 Short Bed		C23Z	24125	6825	7875	9400	11750
2500 Long Bed		C23Z	24315	6600	7625	9150	11450
3500 Long Bed		C33Z	26915	6825	7875	9400	11750
4WD		F		1400	1400	1865	1865
6-Cyl. 5.9L Turbo Dsl		6		4425	4425	5900	5900
V8 5.9 Liter		5,Z		325	325	435	435
V10 8.0 Liter		W		250	250	335	335

2000 DODGE/PLYM—(1,2,3or4)B4—(S28N)—Y—#

Body	Type	VIN	List	Trade-In Fair	Good	Pvt-Party Good	Retail Excellent
DURANGO 4WD—V8—Truck Equipment Schedule T1							
SLT Sport Utility 4D		S28N	29060	6075	7050	9650	13150
R/T Sport Utility 4D		S28Z	33810	6650	7675	10300	13900
w/o Third Seat				(675)	(675)	(900)	(900)
2WD		R		(725)	(725)	(965)	(965)
V8 5.2 Liter		R		0	0	0	0
V8 5.9 Liter (ex. R/T)		Z		350	350	465	465
CARAVAN/VOYAGER—V6—Truck Equipment Schedule T1							
Minivan 4D		P243	21905	3775	4500	6000	8150
SE Minivan 4D		P443	23675	4275	5075	6600	8825
Grand Minivan 4D		P243	22380	4525	5350	6900	9175
SE Grand Minivan 4D		P443	24670	4900	5750	7350	9650
LE Grand Minivan 4D		P54R	27785	5650	6550	8175	10600
ES Grand Minivan 4D		P54L	29995	6050	7000	8700	11200
5 Passenger				(550)	(550)	(735)	(735)
w/o 2nd Sliding Door				(600)	(600)	(800)	(800)
AWD		T		750	750	1000	1000
4-Cyl. 2.4 Liter		B		(1025)	(1025)	(1365)	(1365)
V6 3.8 Liter		L		175	175	235	235
GRAND CARAVAN AWD—V6—Truck Equipment Schedule T1							
Sport Minivan 4D		T44L	28670	6775	7800	9525	12100
5 Passenger				(550)	(550)	(735)	(735)
RAM WAGON—V8—Truck Equipment Schedule T1							
1500 Passenger Van		B15Y	22245	4050	4825	6775	9450
2500 Passenger Van		B25Y	23670	4300	5075	7025	9750
3500 Maxi Passenger		B35Y	26675	4600	5450	7425	10200
V6 3.9 Liter		X		(550)	(550)	(735)	(735)
V8 5.9 Liter		Z		150	150	200	200
RAM VAN—V6—Truck Equipment Schedule T1							
1500 Cargo Van		B11X	19575	4025	4800	6250	8350

2000 DODGE/PLYMOUTH

TRUCKS & VANS

Body Type	VIN	List	Trade-In Fair	Good	Pvt-Party Good	Retail Excellent
110" W.B.			0	0	0	0
Maxi-Van			175	175	235	235
V8 5.2 Liter	T,Y		275	275	365	365
V8 5.9 Liter	Z		550	550	735	735
RAM VAN—V8—Truck Equipment Schedule T1						
2500 Cargo Van	B21Y	21075	4600	5450	6925	9125
3500 Cargo Van	B31Y	23260	4750	5600	7100	9300
Maxi-Van			175	175	235	235
V8 5.9 Liter	Z		150	150	200	200
DAKOTA PICKUP—4-Cyl.—Truck Equipment Schedule T1						
Short Bed	L26P	15850	4500	5300	6550	8450
R/T Short Bed	L26Z	20090	5350	6250	7525	9550
4WD	G		1625	1625	2165	2165
V6 3.9 Liter	X		350	350	465	465
V8 4.7 Liter	N		575	575	765	765
V8 5.9 Liter (ex. R/T)	Z		825	825	1100	1100
DAKOTA PICKUP—V6—Truck Equipment Schedule T1						
Club Cab	L22X	19045	6175	7150	8525	10650
R/T Club Cab	L22Z	22340	6925	8000	9400	11650
Quad Cab	L2AX	20290	6675	7725	9125	11350
4WD	G		1625	1625	2165	2165
4-Cyl. 2.5 Liter	P		(400)	(400)	(535)	(535)
V8 4.7 Liter	N		300	300	400	400
V8 5.9 Liter (ex. R/T)	Z		550	550	735	735
REGULAR CAB PICKUP—V8—Truck Equipment Schedule T1						
1500 Short Bed	C16Y	19695	4900	5725	7050	9100
1500 Long Bed	C16Y	19980	4550	5375	6675	8675
2500 Long Bed	C26Z	22570	5400	6300	7675	9800
3500 Long Bed	C36Z	24330	5700	6625	8025	10200
Work Special			(825)	(825)	(1100)	(1100)
4WD	F		1575	1575	2100	2100
V6 3.9 Liter	X		(625)	(625)	(835)	(835)
6-Cyl. 5.9L Turbo Diesel	6		4625	4625	6165	6165
V8 5.9 Liter	Z,5		350	350	465	465
V10 8.0 Liter	W		275	275	365	365
CLUB CAB PICKUP—V8—Truck Equipment Schedule T1						
1500 Short Bed	C12Y	21890	6575	7600	9050	11350
4WD	F		1575	1575	2100	2100
V8 5.9 Liter	Z		350	350	465	465
QUAD CAB PICKUP—V8—Truck Equipment Schedule T1						
1500 Short Bed	C13Y	22750	7025	8100	9575	11900
1500 Long Bed	C13Y	23030	6700	7750	9200	11450
2500 Short Bed	C23Z	24335	7850	9025	10550	13000
2500 Long Bed	C23Z	24525	7550	8700	10200	12650
3500 Long Bed	C33Z	27125	7850	9025	10550	13000
4WD	F		1575	1575	2100	2100
6-Cyl. 5.9L Turbo Dsl	6		4625	4625	6165	6165
V8 5.9 Liter	Z,5		350	350	465	465
V10 8.0 Liter	W		275	275	365	365

2001 DODGE—(1or2)B(4,7or8)—(S28N)-1

Body Type	VIN	List	Trade-In Fair	Good	Pvt-Party Good	Retail Excellent
DURANGO 4WD—V8—Truck Equipment Schedule T1						
SLT Sport Utility 4D	S28N	30740	7275	8375	11150	14950
R/T Sport Utility 4D	S28Z	30990	7900	9075	11850	15700
w/o Third Seat			(750)	(750)	(1000)	(1000)
2WD	R		(800)	(800)	(1065)	(1065)
V8 5.9 Liter	Z		400	400	535	535
CARAVAN—V6—Truck Equipment Schedule T1						
SE Minivan 4D	P44B	19800	5125	6000	7625	10050
Sport Minivan 4D	P64G	24165	5675	6600	8250	10700
SE Grand Minivan 4D	P44G	22440	6125	7100	8800	11350
Sport Grand 4D	P64G	24915	6375	7400	9125	11650
EX Grand Minivan 4D	P44L	26725	7500	8650	10400	13100
ES Grand Minivan 4D	P54L	29750	7650	8775	10550	13300
5 Passenger			(600)	(600)	(800)	(800)
AWD	T		825	825	1100	1100
4-Cyl. 2.4 Liter			(1125)	(1125)	(1500)	(1500)
V6 3.8 Liter	L		750	750	1000	1000
RAM WAGON—V8—Truck Equipment Schedule T1						
1500 Passenger Van	B15Y	22615	5200	6075	8175	11150
2500 Passenger Van	B25Y	24040	5450	6350	8500	11450
3500 Maxi Passenger	B35Y	27055	5775	6750	8875	11900
V6 3.9 Liter	X		(600)	(600)	(800)	(800)

Body	Type	VIN	List	Trade-In Fair	Trade-In Good	Pvt-Party Good	Retail Excellent
	V8 5.9 Liter	Z		200	200	265	265
RAM VAN—V6—Truck Equipment Schedule T1							
1500 Cargo Van		B11X	19890	5125	6000	7550	9850
2500 Cargo Van		B21X	21390	5325	6225	7775	10100
110" W.B.				0	0	0	0
Maxi-Van				200	200	265	265
V8 5.2 Liter		Y		300	300	400	400
V8 5.9 Liter		Z		600	600	800	800
RAM VAN—V8—Truck Equipment Schedule T1							
3500 Cargo Van		B31Y	23575	5925	6900	8500	10900
Maxi-Van				200	200	265	265
V8 5.9 Liter		Z		200	200	265	265
DAKOTA PICKUP—4-Cyl.—Truck Equipment Schedule T1							
Short Bed		L26P	16255	5350	6250	7500	9525
R/T Short Bed		L26Z	20505	6275	7275	8625	10750
4WD		G		1800	1800	2400	2400
V6 3.9 Liter		X		400	400	535	535
V8 4.7 Liter		N		650	650	865	865
V8 5.9 Liter (ex. R/T)		Z		925	925	1235	1235
DAKOTA PICKUP—V6—Truck Equipment Schedule T1							
Club Cab		L22X	19580	7150	8250	9650	11900
R/T Club Cab		L22Z	22885	8075	9250	10700	13050
Quad Cab		L23X	21950	7775	8925	10350	12700
4WD		G		1800	1800	2400	2400
4-Cyl. 2.5 Liter		P		(450)	(450)	(600)	(600)
V8 4.7 Liter		N		350	350	465	465
V8 5.9 Liter (ex. R/T)		Z		600	600	800	800
REGULAR CAB PICKUP—V8—Truck Equipment Schedule T1							
1500 Short Bed		C16Y	20145	5700	6625	7975	10100
1500 Long Bed		C16Y	20430	5350	6250	7575	9650
2500 Long Bed		C26Z	23475	6300	7300	8700	10900
3500 Long Bed		C36Z	25360	6600	7625	9050	11300
Work Special		F		(975)	(975)	(1300)	(1300)
4WD		F		1750	1750	2335	2335
V6 3.9 Liter		X		(700)	(700)	(935)	(935)
6-Cyl. 5.9L Turbo Diesel		6		4825	4825	6430	6430
6-Cyl. 5.9L HO Turbo Dsl		7		5850	5850	7800	7800
V8 5.9 Liter		Z		375	375	500	500
V10 8.0 Liter		W		300	300	400	400
CLUB CAB PICKUP—V8—Truck Equipment Schedule T1							
1500 Short Bed		C12Y	21465	7625	8750	10250	12600
4WD		F		1750	1750	2335	2335
V8 5.9 Liter		Z		375	375	500	500
QUAD CAB PICKUP—V8—Truck Equipment Schedule T1							
1500 Short Bed		C13Y	23375	8125	9325	10850	13250
1500 Long Bed		C13Y	23655	7775	8925	10400	12800
2500 Short Bed		C23Z	25440	9050	10325	11900	14450
2500 Long Bed		C23Z	25630	8725	9975	11500	14050
3500 Long Bed		C33Z	28155	9050	10325	11900	14450
4WD		F		1750	1750	2335	2335
6-Cyl. 5.9L Turbo Dsl		6		4825	4825	6430	6430
6-Cyl. 5.9L HO Turbo Dsl		7		5850	5850	7800	7800
V8 5.9 Liter		Z		375	375	500	500
V10 8.0 Liter		W		300	300	400	400

2002 DODGE — 1B(4,7or8)–(S38N)–2–#

Body	Type	VIN	List	Trade-In Fair	Trade-In Good	Pvt-Party Good	Retail Excellent
DURANGO 4WD—V8—Truck Equipment Schedule T1							
Sport Utility 4D		S38N	27595	8700	9925	12850	16950
R/T Sport Utility 4D		S78Z	37070	9475	10800	13800	17950
w/o Third Seat				(825)	(825)	(1100)	(1100)
2WD		R		(875)	(875)	(1165)	(1165)
V8 5.9 Liter (ex. R/T)		Z		425	425	565	565
CARAVAN—Truck Equipment Schedule T1							
eC Minivan 4D		P15B	16995	5025	5875	7550	9975
SE Minivan 4D		P44B	19795	6350	7350	9100	11650
Sport Minivan 4D		P64G	24060	6925	8000	9800	12450
SE Grand Minivan 4D		P44G	22440	7450	8575	10350	13100
eL Grand Minivan 4D		P343	24175	7700	8825	10650	13400
Sport Grand 4D		P64G	24930	7725	8875	10700	13450
EX Grand Minivan 4D		P44L	26725	8975	10275	12100	15000
ES Grand Minivan 4D		P54L	30135	9150	10425	12300	15200
5 Passenger				(650)	(650)	(865)	(865)
AWD				900	900	1200	1200

TRUCKS & VANS

Body	Type	VIN	List	Trade-In Fair	Trade-In Good	Pvt-Party Good	Retail Excellent
4-Cyl. 2.4 Liter		B		(1225)	(1225)	(1635)	(1635)
V6 3.8 Liter		L		825	825	1100	1100
RAM WAGON—V8—Truck Equipment Schedule T1							
1500 Passenger Van		B15Y	22035	6675	7725	10050	13350
2500 Passenger Van		B25Y	24050	6950	8025	10350	13750
3500 Maxi Passenger		B35Y	27055	7325	8425	10800	14200
V6 3.9 Liter		X		(650)	(650)	(865)	(865)
V8 5.9 Liter		Z		250	250	335	335
RAM VAN—V6—Truck Equipment Schedule T1							
1500 Cargo Van		B11X	20050	6550	7575	9225	11700
2500 Cargo Van		B21X	21595	6775	7800	9475	12000
110" W.B.				0	0	0	0
Maxi-Van				225	225	300	300
V8 5.2 Liter		Y		325	325	435	435
V8 5.9 Liter		Z		650	650	865	865
RAM VAN—V8—Truck Equipment Schedule T1							
3500 Cargo Van		B31Y	23780	7450	8575	10250	12850
Maxi-Van				225	225	300	300
V8 5.9 Liter		Z		250	250	335	335
DAKOTA PICKUP—4-Cyl.—Truck Equipment Schedule T1							
Short Bed		L26P	16370	6300	7325	8700	10850
R/T Short Bed		L26Z	21290	7325	8425	9850	12100
4WD		G		1975	1975	2635	2635
V6 3.9 Liter		X		450	450	600	600
V8 4.7 Liter		N		700	700	935	935
V8 5.9 Liter (ex. R/T)		Z		1000	1000	1335	1335
DAKOTA PICKUP—V6—Truck Equipment Schedule T1							
Club Cab		L22X	19695	8275	9475	10950	13350
R/T Club Cab		L22Z	23585	9300	10600	12150	14650
Quad Cab		L23X	21985	8975	10275	11750	14250
4WD		G		1975	1975	2635	2635
4-Cyl. 2.5 Liter		P		(500)	(500)	(665)	(665)
V8 4.7 Liter		N		375	375	500	500
V8 5.9 Liter (ex. R/T)		Z		650	650	865	865
REGULAR CAB PICKUP—V8—Truck Equipment Schedule T1							
1500 Short Bed		C16Y	19620	8175	9375	10850	13250
1500 Long Bed		C16Y	19905	7750	8900	10350	12700
2500 HD Long Bed		C26Z	23490	7425	8550	9975	12300
3500 Long Bed		C36Z	25375	7750	8900	10350	12700
4WD		F		1925	1925	2565	2565
V6 3.7 Liter		K		(750)	(750)	(1000)	(1000)
6-Cyl. 5.9L Turbo Diesel		6		5025	5025	6700	6700
6-Cyl. 5.9L HO Turbo Dsl		7		6075	6075	8100	8100
V8 5.9 Liter		Z		400	400	535	535
V10 8.0 Liter		W		300	300	400	400
QUAD CAB PICKUP—V8—Truck Equipment Schedule T1							
1500 Short Bed		C13Y	23840	10750	12200	13800	16500
1500 Long Bed		C13Y	24120	10375	11800	13400	16050
2500 Short Bed		C23Z	25455	10500	11950	13550	16200
2500 Long Bed		C23Z	25645	10125	11525	13100	15750
3500 Long Bed		C33Z	28170	10500	11950	13550	16200
4WD		F		1925	1925	2565	2565
6-Cyl. 5.9L Turbo Dsl		6		5025	5025	6700	6700
6-Cyl. 5.9L HO Turbo Dsl		7		6075	6075	8100	8100
V8 5.9 Liter		Z		400	400	535	535
V10 8.0 Liter		W		300	300	400	400

2003 DODGE — (1,2or3)D(3,4,7or8)-(S38N)-3

Body	Type	VIN	List	Trade-In Fair	Trade-In Good	Pvt-Party Good	Retail Excellent
DURANGO 4WD—V8—Truck Equipment Schedule T1							
Sport Utility 4D		S38N	28875	10275	11700	14800	19100
R/T Sport Utility 4D		S78Z	38670	11175	12675	15800	20300
w/o Third Seat				(700)	(700)	(935)	(935)
2WD		R		(950)	(950)	(1265)	(1265)
V8 5.9 Liter (ex. R/T)		Z		450	450	600	600
CARAVAN—V6—Truck Equipment Schedule T2							
Cargo Minivan		P253	21965	6925	8000	9700	12300
Grand Cargo Minivan		P253	23565	7325	8425	10150	12700
CARAVAN—V6—Truck Equipment Schedule T1							
SE Minivan 4D		P25B	21440	8525	9750	11500	14250
Sport Minivan 4D		P453	25110	9700	11100	12900	15800
SE Grand Minivan 4D		P24R	22890	9100	10375	12200	15000
eL Grand Minivan 4D		P343	24425	9375	10700	12550	15350
Sport Grand 4D		P44R	28040	9425	10750	12600	15400

TRUCKS & VANS

Body	Type	VIN	List	Trade-In Fair	Trade-In Good	Pvt-Party Good	Retail Excellent
EX Grand Minivan 4D	P74L	26400	10750	12200	14100	17150
ES Grand Minivan 4D	P54L	33335	10900	12375	14300	17350
5 Passenger			(700)	(700)	(935)	(935)
AWD	T		975	975	1300	1300
4-Cyl. 2.4 Liter	B		(1325)	(1325)	(1765)	(1765)
V6 3.8 Liter	L		900	900	1200	1200
RAM VAN—V6—Truck Equipment Schedule T1						
1500 Cargo Van	B11X	20685	9025	10325	12000	14700
2500 Cargo Van	B21X	21640	9225	10500	12250	15000
110" W.B.			0	0	0	0
Maxi-Van			250	250	335	335
V8 5.2 Liter	Y		350	350	465	465
V8 5.9 Liter	Z		700	700	935	935
RAM VAN—V8—Truck Equipment Schedule T1						
3500 Cargo Van	B31Y	24415	9975	11375	13150	15950
Maxi-Van			250	250	335	335
V8 5.9 Liter	Z		300	300	400	400
SPRINTER WAGON—5-Cyl. Turbo Diesel—Truck Equip Sch T1						
2500 High Ceiling	D143	28985				
2500 Super High	D143-	30696				
2500 Super High	D243	31230				
2500 Super High	D243	32940				
2500 Super High	D343	34777				
SPRINTER CARGO VAN—5-Cyl. Turbo Diesel—Truck Sch T1						
2500 High Ceiling Van	D143	27490				
2500 Super High Van	D143-	29210				
2500 High Ceiling Van	D243	29206				
2500 Super High Van	D243-	29206				
2500 Super High Van	D343	32753				
3500 High Ceiling Van	D443	30375				
3500 Super High Van	D443	32085				
3500 Super High Van	D343	33917				
DAKOTA PICKUP—V6—Truck Equipment Schedule T1						
Short Bed	L16X	17680	7500	8650	9975	12150
R/T Short Bed	L76Z	22800	8600	9850	11250	13600
Club Cab	L22X	19375	9600	10950	12450	14900
R/T Club Cab	L22Z	25100	10750	12200	13800	16350
Quad Cab	L23X	22550	10425	11850	13350	15900
4WD	G		2150	2150	2865	2865
V8 4.7 Liter	N		400	400	535	535
V8 5.9 Liter (ex. R/T)	Z		700	700	935	935
REGULAR CAB PICKUP—V8—Truck Equipment Schedule T1						
1500 Short Bed	A16N	20225	9700	11100	12450	14800
1500 Long Bed	A16N	20510	9300	10600	11950	14250
4WD	U		2100	2100	2800	2800
V6 3.7 Liter	K		(800)	(800)	(1065)	(1065)
V8 5.7 Liter HEMI	D		1200	1200	1600	1600
V8 5.9 Liter	Z,5		350	350	465	465
REGULAR CAB PICKUP—V8 HEMI—Truck Equipment Schedule T1						
2500 Long Bed	A26D	24255	10475	11900	13300	15750
3500 Long Bed	A36D	26140	10800	12250	13700	16200
4WD	U		2100	2100	2800	2800
6-Cyl. 5.9L Turbo Diesel	6		5225	5225	6965	6965
6-Cyl. 5.9L HO Turbo Dsl	C		6300	6300	8400	8400
V10 8.0 Liter	W		300	300	400	400
QUAD CAB PICKUP—V8—Truck Equipment Schedule T1						
1500 Short Bed	A18N	24960	12100	13725	15200	17850
1500 Long Bed	A18N	25240	11675	13200	14700	17300
4WD	U		2100	2100	2800	2800
V6 3.7 Liter	K		(800)	(800)	(1065)	(1065)
V8 5.7 Liter HEMI	D		1200	1200	1600	1600
V8 5.9 Liter	Z,5		350	350	465	465
QUAD CAB PICKUP—V8 HEMI—Truck Equipment Schedule T1						
2500 Short Bed	A28D	26600	13250	14925	16500	19300
2500 Long Bed	A28D	26790	12875	14550	16100	18750
3500 Short Bed	A386	32455	13250	14925	16500	19800
3500 Long Bed	A38D	29315	13250	14925	16500	19300
4WD	U		2100	2100	2800	2800
6-Cyl. 5.9L Turbo Dsl	6		5225	5225	6965	6965
6-Cyl. 5.9L HO Turbo Dsl	C		6300	6300	8400	8400
V10 8.0 Liter	W		300	300	400	400

Body	Type	VIN	List	Trade-In Fair	Trade-In Good	Pvt-Party Good	Retail Excellent

2004 DODGE–(1,3orW)D(2,3,4,5,7or8)–(S38N)–4

DURANGO 4WD—V8—Truck Equipment Schedule T1
Sport Utility 4D		S38N	29350	14350	16175	18800	22900
w/o Third Seat				(750)	(750)	(1000)	(1000)
2WD		R		(1000)	(1000)	(1335)	(1335)
V6 3.7 Liter		K		(1225)	(1225)	(1635)	(1635)
V8 5.7 Liter		D		1150	1150	1535	1535

CARAVAN—V6 Flex Fuel—Truck Equipment Schedule T2
Cargo Minivan		P21R	22585	8800	10075	11850	14700
Grand Cargo Minivan		P23R	23455	9225	10500	12400	15250

CARAVAN—V6—Truck Equipment Schedule T1
SE Minivan 4D		P25B	21795	10500	11950	13850	16900
SXT Minivan 4D		P45R	24850	11750	13350	15350	18600
SE Grand Minivan 4D		P24R	24975	11125	12625	14600	17700
EX Grand Minivan 4D		P74L	27225	12900	14600	16700	20100
SXT Grand Minivan		P44L	30335	13875	15700	17800	21300
5 Passenger				(750)	(750)	(1000)	(1000)
AWD		T		1050	1050	1400	1400
4-Cyl. 2.4 Liter		B		(1425)	(1425)	(1900)	(1900)
V6 3.8 Liter		L		950	950	1265	1265

SPRINTER WAGON—5-Cyl. Turbo Diesel—Truck Equip Sch T1
2500 High Ceiling		D143	29481				
2500 Super High		D243	31171				
2500 Super Ceiling		D143	31737				
2500 Super High		D343	33428				
2500 Super High		D343-	35302				

SPRINTER CARGO VAN—5-Cyl. Turbo Diesel—Truck Sch T1
2500 High Ceiling		D143	27978				
2500 Super High		D143	29668				
2500 High Ceiling		D243	29703				
2500 Super High		PD143	31393				
2500 Super High		D343	33268				
3500 High Ceiling		D443-	30628				
3500 Super High		D643	32318				
3500 Super High		D543-	34187				

DAKOTA PICKUP—V6—Truck Equipment Schedule T1
Short Bed		L16X	18725	9175	10475	11900	14300
Club Cab		L22X	21395	11425	12950	14550	17300
Quad Cab		L23X	23595	12325	13975	15550	18400
4WD		G		2325	2325	3100	3100
V8 4.7 Liter		N		800	800	1065	1065

REGULAR CAB PICKUP—V8—Truck Equipment Schedule T1
1500 Short Bed		A16N	21900	11675	13200	14550	17000
1500 Long Bed		A16N	22185	11175	12675	13950	16350
4WD		U		2275	2275	3035	3035
V6 3.7 Liter		K		(850)	(850)	(1135)	(1135)
V8 5.7 Liter HEMI		D		1250	1250	1665	1665

REGULAR CAB PICKUP—V8 HEMI—Truck Equipment Schedule T1
2500 Long Bed		A26D	25695	12425	14075	15450	18000
3500 Long Bed		A36D	27715	12825	14500	15900	18500
4WD		U		2275	2275	3035	3035
6-Cyl. 5.9L Turbo Diesel		6		6525	6525	8700	8700
6-Cyl. 5.9L HO Turbo Dsl		C		6525	6525	8700	8700

REGULAR CAB PICKUP—V10—Truck Equipment Schedule T1
SRT/10 1500 Short		A16H	45795				
6-Spd Manual Trans							

QUAD CAB PICKUP—V8—Truck Equipment Schedule T1
1500 Short Bed		A18N	26060	14250	16075	17550	20400
1500 Long Bed		A18N	26415	13825	15600	17050	19800
4WD		U		2275	2275	3035	3035
V6 3.7 Liter		K		(850)	(850)	(1135)	(1135)
V8 5.7 Liter HEMI		D		1250	1250	1665	1665

QUAD CAB PICKUP—V8 HEMI—Truck Equipment Schedule T1
2500 Short Bed		A28D	28150	15450	17425	18950	21900
2500 Long Bed		A28D	28340	15025	16950	18550	21400
3500 Short Bed		A386	34530	15850	17800	19500	22500
3500 Long Bed		A38D	30790	15450	17425	18950	21900
4WD		U		2275	2275	3035	3035
6-Cyl. 5.9L Turbo Dsl		6		5425	5425	7230	7230
6-Cyl. 5.9L HO Turbo Dsl		C		6525	6525	8700	8700

Body	Type	VIN	List	Trade-In Fair	Good	Pvt-Party Good	Retail Excellent

TRUCKS & VANS

FORD

1990 FORD — 1F(MorT)–(U14T)–L–#

BRONCO II 4WD—V6—Truck Equipment Schedule T1
Sport Utility 2D	U14T	16859	525	750	1375	2400
2WD	2		(350)	(350)	(465)	(465)

BRONCO 4WD—V8—Truck Equipment Schedule T1
Sport Utility 2D	U15N	19064	1375	1875	3000	4625
6-Cyl. 4.9 Liter	Y		(350)	(350)	(465)	(465)
V8 5.8 Liter	H		75	75	100	100

AEROSTAR—V6—Truck Equipment Schedule T2
Cargo Minivan	A14U	12542	550	775	1300	2125
Extended Cargo	A34U	13289	550	775	1300	2175
Window Minivan	A15U	12926	550	775	1300	2175
Extended Window	A35U	13673	550	775	1300	2175
4WD	2,4		250	250	335	335
V6 4.0 Liter	X		50	50	65	65

AEROSTAR—V6—Truck Equipment Schedule T1
Minivan	A11U	14487	600	875	1425	2350
Extended Minivan	A31U	15385	675	950	1550	2575
5 Passenger			(200)	(200)	(265)	(265)
4WD	2,4		250	250	335	335
V6 4.0 Liter	X		50	50	65	65

CLUB WAGON—V8—Truck Equipment Schedule T1
E150 Passenger Van	E11N,H	18883	825	1150	1925	3150
E250 Passenger Van	E21H	20104	850	1175	2000	3250
E350 Passenger Van	S31H	21082	900	1250	2100	3350
5 Passenger			(200)	(200)	(265)	(265)
6-Cyl. 4.9 Liter	Y		(200)	(200)	(265)	(265)
V8 460/7.5 Liter	G		100	100	135	135
V8 7.3 Liter Diesel	M		200	200	265	265

ECONOLINE—6-Cyl.—Truck Equipment Schedule T1
E150 Cargo Van	E14V	14589	775	1100	1725	2750
E250 Cargo Van	E24V	14878	825	1150	1825	2900
E350 Cargo Van	E34V	15690	900	1275	1975	3100
Super Van	S		50	50	65	65
V8 5.0, 5.8 Liter	N		100	100	135	135
V8 460/7.5 Liter	G		200	200	265	265
V8 7.3 Liter Diesel	M		200	200	265	265

RANGER PICKUP—4-Cyl.—Truck Equipment Schedule T1
S Short Bed	R10A	8354	250	325	725	1350
S Long Bed	R10A	8510	175	225	575	1125
Short Bed	R10A	9722	275	350	775	1425
Long Bed	R10A	9885	200	300	650	1225
Super Cab	R14A	11269	450	650	1200	2075
4WD	1,5		500	500	665	665
V6 2.9 Liter	T		125	125	165	165
V6 4.0 Liter	X		150	150	200	200

REGULAR CAB PICKUP—V8—Truck Equipment Schedule T1
F150 Short Bed	F15N	14163	1200	1650	2650	4050
F150 Long Bed	F15N	14387	1150	1600	2600	4000
F250 Long Bed	F25H	15550	1225	1700	2700	4125
F350 Long Bed	F35H	16754	1250	1725	2700	4150
Special			(250)	(250)	(335)	(335)
4WD	4,6		500	500	665	665
6-Cyl. 4.9 Liter	Y		(350)	(350)	(465)	(465)
V8 5.8 Liter	H		75	75	100	100
V8 460/7.5 Liter	G		150	150	200	200
V8 7.3 Liter Diesel	M		200	200	265	265

SUPER CAB PICKUP—V8—Truck Equipment Schedule T1
F150 Short Bed	X15N	15513	1500	2025	3050	4550
F150 Long Bed	X15N	15737	1500	1975	3025	4500
F250 Long Bed	X25H	17066	1775	2300	3375	4975
F350 Long Bed	X35G	18577	1650	2150	3250	4775
4WD	4,6		500	500	665	665
6-Cyl. 4.9 Liter	Y		(350)	(350)	(465)	(465)
V8 5.8 Liter	H		75	75	100	100
V8 460/7.5 Liter	G		150	150	200	200
V8 7.3 Liter Diesel	M		200	200	265	265

CREW CAB PICKUP—V8—Truck Equipment Schedule T1
F350 Long Bed	W35H	18571	1875	2400	3525	5125

TRUCKS & VANS

Body Type	VIN	List	Trade-In Fair	Trade-In Good	Pvt-Party Good	Retail Excellent
4WD	6	......	500	500	665	665
V8 460/7.5 Liter	G	......	150	150	200	200
V8 7.3 Liter Diesel	M	......	200	200	265	265

1991 FORD — 1F(MorT)–(U24X)–M–#

Body Type	VIN	List	Trade-In Fair	Trade-In Good	Pvt-Party Good	Retail Excellent
EXPLORER 4WD—V6—Truck Equipment Schedule T1						
Sport Utility 2D	U24X	18340	975	1425	2450	3925
Sport Utility 4D	U34X	19319	1475	1950	3125	4750
2WD	2	......	(375)	(375)	(500)	(500)
BRONCO 4WD—V8—Truck Equipment Schedule T1						
Sport Utility 2D	U15N	20599	1575	2100	3275	4950
6-Cyl. 4.9 Liter		......	(350)	(350)	(465)	(465)
V8 5.8 Liter	H	......	100	100	135	135
AEROSTAR—V6—Truck Equipment Schedule T2						
Cargo Minivan	A14U	13310	600	875	1425	2350
Extended Cargo	A34U	14057	625	900	1450	2400
Window Minivan	A15U	13693	625	900	1450	2400
Extended Window	A35U	14440	625	900	1475	2425
4WD	2,4	......	275	275	365	365
V6 4.0 Liter	X	......	50	50	65	65
AEROSTAR—V6—Truck Equipment Schedule T1						
Minivan	A11U	15466	675	950	1550	2600
Extended Minivan	A31U	16363	775	1075	1750	2850
5 Passenger		......	(225)	(225)	(300)	(300)
4WD	2,4	......	275	275	365	365
V6 4.0 Liter	X	......	50	50	65	65
CLUB WAGON—V8—Truck Equipment Schedule T1						
E150 Passenger Van	E11N,H	19461	900	1300	2150	3475
E250 Passenger Van	E21H	20408	925	1325	2225	3575
E350 Passenger Van	E31H	22390	975	1425	2425	3900
5 Passenger		......	(225)	(225)	(300)	(300)
6-Cyl. 4.9 Liter	Y	......	(225)	(225)	(300)	(300)
V8 460/7.5 Liter	G	......	100	100	135	135
V8 7.3 Liter Diesel	M	......	200	200	265	265
ECONOLINE—6-Cyl.—Truck Equipment Schedule T1						
E150 Cargo Van	E14Y	15366	900	1275	2000	3150
E250 Cargo Van	E24Y	15716	925	1325	2100	3275
E350 Cargo Van	E34Y	16767	1000	1450	2250	3525
Super Van	S	......	50	50	65	65
V8 5.0, 5.8 Liter	N,H	......	100	100	135	135
V8 460/7.5 Liter	G	......	225	225	300	300
V8 7.3 Liter Diesel	M	......	200	200	265	265
RANGER PICKUP—4-Cyl.—Truck Equipment Schedule T2						
S Short Bed	R10A	8729	275	375	825	1475
Sport Short Bed	R10A	8834	300	425	875	1550
Sport Long Bed	R10A	8990	250	425	725	1350
Custom Short Bed	R10A	10213	300	425	875	1550
Custom Long Bed	R10A	10376	250	425	725	1350
Custom Super Cab	R14A	11741	525	750	1325	2250
4WD	1,5	......	550	550	735	735
V6 2.9, 3.0 Liter	T,U	......	125	125	165	165
V6 4.0 Liter	X	......	175	175	235	235
REGULAR CAB PICKUP—V8—Truck Equipment Schedule T1						
F150 Short Bed	F15N	14977	1425	1900	2900	4375
F150 Long Bed	F15N	15221	1375	1875	2850	4325
F250 Long Bed	F25H	16650	1500	1975	3000	4475
F350 Long Bed	F35H	17636	1500	2000	3025	4500
Special		......	(275)	(275)	(365)	(365)
4WD	4,6	......	550	550	735	735
6-Cyl. 4.9 Liter	Y	......	(350)	(350)	(465)	(465)
V8 5.8 Liter	H	......	100	100	135	135
V8 460/7.5 Liter	G	......	150	150	200	200
V8 7.3 Liter Diesel	M	......	200	200	265	265
SUPER CAB PICKUP—V8—Truck Equipment Schedule T1						
F150 Short Bed	X15N	16361	1775	2300	3350	4900
F150 Long Bed	X15N	16595	1725	2250	3300	4850
F250 Long Bed	X25H	19059	2100	2650	3775	5400
F350 Long Bed	X35G	19756	1950	2500	3600	5175
Special		......	(275)	(275)	(365)	(365)
4WD	4,6	......	550	550	735	735
6-Cyl. 4.9 Liter	Y	......	(350)	(350)	(465)	(465)
V8 5.8 Liter	H	......	100	100	135	135
V8 460/7.5 Liter	G	......	150	150	200	200

Body Type	VIN	List	Trade-In Fair	Good	Pvt-Party Good	Retail Excellent
V8 7.3 Liter Diesel	M		200	200	265	265
CREW CAB PICKUP—V8—Truck Equipment Schedule T1						
F350 Long Bed	W35H	19588	2225	2775	3950	5675
4WD	6		550	550	735	735
V8 460/7.5 Liter	G		150	150	200	200
V8 7.3 Liter Diesel	M		200	200	265	265

1992 FORD — 1F(MorT)—(U24X)—N—#

Body Type	VIN	List	Trade-In Fair	Good	Pvt-Party Good	Retail Excellent
EXPLORER 4WD—V6—Truck Equipment Schedule T1						
Sport Utility 2D	U24X	19799	1000	1450	2500	4025
Sport Utility 4D	U34X	20660	1550	2075	3275	4950
2WD	2		(400)	(400)	(535)	(535)
BRONCO 4WD—V8—Truck Equipment Schedule T1						
Sport Utility 2D	U15N	21879	2400	3000	4350	6250
6-Cyl. 4.9 Liter	Y		(375)	(375)	(500)	(500)
V8 7.3 Liter	H		150	150	200	200
AEROSTAR—V6—Truck Equipment Schedule T2						
Cargo Minivan	A14U	14478	550	775	1325	2225
Extended Cargo	A34U	15275	575	825	1375	2300
Window Minivan	A15U	14855	575	825	1400	2350
Extended Window	A35U	15602	600	850	1425	2400
4WD	X		325	325	435	435
V6 4.0 Liter	X		75	75	100	100
AEROSTAR—V6—Truck Equipment Schedule T1						
Minivan	A11U	15881	675	925	1550	2600
Extended Minivan	A31U	17673	775	1075	1775	2900
5 Passenger			(250)	(250)	(335)	(335)
4WD	4		325	325	435	435
V6 4.0 Liter	X		75	75	100	100
CLUB WAGON—V8—Truck Equipment Schedule T1						
Passenger Van	E11N,H	19154	975	1425	2450	3950
Heavy Duty Van	E31H	20363	1050	1500	2600	4125
Super Passenger Van	S31H	22413	1100	1550	2675	4200
5 Passenger			(250)	(250)	(335)	(335)
6-Cyl. 4.9 Liter	Y		(250)	(250)	(335)	(335)
V8 460/7.5 Liter	G		125	125	165	165
V8 7.3 Liter Diesel	M		225	225	300	300
ECONOLINE—6-Cyl.—Truck Equipment Schedule T1						
E150 Cargo Van	E14Y	16636	975	1400	2200	3475
E250 Cargo Van	E24Y	17050	1025	1475	2350	3650
E350 Cargo Van	E34Y	18150	1125	1575	2600	4025
Super Van	S		75	75	100	100
V8 5.0, 5.8 Liter	N,H		125	125	165	165
V8 460/7.5 Liter	G		250	250	335	335
V8 7.3 Liter Diesel	M		225	225	300	300
RANGER PICKUP—4-Cyl.—Truck Equipment Schedule T2						
S Short Bed	R10A	9190	300	400	850	1500
Sport Short Bed	R10A	9306	325	475	900	1625
Sport Long Bed	R10A	9463	250	325	775	1400
Custom Short Bed	R10A	10723	325	475	900	1625
Custom Long Bed	R10A	11048	250	325	775	1400
Custom Super Cab	R14A	12144	600	850	1450	2425
4WD	1,5		675	675	900	900
V6 2.9, 3.0 Liter	T,U		150	150	200	200
V6 4.0 Liter	X		200	200	265	265
REGULAR CAB PICKUP—V8—Truck Equipment Schedule T1						
F150 Short Bed	F15N	15853	1700	2225	3250	4725
F150 Long Bed	F15N	16097	1650	2150	3175	4625
F250 Long Bed	F25H	17699	1800	2325	3325	4850
F350 Long Bed	F35H	18963	1825	2350	3400	4925
Special			(325)	(325)	(435)	(435)
4WD	4,6		650	650	865	865
6-Cyl. 4.9 Liter	Y		(375)	(375)	(500)	(500)
V8 5.8 Liter	H		150	150	200	200
V8 460/7.5 Liter	G		175	175	235	235
V8 7.3 Liter Diesel	M		225	225	300	300
SUPER CAB PICKUP—V8—Truck Equipment Schedule T1						
F150 Short Bed	X15N	17219	2100	2700	3775	5350
F150 Long Bed	X15N	17453	2075	2625	3700	5250
F250 Long Bed	X25H	19237	2525	3125	4275	5975
F350 Long Bed	X35G	20829	2325	2900	4025	5675
Special			(325)	(325)	(435)	(435)
4WD	4,6		650	650	865	865

TRUCKS & VANS

Body	Type	VIN	List	Trade-In Fair	Trade-In Good	Pvt-Party Good	Retail Excellent
6-Cyl. 4.9 Liter		Y		(375)	(375)	(500)	(500)
V8 5.8 Liter		H		150	150	200	200
V8 460/7.5 Liter		G		175	175	235	235
V8 7.3 Liter Diesel		M		225	225	300	300
CREW CAB PICKUP—V8—Truck Equipment Schedule T1							
F350 Long Bed		W35H	20322	2700	3300	4525	6300
4WD		6		650	650	865	865
V8 460/7.5 Liter		G		175	175	235	235
V8 7.3 Liter Diesel		M		225	225	300	300

1993 FORD — 1F(MorT)–(U24X)–P–#

Body	Type	VIN	List	Trade-In Fair	Trade-In Good	Pvt-Party Good	Retail Excellent
EXPLORER 4WD—V6—Truck Equipment Schedule T1							
Sport Utility 2D		U24X	20613	1050	1500	2625	4200
Sport Utility 4D		U34X	21401	1700	2225	3475	5225
Limited				275	275	365	365
2WD		2		(425)	(425)	(565)	(565)
BRONCO 4WD—V8—Truck Equipment Schedule T1							
Sport Utility		U15N	22589	2575	3200	4575	6550
V8 5.8 Liter		H		175	175	235	235
AEROSTAR—V6—Truck Equipment Schedule T2							
Cargo Minivan		A14U	14977	525	750	1300	2225
Extended Cargo		A34U	15724	550	800	1400	2350
Window Minivan		A15U	15272	575	825	1425	2425
Extended Window		A35U	16020	600	850	1475	2475
4WD		2,4		375	375	500	500
V6 4.0 Liter		X		100	100	135	135
AEROSTAR—V6—Truck Equipment Schedule T1							
Minivan		A11U	15682	675	950	1625	2725
Extended Minivan		A31U	17081	800	1125	1875	3075
5 Passenger				(275)	(275)	(365)	(365)
4WD		2,4		375	375	500	500
V6 4.0 Liter		X		100	100	135	135
CLUB WAGON—V8—Truck Equipment Schedule T1							
Passenger Van		E11N	18925	1100	1550	2675	4225
Heavy Duty Van		E31H	20850	1225	1675	2800	4425
Super Passenger Van		S31H	21652	1275	1750	2900	4500
Chateau				275	275	365	365
5 Passenger				(275)	(275)	(365)	(365)
6-Cyl. 4.9 Liter		Y		(275)	(275)	(365)	(365)
V8 460/7.5 Liter		G		150	150	200	200
V8 7.3 Liter Diesel		M		250	250	335	335
ECONOLINE—6-Cyl.—Truck Equipment Schedule T1							
E150 Cargo Van		E14Y	17022	1100	1550	2600	4025
E250 Cargo Van		E24Y	17437	1200	1650	2700	4150
E350 Cargo Van		E34Y	18536	1350	1825	2850	4375
Super Van		S		100	100	135	135
V8 5.0, 5.8 Liter		N,H		150	150	200	200
V8 460/7.5 Liter		G		275	275	365	365
V8 7.3 Liter Diesel		M		250	250	335	335
RANGER PICKUP—4-Cyl.—Truck Equipment Schedule T2							
XL Short Bed		R10A	9190	600	850	1475	2475
XL Long Bed		R10A	9903	475	700	1275	2175
XL Super Cab		R14A	12346	900	1250	2100	3350
Splash Short Bed		R10A	12635	850	1175	2000	3250
4WD		1,5		800	800	1065	1065
V6 3.0 Liter		U		175	175	235	235
V6 4.0 Liter		X		225	225	300	300
REGULAR CAB PICKUP—V8—Truck Equipment Schedule T1							
F150 Short Bed		F15N	15407	1875	2400	3425	4950
F150 Lightning		F15R	21669	2900	3550	4750	6525
F150 Long Bed		F15N	15651	1800	2325	3325	4825
F250 Long Bed		F25H	17160	1975	2525	3550	5100
F350 Long Bed		F35H	19390	2000	2550	3575	5100
Special				(375)	(375)	(500)	(500)
4WD		4,6		750	750	1000	1000
6-Cyl. 4.9 Liter		Y		(400)	(400)	(535)	(535)
V8 5.8 Liter		H,R		175	175	235	235
V8 460/7.5 Liter		G		200	200	265	265
V8 7.3 Liter Diesel		M		250	250	335	335
V8 7.3L Turbo Diesel		K		850	850	1135	1135
SUPER CAB PICKUP—V8—Truck Equipment Schedule T1							
F150 Short Bed		X15N	17483	2350	2925	4025	5650
F150 Long Bed		X15N	17717	2250	2825	3925	5525

0105

Body	Type	VIN	List	Trade-In Fair	Good	Pvt-Party Good	Retail Excellent
F250 Long Bed	X25H	19616	2825	3450	4625	6350
F350 Long Bed	X35G	21572	2950	3600	4800	6575
4WD		4,6		750	750	1000	1000
6-Cyl. 4.9 Liter	Y		(400)	(400)	(535)	(535)
V8 5.8 Liter	H		175	175	235	235
V8 460/7.5 Liter	G		200	200	265	265
V8 7.3 Liter Diesel	M		250	250	335	335
V8 7.3L Turbo Diesel	K		850	850	1135	1135
CREW CAB PICKUP—V8—Truck Equipment Schedule T1							
F350 Long Bed	W35H	20641	3050	3700	4925	6725
4WD		6		750	750	1000	1000
V8 460/7.5 Liter	G		200	200	265	265
V8 7.3 Liter Diesel	M		250	250	335	335
V8 7.3L Turbo Diesel	K		850	850	1135	1135

1994 FORD — 1F(MorT)–(U24X)–R–#

Body	Type	VIN	List	Trade-In Fair	Good	Pvt-Party Good	Retail Excellent
EXPLORER 4WD—V6—Truck Equipment Schedule T1							
Sport Utility 2D	U24X	21145	1125	1575	2775	4475
Sport Utility 4D	U34X	22055	1900	2425	3775	5625
2WD			(450)	(450)	(600)	(600)
BRONCO 4WD—V8—Truck Equipment Schedule T1							
Sport Utility 2D	U15N	24036	2800	3425	4900	6950
V8 5.8 Liter	H		200	200	265	265
AEROSTAR—V6—Truck Equipment Schedule T2							
Cargo Minivan	A14U	15796	525	750	1375	2350
Extended Cargo	A34U	16346	600	850	1500	2525
Window Minivan	A15U	16091	625	900	1525	2650
Extended Window	A35U	16641	625	900	1575	2700
4WD		2,4		425	425	565	565
V6 4.0 Liter	X		100	100	135	135
AEROSTAR—V6—Truck Equipment Schedule T1							
Minivan	A11U	16302	750	1025	1775	2975
Extended Minivan	A31U	17747	875	1225	2075	3350
5 Passenger			(300)	(300)	(400)	(400)
4WD		2,4		425	425	565	565
V6 4.0 Liter	X		100	100	135	135
CLUB WAGON—V8—Truck Equipment Schedule T1							
Passenger Van	E11N	19790	1300	1775	2950	4600
Heavy Duty Van	E31H	21739	1450	1925	3150	4825
Super Passenger Van	S31H	22925	1500	2000	3225	4925
5 Passenger			(300)	(300)	(400)	(400)
6-Cyl. 4.9 Liter	Y		(300)	(300)	(400)	(400)
V8 460/7.5 Liter	G		175	175	235	235
V8 7.3 Liter Diesel	M		(175)	(175)	(235)	(235)
ECONOLINE—6-Cyl.—Truck Equipment Schedule T1							
E150 Cargo Van	E14Y	17806	1350	1825	2875	4425
E250 Cargo Van	E24Y	18201	1425	1900	3000	4525
E350 Cargo Van	E34Y	19299	1575	2100	3200	4775
Super Van			100	100	135	135
V8 5.0, 5.8 Liter	N,H		175	175	235	235
V8 460/7.5 Liter	G		300	300	400	400
V8 7.3 Liter Diesel	M		250	250	335	335
RANGER PICKUP—4-Cyl.—Truck Equipment Schedule T2							
XL Short Bed	R10A	9826	675	925	1625	2750
XL Long Bed	R10A	10200	550	775	1425	2425
XL Super Cab	R14A	12469	975	1400	2400	3900
Splash Short Bed	R10A	13305	950	1375	2375	3875
Splash Super Cab	R14A	14774	1325	1800	2900	4475
4WD		1,5		900	900	1200	1200
V6 3.0 Liter	U		200	200	265	265
V6 4.0 Liter	X		250	250	335	335
REGULAR CAB PICKUP—V8—Truck Equipment Schedule T1							
F150 Short Bed	F15N	16434	2100	2675	3725	5275
F150 Lightning	F15R	23127	3300	3975	5225	7075
F150 Long Bed	F15N	16658	2000	2550	3600	5125
F250 Long Bed	F25H	17480	2225	2775	3875	5450
F350 Long Bed	F35H	20088	2275	2850	3925	5550
Special			(400)	(400)	(535)	(535)
4WD		4,6		850	850	1135	1135
6-Cyl. 4.9 Liter	Y		(425)	(425)	(565)	(565)
V8 5.8 Liter	H,R		200	200	265	265
V8 460/7.5 Liter	G		225	225	300	300
V8 7.3 Liter Diesel	M		250	250	335	335

TRUCKS & VANS

Body	Type	VIN	List	Trade-In Fair	Trade-In Good	Pvt-Party Good	Retail Excellent
	V8 7.3L Turbo Diesel	K		950	950	1265	1265
	V8 7.3L Power Stroke	F		2800	2800	3730	3730
SUPER CAB PICKUP—V8—Truck Equipment Schedule T1							
F150 Short Bed		X15N	18040	2650	3250	4375	6050
F150 Long Bed		X15N	18283	2550	3150	4250	5900
F250 Long Bed		X25H	20578	3200	3875	5100	6900
F350 Long Bed		X35G	22410	3325	4025	5275	7125
Special				(400)	(400)	(535)	(535)
4WD		4,6		850	850	1135	1135
6-Cyl. 4.9 Liter		Y		(425)	(425)	(565)	(565)
V8 5.8 Liter		H		200	200	265	265
V8 460/7.5 Liter		G		225	225	300	300
V8 7.3 Liter Diesel		M		250	250	335	335
V8 7.3L Turbo Diesel		K		950	950	1265	1265
V8 7.3L Power Stroke		F		2800	2800	3730	3730
CREW CAB PICKUP—V8—Truck Equipment Schedule T1							
F350 Long Bed		W35H	21591	3450	4150	5450	7325
4WD		6		850	850	1135	1135
V8 460/7.5 Liter		G		225	225	300	300
V8 7.3 Liter Diesel		M		250	250	335	335
V8 7.3L Turbo Diesel		K		950	950	1265	1265
V8 7.3L Power Stroke		F		2800	2800	3730	3730

1995 FORD—(1or2)F(B,MorT)—(U24X)—S—#

Body	Type	VIN	List	Trade-In Fair	Trade-In Good	Pvt-Party Good	Retail Excellent
EXPLORER 4WD—V6—Truck Equipment Schedule T1							
Sport Utility 2D		U24X	22380	1500	1975	3300	5125
Sport Utility 4D		U34X	23735	2300	2875	4325	6325
2WD		2		(475)	(475)	(635)	(635)
BRONCO 4WD—V8—Truck Equipment Schedule T1							
Sport Utility 2D		U15N	24305	3125	3775	5325	7500
V8 5.8 Liter		H		225	225	300	300
AEROSTAR—V6—Truck Equipment Schedule T2							
Cargo Minivan		A14U	17486	600	850	1525	2650
AEROSTAR—V6—Truck Equipment Schedule T1							
Minivan		A11U	17895	950	1375	2425	3925
Extended Minivan		A31U	22261	1100	1550	2700	4250
5 Passenger		4		(325)	(325)	(435)	(435)
4WD		4		475	475	635	635
V6 4.0 Liter		X		100	100	135	135
WINDSTAR—V6—Truck Equipment Schedule T2							
Cargo Minivan		A544	18655	900	1250	2150	3525
WINDSTAR—V6—Truck Equipment Schedule T1							
GL Minivan		A514	19995	1650	2150	3325	5025
LX Minivan		A524	24080	1925	2450	3675	5400
CLUB WAGON—V8—Truck Equipment Schedule T1							
Passenger Van		E11N	21286	1550	2075	3325	5100
Heavy Duty Van		E31H	22967	1725	2250	3550	5350
Super Passenger Van		S31H	24780	1800	2325	3600	5425
6-Cyl. 4.9 Liter		Y		(325)	(325)	(435)	(435)
V8 460/7.5 Liter		G		200	200	265	265
V8 7.3L Turbo Diesel		F		1650	1650	2200	2200
ECONOLINE—6-Cyl.—Truck Equipment Schedule T1							
E150 Cargo Van		E14Y	18676	1650	2150	3300	4900
E250 Cargo Van		E24Y	19098	1725	2250	3375	5025
E350 Cargo Van		E34Y	20624	1925	2450	3625	5275
Super Van		S		100	100	135	135
V8 5.0, 5.8 Liter		N,H		200	200	265	265
V8 460/7.5 Liter		G		325	325	435	435
V8 7.3L Turbo Diesel		F		1825	1825	2435	2435
RANGER PICKUP—4-Cyl.—Truck Equipment Schedule T2							
XL Short Bed		R10A	10746	775	1100	1900	3150
XL Long Bed		R10A	11130	650	900	1600	2750
XL Super Cab		R14A	13298	1125	1575	2700	4225
Splash Short Bed		R10A	13825	1150	1600	2700	4250
Splash Super Cab		R14A	15400	1575	2100	3250	4875
4WD		1,5		1000	1000	1335	1335
V6 3.0 Liter		U		225	225	300	300
V6 4.0 Liter		X		275	275	365	365
REGULAR CAB PICKUP—V8—Truck Equipment Schedule T1							
F150 Short Bed		F15N	17418	2400	3000	4075	5700
F150 Lightning		F15E		3775	4500	5775	7700
F150 Long Bed		F15N	17642	2275	2850	3925	5525
F250 Long Bed		F25H	18264	2550	3175	4275	5900

Body	Type	VIN	List	Trade-In Fair	Trade-In Good	Pvt-Party Good	Retail Excellent
F350 Long Bed		F35H	20236	**2675**	**3275**	**4400**	**6050**
Special				**(425)**	**(425)**	**(565)**	**(565)**
4WD		4,6		**950**	**950**	**1265**	**1265**
6-Cyl. 4.9 Liter		Y,Z		**(450)**	**(450)**	**(600)**	**(600)**
V8 5.8 Liter		H,R		**225**	**225**	**300**	**300**
V8 460/7.5 Liter		G		**250**	**250**	**335**	**335**
V8 7.3L Turbo Diesel		F		**3100**	**3100**	**4130**	**4130**
SUPER CAB PICKUP—V8—Truck Equipment Schedule T1							
F150 Short Bed		X15N	19297	**3025**	**3700**	**4850**	**6575**
F150 Long Bed		X15N	19540	**2900**	**3550**	**4700**	**6400**
F250 Long Bed		X25H	20670	**3650**	**4375**	**5625**	**7500**
F350 Long Bed		X35G	22730	**3825**	**4550**	**5825**	**7750**
Special				**(425)**	**(425)**	**(565)**	**(565)**
4WD		4,6		**950**	**950**	**1265**	**1265**
6-Cyl. 4.9 Liter		Y		**(450)**	**(450)**	**(600)**	**(600)**
V8 5.8 Liter		H		**225**	**225**	**300**	**300**
V8 460/7.5 Liter		G		**250**	**250**	**335**	**335**
V8 7.3L Turbo Diesel		F		**3100**	**3100**	**4130**	**4130**
CREW CAB PICKUP—V8—Truck Equipment Schedule T1							
F350 Long Bed		W35H	21938	**3925**	**4675**	**6000**	**7950**
4WD		6		**950**	**950**	**1265**	**1265**
V8 460/7.5 Liter		G		**250**	**250**	**335**	**335**
V8 7.3L Turbo Diesel		F		**3100**	**3100**	**4130**	**4130**

1996 FORD—(1or2)F(B,MorT)—(U24X)—T—#

Body	Type	VIN	List	Trade-In Fair	Trade-In Good	Pvt-Party Good	Retail Excellent
EXPLORER 4WD—V6—Truck Equipment Schedule T1							
Sport Utility 2D		U24X	22980	**1900**	**2425**	**3875**	**5825**
XL Sport Utility 4D		U34X	24335	**2775**	**3400**	**4975**	**7125**
2WD		2		**(500)**	**(500)**	**(665)**	**(665)**
AWD		5		**0**	**0**	**0**	**0**
V8 5.0 Liter		P		**200**	**200**	**265**	**265**
BRONCO 4WD—V8—Truck Equipment Schedule T1							
XL Sport Utility 2D		U15N	25375	**3500**	**4200**	**5825**	**8125**
V8 5.8 Liter		H		**250**	**250**	**335**	**335**
AEROSTAR—V6—Truck Equipment Schedule T2							
Cargo Minivan		A14U	17966	**675**	**950**	**1775**	**3075**
AEROSTAR—V6—Truck Equipment Schedule T1							
XLT Minivan		A11U	18375	**1100**	**1550**	**2700**	**4300**
XLT Extended		A31U	22840	**1325**	**1800**	**2975**	**4650**
5 Passenger				**(350)**	**(350)**	**(465)**	**(465)**
4WD		4		**500**	**500**	**665**	**665**
V6 4.0 Liter		X		**100**	**100**	**135**	**135**
WINDSTAR—V6—Truck Equipment Schedule T2							
Cargo Minivan		A544	18825	**1050**	**1500**	**2625**	**4225**
V6 3.0 Liter		U		**(225)**	**(225)**	**(300)**	**(300)**
WINDSTAR—V6—Truck Equipment Schedule T1							
GL Minivan		A514	20785	**1950**	**2500**	**3775**	**5550**
LX Minivan		A514	25340	**2250**	**2800**	**4100**	**5950**
V6 3.0 Liter		U		**(225)**	**(225)**	**(300)**	**(300)**
CLUB WAGON—V8—Truck Equipment Schedule T1							
XL Passenger Van		E11N	22224	**1925**	**2450**	**3825**	**5700**
XL Heavy Duty Van		E31H	23925	**2100**	**2650**	**4000**	**5925**
XL Super Pass Van		S31H	25764	**2150**	**2725**	**4100**	**6050**
6-Cyl. 4.9 Liter		Y		**(350)**	**(350)**	**(465)**	**(465)**
V8 460/7.5 Liter		G		**200**	**200**	**265**	**265**
V8 7.3L Turbo Diesel		F		**1800**	**1800**	**2400**	**2400**
ECONOLINE—6-Cyl.—Truck Equipment Schedule T1							
E150 Cargo Van		E14Y	19346	**2000**	**2550**	**3775**	**5500**
E250 Cargo Van		E24X	19771	**2100**	**2650**	**3875**	**5625**
E350 Cargo Van		E34X	21396	**2275**	**2850**	**4100**	**5900**
Super Van				**100**	**100**	**135**	**135**
V8 5.0, 5.8 Liter		N,H		**200**	**200**	**265**	**265**
V8 460/7.5 Liter		G		**350**	**350**	**465**	**465**
V8 7.3L Turbo Diesel		F		**1950**	**1950**	**2600**	**2600**
RANGER PICKUP—4-Cyl.—Truck Equipment Schedule T2							
XL Short Bed		R10A	11087	**900**	**1300**	**2200**	**3600**
XL Long Bed		R10A	11472	**775**	**1075**	**1925**	**3200**
XL Super Cab		R14A	14217	**1375**	**1850**	**2975**	**4575**
Splash Short Bed		R10A	14645	**1425**	**1900**	**3050**	**4675**
Splash Super Cab		R14U	16305	**1875**	**2400**	**3625**	**5325**
4WD		1,5		**1100**	**1100**	**1465**	**1465**
V6 3.0 Liter		U		**250**	**250**	**335**	**335**
V6 4.0 Liter		X		**300**	**300**	**400**	**400**

TRUCKS & VANS

Body Type	VIN	List	Trade-In Fair	Trade-In Good	Pvt-Party Good	Retail Excellent
REGULAR CAB PICKUP—V8—Truck Equipment Schedule T1						
F150 Short Bed	F15N	18327	2775	3400	4550	6250
F150 Long Bed	F15N	18552	2650	3250	4375	6050
F250 Long Bed	F25H	19017	2975	3625	4775	6500
F350 Long Bed	F35H	20157	3125	3775	4975	6725
Special			(450)	(450)	(600)	(600)
4WD	4,6		1050	1050	1400	1400
6-Cyl. 4.9 Liter	Y		(450)	(450)	(600)	(600)
V8 5.8 Liter	H		250	250	335	335
V8 460/7.5 Liter	G		275	275	365	365
V8 7.3L Turbo Diesel	F		3400	3400	4530	4530
SUPER CAB PICKUP—V8—Truck Equipment Schedule T1						
F150 Short Bed	X15N	20352	3475	4175	5400	7225
F150 Long Bed	X15N	20597	3325	4025	5225	7025
F250 Short Bed	X25H	21667	4350	5125	6500	8525
F250 Long Bed	X25H	21487	4175	4950	6275	8225
F350 Long Bed	X35G	23485	4350	5125	6500	8525
Special			(450)	(450)	(600)	(600)
4WD	4,6		1050	1050	1400	1400
6-Cyl. 4.9 Liter	Y		(450)	(450)	(600)	(600)
V8 5.8 Liter	H		250	250	335	335
V8 460/7.5 Liter	G		275	275	365	365
V8 7.3L Turbo Diesel	F		3400	3400	4530	4530
CREW CAB PICKUP—V8—Truck Equipment Schedule T1						
F250 Short Bed	W25G	23422	4825	5675	7050	9175
F350 Long Bed	W35H	23482	4475	5275	6650	8700
4WD	6		1050	1050	1400	1400
V8 460/7.5 Liter	G		275	275	365	365
V8 7.3L Turbo Diesel	F		3400	3400	4530	4530

1997 FORD—(1or2)F(B,M,orT)—(U24X)—V—#

Body Type	VIN	List	Trade-In Fair	Trade-In Good	Pvt-Party Good	Retail Excellent
EXPLORER 4WD—V6—Truck Equipment Schedule T1						
Sport Utility 2D	U24X	24065	2400	2975	4525	6700
XL Sport Utility 4D	U34X	25420	3325	4025	5700	8050
2WD	2		(525)	(525)	(700)	(700)
AWD	5		0	0	0	0
V6 4.0 Liter SOHC	E		150	150	200	200
V8 5.0 Liter	P		200	200	265	265
EXPEDITION 4WD—V8—Truck Equipment Schedule T1						
XLT Sport Utility 4D	U18W	30510	4875	5700	7850	10800
w/o Third Seat			(575)	(575)	(765)	(765)
2WD	7		(1175)	(1175)	(1565)	(1565)
V8 5.4 Liter	L		275	275	365	365
AEROSTAR—V6—Truck Equipment Schedule T2						
Cargo Minivan	A14U	17995	825	1150	2150	3650
AEROSTAR—V6—Truck Equipment Schedule T1						
XLT Minivan	A11U	18405	1375	1850	3075	4775
XLT Extended	A31U	21170	1600	2100	3375	5125
5 Passenger			(375)	(375)	(500)	(500)
4WD	4		525	525	700	700
V6 4.0 Liter	X		100	100	135	135
WINDSTAR—V6—Truck Equipment Schedule T2						
Cargo Minivan	A544	19600	1375	1850	3075	4775
V6 3.0 Liter	U		(250)	(250)	(335)	(335)
WINDSTAR—V6—Truck Equipment Schedule T1						
Minivan	A514	19995	1925	2450	3775	5600
GL Minivan	A514	23070	2350	2925	4275	6200
LX Minivan	A514	26195	2675	3275	4650	6600
V6 3.0 Liter	U		(250)	(250)	(335)	(335)
CLUB WAGON—V8—Truck Equipment Schedule T1						
XL Passenger Van	E11N	23210	2375	2950	4425	6425
XL Heavy Duty Van	E31L	25255	2550	3150	4600	6675
XL Super Pass Van	S31L	27135	2650	3250	4725	6825
V6 4.2 Liter	2		(375)	(375)	(500)	(500)
V8 7.3L Turbo Diesel	F		1925	1925	2565	2565
V10 6.8 Liter	S		575	575	765	765
ECONOLINE—V6—Truck Equipment Schedule T1						
E150 Cargo Van	E142	20505	2450	3050	4350	6200
E250 Cargo Van	E242	20930	2550	3150	4450	6300
E350 Cargo Van	E34L	23565	2750	3375	4700	6600
Super Van	S		100	100	135	135
V8 4.6, 5.4 Liter	6,L		200	200	265	265
V8 7.3L Turbo Diesel	F		2075	2075	2765	2765

Body	Type	VIN	List	Trade-In Fair	Trade-In Good	Pvt-Party Good	Retail Excellent
V10 6.8 Liter		S		1150	1150	1535	1535
RANGER PICKUP—4-Cyl.—Truck Equipment Schedule T2							
XL Short Bed		R10A	11060	1075	1525	2650	4200
XL Long Bed		R10A	11445	925	1325	2400	3925
XL Super Cab		R14A	14905	1650	2150	3350	5050
Splash Short Bed		R10A	15385	1725	2250	3450	5150
Splash Super Cab		R14U	17010	2225	2775	4050	5825
4WD		1,5		1200	1200	1600	1600
V6 3.0 Liter		U		250	250	335	335
V6 4.0 Liter		X		325	325	435	435
REGULAR CAB PICKUP—V8—Truck Equipment Schedule T1							
F150 Short Bed		F176,W	17480	3425	4150	5350	7175
F150 Long Bed		F176,W	17750	3225	3900	5100	6875
F250 Short Bed		F276,W	18770	3850	4575	5825	7725
F250 H.D. Long Bed		F25H	20265	4375	5150	6475	8475
F350 Long Bed		F35H	20775	4750	5575	6925	9000
Standard (Work Truck)				(475)	(475)	(635)	(635)
4WD		6,8		1150	1150	1535	1535
V6 4.2 Liter		2		(450)	(450)	(600)	(600)
V8 5.4 Liter		L		275	275	365	365
V8 460/7.5 Liter		G		300	300	400	400
V8 7.3L Turbo Diesel		F		3700	3700	4930	4930
SUPER CAB PICKUP—V8—Truck Equipment Schedule T1							
F150 Short Bed		X176,W	19635	4775	5625	7000	9075
F150 Long Bed		X176,W	19920	4550	5375	6725	8750
F250 Short Bed		X276,W	20620	5350	6275	7700	9900
F250 H.D. Short Bed		X25H	22285	4750	5575	6925	9000
F250 H.D. Long Bed		X25H	22105	4550	5375	6725	8750
F350 Long Bed		X35G	23875	5100	5975	7375	9500
Standard (Work Truck)				(475)	(475)	(635)	(635)
4WD		6,8		1150	1150	1535	1535
V6 4.2 Liter		2		(450)	(450)	(600)	(600)
V8 5.4 Liter		L		275	275	365	365
V8 460/7.5 Liter		G		300	300	400	400
V8 7.3L Turbo Diesel		F		3700	3700	4930	4930
CREW CAB PICKUP—V8—Truck Equipment Schedule T1							
F250 Short Bed		W25G	24160	5325	6225	7650	9850
F350 Long Bed		W35H	24220	5525	6425	7900	10150
4WD		6		1150	1150	1535	1535
V8 460/7.5 Liter		G		300	300	400	400
V8 7.3L Turbo Diesel		F		3700	3700	4930	4930

1998 FORD —(1or2)F(B,MorT)–(U24X)–W–#

Body	Type	VIN	List	Trade-In Fair	Trade-In Good	Pvt-Party Good	Retail Excellent
EXPLORER 4WD—V6—Truck Equipment Schedule T1							
Sport Utility 2D		U24X	24315	3000	3675	5300	7575
XL Sport Utility 4D		U34X	24995	4000	4775	6525	8975
2WD		2		(575)	(575)	(765)	(765)
AWD		5		0	0	0	0
V6 4.0 Liter SOHC		E		150	150	200	200
V8 5.0 Liter		P		200	200	265	265
EXPEDITION 4WD—V8—Truck Equipment Schedule T1							
XLT Sport Utility 4D		U18W	31225	5775	6750	8875	11900
w/o Third Seat				(625)	(625)	(835)	(835)
2WD		7		(1225)	(1225)	(1635)	(1635)
V8 5.4 Liter		L		300	300	400	400
WINDSTAR—V6—Truck Equipment Schedule T2							
Cargo Minivan		A544	18590	1750	2275	3525	5275
V6 3.0 Liter		U		(250)	(250)	(335)	(335)
WINDSTAR—V6—Truck Equipment Schedule T1							
Minivan		A514	20970	2350	2925	4250	6100
GL Minivan		A514	24025	2825	3450	4800	6750
LX Minivan		A514	28365	3175	3850	5225	7225
Limited Minivan		A514	30085	3875	4600	6050	8150
V6 3.0 Liter		U		(250)	(250)	(335)	(335)
CLUB WAGON—V8—Truck Equipment Schedule T1							
XL Passenger Van		E11N	23090	2975	3625	5150	7325
XL Heavy Duty Van		E31L	25255	3150	3800	5350	7550
XL Super Pass Van		S31L	26970	3300	3950	5550	7750
V6 4.2 Liter		2		(425)	(425)	(565)	(565)
V8 7.3L Turbo Diesel		F		2050	2050	2735	2735
V10 6.8 Liter		S		600	600	800	800
ECONOLINE—V6—Truck Equipment Schedule T1							
E150 Cargo Van		E142	19795	3050	3700	5025	6900

TRUCKS & VANS

1998 FORD

Body	Type	VIN	List	Trade-In Fair	Trade-In Good	Pvt-Party Good	Retail Excellent
E250 Cargo Van		E242	20105	3150	3800	5100	7025
E350 Cargo Van		E34L	22705	3400	4100	5425	7400
Super Van		S		100	100	135	135
V8 4.6, 5.4 Liter		6,L		200	200	265	265
V8 7.3L Turbo Diesel		F		2200	2200	2935	2935
V10 6.8 Liter		S		1225	1225	1635	1635
RANGER PICKUP—4-Cyl.—Truck Equipment Schedule T2							
XL Short Bed		R10C	11575	1400	1875	3000	4575
XL Long Bed		R10C	12045	1200	1650	2750	4300
Splash Short Bed		R10C	15195	2100	2675	3850	5525
XL Super Cab 2D		R14C	15030	2050	2600	3775	5450
XLT Super Cab 4D		R14C	15625	3000	3675	4925	6775
Splash Super Cab 2D		R14U	16825	2675	3275	4500	6300
Splash Super Cab 4D		R14U	17420	3100	3750	5025	6900
4WD		1,5		1275	1275	1700	1700
V6 3.0 Liter		U		250	250	335	335
V6 4.0 Liter		X		375	375	500	500
REGULAR CAB PICKUP—V8—Truck Equipment Schedule T1							
F150 Short Bed		F176,W	18815	4000	4750	6050	7975
F150 Long Bed		F176,W	19115	3750	4500	5725	7625
F250 Long Bed		F276,W	20225	4450	5225	6550	8575
Standard (Work Truck)				(525)	(525)	(700)	(700)
4WD		6,8		1225	1225	1635	1635
V6 4.2 Liter		2		(475)	(475)	(635)	(635)
V8 5.4 Liter		L		300	300	400	400
SUPER CAB PICKUP—V8—Truck Equipment Schedule T1							
F150 Short Bed		X176,W	21255	5450	6350	7775	9925
F150 Long Bed		X176,W	21555	5200	6075	7475	9600
F250 Short Bed		X276,W	22300	6075	7050	8550	10800
Standard (Work Truck)				(525)	(525)	(700)	(700)
4WD		6,8		1225	1225	1635	1635
V6 4.2 Liter		2		(475)	(475)	(635)	(635)
V8 5.4 Liter		L		300	300	400	400

1999 FORD—(1,2or3)F(B,MorT)–(U24X)–X–

Body	Type	VIN	List	Trade-In Fair	Trade-In Good	Pvt-Party Good	Retail Excellent
EXPLORER 4WD—V6—Truck Equipment Schedule T1							
Sport Utility 2D		U24X	24535	3675	4400	6150	8600
XL Sport Utility 4D		U34X	25310	4825	5675	7525	10200
2WD		2		(650)	(650)	(865)	(865)
AWD		5		0	0	0	0
V6 4.0 Liter SOHC		E		175	175	235	235
V8 5.0 Liter		P		250	250	335	335
EXPEDITION 4WD—V8—Truck Equipment Schedule T1							
XLT Sport Utility 4D		U18W	32610	6850	7900	10200	13500
w/o Third Seat				(725)	(725)	(965)	(965)
2WD		7		(1300)	(1300)	(1735)	(1735)
V8 5.4 Liter		L		325	325	435	435
WINDSTAR—V6—Truck Equipment Schedule T2							
Cargo Minivan		A544	18955	2100	2675	3975	5825
V6 3.0 Liter		U		(275)	(275)	(365)	(365)
WINDSTAR—V6—Truck Equipment Schedule T1							
Minivan		A51U	21300	2800	3425	4800	6775
LX Minivan		A514	24590	3350	4050	5475	7500
SE Minivan		A524	28075	3775	4500	5975	8100
SEL Minivan		A534	30995	4550	5375	6900	9125
w/o 2nd Sliding Door				(550)	(550)	(735)	(735)
ECONOLINE WAGON—V8—Truck Equipment Schedule T1							
E150 XL Passenger		E112	22710	3725	4475	6150	8525
E350 XL Super Duty		S31L	25595	3925	4675	6400	8800
E350 XL S.D. Ext		S31L	27285	4125	4900	6625	9050
V6 4.2 Liter		2		(500)	(500)	(665)	(665)
V8 7.3L Turbo Diesel		F		2275	2275	3035	3035
V10 6.8 Liter		S		650	650	865	865
ECONOLINE VAN—V6—Truck Equipment Schedule T1							
E150 Cargo Van		E142	20025	3800	4525	5925	7975
E250 Cargo Van		E24L	21325	3900	4625	6050	8100
E350 Super Cargo		E34L	24085	4200	5000	6400	8525
Super Van (E250)		S		150	150	200	200
V8 4.6, 5.4 Liter		W,L		250	250	335	335
V8 7.3L Turbo Diesel		F		2525	2525	3365	3365
V10 6.8 Liter		S		1300	1300	1735	1735
RANGER PICKUP—4-Cyl.—Truck Equipment Schedule T2							
XL Short Bed		R10C	11795	1800	2325	3475	5150

TRUCKS & VANS

Body Type	VIN	List	Trade-In Fair	Good	Pvt-Party Good	Retail Excellent
XL Long Bed	R10C	12265	1525	2050	3225	4850
XL Super Cab 2D	R14C	15250	2550	3150	4375	6175
XLT Super Cab 4D	R14X	15910	3625	4350	5675	7625
4WD	1,5		1450	1450	1935	1935
V6 3.0L Flex Fuel	V		300	300	400	400
V6 4.0 Liter	X		450	450	600	600
REGULAR CAB PICKUP—V8—Truck Equipment Schedule T1						
F150 Short Bed	F17W	19205	4575	5400	6725	8725
F150 Long Bed	F17W	19505	4300	5075	6375	8350
F250 Long Bed	F276,W	20575	5075	5950	7325	9400
Work Truck			(675)	(675)	(900)	(900)
4WD	6,8		1400	1400	1865	1865
V6 4.2 Liter	2		(550)	(550)	(735)	(735)
V8 5.4 Liter	L		325	325	435	435
REGULAR CAB PICKUP—V8 Supercharged—Truck Sch T1						
F150 Lightning	F073	29355	9800	11175	12900	15750
SUPER CAB PICKUP—V8—Truck Equipment Schedule T1						
F150 Short Bed	X17W	21985	6250	7225	8700	10950
F150 Long Bed	X17W	22285	5925	6900	8325	10550
F250 Short Bed	X276,W	23355	6950	8050	9575	11950
Work Truck			(675)	(675)	(900)	(900)
4WD	6,8		1400	1400	1865	1865
V6 4.2 Liter	2		(550)	(550)	(735)	(735)
V8 5.4 Liter	L		325	325	435	435
SUPER DUTY REGULAR CAB—V8—Truck Equipment Sch T1						
F250 Long Bed	F20L	21505	6075	7050	8525	10750
F350 Long Bed	F30L	22150	6325	7350	8800	11100
4WD	1		1400	1400	1865	1865
V10 6.8 Liter	S		550	550	735	735
V8 7.3L Turbo Diesel	F		4200	4200	5600	5600
SUPER DUTY SUPER CAB—V8—Truck Equipment Sch T1						
F250 Short Bed	X20L	23260	8000	9175	10750	13300
F250 Long Bed	X20L	23460	7725	8875	10450	12950
F350 Short Bed	X30L	24245	8225	9425	11050	13650
F350 Long Bed	X30L	24445	8000	9175	10750	13300
4WD	1		1400	1400	1865	1865
V8 7.3L Turbo Diesel	F		4200	4200	5600	5600
V10 6.8 Liter	S		550	550	735	735
SUPER DUTY CREW CAB—V8—Truck Equipment Sch T1						
F250 Short Bed	W20L	24985	8975	10275	11950	14650
F250 Long Bed	W20L	25185	8725	9975	11650	14300
F350 Short Bed	W30L	25835	9225	10500	12250	15000
F350 Long Bed	W30L	26035	8975	10275	11950	14650
4WD	1		1400	1400	1865	1865
V8 7.3L Turbo Diesel	F		4200	4200	5600	5600
V10 6.8 Liter	S		550	550	735	735

2000 FORD—(1,2or3)F(B,MorT)—(U70X)—Y–

Body Type	VIN	List	Trade-In Fair	Good	Pvt-Party Good	Retail Excellent
EXPLORER SPORT 4WD—V6—Truck Equipment Schedule T1						
Sport Utility 2D	U70X	24690	4475	5275	7175	9850
2WD			(725)	(725)	(965)	(965)
V6 4.0 Liter SOHC	E		200	200	265	265
EXPLORER 4WD—V6—Truck Equipment Schedule T1						
XL Sport Utility 4D	U72X	26790	5775	6725	8700	11550
2WD			(725)	(725)	(965)	(965)
AWD	5		0	0	0	0
V6 4.0 Liter SOHC	E		200	200	265	265
V8 5.0 Liter	P		300	300	400	400
EXPEDITION 4WD—V8—Truck Equipment Schedule T1						
XLT Sport Utility 4D	U166	33165	8100	9300	11750	15300
w/o Third Seat			(825)	(825)	(1100)	(1100)
2WD			(1350)	(1350)	(1800)	(1800)
V8 5.4 Liter	L		350	350	465	465
EXCURSION 4WD—V10—Truck Equipment Schedule T1						
XLT Sport Utility 4D	U41S	38090	9975	11375	13850	17450
w/o Third Seat			(825)	(825)	(1100)	(1100)
2WD			(1350)	(1350)	(1800)	(1800)
V8 5.4 Liter			(500)	(500)	(665)	(665)
V8 7.3L Turbo Diesel	F		4450	4450	5930	5930
WINDSTAR—V6—Truck Equipment Schedule T2						
Cargo Minivan	A544	20395	2625	3250	4650	6650
WINDSTAR—V6—Truck Equipment Schedule T1						
Minivan	A504	23080	3425	4125	5600	7700

Body	Type	VIN	List	Trade-In Fair	Trade-In Good	Pvt-Party Good	Retail Excellent
LX Minivan		A514	25045	4025	4800	6300	8525
SE Minivan		A524	28195	4500	5300	6875	9125
SEL Minivan		A534	31095	5400	6300	7925	10300
Limited Minivan		A534	33990	6850	7900	9650	12250
w/o 2nd Sliding Door		0		(600)	(600)	(800)	(800)
V6 3.0 Liter		U		(300)	(300)	(400)	(400)
ECONOLINE WAGON—V8—Truck Equipment Schedule T1							
E150 Passenger Van		E112	23810	4725	5550	7425	10050
E350 Super Duty Van		E31L	25900	4950	5800	7675	10300
E350 Super Duty Ext		S31L	27570	5175	6050	7950	10600
V6 4.2 Liter		2		(550)	(550)	(735)	(735)
V8 7.3L Turbo Diesel		F		2500	2500	3335	3335
V10 6.8 Liter		S		675	675	900	900
ECONOLINE VAN—V6—Truck Equipment Schedule T1							
E150 Cargo Van		E142	11995	4725	5550	7050	9275
E250 Cargo Van		E24L	21835	4850	5700	7200	9425
E350 Super Cargo		E34L	24355	5175	6050	7575	9850
Super Van		S		175	175	235	235
V8 4.6, 5.4 Liter		W,L		275	275	365	365
V8 7.3L Turbo Diesel		F		2850	2850	3800	3800
V10 6.8 Liter		S		1350	1350	1800	1800
RANGER PICKUP—4-Cyl.—Truck Equipment Schedule T2							
XL Short Bed		R10C	11995	2250	2825	4075	5875
XL Long Bed		R10C	12465	1975	2525	3750	5500
XL Super Cab 2D		R14C	15655	3125	3775	5100	7000
XL Super Cab 4D		R14C	16230	3900	4650	6050	8075
4WD		1,5		1625	1625	2165	2165
V6 3.0L Flex Fuel				350	350	465	465
V6 4.0 Liter		X		500	500	665	665
REGULAR CAB PICKUP—V8—Truck Equipment Schedule T1							
F150 Short Bed		F17W	19510	5350	6250	7600	9700
F150 Long Bed		F17W	19810	5025	5875	7225	9275
4WD		6,8		1575	1575	2100	2100
Work Truck				(825)	(825)	(1100)	(1100)
V6 4.2 Liter		2		(625)	(625)	(835)	(835)
V8 5.4 Liter		L		350	350	465	465
REGULAR CAB—V8 Supercharged—Truck Equip Sch T1							
F150 Lightning		F073	30895	11225	12775	14600	17500
SUPER CAB PICKUP—V8—Truck Equipment Schedule T1							
F150 Short Bed		X17W	22195	7200	8275	9800	12150
F150 Harley Davidson		X17L	33800	10650	12150	13850	16750
F150 Long Bed		X17W	22495	6875	7925	9400	11700
4WD		6,8		1575	1575	2100	2100
Work Truck				(825)	(825)	(1100)	(1100)
V6 4.2 Liter		2		(625)	(625)	(835)	(835)
V8 5.4 Liter		L		350	350	465	465
SUPER DUTY REGULAR CAB PICKUP—V8—Truck Equip Sch T1							
F250 Short Bed		F20L	22450	7000	8100	9575	11900
F350 Short Bed		F30L	23175	7275	8375	9900	12300
4WD		1		1575	1575	2100	2100
V8 7.3L Turbo Diesel		F		4450	4450	5930	5930
V10 6.8 Liter		S		575	575	765	765
SUPER DUTY SUPER CAB PICKUP—V8—Truck Equip Sch T1							
F250 Short Bed		X20L	24620	9150	10425	12100	14750
F250 Long Bed		X20L	24820	8850	10125	11750	14350
F350 Short Bed		X30L	25410	9425	10750	12450	15100
F350 Long Bed		X30L	25610	9150	10425	12100	14750
4WD		1		1575	1575	2100	2100
V8 7.3L Turbo Diesel		F		4450	4450	5930	5930
V10 6.8 Liter		S		575	575	765	765
SUPER DUTY CREW CAB PICKUP—V8—Truck Equip Sch T1							
F250 Short Bed		W20L	25930	10275	11675	13400	16200
F250 Long Bed		W20L	26130	9975	11375	13100	15900
F350 Short Bed		W30L	26590	10550	11950	13700	16500
F350 Long Bed		W30L	26790	10275	11675	13400	16200
4WD		1		1575	1575	2100	2100
V8 7.3L Turbo Diesel		F		4450	4450	5930	5930
V10 6.8 Liter		S		575	575	765	765

2001 FORD — (1or2)F(B,MorT)–(U021)–1–#

Body	Type	VIN	List	Trade-In Fair	Trade-In Good	Pvt-Party Good	Retail Excellent
ESCAPE 4WD—V6—Truck Equipment Schedule T1							
XLS Sport Utility 4D		U021	21185	6425	7450	9475	12400
XLT Sport Utility 4D		U041	22815	7100	8200	10350	13500

TRUCKS & VANS

Body	Type	VIN	List	Trade-In Fair	Good	Pvt-Party Good	Retail Excellent
2WD				(800)	(800)	(1065)	(1065)
4-Cyl. 2.0 Liter		B		(825)	(825)	(1100)	(1100)
EXPLORER SPORT 4WD—V6—Truck Equipment Schedule T1							
Sport Utility 2D		U70E	24435	5500	6400	8450	11350
2WD		6		(800)	(800)	(1065)	(1065)
EXPLORER 4WD—V6—Truck Equipment Schedule T1							
XLS Sport Utility 4D		U71E	27570	6925	8000	10150	13200
2WD		6		(800)	(800)	(1065)	(1065)
AWD		8		0	0	0	0
V8 5.0 Liter		P		350	350	465	465
EXPLORER SPORT TRAC 4WD—V6—Truck Equipment Sch T1							
Utility Pickup 4D		U77E	25010	7775	8925	11150	14350
2WD		6		(800)	(800)	(1065)	(1065)
EXPEDITION 4WD—V8—Truck Equipment Schedule T1							
XLT Sport Utility 4D		U16W	33405	9700	11050	13700	17500
w/o Third Seat				(925)	(925)	(1235)	(1235)
2WD		5		(1400)	(1400)	(1865)	(1865)
V8 5.4 Liter		L		375	375	500	500
EXCURSION 4WD—V10—Truck Equipment Schedule T1							
XLT Sport Utility 4D		U41S	38925	11750	13300	15950	19850
w/o Third Seat				(925)	(925)	(1235)	(1235)
2WD		0		(1400)	(1400)	(1865)	(1865)
V8 5.4 Liter		L		(500)	(500)	(665)	(665)
V8 7.3L Turbo Diesel		F		4700	4700	6265	6265
WINDSTAR—V6—Truck Equipment Schedule T1							
Cargo Minivan		A544	20540	3325	4025	5550	7700
WINDSTAR—V6—Truck Equipment Schedule T1							
LX Minivan		A514	25320	4925	5775	7400	9750
SE Sport Minivan		A574	27755	5300	6200	7825	10200
SE Minivan		A524	28915	5425	6325	8000	10400
SEL Minivan		A534	31435	6450	7475	9175	11700
Limited Minivan		A584	34085	8075	9250	11050	13800
w/o 2nd Sliding Door		0		(650)	(650)	(865)	(865)
ECONOLINE WAGON—V8—Truck Equipment Schedule T1							
E150 Passenger Van		E11W	24060	6000	6950	8975	11850
E350 Super Duty		E31L	26350	6250	7250	9275	12200
E350 Super Duty Ext.		S31L	27970	6525	7525	9600	12600
V6 4.2 Liter		2		(600)	(600)	(800)	(800)
V8 7.3L Turbo Diesel		F		2725	2725	3630	3630
V10 6.8 Liter		S		700	700	935	935
ECONOLINE VAN—V6—Truck Equipment Schedule T1							
E150 Cargo Van		E142	21175	5925	6900	8475	10850
E250 Cargo Van		E24L	22445	6050	7000	8600	11000
E350 Super Cargo		E34L	24875	6400	7425	9025	11450
Super Van		S		200	200	265	265
Crew Van Pkg				300	300	400	400
V8 4.6, 5.4 Liter		W,L		300	300	400	400
V8 7.3L Turbo Diesel		F		3150	3150	4200	4200
V10 6.8 Liter		S		1400	1400	1865	1865
RANGER PICKUP—4-Cyl.—Truck Equipment Schedule T2							
XL Short Bed		R10C	12400	2875	3525	4850	6775
XL Long Bed		R10C	13515	2550	3175	4475	6325
XL Super Cab 2D		R16C	16465	3825	4550	5925	7975
XL Super Cab 4D		R14C	20960	4725	5550	6975	9150
4WD		1,5		1800	1800	2400	2400
V6 3.0 Liter		U		400	400	535	535
V6 4.0 Liter		E		550	550	735	735
REGULAR CAB PICKUP—V8—Truck Equipment Schedule T1							
F150 Short Bed		F17W	20170	6300	7300	8700	10900
F150 Long Bed		F17W	20470	5925	6900	8250	10400
4WD		6,8		1750	1750	2335	2335
Work Truck				(975)	(975)	(1300)	(1300)
V6 4.2 Liter		2		(700)	(700)	(935)	(935)
V8 5.4 Liter		L,Z		375	375	500	500
REGULAR CAB PICKUP—V8 Supercharged—Truck Sch T1							
F150 Lightning		F073	32460	12900	14600	16400	19500
SUPER CAB PICKUP—V8—Truck Equipment Schedule T1							
F150 Short Bed		X17W	22855	8350	9575	11100	13600
F150 Long Bed		X17W	23155	8000	9175	10650	13100
4WD		6,8		1750	1750	2335	2335
Work Truck				(975)	(975)	(1300)	(1300)
V6 4.2 Liter		2		(700)	(700)	(935)	(935)
V8 5.4 Liter		L,Z		375	375	500	500

Body Type	VIN	List	Trade-In Fair	Trade-In Good	Pvt-Party Good	Retail Excellent
SUPERCREW PICKUP—V8—Truck Equipment Schedule T1						
F150 Short Bed 4D	W07W	26940	9600	10950	12550	15150
F150 King Ranch	W07W	31455	11125	12625	14350	17200
F150 HarleyDavidson	W07L	34495	14825	16700	18650	22000
4WD	8		1750	1750	2335	2335
V8 5.4 Liter	L		375	375	500	500
SUPER DUTY REGULAR CAB—V8—Truck Equipment Sch T1						
F250 Long Bed	F20L	23155	8125	9325	10850	13300
F350 Long Bed	F30L	23580	8450	9650	11200	13700
4WD	1		1750	1750	2335	2335
V8 7.3L Turbo Diesel	F		4700	4700	6265	6265
V10 6.8 Liter	S		600	600	800	800
SUPER DUTY SUPER CAB—V8—Truck Equipment Schedule T1						
F250 Short Bed	X20L	25295	10500	11950	13650	16350
F250 Long Bed	X20L	25495	10175	11575	13250	15950
F350 Short Bed	X30L	26085	10850	12300	14000	16800
F350 Long Bed	X30L	26285	10500	11950	13650	16350
4WD	1		1750	1750	2335	2335
V8 7.3L Turbo Diesel	F		4700	4700	6265	6265
V10 6.8 Liter	S		600	600	800	800
SUPER DUTY CREW CAB—V8—Truck Equipment Schedule T1						
F250 Short Bed	W20L	25295	11750	13300	15050	17950
F250 Long Bed	W20L	26805	11475	13000	14750	17600
F350 Short Bed	W30L	27265	12050	13625	15400	18350
F350 Long Bed	W30L	27465	11750	13300	15050	17950
Platinum Edition			350	350	465	465
4WD	1		1750	1750	2335	2335
V8 7.3L Turbo Diesel	F		4700	4700	6265	6265
V10 6.8 Liter	S		600	600	800	800

2002 FORD — (1or2)F(B,MorT)–(U021)–2–#

Body Type	VIN	List	Trade-In Fair	Trade-In Good	Pvt-Party Good	Retail Excellent
ESCAPE 4WD—V6—Truck Equipment Schedule T1						
XLS Sport Utility 4D	U021	21910	7725	8875	11050	14200
XLT Sport Utility 4D	U041	23935	8450	9650	11950	15300
2WD			(875)	(875)	(1165)	(1165)
4-Cyl. 2.0 Liter	B		(925)	(925)	(1235)	(1235)
EXPLORER SPORT 4WD—V6—Truck Equipment Schedule T1						
Sport Utility 2D	U70E	24785	7625	8750	11000	14250
2WD	6		(875)	(875)	(1165)	(1165)
EXPLORER 4WD—V6—Truck Equipment Schedule T1						
XLS Sport Utility 4D	U71E	27775	9225	10500	12800	16200
Third Seat			650	650	865	865
2WD	6		(875)	(875)	(1165)	(1165)
V8 4.6 Liter	W		400	400	535	535
EXPLORER SPORT TRAC 4WD—V6—Truck Equipment Sch T1						
Utility Pickup 4D	U77E	25410	9900	11225	13600	17100
2WD			(875)	(875)	(1165)	(1165)
EXPEDITION 4WD—V8—Truck Equipment Schedule T1						
XLT Sport Utility 4D	U16W	33810	11525	13050	15950	20200
w/o Third Seat			(1000)	(1000)	(1335)	(1335)
2WD	5		(1450)	(1450)	(1935)	(1935)
V8 5.4 Liter	L		400	400	535	535
EXCURSION 4WD—V10—Truck Equipment Schedule T1						
XLT Sport Utility 4D	U41S	38985	13825	15600	18350	22600
w/o Third Seat			(1000)	(1000)	(1335)	(1335)
2WD			(1450)	(1450)	(1935)	(1935)
V8 5.4 Liter	L		(500)	(500)	(665)	(665)
V8 7.3L Turbo Diesel	F		4950	4950	6600	6600
WINDSTAR—V6—Truck Equipment Schedule T2						
Cargo Minivan	A544	20905	4350	5125	6775	9125
WINDSTAR—V6—Truck Equipment Schedule T1						
LX Minivan	A514	22995	6100	7075	8800	11400
SE Minivan	A524	29280	6650	7675	9425	12050
SEL Minivan	A534	31950	7825	8975	10800	13550
Limited Minivan	A584	34360	9600	10950	12800	15800
w/ 2nd Sliding Door	0		(700)	(700)	(935)	(935)
ECONOLINE WAGON—V8—Truck Equipment Schedule T1						
E150 Passenger Van	E1W	24660	7600	8725	11000	14200
E350 Super Duty	E31L	26950	7900	9075	11300	14550
E350 Super Duty Ext	S31L	28370	8175	9375	11650	14950
V6 4.2 Liter	2		(650)	(650)	(865)	(865)
V8 7.3L Turbo Diesel	F		2925	2925	3900	3900
V10 6.8 Liter	S		725	725	965	965

Body	Type	VIN	List	Trade-In Fair	Good	Pvt-Party Good	Retail Excellent
ECONOLINE VAN—V6—Truck Equipment Schedule T1							
E150 Cargo Van		E142	21880	7450	8575	10250	12850
E250 Cargo Van		E242	22750	7550	8700	10400	13050
E350 Super Cargo		E34L	25230	8000	9175	10900	13600
Super Van		S		225	225	300	300
Crew Van Pkg				325	325	435	435
V8 4.6, 5.4 Liter		W,L		325	325	435	435
V8 7.3L Turbo Diesel		F		3450	3450	4600	4600
V10 6.8 Liter				1450	1450	1935	1935
RANGER PICKUP—4-Cyl.—Truck Equipment Schedule T2							
XL Short Bed		R10C	12725	3625	4350	5750	7825
XL Long Bed		R10C	13655	3300	3950	5375	7400
XL Super Cab 2D		R14C	16400	6625	5475	6925	9125
XL Super Cab 4D		R14C	18075	5650	6550	8100	10350
4WD		1,5		1975	1975	2635	2635
V6 3.0 Liter		U		450	450	600	600
V6 4.0 Liter		E		600	600	800	800
REGULAR CAB PICKUP—V8—Truck Equipment Schedule T1							
F150 Short Bed		F17W	20640	7525	8675	10100	12350
F150 Long Bed		F17W	20940	7125	8225	9600	11850
4WD		6,8		1925	1925	2565	2565
Work Truck				(1125)	(1125)	(1500)	(1500)
V6 4.2 Liter		2		(750)	(750)	(1000)	(1000)
V8 5.4 Liter		L,Z		400	400	535	535
REGULAR CAB PICKUP—V8 Supercharged—Truck Sch T1							
F150 Lightning		F073	32490	14825	16700	18550	21700
SUPER CAB PICKUP—V8—Truck Equipment Schedule T1							
F150 Short Bed		X17W	23290	9800	11175	12700	15250
F150 Long Bed		X17W	22840	9375	10700	12250	14750
F150 King Ranch		X17W	29735	10900	12375	13950	16650
4WD		6,8		1925	1925	2565	2565
Work Truck				(1125)	(1125)	(1500)	(1500)
V6 4.2 Liter		2		(750)	(750)	(1000)	(1000)
V8 5.4 Liter		L,Z		400	400	535	535
SUPERCREW PICKUP—V8—Truck Equipment Schedule T1							
F150 Short Bed 4D		W07W	27660	11175	12675	14250	17000
F150 King Ranch 4D		W07W	32135	12875	14550	16200	19150
4WD		8		1925	1925	2565	2565
V8 5.4 Liter		L		400	400	535	535
SUPERCREW PICKUP—V8 Supercharged—Truck Equip Sch T1							
F150 HarleyDavidson		W073	36520	17050	19150	21000	24500
SUPER DUTY REGULAR CAB PICKUP—V8—Truck Equip Sch T1							
F250 Long Bed		F20L	22725	9550	10900	12450	15000
F350 Long Bed		F30L	23985	9850	11225	12750	15350
4WD		1		1925	1925	2565	2565
V8 7.3L Turbo Diesel		F		4950	4950	6600	6600
V10 6.8 Liter		S		625	625	835	835
SUPER DUTY SUPER CAB PICKUP—V8—Truck Equip Sch T1							
F250 Short Bed		X20L	25715	12100	13725	15400	18250
F250 Long Bed		X20L	25915	11750	13350	15000	17800
F350 Short Bed		X30L	26505	12475	14100	15850	18700
F350 Long Bed		X30L	26705	12100	13725	15400	18250
4WD		1		1925	1925	2565	2565
V8 7.3L Turbo Diesel		F		4950	4950	6600	6600
V10 6.8 Liter		S		625	625	835	835
SUPER DUTY CREW CAB PICKUP—V8—Truck Equipment Sch T1							
F250 Short Bed		W20L	27025	13500	15225	16950	19950
F250 Long Bed		W20L	27225	13150	14875	16600	19600
F350 Short Bed		W30L	27685	13775	15550	17350	20400
F350 Long Bed		W30L	27885	13500	15225	16950	19950
4WD		1		1925	1925	2565	2565
V8 7.3L Turbo Diesel		F		4950	4950	6600	6600
V10 6.8 Liter		S		625	625	835	835

2003 FORD — (1or2)F(B,MorT)—(U921)–3–#

Body	Type	VIN	List	Trade-In Fair	Good	Pvt-Party Good	Retail Excellent
ESCAPE 4WD—V6 Flex Fuel—Truck Equipment Schedule T1							
XLS Sport Utility 4D		U921	22550	9300	10600	12850	16200
XLT Sport Utility 4D		U931	25475	10025	11425	13800	17350
Limited Sport Util 4D		U941	27475	10800	12250	14700	18300
2WD		0		(950)	(950)	(1265)	(1265)
4-Cyl. 2.0 Liter		B		(1025)	(1025)	(1365)	(1365)
EXPLORER SPORT 4WD—V6—Truck Equipment Schedule T1							
Sport Utility 2D		U70E	25825	9150	10425	12750	16200

SEE BACK PAGES FOR TRUCK EQUIPMENT

Body Type	VIN	List	Trade-In Fair	Trade-In Good	Pvt-Party Good	Retail Excellent
2WD	6		(950)	(950)	(1265)	(1265)
EXPLORER 4WD—V6 Flex Fuel—Truck Equipment Schedule T1						
XLS Sport Utility 4D	U72K	28470	10900	12325	14800	18400
Third Seat			700	700	935	935
2WD	6		(950)	(950)	(1265)	(1265)
AWD	8		0	0	0	0
V8 4.6 Liter	W		450	450	600	600
EXPLORER SPORT TRAC 4WD—V6—Truck Equipment Sch T1						
XLS Util Pickup 4D	U77E	26185	11625	13150	15600	19300
2WD	6		(950)	(950)	(1265)	(1265)
EXPEDITION 4WD—V8—Truck Equipment Schedule T1						
XLT Sport Utility 4D	U16W	34145	14450	16425	19600	24300
w/o Third Seat			(1075)	(1075)	(1435)	(1435)
2WD	5,7		(1500)	(1500)	(2000)	(2000)
V8 5.4 Liter	L		400	400	535	535
EXCURSION 4WD—V10—Truck Equipment Schedule T1						
XLT Sport Utility 4D	U41S	39635	16175	18250	21200	25800
w/o Third Seat			(700)	(700)	(935)	(935)
2WD	0,2,4		(1500)	(1500)	(2000)	(2000)
V8 5.4 Liter	L		(500)	(500)	(665)	(665)
V8 6.0L Turbo Diesel	P		5500	5500	7330	7330
V8 7.3L Turbo Diesel	F		5200	5200	6930	6930
WINDSTAR—V6—Truck Equipment Schedule T2						
Cargo Minivan	A544	21360	5675	6600	8225	10650
WINDSTAR—V6—Truck Equipment Schedule T1						
LX Minivan	A514	23365	7575	8700	10450	13100
SE Minivan	A524	29675	8175	9375	11150	13800
SEL Minivan	A534	32405	9425	10750	12600	15500
Limited Minivan	A584	35110	11425	12950	14900	17950
w/o 2nd Sliding Door	0		(750)	(750)	(1000)	(1000)
ECONOLINE WAGON—V8—Truck Equipment Schedule T1						
E150 Passenger Van	E11W	25250	9700	11100	13450	16950
E350 Super Duty	E31L	24790	9975	11375	13800	17350
E350 Super Duty Ext	S31L	28910	10375	11800	14200	17800
V6 4.2 Liter	2		(700)	(700)	(935)	(935)
V8 7.3L Turbo Diesel	F		3125	3125	4165	4165
V10 6.8 Liter	S		750	750	1000	1000
ECONOLINE VAN—V6—Truck Equipment Schedule T1						
E150 Super Cargo	E142	22420	9425	10750	12500	15200
E250 Super Cargo	E242	23390	9550	10900	12600	15350
E350 Super Cargo	E34L	25770	9975	11375	13150	15950
Super Van	S		250	250	335	335
Crew Van Pkg			350	350	465	465
V8 4.6, 5.4 Liter	W,L		350	350	465	465
V8 7.3L Turbo Diesel	F		3750	3750	5000	5000
V10 6.8 Liter	S		1500	1500	2000	2000
RANGER PICKUP—4-Cyl.—Truck Equipment Schedule T2						
XL Short Bed	R10D	13620	4600	5425	6800	8875
XL Long Bed	R10D	14370	4225	5025	6350	8400
XL Super Cab 2D	R14U	17320	5700	6625	8075	10250
XL Super Cab 4D	R44E	18605	6775	7800	9300	11650
4WD	1,5		2150	2150	2865	2865
V6 3.0 Liter	U		500	500	665	665
V6 4.0 Liter	E		650	650	865	865
REGULAR CAB PICKUP—V8—Truck Equipment Schedule T1						
F150 Short Bed	F17W	21300	9050	10325	11650	13900
F150 Long Bed	F17W	21600	8650	9900	11200	13400
4WD	6,8		2100	2100	2800	2800
Work Truck			(1275)	(1275)	(1700)	(1700)
V6 4.2 Liter	2		(800)	(800)	(1065)	(1065)
V8 5.4 Liter	L,Z		400	400	535	535
REGULAR CAB PICKUP—V8 Supercharged—Truck Sch T1						
F150 Lightning	F073	33255	17100	19200	20900	24100
SUPER CAB PICKUP—V8—Truck Equipment Schedule T1						
F150 Short Bed	X17W	23950	11525	13050	14500	17050
F150 Long Bed	X17W	24250	11100	12575	13950	16450
F150 King Ranch 4D	X17W	31660	12725	14400	15900	18600
4WD	6,8		2100	2100	2800	2800
Work Truck			(1275)	(1275)	(1700)	(1700)
V6 4.2 Liter	2		(800)	(800)	(1065)	(1065)
V8 5.4 Liter	L,Z		400	400	535	535
SUPERCREW PICKUP—V8—Truck Equipment Schedule T1						
F150 Short Bed 4D	W07W	28320	13000	14725	16200	18950

Body	Type	VIN	List	Trade-In Fair	Trade-In Good	Pvt-Party Good	Retail Excellent
F150 King Ranch 4D	W07W	33115	14825	16700	18350	21200
4WD		8		2100	2100	2800	2800
V8 5.4 Liter		L		400	400	535	535
SUPERCREW PICKUP—V8 Supercharged—Truck Equip Sch T1							
F150 HarleyDavidson	W073	37295	19500	21900	23700	27200
SUPER DUTY REGULAR CAB PICKUP—V8—Truck Sch T1							
F250 Long Bed	F20L	23760	11225	12775	14200	16700
F350 Long Bed	F30L	24215	11575	13100	14550	17100
4WD		1		2100	2100	2800	2800
V8 6.0L Turbo Diesel		P		5500	5500	7330	7330
V8 7.3L Turbo Diesel		F		5200	5200	6930	6930
V10 6.8 Liter		S		650	650	865	865
SUPER DUTY SUPER CAB PICKUP—V8—Truck Sch T1							
F250 Short Bed	X20L	25945	14075	15850	17400	20300
F250 Long Bed	X20L	26145	13675	15450	17000	19800
F350 Short Bed	X30L	26735	14400	16275	17850	20700
F350 Long Bed	X30L	26935	14075	15850	17400	20300
4WD		1		2100	2100	2800	2800
V8 6.0L Turbo Diesel		P		5500	5500	7330	7330
V8 7.3L Turbo Diesel		F		5200	5200	6930	6930
V10 6.8 Liter		S		650	650	865	865
SUPER DUTY CREW CAB PICKUP—V8—Truck Equipment Sch T1							
F250 Short Bed	W20L	27355	15550	17525	19150	22200
F250 King Ranch 6'	W20L	36460	16700	18775	20400	23600
F250 Long Bed	W20L	27555	15175	17100	18700	21700
F250 King Ranch 8'	W20L	36660	16275	18325	19950	23000
F350 Short Bed	W30L	28015	15900	17850	19500	22600
F350 King Ranch 6'	W30L	37325	17050	19150	20800	24000
F350 Long Bed	W30L	28215	15550	17525	19150	22200
F350 King Ranch 8'	W30L	37525	16700	18775	20400	23600
4WD		1		2100	2100	2800	2800
V8 6.0L Turbo Diesel		P		5500	5500	7330	7330
V8 7.3L Turbo Diesel		F		5200	5200	6930	6930
V10 6.8 Liter		S		650	650	865	865

2004 FORD—(1or2)F(B,MorT)–(U921)–4–#

Body	Type	VIN	List	Trade-In Fair	Trade-In Good	Pvt-Party Good	Retail Excellent
ESCAPE 4WD—V6—Truck Equipment Schedule T1							
XLS Sport Utility 4D	U921	22515	11175	12675	15050	18700
XLT Sport Utility 4D	U931	24770	11900	13500	16050	19850
Limited Sport Util 4D	U941	26830	12725	14400	17000	20900
2WD		0		(1000)	(1000)	(1335)	(1335)
4-Cyl. 2.0 Liter		B		(1125)	(1125)	(1500)	(1500)
EXPLORER 4WD—V6 Flex Fuel—Truck Equipment Schedule T1							
XLS Sport Utility 4D	U72K	29155	12875	14550	17150	21100
Third Seat				750	750	1000	1000
2WD		6		(1000)	(1000)	(1335)	(1335)
AWD		8		0	0	0	0
V8 4.6 Liter		W		475	475	635	635
EXPLORER SPORT TRAC 4WD—V6 Flex Fuel—Truck Sch T1							
XLS Utility Pickup	U77K	26460	13625	15400	18050	22100
2WD		6		(1000)	(1000)	(1335)	(1335)
EXPEDITION 4WD—V8—Truck Equipment Schedule T1							
XLS Sport Utility 4D	U16W	35305	17425	19575	22900	28000
w/o Third Seat				(1150)	(1150)	(1535)	(1535)
2WD		3,5,7		(1550)	(1550)	(2065)	(2065)
V8 5.4 Liter		L		400	400	535	535
EXCURSION 4WD—V10—Truck Equipment Schedule T1							
XLS Sport Utility 4D	U41S	40485	19100	21400	24700	29700
w/o Third Seat				(1150)	(1150)	(1535)	(1535)
2WD		0,2,4		(1550)	(1550)	(2065)	(2065)
V8 5.4 Liter		L		(500)	(500)	(665)	(665)
V8 6.0L Turbo Diesel		P		5775	5775	7700	7700
FREESTAR—V6—Truck Equipment Schedule T2							
Cargo Minivan	A546	22070	9700	11100	12900	15850
FREESTAR—V6—Truck Equipment Schedule T1							
S Minivan	A546	24460	11275	12825	14800	17900
SE Minivan	A526	26930	11700	13250	15250	18450
SES Minivan	A576	28750	12050	13675	15700	18900
SEL Minivan	A532	29995	12475	14100	16200	19500
Limited Minivan	A582	33630	12875	14550	16600	19950
ECONOLINE WAGON—V8—Truck Equipment Schedule T1							
E150 Passenger Van	E11W	25255	12425	14075	16800	20800
E350 Super Duty	E31L	27995	12775	14450	17200	21300

TRUCKS & VANS

Body / Type	VIN	List	Trade-In Fair	Trade-In Good	Pvt-Party Good	Retail Excellent
E350 Super Duty Ext.	S31L	29415	13150	14875	17550	21700
V8 6.0L Turbo Diesel	P		3325	3325	4430	4430
V10 6.8 Liter	S		775	775	1035	1035
ECONOLINE VAN—V8—Truck Equipment Schedule T1						
E150 Super Cargo	E14W	23060	12000	13575	15450	18550
E250 Super Cargo	E24W	24105	12100	13725	15600	18700
E350 Super Cargo	E34L	26110	12625	14250	16200	19400
Super Van	S		275	275	365	365
Crew Van Pkg.			375	375	500	500
V8 5.4 Liter	L		375	375	500	500
V8 6.0L Turbo Diesel	P		5775	5775	7700	7700
V10 6.8 Liter	S		1550	1550	2065	2065
RANGER PICKUP—4-Cyl.—Truck Equipment Schedule T2						
XL Short Bed	R10D	14385	6050	7000	8450	10650
XL Long Bed	R10D	15135	5650	6575	7975	10150
XL Super Cab 2D	R14U	18120	7225	8300	9850	12200
XL Super Cab 4D	R44E	19405	8400	9600	11200	13750
4WD	1,5		2325	2325	3100	3100
V6 3.0 Liter	U		525	525	700	700
V6 4.0 Liter	E		700	700	935	935
HERITAGE REGULAR CAB PICKUP—V8—Truck Equipment Schedule T1						
F150 Short Bed	F17W	21765	11675	13200	14450	16800
F150 Long Bed	F17W	22065	11125	12625	13800	16100
Work Truck			(1400)	(1400)	(1865)	(1865)
4WD	6,8		2275	2275	3035	3035
V6 4.2 Liter	2		(850)	(850)	(1135)	(1135)
V8 5.4L Bi-Fuel			400	400	535	535
REGULAR CAB PICKUP—V8 Supercharged—Truck Equip Sch T1						
F150 Lightning	F073	33560	21600	24300	26000	29500
HERITAGE SUPER CAB PICKUP—V8—Truck Equipment Sch T1						
F150 Short Bed	X17W	24115	14250	16075	17450	20200
F150 Long Bed	X17W	24715	13825	15600	17000	19600
Work Truck			(1400)	(1400)	(1865)	(1865)
4WD	8		2275	2275	3035	3035
V6 4.2 Liter	2		(850)	(850)	(1135)	(1135)
V8 5.4L Bi-Fuel			400	400	535	535
REGULAR CAB PICKUP—V8—Truck Equipment Schedule T1						
F150 Short Bed	F12W	22010	12950	14600	15950	18450
F150 Long Bed	F12W	22310	12475	14100	15400	17850
4WD	4		2275	2275	3035	3035
V8 5.4 Liter	5		400	400	535	535
SUPER CAB PICKUP—V8—Truck Equipment Schedule T1						
F150 5 1/2'	X12W	25010	15600	17575	19000	21800
F150 6 1/2'	X12W	24660	15600	17575	19000	21800
F150 8'	X12W	24960	15125	17050	18500	21200
4WD	4		2275	2275	3035	3035
V8 5.4 Liter	5		400	400	535	535
SUPERCREW PICKUP—V8—Truck Equipment Schedule T1						
F150 Short Bed 4D	W12W	29815	17175	19300	20800	23800
4WD	4		2275	2275	3035	3035
V8 5.4 Liter	5		400	400	535	535
SUPER DUTY REGULAR CAB PICKUP—V8—Truck Equip Sch T1						
F250 Long Bed	F20L	24430	13350	15075	16450	19000
F350 Long Bed	F30L	24885	13725	15500	16900	19500
4WD			2275	2275	3035	3035
V8 6.0L Turbo Diesel	P		5775	5775	7700	7700
V10 6.8 Liter	S		675	675	900	900
SUPER DUTY SUPER CAB PICKUP—V8—Truck Equipment Sch T1						
F250 Short Bed	X20L	26615	16375	18425	19950	22800
F250 Harley 6'	X20S	39890	24100	26975	28900	32600
F250 Long Bed	X20L	26815	15975	18000	19500	22400
F250 Harley 8'	X20S	40090	23700	26500	28400	32200
F350 Short Bed	X30L	27405	16750	18875	20400	23400
F350 Harley 6'	X31S	40895	24575	27450	29300	33100
F350 Long Bed	X30L	27605	16375	18425	19950	22800
F350 Harley 8'	X31S	41095	24100	26975	28900	32600
4WD			2275	2275	3035	3035
V8 6.0L Turbo Diesel	P		5775	5775	7700	7700
V10 6.8 Liter	S		675	675	900	900
SUPER DUTY CREW CAB PICKUP—V8—Truck Equipment Sch T1						
F250 Short Bed	W20L	28025	17950	20150	21800	24900
F250 King Ranch 6'	W20L	37350	19150	21500	23200	26500
F250 Harley 6'	W21S	42385	25725	28700	30600	34600

Body	Type	VIN	List	Trade-In Fair	Trade-In Good	Pvt-Party Good	Retail Excellent
F250	Long Bed	W20L	28225	17525	19675	21300	24400
F250	King Ranch 8'	W20L	37550	18775	21025	22800	25900
F250	Harley 8'	W21S	42585	25250	28225	30100	34100
F350	Short Bed	W30L	28685	18325	20650	22300	25400
F350	King Ranch 6'	W30L	38215	19575	21975	23700	27100
F350	Harley 6'	W35S	43000	26100	29175	31100	35000
F350	Long Bed	W30L	28885	17950	20150	21800	24900
F350	King Ranch 8'	W30L	38415	19150	21500	23200	26500
F350	Harley 8'	W35S	43200	25725	28700	30600	34600
4WD		1		2275	2275	3035	3035
V8 6.0L Turbo Diesel		P		5775	5775	7700	7700
V10 6.8 Liter		S		675	675	900	900

GMC — See CHEVROLET TRUCKS

GEO

1990 GEO — JGC-(J18U)-L-#

TRACKER 4WD—4-Cyl.—Truck Equipment Schedule T2

Type	VIN	List	Fair	Good	P-P Good	Retail
Sport Utility 2D	J18U	11607	325	475	1050	1925
Spt Utility Conv 2D	J18U	11297	325	475	1025	1925
LSi Sport Utility 2D	J18U	12515	450	650	1275	2250
LSi Spt Util Conv 2D	J18U	12065	425	625	1225	2175

1991 GEO — JGC-(J18U)-M-#

TRACKER 4WD—4-Cyl.—Truck Equipment Schedule T2

Type	VIN	List	Fair	Good	P-P Good	Retail
Sport Utility 2D	J18U	11867	375	550	1200	2175
Spt Utility Conv 2D	J18U	11467	375	525	1150	2125
LSi Sport Utility 2D	J18U	12865	500	725	1425	2525
LSi Spt Util Conv 2D	J18U	12275	475	675	1350	2425
2WD	E		(325)	(325)	(435)	(435)

1992 GEO — JGC-(J18U)-N-#

TRACKER 4WD—4-Cyl.—Truck Equipment Schedule T2

Type	VIN	List	Fair	Good	P-P Good	Retail
Sport Utility 2D	J18U	12502	375	525	1200	2250
Spt Utility Conv 2D	J18U	12102	350	500	1200	2225
LSi Sport Utility 2D	J18U	13500	525	750	1500	2700
LSi Spt Util Conv 2D	J18U	12900	475	700	1450	2600
2WD	E		(350)	(350)	(465)	(465)

1993 GEO — 2CC-(J18U)-P-#

TRACKER 4WD—4-Cyl.—Truck Equipment Schedule T2

Type	VIN	List	Fair	Good	P-P Good	Retail
Sport Utility 2D	J18U	12351	375	525	1275	2400
Spt Utility Conv 2D	J18U	12186	350	500	1250	2350
LSi Sport Utility 2D	J18U	13250	550	775	1600	2900
LSi Spt Util Conv 2D	J18U	12985	525	750	1525	2800
2WD	E		(375)	(375)	(500)	(500)

1994 GEO — 2CC-(J18U)-R-#

TRACKER 4WD—4-Cyl.—Truck Equipment Schedule T2

Type	VIN	List	Fair	Good	P-P Good	Retail
Sport Utility 2D	J18U	12901	400	600	1400	2650
Spt Utility Conv 2D	J18U	12741	400	575	1375	2600
LSi Sport Utility 2D	J18U	14065	625	900	1825	3250
LSi Spt Util Conv 2D	J18U	13800	575	825	1700	3100
2WD	E		(400)	(400)	(535)	(535)

1995 GEO — 2C(CorN)-(J186)-S-#

TRACKER 4WD—4-Cyl.—Truck Equipment Schedule T2

Type	VIN	List	Fair	Good	P-P Good	Retail
Sport Utility 2D	J186	13631	500	725	1625	3025
Spt Utility Conv 2D	J186	13551	475	700	1575	2975
LSi Sport Utility 2D	J186	14795	750	1025	2200	3875
LSi Spt Util Conv 2D	J186	14615	675	950	2000	3525
2WD	E		(425)	(425)	(565)	(565)

1996 GEO — 2C(CorN)-(J186)-T-#

TRACKER 4WD—4-Cyl.—Truck Equipment Schedule T2

Type	VIN	List	Fair	Good	P-P Good	Retail
Spt Utility Conv 2D	J186	15071	625	900	1900	3425
Sport Utility 4D	J136	15941	975	1425	2700	4450

TRUCKS & VANS

Body	Type	VIN	List	Trade-In Fair	Good	Pvt-Party Good	Retail Excellent
LSi Spt Util Conv 2D		J186	15501	**825**	**1150**	**2375**	**4100**
LSi Sport Utility 4D		J136	16331	**1275**	**1750**	**3100**	**4950**
2WD		E		**(450)**	**(450)**	**(600)**	**(600)**

1997 GEO — 2C(CorN)–(J186)–V–#

TRACKER 4WD—4-Cyl.—Truck Equipment Schedule T2
Spt Utility Conv 2D		J186	15096	**800**	**1125**	**2375**	**4150**
Sport Utility 4D		J136	15966	**1225**	**1700**	**3075**	**4950**
LSi Sport Utility 4D		J186	16356	**1575**	**2100**	**3525**	**5475**
2WD		E		**(475)**	**(475)**	**(635)**	**(635)**

HONDA

1994 HONDA — 4S6(CG58E)–R–#

PASSPORT—4-Cyl.—Truck Equipment Schedule T1
DX Sport Utility 4D		CG58E	16035	**1175**	**1625**	**2850**	**4550**
Manual Trans				**(175)**	**(175)**	**(235)**	**(235)**

PASSPORT 4WD—V6—Truck Equipment Schedule T1
LX Sport Utility 4D		CY58V	22825	**2200**	**2775**	**4150**	**6100**
EX Sport Utility 4D		CY58V	25375	**2625**	**3250**	**4675**	**6725**
2WD		G		**(400)**	**(400)**	**(535)**	**(535)**

1995 HONDA — (JHMor4S6)(CG58E)–S–#

PASSPORT—4-Cyl.—Truck Equipment Schedule T1
DX Sport Utility 4D		CG58E	16610	**1400**	**1875**	**3200**	**5025**
Dual Air Bags				**0**	**0**	**0**	**0**
Manual Trans				**(200)**	**(200)**	**(265)**	**(265)**

PASSPORT 4WD—V6—Truck Equipment Schedule T1
LX Sport Utility 4D		CY58V	23580	**2550**	**3150**	**4600**	**6675**
EX Sport Utility 4D		CY58V	26930	**2975**	**3650**	**5175**	**7350**
2WD		G		**(425)**	**(425)**	**(565)**	**(565)**
Dual Air Bags				**0**	**0**	**0**	**0**

ODYSSEY—4-Cyl.—Truck Equipment Schedule T1
LX Minivan 4D		RA184	23380	**3475**	**4175**	**5625**	**7700**
EX Minivan 4D		RA187	25390	**3675**	**4400**	**5850**	**7975**

1996 HONDA — (JHMor4S6)(CK58E)–T–#

PASSPORT—4-Cyl.—Truck Equipment Schedule T1
DX Sport Utility 4D		CK58E	18385	**1700**	**2225**	**3650**	**5600**
Manual Trans				**(225)**	**(225)**	**(300)**	**(300)**

PASSPORT 4WD—V6—Truck Equipment Schedule T1
LX Sport Utility 4D		CM58V	25380	**2950**	**3600**	**5150**	**7350**
EX Sport Utility 4D		CM58V	29425	**3425**	**4150**	**5775**	**8100**
2WD		G		**(450)**	**(450)**	**(600)**	**(600)**

ODYSSEY—4-Cyl.—Truck Equipment Schedule T1
LX Minivan 4D		RA184	23955	**3900**	**4650**	**6200**	**8375**
EX Minivan 4D		RA187	25945	**4125**	**4900**	**6425**	**8675**

1997 HONDA–(JHL,JHMor4S6)(RD184)–V

CR-V 4WD—4-Cyl.—Truck Equipment Schedule T2
Sport Utility 4D		RD184	19695	**4550**	**5375**	**6875**	**9075**

PASSPORT 4WD—V6—Truck Equipment Schedule T1
LX Sport Utility 4D		CM58V	25895	**3425**	**4150**	**5825**	**8175**
EX Sport Utility 4D		CM58V	29425	**3975**	**4725**	**6475**	**8950**
2WD		G		**(475)**	**(475)**	**(635)**	**(635)**

ODYSSEY—4-Cyl.—Truck Equipment Schedule T1
LX Minivan 4D		RA184	23955	**4450**	**5225**	**6825**	**9125**
EX Minivan 4D		RA187	25945	**4625**	**5475**	**7075**	**9400**

1998 HONDA–(JHL,JHMor4S6)(RD174)–W

CR-V 4WD—4-Cyl.—Truck Equipment Schedule T2
LX Sport Utility 4D		RD174	19145	**4800**	**5650**	**7025**	**9150**
EX Sport Utility 4D		RD176	20645	**5150**	**6025**	**7450**	**9600**
2WD		2		**(525)**	**(525)**	**(700)**	**(700)**

PASSPORT 4WD—V6—Truck Equipment Schedule T1
LX Sport Utility 4D		CM58W	26995	**4300**	**5075**	**6850**	**9325**
EX Sport Utility 4D		CM58W	29345	**4900**	**5725**	**7525**	**10150**
2WD		K		**(525)**	**(525)**	**(700)**	**(700)**

ODYSSEY—4-Cyl.—Truck Equipment Schedule T1
LX Minivan 4D		RA386	24205	**5075**	**5950**	**7500**	**9800**

Body	Type	VIN	List	Trade-In Fair	Trade-In Good	Pvt-Party Good	Retail Excellent
EX Minivan 4D		RA387	26195	5275	6175	7750	10100

1999 HONDA—(JHL,2HKor4S6)(RD174)—X

CR-V 4WD—4-Cyl.—Truck Equipment Schedule T2

LX Sport Utility 4D		RD174	19365	5650	6550	8025	10200
EX Sport Utility 4D		RD176	20865	6050	7000	8525	10800
2WD		2		(600)	(600)	(800)	(800)

PASSPORT 4WD—V6—Truck Equipment Schedule T1

LX Sport Utility 4D		CM58W	27015	5200	6075	7975	10650
EX Sport Utility 4D		CM58W	29365	5900	6875	8800	11600
2WD		K		(600)	(600)	(800)	(800)

ODYSSEY—V6—Truck Equipment Schedule T1

LX Minivan 4D		RL184	23615	7275	8375	10150	12800
EX Minivan 4D		RL186	26215	8000	9175	11000	13800

2000 HONDA—(JHL,2HKor4S6)(RD174)—Y-

CR-V 4WD—4-Cyl.—Truck Equipment Schedule T2

LX Sport Utility 4D		RD174	19465	6575	7600	9100	11400
EX Sport Utility 4D		RD176	20965	7025	8100	9650	12050
SE Sport Utility 4D		RD187	23015	7275	8350	9900	12350
2WD		2		(675)	(675)	(900)	(900)

PASSPORT 4WD—V6—Truck Equipment Schedule T1

LX Sport Utility 4D		CM58V	27515	6250	7250	9275	12200
EX Sport Utility 4D		CM58V	29465	7050	8125	10200	13250
2WD		K		(675)	(675)	(900)	(900)

ODYSSEY—V6—Truck Equipment Schedule T1

LX Minivan 4D		RL185	23615	8475	9700	11550	14400
EX Minivan 4D		RL186	26415	9275	10550	12500	15450

2001 HONDA—(JHL,2HKor4S6)(RD174)—1-

CR-V 4WD—4-Cyl.—Truck Equipment Schedule T2

LX Sport Utility 4D		RD174	19590	7675	8800	10350	12800
EX Sport Utility 4D		RD176	21190	8175	9375	11000	13500
SE Sport Utility 4D		RD187	23240	8450	9650	11300	13800
2WD		2		(750)	(750)	(1000)	(1000)

PASSPORT 4WD—V6—Truck Equipment Schedule T1

LX Sport Utility 4D		CM58W	27740	7500	8650	10800	13950
EX Sport Utility 4D		CM58W	29690	8450	9650	11850	15100
2WD		K		(750)	(750)	(1000)	(1000)

ODYSSEY—V6—Truck Equipment Schedule T1

LX Minivan 4D		RL185	24340	9900	11225	13200	16200
EX Minivan 4D		RL186	26840	10750	12200	14200	17350

2002 HONDA—(JHL,2HKor4S6)(RD784)—2-

CR-V 4WD—4-Cyl.—Truck Equipment Schedule T2

LX Sport Utility 4D		RD784	19640	8925	10225	11800	14350
EX Sport Utility 4D		RD788	21940	9475	10800	12400	15000
2WD		2		(825)	(825)	(1100)	(1100)

PASSPORT 4WD—V6—Truck Equipment Schedule T1

LX Sport Utility 4D		CM58W	28040	8975	10275	12550	15950
EX Sport Utility 4D		CM58W	29990	9975	11375	13750	17250
2WD		K		(825)	(825)	(1100)	(1100)

ODYSSEY—V6—Truck Equipment Schedule T1

LX Minivan 4D		RL185	24690	11575	13100	15100	18300
EX Minivan 4D		RL186	27190	12525	14150	16200	19500

2003 HONDA—(Jor5)HorJ(L,Kor6)(YH282)—3

ELEMENT 4WD—4-Cyl.—Truck Equipment Schedule T2

DX Sport Utility 4D		YH282	18760	9275	10550	12000	14350
EX Sport Utility 4D		YH285	21310	10375	11800	13250	15750
2WD				(900)	(900)	(1200)	(1200)

CR-V 4WD—4-Cyl.—Truck Equipment Schedule T2

LX Sport Utility 4D		RD774	19760	10425	11850	13300	15800
EX Sport Utility 4D		RD778	22060	11000	12475	13950	16500
2WD		2		(900)	(900)	(1200)	(1200)

PILOT 4WD—V6—Truck Equipment Schedule T1

LX Sport Utility 4D		YF181	27360	16950	19050	20800	24000
EX Sport Utility 4D		YF184	29730	18100	20350	22100	25400

ODYSSEY—V6—Truck Equipment Schedule T1

LX Minivan 4D		RL185	24360	13525	15300	17300	20500
EX Minivan 4D		RL186	27360	14600	16475	18500	21900

TRUCKS & VANS

Body	Type	VIN	List	Trade-In Fair	Trade-In Good	Pvt-Party Good	Retail Excellent

TRUCKS & VANS

2004 HONDA—(J,2or5)F,HorJ(K,L,Nor6)(YH282)—4

ELEMENT 4WD—4-Cyl.—Truck Equipment Schedule T2

Body	Type	VIN	List	Fair	Good	Good	Excellent
DX Sport Utility 4D		YH282	17990	10900	12325	13700	16050
LX Sport Utility 4D		YH273	18990	11675	13200	14600	17050
EX Sport Utility 4D		YH285	20790	12050	13675	15050	17550
2WD				(950)	(950)	(1265)	(1265)

CR-V 4WD—4-Cyl.—Truck Equipment Schedule T2

LX Sport Utility 4D		RD774	19890	12100	13725	15100	17600
EX Sport Utility 4D		RD778	22240	12725	14400	15850	18450
2WD		2		(950)	(950)	(1265)	(1265)

PILOT 4WD—V6—Truck Equipment Schedule T1

LX Sport Utility 4D		YF181	27590	19400	21800	23600	27000
EX Sport Utility 4D		YF184	29960	20650	23125	25000	28500

ODYSSEY—V6—Truck Equipment Schedule T1

LX Minivan 4D		RL185	24980	15925	17950	20100	23600
EX Minivan 4D		RL186	27480	17050	19150	21300	25100

HUMMER

1993 HUMMER—137(XE82)--P-#

H1 4WD—V8 DIESEL—Truck Equipment Schedule T3

Hard Top 2D		XE82	48620	15800	17750	21300	26500
Open Top 4D		XE85	50570	16850	18950	22700	28000
Hard Top 4D		XE83	52020	17425	19575	23300	28900
Wagon 4D		XE84	55020	18000	20250	24100	29800
GA Pkg				1350	1350	1800	1800
GC Pkg				2075	2075	2765	2765
Winch				575	575	765	765

1994 HUMMER—137(YA82)--R-#

H1 4WD—V8 DIESEL—Truck Equipment Schedule T3

Hard Top 2D		YA82	42706	16700	18775	22200	27400
Open Top 4D		YA85	47440	17850	20075	23700	29100
Hard Top 4D		YA83	53960	18575	20825	24600	30000
Wagon 4D		YA84	57019	19150	21500	25300	31000
GA Pkg				1500	1500	2000	2000
GC Pkg				2300	2300	3065	3065
Winch				625	625	835	835

1995 HUMMER—137(YA82)--S-#

H1 4WD—V8 DIESEL—Truck Equipment Schedule T3

Hard Top 2D		YA82	43265	17675	19875	23300	28500
HardTop Enlarged 2D		YA82	46970	18325	20650	24100	29500
OpenTop Recruit 4D		YA85	50317	19000	21300	24900	30300
Open Top 4D		YA85	53239	19000	21300	24900	30300
Hard Top 4D		YA83	57652	19775	22175	25900	31600
Wagon 4D		YA84	60858	20450	22850	26700	32500
GA Pkg				1650	1650	2200	2200
GC Pkg				2525	2525	3365	3365
Winch				675	675	900	900
V8 5.7 Liter		D		(1350)	(1350)	(1800)	(1800)

1996 HUMMER — 137(YA82)--T-#

H1 4WD—V8 DIESEL—Truck Equipment Schedule T3

Hard Top 2D		YA82	46765	18675	20925	24500	29800
HardTop Enlarged 2D		YA82	50649	19400	21800	25300	30800
OpenTop Recruit 4D		YA85	54230	20150	22650	26200	31800
Open Top 4D		YA85	57346	20150	22650	26200	31800
Hard Top 4D		YA83	62037	21025	23525	27300	32900
Wagon 4D		YA84	65421	21700	24375	28100	34000
GA Pkg				1800	1800	2400	2400
GC Pkg				2750	2750	3665	3665
Winch				725	725	965	965
V8 5.7 Liter		D		(1425)	(1425)	(1900)	(1900)
V8 6.5L Turbo Diesel		Z		1350	1350	1800	1800

1997 HUMMER — 137(YA82)--V-#

H1 4WD—V8 DIESEL—Truck Equipment Schedule T3

Hard Top 2D		YA82	55749	20650	23125	26700	32200

Body Type	VIN	List	Trade-In Fair	Good	Pvt-Party Good	Retail Excellent
Open Top 4D	YA85	61954	21400	24000	27600	33300
Hard Top 4D	YA83	67330	22375	25050	28800	34600
Wagon 4D	YA84	70614	23125	25925	29800	35700
GA Pkg			1925	1925	2565	2565
GC Pkg			2975	2975	3965	3965
Winch			775	775	1035	1035
V8 6.5L Turbo Diesel	Z		1450	1450	1935	1935

1998 HUMMER — 137(YA82)--W-#

H1 4WD—V8 DIESEL—Truck Equipment Schedule T3

Body Type	VIN	List	Fair	Good	Good	Excellent
Hard Top 2D	YA82	57859	22275	24950	28600	34400
Open Top 4D	YA85	64451	23325	26100	29900	35700
Hard Top 4D	YA83	70174	24375	27275	31200	37200
Wagon 4D	YA84	73605	25150	28125	32100	38300
GA Pkg			2050	2050	2735	2735
GC Pkg			3175	3175	4230	4230
Winch			825	825	1100	1100
V8 6.5L Turbo Diesel	Z		1550	1550	2065	2065

1999 HUMMER — 137(YA82)--X-#

H1 4WD—V8 DIESEL—Truck Equipment Schedule T3

Body Type	VIN	List	Fair	Good	Good	Excellent
Hard Top 2D	YA82	66522	25725	28700	32500	38700
Open Top 4D	YA85	73580	27175	30325	34400	40700
Hard Top 4D	YA83	79677	28500	31775	35900	42500
Wagon 4D	YA84	83211	29675	33125	37300	44100
GA Pkg			2350	2350	3135	3135
GC Pkg			3625	3625	4830	4830
Winch			950	950	1265	1265

2000 HUMMER — 137(ZA89)--Y-#

H1 4WD—V8 Turbo Diesel—Truck Equipment Sch T3

Body Type	VIN	List	Fair	Good	Good	Excellent
Hard Top 2D	ZA89	70819	29275	32650	36600	43100
Open Top 4D	ZA90	80499	31300	34950	39100	45900
Hard Top 4D	ZA83	87058	32825	36675	40900	47900
Wagon 4D	ZA84	90844	34275	38200	42600	49800
Slantback 4D	ZA91	93197	34750	38775	43100	50400
GA Pkg			2650	2650	3530	3530
GC Pkg			4075	4075	5430	5430
Winch			1075	1075	1435	1435

2001 HUMMER — 137(ZA82)--1-#

H1 4WD—V8 Turbo Diesel—Truck Equipment Sch T3

Body Type	VIN	List	Fair	Good	Good	Excellent
Hard Top 2D	ZA82	76862	33800	37625	41900	48800
Open Top 4D	ZA85	84608	36375	40600	44900	52200
Hard Top 4D	ZA83	91553	38200	42625	47000	54500
Wagon 4D	ZA84	95404	39925	44450	49000	56700
GA Pkg			2950	2950	3930	3930
GC Pkg			4525	4525	6030	6030
Winch			1200	1200	1600	1600

2002 HUMMER — 137(ZA85)--2-#

H1 4WD—V8 Turbo Diesel—Truck Equipment Sch T3

Body Type	VIN	List	Fair	Good	Good	Excellent
Open Top 4D	ZA85	98681	41475	46175	50500	58200
Enclosed Wagon 4D	ZA84	109834	45400	50500	55100	63300
Winch			1325	1325	1765	1765

2003 HUMMER — 5GR-(A903)-3-#

H1 4WD—V8 Turbo Diesel—Truck Equipment Sch T3

Body Type	VIN	List	Fair	Good	Good	Excellent
Open Top 4D	A903	106185	46850	52025	56500	64700
Wagon 4D	A843	117508	51275	57025	61700	70300
Winch			1425	1425	1900	1900

H2 4WD—V8—Truck Equipment Schedule T3

Body Type	VIN	List	Fair	Good	Good	Excellent
Sport Utility 4D	N23U	50200	27450	30625	34400	40400
Third Seat			700	700	935	935
Adventure Pkg			450	450	600	600
Lux Pkg			450	450	600	600
Air Suspension			400	400	535	535

2004 HUMMER — 5GR-(A903)-4-#

H1 4WD—V8 Turbo Diesel—Truck Equipment Sch T3

Body Type	VIN	List	Fair	Good	Good	Excellent
Open Top 4D	A903	106185	52800	58650	63100	71400

Body	Type	VIN	List	Trade-In Fair	Good	Pvt-Party Good	Retail Excellent
Wagon 4D		ZA84	117508	57700	64125	68700	77600
Winch				1525	1525	2035	2035
Adventure Pkg				475	475	635	635
H2 4WD—V8—Truck Equipment Schedule T3							
Sport Utility 4D		N23U	51395	31400	35050	38900	45300
Limited Ed Spt Util		N23U	59840	31775	35425	39300	45800
Third Seat				750	750	1000	1000
Adventure Pkg				475	475	635	635
Lux Pkg				475	475	635	635
Air Suspension				400	400	535	535

HYUNDAI

2001 HYUNDAI — KM8S(B72D)–1–#

SANTA FE 4WD—V6—Truck Equipment Schedule T2

Body	Type	VIN	List	Trade-In Fair	Good	Pvt-Party Good	Retail Excellent
GL Sport Utility 4D		B72D	20234	5400	6300	7875	10200
GLS Sport Utility 4D		C72D	21234	6325	7350	8950	11400
LX Sport Utility 4D		C72D	22434	6825	7875	9700	12400
2WD		8		(750)	(750)	(1000)	(1000)
4-Cyl. 2.4 Liter		B		(600)	(600)	(800)	(800)

2002 HYUNDAI — KM8S(B82B)–2–#

SANTA FE—4-Cyl.—Equipment Schedule T2

Body	Type	VIN	List	Trade-In Fair	Good	Pvt-Party Good	Retail Excellent
Sport Utility 4D		B82B	17694	6375	7400	9050	11500
SANTA FE 4WD—V6—Truck Equipment Schedule T2							
GLS Sport Utility 4D		C72D	21594	7425	8550	10250	12850
LX Sport Utility 4D		C72D	23794	8000	9175	11050	13900
2WD		8		(825)	(825)	(1100)	(1100)

2003 HYUNDAI — KM8S(B82B)–3–#

SANTA FE—4-Cyl.—Truck Equipment Schedule T2

Body	Type	VIN	List	Trade-In Fair	Good	Pvt-Party Good	Retail Excellent
Sport Utility 4D		B82B	17894	7575	8700	10300	12850
SANTA FE 4WD—V6—Truck Equipment Schedule T2							
GLS Sport Utility 4D		C72D	21894	8725	9975	11650	14300
LX Sport Utility 4D		C72D	24394	9325	10650	12600	15500
2WD		8		(900)	(900)	(1200)	(1200)
V6 3.5 Liter		E		500	500	665	665

2004 HYUNDAI — KM8S(B82B)–4–#

SANTA FE—4-Cyl.—Truck Equipment Schedule T2

Body	Type	VIN	List	Trade-In Fair	Good	Pvt-Party Good	Retail Excellent
Sport Utility 4D		B82B	18589	9025	10325	11900	14550
SANTA FE 4WD—V6—Truck Equipment Schedule T2							
GLS Sport Utility 4D		C72D	23089	10275	11675	13400	16200
LX Sport Utility 4D		C72E	26089	10950	12425	14400	17500
2WD		8		(950)	(950)	(1265)	(1265)
V6 3.5 Liter		E		500	500	665	665

INFINITI

1997 INFINITI — JN6(AR05Y)–V–#

QX4 4WD—V6—Truck Equipment Schedule T3

Body	Type	VIN	List	Trade-In Fair	Good	Pvt-Party Good	Retail Excellent
Sport Utility 4D		AR05Y	36045	6725	7775	9400	11900

1998 INFINITI — JN6(AR05Y)–W–#

QX4 4WD—V6—Truck Equipment Schedule T3

Body	Type	VIN	List	Trade-In Fair	Good	Pvt-Party Good	Retail Excellent
Sport Utility 4D		AR05Y	36045	7650	8775	10450	13050

1999 INFINITI — JN6(AR05Y)–X–#

QX4 4WD—V6—Truck Equipment Schedule T3

Body	Type	VIN	List	Trade-In Fair	Good	Pvt-Party Good	Retail Excellent
Sport Utility 4D		AR05Y	36075	8750	10025	11850	14700

2000 INFINITI — JNR(AR05Y)–Y–#

QX4 4WD—V6—Truck Equipment Schedule T3

Body	Type	VIN	List	Trade-In Fair	Good	Pvt-Party Good	Retail Excellent
Sport Utility 4D		AR05Y	36075	10125	11525	13600	16750

TRUCKS & VANS

Body	Type	VIN	List	Trade-In Fair	Good	Pvt-Party Good	Retail Excellent

2001 INFINITI — JNR(DR07Y)-1-#

QX4 4WD—V6—Truck Equipment Schedule T3

Sport Utility 4D		DR07Y	36075	13100	14825	17050	20500
2WD		X		(800)	(800)	(1065)	(1065)

2002 INFINITI — JNR(DR07Y)-2-#

QX4 4WD—V6—Truck Equipment Schedule T3

Sport Utility 4D		DR07Y	36095	15025	16950	19200	22900
2WD		X		(875)	(875)	(1165)	(1165)

2003 INFINITI — JNR(AS08W)-3-#

FX35 AWD—V6—Truck Equipment Schedule T3

Sport Utility 4D		AS08W	36245	22650	25350	28200	33000
2WD		U		(950)	(950)	(1265)	(1265)
Sport Pkg				1000	1000	1335	1335

FX45 AWD—V8—Truck Equipment Schedule T3

Sport Utility 4D		BS08W	44770	26975	30150	33200	38500

QX4 4WD—V6—Truck Equipment Schedule T3

Sport Utility 4D		DR09Y	36695	17275	19400	21800	25700
2WD		X		(950)	(950)	(1265)	(1265)

2004 INFINITI — JNR(AS08W)-4-#

FX35 AWD—V6—Truck Equipment Schedule T3

Sport Utility 4D		AS08W	36395				
2WD		U					

FX45 AWD—V8—Truck Equipment Schedule T3

Sport Utility 4D		BS08W	44920				

QX56 AWD—V8—Truck Equipment Schedule T3

Sport Utility 4D		AA08C	51080				
2WD							

ISUZU

1990 ISUZU — JA(AorC)-(H01E)-L-#

AMIGO 4WD—4-Cyl.—Truck Equipment Schedule T2

S Sport Utility 2D		H01E	12558	500	725	1200	2025
XS Sport Utility 2D		H01E	13798	550	775	1300	2125
Rear Seat				100	100	135	135
2WD		G		(300)	(300)	(400)	(400)
4-Cyl. 2.3 Liter				(100)	(100)	(135)	(135)

TROOPER II 4WD—4-Cyl.—Truck Equipment Schedule T1

S Sport Utility 4D		H58E	14698	600	850	1500	2600
V6 2.8 Liter		R		150	150	200	200

TROOPER II 4WD—V6—Truck Equipment Schedule T1

XS Sport Utility 4D		H58R	17048	850	1200	2100	3425
LS Sport Utility 4D		H58R	19148	900	1250	2150	3525

PICKUP—4-Cyl.—Truck Equipment Schedule T2

S Short Bed		L11E	8708	300	450	900	1575
S Long Bed		L14E	10128	325	475	900	1625
S 1 Ton Long Bed		L34E	10108	400	600	1100	1925
XS Short Bed		L11E	8828	325	475	900	1625
LS Short Bed		L11E	11128	400	600	1100	1925
S Spacecab		L16E	9988	600	850	1475	2475
XS Spacecab		L16E	10828	775	1100	1850	3025
LS Spacecab		L16E	12358	825	1150	1900	3100
4WD		R		500	500	665	665
4-Cyl. 2.3 Liter				(100)	(100)	(135)	(135)

1991 ISUZU — (JAA,JACor4S2)-(Y01E)-M

AMIGO 4WD—4-Cyl.—Truck Equipment Schedule T2

S Sport Utility 2D		Y01E	12988	575	825	1375	2300
XS Sport Utility 2D		Y01E	14268	625	900	1475	2425
Rear Seat				100	100	135	135
2WD		G		(325)	(325)	(435)	(435)
4-Cyl. 2.3 Liter		L		(100)	(100)	(135)	(135)

RODEO 4WD—V6—Truck Equipment Schedule T1

S Sport Utility 4D		Y58Z	15498	1400	1875	3025	4650
XS Sport Utility 4D		Y58Z	18098	1600	2100	3300	5000
LS Sport Utility 4D		Y58Z	18998	1750	2275	3475	5200

Body	Type	VIN	List	Trade-In Fair	Trade-In Good	Pvt-Party Good	Retail Excellent
2WD		G	___	(375)	(375)	(500)	(500)
4-Cyl. 2.6 Liter		E	___	(325)	(325)	(435)	(435)
TROOPER 4WD—4-Cyl.—Truck Equipment Schedule T1							
S Sport Utility 4D		H58E	16068	675	950	1675	2850
V6 2.8 Liter		R	___	175	175	235	235
TROOPER 4WD—V6—Truck Equipment Schedule T1							
XS Sport Utility 4D		H58R	18688	975	1400	2425	3925
SE Sport Utility 4D		H58R	18838	975	1400	2425	3925
LS Sport Utility 4D		H58R	20838	1000	1450	2500	4000
PICKUP—4-Cyl.—Truck Equipment Schedule T2							
S Short Bed		L11E	8818	325	475	950	1675
S Long Bed		L14E	10258	350	500	975	1725
S 1 Ton Long Bed		L34E	10218	450	650	1175	2025
S Spacecab		L16E	10068	650	900	1525	2600
LS Spacecab		L16E	12548	900	1250	2050	3275
4WD		R	___	550	550	735	735
4-Cyl. 2.3 Liter		L	___	(100)	(100)	(135)	(135)
V6 3.1 Liter			___	150	150	200	200
PICKUP 4WD—V6—Truck Equipment Schedule T2							
LS Short Bed		L16E	11988	950	1350	2175	3475

1992 ISUZU — (JAA,4S1or4S2)–(Y01E)–N

Body	Type	VIN	List	Trade-In Fair	Trade-In Good	Pvt-Party Good	Retail Excellent
AMIGO 4WD—4-Cyl.—Truck Equipment Schedule T2							
S Sport Utility 2D		Y01E	14318	650	900	1525	2725
XS Sport Utility 2D		Y01E	15668	700	1000	1650	2725
2WD		G	___	(350)	(350)	(465)	(465)
4-Cyl. 2.3 Liter		L	___	(125)	(125)	(165)	(165)
RODEO 4WD—V6—Truck Equipment Schedule T1							
S Sport Utility 4D		Y58Z	16668	1400	1875	3050	4700
XS Sport Utility 4D		Y58Z	19748	1650	2150	3375	5100
LS Sport Utility 4D		Y58Z	20068	1800	2325	3600	5350
2WD		G	___	(400)	(400)	(535)	(535)
4-Cyl. 2.6 Liter		E	___	(350)	(350)	(465)	(465)
TROOPER 4WD—V6—Truck Equipment Schedule T1							
S Sport Utility 4D		H58V	21169	1575	2100	3350	5100
LS Sport Utility 4D		H58W	25769	2125	2700	4050	5975
PICKUP—4-Cyl.—Truck Equipment Schedule T2							
S Short Bed		L11E	9438	350	500	975	1725
S Long Bed		L14E	9718	375	550	1025	1800
S 1 Ton Long Bed		L34E	10958	475	700	1225	2100
S Spacecab		L16E	10758	700	1000	1650	2750
LS Spacecab		L16E	13438	925	1325	2150	3425
4WD		R	___	675	675	900	900
4-Cyl. 2.3 Liter		L	___	(125)	(125)	(165)	(165)
V6 3.1 Liter		Z	___	225	225	300	300

1993 ISUZU — (JAA,4S1or4S2)–(Y01E)–P

Body	Type	VIN	List	Trade-In Fair	Trade-In Good	Pvt-Party Good	Retail Excellent
AMIGO 4WD—4-Cyl.—Truck Equipment Schedule T2							
S Sport Utility 2D		Y01E	14988	750	1025	1725	2850
XS Sport Utility 2D		Y01E	16338	825	1150	1900	3075
2WD		G	___	(375)	(375)	(500)	(500)
4-Cyl. 2.3 Liter		L	___	(150)	(150)	(200)	(200)
RODEO 4WD—V6—Truck Equipment Schedule T1							
S Sport Utility 4D		Y58V	20158	1375	1850	3050	4750
LS Sport Utility 4D		Y58V	23258	1825	2350	3650	5475
2WD		G	___	(425)	(425)	(565)	(565)
4-Cyl. 2.6 Liter		E	___	(375)	(375)	(500)	(500)
TROOPER 4WD—V6—Truck Equipment Schedule T1							
S Sport Utility 4D		H58V	22119	1650	2150	3475	5300
RS Sport Utility 2D		H57W	23869	1750	2275	3600	5450
LS Sport Utility 4D		H58W	26519	2250	2825	4250	6250
PICKUP—4-Cyl.—Truck Equipment Schedule T2							
S Short Bed		L11E	9338	375	550	1050	1850
S Long Bed		L14E	10438	400	600	1100	1925
S Spacecab		L16E	11888	775	1100	1850	3025
4WD		R	___	800	800	1065	1065
4-Cyl. 2.3 Liter		L	___	(150)	(150)	(200)	(200)
V6 3.1 Liter		Z	___	300	300	400	400

1994 ISUZU — (JAA,4S1or4S2)–(Y07E)–R

Body	Type	VIN	List	Trade-In Fair	Trade-In Good	Pvt-Party Good	Retail Excellent
AMIGO 4WD—4-Cyl.—Truck Equipment Schedule T2							
S Sport Utility 2D		Y07E	17149	850	1200	2025	3275

TRUCKS & VANS

Body	Type	VIN	List	Trade-In Fair	Trade-In Good	Pvt-Party Good	Retail Excellent
XS Sport Utility 2D		Y07E	17549	**925**	**1325**	**2200**	**3525**
2WD		G		**(400)**	**(400)**	**(535)**	**(535)**
RODEO 4WD—V6—Truck Equipment Schedule T1							
S Sport Utility 4D		Y58V	21574	**1425**	**1900**	**3200**	**4975**
LS Sport Utility 4D		Y58V	25274	**1950**	**2500**	**3875**	**5775**
2WD		G		**(450)**	**(450)**	**(600)**	**(600)**
4-Cyl. 2.6 Liter		E		**(400)**	**(400)**	**(535)**	**(535)**
TROOPER 4WD—V6—Truck Equipment Schedule T1							
S Sport Utility 4D		H58V	23700	**1750**	**2275**	**3650**	**5575**
RS Sport Utility 2D		H57W	25550	**1875**	**2400**	**3825**	**5750**
LS Sport Utility 4D		H58W	28400	**2425**	**3025**	**4500**	**6600**
SE Sport Utility 4D		H58W	33200	**2975**	**3625**	**5175**	**7375**
PICKUP—4-Cyl.—Truck Equipment Schedule T2							
S Short Bed		L11E	12349	**400**	**600**	**1150**	**2025**
S Long Bed		L14E	11159	**450**	**625**	**1200**	**2100**
S Spacecab		L16E	13059	**850**	**1175**	**2000**	**3275**
4WD		R		**900**	**900**	**1200**	**1200**
4-Cyl. 2.3 Liter		L		**(175)**	**(175)**	**(235)**	**(235)**
V6 3.1 Liter		Z		**375**	**375**	**500**	**500**

Body	Type	VIN	List	Trade-In Fair	Trade-In Good	Pvt-Party Good	Retail Excellent
RODEO 4WD—V6—Truck Equipment Schedule T1							
S Sport Utility 4D		Y58V	22750	**1550**	**2075**	**3450**	**5350**
LS Sport Utility 4D		Y58V	26670	**2150**	**2725**	**4200**	**6250**
2WD		G,K		**(475)**	**(475)**	**(635)**	**(635)**
4-Cyl. 2.6 Liter		E		**(425)**	**(425)**	**(565)**	**(565)**
TROOPER 4WD—V6—Truck Equipment Schedule T1							
S Sport Utility 4D		J58V	26270	**1950**	**2475**	**3950**	**6000**
RS Sport Utility 2D		J57W	29220	**2075**	**2625**	**4100**	**6175**
LS Sport Utility 4D		J58V	30400	**2700**	**3300**	**4875**	**7075**
SE Sport Utility 4D		J58V	34445	**3300**	**3950**	**5625**	**7950**
Ltd Sport Utility 4D		J58V	37220	**3575**	**4300**	**6000**	**8375**
PICKUP—4-Cyl.—Truck Equipment Schedule T2							
S Short Bed		L11L	10399	**475**	**700**	**1300**	**2250**
S Long Bed		L14L	11809	**525**	**750**	**1350**	**2350**
PICKUP 4WD—4-Cyl.—Truck Equipment Schedule T2							
S Short Bed		R11E	14519	**1500**	**1975**	**3100**	**4700**

Body	Type	VIN	List	Trade-In Fair	Trade-In Good	Pvt-Party Good	Retail Excellent
RODEO 4WD—V6—Truck Equipment Schedule T1							
S Sport Utility 4D		M58V	25085	**1800**	**2325**	**3800**	**5800**
LS Sport Utility 4D		M58V	28705	**2450**	**3050**	**4600**	**6775**
2WD		K		**(500)**	**(500)**	**(665)**	**(665)**
4-Cyl. 2.6 Liter		E		**(450)**	**(450)**	**(600)**	**(600)**
OASIS—4-Cyl.—Truck Equipment Schedule T1							
S Minivan 4D		J184	23940	**3275**	**3925**	**5375**	**7425**
LS Minivan 4D		J187	26435	**3550**	**4250**	**5725**	**7850**
TROOPER 4WD—V6—Truck Equipment Schedule T1							
S Sport Utility 4D		J58V	28585	**2200**	**2775**	**4350**	**6500**
LS Sport Utility 4D		J58V	32015	**3000**	**3675**	**5350**	**7675**
Ltd Sport Utility 4D		J58V	38435	**4000**	**4750**	**6550**	**9075**
SE Sport Utility 4D		J58V	38945	**3675**	**4400**	**6150**	**8600**
HOMBRE—4-Cyl.—Truck Equipment Schedule T2							
S Short Bed		S144	11719	**900**	**1300**	**2250**	**3650**
XS Short Bed		S144	12548	**950**	**1350**	**2375**	**3900**

Body	Type	VIN	List	Trade-In Fair	Trade-In Good	Pvt-Party Good	Retail Excellent
RODEO 4WD—V6—Truck Equipment Schedule T1							
S Sport Utility 4D		M58V	25235	**2100**	**2675**	**4250**	**6425**
LS Sport Utility 4D		M58V	28855	**2800**	**3425**	**5100**	**7450**
2WD		K		**(525)**	**(525)**	**(700)**	**(700)**
4-Cyl. 2.6 Liter		E		**(475)**	**(475)**	**(635)**	**(635)**
OASIS—4-Cyl.—Truck Equipment Schedule T1							
S Minivan 4D		J184	24175	**3725**	**4475**	**5950**	**8100**
LS Minivan 4D		J187	26435	**4025**	**4800**	**6325**	**8575**
TROOPER 4WD—V6—Truck Equipment Schedule T1							
S Sport Utility 4D		J58V	28245	**2550**	**3175**	**4850**	**7175**
LS Sport Utility 4D		J58V	32715	**3425**	**4125**	**5900**	**8400**
Ltd Sport Utility 4D		J58V	38435	**4500**	**5300**	**7225**	**9900**
HOMBRE—4-Cyl.—Truck Equipment Schedule T2							
S Short Bed		S144	11992	**1100**	**1550**	**2675**	**4250**
XS Short Bed		S144	12419	**1125**	**1575**	**2700**	**4300**

SEE BACK PAGES FOR TRUCK EQUIPMENT

Body	Type	VIN	List	Trade-In Fair	Trade-In Good	Pvt-Party Good	Retail Excellent
XS Spacecab		S194	14774	**1875**	**2400**	**3625**	**5350**
V6 4.3 Liter		X		**250**	**250**	**335**	**335**

1998 ISUZU–(JR2,1GG,4S2orJAC)–(M57D)–W

AMIGO 4WD—4-Cyl.—Truck Equipment Schedule T2
S Sport Utility 2D		M57D	17945	**3000**	**3675**	**4900**	**6700**
2WD		K		**(525)**	**(525)**	**(700)**	**(700)**
V6 3.2 Liter		W		**625**	**625**	**835**	**835**

RODEO 4WD—V6—Truck Equipment Schedule T1
S Sport Utility 4D		M58W	25635	**2650**	**3250**	**4950**	**7250**
LS Sport Utility 4D		M58W	29355	**3400**	**4100**	**5850**	**8275**
2WD		K		**(575)**	**(575)**	**(765)**	**(765)**
4-Cyl. 2.2 Liter		D		**(525)**	**(525)**	**(700)**	**(700)**

OASIS—4-Cyl.—Truck Equipment Schedule T1
S Minivan 4D		J286	23977	**4325**	**5100**	**6575**	**8750**
LS Minivan 4D		J287	26247	**4625**	**5475**	**6975**	**9225**

TROOPER 4WD—V6—Truck Equipment Schedule T1
S Sport Utility 4D		J58X	28245	**3150**	**3800**	**5525**	**7925**

HOMBRE—4-Cyl.—Truck Equipment Schedule T2
S Short Bed		S144	12169	**1375**	**1875**	**2975**	**4525**
XS Short Bed		S144	12704	**1450**	**1925**	**3050**	**4625**
XS Spacecab		S194	15650	**2225**	**2775**	**3975**	**5700**
4WD		T		**1275**	**1275**	**1700**	**1700**
V6 4.3 Liter		X		**250**	**250**	**335**	**335**

1999 ISUZU–(JAC,JR2,4S2or1GG)–(M57D)–X–

AMIGO 4WD—4-Cyl.—Truck Equipment Schedule T2
S Sport Utility 2D		M57D	18825	**3600**	**4325**	**5625**	**7500**
2WD		K		**(600)**	**(600)**	**(800)**	**(800)**
Hard Top				**125**	**125**	**165**	**165**
V6 3.2 Liter		W		**700**	**700**	**935**	**935**

RODEO 4WD—V6—Truck Equipment Schedule T1
S Sport Utility 4D		M58W	26135	**3250**	**3900**	**5700**	**8200**
LS Sport Utility 4D		M58W	27985	**4100**	**4875**	**6775**	**9375**
LSE Sport Utility 4D		M58W	31145	**4725**	**5550**	**7500**	**10200**
2WD				**(650)**	**(650)**	**(865)**	**(865)**
4-Cyl. 2.2 Liter		D		**(600)**	**(600)**	**(800)**	**(800)**

VEHICROSS 4WD—V6—Truck Equipment Schedule T1
Sport Utility 2D		N57X	29595	**5425**	**6325**	**8225**	**10950**

OASIS—4-Cyl.—Truck Equipment Schedule T1
S Minivan 4D		J286	24175	**5175**	**6050**	**7600**	**9925**

TROOPER 4WD—V6—Truck Equipment Schedule T1
S Sport Utility 4D		J58X	27595	**3825**	**4550**	**6400**	**9000**
Performance Pkg				**250**	**250**	**335**	**335**

HOMBRE—4-Cyl.—Truck Equipment Schedule T2
S Short Bed		S144	12040	**1750**	**2275**	**3425**	**5100**
XS Short Bed		S144	12575	**1875**	**2400**	**3600**	**5275**
XS Spacecab		S194	15695	**2700**	**3325**	**4575**	**6400**
Third Door				**225**	**225**	**300**	**300**
4WD		T		**1450**	**1450**	**1935**	**1935**
V6 4.3 Liter		X		**300**	**300**	**400**	**400**

2000 ISUZU–(JAC,4S2or1GG)–(M57D)–Y–#

AMIGO 4WD—4-Cyl.—Truck Equipment Schedule T2
S Sport Utility 2D		M57D	20190	**4325**	**5100**	**6450**	**8475**
2WD		K		**(675)**	**(675)**	**(900)**	**(900)**
Hard Top				**150**	**150**	**200**	**200**
V6 3.2 Liter		W		**750**	**750**	**1000**	**1000**

RODEO 4WD—V6—Truck Equipment Schedule T1
S Sport Utility 4D		M58W	24935	**3975**	**4725**	**6700**	**9375**
LS Sport Utility 4D		M58W	27815	**4950**	**5800**	**7825**	**10650**
LSE Sport Utility 4D		M58W	31760	**5650**	**6575**	**8675**	**11600**
2WD				**(725)**	**(725)**	**(965)**	**(965)**
4-Cyl. 2.2 Liter		D		**(675)**	**(675)**	**(900)**	**(900)**

VEHICROSS 4WD—V6—Truck Equipment Schedule T1
Sport Utility 2D		N57X	31045	**6450**	**7475**	**9500**	**12450**

TROOPER 4WD—V6—Truck Equipment Schedule T1
S Sport Utility 4D		J58X	29445	**4625**	**5475**	**7475**	**10250**
LS Sport Utility 4D		J58X	31145	**5850**	**6825**	**8900**	**11850**
Limited Sport Util 4D		J58X	35193	**7250**	**8325**	**10500**	**13700**
2WD				**(1075)**	**(1075)**	**(1435)**	**(1435)**

Body	Type	VIN	List	Trade-In Fair	Good	Pvt-Party Good	Retail Excellent
HOMBRE—4-Cyl.—Truck Equipment Schedule T2							
S	Short Bed	S144	11855	2225	2775	4050	5825
XS	Short Bed	S144	13355	2400	3000	4275	6075
S	Spacecab	S194	14180	3075	3725	5050	6925
XS	Spacecab	S194	16005	3300	4000	5325	7275
	Third Door			250	250	335	335
	4WD	T		1625	1625	2165	2165
	V6 4.3 Liter	W		350	350	465	465

2001 ISUZU—(JACor4S2)—(M57W)—1—#

Body	Type	VIN	List	Fair	Good	Good	Excellent
RODEO SPORT 4WD—V6—Truck Equipment Schedule T2							
	Soft Top 2D	M57W	20270	5275	6175	7550	9700
	Hard Top 2D	M57W	20880	5450	6350	7775	9925
	2WD	K		(800)	(800)	(1065)	(1065)
	4-Cyl. 2.2 Liter	D		(750)	(750)	(1000)	(1000)
RODEO 4WD—V6—Truck Equipment Schedule T1							
S	Sport Utility 4D	M58W	26025	4925	5775	7875	10800
LS	Sport Utility 4D	M58W	27480	6000	6950	9150	12200
LSE	Sport Utility 4D	M58W	31950	6800	7825	10100	13250
	2WD	K		(800)	(800)	(1065)	(1065)
	4-Cyl. 2.2 Liter	D		(750)	(750)	(1000)	(1000)
VEHICROSS 4WD—V6—Truck Equipment Schedule T1							
	Sport Utility 2D	N57X	31045	7700	8825	11000	14150
TROOPER 4WD—V6—Truck Equipment Schedule T1							
S	Sport Utility 4D	J58X	29690	5675	6600	8750	11800
LS	Sport Utility 4D	J58X	31285	7000	8100	10300	13550
Limited	Sport Utility 4D	J58X	35333	8525	9750	12100	15500
	2WD			(1200)	(1200)	(1600)	(1600)

2002 ISUZU—(JACor4S2)—(M57W)—2—#

Body	Type	VIN	List	Fair	Good	Good	Excellent
RODEO SPORT 4WD—V6—Truck Equipment Schedule T2							
	Soft Top 2D	M57W	22655	6325	7350	8750	11000
	Hard Top 2D	M57W	22380	6525	7525	8975	11250
	2WD	K		(875)	(875)	(1165)	(1165)
	4-Cyl. 2.2 Liter	D		(825)	(825)	(1100)	(1100)
RODEO 4WD—V6—Truck Equipment Schedule T1							
S	Sport Utility 4D	M58W	25305	6075	7050	9325	12550
LS	Sport Utility 4D	M58W	28355	7275	8350	10700	14000
LSE	Sport Utility 4D	M58W	32340	8125	9325	11700	15100
	2WD	K		(875)	(875)	(1165)	(1165)
	4-Cyl. 2.2 Liter	D		(825)	(825)	(1100)	(1100)
AXIOM 4WD—V6—Truck Equipment Schedule T1							
	Sport Utility 4D	F58X	29625	7075	8150	10350	13600
XS	Sport Utility 4D	F58X	31945	7350	8450	10700	13900
	2WD			(875)	(875)	(1165)	(1165)
TROOPER 4WD—V6—Truck Equipment Schedule T1							
S	Sport Utility 4D	J58X	30015	6900	7975	10300	13650
LS	Sport Utility 4D	J58X	33300	8400	9600	12050	15500
Limited	Sport Utility 4D	J58X	37270	9975	11375	13850	17550
	2WD			(1325)	(1325)	(1765)	(1765)

2003 ISUZU — (4NUor4S2)—(K57D)—3—#

Body	Type	VIN	List	Fair	Good	Good	Excellent
RODEO SPORT—4-Cyl.—Truck Equipment Schedule T2							
S	Soft Top 2D	K57D	14624	6300	7300	8600	10650
RODEO SPORT 4WD—V6—Truck Equipment Schedule T2							
S	Hard Top 2D	M57W	20040	7825	8975	10300	12600
	2WD	K		(950)	(950)	(1265)	(1265)
	4-Cyl. 2.2 Liter	D		(900)	(900)	(1200)	(1200)
RODEO 4WD—V6—Truck Equipment Schedule T1							
S	Sport Utility 4D	M58W	22004	7500	8625	10950	14300
	2WD	K		(950)	(950)	(1265)	(1265)
	4-Cyl. 2.2 Liter	D		(900)	(900)	(1200)	(1200)
AXIOM 4WD—V6—Truck Equipment Schedule T1							
S	Sport Utility 4D	F58X	27620	8575	9800	12100	15400
XS	Sport Utility 4D	F58X	30620	8850	10125	12450	15800
	2WD	E		(950)	(950)	(1265)	(1265)
ASCENDER 4WD—6-Cyl.—Truck Equipment Schedule T1							
S	Sport Utility 4D	T16S	31974	11325	12875	15950	20400
LS	Sport Utility 4D	T16S	35074	11700	13250	16350	20800
Limited	Sport Utility 4D	T16T	38674	12050	13675	16800	21300
	2WD	S		(1500)	(1500)	(2000)	(2000)
	V8 5.3 Liter	T		550	550	735	735

Body	Type	VIN	List	Trade-In Fair	Good	Pvt-Party Good	Retail Excellent

2004 ISUZU — (4NUor4S2)–(M58W)–4–#

RODEO 4WD—V6—Truck Equipment Schedule T1

S Sport Utility 4D	M58W	23479	**9225**	10500	13000	16650
2WD	K		**(1000)**	(1000)	(1335)	(1335)
V6 3.5 Liter			**500**	500	665	665

AXIOM 4WD—V6—Truck Equipment Schedule T1

S Sport Utility 4D	F58X	28149				
XS Sport Utility 4D	F58X	31149				
2WD	E					

ASCENDER 4WD—6-Cyl.—Truck Equipment Schedule T1

S Sport Utility 4D	T16S	31849	**13675**	15450	18700	23500
LS Sport Utility 4D	T16S	34448	**14100**	15900	19200	24000
Limited Sport Util 4D	T16T	38446	**14450**	16325	19600	24500
w/o Third Seat			**(900)**	(900)	(1200)	(1200)
2WD	S		**(1550)**	(1550)	(2065)	(2065)
V8 5.3 Liter	T		**575**	575	765	765

JEEP

1990 JEEP — 1J(4or7)–(Y19E)–L–#

WRANGLER 4WD—4-Cyl.—Truck Equipment Schedule T2

S Sport Utility 2D	Y19E	10116	**1575**	2100	3150	4675
Sport Utility 2D	Y29E	12049	**1725**	2250	3350	4950
Islander Spt Util 2D	Y39E	12773	**1825**	2375	3475	5100
Sahara Spt Util 2D	Y49E	13872	**1850**	2375	3525	5150
Hard Top			**250**	250	335	335
6-Cyl. 4.2 Liter	T		**500**	500	665	665

WRANGLER 4WD—6-Cyl.—Truck Equipment Schedule T2

Laredo Sport Utility	Y59T	16072	**2400**	2975	4200	5975
Hard Top			**250**	250	335	335

CHEROKEE 4WD—4-Cyl.—Truck Equipment Schedule T1

Sport Utility 2D	J27E	16609	**950**	1375	2400	3900
Sport Utility 4D	J28E	17484	**1050**	1500	2575	4075
2WD	T		**(350)**	(350)	(465)	(465)
6-Cyl. 4.0 Liter	L		**150**	150	200	200

CHEROKEE 4WD—6-Cyl.—Truck Equipment Schedule T3

Limited Sport Util 2D	J77S	25000	**1575**	2100	3300	5050
Limited Sport Util 4D	J78S	26125	**1900**	2425	3700	5500

WAGONEER 4WD—6-Cyl.—Truck Equipment Schedule T3

Limited Spt Utl 4D	N78L	25145	**1675**	2200	3425	5150

GRAND WAGONEER 4WD—V8—Truck Equipment Schedule T3

Sport Utility 4D	S587	28455	**1300**	1775	2900	4500

COMANCHE PICKUP 4WD—4-Cyl.—Truck Equipment Sch T2

Short Bed	J26E	12001	**325**	475	950	1675
Long Bed	J26E	12411	**300**	450	900	1575
2WD	T		**(300)**	(300)	(400)	(400)
6-Cyl. 4.0 Liter	T		**300**	300	400	400

1991 JEEP — 1J(4or7)–(Y19P)–M–#

WRANGLER 4WD—4-Cyl.—Truck Equipment Schedule T2

S Sport Utility 2D	Y19P	10645	**1775**	2300	3400	5000
Sport Utility 2D	Y29P	12673	**1950**	2475	3625	5275
Islander Spt Util 2D	Y39P	13681	**2050**	2600	3775	5475
Sahara Spt Util 2D	Y49P	14829	**2100**	2650	3850	5550
Hard Top			**250**	250	335	335
6-Cyl. 4.0 Liter	S		**550**	550	735	735

WRANGLER 4WD—6-Cyl.—Truck Equipment Schedule T2

Renegade Spt Util 2D	Y59S	17209	**2675**	3275	4550	6400
Hard Top			**250**	250	335	335

CHEROKEE 4WD—4-Cyl.—Truck Equipment Schedule T1

Sport Utility 2D	J27E	16632	**1050**	1500	2575	4075
Sport Utility 4D	J28P	17615	**1200**	1650	2750	4325
2WD	T		**(375)**	(375)	(500)	(500)
6-Cyl. 4.0 Liter	S		**175**	175	235	235

CHEROKEE 4WD—6-Cyl.—Truck Equipment Schedule T3

Briarwood Spt Util 4D	J78S	24643	**2100**	2700	3950	5775
Limited Sport Util 4D	J78S	25164	**2150**	2725	4025	5850

GRAND WAGONEER 4WD—V8—Truck Equipment Schedule T3

Sport Utility 4D	S587	29819	**1500**	2000	3175	4825

1991 JEEP

Body	Type	VIN	List	Trade-In Fair	Trade-In Good	Pvt-Party Good	Retail Excellent
COMANCHE PICKUP 4WD—4-Cyl.—Truck Equipment Sch T2							
Short Bed	J26P	12588	400	575	1075	1925
Long Bed	J26P	13000	375	525	1025	1850
2WD	T		(325)	(325)	(435)	(435)
6-Cyl. 4.0 Liter	S		325	325	435	435

1992 JEEP — 1J(4or7)-(Y19P)-N-#

Body	Type	VIN	List	Trade-In Fair	Trade-In Good	Pvt-Party Good	Retail Excellent
WRANGLER 4WD—4-Cyl.—Truck Equipment Schedule T2							
S Sport Utility 2D	Y19P	11250	1950	2500	3675	5325
Sport Utility 2D	Y29P	13324	2150	2725	3900	5650
Hard Top			275	275	365	365
6-Cyl. 4.0 Liter	S		625	625	835	835
WRANGLER 4WD—6-Cyl.—Truck Equipment Schedule T2							
Islander Spt Util 2D	Y39S	14674	2750	3375	4675	6550
Sahara Spt Util 2D	Y49S	15823	2900	3550	4875	6775
Renegade Spt Util 2D	Y69S	17590	3075	3650	4975	6900
Hard Top			275	275	365	365
CHEROKEE 4WD—4-Cyl.—Truck Equipment Schedule T1							
Sport Utility 2D	J27P	18030	1000	1450	2500	4025
Sport Utility 4D	J28P	19040	1125	1575	2700	4275
Laredo			75	75	100	100
Sport			75	75	100	100
2WD	T		(400)	(400)	(535)	(535)
6-Cyl. 4.0 Liter	S		225	225	300	300
CHEROKEE 4WD—6-Cyl.—Truck Equipment Schedule T3							
Briarwood Spt Utl 4D	N78S	25284	2225	2775	4100	5975
Limited Sport Util 4D	J78S	25819	2250	2825	4150	6025
COMANCHE PICKUP 4WD—4-Cyl.—Truck Equipment Sch T2							
Short Bed	J26P	13108	475	700	1250	2125
Long Bed	J26P	13839	450	625	1150	2025
Eliminator or Sport			75	75	100	100
Pioneer			75	75	100	100
2WD	T		(350)	(350)	(465)	(465)
6-Cyl. 4.0 Liter	S		375	375	500	500

1993 JEEP — 1J4-(Y19P)-P-#

Body	Type	VIN	List	Trade-In Fair	Trade-In Good	Pvt-Party Good	Retail Excellent
WRANGLER 4WD—4-Cyl.—Truck Equipment Schedule T2							
S Sport Utility 2D	Y19P	11680	2175	2750	3925	5675
Sport Utility 2D	Y29P	13828	2400	3000	4225	6000
Hard Top			300	300	400	400
6-Cyl. 4.0 Liter	S		700	700	935	935
WRANGLER 4WD—6-Cyl.—Truck Equipment Schedule T2							
Sahara Spt Util 2D	Y49S	16327	3275	3925	5300	7275
Renegade Spt Util 2D	Y69S	18094	3325	4025	5400	7400
Hard Top			300	300	400	400
CHEROKEE 4WD—6-Cyl.—Truck Equipment Schedule T1							
Sport Utility 2D	J27S	16432	1375	1850	2975	4550
Sport Utility 4D	J28S	17442	1550	2075	3250	4900
Sport 2D	J67S	18033	1350	1825	2950	4525
Sport 4D	J68S	19043	1600	2100	3300	4975
Country Sport Util 2D	J77S	19721	1375	1850	2975	4550
Country Sport Util 4D	J78S	20731	1550	2075	3250	4900
2WD	T		(425)	(425)	(565)	(565)
4-Cyl. 2.5 Liter	P		(375)	(375)	(500)	(500)
GRAND CHEROKEE 4WD—6-Cyl.—Truck Equipment Sch T1							
Sport Utility 4D	Z68S	21898	2225	2775	4100	5975
Sport Utility 4D	Z88S	21898	2225	2775	4100	5975
Laredo Sport Util 4D	Z58S	23082	2550	3175	4525	6475
2WD	X		(425)	(425)	(565)	(565)
V8 5.2 Liter	Y		325	325	435	435
GRAND CHEROKEE 4WD—V8—Truck Equipment Schedule T3							
Wagoneer Spt Util 4D	Z88Y	29826	3875	4600	6175	8425
Limited Sport Util 4D	Z78Y	28925	3975	4725	6325	8650
6-Cyl. 4.0L (Limited)	S		(325)	(325)	(435)	(435)

1994 JEEP — 1J4-(Y19P)-R-#

Body	Type	VIN	List	Trade-In Fair	Trade-In Good	Pvt-Party Good	Retail Excellent
WRANGLER 4WD—4-Cyl.—Truck Equipment Schedule T2							
S Sport Utility 2D	Y19P	12610	2450	3050	4300	6100
w/o Rear Seat			(100)	(100)	(135)	(135)
Hard Top			325	325	435	435
WRANGLER 4WD—6-Cyl.—Truck Equipment Schedule T2							
SE Sport Utility 2D	Y29S	14949	3500	4200	5625	7650

TRUCKS & VANS

TRUCKS & VANS

Body Type	VIN	List	Trade-In Fair	Trade-In Good	Pvt-Party Good	Retail Excellent
Sahara Spt Util 2D	Y49S	17372	3625	4350	5750	7825
Renegade Spt Util 2D	Y69S	19201	3725	4475	5875	7975
w/o Rear Seat			(100)	(100)	(135)	(135)
Hard Top			325	325	435	435
CHEROKEE 4WD—6-Cyl.—Truck Equipment Schedule T1						
SE Sport Utility 2D	J27S	17402	1475	1950	3150	4800
SE Sport Utility 4D	J28S	18412	1700	2225	3425	5150
Sport 2D	J67S	18947	1450	1925	3100	4725
Sport 4D	J68S	19957	1750	2275	3475	5200
Country Sport Util 2D	J77S	20584	1475	1950	3150	4800
Country Sport Util 4D	J78S	21594	1700	2225	3425	5150
2WD	T		(450)	(450)	(600)	(600)
4-Cyl. 2.5 Liter	P		(400)	(400)	(535)	(535)
GRAND CHEROKEE 4WD—6-Cyl.—Truck Equipment Sch T1						
SE Sport Utility 4D	Z68S	23488	2350	2925	4300	6250
Laredo Sport Util 4D	Z58S	23627	2700	3325	4775	6825
2WD	X		(450)	(450)	(600)	(600)
V8 5.2 Liter	Y		375	375	500	500
GRAND CHEROKEE 4WD—V8—Truck Equipment Schedule T3						
Limited Sport Util 4D	Z78Y	30113	4225	5025	6825	9350
6-Cyl. 4.0 Liter	S		(375)	(375)	(500)	(500)

Body Type	VIN	List	Trade-In Fair	Trade-In Good	Pvt-Party Good	Retail Excellent
WRANGLER 4WD—4-Cyl.—Truck Equipment Schedule T2						
S Sport Utility 2D	Y19P	13038	2775	3400	4700	6575
w/o Rear Seat			(100)	(100)	(135)	(135)
Rio Grande Pkg			425	425	565	565
Hard Top			350	350	465	465
WRANGLER 4WD—6-Cyl.—Truck Equipment Schedule T2						
SE Sport Utility 2D	Y29S	15932	3925	4675	6150	8250
Sahara Spt Util 2D	Y49S	17957	4050	4825	6300	8450
w/o Rear Seat			(100)	(100)	(135)	(135)
Hard Top			350	350	465	465
CHEROKEE 4WD—6-Cyl.—Truck Equipment Schedule T1						
SE Sport Utility 2D	J27S	18194	1650	2175	3400	5150
SE Sport Utility 4D	J28S	19228	1950	2475	3750	5550
Sport 2D	J67S	19800	1625	2125	3350	5100
Sport 4D	J68S	20834	1975	2525	3825	5625
Country Sport Util 4D	J78S	22398	1950	2475	3750	5550
2WD	T		(475)	(475)	(635)	(635)
4-Cyl. 2.5 Liter	P		(425)	(425)	(565)	(565)
GRAND CHEROKEE 4WD—6-Cyl.—Truck Equipment Sch T1						
SE Sport Utility 4D	Z68S	25075	2550	3175	4600	6650
Laredo Sport Util 4D	Z58S	25706	2975	3625	5125	7275
2WD	X		(475)	(475)	(635)	(635)
V8 5.2 Liter	Y		425	425	565	565
GRAND CHEROKEE 4WD—V8—Truck Equipment Schedule T3						
Limited/Orvis 4D	Z78Y	31182	4575	5400	7300	9975
2WD	X		(475)	(475)	(635)	(635)
6-Cyl. 4.0 Liter	S		(425)	(425)	(565)	(565)

Body Type	VIN	List	Trade-In Fair	Trade-In Good	Pvt-Party Good	Retail Excellent
CHEROKEE 4WD—6-Cyl.—Truck Equipment Schedule T1						
SE Sport Utility 2D	J27S	18369	1950	2500	3825	5650
SE Sport Utility 4D	J28S	19403	2250	2800	4150	6050
Sport 2D	J67S	19908	1900	2425	3725	5550
Sport 4D	J68S	20942	2275	2850	4200	6100
Country Sport Util 4D	J78S	22476	2250	2800	4150	6050
2WD	T		(500)	(500)	(665)	(665)
4-Cyl. 2.5 Liter	P		(450)	(450)	(600)	(600)
GRAND CHEROKEE 4WD—6-Cyl.—Truck Equipment Sch T1						
Laredo Sport Util 4D	Z58S	27071	2725	3350	4925	7075
2WD	X		(500)	(500)	(665)	(665)
V8 5.2 Liter	Y		475	475	635	635
GRAND CHEROKEE 4WD—V8—Truck Equipment Schedule T3						
Limited/Orvis 4D	Z78Y	33406	4475	5250	7250	10050
2WD	X		(500)	(500)	(665)	(665)
6-Cyl. 4.0 Liter	S		(475)	(475)	(635)	(635)

Body Type	VIN	List	Trade-In Fair	Trade-In Good	Pvt-Party Good	Retail Excellent
WRANGLER 4WD—4-Cyl.—Truck Equipment Schedule T2						
SE Sport Utility 2D	Y29P	14857	3900	4650	6075	8150

Body	Type	VIN	List	Trade-In Fair	Trade-In Good	Pvt-Party Good	Retail Excellent
	w/o Rear Seat			(100)	(100)	(135)	(135)
	Hard Top			400	400	535	535

WRANGLER 4WD—6-Cyl.—Truck Equipment Schedule T2

Body	Type	VIN	List	Fair	Good	Good	Excellent
Sport Utility 2D		Y19S	17665	4875	5700	7250	9500
Sahara Spt Util 2D		Y49S	19363	4900	5750	7300	9550
	w/o Rear Seat			(100)	(100)	(135)	(135)
	Hard Top			400	400	535	535

CHEROKEE 4WD—6-Cyl.—Truck Equipment Schedule T1

Body	Type	VIN	List	Fair	Good	Good	Excellent
SE Sport Utility 2D		J27S	19280	2325	2900	4300	6275
SE Sport Utility 4D		J28S	20315	2650	3250	4675	6700
Sport 2D		J67S	20895	2250	2825	4250	6200
Sport 4D		J68S	21305	2700	3300	4725	6750
Country Sport Util 4D		J78S	23945	2650	3250	4675	6700
2WD		T		(525)	(525)	(700)	(700)
4-Cyl. 2.5 Liter		P		(475)	(475)	(635)	(635)

GRAND CHEROKEE 4WD—6-Cyl.—Truck Equipment Sch T1

Body	Type	VIN	List	Fair	Good	Good	Excellent
Laredo Sport Util 4D		Z58S	28040	3300	4000	5700	8050
TSi Sport Util 4D		Z58Y	30190	3550	4250	5950	8350
2WD		X		(525)	(525)	(700)	(700)
V8 5.2 Liter		Y		525	525	700	700

GRAND CHEROKEE 4WD—V8—Truck Equipment Schedule T3

Body	Type	VIN	List	Fair	Good	Good	Excellent
Limited/Orvis 4D		Z78Y	34315	5125	6000	8150	11150
2WD		X		(525)	(525)	(700)	(700)
6-Cyl. 4.0 Liter		S		(525)	(525)	(700)	(700)

WRANGLER 4WD—4-Cyl.—Truck Equipment Schedule T2

Body	Type	VIN	List	Fair	Good	Good	Excellent
SE Sport Utility 2D		Y29P	15480	4475	5250	6625	8675
	w/o Rear Seat			(100)	(100)	(135)	(135)
	Hard Top			425	425	565	565

WRANGLER 4WD—6-Cyl.—Truck Equipment Schedule T2

Body	Type	VIN	List	Fair	Good	Good	Excellent
Sport Utility 2D		Y19S	18030	5475	6375	7825	10050
Sahara Spt Util 2D		Y49S	20140	5525	6425	7900	10150
	w/o Rear Seat			(100)	(100)	(135)	(135)
	Hard Top			425	425	565	565

CHEROKEE 4WD—6-Cyl.—Truck Equipment Schedule T1

Body	Type	VIN	List	Fair	Good	Good	Excellent
SE Sport Utility 2D		J27S	20270	2825	3475	4925	6925
SE Sport Utility 4D		J28S	21305	3200	3875	5325	7425
Sport 2D		J67S	21885	2825	3450	4900	6900
Sport 4D		J68S	22920	3275	3925	5400	7500
Classic Sport Util 4D		J68S	23370	3225	3900	5350	7450
Limited Sport Util 4D		J78S	24885	4025	4800	6600	9150
2WD		T		(575)	(575)	(765)	(765)
4-Cyl. 2.5 Liter		P		(525)	(525)	(700)	(700)

GRAND CHEROKEE 4WD—6-Cyl.—Truck Equipment Sch T1

Body	Type	VIN	List	Fair	Good	Good	Excellent
Laredo Sport Util 4D		Z58S	28340	4000	4775	6525	8975
Special Ed Sport Util		Z48S	30040	4150	4925	6675	9150
TSi Sport Utility 4D		Z58S	30490	4250	5050	6800	9275
2WD		X		(575)	(575)	(765)	(765)
V8 5.2 Liter		Y		575	575	765	765

GRAND CHEROKEE 4WD—V8—Truck Equipment Schedule T3

Body	Type	VIN	List	Fair	Good	Good	Excellent
Limited Sport Util 4D		Z78Y	35195	5950	6900	9150	12250
5.9 Limited Sport Util		Z88Z	38700	6150	7125	9500	12800
2WD		X		(575)	(575)	(765)	(765)
6-Cyl. 4.0 Liter		S		(575)	(575)	(765)	(765)

WRANGLER 4WD—4-Cyl.—Truck Equipment Schedule T2

Body	Type	VIN	List	Fair	Good	Good	Excellent
SE Sport Utility 2D		Y29P	15670	4975	5825	7225	9350
	w/o Rear Seat			(150)	(150)	(200)	(200)
	Hard Top			500	500	665	665

WRANGLER 4WD—6-Cyl.—Truck Equipment Schedule T2

Body	Type	VIN	List	Fair	Good	Good	Excellent
Sport Utility 2D		Y19S	18335	6125	7100	8600	10900
Sahara Spt Util 2D		Y49S	20495	6250	7250	8750	11100
	w/o Rear Seat			(150)	(150)	(200)	(200)
	Hard Top			500	500	665	665

CHEROKEE 4WD—6-Cyl.—Truck Equipment Schedule T1

Body	Type	VIN	List	Fair	Good	Good	Excellent
SE Sport Utility 2D		F27P	20815	3500	4200	5725	7925
SE Sport Utility 4D		F28P	21850	3900	4625	6225	8450
Sport 2D		F67S	22540	3600	4325	5850	8050
Sport 4D		F68S	23375	4100	4875	6450	8700
Classic Sport Util 4D		F68S	23945	4100	4875	6450	8700
Limited Sport Util 4D		F78S	25505	4900	5725	7650	10350

1999 JEEP

Body Type	VIN	List	Trade-In Fair	Trade-In Good	Pvt-Party Good	Retail Excellent
2WD	T		(650)	(650)	(865)	(865)
4-Cyl. 2.5 Liter	P		(600)	(600)	(800)	(800)
GRAND CHEROKEE 4WD—6-Cyl.—Truck Equipment Sch T1						
Laredo Sport Util 4D	W58S	28225	5525	6425	8350	11100
2WD	2		(650)	(650)	(865)	(865)
V8 4.7 Liter	N		675	675	900	900
GRAND CHEROKEE 4WD—V8—Truck Equipment Schedule T3						
Limited Sport Util	W68N	35480	7750	8900	11350	14800
2WD	X		(650)	(650)	(865)	(865)
6-Cyl. 4.0 Liter	S		(700)	(700)	(935)	(935)

2000 JEEP — 1J4-(A29P)-Y-#

Body Type	VIN	List	Trade-In Fair	Trade-In Good	Pvt-Party Good	Retail Excellent
WRANGLER 4WD—4-Cyl.—Truck Equipment Schedule T2						
SE Sport Utility 2D	A29P	16305	5650	6550	8000	10200
w/o Rear Seat			(175)	(175)	(235)	(235)
Hard Top			550	550	735	735
WRANGLER 4WD—6-Cyl.—Truck Equipment Schedule T2						
Sport Utility 2D	A49S	18995	6925	8000	9525	11900
Sahara Spt Util 2D	A59S	20925	7100	8200	9750	12150
w/o Rear Seat			(175)	(175)	(235)	(235)
Hard Top			550	550	735	735
CHEROKEE 4WD—6-Cyl.—Truck Equipment Schedule T1						
SE Sport Utility 2D	F27P	21285	4325	5100	6750	9100
SE Sport Utility 4D	F28P	22320	4750	5575	7250	9650
Sport 2D	F47S	21860	4525	5350	7000	9375
Sport 4D	F48S	22895	5100	5975	7650	10150
Classic Sport Util 4D	F58S	23420	5100	5975	7700	10200
Limited Sport Util 4D	F68S	25745	5850	6825	8875	11800
2WD	T		(725)	(725)	(965)	(965)
4-Cyl. 2.5 Liter	P		(675)	(675)	(900)	(900)
GRAND CHEROKEE 4WD—6-Cyl.—Truck Equipment Sch T1						
Laredo Sport Util 4D	W48S	29075	6550	7575	9650	12600
2WD	X		(725)	(725)	(965)	(965)
V8 4.7 Liter	N		750	750	1000	1000
GRAND CHEROKEE 4WD—V8—Truck Equipment Schedule T3						
Limited Spt Util 4D	258N	35950	9050	10325	12950	16750
2WD	X		(725)	(725)	(965)	(965)
6-Cyl. 4.0 Liter	S		(825)	(825)	(1100)	(1100)

2001 JEEP — 1J4-(A29P)-1-#

Body Type	VIN	List	Trade-In Fair	Trade-In Good	Pvt-Party Good	Retail Excellent
WRANGLER 4WD—4-Cyl.—Truck Equipment Schedule T2						
SE Sport Utility 2D	A29P	16095	6425	7450	8900	11200
w/o Rear Seat			(200)	(200)	(265)	(265)
Hard Top			600	600	800	800
WRANGLER 4WD—6-Cyl.—Truck Equipment Schedule T2						
Sport Utility 2D	A49S	19615	7900	9075	10600	13100
Sahara Spt Util 2D	A59S	22895	8125	9325	10950	13450
Hard Top			600	600	800	800
CHEROKEE 4WD—6-Cyl.—Truck Equipment Schedule T1						
SE Sport Utility 2D	F27S	21780	5325	6225	7975	10500
SE Sport Utility 4D	F28S	22815	5775	6750	8525	11150
Sport Utility 2D	F47S	22410	5675	6600	8400	11000
Sport Utility 4D	F48S	23445	6300	7300	9125	11800
Classic Sport Util 4D	F58S	23835	6325	7350	9175	11850
Limited Sport Util 4D	F68S	23970	7025	8100	10300	13550
2WD			(800)	(800)	(1065)	(1065)
GRAND CHEROKEE 4WD—6-Cyl.—Truck Equipment Sch T1						
Laredo Sport Util 4D	W48S	29855	7825	8975	11200	14350
2WD	X		(800)	(800)	(1065)	(1065)
V8 4.7 Liter	N		825	825	1100	1100
GRAND CHEROKEE 4WD—V8—Truck Equipment Schedule T3						
Limited Spt Util 4D	W58N	35870	10550	12050	14800	18800
2WD	X		(800)	(800)	(1065)	(1065)
6-Cyl. 4.0 Liter	S		(925)	(925)	(1235)	(1235)

2002 JEEP — 1J(4or8)-(A29P)-2-#

Body Type	VIN	List	Trade-In Fair	Trade-In Good	Pvt-Party Good	Retail Excellent
WRANGLER 4WD—4-Cyl.—Truck Equipment Schedule T2						
SE Sport Utility 2D	A29P	16410	7425	8525	10050	12450
w/o Rear Seat			(225)	(225)	(300)	(300)
Hard Top			650	650	865	865
WRANGLER 4WD—6-Cyl.—Truck Equipment Schedule T2						
X Sport Utility 2D	A49S	18995	8600	9850	11400	13900

TRUCKS & VANS

Body Type	VIN	List	Trade-In Fair	Good	Pvt-Party Good	Retail Excellent
Sport Utility 2D	A49S	20665	9025	10325	11900	14450
Sahara Spt Util 2D	A59S	24035	9300	10600	12250	14850
Hard Top			650	650	865	865
LIBERTY 4WD—V6—Truck Equipment Schedule T1						
Sport Utility 4D	L48K	21070	7825	8975	10900	13750
Limited Utility 4D	L58K	23305	8925	10225	12150	15100
Renegade Utility 4D	L38K	23855	9425	10750	12700	15800
2WD			(875)	(875)	(1165)	(1165)
4-Cyl. 2.4 Liter	1		(925)	(925)	(1235)	(1235)
GRAND CHEROKEE 4WD—6-Cyl.—Truck Equipment Schedule T1						
Laredo Sport Util 4D	W48S	27995	9225	10500	12850	16300
Sport Utility 4D	W38S	29140	9500	10850	13200	16650
2WD	X		(875)	(875)	(1165)	(1165)
V8 4.7 Liter	N		900	900	1200	1200
GRAND CHEROKEE 4WD—V8—Truck Equipment Schedule T3						
Limited Spt Util 4D	W58N	33300	12300	13925	16850	21100
Overland Spt Utl 4D	W68N	37430	14025	15800	18400	22400
2WD	X		(875)	(875)	(1165)	(1165)
6-Cyl. 4.0 Liter	S		(1025)	(1025)	(1365)	(1365)

2003 JEEP — 1J(4or8)-(A291)-3-#

Body Type	VIN	List	Trade-In Fair	Good	Pvt-Party Good	Retail Excellent
WRANGLER 4WD—4-Cyl.—Truck Equipment Schedule T2						
SE Sport Utility 2D	A291	16910	8600	9850	11250	13550
w/o Rear Seat			(250)	(250)	(335)	(335)
Hard Top			700	700	935	935
WRANGLER 4WD—6-Cyl.—Truck Equipment Schedule T2						
X Sport Utility 2D	A39S	19295	9975	11325	12800	15250
Sport Utility 2D	A49S	21105	10325	11750	13250	15750
Sahara Spt Util 2D	A59S	24695	10700	12150	13700	16200
Rubicon Spt Utl 2D	A59S	24995	11475	13050	14600	17250
Hard Top			700	700	935	935
LIBERTY 4WD—V6—Truck Equipment Schedule T1						
Sport Utility 4D	L48K	22880	9375	10700	12650	15650
Limited Utility 4D	L58K	24045	10550	12050	14000	17200
Renegade Utility 4D	L38K	24630	11125	12625	14650	17850
2WD			(950)	(950)	(1265)	(1265)
4-Cyl. 2.4 Liter	1		(1025)	(1025)	(1365)	(1365)
GRAND CHEROKEE 4WD—6-Cyl.—Truck Equipment Schedule T1						
Laredo Sport Util 4D	W48S	28640	10900	12375	14800	18450
2WD	X		(950)	(950)	(1265)	(1265)
V8 4.7 Liter	N		975	975	1300	1300
GRAND CHEROKEE 4WD—V8—Truck Equipment Schedule T3						
Limited Spt Util 4D	W58N	34920	14200	16025	19100	23600
Overland Spt Utl 4D	W68J	37975	16125	18150	20800	25100
2WD	X		(950)	(950)	(1265)	(1265)
6-Cyl. 4.0 Liter	S		(1125)	(1125)	(1500)	(1500)

2004 JEEP — 1J(4or8)-(A291)-4-#

Body Type	VIN	List	Trade-In Fair	Good	Pvt-Party Good	Retail Excellent
WRANGLER 4WD—4-Cyl.—Truck Equipment Schedule T2						
SE Sport Utility 2D	A291	17515	9975	11375	12700	15050
w/o Rear Seat			(275)	(275)	(365)	(365)
Hard Top			750	750	1000	1000
WRANGLER 4WD—6-Cyl.—Truck Equipment Schedule T2						
X Sport Utility 2D	A49S	19945	11525	13050	14500	17050
Sport Utility 2D	A49S	21930	11900	13500	14950	17500
Unlimited Spt Util 2D	A49S	24995				
Sahara Spt Util 2D	A59S	25520	12325	13975	15400	18050
Rubicon Spt Utl 2D	A59S	25695	13150	14875	16400	19150
Hard Top			750	750	1000	1000
LIBERTY 4WD—V6—Truck Equipment Schedule T1						
Sport Utility 4D	L48K	21855	11225	12775	14850	18100
Limited Utility 4D	L58K	24870	12525	14150	16300	19800
Renegade Utility 4D	L38K	25455	13150	14875	17050	20500
2WD	K		(1000)	(1000)	(1335)	(1335)
4-Cyl. 2.4 Liter			(1125)	(1125)	(1500)	(1500)
GRAND CHEROKEE 4WD—6-Cyl.—Truck Equipment Schedule T1						
Laredo Sport Util 4D	W48S	29875	12900	14600	17200	21100
2WD	X		(1000)	(1000)	(1335)	(1335)
V8 4.7 Liter	N,J		1050	1050	1400	1400
GRAND CHEROKEE 4WD—V8—Truck Equipment Schedule T3						
Limited Spt Util 4D	W58N	35655	16475	18525	21700	26600
Overland Spt Utl 4D	W68J	39920	18525	20825	23500	27900
2WD	X		(1000)	(1000)	(1335)	(1335)

Body	Type	VIN	List	Trade-In Fair	Good	Pvt-Party Good	Retail Excellent
6-Cyl. 4.0 Liter		S		(1225)	(1225)	(1635)	(1635)

KIA

1995 KIA — KND(JA721)–S–#

SPORTAGE 4WD—4-Cyl.—Truck Equipment Schedule T2

Sport Utility 4D		JA721	14895	1025	1450	2500	3975
EX Sport Utility 4D		JA721	15895	1225	1675	2775	4325
2WD				(425)	(425)	(565)	(565)
4-Cyl. 2.0L DOHC		3		100	100	135	135

1996 KIA — KND(JA723)–T–#

SPORTAGE 4WD—4-Cyl.—Truck Equipment Schedule T2

Sport Utility 4D		JA723	15720	1275	1750	2850	4425
EX Sport Utility 4D		JA723	16420	1500	2025	3175	4775
2WD				(450)	(450)	(600)	(600)

1997 KIA — KND(JA723)–V–#

SPORTAGE 4WD—4-Cyl.—Truck Equipment Schedule T2

Sport Utility 4D		JA723	16420	1625	2125	3300	4950
EX Sport Utility 4D		JA723	17040	1900	2425	3625	5325
2WD				(475)	(475)	(635)	(635)

1998 KIA — KND(JA723)–W–#

SPORTAGE 4WD—4-Cyl.—Truck Equipment Schedule T2

Sport Utility 4D		JA723	17845	2100	2650	3775	5425
EX Sport Utility 4D		JA723	18945	2375	2950	4125	5800
2WD				(525)	(525)	(700)	(700)

1999 KIA — KNM(JA623)–X–#

SPORTAGE 4WD—4-Cyl.—Truck Equipment Schedule T2

Sport Util Conv 2D		JA623	14945	2100	2700	3850	5525
Sport Utility 4D		JA723	16745	2550	3150	4350	6075
EX Sport Utility 4D		JA723	19045	2850	3500	4725	6525
2WD		B		(600)	(600)	(800)	(800)

2000 KIA — KNM(JA623)–Y–#

SPORTAGE 4WD—4-Cyl.—Truck Equipment Schedule T2

Sport Util Conv 2D		JA623	14945	2675	3275	4500	6275
Sport Utility 4D		JA723	16745	3125	3775	5025	6875
EX Sport Utility 4D		JA723	19045	3475	4175	5450	7350
2WD		B		(675)	(675)	(900)	(900)

2001 KIA — KND(JB623)–1–#

SPORTAGE 4WD—4-Cyl.—Truck Equipment Schedule T2

Sport Util Conv 2D		JB623	15345	3325	4025	5300	7175
Sport Utility 4D		JB723	17245	3850	4575	5875	7825
EX Sport Utility 4D		JB723	19545	4250	5050	6350	8350
Limited Spt Util 4D		JB723	20090	4825	5675	7025	9125
2WD				(750)	(750)	(1000)	(1000)

2002 KIA — KND(JA623)–2–#

SPORTAGE 4WD—4-Cyl.—Truck Equipment Schedule T2

Sport Util Conv 2D		JA623	15640	4200	5000	6300	8300
Sport Utility 4D		JA723	18715	4750	5575	6925	9000
2WD		B		(825)	(825)	(1100)	(1100)

SEDONA—V6—Truck Equipment Schedule T1

LX Minivan		UP131	21590	6850	7900	9575	12100
EX Minivan		UP131	21590	7525	8675	10350	13000

2003 KIA — KND(UP131)–3–#

SEDONA—V6—Truck Equipment Schedule T1

LX Minivan		UP131	19965	8450	9650	11400	14000
EX Minivan		UP131	22180	9175	10475	12250	15000

SORENTO 4WD—V6—Truck Equipment Schedule T1

LX Sport Utility 4D		JC733	21795	8300	9525	11800	15100
EX Sport Utility 4D		JC733	24595	9050	10325	12650	16100
2WD				(950)	(950)	(1265)	(1265)

2004 KIA

Body	Type	VIN	List	Trade-In Fair	Trade-In Good	Pvt-Party Good	Retail Excellent
2004 KIA — KND(UP131)–4–#							
SEDONA—V6—Truck Equipment Schedule T1							
LX Minivan		UP131	20615	**10475**	**11900**	**13750**	**16650**
EX Minivan		UP131	22725	**11225**	**12775**	**14650**	**17650**
SORENTO 4WD—V6—Truck Equipment Schedule T1							
LX Sport Utility 4D		JC733	23290	**10125**	**11525**	**13950**	**17550**
EX Sport Utility 4D		JC733	25490	**10900**	**12375**	**14900**	**18600**
2WD		D		**(1000)**	**(1000)**	**(1335)**	**(1335)**

LAND ROVER

1990 LAND ROVER — SAL(HV124)–L–#

RANGE ROVER 4WD—V8—Truck Equipment Schedule T3

Body	Type	VIN	List	Fair	Good	Good	Excellent
Sport Utility 4D		HV124	38575	**1250**	**1725**	**2950**	**4625**
County Sport Util 4D		HV124	40675	**1625**	**2125**	**3425**	**5225**

1991 LAND ROVER — SAL(HV124)–M–#

RANGE ROVER 4WD—V8—Truck Equipment Schedule T3

Hunter Sport Util 4D		HV124	36525	**800**	**1125**	**2100**	**3600**
Sport Utility 4D		HV124	44475	**1500**	**2000**	**3300**	**5125**
Great Divide Util 4D		HV124	45075	**1625**	**2125**	**3450**	**5300**
County SE Util 4D		HV124	46975	**1625**	**2475**	**3875**	**5800**

1992 LAND ROVER — SAL(HV124)–N–#

RANGE ROVER 4WD—V8—Truck Equipment Schedule T3

Sport Utility 4D		HV124	39475	**1500**	**2025**	**3375**	**5250**
County Sport Util 4D		HV124	45075	**2025**	**2575**	**4000**	**6025**

1993 LAND ROVER — SAL(DH128)–P–#

DEFENDER 110 4WD—V8—Truck Equipment Schedule T2

Sport Utility 4D		DH128	40575	********	********	********	**25800**

RANGE ROVER 4WD—V8—Truck Equipment Schedule T3

County Sport Util 4D		HC124	45125	**2175**	**2750**	**4275**	**6350**
County LWB Util 4D		HC134	49825	**2825**	**3475**	**5100**	**7350**

1994 LAND ROVER — SAL(DV228)–R–#

DEFENDER 90 4WD—V8—Truck Equipment Schedule T2

Sport Utility 2D		DV228	28495	********	********	********	**26500**

DISCOVERY 4WD—V8—Truck Equipment Schedule T3

Sport Utility 4D		JY124	30725	**2150**	**2725**	**4150**	**6150**
Dual Moon Roofs				**600**	**600**	**800**	**800**
Rear Jump Seats				**300**	**300**	**400**	**400**
Manual Trans				**(300)**	**(300)**	**(400)**	**(400)**
Rear Air Conditioning				**175**	**175**	**235**	**235**

RANGE ROVER 4WD—V8—Truck Equipment Schedule T3

County Sport Util 4D		HV124	47525	**2150**	**2725**	**4375**	**6575**
County LWB 4D		HC134	50825	**2875**	**3525**	**5250**	**7600**

1995 LAND ROVER — SAL(DV228)–S–#

DEFENDER 90 4WD—V8—Truck Equipment Schedule T2

Soft Top Spt Util 2D		DV228	29275	********	********	********	**27900**
Hard Top Spt Util 2D		DV228		********	********	********	**29100**

DISCOVERY 4WD—V8—Truck Equipment Schedule T3

Sport Utility 4D		JY124	32375	**2650**	**3250**	**4800**	**6950**
Dual Moon Roofs				**625**	**625**	**835**	**835**
Rear Jump Seats				**325**	**325**	**435**	**435**
Rear Air Conditioning				**200**	**200**	**265**	**265**
Manual Trans				**(325)**	**(325)**	**(435)**	**(435)**

RANGE ROVER 4WD—V8—Truck Equipment Schedule T3

County Classic 4D		HV124	45625	**2625**	**3250**	**4975**	**7325**
County LWB 4D		HC134	53125	**3275**	**3925**	**5725**	**8225**
4.0 SE Sport Util 4D		PV124	54625	**5525**	**6425**	**8550**	**11500**

1996 LAND ROVER — SAL(JY124)–T–#

DISCOVERY 4WD—V8—Truck Equipment Schedule T3

SD Sport Utility 4D		JY124	32975	**3200**	**3875**	**5550**	**7875**
SE Sport Utility 4D		JY124	35975	**4175**	**4975**	**6775**	**9300**
SE7 Sport Util 4D		JY124	38550	**4425**	**5200**	**7025**	**9600**

TRUCKS & VANS

1996 LAND ROVER

Body	Type	VIN	List	Trade-In Fair	Trade-In Good	Pvt-Party Good	Retail Excellent
	Rear Jump Seats (Ex SE7)			350	350	465	465
	Dual Moon Roofs			650	650	865	865
	Manual Trans	8		(350)	(350)	(465)	(465)
RANGE ROVER 4WD—V8—Truck Equipment Schedule T3							
4.0 SE Spt Util 4D		PV124	55625	6200	7175	9375	12550
4.6 SE Spt Util 4D		PV144	62625	8925	10225	12750	16400

1997 LAND ROVER — SAL(DV224)-V-#

DEFENDER 90 4WD—V8—Truck Equipment Schedule T2							
Soft Top Spt Util 2D		DV224	32625	****	****	****	31000
Hard Top Spt Util 2D		DV324	34625	****	****	****	32500
DISCOVERY 4WD—V8—Truck Equipment Schedule T3							
SD Sport Utility 4D		JY124	34625	3825	4550	6375	8925
XD Sport Utility 4D		JY124	36125	4800	5650	7575	10300
SE Sport Utility 4D		JY124	36625	4900	5725	7675	10400
SE7 Sport Utility 4D		JY124	39125	5125	6000	8000	10800
	Rear Jump Seats (Ex SE7)			375	375	500	500
	Dual Moon Roofs			675	675	900	900
	Manual Trans	8		(375)	(375)	(500)	(500)
RANGE ROVER 4WD—V8—Truck Equipment Schedule T3							
4.0 SE Spt Util 4D		PV124	56125	6975	8075	10400	13750
4.6 HSE Spt Util 4D		PV144	63625	9975	11325	14000	17900

1998 LAND ROVER — SAL(JY124)-W-#

DISCOVERY 4WD—V8—Truck Equipment Schedule T3							
LE Sport Utility 4D		JY124	35125	5750	6700	8700	11550
LSE Sport Utility 4D		JY124	38625	6025	6975	9025	11950
	Rear Jump Seats			425	425	565	565
	Rear Air Conditioning			250	250	335	335
	Dual Moon Roofs			700	700	935	935
RANGE ROVER 4WD—V8—Truck Equipment Schedule T3							
4.0 SE Spt Util 4D		PV124	56625	8000	9175	11400	14600
4.6 HSE Spt Util 4D		PV144	64125	11175	12725	15200	19000

1999 LAND ROVER — SAL(JY124)-X-#

DISCOVERY 4WD—V8—Truck Equipment Schedule T3							
SD Sport Utility 4D		JY124	33625	6950	8050	9975	12850
	Rear Jump Seats			500	500	665	665
	Dual Moon Roofs			750	750	1000	1000
DISCOVERY SERIES II 4WD—V8—Truck Equipment Schedule T3							
Sport Utility 4D		TY124	36725	8175	9375	11400	14500
	Rear Jump Seats			500	500	665	665
	Rear Air Conditioning			300	300	400	400
	Dual Moon Roofs			750	750	1000	1000
	Performance Pkg			725	725	965	965
RANGE ROVER 4WD—V8—Truck Equipment Schedule T3							
4.0 Sport Utility 4D		PA124	57625	9900	11225	13800	17550
4.0 S Sport Utility 4D		PA124	57625	9900	11225	13800	17550
4.0 SE Sport Util 4D		PV124	58525	10500	11950	14550	18350
4.6 HSE Sport Util 4D		PV144	66625	14150	15975	18850	23200

2000 LAND ROVER — SAL(TY124)-Y-#

DISCOVERY SERIES II 4WD—V8—Truck Equipment Schedule T3							
SD Sport Utility 4D		TY124	33975	8800	10075	12150	15200
SD7 Sport Utility 4D		TY124	35725	9600	10950	13050	16250
Sport Utility 4D		TY124	36725	10125	11525	13700	16950
	Rear Jump Seats			550	550	735	735
	Rear Air Conditioning			350	350	465	465
	Dual Moon Roofs			775	775	1035	1035
	Performance Pkg			825	825	1100	1100
RANGE ROVER 4WD—V8—Truck Equipment Schedule T3							
County Sport Util 4D		PA124	58925	11575	13100	15850	19850
4.0 Sport Util 4D		PA124	59625	12100	13725	16500	20600
4.0 SE Sport Util 4D		PV124	59625	12775	14450	17300	21500
4.6 HSK Spt Util 4D		PF164	67625	16475	18525	21600	26400
4.6 HSE Spt Util 4D		PV144	67925	16950	19050	22200	26900
4.6 Vitesse Spt Util 4D		PF164	68625	16950	19050	22300	27100
4.6 Holland Holland		PV164	79625	19675	22075	25400	30600

Body	Type	VIN	List	Trade-In Fair	Trade-In Good	Pvt-Party Good	Retail Excellent

2001 LAND ROVER — SAL(TY124)-1-#

DISCOVERY SERIES II 4WD—V8—Truck Equipment Schedule T3

SD Sport Utility 4D		TY124	33975	10850	12300	14450	17750
SD7 Sport Utility 4D		TY124	35725	11700	13250	15450	18850
LE Sport Utility 4D		TY124	34975	12425	14075	16300	19850
LE7 Sport Utility 4D		TY124	36725	12675	14350	16600	20200
SE Sport Utility 4D		TY124	36975	12950	14700	16950	20500
SE7 Sport Utility 4D		TY124	38725	13150	14875	17150	20700
Rear Jump Seats				600	600	800	800
Rear Air Conditioning				400	400	535	535
Dual Moon Roofs				800	800	1065	1065
Performance Pkg				925	925	1235	1235

RANGE ROVER 4WD—V8—Truck Equipment Schedule T3

4.6 SE Sport Util 4D		PV164	62625	15350	17325	20400	25000
4.6 HSE Sport Util		PV164	19875	22375	25700	30900	

2002 LAND ROVER — SAL(NM222)-2-#

FREELANDER AWD—V6—Truck Equipment Schedule T3

S Sport Utility 4D		NM222	25600	9425	10750	12400	15000
SE Sport Utility 4D		NY222	28400	10800	12250	13950	16750
HSE Sport Util 4D		NE222	32200	12100	13725	15500	18450

DISCOVERY SERIES II 4WD—V8—Truck Equipment Schedule T3

SD Sport Utility 4D		TL144	33995	13050	14775	17000	20500
SD7 Sport Utility 4D		TK144	34995	14025	15800	18050	21700
SE Sport Utility 4D		TY144	37795	15500	17475	19800	23600
SE7 Sport Utility 4D		TW124	38875	15600	17575	19850	23700
Rear Jump Seats				650	650	865	865
Rear Air Conditioning				425	425	565	565
Dual Moon Roofs				825	825	1100	1100
Performance Pkg				1000	1000	1335	1335

RANGE ROVER 4WD—V8—Truck Equipment Schedule T3

4.6 HSE Sport Util 4D		PL162	68665	23325	26100	29600	35100

2003 LAND ROVER — SAL(NM222)-3-#

FREELANDER AWD—V6—Truck Equipment Schedule T3

S Sport Utility 4D		NM222	25600	11525	13050	14850	17700
SE3 Sport Utility 2D		NY122	26995	12625	14300	16150	19150
SE Sport Utility 4D		NY222	28400	13000	14725	16500	19600
HSE Sport Util 4D		NE222	32200	14400	16275	18200	21400

DISCOVERY 4WD—V8—Truck Equipment Schedule T3

S Sport Utility 4D		TL144	34995	15500	17475	19700	23400
SE Sport Utility 4D		TY144	38995	18200	20450	22800	26900
HSE Sport Utility 4D		TP144	40995	19975	22475	25000	29200
Rear Jump Seats				700	700	935	935
Rear Air Conditioning				450	450	600	600
Dual Moon Roofs				850	850	1135	1135
Suspension Pkg				1075	1075	1435	1435

RANGE ROVER 4WD—V8—Truck Equipment Schedule T3

HSE Sport Util 4D		MB114	71865	44650	49725	53300	60300

2004 LAND ROVER — SAL(NY222)-4-#

FREELANDER AWD—V6—Truck Equipment Schedule T3

SE Sport Utility 4D		NY222	25995	15700	17675	19800	23200
SE3 Sport Utility 2D		NY222	28195	15300	17275	19300	22700
HSE Sport Util 4D		NE222	28995	17275	19400	21600	25200

DISCOVERY 4WD—V8—Truck Equipment Schedule T3

S Sport Utility 4D		TL194	34995	18250	20550	22800	26900
SE Sport Utility 4D		TY194	39250	21125	23700	26200	30400
HSE Sport Utility 4D		TP194	41250	23050	25825	28300	32700
G4 Sport Utility 4D		TL194	39995	21900	24475	27000	31300
Rear Jump Seats				750	750	1000	1000
Rear Air Conditioning				475	475	635	635
Dual Moon Roofs				875	875	1165	1165
Suspension Pkg				1150	1150	1535	1535

RANGE ROVER 4WD—V8—Truck Equipment Schedule T3

HSE Sport Util 4D		ME114	72250	49925	55500	59100	66400
Westminister Util		MH114	84700				

TRUCKS & VANS

Body	Type	VIN	List	Trade-In Fair	Good	Pvt-Party Good	Retail Excellent

LEXUS

1996 LEXUS — JT6(HJ88J)-T-#

LX 450 4WD—6-Cyl.—Truck Equipment Schedule T3
| Sport Utility 4D | HJ88J | 47995 | 9425 | 10750 | 13400 | 17200 |

1997 LEXUS — JT6(HJ88J)-V-#

LX 450 4WD—6-Cyl.—Truck Equipment Schedule T3
| Sport Utility 4D | HJ88J | 48945 | 10650 | 12150 | 14900 | 18850 |

1998 LEXUS — JT6(HT00W)-W-#

LX 470 4WD—V8—Truck Equipment Schedule T3
| Sport Utility 4D | HT00W | 55445 | 15450 | 17425 | 20400 | 25200 |

1999 LEXUS — JT6(HF10U)-X-#

RX 300 4WD—V6—Truck Equipment Schedule T3
| Sport Utility 4D | HF10U | 34980 | 12150 | 13775 | 15850 | 19200 |
| 2WD | G | | (950) | (950) | (1265) | (1265) |

LX 470 4WD—V8—Truck Equipment Schedule T3
| Sport Utility 4D | HT00W | 56400 | 18775 | 21025 | 24400 | 29500 |

2000 LEXUS — JT6(HF10U)-Y-#

RX 300 4WD—V6—Truck Equipment Schedule T3
| Sport Utility 4D | HF10U | 35680 | 14350 | 16175 | 18400 | 22000 |
| 2WD | G | | (1075) | (1075) | (1435) | (1435) |

LX 470 4WD—V8—Truck Equipment Schedule T3
| Sport Utility 4D | HT00W | 59500 | 22275 | 24875 | 28400 | 34000 |

2001 LEXUS — JTJ(HF10U)-1-#

RX 300 4WD—V6—Truck Equipment Schedule T3
Sport Utility 4D	HF10U	37430	16750	18875	21200	25100
2WD	G		(1200)	(1200)	(1600)	(1600)
Silversport Edition			300	300	400	400

LX 470 4WD—V8—Truck Equipment Schedule T3
| Sport Utility 4D | HT00W | 61950 | 26025 | 29100 | 32700 | 38700 |

2002 LEXUS — JTJ(HF10U)-2-#

RX 300 4WD—V6—Truck Equipment Schedule T3
Sport Utility 4D	HF10U	37580	19575	21975	24400	28400
2WD	G		(1325)	(1325)	(1765)	(1765)
Coach Edition			425	425	565	565

LX 470 4WD—V8—Truck Equipment Schedule T3
| Sport Utility 4D | HT00W | 63051 | 30150 | 33600 | 37400 | 43800 |

2003 LEXUS — JTJ(HF10U)-3-#

RX 300 4WD—V6—Truck Equipment Schedule T3
| Sport Utility 4D | HF10U | 38800 | 22750 | 25450 | 27900 | 32300 |
| 2WD | G | | (1425) | (1425) | (1900) | (1900) |

GX 470 4WD—V8—Truck Equipment Schedule T3
| Sport Utility 4D | BT20X | 45500 | 28800 | 32150 | 35900 | 42100 |
| Third Row Seat | | | 800 | 800 | 1065 | 1065 |

LX 470 4WD—V8—Truck Equipment Schedule T3
| Sport Utility 4D | HT00W | 63700 | 34550 | 38500 | 42400 | 49200 |

2004 LEXUS — JTJ(HA31U)-4-#

RX 330 AWD—V6—Truck Equipment Schedule T3
Sport Utility 4D	HA31U	39195	26400	29575	32100	36800
2WD	G		(1525)	(1525)	(2035)	(2035)
Performance Pkg			2500	2500	3335	3335

GX 470 4WD—V8—Truck Equipment Schedule T3
| Sport Utility 4D | BT20X | 45700 | | | | |
| Third Row Seat | | | | | | |

LX 470 4WD—V8—Truck Equipment Schedule T3
| Sport Utility 4D | HT00W | 64800 | | | | |

Body	Type	VIN	List	Trade-In Fair	Good	Pvt-Party Good	Retail Excellent

LINCOLN

1998 LINCOLN — 5LM-(U28L)-W-#

NAVIGATOR 4WD—V8—Truck Equipment Schedule T3
Sport Utility 4D	U28L	43300	**10175**	**11575**	**14100**	**17850**
w/o Rear Air Conditioning			(250)	(250)	(335)	(335)
2WD	7		(1225)	(1225)	(1635)	(1635)

1999 LINCOLN — 5LM-(U28L)-X-#

NAVIGATOR 4WD—V8—Truck Equipment Schedule T3
Sport Utility 4D	U28L	43800	**11850**	**13450**	**16200**	**20300**
w/o Rear Air Conditioning			(300)	(300)	(400)	(400)
2WD	7		(1300)	(1300)	(1735)	(1735)

2000 LINCOLN — 5LM-(U28A)-Y-#

NAVIGATOR 4WD—V8—Truck Equipment Schedule T3
Sport Utility 4D	U28A	46500	**13825**	**15600**	**18500**	**22800**
w/o Rear Air Conditioning			(350)	(350)	(465)	(465)
2WD	7		(1350)	(1350)	(1800)	(1800)

2001 LINCOLN — 5LM-(U28A,R)-1-#

NAVIGATOR 4WD—V8—Truck Equipment Schedule T3
Sport Utility 4D	U28A,R	48085	**16025**	**18050**	**21100**	**25800**
2WD	7		(1400)	(1400)	(1865)	(1865)

2002 LINCOLN — 5LM-(U28R)-2-#

NAVIGATOR 4WD—V8—Truck Equipment Schedule T3
Sport Utility 4D	U28R	48680	**18525**	**20825**	**24000**	**29100**
2WD	7		(1450)	(1450)	(1935)	(1935)

BLACKWOOD—V8—Truck Equipment Schedule T3
Sport Util Pickup 4D	W05A	52500	**19300**	**21600**	**23600**	**27300**

2003 LINCOLN — 5LM-(U88H)-3-#

AVIATOR AWD—V8—Truck Equipment Schedule T3
Sport Utility 4D	U88H	42945	**20725**	**23225**	**26100**	**30900**
2WD	6		(1500)	(1500)	(2000)	(2000)

NAVIGATOR 4WD—V8—Truck Equipment Schedule T3
Sport Utility 4D	U28R	52425	**24375**	**27275**	**30800**	**36600**
2WD			(1500)	(1500)	(2000)	(2000)

2004 LINCOLN — 5LM-(U88H)-4-#

AVIATOR AWD—V8—Truck Equipment Schedule T3
Sport Utility 4D	U88H	43400	**23900**	**26700**	**29700**	**34600**
2WD	6		(1550)	(1550)	(2065)	(2065)

NAVIGATOR 4WD—V8—Truck Equipment Schedule T3
Sport Utility 4D	U28R	52775	**28225**	**31575**	**35200**	**41400**
2WD			(1550)	(1550)	(2065)	(2065)

MAZDA

1990 MAZDA — JM(2or3)(LV521)-L-#

MPV—4-Cyl.—Truck Equipment Schedule T1
Minivan	LV521	16822	**675**	**925**	**1525**	**2525**
V6 3.0 Liter	2		200	200	265	265

MPV 4WD—V6—Truck Equipment Schedule T1
Minivan	LV523	20572	**950**	**1350**	**2150**	**3400**

B2200 PICKUP—4-Cyl.—Truck Equipment Schedule T2
Short Bed	UF113	8378	325	475	925	1625
Long Bed	UF213	9028	375	550	1025	1800
Cab Plus	UF313	9778	675	925	1575	2650
SE-5 Sport Pkg			100	100	135	135
LE-5 Luxury Pkg			100	100	135	135

B2600i PICKUP—4-Cyl.—Truck Equipment Schedule T2
Short Bed	UF114	9028	400	600	1075	1900
Cab Plus	UF314	10428	750	1050	1775	2900
SE-5 Sport Pkg			100	100	135	135
LE-5 Luxury Pkg			100	100	135	135

TRUCKS & VANS

Body Type	VIN	List	Trade-In Fair	Trade-In Good	Pvt-Party Good	Retail Excellent
4WD	4,6		500	500	665	665

1991 MAZDA — JM(2or3)(LV521)–M–#

MPV—4-Cyl.—Truck Equipment Schedule T1
Minivan	LV521	18073	750	1050	1750	2850
V6 3.0 Liter	2		225	225	300	300

MPV 4WD—V6—Truck Equipment Schedule T1
Minivan	LV523	20743	1075	1525	2550	4000

NAVAJO 4WD—V6—Truck Equipment Schedule T1
Sport Utility 2D	CU44X	20000	975	1425	2450	3925

B2200 PICKUP—4-Cyl.—Truck Equipment Schedule T2
Short Bed	UF113	8748	375	550	1025	1800
Long Bed	UF213	9408	450	625	1150	2025
Cab Plus	UF313	10268	775	1075	1800	2975
SE-5 Sport Pkg			100	100	135	135
LE-5 Luxury Pkg			100	100	135	135

B2600i PICKUP—4-Cyl.—Truck Equipment Schedule T2
Short Bed	UF414	9108	475	675	1225	2100
Cab Plus	UF314	10358	875	1225	2025	3275
SE-5 Sport Pkg			100	100	135	135
LE-5 Luxury Pkg			100	100	135	135
4WD	4,6		550	550	735	735

1992 MAZDA — (4ForJM)(2or3)(LV521)–N–#

MPV—4-Cyl.—Truck Equipment Schedule T1
Minivan	LV521	17844	825	1150	1925	3100
V6 3.0 Liter	2		275	275	365	365

MPV 4WD—V6—Truck Equipment Schedule T1
Minivan	LV523	21394	1300	1775	2825	4375

NAVAJO 4WD—V6—Truck Equipment Schedule T1
DX Sport Utility 2D	CU44X	18680	1000	1450	2500	4025
LX Sport Utility 2D	CU44X	19785	1150	1600	2725	4300
2WD	2		(400)	(400)	(535)	(535)

B2200 PICKUP—4-Cyl.—Truck Equipment Schedule T2
Short Bed	UF113	8845	400	575	1075	1900
Long Bed	UF213	9560	475	700	1250	2125
Cab Plus	UF313	10345	850	1175	1975	3200
SE-5 Pkg			125	125	165	165
LE-5 Pkg			125	125	165	165

B2600i PICKUP—4-Cyl.—Truck Equipment Schedule T2
Short Bed	UF114	9470	525	750	1325	2250
Cab Plus	UF314	10695	950	1350	2200	3525
SE-5 Pkg			125	125	165	165
LE-5 Pkg			125	125	165	165
4WD	4,6		675	675	900	900

1993 MAZDA — (JMor4F)(2or3)(LV521)–P

MPV—4-Cyl.—Truck Equipment Schedule T1
Minivan	LV521	19255	900	1300	2175	3475
Air Bag			0	0	0	0
V6 3.0 Liter	2		325	325	435	435

MPV 4WD—V6—Truck Equipment Schedule T1
Minivan	LV523	22960	1550	2075	3225	4825
Air Bag			0	0	0	0

NAVAJO 4WD—V6—Truck Equipment Schedule T1
DX Sport Utility 2D	CU44X	20700	1050	1500	2625	4200
LX Sport Utility 2D	CU44X	22470	1250	1725	2900	4525
2WD	2		(425)	(425)	(565)	(565)

B2200 PICKUP—4-Cyl.—Truck Equipment Schedule T2
Short Bed	UF113	9275	450	650	1200	2100
Long Bed	UF213	9990	550	800	1425	2400
Cab Plus	UF313	10935	925	1325	2200	3525
SE-5 Sport Pkg			150	150	200	200
LE-5 Luxury Pkg			150	150	200	200

B2600i PICKUP—4-Cyl.—Truck Equipment Schedule T2
Cab Plus	UF314	11785	1050	1500	2550	4025
SE-5 Pkg			150	150	200	200
LE-5 Pkg			150	150	200	200
4WD	4,6		800	800	1065	1065

B2600i PICKUP 4WD—4-Cyl.—Truck Equipment Schedule T2
Short Bed	UF114	12235	1025	1475	2500	3950
SE-5 Sport Pkg			150	150	200	200

Body	Type	VIN	List	Trade-In Fair	Trade-In Good	Pvt-Party Good	Retail Excellent
LE-5 Luxury Pkg				150	150	200	200

1994 MAZDA — (JMor4F)(2or3)–(V521)–R

MPV—4-Cyl.—Truck Equipment Schedule T1
| Minivan | | V521 | 20900 | 1050 | 1500 | 2550 | 4050 |
| V6 3.0 Liter | | U | | 375 | 375 | 500 | 500 |

MPV 4WD—V6—Truck Equipment Schedule T1
| Minivan | | V523 | 24700 | 1875 | 2400 | 3600 | 5300 |

NAVAJO 4WD—V6—Truck Equipment Schedule T1
DX Sport Utility 2D		U44X	20350	1125	1575	2775	4475
LX Sport Utility 2D		U44X	23260	1400	1875	3125	4850
2WD		2		(450)	(450)	(600)	(600)

B2300 PICKUP—4-Cyl.—Truck Equipment Schedule T2
Short Bed		R12A	10025	750	1025	1775	2975
Cab Plus		R16A	12480	1125	1575	2675	4200
SE Short Bed		R12A	11670	850	1175	2000	3275

B3000 PICKUP—V6—Truck Equipment Schedule T2
SE Short Bed		R12U	12140	950	1375	2375	3875
SE Long Bed		R21U	12785	975	1425	2450	3925
Cab Plus		R16U	12950	1375	1875	2975	4550
SE Cab Plus		R16U	13630	1500	2025	3175	4775

B3000 PICKUP 4WD—V6—Truck Equipment Schedule T2
| Short Bed | | R13U | 14895 | 1300 | 1775 | 2875 | 4450 |
| Cab Plus | | R17U | 15955 | 1850 | 2375 | 3575 | 5250 |

B4000 PICKUP—V6—Truck Equipment Schedule T2
| SE Long Bed | | R21X | 12965 | 975 | 1425 | 2450 | 3925 |
| LE Cab Plus | | R16X | 15815 | 1300 | 1775 | 2875 | 4450 |

B4000 PICKUP 4WD—V6—Truck Equipment Schedule T2
SE Short Bed		R13X	16885	1350	1825	2925	4500
SE Cab Plus		R17X	17755	1825	2350	3525	5200
LE Cab Plus		R17X	19960	2100	2650	3875	5625

1995 MAZDA — (JM3or4F4)–(V522)–S–#

MPV—V6—Truck Equipment Schedule T1
L Minivan		V522	22505	1250	1725	2850	4475
LX Minivan		V522	23155	1425	1900	3075	4700
LXE Minivan		V522	24845	1650	2175	3375	5100
4WD		3		475	475	635	635

B2300 PICKUP—4-Cyl.—Truck Equipment Schedule T2
Short Bed		R12A	10765	850	1200	2075	3350
Long Bed		R12A	11155	900	1250	2100	3425
Cab Plus		R16A	13485	1350	1825	2925	4500
SE Short Bed		R12A	12485	950	1375	2375	3875
SE Cab Plus		R16A	14185	1625	2125	3300	4925
4WD		3		1000	1000	1335	1335

B3000 PICKUP—V6—Truck Equipment Schedule T2
| SE Short Bed | | R12U | 13155 | 1100 | 1550 | 2675 | 4200 |
| SE Cab Plus | | R16U | 14855 | 1800 | 2325 | 3475 | 5150 |

B3000 PICKUP 4WD—V6—Truck Equipment Schedule T2
| Cab Plus | | R17U | 17715 | 2150 | 2725 | 3925 | 5700 |

B4000 PICKUP—V6—Truck Equipment Schedule T2
| SE Cab Plus | | R16X | 15400 | 1475 | 1950 | 3100 | 4700 |
| LE Cab Plus | | R16X | 16925 | 1500 | 2025 | 3175 | 4775 |

B4000 PICKUP 4WD—V6—Truck Equipment Schedule T2
SE Short Bed		R13X	18360	1575	2100	3250	4875
SE Cab Plus		R17X	19485	2100	2700	3900	5650
LE Cab Plus		R17X	20640	2400	3000	4275	6075

1996 MAZDA — (JM3or4F4)(LV522)–T–#

MPV—V6—Truck Equipment Schedule T1
DX Minivan		LV522	22845	2050	2600	3900	5750
LX Minivan		LV522	22735	2200	2775	4100	5975
ES Minivan		LV522	25135	2500	3100	4475	6375
4WD		3		500	500	665	665

B2300 PICKUP—4-Cyl.—Truck Equipment Schedule T2
Short Bed		R12A	10600	975	1400	2450	3950
Long Bed		R12A	10985	1000	1450	2500	4000
Cab Plus		R16A	13720	1525	2075	3250	4900
SE Short Bed		R12A	12545	1100	1550	2650	4200
SE Cab Plus		R16A	14840	1900	2425	3650	5350
4WD		3,7		1100	1100	1465	1465

Body	Type	VIN	List	Trade-In Fair	Good	Pvt-Party Good	Retail Excellent
B3000 PICKUP—V6—Truck Equipment Schedule T2							
SE Cab Plus	R16U	15675	2100	2650	3875	5625
B3000 PICKUP 4WD—V6—Truck Equipment Schedule T2							
Cab Plus	R17U	18170	2500	3100	4375	6200
B4000 PICKUP—V6—Truck Equipment Schedule T2							
LE Cab Plus	R16X	17845	1775	2300	3475	5175
B4000 PICKUP 4WD—V6—Truck Equipment Schedule T2							
SE Short Bed	R13X	18810	1850	2375	3575	5275
SE Cab Plus	R17X	20065	2425	3025	4300	6100
SE Cab Plus	R17X	22440	2750	3375	4700	6600

1997 MAZDA — (JM3or4F4)(LV522)–V–#

Body	Type	VIN	List	Trade-In Fair	Good	Pvt-Party Good	Retail Excellent
MPV—V6—Truck Equipment Schedule T1							
LX Minivan	LV522	24370	2600	3225	4625	6650
ES Minivan	LV522	28270	2900	3550	5000	7050
4WD		3	525	525	700	700
B2300 PICKUP—4-Cyl.—Truck Equipment Schedule T2							
Short Bed	R12A	11060	1175	1625	2750	4350
SE Short Bed	R12A	13225	1350	1825	2975	4575
SE Cab Plus	R16A	15480	2225	2775	4050	5825
B4000 PICKUP—V6—Truck Equipment Schedule T2							
SE Cab Plus	R16X	16225	2550	3175	4450	6300
B4000 PICKUP 4WD—V6—Truck Equipment Schedule T2							
Short Bed	R13X	16775	2175	2750	4000	5775
SE Cab Plus	R17X	18660	2725	3350	4675	6550
SE Cab Plus	R17X	20275	2800	3425	4750	6650

1998 MAZDA — (JM3or4F4)(LV522)–W–#

Body	Type	VIN	List	Trade-In Fair	Good	Pvt-Party Good	Retail Excellent
MPV—V6—Truck Equipment Schedule T1							
LX Minivan	LV522	24370	3100	3750	5175	7225
ES Minivan	LV522	28270	3425	4150	5600	7700
4WD		3	575	575	765	765
B2500 PICKUP—4-Cyl.—Truck Equipment Schedule T2							
SX Short Bed	R12C	11575	1400	1875	3100	4800
SE Short Bed	R12C	13215	1575	2100	3300	5050
SE Cab Plus 2D	R16C	15355	2150	2725	4000	5825
SE Cab Plus 4D	R16C	15950	2725	3350	4700	6625
B3000 PICKUP—V6—Truck Equipment Schedule T2							
SE Cab Plus 2D	R16U	16305	2550	3150	4475	6325
SE Cab Plus 4D	R14U	16900	2800	3425	4775	6725
B3000 PICKUP 4WD—V6—Truck Equipment Schedule T2							
SX Short Bed	R13U	15925	2100	2700	3950	5775
SE Short Bed	R13U	17455	2375	2950	4275	6125
SE Cab Plus 2D	R17U	18940	3250	3900	5300	7300
SE Cab Plus 4D	R15U	19535	3575	4300	5700	7775
B4000 PICKUP—V6—Truck Equipment Schedule T2							
SE Cab Plus 2D	R16X	17155	2900	3550	4925	6875
SE Cab Plus 4D	R14X	17750	3150	3825	5200	7200
B4000 PICKUP 4WD—V6—Truck Equipment Schedule T2							
SE Cab Plus 2D	R17X	19840	3200	3875	5250	7250
SE Cab Plus 4D	R15X	20435	3700	4425	5825	7925

1999 MAZDA — (JM3or4F4)–(R12C)–X–#

Body	Type	VIN	List	Trade-In Fair	Good	Pvt-Party Good	Retail Excellent
B2500 PICKUP—4-Cyl.—Truck Equipment Schedule T2							
SX Short Bed	R12C	11795	1800	2325	3625	5450
SE Short Bed	R12C	14170	2075	2625	3925	5775
Troy Lee Short Bed	R12C	15130	2250	2825	4175	6050
SE Cab Plus	R16C	16225	2725	3350	4725	6700
SE Cab Plus 4D	R16C	16885	3325	4025	5450	7500
B3000 PICKUP—V6—Truck Equipment Schedule T2							
SE Cab Plus 2D	R16U	16800	3125	3775	5175	7200
SE Cab Plus 4D	R16U	17460	3450	4150	5600	7650
Troy Lee Cab Plus 4D	R16U	18955	3750	4500	5925	8050
B3000 PICKUP 4WD—V6—Truck Equipment Schedule T2							
SE Short Bed	R13U	18060	2925	3575	4950	6925
SE Cab Plus 2D	R17U	19715	3900	4625	6100	8225
SE Cab Plus 4D	R17U	20375	4325	5100	6625	8825
B4000 PICKUP—V6—Truck Equipment Schedule T2							
SE Short Bed	R12X	18090	2525	3125	4475	6375
SE Cab Plus 2D	R16X	20145	3525	4225	5675	7750
SE Cab Plus 4D	R16X	20805	3850	4575	6050	8150

Body Type	VIN	List	Trade-In Fair	Good	Pvt-Party Good	Retail Excellent
B4000 PICKUP 4WD—V6—Truck Equipment Schedule T2						
SE Cab Plus 2D	R17X	21140	4000	4750	6250	8375
SE Cab Plus 4D	R17X	22800	4475	5250	6775	9000
Troy Lee Cab Plus 4D	R17X	23995	4800	5650	7175	9450

2000 MAZDA–(JM3,4F2or4F4)–(LW28)–Y–

Body Type	VIN	List	Trade-In Fair	Good	Pvt-Party Good	Retail Excellent
MPV—V6—Truck Equipment Schedule T1						
DX Minivan 4D	LW28	20475	5650	6550	8025	10200
LX Minivan 4D	LW28	22530	5850	6825	8300	10550
ES Minivan 4D	LW28	26030	6300	7325	8800	11150
B2500 PICKUP—4-Cyl.—Truck Equipment Schedule T2						
SX Short Bed	R12C	12005	2300	2875	4275	6225
SE Short Bed	R12C	14315	2600	3225	4600	6600
SE Cab Plus 2D	R16C	16505	3400	4100	5575	7650
B3000 PICKUP—V6—Truck Equipment Schedule T2						
SX Short Bed	R12V	12400	2750	3375	4800	6825
SE Short Bed	R12V	14710	2925	3575	5000	7025
SE Cab Plus 2D	R16V	16975	3775	4500	6000	8125
SE Cab Plus 4D	R16V	17715	4200	5000	6500	8700
Troy Lee Cab Plus 4D	R16V	19120	4475	5275	6825	9075
B3000 PICKUP 4WD—V6—Truck Equipment Schedule T2						
SE Short Bed	R13V	18235	3575	4275	5750	7875
SE Cab Plus 4D	R17V	20720	5075	6025	7625	9975
B4000 PICKUP—V6—Truck Equipment Schedule T2						
SE Cab Plus 4D	R16X	21140	4575	5400	6925	9200
B4000 PICKUP 4WD—V6—Truck Equipment Schedule T2						
SE Cab Plus 4D	R17X	23050	5300	6200	7800	10200
Troy Lee Cab Plus 4D	R17X	24150	5675	6600	8225	10650

2001 MAZDA–(JM3,4F2or4F4)–(U06B)–1–

Body Type	VIN	List	Trade-In Fair	Good	Pvt-Party Good	Retail Excellent
TRIBUTE 4WD—V6—Truck Equipment Schedule T1						
DX Sport Utility 4D	U06B	21055	5800	6775	8825	11750
LX Sport Utility 4D	U08B	22535	6100	7075	9175	12150
ES Sport Utility 4D	U081	23540	6425	7450	9550	12600
2WD			(800)	(800)	(1065)	(1065)
4-Cyl. 2.0 Liter	B		(825)	(825)	(1100)	(1100)
MPV—V6—Truck Equipment Schedule T1						
DX Minivan 4D	LW28	21155	6825	7850	9375	11750
LX Minivan 4D	LW28	23280	7050	8125	9700	12100
ES Minivan 4D	LW28	26760	7550	8700	10250	12750
B2300 PICKUP—4-Cyl.—Truck Equipment Schedule T2						
SX Short Bed	R12D	12930	3025	3700	5150	7250
SE Short Bed	R12D	15130	3350	4050	5550	7650
B2500 PICKUP—4-Cyl.—Truck Equipment Schedule T2						
SX Short Bed	R12C	12785	2950	3600	5075	7125
SE Short Bed	R12C	14985	3300	3950	5450	7500
B3000 PICKUP—V6—Truck Equipment Schedule T2						
SE Short Bed	R12V	15280	3625	4350	5850	8025
Dual Sport Short Bed	R12V	15315	3725	4450	5950	8100
SE Cab Plus 2D	R16V	17515	4575	5400	6950	9250
SE Cab Plus 4D	R16V	18180	5100	5975	7575	9925
Dual Sport Cab + 2D	R16V	17735	5100	5975	7575	9925
B3000 PICKUP 4WD—V6—Truck Equipment Schedule T2						
SE Short Bed	R13V	18810	4350	5125	6700	8950
SE Cab Plus 2D	R13V	20480	5525	6425	8075	10450
B4000 PICKUP—V6—Truck Equipment Schedule T2						
Dual Sport Cab + 4D	R17X	19935	5475	6375	8025	10400
B4000 PICKUP 4WD—V6—Truck Equipment Schedule T2						
SE Cab Plus 4D	R17X	22780	6300	7300	8950	11450

2002 MAZDA–(JM3,4F2or4F4)–(U06B)–2

Body Type	VIN	List	Trade-In Fair	Good	Pvt-Party Good	Retail Excellent
TRIBUTE 4WD—V6—Truck Equipment Schedule T1						
DX Sport Utility 4D	U06B	22575	7050	8125	10350	13600
LX Sport Utility 4D	U08B	23225	7400	8500	10750	13950
ES Sport Utility 4D	U081	24455	7725	8875	11150	14400
2WD			(875)	(875)	(1165)	(1165)
4-Cyl. 2.0 Liter	B		(925)	(925)	(1235)	(1235)
MPV—V6—Truck Equipment Schedule T1						
LX Minivan 4D	LW28	22770	8575	9800	11400	13950
ES Minivan 4D	LW28	27712	9100	10375	12050	14700
B2300 PICKUP—4-Cyl.—Truck Equipment Schedule T2						
Short Bed	R12D	13240	3800	4525	6100	8350

2002 MAZDA

Body Type	VIN	List	Trade-In Fair	Trade-In Good	Pvt-Party Good	Retail Excellent
B3000 PICKUP—V6—Truck Equipment Schedule T2						
Dual Sport Short Bed	R12V	15870	4525	5350	6950	9300
Dual Sport Cab + 2D	R16V	18290	6075	7025	8700	11250
B3000 PICKUP 4WD—V6—Truck Equipment Schedule T2						
Cab Plus 2D	R13V	20775	6525	7550	9300	11850
B4000 PICKUP—V6—Truck Equipment Schedule T2						
Dual Sport Cab + 4D	R17X	20085	6475	7500	9200	11750
B4000 PICKUP 4WD—V6—Truck Equipment Schedule T2						
Cab Plus 4D	R17X	22830	7425	8525	10300	13000

2003 MAZDA—(JM3,4F2or4F4)—(Z92B)—3

Body Type	VIN	List	Trade-In Fair	Trade-In Good	Pvt-Party Good	Retail Excellent
TRIBUTE 4WD—4-Cyl.—Truck Equipment Schedule T1						
DX Sport Utility 4D	Z92B	20440	7250	8325	10550	13750
2WD	0		(950)	(950)	(1265)	(1265)
Manual Trans			0	0	0	0
TRIBUTE 4WD—V6—Truck Equipment Schedule T1						
LX Sport Utility 4D	Z941	22125	8925	10225	12550	15900
ES Sport Utility 4D	Z961	24885	9300	10600	12950	16350
2WD	0		(950)	(950)	(1265)	(1265)
MPV—V6—Truck Equipment Schedule T1						
LX S-V Minivan 4D	LW28A	21895	9650	11000	12600	15200
LX Minivan 4D	LW28A	23120	10275	11700	13350	16100
ES Minivan 4D	LW28A	26520	10900	12375	14050	16850
B2300 PICKUP—4-Cyl.—Truck Equipment Schedule T2						
Short Bed	R12D	13740	4775	5625	7175	9450
SE Cab Plus	R16D	17960	5925	6900	8525	10950
B3000 PICKUP—V6—Truck Equipment Schedule T2						
Dual Sport Short Bed	R12U	16590	5600	6500	8100	10500
Dual Sport Cab + 2D	R16V	18700	7275	8350	10050	12600
SE Cab Plus 4D	R46V	18935	7225	8300	9975	12600
B4000 PICKUP—V6—Truck Equipment Schedule T2						
Dual Sport Cab + 4D	R17E	20495	7700	8850	10550	13200
B4000 PICKUP 4WD—V6—Truck Equipment Schedule T2						
Cab Plus 2D	R17X	20260	7575	8700	10400	13050
SE Cab Plus 2D	R17X	21705	8300	9525	11300	13950
SE Cab Plus 4D	R17X	23240	8750	10025	11800	14550

2004 MAZDA—(JM3,4F2or4F4)—(Z92B)—4

Body Type	VIN	List	Trade-In Fair	Trade-In Good	Pvt-Party Good	Retail Excellent
TRIBUTE 4WD—4-Cyl.—Truck Equipment Schedule T1						
DX Sport Utility 4D	Z92B	21087	8925	10225	12550	16000
2WD	0		(1000)	(1000)	(1335)	(1335)
Manual Trans			0	0	0	0
TRIBUTE 4WD—V6—Truck Equipment Schedule T1						
LX Sport Utility 4D	Z941	23972	10800	12250	14750	18450
ES Sport Utility 4D	Z961	25562	11175	12675	15150	18900
2WD	0		(1000)	(1000)	(1335)	(1335)
MPV—V6—Truck Equipment Schedule T1						
LX Minivan 4D	W28A	23780	12525	14150	15950	18950
ES Minivan 4D	W28A	28750	13150	14875	16700	19800
B2300 PICKUP—4-Cyl.—Truck Equipment Schedule T2						
Short Bed	R12D	14840	6250	7250	8850	11300
SE Cab Plus	R16D	18980	7500	8650	10300	12950
B3000 PICKUP—V6—Truck Equipment Schedule T2						
Dual Sport Short Bed	R12U	17915	7100	8200	9900	12500
Dual Sport Cab + 2D	R16V	19871	8925	10225	12050	14900
SE Cab Plus 4D	R46V	20140	8875	10175	12000	14850
B4000 PICKUP—V6—Truck Equipment Schedule T2						
Dual Sport Cab + 4D	R17E	21865	9425	10750	12600	15450
B4000 PICKUP 4WD—V6—Truck Equipment Schedule T2						
Cab Plus 2D	R17X	20850	9300	10600	12450	15300
SE Cab Plus 2D	R17X	22350	10025	11425	13350	16350
SE Cab Plus 4D	R17X	24090	10550	12050	13950	17000

MERCEDES-BENZ

1998 MERCEDES-BENZ — 4JG(AB54E)—W—#

Body Type	VIN	List	Trade-In Fair	Trade-In Good	Pvt-Party Good	Retail Excellent
ML-CLASS 4WD—V6—Truck Equipment Schedule T3						
ML320 Sport Utl 4D	AB54E	38590	8750	10025	12100	15150
Third Seat			300	300	400	400

0105

Body Type	VIN	List	Trade-In Fair	Good	Pvt-Party Good	Retail Excellent

1999 MERCEDES-BENZ — 4JG(AB54E)-X-#

ML-CLASS 4WD—V6—Truck Equipment Schedule T3
| ML320 Sport Utl 4D | AB54E | 39590 | 10600 | 12100 | 14300 | 17650 |
| Third Seat | | | 350 | 350 | 465 | 465 |

ML-CLASS 4WD—V8—Truck Equipment Schedule T3
| ML430 Sport Utl 4D | AB72E | 44345 | 12325 | 13975 | 16300 | 19950 |
| Third Seat | | | 350 | 350 | 465 | 465 |

2000 MERCEDES-BENZ — 4JG(AB54E)-Y-#

ML-CLASS 4WD—V6—Truck Equipment Schedule T3
| ML320 Sport Utl 4D | AB54E | 36895 | 12675 | 14350 | 16700 | 20400 |
| Third Seat | | | 400 | 400 | 535 | 535 |

ML-CLASS 4WD—V8—Truck Equipment Schedule T3
ML430 Sport Utl 4D	AB72E	44345	14600	16475	18950	22900
ML55 Sport Util 4D	AB74E	65495	23625	26400	29900	35400
Third Seat			400	400	535	535

2001 MERCEDES-BENZ — 4JG(AB54E)-1-#

ML-CLASS 4WD—V6—Truck Equipment Schedule T3
ML320 Sport Utl 4D	AB54E	38045	15025	16950	19500	23400
Sport Pkg			300	300	400	400
Third Seat			450	450	600	600
designo Edition			600	600	800	800

ML-CLASS 4WD—V8—Truck Equipment Schedule T3
ML430 Sport Utl 4D	AB72E	44845	17175	19300	22000	26200
ML55 Sport Util 4D	AB74E	66545	27175	30325	33900	39800
Sport Pkg			300	300	400	400
Third Seat			450	450	600	600
designo Edition			600	600	800	800

2002 MERCEDES-BENZ — WDCor4JG(AB54E)-2-#

ML-CLASS 4WD—V6—Truck Equipment Schedule T3
ML320 Sport Utl 4D	AB54E	36945	17675	19875	22600	26900
Sport Pkg			325	325	435	435
Third Seat			500	500	665	665
Design Edition			725	725	965	965

ML-CLASS 4WD—V8—Truck Equipment Schedule T3
ML500 Sport Utl 4D	AB75E	45595	21300	23900	26800	31500
ML55 Sport Util 4D	AB74E	66545	31000	34550	38300	44500
Sport Pkg			325	325	435	435
Third Seat			500	500	665	665
designo Edition			725	725	965	965

G-CLASS AWD—V8—Truck Equipment Schedule T3
| G500 Sport Utl 4D | YR49E | 73145 | 37625 | 41950 | 46200 | 53500 |
| designo Edition | | | 725 | 725 | 965 | 965 |

2003 MERCEDES-BENZ — WDCor4JG(AB54E)-3-#

ML-CLASS 4WD—V6—Truck Equipment Schedule T3
ML320 Sport Utl 4D	AB54E	40315	20725	23225	26000	30700
ML350 Sport Utl 4D	AB57E	40665	21500	24100	26900	31700
Sport Pkg			350	350	465	465
Inspiration Edition			750	750	1000	1000
designo Edition			825	825	1100	1100
Third Seat			550	550	735	735

ML-CLASS 4WD—V8—Truck Equipment Schedule T3
ML500 Sport Utl 4D	AB75E	46015	24675	27650	30600	35700
ML55 Sport Util 4D	AB74E	66565	35225	39175	43000	49700
Sport Pkg			350	350	465	465
Inspiration Edition			750	750	1000	1000
designo Edition			825	825	1100	1100
Third Seat			550	550	735	735

G-CLASS AWD—V8—Truck Equipment Schedule T3
G500 Sport Utility 4D	YR49	74265	42250	47050	51300	58800
G55 Sport Utility 4D	YR46	90565	50200	55775	60400	68800
designo Edition			825	825	1100	1100

2004 MERCEDES-BENZ — WDCor4JG(AB57E)-4-#

ML-CLASS 4WD—V6—Truck Equipment Schedule T3
| ML350 Sport Utl 4D | AB57E | 39720 | 25150 | 28125 | 31100 | 36200 |
| Inspiration Edition | | | 775 | 775 | 1035 | 1035 |

Body	Type	VIN	List	Trade-In Fair	Trade-In Good	Pvt-Party Good	Retail Excellent
designo Edition				925	925	1235	1235
Third Seat				575	575	765	765
ML-CLASS 4WD—V8—Truck Equipment Schedule T3							
ML500 Sport Utl 4D	AB75E	46470	28600	31875	35000	40400
Inspiration Edition				775	775	1035	1035
designo Edition				925	925	1235	1235
Third Seat				575	575	765	765
G-CLASS AWD—V8—Truck Equipment Schedule T3							
G500 Sport Utility 4D	YR49	76870					
G55 Sport Utility 4D	YR46	93420					
designo Edition							

MERCURY

1993 MERCURY — 4M2-(V11W)-P-#

VILLAGER—V6—Truck Equipment Schedule T1

Body	Type	VIN	List	Fair	Good	Good	Excellent
GS Minivan		V11W	18851	1375	1875	2975	4525
LS Minivan		V11W	22683	1800	2325	3500	5175
5 Passenger				(275)	(275)	(365)	(365)

1994 MERCURY — 4M2-(V11W)-R-#

VILLAGER—V6—Truck Equipment Schedule T1

GS Minivan		V11W	19292	1625	2125	3300	4950
LS Minivan		V11W	22975	2100	2650	3875	5650
Nautica Minivan		V11W	26238	2350	2925	4200	6025
5 Passenger				(300)	(300)	(400)	(400)

1995 MERCURY — 4M2-(V11W)-S-#

VILLAGER—V6—Truck Equipment Schedule T1

GS Minivan		V11W	21090	1925	2450	3675	5425
LS Minivan		V11W	24650	2400	3000	4300	6175
Nautica Minivan		V11W	27535	2700	3300	4650	6575
5 Passenger				(325)	(325)	(435)	(435)

1996 MERCURY — 4M2-(V11W)-T-#

VILLAGER—V6—Truck Equipment Schedule T1

GS Minivan		V11W	21745	2250	2800	4125	5975
LS Minivan		V11W	25595	2775	3400	4800	6775
Nautica Minivan		V11W	28375	3100	3750	5150	7200
5 Passenger				(350)	(350)	(465)	(465)

1997 MERCURY — 4M(2or4)-(U55P)-V-#

MOUNTAINEER AWD—V8—Truck Equipment Schedule T1

Sport Utility 4D		U55P	29995	3650	4375	6075	8475
2WD		2		(525)	(525)	(700)	(700)

VILLAGER—V6—Truck Equipment Schedule T1

GS Minivan		V111	22395	2675	3275	4675	6650
LS Minivan		V111	27595	3250	3900	5375	7475
Nautica Minivan		V111	28995	3575	4275	5775	7925
5 Passenger				(375)	(375)	(500)	(500)

1998 MERCURY — 4M(2or4)-(U55P)-W-#

MOUNTAINEER AWD—V8—Truck Equipment Schedule T1

Sport Utility 4D		U55P	29785	4375	5150	6925	9425
2WD		4		(575)	(575)	(765)	(765)
4WD		4		0	0	0	0
V6 4.0 Liter		E		(300)	(300)	(400)	(400)

VILLAGER—V6—Truck Equipment Schedule T1

GS Minivan		V111	22885	3175	3850	5225	7225
LS Minivan		V111	27485	3825	4550	6000	8100
Nautica Minivan		V111	28885	4150	4925	6375	8550
5 Passenger				(425)	(425)	(565)	(565)

1999 MERCURY — 4M2-(U55P)-X-#

MOUNTAINEER AWD—V8—Truck Equipment Schedule T1

Sport Utility 4D		U55P	30015	5250	6150	8050	10750
2WD		2		(650)	(650)	(865)	(865)
4WD		4		0	0	0	0
V6 4.0 Liter		E		(350)	(350)	(465)	(465)

TRUCKS & VANS

Body	Type	VIN	List	Trade-In Fair	Trade-In Good	Pvt-Party Good	Retail Excellent
VILLAGER—V6—Truck Equipment Schedule T1							
Minivan 4D		V11T	22995	4150	4925	6225	8150
Sport Minivan 4D		V11T	25595	5250	6150	7525	9650
Estate Minivan 4D		V11T	25595	5300	6200	7575	9700

2000 MERCURY — 4M2–(U86P)–Y–#

MOUNTAINEER AWD—V8—Truck Equipment Schedule T1							
Sport Utility 4D		U86P	30360	6300	7300	9300	12250
Premier				750	750	1000	1000
2WD		6		(725)	(725)	(965)	(965)
4WD		7		0	0	0	0
V6 4.0 Liter		E		(400)	(400)	(535)	(535)
VILLAGER—V6—Truck Equipment Schedule T1							
Minivan 4D		V11T	22995	4950	5800	7200	9300
Sport Minivan 4D		V12T	25995	6225	7200	8675	10950
Estate Minivan 4D		V14T	27695	6300	7325	8775	11100

2001 MERCURY — 4M2–(U86P)–1–#

MOUNTAINEER AWD—V8—Truck Equipment Schedule T1							
Sport Utility 4D		U86P	30695	7525	8675	10850	14000
Premier				825	825	1100	1100
2WD		6		(800)	(800)	(1065)	(1065)
4WD		7		0	0	0	0
V6 4.0 Liter		E		(450)	(450)	(600)	(600)
VILLAGER—V6—Truck Equipment Schedule T1							
Minivan 4D		V11T	23140	5950	6900	8400	10650
Sport Minivan 4D		V12T	26365	7375	8475	10050	12450
Estate Minivan 4D		V14T	27840	7475	8600	10200	12600

2002 MERCURY — 4M2–(U86W)–2–#

MOUNTAINEER AWD—V8—Truck Equipment Schedule T1							
Sport Utility 4D		U86W	31310	10225	11625	13950	17500
Premier				900	900	1200	1200
2WD		6		(875)	(875)	(1165)	(1165)
V6 4.0 Liter		E		(500)	(500)	(665)	(665)
VILLAGER—V6—Truck Equipment Schedule T1							
Minivan 4D		V11T	19995	7250	8325	9900	12300
Sport Minivan 4D		V12T	24995	8800	10075	11700	14300
Estate Minivan 4D		V14T	26995	8875	10175	11800	14400

2003 MERCURY — 4M2–(U86W)–3–#

MOUNTAINEER AWD—V8—Truck Equipment Schedule T1							
Sport Utility 4D		U86W	32605	11950	13525	16050	19800
Premier				975	975	1300	1300
w/o Third Seat				(800)	(800)	(1065)	(1065)
2WD		6		(950)	(950)	(1265)	(1265)
V6 4.0L Flex Fuel		K		(550)	(550)	(735)	(735)

2004 MERCURY — (2MRor4M2)–(A202)–4–#

MONTEREY—V6—Truck Equipment Schedule T1							
Minivan		A202	29995	11275	12825	14800	17900
Premier				775	775	1035	1035
MOUNTAINEER AWD—V8—Truck Equipment Schedule T1							
Sport Utility 4D		U86W	32855	14025	15800	18450	22500
Premier				1050	1050	1400	1400
w/o Third Seat				(800)	(800)	(1065)	(1065)
2WD		6		(1000)	(1000)	(1335)	(1335)
V6 4.0L Flex Fuel		K		(575)	(575)	(765)	(765)

MITSUBISHI

1990 MITSUBISHI — JA(4or7)–(J43S)–L–#

MONTERO 4WD—V6—Truck Equipment Schedule T1							
SP Sport Utility 2D		J43S	15827	950	1350	2375	3875
Sport Utility 2D		J53S	16517	1000	1450	2475	3950
Sport Utility 4D		J31S	17497	1400	1875	3025	4650
RS Sport Utility 4D		J41S	20607	1400	1875	3050	4675
LS Sport Utility 4D		J51S	20607	1475	1950	3125	4775
MINIVAN—4-Cyl.—Truck Equipment Schedule T2							
Cargo Minivan		N23W	11527	275	350	725	1300

TRUCKS & VANS

Body	Type	VIN	List	Trade-In Fair	Trade-In Good	Pvt-Party Good	Retail Excellent
MINIVAN—4-Cyl.—Truck Equipment Schedule T1							
Minivan		N44W	16921	575	825	1350	2250
LS Minivan		N54W	18303	675	950	1550	2575
MIGHTY MAX PICKUP—4-Cyl.—Truck Equipment Schedule T2							
Short Bed		L24W	8284	300	450	900	1575
1 Ton Short Bed		L29W	9574	375	550	1025	1800
Macro Cab Short Bed		L25W	9514	700	975	1650	2750
MIGHTY MAX PICKUP 4WD—Truck Equipment Sch T2							
Short Bed		M24S	12054	550	775	1350	2300

1991 MITSUBISHI—JA(4or7)–(J31S)–M–#

Body	Type	VIN	List	Trade-In Fair	Trade-In Good	Pvt-Party Good	Retail Excellent
MONTERO 4WD—V6—Truck Equipment Schedule T1							
Sport Utility 4D		J31S	17342	1625	2125	3300	4975
RS Sport Utility 4D		J31S	17822	1625	2125	3300	5000
LS Sport Utility 4D		J51S	20652	1675	2200	3400	5100
MIGHTY MAX PICKUP—4-Cyl.—Truck Equipment Schedule T2							
Short Bed		L24W	8329	350	500	975	1725
1 Ton Long Bed		L29W	9322	450	625	1150	1975
Macro Cab Short Bed		L25W	9559	800	1125	1850	3025
MIGHTY MAX PICKUP 4WD—Truck Equipment Sch T2							
Short Bed		M24S	12339	625	900	1500	2525

1992 MITSUBISHI—JA(4or7)–(K31S)–N–#

Body	Type	VIN	List	Trade-In Fair	Trade-In Good	Pvt-Party Good	Retail Excellent
MONTERO 4WD—V6—Truck Equipment Schedule T1							
Sport Utility 4D		K31S	19967	2100	2700	3950	5775
RS Sport Utility 4D		K41S	21627	2150	2725	4025	5875
LS Sport Utility 4D		K41S	24247	2250	2800	4125	6000
SR Sport Utility 4D		K51S	23657	2275	2850	4200	6075
MIGHTY MAX PICKUP—4-Cyl.—Truck Equipment Schedule T2							
Short Bed		L24W	8744	375	550	1025	1800
1 Ton Long Bed		L29W	10094	475	700	1225	2100
Macro Cab Short Bed		L25W	10044	850	1200	1975	3150
MIGHTY MAX PICKUP 4WD—V6—Truck Equipment Sch T2							
Short Bed		M24S	12954	675	950	1600	2700

1993 MITSUBISHI—JA(4or7)–(R31H)–P–#

Body	Type	VIN	List	Trade-In Fair	Trade-In Good	Pvt-Party Good	Retail Excellent
MONTERO 4WD—V6—Truck Equipment Schedule T1							
Sport Utility 4D		R31H	21037	2250	2800	4150	6025
RS Sport Utility 4D		R41H	22887	2300	2875	4250	6150
LS Sport Utility 4D		R41H	25928	2400	3000	4375	6300
SR Sport Utility 4D		R51H	26528	2450	3050	4425	6350
MIGHTY MAX PICKUP—4-Cyl.—Truck Equipment Schedule T2							
Short Bed		S21G	9253	425	625	1125	1975
Macro Cab Short Bed		S23G	10623	900	1300	2100	3350
MIGHTY MAX PICKUP 4WD—V6—Truck Equipment Sch T2							
Short Bed		T21H	13693	750	1050	1775	2925

1994 MITSUBISHI—JA(4or7)–(R41H)–R–#

Body	Type	VIN	List	Trade-In Fair	Trade-In Good	Pvt-Party Good	Retail Excellent
MONTERO 4WD—V6—Truck Equipment Schedule T1							
LS Sport Utility 4D		R41H	26024	2625	3250	4675	6700
SR Sport Utility 4D		R51M	31920	3600	4325	5900	8150
MIGHTY MAX PICKUP—4-Cyl.—Truck Equipment Schedule T2							
Short Bed		S21G	10170	475	675	1250	2175
Macro Cab Short Bed		S23G	11640	950	1375	2250	3600
MIGHTY MAX PICKUP 4WD—V6—Truck Equipment Sch T2							
Short Bed		T21H	14639	825	1150	1975	3250

1995 MITSUBISHI—JA(4or7)–(R41H)–S–#

Body	Type	VIN	List	Trade-In Fair	Trade-In Good	Pvt-Party Good	Retail Excellent
MONTERO 4WD—V6—Truck Equipment Schedule T1							
LS Sport Utility 4D		R41H	28920	2925	3575	5100	7225
SR Sport Utility 4D		R51M	35070	4000	4775	6450	8825
MIGHTY MAX PICKUP—4-Cyl.—Truck Equipment Schedule T2							
Short Bed		S21G	10779	550	800	1450	2475

1996 MITSUBISHI — JA4–(R41H)–T–#

Body	Type	VIN	List	Trade-In Fair	Trade-In Good	Pvt-Party Good	Retail Excellent
MONTERO 4WD—V6—Truck Equipment Schedule T1							
LS Sport Utility 4D		R41H	31458	3300	4000	5625	7875
SR Sport Utility 4D		R51M	38200	4500	5300	7050	9550
MIGHTY MAX PICKUP—4-Cyl.—Truck Equipment Schedule T2							
Short Bed		S21G	11590	675	925	1675	2850

Body Type	VIN	List	Trade-In Fair	Trade-In Good	Pvt-Party Good	Retail Excellent

TRUCKS & VANS

1997 MITSUBISHI — JA4–(S21G)–V–#

MONTERO SPORT 2WD—4-Cyl.—Truck Equipment Schedule T1
ES Utility 4D	S21G	18980	1600	2100	3600	5650

MONTERO SPORT 4WD—V6—Truck Equipment Schedule T1
LS Utility 4D	T31P	25452	3350	4050	5725	8100
XLS Utility 4D	T41P	31555	3525	4225	5950	8325
2WD	S		(525)	(525)	(700)	(700)

MONTERO 4WD—V6—Truck Equipment Schedule T1
LS Sport Util 4D	R41R	31040	3800	4525	6250	8675
SR Sport Util 4D	R51R	38827	5050	5925	7775	10400

1998 MITSUBISHI — JA4–(S21G)–W–#

MONTERO SPORT 2WD—4-Cyl.—Truck Equipment Schedule T1
ES Utility 4D	S21G	19390	2150	2725	4300	6425

MONTERO SPORT 4WD—V6—Truck Equipment Schedule T1
LS Utility 4D	T31P	26140	4050	4825	6575	9025
XLS Utility 4D	T41P	32695	4225	5025	6775	9250
2WD	S		(575)	(575)	(765)	(765)

MONTERO 4WD—V6—Truck Equipment Schedule T1
Sport Utility 4D	R51R	33975	5200	6100	7950	10600

1999 MITSUBISHI — JA4–(S21G)–X–#

MONTERO SPORT 2WD—4-Cyl.—Truck Equipment Schedule T1
ES Utility 4D	S21G	19680	2625	3250	4900	7200

MONTERO SPORT 4WD—V6—Truck Equipment Schedule T1
LS Utility 4D	T31H	27445	4775	5625	7475	10100
XLS Utility 4D	T31H	29355	5000	5850	7700	10350
Limited Utility 4D	T41R	33085	5850	6825	8725	11500
2WD	S		(650)	(650)	(865)	(865)

MONTERO 4WD—V6—Truck Equipment Schedule T1
Sport Utility 4D	R51R	31825	6250	7250	9225	12050

2000 MITSUBISHI — JA4–(S21H)–Y–#

MONTERO SPORT 2WD—V6—Truck Equipment Schedule T1
ES Utility 4D	S21H	22982	3550	4250	5800	8050

MONTERO SPORT 4WD—V6—Truck Equipment Schedule T1
LS Utility 4D	T31H	27262	5975	6925	8700	11250
XLS Utility 4D	T31H	29782	6225	7200	8950	11550
Limited Utility 4D	T41H	31812	7200	8275	10150	12850
2WD	S		(725)	(725)	(965)	(965)

MONTERO 4WD—V6—Truck Equipment Schedule T1
Sport Utility 4D	R51R	32262	7425	8550	10650	13750
Endeavor Pkg			275	275	365	365

2001 MITSUBISHI — JA4–(T21H)–1–#

MONTERO SPORT 4WD—V6—Truck Equipment Schedule T1
ES Utility 4D	T21H	25467	6125	7100	8875	11500
LS Utility 4D	T31H	28177	7050	8125	9975	12700
XS Sport Utility 4D	T31H	29187	7200	8275	10200	12950
XLS Utility 4D	T31H	29827	7300	8400	10250	13050
Limited Utility 4D	T41H	33297	8400	9600	11550	14500
2WD	S		(800)	(800)	(1065)	(1065)

MONTERO 4WD—V6—Truck Equipment Schedule T1
XLS Sport Utility 4D	W31R	31817	9375	10700	12650	15700
Limited Spt Util 4D	W51R	35817	10175	11575	13600	16750

2002 MITSUBISHI — JA4–(T21H)–2–#

MONTERO SPORT 4WD—V6—Truck Equipment Schedule T1
ES Utility 4D	T21H	25647	7300	8400	10300	13200
LS Utility 4D	T31H	28337	8300	9525	11450	14450
XLS Utility 4D	T31H	30187	8600	9850	11800	14850
Limited Utility 4D	T41R	33447	9800	11175	13200	16350
2WD	S		(875)	(875)	(1165)	(1165)

MONTERO 4WD—V6—Truck Equipment Schedule T1
XLS Sport Utility 4D	W31R	32247	11000	12475	14550	17800
Limited Spt Util 4D	W51R	36357	11800	13400	15500	18850

2003 MITSUBISHI — JA4–(Z31G)–3–#

OUTLANDER AWD—4-Cyl.—Truck Equipment Schedule T1
LS Sport Utility 4D	Z31G	19877	8725	9975	11200	13300

TRUCKS & VANS

Body Type	VIN	List	Trade-In Fair	Good	Pvt-Party Good	Retail Excellent
XLS Sport Utility 4D	Z41G	21370	9475	10800	12050	14250
2WD			(900)	(900)	(1200)	(1200)
MONTERO SPORT 4WD—V6—Truck Equipment Schedule T1						
ES Utility 4D	T21H	25802	8750	10025	12000	15000
LS Utility 4D	T21H	28362	9850	11225	13200	16300
XLS Utility 4D	T31H	30212	10125	11525	13600	16700
Limited Utility 4D	T41R	33472	11475	13000	15050	18400
S			(950)	(950)	(1265)	(1265)
MONTERO 4WD—V6—Truck Equipment Schedule T1						
XLS Sport Utility 4D	W31S	33072	12875	14550	16700	20200
Limited Spt Util 4D	W51S	37182	13775	15550	17750	21300

2004 MITSUBISHI — (Jor4)A4–(Z31G)–4–#

OUTLANDER AWD—4-Cyl.—Truck Equipment Schedule T1						
LS Sport Utility 4D	Z31G	20692	10275	11700	12900	15050
XLS Sport Utility 4D	Z41G	22792	11100	12575	13800	16150
2WD			(950)	(950)	(1265)	(1265)
MONTERO SPORT 4WD—V6—Truck Equipment Schedule T1						
LS Utility 4D	T31R	26392	11675	13200	15350	18750
XLS Utility 4D	T31R	28592	12000	13575	15800	19200
S			(1000)	(1000)	(1335)	(1335)
ENDEAVOR AWD—V6—Truck Equipment Schedule T1						
LS Sport Utility 4D	N21S	28192	12675	14350	16950	20800
XLS Sport Utility 4D	N31S	30492	14075	15850	18500	22600
Limited Sport Util 4D	N41S	33792	15350	17325	19950	24100
2WD	M		(1000)	(1000)	(1335)	(1335)
MONTERO 4WD—V6—Truck Equipment Schedule T1						
Limited Spt Util 4D	W51S	35624	15975	18000	20400	24200

NISSAN

1990 NISSAN — (JN8or1N6)(HD17Y)–L–#

PATHFINDER 4WD—V6—Truck Equipment Schedule T1						
XE Sport Utility 4D	HD17Y	19550	1650	2150	3350	5050
SE Sport Utility 2D	HD16Y	23844	1900	2425	3675	5450
SE Sport Utility 4D	HD17Y	22179	1975	2525	3800	5575
2WD	S		(350)	(350)	(465)	(465)
MINIVAN—4-Cyl.—Truck Equipment Schedule T1						
XE Minivan	SC26S	16009	400	575	1000	1725
GXE Minivan	SC26S	17709	450	650	1125	1900
PICKUP—4-Cyl.—Truck Equipment Schedule T2						
Short Bed	SD11S	8409	400	600	1075	1850
E King Cab	SD16S	10009	825	1150	1900	3075
4WD	Y		500	500	665	665
PICKUP—V6—Truck Equipment Schedule T2						
Long Bed	HD12S	9784	525	750	1325	2225
SE King Cab	HD16S	12859	850	1175	1950	3150
4WD	Y		500	500	665	665

1991 NISSAN — (JN8or1N6)(HD17Y)–M–#

PATHFINDER 4WD—V6—Truck Equipment Schedule T1						
XE Sport Utility 4D	HD17Y	19950	1925	2450	3700	5450
SE Sport Utility 4D	HD17Y	22579	2275	2850	4175	6025
2WD	S		(375)	(375)	(500)	(500)
PICKUP—4-Cyl.—Truck Equipment Schedule T2						
Short Bed	SD11S	8554	450	650	1175	2025
King Cab	SD16S	10124	900	1300	2100	3350
4WD	Y		550	550	735	735
PICKUP—V6—Truck Equipment Schedule T2						
Long Bed	HD12H	9899	600	850	1450	2425
SE King Cab	HD16S	12974	925	1325	2175	3475
4WD	Y		550	550	735	735

1992 NISSAN — (JN8or1N6)(HD17Y)–N–#

PATHFINDER 4WD—V6—Truck Equipment Schedule T1						
XE Sport Utility 4D	HD17Y	21275	2025	2575	3850	5650
SE Sport Utility 4D	HD17Y	23225	2450	3050	4400	6300
2WD			(400)	(400)	(535)	(535)
PICKUP—4-Cyl.—Truck Equipment Schedule T2						
Short Bed	SD11S	9165	500	725	1275	2175
King Cab	SD16S	10825	975	1425	2275	3600

1992 NISSAN

Body	Type	VIN	List	Trade-In Fair	Trade-In Good	Pvt-Party Good	Retail Excellent
4WD		Y		675	675	900	900
PICKUP—V6—Truck Equipment Schedule T2							
Long Bed		HD12S	10580	675	950	1600	2700
SE King Cab		HD16S	13805	1050	1500	2525	3975
4WD		Y		675	675	900	900

1993 NISSAN — (JN8or1N6)(HD17Y)–P–#

Body	Type	VIN	List	Trade-In Fair	Trade-In Good	Pvt-Party Good	Retail Excellent
PATHFINDER 4WD—V6—Truck Equipment Schedule T1							
XE Sport Utility 4D		HD17Y	22380	2150	2725	4050	5900
SE Sport Utility 4D		HD17Y	24680	2675	3275	4675	6675
2WD		S		(425)	(425)	(565)	(565)
QUEST—V6—Truck Equipment Schedule T1							
XE Minivan		DN11W	17895	1700	2225	3400	5075
GXE Minivan		DN11W	21800	2100	2675	3900	5650
5 Passenger				(275)	(275)	(365)	(365)
PICKUP—4-Cyl.—Truck Equipment Schedule T1							
Short Bed		SD11S	9545	575	825	1425	2425
King Cab		SD16S	11845	1100	1550	2575	4050
4WD		Y		800	800	1065	1065
PICKUP—V6—Truck Equipment Schedule T2							
Long Bed		HD12S	11015	775	1100	1850	3025
SE King Cab		HD16S	14405	1250	1725	2775	4325
4WD		Y		800	800	1065	1065

1994 NISSAN — (JN8or1N6)(HD17Y)–R–#

Body	Type	VIN	List	Trade-In Fair	Trade-In Good	Pvt-Party Good	Retail Excellent
PATHFINDER 4WD—V6—Truck Equipment Schedule T1							
XE Sport Utility 4D		HD17Y	23844	2375	2950	4350	6300
SE Sport Utility 4D		HD17Y	27484	2900	3550	5025	7100
LE Sport Utility 4D		HD17Y	29379	3425	4150	5700	7925
2WD				(450)	(450)	(600)	(600)
QUEST—V6—Truck Equipment Schedule T1							
XE Minivan		DN11W	18909	2000	2550	3775	5525
GXE Minivan		DN11W	23419	2425	3025	4300	6150
PICKUP—4-Cyl.—Truck Equipment Schedule T2							
Short Bed		SD11S	9739	750	1050	1825	3025
XE Short Bed		SD11S	10509	825	1150	1975	3250
XE King Cab		SD16S	12059	1425	1900	3050	4650
4WD		Y		900	900	1200	1200
V6 3.0 Liter		H		200	200	265	265
PICKUP—V6—Truck Equipment Schedule T2							
Long Bed		HD12S	11569	1050	1500	2575	4075
SE King Cab		HD16S	14659	1750	2275	3450	5125
4WD		Y		900	900	1200	1200

1995 NISSAN — (JN8or4N2)(HD17Y)–S–#

Body	Type	VIN	List	Trade-In Fair	Trade-In Good	Pvt-Party Good	Retail Excellent
PATHFINDER 4WD—V6—Truck Equipment Schedule T1							
XE Sport Utility 4D		HD17Y	24988	2675	3275	4750	6825
SE Sport Utility 4D		HD17Y	29028	3250	3900	5475	7675
LE Sport Utility 4D		HD17Y	30749	3825	4550	6200	8525
2WD				(475)	(475)	(635)	(635)
QUEST—V6—Truck Equipment Schedule T1							
XE Minivan		DN11W	20229	2325	2900	4200	6050
GXE Minivan		DN11W	24999	2800	3425	4775	6725
PICKUP—4-Cyl.—Truck Equipment Schedule T2							
Short Bed		SD11S	10319	875	1225	2100	3400
XE Short Bed		SD11S	11399	925	1325	2225	3600
XE King Cab		SD16S	13079	1700	2225	3440	5100
4WD		Y		1000	1000	1335	1335
V6 3.0 Liter		H		225	225	300	300
PICKUP—V6—Truck Equipment Schedule T2							
Long Bed		HD11S	12479	1300	1775	2875	4475
4WD		Y		1000	1000	1335	1335
PICKUP 4WD—V6—Truck Equipment Schedule T2							
SE King Cab		HD16Y	20989	2850	3500	4825	6725

1996 NISSAN — (JN8or4N2)(AR05Y)–T–#

Body	Type	VIN	List	Trade-In Fair	Trade-In Good	Pvt-Party Good	Retail Excellent
PATHFINDER 4WD—V6—Truck Equipment Schedule T1							
XE Sport Utility 4D		AR05Y	26803	3075	3725	5325	7525
SE Sport Utility 4D		AR05Y	29748	3700	4425	6075	8425
LE Sport Utility 4D		AR05Y	32129	4325	5100	6850	9325
2WD				(500)	(500)	(665)	(665)

TRUCKS & VANS

0105   SEE BACK PAGES FOR TRUCK EQUIPMENT   343

Body	Type	VIN	List	Trade-In Fair	Good	Pvt-Party Good	Retail Excellent

TRUCKS & VANS

QUEST—V6—Truck Equipment Schedule T1
| XE Minivan | DN11W | 21304 | **2700** | **3300** | **4675** | **6625** |
| GXE Minivan | DN11W | 26104 | **3225** | **3900** | **5325** | **7400** |

PICKUP—4-Cyl.—Truck Equipment Schedule T2
Short Bed	SD11S	11404	**975**	**1425**	**2475**	**3975**
XE Short Bed	SD11S	12904	**1050**	**1500**	**2600**	**4125**
XE King Cab	SD16S	14554	**2025**	**2575**	**3800**	**5550**
SE King Cab	SD16S	17004	**2550**	**3150**	**4450**	**6300**
4WD	Y		**1100**	**1100**	**1465**	**1465**

PATHFINDER 4WD—V6—Truck Equipment Schedule T1
XE Sport Utility 4D	AR05Y	27318	**3650**	**4375**	**6075**	**8475**
SE Sport Utility 4D	AR05Y	30568	**4325**	**5100**	**6900**	**9400**
LE Sport Utility 4D	AR05Y	32719	**4975**	**5825**	**7700**	**10350**
2WD	S		**(525)**	**(525)**	**(700)**	**(700)**

QUEST—V6—Truck Equipment Schedule T1
| XE Minivan | DN111 | 21669 | **3150** | **3800** | **5225** | **7300** |
| GXE Minivan | DN111 | 26469 | **3700** | **4425** | **5925** | **8100** |

PICKUP—4-Cyl.—Truck Equipment Schedule T2
Short Bed	SD11S	11469	**1200**	**1650**	**2775**	**4400**
XE Short Bed	SD11S	13469	**1300**	**1775**	**2925**	**4525**
XE King Cab	SD16S	15119	**2400**	**2975**	**4275**	**6100**
SE King Cab	SD16S	17519	**2975**	**3650**	**4975**	**6900**
4WD	Y		**1200**	**1200**	**1600**	**1600**

PATHFINDER 4WD—V6—Truck Equipment Schedule T1
XE Sport Utility 4D	AR05Y	27489	**4350**	**5125**	**6900**	**9400**
SE Sport Utility 4D	AR05Y	30589	**5075**	**5950**	**7775**	**10400**
LE Sport Utility 4D	AR05Y	33339	**5775**	**6750**	**8650**	**11400**
2WD	S		**(575)**	**(575)**	**(765)**	**(765)**

QUEST—V6—Truck Equipment Schedule T1
XE Minivan	DN111	23589	**3700**	**4425**	**5825**	**7925**
GXE Minivan	DN111	26539	**4275**	**5075**	**6525**	**8700**
GLE Minivan	DN111	27838	**4525**	**5350**	**6875**	**9075**

FRONTIER PICKUP—4-Cyl.—Truck Equipment Schedule T2
Short Bed	DD21S	12480	**1875**	**2400**	**3500**	**5100**
XE Short Bed	DD21S	13680	**1975**	**2525**	**3650**	**5250**
XE King Cab	DD26S	15130	**3175**	**3850**	**5075**	**6900**
SE King Cab	DD26S	18480	**3850**	**4575**	**5850**	**7775**
4WD	Y		**1275**	**1275**	**1700**	**1700**

PATHFINDER 4WD—V6—Truck Equipment Schedule T1
XE Sport Utility 4D	AR05Y	27669	**5175**	**6050**	**7950**	**10600**
SE Sport Utility 4D	AR05Y	30769	**6000**	**6950**	**8900**	**11700**
LE Sport Utility 4D	AR05Y	33469	**6850**	**7900**	**9925**	**12850**
2WD	S		**(650)**	**(650)**	**(865)**	**(865)**

PATHFINDER 4WD (1999.5)—V6—Truck Equip Schedule T1
XE Sport Utility 4D	AR07Y	28819	**5675**	**6600**	**8525**	**11300**
SE Sport Utility 4D	AR07Y	30769	**6500**	**7500**	**9500**	**12400**
LE Sport Utility 4D	AR07Y	31719	**7350**	**8450**	**10500**	**13550**
2WD	S		**(650)**	**(650)**	**(865)**	**(865)**

QUEST—V6—Truck Equipment Schedule T1
GXE Minivan	XN11T	22679	**4750**	**5575**	**6900**	**8950**
SE Minivan	XN11T	24419	**5400**	**6300**	**7700**	**9850**
GLE Minivan	XN11T	26819	**5700**	**6650**	**8100**	**10250**

FRONTIER—4-Cyl.—Truck Equipment Schedule T2
XE Short Bed	DD21S	12010	**2600**	**3225**	**4400**	**6125**
XE King Cab	DD26S	14010	**3850**	**4575**	**5850**	**7775**
SE King Cab	DD26S	15510	**4475**	**5250**	**6575**	**8600**
4WD	Y		**1450**	**1450**	**1935**	**1935**
V6 3.3 Liter	E		**300**	**300**	**400**	**400**

XTERRA 4WD—V6—Truck Equipment Schedule T1
XE Sport Utility 4D	ED28Y	22019	**6500**	**7500**	**9000**	**11350**
SE Sport Utility 4D	ED28Y	26069	**7625**	**8750**	**10300**	**12800**
2WD	D		**(675)**	**(675)**	**(900)**	**(900)**
4-Cyl. 2.4 Liter	T		**(550)**	**(550)**	**(735)**	**(735)**

Body	Type	VIN	List	Trade-In Fair	Good	Pvt-Party Good	Retail Excellent
PATHFINDER 4WD—V6—Truck Equipment Schedule T1							
XE Sport Utility 4D	AR05Y	28919	6300	7300	9300	12250
SE Sport Utility 4D	AR05Y	30869	7225	8300	10400	13500
LE Sport Utility 4D	AR05Y	31819	8175	9375	11550	14800
2WD	S		(725)	(725)	(965)	(965)
QUEST—V6—Truck Equipment Schedule T1							
GXE Minivan	XN11T	22779	5650	6550	8000	10200
SE Minivan	XN11T	24919	6375	7375	8875	11200
GLE Minivan	XN11T	26919	6725	7775	9275	11600
FRONTIER—4-Cyl.—Truck Equipment Schedule T2							
XE Short Bed	DD21S	12110	3300	3950	5200	7050
XE King Cab	DD26S	14060	4575	5400	6750	8750
4WD	Y		1625	1625	2165	2165
V6 3.3 Liter	E		350	350	465	465
FRONTIER—V6—Truck Equipment Schedule T2							
Desrt Rnr XE King	ED26S	16260	5000	5850	7225	9300
Desrt Rnr SE King	ED26S	18410	5325	6225	7600	9750
SE King Cab	DD26Y	21010	5350	6250	7650	9800
XE Crew Cab 4D	ED27S	17810	5700	6625	8050	10200
SE Crew Cab 4D	ED27S	19110	6100	7075	8550	10800
4WD	Y		1625	1625	2165	2165

Body	Type	VIN	List	Trade-In Fair	Good	Pvt-Party Good	Retail Excellent
XTERRA 4WD—V6—Truck Equipment Schedule T1							
XE Sport Utility 4D	ED28Y	22569	7525	8675	10200	12600
SE Sport Utility 4D	ED28Y	26619	8800	10075	11650	14250
2WD			(750)	(750)	(1000)	(1000)
4-Cyl. 2.4 Liter	D		(600)	(600)	(800)	(800)
PATHFINDER 4WD—V6—Truck Equipment Schedule T1							
XE Sport Utility 4D	DR07Y	30169	7550	8700	10850	14000
SE Sport Utility 4D	DR07Y	30869	8575	9800	12050	15300
LE Sport Utility 4D	DR07Y	31819	9700	11050	13350	16750
2WD	X		(800)	(800)	(1065)	(1065)
4WD	Y		0	0	0	0
QUEST—V6—Truck Equipment Schedule T1							
GXE Minivan	ZN15T	22959	6725	7775	9275	11600
SE Minivan	ZN16T	24919	7550	8700	10250	12700
GLE Minivan	ZN17T	27569	7950	9125	10700	13200
FRONTIER—4-Cyl.—Truck Equipment Schedule T2							
XE Short Bed	DD21S	12219	4100	4875	6175	8125
XE King Cab	DD26S	14169	5450	6350	7750	9900
4WD	Y		1800	1800	2400	2400
V6 3.3 Liter	E		400	400	535	535
FRONTIER—V6—Truck Equipment Schedule T2							
Desrt Rnr XE King	ED26T	16469	5900	6875	8275	10450
Desrt Rnr SE King	ED26T	18619	6300	7325	8750	11000
SE King Cab	DD26Y	21219	6375	7375	8825	11100
XE Crew Cab 4D	ED27T	18569	6700	7750	9225	11500
SE Crew Cab 4D	ED27T	20719	7225	8300	9850	12200
4WD	Y		1800	1800	2400	2400
FRONTIER—V6 Supercharged—Truck Equipment Schedule T2							
King Cab	MD26T	20519	6375	7400	8850	11150
Crew Cab 4D	MD27T	21969	7350	8450	9925	12350
4WD	Y		1800	1800	2400	2400

Body	Type	VIN	List	Trade-In Fair	Good	Pvt-Party Good	Retail Excellent
XTERRA 4WD—V6—Truck Equipment Sch T1							
XE Sport Utility 4D	ED28Y	22739	8725	9975	11550	14100
SE Sport Utility 4D	ED28Y	26739	10175	11575	13250	15950
2WD	T		(825)	(825)	(1100)	(1100)
4-Cyl. 2.4 Liter	D		(650)	(650)	(865)	(865)
XTERRA 4WD—V6 Supercharged—Truck Equipment Sch T1							
XE S/C Spt Util 4D	MD28T	26239	9425	10750	12400	15000
SE S/C Spt Util 4D	MD28T	28039	10850	12300	13950	16750
2WD	T		(825)	(825)	(1100)	(1100)
PATHFINDER 4WD—V6—Truck Equipment Schedule T1							
SE Sport Utility 4D	DR07Y	29189	10025	11425	13800	17350
LE Sport Utility 4D	DR07Y	32039	11225	12775	15200	18850
2WD	X		(875)	(875)	(1165)	(1165)
QUEST—V6—Truck Equipment Schedule T1							
GXE Minivan	ZN15T	23279	8100	9300	10900	13400
SE Minivan	ZN16T	25039	9025	10325	11900	14550
GLE Minivan	ZN17T	27689	9425	10750	12400	15050

Body Type	VIN	List	Trade-In Fair	Trade-In Good	Pvt-Party Good	Retail Excellent
FRONTIER KING CAB—4-Cyl.—Truck Equipment Sch T2						
Short Bed	ED27S	13339	6075	7050	8550	10800
XE Short Bed	DD26S	14339	6400	7425	8900	11200
4WD	Y	......	1975	1975	2635	2635
V6 3.3 Liter	E	......	450	450	600	600
FRONTIER KING CAB—V6—Truck Equipment Schedule T2						
Desert Runner XE	ED26T	16539	6900	7975	9450	11800
Desert Runner SE	ED26T	19739	7425	8525	10100	12500
SE Short Bed	ED26Y	22339	7500	8650	10200	12600
4WD	Y	......	1975	1975	2635	2635
FRONTIER CREW CAB—V6—Truck Equipment Schedule T2						
XE Short Bed	ED27T	18739	7825	8975	10550	13000
XE Long Bed	ED27T	19299	7850	9025	10550	13050
SE Short Bed	ED27T	22239	8450	9650	11250	13800
SE Long Bed	ED27T	22799	8475	9700	11300	13800
4WD	Y	......	1975	1975	2635	2635
FRONTIER KING CAB—V6 Supercharged—Truck Equip Sch T2						
Short Bed	MD26T	20889	7575	8700	10250	12700
4WD	Y	......	1975	1975	2635	2635
FRONTIER CREW CAB—V6 Supercharged—Truck Equip Sch T2						
Short Bed	MD27T	23739	8700	9925	11500	14100
Long Bed	MD27T	24299	8700	9925	11500	14100
4WD	Y	......	1975	1975	2635	2635

2003 NISSAN—(1N6,5N1orJN8)(ED28Y)-3-#

Body Type	VIN	List	Trade-In Fair	Trade-In Good	Pvt-Party Good	Retail Excellent
XTERRA 4WD—V6—Truck Equipment Schedule T1						
XE Sport Utility 4D	ED28Y	23939	10125	11525	13050	15600
SE Sport Utility 4D	ED28Y	27239	11700	13250	14850	17550
2WD	T	......	(900)	(900)	(1200)	(1200)
4-Cyl. 2.4 Liter	D	......	(700)	(700)	(935)	(935)
XTERRA 4WD—V6 Supercharged—Truck Equipment Schedule T1						
SE S/C Spt Util 4D	MD28T	28539	12425	14075	15700	18550
2WD	T	......	(900)	(900)	(1200)	(1200)
MURANO AWD—V6—Equipment Schedule T1						
SL Sport Utility 4D	AZ08W	30339	15350	17325	19600	23200
SE Sport Utility 4D	AZ08W	31139	15750	17700	19950	23700
2WD		......	(950)	(950)	(1265)	(1265)
PATHFINDER 4WD—V6—Truck Equipment Schedule T1						
SE Sport Utility 4D	DR09Y	29339	11800	13400	15850	19600
LE Sport Utility 4D	DR09Y	34339	13150	14875	17400	21300
2WD	X	......	(950)	(950)	(1265)	(1265)
FRONTIER KING CAB—4-Cyl.—Truck Equipment Schedule T2						
Short Bed	ED27S	13529	7275	8350	9800	12050
XE Short Bed	DD26S	14579	7600	8725	10200	12500
4WD		......	2150	2150	2865	2865
V6 3.3 Liter	E	......	500	500	665	665
FRONTIER KING CAB—V6—Truck Equipment Schedule T2						
Desert Runner XE	ED26T	16709	8125	9325	10800	13150
Desert Runner SE	ED26T	21109	8725	9975	11450	13900
FRONTIER KING CAB 4WD—V6—Truck Equipment Schedule T2						
SE Short Bed	ED26Y	23709	8875	10175	11650	14100
FRONTIER CREW CAB—V6—Truck Equipment Schedule T2						
XE Short Bed	ED27T	18979	9175	10475	12000	14500
XE Long Bed	ED27T	19529	9275	10550	12100	14600
SE Short Bed	ED27T	22829	9850	11225	12750	15300
SE Long Bed	ED27T	23379	9975	11325	12900	15500
4WD		......	2150	2150	2865	2865
FRONTIER KING CAB—V6 Supercharged—Truck Equip Sch T2						
Short Bed	MD26T	21359	9025	10325	11800	14250
4WD		......	2150	2150	2865	2865
FRONTIER CREW CAB—V6 Supercharged—Truck Equip Sch T2						
Short Bed	MD27T	24329	10225	11625	13200	15800
Long Bed	MD27T	24879	10275	11700	13300	15900
4WD	Y	......	2150	2150	2865	2865

2004 NISSAN—(1N6,5N1orJN8)(ED28Y)-4-#

Body Type	VIN	List	Trade-In Fair	Trade-In Good	Pvt-Party Good	Retail Excellent
XTERRA 4WD—V6—Truck Equipment Schedule T1						
XE Sport Utility 4D	ED28Y	22940	11750	13350	14900	17500
SE Sport Utility 4D	ED28Y	27240	13525	15275	16900	19800
2WD	T	......	(950)	(950)	(1265)	(1265)
4-Cyl. 2.4 Liter	D	......	(750)	(750)	(1000)	(1000)
XTERRA 4WD—V6 Supercharged—Truck Equipment Schedule T1						
SE S/C Spt Util 4D	MD28T	28540	14300	16125	17800	20700

0105

Body	Type	VIN	List	Trade-In Fair	Trade-In Good	Pvt-Party Good	Retail Excellent
2WD		T		**(950)**	**(950)**	**(1265)**	**(1265)**
MURANO AWD—V6—Truck Equipment Schedule T1							
	SL Sport Utility 4D	AZ08W	30340	17750	19975	22300	26100
	SE Sport Utility 4D	AZ08W	31290	18200	20450	22800	26700
2WD		T		**(1000)**	**(1000)**	**(1335)**	**(1335)**
QUEST—V6—Truck Equipment Schedule T1							
	S Minivan	BV28U	24780				
	SL Minivan	BV28U	27280				
	SE Minivan	BV28U	32780				
PATHFINDER 4WD—V6—Truck Equipment Schedule T1							
	SE Sport Utility 4D	DR09Y	29440	13875	15700	18300	22300
	LE Sport Utility 4D	DR09Y	34590	15300	17225	19850	24000
2WD		X		**(1000)**	**(1000)**	**(1335)**	**(1335)**
PATHFINDER ARMADA 4WD—V8—Truck Equipment Schedule T1							
	SE Sport Utility 4D	AA08B	36750				
	LE Sport Utility 4D	AA08B	41250				
2WD		A					
FRONTIER KING CAB—4-Cyl.—Truck Equipment Schedule T2							
	Short Bed	ED27S	13830	8875	10175	11600	14000
	XE Short Bed	DD26S	14880	9300	10600	12100	14550
4WD		Y		2325	2325	3100	3100
	V6 3.3 Liter	E		525	525	700	700
FRONTIER KING CAB—V6—Truck Equipment Schedule T2							
	Desert Runner XE	ED26T	17030	9900	11225	12750	15300
FRONTIER KING CAB 4WD—V6 Supercharged—Truck Sch T2							
	Short Bed	MD26T	25430	10900	12375	13950	16650
FRONTIER CREW CAB—V6—Truck Equipment Schedule T2							
	XE Short Bed	ED27T	19360	11000	12475	14050	16750
	XE Long Bed	ED27T	19910	11125	12625	14200	16900
	LE Short Bed	ED27T	24900	11750	13300	14950	17700
	LE Long Bed	ED27T	25450	11950	13525	15150	18000
4WD		Y		2325	2325	3100	3100
FRONTIER CREW CAB—V6 Supercharged—Truck Equip Sch T2							
	Short Bed	MD27T	24810	12250	13875	15550	18400
	Long Bed	MD27T	25360	12325	13975	15650	18550
4WD				2325	2325	3100	3100
TITAN KING CAB—V8—Truck Equipment Schedule T1							
	XE Short Bed	AA06A	23050				
	SE Short Bed	AA06A	25050				
	LE Short Bed	AA06A	29450				
4WD		B					
TITAN CREW CAB—V8—Truck Equipment Schedule T1							
	XE Short Bed	AA07A	25750				
	SE Short Bed	AA07A	27350				
	LE Short Bed	AA07A	31750				
4WD							

OLDSMOBILE

1990 OLDSMOBILE — 1GH–(U06D)–L–#

SILHOUETTE—V6—Truck Equipment Schedule T1							
	Minivan	U06D	17695	500	725	1225	2075

1991 OLDSMOBILE — 1GH–(U06D)–M–#

SILHOUETTE—V6—Truck Equipment Schedule T1							
	Minivan	U06D	18705	575	825	1400	2350
BRAVADA AWD—V6—Truck Equipment Schedule T3							
	Sport Utility 4D	T13Z	24250	1650	2175	3375	5075

1992 OLDSMOBILE — 1GH–(U06D)–N–#

SILHOUETTE—V6—Truck Equipment Schedule T1							
	Minivan	U06D	19625	625	900	1500	2525
	V6 3.8 Liter	L		75	75	100	100
BRAVADA AWD—V6—Truck Equipment Schedule T3							
	Sport Utility 4D	T13Z	25070	1725	2250	3475	5200
	V6 4.3L High Output	W		125	125	165	165

1993 OLDSMOBILE — 1GH–(U06D)–P–#

SILHOUETTE—V6—Truck Equipment Schedule T1							
	Minivan	U06D	20029	700	1000	1700	2850
	V6 3.8 Liter	L		100	100	135	135

1993 OLDSMOBILE

Body	Type	VIN	List	Trade-In Fair	Good	Pvt-Party Good	Retail Excellent
BRAVADA AWD—V6—Truck Equipment Schedule T3							
Sport Utility 4D		T13W	26474	1825	2350	3625	5425

1994 OLDSMOBILE — 1GH–(U06D)–R–#

SILHOUETTE—V6—Truck Equipment Schedule T1							
Minivan		U06D	20625	1100	1550	2625	4125
V6 3.8 Liter		L		100	100	135	135
BRAVADA AWD—V6—Truck Equipment Schedule T3							
Sport Utility 4D		T13W	27120	1975	2525	3875	5725

1995 OLDSMOBILE — 1GH–(U06L)–S–#

SILHOUETTE—V6—Truck Equipment Schedule T1							
Minivan		U06L	20795	1300	1775	2900	4500

1996 OLDSMOBILE — 1GH–(U06E)–T–#

SILHOUETTE—V6—Truck Equipment Schedule T1							
Minivan		U06E	21900	1525	2050	3275	4975
BRAVADA AWD—V6—Truck Equipment Schedule T3							
Sport Utility 4D		T13W	29995	3100	3750	5325	7550

1997 OLDSMOBILE — 1GH–(U06E)–V–#

SILHOUETTE—V6—Truck Equipment Schedule T1							
Minivan		U06E	22245	2350	2925	4300	6225
Extended Minivan		X06E	23075	2725	3350	4750	6750
GL Extended		X06E	25145	2900	3550	4975	6975
GLS Extended		X06E	26805	2975	3650	5075	7100
w/o 2nd Sliding Door				(475)	(475)	(635)	(635)
BRAVADA AWD—V6—Truck Equipment Schedule T3							
Sport Utility 4D		T13W	30800	3575	4275	5975	8350

1998 OLDSMOBILE — 1GH–(U03E)–W–#

SILHOUETTE—V6—Truck Equipment Schedule T1							
GS Minivan		U03E	25000	2875	3525	4875	6825
GL Extended		X03E	24535	3475	4175	5600	7625
GLS Extended		X03E	27735	3575	4275	5700	7750
BRAVADA AWD—V6—Truck Equipment Schedule T3							
Sport Utility 4D		T13W	31160	4200	5000	6750	9225

1999 OLDSMOBILE — 1GH–(U03E)–X–#

SILHOUETTE—V6—Truck Equipment Schedule T1							
GS Minivan		U03E	25370	3550	4250	5700	7775
GL Extended		X03E	24990	4050	5050	6525	8700
GLS Extended		X03E	28665	4325	5100	6625	8825
Premiere Ed Ext		X03E	31580	5100	5975	7550	9900
BRAVADA AWD—V6—Truck Equipment Schedule T3							
Sport Utility 4D		T13W	31568	5200	6075	7975	10650

2000 OLDSMOBILE — 1GH–(X03E)–Y–#

SILHOUETTE—V6—Truck Equipment Schedule T1							
GL Extended		X03E	25530	5100	5975	7575	9925
GLS Extended		X03E	29220	5200	6100	7700	10100
Premiere Ed Ext		X03E	32130	6075	7050	8725	11250
BRAVADA AWD—V6—Truck Equipment Schedule T3							
Sport Utility 4D		T13W	31923	5975	6925	8950	11800

2001 OLDSMOBILE — 1GH–(X03E)–1–#

SILHOUETTE—V6—Truck Equipment Schedule T1							
GL Extended		X03E	26920	6200	7175	8850	11400
GLS Extended		X03E	31055	6300	7325	9025	11550
Premiere Ed Ext		X03E	33855	7275	8350	10150	12750
BRAVADA AWD—V6—Truck Equipment Schedule T3							
Sport Utility 4D		T13W	32335	7150	8250	10350	13500

2002 OLDSMOBILE — 1GH–(X23E)–2–#

SILHOUETTE—V6—Truck Equipment Schedule T1							
GL Extended		X23E	27560	7525	8675	10450	13200
GLS Extended		X03E	31635	7675	8800	10600	13350
Premiere Ext		X13E	33535	8725	9975	11800	14700
AWD		V		900	900	1200	1200

Body	Type	VIN	List	Trade-In Fair	Good	Pvt-Party Good	Retail Excellent
BRAVADA AWD—6-Cyl.—Truck Equipment Schedule T3							
Sport Utility 4D		T13W	34967	**9800**	**11175**	**13700**	**17350**
2WD		S		(875)	(875)	(1165)	(1165)

2003 OLDSMOBILE — 1GH-(X23E)-3-#

SILHOUETTE—V6—Truck Equipment Schedule T1							
GL Extended		X23E	28510	**9225**	**10500**	**12350**	**15150**
GLS Extended		X03E	32175	**9375**	**10700**	**12550**	**15350**
Premiere Extended		X13E	34225	**10500**	**11950**	**13800**	**16800**
AWD		V		975	975	1300	1300
BRAVADA AWD—6-Cyl.—Truck Equipment Schedule T3							
Sport Utility 4D		T13S	35145	**11475**	**13050**	**15650**	**19600**
2WD		S		(950)	(950)	(1265)	(1265)

2004 OLDSMOBILE — 1GH-(X23E)-4-#

SILHOUETTE—V6—Truck Equipment Schedule T1							
GL Extended		X23E	28790	**11225**	**12775**	**14750**	**17900**
GLS Extended		X03E	32450	**11450**	**12950**	**14950**	**18100**
Premiere Extended		X13E	34510	**12625**	**14300**	**16350**	**19700**
AWD		V		1050	1050	1400	1400
BRAVADA AWD—6-Cyl.—Truck Equipment Schedule T3							
Sport Utility 4D		T13S	36245	**13525**	**15275**	**18050**	**22300**
2WD		S		(1000)	(1000)	(1335)	(1335)

PLYMOUTH — See DODGE TRUCKS

PONTIAC

1990 PONTIAC — 1GM-(U06D)-L-#

TRANS SPORT—V6—Truck Equipment Schedule T1							
Minivan		U06D	16300	**475**	**675**	**1150**	**1975**
SE Minivan		U06D	18625	**525**	**750**	**1250**	**2100**
5 Passenger				(200)	(200)	(265)	(265)

1991 PONTIAC — 1GM-(U06D)-M-#

TRANS SPORT—V6—Truck Equipment Schedule T1							
Minivan		U06D	17609	**550**	**775**	**1350**	**2250**
SE Minivan		U06D	19509	**600**	**850**	**1425**	**2400**
5 Passenger				(225)	(225)	(300)	(300)

1992 PONTIAC — 1GM-(U06D)-N-#

TRANS SPORT—V6—Truck Equipment Schedule T1							
SE Minivan		U06D	17585	**425**	**625**	**1125**	**1975**
GT Minivan		U06L	21465	**975**	**1425**	**2300**	**3650**
5 Passenger				(250)	(250)	(335)	(335)
V6 3.8 Liter		L		75	75	100	100

1993 PONTIAC — 1G(YorM)-(U06D)-P-#

TRANS SPORT—V6—Truck Equipment Schedule T1							
SE Minivan		U06D	18049	**475**	**700**	**1275**	**2225**
5 Passenger				(275)	(275)	(365)	(365)
V6 3.8 Liter		L		100	100	135	135

1994 PONTIAC — 1G(YorM)-(U06D)-R-#

TRANS SPORT—V6—Truck Equipment Schedule T1							
SE Minivan		U06D	18279	**875**	**1225**	**2100**	**3400**
5 Passenger				(300)	(300)	(400)	(400)
V6 3.8 Liter		L		100	100	135	135

1995 PONTIAC — 1G(YorM)-(U06D)-S-#

TRANS SPORT—V6—Truck Equipment Schedule T1							
SE Minivan		U06D	19964	**975**	**1425**	**2475**	**4000**
5 Passenger				(325)	(325)	(435)	(435)
V6 3.8 Liter		L		100	100	135	135

TRUCKS & VANS

TRUCKS & VANS

Body	Type	VIN	List	Trade-In Fair	Good	Pvt-Party Good	Retail Excellent

1996 PONTIAC — 1GM-(U06E)-T-#

TRANS SPORT—V6—Truck Equipment Schedule T1

Body	Type	VIN	List	Fair	Good	Good	Excellent
SE Minivan		U06E	21595	**1175**	**1625**	**2800**	**4450**
5 Passenger				**(350)**	**(350)**	**(465)**	**(465)**

1997 PONTIAC — 1GM-(U06E)-V-#

TRANS SPORT—V6—Truck Equipment Schedule T1

Body	Type	VIN	List	Fair	Good	Good	Excellent
SE Minivan		U06E	21049	**2475**	**3075**	**4450**	**6375**
SE Extended Minivan		X09E	23939	**3175**	**3850**	**5300**	**7400**
Montana				**375**	**375**	**500**	**500**
w/o 2nd Sliding Door				**(475)**	**(475)**	**(635)**	**(635)**

1998 PONTIAC — 1GM-(U03E)-W-#

TRANS SPORT—V6—Truck Equipment Schedule T1

Body	Type	VIN	List	Fair	Good	Good	Excellent
Minivan		U03E	22950	**3000**	**3675**	**5025**	**6975**
Extended Minivan		X03E	23660	**3775**	**4500**	**5950**	**8050**
Montana				**400**	**400**	**535**	**535**
w/o 2nd Sliding Door				**(500)**	**(500)**	**(665)**	**(665)**

1999 PONTIAC — 1GM-(U03E)-X-#

MONTANA—V6—Truck Equipment Schedule T1

Body	Type	VIN	List	Fair	Good	Good	Excellent
Minivan		U03E	23455	**3700**	**4425**	**5850**	**7975**
Extended Minivan		X03E	24455	**4575**	**5400**	**6925**	**9175**
w/o 2nd Sliding Door				**(550)**	**(550)**	**(735)**	**(735)**

2000 PONTIAC — 1GM-(U03E)-Y-#

MONTANA—V6—Truck Equipment Schedule T1

Body	Type	VIN	List	Fair	Good	Good	Excellent
Minivan		U03E	24255	**4500**	**5300**	**6875**	**9125**
Extended Minivan		X03E	25365	**5500**	**6400**	**8025**	**10400**

2001 PONTIAC — (1GMor3G7)-(A03E)-1-#

AZTEK—V6—Truck Equipment Schedule T1

Body	Type	VIN	List	Fair	Good	Good	Excellent
Sport Utility 4D		A03E	21995	**4475**	**5275**	**6900**	**9225**
GT Sport Utility 4D		A03E	24995	**5225**	**6125**	**7800**	**10200**
AWD		B		**825**	**825**	**1100**	**1100**

MONTANA—V6—Truck Equipment Schedule T1

Body	Type	VIN	List	Fair	Good	Good	Excellent
Minivan 4D		U03E	24810	**5500**	**6425**	**8075**	**10500**
Extended Minivan 4D		X03E	27150	**6600**	**7625**	**9325**	**11900**

2002 PONTIAC — (1GMor3G7)-(A03E)-2-#

AZTEK—V6—Truck Equipment Schedule T1

Body	Type	VIN	List	Fair	Good	Good	Excellent
Sport Utility 4D		A03E	20545	**5600**	**6500**	**8250**	**10800**
AWD		B		**900**	**900**	**1200**	**1200**

MONTANA—V6—Truck Equipment Schedule T1

Body	Type	VIN	List	Fair	Good	Good	Excellent
Minivan 4D		U03E	24990	**6800**	**7825**	**9600**	**12250**
Extended Minivan 4D		X03E	27390	**8000**	**9175**	**11000**	**13800**

2003 PONTIAC — (1GMor3G7)-(A03E)-3-#

AZTEK—V6—Truck Equipment Schedule T1

Body	Type	VIN	List	Fair	Good	Good	Excellent
Sport Utility 4D		A03E	20870	**6950**	**8025**	**9800**	**12500**
AWD		B		**975**	**975**	**1300**	**1300**

MONTANA—V6—Truck Equipment Schedule T1

Body	Type	VIN	List	Fair	Good	Good	Excellent
Minivan 4D		U03E	24845	**8400**	**9600**	**11400**	**14100**
Extended Minivan 4D		X03E	26645	**9700**	**11100**	**12900**	**15800**
AWD		V		**1000**	**1000**	**1335**	**1335**

2004 PONTIAC — (1GMor3G7)-(A03E)-4-#

AZTEK—V6—Truck Equipment Schedule T1

Body	Type	VIN	List	Fair	Good	Good	Excellent
Sport Utility 4D		A03E	21595	**8650**	**9900**	**11750**	**14600**
AWD		B		**1050**	**1050**	**1400**	**1400**

MONTANA—V6—Truck Equipment Schedule T1

Body	Type	VIN	List	Fair	Good	Good	Excellent
Minivan 4D		U03E	23845	**10375**	**11800**	**13750**	**16750**
Extended Minivan 4D		X03E	26220	**11750**	**13350**	**15350**	**18600**
AWD		V		**1000**	**1000**	**1335**	**1335**

Body	Type	VIN	List	Trade-In Fair	Good	Pvt-Party Good	Retail Excellent

PORSCHE

2003 PORSCHE — WP1-(AB29P)-3-#

CAYENNE AWD—V8—Truck Equipment Schedule T3
S Sport Utility 4D AB29P 56665 **35900 40025 43600 50000**
CAYENNE AWD—V8 Turbo—Truck Equipment Schedule T3
Sport Utility 4D AC29P 89665 **57125 63450 67900 76500**

2004 PORSCHE — WP1-(AB29P)-4-#

CAYENNE AWD—V6—Truck Equipment Schedule T3
Sport Utility 4D AB29P 43665
CAYENNE AWD—V8—Truck Equipment Schedule T3
S Sport Utility 4D AB29P 56665
CAYENNE AWD—V8 Turbo—Truck Equipment Schedule T3
Sport Utility 4D AC29P 89665

SATURN

2002 SATURN — 5GZ-(Z23D)-2-#

VUE—4-Cyl.—Truck Equipment Schedule T1
Sport Utility 4D Z23D 17775 **7375 8475 10200 12850**
AWD .... ------ **900 900 1200 1200**
V6 3.0 Liter .... B **650 650 865 865**

2003 SATURN — 5GZ-(Z23D)-3-#

VUE—4-Cyl.—Truck Equipment Schedule T1
Sport Utility 4D Z23D 18295 **8725 9975 11650 14350**
AWD 4,6 **975 975 1300 1300**
V6 3.0 Liter .... B **700 700 935 935**

2004 SATURN — 5GZ-(Z23D)-4-#

VUE—4-Cyl.—Truck Equipment Schedule T1
Sport Utility 4D Z23D 19135 **10275 11700 13450 16200**
AWD 4,6 **1050 1050 1400 1400**
V6 3.5 Liter .... B **750 750 1000 1000**

SUBARU

1998 SUBARU — JF1(SF615)-W-#

FORESTER AWD—4-Cyl.—Truck Equipment Schedule T1
Sport Utility 4D SF615 19190 **4850 5700 7075 9200**
L Sport Utility 4D SF635 21290 **5275 6175 7600 9800**
S Sport Utility 4D SF655 23490 **5700 6625 8100 10350**

1999 SUBARU — JF1(SF615)-X-#

FORESTER AWD—4-Cyl.—Truck Equipment Schedule T1
Sport Utility 4D SF615 19190 **5750 6700 8150 10400**
L Sport Utility 4D SF635 21290 **6250 7250 8750 11100**
S Sport Utility 4D SF655 23790 **6725 7775 9300 11700**

2000 SUBARU — JF1(SF635)-Y-#

FORESTER AWD—4-Cyl.—Truck Equipment Schedule T1
L Sport Utility 4D SF635 21390 **7325 8425 9975 12450**
S Sport Utility 4D SF655 23890 **7850 9025 10600 13150**

2001 SUBARU — JF1(SF635)-1-#

FORESTER AWD—4-Cyl.—Truck Equipment Schedule T1
L Sport Utility 4D SF635 21590 **8575 9800 11400 13950**
S Sport Utility 4D SF655 24190 **9175 10475 12100 14750**

2002 SUBARU — JF1(SF635)-2-#

FORESTER AWD—4-Cyl.—Truck Equipment Schedule T1
L Sport Utility 4D SF635 21625 **9975 11325 12950 15600**
S Sport Utility 4D SF655 24220 **10600 12100 13750 16450**

TRUCKS & VANS

Body	Type	VIN	List	Trade-In Fair	Good	Pvt-Party Good	Retail Excellent
2003 SUBARU–(JF1or4S4)(BorS)(G636)–3							
FORESTER AWD—4-Cyl.—Truck Equipment Schedule T1							
X Sport Utility 4D		G638	21870	**11525**	**13050**	**14650**	**17300**
XS Sport Utility 4D		G656	24220	**12300**	**13925**	**15450**	**18200**
BAJA AWD—4-Cyl.—Truck Equipment Schedule T1							
Sport Util Pickup 4D		T61C	24520	**8725**	**9975**	**12450**	**15950**
2004 SUBARU–(JF1or4S4)(BorS)(G636)–4							
FORESTER AWD—4-Cyl.—Truck Equipment Schedule T1							
X Sport Utility 4D		G638	22245	**13300**	**15025**	**16550**	**19300**
XS Sport Utility 4D		G656	24495	**14100**	**15900**	**17450**	**20400**
FORESTER AWD—4-Cyl. Turbo—Truck Equipment Schedule T1							
XT Sport Utility 4D		G696	26320	**14875**	**16750**	**18450**	**21400**
BAJA AWD—4-Cyl.—Truck Equipment Schedule T1							
Sport Util Pickup 4D		T61C	22545	**10850**	**12300**	**14950**	**18800**
BAJA AWD—4-Cyl. Turbo—Truck Equipment Schedule T1							
Sport Util Pickup 4D		T63C	24545	**12375**	**14025**	**16750**	**20800**

SUZUKI

Body	Type	VIN	List	Trade-In Fair	Good	Pvt-Party Good	Retail Excellent
1990 SUZUKI — JS(3or4)(JC3–C)–L–#							
SAMURAI 4WD—4-Cyl.—Truck Equipment Schedule T2							
JL Convertible		JC3–C	8259	**500**	**725**	**1200**	**2025**
Fiberglass Hard Top				**50**	**50**	**65**	**65**
SIDEKICK—4-Cyl.—Truck Equipment Schedule T2							
JS Convertible		TA0–C	10259	**325**	**475**	**1025**	**1900**
SIDEKICK 4WD—4-Cyl.—Truck Equipment Schedule T2							
JX Deluxe Conv		TA0–C	11059	**325**	**475**	**1050**	**1925**
JX Deluxe Sport Util		TA0–V	11359	**375**	**525**	**1100**	**2025**
JLX Custom Conv		TA0–C	12559	**375**	**525**	**1100**	**2025**
JLX Cstm Sport Util		TA0–V	12759	**425**	**625**	**1225**	**2175**
1991 SUZUKI — JS(3or4)(JD31C)–M–#							
SAMURAI—4-Cyl.—Truck Equipment Schedule T2							
JA Convertible		JD31C	6279	**450**	**625**	**1100**	**1850**
JS Convertible		JD31C	7279	**450**	**625**	**1100**	**1850**
SAMURAI 4WD—4-Cyl.—Truck Equipment Schedule T2							
JL Convertible		JC31C	8579	**525**	**750**	**1250**	**2100**
Fiberglass Hard Top				**50**	**50**	**65**	**65**
SIDEKICK—4-Cyl.—Truck Equipment Schedule T2							
JS Convertible 2D		TC01C	10579	**200**	**300**	**825**	**1575**
SIDEKICK 4WD—4-Cyl.—Truck Equipment Schedule T2							
JL Convertible 2D		TA01C	11279	**375**	**550**	**1200**	**2175**
JX Convertible 2D		TA01C	12079	**400**	**600**	**1250**	**2250**
JX Sport Utility 4D		TD01V	12294	**600**	**850**	**1600**	**2800**
JLX Sport Util 4D		TD01V	13294	**725**	**1025**	**1875**	**3200**
1992 SUZUKI — JS(3or4)(JD31C)–N–#							
SAMURAI—4-Cyl.—Truck Equipment Schedule T2							
JA Convertible		JD31C	6599	**350**	**500**	**925**	**1625**
SAMURAI 4WD—4-Cyl.—Truck Equipment Schedule T2							
JL Convertible		JC31C	8499	**450**	**650**	**1125**	**1925**
Fiberglass Hard Top				**75**	**75**	**100**	**100**
SIDEKICK—4-Cyl.—Truck Equipment Schedule T2							
JS-Plus Conv 2D		TC01C	10999	**175**	**225**	**775**	**1575**
JS Sport Utility 4D		TE01C	11959	**450**	**625**	**1350**	**2475**
SIDEKICK 4WD—4-Cyl.—Truck Equipment Schedule T2							
JX Convertible 2D		TA01C	12299	**375**	**525**	**1200**	**2300**
JX Limited Conv 2D		TA01C	13599	**375**	**550**	**1250**	**2300**
JX Sport Utility 4D		TD01V	12809	**625**	**900**	**1700**	**3025**
JLX Sport Util 4D		TD01V	14009	**775**	**1075**	**2025**	**3425**
JLX Ltd Spt Util 4D		TD01V	15509	**800**	**1125**	**2100**	**3525**
1993 SUZUKI — (JSor2S)(3or4)(JD31C)–P							
SAMURAI—4-Cyl.—Truck Equipment Schedule T2							
JA Convertible		JD31C	7019	**300**	**400**	**825**	**1475**
SAMURAI 4WD—4-Cyl.—Truck Equipment Schedule T2							
JL Convertible		JC31C	8919	**400**	**575**	**1025**	**1800**
Fiberglass Hard Top				**100**	**100**	**135**	**135**

1993 SUZUKI

Body	Type	VIN	List	Trade-In Fair	Good	Pvt-Party Good	Retail Excellent
SIDEKICK—4-Cyl.—Truck Equipment Schedule T2							
JS Convertible 2D		TC01C	11319	150	225	800	1675
JS Sport Utility 4D		TE01C	12229	450	650	1450	2650
SIDEKICK 4WD—4-Cyl.—Truck Equipment Schedule T2							
JX Convertible 2D		TA01C	12719	375	525	1275	2400
JX Sport Utility 4D		TD01V	13329	675	925	1875	3275
JLX Sport Util 4D		TD01V	14529	825	1150	2275	3900

1994 SUZUKI — (JSor2S)(3or4)(JC31C)-R

Body	Type	VIN	List	Trade-In Fair	Good	Pvt-Party Good	Retail Excellent
SAMURAI 4WD—4-Cyl.—Truck Equipment Schedule T2							
JL Convertible		JC31C	9799	375	525	1025	1800
Fiberglass Hard Top				100	100	135	135
SIDEKICK—4-Cyl.—Truck Equipment Schedule T2							
JS Convertible 2D		TC01C	11779	175	250	900	1900
JS Sport Utility 4D		TE01C	13199	525	750	1575	2925
SIDEKICK 4WD—4-Cyl.—Truck Equipment Schedule T2							
JX Convertible 2D		TA01C	13179	400	600	1400	2650
JX Sport Utility 4D		TD01V	14429	750	1050	2100	3600
JLX Sport Util 4D		TD01V	15779	900	1300	2500	4200

1995 SUZUKI — (JS3,JS4or2S3)(JC31C)-S

Body	Type	VIN	List	Trade-In Fair	Good	Pvt-Party Good	Retail Excellent
SAMURAI 4WD—4-Cyl.—Truck Equipment Schedule T2							
JL Convertible		JC31C	10234	375	550	1075	1925
Fiberglass Hard Top				100	100	135	135
SIDEKICK—4-Cyl.—Truck Equipment Schedule T2							
JS Convertible 2D		TC01C	12344	250	325	1100	2225
JS Sport Utility 4D		TE02V	13869	625	900	1875	3350
Limited				100	100	135	135
SIDEKICK 4WD—4-Cyl.—Truck Equipment Schedule T2							
JX Convertible 2D		TA02C	13844	500	725	1625	3025
JX Sport Utility 4D		TD03V	15179	875	1225	2425	4125
JLX Sport Util 4D		TD03V	16689	1050	1500	2800	4575
Limited				100	100	135	135

1996 SUZUKI — (2SorJS)3(TC02C)-T-#

Body	Type	VIN	List	Trade-In Fair	Good	Pvt-Party Good	Retail Excellent
SIDEKICK—4-Cyl.—Truck Equipment Schedule T2							
JS Convertible 2D		TC02C	13274	350	500	1375	2650
JS Utility 4D		TE02V	14789	775	1075	2275	3975
SIDEKICK 4WD—4-Cyl.—Truck Equipment Schedule T2							
JX Convertible 2D		TA02C	15044	650	900	1975	3525
JX Utility 4D		TD03V	16389	1025	1450	2725	4500
Sport JX Utility 4D		TD21V	18389	1800	2325	3725	5675
Sport JLX Util 4D		TD21V	19389	1850	2375	3800	5750
X-90 4WD—4-Cyl.—Truck Equipment Schedule T2							
Sport Utility 2D		LB11S	15389	825	1150	1975	3275
2WD		A		(450)	(450)	(600)	(600)

1997 SUZUKI — (2SorJS)3(TC02C)-V-#

Body	Type	VIN	List	Trade-In Fair	Good	Pvt-Party Good	Retail Excellent
SIDEKICK—4-Cyl.—Truck Equipment Schedule T2							
JS Convertible 2D		TC02C	13299	525	750	1750	3275
JS Utility 4D		TE02V	14819	950	1350	2675	4475
Sport JS Utility 4D		TE21V	17119	1000	1450	2750	4575
SIDEKICK 4WD—4-Cyl.—Truck Equipment Schedule T2							
JX Convertible 2D		TA02C	15069	850	1175	2450	4250
JX Utility 4D		TD03V	16419	1275	1750	3125	5025
Sport JX Utility 4D		TD21V	18119	2125	2700	4200	6250
Sport JLX Util 4D		TD21V	19619	2275	2900	4300	6350
X-90 4WD—4-Cyl.—Truck Equipment Schedule T2							
Sport Utility 2D		LB11S	15019	1025	1475	2550	4100
2WD		A		(475)	(475)	(635)	(635)

1998 SUZUKI — (2SorJS)3(TC02C)-W-#

Body	Type	VIN	List	Trade-In Fair	Good	Pvt-Party Good	Retail Excellent
SIDEKICK—4-Cyl.—Truck Equipment Schedule T2							
JS Convertible 2D		TC02C	13519	725	1025	2225	3925
JS Utility 4D		TE02V	14829	1225	1700	3025	4850
Sport JS Utility 4D		TE02V	17329	1325	1800	3150	4975
SIDEKICK 4WD—4-Cyl.—Truck Equipment Schedule T2							
JX Convertible 2D		TA02C	15289	1075	1525	2825	4625
JX Utility 4D		TD03V	16429	1650	2175	3550	5450
Sport JX Utility 4D		TD21V	18329	2600	3225	4675	6725
Sport JLX Util 4D		TD21V	19829	2700	3300	4750	6825

TRUCKS & VANS

Body Type	VIN	List	Trade-In Fair	Good	Pvt-Party Good	Retail Excellent
X-90 4WD—4-Cyl.—Truck Equipment Schedule T2						
Sport Utility 2D	LB11S	15229	**1400**	**1875**	**2950**	**4500**
2WD	A		**(525)**	**(525)**	**(700)**	**(700)**

1999 SUZUKI — (Jor2)S3(TC52C)-X-#

Body Type	VIN	List	Trade-In Fair	Good	Pvt-Party Good	Retail Excellent
VITARA—4-Cyl.—Truck Equipment Schedule T2						
JS Convertible 2D	TC52C	14719	**900**	**1250**	**2575**	**4400**
JS Hard Top 4D	TE52V	15829	**1525**	**2050**	**3475**	**5425**
4-Cyl. 1.6 Liter			**(225)**	**(225)**	**(300)**	**(300)**
VITARA 4WD—4-Cyl.—Truck Equipment Schedule T2						
JX Convertible 2D	TA52C	16519	**1125**	**1575**	**2975**	**4875**
JX Hard Top 4D	TD52V	17429	**1875**	**2400**	**3875**	**5850**
4-Cyl. 1.6 Liter			**(225)**	**(225)**	**(300)**	**(300)**
GRAND VITARA—V6—Truck Equipment Schedule T1						
JS Utility 4D	TE62V	18429	**2750**	**3375**	**4925**	**7050**
GRAND VITARA 4WD—V6—Truck Equipment Schedule T1						
JLX Utility 4D	TD62V	19429	**3250**	**3900**	**5475**	**7675**

2000 SUZUKI — (Jor2)S3(TC03C)-Y-#

Body Type	VIN	List	Trade-In Fair	Good	Pvt-Party Good	Retail Excellent
VITARA—4-Cyl.—Truck Equipment Schedule T2						
JS Convertible 2D	TC03C	13939	**1125**	**1575**	**3050**	**5000**
JS Hard Top 4D	TE52V	15949	**1975**	**2525**	**4025**	**6100**
JLS Convertible 2D	TC52C	15439	**1675**	**2200**	**3700**	**5700**
JLS Hard Top 4D	TE52V	16749	**2250**	**2825**	**4375**	**6475**
VITARA 4WD—4-Cyl.—Truck Equipment Schedule T2						
JX Convertible 2D	TA03C	15739	**1500**	**2025**	**3500**	**5500**
JX Hard Top 4D	TD52V	17549	**2350**	**2925**	**4475**	**6600**
JLX Convertible 2D	TA52C	17239	**3075**	**3725**	**5325**	**7525**
JLX Hard Top 4D	TD52V	18349	**3325**	**4025**	**5650**	**7900**
GRAND VITARA—V6—Truck Equipment Schedule T1						
JLS Hard Top 4D	TE62V	19749	**3375**	**4075**	**5700**	**7950**
Ltd Hard Top 4D	TE62V	22149	**3575**	**4275**	**5900**	**8175**
GRAND VITARA 4WD—V6—Truck Equipment Schedule T1						
JLX Hard Top 4D	TD62V	20749	**3900**	**4650**	**6300**	**8675**
Ltd Hard Top 4D	TD62V	23149	**4000**	**4750**	**6400**	**8750**

2001 SUZUKI — (Jor2)S3(TC03C)-1-#

Body Type	VIN	List	Trade-In Fair	Good	Pvt-Party Good	Retail Excellent
VITARA—4-Cyl.—Truck Equipment Schedule T2						
JS Convertible 2D	TC03C	14369	**1625**	**2125**	**3675**	**5750**
JS Hard Top 4D	TE03C	16079	**2550**	**3175**	**4750**	**6950**
JLS Convertible 2D	TC52C	15869	**2225**	**2775**	**4400**	**6550**
JLS Hard Top 2D	TE52V	16869	**2725**	**3350**	**4975**	**7200**
JLS Hard Top 4D	TE52V	17079	**2875**	**3525**	**5125**	**7400**
VITARA 4WD—4-Cyl.—Truck Equipment Schedule T2						
JX Convertible 2D	TA03C	15969	**2075**	**2625**	**4175**	**6325**
JX Hard Top 4D	TD52V	17579	**2975**	**3625**	**5250**	**7500**
JLX Convertible 2D	TA52C	17469	**3775**	**4500**	**6200**	**8550**
JLX Hard Top 2D	TD52V	18459	**4225**	**5025**	**6725**	**9150**
JLX Hard Top 4D	TD52V	18579	**4050**	**4825**	**6525**	**8925**
GRAND VITARA—V6—Truck Equipment Schedule T1						
JLS Hard Top 4D	TE62V	19879	**4150**	**4925**	**6625**	**9025**
Ltd Hard Top 4D	TE62V	22279	**4325**	**5100**	**6825**	**9250**
GRAND VITARA 4WD—V6—Truck Equipment Schedule T1						
JLX Hard Top 4D	TD62V	21079	**4750**	**5575**	**7325**	**9800**
Ltd Hard Top 4D	TD62V	23479	**4825**	**5675**	**7425**	**9925**
XL-7 4WD—V6—Truck Equipment Schedule T1						
Sport Utility 4D	TX92V	21499	**5025**	**5875**	**7550**	**10050**
Plus Sport Util 4D	TX92V	23999	**5250**	**6150**	**7875**	**10350**
Touring Spt Util 4D	TX92V	24999	**5350**	**6250**	**7975**	**10450**
Limited Spt Util 4D	TX92V	26499	**5375**	**6300**	**8000**	**10500**
2WD			**(800)**	**(800)**	**(1065)**	**(1065)**

2002 SUZUKI — (Jor2)S3(TC52C)-2-#

Body Type	VIN	List	Trade-In Fair	Good	Pvt-Party Good	Retail Excellent
VITARA—4-Cyl.—Truck Equipment Schedule T2						
JLS Convertible 2D	TC52C	16089	**2950**	**3600**	**5275**	**7575**
JLS Hard Top 4D	TE52V	17299	**3650**	**4375**	**6075**	**8475**
VITARA 4WD—4-Cyl.—Truck Equipment Schedule T2						
JLX Convertible 2D	TA52C	17489	**4625**	**5475**	**7225**	**9750**
JLX Hard Top 4D	TD52V	18659	**4950**	**5800**	**7575**	**10150**
GRAND VITARA—V6—Truck Equipment Schedule T1						
JLS Hard Top 4D	TE62V	19099	**5050**	**5925**	**7700**	**10250**
Ltd Hard Top 4D	TE62V	22299	**5200**	**6100**	**7900**	**10450**

Body	Type	VIN	List	Trade-In Fair	Good	Pvt-Party Good	Retail Excellent
GRAND VITARA 4WD—V6—Truck Equipment Schedule T1							
JLX Hard Top 4D		TD62V	20299	5700	6650	8450	11100
Ltd Hard Top 4D		TD62V	23499	5800	6775	8600	11250
XL-7 4WD—V6—Truck Equipment Schedule T1							
Sport Utility 4D		TX92V	22319	6250	7250	9100	11800
Plus Spt Util 4D		TX92V	23819	6525	7525	9400	12150
Touring Spt Utl 4D		TX92V	25319	6600	7625	9500	12250
Limited Spt Utl 4D		TX92V	26519	6675	7700	9575	12350
2WD		Y		(875)	(875)	(1165)	(1165)

Body	Type	VIN	List	Trade-In Fair	Good	Pvt-Party Good	Retail Excellent
VITARA—4-Cyl.—Truck Equipment Schedule T2							
Convertible 2D		TC52C	16109	3900	4625	6250	8525
Hard Top 4D		TE52V	17319	4625	5475	7100	9475
VITARA 4WD—4-Cyl.—Truck Equipment Schedule T2							
Convertible 2D		TA52C	17509	5725	6675	8350	10850
Hard Top 4D		TD52V	18719	6075	7025	8725	11300
GRAND VITARA—V6—Truck Equipment Schedule T1							
Hard Top 4D		TE62V	20119	6200	7175	8900	11450
GRAND VITARA 4WD—V6—Truck Equipment Schedule T1							
Hard Top 4D		TD62V	20319	6900	7975	9750	12400
XL-7 4WD—V6—Truck Equipment Schedule T1							
Touring Spt Utl 4D		TX92V	22339	8100	9300	11250	14100
Limited Spt Utl 4D		TX92V	25399	8175	9375	11350	14200
w/o Third Seat				(550)	(550)	(735)	(735)
2WD		Y		(950)	(950)	(1265)	(1265)

Body	Type	VIN	List	Trade-In Fair	Good	Pvt-Party Good	Retail Excellent
VITARA—V6—Truck Equipment Schedule T2							
LX Hard Top 4D		TE52V	16799	5850	6825	8400	10800
VITARA 4WD—V6—Truck Equipment Schedule T2							
LX Hard Top 4D		TD52V	17999	7425	8525	10200	12800
GRAND VITARA—V6—Truck Equipment Schedule T1							
LX Hard Top 4D		TE62V	18999	7550	8700	10350	13000
EX Hard Top 4D		TE62V	20799	8175	9375	11150	13800
GRAND VITARA 4WD—V6—Truck Equipment Schedule T1							
EX Hard Top 4D		TD62V	22499	8350	9575	11350	14050
LX Hard Top 4D		TD62V	19499	8975	10275	12050	14900
XL-7 4WD—V6—Truck Equipment Schedule T1							
LX Sport Utility 4D		TX92V	22899	9975	11325	13400	16550
EX Sport Utility 4D		TX92V	25399	10025	11425	13500	16650
w/o Third Seat				(750)	(750)	(1000)	(1000)
2WD		Y		(1000)	(1000)	(1335)	(1335)

TOYOTA

Body	Type	VIN	List	Trade-In Fair	Good	Pvt-Party Good	Retail Excellent
4RUNNER 4WD—4-Cyl.—Truck Equipment Schedule T1							
SR5 Sport Util 2D		RN37J	18908	1975	2525	3775	5550
SR5 Sport Util 4D		RN39W	18408	2175	2750	4025	5850
2WD		2		(350)	(350)	(465)	(465)
V6 3.0 Liter		V		150	150	200	200
LAND CRUISER 4WD—6-Cyl.—Truck Equipment Schedule T1							
Sport Utility 4D		FJ62W	22053	1825	2350	3725	5600
PICKUP—4-Cyl.—Truck Equipment Schedule T2							
Short Bed 4S		RN81A	8473	1025	1475	2450	3875
Deluxe Short Bed		RN81P	9213	1075	1525	2550	4000
Deluxe Long Bed		RN82P	9743	1100	1550	2600	4050
Deluxe Xtra Cab		RN93P	10453	1600	2100	3250	4850
Dlx 1 Ton Long Bed		VN82P	11513	1150	1600	2650	4125
SR5 Long Bed		RN82S	10463	1150	1600	2650	4125
SR5 Xtra Cab		RN93S	11463	1700	2225	3350	5000
4WD		0,1		500	500	665	665
V6 3.0 Liter		V		100	100	135	135
PICKUP 4WD—4-Cyl.—Truck Equipment Schedule T2							
SR5 Short Bed		RN01S	12323	1675	2200	3325	4950
V6 3.0 Liter		M,V		100	100	135	135

Body	Type	VIN	List	Trade-In Fair	Good	Pvt-Party Good	Retail Excellent
4RUNNER 4WD—4-Cyl.—Truck Equipment Schedule T1							
SR5 Sport Util 2D		RN37J	18918	2250	2825	4125	5975

TRUCKS & VANS

TRUCKS & VANS

Body	Type	VIN	List	Trade-In Fair	Trade-In Good	Pvt-Party Good	Retail Excellent
SR5 Sport Util 4D	RN37W	18908	**2500**	**3100**	**4425**	**6300**
2WD	2		(375)	(375)	(500)	(500)
V6 3.0 Liter	V		175	175	235	235
LAND CRUISER 4WD—6-Cyl.—Truck Equipment Schedule T1							
Sport Utility 4D	FJ80W	23953	**3625**	**4350**	**6100**	**8525**
PREVIA—4-Cyl.—Truck Equipment Schedule T1							
Deluxe Minivan	AC11R	17173	**1625**	**2125**	**3325**	**5050**
LE Minivan	AC12R	19573	**1950**	**2475**	**3750**	**5550**
4WD	2		275	275	365	365
PICKUP—4-Cyl.—Truck Equipment Schedule T1							
Short Bed	RN81A	8683	**1125**	**1575**	**2625**	**4075**
Deluxe Short Bed	RN81P	9503	**1200**	**1650**	**2700**	**4225**
Deluxe Long Bed	RN82P	10033	**1225**	**1700**	**2750**	**4275**
Deluxe Xtra Cab	RN93P	10743	**1775**	**2300**	**3450**	**5125**
4WD	0,1		550	550	735	735
V6 3.0 Liter	V		150	150	200	200
PICKUP—V6—Truck Equipment Schedule T2							
1 Ton Long Bed	VN82N	11803	**1375**	**1850**	**2925**	**4500**
SR5 Xtra Cab	VN93G	13533	**2050**	**2600**	**3825**	**5550**
4WD	0,1		550	550	735	735

1992 TOYOTA — (JT3or1N4)(RN37J)–N–#

Body	Type	VIN	List	Trade-In Fair	Trade-In Good	Pvt-Party Good	Retail Excellent
4RUNNER 4WD—4-Cyl.—Truck Equipment Schedule T1							
SR5 Sport Util 2D	RN37J	20723	**2400**	**2975**	**4300**	**6200**
SR5 Sport Util 4D	RN37W	20593	**2650**	**3250**	**4625**	**6600**
2WD	2		(400)	(400)	(535)	(535)
V6 3.0 Liter	V		225	225	300	300
LAND CRUISER 4WD—6-Cyl.—Truck Equipment Schedule T1							
Sport Utility 4D	FJ80W	25923	**4225**	**5025**	**6875**	**9450**
PREVIA—4-Cyl.—Truck Equipment Schedule T1							
Deluxe Minivan	AC11R	19453	**1825**	**2350**	**3625**	**5375**
LE Minivan	AC12R	21743	**2200**	**2775**	**4100**	**5975**
All-Trac AWD	2		325	325	435	435
PICKUP—4-Cyl.—Truck Equipment Schedule T2							
Short Bed	RN81A	9503	**1175**	**1625**	**2675**	**4125**
Deluxe Short Bed	RN81P	10373	**1300**	**1775**	**2825**	**4350**
Deluxe Long Bed	RN82P	10903	**1375**	**1875**	**2925**	**4475**
Deluxe Xtra Cab	RN93P	11613	**1950**	**2500**	**3675**	**5350**
4WD	0		675	675	900	900
V6 3.0 Liter	V		225	225	300	300
PICKUP—V6—Truck Equipment Schedule T2							
1 Ton Long Bed	VN82N	12593	**1500**	**2025**	**3125**	**4700**
SR5 Xtra Cab	VN93G	14353	**2250**	**2825**	**4050**	**5800**
4WD	0		675	675	900	900

1993 TOYOTA — (JT3or1N4)(RN37W)–P–#

Body	Type	VIN	List	Trade-In Fair	Trade-In Good	Pvt-Party Good	Retail Excellent
4RUNNER 4WD—4-Cyl.—Truck Equipment Schedule T1							
SR5 Spt Utility 4D	RN37W	20143	**2825**	**3475**	**4925**	**6925**
2WD	2		(425)	(425)	(565)	(565)
V6 3.0 Liter	V		275	275	365	365
LAND CRUISER 4WD—6-Cyl.—Truck Equipment Schedule T1							
Sport Utility 4D	DJ81W	31503	**4900**	**5750**	**7725**	**10500**
Third Seat Pkg			275	275	365	365
PREVIA—4-Cyl.—Truck Equipment Schedule T1							
Deluxe Minivan	AC11R	21198	**2100**	**2675**	**3975**	**5850**
LE Minivan	AC12R	23583	**2525**	**3125**	**4500**	**6475**
All-Trac AWD	2		375	375	500	500
PICKUP—4-Cyl.—Truck Equipment Schedule T2							
Short Bed	RN81A	9723	**1225**	**1700**	**2725**	**4225**
Deluxe Short Bed	RN81P	10743	**1425**	**1900**	**3000**	**4525**
Deluxe Long Bed	RN82P	11283	**1500**	**2000**	**3100**	**4650**
Deluxe Xtra Cab	RN93P	12203	**2125**	**2700**	**3900**	**5650**
4WD	0,1		800	800	1065	1065
V6 3.0 Liter	V		300	300	400	400
PICKUP—V6—Truck Equipment Schedule T2							
SR5 Xtra Cab	VN93G	14963	**2500**	**3100**	**4350**	**6150**
4WD	1		800	800	1065	1065
T100 PICKUP—V6—Truck Equipment Schedule T2							
Long Bed	VD10A	14533	**1550**	**2075**	**3200**	**4775**
1 Ton Long Bed	VD10B	15253	**1850**	**2375**	**3550**	**5225**
SR5 Long Bed	VD10C	16043	**1850**	**2375**	**3550**	**5225**
4WD			800	800	1065	1065

TRUCKS & VANS

Body	Type	VIN	List	Trade-In Fair	Trade-In Good	Pvt-Party Good	Retail Excellent
1994 TOYOTA — (JT3orR1N4)(RN37W)–R–#							
4RUNNER 4WD—4-Cyl.—Truck Equipment Schedule T1							
SR5 Spt Utility 4D		RN37W	21338	3100	3750	5250	7375
2WD		2		(450)	(450)	(600)	(600)
V6 3.0 Liter		V		325	325	435	435
LAND CRUISER 4WD—6-Cyl.—Truck Equipment Schedule T1							
Sport Utility 4D		DJ81W	34653	6675	7700	9925	13150
Third Seat Pkg				300	300	400	400
PREVIA—4-Cyl.—Truck Equipment Schedule T1							
DX Minivan		AC11R	24218	2400	3000	4400	6325
LE Minivan		AC12R	26183	2850	3500	4950	7000
All-Trac AWD		2		425	425	565	565
PREVIA—4-Cyl. Supercharged—Truck Equipment Schedule T1							
LE S/C Minivan		AC14R	28543	3450	4150	5700	7875
All-Trac AWD		2		425	425	565	565
PICKUP—4-Cyl.—Truck Equipment Schedule T2							
Short Bed		RN81A	10443	1300	1775	2825	4375
DX Short Bed		RN81L	11533	1525	2050	3175	4775
DX Xtra Cab		RN93P	13083	2325	2900	4150	5925
4WD		0,1		900	900	1200	1200
V6 3.0 Liter		V		375	375	500	500
PICKUP—V6—Truck Equipment Schedule T2							
SR5 Xtra Cab		VN93G	15943	2700	3325	4625	6500
4WD		1		900	900	1200	1200
T100 PICKUP—4-Cyl.—Truck Equipment Schedule T2							
Long Bed		UD10D	13623	1550	2075	3225	4825
T100 PICKUP—6-Cyl.—Truck Equipment Schedule T2							
DX Long Bed		VD10A	15323	1800	2325	3500	5175
DX 1 Ton Long Bed		VD10B	16063	2125	2700	3900	5675
SR5 Long Bed		VD10C	17153	2125	2700	3900	5675
4WD				850	850	1135	1135
1995 TOYOTA—(JT3,JT4or4TA)(RN37W)–S–#							
4RUNNER 4WD—4-Cyl.—Truck Equipment Schedule T1							
SR5 Spt Utility 4D		RN37W	22450	3425	4125	5700	7950
Limited				475	475	635	635
2WD		2		(475)	(475)	(635)	(635)
V6 3.0 Liter		V		375	375	500	500
LAND CRUISER 4WD—6-Cyl.—Truck Equipment Schedule T1							
Sport Utility 4D		DJ81W	39085	7550	8700	11100	14500
Third Seat Pkg				325	325	435	435
PREVIA—4-Cyl.—Truck Equipment Schedule T1							
DX Minivan		AC11R	24400	2750	3325	4850	6900
LE Minivan		AC12R	26975	3275	3925	5450	7600
All-Trac AWD		2		475	475	635	635
PREVIA—4-Cyl. Supercharged—Truck Equipment Schedule T1							
DX S/C Minivan		AC13R	24900	3425	4150	5700	7875
LE S/C Minivan		AC14R	27475	3925	4675	6300	8600
All-Trac AWD		2		475	475	635	635
PICKUP—4-Cyl.—Truck Equipment Schedule T2							
Short Bed		RN81A	10985	1425	1900	3000	4575
DX Short Bed		RN81P	11885	1725	2250	3400	5050
DX Xtra Cab		RN93P	13495	2550	3175	4450	6275
4WD		0,1		1000	1000	1335	1335
V6 3.0 Liter		V		450	450	600	600
PICKUP—V6—Truck Equipment Schedule T2							
SR5 Xtra Cab		VN93G	16455	3000	3675	5000	6900
4WD		1		1000	1000	1335	1335
TACOMA—4-Cyl.—Truck Equipment Sch T2							
Short Bed		UN41B	12435	1975	2525	3725	5425
Xtra Cab		UN53B	14545	2550	3175	4450	6300
4WD		6,7		1000	1000	1335	1335
V6 3.4 Liter				450	450	600	600
TACOMA 4WD—V6—Truck Equipment Sch T2							
SR5 Xtra Cab		VN73K	21715	4500	5300	6875	9125
T100 PICKUP—V6—Truck Equipment Schedule T2							
Long Bed		VD10D	15135	1850	2375	3575	5250
DX Long Bed		VD11E	16155	2100	2700	3900	5650
DX 1 Ton Long Bed		VD11G	16935	2475	3075	4325	6150
DX Xtra Cab		VD12E	18000	3150	3800	5150	7100
SR5 Xtra Cab		VD12F	19275	3725	4475	5875	7975
4WD				1000	1000	1335	1335

Body	Type	VIN	List	Trade-In Fair	Trade-In Good	Pvt-Party Good	Retail Excellent
4-Cyl. 2.7 Liter		U		(225)	(225)	(300)	(300)

1996 TOYOTA—(JT3,JT4or4TA)(YP10V)—T—#

RAV4 4WD—4-Cyl.—Truck Equipment Schedule T2
Sport Utility 2D		YP10V	17058	3000	3675	4925	6775
Sport Utility 4D		HP10V	17758	3450	4150	5475	7425
2WD		G,X		(450)	(450)	(600)	(600)
Dual Sun Roofs				50	50	65	65

4RUNNER 4WD—4-Cyl.—Truck Equipment Schedule T1
| Sport Utility 4D | | HM84R | 23853 | 4175 | 4950 | 6375 | 8525 |
| 2WD | | G | | (500) | (500) | (665) | (665) |

4RUNNER 4WD—V6—Truck Equipment Schedule T1
SR5 Spt Utility 4D		HN86R	27453	5675	6600	8225	10650
Limited Spt Util 4D		HN87R	33408	6700	7750	9500	12150
2WD		G		(500)	(500)	(665)	(665)

LAND CRUISER 4WD—6-Cyl.—Truck Equipment Schedule T3
| Sport Utility 4D | | HJ85J | 45483 | 8575 | 9800 | 12350 | 16000 |
| Third Seat Pkg | | | | 350 | 350 | 465 | 465 |

PREVIA—4-Cyl. Supercharged—Truck Equipment Schedule T1
DX S/C Minivan		GK12M	26473	3900	4650	6300	8600
LE S/C Minivan		GK13M	29278	4475	5250	6925	9350
AWD				500	500	665	665

TACOMA—4-Cyl.—Truck Equipment Schedule T2
Short Bed		NL42N	12643	2275	2850	4100	5900
Xtra Cab		VL52M	14793	2925	3575	4925	6850
4WD		6,7		1100	1100	1465	1465
V6 3.4 Liter		N		525	525	700	700

TACOMA—4WD—V6—Truck Equipment Schedule T2
| SR5 Xtra Cab | | WN74N | 22648 | 5150 | 6025 | 7650 | 10050 |

T100 PICKUP—4-Cyl.—Truck Equipment Schedule T2
| Long Bed | | JM11D | 15113 | 2150 | 2725 | 3950 | 5725 |

T100 PICKUP—V6—Truck Equipment Schedule T2
Xtra Cab		TN12D	18683	3550	4250	5675	7700
SR5 Xtra Cab		UN14D	20158	4200	5000	6475	8650
4WD		2		1050	1050	1400	1400

1997 TOYOTA—(JT3,JT4or4TA)(YP10V)—V

RAV4 4WD—4-Cyl.—Truck Equipment Schedule T2
Sport Utility 2D		YP10V	17128	3550	4250	5575	7500
Sport Utility 4D		HP10V	17828	4000	4775	6150	8150
2WD		G,X		(475)	(475)	(635)	(635)
Dual Sun Roofs				50	50	65	65

4RUNNER 4WD—4-Cyl.—Truck Equipment Schedule T1
| Sport Utility 4D | | HM84R | 24293 | 4825 | 5675 | 7225 | 9500 |
| 2WD | | G | | (525) | (525) | (700) | (700) |

4RUNNER 4WD—V6—Truck Equipment Schedule T1
SR5 Sport Util 4D		HN86R	27983	6450	7475	9200	11750
Limited Spt Util 4D		HN87R	34158	7550	8700	10500	13300
2WD		G		(525)	(525)	(700)	(700)

LAND CRUISER 4WD—6-Cyl.—Truck Equipment Schedule T3
| Sport Utility 4D | | HJ85J | 46293 | 9700 | 11100 | 13750 | 17550 |
| Third Seat Pkg | | | | 475 | 475 | 635 | 635 |

PREVIA—4-Cyl. Supercharged—Truck Equipment Schedule T1
DX S/C Minivan		GK12M	26963	4475	5250	6950	9375
LE S/C Minivan		GK13M	29858	5050	5925	7675	10200
All-Trac AWD		2		525	525	700	700

TACOMA—4-Cyl.—Truck Equipment Schedule T2
Short Bed		NL42N	12813	2675	3275	4575	6425
Xtra Cab		VL52M	14983	3350	4050	5425	7450
4WD				1200	1200	1600	1600
V6 3.4 Liter		N		575	575	765	765

TACOMA—4WD—V6—Truck Equipment Schedule T2
| SR5 Xtra Cab | | WN74N | 22868 | 5850 | 6825 | 8475 | 10950 |

T100—4-Cyl.—Truck Equipment Schedule T2
| Long Bed | | JM11D | 15303 | 2550 | 3150 | 4425 | 6275 |

T100—V6—Truck Equipment Schedule T2
DX Xtra Cab		TN12D	19213	4000	4775	6250	8350
SR5 Xtra Cab		UN14D	20428	4750	5575	7100	9350
4WD		2		1150	1150	1535	1535

0105

1998 TOYOTA

Body	Type	VIN	List	Trade-In Fair	Good	Pvt-Party Good	Retail Excellent
1998 TOYOTA—(JT3, JT4or4TA)(YP10V)—W							
RAV4 4WD—4-Cyl.—Truck Equipment Schedule T2							
Sport Util Conv 2D	YP10V	17218	4250	5050	6300	8175
Sport Utility 2D	YP10V	17218	4175	4950	6175	8075
Sport Utility 4D	HP10V	18078	4675	5525	6800	8750
2WD	G,X		(525)	(525)	(700)	(700)
4RUNNER 4WD—4-Cyl.—Truck Equipment Schedule T1							
Sport Utility 4D	HM84R	25013	5625	6525	8100	10450
2WD	G		(575)	(575)	(765)	(765)
4RUNNER 4WD—V6—Truck Equipment Schedule T1							
SR5 Sport Util 4D	HN86R	28573	7400	8500	10250	12900
Limited Spt Util 4D	HN87R	35038	8600	9850	11950	14550
2WD	G		(575)	(575)	(765)	(765)
LAND CRUISER 4WD—V8—Truck Equipment Schedule T3							
Sport Utility 4D	HT05J	46413	13150	14875	17650	21900
Third Seat Pkg			525	525	700	700
SIENNA—V6—Truck Equipment Schedule T1							
CE Minivan	GF19C	21560	4700	5525	7050	9300
LE Minivan	ZF13C	24395	5300	6200	7775	10150
XLE Minivan	ZF13C	27520	6025	6975	8650	11100
w/o 2nd Sliding Door			(500)	(500)	(665)	(665)
TACOMA—4-Cyl.—Truck Equipment Schedule T2							
Short Bed	NL42N	13228	3075	3725	5000	6875
Xtra Cab	VL52N	15128	3850	4575	5900	7900
PreRunner Xtra	SM92N	17658	4750	5600	7025	9175
4WD	6,7		1275	1275	1700	1700
V6 3.4 Liter	N		625	625	835	835
TACOMA 4WD—V6—Truck Equipment Schedule T2							
Limited Xtra Cab	WN74N	24448	6300	7300	8850	11250
T100—4-Cyl.—Truck Equipment Schedule T2							
Long Bed	JM11D	15248	2975	3650	4900	6750
T100—V6—Truck Equipment Schedule T2							
DX Xtra Cab	TN12D	19218	4600	5450	6875	8975
SR5 Xtra Cab	TN14D	20848	5375	6300	7750	9975
4WD	2		1225	1225	1635	1635
1999 TOYOTA—(4,5orJ)T(3,AorB)(YP10V)—X							
RAV4 4WD—4-Cyl.—Truck Equipment Schedule T2							
Sport Util Conv 2D	YP10V	17508	5650	6550	7925	10050
Sport Utility 4D	HP10V	18198	5525	6425	7800	9900
2WD	G,X		(600)	(600)	(800)	(800)
4RUNNER 4WD—4-Cyl.—Truck Equipment Schedule T1							
Sport Utility 4D	HM84R	25443	6500	7500	9150	11600
2WD	G		(650)	(650)	(865)	(865)
4RUNNER 4WD—V6—Truck Equipment Schedule T1							
SR5 Sport Util 4D	HN86R	28773	8525	9750	11500	14300
Limited Spt Util 4D	HN87R	36088	9925	11275	13200	16200
2WD	G		(650)	(650)	(865)	(865)
LAND CRUISER 4WD—V8—Truck Equipment Schedule T3							
Sport Utility 4D	HT05J	48718	15900	17900	20900	25600
Third Seat Pkg			600	600	800	800
SIENNA—V6—Truck Equipment Schedule T1							
CE Minivan	GF19C	22738	5700	6650	8250	10650
LE Minivan	ZF13C	24778	6400	7425	9100	11600
XLE Minivan	ZF13C	28099	7225	8300	10100	12700
w/o 2nd Sliding Door			(550)	(550)	(735)	(735)
TACOMA—4-Cyl.—Truck Equipment Schedule T2							
Short Bed	NL42N	13388	3600	4325	5650	7600
Xtra Cab	VL52N	15288	4475	5250	6650	8725
PreRunner Short	NM92N	15188	4450	5225	6625	8700
PreRunner Xtra	SM92N	18028	5500	6425	7925	10200
4WD	6,7		1450	1450	1935	1935
V6 3.4 Liter	N		725	725	965	965
TACOMA 4WD—V6—Truck Equipment Schedule T2							
Limited Xtra Cab	WN74N	25108	7425	8550	10200	12750
2000 TOYOTA—(4,5orJ)T(3,AorB)(HP10V)—Y							
RAV4 4WD—4-Cyl.—Truck Equipment Schedule T2							
Sport Utility 4D	HP10V	18558	6475	7500	8875	11100
2WD			(675)	(675)	(900)	(900)

TRUCKS & VANS

Body Type	VIN	List	Trade-In Fair	Good	Pvt-Party Good	Retail Excellent
4RUNNER 4WD—4-Cyl.—Truck Equipment Schedule T1						
Sport Utility 4D	HM84R	26046	7525	8675	10350	13000
2WD	G		(725)	(725)	(965)	(965)
4RUNNER 4WD—V6—Truck Equipment Schedule T1						
SR5 Sport Util 4D	HN86R	29786	9800	11175	13050	16000
Limited Spt Util 4D	HN87R	36948	11375	12900	14900	18050
2WD	G		(725)	(725)	(965)	(965)
LAND CRUISER 4WD—V8—Truck Equipment Schedule T3						
Sport Utility 4D	HT05J	51308	18900	21225	24600	29700
Third Seat Pkg			675	675	900	900
SIENNA—V6—Truck Equipment Schedule T1						
CE Minivan	ZF19C	23338	6850	7900	9650	12250
LE Minivan	ZF13C	25378	7650	8775	10550	13300
XLE Minivan	ZF13C	27414	8575	9800	11600	14450
w/o 2nd Sliding Door			(600)	(600)	(800)	(800)
TACOMA—4-Cyl.—Truck Equipment Schedule T2						
Short Bed	NL42N	12208	4225	5025	6400	8475
Xtra Cab	VL52N	14458	5150	6025	7500	9700
PreRunner Short	NM92N	14298	5150	6025	7500	9700
PreRunner Xtra	SM92N	17418	6325	7350	8875	11250
4WD			1625	1625	2165	2165
V6 3.4 Liter	N		825	825	1100	1100
TACOMA 4WD—V6—Truck Equipment Schedule T2						
Limited Xtra Cab	WN74N	24758	8650	9900	11600	14300
TUNDRA—V6—Truck Equipment Schedule T2						
Long Bed	JN321	15475	5700	6650	8000	10100
TUNDRA 4WD—V8—Truck Equipment Schedule T2						
SR5 Long Bed	KT441	23190	7500	8625	10100	12450
V6 3.4 Liter			(675)	(675)	(900)	(900)
TUNDRA—V8—Truck Equipment Schedule T2						
SR5 Access Cab 4D	RT341	22730	8300	9525	11050	13550
Ltd Access Cab 4D	RT381	24975	8700	9925	11450	14000
4WD	4		1575	1575	2100	2100
V6 3.4 Liter	N		(675)	(675)	(900)	(900)

Body Type	VIN	List	Trade-In Fair	Good	Pvt-Party Good	Retail Excellent
RAV4 4WD—4-Cyl.—Truck Equipment Schedule T1						
Sport Utility 4D	HH20V	18095	7850	9025	10400	12700
2WD	G,Z		(750)	(750)	(1000)	(1000)
HIGHLANDER 4WD—V6—Truck Equipment Schedule T1						
Sport Utility 4D	HF21A	26950	10850	12300	14100	17000
Limited Spt Util 4D	HF21A	30445	11750	13350	15200	18250
2WD			(800)	(800)	(1065)	(1065)
4-Cyl. 2.4 Liter			(825)	(825)	(1100)	(1100)
4RUNNER 4WD—V6—Truck Equipment Schedule T1						
SR5 Sport Util 4D	HN86R	29375	11275	12825	14800	17900
Limited Spt Util 4D	HN87R	38085	13000	14725	16800	20200
2WD	G		(800)	(800)	(1065)	(1065)
SEQUOIA 4WD—V8—Truck Equipment Schedule T1						
SR5 Spt Util 4D	BT44A	34825	14775	16700	18950	22700
Limited Spt Util 4D	BT48A	42755	15750	17700	20400	24600
2WD			(800)	(800)	(1065)	(1065)
LAND CRUISER 4WD—V8—Truck Equipment Schedule T3						
Sport Utility 4D	HT05J	53375	22275	24875	28300	33800
Third Seat Pkg			750	750	1000	1000
SIENNA—V6—Truck Equipment Schedule T1						
CE Minivan	ZF19C	24385	8175	9375	11250	14000
LE Minivan	ZF13C	26235	9100	10375	12300	15150
XLE Minivan	ZF13C	28916	10075	11475	13450	16450
TACOMA—4-Cyl.—Truck Equipment Schedule T2						
Short Bed	NL42N	12325	5300	6200	7500	9475
Xtra Cab	VL52N	14965	6300	7325	8675	10800
PreRunner Short	NM92N	14215	6325	7350	8675	10800
PreRunner Xtra	SM92N	16815	7600	8725	10200	12550
PreRunner 4D	GM92N	18335	8750	10025	11500	13950
PreRunner Ltd 4D	GM92N	22690	9475	10800	12400	14950
4WD			1800	1800	2400	2400
V6 3.4 Liter	N		925	925	1235	1235
TACOMA—V6—Truck Equipment Schedule T2						
S-Runner Xtra Cab	VN52N	18385	7625	8750	10200	12550
TACOMA 4WD—V6—Truck Equipment Schedule T2						
Limited Xtra Cab	WN74N	24895	10275	11700	13300	15950
Double Cab 4D	HN72N	22345	9925	11275	12850	15450

Body	Type	VIN	List	Trade-In Fair	Trade-In Good	Pvt-Party Good	Retail Excellent
Ltd Double Cab 4D		HN72N	25840	10425	11850	13450	16150
4-Cyl. 2.7 Liter		M		(825)	(825)	(1100)	(1100)
TUNDRA—V6—Truck Equipment Schedule T2							
Long Bed		JN321	16085	6725	7775	9175	11400
TUNDRA 4WD—V8—Truck Equipment Schedule T2							
SR5 Long Bed		RT441	23885	8650	9900	11400	13900
TUNDRA—V8—Truck Equipment Schedule T2							
SR5 Access Cab 4D		RT341	23455	9600	10950	12550	15100
Ltd Access Cab 4D		RT381	26205	9975	11375	13000	15650
4WD		4		1750	1750	2335	2335
V6 3.4 Liter		N		(750)	(750)	(1000)	(1000)

Body	Type	VIN	List	Trade-In Fair	Trade-In Good	Pvt-Party Good	Retail Excellent
RAV4 4WD—4-Cyl.—Truck Equipment Schedule T2							
Sport Utility 4D		HH20V	18435	9225	10500	11950	14350
2WD		G		(825)	(825)	(1100)	(1100)
HIGHLANDER 4WD—V6—Truck Equipment Schedule T1							
Sport Utility 4D		HF21A	27370	12575	14200	16150	19300
Limited Spt Util 4D		HF21A	31305	13575	15350	17350	20600
2WD		D		(875)	(875)	(1165)	(1165)
4-Cyl. 2.4 Liter		D		(925)	(925)	(1235)	(1235)
4RUNNER 4WD—V6—Truck Equipment Schedule T1							
SR5 Sport Util 4D		HN86R	29385	12950	14700	16750	20100
Limited Spt Util 4D		HN87R	36615	14875	16750	18900	22500
2WD		G		(875)	(875)	(1165)	(1165)
SEQUOIA 4WD—V8—Truck Equipment Schedule T1							
SR5 Spt Util 4D		BT44A	35305	17050	19150	21500	25400
Limited Spt Util 4D		BT48A	43235	18100	20350	23100	27600
2WD		Z		(875)	(875)	(1165)	(1165)
LAND CRUISER 4WD—V8—Truck Equipment Schedule T3							
Sport Utility 4D		HT05J	53105	25825	28900	32400	38300
SIENNA—V6—Truck Equipment Schedule T1							
CE Minivan		ZF19C	24415	9800	11175	13100	16100
LE Minivan		ZF13C	26265	10800	12250	14200	17350
XLE Minivan		ZF13C	28522	11850	13450	15450	18700
TACOMA—4-Cyl.—Truck Equipment Schedule T2							
Short Bed		NL42N	12410	6225	7200	8575	10700
Xtra Cab		VL52N	15050	7275	8375	9800	12050
PreRunner Short		NM92N	14400	7350	8450	9900	12150
PreRunner Xtra		SM92N	17000	8725	9975	11450	13900
PreRunner 4D		GM92N	18620	9975	11375	12900	15500
4WD		N		1975	1975	2635	2635
V6 3.4 Liter		N		1025	1025	1365	1365
TACOMA—4-Cyl.—Truck Equipment Schedule T2							
S-Runner Xtra Cab		VN52N	18570	8925	10225	11700	14150
PreRunner Ltd 4D		GM92N	23000	10800	12250	13850	16550
TACOMA 4WD—V6—Truck Equipment Schedule T2							
Limited Xtra Cab		WN72N	23655	11750	13350	15000	17750
Double Cab 4D		HN72N	22630	11275	12825	14400	17150
Ltd Double Cab 4D		HN72N	26150	11950	13525	15200	18050
TUNDRA—V6—Truck Equipment Schedule T2							
Long Bed		JN321	16115	7850	9025	10500	12850
TUNDRA 4WD—V8—Truck Equipment Schedule T2							
SR5 Long Bed		KT441	23915	9925	11275	12850	15500
TUNDRA—V8—Truck Equipment Schedule T2							
SR5 Access Cab 4D		RT341	23485	11000	12475	14150	16900
Ltd Access Cab 4D		RT230	27230	11475	13000	14650	17450
4WD		4		1925	1925	2565	2565
V6 3.4 Liter		N		(825)	(825)	(1100)	(1100)

Body	Type	VIN	List	Trade-In Fair	Trade-In Good	Pvt-Party Good	Retail Excellent
RAV4 4WD—4-Cyl.—Truck Equipment Schedule T2							
Sport Utility 4D		HH20V	18435	10750	12200	13550	15900
2WD		G,Z		(900)	(900)	(1200)	(1200)
HIGHLANDER 4WD—V6—Truck Equipment Schedule T1							
Sport Utility 4D		HF21A	25790	14550	16425	18350	21600
Limited Spt Util 4D		HF21A	31305	15650	17625	19600	22900
2WD		D		(950)	(950)	(1265)	(1265)
4-Cyl. 2.4 Liter		D		(1025)	(1025)	(1365)	(1365)
4RUNNER 4WD—V6—Truck Equipment Schedule T1							
SR5 Sport Util 4D		BU14R	29990	14600	16475	18850	22700
Sport Utility 4D		BU14R	31785	14700	16600	19000	22800
Limited Spt Util 4D		BU17R	36190	16600	18675	21200	25200

TRUCKS & VANS

TRUCKS & VANS

Body Type	VIN	List	Trade-In Fair	Good	Pvt-Party Good	Retail Excellent
2WD	Z	....	(950)	(950)	(1265)	(1265)
V8 4.7 Liter	T	....	450	450	600	600
SEQUOIA 4WD—V8—Truck Equipment Schedule T1						
SR5 Spt Util 4D	BT44A	35565	19400	21800	24200	28200
Limited Spt Util 4D	BT48A	44030	20650	23125	26000	30700
2WD	Z	....	(950)	(950)	(1265)	(1265)
LAND CRUISER 4WD—V8—Truck Equipment Schedule T3						
Sport Utility 4D	HT05J	53915	29750	33225	37000	43300
SIENNA—V6—Truck Equipment Schedule T1						
CE Minivan	ZF19C	24415	11750	13300	15150	18250
LE Minivan	ZF13C	26265	12825	14500	16400	19600
XLE Minivan	ZF13C	28522	14025	15800	17800	21100
TACOMA—4-Cyl.—Truck Equipment Schedule T2						
Short Bed	NL42N	12610	6825	7875	9125	11150
Xtra Cab	VL52N	15250	8000	9175	10450	12600
PreRunner Short	NM92N	14525	8075	9250	10550	12700
PreRunner Xtra	SM92N	17200	9550	10900	12250	14600
PreRunner 4D	GM92N	18820	10950	12425	13850	16350
4WD			2150	2150	2865	2865
V6 3.4 Liter	N		1125	1125	1500	1500
TACOMA—V6—Truck Equipment Schedule T2						
PreRunner Ltd 4D	GN92N	23430	11800	13400	14900	17450
TACOMA 4WD—V6—Truck Equipment Schedule T2						
Limited Xtra Cab	WN72N	24085	12950	14700	16200	18950
Double Cab 4D	HN72N	22830	12325	13975	15450	18100
Ltd Double Cab 4D	HN72N	26580	13200	14875	16450	19200
TUNDRA—V6—Truck Equipment Schedule T2						
Long Bed	JN321	16465	9225	10500	11900	14250
TUNDRA 4WD—V8—Truck Equipment Schedule T2						
SR5 Long Bed	KT441	24265	11475	13000	14500	17100
TUNDRA—V8—Truck Equipment Schedule T2						
SR5 Access Cab 4D	RT341	23835	12625	14250	15850	18600
Ltd Access Cab 4D	RT381	27465	13150	14875	16450	19300
4WD	4		2100	2100	2800	2800
V6 3.4 Liter			(900)	(900)	(1200)	(1200)

2004 TOYOTA–(5orJ)T(B,DorE)(HD20V)–4–#

Body Type	VIN	List	Trade-In Fair	Good	Pvt-Party Good	Retail Excellent
RAV4 4WD—4-Cyl.—Truck Equipment Schedule T2						
Sport Utility 4D	HD20V	20290	12525	14150	15400	17800
2WD	Z	....	(950)	(950)	(1265)	(1265)
HIGHLANDER 4WD—V6—Truck Equipment Schedule T1						
Sport Utility 4D	HD21A	27930	16850	18950	20900	24500
Limited Spt Utl 4D	HF21A	31920	18000	20250	22300	25900
2WD	Z		(1000)	(1000)	(1335)	(1335)
4-Cyl. 2.4 Liter	D		(1125)	(1125)	(1500)	(1500)
4RUNNER 4WD—V6—Truck Equipment Schedule T2						
SR5 Sport Util 4D	BU14R	29985	16850	18950	21500	25500
Sport Utility 4D	BU14R	31225	16950	19050	21600	25600
Limited Spt Utl 4D	BU17R	36260	19000	21300	24000	28300
2WD	Z		(1000)	(1000)	(1335)	(1335)
V8 4.7 Liter	T		475	475	635	635
SEQUOIA 4WD—V8—Truck Equipment Schedule T1						
SR5 Spt Util 4D	BT44A	35695	22275	24875	27300	31600
Limited Spt Util 4D	BT48A	44760	23625	26400	29400	34300
2WD	Z		(1000)	(1000)	(1335)	(1335)
LAND CRUISER 4WD—V8—Truck Equipment Schedule T3						
Sport Utility 4D	HT05J	54765	34275	38200	42000	48800
SIENNA—V6—Truck Equipment Schedule T1						
CE Minivan	ZA23C	23495	13875	15700	17650	21000
LE Minivan	ZA23C	24800	15025	16950	19000	22500
XLE Minivan	ZA22C	28800	16275	18325	20400	24100
XLE Limited	ZA22C	35020	16950	19050	21200	24900
AWD			1050	1050	1400	1400
TACOMA PICKUP—4-Cyl.—Truck Equipment Schedule T2						
Short Bed	NL42N	12800	8350	9575	10750	12800
Xtra Cab	VL52N	15460	9550	10900	12150	14350
PreRunner Short	NM92N	14715	9700	11100	12350	14550
PreRunner Xtra	SM92N	17410	11275	12825	14150	16550
PreRunner 4D	GM92N	19030	12825	14500	15950	18550
4WD	W,H		2325	2325	3100	3100
V6 3.4 Liter	N		1225	1225	1635	1635
TACOMA PICKUP—V6—Truck Equipment Schedule T2						
S-Runner Xtra Cab	VN52N	20700	11750	13350	14750	17250

Body	Type	VIN	List	Trade-In Fair	Good	Pvt-Party Good	Retail Excellent
PreRunner Ltd 4D		GN92N	23640	13775	15550	17050	19800
TACOMA PICKUP 4WD—V6—Truck Equipment Schedule T2							
Limited Xtra Cab		WN72N	24295	15075	17000	18600	21500
Double Cab 4D		HN72N	23040	14350	16175	17700	20500
Ltd Double Cab 4D		HN72N	26790	15300	17275	18850	21800
TUNDRA—V6—Truck Equipment Schedule T2							
Long Bed		JN321	16495	11100	12575	13950	16450
TUNDRA 4WD—V8—Truck Equipment Schedule T2							
SR5 Long Bed		KT441	24415	13450	15175	16700	19500
TUNDRA—V8—Truck Equipment Schedule T2							
SR5 Access Cab 4D		RN341	23985	14700	16600	18200	21100
Ltd Access Cab 4D		RT381	27615	15300	17225	18850	21900
SR5 Double Cab 4D		ET341	26185	16700	18775	20500	23700
Ltd Double Cab 4D		ET381	29810	17275	19400	21100	24400
4WD		4		2275	2275	3035	3035
V6 3.4 Liter		N		(950)	(950)	(1265)	(1265)

VOLKSWAGEN

1990 VOLKSWAGEN — WV2(YB025)-L-#

VANAGON—4-Cyl.—Truck Equipment Schedule T2							
Minivan		YB025	14400	1350	1825	2900	4475
GL Minivan		YB025	16810	1375	1850	2950	4500
Carat Minivan		YB025	18990	1575	2100	3250	4875
Multi-Van		XB025	20750	4525	5350	7000	9400
GL Camper		ZB025	21310	5000	5850	7575	10100
4WD Syncro				2000	2000	2665	2665

1991 VOLKSWAGEN — WV2(YB025)-M-#

VANAGON—4-Cyl.—Truck Equipment Schedule T2							
Minivan		YB025	14680	1575	2100	3275	4950
GL Minivan		YB025	17140	1600	2100	3300	4975
Carat Minivan		YB025	18780	1875	2400	3650	5400
Multi-Van		TB025	21160	5200	6100	7950	10550
GL Camper		ZB025	21730	5725	6675	8600	11400
4WD Syncro				2000	2000	2665	2665

1992 VOLKSWAGEN — Not Imported

1993 VOLKSWAGEN — WV2(HD070)-P-#

EUROVAN—5-Cyl.—Truck Equipment Schedule T2							
CL Minivan		HD070	17130	1500	2000	3200	4875
GL Minivan		KD070	20910	1800	2325	3575	5325
MV Minivan		MD070	22340	2250	2825	4150	6025
Weekender Pkg				1700	1700	2265	2265

1994 - 1998 VOLKSWAGEN — Not Imported

1999 VOLKSWAGEN — WV2(KH270)-X-#

EUROVAN—V6—Truck Equipment Schedule T1							
GLS Minivan		KH270	30465	6775	7800	9200	11400
MV Minivan		MH270	31965	7325	8425	9850	12150
Weekender Pkg				6000	6000	8000	8000

2000 VOLKSWAGEN — WV2(KH270)-Y-#

EUROVAN—V6—Truck Equipment Schedule T1							
GLS Minivan		KH270	31890	8100	9300	10800	13200
MV Minivan		MH270	33390	8750	10025	11550	14050
Weekender Pkg				6000	6000	8000	8000

2001 VOLKSWAGEN — WV2(KH470)-1-#

EUROVAN—V6—Truck Equipment Schedule T1							
Minivan		KH470	26815	9750	11125	12700	15300
MV Minivan		MH470	28315	10500	11950	13600	16250
Weekender Pkg				6000	6000	8000	8000

2002 VOLKSWAGEN — WV2(KB470)-2-#

EUROVAN—V6—Truck Equipment Schedule T1							
GLS Minivan		KB470	26815	11700	13250	15000	17850

TRUCKS & VANS

Body	Type	VIN	List	Trade-In Fair	Good	Pvt-Party Good	Retail Excellent
MV Minivan		MB470	28315	**12525**	**14150**	**15950**	**18900**
Weekender Pkg.				**6000**	**6000**	**8000**	**8000**

2003 VOLKSWAGEN — WV2(KB470)-3-#

EUROVAN—V6—Truck Equipment Schedule T1

Body	Type	VIN	List	Trade-In Fair	Good	Pvt-Party Good	Retail Excellent
GLS Minivan		KB470	26815	**14100**	**15925**	**17750**	**20900**
MV Minivan		MB470	28315	**15025**	**16950**	**18800**	**22100**
Weekender Pkg.				**6000**	**6000**	**8000**	**8000**

2004 VOLKSWAGEN — USED DATA NOT YET AVAILABLE

VOLVO

2003 VOLVO — YV1(CN59H)-3-#

XC90—5-Cyl. Turbo—Truck Equipment Schedule T3

Body	Type	VIN	List	Trade-In Fair	Good	Pvt-Party Good	Retail Excellent
Sport Utility 4D		CN59H	36610	**23125**	**25925**	**29100**	**34400**
Third Row Seat				**550**	**550**	**735**	**735**

XC90 AWD—5-Cyl. Turbo—Truck Equipment Schedule T3

Body	Type	VIN	List	Trade-In Fair	Good	Pvt-Party Good	Retail Excellent
Sport Utility 4D		CM59H	38360	**24000**	**26875**	**30100**	**35500**
Third Row Seat				**550**	**550**	**735**	**735**

XC90 AWD—6-Cyl. Twin Turbo—Truck Equipment Schedule T3

Body	Type	VIN	List	Trade-In Fair	Good	Pvt-Party Good	Retail Excellent
T6 Sport Utility 4D		CM91H	40660	**25625**	**28600**	**32000**	**37500**
Third Row Seat				**550**	**550**	**735**	**735**

2004 VOLVO — USED DATA NOT YET AVAILABLE

Equipment	90-91	92	93	94	95	96	97

MODEL PACKAGES (Truck Schedules T1 & T2)
(Add Only If Not Listed on Individual Vehicle Listing)

CHEVROLET/GMC:

LT (Astro)/SLT (Safari)							
	100	100	100	100	125	150	175

FORD:

Limited, Chateau	—	200	275	350	425	500	575
Eddie Bauer, Silver Anniversary							
	125	150	175	225	275	325	375

ALL MAKES: (All Other Model Pkgs Not Listed)

	75	75	75	75	75	75	100

TRUCK SCHEDULE T1 (Deduct For)

Manual Trans	(225)	(250)	(275)	(300)	(325)	(350)	(375)
w/o Pwr Steering	(100)	(125)	(150)	(150)	(150)	(150)	(150)
w/o Air Cond	(150)	(175)	(200)	(225)	(250)	(250)	(250)

TRUCK SCHEDULE T2 (Add For)

Auto Trans	175	200	225	250	275	300	325
Power Steering	50	75	75	75	75	75	75
Air Cond	150	175	200	200	200	200	200
TOTAL	**375**	**450**	**500**	**525**	**550**	**575**	**600**

TRUCK SCHEDULE T3 (See Page 366)

OTHER OPTIONS (Truck Schedules T1 & T2)

Cassette	25	25	25	25	25	50	75
Power Windows	50	75	100	100	100	100	100
Pwr Door Locks	25	50	50	50	50	50	50
Tilt Wheel	25	50	75	75	75	75	75
Cruise Control	25	25	25	25	25	25	25
TOTAL	**150**	**225**	**275**	**275**	**275**	**300**	**325**

w/o AM/FM	(25)	(50)	(50)	(50)	(50)	(50)	(50)
CD (Single Disc)	50	50	50	100	100	100	100
CD (Multi Disc)	100	100	100	175	200	200	200
Premium Sound	25	50	50	50	50	50	50
Air Cond, Rear	100	125	150	175	200	225	250
Leather	25	50	75	100	125	150	175
Quad Seating (4 Buckets)	100	125	150	150	150	150	150

SEE PAGE 9 FOR PVT PARTY & RETAIL EQUIPMENT 365

TRUCKS & VANS

Equipment	90-91	92	93	94	95	96	97
Van Seating Pkgs							
(11/12 Pass)	250	275	300	325	350	375	400
(15 Passenger)	400	425	450	475	500	525	550
Privacy Glass (Vans/Wagons/Sport Utilities)							
	25	50	50	50	50	50	50
Sliding Rear Window (Pickups)							
	25	25	25	25	25	25	25
Roof Rack	25	25	25	25	25	25	25
Sun Roof or Moon Roof							
(Flip-Up)	50	50	50	50	50	50	50
(Sliding)	125	150	175	200	225	250	275
Pickup Shell/Cap	50	75	100	100	100	100	100
Bed Liner	50	50	50	50	50	50	75
Grille Guard	25	50	50	50	50	50	50
Winch	50	50	50	50	75	100	125
Custom Bumper	25	50	50	50	50	50	50
Stepside							
(Short Bed PU)	25	50	75	100	125	150	150
(Long Bed PU)	(250)	(250)	(250)	(250)	(250)	(250)	(250)
Running Boards	25	50	50	50	50	50	50
Alloy Wheels	50	75	100	125	150	150	150
Premium Wheels	125	150	175	200	225	250	275
Wide Tires or Oversize Off-Road Tires							
	50	50	50	50	50	50	75
ABS (4-Wheel)	50	75	100	125	150	150	150
Opt Fuel Tank	25	50	50	50	50	50	50
Towing Pkg	100	125	150	175	200	200	200
Dual Rear Wheels (Add Only on Models Not Listed as DR)							
	575	625	675	700	725	750	775

TRUCK SCHEDULE T3 (This Equipment Only)

CD (Single Disc)	50	50	50	125	150	150	150
CD (Multi Disc)	100	100	125	175	200	225	250
Premium Sound	50	75	100	125	150	150	150
Integrated Phone	—	25	50	50	50	50	50
Sun/Moon Roof	125	150	175	200	225	250	275
Grille Guard	25	50	50	50	50	50	50
Running Boards	25	50	50	50	50	50	50
Premium Wheels	125	150	175	200	225	250	275
Towing Pkg	100	125	150	175	200	200	200
w/o Leather	—	(25)	(50)	(75)	(100)	(125)	(175)

FOR MILEAGE ADJUSTMENT — SEE PAGE 9

Equipment	98	99	00	01	02	03	04

TRUCKS & VANS

MODEL & TRIM PACKAGES (Truck Schedules T1 & T2)
(Add Only If Not Listed on Individual Vehicle Listing)

CHEVROLET/GMC:

	98	99	00	01	02	03	04
Silverado, LS, LT, LTZ, TrailBlazer, Xtreme, SLE (Full-Size), SLT, Diamond, Warner Bros Ed	400	450	500	550	600	675	750
SLE (Sonoma/Jimmy/Safari), Sport, SS, LS (S10/Colorado), ZR2 Suspension	250	275	300	325	375	425	475
SLS	200	225	250	275	300	325	—
SL, Z71 Off-Road, Cheyenne	125	125	125	125	150	175	200

DODGE/PLYMOUTH:

	98	99	00	01	02	03	04
SLT, SXT, Laramie, Limited	300	325	375	425	475	525	575
SS/T, Expresso	250	275	—	—	—	—	—
ST, Sport, Off-Road	125	125	125	125	150	175	200

FORD:

	98	99	00	01	02	03	04
Eddie Bauer (Explorer/Expedition), Limited, Chateau	825	950	1075	1225	1375	1525	1675
Lariat, Lariat LE	600	675	750	825	900	975	1050
XLT, Edge Plus, Adrenaline	400	450	500	550	600	675	750
STX, XLS, Edge	250	275	300	325	375	425	475
XL, Sport, Off-Road, Tremor, LE, FX4, Heritage, NBX	125	125	125	125	150	175	200

ALL MAKES: (All Other Model Pkgs Not Listed)

	98	99	00	01	02	03	04
	125	125	125	125	150	175	200

TRUCK SCHEDULE T1 (Deduct For)

	98	99	00	01	02	03	04
5-Spd Manual	(425)	(500)	(550)	(600)	(650)	(700)	(750)
6-Spd Manual	—	(300)	(350)	(400)	(425)	(450)	(475)
w/o Pwr Steering	(150)	(175)	(200)	(225)	(250)	(275)	(300)
w/o Air Cond	(250)	(300)	(350)	(400)	(450)	(500)	(550)

TRUCK SCHEDULE T2 (Add For)

	98	99	00	01	02	03	04
Auto Trans	350	400	450	500	550	600	650
Power Steering	75	100	125	150	150	150	150
Air Cond	200	250	300	350	400	450	475
TOTAL	625	750	875	1000	1100	1200	1275

SEE PAGE 9 FOR PVT PARTY & RETAIL EQUIPMENT 367

Equipment	98	99	00	01	02	03	04
TRUCK SCHEDULE T3 (See Page 369)							
OTHER OPTIONS (Truck Schedules T1 & T2)							
Cassette	100	100	100	100	100	125	150
Power Windows	100	125	150	175	200	225	250
Pwr Door Locks	50	75	100	125	150	175	175
Tilt Wheel	75	100	125	150	175	200	200
Cruise Control	25	50	75	100	125	150	150
TOTAL	350	450	550	650	750	875	925
w/o AM/FM	(50)	(75)	(100)	(100)	(100)	(100)	(100)
CD (Single Disc)	100	125	150	175	200	225	250
CD (Multi Disc)	200	250	275	300	325	350	375
Premium Sound	50	100	125	150	175	200	225
Integrated Phone	50	75	100	125	150	175	200
Video/DVD	200	250	275	300	325	350	375
NavigationSystm	400	450	475	500	525	550	575
Air Cond, Rear	250	300	350	400	425	450	475
Leather	200	250	275	300	325	350	375
Power Seat	25	25	25	50	75	100	125
Dual Pwr Seats	75	100	125	150	175	200	225
Quad Seating							
(4 Buckets)	150	200	250	300	325	350	375
Van Seating Packages							
(11/12 Pass)	400	450	500	550	600	650	700
(14/15 Pass)	550	600	650	700	750	800	850
Power Sliding Doors (Minivans)							
Single	25	25	25	25	25	50	75
Dual	50	50	75	100	125	150	175
Privacy Glass (Vans/Wagons/Sport Utilities)							
	50	75	100	100	100	100	100
Sliding Rear Window (Pickups)							
	25	50	75	75	75	75	75
Roof Rack	25	50	75	100	100	100	100
Sun Roof or Moon Roof							
(Flip-Up)	50	75	100	125	150	175	200
(Sliding)	300	350	400	450	500	550	575
Pickup Shell/Cap	100	150	175	200	225	250	275
Hard Tonneau	50	100	125	150	175	200	225
Bed Liner	100	100	100	130	125	150	175
Grille Guard	50	75	75	75	75	75	75
Winch	150	150	175	200	225	250	275
Custom Bumper	50	75	100	100	100	100	100
Custom Paint	25	25	25	50	75	100	125
Two-Tone Paint	25	25	25	50	75	100	125
Stepside Bed	150	200	250	300	325	350	375
Running Boards	50	75	100	100	100	100	100

TRUCKS & VANS

Equipment	98	99	00	01	02	03	04
Alloy Wheels	150	175	200	225	250	275	300
Premium Wheels	300	350	375	400	425	450	475
Wide Tires or Oversize Off-Road Tires							
	100	100	100	100	125	150	175
ABS (4 Wheel)	150	175	200	200	200	200	200
Opt Fuel Tank	50	—	—	—	—	—	—
Towing Pkg	200	225	250	275	300	300	300
Dual Rear Wheels (Add Only on Models Not Listed as DR)							
	825	950	1075	1200	1325	1450	1575

TRUCK SCHEDULE T3 (This Equipment Only)

	98	99	00	01	02	03	04
CD (Single Disc)	150	175	200	225	250	275	300
CD (Multi Disc)	250	300	350	400	425	450	475
Premium Sound	150	200	250	300	325	350	375
Integrated Phone	50	75	100	125	150	175	200
Video/DVD	200	250	275	300	325	350	375
NavigationSystm	400	450	475	500	525	550	575
Sun/Moon Roof	300	350	400	450	500	550	575
Premium Wheels	300	350	375	400	425	450	475
Grille Guard	50	75	75	75	75	75	75
Running Boards	50	75	100	100	100	100	100
Power Sliding Doors (Minivans)							
Single	25	25	25	25	25	50	75
Dual	50	50	75	100	125	150	175
Towing Pkg	200	225	250	275	300	300	300
w/o Leather	(200)	(250)	(300)	(350)	(400)	(475)	(550)

FOR MILEAGE ADJUSTMENT — SEE PAGE 9